T0180373

Lecture Notes in Computer Science

Lecture Notes in Artificial Intelligence 14170

Founding Editor

Jörg Siekmann

Series Editors

Randy Goebel, *University of Alberta, Edmonton, Canada*
Wolfgang Wahlster, *DFKI, Berlin, Germany*
Zhi-Hua Zhou, *Nanjing University, Nanjing, China*

The series Lecture Notes in Artificial Intelligence (LNAI) was established in 1988 as a topical subseries of LNCS devoted to artificial intelligence.

The series publishes state-of-the-art research results at a high level. As with the LNCS mother series, the mission of the series is to serve the international R & D community by providing an invaluable service, mainly focused on the publication of conference and workshop proceedings and postproceedings.

Danai Koutra · Claudia Plant ·
Manuel Gomez Rodriguez · Elena Baralis ·
Francesco Bonchi
Editors

Machine Learning and Knowledge Discovery in Databases

Research Track

European Conference, ECML PKDD 2023
Turin, Italy, September 18–22, 2023
Proceedings, Part II

Springer

Editors
Danai Koutra
University of Michigan
Ann Arbor, MI, USA

Claudia Plant
University of Vienna
Vienna, Austria

Manuel Gomez Rodriguez
Max Planck Institute for Software Systems
Kaiserslautern, Germany

Elena Baralis
Politecnico di Torino
Turin, Italy

Francesco Bonchi
CENTAI
Turin, Italy

ISSN 0302-9743 ISSN 1611-3349 (electronic)
Lecture Notes in Artificial Intelligence
ISBN 978-3-031-43414-3 ISBN 978-3-031-43415-0 (eBook)
https://doi.org/10.1007/978-3-031-43415-0

LNCS Sublibrary: SL7 – Artificial Intelligence

© The Editor(s) (if applicable) and The Author(s), under exclusive license
to Springer Nature Switzerland AG 2023

This work is subject to copyright. All rights are reserved by the Publisher, whether the whole or part of the material is concerned, specifically the rights of translation, reprinting, reuse of illustrations, recitation, broadcasting, reproduction on microfilms or in any other physical way, and transmission or information storage and retrieval, electronic adaptation, computer software, or by similar or dissimilar methodology now known or hereafter developed.
The use of general descriptive names, registered names, trademarks, service marks, etc. in this publication does not imply, even in the absence of a specific statement, that such names are exempt from the relevant protective laws and regulations and therefore free for general use.
The publisher, the authors, and the editors are safe to assume that the advice and information in this book are believed to be true and accurate at the date of publication. Neither the publisher nor the authors or the editors give a warranty, expressed or implied, with respect to the material contained herein or for any errors or omissions that may have been made. The publisher remains neutral with regard to jurisdictional claims in published maps and institutional affiliations.

This Springer imprint is published by the registered company Springer Nature Switzerland AG
The registered company address is: Gewerbestrasse 11, 6330 Cham, Switzerland

Paper in this product is recyclable.

Preface

The 2023 edition of the European Conference on Machine Learning and Principles and Practice of Knowledge Discovery in Databases (ECML PKDD 2023) was held in Turin, Italy, from September 18 to 22, 2023.

The ECML PKDD conference, held annually, acts as a worldwide platform showcasing the latest advancements in machine learning and knowledge discovery in databases, encompassing groundbreaking applications. With a history of successful editions, ECML PKDD has established itself as the leading European machine learning and data mining conference, offering researchers and practitioners an unparalleled opportunity to exchange knowledge and ideas.

The main conference program consisted of presentations of 255 accepted papers and three keynote talks (in order of appearance):

- Max Welling (University of Amsterdam): Neural Wave Representations
- Michael Bronstein (University of Oxford): Physics-Inspired Graph Neural Networks
- Kate Crawford (USC Annenberg): Mapping Generative AI

In addition, there were 30 workshops, 9 combined workshop-tutorials, 5 tutorials, 3 discovery challenges, and 16 demonstrations. Moreover, the PhD Forum provided a friendly environment for junior PhD students to exchange ideas and experiences with peers in an interactive atmosphere and to get constructive feedback from senior researchers. The conference included a Special Day on Artificial Intelligence for Financial Crime Fight to discuss, share, and present recent developments in AI-based financial crime detection.

In recognition of the paramount significance of ethics in machine learning and data mining, we invited the authors to include an ethical statement in their submissions. We encouraged the authors to discuss the ethical implications of their submission, such as those related to the collection and processing of personal data, the inference of personal information, or the potential risks. We are pleased to report that our call for ethical statements was met with an overwhelmingly positive response from the authors.

The ECML PKDD 2023 Organizing Committee supported Diversity and Inclusion by awarding some grants that enable early career researchers to attend the conference, present their research activities, and become part of the ECML PKDD community. A total of 8 grants covering all or part of the registration fee (4 free registrations and 4 with 50% discount) were awarded to individuals who belong to underrepresented communities, based on gender and role/position, to attend the conference and present their research activities. The goal of the grants was to provide financial support to early-career (women) scientists and Master and Ph.D. students from developing countries. The Diversity and Inclusion action also includes the SoBigData Award, fully sponsored by the SoBigData++ Horizon2020 project, which aims to encourage more diverse participation in computer science and machine learning events. The award is intended to cover expenses for transportation and accommodation.

The papers presented during the three main conference days were organized in four different tracks:

- Research Track: research or methodology papers from all areas in machine learning, knowledge discovery, and data mining;
- Applied Data Science Track: papers on novel applications of machine learning, data mining, and knowledge discovery to solve real-world use cases, thereby bridging the gap between practice and current theory;
- Journal Track: papers published in special issues of the journals Machine Learning and Data Mining and Knowledge Discovery;
- Demo Track: short papers introducing new prototypes or fully operational systems that exploit data science techniques and are presented via working demonstrations.

We received 829 submissions for the Research track and 239 for the Applied Data Science Track.

We accepted 196 papers (24%) in the Research Track and 58 (24%) in the Applied Data Science Track. In addition, there were 44 papers from the Journal Track and 16 demo papers (out of 28 submissions).

We want to thank all participants, authors, all chairs, all Program Committee members, area chairs, session chairs, volunteers, co-organizers, and organizers of workshops and tutorials for making ECML PKDD 2023 an outstanding success. Thanks to Springer for their continuous support and Microsoft for allowing us to use their CMT software for conference management and providing support throughout. Special thanks to our sponsors and the ECML PKDD Steering Committee for their support. Finally, we thank the organizing institutions: CENTAI (Italy) and Politecnico di Torino (Italy).

September 2023

Elena Baralis
Francesco Bonchi
Manuel Gomez Rodriguez
Danai Koutra
Claudia Plant
Gianmarco De Francisci Morales
Claudia Perlich

Organization

General Chairs

Elena Baralis	Politecnico di Torino, Italy
Francesco Bonchi	CENTAI, Italy and Eurecat, Spain

Research Track Program Chairs

Manuel Gomez Rodriguez	Max Planck Institute for Software Systems, Germany
Danai Koutra	University of Michigan, USA
Claudia Plant	University of Vienna, Austria

Applied Data Science Track Program Chairs

Gianmarco De Francisci Morales	CENTAI, Italy
Claudia Perlich	NYU and TwoSigma, USA

Journal Track Chairs

Tania Cerquitelli	Politecnico di Torino, Italy
Marcello Restelli	Politecnico di Milano, Italy
Charalampos E. Tsourakakis	Boston University, USA and ISI Foundation, Italy
Fabio Vitale	CENTAI, Italy

Workshop and Tutorial Chairs

Rosa Meo	University of Turin, Italy
Fabrizio Silvestri	Sapienza University of Rome, Italy

Demo Chairs

Nicolas Kourtellis — Telefonica, Spain
Natali Ruchansky — Netflix, USA

Local Chairs

Daniele Apiletti — Politecnico di Torino, Italy
Paolo Bajardi — CENTAI, Italy
Eliana Pastor — Politecnico di Torino, Italy

Discovery Challenge Chairs

Danilo Giordano — Politecnico di Torino, Italy
André Panisson — CENTAI, Italy

PhD Forum Chairs

Yllka Velaj — University of Vienna, Austria
Matteo Riondato — Amherst College, USA

Diversity and Inclusion Chair

Tania Cerquitelli — Politecnico di Torino, Italy

Proceedings Chairs

Eliana Pastor — Politecnico di Torino, Italy
Giulia Preti — CENTAI, Italy

Sponsorship Chairs

Daniele Apiletti — Politecnico di Torino, Italy
Paolo Bajardi — CENTAI, Italy

Web Chair

Alessandro Fiori	Flowygo, Italy

Social Media and Publicity Chair

Flavio Giobergia	Politecnico di Torino, Italy

Online Chairs

Alkis Koudounas	Politecnico di Torino, Italy
Simone Monaco	Politecnico di Torino, Italy

Best Paper Awards Chairs

Peter Flach	University of Bristol, UK
Katharina Morik	TU Dortmund, Germany
Arno Siebes	Utrecht University, The Netherlands

ECML PKDD Steering Committee

Massih-Reza Amini	Université Grenoble Alpes, France
Annalisa Appice	University of Bari, Aldo Moro, Italy
Ira Assent	Aarhus University, Denmark
Tania Cerquitelli	Politecnico di Torino, Italy
Albert Bifet	University of Waikato, New Zealand
Francesco Bonchi	CENTAI, Italy and Eurecat, Spain
Peggy Cellier	INSA Rennes, France
Saso Dzeroski	Jožef Stefan Institute, Slovenia
Tias Guns	KU Leuven, Belgium
Alípio M. G. Jorge	University of Porto, Portugal
Kristian Kersting	TU Darmstadt, Germany
Jefrey Lijffijt	Ghent University, Belgium
Luís Moreira-Matias	Sennder GmbH, Germany
Katharina Morik	TU Dortmund, Germany
Siegfried Nijssen	Université catholique de Louvain, Belgium
Andrea Passerini	University of Trento, Italy

Fernando Perez-Cruz	ETH Zurich, Switzerland
Alessandra Sala	Shutterstock, Ireland
Arno Siebes	Utrecht University, The Netherlands
Grigorios Tsoumakas	Aristotle University of Thessaloniki, Greece
Isabel Valera	Universität des Saarlandes, Germany

Program Committee

Guest Editorial Board, Journal Track

Richard Allmendinger	University of Manchester, UK
Marie Anastacio	RWTH Aachen University, Germany
Giuseppina Andresini	University of Bari, Aldo Moro, Italy
Annalisa Appice	University of Bari, Aldo Moro, Italy
Ira Assent	Aarhus University, Denmark
Martin Atzmueller	Osnabrück University, Germany
Jaume Bacardit	Newcastle University, UK
Anthony Bagnall	University of East Anglia, UK
Mitra Baratchi	Leiden University, The Netherlands
Nicola Basilico	University of Milan, Italy
Franka Bause	University of Vienna, Austria
Viktor Bengs	LMU Munich, Germany
Anna Bernasconi	Politecnico di Milano, Italy
Lorenzo Bisi	ML cube, Italy
Veronica Bolon-Canedo	University of A Coruña, Spain
Paolo Bonetti	Politecnico di Milano, Italy
Ilaria Bordino	UniCredit, Italy
Claudio Borile	CENTAI, Italy
Luca Cagliero	Politecnico di Torino, Italy
Ricardo Campello	University of Newcastle, Australia
Barbara Catania	University of Genoa, Italy
Michelangelo Ceci	University of Bari, Aldo Moro, Italy
Loïc Cerf	Universidade Federal de Minas Gerais, Brazil
Julen Cestero	Politecnico di Milano, Italy
Sudhanshu Chanpuriya	University of Massachusetts, Amherst, USA
Tianyi Chen	Boston University, USA
Federico Cinus	Sapienza University of Rome, Italy
Gabriele Ciravegna	Politecnico di Torino, Italy
Luca Colomba	Politecnico di Torino, Italy
Silvia Corchs	University of Milan, Italy

Marco Cotogni	University of Pavia, Italy
Gabriele D'Acunto	Sapienza University of Rome, Italy
Cassio Fraga Dantas	TETIS, Université Montpellier, INRAE, France
Jérôme Darmont	Université Lumière Lyon 2, France
George Dasoulas	Harvard University, USA
Sébastien Destercke	Université de Technologie de Compiègne, France
Shridhar Devamane	Global Academy of Technology, India
Claudia Diamantini	Università Politecnica delle Marche, Italy
Gianluca Drappo	Politecnico di Milano, Italy
Pedro Ferreira	University of Lisbon, Portugal
Cèsar Ferri	Universitat Politècnica de València, Spain
M. Julia Flores	Universidad de Castilla-La Mancha, Spain
Germain Forestier	University of Haute-Alsace, France
Elisa Fromont	Université de Rennes 1, France
Emanuele Frontoni	University of Macerata, Italy
Esther Galbrun	University of Eastern Finland, Finland
Joao Gama	University of Porto, Portugal
Jose A. Gamez	Universidad de Castilla-La Mancha, Spain
David García Soriano	ISI Foundation, Italy
Paolo Garza	Politecnico di Torino, Italy
Salvatore Greco	Politecnico di Torino, Italy
Riccardo Guidotti	University of Pisa, Italy
Francesco Gullo	UniCredit, Italy
Shahrzad Haddadan	Rutgers Business School, USA
Martin Holena	Czech Academy of Sciences, Czech Republic
Jaakko Hollmén	Stockholm University, Sweden
Dino Ienco	INRAE, France
Georgiana Ifrim	University College Dublin, Ireland
Felix Iglesias	TU Vienna, Austria
Angelo Impedovo	Niuma, Italy
Manfred Jaeger	Aalborg University, Denmark
Szymon Jaroszewicz	Warsaw University of Technology, Poland
Panagiotis Karras	Aarhus University, Denmark
George Katsimpras	National Center for Scientific Research Demokritos, Greece
Mehdi Kaytoue	Infologic R&D, France
Dragi Kocev	Jožef Stefan Institute, Slovenia
Yun Sing Koh	University of Auckland, New Zealand
Sotiropoulos Konstantinos	Boston University, USA
Lars Kotthoff	University of Wyoming, USA
Alkis Koudounas	Politecnico di Torino, Italy
Tommaso Lanciano	Sapienza University of Rome, Italy

Helge Langseth	Norwegian University of Science and Technology, Norway
Thien Le	MIT, USA
Hsuan-Tien Lin	National Taiwan University, Taiwan
Marco Lippi	University of Modena and Reggio Emilia, Italy
Corrado Loglisci	University of Bari, Aldo Moro, Italy
Manuel López-ibáñez	University of Manchester, UK
Nuno Lourenço	CISUC, Portugal
Claudio Lucchese	Ca' Foscari University of Venice, Italy
Brian Mac Namee	University College Dublin, Ireland
Gjorgji Madjarov	Ss. Cyril and Methodius University in Skopje, North Macedonia
Luigi Malagò	Transylvanian Institute of Neuroscience, Romania
Sagar Malhotra	Fondazione Bruno Kessler, Italy
Fragkiskos Malliaros	CentraleSupélec, Université Paris-Saclay, France
Giuseppe Manco	ICAR-CNR, Italy
Basarab Matei	Sorbonne Université Paris Nord, France
Michael Mathioudakis	University of Helsinki, Finland
Rosa Meo	University of Turin, Italy
Mohamed-Lamine Messai	Université Lumière Lyon 2, France
Sara Migliorini	University of Verona, Italy
Alex Mircoli	Università Politecnica delle Marche, Italy
Atsushi Miyauchi	University of Tokyo, Japan
Simone Monaco	Politecnico di Torino, Italy
Anna Monreale	University of Pisa, Italy
Corrado Monti	CENTAI, Italy
Katharina Morik	TU Dortmund, Germany
Lia Morra	Politecnico di Torino, Italy
Arsenii Mustafin	Boston University, USA
Mirco Mutti	Politecnico di Milano/University of Bologna, Italy
Amedeo Napoli	University of Lorraine, CNRS, LORIA, France
Kleber Oliveira	CENTAI, Italy
Gabriella Olmo	Politecnico di Torino, Italy
Marios Papachristou	Cornell University, USA
Panagiotis Papapetrou	Stockholm University, Sweden
Matteo Papini	Universitat Pompeu Fabra, Spain
Vincenzo Pasquadibisceglie	University of Bari, Aldo Moro, Italy
Eliana Pastor	Politecnico di Torino, Italy
Andrea Paudice	University of Milan, Italy
Charlotte Pelletier	IRISA - Université Bretagne-Sud, France
Ruggero G. Pensa	University of Turin, Italy
Simone Piaggesi	University of Bologna/ISI Foundation, Italy

Matteo Pirotta	Meta, France
Marc Plantevit	EPITA, France
Konstantinos Pliakos	KU Leuven, Belgium
Kai Puolamäki	University of Helsinki, Finland
Jan Ramon	Inria, France
Rita P. Ribeiro	INESC TEC/University of Porto, Portugal
Matteo Riondato	Amherst College, USA
Antonio Riva	Politecnico di Milano, Italy
Shota Saito	University College London, UK
Flora Salim	University of New South Wales, Australia
Roberto Santana	University of the Basque Country, Spain
Lars Schmidt-Thieme	University of Hildesheim, Germany
Thomas Seidl	LMU Munich, Germany
Kijung Shin	KAIST, South Korea
Shinichi Shirakawa	Yokohama National University, Japan
Konstantinos Sotiropoulos	Boston University, USA
Fabian Spaeh	Boston University, USA
Gerasimos Spanakis	Maastricht University, The Netherlands
Myra Spiliopoulou	Otto-von-Guericke-University Magdeburg, Germany
Jerzy Stefanowski	Poznan University of Technology, Poland
Mahito Sugiyama	National Institute of Informatics, Japan
Nikolaj Tatti	University of Helsinki, Finland
Maximilian Thiessen	TU Vienna, Austria
Josephine Thomas	University of Kassel, Germany
Kiran Tomlinson	Cornell University, USA
Leonardo Trujillo	Tecnológico Nacional de México, Mexico
Grigorios Tsoumakas	Aristotle University of Thessaloniki, Greece
Genoveva Vargas-Solar	CNRS, LIRIS Lab, France
Edoardo Vittori	Politecnico di Milano/Intesa Sanpaolo, Italy
Christel Vrain	University of Orléans, France
Willem Waegeman	Ghent University, Belgium
Yanbang Wang	Cornell University, USA
Pascal Welke	University of Bonn, Germany
Marcel Wever	LMU Munich, Germany
Stefan Wrobel	University of Bonn/Fraunhofer IAIS, Germany
Guoxian Yu	Shandong University, China
Ilias Zavitsanos	National Center for Scientific Research Demokritos, Greece
Ye Zhu	Deakin University, Australia
Albrecht Zimmermann	Université de Caen Normandie, France

Area Chairs, Research Track

Fabrizio Angiulli	University of Calabria, Italy
Annalisa Appice	University of Bari, Aldo Moro, Italy
Antonio Artés	Universidad Carlos III de Madrid, Spain
Martin Atzmueller	Osnabrück University, Germany
Christian Böhm	University of Vienna, Austria
Michael R. Berthold	KNIME, Switzerland
Albert Bifet	Université Paris-Saclay, France
Hendrik Blockeel	KU Leuven, Belgium
Ulf Brefeld	Leuphana University, Germany
Paula Brito	INESC TEC - LIAAD/University of Porto, Portugal
Wolfram Burgard	University of Technology Nuremberg, Germany
Seshadhri C.	UCSC, USA
Michelangelo Ceci	University of Bari, Aldo Moro, Italy
Peggy Cellier	IRISA - INSA Rennes, France
Duen Horng Chau	Georgia Institute of Technology, USA
Nicolas Courty	IRISA - Université Bretagne-Sud, France
Bruno Cremilleux	Université de Caen Normandie, France
Jesse Davis	KU Leuven, Belgium
Abir De	IIT Bombay, India
Tom Diethe	AstraZeneca, UK
Yuxiao Dong	Tsinghua University, China
Kurt Driessens	Maastricht University, The Netherlands
Tapio Elomaa	Tampere University, Finland
Johannes Fürnkranz	JKU Linz, Austria
Sophie Fellenz	RPTU Kaiserslautern-Landau, Germany
Elisa Fromont	IRISA/Inria rba - Université de Rennes 1, France
Thomas Gärtner	TU Vienna, Austria
Patrick Gallinari	Criteo AI Lab - Sorbonne Université, France
Joao Gama	INESC TEC - LIAAD, Portugal
Rayid Ghani	Carnegie Mellon University, USA
Aristides Gionis	KTH Royal Institute of Technology, Sweden
Chen Gong	Nanjing University of Science and Technology, China
Francesco Gullo	UniCredit, Italy
Eyke Hüllermeier	LMU Munich, Germany
Junheng Hao	University of California, Los Angeles, USA
José Hernández-Orallo	Universitat Politècnica de Valencia, Spain
Daniel Hernández-Lobato	Universidad Autonoma de Madrid, Spain
Sibylle Hess	TU Eindhoven, The Netherlands

Jaakko Hollmén	Aalto University, Finland
Andreas Hotho	University of Würzburg, Germany
Georgiana Ifrim	University College Dublin, Ireland
Jayaraman J. Thiagarajan	Lawrence Livermore, USA
Alipio M. G. Jorge	INESC TEC/University of Porto, Portugal
Ross King	Chalmers University of Technology, Sweden
Yun Sing Koh	University of Auckland, New Zealand
Lars Kotthoff	University of Wyoming, USA
Peer Kröger	Christian-Albrechst University of Kiel, Germany
Stefan Kramer	JGU Mainz, Germany
Jörg Lücke	University of Oldenburg, Germany
Niklas Lavesson	Blekinge Institute of Technology, Sweden
Bruno Lepri	Fondazione Bruno Kessler, Italy
Jefrey Lijffijt	Ghent University, Belgium
Marius Lindauer	Leibniz University Hannover, Germany
Patrick Loiseau	Inria, France
Jose A. Lozano	UPV/EHU, Spain
Emmanuel Müller	TU Dortmund, Germany
Donato Malerba	University of Bari, Aldo Moro, Italy
Fragkiskos Malliaros	CentraleSupelec, France
Giuseppe Manco	ICAR-CNR, Italy
Pauli Miettinen	University of Eastern Finland, Finland
Dunja Mladenic	Jožef Stefan Institute, Slovenia
Anna Monreale	University of Pisa, Italy
Luis Moreira-Matias	Sennder GmbH, Germany
Katharina J. Morik	TU Dortmund, Germany
Siegfried Nijssen	Université catholique de Louvain, Belgium
Evangelos Papalexakis	UC, Riverside, USA
Panagiotis Papapetrou	Stockholm University, Sweden
Andrea Passerini	University of Trento, Italy
Mykola Pechenizkiy	TU Eindhoven, The Netherlands
Jaakko Peltonen	Tampere University, Finland
Franz Pernkopf	TU Graz, Austria
Bernhard Pfahringer	University of Waikato, New Zealand
Fabio Pinelli	IMT Lucca, Italy
Goran Radanovic	Max Planck Institute for Software Systems, Germany
Jesse Read	École Polytechnique, France
Matthias Renz	Christian-Albrechst University of Kiel, Germany
Marian-Andrei Rizoiu	University of Technology, Sydney, Australia
Celine Robardet	INSA Lyon, France
Juho Rousu	Aalto University, Finland

Sriparna Saha	IIT Patna, India
Ute Schmid	University of Bamberg, Germany
Lars Schmidt-Thieme	University of Hildesheim, Germany
Michele Sebag	LISN CNRS, France
Thomas Seidl	LMU Munich, Germany
Junming Shao	University of Electronic Science and Technology of China, China
Arno Siebes	Utrecht University, The Netherlands
Fabrizio Silvestri	Sapienza University of Rome, Italy
Carlos Soares	University of Porto, Portugal
Christian Sohler	University of Cologne, Germany
Myra Spiliopoulou	Otto-von-Guericke-University Magdeburg, Germany
Jie Tang	Tsinghua University, China
Nikolaj Tatti	University of Helsinki, Finland
Evimaria Terzi	Boston University, USA
Marc Tommasi	Lille University, France
Heike Trautmann	University of Münster, Germany
Herke van Hoof	University of Amsterdam, The Netherlands
Celine Vens	KU Leuven, Belgium
Christel Vrain	University of Orleans, France
Jilles Vreeken	CISPA Helmholtz Center for Information Security, Germany
Wei Ye	Tongji University, China
Jing Zhang	Renmin University of China, China
Min-Ling Zhang	Southeast University, China

Area Chairs, Applied Data Science Track

Annalisa Appice	University of Bari, Aldo Moro, Italy
Ira Assent	Aarhus University, Denmark
Martin Atzmueller	Osnabrück University, Germany
Michael R. Berthold	KNIME, Switzerland
Hendrik Blockeel	KU Leuven, Belgium
Michelangelo Ceci	University of Bari, Aldo Moro, Italy
Peggy Cellier	IRISA - INSA Rennes, France
Yi Chang	Jilin University, China
Nicolas Courty	IRISA - UBS, France
Bruno Cremilleux	Université de Caen Normandie, France
Peng Cui	Tsinghua University, China
Anirban Dasgupta	IIT Gandhinagar, India

Tom Diethe	AstraZeneca, UK
Carlotta Domeniconi	George Mason University, USA
Dejing Dou	BCG, USA
Kurt Driessens	Maastricht University, The Netherlands
Johannes Fürnkranz	JKU Linz, Austria
Faisal Farooq	Qatar Computing Research Institute, Qatar
Paolo Frasconi	University of Florence, Italy
Elisa Fromont	IRISA/Inria rba - Université de Rennes 1, France
Glenn Fung	Liberty Mutual, USA
Joao Gama	INESC TEC - LIAAD, Portugal
Jose A. Gamez	Universidad de Castilla-La Mancha, Spain
Rayid Ghani	Carnegie Mellon University, USA
Aristides Gionis	KTH Royal Institute of Technology, Sweden
Sreenivas Gollapudi	Google, USA
Francesco Gullo	UniCredit, Italy
Eyke Hüllermeier	LMU Munich, Germany
Jingrui He	University of Illinois at Urbana-Champaign, USA
Jaakko Hollmén	Aalto University, Finland
Andreas Hotho	University of Würzburg, Germany
Daxin Jiang	Microsoft, Beijing, China
Alipio M. G. Jorge	INESC TEC/University of Porto, Portugal
George Karypis	University of Minnesota, USA
Eamonn Keogh	UC, Riverside, USA
Yun Sing Koh	University of Auckland, New Zealand
Parisa Kordjamshidi	Michigan State University, USA
Lars Kotthoff	University of Wyoming, USA
Nicolas Kourtellis	Telefonica Research, Spain
Stefan Kramer	JGU Mainz, Germany
Balaji Krishnapuram	Pinterest, USA
Niklas Lavesson	Blekinge Institute of Technology, Sweden
Chuan Lei	Amazon Web Services, USA
Marius Lindauer	Leibniz University Hannover, Germany
Patrick Loiseau	Inria, France
Giuseppe Manco	ICAR-CNR, Italy
Gabor Melli	PredictionWorks, USA
Anna Monreale	University of Pisa, Italy
Luis Moreira-Matias	Sennder GmbH, Germany
Nuria Oliver	ELLIS Alicante, Spain
Panagiotis Papapetrou	Stockholm University, Sweden
Mykola Pechenizkiy	TU Eindhoven, The Netherlands
Jian Pei	Simon Fraser University, Canada
Julien Perez	Naver Labs Europe, France

Fabio Pinelli	IMT Lucca, Italy
Zhiwei (Tony) Qin	Lyft, USA
Visvanathan Ramesh	Goethe University, Germany
Zhaochun Ren	Shandong University, China
Sriparna Saha	IIT Patna, India
Ute Schmid	University of Bamberg, Germany
Lars Schmidt-Thieme	University of Hildesheim, Germany
Thomas Seidl	LMU Munich, Germany
Fabrizio Silvestri	Sapienza University of Rome, Italy
Myra Spiliopoulou	Otto-von-Guericke-University Magdeburg, Germany
Karthik Subbian	Amazon, USA
Liang Sun	Alibaba Group, China
Jie Tang	Tsinghua University, China
Jiliang Tang	Michigan State University, USA
Sandeep Tata	Google, USA
Nikolaj Tatti	University of Helsinki, Finland
Marc Tommasi	Lille University, France
Yongxin Tong	Beihang University, China
Vincent S. Tseng	National Yang Ming Chiao Tung University, Taiwan
Antti Ukkonen	University of Helsinki, Finland
Willem Waegeman	Ghent University, Belgium
Fei Wang	Cornell University, USA
Jie Wang	University of Science and Technology of China, China
Sinong Wang	Meta AI, USA
Zheng Wang	Alibaba DAMO Academy, China
Lingfei Wu	Pinterest, USA
Yinglong Xia	Meta, USA
Hui Xiong	Rutgers University, USA
Hongxia Yang	Alibaba Group, China
Min-Ling Zhang	Southeast University, China
Jiayu Zhou	Michigan State University, USA
Xingquan Zhu	Florida Atlantic University, USA
Fuzhen Zhuang	Institute of Artificial Intelligence, China
Albrecht Zimmermann	Université de Caen Normandie, France

Program Committee, Research Track

Matthias Aßenmacher	LMU Munich, Germany
Sara Abdali	Microsoft, USA
Evrim Acar	Simula Metropolitan Center for Digital Engineering, Norway
Homayun Afrabandpey	Nokia Technologies, Finland
Reza Akbarinia	Inria, France
Cuneyt G. Akcora	University of Manitoba, Canada
Ranya Almohsen	West Virginia University, USA
Thiago Andrade	INESC TEC/University of Porto, Portugal
Jean-Marc Andreoli	Naverlabs Europe, France
Giuseppina Andresini	University of Bari, Aldo Moro, Italy
Alessandro Antonucci	IDSIA, Switzerland
Xiang Ao	Institute of Computing Technology, CAS, China
Héber H. Arcolezi	Inria/École Polytechnique, France
Jerónimo Arenas-García	Universidad Carlos III de Madrid, Spain
Yusuf Arslan	University of Luxembourg, Luxemburg
Ali Ayadi	University of Strasbourg, France
Steve Azzolin	University of Trento, Italy
Pierre-Luc Bacon	Mila, Canada
Bunil K. Balabantaray	NIT Meghalaya, India
Mitra Baratchi	LIACS/Leiden University, The Netherlands
Christian Bauckhage	Fraunhofer IAIS, Germany
Anna Beer	Aarhus University, Denmark
Michael Beigl	Karlsruhe Institute of Technology, Germany
Khalid Benabdeslem	Université de Lyon, Lyon 1, France
Idir Benouaret	Epita Research Laboratory, France
Paul Berg	IRISA, France
Christoph Bergmeir	Monash University, Australia
Gilberto Bernardes	INESC TEC/University of Porto, Portugal
Eva Besada-Portas	Universidad Complutense de Madrid, Spain
Jalaj Bhandari	Columbia University, USA
Asmita Bhat	TU Kaiserslautern, Germany
Monowar Bhuyan	Umeå University, Sweden
Adrien Bibal	University of Colorado Anschutz Medical Campus, USA
Manuele Bicego	University of Verona, Italy
Przemyslaw Biecek	Warsaw University of Technology, Poland
Alexander Binder	University of Oslo, Norway
Livio Bioglio	University of Turin, Italy
Patrick Blöbaum	Amazon Web Services, USA

Thomas Bonald	Télécom Paris, France
Ludovico Boratto	University of Cagliari, Italy
Stefano Bortoli	Huawei Research Center, Germany
Tassadit Bouadi	Université de Rennes 1, France
Ahcène Boubekki	UiT, Arctic University of Norway, Norway
Luc Brogat-Motte	Télécom Paris, France
Jannis Brugger	TU Darmstadt, Germany
Nhat-Tan Bui	University of Science - VNUHCM, Vietnam
Mirko Bunse	TU Dortmund, Germany
John Burden	University of Cambridge, UK
Wolfram Burgard	University of Technology, Germany
Julian Busch	Siemens Technology, Germany
Sebastian Buschjäger	TU Dortmund, Germany
Oswald C.	NIT Trichy, India
Seshadhri C.	UCSC, USA
Xin-Qiang Cai	University of Tokyo, Japan
Zekun Cai	University of Tokyo, Japan
Xiaofeng Cao	University of Technology, Sydney, Australia
Giuseppe Casalicchio	LMU Munich, Germany
Guilherme Cassales	University of Waikato, New Zealand
Oded Cats	TU Delft, The Netherlands
Remy Cazabet	Université de Lyon, Lyon 1, France
Mattia Cerrato	JGU Mainz, Germany
Ricardo Cerri	Federal University of Sao Carlos, Brazil
Prithwish Chakraborty	IBM Research, USA
Harry Kai-Ho Chan	University of Sheffield, UK
Joydeep Chandra	IIT Patna, India
Vaggos Chatziafratis	Stanford University, USA
Zaineb Chelly Dagdia	UVSQ - Université Paris-Saclay, France
Hongyang Chen	Zhejiang Lab, China
Huaming Chen	University of Sydney, Australia
Hung-Hsuan Chen	National Central University, Taiwan
Jin Chen	University of Electronic Science and Technology of China, China
Kuan-Hsun Chen	University of Twente, The Netherlands
Ling Chen	University of Technology, Australia
Lingwei Chen	Wright State University, USA
Minyu Chen	Shanghai Jiaotong University, China
Xi Chen	Ghent University, Belgium
Xiaojun Chen	Institute of Information Engineering, CAS, China
Xuefeng Chen	Chongqing University, China
Ying Chen	RMIT University, Australia

Yueguo Chen	Renmin University of China, China
Yuzhou Chen	Temple University, USA
Zheng Chen	Osaka University, Japan
Ziheng Chen	Walmart, USA
Lu Cheng	University of Illinois, Chicago, USA
Xu Cheng	Shanghai Jiao Tong University, China
Zhiyong Cheng	Shandong Academy of Sciences, China
Yann Chevaleyre	Université Paris Dauphine, France
Chun Wai Chiu	Keele University, UK
Silvia Chiusano	Politecnico di Torino, Italy
Satyendra Singh Chouhan	MNIT Jaipur, India
Hua Chu	Xidian University, China
Sarel Cohen	Academic College of Tel Aviv-Yaffo, Israel
J. Alberto Conejero	Universitat Politècnica de València, Spain
Lidia Contreras-Ochando	Universitat Politècnica de València, Spain
Giorgio Corani	IDSIA, Switzerland
Luca Corbucci	University of Pisa, Italy
Roberto Corizzo	American University, USA
Baris Coskunuzer	University of Texas at Dallas, USA
Fabrizio Costa	Exeter University, UK
Gustavo de Assis Costa	Instituto Federal de Goiás, Brazil
Evan Crothers	University of Ottawa, Canada
Pádraig Cunningham	University College Dublin, Ireland
Jacek Cyranka	University of Warsaw, Poland
Tianxiang Dai	Huawei European Research Institute, Germany
Xuan-Hong Dang	IBM T.J. Watson Research Center, USA
Thi-Bich-Hanh Dao	University of Orleans, France
Debasis Das	Indian Institute of Technology Jodhpur, India
Paul Davidsson	Malmö University, Sweden
Marcilio de Souto	LIFO, University of Orleans, France
Klest Dedja	KU Leuven, Belgium
Elena Demidova	University of Bonn, Germany
Caglar Demir	Paderborn University, Germany
Difan Deng	Leibniz University Hannover, Germany
Laurens Devos	KU Leuven, Belgium
Nicola Di Mauro	University of Bari, Aldo Moro, Italy
Jingtao Ding	Tsinghua University, China
Yao-Xiang Ding	Nanjing University, China
Lamine Diop	EPITA, France
Gillian Dobbie	University of Auckland, New Zealand
Stephan Doerfel	Kiel University of Applied Sciences, Germany
Carola Doerr	Sorbonne Université, France

Nanqing Dong	University of Oxford, UK
Haizhou Du	Shanghai University of Electric Power, China
Qihan Du	Renmin University of China, China
Songlin Du	Southeast University, China
Xin Du	University of Edinburgh, UK
Wouter Duivesteijn	TU Eindhoven, The Netherlands
Inês Dutra	University of Porto, Portugal
Sourav Dutta	Huawei Research Centre, Ireland
Saso Dzeroski	Jožef Stefan Institute, Slovenia
Nabil El Malki	IRIT, France
Mohab Elkaref	IBM Research Europe, UK
Tapio Elomaa	Tampere University, Finland
Dominik M. Endres	University of Marburg, Germany
Georgios Exarchakis	University of Bath, UK
Lukas Faber	ETH Zurich, Switzerland
Samuel G. Fadel	Leuphana University, Germany
Haoyi Fan	Zhengzhou University, China
Zipei Fan	University of Tokyo, Japan
Hadi Fanaee-T	Halmstad University, Sweden
Elaine Ribeiro Faria	UFU, Brazil
Fabio Fassetti	University of Calabria, Italy
Anthony Faustine	ITI/LARSyS - Técnico Lisboa, Portugal
Sophie Fellenz	RPTU Kaiserslautern-Landau, Germany
Wenjie Feng	National University of Singapore, Singapore
Zunlei Feng	Zhejiang University, China
Daniel Fernández-Sánchez	Universidad Autónoma de Madrid, Spain
Luca Ferragina	University of Calabria, Italy
Emilio Ferrara	USC ISI, USA
Cèsar Ferri	Universitat Politècnica València, Spain
Flavio Figueiredo	Universidade Federal de Minas Gerais, Brazil
Lucie Flek	University of Marburg, Germany
Michele Fontana	University of Pisa, Italy
Germain Forestier	University of Haute-Alsace, France
Raphaël Fournier-S'niehotta	CNAM, France
Benoît Frénay	University of Namur, Belgium
Kary Främling	Umeå University, Sweden
Holger Froening	University of Heidelberg, Germany
Fabio Fumarola	Prometeia, Italy
María José Gómez-Silva	Universidad Complutense de Madrid, Spain
Vanessa Gómez-Verdejo	Universidad Carlos III de Madrid, Spain
Pratik Gajane	TU Eindhoven, The Netherlands
Esther Galbrun	University of Eastern Finland, Finland

Claudio Gallicchio	University of Pisa, Italy
Chen Gao	Tsinghua University, China
Shengxiang Gao	Kunming University of Science and Technology, China
Yifeng Gao	University of Texas Rio Grande Valley, USA
Luis Garcia	University of Brasilia, Brazil
Dominique Gay	Université de La Réunion, France
Suyu Ge	University of Illinois at Urbana-Champaign, USA
Zhaocheng Ge	Huazhong University of Science and Technology, China
Alborz Geramifard	Facebook AI, USA
Ahana Ghosh	Max Planck Institute for Software Systems, Germany
Shreya Ghosh	Penn State University, USA
Flavio Giobergia	Politecnico di Torino, Italy
Sarunas Girdzijauskas	KTH Royal Institute of Technology, Sweden
Heitor Murilo Gomes	University of Waikato, Sweden
Wenwen Gong	Tsinghua University, China
Bedartha Goswami	University of Tübingen, Germany
Anastasios Gounaris	Aristotle University of Thessaloniki, Greece
Michael Granitzer	University of Passau, Germany
Derek Greene	University College Dublin, Ireland
Moritz Grosse-Wentrup	University of Vienna, Austria
Marek Grzes	University of Kent, UK
Xinyu Guan	Xian Jiaotong University, China
Massimo Guarascio	ICAR-CNR, Italy
Riccardo Guidotti	University of Pisa, Italy
Lan-Zhe Guo	Nanjing University, China
Lingbing Guo	Zhejiang University, China
Shanqing Guo	Shandong University, China
Karthik S. Gurumoorthy	Walmart, USA
Thomas Guyet	Inria, France
Huong Ha	RMIT University, Australia
Benjamin Halstead	University of Auckland, New Zealand
Massinissa Hamidi	LIPN-UMR CNRS 7030, France
Donghong Han	Northeastern University, USA
Marwan Hassani	TU Eindhoven, The Netherlands
Rima Hazra	Indian Institute of Technology, Kharagpur, India
Mark Heimann	Lawrence Livermore, USA
Cesar Hidalgo	University of Toulouse, France
Martin Holena	Institute of Computer Science, Czech Republic
Mike Holenderski	TU Eindhoven, The Netherlands

Adrian Horzyk	AGH University of Science and Technology, Poland
Shifu Hou	Case Western Reserve University, USA
Hongsheng Hu	CSIRO, Australia
Yaowei Hu	University of Arkansas, USA
Yang Hua	Queen's University Belfast, UK
Chao Huang	University of Hong Kong, China
Guanjie Huang	Penn State University, USA
Hong Huang	Huazhong University of Science and Technology, China
Nina C. Hubig	Clemson University, USA
Dino Ienco	Irstea Institute, France
Angelo Impedovo	Niuma, Italy
Roberto Interdonato	CIRAD, France
Stratis Ioannidis	Northeastern University, USA
Nevo Itzhak	Ben-Gurion University, Israel
Raghav Jain	IIT Patna, India
Kuk Jin Jang	University of Pennsylvania, USA
Szymon Jaroszewicz	Polish Academy of Sciences, Poland
Shaoxiong Ji	University of Helsinki, Finland
Bin-Bin Jia	Lanzhou University of Technology, China
Caiyan Jia	School of Computer and Information Technology, China
Xiuyi Jia	Nanjing University of Science and Technology, China
Nan Jiang	Purdue University, USA
Renhe Jiang	University of Tokyo, Japan
Song Jiang	University of California, Los Angeles, USA
Pengfei Jiao	Hangzhou Dianzi University, China
Di Jin	Amazon, USA
Guangyin Jin	National University of Defense Technology, China
Jiahui Jin	Southeast University, China
Ruoming Jin	Kent State University, USA
Yilun Jin	The Hong Kong University of Science and Technology, Hong Kong
Hugo Jonker	Open University of the Netherlands, The Netherlands
Adan Jose-Garcia	Lille University, France
Marius Köppel	JGU Mainz, Germany
Vana Kalogeraki	Athens University of Economics and Business, Greece
Konstantinos Kalpakis	University of Maryland Baltimore County, USA

Andreas Kaltenbrunner	ISI Foundation, Italy
Shivaram Kalyanakrishnan	IIT Bombay, India
Toshihiro Kamishima	National Institute of Advanced Industrial Science and Technology, Japan
Bo Kang	Ghent University, Belgium
Murat Kantarcioglu	UT Dallas
Thommen Karimpanal George	Deakin University, Australia
Saurav Karmakar	University of Galway, Ireland
Panagiotis Karras	Aarhus University, Denmark
Dimitrios Katsaros	University of Thessaly, Greece
Eamonn Keogh	UC, Riverside, USA
Jaleed Khan	University of Galway, Ireland
Irwin King	Chinese University of Hong Kong, China
Mauritius Klein	LMU Munich, Germany
Tomas Kliegr	Prague University of Economics and Business, Czech Republic
Dmitry Kobak	University of Tübingen, Germany
Dragi Kocev	Jožef Stefan Institute, Slovenia
Lars Kotthoff	University of Wyoming, USA
Anna Krause	University of Würzburg, Germany
Amer Krivosija	TU Dortmund, Germany
Daniel Kudenko	L3S Research Center, Germany
Meelis Kull	University of Tartu, Estonia
Sergey O. Kuznetsov	HSE, Russia
Beatriz López	University of Girona, Spain
Jörg Lücke	University of Oldenburg, Germany
Firas Laakom	Tampere University, Finland
Mateusz Lango	Poznan University of Technology, Poland
Hady Lauw	Singapore Management University, Singapore
Tuan Le	New Mexico State University, USA
Erwan Le Merrer	Inria, France
Thach Le Nguyen	Insight Centre, Ireland
Tai Le Quy	L3S Research Center, Germany
Mustapha Lebbah	UVSQ - Université Paris-Saclay, France
Dongman Lee	KAIST, South Korea
Yeon-Chang Lee	Georgia Institute of Technology, USA
Zed Lee	Stockholm University, Sweden
Mathieu Lefort	Université de Lyon, France
Yunwen Lei	University of Birmingham, UK
Vincent Lemaire	Orange Innovation, France
Daniel Lemire	TÉLUQ University, Canada
Florian Lemmerich	RWTH Aachen University, Germany

Youfang Leng	Renmin University of China, China
Carson K. Leung	University of Manitoba, Canada
Dan Li	Sun Yat-Sen University, China
Gang Li	Deakin University, Australia
Jiaming Li	Huazhong University of Science and Technology, China
Mark Junjie Li	Shenzhen University, China
Nian Li	Tsinghua University, China
Shuai Li	University of Cambridge, UK
Tong Li	Hong Kong University of Science and Technology, China
Xiang Li	East China Normal University, China
Yang Li	University of North Carolina at Chapel Hill, USA
Yingming Li	Zhejiang University, China
Yinsheng Li	Fudan University, China
Yong Li	Huawei European Research Center, Germany
Zhihui Li	University of New South Wales, Australia
Zhixin Li	Guangxi Normal University, China
Defu Lian	University of Science and Technology of China, China
Yuxuan Liang	National University of Singapore, Singapore
Angelica Liguori	University of Calabria, Italy
Nick Lim	University of Waikato, Sweden
Baijiong Lin	The Hong Kong University of Science and Technology, Hong Kong
Piotr Lipinski	University of Wrocław, Poland
Marco Lippi	University of Modena and Reggio Emilia, Italy
Bowen Liu	Stanford University, USA
Chien-Liang Liu	National Chiao Tung University, Taiwan
Fenglin Liu	University of Oxford, UK
Junze Liu	University of California, Irvine, USA
Li Liu	Chongqing University, China
Ninghao Liu	University of Georgia, USA
Shenghua Liu	Institute of Computing Technology, CAS, China
Xiao Fan Liu	City University of Hong Kong, Hong Kong
Xu Liu	National University of Singapore, Singapore
Yang Liu	Institute of Computing Technology, CAS, China
Zihan Liu	Zhejiang University/Westlake University, China
Robert Loftin	TU Delft, The Netherlands
Corrado Loglisci	University of Bari, Aldo Moro, Italy
Mingsheng Long	Tsinghua University, China
Antonio Longa	Fondazione Bruno Kessler, Italy

Grigorios Loukides	King's College London, UK
Tsai-Ching Lu	HRL Laboratories, USA
Zhiwu Lu	Renmin University of China, China
Pedro Henrique Luz de Araujo	University of Vienna, Austria
Marcos M. Raimundo	University of Campinas, Brazil
Maximilian Münch	University of Applied Sciences Würzburg-Schweinfurt, Germany
Fenglong Ma	Pennsylvania State University, USA
Pingchuan Ma	The Hong Kong University of Science and Technology, Hong Kong
Yao Ma	New Jersey Institute of Technology, USA
Brian Mac Namee	University College Dublin, Ireland
Henryk Maciejewski	Wrocław University of Science and Technology, Poland
Ayush Maheshwari	IIT Bombay, India
Ajay A. Mahimkar	AT&T, USA
Ayan Majumdar	Max Planck Institute for Software Systems, Germany
Donato Malerba	University of Bari, Aldo Moro, Italy
Aakarsh Malhotra	IIIT-Delhi, India
Fragkiskos Malliaros	CentraleSupelec, France
Pekka Malo	Aalto University, Finland
Hiroshi Mamitsuka	Kyoto University, Japan/Aalto University, Finland
Domenico Mandaglio	University of Calabria, Italy
Robin Manhaeve	KU Leuven, Belgium
Silviu Maniu	Université Paris-Saclay, France
Cinmayii G. Manliguez	National Sun Yat-Sen University, Taiwan
Naresh Manwani	IIIT Hyderabad, India
Giovanni Luca Marchetti	KTH Royal Institute of Technology, Sweden
Koji Maruhashi	Fujitsu Research, Fujitsu Limited, Japan
Florent Masseglia	Inria, France
Sarah Masud	IIIT-Delhi, India
Timothée Mathieu	Inria, France
Amir Mehrpanah	KTH Royal Institute of Technology, Sweden
Wagner Meira Jr.	Universidade Federal de Minas Gerais, Brazil
Joao Mendes-Moreira	INESC TEC, Portugal
Rui Meng	BNU-HKBU United International College, China
Fabio Mercorio	University of Milan-Bicocca, Italy
Alberto Maria Metelli	Politecnico di Milano, Italy
Carlo Metta	CNR-ISTI, Italy
Paolo Mignone	University of Bari, Aldo Moro, Italy
Tsunenori Mine	Kyushu University, Japan

Nuno Moniz	INESC TEC, Portugal
Pierre Monnin	Université Côte d'Azur, Inria, CNRS, I3S, France
Carlos Monserrat-Aranda	Universitat Politècnica de València, Spain
Raha Moraffah	Arizona State University, USA
Davide Mottin	Aarhus University, Denmark
Hamid Mousavi	University of Oldenburg, Germany
Abdullah Mueen	University of New Mexico, USA
Shamsuddeen Hassan Muhamamd	University of Porto, Portugal
Koyel Mukherjee	Adobe Research, India
Yusuke Mukuta	University of Tokyo, Japan
Pranava Mummoju	University of Vienna, Austria
Taichi Murayama	NAIST, Japan
Ankur Nahar	IIT Jodhpur, India
Felipe Kenji Nakano	KU Leuven, Belgium
Hideki Nakayama	University of Tokyo, Japan
Géraldin Nanfack	University of Namur, Belgium
Mirco Nanni	CNR-ISTI, Italy
Franco Maria Nardini	CNR-ISTI, Italy
Usman Naseem	University of Sydney, Australia
Reza Nasirigerdeh	TU Munich, Germany
Rajashree Nayak	MIT ADT University, India
Benjamin Negrevergne	Université Paris Dauphine, France
Stefan Neumann	KTH Royal Institute of Technology, Sweden
Anna Nguyen	IBM, USA
Shiwen Ni	SIAT, CAS, China
Siegfried Nijssen	Université catholique de Louvain, Belgium
Iasonas Nikolaou	Boston University, USA
Simona Nisticò	University of Calabria, Italy
Hao Niu	KDDI Research, Japan
Mehdi Nourelahi	University of Wyoming, USA
Slawomir Nowaczyk	Halmstad University, Sweden
Eirini Ntoutsi	Bundeswehr University Munich, Germany
Barry O'Sullivan	University College Cork, Ireland
Nastaran Okati	Max Planck Institute for Software Systems, Germany
Tsuyoshi Okita	Kyushu Institute of Technology, Japan
Pablo Olmos	Universidad Carlos III de Madrid, Spain
Luis Antonio Ortega Andrés	Autonomous University of Madrid, Spain
Abdelkader Ouali	Université de Caen Normandie, France
Latifa Oukhellou	IFSTTAR, France
Chun Ouyang	Queensland University of Technology, Australia
Andrei Paleyes	University of Cambridge, UK

Menghai Pan	Visa Research, USA
Shirui Pan	Griffith University, Australia
Apostolos N. Papadopoulos	Aristotle University of Thessaloniki, Greece
Chanyoung Park	KAIST, South Korea
Emilio Parrado-Hernandez	Universidad Carlos III de Madrid, Spain
Vincenzo Pasquadibisceglie	University of Bari, Aldo Moro, Italy
Eliana Pastor	Politecnico di Torino, Italy
Anand Paul	Kyungpook National University, South Korea
Shichao Pei	University of Notre Dame, USA
Yulong Pei	TU Eindhoven, The Netherlands
Leonardo Pellegrina	University of Padua, Italy
Ruggero Pensa	University of Turin, Italy
Fabiola Pereira	UFU, Brazil
Lucas Pereira	ITI/LARSyS - Técnico Lisboa, Portugal
Miquel Perello-Nieto	University of Bristol, UK
Lorenzo Perini	KU Leuven, Belgium
Matej Petkovifá	University of Ljubljana, Slovenia
Lukas Pfahler	TU Dortmund, Germany
Ninh Pham	University of Auckland, New Zealand
Guangyuan Piao	Maynooth University, Ireland
Francesco Piccialli	University of Naples Federico II, Italy
Martin Pilát	Charles University, Czech Republic
Gianvito Pio	University of Bari, Aldo Moro, Italy
Giuseppe Pirrò	Sapienza University of Rome, Italy
Francesco S. Pisani	ICAR-CNR, Italy
Srijith P. K.	IIIT Hyderabad, India
Marc Plantevit	EPITA, France
Mirko Polato	University of Turin, Italy
Axel Polleres	Vienna University of Economics and Business, Austria
Giovanni Ponti	ENEA, Italy
Paul Prasse	University of Potsdam, Germany
Mahardhika Pratama	University of South Australia, Australia
Philippe Preux	Inria, France
Ricardo B. Prudencio	Universidade Federal de Pernambuco, Brazil
Chiara Pugliese	CNR-ISTI, Italy
Erasmo Purificato	Otto-von-Guericke-University Magdeburg, Germany
Abdulhakim Qahtan	Utrecht University, The Netherlands
Lianyong Qi	China University of Petroleum, China
Kun Qian	Amazon Web Services, USA
Tieyun Qian	Wuhan University, China

Chuan Qin	BOSS Zhipin, China
Yumou Qiu	Iowa State University, USA
Dimitrios Rafailidis	University of Thessaly, Greece
Edward Raff	Booz Allen Hamilton, USA
Chang Rajani	University of Helsinki, Finland
Herilalaina Rakotoarison	Inria, France
M. José Ramírez-Quintana	Universitat Politècnica de Valencia, Spain
Jan Ramon	Inria, France
Rajeev Rastogi	Amazon, India
Domenico Redavid	University of Bari, Aldo Moro, Italy
Qianqian Ren	Heilongjiang University, China
Salvatore Rinzivillo	CNR-ISTI, Italy
Matteo Riondato	Amherst College, USA
Giuseppe Rizzo	Niuma, Italy
Marko Robnik-Sikonja	University of Ljubljana, Slovenia
Christophe Rodrigues	Pôle Universitaire Léonard de Vinci, France
Federica Rollo	University of Modena and Reggio Emilia, Italy
Luca Romeo	University of Macerata, Italy
Benjamin Roth	University of Vienna, Austria
Céline Rouveirol	LIPN - Université Sorbonne Paris Nord, France
Salvatore Ruggieri	University of Pisa, Italy
Pietro Sabatino	ICAR-CNR, Italy
Luca Sabbioni	Politecnico di Milano, Italy
Tulika Saha	University of Manchester, UK
Pablo Sanchez Martin	Max Planck Institute for Intelligent Systems, Germany
Parinya Sanguansat	Panyapiwat Institute of Management, Thailand
Shreya Saxena	Quantiphi, India
Yücel Saygin	Sabanci Universitesi, Turkey
Patrick Schäfer	Humboldt-Universität zu Berlin, Germany
Kevin Schewior	University of Southern Denmark, Denmark
Rainer Schlosser	Hasso Plattner Institute, Germany
Johannes Schneider	University of Liechtenstein, Liechtenstein
Matthias Schubert	LMU Munich, Germany
Alexander Schulz	CITEC - Bielefeld University, Germany
Andreas Schwung	Fachhoschschule Südwestfalen, Germany
Raquel Sebastião	IEETA/DETI-UA, Portugal
Pierre Senellart	ENS, PSL University, France
Edoardo Serra	Boise State University, USA
Mattia Setzu	University of Pisa, Italy
Ammar Shaker	NEC Laboratories Europe, Germany
Shubhranshu Shekhar	Carnegie Mellon University, USA

Jiaming Shen	Google Research, USA
Qiang Sheng	Institute of Computing Technology, CAS, China
Bin Shi	Xi'an Jiaotong University, China
Jimeng Shi	Florida International University, USA
Laixi Shi	Carnegie Mellon University, USA
Rongye Shi	Columbia University, USA
Harsh Shrivastava	Microsoft Research, USA
Jonathan A. Silva	Universidade Federal de Mato Grosso do Sul, Brazil
Esther-Lydia Silva-Ramírez	Universidad de Cádiz, Spain
Kuldeep Singh	Cerence, Germany
Moshe Sipper	Ben-Gurion University of the Negev, Israel
Andrzej Skowron	University of Warsaw, Poland
Krzysztof Slot	Lodz University of Technology, Poland
Marek Smieja	Jagiellonian University, Poland
Gavin Smith	University of Nottingham, UK
Carlos Soares	University of Porto, Portugal
Cláudia Soares	NOVA LINCS, Portugal
Andy Song	RMIT University, Australia
Dongjin Song	University of Connecticut, USA
Hao Song	Seldon, UK
Jie Song	Zhejiang University, China
Linxin Song	Waseda University, Japan
Liyan Song	Southern University of Science and Technology, China
Zixing Song	Chinese University of Hong Kong, China
Arnaud Soulet	University of Tours, France
Sucheta Soundarajan	Syracuse University, USA
Francesca Spezzano	Boise State University, USA
Myra Spiliopoulou	Otto-von-Guericke-University Magdeburg, Germany
Janusz Starzyk	WSIZ, Poland
Jerzy Stefanowski	Poznan University of Technology, Poland
Julian Stier	University of Passau, Germany
Michiel Stock	Ghent University, Belgium
Eleni Straitouri	Max Planck Institute for Software Systems, Germany
Łukasz Struski	Jagiellonian University, Poland
Jinyan Su	University of Electronic Science and Technology of China, China
David Q. Sun	Apple, USA
Guangzhong Sun	University of Science and Technology of China, China

Mingxuan Sun	Louisiana State University, USA
Peijie Sun	Tsinghua University, China
Weiwei Sun	Shandong University, China
Xin Sun	TU Munich, Germany
Maryam Tabar	Pennsylvania State University, USA
Anika Tabassum	Virginia Tech, USA
Shazia Tabassum	INESC TEC, Portugal
Andrea Tagarelli	University of Calabria, Italy
Acar Tamersoy	NortonLifeLock Research Group, USA
Chang Wei Tan	Monash University, Australia
Cheng Tan	Zhejiang University/Westlake University, China
Garth Tarr	University of Sydney, Australia
Romain Tavenard	LETG-Rennes/IRISA, France
Maguelonne Teisseire	INRAE - UMR Tetis, France
Evimaria Terzi	Boston University, USA
Stefano Teso	University of Trento, Italy
Surendrabikram Thapa	Virginia Tech, USA
Maximilian Thiessen	TU Vienna, Austria
Steffen Thoma	FZI Research Center for Information Technology, Germany
Simon Tihon	Euranova, Belgium
Kai Ming Ting	Nanjing University, China
Abhisek Tiwari	IIT Patna, India
Gabriele Tolomei	Sapienza University of Rome, Italy
Guangmo Tong	University of Delaware, USA
Sunna Torge	TU Dresden, Germany
Giovanni Trappolini	Sapienza University of Rome, Italy
Volker Tresp	Siemens AG/LMU Munich, Germany
Sofia Triantafillou	University of Crete, Greece
Sebastian Trimpe	RWTH Aachen University, Germany
Sebastian Tschiatschek	University of Vienna, Austria
Athena Vakal	Aristotle University of Thessaloniki, Greece
Peter van der Putten	Leiden University, The Netherlands
Fabio Vandin	University of Padua, Italy
Aparna S. Varde	Montclair State University, USA
Julien Velcin	Université Lumière Lyon 2, France
Bruno Veloso	INESC TEC/University of Porto, Portugal
Rosana Veroneze	LBiC, Brazil
Gennaro Vessio	University of Bari, Aldo Moro, Italy
Tiphaine Viard	Télécom Paris, France
Herna L. Viktor	University of Ottawa, Canada

Joao Vinagre	Joint Research Centre - European Commission, Belgium
Jordi Vitria	Universitat de Barcelona, Spain
Jean-Noël Vittaut	LIP6 - CNRS - Sorbonne Université, France
Marco Viviani	University of Milan-Bicocca, Italy
Paola Vocca	Tor Vergata University of Rome, Italy
Tomasz Walkowiak	Wrocław University of Science and Technology, Poland
Ziwen Wan	University of California, Irvine, USA
Beilun Wang	Southeast University, China
Chuan-Ju Wang	Academia Sinica, Taiwan
Deng-Bao Wang	Southeast University, China
Di Wang	KAUST, Saudi Arabia
Dianhui Wang	La Trobe University, Australia
Hongwei Wang	University of Illinois at Urbana-Champaign, USA
Huandong Wang	Tsinghua University, China
Hui (Wendy) Wang	Stevens Institute of Technology, USA
Jiaqi Wang	Penn State University, USA
Puyu Wang	City University of Hong Kong, China
Qing Wang	Australian National University, Australia
Ruijie Wang	University of Illinois at Urbana-Champaign, USA
Senzhang Wang	Central South University, China
Shuo Wang	University of Birmingham, UK
Suhang Wang	Pennsylvania State University, USA
Wei Wang	Fudan University, China
Wenjie Wang	Shanghai Tech University, China
Yanhao Wang	East China Normal University, China
Yimu Wang	University of Waterloo, Canada
Yue Wang	Microsoft Research, USA
Yue Wang	Waymo, USA
Zhaonan Wang	University of Tokyo, Japan
Zhi Wang	Southwest University, China
Zijie J. Wang	Georgia Tech, USA
Roger Wattenhofer	ETH Zurich, Switzerland
Pascal Weber	University of Vienna, Austria
Jörg Wicker	University of Auckland, New Zealand
Michael Wilbur	Vanderbilt University, USA
Weng-Fai Wong	National University of Singapore, Singapore
Bin Wu	Zhengzhou University, China
Chenwang Wu	University of Science and Technology of China, China

Di Wu	Chongqing Institute of Green and Intelligent Technology, CAS, China
Guoqiang Wu	Shandong University, China
Peng Wu	Shanghai Jiao Tong University, China
Xiaotong Wu	Nanjing Normal University, China
Yongkai Wu	Clemson University, USA
Danyang Xiao	Sun Yat-Sen University, China
Zhiwen Xiao	Southwest Jiaotong University, China
Cheng Xie	Yunnan University, China
Hong Xie	Chongqing Institute of Green and Intelligent Technology, CAS, China
Yaqi Xie	Carnegie Mellon University, USA
Huanlai Xing	Southwest Jiaotong University, China
Ning Xu	Southeast University, China
Xiaolong Xu	Nanjing University of Information Science and Technology, China
Hao Xue	University of New South Wales, Australia
Yexiang Xue	Purdue University, USA
Sangeeta Yadav	Indian Institute of Science, India
Qiao Yan	Shenzhen University, China
Yan Yan	Carleton University, Canada
Yu Yan	People's Public Security University of China, China
Yujun Yan	Dartmouth College, USA
Jie Yang	University of Wollongong, Australia
Shaofu Yang	Southeast University, China
Yang Yang	Nanjing University of Science and Technology, China
Liang Yao	Tencent, China
Muchao Ye	Pennsylvania State University, USA
Michael Yeh	Visa Research, USA
Kalidas Yeturu	Indian Institute of Technology Tirupati, India
Hang Yin	University of Copenhagen, Denmark
Hongwei Yong	Hong Kong Polytechnic University, China
Jaemin Yoo	KAIST, South Korea
Mengbo You	Iwate University, Japan
Hang Yu	Shanghai University, China
Weiren Yu	University of Warwick, UK
Wenjian Yu	Tsinghua University, China
Jidong Yuan	Beijing Jiaotong University, China
Aras Yurtman	KU Leuven, Belgium
Claudius Zelenka	Christian-Albrechts University of Kiel, Germany

Akka Zemmari	University of Bordeaux, France
Bonan Zhang	Princeton University, USA
Chao Zhang	Zhejiang University, China
Chuang Zhang	Nanjing University of Science and Technology, China
Danqing Zhang	Amazon, USA
Guoqiang Zhang	University of Technology, Sydney, Australia
Guoxi Zhang	Kyoto University, Japan
Hao Zhang	Fudan University, China
Junbo Zhang	JD Intelligent Cities Research, China
Le Zhang	Baidu Research, China
Ming Zhang	National Key Laboratory of Science and Technology on Information System Security, China
Qiannan Zhang	KAUST, Saudi Arabia
Tianlin Zhang	University of Manchester, UK
Wenbin Zhang	Michigan Tech, USA
Xiang Zhang	National University of Defense Technology, China
Xiao Zhang	Shandong University, China
Xiaoming Zhang	Beihang University, China
Xinyang Zhang	University of Illinois at Urbana-Champaign, USA
Yaying Zhang	Tongji University, China
Yin Zhang	University of Electronic Science and Technology of China, China
Yongqi Zhang	4Paradigm, China
Zhiwen Zhang	University of Tokyo, Japan
Mia Zhao	Airbnb, USA
Sichen Zhao	RMIT University, Australia
Xiaoting Zhao	Etsy, USA
Tongya Zheng	Zhejiang University, China
Wenhao Zheng	Shopee, Singapore
Yu Zheng	Tsinghua University, China
Yujia Zheng	Carnegie Mellon University, USA
Jiang Zhong	Chongqing University, China
Wei Zhou	School of Cyber Security, CAS, China
Zhengyang Zhou	University of Science and Technology of China, China
Chuang Zhu	Beijing University of Posts and Telecommunications, China
Jing Zhu	University of Michigan, USA
Jinjing Zhu	Hong Kong University of Science and Technology, China

Junxing Zhu	National University of Defense Technology, China
Yanmin Zhu	Shanghai Jiao Tong University, China
Ye Zhu	Deakin University, Australia
Yichen Zhu	Midea Group, China
Zirui Zhuang	Beijing University of Posts and Telecommunications, China
Tommaso Zoppi	University of Florence, Italy
Meiyun Zuo	Renmin University of China, China

Program Committee, Applied Data Science Track

Jussara Almeida	Universidade Federal de Minas Gerais, Brazil
Mozhdeh Ariannezhad	University of Amsterdam, The Netherlands
Renato M. Assuncao	ESRI, USA
Hajer Ayadi	York University, Canada
Ashraf Bah Rabiou	University of Delaware, USA
Amey Barapatre	Microsoft, USA
Patrice Bellot	Aix-Marseille Université - CNRS LSIS, France
Ludovico Boratto	University of Cagliari, Italy
Claudio Borile	CENTAI, Italy
Yi Cai	South China University of Technology, China
Lei Cao	University of Arizona/MIT, USA
Shilei Cao	Tencent, China
Yang Cao	Hokkaido University, Japan
Aniket Chakrabarti	Amazon, USA
Chaochao Chen	Zhejiang University, China
Chung-Chi Chen	National Taiwan University, Taiwan
Meng Chen	Shandong University, China
Ruey-Cheng Chen	Canva, Australia
Tong Chen	University of Queensland, Australia
Yi Chen	NJIT, USA
Zhiyu Chen	Amazon, USA
Wei Cheng	NEC Laboratories America, USA
Lingyang Chu	McMaster University, Canada
Xiaokai Chu	Tencent, China
Zhendong Chu	University of Virginia, USA
Federico Cinus	Sapienza University of Rome/CENTAI, Italy
Francisco Claude-Faust	LinkedIn, USA
Gabriele D'Acunto	Sapienza University of Rome, Italy
Ariyam Das	Google, USA

Jingtao Ding	Tsinghua University, China
Kaize Ding	Arizona State University, USA
Manqing Dong	eBay, Australia
Yushun Dong	University of Virginia, USA
Yingtong Dou	University of Illinois, Chicago, USA
Yixiang Fang	Chinese University of Hong Kong, China
Kaiyu Feng	Beijing Institute of Technology, China
Dayne Freitag	SRI International, USA
Yanjie Fu	University of Central Florida, USA
Matteo Gabburo	University of Trento, Italy
Sabrina Gaito	University of Milan, Italy
Chen Gao	Tsinghua University, China
Liangcai Gao	Peking University, China
Yunjun Gao	Zhejiang University, China
Lluis Garcia-Pueyo	Meta, USA
Mariana-Iuliana Georgescu	University of Bucharest, Romania
Aakash Goel	Amazon, USA
Marcos Goncalves	Universidade Federal de Minas Gerais, Brazil
Francesco Guerra	University of Modena e Reggio Emilia, Italy
Huifeng Guo	Huawei Noah's Ark Lab, China
Ruocheng Guo	ByteDance, China
Zhen Hai	Alibaba DAMO Academy, China
Eui-Hong (Sam) Han	The Washington Post, USA
Jinyoung Han	Sungkyunkwan University, South Korea
Shuchu Han	Stellar Cyber, USA
Dongxiao He	Tianjin University, China
Junyuan Hong	Michigan State University, USA
Yupeng Hou	UC San Diego, USA
Binbin Hu	Ant Group, China
Jun Hu	National University of Singapore, Singapore
Hong Huang	Huazhong University of Science and Technology, China
Xin Huang	Hong Kong Baptist University, China
Yizheng Huang	York University, Canada
Yu Huang	University of Florida, USA
Stratis Ioannidis	Northeastern University, USA
Radu Tudor Ionescu	University of Bucharest, Romania
Murium Iqbal	Etsy, USA
Shoaib Jameel	University of Southampton, UK
Jian Kang	University of Rochester, USA
Pinar Karagoz	METU, Turkey
Praveen C. Kolli	Carnegie Mellon University, USA

Deguang Kong	Yahoo Research, USA
Adit Krishnan	University of Illinois at Urbana-Champaign, USA
Mayank Kulkarni	Amazon, USA
Susana Ladra	University of A Coruña, Spain
Renaud Lambiotte	University of Oxford, UK
Tommaso Lanciano	KTH Royal Institute of Technology, Sweden
Md Tahmid Rahman Laskar	Dialpad, Canada
Matthieu Latapy	CNRS, France
Noah Lee	Meta, USA
Wang-Chien Lee	Pennsylvania State University, USA
Chang Li	Apple, USA
Chaozhuo Li	Microsoft Research Asia, China
Daifeng Li	Sun Yat-Sen University, China
Lei Li	Hong Kong University of Science and Technology, China
Shuai Li	University of Cambridge, UK
Xiang Lian	Kent State University, USA
Zhaohui Liang	National Library of Medicine, NIH, USA
Bang Liu	University of Montreal, Canada
Ji Liu	Baidu Research, China
Jingjing Liu	MD Anderson Cancer Center, USA
Tingwen Liu	Institute of Information Engineering, CAS, China
Weiwen Liu	Huawei Noah's Ark Lab, China
Andreas Lommatzsch	TU Berlin, Germany
Jiyun Luo	Pinterest, USA
Ping Luo	CAS, China
Xin Luo	Shandong University, China
Jing Ma	University of Virginia, USA
Xian-Ling Mao	Beijing Institute of Technology, China
Mirko Marras	University of Cagliari, Italy
Zoltan Miklos	Université de Rennes 1, France
Ahmed K. Mohamed	Meta, USA
Mukesh Mohania	IIIT Delhi, India
Corrado Monti	CENTAI, Italy
Sushant More	Amazon, USA
Jose G. Moreno	University of Toulouse, France
Aayush Mudgal	Pinterest, USA
Sepideh Nahali	York University, Canada
Wolfgang Nejdl	L3S Research Center, Germany
Yifan Nie	University of Montreal, Canada
Di Niu	University of Alberta, Canada
Symeon Papadopoulos	CERTH/ITI, Greece

Manos Papagelis	York University, Canada
Leonardo Pellegrina	University of Padua, Italy
Claudia Perlich	TwoSigma, USA
Fabio Pinelli	IMT Lucca, Italy
Giulia Preti	CENTAI, Italy
Buyue Qian	Xi'an Jiaotong University, China
Chuan Qin	BOSS Zhipin, China
Xiao Qin	Amazon Web Services AI/ML, USA
Yanghui Rao	Sun Yat-Sen University, China
Yusuf Sale	LMU Munich, Germany
Eric Sanjuan	Avignon University, France
Maria Luisa Sapino	University of Turin, Italy
Emmanouil Schinas	CERTH/ITI, Greece
Nasrullah Sheikh	IBM Research, USA
Yue Shi	Meta, USA
Gianmaria Silvello	University of Padua, Italy
Yang Song	Apple, USA
Francesca Spezzano	Boise State University, USA
Efstathios Stamatatos	University of the Aegean, Greece
Kostas Stefanidis	Tampere University, Finland
Ting Su	Imperial College London, UK
Munira Syed	Procter & Gamble, USA
Liang Tang	Google, USA
Ruiming Tang	Huawei Noah's Ark Lab, China
Junichi Tatemura	Google, USA
Mingfei Teng	Amazon, USA
Sofia Tolmach	Amazon, Israel
Ismail Hakki Toroslu	METU, Turkey
Kazutoshi Umemoto	University of Tokyo, Japan
Yao Wan	Huazhong University of Science and Technology, China
Chang-Dong Wang	Sun Yat-Sen University, China
Chong Wang	Amazon, USA
Chuan-Ju Wang	Academia Sinica, Taiwan
Hongzhi Wang	Harbin Institute of Technology, China
Kai Wang	Shanghai Jiao Tong University, China
Ning Wang	Beijing Jiaotong University, China
Pengyuan Wang	University of Georgia, USA
Senzhang Wang	Central South University, China
Sheng Wang	Wuhan University, China
Shoujin Wang	Macquarie University, Australia
Wentao Wang	Michigan State University, USA

Yang Wang	University of Science and Technology of China, China
Zhihong Wang	Tsinghua University, China
Zihan Wang	Shandong University, China
Shi-ting Wen	Ningbo Tech University, China
Song Wen	Rutgers University, USA
Zeyi Wen	Hong Kong University of Science and Technology, China
Fangzhao Wu	Microsoft Research Asia, China
Jun Wu	University of Illinois at Urbana-Champaign, USA
Wentao Wu	Microsoft Research, USA
Yanghua Xiao	Fudan University, China
Haoyi Xiong	Baidu, China
Dongkuan Xu	North Carolina State University, USA
Guandong Xu	University of Technology, Sydney, Australia
Shan Xue	Macquarie University, Australia
Le Yan	Google, USA
De-Nian Yang	Academia Sinica, Taiwan
Fan Yang	Rice University, USA
Yu Yang	City University of Hong Kong, China
Fanghua Ye	University College London, UK
Jianhua Yin	Shandong University, China
Yifang Yin	A*STAR-I2R, Singapore
Changlong Yu	Hong Kong University of Science and Technology, China
Dongxiao Yu	Shandong University, China
Ye Yuan	Beijing Institute of Technology, China
Daochen Zha	Rice University, USA
Feng Zhang	Renmin University of China, China
Mengxuan Zhang	University of North Texas, USA
Xianli Zhang	Xi'an Jiaotong University, China
Xuyun Zhang	Macquarie University, Australia
Chen Zhao	Baylor University, USA
Di Zhao	University of Auckland, New Zealand
Yanchang Zhao	CSIRO, Australia
Kaiping Zheng	National University of Singapore, Singapore
Yong Zheng	Illinois Institute of Technology, USA
Jingbo Zhou	Baidu, China
Ming Zhou	University of Technology, Sydney, Australia
Qinghai Zhou	University of Illinois at Urbana-Champaign, USA
Tian Zhou	Alibaba DAMO Academy, China
Xinyi Zhou	University of Washington, USA

Yucheng Zhou	University of Macau, China
Jiangang Zhu	ByteDance, China
Yongchun Zhu	CAS, China
Ziwei Zhu	George Mason University, USA
Jia Zou	Arizona State University, USA

Program Committee, Demo Track

Ferran Diego	Telefonica Research, Spain
Jan Florjanczyk	Netflix, USA
Mikko Heikkila	Telefonica Research, Spain
Jesus Omaña Iglesias	Telefonica Research, Spain
Nicolas Kourtellis	Telefonica Research, Spain
Eduard Marin	Telefonica Research, Spain
Souneil Park	Telefonica Research, Spain
Aravindh Raman	Telefonica Research, Spain
Ashish Rastogi	Netflix, USA
Natali Ruchansky	Netflix, USA
David Solans	Telefonica Research, Spain

Sponsors

AFC DIGITAL HUB

Platinum

ASML

ThermoFisher SCIENTIFIC

VOLKSWAGEN GROUP

Gold

Silver

Bronze

PhD Forum Sponsor

Publishing Partner

Invited Talks Abstracts

Neural Wave Representations

Max Welling

University of Amsterdam, The Netherlands

Abstract. Good neural architectures are rooted in good inductive biases (a.k.a. priors). Equivariance under symmetries is a prime example of a successful physics-inspired prior which sometimes dramatically reduces the number of examples needed to learn predictive models. In this work, we tried to extend this thinking to more flexible priors in the hidden variables of a neural network. In particular, we imposed wavelike dynamics in hidden variables under transformations of the inputs, which relaxes the stricter notion of equivariance. We find that under certain conditions, wavelike dynamics naturally arises in these hidden representations. We formalize this idea in a VAE-over-time architecture where the hidden dynamics is described by a Fokker-Planck (a.k.a. drift-diffusion) equation. This in turn leads to a new definition of a disentangled hidden representation of input states that can easily be manipulated to undergo transformations. I also discussed very preliminary work on how the Schrödinger equation can also be used to move information in the hidden representations.

Biography. Prof. Dr. Max Welling is a research chair in Machine Learning at the University of Amsterdam and a Distinguished Scientist at MSR. He is a fellow at the Canadian Institute for Advanced Research (CIFAR) and the European Lab for Learning and Intelligent Systems (ELLIS) where he also serves on the founding board. His previous appointments include VP at Qualcomm Technologies, professor at UC Irvine, postdoc at the University of Toronto and UCL under the supervision of Prof. Geoffrey Hinton, and postdoc at Caltech under the supervision of Prof. Pietro Perona. He finished his PhD in theoretical high energy physics under the supervision of Nobel laureate Prof. Gerard 't Hooft. Max Welling served as associate editor-in-chief of IEEE TPAMI from 2011–2015, he has served on the advisory board of the NeurIPS Foundation since 2015 and was program chair and general chair of NeurIPS in 2013 and 2014 respectively. He was also program chair of AISTATS in 2009 and ECCV in 2016 and general chair of MIDL in 2018. Max Welling was a recipient of the ECCV Koenderink Prize in 2010 and the ICML Test of Time Award in 2021. He directs the Amsterdam Machine Learning Lab (AMLAB) and co-directs the Qualcomm-UvA deep learning lab (QUVA) and the Bosch-UvA Deep Learning lab (DELTA).

Physics-Inspired Graph Neural Networks

Michael Bronstein

University of Oxford, UK

Abstract. The message-passing paradigm has been the "battle horse" of deep learning on graphs for several years, making graph neural networks a big success in a wide range of applications, from particle physics to protein design. From a theoretical viewpoint, it established the link to the Weisfeiler-Lehman hierarchy, allowing us to analyse the expressive power of GNNs. We argue that the very "node-and-edge"-centric mindset of current graph deep learning schemes may hinder future progress in the field. As an alternative, we propose physics-inspired "continuous" learning models that open up a new trove of tools from the fields of differential geometry, algebraic topology, and differential equations so far largely unexplored in graph ML.

Biography. Michael Bronstein is the DeepMind Professor of AI at the University of Oxford. He was previously a professor at Imperial College London and held visiting appointments at Stanford, MIT, and Harvard, and has also been affiliated with three Institutes for Advanced Study (at TUM as a Rudolf Diesel Fellow (2017–2019), at Harvard as a Radcliffe fellow (2017–2018), and at Princeton as a short-time scholar (2020)). Michael received his PhD from the Technion in 2007. He is the recipient of the Royal Society Wolfson Research Merit Award, Royal Academy of Engineering Silver Medal, five ERC grants, two Google Faculty Research Awards, and two Amazon AWS ML Research Awards. He is a Member of the Academia Europaea, Fellow of the IEEE, IAPR, BCS, and ELLIS, ACM Distinguished Speaker, and World Economic Forum Young Scientist. In addition to his academic career, Michael is a serial entrepreneur and founder of multiple startup companies, including Novafora, Invision (acquired by Intel in 2012), Videocites, and Fabula AI (acquired by Twitter in 2019).

Mapping Generative AI

Kate Crawford

USC Annenberg, USA

Abstract. Training data is foundational to generative AI systems. From Common Crawl's 3.1 billion web pages to LAION-5B's corpus of almost 6 billion image-text pairs, these vast collections – scraped from the internet and treated as "ground truth" – play a critical role in shaping the epistemic boundaries that govern generative AI models. Yet training data is beset with complex social, political, and epistemological challenges. What happens when data is stripped of context, meaning, and provenance? How does training data limit what and how machine learning systems interpret the world? What are the copyright implications of these datasets? And most importantly, what forms of power do these approaches enhance and enable? This keynote is an invitation to reflect on the epistemic foundations of generative AI, and to consider the wide-ranging impacts of the current generative turn.

Biography. Professor Kate Crawford is a leading international scholar of the social implications of artificial intelligence. She is a Research Professor at USC Annenberg in Los Angeles, a Senior Principal Researcher at MSR in New York, an Honorary Professor at the University of Sydney, and the inaugural Visiting Chair for AI and Justice at the École Normale Supérieure in Paris. Her latest book, *Atlas of AI* (Yale, 2021) won the Sally Hacker Prize from the Society for the History of Technology, the ASIS&T Best Information Science Book Award, and was named one of the best books in 2021 by *New Scientist* and the *Financial Times*. Over her twenty-year research career, she has also produced groundbreaking creative collaborations and visual investigations. Her project *Anatomy of an AI System* with Vladan Joler is in the permanent collection of the Museum of Modern Art in New York and the V&A in London, and was awarded with the Design of the Year Award in 2019 and included in the Design of the Decades by the Design Museum of London. Her collaboration with the artist Trevor Paglen, *Excavating AI*, won the Ayrton Prize from the British Society for the History of Science. She has advised policymakers in the United Nations, the White House, and the European Parliament, and she currently leads the Knowing Machines Project, an international research collaboration that investigates the foundations of machine learning.

Contents – Part II

Computer Vision

Sample Prior Guided Robust Model Learning to Suppress Noisy Labels

Wenkai Chen, Chuang Zhu(✉), and Mengting Li

School of Artificial Intelligence, Beijing University of Posts and Telecommunications, Beijing, China
{wkchen,czhu,mtli}@bupt.edu.com

Abstract. Imperfect labels are ubiquitous in real-world datasets and seriously harm the model performance. Several recent effective methods for handling noisy labels have two key steps: 1) dividing samples into cleanly labeled and wrongly labeled sets by training loss, 2) using semi-supervised methods to generate pseudo-labels for samples in the wrongly labeled set. However, current methods always hurt the informative hard samples due to the similar loss distribution between the hard samples and the noisy ones. In this paper, we proposed PGDF (Prior Guided Denoising Framework), a novel framework to learn a deep model to suppress noisy label by using the training history to generate the sample prior knowledge, which is integrated into both sample dividing step and semi-supervised step. Our framework can save more informative hard clean samples into the cleanly labeled set. Besides, our framework also promotes the quality of pseudo-labels during the semi-supervised step by suppressing the noise in the current pseudo-labels generating scheme. To further enhance the hard samples, we reweight the samples in the cleanly labeled set during training. We evaluated our method using synthetic datasets based on CIFAR-10 and CIFAR-100, as well as on the real-world datasets WebVision and Clothing1M. The results demonstrate substantial improvements over state-of-the-art methods. The code is available at https://github.com/bupt-ai-cz/PGDF.

Keywords: Noisy label · Hard sample · Semi-supervised learning · Pseudo-label

1 Introduction

Deep learning techniques, such as convolutional neural networks (CNNs), have recently achieved great success in object recognition [20], image classification [15], and natural language processing (NLP) [39]. Most existing CNN deep models mainly rely on collecting large scale labeled datasets, such as ImageNet [24]. However, it is very expensive and difficult to collect a large scale dataset with clean labels [38]. Moreover, in the real world, noisy labels are often inevitable in manual annotation [27]. Therefore, research on designing robust algorithms with noisy labels is of great significance [33].

© The Author(s), under exclusive license to Springer Nature Switzerland AG 2023
D. Koutra et al. (Eds.): ECML PKDD 2023, LNAI 14170, pp. 3–19, 2023.
https://doi.org/10.1007/978-3-031-43415-0_1

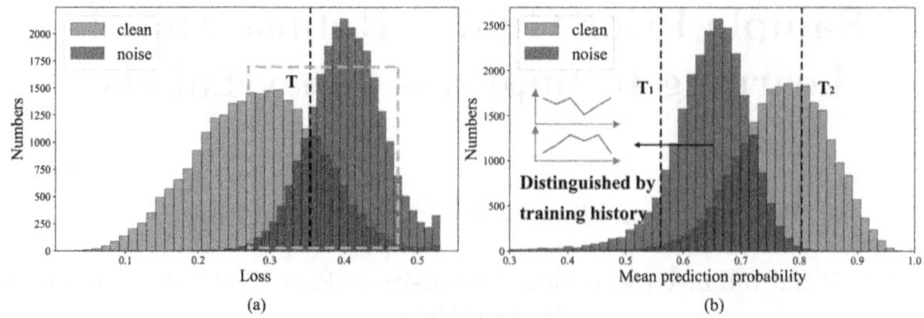

Fig. 1. (a) Loss distribution of the clean and noise samples in CIFAR-100 with 50% symmetric noise ratio, samples in the yellow dotted box are indistinguishable by training loss. (b) Mean prediction probability distribution of the clean and noisy samples in CIFAR-100 with 50% symmetric noise ratio, we used training history to distinguish the clean/noisy samples between threshold T_1 and T_2. (Color figure online)

In the literature, a lot of approaches were proposed to improve the learning performance with label noise, such as estimating the noise transition matrix [8,22], designing noise-robust loss functions [7,19,37], designing noise-robust regularization [18,29], sample selection [4,9], and semi-supervised learning [6,16]. Recently, methods of semi-supervised learning achieve the state-of-the-art performance. They always first divide samples into cleanly labeled and wrongly labeled sets by training loss, and then use semi-supervised methods to generate pseudo-labels for samples in the wrongly labeled set. Since the noisy samples tend to have larger training loss than the clean one, the sample dividing step is generally based on the small-loss strategy [40]. At each epoch, samples with small loss are classified as clean data, and large loss as noise. However, the above methods fail in distinguishing informative hard samples from noisy ones due to their similar loss distributions (as depicted in Fig. 1(a), samples in the yellow dotted box are indistinguishable), and thus may neglect the important information of the hard samples [36]. To the best of our knowledge, there are very few works studying hard samples under noisy label scenarios. Work [32] mentioned the hard samples in learning with noisy labels, but that work did not explicitly identify hard samples. Work [2] proposed an approach which alternatively optimized the classifier and updated the training sample to rescue hard samples. However, this approach still only uses the information of training loss and those hard samples that cannot be distinguished by training loss are seriously injured.

Although the hard samples and noisy samples cannot be directly distinguished by training loss, we observed that they have different behaviors in training history, and our previous work [46] conducted some preliminary research on this in medical images. Through this intuition, based on a popular semi-supervised denoising framework "DivideMix", we propose PGDF (Prior Guided Denoising Framework), a novel framework to learn a deep model to suppress noise while avoid the misinjury of hard clean samples. We first use the training history to distinguish the hard samples from the noisy ones (as depicted in Fig. 1(b), samples between two thresholds are distinguished by training history).

Thus, we classify the samples into an easy set, a hard set, and a noisy set by using the prior knowledge. The divided dataset is then guiding the subsequent training process. Our key findings and contributions are summarized as follows:

- Hard samples and noisy samples can be recognized using training history. We first propose a Prior Generation Module, which generates the prior knowledge to pre-classify the samples into an easy set, a hard set, and a noisy set. Compared to the existing sample dividing scheme (small-loss strategy), ours can save more informative hard clean samples. We further optimize the pre-classification result at each epoch with adaptive sample attribution obtained by Gaussian Mixture Model.
- We realize robust noisy labels suppression based on the divided sets. On one hand, we generate high-quality pseudo-labels with the help of the estimated pseudo-label distribution transition matrix. On the other hand, we further safely enhance the informative samples in the hard set, while previous existing noisy labels processing methods cannot achieve this because they fail to distinguish the hard samples and noisy ones.
- We experimentally show that our PGDF significantly advances state-of-the-art results on multiple benchmarks with different types and levels of label noise. We also provide the ablation study to examine the effect of different components.

2 Related Work

In this section we describe existing works on learning with noisy labels. Typically, the noisy-label processing algorithms can be classified into five categories by exploring different strategies: estimating the noise transition matrix [8,22], designing noise-robust loss functions [7,19,37,44,45], adding noise-robust regularization [18,29], selecting sample subset [4,9,12], and semi-supervised learning [6,16].

In the first category, different transition matrix estimation methods were proposed in [8,22], such as using additional softmax layer [8], and two-step estimating scheme [22]. However, these transition matrix estimations fail in real-world datasets where the utilized prior assumption is no longer valid [10]. Being free of transition matrix estimation, the second category targets at designing loss functions that have more noise-tolerant power. Work in [7] adopted mean absolute error (MAE) which demonstrates more noise-robust ability than cross-entropy loss. The authors in work [37] proposed determinant-based mutual information loss which can be applied to any existing classification neural networks regardless of the noise pattern. Recently, work [45] proposed a novel strategy to restrict the model output and thus made any loss robust to noisy labels. Nevertheless, it has been reported that performances with such losses are significantly affected by noisy labels [23]. Such implementations perform well only in simple cases where learning is easy or the number of classes is small. For designing noise-robust regularization, work in [29] assumed the existence of multiple annotators and introduced a regularized EM-based approach to model the label transition probability. In work [18], a regularization term was proposed to implicitly prevent memorization of the false labels.

Most recent successful sample selection strategies in the fourth category conducted noisy label processing by selecting clean samples through "small-loss" strategy. Work [13] pre-trained an extra network, and then used the extra network for selecting clean instances to guide the training. The authors in work [9] proposed a Co-teaching scheme with two models, where each model selected a certain number of small-loss samples and fed them to its peer model for further training. Based on this scheme, work [4] tried to improve the performance by proposing an Iterative Noisy Cross-Validation (INCV) method. Work [12] adjusted the hyper-parameters of model to make its status transfer from overfitting to underfitting cyclically, and recorded the history of sample training loss to select clean samples. This family of methods effectively avoids the risk of false correction by simply excluding unreliable samples. However, they may eliminate numerous useful samples. To solve this shortcoming, the methods of the fifth category based on semi-supervised learning treated the noisy samples as unlabeled samples, and used the outputs of classification models as pseudo-labels for subsequent loss calculations. The authors in [16] proposed DivideMix, which relied on MixMatch [3] to linearly combine training samples classified as clean or noisy. Work [6] designed a two-stage method called LongReMix, which first found the high confidence samples and then used the high confidence samples to update the predicted clean set and trained the model. Recently, work [21] used different data augmentation strategies in different steps to improve the performance of DivideMix, and work [43] used a self-supervised pre-training method to improve the performance of DivideMix.

The above sample selection strategy and semi-supervised learning strategy both select the samples with clean labels for the subsequent training process. All of their selecting strategies are based on the training loss because the clean samples tend to have small loss during training. However, they will hurt the informative hard samples due to the similar loss distribution between the hard samples and the noisy ones. Our work strives to reconcile this gap by distinguishing the hard samples from the noisy ones by introducing a sample prior knowledge generated by training history.

3 Method

The overview of our proposed PGDF is shown in Fig. 2. The first stage (Prior Guided Sample Dividing) of PGDF is dividing the samples into an easy set, a hard set, and a noisy set. The Prior Generation Module first pre-classifies the samples into three sets as prior knowledge; then, at each epoch, the pre-classification result is optimized by the Gaussian Mixture Model (Sample Dividing Optimization). With the divided sets, the second stage (Denoising with the Divided Sets) conducts label correction for samples with the help of the estimated distribution transition matrix (Pseudo-labels Refining), and then the hard

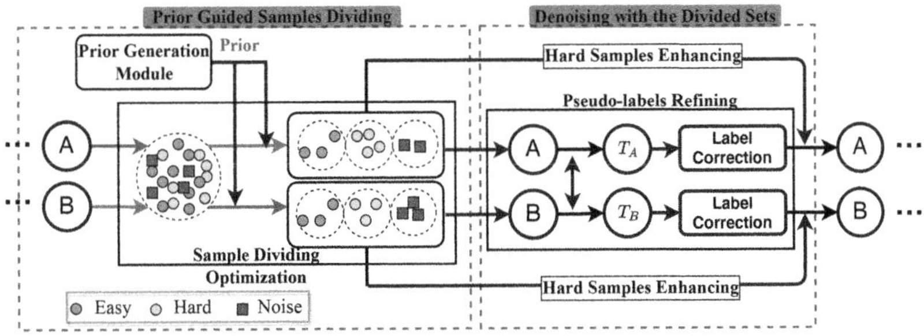

Fig. 2. PGDF first generates the prior knowledge by the Prior Generation Module. Then, it trains two models (A and B) simultaneously. At each epoch, a model divides the original dataset into an easy set, a hard set, and a noisy set by combining the prior knowledge and the loss value of each sample. The divided dataset is used by the other network. After the first stage, the models conduct label correction for samples with the help of the estimated distribution transition matrix. Finally, the training loss is reweighted by the dividing result to further enhance the hard samples.

samples are further enhanced (Hard Samples Enhancing). The details of each component are described in the following.

3.1 Prior Guided Sample Dividing

Prior Generation Module. Many previous work methods use the "small-loss" strategy to detect noisy samples, where at each epoch, samples with small loss are classified as clean data and large loss as noise. Sample with small loss means the prediction probability of the model output is closer to the supervising label. We directly used the normalized probability for analysis since the loss value is just calculated by the normalized probability and the ground truth label. We first train a CNN classification model with the data, and record the probability history of the model output for each sample on the class of its corresponding label. Then, we calculate the mean prediction probability value of the sample training history which is shown in Fig. 1(b). The figure shows the clean sample tends to have a higher mean prediction probability than the noisy one. Therefore, we can set two thresholds (such as the black dotted lines in Fig. 1(b)). Samples with mean prediction probability lower than T_1 are almost noisy, while higher than T_2 are almost clean. However, we still cannot distinguish the samples with mean prediction probability between two thresholds. We define this part of clean data as hard samples in our work.

In order to distinguish the hard samples from the noisy ones, we construct the Prior Generation Module based on the prediction history of the training samples, as depicted by Fig. 3. For the training set D with N samples, we gradually obtain the corresponding N prediction probability maps through the training of a CNN classification model for k epochs. This module first selects easy samples D_e and part of noisy samples D_{n1} by using the mean prediction probability values. Then we manually add noise to the D_e as D_a and record whether the sample is noise

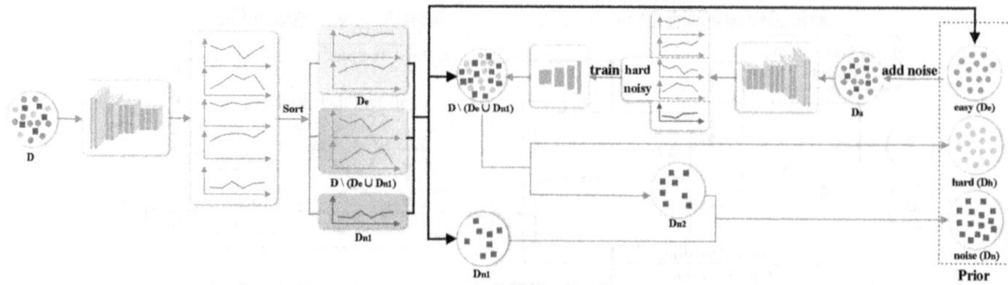

Fig. 3. The overview of the Prior Generation Module. It takes training history as input and pre-classifies the samples into an easy set, a hard set, and a noisy set.

or not. The noise ratio of the adding noise is the same as the original dataset, which can be known or estimated by the noise cross-validation algorithm of work [4]. After that, we train the same classification model by using D_a and record training history again. Then we discard the "easy samples" and part of "noisy samples" of D_a according to mean prediction probability, and utilize the rest samples as training data to train the classifier. We use a simple one dimension CNN which contains 3 one dimension convolution layers and a fully connected layer as the classifier here. So far, we will obtain a classifier that takes the prediction probability map of training history as input, and output whether it is a hard sample or a noisy one. Finally, we put the samples in $D \setminus (D_e \cup D_{n1})$ into the classifier to get the hard sample set D_h and a part of the noisy set D_{n2}, and we combine D_{n1} and D_{n2} as the noisy set D_n. Algorithm 1 shows the details of this module.

Algorithm 1. Prior Generation Module.

Input: $D = [d_1, d_2, ..., d_n]$, d_i is input image, label $Y = [y_1, y_2, ..., y_n]$, y_i is label for d_i, easy samples ratio τ_e, part of noisy samples ratio τ_{n1}

Output: easy set D_e, hard set D_h, noise set D_n

1: Train classification model M_c by using D and Y, record training history $H = [h_1, h_2, ..., h_n]$, where h_i is a vector with shape of $1 * k(epoch)$

2: Calculate the mean value of H as H_m, $H_m = [mean(h_1), mean(h_2), ..., mean(h_n)]$, sort D descending by H_m, select easy samples $D_e = D[0 : len(D) * \tau_e]$, select part of noisy samples $D_{n1} = D[len(D) * (1 - \tau_{n1}) : len(D)]$

3: Add noise to D_e as D_a, get noisy label Y_n and record whether it is noise or not $R = [r_1, r_2, ..., r_n]$

4: Retrain M_c by D_a and Y_n, record training history H_n

5: Sort H_n descending by mean, select training history $H'_n = H_n[len(H_n) * \tau_e : len(H_n) * (1 - \tau_{n1})]$

6: Train classifier M_m by using H'_n and R

7: Put the samples in $D \setminus (D_e \cup D_{n1})$ into M_m and get D_h and D_{n2}

8: $D_n = D_{n1} \cup D_{n2}$

9: **return** D_e, D_h, D_n

Sample Dividing Optimization. Considering the online training loss at each epoch is also important information to help sample dividing, we apply this information to optimize the pre-classification result. Specifically, as shown in Fig. 2, at each epoch, we get the clean probability w_{it} of each sample from training loss by using Gaussian Mixture Model (GMM) following previous work [16]. And we have already got the prior knowledge of each sample, we set the clean probability of prior knowledge as w_{ip} from Eq. (1),

$$w_{ip} = \begin{cases} 1, & d_i \in D_e \\ p_h, & d_i \in D_h \\ 1-p_n, & d_i \in D_{n_2} \\ 0, & d_i \in D_{n_1} \end{cases}, \tag{1}$$

where p_h is the classifier (M_m) prediction probability for d_i to be hard sample and p_n is the classifier prediction probability for d_i to be noisy sample. Then, we combine w_{it} and w_{ip} to get the clean probability w_i by Eq. (2),

$$w_i = \begin{cases} 1, & d_i \in D_e \\ m w_{it} + (1-m) w_{ip}, & d_i \in D_h \cup D_n \end{cases}, \tag{2}$$

where m is a hyper-parameter. Finally, we divide samples with w_i equal to 1 into the easy set $\tilde{D_e}$, the samples with $0.5 < w_i < 1$ are divided into the hard set $\tilde{D_h}$, and the rest samples are divided into the noisy set $\tilde{D_n}$. Each network divides the original dataset for the other network to use to avoid confirmation bias of self-training similar to previous works [4,9,16].

3.2 Denoising with the Divided Sets

Pseudo-labels Refining. After the sample dividing phase, we combine the outputs of the two models to generate the pseudo-labels P to conduct label correction, similar to "co-guessing" in DivideMix [16]. Considering the samples in the easy set are highly reliable, we can use this part of data to estimate the distribution difference between pseudo-label and the ground truth, which can then be used to refine the pseudo-labels. Given the ground truth label Y, we use a square matrix T to denote the differences between ground truth label distribution $\hat{Y}$ and pseudo-label distribution $\hat{P}$, thus $\hat{P} = \hat{Y}T$ and $\hat{Y} = \hat{P}T^{-1}$.

Specifically, we use the easy set $\tilde{D_e}$ and its label $Y_{\tilde{D_e}}$ to estimate the T to refine P. We first pass the easy set $\tilde{D_e}$ to the model and get $P_{\tilde{D_e}}$, where $P_{\tilde{D_e}}$ denotes the model outputs of $\tilde{D_e}$. Then we obtain T, of which the element $T_{i,j}$ can be calculated by Eq. (3),

$$T_{i,j} = \frac{1}{|N_i|} \sum_{n \in N_i} p_j^n, \tag{3}$$

where N_i consists of samples with the same label of class i in D_e, $|N_i|$ is the sample number of N_i, p_j^n is the model output softmax probability for class j of the sample n. After that, we refine the pseudo-labels P by Eq. (4),

$$\tilde{P} = PT^{-1}, \tag{4}$$

where $\tilde{P}$ is the refined pseudo-labels. Because $\tilde{P}$ may contain negative values, we first utilize Eq. (5) to enable the non-negative matrix, and then perform normalization along the row direction by Eq. (6) to ensure the summation of elements in each pseudo-label probability vector equal to 1.

$$\tilde{P} = \max\left(\tilde{P}, 0\right). \tag{5}$$

$$\tilde{P}_{ij} = \tilde{P}_{ij} / \sum_{j} \tilde{P}_{ij}. \tag{6}$$

Finally, the labels of samples in noisy set $\tilde{D_n}$ are replaced by the refined pseudo-labels $\tilde{P}$. And the label of sample i in hard set $\tilde{D_h}$ is replaced by the combination of the refined pseudo-label p_i in $\tilde{P}$ and original label y_i in Y as Eq. (7), where w_i is the clean probability of sample i.

$$y_i = w_i y_i + (1 - w_i) p_i. \tag{7}$$

Hard Sample Enhancing. After generating the pseudo-labels, the samples in easy set and hard set are grouped in labeled set $\hat{\mathcal{X}}$, and the noisy set is considered as unlabeled set $\hat{\mathcal{U}}$. We followed MixMatch [3] to "mix" the data, where each sample is randomly interpolated with another sample to generate mixed input x and label p. MixMatch transforms $\hat{\mathcal{X}}$ and $\hat{\mathcal{U}}$ to $\mathcal{X}'$ and $\mathcal{U}'$. To further enhance the informative hard samples, the loss on $\mathcal{X}'$ is reweighted by w_i as shown in Eq. (8), where r is a hyper-parameter. Similar to DivideMix [16], the loss on $\mathcal{U}'$ is the mean squared error as shown in Eq. (9), and the regularization term is shown in Eq. (10).

$$\mathcal{L}_{\mathcal{X}} = -\frac{1}{|\mathcal{X}'|} \sum_{x_i \in \mathcal{X}'} \frac{1}{w_i^r} \sum_c p_c \log\left(\mathrm{p}_{\mathrm{model}}^{\mathrm{c}}(x_i; \theta)\right). \tag{8}$$

$$\mathcal{L}_{\mathcal{U}} = \frac{1}{|\mathcal{U}'|} \sum_{x_i \in \mathcal{U}'} \|p - \mathrm{p}_{\mathrm{model}}(x_i; \theta)\|_2^2. \tag{9}$$

$$\mathcal{L}_{\mathrm{reg}} = \sum_c \pi_c \log\left(\pi_c / \frac{1}{|\mathcal{X}'| + |\mathcal{U}'|} \sum_{x_i \in \mathcal{X}' + \mathcal{U}'} \mathrm{p}_{\mathrm{model}}^{\mathrm{c}}(x_i; \theta)\right). \tag{10}$$

Finally the total loss is defined in Eq. (11). λ_u and λ_r follow the same settings in DivideMix.

$$\mathcal{L} = \mathcal{L}_{\mathcal{X}} + \lambda_u \mathcal{L}_{\mathcal{U}} + \lambda_r \mathcal{L}_{\mathrm{reg}}. \tag{11}$$

4 Experiment

4.1 Datasets and Implementation Details

We compare our PGDF with related approaches on four benchmark datasets, namely CIFAR-10 [14], CIFAR-100 [14], WebVision [34], and Clothing1M [31].

Both CIFAR-10 and CIFAR-100 have 50000 training and 10000 testing images of size 32 × 32 pixels. CIFAR-10 contains 10 classes and CIFAR-100 contains 100 classes for classification. As CIFAR-10 and CIFAR-100 datasets originally do not contain label noise, following previous works [16,21], we experiment with two types of label noise: symmetric and asymmetric. Symmetric noise is generated by randomly replacing the labels for a percentage of the training data with all possible labels, and asymmetric noise is designed to mimic the structure of real-world label noise, where labels are only replaced by similar classes (e.g. deer→horse, dog↔cat) [16]. WebVision contains 2.4 million images in 1000 classes. Since the dataset is quite large, for quick experiments, we follow the previous works [4,16,35] and only use the first 50 classes of the Google image subset. Its noise level is estimated at 20% [26]. Clothing1M is a real-world dataset that consists of 1 million training images acquired from online shopping websites and it is composed of 14 classes. Its noise level is estimated at 38.5% [26].

Table 1. Comparison with state-of-the-art methods in test accuracy (%) on CIFAR-10 with symmetric noise (ranging from 20% to 90%) and 40% asymmetric noise.

Noise type		sym.				asym.
Method/Ratio		20%	50%	80%	90%	40%
Cross-Entropy	best	86.8	79.4	62.9	42.7	85.0
	last	82.7	57.9	26.1	16.8	72.3
Mixup	best	95.6	87.1	71.6	52.2	-
[41]	last	92.3	77.3	46.7	43.9	-
M-correction	best	94.0	92.0	86.8	69.1	87.4
[1]	last	93.8	91.9	86.6	68.7	86.3
Meta-Learning	best	92.9	89.3	77.4	58.7	89.2
[17]	last	92.0	88.8	76.1	58.3	88.6
ELR+	best	95.8	94.8	93.3	78.7	93.0
[18]	last	-	-	-	-	-
LongReMix	best	96.2	95.0	93.9	82.0	94.7
[6]	last	96.0	94.7	93.4	81.3	94.3
DivideMix	best	96.1	94.6	93.2	76.0	93.4
[16]	last	95.7	94.4	92.9	75.4	92.1
DM-AugDesc-WS-SAW	best	96.3	95.6	93.7	35.3	94.4
[21]	last	96.2	95.4	93.6	10.0	94.1
PGDF (ours)	best	**96.7**	**96.3**	**94.7**	**84.0**	**94.8**
	last	**96.6**	**96.2**	**94.6**	**83.1**	**94.5**

In our experiment, we use the same backbones as previous methods to make our results comparable. For CIFAR-10 and CIFAR-100, we use an 18-layer PreAct ResNet [11] as the backbone and train it using SGD with a batch size of 128, a momentum of 0.9, a weight decay of 0.0005, and the models are trained for roughly 300 epochs depending on the speed of convergence. We set the initial learning rate as 0.02, and reduce it by a factor of 10 after 150 epochs. The warm up period is 10 epochs for CIFAR-10 and 30 epochs for CIFAR-100.

For WebVision, we use the Inception-ResNet v2 [28] as the backbone, and train it using SGD with a momentum of 0.9, a learning rate of 0.01, and a batch size of 32. The networks are trained for 80 epochs and the warm up period is 1 epoch.

For Clothing1M, we use a ResNet-50 with pre-trained ImageNet weights. We train the network using SGD for 80 epochs with a momentum of 0.9, a weight decay of 0.001, and a batch size of 32. The initial learning rate is set as 0.002 and reduced by a factor of 10 after 40 epochs.

The hyper-parameters proposed in this paper are set in the same manner for all datasets. We set $m = 0.5$, $r = 2$, $\tau_e = 0.5 * (1 - \tau)$, and $\tau_{n1} = 0.5 * \tau$ (τ is the estimated noise ratio).

4.2 Comparison with State-of-the-Art Methods

We compare the performance of PGDF with recent state-of-the-art methods: Mixup [41], M-correction [1], Meta-Learning [17], NCT [25], ELR+ [18], DivideMix [16], NGC [35], LongReMix [6], and DM-AugDesc-WS-SAW Results for those techniques were directly copied from their respective papers.

Table 2. Comparison with state-of-the-art methods in test accuracy (%) on CIFAR-100 with symmetric noise (ranging from 20% to 90%).

Method/Ratio		20%	50%	80%	90%
Cross-Entropy	best	62.0	46.7	19.9	10.1
	last	61.8	37.3	8.8	3.5
Mixup	best	67.8	57.3	30.8	14.6
[41]	last	66.0	46.6	17.6	8.1
M-correction	best	73.9	66.1	48.2	24.3
[1]	last	73.4	65.4	47.6	20.5
Meta-Learning	best	68.5	59.2	42.4	19.5
[17]	last	67.7	58.0	40.1	14.3
ELR+	best	77.6	73.6	60.8	33.4
[18]	last	-	-	-	-
LongReMix	best	77.8	75.6	62.9	33.8
[6]	last	77.5	75.1	62.3	33.2
DivideMix	best	77.3	74.6	60.2	31.5
[16]	last	76.9	74.2	59.6	31.0
DM-AugDesc-WS-SAW	best	79.6	77.6	61.8	17.3
[21]	last	79.5	77.5	61.6	15.1
PGDF (ours)	best	**81.3**	**78.0**	**66.7**	**42.3**
	last	**81.2**	**77.6**	**65.9**	**41.7**

Table 3. Comparison with state-of-the-art methods trained on (mini) WebVision dataset in top-1/top-5 accuracy (%) on the WebVision validation set and the ImageNet ILSVRC12 validation set.

Method	WebVision		ILSVRC12	
	top1	top5	top1	top5
NCT [25]	75.16	90.77	71.73	91.61
ELR+ [18]	77.78	91.68	70.29	89.76
LongReMix [6]	78.92	92.32	-	-
NGC [35]	79.16	91.84	74.44	91.04
DivideMix [16]	77.32	91.64	75.20	90.84
PGDF (ours)	**81.47**	**94.03**	**75.45**	**93.11**

Table 4. Comparison with state-of-the-art methods in test accuracy (%) on the Clothing1M dataset.

Method	Test Accuracy
Cross-Entropy	69.21
M-correction [1]	71.00
Meta-Learning [17]	73.47
NCT [25]	74.02
ELR+ [18]	74.81
LongReMix [6]	74.38
DivideMix [16]	74.76
DM-AugDesc-WS-SAW [21]	75.11
PGDF (ours)	**75.19**

Table 1 shows the results on CIFAR-10 with different levels of symmetric label noise ranging from 20% to 90% and with 40% asymmetric noise. Table 2 shows the results on CIFAR-100 with different levels of symmetric label noise ranging from 20% to 90%. Following the same metrics in previous works [6,16,18,21], we report both the best test accuracy across all epochs and the averaged test accuracy over the last 10 epochs of training. Our PGDF outperforms the state-of-the-art methods across all noise ratios.

Table 3 compares PGDF with state-of-the-art methods on (mini) WebVision dataset. Our method outperforms all other methods by a large margin. Table 4 shows the result on Clothing1M dataset. Our method also achieves state-of-the-art performance. The result shows our method also works in real-world situations.

4.3 Ablation Study

We study the effect of removing different components to provide insights into what makes our method successful. The result is shown in Table 5.

To study the effect of the prior knowledge, we divide the dataset only by w_{it} and change the easy set threshold to 0.95 because there is no value equal to 1

Table 5. Ablation study results in terms of average test accuracy (%, 3 runs) with standard deviation on CIFAR-10 with 50% and 80% symmetric noise.

Method/Noise ratio		50%	80%
PGDF	best	**96.26 ± 0.09**	**94.69 ± 0.46**
	last	**96.15 ± 0.13**	**94.55 ± 0.25**
PGDF w/o prior knowledge	best	95.55 ± 0.11	93.77 ± 0.19
	last	95.12 ± 0.19	93.51 ± 0.23
PGDF w/o sample dividing optimization	best	95.73 ± 0.09	93.51 ± 0.28
	last	95.50 ± 0.12	93.20 ± 0.32
PGDF w/o pseudo-labels refining	best	95.78 ± 0.26	94.06 ± 0.68
	last	95.35 ± 0.27	93.71 ± 0.52
PGDF w/o hard samples enhancing	best	96.01 ± 0.19	94.39 ± 0.28
	last	95.78 ± 0.07	94.21 ± 0.23

in w_{it}. The result shows the prior knowledge is very effective to save more hard samples and filter more noisy ones. By removing the prior generation module, the test accuracy decreases by an average of about 0.93%.

To study the effect of the sample dividing optimization, we divide the dataset only by the prior knowledge w_{ip}. The result shows that whether a sample is noisy or not depends not only on the training history, but also on the information of the image itself and the corresponding label. Integrating this information can make judgments more accurate. By removing the sample dividing optimization phase, the test accuracy decreases by an average of about 0.68%.

To study the effect of the pseudo-labels refining phase, we use the pseudo-labels without being refined by the estimated transition matrix. By removing the pseudo-labels refining phase, the test accuracy decreases by an average of about 0.69%. We also evaluate the pseudo-labels refinement method in DivideMix [16] by replacing our scheme with "co-refinement" and "co-guessing". By replacing our pseudo-labels refining phase with "co-refinement" and "co-guessing", the test accuracy decreases by an average of about 0.49%.

To study the effect of the hard samples enhancing, we remove the hard enhancing component. The decrease in accuracy suggests that by enhancing the informative hard samples, the method yields better performance by an average of 0.32%.

Among the prior knowledge, sample dividing optimizations, pseudo-labels refining, and hard enhancing, the prior knowledge introduces the maximum performance gain. All components have a certain gain.

4.4 Generalization to Instance-Dependent Label Noise

Note that the instance-dependent label noise is a new challenging synthetic noise type and would introduce many hard confident samples. We conducted additional experiments on this noise type to better illustrate the superiority of our method. In order to make the comparison fair, we followed the same metrics and used the same noisy label files in work [5]. We compared the recent state-of-the-art methods in learning with instance-dependent label noise: CAL [47], SEAL [5]; and some other baselines [9,22,30,37,42]. Table 6 shows the experimental result. Result for "CAL" was re-implemented based on the public code of work [47]. Other results for previous methods were directly copied from work [5].

Table 6. Comparison with state-of-the-art methods in terms of average test accuracy (%, 3 runs) on CIFAR-10 with instance-dependent label noise (ranging from 10% to 40%).

Method	10%	20%	30%	40%
Cross-Entropy	91.25 ± 0.27	86.34 ± 0.11	80.87 ± 0.05	75.68 ± 0.29
Forward [22]	91.06 ± 0.02	86.35 ± 0.11	78.87 ± 2.66	71.12 ± 0.47
Co-teaching [9]	91.22 ± 0.25	87.28 ± 0.20	84.33 ± 0.17	78.72 ± 0.47
GCE [42]	90.97 ± 0.21	86.44 ± 0.23	81.54 ± 0.15	76.71 ± 0.39
DAC [30]	90.94 ± 0.09	86.16 ± 0.13	80.88 ± 0.46	74.80 ± 0.32
DMI [37]	91.26 ± 0.06	86.57 ± 0.16	81.98 ± 0.57	77.81 ± 0.85
CAL [47]	90.55 ± 0.02	87.42 ± 0.13	84.85 ± 0.07	82.18 ± 0.18
SEAL [5]	91.32 ± 0.14	87.79 ± 0.09	85.30 ± 0.01	82.98 ± 0.05
PGDF	**94.09 ± 0.27**	**91.85 ± 0.09**	**90.64 ± 0.50**	**87.67 ± 0.32**

According to the experimental results, our method outperforms all other methods by a large margin. This shows the generalization ability of our method is well since it also works in complex synthetic label noise.

4.5 Hyper-parameters Analysis

Table 7. Results in terms of average test accuracy (%, 3 runs) with standard deviation on different "τ_e" and "τ_{n1}" on CIFAR-10 with 50% symmetric noise ratio.

τ_e	0.2	0.25	0.3	0.35
best	96.09 ± 0.04	96.26 ± 0.09	96.14 ± 0.08	96.11 ± 0.06
last	95.98 ± 0.06	96.15 ± 0.13	95.99 ± 0.10	95.93 ± 0.09
τ_{n1}	0.2	0.25	0.3	0.35
best	96.26 ± 0.12	96.26 ± 0.09	96.25 ± 0.13	96.02 ± 0.07
last	96.08 ± 0.11	96.15 ± 0.13	96.11 ± 0.16	95.82 ± 0.10

In order to analyze how sensitive PGDF is to the hyper-parameters τ_e and τ_{n1}, we trained on different τ_e and τ_{n1} in CIFAR-10 dataset with 50% symmetric noise ratio. Specifically, we first adjusted the value of τ_e with fixed $\tau_{n1} = 0.25$, and thus obtained the sensitivity of PGDF to τ_e. Then we adjusted the value of τ_{n1} with fixed $\tau_e = 0.25$, and thus obtained the sensitivity of PGDF to τ_{n1}. We report both the best test accuracy across all epochs and the averaged test accuracy over the last 10 epochs of training, as shown in Table 7. The result shows that the performance is stable when changing τ_e and τ_{n1} in a reasonable range. Thus, the performance does not highly rely on the pre-defined settings of τ_e and τ_{n1}. Although their settings depend on the noise ratio, they are still easy to set due to the insensitivity. In fact, we set hyper-parameter τ_e to select a part of samples which are highly reliable to train the M_m (the classifier to distinguish the hard and noisy samples). The settings of τ_e and τ_{n1} are not critical, they just support the algorithm. Analysis of other hyper-parameters is shown in Appendix.

4.6 Discussion for Prior Generation Module

To better discuss and verify the performance of our Prior Generation Module, we calculated the pre-classification accuracy of our Prior Generation Module on the CIFAR-10 and CIFAR-100 datasets compared to the strategy of directly using loss to dividing samples. The result is shown in Table 8. According to the result, the identification performance of our strategy is much better than the strategy that only used the training loss. Our Prior Generation Module indeed improves the accuracy of sample division and avoids hurting the hard samples.

Table 8. Comparison of samples classification accuracy (%, clean/noisy) between the Prior Generation Module (PGM) and the strategy that directly using training loss.

Method	CIFAR-10 Sym-20%	CIFAR-10 Sym-50%	CIFAR-100 Sym-20%	CIFAR-100 Sym-50%
By training loss	88.80	78.16	81.12	68.99
PGM	**97.66**	**94.71**	**94.77**	**90.80**

5 Limitations

The quantifiable behavioral differences between hard and noisy samples are not clear. There could exist other better metrics that can be used to directly distinguish them and thus can simplify the dividing phase. We conducted some preliminary experiments for hard and noisy sample behavior analysis in appendix. Our subsequent work will continue to investigate specific quantifiable metrics to simplify the process of the Prior Generation Module, and how to strengthen hard samples more reasonably is a direction worth studying in the future.

6 Conclusions

The existing methods for learning with noisy labels fail to distinguish the hard samples from the noisy ones and thus ruin the model performance. In this paper, we propose PGDF to learn a deep model to suppress noise. We found that the training history can be used to distinguish the hard samples and noisy samples. By integrating our Prior Generation, more hard clean samples can be saved. Besides, our pseudo-labels refining and hard enhancing phase further boost the performance. Through extensive experiments show that PGDF outperforms state-of-the-art performance.

Acknowledgement. This work was supported by BUPT innovation and entrepreneurship support program (2023-YC-A185).

Ethical Statement. As far as we know, this paper may not have any potential ethical risk.

References

1. Arazo, E., Ortego, D., Albert, P., O'Connor, N., McGuinness, K.: Unsupervised label noise modeling and loss correction. In: International Conference on Machine Learning, pp. 312–321. PMLR (2019)
2. Bai, Y., Liu, T.: Me-momentum: Extracting hard confident examples from noisily labeled data. In: Proceedings of the IEEE/CVF International Conference on Computer Vision, pp. 9312–9321 (2021)
3. Berthelot, D., Carlini, N., Goodfellow, I., Papernot, N., Oliver, A., Raffel, C.: Mixmatch: A holistic approach to semi-supervised learning. In: Advances in Neural Information Processing Systems 32: Annual Conference on Neural Information Processing Systems (2019)
4. Chen, P., Liao, B., Chen, G., Zhang, S.: Understanding and utilizing deep neural networks trained with noisy labels. arXiv preprint arXiv:1905.05040 (2019)
5. Chen, P., Ye, J., Chen, G., Zhao, J., Heng, P.A.: Beyond class-conditional assumption: A primary attempt to combat instance-dependent label noise. In: Proceedings of the AAAI Conference on Artificial Intelligence (2021)
6. Cordeiro, F.R., Sachdeva, R., Belagiannis, V., Reid, I., Carneiro, G.: Longremix: Robust learning with high confidence samples in a noisy label environment. arXiv preprint arXiv:2103.04173 (2021)
7. Ghosh, A., Kumar, H., Sastry, P.: Robust loss functions under label noise for deep neural networks. In: Thirty-First AAAI Conference on Artificial Intelligence (2017)
8. Goldberger, J., Ben-Reuven, E.: Training deep neural-networks using a noise adaptation layer. In: 5th International Conference on Learning Representations (2017)
9. Han, B., et al.: Co-teaching: Robust training of deep neural networks with extremely noisy labels. Adv. Neural Inform. Process. syst. **31** 8527–8537 (2018)
10. Han, J., Luo, P., Wang, X.: Deep self-learning from noisy labels. In: Proceedings of the IEEE/CVF International Conference on Computer Vision, pp. 5138–5147 (2019)
11. He, K., Zhang, X., Ren, S., Sun, J.: Identity mappings in deep residual networks. In: European Conference on Computer Vision (2016)
12. Huang, J., Qu, L., Jia, R., Zhao, B.: O2u-net: A simple noisy label detection approach for deep neural networks. In: Proceedings of the IEEE/CVF International Conference on Computer Vision, pp. 3326–3334 (2019)
13. Jiang, L., Zhou, Z., Leung, T., Li, L.J., Fei-Fei, L.: Mentornet: Learning data-driven curriculum for very deep neural networks on corrupted labels. In: International Conference on Machine Learning, pp. 2304–2313. PMLR (2018)

14. Krizhevsky, A., Hinton, G.: Learning multiple layers of features from tiny images. Handbook of Systemic Autoimmune Diseases **1**(4) (2009)
15. Krizhevsky, A., Sutskever, I., Hinton, G.E.: Imagenet classification with deep convolutional neural networks. Adv. Neural Inform. Process. Syst. **25** 1097–1105 (2012)
16. Li, J., Socher, R., Hoi, S.: Dividemix: Learning with noisy labels as semi-supervised learning (2020)
17. Li, J., Wong, Y., Zhao, Q., Kankanhalli, M.S.: Learning to learn from noisy labeled data. In: 2019 IEEE/CVF Conference on Computer Vision and Pattern Recognition (CVPR) (2019)
18. Liu, S., Niles-Weed, J., Razavian, N., Fernandez-Granda, C.: Early-learning regularization prevents memorization of noisy labels (2020)
19. Lyu, Y., Tsang, I.W.: Curriculum loss: Robust learning and generalization against label corruption (2019)
20. Montserrat, D.M., Lin, Q., Allebach, J., Delp, E.J.: Training object detection and recognition CNN models using data augmentation. Electronic Imaging **2017**(10), 27–36 (2017)
21. Nishi, K., Ding, Y., Rich, A., Hllerer, T.: Augmentation strategies for learning with noisy labels. In: Proceedings of the IEEE/CVF Conference on Computer Vision and Pattern Recognition (CVPR) (2021)
22. Patrini, G., Rozza, A., Krishna Menon, A., Nock, R., Qu, L.: Making deep neural networks robust to label noise: A loss correction approach. In: Proceedings of the IEEE Conference on Computer Vision and Pattern Recognition, pp. 1944–1952 (2017)
23. Ren, M., Zeng, W., Yang, B., Urtasun, R.: Learning to reweight examples for robust deep learning (2018)
24. Russakovsky, O., et al.: Imagenet large scale visual recognition challenge. Int. J. Comput. Vision **115**(3), 211–252 (2015)
25. Sarfraz, F., Arani, E., Zonooz, B.: Noisy concurrent training for efficient learning under label noise. In: Proceedings of the IEEE/CVF Winter Conference on Applications of Computer Vision, pp. 3159–3168 (2021)
26. Song, H., Kim, M., Park, D., Lee, J.G.: Prestopping: How does early stopping help generalization against label noise? (2019)
27. Sun, Y., Tian, Y., Xu, Y., Li, J.: Limited gradient descent: Learning with noisy labels. IEEE Access **7**, 168296–168306 (2019)
28. Szegedy, C., Ioffe, S., Vanhoucke, V., Alemi, A.A.: Inception-v4, inception-resnet and the impact of residual connections on learning (2017)
29. Tanno, R., Saeedi, A., Sankaranarayanan, S., AleXaNder, D.C., Silberman, N.: Learning from noisy labels by regularized estimation of annotator confusion. In: 2019 IEEE/CVF Conference on Computer Vision and Pattern Recognition (CVPR) (2020)
30. Thulasidasan, S., Bhattacharya, T., Bilmes, J., Chennupati, G., Mohd-Yusof, J.: Combating label noise in deep learning using abstention. arXiv preprint arXiv:1905.10964 (2019)
31. Tong, X., Tian, X., Yi, Y., Chang, H., Wang, X.: Learning from massive noisy labeled data for image classification. In: 2015 IEEE Conference on Computer Vision and Pattern Recognition (CVPR) (2015)
32. Wang, Y., Ma, X., Chen, Z., Luo, Y., Yi, J., Bailey, J.: Symmetric cross entropy for robust learning with noisy labels. In: Proceedings of the IEEE/CVF International Conference on Computer Vision, pp. 322–330 (2019)

33. Wei, Y., Gong, C., Chen, S., Liu, T., Yang, J., Tao, D.: Harnessing side information for classification under label noise. IEEE Trans. Neural Netw. Learn. Syst. **31**(9), 3178–3192 (2019)
34. Wen, L., Wang, L., Wei, L., Agustsson, E., Gool, L.V.: Webvision database: Visual learning and understanding from web data (2017)
35. Wu, Z.F., Wei, T., Jiang, J., Mao, C., Tang, M., Li, Y.F.: Ngc: A unified framework for learning with open-world noisy data. arXiv preprint arXiv:2108.11035 (2021)
36. Xiao, T., Xia, T., Yang, Y., Huang, C., Wang, X.: Learning from massive noisy labeled data for image classification. In: Proceedings of the IEEE Conference On Computer Vision and Pattern Recognition, pp. 2691–2699 (2015)
37. Xu, Y., Cao, P., Kong, Y., Wang, Y.: L_dmi: An information-theoretic noise-robust loss function. arXiv preprint arXiv:1909.03388 (2019)
38. Yi, K., Wu, J.: Probabilistic end-to-end noise correction for learning with noisy labels. arXiv preprint arXiv:1903.07788 (2019)
39. Young, T., Hazarika, D., Poria, S., Cambria, E.: Recent trends in deep learning based natural language processing. IEEE Comput. Intell. Mag. **13**(3), 55–75 (2018)
40. Yu, X., Han, B., Yao, J., Niu, G., Tsang, I.W., Sugiyama, M.: How does disagreement help generalization against label corruption? (2019)
41. Zhang, H., Cisse, M., Dauphin, Y.N., Lopez-Paz, D.: mixup: Beyond empirical risk minimization (2018)
42. Zhang, Z., Sabuncu, M.: Generalized cross entropy loss for training deep neural networks with noisy labels. Adv. Neural Inform. Process. Syst. **31** 8778–8788 (2018)
43. Zheltonozhskii, E., Baskin, C., Mendelson, A., Bronstein, A.M., Litany, O.: Contrast to divide: Self-supervised pre-training for learning with noisy labels. In: Proceedings of the IEEE/CVF Winter Conference on Applications of Computer Vision, pp. 1657–1667 (2022)
44. Zhou, X., Liu, X., Jiang, J., Gao, X., Ji, X.: Asymmetric loss functions for learning with noisy labels. arXiv preprint arXiv:2106.03110 (2021)
45. Zhou, X., Liu, X., Wang, C., Zhai, D., Jiang, J., Ji, X.: Learning with noisy labels via sparse regularization. In: Proceedings of the IEEE/CVF International Conference on Computer Vision, pp. 72–81 (2021)
46. Zhu, C., Chen, W., Peng, T., Wang, Y., Jin, M.: Hard sample aware noise robust learning for histopathology image classification. IEEE Trans. Med. Imaging **41**(4), 881–894 (2021)
47. Zhu, Z., Liu, T., Liu, Y.: A second-order approach to learning with instance-dependent label noise. In: Proceedings of the IEEE/CVF Conference on Computer Vision and Pattern Recognition, pp. 10113–10123 (2021)

DCID: Deep Canonical Information Decomposition

Alexander Rakowski[1](✉) and Christoph Lippert[1,2]

[1] Hasso Plattner Institute for Digital Engineering, University of Potsdam, Potsdam, Germany
{alexander.rakowski,christoph.lippert}@hpi.de
[2] Hasso Plattner Institute for Digital Health at Mount Sinai, New York, USA

Abstract. We consider the problem of identifying the signal shared between two one-dimensional *target* variables, in the presence of additional multivariate observations. Canonical Correlation Analysis (CCA)-based methods have traditionally been used to identify shared variables, however, they were designed for multivariate targets and only offer trivial solutions for univariate cases. In the context of Multi-Task Learning (MTL), various models were postulated to learn features that are sparse and shared across multiple tasks. However, these methods were typically evaluated by their predictive performance. To the best of our knowledge, no prior studies systematically evaluated models in terms of correctly recovering the shared signal. Here, we formalize the setting of univariate shared information retrieval, and propose ICM, an evaluation metric which can be used in the presence of ground-truth labels, quantifying 3 aspects of the learned shared features. We further propose Deep Canonical Information Decomposition (DCID) - a simple, yet effective approach for learning the shared variables. We benchmark the models on a range of scenarios on synthetic data with known ground-truths and observe DCID outperforming the baselines in a wide range of settings. Finally, we demonstrate a real-life application of DCID on brain Magnetic Resonance Imaging (MRI) data, where we are able to extract more accurate predictors of changes in brain regions and obesity. The code for our experiments as well as the supplementary materials are available at https://github.com/alexrakowski/dcid.

Keywords: Shared Variables Retrieval · CCA · Canonical Correlation Analysis

1 Introduction

In this paper, we approach the problem of isolating the *shared* signal $\mathbf{Z}$ associated with two scalar *target variables* Y_1 and Y_2, from their *individual* signals $\mathbf{Z_1}$ and $\mathbf{Z_2}$, by leveraging additional, high-dimensional observations $\mathbf{X}$ (see Fig. 1 for the corresponding graphical model). Analyzing the relationships between pairs of variables is ubiquitous in biomedical or healthcare studies. However,

© The Author(s), under exclusive license to Springer Nature Switzerland AG 2023
D. Koutra et al. (Eds.): ECML PKDD 2023, LNAI 14170, pp. 20–35, 2023.
https://doi.org/10.1007/978-3-031-43415-0_2

while biological traits are often governed by complex processes and can have a wide range of causes, we rarely have access to the fine-grained, low-level signals constituting the phenomena of interest. Instead, we have to either develop hand-crafted quantities based on prior knowledge, which is often a costly process, or resort to high-level, "aggregate" measurements of the world. If the underlying signal is weak, it might prove challenging to detect associations between such aggregated variables. On the other hand, in many fields, we have access to high-dimensional measurements, such as medical scans or genome sequencing data, which provide rich, albeit "unlabeled" signal. We propose to leverage such data to **decompose** the traits of interest into their **shared** and **individual** parts, allowing us to better quantify the relationships between them.

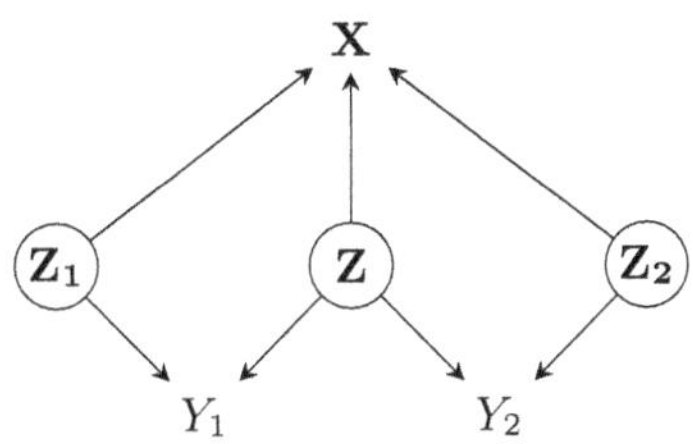

Fig. 1. A Directed Acyclic Graph (DAG) representing the graphical model used in our setting. Unobserved variables are denoted in circles. The two univariate random variables Y_1, Y_2 are generated by their **individual** ancestors $\mathbf{Z_1}, \mathbf{Z_2}$, and a **shared** ancestor $\mathbf{Z}$. The multivariate $\mathbf{X}$ is generated by all 3 latent variables. The following pairs of variables are independent under this model: $\mathbf{Z} \perp \mathbf{Z_1}$, $\mathbf{Z} \perp \mathbf{Z_2}$, $\mathbf{Z_1} \perp \mathbf{Z_2}$, $\mathbf{Z_1} \perp Y_2$ and $\mathbf{Z_2} \perp Y_1$.

Probabilistic CCA (pCCA) was one of the early approaches to learning the shared signal between pairs of random variables (r.v.s) [4,23]. However, its effectiveness is limited to multivariate observations - for scalar variables we can only learn the variables themselves, up to multiplication by a constant. A variety of methods from the field of Multi-Task Feature Learning (MTFL) learn feature representations of $\mathbf{X}$, which should be sparse and shared across tasks [2,25,41]. These models are typically evaluated by their predictive performance, and the shared features are rather a means of improving predictions, than a goal itself. To the best of our knowledge, no studies exist which systematically quantify how accurate are such models in recovering the signal shared between tasks.

To this end, we define the ICM score, which evaluates 3 aspects of learned shared features: *informativeness*, *completeness*, and *minimality*, when ground-truth labels are available. Furthermore, we propose Deep Canonical Information Decomposition (DCID), an approach utilizing Deep Neural Network (DNN) feature extractors and Canonical Correlation Analysis (CCA) to learn the variables $\mathbf{Z}$ shared between traits. DCID approximates the traits of interest with DNN classifiers and utilizes their latent features as multivariate decompositions of the traits. It then identifies the shared factors by performing CCA between the two sets of latent representations and retaining the most correlated components (see Fig. 3 for a graphical overview of the method).

Our contributions can be summarized as follows:

1. We define the ICM score, which allows evaluation of learned shared features in the presence of ground-truth labels (Sect. 3)
2. We propose DCID, a method leveraging DNN classifiers and CCA to learn the shared signal (Sect. 4).
3. We benchmark the proposed model, along several baselines, on a range of scenarios with synthetic data, and analyze their performance wrt. different properties of the underlying ground-truth (Sects. 5.3 and 5.4).
4. Finally, we demonstrate a real-life use-case of the proposed method, by applying it on a dataset of brain Magnetic Resonance Imaging (MRI) data to better quantify the relationships between brain structures and obesity (Sect. 5.5).

2 Related Work

2.1 Canonical Correlation Analysis (CCA)

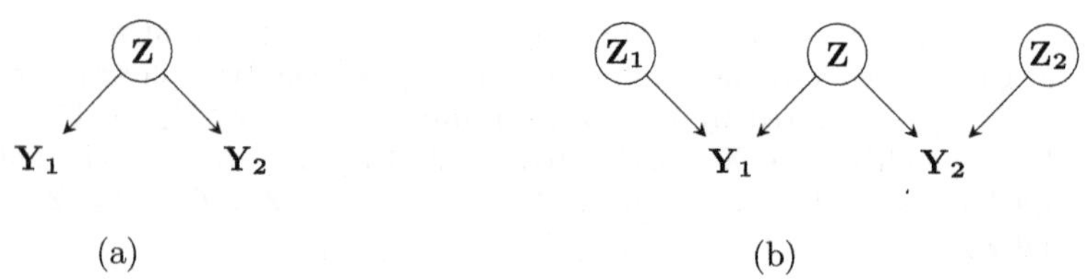

Fig. 2. Two probabilistic interpretations of Canonical Correlation Analysis (CCA). In (a), the observed variables are different, noisy views (linear transformations) of the same underlying variable $\mathbf{Z}$. In (b), two additional, view-specific latent variables $\mathbf{Z_1}$ and $\mathbf{Z_2}$ are introduced, which can be interpreted as modeling the uncertainty of $p(\mathbf{Y}|\mathbf{Z})$.

CCA is a statistical technique operating on pairs of multivariate observations [19, 21]. It is similar to Principal Component Analysis (PCA) [30], in that it finds linear transformations of the observations, such that the resulting variables are uncorrelated. Specifically, for a pair of observations $\mathbf{Y_1} \in \mathbb{R}^{n \times p}$ and $\mathbf{Y_2} \in \mathbb{R}^{n \times q}$, it finds linear transformations $U \in \mathbb{R}^{p \times d}$, $V \in \mathbb{R}^{q \times d}$, $d = min\{p, q\}$ which maximize the correlation between the consecutive pairs of the resulting variables $\mathbf{C_1} = \mathbf{Y_1}U$, $\mathbf{C_2} = \mathbf{Y_2}V$. In the probabilistic interpretation of CCA [4], one can interpret the observed variables as two different views of the latent variable $\mathbf{Z}$ (Fig. 2a). This interpretation is extended in [23] to include view-specific variables $\mathbf{Z_1}$ and $\mathbf{Z_2}$ (Fig. 2b), which is the closest to our setting.

2.2 Multi-Task Learning (MTL)

MTL is a machine learning paradigm, where models are fitted to several tasks simultaneously, with the assumption that such joint optimization will lead to better generalization for each task [9,33,42]. In Multi-Task Feature Learning (MTFL), one aims to learn a low-dimensional representation of the input data, that is shared across tasks [2,34]. The early approaches for MTFL worked with linear models and were based on imposing constraints on the matrix of model parameters, such as sparsity or low-rank factorization [2,3,25]. Modern approaches extend MTFL to DNN models by using tensor factorization in place of matrix factorization [40,41] or by employing adversarial training to learn task-invariant, and task-specific features [7,26,36].

3 Univariate Shared Information Retrieval

In this section, we formalize the problem setting (Sect. 3.1) and define 3 quantities measuring different aspects of the learned shared representations, which constitute the model evaluation procedure (Sect. 3.2).

3.1 Problem Setting

In our setting, we observe two univariate r.v.s $Y_1, Y_2 \in \mathbb{R}$, which we will refer to as the *target variables*, and a multivariate r.v. $\mathbf{X} \in \mathbb{R}^l$. We further define 3 unobserved, multivariate, and pairwise-independent *latent variables* $\mathbf{Z}, \mathbf{Z_1}, \mathbf{Z_2} \in \mathbb{R}^k$, which generate the observed variables. We will refer to $\mathbf{Z_1}$ and $\mathbf{Z_2}$ as the *individual variables*, and to $\mathbf{Z}$ as the *shared variables*. The main assumption of the model is that the individual variables $\mathbf{Z_1}$ and $\mathbf{Z_2}$ are each independent from one of the target variables, i.e., $\mathbf{Z_1} \perp Y_2$ and $\mathbf{Z_2} \perp Y_1$, while the shared variable $\mathbf{Z}$ is generating all the observed r.v.s, i.e., Y_1, Y_2 and $\mathbf{X}$. The corresponding graphical model is shown in Fig. 1. Similar to the pCCA setting, we assume additivity of the effects of the shared and individual variables on Y_i, i.e.:

$$Y_i = \psi_i(\mathbf{Z}) + \phi_i(\mathbf{Z_i}),\ i \in \{1,2\} \tag{1}$$

where ψ_i and ϕ_i are arbitrary functions $\mathbb{R}^k \mapsto \mathbb{R}$.

Our task of interest is then predicting the shared variable $\mathbf{Z}$ given the observed r.v.s, i.e., learning an accurate model of $p(\mathbf{Z}|Y_1, Y_2, X)$, **without access to $\mathbf{Z}, \mathbf{Z_1}, \mathbf{Z_2}$ during training**.

3.2 Evaluating the Shared Representations

While in practical scenarios we assume that the latent variables remain unobserved, to benchmark how well do different algorithms recover $\mathbf{Z}$, we need to test them in a controlled setting, where all ground-truth variables are available at least during test time. Let $\mathcal{D} = \{\mathbf{x}^{(i)}, y_1^{(i)}, y_2^{(i)}, \mathbf{z}^{(i)}, \mathbf{z}_1^{(i)}, \mathbf{z}_2^{(i)}\}_{i=1}^N$ be a ground-truth dataset, and $\hat{\mathbf{z}} = \{\hat{\mathbf{z}}^{(i)}\}_{i=1}^N$ be the learned shared representations. We will denote by $[\mathbf{x}, \mathbf{y}]$ the column-wise concatenation of $\mathbf{x}$ and $\mathbf{y}$, and by $R^2(\mathbf{x}, \mathbf{y})$ the ratio of variance explained (i.e., the coefficient of determination) by fitting a linear regression model of $\mathbf{x}$ to $\mathbf{y}$:

$$R^2(\mathbf{x}, \mathbf{y}) = 1 - \frac{1}{d} \sum_{j=1}^{d} \frac{\sum_i (e_j^{(i)})^2}{\sum_i (y_j^{(i)} - \bar{y}_j)^2} \tag{2}$$

where $e_j^{(i)} = \hat{y_j}^{(i)} - y_j^{(i)}$ are residuals of the model of the j-th dimension of $\mathbf{y}$.

Inspired by the DCI score [15] from the field of disentangled representation learning, we define the following requirements for a learned representation $\hat{\mathbf{Z}}$ as correctly identifying the shared variable $\mathbf{Z}$:

1. **Informativeness**: $\mathbf{Z}$ should be predictable from $\hat{\mathbf{Z}}$. We measure this as the ratio of variance explained by a model fitted to predict $\mathbf{Z}$ from $\hat{\mathbf{Z}}$:

$$\mathcal{L}_{info}(\hat{\mathbf{z}}, \mathbf{z}) = R^2(\hat{\mathbf{z}}, \mathbf{z}) \tag{3}$$

2. **Compactness**: $\mathbf{Z}$ should be sufficient to predict $\hat{\mathbf{Z}}$. We measure this as the ratio of variance explained by a model fitted to predict $\hat{\mathbf{Z}}$ from $\mathbf{Z}$:

$$\mathcal{L}_{comp}(\mathbf{z}, \hat{\mathbf{z}}) = R^2(\mathbf{z}, \hat{\mathbf{z}}) \tag{4}$$

3. **Minimality**: $\hat{\mathbf{Z}}$ should only contain information about $\mathbf{Z}$. We measure this as one minus the ratio of variance explained by a model fitted to predict the individual variables $\mathbf{Z_1}$ and $\mathbf{Z_2}$ from $\hat{\mathbf{Z}}$:

$$\mathcal{L}_{min}(\hat{\mathbf{z}}, \mathbf{z_1}, \mathbf{z_2}) = 1 - R^2(\hat{\mathbf{z}}, [\mathbf{z_1}, \mathbf{z_2}]) \tag{5}$$

The final score, ICM, is given as the product of the individual scores:

$$ICM(\hat{\mathbf{z}}, \mathcal{D}) = \mathcal{L}_{info}(\hat{\mathbf{z}}, \mathbf{z}) \cdot \mathcal{L}_{comp}(\mathbf{z}, \hat{\mathbf{z}}) \cdot \mathcal{L}_{min}(\hat{\mathbf{z}}, \mathbf{z_1}, \mathbf{z_2}) \tag{6}$$

and takes values in $[0, 1]$, with 1 being a perfect score, identifying $\mathbf{Z}$ up to a rotation.

Note that minimality might seem redundant given compactness - if $\mathbf{Z}$ explains all the variance in $\hat{\mathbf{Z}}$, then, since $\mathbf{Z} \perp \mathbf{Z_1}, \mathbf{Z_2}$, $\hat{\mathbf{Z}}$ would contain no information about $\mathbf{Z_1}$ or $\mathbf{Z_2}$. However, if we accidentally choose the dimensionality of $\hat{\mathbf{Z}}$ to be much higher than that of $\mathbf{Z}$, a model can "hide" information about $\mathbf{Z_1}$ and $\mathbf{Z_2}$ by replicating the information about $\mathbf{Z}$ multiple times, e.g., $\hat{\mathbf{Z}} = \{\mathbf{Z_1}, \mathbf{Z_2}, \mathbf{Z}, \ldots \mathbf{Z}\}$. This would result in a perfect informativeness and an almost perfect compactness score, but a low minimality score.

4 Method: Deep Canonical Information Decomposition

In this section, we outline the difficulty in tackling the problem formulated above with CCA (Sect. 4.1), and describe an algorithm for solving it by exploiting the additional observed variable $\mathbf{X}$ (Sect. 4.2).

4.1 Limitations of the CCA Setting

Without $\mathbf{X}$, our setting can be seen as a special case of Probabilistic CCA (pCCA) [23], where the observed variables ("views" of the data) have a dimensionality of one (see Fig. 2b). If we assume non-empty $\mathbf{Z}$, then, by the pCCA model, $\mathbf{Z_1}$ and $\mathbf{Z_2}$ would have a dimensionality of zero, resulting in degenerate solutions in form of:

$$\begin{gathered} \hat{Z} = \alpha Y_1 \\ \vee \\ \hat{Z} = \alpha Y_2 \\ \alpha \neq 0 \end{gathered} \tag{7}$$

as the only linear transformations of univariate Y_1 and Y_2 are the variables themselves, up to scalar multiplication.

4.2 Deep Canonical Information Decomposition (DCID)

In order to find $\mathbf{Z}$, we need "unaggregated", multivariate views of Y_1 and Y_2. To achieve this, we leverage the high-dimensional observations $\mathbf{X}$, e.g., images, to learn decompositions of Y_1, Y_2 as transformations of $\mathbf{X}$. Specifically, we assume that both Y_i can be approximated as transformations of $\mathbf{X}$ with functions $h_i(\mathbf{X}) = \hat{Y}_i$. We further assume they can be decomposed as $h_i = g_i \circ f_i$, where $f_i : \mathbb{R}^l \mapsto \mathbb{R}^k$, called the *representation function*, can be an arbitrary, potentially nonlinear mapping, and $g_i : \mathbb{R}^k \mapsto \mathbb{R}$, called the *classifier function*, is a linear combination. The k-dimensional outputs of $f_i(\mathbf{X}) = \mathbf{B_i}$ constitute the multivariate decompositions of Y_i. Since these are no longer univariate, we can now apply the standard CCA algorithm on $\mathbf{B_1}, \mathbf{B_2}$ to obtain pairs of canonical variables $\mathbf{C_1}, \mathbf{C_2} \in \mathbb{R}^k$, sorted by the strength of their pairwise correlations, i.e.,

$$\forall i, j \in |k| : i < j \Rightarrow corr(\mathbf{C}_{1,i}, \mathbf{C}_{2,i}) \leq corr(\mathbf{C}_{1,j}, \mathbf{C}_{2,j}) \tag{8}$$

In order to extract the most informative features, we can select the n pairs of canonical variables with correlations above a certain threshold T:

$$n = \operatorname*{argmax}_{i \in |k|} corr(\mathbf{C}_{1,i}, \mathbf{C}_{2,i}) > T \tag{9}$$

We then take the $\hat{\mathbf{Z}} = \frac{1}{2}(\mathbf{C}_{1,1:n} + \mathbf{C}_{2,1:n})$ as our estimate of the shared $\mathbf{Z}$. The complete process is illustrated in Fig. 3 and described step-wise in Algorithm 1.

Modeling the $\mathbf{h_i}$. In practice, we approximate each h_i by training DNN models to minimize $\mathbb{E}[Y_i - h_i(\mathbf{X})]^2$, i.e., a standard Mean Squared Error (MSE) objective. DNNs are a fitting choice for modeling h_i, since various popular architectures, e.g., ResNet [20], can naturally be decomposed into a nonlinear *feature extractor* (our f_i) and a linear *prediction head* (our g_i).

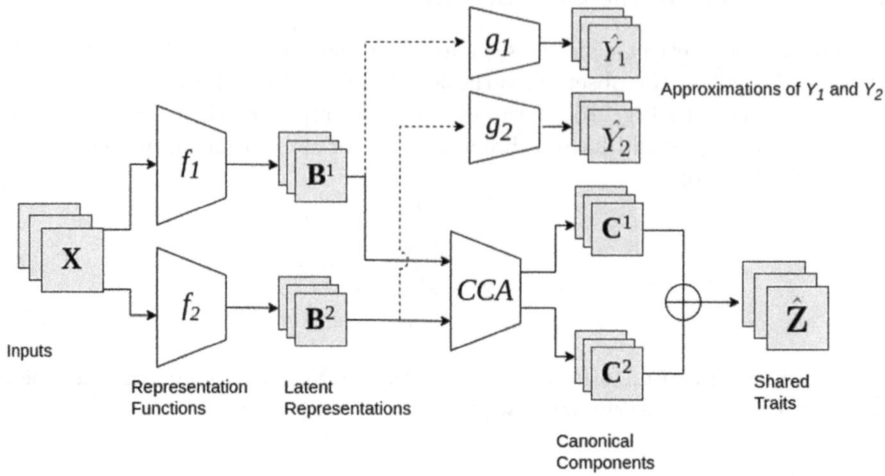

Fig. 3. A visual illustration of the Deep Canonical Information Decomposition (DCID) model. The target variables Y_1 and Y_2 are approximated by fitting DNN predictors on the high-dimensional data $\mathbf{X}$. Outputs of the penultimate layers of the networks are then used as multivariate decompositions of Y_1 and Y_2, and fed into CCA to estimate the shared signal $\hat{\mathbf{Z}}$.

Algorithm 1: DCID: Computing the shared features $\hat{\mathbf{z}}$ and the prediction function $f^\star$

Input: $\mathcal{D} = \{\mathbf{x}^{(i)}, y_1^{(i)}, y_2^{(i)}\}_{i=1}^N$; /* Training dataset */
Input: $\mathcal{L}(\cdot,\cdot)$; /* Loss function to optimize the DNNs, e.g., L_2 */
Input: T ; /* Canonical correlation threshold */
Output: $\hat{\mathbf{Z}}$; /* Features shared between Y_1 and Y_2 */
Output: $f^\star$; /* Function to predict $\hat{\mathbf{Z}}$ from new data */
$f_1, g_1 \leftarrow \text{argmin}_{h=g\circ f} \mathcal{L}(\mathbf{y}_1, h(\mathbf{x}))$; /* Fit a DNN to predict $\mathbf{y}_1$ from x */
$f_2, g_2 \leftarrow \text{argmin}_{h=g\circ f} \mathcal{L}(\mathbf{y}_2, h(\mathbf{x}))$; /* Fit a DNN to predict $\mathbf{y}_2$ from x */
$\mathbf{b}_1 \leftarrow f_1(\mathbf{x})$;
$\mathbf{b}_2 \leftarrow f_2(\mathbf{x})$;
$U, V \leftarrow \text{CCA}(\mathbf{b}_1, \mathbf{b}_2)$; /* Compute the CCA projection matrices U, V */
$\hat{\mathbf{z}} \leftarrow \emptyset$;
$n \leftarrow 1$;
while $corr(U_n^\top \mathbf{b}_1, V_n^\top \mathbf{b}_2) > T$ **do**
  $\mathbf{b}^n \leftarrow \frac{1}{2}(U_n^\top \mathbf{b}_1 + V_n^\top \mathbf{b}_2)$;
  $\hat{\mathbf{z}} \leftarrow \hat{\mathbf{z}} \cup \{\mathbf{b}^n\}$; /* Add a new shared component S^n */
  $n \leftarrow n + 1$;
end
$n \leftarrow n - 1$;
$f^\star(\cdot) \leftarrow \frac{1}{2}[U_{1:n}^\top f_1(\cdot) + V_{1:n}^\top f_2(\cdot)]$; /* Save the function $f^\star$ */

5 Experiments

In Sect. 5.1 we describe the baseline models we compare against, and in Sect. 5.2 we describe the settings of the conducted experiments, such as model hyper-parameters or datasets used. In Sects. 5.3 and 5.4 we conduct experiments on synthetic data with know ground-truth - in Sect. 5.3 we benchmark the models in terms of retrieving the shared variables $\mathbf{Z}$, and in Sects. 5.4 we evaluate how the performance of the models degrades when the variance explained by the shared variables changes. Finally, in Sect. 5.5 we demonstrate a real-life use case of the proposed DCID method on brain MRI data, where the underlying ground-truth is not known.

5.1 Baselines

Multi-Task Learning (MTL). We train a DNN model in a standard multi-task setting, i.e., to predict both Y_1 and Y_2 with a shared feature extractor $f : \mathbb{R}^l \mapsto \mathbb{R}^k$ and task-specific linear heads $g_1, g_2 : \mathbb{R}^k \mapsto \mathbb{R}$. We then select as $\hat{\mathbf{Z}}$ the set of features of f, for which the magnitude of normalized weights of the task-specific heads exceeds a certain threshold T_{MTL} for both heads, i.e.:

$$f(\cdot)_i \in \hat{\mathbf{Z}} \implies T_{MTL} \leq \frac{|G_{1,i}|}{max|G_{1,:}|} \wedge T_{MTL} \leq \frac{|G_{2,i}|}{max|G_{2,:}|} \tag{10}$$

where G_1, G_2 are weight vectors of the linear heads g_1, g_2.

Multi-Task Feature Learning (MTFL). We train a multi-task DNN as in the MTL setting, and apply the algorithm for *sparse common feature learning* of [3] on the features of f. This results in new sparse features f' and their corresponding new prediction heads g'_1, g'_2. As in the above setting, we select features of f' with the magnitude of normalized weights for g'_i above a threshold T_{MTL}.

Adversarial Multi-Task Learning (Adv. MTL). Introduced in [26], this model learns 3 disjoint feature spaces: 2 task-specific, *private* feature spaces, and a *shared* space, with features common for both tasks. The model is trained in an adversarial manner, with the discriminator trying to predict the task from the shared features. Additionally, it imposes an orthogonality constraint on the shared and individual spaces, forcing them to contain different information.

5.2 Experimental Settings

Synthetic Data. For experiments with known ground-truth, we employed the Shapes3D dataset [8], which contains synthetic 64×64 pixel RGB images of simple 3-dimensional objects against a background, generated from 6 independent latent factors: floor hue, wall hue, object hue, scale, shape and orientation of the object, resulting in 480,000 samples total. We take the images as $\mathbf{X}$, and select different factors as the unobserved variables $\mathbf{Z}, \mathbf{Z_1}, \mathbf{Z_2}$. As the 6 factors are the only sources of variation in the observed data $\mathbf{X}$, it allows for an accurate evaluation of model performance in terms of retrieving $\mathbf{Z}$.

We employed the encoder architecture from [27] as the DNN backbone used to learn f_1 and f_2. The models were trained for a single pass over the dataset, with a mini-batch of size 128 using the Adam optimizer [22] with a learning rate of 10^{-4}. We repeated each experimental setting over 3 random seeds, each time splitting the dataset into different train/validation/test split with ratios of (70/15/15)%. For the hyperparameter sweep performed in Sect. 5.3 we considered: 10 values evenly spread on $[0, 1]$ for T of DCID, 10 values evenly spaced on $[0, 1]$ for T_{MTL} of MTL, MTFL, and Adv. MTL, 10 values evenly spread on a logarithmic scale of $[10^{-4}, 10]$ for the γ parameter of MTFL, and $\gamma, \lambda \in \{0.01, 0.05, 0.1, 0.5, 1\}$ and a learning rate of the discriminator in $\{10^{-4}, 10^{-3}\}$ for Adv. MTL.

Brain MRI Data. For the experiments on brain MRI scans (Sect. 5.5) we employed data from the UK Biobank (UKB) medical database [39]. Specifically, we selected data for participants who underwent the brain scanning procedure, self-identified as "white-British", and have a similar genetic ancestry, which resulted in 34, 314 data points. As the input data $\mathbf{X}$ we took the T1-weighted structural scans, which were non-linearly registered to an MNI template [1,28], and downsampled them to a size of $96 \times 96 \times 96$ voxels. For Y_2, we selected body mass-related measurements available in the dataset, such as the total body fat mass (BFM), weight, or body mass index (BMI). For Y_1, we computed the total volumes of several brain Regions of Interest (ROIs), e.g., the total volume of hippocampi or lateral ventricles, using the Synthseg software [6].

We employed a 3D MobileNetV2 [24], with a width parameter of 2, as the DNN architecture used to learn f_1 and f_2. The models were trained for 40 epochs with a mini-batch size of 12 using the Adam optimizer with a learning rate of 10^{-4}. For each possible pair of Y_1 and Y_2 we repeated the experiments across 3 random seeds, each time selecting a different 30% of the samples as the test set.

5.3 Learning the Shared Features Z

To evaluate how accurately do different models learn the underlying shared features $\mathbf{Z}$, we trained them in controlled settings with known ground-truth. We created the latent variables from the 6 factors of the Shapes3D dataset, by randomly selecting two individual factors Z_1, Z_2 and one shared factor Z, and constructed the target variables as $Y_1 = Z_1 + Z$ and $Y_2 = Z_2 + Z$. This resulted in 60 possible scenarios with different underlying latent variables. To ensure a fair comparison, for each model we performed a grid search over all hyperparameters on 30 random scenarios, and evaluated it on the remaining 30 scenarios using the best found hyperparameter setting.

The resulting ICM scores are shown in Table 1. The proposed DCID model performed best both in terms of the final ICM score, as well as the individual scores. The MTL and MTFL methods performed similarly in terms of the ICM

score, with MTL achieving higher *informativeness*, and MTFL a lower *minimality* score. The Adv. MTL model had the lowest ICM, performing well only in terms of *minimality*.

Table 1. ICM scores of models trained on the Shapes3D dataset to retrieve the shared **Z**. Reported are the mean and standard deviation of each score over 90 runs per model (30 scenarios × 3 random seeds).

Model	ICM ↑	Informativeness ↑	Compactness ↑	Minimality ↓
Adv. MTL	0.06 (±0.05)	0.22 (±0.11)	0.22 (±0.11)	0.03 (±0.02)
MTL	0.18 (±0.14)	0.65 (±0.19)	0.33 (±0.19)	0.23 (±0.12)
MTFL	0.19 (±0.15)	0.47 (±0.23)	0.37 (±0.22)	0.12 (±0.08)
DCID (ours)	**0.62** (±0.15)	**0.85** (±0.07)	**0.73** (±0.17)	**0.01** (±0.02)

5.4 Variance Explained by Z and Model Performance

We further investigated how the amount of variance in Y_1, Y_2 explained by $\mathbf{Z}$ influences model performance, with two series of experiments. In the first one, we controlled τ, the ratio of variance in Y_1, Y_2 explained by the shared variables $\mathbf{Z}$ to the variance explained by the individual variables $\mathbf{Z_1}, \mathbf{Z_2}$, i.e.:

$$\tau = \frac{R^2(\mathbf{Z}, [Y_1, Y_2])}{R^2([\mathbf{Z_1}, \mathbf{Z_2}], [Y_1, Y_2])} \tag{11}$$

We created 15 different base scenarios, each time selecting a different pair of variables as $\mathbf{Z_1}, \mathbf{Z_2}$, and the remaining 4 as $\mathbf{Z}$. For each scenario we then varied τ 17 times on a logarithmic scale from 0.1 to 10, and trained models using their best hyperparameter settings from Sect. 5.3.

We plot the resulting ICM scores against τ in Fig. 4. Firstly, all the models fail to recover $\mathbf{Z}$ for $\tau \leq 0.3$, i.e., when the signal of $\mathbf{Z}$ is weak. For $\tau \in [0.3, 2.3]$ the DCID model outperforms the baselines by a wide margin, even for $\tau < 1$. The MTL models begin to recover $\mathbf{Z}$ only when it dominates the signal in the target variables. Interestingly, the performance of DCID drops suddenly for $\tau = 2.37$, and is outperformed by the MTL and MTFL models for $\tau > 2.8$. This is a surprising behavior, and we observed it occur independently of values of the threshold T (see Fig. 1 of the supplementary material).

In the second scenario, we controlled κ, the ratio of variance explained by $\mathbf{Z}$ in Y_1 to the variance explained in Y_2, i.e.:

$$\kappa = \frac{R^2(\mathbf{Z}, Y_1)}{R^2(\mathbf{Z}, Y_2)} \tag{12}$$

We created 60 base scenarios, similarly as in Sect. 5.3, and for each we varied κ 6 times evenly on the scale from 0.1 to 1. Again, we selected the model hyperparameters that performed best in Sect. 5.3.

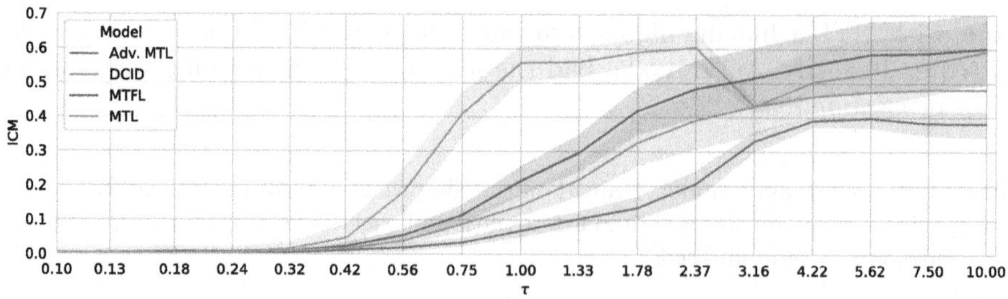

Fig. 4. *ICM* scores (y-axis) of different models plotted against τ, the ratio of variance in Y_1, Y_2 explained by $\mathbf{Z}$ to the variance explained by $\mathbf{Z_1}, \mathbf{Z_2}$ (x-axis, logarithmic scale).

We plot the resulting *ICM* scores against κ in Fig. 5. For $\kappa \in [0.5, 1]$ the DCID model retains a consistent performance. For values of κ below 0.5 its performance decreases linearly, for $\kappa \leq 0.2$ achieving lower *ICM* scores than the MTL and MTFL models. The scores in the low κ regime are higher, however, than the scores for low τ values, indicating that while DCID performs best when $\mathbf{Z}$ explains a large amount of variance in both target variables, it is also beneficial if at least one of the target variables is strongly associated with $\mathbf{Z}$. The baseline models, while achieving lower scores overall, seem to have their performance hardly affected by changes in κ.

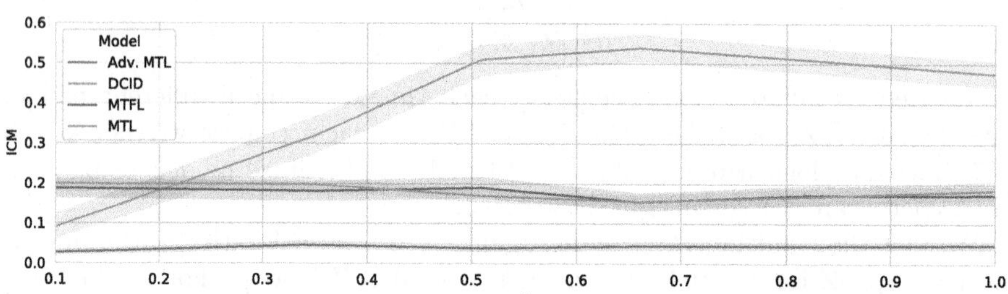

Fig. 5. *ICM* scores (y-axis) of different models plotted against κ, the ratio of variance explained by $\mathbf{Z}$ in Y_1 to the variance explained in Y_2 (x-axis). For $\kappa = 1$ the shared variables explain the same amount of variance in both target variables.

5.5 Obesity and the Volume of Brain Regions of Interest (ROIs)

Background. The occurrence of neuropsychiatric disorders is associated with a multitude of factors. For example, the risk of developing dementia can depend on age [11,37], ethnicity [10,35], or genetic [16,38], vascular [12,31], and even dietary [17,42] factors. However, only a subset of these factors are modifiable.

Being aware of the genetic predisposition of an individual for developing a disorder does not directly translate into possible preventive actions. On the other hand, mid-life obesity is a known factor for dementia, which can be potentially acted upon [5,18]. Several studies analyzed the statistical relations between brain ROIs and obesity [13,14,32]. A natural limitation of these studies is the fact that they work with "aggregated" variables, quantifying obesity or ROI volumes as single values, potentially losing information about the complex traits. Phenomena such as the "obesity paradox", where obesity can have both adverse and positive effects [29], indicate the need for deeper dissecting the variables of interest and the connections between them.

Analysis Using DCID. We approach this problem by estimating the shared signal $\mathbf{Z}$ between Y_1, the body fat mass (BFM), and Y_2, the volume of different brain ROIs. We trained several DCID models on the UKB data to predict BFM and volumes of the following ROIs: brain stem, cerebrospinal fluid (CSF), subcortical gray matter, ventricles, and the hippocampus. Additionally, we trained models for Y_1 being the body weight, or BMI, and report results for these in Sect. 2 of the supplementary material. Since the main interest lies in the effect of obesity on the ROIs, we constructed "surrogate" variables of Y_1, denoted by $\psi_1(\mathbf{Z})$ (see Eq. 1), which isolate the shared signal in Y_1 from the individual one. This is a conservative approach since it only utilizes features of the model trained to predict Y_1, with the information about Y_2 used only to rotate the features and extract the shared dimensions.

First, we demonstrate how $\psi_1(\mathbf{Z})$ allows for more accurate estimates of change in the ROIs, since it ignores the signal in Y_1 which is independent of Y_2. We fitted $\mathbf{Z}$ on the training data by selecting shared components with a threshold $T > 0.2$. We then obtained predictions of $\psi_1(\mathbf{Z})$ on the test set and computed their correlation with the ROI. We report the results for all the ROIs in Table 2, and plot BFM and $\psi_1(\mathbf{Z})$ against the volume of the subcortical gray matter for a single model in Fig. 6. For all ROIs the surrogate variable is correlated stronger than BFM, up to 8-fold for the ventricles, while retaining the sign of the coefficient. The smallest gains seem to be achieved for CSF, where the spread of coefficients over different runs is also the highest.

Secondly, we show how obtaining $\psi_1(\mathbf{Z})$ allows us to estimate the variance explained separately in Y_1 and Y_2, which is not possible by merely computing the correlation coefficient between Y_1 and Y_2. We plot the ratio of explained variance for each ROI in Fig. 7. While $\psi_1(\mathbf{Z})$ explains a similar amount of variance for ventricles and BFM, we can see bigger disparities for other ROIs, especially for the brain stem, where the variance explained in BFM is negligible. This might indicate that predictions of the the brain stem volume from BFM would be less reliable than predictions of other ROIs.

Table 2. Pearson correlation coefficients between volumes of Regions of Interest (ROIs) in brain MRI scans (columns) and two variables - Y_1, being the measurements of total body fat mass (first row), and a surrogate variable $\psi_1(\mathbf{Z})$, isolating the signal of the shared variables $\mathbf{Z}$ contributing to Y_1. In parentheses, we report the standard deviation of the coefficients over 3 training runs over different subsets of data.

Variable	Brain Stem	CSF	Gray Matter	Hippocampus	Ventricles
Y_1	−0.03 (±0.01)	0.01 (±0.00)	0.04 (±0.00)	0.05 (±0.00)	−0.02 (±0.00)
$\psi_1(\mathbf{Z})$	−0.20 (±0.07)	0.06 (±0.22)	0.25 (±0.04)	0.22 (±0.05)	−0.17 (±0.08)

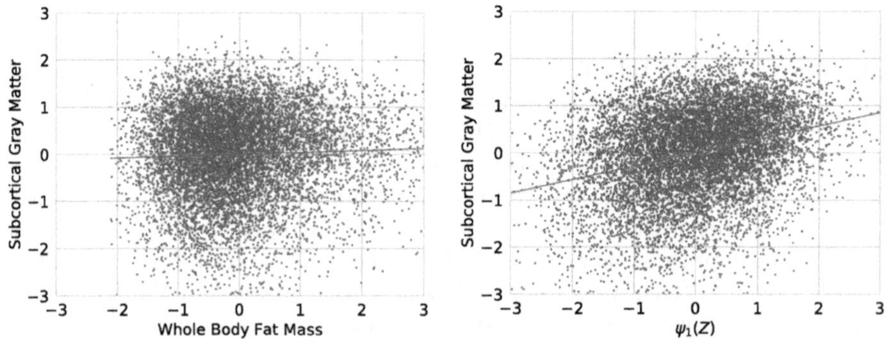

(a) (b)

Fig. 6. Volumes of subcortical gray matter plotted against body fat mass (*a*) and against the surrogate variable $\psi_1(\mathbf{Z})$ (*b*), for a single trained model. All variables were standardized to a z-score before plotting. (Color figure online)

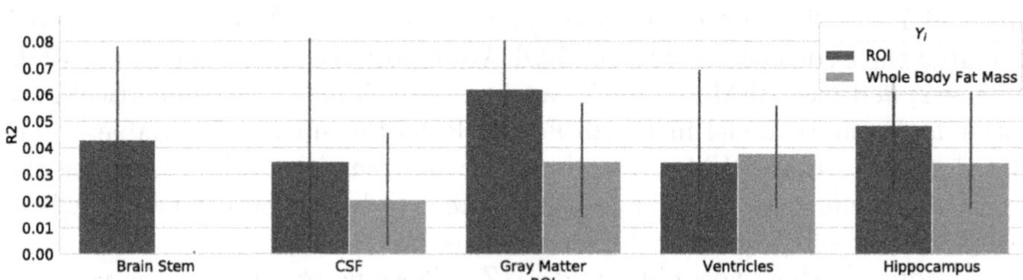

Fig. 7. Ratio of total variance explained by the surrogate variable $\psi_1(\mathbf{Z})$ in different brain Regions of Interest (ROIs) (blue bars) and in BFM (yellow bars). (Color figure online)

6 Discussion

In this work, we approached in a systematic manner the task of recovering the latent signal shared between scalar variables, by formalizing the problem setting and defining an evaluation procedure for model benchmarking, and proposed a new method, DCID, for solving the task.

6.1 Results Summary

By conducting experiments in controlled settings on synthetic data we could analyze model performance wrt. properties of the latent variables. Notably, we observed that the baseline models performed poorly when the shared variables were not strongly dominating the signal in the data, which is arguably the more realistic setting. The DCID model proved more robust in these scenarios, outperforming the baselines in most cases. We note, however, that it was still sensitive to the magnitude of the shared signal, and, interestingly, exhibited a loss of performance when the shared signal was strongly dominating. Investigating the loss of performance in the strong-signal regime, and improving robustness in the low-signal one are thus two natural directions for future work. Nevertheless, we believe that DCID can serve as an easy-to-implement, yet effective baseline.

6.2 Limitations

A main assumption of the method is that the observed variables $\mathbf{X}$ are rich in information, preserving the signal about the latent variables. Since, in practice, we do not observe the latent variables, we cannot test whether this assumption holds. As a substitute safety measure, we can assess the performance in predicting the observed target variables Y. If these cannot be predicted accurately, then it is unlikely that the model will correctly recover the latent variables either. Furthermore, we note that the method should not be mistaken as allowing to reason about causal relations between variables. It could, however, be used as part of a preprocessing pipeline in a causal inference setting, e.g., for producing candidate variables for mediation analysis.

Acknowledgements. This research was funded by the HPI research school on Data Science and Engineering. Data used in the preparation of this article were obtained from the UK Biobank Resource under Application Number 40502.

Ethical Considerations. As mentioned in the main text (Sect. 5.2), we conducted the brain MRI experiments on the "white-British" subset of the UKB dataset. This was done to avoid unnecessary confounding, as the experiments were meant as a proof of concept, rather than a strict medical study. When conducting the latter, measures should be taken to include all available ethnicities whenever possible, in order to avoid increasing the already existing disparities in representations of ethnic minorities in medical studies.

References

1. Alfaro-Almagro, F., et al.: Image processing and quality control for the first 10,000 brain imaging datasets from UK biobank. Neuroimage **166**, 400–424 (2018)
2. Argyriou, A., Evgeniou, T., Pontil, M.: Multi-task feature learning. Adv. Neural Inform. Process. Syst. **19** (2006)
3. Argyriou, A., Evgeniou, T., Pontil, M.: Convex multi-task feature learning. Mach. Learn. **73**, 243–272 (2008)

4. Bach, F.R., Jordan, M.I.: A probabilistic interpretation of canonical correlation analysis (2005)
5. Baumgart, M., Snyder, H.M., Carrillo, M.C., Fazio, S., Kim, H., Johns, H.: Summary of the evidence on modifiable risk factors for cognitive decline and dementia: a population-based perspective. Alzheimer's and Dementia **11**(6), 718–726 (2015)
6. Billot, B., et al.: Synthseg: Domain Randomisation for Segmentation of Brain MRI Scans of any Contrast and Resolution. arXiv:2107.09559 [cs] (2021)
7. Bousmalis, K., Trigeorgis, G., Silberman, N., Krishnan, D., Erhan, D.: Domain separation networks. Adv. Neural Inform. Process. Syst. **29** (2016)
8. Burgess, C., Kim, H.: 3d shapes dataset (2018)
9. Caruana, R.: Multitask learning. Springer (1998)
10. Chen, C., Zissimopoulos, J.M.: Racial and ethnic differences in trends in dementia prevalence and risk factors in the united states. Alzheimer's and Dementia: Trans. Res. and Clin. Intervent. **4**, 510–520 (2018)
11. Chen, J.H., Lin, K.P., Chen, Y.C.: Risk factors for dementia. J. Formos. Med. Assoc. **108**(10), 754–764 (2009)
12. Cherbuin, N., Mortby, M.E., Janke, A.L., Sachdev, P.S., Abhayaratna, W.P., Anstey, K.J.: Blood pressure, brain structure, and cognition: opposite associations in men and women. Am. J. Hypertens. **28**(2), 225–231 (2015)
13. Dekkers, I.A., Jansen, P.R., Lamb, H.J.: Obesity, brain volume, and white matter microstructure at MRI: a cross-sectional UK biobank study. Radiology **291**(3), 763–771 (2019)
14. Driscoll, I.: Midlife obesity and trajectories of brain volume changes in older adults. Hum. Brain Mapp. **33**(9), 2204–2210 (2012)
15. Eastwood, C., Williams, C.K.: A framework for the quantitative evaluation of disentangled representations. In: International Conference on Learning Representations (2018)
16. Emrani, S., Arain, H.A., DeMarshall, C., Nuriel, T.: Apoe4 is associated with cognitive and pathological heterogeneity in patients with Alzheimer's disease: a systematic review. Alzheimer's Res. Therapy **12**(1), 1–19 (2020)
17. Frausto, D.M., Forsyth, C.B., Keshavarzian, A., Voigt, R.M.: Dietary regulation of gut-brain axis in Alzheimer's disease: Importance of microbiota metabolites. Front. Neurosci. **15**, 736814 (2021)
18. Gorospe, E.C., Dave, J.K.: The risk of dementia with increased body mass index The risk of dementia with increased body mass index. Age Ageing **36**(1), 23–29 (2007) The risk of dementia with increased body mass index. Age Ageing **36**(1), 23–29 (2007)
19. Hardoon, D.R., Szedmak, S., Shawe-Taylor, J.: Canonical correlation analysis: an overview with application to learning methods. Neural Comput. **16**(12), 2639–2664 (2004)
20. He, K., Zhang, X., Ren, S., Sun, J.: Deep residual learning for image recognition. In: Proceedings of the IEEE Conference on Computer Vision and Pattern Recognition, pp. 770–778 (2016)
21. Hotelling, H.: Relations between two sets of variates. In: Breakthroughs in statistics, pp. 162–190. Springer (1992). https://doi.org/10.1007/978-1-4612-4380-9_14
22. Kingma, D.P., Ba, J.: Adam: A method for stochastic optimization. arXiv preprint arXiv:1412.6980 (2014)
23. Klami, A., Kaski, S.: Probabilistic approach to detecting dependencies between data sets. Neurocomputing **72**(1–3), 39–46 (2008)

24. Köpüklü, O., Kose, N., Gunduz, A., Rigoll, G.: Resource efficient 3d convolutional neural networks. In: 2019 IEEE/CVF International Conference on Computer Vision Workshop (ICCVW), pp. 1910–1919. IEEE (2019)
25. Kumar, A., Daume III, H.: Learning task grouping and overlap in multi-task learning. arXiv preprint arXiv:1206.6417 (2012)
26. Liu, P., Qiu, X., Huang, X.J.: Adversarial multi-task learning for text classification. In: Proceedings of the 55th Annual Meeting of the Association for Computational Linguistics (Volume 1: Long Papers), pp. 1–10 (2017)
27. Locatello, F., et al.: Challenging common assumptions in the unsupervised learning of disentangled representations. In: International Conference on Machine Learning, pp. 4114–4124. PMLR (2019)
28. Miller, K.L.: Multimodal population brain imaging in the UK biobank prospective epidemiological study. Nat. Neurosci. **19**(11), 1523–1536 (2016)
29. Monda, V., et al: Obesity and brain illness: from cognitive and psychological evidences to obesity paradox. Diabetes, Metab. Syndr. Obesity: Targets Therapy, pp. 473–479 (2017)
30. Pearson, K.: Liii. on lines and planes of closest fit to systems of points in space. London, Edinburgh, Dublin philosophical Mag. J. Sci. **2**(11), 559–572 (1901)
31. Prabhakaran, S.: Blood pressure, brain volume and white matter hyperintensities, and dementia risk. JAMA **322**(6), 512–513 (2019)
32. Raji, C.A.: Brain structure and obesity. Hum. Brain Mapp. **31**(3), 353–364 (2010)
33. Ruder, S.: An overview of multi-task learning in deep neural networks. arXiv preprint arXiv:1706.05098 (2017)
34. Schölkopf, B., Platt, J., Hofmann, T.: Multi-task feature learning (2007)
35. Shiekh, S.I., Cadogan, S.L., Lin, L.Y., Mathur, R., Smeeth, L., Warren-Gash, C.: Ethnic differences in dementia risk: a systematic review and meta-analysis. J. Alzheimers Dis. **80**(1), 337–355 (2021)
36. Shinohara, Y.: Adversarial multi-task learning of deep neural networks for robust speech recognition. In: Interspeech, pp. 2369–2372. San Francisco, CA, USA (2016)
37. Stephan, Y., Sutin, A.R., Luchetti, M., Terracciano, A.: Subjective age and risk of incident dementia: evidence from the national health and aging trends survey. J. Psychiatr. Res. **100**, 1–4 (2018)
38. Strittmatter, W.J., et al.: Apolipoprotein e: high-avidity binding to beta-amyloid and increased frequency of type 4 allele in late-onset familial alzheimer disease. Proc. Natl. Acad. Sci. **90**(5), 1977–1981 (1993)
39. Sudlow, C., et al.: UK biobank: an open access resource for identifying the causes of a wide range of complex diseases of middle and old age. PLoS Med. **12**(3), e1001779 (2015)
40. Wimalawarne, K., Sugiyama, M., Tomioka, R.: Multitask learning meets tensor factorization: task imputation via convex optimization. Adv. Neural Inform. Process. Syst. vol. 27 (2014)
41. Yang, Y., Hospedales, T.: Deep multi-task representation learning: A tensor factorisation approach. arXiv preprint arXiv:1605.06391 (2016)
42. Zhang, H., Greenwood, D.C., Risch, H.A., Bunce, D., Hardie, L.J., Cade, J.E.: Meat consumption and risk of incident dementia: cohort study of 493,888 UK biobank participants. Am. J. Clin. Nutr. **114**(1), 175–184 (2021)

Negative Prototypes Guided Contrastive Learning for Weakly Supervised Object Detection

Yu Zhang, Chuang Zhu(✉), Guoqing Yang, and Siqi Chen

School of Artificial Intelligence, Beijing University of Posts and Telecommunications, Beijing, China
czhu@bupt.edu.cn

Abstract. Weakly Supervised Object Detection (WSOD) with only image-level annotation has recently attracted wide attention. Many existing methods ignore the inter-image relationship of instances which share similar characteristics while can certainly be determined not to belong to the same category. Therefore, in order to make full use of the weak label, we propose the Negative Prototypes Guided Contrastive learning (NPGC) architecture. Firstly, we define Negative Prototype as the proposal with the highest confidence score misclassified for the category that does not appear in the label. Unlike other methods that only utilize category positive feature, we construct an online updated global feature bank to store both positive prototypes and negative prototypes. Meanwhile, we propose a pseudo label sampling module to mine reliable instances and discard the easily misclassified instances based on the feature similarity with corresponding prototypes in global feature bank. Finally, we follow the contrastive learning paradigm to optimize the proposal's feature representation by attracting same class samples closer and pushing different class samples away in the embedding space. Extensive experiments have been conducted on VOC07, VOC12 datasets, which shows that our proposed method achieves the state-of-the-art performance.

Keywords: Weakly supervised learning · Object detection · Contrastive learning

1 Introduction

Object detection is a classic computer vision task that jointly estimates class labels and bounding boxes of individual objects. In the last few decades, supervised learning of object detection has achieved remarkable progress thanks to the advances of Convolutional Neural Networks (CNNs) [12,13,23]. However, the supervision of object detection training process often requires precise bounding boxes labels at a large scale, which is very labor-intensive and time-consuming.

Weakly supervised object detection (WSOD) [2] has recently attracted wide attention due to its greatly substitution of only image-level annotated datasets for precise annotated datasets in training process. Most existing methods are

© The Author(s), under exclusive license to Springer Nature Switzerland AG 2023
D. Koutra et al. (Eds.): ECML PKDD 2023, LNAI 14170, pp. 36–51, 2023.
https://doi.org/10.1007/978-3-031-43415-0_3

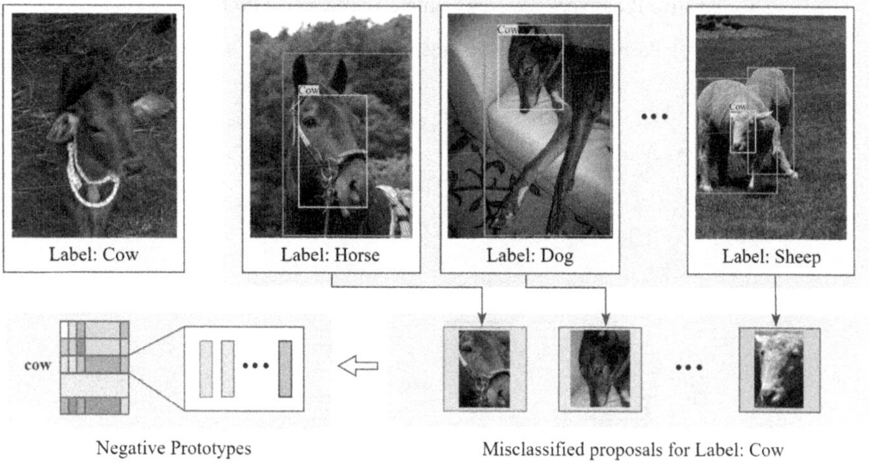

Fig. 1. Illustration for negative prototypes. The green box in each of the three top-right images refers to the ground truth bounding box of the category "Horse", "Dog" and "Sheep", respectively. The yellow boxes refer to the misclassified proposals for the category "Cow". It is clear that "Cow" does not appear in any of the three images, while there are still proposals mistakenly detected as "Cow". We consider such proposals as negative prototypes for the category "Cow". We then extract the feature representations of these proposals and store them in the negative prototypes bank. (Color figure online)

based on Multiple Instance Learning (MIL) [2,17,24,29,30] to transform WSOD into a multi-label classification task. [30] tended to select the proposal with high confidence as the pseudo label and adopted multiple branch to refine the original proposal to gain more precise bounding-box, which has become the pipeline for numerous subsequent studies.

However, with only image-level supervision, the classifier always faces the problem of **instance ambiguity** and **partial detection**. Instance ambiguity refers to the tendency to have missing instances or multiple grouped instances. Partial detection means that the detector tends to detect the most discriminative part of the target objects, which is also an inherent defect of the CNN network [9]. Thus, there is still a large performance gap between weakly (mAP=56.8% in VOC07) [17] and fully (mAP=89.3% in VOC07) [11] supervised object detectors. Different methods [6,17,20,21,24–26,28,33,39,40] have been introduced to mitigate the above mentioned problems of WSOD. However, these methods generally lack full exploitation of the given limited annotation information. They mainly focus on the single input image itself, ignoring the corresponding relationship of instances in the whole dataset.

Therefore, we think of mining the hidden inter-image category information in the whole dataset. Instances belonging to the same category share similar characteristics, and we consider the typical features of the same category in the whole dataset as class positive prototypes. In contrast, we propose the concept of negative prototypes as the proposals with high confidence score misclassified for

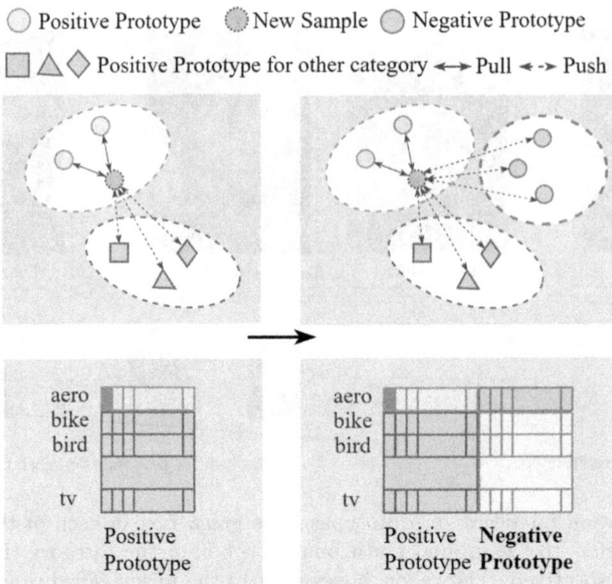

Fig. 2. Comparison of classic contrastive learning (left) and our contrastive learning (right). We proposed the concept of Negative Prototypes (proposal mis-classified for category which has similar characteristics to current category while can certainly be determined not to belong to) and construct a global feature bank to store both positive prototype and negative prototype.

the category that does not appear in image label, which is illustrated in detail in Fig. 1. Observation reveals that negative prototypes always contain valuable category-specific discriminative features. The detector tends to produce false predictions in the regions containing category discriminative features due to the overfitting of discriminative regions (e.g. the heads of the dog and the horse). By leveraging the positive prototypes, we can retrieve several missing instances, and likewise, by leveraging the negative prototypes, we are also able to alleviate the problem of partial detection.

In this paper, we propose a global negative prototypes guided contrastive learning weakly supervised object detection framework (NPGC). Our intuition is to fully exploit both visually correlated and visually discriminative category information in the whole dataset to improve the object classification ability of the weakly supervised detector. We construct an online updated global feature bank to store multiple class Positive Prototypes (PP) and Negative Prototypes (NP) from the whole dataset. Meanwhile, we design a novel Pseudo Label Sampling (PLS) module, which is used to mine the missing instances and punish overfitted instances that are prone to be partially detected. Based on the average feature similarity of candidate proposals and the positive prototypes of the same category, we can obtain a threshold τ_{pos} to mine proposals that might be omitted. Similarly, according to the average feature distance of candidate proposals and the negative prototypes of the same category with maximum similarity, a threshold τ_{neg} can also be obtained so as to discard the partial overfitted instances. Afterwards, as shown in Fig. 2, we leverages a contrastive learning paradigm to narrow the distance in representation space between positive sample pairs and push the distance between negative sample pairs.

Our key contributions can be summarized as follows:

- First, we construct an elaborate global negative prototypes guided contrastive learning weakly supervised object detection framework.
- Second, we propose negative prototypes which contain valuable category-specific discriminative features. We construct an online updated global feature bank to store both class positive prototypes and negative prototypes, and then leverage contrast learning loss to optimize it.
- Third, we devise a pseudo label sampling module, which utilized inter-image information from the global feature bank into pseudo proposal selection. This module effectively enables detector to mine the missing instances and simultaneously punish overfitted instances to alleviate the discriminal part detection problem.

2 Related Work

2.1 Weakly Supervised Object Detection

Bilen [2] unifies deep convolutional network and Multi-Instance Learning (MIL) in an end-to-end WSOD network called Weakly Supervised Deep Detection Network (WSDDN) for the first time. As an improvement to WSDDN, Tang *et al.* [30] gradually optimizes the predict bounding boxes by selecting high confidence region as pseudo label and adding an Online Instance Classifier Refinement module (OICR). Based on [30], in order to further improve detector's performance, Tang *et al.* [29] introduces a Proposal Clustering Learning (PCL) method for candidate proposals, so that proposals with similar features could be clustered together as much as possible. More recently, Huang *et al.* [17] proposes Comprehensive Attention Self-Distillation (CASD) framework that aggregate attention maps of input-wise and layer-wise to reach more balanced feature learning. Yin *et al.* [37] devises an Instance Mining framework with Class Feature Bank (IM-CFB), which uses the uses the top-similarity scored instance to improve proposal selection. Seo *et al.* [25] proposes a minibatch-level instance labeling and Weakly Supervised Contrastive Learning (WSCL) method with feature bank, while it may encounter the situation that the same category does not appear in the same minibatch. Inspired by [25], we propose a global class feature bank strategy and innovatively merge the prototypes of category negative samples, instead of solely employing the positive prototypes.

2.2 Contrastive Learning

Recently, there has been a trend towards exploring contrastive loss for representation learning. The idea of contrastive learning is to pull the samples from the positive pair closer together and push the samples from the negative pair apart. For instance, Hjelm *et al.* [16] propose Deep InfoMax to maximize the mutual information between the input and output of a deep network for unsupervised representation learning. More recently, Chen *et al.* [3] presents a method for learning visual representations, which maximizes the agreement between different augmented views of the same image via a contrastive loss. He *et al.* [15] proposes Momentum Contrast (MoCo), which utilizes a memory bank to store instance features. The purpose is to learn the representation by matching features of the same instance in different augmented views. Tian *et al.* [31] extends the input to more than two views. These methods are all based on a similar contrastive loss associated with Noise Contrastive Estimation (NCE) [14]. Oord *et al.* [22] proposed Contrastive Predictive Coding (CPC) that learns representations for sequential data. We choose the InfoNCE loss from [22] to minimize the distance between samples of the same category and maximize the distance between samples of different categories.

3 Proposed Method

In this paper, we introduce a negative prototypes guided contrastive learning weakly supervised object detection framework. The overall architecture of the proposed network is shown in Fig 3. We employ a MIL branch and an instance refinement branch as the basic network. On this basis we utilised a context-based feature extraction module to obtain more effective feature representation and designed a novel contrastive branch to employ the hidden inter-image information.

3.1 Preliminaries

Formally, given a weakly supervised dataset D, we denote $I \in \mathbb{R}^{h\times w\times 3}$ as an input image from D. The image-level category label $y = \{y_1, \ldots, y_C\} \in \mathbb{R}^{C\times 1}$, where C is the number of weakly supervised dataset categories. The corresponding region proposals pre-generated are $R = \{r_1, \ldots, r_N\}$, where N is total number of proposals.

MIL Branch. For an input image I and its region proposals R, a CNN backbone firstly extracts the image feature map F. F is then fed into the feature extractor module containing different pooling layers and two Fully-Connected (FC) layers to obtain proposal feature vectors fc_{cls} and fc_{det}. Subsequently, proposal features fc_{cls} and fc_{det} pass through MIL branch according to WSDDN [2], which includes two streams to produce classification score matrices $X_{cls} \in \mathbb{R}^{C\times N}$ and detection score matrices $X_{det} \in \mathbb{R}^{C\times N}$, respectively. X_{cls} normalized by a softmax layer $\sigma(\cdot)$ along the classes (rows) representing the probability of a region r being classified as category c, whereas X_{det} computed along the regions (columns) representing the probability of whether detecting region r for category

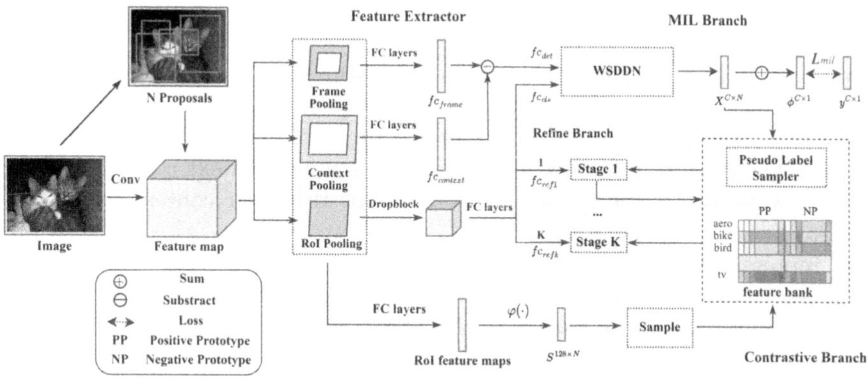

Fig. 3. Overall architecture of the proposed method. NPGC consists of four major components: Feature extractor, MIL branch, Contrastive branch, and Online instance refine branch. We constructed a global feature bank to store both positive prototypes and negative prototypes, which utilized contrastive learning to pull close the samples from the positive pair and to push apart the samples from the negative pair. We employ a pseudo label sampling module to mine the missing instances and punish overfitted instances.

c are obtained. The final proposal score $X \in \mathbb{R}^{C \times N}$ is computed via an element-wise product $X = \sigma(X_{cls}) \odot \sigma(X_{det})$. The image score $\phi \in \mathbb{R}^{C \times 1}$ is obtained by the sum over all proposals, $\phi = \sum_{r=1}^{N} X_r$, and the following multi class cross entropy is minimized,

$$L_{mil} = -\sum_{c=1}^{C} \{y_c \log \phi_c + (1 - y_c) \log(1 - \phi_c)\} \tag{1}$$

where ϕ_c equals to image score ϕ for the c-th class, y_c represents whether an object of category c is presented in the image.

Online Instance Refine Branch. For the k-th refine branch ($k \in \{1, \ldots, K\}$), $fc_{ref^k} \in \mathbb{R}^{(C+1) \times N}$ is the input proposal feature vector (The (C+1)-th category refers to background class). Each refinement stage is supervised by the previous stage, thus the pseudo ground truth label $\hat{y}^k_{c,r} \in \mathbb{R}^{(C+1) \times N}$ for stage k is generated from the last stage's output. Following the general pipeline [36] an extra regression stream is added to regress bounding boxes online. Overall, the instance refinement loss L^k_{ref} is defined as,

$$L^k_{ref} = -\{\frac{1}{N^k} \sum_{r=1}^{N^k} \sum_{c=1}^{C+1} \hat{y}^k_{c,r} \log x^k_{c,r} - \frac{1}{G^k} \sum_{r=1}^{G^k} Smooth_{L1}(t^k_r, \hat{t^k_r})\} \tag{2}$$

where N^k is the number of proposals and G^k is the total number of positive proposals in the k-th branch. t_r and $\hat{t_r}$ are the coordinate offsets and sizes of the r-th predicted and ground truth bounding-box.

3.2 Feature Extractor

Inspired by [18], we extract three different features to represent each object proposal, which are the RoI feature, the context feature, and the frame feature, respectively. Specifically, the RoI feature is to represent the content of each proposal. The context feature is to represent the outer context content of each proposal, while the frame feature is to represent the inner context content of each proposal.

To represent the location of each proposal, we follow [18,39] to subtract the pooled context feature $fc_{context}$ from the frame feature fc_{frame} to obtain the input representation of the detection branch fc_{det}. Meanwhile, we leverage a dropblock to randomly mask out some blocks of the RoI feature map. We then let it go through two fc layers and serve as the input representation of the classification fc_{cls} and refine branch $fc_{ref^k}, k \in \{1, \cdots, K\}$. By considering more information of the surrounding parts of the proposal, the extracted feature contains more location information and can effectively alleviate the problem of partial detection.

3.3 Contrastive Branch

For each image, all we know is its corresponding image level label, thus we intend to make as much use of this information as possible. Instances of the same category share similar characteristics, thus it is possible for us to extract several positive instance prototypes of each category from the entire data set, which is useful for alleviating the problem of missing instances. At the same time, we can also extract the mis-classified instances corresponding to certain category from the whole data set and treat them as negative instance prototypes, which share the similar discriminative features of the highly overfitted region. We can leverage this property to mitigate the problem of partial detection.

Following [25], we construct a similarity head $\varphi(\cdot)$ as shown in Fig 3, which maps the input RoI feature vectors to $S \in \mathbb{R}^{128\times N}$ a 128-dimensional embedding space. For each ground truth category c from image I, we choose the top ranking proposal $\tilde{r}_{c,m} = \arg\max_N(X_c)$ from the final proposal score $X \in \mathbb{R}^{C\times N}$, where m is the proposal index. And $\tilde{s}_{c,m}$ denoted as the corresponding feature representation of the top ranking proposal in the embedding space. And we store it into the positive feature bank.

Negative Prototypes. Our objective is to discover the negative prototypes of each category, so as to drive the detector's predictions away from the corresponding negative prototypes.

It can be calculated from the final proposal score matrix $X \in \mathbb{R}^{C\times N}$ that each image, except for categories in its ground truth label, gives out the index of the highest confidence score proposal mis-classified for other categories. This instance exactly is the negative prototype of its predicted category. Since we know explicitly that this proposal's prediction category is by no means exist in this image, yet it appears to be this category with high confidence. For example, in an input image labeled with "cat", one of the proposals is predicted to be "dog" with high confidence, but obviously "dog" shouldn't have been existed in this image. Therefore, we can conclude that this proposal has feature expression which tends to be mis-classified with "dog" while it is certainly not "dog". In this case, we suppose such proposal a negative prototype of category "dog", then we take its representation feature and store it into the negative feature bank.

The total global feature bank is denoted as $M = \bigcup_{c=1}^{C} S_c^{pos} \cup S_c^{neg}$, where S^{pos} is the positive prototype bank and S^{neg} is the negative prototype bank. For each selected negative prototype representation $s_{c,i}$, we select the most similar feature $s_{c,j}^{neg}$ from S_c^{neg} to maximize the assistance of the current instance.

$$s_{c,j}^{neg} = r \cdot s_{c,j}^{neg} + (1 - r) \cdot s_{c,i} \tag{3}$$

where r is the momentum coefficient [15], $s_{c,i}$ refers to the newly selected negative prototype, $s_{c,j}^{neg}$ refers to the the most similar feature with $s_{c,i}$ from S_c^{neg}. And the bank updating strategy is the same for the positive prototype bank.

Pseudo Label Sampling Module. As shown in Fig. 4, we construct a pseudo label sampling module to mine the missing instances and discard the overfitted instances.

We first calculate the representation feature similarity $sim(\cdot)$ between the top ranking proposal $\tilde{s}_{c,m}$ and the positive prototypes s_c^{pos} from the positive prototype bank. The average similarity is regarded as the threshold τ_{pos} for mining positive samples.

$$\tau_{pos} = \frac{1}{|S_c^{pos}|} \sum_{i=1}^{|S_c^{pos}|} sim(\tilde{s}_{c,m}, s_{c,i}^{pos}) \tag{4}$$

For each candidate proposal $r \in R$, we calculate the similarity between s_r and the top ranking proposal feature $\tilde{s}_{c,m}$, from which we can mine proposals might be omitted by selecting candidate proposals whose similarity exceed τ_{pos}.

$$sim(s_r, \tilde{s}_{c,m}) > \tau_{pos} \tag{5}$$

Accordingly, we calculate the similarity between each candidate proposal feature s_r and its corresponding negative prototype $\tilde{s}_{c,r}^{neg}$ with maximum similarity, where $\tilde{s}_{c,r}^{neg} = \arg\max_i(sim(s_r, s_{c,i}^{neg})), i = \{1, \cdots, |S_c^{neg}|\}$. The average similarity is regarded as the threshold τ_{neg} for discarding negative samples

$$\tau_{neg} = \frac{1}{|R|} \sum_{r=1}^{|R|} sim(s_r, \tilde{s}_{c,r}^{neg}) \tag{6}$$

The feature similarity between current instance and its negative prototype represents the probability of belonging to easily mis-classified discriminal regions.

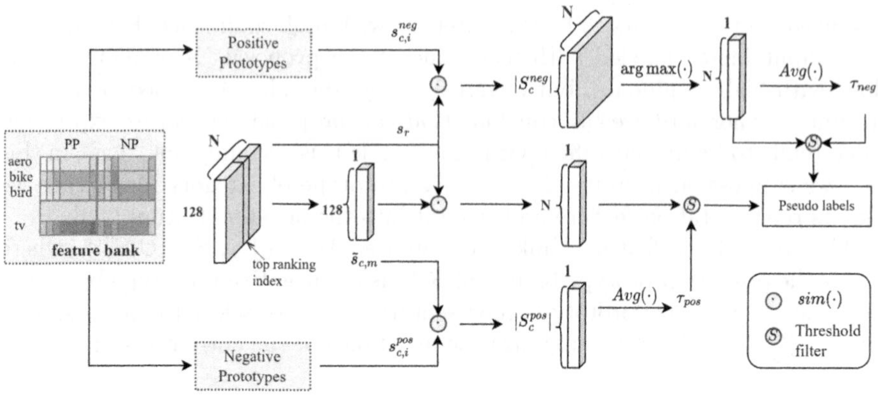

Fig. 4. Pseudo Label Sampling Module

Instances with low feature similarity , i.e. those below the threshold τ_{neg}, means that the instance is less likely overfitted and should be reserved.

$$sim(s_r, \tilde{s}_{c,r}^{neg}) < \tau_{neg} \tag{7}$$

Contrastive Learning: We use contrastive learning to optimize the feature representations for the proposals by attracting positive samples closer together and repelling negative samples away from positives samples in the embedding space. To obtain more views of samples for contrastive learning, we apply the same feature augmentation methods following [25].

$$L_{cont} = -\frac{1}{|M|}\sum_{i=1}^{|M|}\log\frac{exp(s_i \cdot s_+/\varepsilon)}{exp(s_i \cdot s_+/\varepsilon) + \sum_{S_-} exp(s_i \cdot s_+/\varepsilon)} \tag{8}$$

where $M = \bigcup_{c=1}^{C} S_c^{pos} \cup S_c^{neg}$, and ε is a temperature parameter introduced in [19]. We use the contrastive loss to pull s_i close to s_+ of the same class while pushing it away from s_- both positive prototypes from other classes and its negative prototypes, and thus enhance the discrimination and generalization of current instance representation

Finally, the total loss of training the network is the combination of all the loss functions mentioned before.

$$L_{total} = L_{mil} + \sum_{k=1}^{K} L_{ref}^{k} + \lambda L_{cont} \tag{9}$$

4 Experimental Results

4.1 Datasets

We evaluate our proposed method on both Pascal VOC 2007 and Pascal VOC 2012 [7] , which are commonly used to assess WSOD performance. For the VOC datasets, we employ the trainval set (5,011 images in VOC 2007, 11,540 images in VOC 2012) for training and evaluate the model's performance on the test set. VOC 2007 and 2012 both contain 20 categories. We apply Mean average precision (mAP) with standard IoU threshold (0.5) to evaluate the object detection accuracy on the testing set.

4.2 Implementation Details

We adopt the Imagenet [5] pretrained model VGG16 [27] as the backbone. For VGG16, following the previous methods [25], we replace a global average pooling layer with a RoI pooling layer, and remove the last FC layer leaving two FC layers, which all the heads including the similarity head are attached to. Proposal generating method such as Selective Search [32] and MCG [1] are used for VOC dataset to generate initial proposals, and we use around 2,000 proposals per image. Then, the whole model is trained on 4 NVIDIA GeForce GTX 3090 with 24 GB GPU memory using a SGD optimizer with an initial learning rate of 0.01, weight decay of 0.0001 and momentum of 0.9 are used to optimize the model.

The overall iteration numbers are set to 35,000, 70,000 for VOC 2007, VOC 2012. Following the previous methods [17,24,30], the inputs are multi-scaled to {480, 576, 688, 864, 1000, 1200} for both training and inference time. The final predictions are made after applying NMS of which threshold is set to 0.4 for both datasets. In the refinement branch, we set the number of refinement stages $K = 3$. The bank size M is set to 6, which is experimentally illustrated in Table. 6. The hyperparameter ε from Eq. (8) is set to 0.2 following the experiments conducted in [3,19]. And hyperparameter λ from Eq. (9) is set to 0.03 as explained in Sect.4.5.

Table 1. Comparison of the State-of-the-arts methods on VOC07 and VOC12 of mAP(%).

Method	mAP(%) VOC07	mAP(%) VOC12
WSDDN [2] CVPR'16	34.8	-
OICR [30] CVPR'17	41.2	37.9
PCL [29] TPAMI'18	43.5	40.6
C-WSL [8] ECCV'18	46.8	43.0
C-MIL [34] CVPR'18	50.5	46.7
C-MIDN [10] ICCV'19	52.6	50.2
WSOD2 [38] ICCV'19	53.6	47.2
SLV [4] CVPR'20	53.5	49.2
MIST [24] CVPR'20	54.9	52.1
CASD [17] NIPS'20	56.8	53.6
IM-CFB [37] AAAI'21	54.3	49.4
CPE [21] TIP'22	55.9	54.3
NDI [35] IJCAI'22	56.8	53.9
Ours	**57.7**	**54.3**

4.3 Comparison with State-of-the-Arts

In Tables 1, 2 and 3, we compare our proposed method with other state-of-the-art algorithms on PASCAL VOC07 and VOC12. Regardless of backbone structure, the results show that our method achieves the 57.7% mAP and 54.3% mAP in VOC07 and VOC12, respectively, which outperforms the other methods and reach the new state-of-the-art performance.

More qualitative results are shown in Fig. 6, from which it can be seen that our model is able to mine the easily omitted multiple instances of the same category (car, person) and detect various objects of different classes (tvmoniter, pottleplant) in relatively complicated scenes.

Table 2. Comparison with the state-of-the-arts methods in terms of Per-class AP results on VOC07.

Method	Aero	Bike	Bird	Boat	Bottle	Bus	Car	Cat	Chair	Cow	Table	Dog	Horse	Motor	Person	Plant	Sheep	Sofa	Train	TV	**mAP**
WSDDN	39.4	50.1	31.5	16.3	12.6	64.5	42.8	42.6	10.1	35.7	24.9	38.2	34.4	56.6	9.4	14.7	30.2	40.7	54.7	46.9	34.8
OICR	58.0	62.4	31.1	19.4	13.0	65.1	62.2	28.4	24.8	44.7	30.6	25.3	37.8	65.5	15.7	24.1	41.7	46.9	64.3	62.6	41.2
PCL	54.4	69.0	39.3	19.2	15.7	62.9	64.4	30.0	25.1	52.5	44.4	19.6	39.3	67.7	17.8	22.9	46.6	57.5	58.6	63.0	43.5
C-WSL	62.9	64.8	39.8	28.1	16.4	69.5	68.2	47.0	27.9	55.8	43.7	31.2	43.8	65.0	10.9	26.1	52.7	55.3	60.2	66.6	46.8
C-MIL	62.5	58.4	49.5	32.1	19.8	70.5	66.1	63.4	20.0	60.5	**52.9**	53.5	57.4	68.9	8.4	24.6	51.8	58.7	66.7	63.5	50.5
C-MIDN	53.3	71.5	49.8	26.1	20.3	70.3	69.9	68.3	28.7	65.3	45.1	64.6	58.0	71.2	20.0	27.5	54.9	54.9	69.4	63.5	52.6
WSOD2	65.1	64.8	57.2	**39.2**	24.3	69.8	66.2	61.0	29.8	64.6	42.5	60.1	71.2	70.7	21.9	28.1	58.6	59.7	52.2	64.8	53.6
SLV	65.6	71.4	49.0	37.1	24.6	69.6	70.3	70.6	30.8	63.1	36.0	61.4	65.3	68.4	12.4	**29.9**	52.4	60.0	67.6	64.5	53.5
MIST	68.8	**77.7**	57.0	27.7	28.9	69.1	74.5	67.0	32.1	**73.2**	48.1	45.2	54.4	73.7	35.0	29.3	**64.1**	53.8	65.3	65.2	54.9
CASD	-	-	-	-	-	-	-	-	-	-	-	-	-	-	-	-	-	-	-	-	56.8
IM-CFB	64.1	74.6	44.7	29.4	26.9	73.3	72.0	71.2	28.1	66.7	48.1	63.8	55.5	68.3	17.8	27.7	54.4	62.7	70.5	66.6	54.3
CPE	62.4	76.4	**59.7**	33.8	28.7	71.7	66.1	**72.2**	**33.9**	67.7	47.6	**67.2**	60.0	71.7	18.1	29.9	53.8	58.9	**74.3**	64.1	55.9
NDI	-	-	-	-	-	-	-	-	-	-	-	-	-	-	-	-	-	-	-	-	56.8
Ours	**69.1**	77.1	54.7	31.8	**29.7**	**74.3**	**78.6**	71.5	20.1	72.6	34.5	61.6	**75.3**	**78.4**	**35.7**	24.1	59.1	**66.4**	72.9	**67.1**	**57.7**

Table 3. Comparison with the state-of-the-arts methods in terms of Per-class AP results on VOC12.

Method	Aero	Bike	Bird	Boat	Bottle	Bus	Car	Cat	Chair	Cow	Table	Dog	Horse	Motor	Person	Plant	Sheep	Sofa	Train	TV	**mAP**
OICR	67.7	61.2	41.5	25.6	22.2	54.6	49.7	25.4	19.9	47.0	18.1	26.0	38.9	67.7	2.0	22.6	41.1	34.3	37.9	55.3	37.9
PCL	-	-	-	-	-	-	-	-	-	-	-	-	-	-	-	-	-	-	-	-	40.6
C-WSL	74.0	67.3	45.6	29.2	26.8	62.5	54.8	21.5	22.6	50.6	24.7	25.6	57.4	71.0	2.4	22.8	44.5	44.2	45.2	66.9	43.0
C-MIL	-	-	-	-	-	-	-	-	-	-	-	-	-	-	-	-	-	-	-	-	46.7
C-MIDN	72.9	68.9	53.9	25.3	29.7	60.9	56.0	**78.3**	23.0	57.8	**25.7**	**73.0**	63.5	73.7	13.1	28.7	51.5	35.0	56.1	57.5	50.2
WSOD2	-	-	-	-	-	-	-	-	-	-	-	-	-	-	-	-	-	-	-	-	47.2
SLV	-	-	-	-	-	-	-	-	-	-	-	-	-	-	-	-	-	-	-	-	49.2
MIST	**78.3**	73.9	56.5	**30.4**	**37.4**	64.2	**59.3**	60.3	**26.6**	66.8	25.0	55.0	61.8	**79.3**	14.5	**30.3**	**61.5**	40.7	56.4	63.5	52.1
CASD	-	-	-	-	-	-	-	-	-	-	-	-	-	-	-	-	-	-	-	-	53.6
IM-CFB	-	-	-	-	-	-	-	-	-	-	-	-	-	-	-	-	-	-	-	-	49.4
CPE	-	-	-	-	-	-	-	-	-	-	-	-	-	-	-	-	-	-	-	-	54.3
NDI	-	-	-	-	-	-	-	-	-	-	-	-	-	-	-	-	-	-	-	-	53.9
Ours	75.4	**75.3**	**59.1**	29.6	30.6	**69.9**	56.8	63.0	23.3	**71.3**	25.3	63.1	**66.4**	76.7	**19.0**	25.5	61.4	**56.7**	**66.6**	**70.5**	**54.3**

4.4 Qualitative Results

It is shown in Fig. 5 that our method effectively addresses on the main challenges of WSOD compared to OICR [30]. The left columns show the results from OICR whereas the right columns show the results from our method. In (a) and (b), we investigate the effectiveness of our model in resolving the instance ambiguity problem which consists of missing instances and grouped instances, respectively. We can observe that many instances that have been ignored previously can be detected via our model. Meanwhile, in (b) we can also observe that grouped instances are separated into multiple bounding boxes. Moreover, the partial detection problem is largely alleviated shown in (c), especially for the categories with various poses such as dog, cat and person.

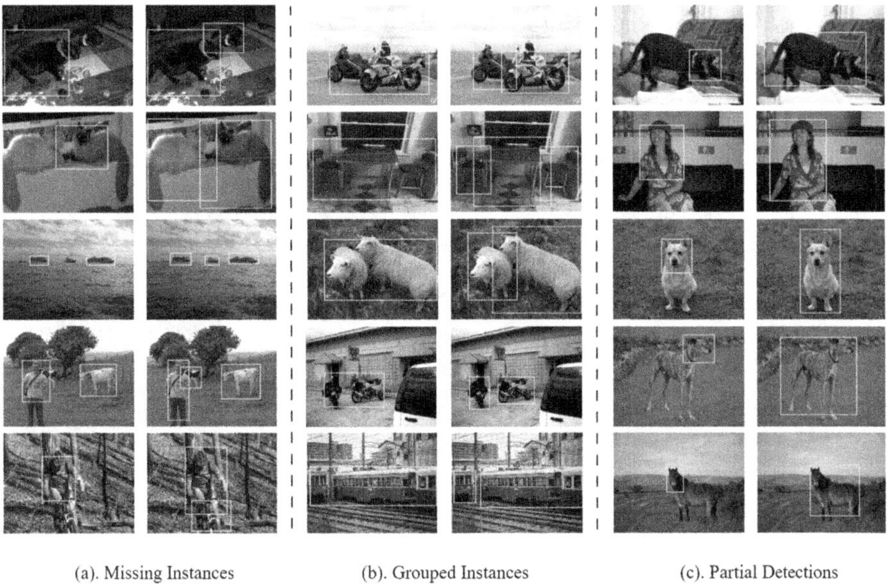

Fig. 5. Qualitative results on VOC 2007 test set. The left columns show the results from OICR whereas the right columns show the results from our method.

4.5 Ablation Study

In this section, we make a comprehensive ablation study of the effect gains from different components, the sensitivity of hyperparameters, and the length of feature bank. The experiments are implemented on the VOC 2007 dataset.

Components Effect. We conduct experiments to prove the effectiveness of each component in our proposed method as shown in Table 5, where PLS, CL, NP means the pseudo label sampling module, contrastive learning, negative prototypes mentioned in Sect. 3.3, respectively. Our Baseline is the framework in Fig. 3 without contrastive branch, which achieves 56.1% mAP.

Table 4. Ablation study on VOC 2007 dataset of different components in our method.

Baseline	PLS	CL	NP	mAP(%)
√				56.1
√	√			56.8(+0.7)
√	√	√		57.2(+1.1)
√	√	√	√	**57.7**(+1.6)

We firstly analyze the effect of PLS and CL algorithm on our method NPGC. As shown in Table 4, after applying PLS, our method achieves 56.8% mAP with

0.7% gains. After applyig both PLS and CL, it brings 1.1% gains in mAP. Based on this, we append the nagative prototyes into former structure, and it reach 57.7% mAP, which shows the effectiveness of our method.

Fig. 6. More detection results on VOC 2007 test set. Boxes in light green represent ground-truth boxes, and boxes in other colors represent the predicted bounding boxes and the confidence scores. (Color figure online)

Table 5. Ablation study on different hyperparameters' value in our method.

λ	0.01	0.02	0.03	0.04	0.05
mAP(%)	56.6	57.0	**57.7**	56.1	56.3

Hyperparameters. We provide the experiment results with different values of the hyperparameters we introduce. We conduct experiments on how to choose the loss parameter λ from Eq. (9) in Table 5, and $\lambda = 0.03$ achieves the best result. In Eq. (8), we use the same values of $\varepsilon = 0.2$ following the experiments conducted in other contrastive learning methods [3,19].

Length of Feature Bank. We finally analyze the effect of the length of feature bank. If the length is too small, the feature bank is difficult to store the diversity of instance representations well, resulting in less kind of objects collected. And if the length is too large, it is easy to absorb some noisy information during the learning of instance representations and background proposals will be selected incorrectly. In this paper, we recommend setting $M = 6$ to balance the number of stored instance features.

Table 6. Ablation study on the length of feature bank in our method.

M	2	4	6	8
mAP(%)	55.6	57.0	**57.7**	56.4

5 Conclusion

In conclusion, we presented a global negative prototypes guided contrastive learning weakly supervised object detection framework. We novelly introduce the concept of Negative Prototypes. Meanwhile, we construct a global feature bank to store both positive prototypes and negative prototypes, using contrastive learning to mine the hidden inter-image category information in the whole dataset.

Acknowledgements. This work was supported by the National Key R&D Program of China (2021ZD0109800), the National Natural Science Foundation of China (81972248) and BUPT innovation and entrepreneurship support program 2023-YC-A185.

Ethical Statement. This research was conducted in accordance with ethical guidelines and regulations. The paper aims to contribute to knowledge while upholding ethical standards.

References

1. Arbeláez, P., Pont-Tuset, J., Barron, J.T., Marques, F., Malik, J.: Multiscale combinatorial grouping. In: Proceedings of the IEEE Conference on Computer Vision and Pattern Recognition, pp. 328–335 (2014)
2. Bilen, H., Vedaldi, A.: Weakly supervised deep detection networks. In: Proceedings of the IEEE Conference on Computer Vision and Pattern Recognition, pp. 2846–2854 (2016)
3. Chen, T., Kornblith, S., Norouzi, M., Hinton, G.: A simple framework for contrastive learning of visual representations. In: International Conference on Machine Learning, pp. 1597–1607. PMLR (2020)
4. Chen, Z., Fu, Z., Jiang, R., Chen, Y., Hua, X.S.: Slv: Spatial likelihood voting for weakly supervised object detection. In: Proceedings of the IEEE/CVF Conference on Computer Vision and Pattern Recognition, pp. 12995–13004 (2020)
5. Deng, J., Dong, W., Socher, R., Li, L.J., Li, K., Fei-Fei, L.: Imagenet: A large-scale hierarchical image database. In: 2009 IEEE Conference on Computer Vision and Pattern Recognition, pp. 248–255. IEEE (2009)
6. Dong, B., Huang, Z., Guo, Y., Wang, Q., Niu, Z., Zuo, W.: Boosting weakly supervised object detection via learning bounding box adjusters. In: Proceedings of the IEEE/CVF International Conference on Computer Vision, pp. 2876–2885 (2021)
7. Everingham, M., Van Gool, L., Williams, C.K., Winn, J., Zisserman, A.: The pascal visual object classes (voc) challenge. Int. J. Comput. Vision **88**, 303–338 (2010)
8. Gao, M., Li, A., Yu, R., Morariu, V.I., Davis, L.S.: C-wsl: Count-guided weakly supervised localization. In: Proceedings of the European Conference on Computer Vision (ECCV), pp. 152–168 (2018)

9. Gao, W., et al.: Ts-cam: Token semantic coupled attention map for weakly supervised object localization. In: Proceedings of the IEEE/CVF International Conference on Computer Vision, pp. 2886–2895 (2021)
10. Gao, Y., et al.: C-midn: Coupled multiple instance detection network with segmentation guidance for weakly supervised object detection. In: Proceedings of the IEEE/CVF International Conference on Computer Vision, pp. 9834–9843 (2019)
11. Ghiasi, G., et al.: Simple copy-paste is a strong data augmentation method for instance segmentation. In: Proceedings of the IEEE/CVF Conference on Computer Vision And Pattern Recognition, pp. 2918–2928 (2021)
12. Girshick, R.: Fast r-CNN. In: Proceedings of the IEEE International Conference On Computer Vision, pp. 1440–1448 (2015)
13. Girshick, R., Donahue, J., Darrell, T., Malik, J.: Rich feature hierarchies for accurate object detection and semantic segmentation. In: Proceedings of the IEEE Conference On Computer Vision And Pattern Recognition, pp. 580–587 (2014)
14. Gutmann, M., Hyvärinen, A.: Noise-contrastive estimation: A new estimation principle for unnormalized statistical models. In: Proceedings of the Thirteenth International Conference on Artificial Intelligence and Statistics, pp. 297–304. JMLR Workshop and Conference Proceedings (2010)
15. He, K., Fan, H., Wu, Y., Xie, S., Girshick, R.: Momentum contrast for unsupervised visual representation learning. In: Proceedings of the IEEE/CVF Conference On Computer Vision and Pattern Recognition, pp. 9729–9738 (2020)
16. Hjelm, R.D., et al.: Learning deep representations by mutual information estimation and maximization. arXiv preprint arXiv:1808.06670 (2018)
17. Huang, Z., Ke, W., Huang, D.: Improving object detection with inverted attention. In: 2020 IEEE Winter Conference on Applications of Computer Vision (WACV), pp. 1294–1302. IEEE (2020)
18. Kantorov, V., Oquab, M., Cho, M., Laptev, I.: Contextlocnet: Context-aware deep network models for weakly supervised localization. In: Computer Vision-ECCV 2016: 14th European Conference, Amsterdam, The Netherlands, October 11–14, 2016, Proceedings, Part V 14. pp. 350–365. Springer (2016). https://doi.org/10.1007/978-3-319-46454-1_22
19. Khosla, P., et al.: Supervised contrastive learning. Adv. Neural. Inf. Process. Syst. **33**, 18661–18673 (2020)
20. Kosugi, S., Yamasaki, T., Aizawa, K.: Object-aware instance labeling for weakly supervised object detection. In: Proceedings of the IEEE/CVF International Conference on Computer Vision, pp. 6064–6072 (2019)
21. Lv, P., Hu, S., Hao, T.: Contrastive proposal extension with LSTM network for weakly supervised object detection. IEEE Trans. Image Process. **31**, 6879–6892 (2022)
22. Oord, A.v.d., Li, Y., Vinyals, O.: Representation learning with contrastive predictive coding. arXiv preprint arXiv:1807.03748 (2018)
23. Ren, S., He, K., Girshick, R., Sun, J.: Faster r-cnn: Towards real-time object detection with region proposal networks. Adv. Neural Inform. Process. Syst. **28** (2015)
24. Ren, Z., et al..: Instance-aware, context-focused, and memory-efficient weakly supervised object detection. In: Proceedings of the IEEE/CVF Conference on Computer Vision and Pattern Recognition, pp. 10598–10607 (2020)
25. Seo, J., Bae, W., Sutherland, D.J., Noh, J., Kim, D.: Object discovery via contrastive learning for weakly supervised object detection. In: Computer Vision-ECCV 2022: 17th European Conference, Tel Aviv, Israel, October 23–27, 2022, Proceedings, Part XXXI. pp. 312–329. Springer (2022). https://doi.org/10.1007/978-3-031-19821-2_18

26. Shen, Y., Ji, R., Chen, Z., Wu, Y., Huang, F.: Uwsod: toward fully-supervised-level capacity weakly supervised object detection. Adv. Neural. Inf. Process. Syst. **33**, 7005–7019 (2020)
27. Simonyan, K., Zisserman, A.: Very deep convolutional networks for large-scale image recognition. arXiv preprint arXiv:1409.1556 (2014)
28. Sui, L., Zhang, C.L., Wu, J.: Salvage of supervision in weakly supervised object detection. In: Proceedings of the IEEE/CVF Conference on Computer Vision and Pattern Recognition, pp. 14227–14236 (2022)
29. Tang, P., et al.: PCL: Proposal cluster learning for weakly supervised object detection. IEEE Trans. Pattern Anal. Mach. Intell. **42**(1), 176–191 (2018)
30. Tang, P., Wang, X., Bai, X., Liu, W.: Multiple instance detection network with online instance classifier refinement. In: Proceedings of the IEEE Conference on Computer Vision and Pattern Recognition, pp. 2843–2851 (2017)
31. Tian, Y., Krishnan, D., Isola, P.: Contrastive multiview coding. In: Vedaldi, A., Bischof, H., Brox, T., Frahm, J.-M. (eds.) ECCV 2020. LNCS, vol. 12356, pp. 776–794. Springer, Cham (2020). https://doi.org/10.1007/978-3-030-58621-8_45
32. Uijlings, J.R.R., van de Sande, K.E.A., Gevers, T., Smeulders, A.W.M.: Selective search for object recognition. Int. J. Comput. Vision **104**, 154–171 (2013)
33. Wan, F., Liu, C., Ke, W., Ji, X., Jiao, J., Ye, Q.: C-mil: Continuation multiple instance learning for weakly supervised object detection. In: Proceedings of the IEEE/CVF Conference on Computer Vision and Pattern Recognition, pp. 2199–2208 (2019)
34. Wan, F., Wei, P., Jiao, J., Han, Z., Ye, Q.: Min-entropy latent model for weakly supervised object detection. In: Proceedings of the IEEE Conference on Computer Vision and Pattern Recognition, pp. 1297–1306 (2018)
35. Wang, G., Zhang, X., Peng, Z., Tang, X., Zhou, H., Jiao, L.: Absolute wrong makes better: Boosting weakly supervised object detection via negative deterministic information. arXiv preprint arXiv:2204.10068 (2022)
36. Yang, K., Li, D., Dou, Y.: Towards precise end-to-end weakly supervised object detection network. In: Proceedings of the IEEE/CVF International Conference on Computer Vision, pp. 8372–8381 (2019)
37. Yin, Y., Deng, J., Zhou, W., Li, H.: Instance mining with class feature banks for weakly supervised object detection. In: Proceedings of the AAAI Conference on Artificial Intelligence. vol. 35, pp. 3190–3198 (2021)
38. Zeng, Z., Liu, B., Fu, J., Chao, H., Zhang, L.: Wsod2: Learning bottom-up and top-down objectness distillation for weakly-supervised object detection. In: Proceedings of the IEEE/CVF International Conference On Computer Vision, pp. 8292–8300 (2019)
39. Zhang, D., Zeng, W., Yao, J., Han, J.: Weakly supervised object detection using proposal-and semantic-level relationships. IEEE Trans. Pattern Anal. Mach. Intell. **44**(6), 3349–3363 (2020)
40. Zhong, Y., Wang, J., Peng, J., Zhang, L.: Boosting weakly supervised object detection with progressive knowledge transfer. In: Vedaldi, A., Bischof, H., Brox, T., Frahm, J.-M. (eds.) ECCV 2020. LNCS, vol. 12371, pp. 615–631. Springer, Cham (2020). https://doi.org/10.1007/978-3-030-58574-7_37

Voting from Nearest Tasks: Meta-Vote Pruning of Pre-trained Models for Downstream Tasks

Haiyan Zhao[1(✉)], Tianyi Zhou[2], Guodong Long[1], Jing Jiang[1], and Chengqi Zhang[1]

[1] Australian Artificial Intelligence Institute, University of Technology Sydney, Sydney, Australia
Haiyan.Zhao-2@student.uts.edu.au,
{guodong.long,jing.jiang,chengqi.zhang}@uts.edu.au
[2] University of Maryland, College Park, College Park, USA
tianyi@umd.edu

Abstract. As large-scale pre-trained models have become the major choices of various applications, new challenges arise for model pruning, e.g., can we avoid pruning the same model from scratch for downstream tasks? How to reuse the pruning results of previous tasks to accelerate the pruning for new tasks? To address these challenges, we create a small model for a new task from the pruned models of similar tasks. We show that a few fine-tuning steps on this model suffice to produce a promising pruned model for the new task. We study this "meta-pruning" from nearest tasks on two major classes of pre-trained models, convolutional neural network and vision transformer, under a limited budget of pruning iterations. Our study begins by investigating the overlap of pruned models for similar tasks and how the overlap changes over different layers and blocks. Inspired by these discoveries, we develop a simple but effective "Meta-Vote Pruning" method that significantly reduces the pruning iterations for a new task by initializing a sub-network from the pruned models of its nearest tasks. In experiments, we demonstrate MVP's accuracy, efficiency, and generalization advantages through extensive empirical studies and comparisons with popular pruning methods over several datasets.

Keywords: Model pruning · Meta learning · Pre-trained model

1 Introduction

Large-scale pre-trained models usually contain tens of millions or even billions of parameters for promising generalization performance. The computation and memory of modern GPUs or clusters can support to train such models, but directly deploying them to edge devices can easily violate the hardware limits on memory and computation. Network pruning [3,11,19,41] has been widely studied to compress neural nets by removing redundant connections and nodes. Numerous empirical results have verified that pruning can compress the original network into smaller sub-networks that still enjoy comparable performance. Instead

© The Author(s), under exclusive license to Springer Nature Switzerland AG 2023
D. Koutra et al. (Eds.): ECML PKDD 2023, LNAI 14170, pp. 52–68, 2023.
https://doi.org/10.1007/978-3-031-43415-0_4

of reducing the network to the target size by one-time pruning, iterative pruning that alternates between pruning and fine-tuning for iterations usually achieves better performance [12,18]. Theoretically, a line of recent works [8,26,36,49] attempts to prove the lottery ticket hypothesis, i.e., the existence of such sub-networks, for different pruning settings.

Large-scale pre-trained models are widely used in various domains [39,46,47]. In a variety of practical applications, a large-scale pre-trained network like ResNet-50 [13] or Vision Transformer (ViT) [6] usually needs to be pruned for a wide variety of devices and adapted to different downstream tasks. Running an iterative pruning algorithm for every device or task from the same pre-trained network can create an enormous carbon footprint overload in our biosphere and waste a lot of computational power. On the other hand, the wide applications of a few pre-trained models have already created thousands of pruned models for different downstream tasks. Can we reuse these pruned models as prior knowledge to save the pruning computation on new tasks? We call this problem "meta-pruning". In this paper, we mainly focus on a special case of it, which initializes a sub-network for a given new task based on the pruned models of similar tasks. Meta-pruning is non-parametric if no parametric model is trained to produce the initialization. It is analogous to MAML [7] in that the meta-objective optimizes the initialization of a network. It differs from MAML in that (1) both the sub-network's architecture and weights are initialized; (2) the initialization is not universal but task-specific.

Since meta-pruning aims to find better sub-network initialization for new tasks, we limit the iterations during meta-pruning to strengthen the impact of initialization on the final pruned model. This also controls the computational cost and carbon footprint of meta-pruning much less than conventional pruning, that requires many iterations. Under this constraint, a well-performed pre-trained model is critical to the meta-pruning performance because (1) it needs to provide initialized sub-networks for different tasks; and (2) a few iterations of fine-tuning to the sub-networks should suffice to produce high-quality pruned models for targeted tasks. Meta-pruning follows a practical setting where one single pre-trained model is tailored for different tasks using limited iterations. We study two classes of the most widely used pre-trained models, i.e., convolutional neural networks (CNN) and ViT.

The primary contribution of this paper is two folds. In the first part, we conduct a thorough empirical study that applies different pruning methods to CNN and ViT and compares their produced sub-networks for hundreds of downstream tasks. No meta-pruning is studied in this part. Its primary purpose is to (1) find the nearest tasks for a new task using different similarity metrics; (2) compare the pruned models for different but similar tasks. To this end, we build a dataset of tasks and their sub-networks pruned from the same pre-trained models. Statistics and evaluations on this dataset indicate similar tasks with high similarity tend to share more nodes/filters/heads preserved in their pruned models, especially in deeper layers that notably capture high-level task-specific features.

Motivated by the empirical study, the second part of this paper proposes a simple yet strong meta-pruning method called "meta-vote pruning (MVP)".

It can significantly reduce the pruning cost and memory required by previous pruning approaches yet still produce pruned models with promising performance. Given a pre-trained model, MVP finds a sub-network for a new task by selecting nodes/filters/heads through majority voting among its nearest tasks, e.g., a filter will be sampled with a higher chance if it is selected into more sub-networks of similar tasks. To simplify the method, we sample the same proportion of nodes/filters/heads as the targeted pruning ratio. Then we apply a few iterations of fine-tuning to the initialized sub-network using training data of the new task. Although a more sophisticated procedure can be developed, the proposed method saves substantial computation and memory while maintaining a high test accuracy of pruned models. We demonstrate these via experiments over tasks from CIFAR-100 [17], ImageNet [4], Caltech-256 [10] and several fine-grained datasets. The pruned models extracted from an ImageNet pre-trained model can also vote for tasks drawn from the unseen datasets with great performance, which shows the generalization of MVP.

2 Related Works

Network pruning Network pruning has been widely studied to compress a network and accelerate its inference for a single task. We mainly summarize structure pruning below. In CNN, to encourage the sparsity of the pruned network, L_0 [25], L_1 [24] or L_2 [12] regularization have been used. Polarization regularization [56] shrinks some nodes towards 0 and strengthens the others to keep important nodes intact. Different criteria have been proposed to evaluate the importance of nodes/filters. Li et al. [18] prune filters with the smallest sum of parameters' absolute values. Lin et al. [20] prune filters according to the second-order Taylor expansion of the loss. Methods [1,8] based on the lottery ticket hypothesis, try to find a well-performed sparse initialization for each task.

ViT has been widely used in computer vision and achieved SOTA performance in many tasks. The input patches for each block can be pruned to save computation for the transformer [9,15,40]. Goyal et al. [9] propose a metric to measure the importance of each patch and dynamically prune patches in each layer. PatchSlimming [40] retains patches critical to preserving the original final output. HVT [33] is a CNN-like method that shortens the patch sequence by max-pooling. Another line of works [50,51,55] automatically prunes the unimportant heads, nodes and blocks in ViT. These methods excel on single-task pruning, but their cost linearly increases for multiple tasks (and thus more expensive than meta-pruning) because: (1) a large model needs to be trained for every task; (2) every task requires pruning its large pre-trained model from scratch. For both CNN and ViT, it is time-consuming for these pruning methods to build a pruned model for each unseen target task from a large pre-trained model. Our proposed method can borrow the knowledge of the existing pruned models extracted by these pruning methods and use them to generate a well-performed pruned model for the unseen task with a few fine-tuning iterations.

Meta-pruning. To our knowledge, the non-parametric meta-pruning problem, i.e., how to prune a model for a target task using the pruned models of other tasks, has not been specifically studied in previous work. However, several recent studies aim at learning meta(prior) knowledge that can improve pruning in other scenarios. MetaPruning [23] trains a weight-generation meta-network to prune the same network for the same task under different constraints, e.g., user/hardware-defined pruning ratios. DHP [19] addresses the same problem but does not rely on any reinforcement learning or evolutionary algorithm since it makes the pruning procedure differentiable. Meta-learning has been studied to find better weight-initialization for pruning on different tasks, e.g., Tian et al. [41] apply Reptile [31] for overfitting reduction. Meta-learning has also been studied to select the best pruning criterion for different tasks [14]. In [37], a shared sparse backbone network is trained for multi-task learning, but it cannot be adapted to new tasks. Our method is the first to use meta-learning to extract a pruned model for a new task. The main differences between our approach to them are: (1) we do not train a parametric meta-learner but instead use majority voting from similar tasks; and (2) our meta-voting generates a pruned small sub-network to initialize the target task training, which significantly reduces the pruning cost.

3 Empirical Study: Pruning a Pre-trained Model for Different Tasks

In this section, we conduct an empirical study that applies different methods to prune a CNN or ViT pre-trained model for hundreds of tasks. Our study focuses on the overlap between the pruned models for different tasks and whether/how it relates to their similarity. To this end, we introduce different task similarities and compare the overlap associated with different similarity groups. The results show that more similar tasks tend to share more nodes/filters/heads in their pruned models. And this holds across different pruning methods, datasets and pre-trained models. No meta-pruning is used in the study.

3.1 A Dataset of Pruned Models

While the number of possible downstream tasks and users can be huge in practice, the current progress on foundation models shows that one or a few large-scale pre-trained models with light fine-tuning usually achieve the SOTA performance on most of them. To simulate this scenario on a standard dataset, our empirical study creates a dataset of pruned models for hundreds of tasks from the same pre-trained model. We choose CIFAR-100 and ImageNet for the study due to the many classes in them. We randomly draw 1000 classification tasks for each dataset, each defined on 5 classes sampled without replacement. We adopt ResNet-18 [13] pre-trained on CIFAR-100, ResNet-50 and a small version of DeiT [42] pre-trained on ImageNet. For ResNet-18 and ResNet-50, we prune two types of pre-trained models, i.e., the supervised training following [5] and the self-supervised training following SimSiam [2] (only the encoder is used). For ViT, the training of its pre-trained model follows [6].

Iterative Pruning. We apply iterative filter-pruning (IFP) to ResNet. Unlike magnitude-based pruning [18] with a one-time selection of nodes/weights, iterative pruning alternates between network pruning and fine-tuning of model weights for multiple iterations, each prunes $p\%$ of the remaining nodes/weights so it progressively prunes a large network to the targeted size. It usually performs better than other pruning methods and has been mainly studied in theoretical works about Lottery Ticket Hypothesis [8]. We take the activation values of filters averaged over all training samples to measure the importance of filters [29], referred to as Activation Pruning, in which filters with smaller activation values contain less information of input data.

Automatic Pruning. Inspired by the automatic structured pruning method [53], we prune ViT by automatic head&node pruning (AHNP) for a given task, which parameterizes the sub-network as the pre-trained model with a learnable score multiplied to each prunable head and node. The differentiable scores of all prunable heads and nodes are optimized to encourage sparsity with an additional $L1$ regularization loss. After each optimization step, we apply simple thresholding to these scores to remove heads and nodes with small scores. The optimization stops if the pruned model reaches the targeted size and the model will be fine-tuned for a few iterations.

For tasks of CIFAR-100, we run IFP for all 1000 tasks on ResNet-18. And we apply IFP and AHNP to tasks of ImageNet on ResNet-50 and ViT, respectively. Finally, we create a dataset of pruned models for thousands of tasks over different pre-trained models. For each task i, we record its labels C_i, the set of preserved nodes/filters/heads $\{\Omega_\ell\}_{\ell=1:L-1}$ and the pruned model θ_T. We use the same hyperparameters for different tasks. For IFP on ResNet, we use a learning rate of 0.005, pruning iterations of 1000 and batch size of 128 for both the tasks of CIFAR-100 and ImageNet. When applying AHNP to ViT, we follow the ViT training in [43]. We reduce the pruning iterations to 1000 and use a small learning rate of 0.00005 for parameters inherited from the pre-trained ViT (to preserve its knowledge) and a large learning rate of 0.05 for the learnable scores. The pruning ratio is 90% for all pruned models.

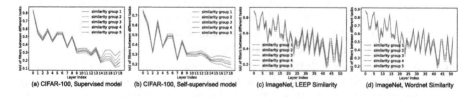

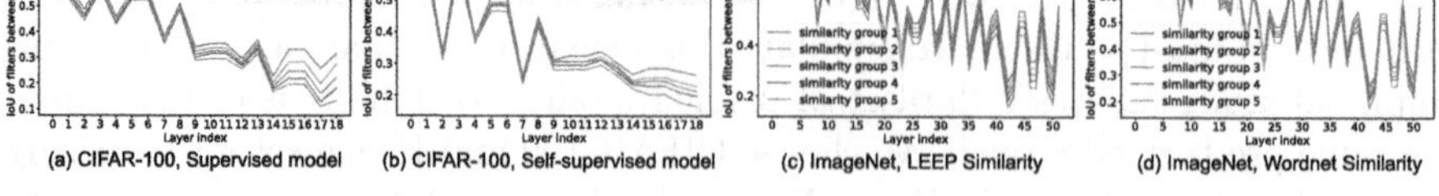

Fig. 1. IoU of layers in ResNet between tasks with different similarities.

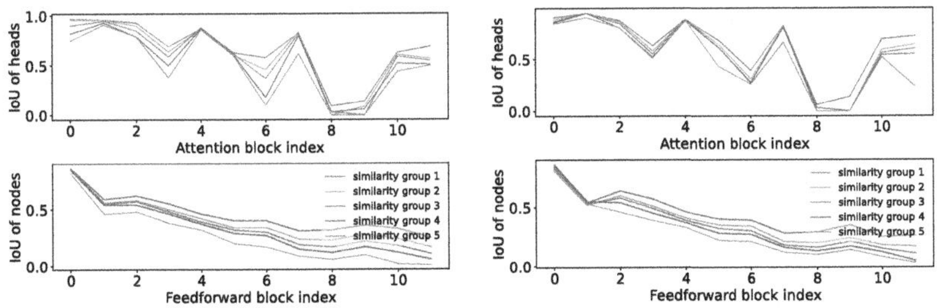

(a) ImageNet, LEEP Similarity (b) ImageNet, Wordnet Similarity

Fig. 2. IoU of blocks in ViT between tasks with different similarities.

3.2 Do Similar Tasks Share More Nodes on Their Pruned Models?

The representations learned for a task can still be helpful to similar tasks. This motivates transfer/multi-task/meta-learning methods [21,22]. But do similar tasks also share more structures in their pruned sub-networks? We apply two metrics to measure the similarity between classification tasks in our dataset and study whether/how the similarity relates to their shared nodes/filters/heads in different layers of their pruned models.

Similarity Metrics. We apply two metrics to compute the similarity between tasks and find the nearest tasks, i.e., the Log Expected Empirical Prediction (LEEP) [30] and the Wordnet wup similarity [35,45]. LEEP score is widely used in transfer learning to estimate the knowledge transferability from a source task to a target task. In our study, for each target task, we can rank the other tasks by their LEEP similarity score from each of them to the target one. Computing the LEEP score only requires a single forward pass of the pruned model on the target task's data. Wordnet wup similarity only requires the semantic labels of classes in each task and it is based on the depths of their corresponding synsets in the Wordnet [27] taxonomies. It does not depend on the pruned model so it is more efficient to compute.

Overlap Between Tasks. Let Ω_ℓ^i and Ω_ℓ^j denote the sets of filters/nodes/heads remained in layer-ℓ after running IFP or AHNP for task i and j (when using the same pre-trained model), we measure the overlap of the two sets by intersection over union (IoU) ratio [16], i.e., IoU $= {|\Omega_\ell^i \cap \Omega_\ell^j|}/{|\Omega_\ell^i \cup \Omega_\ell^j|}$.

Figure 1 (ResNet) and Fig. 2 (ViT) report the IoU of each layer/block for pairs of tasks with different similarities. For each target task, the tasks in the dataset are partitioned into 5 similarity groups according to their LEEP scores or Wordnet similarities to the target task. The similarity decreases from group 1 to group 5. Specifically, for each test task, we compute its similarity scores with its neighbours in the model zoo. We sort these similarity scores and partition them into five groups of equal intervals. Neighbours whose similarity scores fall into a certain interval will be assigned to the corresponding group.

Algorithm 1. META-VOTE PRUNING (MVP)

Input : Target task i and its training set D_i, pruning ratio r, J, N, a dataset of pruned models for different tasks
Output : A pruned model for target task-i
Initialize: $\Omega_\ell \leftarrow \emptyset$, the set of filters in layer-ℓ

```
Sample N similar tasks N^i to task i according to LEEP score or Wordnet similarity;
for ℓ ← 1 to L − 1 do
    Sample (1 − r)n_ℓ filters with probability p(k) (Eq. (1)) and add them to Ω_ℓ;
    for k ∈ Ω_ℓ do
        Initialize filter-k by averaging its parameters of tasks in {j ∈ N^i : k ∈ Ω_ℓ^j};
    end
end
Fine-tune the pruned model for J iterations on D_i.
```

For all the datasets and architectures, **more similar tasks tend to share more filters/nodes/heads** (larger IoU) between their pruned models. Therefore, for a new task, the pruned models of its nearest tasks preserve many important filters for it and combining them might result in a better and much smaller sub-network to initialize the new task. Moreover, for deeper layers/blocks in both ResNet and ViT, the gap between different similarity groups on the IoU increases because the features are more task-specific in deeper layers. Due to the same reason, for every similarity group, IoU decreases with depth in the overall trend (though fluctuating locally). Furthermore, Fig. 2 shows that the IoU gap between similarity groups defined by the LEEP score is larger than that obtained by Wordnet similarity. This indicates that the semantic similarity between class labels might not be as accurate as the LEEP score that takes the pruned model and its learned representations into account.

4 Meta-Vote Pruning (MVP)

Knowledge sharing between tasks has been widely applied in several domains like transfer learning, continual learning and federated learning [38,48,54]. Inspired by the empirical study above, we propose a simple yet strong baseline "meta-vote pruning (MVP)" (Algorithm 1) for non-parametric meta-pruning. The procedure of MVP majority voting is shown in Fig. 3. Given a target task i, MVP draws a sub-network of a pre-trained network by sampling filters/nodes/heads in each layer using majority voting from its nearest tasks N^i and their pruned models. In particular, for each filter-$k \in [n_\ell]$ from layer-ℓ of the pre-trained model, we apply softmax (with temperature τ) to the times of each filter being selected by tasks in N^i, which yields a probability distribution over all the filters $[n_\ell]$, i.e., $\forall k \in [n_\ell]$,

$$p(k) = \frac{\exp(|\{j \in N^i : k \in \Omega_\ell^j\}|/\tau)}{\sum_{h\in[n_\ell]} \exp(|\{j \in N^i : h \in \Omega_\ell^j\}|/\tau)} \tag{1}$$

To initialize layer-ℓ of the sub-network, MVP samples filters from this distribution (without replacement) according to the targeted pruning ratio r. We

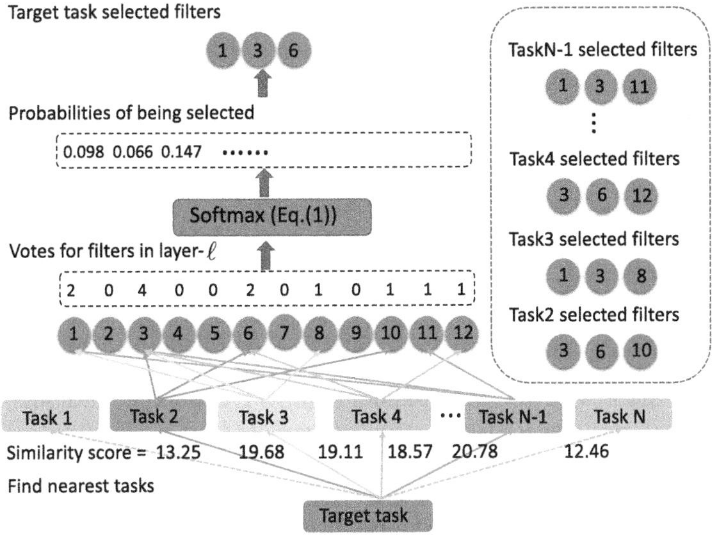

Fig. 3. The example of majority voting in MVP. Each similar neighbour task of the target task vote for filters that are reserved by its pruned model. Then, softmax is applied to the votes of all filters in layer-ℓ and filters with more votes have a higher probability to be selected by the target task.

further initialize the parameters of each filter-k by averaging its parameters in the pruned models of similar tasks which preserve filter-k. MVP then fine-tunes the initialized sub-network for a few iterations on the training set of the target task since MVP targets to keep the computational cost low.

5 Experiments

In this section, we conduct extensive experiments on CIFAR-100 and ImageNet over different pre-trained models, which evaluate MVP (Algorithm 1) and compare it with SOTA methods under different settings. We validate the strong generalization of MVP by applying it to unseen tasks from Caltech-256 and fine-grained datasets. We further study the effect of different pruning iterations, neighbour numbers, task sizes and similarity metrics for MVP. The results show that MVP outperforms other methods with better performance and higher efficiency.

5.1 Implementation Details

The experiments of MVP are mainly based on the tasks from the dataset introduced in Sect. 3.1. For each experiment, we randomly draw 100 test tasks (i.e., the target task in Algorithm 1) from the dataset and treat the rest tasks as training tasks. To evaluate MVP on CNN, we run MVP on the pruned models of ResNet-18 and ResNet-50 for CIFAR-100 and ImageNet, respectively. For both these two experiments, we use the meta-pruning iterations of 100, batch size of 128, the learning rate of 0.01 and optimizer of SGD with the cosine-annealing learning rate schedule. For experiments of ViT, MVP is applied to the pruned models of ViT for ImageNet. The meta-pruning iterations and batch size are also set as 100 and 128, respectively. Following the setting of training ViT in [43], we apply a small learning rate of 0.0002 and optimizer of AdamW with the cosine-annealing learning rate schedule. The small number of meta-pruning iterations demonstrates the efficiency of MVP. The target pruning ratio of MVP for all tasks is 90%. All the accuracy results shown in this section are averaged over the 100 test tasks.

5.2 Baseline Methods

We compare MVP with several baselines and SOTA pruning methods. We first implement two baselines to show the advantages of MVP. (1) Conventional pruning. We apply a larger number of pruning iterations to extract pruned models for each target task by IFP or AHNP introduced in Sect. 3.1. This baseline can be regarded as the upper-bound performance. (2) Random pruning. To validate whether the initialization of MVP makes sense, for each target task, we initialize its sub-network by randomly sampling the same number of nodes/filters/heads as MVP from the pre-trained model. We take this baseline as the lower-bound performance.

We also include other SOTA pruning methods. For MVP on CNN, we compare MVP with IHT-based Reptile [41], a meta-pruning method that uses Reptile [31] and iterative pruning to find better weight-initialization for a pruned meta-model. Given a new task, it fine-tunes the pruned meta-model for a limited number of iterations to obtain the final pruned model. MEST [52] is the SOTA method in the sparse training community, which trains a model from a sparse sub-network so that less computation is required. DLTH [1] is based on a variant of the Lottery Ticket Hypothesis. It transforms random tickets into winning tickets. We compare MVP with UVC [51] and PoWER [9] on ViT pruning. Unlike AHNP, which prunes heads and nodes, UVC also skips the unimportant layers and blocks in ViT. Unlike parameter pruning, PoWER adopts a dynamic method of pruning the input patches of each block for each input sample. For a fair comparison, except for the upper bound baseline, the pruning iterations of all other methods and MVP are set to 100. And the pruning ratios of all methods are set to 90%.

5.3 Main Results

The results of applying MVP to tasks from CIFAR-100(ImageNet) on ResNet-18(ResNet-50) supervised and self-supervised pre-trained model and the baseline methods are reported in Table 1. On both datasets and pre-trained models, MVP outperforms IFP which spends 10× iterations of MVP. Hence, MVP can produce a higher-quality pruned model when using fewer iterations. The results demonstrate that MVP can work well on tasks from both supervised and self-supervised pre-trained models. The random pruning performs much poorer than

Table 1. Comparison between MVP and baseline methods on CNN. '-SSL' behind each method means applying this method to pruned models extracted from self-supervised pre-trained models. **Bold** and Bold gray mark the best and second best accuracy.

Methods	Pruning Iterations	ResNet-18		ResNet-50	
		Acc	FLOPs	Acc	FLOPs
IFP	1000	87.99 ± 0.47	14.88(T)	91.16 ± 0.68	110.06(T)
IFP-SSL	1000	85.22 ± 0.52	14.88(T)	85.84 ± 0.75	110.06(T)
Random Pruning	100	33.12 ± 6.47	0.43(T)	22.42 ± 3.92	3.16(T)
IHT-based Reptile [41]	100	75.23 ± 0.87	0.43(T)	73.40 ± 0.75	3.16(T)
MEST [52]	100	76.28 ± 0.82	0.47(T)	66.25 ± 2.33	3.48(T)
DLTH [1]	100	74.46 ± 1.24	4.28(T)	69.33 ± 1.56	31.64(T)
MVP(**ours**)	100	$\mathbf{88.98 \pm 0.38}$	0.43(T)	$\mathbf{91.80 \pm 0.26}$	3.16(T)
MVP-SSL(**ours**)	100	86.82 ± 0.13	0.43(T)	85.92 ± 0.26	3.16(T)

MVP, which indicates the importance of majority voting from the nearest tasks in selecting filters.

We also compare MVP with SOTA pruning methods for CNN. IHT-based Reptile [41] trains a universal sparse sub-network for all target tasks by applying meta-learning on training tasks. MVP achieves higher accuracy than IHT-based Reptile under the same training iterations, implying that MVP can find an accurate sub-network for each target task as its initialization and improve its performance. MEST [52] can speed up pruning by starting training from a well-designed sub-network. As a variant of Lottery Ticket Hypothesis, DLTH [1] proposes a method to transform any random ticket into the winning ticket. MVP outperforms MEST and DLTH by a large margin because MVP is trained on a sub-network selected using meta knowledge from similar tasks. In contrast, the initial sub-network for MEST or the winning ticket of DLTH does not leverage any prior knowledge about the target task.

Table 2. Comparison between MVP and baseline methods on ViT. **Bold** and Bold gray mark the best and second best accuracy.

Methods	Pruning Iterations	ViT	
		Acc	FLOPs
AHNP	1000	$\mathbf{89.48 \pm 0.62}$	81.50(T)
Random Pruning	100	58.71 ± 4.14	3.25(T)
UVC [51]	100	80.30 ± 0.57	26.73(T)
PoWER [9]	100	77.76 ± 1.18	20.86(T)
MVP(**ours**)	100	89.23 ± 0.49	3.25(T)

Table 2 shows the comparison between MVP and baseline methods on ViT. Similar to the results on pruning CNN, the performance of MVP on ViT is comparable to AHNP which applies much more pruning iterations. The accuracy of random pruning is still much worse. MVP also outperforms SOTA pruning methods developed for ViT. Hence, on ViT, MVP can efficiently produce a small yet high-quality sub-network for each new task by exploiting the nearest tasks' models. The baselines are slower and require more iterations than MVP because they need to re-train the model to achieve a small loss when some parameters or patches are removed. Both UVC and PoWER cannot recover the accuracy under this strong constraint. In contrast, the majority voting in MVP directly produces a small sub-network from similar tasks' models so only a few iterations suffice to reach a downstream task performance comparable to AHNP with 10x iterations.

5.4 Performance on Unseen Dataset

In this section, to validate the generalization of MVP, we apply MVP to produce pruned models for target tasks from unseen dataset Caltech-256 [10] and fine-grained dataset CUB200-2011 [44], Oxford Flowers-102 [32] and Oxford-IIIT Pets [34], using the pruned models of tasks from ResNet-50 training on ImageNet. The data of these datasets are never seen by the pre-trained model and tasks in the pruned model dataset. Each target task is defined on 5 classes sampled without replacement from each dataset.

The performance of MVP on Caltech-256 is shown in Table 3, which is still comparable to the IFP using 10x pruning iterations. When the number of pruning iterations of IFP decreases, its performance becomes much worse. Besides Caltech-256, we also validate the effectiveness of MVP on more difficult fine-grained datasets, i.e., CUB200-2011, Oxford Flowers-102 and Oxford-IIIT Pets where images in different classes are from various species of birds, flowers and animals, which are hard to distinguish. On target tasks from fine-grained datasets, MVP also works better than IFP, which needs much more computation costs.

The results show that MVP can still produce a high-quality initialization for the task from unseen datasets by majority voting of similar tasks so that the pruned model can converge quickly with high accuracy. MVP's great performance on fine-grained datasets implies that MVP can learn from different objects to facilitate the classification of hard-to-distinguish target tasks. This

Table 3. Accuracy of MVP on unseen tasks.

Methods	Caltech-256			CUB200-2011		
	Iters	Acc	FLOPs	Iters	Acc	FLOPs
IFP	800	80.28 ± 1.64	93.06(T)	800	77.09 ± 0.51	23.99(T)
IFP	60	42.90 ± 3.79	6.73(T)	80	52.85 ± 2.95	2.17(T)
MVP(**ours**)	60	$\mathbf{80.72 \pm 0.64}$	1.90(T)	80	$\mathbf{79.54 \pm 0.88}$	0.63(T)

Table 4. Accuracy of MVP on more fine-grained tasks.

Methods	Oxford Flowers-102			Oxford-IIIT Pets		
	Iters	Acc	FLOPs	Iters	Acc	FLOPs
IFP	800	95.20 ± 1.39	47.98(T)	1000	77.38 ± 0.96	59.33(T)
IFP	60	54.20 ± 6.61	3.04(T)	100	55.76 ± 3.86	4.57(T)
MVP(**ours**)	60	$\mathbf{95.40 \pm 1.34}$	0.95(T)	100	$\mathbf{78.29 \pm 0.77}$	1.58(T)

experiment demonstrates that MVP can be applied to various datasets and generalizes well.

Table 5. Results on sub-tasks of different sizes for CIFAR-100.

Methods	10-classification			3-classification		
	Iters	Acc	FLOPs	Iters	Acc	FLOPs
IFP	1500	84.29 ± 0.26	25.48(T)	500	88.75 ± 0.71	5.59(T)
MVP(**ours**)	190	83.53 ± 0.34	1.21(T)	60	89.25 ± 0.23	0.12(T)

5.5 Results of MVP on Sub-tasks of Different Sizes

To evaluate the performance of MVP on sub-tasks of different sizes, we build a dataset of pruned models for 10-classification and 3-classification sub-tasks from CIFAR-100, of which the pruning ratio is set to 85% and 95% respectively. The results are shown in Table 5. From the results, we can find that When changing the size of the sub-tasks, MVP can consistently achieve comparable or better performance than SoTA methods by spending much less computation. MVP is applicable to a variety of tasks of different sizes.

5.6 Ablation Study

Effect of Iteration Numbers. Given a new target task and a pre-trained model, MVP can build a well-performed small model in a few iterations, demonstrating its capability in reducing adaptation costs. In plot (a) of Fig. 4, we compare MVP with conventional pruning methods using different numbers of iterations. On different architectures of pre-trained models, MVP converges to a high accuracy after nearly 100 iteration. On the contrary, the conventional pruning methods need much more iterations(> 500) to be comparable to MVP. With only ≤ 50 pruning iterations, MVP can reach a reasonable accuracy, while conventional pruning methods perform poorly. These imply that the initialized sub-network obtained by majority voting already contains helpful knowledge from its similar tasks to speed up the training of the pruned model.

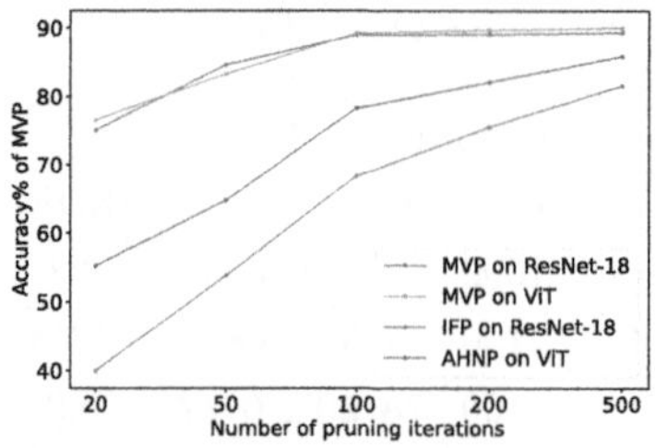

(a) Effect of Pruning Iterations

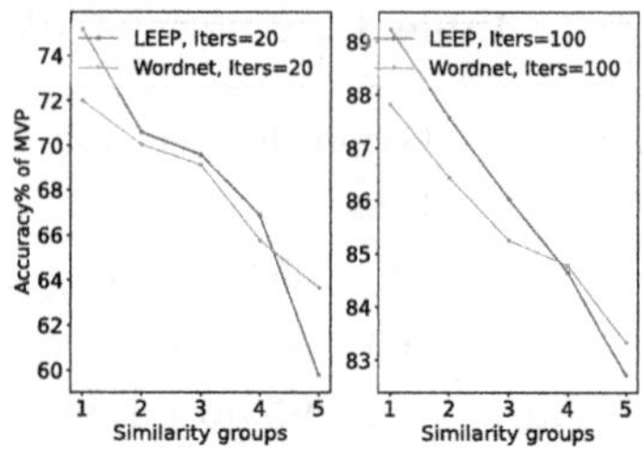

(b) Effect of Task Similarities

Fig. 4. **(a)** Comparison between MVP and conventional pruning methods with different pruning iterations on different architectures. For both ResNet-18 and ViT, MVP converges much faster in a small number of iterations than conventional pruning methods. **(b)** Comparison between LEEP score and Wordnet similarity for MVP with different pruning iterations. From similarity groups 1 to 5, the similarities between tasks decrease. For both similarity metrics, more similar tasks get better performance. LEEP score can better measure similarities between tasks than Wordnet similarity.

Effect of Similarities between Tasks. MVP consistently achieves better performance when applied to the nearest tasks with the highest similarities. In plot (b) of Fig. 4, we compare the LEEP score with the Wordnet similarity and study the effect of applying MVP to neighbour tasks with different similarities. From similarity group 1 to group 5, the similarities between tasks decrease. We find that for both the two similarity metrics, the accuracy of MVP improves significantly when the similarities between tasks increase. When the pruning iterations are small($= 20$), where the initialization of the sub-network is more important, the accuracy of tasks from similarity group 1 leads to similarity group 5 by 15%. Despite the accuracy of similarity group 5 improving when the pruning iterations increase to 100, there is still a gap of 7%. This result indicates that neighbour tasks with high similarities share more knowledge with the target task. In this plot, we also find that tasks in different similarity groups classified by LEEP score show larger differences than Wordnet similarity, implying that LEEP score can better evaluate similarities between tasks. This result is consistent with our observation in the empirical study. The performance of Wordnet similarity is also good and can still be an alternative when time and computational resources are limited.

Comparison between Pruned Models Extracted by Different Pruning Method. In this part, we apply MVP to pruned models extracted by Taylor Pruning [28] on ResNet-18 for CIFAR-100 tasks to prove that MVP works well on pruned models extracted by various pruning methods. Taylor Pruning measures the importance of each filter by the effect of removing this filter on final loss. In plot (a) of Fig. 5, we show the IoU of each layer for pairs of tasks with different task similarities, of which the pruned models are extracted by Taylor Pruning. Consistent with our observation in the empirical study, pruned models with higher similarities share more filters.

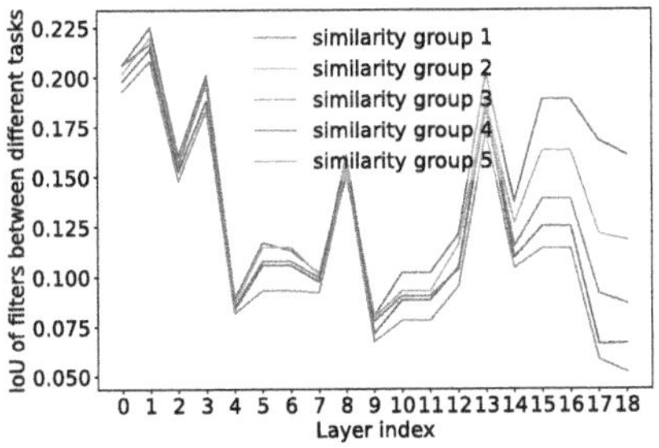

(a) Layers IoU for IFP(Taylor Pruning)

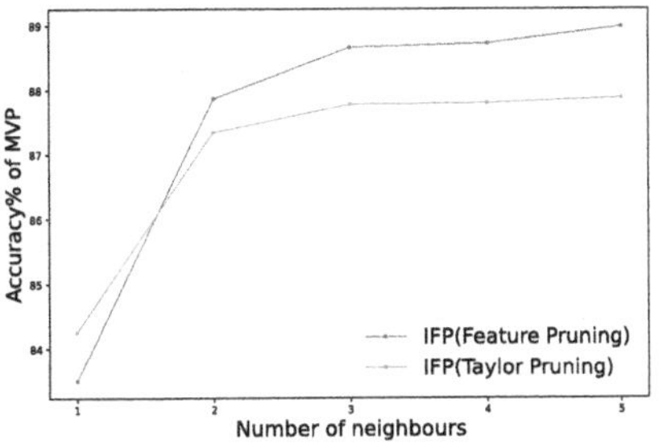

(b) Effect of Neighbour Numbers

Fig. 5. (a) IoU of layers in ResNet-18 between tasks whose pruned models are extracted by IFP (Taylor Pruning) and more similar tasks also share more filters, especially in deeper layers.**(b)** Results of applying MVP to pruned models from Activation Pruning and Taylor Pruning over a different number of neighbours. MVP (neighbour number ≥ 2) can improve the performance of transfer learning (neighbour number $= 1$) by a large margin when applied to pruned models extracted by different pruning methods.

Effect of Number of Neighbours. In plot (b) of Fig. 5, we investigate the effect of the number of neighbours for MVP. When the number $= 1$, MVP reduces to transfer learning which learns from the pruned model of a single similar task. In the plot, when the number of neighbours increases from 1 to 2, the performance improves sharply. This result implies the effectiveness of meta knowledge from different neighbours. When the number of neighbours ≥ 3, for both Activation Pruning and Taylor Pruning, the accuracy improves little, which indicates that 3 neighbours are enough for MVP to produce a high-quality initialization.

6 Conclusion

In this paper, we study "non-parametric meta-pruning" problem that aims to reduce the memory and computational costs of single-task pruning via reusing a pre-trained model and similar tasks' pruned models to find an initialization sub-network for a new task. We conduct an empirical study investigating the relationship between task similarity and the pruned models of two tasks for different datasets and deep neural networks. The empirical study motivates a simple yet strong baseline for meta-pruning, called "meta-vote pruning (MVP)" (Algorithm 1). By extensive experiments on multiple tasks drawn from several datasets under different training settings, we demonstrate the advantages of MVP over other SOTA pruning methods in the region of limited computation and show its potential to reduce the carbon footprint of pruning/fine-tuning large networks for billions of edge devices and tasks.

Ethical Statement. Our study utilizes only publicly available models and data widely used in the deep learning community. As such, we believe that our work is not associated with any potential ethical implications regarding the collection and processing of personal data or the inference of personal information. Our proposed method aims to improve the efficiency of applying large pre-trained models to downstream tasks and is not related to any use in policing or military settings. We are committed to maintaining the highest ethical standards in our research, and we have taken all necessary measures to ensure that our work complies with the ethical principles and values of the research community. Additionally, we want to emphasize that our research is intended for the betterment of society and is not intended to cause any harm.

References

1. Bai, Y., Wang, H., Tao, Z., Li, K., Fu, Y.: Dual lottery ticket hypothesis. arXiv preprint arXiv:2203.04248 (2022)
2. Chen, X., He, K.: Exploring simple siamese representation learning. arXiv preprint arXiv:2011.10566 (2020)
3. Chin, T.W., Ding, R., Zhang, C., Marculescu, D.: Towards efficient model compression via learned global ranking. In: 2020 IEEE/CVF Conference on Computer Vision and Pattern Recognition (CVPR), pp. 1515–1525 (2020)
4. Deng, J., Dong, W., Socher, R., Li, L.J., Li, K., Fei-Fei, L.: Imagenet: a large-scale hierarchical image database. In: 2009 IEEE Conference on Computer Vision and Pattern Recognition, pp. 248–255 (2009). https://doi.org/10.1109/CVPR.2009.5206848
5. Devries, T., Taylor, G.W.: Improved regularization of convolutional neural networks with cutout. arXiv: 1708.04552 (2017)
6. Dosovitskiy, A., et al.: An image is worth 16x16 words: transformers for image recognition at scale. In: International Conference on Learning Representations (2021). https://openreview.net/forum?id=YicbFdNTTy
7. Finn, C., Abbeel, P., Levine, S.: Model-agnostic meta-learning for fast adaptation of deep networks. In: ICML (2017)
8. Frankle, J., Carbin, M.: The lottery ticket hypothesis: Training pruned neural networks. arXiv: 1803.03635 (2018)
9. Goyal, S., Choudhury, A.R., Raje, S., Chakaravarthy, V., Sabharwal, Y., Verma, A.: Power-bert: accelerating bert inference via progressive word-vector elimination. In: International Conference on Machine Learning, pp. 3690–3699. PMLR (2020)
10. Griffin, G., Holub, A., Perona, P.: Caltech-256 object category dataset (2007)
11. Han, S., Mao, H., Dally, W.J.: Deep compression: compressing deep neural networks with pruning, trained quantization and huffman coding. In: International Conference on Learning Representations (ICLR) (2016)
12. Han, S., Pool, J., Tran, J., Dally, W.: Learning both weights and connections for efficient neural network. arXiv: 1506.02626 (2015)
13. He, K., Zhang, X., Ren, S., Sun, J.: Deep residual learning for image recognition. In: 2016 IEEE Conference on Computer Vision and Pattern Recognition (CVPR), pp. 770–778 (2016)
14. He, Y., Liu, P., Zhu, L., Yang, Y.: Meta filter pruning to accelerate deep convolutional neural networks. arXiv: 1904.03961 (2019)
15. Hou, L., Pang, R.Y., Zhou, T., Wu, Y., Song, X., Song, X., Zhou, D.: Token dropping for efficient bert pretraining. arXiv preprint arXiv:2203.13240 (2022)
16. Jaccard, P.: Etude de la distribution florale dans une portion des alpes et du jura. Bull. Soc. Vaud. Sci. Nat. **37**, 547–579 (1901). https://doi.org/10.5169/seals-266450

17. Krizhevsky, A., Hinton, G.: Learning multiple layers of features from tiny images. University of Toronto, Tech. rep. (2009)
18. Li, H., Kadav, A., Durdanovic, I., Samet, H., Graf, H.: Pruning filters for efficient convnets. arXiv: 1608.08710 (2017)
19. Li, Y., Gu, S., Zhang, K., Gool, L., Timofte, R.: Dhp: Differentiable meta pruning via hypernetworks. arXiv: 2003.13683 (2020)
20. Lin, S., Ji, R., Li, Y., Wu, Y., Huang, F., Zhang, B.: Accelerating convolutional networks via global & dynamic filter pruning. In: IJCAI (2018)
21. Liu, L., Zhou, T., Long, G., Jiang, J., Yao, L., Zhang, C.: Prototype propagation networks (ppn) for weakly-supervised few-shot learning on category graph. arXiv preprint arXiv:1905.04042 (2019)
22. Liu, L., Zhou, T., Long, G., Jiang, J., Zhang, C.: Attribute propagation network for graph zero-shot learning. In: Proceedings of the AAAI Conference on Artificial Intelligence, vol. 34, pp. 4868–4875 (2020)
23. Liu, Z., et al.: Metapruning: Meta learning for automatic neural network channel pruning. 2019 IEEE/CVF International Conference on Computer Vision (ICCV), pp. 3295–3304 (2019)
24. Liu, Z., Li, J., Shen, Z., Huang, G., Yan, S., Zhang, C.: Learning efficient convolutional networks through network slimming. In: 2017 IEEE International Conference on Computer Vision (ICCV), pp. 2755–2763 (2017)
25. Louizos, C., Welling, M., Kingma, D.P.: Learning sparse neural networks through l0 regularization. arXiv: 1712.01312 (2018)
26. Malach, E., Yehudai, G., Shalev-Shwartz, S., Shamir, O.: Proving the lottery ticket hypothesis: Pruning is all you need. In: ICML (2020)
27. Miller, G.A.: Wordnet: a lexical database for English. Commun. ACM **38**(11), 39–41 (1995)
28. Molchanov, P., Mallya, A., Tyree, S., Frosio, I., Kautz, J.: Importance estimation for neural network pruning. In: Proceedings of the IEEE/CVF Conference on Computer Vision and Pattern Recognition, pp. 11264–11272 (2019)
29. Molchanov, P., Tyree, S., Karras, T., Aila, T., Kautz, J.: Pruning convolutional neural networks for resource efficient inference. arXiv preprint arXiv:1611.06440 (2016)
30. Nguyen, C., Hassner, T., Seeger, M., Archambeau, C.: Leep: a new measure to evaluate transferability of learned representations. In: International Conference on Machine Learning, pp. 7294–7305. PMLR (2020)
31. Nichol, A., Achiam, J., Schulman, J.: On first-order meta-learning algorithms. arXiv: 1803.02999 (2018)
32. Nilsback, M.E., Zisserman, A.: Automated flower classification over a large number of classes. In: 2008 Sixth Indian Conference on Computer Vision, Graphics & Image Processing, pp. 722–729. IEEE (2008)
33. Pan, Z., Zhuang, B., Liu, J., He, H., Cai, J.: Scalable vision transformers with hierarchical pooling. In: Proceedings of the IEEE/CVF International Conference on Computer Vision, pp. 377–386 (2021)
34. Parkhi, O.M., Vedaldi, A., Zisserman, A., Jawahar, C.: Cats and dogs. In: 2012 IEEE Conference on Computer Vision and Pattern Recognition, pp. 3498–3505. IEEE (2012)
35. Pedersen, T., Patwardhan, S., Michelizzi, J., et al.: Wordnet: Similarity-measuring the relatedness of concepts. In: AAAI, vol. 4, pp. 25–29 (2004)
36. Savarese, P.H.P., Silva, H., Maire, M.: Winning the lottery with continuous sparsification. arXiv: 1912.04427 (2020)

37. Sun, T., et al.: Learning sparse sharing architectures for multiple tasks. arXiv: 1911.05034 (2020)
38. Tan, Y., Liu, Y., Long, G., Jiang, J., Lu, Q., Zhang, C.: Federated learning on non-iid graphs via structural knowledge sharing. arXiv preprint arXiv:2211.13009 (2022)
39. Tan, Y., Long, G., Ma, J., Liu, L., Zhou, T., Jiang, J.: Federated learning from pre-trained models: a contrastive learning approach. arXiv preprint arXiv:2209.10083 (2022)
40. Tang, Y., et al.: Patch slimming for efficient vision transformers. In: Proceedings of the IEEE/CVF Conference on Computer Vision and Pattern Recognition, pp. 12165–12174 (2022)
41. Tian, H., Liu, B., Yuan, X., Liu, Q.: Meta-learning with network pruning. arXiv: 2007.03219 (2020)
42. Touvron, H., Cord, M., Douze, M., Massa, F., Sablayrolles, A., Jégou, H.: Training data-efficient image transformers & distillation through attention. In: International Conference on Machine Learning, pp. 10347–10357. PMLR (2021)
43. Touvron, H., Cord, M., Douze, M., Massa, F., Sablayrolles, A., Jegou, H.: Training data-efficient image transformers & distillation through attention. In: International Conference on Machine Learning, vol. 139, pp. 10347–10357 (July 2021)
44. Wah, C., Branson, S., Welinder, P., Perona, P., Belongie, S.: The caltech-ucsd birds-200-2011 dataset (2011)
45. Wu, Z., Palmer, M.: Verb semantics and lexical selection. arXiv preprint cmp-lg/9406033 (1994)
46. Yang, K., et al.: Adversarial auto-augment with label preservation: a representation learning principle guided approach. arXiv preprint arXiv:2211.00824 (2022)
47. Yang, K., Zhou, T., Tian, X., Tao, D.: Identity-disentangled adversarial augmentation for self-supervised learning. In: International Conference on Machine Learning, pp. 25364–25381. PMLR (2022)
48. Yang, Y., Zhou, T., Jiang, J., Long, G., Shi, Y.: Continual task allocation in meta-policy network via sparse prompting. arXiv preprint arXiv:2305.18444 (2023)
49. Ye, M., Wu, L., Liu, Q.: Greedy optimization provably wins the lottery: logarithmic number of winning tickets is enough. arXiv: 2010.15969 (2020)
50. Yu, F., Huang, K., Wang, M., Cheng, Y., Chu, W., Cui, L.: Width & depth pruning for vision transformers. In: AAAI Conference on Artificial Intelligence (AAAI), vol. 2022 (2022)
51. Yu, S., et al.: Unified visual transformer compression. In: International Conference on Learning Representations (2022). https://openreview.net/forum?id=9jsZiUgkCZP
52. Yuan, G., et al.: Mest: Accurate and fast memory-economic sparse training framework on the edge. In: Advances in Neural Information Processing Systems 34 (2021)
53. Zhao, H., Zhou, T., Long, G., Jiang, J., Zhang, C.: Extracting local reasoning chains of deep neural networks. Trans. Mach. Learn. Res. (2022). https://openreview.net/forum?id=RP6G787uD8
54. Zhao, H., Zhou, T., Long, G., Jiang, J., Zhang, C.: Does continual learning equally forget all parameters? arXiv preprint arXiv:2304.04158 (2023)
55. Zhu, M., Tang, Y., Han, K.: Vision transformer pruning. arXiv preprint arXiv:2104.08500 (2021)
56. Zhuang, T., Zhang, Z., Huang, Y., Zeng, X., Shuang, K., Li, X.: Neuron-level structured pruning using polarization regularizer. In: NeurIPS (2020)

Make a Long Image Short: Adaptive Token Length for Vision Transformers

Qiqi Zhou[1] and Yichen Zhu[2](✉)

[1] Shanghai University of Electric Power, Shanghai, China
zhouqq31@midea.com
[2] Midea Group, Shanghai, China
zhuyc25@midea.com

Abstract. The vision transformer is a model that breaks down each image into a sequence of tokens with a fixed length and processes them similarly to words in natural language processing. Although increasing the number of tokens typically results in better performance, it also leads to a considerable increase in computational cost. Motivated by the saying "A picture is worth a thousand words," we propose an innovative approach to accelerate the ViT model by shortening long images. Specifically, we introduce a method for adaptively assigning token length for each image at test time to accelerate inference speed. First, we train a Resizable-ViT (ReViT) model capable of processing input with diverse token lengths. Next, we extract token-length labels from ReViT that indicate the minimum number of tokens required to achieve accurate predictions. We then use these labels to train a lightweight Token-Length Assigner (TLA) that allocates the optimal token length for each image during inference. The TLA enables ReViT to process images with the minimum sufficient number of tokens, reducing token numbers in the ViT model and improving inference speed. Our approach is general and compatible with modern vision transformer architectures, significantly reducing computational costs. We verified the effectiveness of our methods on multiple representative ViT models on image classification and action recognition.

Keywords: vision transformer · token compression

1 Introduction

The transformer has achieved remarkable success in computer vision since the introduction of ViT [12]. It has demonstrated impressive performance compared to convolutional neural networks (CNNs) on various visual domains, including image classification [10,43], object detection [7,58], semantic segmentation [26], and action recognition [4,13], using both supervised and self-supervised [2,19] training configurations. Despite the development of ViT models, their deployment remains a challenge due to the high computational cost associated with them.

Q. Zhou—Work done during internships at Midea Group.

© The Author(s), under exclusive license to Springer Nature Switzerland AG 2023
D. Koutra et al. (Eds.): ECML PKDD 2023, LNAI 14170, pp. 69–85, 2023.
https://doi.org/10.1007/978-3-031-43415-0_5

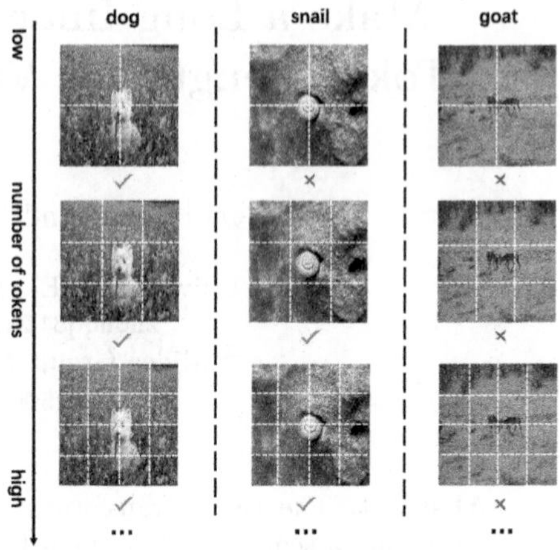

Fig. 1. The motivation for our approach. While some images (right) may need many tokens to predict their category, some images are easy to recognize. Thus, only a small number of tokens is sufficient to classify them correctly.

Accelerating ViT is a crucial yet understudied area. While many techniques like pruning, distillation, and neural architecture search have been applied to accelerate CNNs, these cannot be directly applied to ViT due to significant differences between the models [30,32,36]. As the attention module in the transformer computes the fully-connected relations among all input patches [44], the computational cost becomes quadratic with respect to the length of the input sequence [3,9]. Consequently, the transformer can be computationally expensive, particularly for longer input sequences. In the ViT model, images are divided into a fixed number of tokens; following conventional practice [12], an image is represented by 16×16 tokens. We aim to reduce the computational complexity of ViT by reducing the number of tokens used to split the images. Our motivation is depicted in Fig. 1, which shows three examples predicted by individually trained DeiT-S models [43] with different token lengths. The checkmark denotes correct prediction, and the cross denotes the wrong prediction. We observe that some "easy-to-classify" images only require a few tokens to determine their category accurately, while some images require more tokens to make the right prediction. These observations motivate us to reduce the computational complexity of the existing ViT model by accurately classifying the input using the minimum possible number of tokens.

In an ideal scenario, we would know the minimum number of tokens required to accurately predict an image, and we could train a model to assign the optimal token length to the ViT model. However, training multiple ViT models, each with a fixed token length, would be computationally infeasible. To address this, we propose a modification to the transformer architecture, changing it from "static" to "dynamic," enabling the ViT model to adaptively process images with varying token lengths. This dynamic transformer, called Resizable-ViT (ReViT), identifies the minimum token length required to achieve correct predictions for each image. We then train a lightweight Token-Length Assigner (TLA) to predict the appropriate token length for a given image, with the label obtained from the ReViT. Consequently, the ReViT can process images with lower computational costs based on the assigned token length.

The primary challenge of our approach is training the ReViT to enable the ViT model to process images of any size provided by the TLA. To tackle this challenge, we introduce a token length-aware layer normalization that switches the normalization statistics for each type of token length, and a self-distillation module that enhances the model's performance when using short token lengths in ReViT. Additionally, the ViT model needs to see the images with the corresponding token lengths beforehand to handle various token lengths effectively. However, as the number of predefined token-length choices increases, the training cost linearly increases. To overcome this, we introduce a parallel computing strategy for efficient training that makes the ReViT training almost as inexpensive as a vanilla ViT model's training.

We showcase the efficacy of our approach on several prominent ViT models, such as DeiT [43] and LV-ViT [23] for image classification, and TimesFormer [4] for video recognition. Our experiments demonstrate that our method can significantly reduce computational costs while maintaining performance levels. For instance, we achieve a 50% acceleration in DeiT-S [43] model with an accuracy reduction of only 0.1%. On action recognition, the computational cost of TimesFormer [4] can be reduced up to 33% on Kinetic 400 with only a 0.5% loss in recognition accuracy.

2 Related Works

Vision Transformer. ViT have recently gained much attention in computer vision due to their strong capability to model long-range relations. Many attempts have been made to integrate long-range modeling into CNNs, such as non-local networks [46,52], relation networks [21], among others. Vision Transformer (ViT) [12] introduced a set of pure Transformer backbones for image classification, and its follow-ups have soon modified the vision transformer to dominate many downstream tasks for computer vision, such as object detection [7,58], semantic segmentation [26], action recognition [4,13], 2D/3D human pose estimation [51,57], 3D object detection [34], and even self-supervision [19]. ViT has shown great potential to be an alternative backbone for convolutional neural networks.

Dynamic Vision Transformer. The over-parameterized model is known to have many attractive merits and can achieve better performance than smaller models. However, in real-world scenarios, computational efficiency is critical as executed computation is translated into power consumption or carbon emission. To address this issue, many works have attempted to reduce the computational cost of Convolutional Neural Networks (CNNs) through methods such as neural architecture search [6,25,59,63], knowledge distillation [20,22,56,60–62], and pruning [15,18].

Recent work has shift its attention to reduce the number of tokens used for inference, as the number of tokens can be a computational bottleneck to the vision transformer. There are two major approaches: unstructured token sparsification and structured token division. The majority of works, including PatchSlim [42], TokenSparse [37], GlobalEncoder [40], IA-RED [33], and Tokenlearner [38], focus on the former. TokenLearner [38] uses an MLP to reduce the number of tokens. TokenPooling [31] merges tokens via a k-mean based algorithm. TokenMerge [5] calculates the token similarity and merges tokens via bipartite soft matching.

They aim to remove uninformative tokens, such as those that learn features from the background of the image, thereby boosting inference speed by reserving only informative tokens. These approaches typically need to progressively reduce the number of tokens based on the inputs and can be performed either jointly with ViT training or afterward. However, pruning tokens sparsely can bring unstable training issues, especially when the model is huge [24].

The latter, which is known as unstructured token sparsification, is the most relevant work to our research. Wang et al. [47] proposed Dynamic Vision Transformer (DVT) to dynamically determine the number of patches required to divide an image. They employed a cascade of ViT models, with each ViT responsible for a specific token length. The cascade ViT model makes a sequential decision and stops inference for an input image if it has sufficient confidence in the prediction at the current token length. In contrast to DVT [47], our method is more practical and accessible, as it only requires a *single* ViT model. Additionally, we focus on how to *accurately* determine the minimum number of token lengths required in the transformer to provide correct predictions for each image.

3 Methodology

The vision transformers treat an image as a sentence by dividing the 2D image into 1D tokens and modeling the long-range dependencies between them using the multi-head self-attention mechanism. However, the self-attention is considered the computational bottleneck in the transformer model, as its computational cost increases quadratically with the number of incoming tokens. As mentioned earlier, our approach is motivated by the observation that many "easy-to-recognize" images do not require 16×16 tokens [12] to be correctly classified. Therefore, computational costs can be reduced by processing fewer tokens on "easy" images while using more tokens on "hard" images. It is worth noting that the key to a successful input-dependent token-adaptive ViT model is to determine precisely the minimum number of tokens required to accurately classify the image.

To achieve our goal, we propose a two-stage model training approach. In the first stage, we train a ViT model that can handle images with any predefined token lengths. Usually, a single ViT model can only handle one token length. We describe the model design and training strategy of this ViT model in detail in Sect. 3.2. In the second stage, we train a model to determine the appropriate token length for each image. We first obtain the token-length label, which represents the minimum number of tokens required for accurate classification, from the previously trained ViT model. Then, we train a Token-Length Assigner (TLA) using the training data, where the input is an image and the label is the corresponding token length. This decoupled procedure allows the TLA to make a better decision regarding the number of tokens required for each image. During inference, the TLA guides the ViT model on the optimal number of tokens

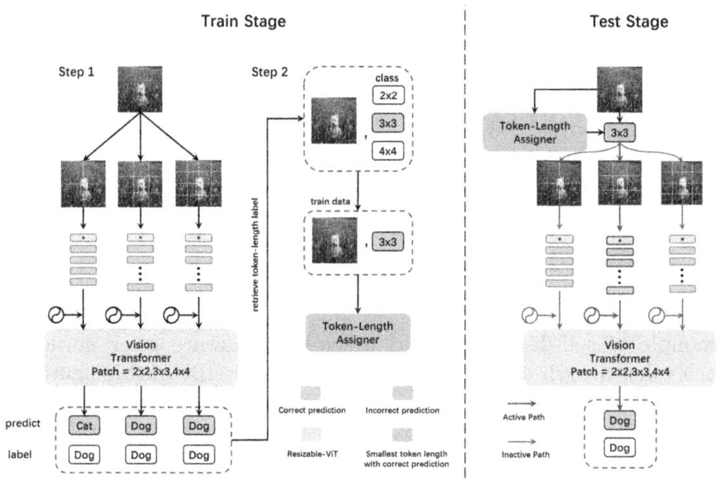

Fig. 2. **Left**: There are two steps in the training procedure. First, we train the Resizable-ViT that can split an image into any predefined token length. Secondly, we train a Token-Length Assigner based on the token-length label that is retrieved from ReViT. It is the smallest number of tokens that can correctly predicate the class of the image. **Right**: In inference, the TLA first assigns a token-length for the image, then ReViT uses this setting to make predication.

required for accurate classification based on the input. The complete training and testing process is illustrated in Fig. 2.

In the following, we first introduce the Token-Label Assigner, then present the training method on the Resizable-ViT model and improved techniques.

3.1 Token-Length Assigner

The purpose of the Token-Length Assigner (TLA) is to make accurate predictions based on the feedback from ReViT. TLA training is performed after ReViT. We first define a list of token lengths $L = [l_1, l_2, \ldots, l_n]$ in descending order. For simplicity, we use a single number to represent the token length, such as $L = [14 \times 14, 10 \times 10, 7 \times 7]$. The model with a token length of 7×7 has the lowest computational cost among the three token lengths.

In order to train a token-length adapter (TLA), it is necessary to obtain a token-length label from the ReViT model at convergence. For an image, the token-length label is defined as the minimum token length required by the ViT model to accurately classify that image. The inference speed of the ReViT model, denoted by M, can be ranked as $Speed(M_{l_1}) < Speed(M_{l_2}) < \cdots < Speed(M_{l_k})$, where $k = len(L)$ represents the total number of options for token length. For each input x, we can obtain the prediction $y_{l_i} = M_{l_i}(X)$ for all $i \in n$. The label of the input x is determined by the smallest token size l_j for which any smaller token length would result in an incorrect prediction, i.e., $y_{l_{j-1}} \neq y^{gt}$,

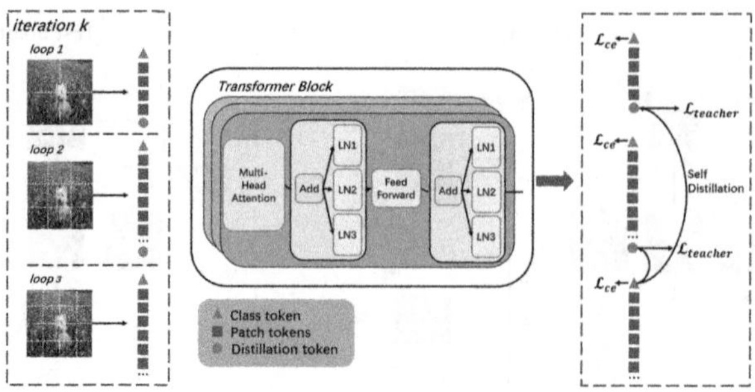

Fig. 3. Example of self-distillation and token-length aware layer normalization in ReViT. Each token length corresponds to a LayerNorm (LN in this figure) and pass-through this LayerNorm during both training and inference. The self-distillation is only conducted in training, where smaller token lengths have an extra distillation token to learn from the teacher's knowledge.

where *gt* is the ground truth label. Therefore, a set of input-output pairs (x, l_j) can be obtained and used to train the TLA. Since token-label assignment is straightforward, the TLA is a lightweight module, with minimal computational overhead introduced. Moreover, since unnecessary tokens are reduced in the ViT model, the additional computational overhead is relatively small.

3.2 Resizable-ViT

In this section, we present the Resizable-ViT (ReViT), a dynamic ViT model capable of accurately classifying images with various token lengths. We introduce two techniques that enhance the performance of ReViT and subsequently present the training strategy. Additionally, we offer an efficient training implementation that accelerates the training process of ReViT.

Token-Aware Layer Normalization. The Layer Normalization (LN/ LayerNorm) layer is a widely used normalization technique that accelerates training and improves the generalization of the Transformer architecture. In both natural language processing and computer vision, it is common to adopt an LN layer after addition in the transformer block. However, as the feature maps of the self-attention matrices and feed-forward networks constantly change, the number of token sizes changes as well. Consequently, inaccurate normalization statistics across different token lengths are shared in the same layer, which impairs test accuracy. Additionally, we found empirically that LN cannot be shared in ReViT.

To address this issue, we propose a Token-Length-Aware LayerNorm (TAL-LN), which uses an independent LayerNorm for each choice of token length in the predefined token length list. In other words, we use *Add* & $\{LN_1, ..., LN_k\}$ as a building block, where k represents the number of predefined token lengths. Each LayerNorm layer calculates layer-wise statistics specifically and learns the parameters of the corresponding feature map. Furthermore, the number of extra

Algorithm 1: Training Resizable-ViT M.

Require: Define Token-Length Assigner T, token-length list $\mathbf{R}$, for example, $\{16, 24, 32\}$. The iterations N_M for training M. The $CE(\cdot)$ denotes cross-entropy loss, and $DisT(\cdot)$ denotes distillation loss.

```
for t = 1, ..., N_M do
    Get data x and class label y_c of current mini-batch.
    Clear gradients for all parameters, optimizer.zero_grad()
    for i = 1, ..., len(R) - 1 do
        Convert ReviT to selected token-length M_i,
        Execute current scaling configuration. ŷ_i = M_i(x).
        if R[i] == 16 then
            set teacher label. ŷ_i^teacher = ŷ_i
            Compute loss loss_i = CE(ŷ_i, y)
        end
        else
            Compute loss loss_i = DisT(ŷ_i^teacher, ŷ_i, y)
        end
        Compute gradients, loss_i.backward()
    end
    Update weights, optimizer.step().
end
Obtain token-length label for all train data (x, y_t).
Train T with (x, y_t).
```

parameters in TAL-LN is negligible since the number of parameters in normalization layers typically takes less than one percent of the total model size [55]. A brief summary is illustrated in Fig. 3.

Self-Distillation. It is aware that the performance of ViT is strongly correlated to the number of patches, and experiments have shown that reducing the token size significantly hampers the accuracy of small token ViT. Directly optimizing via supervision from the ground truth poses a challenge for the small token length sub-model. Motivated by self-attention, a variant of knowledge distillation techniques, where the teacher can be insufficiently trained, or even the student model itself [53–55], we propose a token length-aware self-distillation (TLSD). In the next section, we will show that the model with the largest token length M_1 is always trained first. For M_{l_1}, the training objective is to minimize the cross-entropy loss $\mathcal{L}CE$. When it comes to the model with other token lengths $Ml_i, i \leq k, i \neq 1$, we use a distillation objective to train the target model:

$$\mathcal{L}_{teacher} = (1 - \lambda)\mathcal{L}_{CE}(\phi(Z_s), y) + \lambda\tau^2 KL(\phi(Z_s/\tau), \phi(Z_t/\tau)) \quad (1)$$

where Z_s and Z_t is the logits of the student model M_{l_i} and teacher model M_{l_1}, respectively. τ is the temperature for the distillation, λ is the coefficient balancing the KL loss (Kullack-Leibler divergence) and the CE loss (cross-entropy) on ground truth label y, and ϕ is the softmax function. Similar to DeiT, we add a distillation token for student models. Figure 3 gives an overview. Notably, this distillation scheme is computational-free: we can directly use the predicted label of the model with the largest token length as the training label for other sub-model, while for the largest token length model, we use ground truth.

3.3 Training Strategy

To enable the ViT model to adaptively process various token lengths in the predefined choice list, it is necessary to expose it to images with different token lengths. Inspired by batch gradient accumulation, a technique used to overcome the problem of small batch size by accumulating gradient and batch statistics in a single iteration, we propose a mixing token length training. As shown in Algorithm 1, a batch of images is processed with different token lengths to compute the loss through feed-forward, and individual gradients are obtained. After looping through all token length choices, the gradients of all parameters calculated by feeding different token lengths are accumulated to update the parameters.

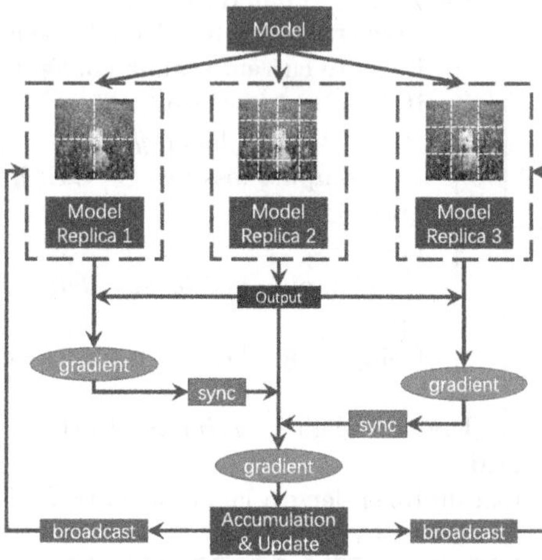

Fig. 4. Efficient training implement for Resizable Transformer through parallel computing. All gradient from the replicate nodes are synchronize on the node where that have the largest token length to save the cost of communication.

Efficient Training Implementation. An issue with the aforementioned training strategy is that the training time increases linearly with the number of predefined token length choices. To address this issue, we propose an efficient implementation strategy that trades memory cost for training time. As shown in Fig. 4, we replicate the model, with each model corresponding to a specific token length. At the end of each iteration, the gradients of the different replicas are synchronized and accumulated. Notably, we always send the gradient of replicas in which the token length is small to the one with a larger token length, as they are the training bottleneck. Thus, the communication cost in the gradient synchronization step is negligible. Then, the model parameters are updated through back-propagation. After the parameter updating is complete, the main process distributes the learned parameters to the rest of the replicas. These steps are repeated until the end of training, after which all replicas except the model in the main process can be removed. As such, the training time of the Resizable Transformer reduces from $O(k)$ to $O(1)$, where k is the number of predefined token lengths. Though the number of k is small, i.e., $k = 3$, in practice, the computational cost of training k ViT is high. Through our designed parallel computing, the training cost for

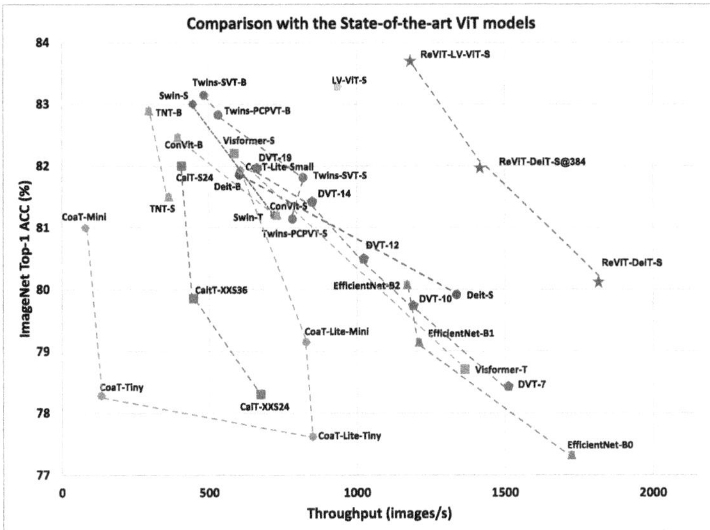

Fig. 5. Comparison of different models with various accuracy-throughput trade-off. The throughput is measured on an NVIDIA RTX 3090 GPU with batch size fixed to 32. The input image size is 224 × 224 unless indicate otherwise. The ReViT (red stare in the figure) achieves better trade-off than other methods, including DVT [47]. (Color figure online)

ReViT is almost the same as that of naive ViT, where the cost of communication between replicas is negligible compared to the model training cost. In exchange for fast training, extra computational power is required for parallel computing.

4 Experiments

Implementation Details. For image classification, we trained all models on the ImageNet [11] training set consisting of around 1.2 million images and reported their accuracy on the 50k test images. The predefined token lengths were set to 14 × 14, 10 × 10, and 7 × 7 by default, with the token length of 4 × 4 excluded due to a significant accuracy drop. We conducted experiments on DeiT-S [43] and LV-ViT-S [23] using an image resolution of 224 × 224, unless otherwise specified. We followed the training settings and optimization methods described in the original papers of DeiT [43] and LV-ViT [23]. For LV-ViT, we obtained token labels for smaller token lengths using their proposed method. We also trained the ReViT on resized images with higher resolutions, such as 384 on DeiT-S. To avoid optimization difficulties caused by large kernel and stride convolutional layers required for patch embedding, we replaced them with consecutive convolutions followed by the method in Xiao et al. [49]. After training the ReViT, we obtained token-length labels for all training data and trained the Token-Length Assigner (TLA), which was a small version of EfficientNet-B0 compared to the ViT model. We also included feature map transfer and

Table 1. Video recognition on Something-Something V2. Our ReViT outperforms state-of-the-art CNN-based and ViT-based methods. IN-21 and K400 are abbreviations for ImageNet-21K and Kinetic-400 datasets.

Method	Backbone	FLOPs (G)	Top-1 (%)	Top-5 (%)	Frames	Extra Data
TEINet [28]	ResNet50	99×10 ×3	66.5	-	8+16	ImageNet-1K
TANet [29]	ResNet50	99 × 2 × 3	66.0	90.1		
TDN [45]	ResNet101	198×1× 3	69.6	92.2		
SlowFast [14]	ResNet101	106×1×3	63.1	87.6	8+32	Kinetics-400
MViTv1 [13]	MViTv1-B	455×1×3	67.7	90.9	64	
TimeSformer [4]	ViT-B	196×1×3	59.5	–	8	ImageNet21K
TimeSformer [4]	ViT-L	5549×1×3	62.4	–	64	
ViViT [1]	ViT-L	995×4×3	65.9	89.9	32	IN-21K + K400
Video Swin [27]	Swin-B	321×1×3	69.6	92.7	32	
Motionformer [35]	ViT-B	370×1×3	66.5	90.1	16	
Motionformer [35]	ViT-L	1185×1×3	68.1	91.2	32	
ReViT_motionformer	ViT-B	183×1×3	66.6	89.9	16	IN-21K + K400
ReViT_motionformer	ViT-L	570×1×3	67.6	90.8	32	

attention transfer as part of self-distillation, which we found empirically useful. We use Something-Something V2 [16] to conduct experiments on action recognition. The Something-Something V2 is another large-scale video dataset, having around 169k videos for training and 20k videos for validation. We follow the training setting of MotionFormer [35]. Specifically, two versions of MotionFormer are tested. The default version operates on 16 × 224 × 224 video clips, and a high spatial resolution variant operates on 32 × 448 × 448 video clips.

4.1 Experimental Results

Main Results on ImageNet Classification. We present the main results of our ReViT based on DeiT-S and LV-ViT-S in Fig. 5. Our approach is compared with several models, including DeiT [43], CaiT [39], LV-ViT [23], CoaT [50], Swin [26], Twins [10], Visformer [8], ConViT [48], TNT [17], and EfficientNet [41]. The results show that our method achieves a favorable accuracy-throughput trade-off. Specifically, ReViT reduces the computational cost of the baseline counterpart by decreasing the token number used for inference. By increasing the input resolution, we manage to outperform the baseline counterpart, given a similar computational cost. We also highlight the experimental results of DVT [47] in red. Our method achieves significantly better performance in terms of both accuracy and throughput. We hypothesize that despite the low FLOPs of DVT, the practical speed of DVT is high due to its multiple cascade ViT structure.

Main Results on Video Recognition. One of the core motivations behind ReViT is to address the issue of high computational costs in extremely long token lengths during inference for image classification tasks. To further explore this idea, we investigate the applicability of our method to video recognition

Fig. 6. Visualization of "hard", "medium", and "easy" samples that predicted by Token-Length Assigner and which the ReViT-DeiT-S got correction prediction. Most of the "easy" images have clear sight on the object, while size of objects is mostly small for "hard" samples.

tasks, where the token length in transformers is typically much longer than that in image classifiers.

To this end, we train the ReViT-MotionFormer models with ViT-B and ViT-L, two different backbones, and compare them with the baseline models, respectively. The results are presented in Table 1. Our method demonstrates a significant speedup over the MotionFormer baseline, with a computational cost reduction of approximately 51% and a 0.1% accuracy increase. By training on larger image resolutions, we correspondingly reduce the model size by 48% with a 0.5% accuracy drop, which is slightly worse than the smaller resolution counterpart. Nonetheless, our experiments demonstrate that ReViT is effective for action recognition tasks.

Visualization of Samples with Different Token-Length. We selected eight classes from the ImageNet validation set and chose three samples from each category, classified as easy, medium, and hard, corresponding to tokens with dimensions of 14×14, 10×10, and 7×7, respectively. The image samples were selected based on the token length assigned by the Token-Length Assigner. The resulting images are displayed in Fig. 6. Notably, some classes do not have all images filled because less than three samples in the validation set belong to those categories. For example, only one image in the dog class requires the largest token length for classification. We observe that the number of tokens required to predict the category is highly correlated with the object's size. For larger objects, only a few tokens are sufficient to predict their category.

Table 2. The ablation study of self-distillation in ReviT. The SD* denotes the self-distillation. We also evaluate the performance with different choices of τ. The self-distillation improves the performance notably, the small token length model outperforms the baseline when $\tau = 0.9$.

Method	SD*	τ	Top-1 Acc (%)		
			14 × 14	10 × 10	7 × 7
Deit-S	✗	-	79.85	74.68	72.41
ReViT	✗	–	80.12	74.24	70.15
	✓	0.5	79.92	76.16	71.33
	✓	0.9	79.83	76.86	74.21

Table 3. The ablation study of shared patch embedding and shared position encoding in ReViT. The Pos denotes the positional encoding module. We notice that sharing these two modules decrease the model accuracy.

Method	Shared		Top-1 Acc (%)		
	Patch	Pos	14 × 14	10 × 10	7 × 7
ReViT	✗	✓	65.14	61.30	58.35
	✓	✗	75.24	71.32	69.73
	✓	✓	79.83	76.85	74.21

4.2 Ablation Study

Shared Patch Embedding and Position Encoding. We conducted an experiment to evaluate the impact of using shared patch embedding and position encoding. As the token number changes during training, we applied some techniques to enable sharing of both operations. To handle position encoding, we followed the approach of ViT [12] and zero-padded the position encoding module whenever the token size changed. This technique was initially used to adjust the positional encoding in the pretrain-finetune paradigm. For shared patch embedding, we used a weight-sharing kernel [6]. A large kernel was constructed to process a large patch size, and when the patch size changed, a smaller kernel with shared weight on the center was adopted to flatten the image patch.

As shown in Table 3, both shared patch embedding and shared positional encoding decreased the model's accuracy. In particular, the accuracy dropped by nearly 14% for the large token length model when using the shared patch strategy. The shared positional encoding module performed better than shared patch embedding but still significantly impacted the performance of ReViT.

The Effect of Self-Distillation and Choice of τ. We conducted experiments to verify the effectiveness of self-distillation in ReViT and investigated the impact of the hyper-parameter τ. We tested two different values of τ, 0.9 and 0.5, for all sub-networks and demonstrated the results in Table 2. Without self-distillation, the accuracy on small token lengths was comparable to tokens of size 10×10, but

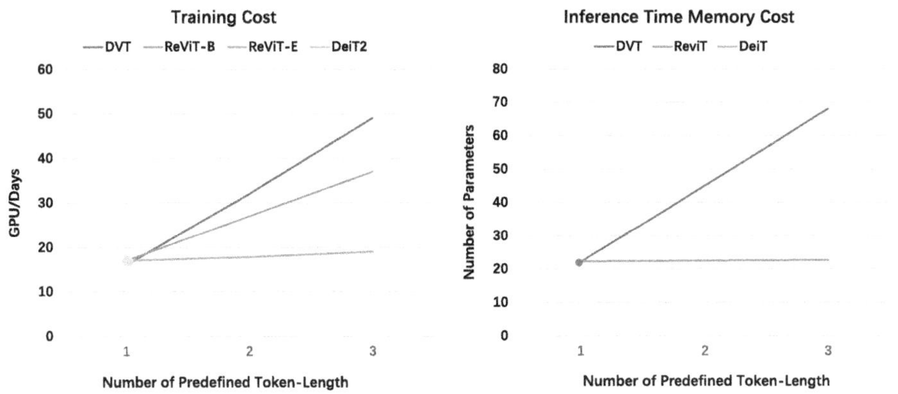

Fig. 7. Compare our approach with DeiT-S [43] and DVT [47] for training cost and memory cost at inference time in terms of the number of predefined token-length. Our proposed ReViT is almost a cheap as training the baseline DeiT-S, while DVT requires linearly increased budget on training and memory.

significantly worse on tokens of size 7×7. When we applied self-distillation with $\tau = 5$, the accuracy of both models increased. To further evaluate the model, we used $\tau = 5$. The higher value of τ negatively impacted the accuracy of the largest token length, dropping the accuracy by around 0.3%, but significantly improving the performance of models with token size 7×7. This highlights the necessity of using self-distillation in our scenario and demonstrates the importance of carefully selecting the hyper-parameter τ for optimal performance.

Training Cost and Memory Consumption. We compared ReViT with DeiT-S and DVT [47] in terms of training cost and memory consumption, as shown in Fig. 7. ReViT-B denotes the baseline approach of ReViT, while ReViT-E is the efficient implementation method. Both ReViT-B and DeiT-S show a linear increase in training cost as the number of choices in s increases. ReViT-B is cheaper because backpropagation of multiple token lengths is merged. However, the training time of ReViT-E slightly increases due to the communication cost between parallel models increasing.

As for memory consumption (number of parameters) during testing, since our method only has a single ViT where most computational heavy components are shared, the memory cost is slightly higher than the baseline. However, compared to DVT, the increase in the number of parameters with respect to the increasing number of token length choices is negligible. This indicates that our approach is more practical than DVT in terms of both training cost and memory cost. Furthermore, our method is easier to apply to existing ViT models than DVT.

Comparison with DVT. We conducted a further investigation of our proposed method based on DeiT-S and compared it with DVT, which was also developed based on DeiT-S. Figure 8 shows that our proposed ReViT achieves superior

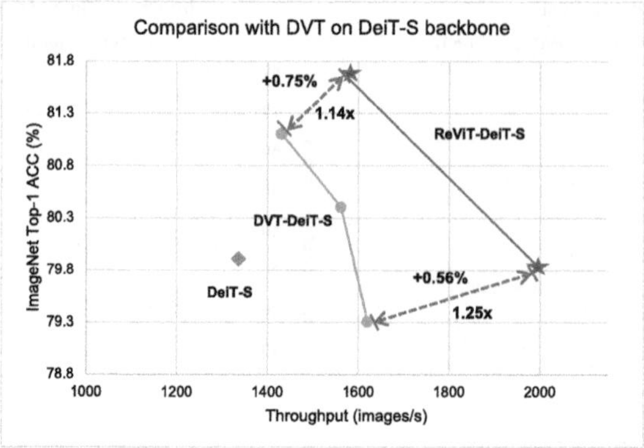

Fig. 8. Comparison with DVT [47] on DeiT-S backbone. Our method outperforms DVT by a large margin.

performance compared to DVT. This could be due to our better selection of the number of patches that achieves the best accuracy-speed tradeoff.

5 Conclusions

This paper aims to reduce the token length to split the image in the ViT model to eliminate unnecessary computational costs. First, we propose the Resizable Transformer (ReViT), which adaptively processes any predefined token size for a given image. Then, we define a Token-Length Assigner to decide the minimum number of tokens that the transformer can use to classify the individual image correctly. Extensive experiments indicate that ReViT can significantly accelerate the state-of-the-art ViT model. Also, compared to the prior SOTA method, our approach achieves better training speed, inference cost, and model performance. Therefore, we believe our paper benefits practitioners who would like to adopt ViT in deployment.

References

1. Arnab, A., Dehghani, M., Heigold, G., Sun, C., Lučić, M., Schmid, C.: Vivit: a video vision transformer. In: Proceedings of the IEEE/CVF International Conference on Computer Vision, pp. 6836–6846 (2021)
2. Bao, H., Dong, L., Wei, F.: Beit: Bert pre-training of image transformers. arXiv preprint arXiv:2106.08254 (2021)
3. Beltagy, I., Peters, M.E., Cohan, A.: Longformer: the long-document transformer. arXiv preprint arXiv:2004.05150 (2020)
4. Bertasius, G., Wang, H., Torresani, L.: Is space-time attention all you need for video understanding? In: ICML, vol. 2, p. 4 (2021)
5. Bolya, D., Fu, C.Y., Dai, X., Zhang, P., Feichtenhofer, C., Hoffman, J.: Token merging: Your vit but faster. In: The Eleventh International Conference on Learning Representations (2023). https://openreview.net/forum?id=JroZRaRw7Eu

6. Cai, H., Gan, C., Wang, T., Zhang, Z., Han, S.: Once-for-all: train one network and specialize it for efficient deployment. arXiv preprint arXiv:1908.09791 (2019)
7. Carion, N., Massa, F., Synnaeve, G., Usunier, N., Kirillov, A., Zagoruyko, S.: End-to-end object detection with transformers. In: Vedaldi, A., Bischof, H., Brox, T., Frahm, J.-M. (eds.) ECCV 2020. LNCS, vol. 12346, pp. 213–229. Springer, Cham (2020). https://doi.org/10.1007/978-3-030-58452-8_13
8. Chen, Z., Xie, L., Niu, J., Liu, X., Wei, L., Tian, Q.: Visformer: the vision-friendly transformer. arXiv preprint arXiv:2104.12533 (2021)
9. Choromanski, K., et al.: Rethinking attention with performers. arXiv preprint arXiv:2009.14794 (2020)
10. Chu, X., et al.: Twins: Revisiting the design of spatial attention in vision transformers, vol. 1(2), p. 3. arXiv preprint arXiv:2104.13840 (2021)
11. Deng, J., Dong, W., Socher, R., Li, L.J., Li, K., Fei-Fei, L.: Imagenet: a large-scale hierarchical image database. In: 2009 IEEE Conference on Computer Vision and Pattern Recognition, pp. 248–255. Ieee (2009)
12. Dosovitskiy, A., et al.: An image is worth 16x16 words: transformers for image recognition at scale. arXiv preprint arXiv:2010.11929 (2020)
13. Fan, H., Xiong, B., Mangalam, K., Li, Y., Yan, Z., Malik, J., Feichtenhofer, C.: Multiscale vision transformers. In: Proceedings of the IEEE/CVF International Conference on Computer Vision, pp. 6824–6835 (2021)
14. Feichtenhofer, C., Fan, H., Malik, J., He, K.: Slowfast networks for video recognition. In: Proceedings of the IEEE/CVF International Conference on Computer Vision, pp. 6202–6211 (2019)
15. Frankle, J., Carbin, M.: The lottery ticket hypothesis: Finding sparse, trainable neural networks. arXiv preprint arXiv:1803.03635 (2018)
16. Goyal, R., et al.: The "something something" video database for learning and evaluating visual common sense. In: Proceedings of the IEEE International Conference on Computer Vision, pp. 5842–5850 (2017)
17. Han, K., Xiao, A., Wu, E., Guo, J., Xu, C., Wang, Y.: Transformer in transformer. arXiv preprint arXiv:2103.00112 (2021)
18. Han, S., Mao, H., Dally, W.J.: Deep compression: compressing deep neural networks with pruning, trained quantization and huffman coding. arXiv preprint arXiv:1510.00149 (2015)
19. He, K., Chen, X., Xie, S., Li, Y., Dollàr, P., Girshick, R.: Masked autoencoders are scalable vision learners (2021)
20. Hinton, G., Vinyals, O., Dean, J.: Distilling the knowledge in a neural network. arXiv preprint arXiv:1503.02531 (2015)
21. Hu, H., Gu, J., Zhang, Z., Dai, J., Wei, Y.: Relation networks for object detection. In: Proceedings of the IEEE Conference on Computer Vision and Pattern Recognition, pp. 3588–3597 (2018)
22. Huang, Y., et al.: Label-guided auxiliary training improves 3d object detector. In: European Conference on Computer Vision, pp. 684–700. Springer (2022). https://doi.org/10.1007/978-3-031-20077-9_40
23. Jiang, Z., et al.: Token labeling: Training a 85.5% top-1 accuracy vision transformer with 56m parameters on imagenet. arXiv preprint arXiv:2104.10858 (2021)
24. Li, Y., Fan, H., Hu, R., Feichtenhofer, C., He, K.: Scaling language-image pre-training via masking. arXiv preprint arXiv:2212.00794 (2022)
25. Liu, H., Simonyan, K., Yang, Y.: Darts: Differentiable architecture search. arXiv preprint arXiv:1806.09055 (2018)
26. Liu, Z., et al.: Swin transformer: Hierarchical vision transformer using shifted windows. arXiv preprint arXiv:2103.14030 (2021)

27. Liu, Z., et al.: Video swin transformer. In: Proceedings of the IEEE/CVF Conference on Computer Vision and Pattern Recognition, pp. 3202–3211 (2022)
28. Liu, Z., et al.: Teinet: Towards an efficient architecture for video recognition. In: Proceedings of the AAAI Conference on Artificial Intelligence, vol. 34, pp. 11669–11676 (2020)
29. Liu, Z., Wang, L., Wu, W., Qian, C., Lu, T.: Tam: temporal adaptive module for video recognition. In: Proceedings of the IEEE/CVF International Conference on Computer Vision, pp. 13708–13718 (2021)
30. Mahmood, K., Mahmood, R., Van Dijk, M.: On the robustness of vision transformers to adversarial examples. arXiv preprint arXiv:2104.02610 (2021)
31. Marin, D., Chang, J.H.R., Ranjan, A., Prabhu, A., Rastegari, M., Tuzel, O.: Token pooling in vision transformers. arXiv preprint arXiv:2110.03860 (2021)
32. Naseer, M., Ranasinghe, K., Khan, S., Hayat, M., Khan, F.S., Yang, M.H.: Intriguing properties of vision transformers. arXiv preprint arXiv:2105.10497 (2021)
33. Pan, B., Panda, R., Jiang, Y., Wang, Z., Feris, R., Oliva, A.: Ia-red^2: interpretability-aware redundancy reduction for vision transformers. arXiv preprint arXiv:2106.12620 (2021)
34. Pan, X., Xia, Z., Song, S., Li, L.E., Huang, G.: 3d object detection with pointformer. In: Proceedings of the IEEE/CVF Conference on Computer Vision and Pattern Recognition, pp. 7463–7472 (2021)
35. Patrick, M., et al.: Keeping your eye on the ball: Trajectory attention in video transformers. Adv. Neural. Inf. Process. Syst. **34**, 12493–12506 (2021)
36. Raghu, M., Unterthiner, T., Kornblith, S., Zhang, C., Dosovitskiy, A.: Do vision transformers see like convolutional neural networks? arXiv preprint arXiv:2108.08810 4 (2021)
37. Rao, Y., Zhao, W., Liu, B., Lu, J., Zhou, J., Hsieh, C.J.: Dynamicvit: efficient vision transformers with dynamic token sparsification. arXiv preprint arXiv:2106.02034 (2021)
38. Ryoo, M.S., Piergiovanni, A., Arnab, A., Dehghani, M., Angelova, A.: Tokenlearner: what can 8 learned tokens do for images and videos? arXiv preprint arXiv:2106.11297 (2021)
39. Sablayrolles, H.T.M.C.A., Jégou, G.S.H.: Going deeper with image transformers
40. Song, L., et al.: Dynamic grained encoder for vision transformers. In: Thirty-Fifth Conference on Neural Information Processing Systems (2021). https://openreview.net/forum?id=gnAIV-EKw2
41. Tan, M., Le, Q.: Efficientnet: Rethinking model scaling for convolutional neural networks. In: International Conference on Machine Learning, pp. 6105–6114. PMLR (2019)
42. Tang, Y., et al.: Patch slimming for efficient vision transformers. arXiv preprint arXiv:2106.02852 (2021)
43. Touvron, H., Cord, M., Douze, M., Massa, F., Sablayrolles, A., Jégou, H.: Training data-efficient image transformers & distillation through attention. In: International Conference on Machine Learning, pp. 10347–10357. PMLR (2021)
44. Vaswani, A., et al.: Attention is all you need. In: Advances in Neural Information Processing Systems, pp. 5998–6008 (2017)
45. Wang, L., Tong, Z., Ji, B., Wu, G.: Tdn: temporal difference networks for efficient action recognition. In: Proceedings of the IEEE/CVF Conference on Computer Vision and Pattern Recognition, pp. 1895–1904 (2021)
46. Wang, X., Girshick, R., Gupta, A., He, K.: Non-local neural networks. In: Proceedings of the IEEE Conference on Computer Vision and Pattern Recognition, pp. 7794–7803 (2018)

47. Wang, Y., Huang, R., Song, S., Huang, Z., Huang, G.: Not all images are worth 16x16 words: Dynamic vision transformers with adaptive sequence length. arXiv preprint arXiv:2105.15075 (2021)
48. Wu, H., et al.: Cvt: introducing convolutions to vision transformers. arXiv preprint arXiv:2103.15808 (2021)
49. Xiao, T., Singh, M., Mintun, E., Darrell, T., Dollár, P., Girshick, R.: Early convolutions help transformers see better. arXiv preprint arXiv:2106.14881 (2021)
50. Xu, W., Xu, Y., Chang, T., Tu, Z.: Co-scale conv-attentional image transformers. arXiv preprint arXiv:2104.06399 (2021)
51. Yang, S., Quan, Z., Nie, M., Yang, W.: Transpose: towards explainable human pose estimation by transformer. arXiv preprint arXiv:2012.14214 (2020)
52. Yin, M., et al.: Disentangled non-local neural networks. In: Vedaldi, A., Bischof, H., Brox, T., Frahm, J.-M. (eds.) ECCV 2020. LNCS, vol. 12360, pp. 191–207. Springer, Cham (2020). https://doi.org/10.1007/978-3-030-58555-6_12
53. Yu, J., Huang, T.S.: Universally slimmable networks and improved training techniques. In: Proceedings of the IEEE/CVF International Conference on Computer Vision, pp. 1803–1811 (2019)
54. Yu, J., et al.: BigNAS: scaling up neural architecture search with big single-stage models. In: Vedaldi, A., Bischof, H., Brox, T., Frahm, J.-M. (eds.) ECCV 2020. LNCS, vol. 12352, pp. 702–717. Springer, Cham (2020). https://doi.org/10.1007/978-3-030-58571-6_41
55. Yu, J., Yang, L., Xu, N., Yang, J., Huang, T.: Slimmable neural networks. arXiv preprint arXiv:1812.08928 (2018)
56. Zhao, B., Cui, Q., Song, R., Qiu, Y., Liang, J.: Decoupled knowledge distillation. In: Proceedings of the IEEE/CVF Conference on Computer Vision and Pattern Recognition, pp. 11953–11962 (2022)
57. Zheng, C., Zhu, S., Mendieta, M., Yang, T., Chen, C., Ding, Z.: 3d human pose estimation with spatial and temporal transformers. arXiv preprint arXiv:2103.10455 (2021)
58. Zhu, X., Su, W., Lu, L., Li, B., Wang, X., Dai, J.: Deformable detr: deformable transformers for end-to-end object detection. arXiv preprint arXiv:2010.04159 (2020)
59. Zhu, Y., Fu, X.: Bnnas++: towards unbiased neural architecture search with batch normalization. IEEE Access **10**, 128424–128432 (2022)
60. Zhu, Y., et al.: Teach less, learn more: on the undistillable classes in knowledge distillation. In: Advances in Neural Information Processing Systems
61. Zhu, Y., Wang, Y.: Student customized knowledge distillation: bridging the gap between student and teacher. In: Proceedings of the IEEE/CVF International Conference on Computer Vision, pp. 5057–5066 (2021)
62. Zhu, Y., et al.: Scalekd: Distilling scale-aware knowledge in small object detector. In: Proceedings of the IEEE/CVF Conference on Computer Vision and Pattern Recognition (CVPR), pp. 19723–19733 (June 2023)
63. Zoph, B., Le, Q.V.: Neural architecture search with reinforcement learning. arXiv preprint arXiv:1611.01578 (2016)

Graph Rebasing and Joint Similarity Reconstruction for Cross-Modal Hash Retrieval

Dan Yao[1,2] and Zhixin Li[1,2](✉)

[1] Key Lab of Education Blockchain and Intelligent Technology, Ministry of Education, Guangxi Normal University, Guilin 541004, China
[2] Guangxi Key Lab of Multi-source Information Mining and Security, Guangxi Normal University, Guilin 541004, China
lizx@gxnu.edu.cn

Abstract. Cross-modal hash retrieval methods improve retrieval speed and reduce storage space at the same time. The accuracy of intra-modal and inter-modal similarity is insufficient, and the large gap between modalities leads to semantic bias. In this paper, we propose a Graph Rebasing and Joint Similarity Reconstruction (GRJSR) method for cross-modal hash retrieval. Particularly, the graph rebasing module is used to filter out graph nodes with weak similarity and associate graph nodes with strong similarity, resulting in fine-grained intra-modal similarity relation graphs. The joint similarity reconstruction module further strengthens cross-modal correlation and implements fine-grained similarity alignment between modalities. In addition, we combine the similarity representation of real-valued and hash features to design the intra-modal and inter-modal training strategies. GRJSR conducted extensive experiments on two cross-modal retrieval datasets, and the experimental results effectively validated the superiority of the proposed method and significantly improved the retrieval performance.

Keywords: Cross-modal retrieval · Unsupervised cross-modal hashing · Similarity matrix · Graph rebasing · Similarity reconstruction

1 Introduction

As the scale of data on the internet continues to expand, the retrieval needs of users increase and retrieval techniques evolve. Cross-modal retrieval has attracted widespread research interest, aiming to use one modality as a query to retrieve relevant data from another modality and explore the relationships between data from different modalities. As information technology continues to develop and multimedia data of all types increases dramatically, the efficiency and accuracy of cross-modal retrieval become ever more important.

Compared with the widely used instance common space methods [6,16,17,21, 28,31,32,36,40,41], the cross-modal hash retrieval methods [27,39,44,45,47] can improve the speed of cross-modal retrieval, reduce the storage space and greatly

© The Author(s), under exclusive license to Springer Nature Switzerland AG 2023
D. Koutra et al. (Eds.): ECML PKDD 2023, LNAI 14170, pp. 86–102, 2023.
https://doi.org/10.1007/978-3-031-43415-0_6

improve the retrieval efficiency while keeping the accuracy within a controlled range, resulting in a better balance between accuracy and efficiency. The basic concept of the cross-modal hash method is to map cross-modal data into a common hamming space, obtaining similar cross-modal content along with similar binary hash codes and preserving intra-modal and inter-modal similarity. Cross-modal hashing methods can be divided into supervised and unsupervised methods. The supervised methods [18,20,22,23,29,33,34,37] require manually annotated semantic labels. While the supervised method can further improve retrieval performance compared to the unsupervised method, it also inevitably increases computational costs. The unsupervised methods [4,10,11,19,26,30,35,42,43] only need to know whether heterogeneous data co-exist, significantly reducing the computational cost and making the method more flexible and feasible. In this paper, we focus on unsupervised cross-modal hashing methods.

Unsupervised cross-modal hash retrieval is label-free and leads to inaccurate semantic data similarity. After constructing the similarity relation graph, certain samples are close to each other in a specific domain, such as cats and dogs, because of the lack of labeling information. So there will be some wrong connections between the nodes of the relation graph, and semantic bias will exist in this case. Some problems with existing methods need further consideration. Firstly, the similarity matrix obtained by the cosine function may integrate meaningless similarity information. Therefore, the process of intra-modal and inter-modal similarity information is critical. The second is the limitation of constructing similarity relation graphs. When constructing the relation graphs, some methods ignore the relation between nodes and their multiple neighbours. Most of them only consider pairs of nodes. This can result in the construction of relation graphs that do not take into account the more comprehensive similarity information. The last point is that some methods construct global relation graphs but ignore locally useful information. This leads to results that do not yield fine-grained similarity information.

To address the above problems, we propose a Graph Rebasing and Joint Similarity Reconstruction(GRJSR) method to facilitate efficient cross-modal retrieval. The main contributions of this paper are as follows:

- We propose a Graph Rebasing (GR) module, which filters out the neighbour nodes with low correlation and computes the neighbour nodes with high correlation. Eventually, we obtain intra-modal relation graphs that exhibit fine-grained similarity. The schematic diagram of our proposed Graph Rebasing (GR) method is shown in Fig. 1.
- With the Joint Similarity Reconstruction (JSR) module proposed in this paper, we reconstruct the inter-modal similarity relation graphs. Finer-grained alignment between modalities is achieved, and more valuable similarity information is obtained.
- We design a combined intra-modal and inter-modal training strategy. We conduct comprehensive experiments with two widely used image and text retrieval datasets to verify that GRJSR significantly improves retrieval performance.

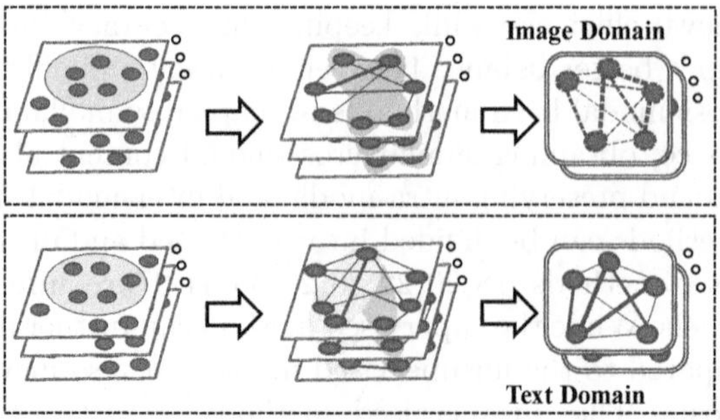

Fig. 1. The schematic diagram of our proposed Graph Rebasing (GR) process. The circles in the shaded part are samples from the same class. Because of the lack of labeling information, these samples may be close to each other but belong to different types, such as dogs, wolves and cats. The thicker the line connecting the samples, the higher the correlation of the samples.

2 Related Work

2.1 Supervised Cross-Modal Hashing Methods

Some supervised methods use label information combined with semantic relations to obtain valid hash codes. SDDH [22] imposes orthogonality and balance constraints to the matrix and embeds it into the hash code in order to better capture the similarity information of the same class. QDCMH [18] proposes a method to construct quadratic loss functions. The method combines them with representation learning and hash codes to effectively capture heterogeneous cross-modal similarity. NSDH [33] constructs a semantic label matrix and combines it with similarity information to enhance the semantic information of the hash code. Finally, a more discriminative hash code is obtained. MSLF [29] uses labels to generate common attributes of different modalities and obtains hash code with lower computational cost. OLCH [34] proposes a learning framework for online semantic representation in order to efficiently handle large-scale and streaming data. Learning hash codes for data increments, updating hash functions in a streaming way, and finally optimizing hash functions.

2.2 Unsupervised Cross-Modal Hashing Methods

Some unsupervised methods focus on computing the similarity between features, using the similarity metric as the optimization objective. DGCPN [35] constructs the retrieved data as a static global KNN graph, calculates the probability of similarity between two nodes, and obtains the graph neighbor coherence. The method improves the accuracy of similarity by maintaining robustness through combined losses. The constructed similarity matrix is further analysed by HNH [43], resulting in a high order similarity matrix between modalities. A common representation is then introduced on the basis of the different modalities, easing the differences between the modalities. SRCH [30] first generates the geometric and semantic graphs within the modalities and then applies hash codes to rebase the edges within the graphs. The method also uses hash autoencoders to maintain and quantify inter-modal similarity. IRGR [10] uses the KNN method to construct global and local similarity relation graphs. The method obtains valid similarity information based on graph reasoning and proposes a step-by-step training strategy to reduce semantic loss.

3 Methodology

The framework of GRJSR is shown in Fig. 2. GRJSR can obtain deep semantic features through feature extraction. In this paper, we employ pre-trained AlexNet [13] to extract image features $F_I \in \mathbb{R}^{m\times dv}$, and use bag-of-words(BOW) model to extract text features $F_T \in \mathbb{R}^{m\times dt}$. The image and text features of the i-th instance are denoted as $\{v_i \mid i \in [1,m], v_i \in \mathbb{R}^{dv}\}$ and $\{t_i \mid i \in [1,m], t_i \in \mathbb{R}^{dt}\}$, which m means there are m training samples, dv and dt denote the dimensions of image and text features respectively. Given the specific hash code length c, we define the hash features as $H_* \in \mathbb{R}^{m\times c}, * \in \{I,T\}$ similar to [3,8,9,14,24,25]. Following [1,15,26], we generate the corresponding binary hash codes $B_* \in \{-1,+1\}^{m\times c}, * \in \{I,T\}$. Similarity matrix calculation by the cosine similarity function:

$$S_{x,y} = cos(S_x, S_y) = \frac{S_x^T S_y}{\|S_x\|_2 \|S_y\|_2} \tag{1}$$

where S_x^T is the transpose of S_x, $\|\cdot\|$ indicates the L2-norm.

3.1 Local Relation Graph Building

Similar to DGCPN [35], intra-modal local relation graph building constructs multiple local relation graphs within image modality and text modality based on the K-nearest neighbor (KNN) method respectively. We denote the image graph and text graph instance set as $G_* = \{*, E\}, * \in \{V,T\}$. $V = \{v_i\}_{i=1}^m$. $T = \{t_i\}_{i=1}^m$. Each instance can be represented as a node in a relation graph, the node sets are denoted as V or T. And the similarity between instances can be indicated by the weights of the edges E in the relation graphs. Our method is to perform conditional probability operations on the two intra-modal instances. The relation between two instances within the same modality is calculated conditional on other instances within the modality, resulting in intra-modal local relation graphs:

$$\begin{aligned} P(l_{*i} = l_{*j}) = \sum_{q=1}^{m} P\left(l_{*i}^F = l_{*q}^F \mid *_i, *_q\right) \\ \times P\left(l_{*j}^F = l_{*q}^F \mid *_j, *_q\right), * \in \{v,t\} \end{aligned} \tag{2}$$

$P(l_{*i} = l_{*j})$ is the probability of similarity between instances, which can also be expressed as local relation graphs. We use virtual labels to analyze the

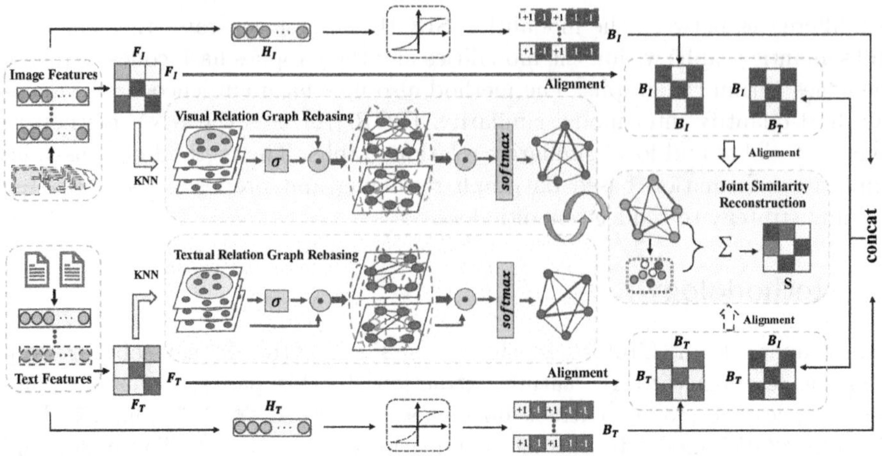

Fig. 2. GRJSR firstly extracts the image and text features, then constructs the similarity matrices of image and text. Followed by the KNN method to obtain the intra-modal local relation graphs and uses our proposed Graph Rebasing (GR) module to process the relation graphs within the two modalities. Next step, we combine the similarity information of two modalities and perform the Joint Similarity Reconstruction (JSR) module on the inter-modal similarity information, which can obtain the fine-grained similarity alignment. Finally, the intra-modal and inter-modal training strategies reduce the semantic gap.

similarity between nodes, where $l_{*i}, * \in v, t$ indicates the label of vi or ti. $P\left(l_{*i}^F = l_{*q}^F \mid *_i, *_q\right)$ indicates that two nodes $*_i$ and $*_q$ have the highest similarity. We assume that each node is related to its k nearest nodes:

$$P\left(l_{*i}^F = l_{*q}^F \mid *_i, *_q\right) = \begin{cases} \frac{d(*_i,*_q)}{\sum_{*_p \in Ne(*_i,k)} d(*_i,*_p)} & *_q \in Ne\left(*_i, k\right) \\ 0 & else \end{cases} \tag{3}$$

l_{vi}^F is the virtual label for nodes between image graphs, l_{ti}^F is the virtual label for nodes between text graphs. Where $Ne\left(*_i, k\right)$ indicates the set of k-nearest neighbors of $*_i$ using $d\left(*_i, *_q\right)$. We calculate the similarity matrices of the original features. $S_{x,x}^F = \cos(F_x, F_x) = \frac{F_x^T F_x}{\|F_x\|_2 \|F_x\|_2}, x \in \{I, T\}$. $S_{x,x}^F(i,q) = S_{x,x}^F(q,i)$ in the matrix represents the similarity of instance i to instance q. When $d\left(v_i, v_p\right) = S_{I,I}^F(i,q) = S_{I,I}^F(q,i)$, calculate $P(l_{vi} = l_{vj})$ to obtain visual relation graph G_I; When $d\left(t_i, t_p\right) = S_{T,T}^F(i,q) = S_{T,T}^F(q,i)$, calculate $P(l_{ti} = l_{tj})$ to obtain textual relation graph G_T.

3.2 Graph Rebasing

The above method of computing the relation graphs does not adequately consider nodes other than the two nodes. Our proposed relation graph rebasing method can comprehensively consider the neighbour nodes and obtain fine-grained similarity information. The above formula using conditional probability mainly constructs a local relation graph by two nodes. Our method uses the gating mechanism to consider other neighbors between two nodes, filters out nodes with fewer similar neighbors, and connects nodes with more common similar neighbors. We generate the gating mask for the image relation graph $Mask^{G_I} \in \mathbb{R}^{m\times d_v}$ and the gating mask for the text relation graph $Mask^{G_T} \in \mathbb{R}^{m\times d_t}$ by the sigmoid function:

$$\begin{cases} Mask^{G_I} = \sigma\left(G_I W_v + b_v\right) \\ Mask^{G_T} = \sigma\left(G_T W_t + b_t\right) \end{cases} \tag{4}$$

where $\sigma(\cdot)$ denotes sigmoid function. W_v and W_t are the learnable projection matrices, while b_v and b_t are the bias vectors. Then we can get the filtered relation graphs $\widetilde{G_*}$:

$$\widetilde{G_*} = M^{G_*} \odot G_* \tag{5}$$

To obtain sufficient semantic similarity information, we fuse the similarities between neighbours by quadratic weighting. The fusion of information from different neighbours can effectively capture fine-grained similarity information to obtain the intra-modal fine-grained similarity relation graphs:

$$R_* = softmax\left(\widetilde{G_*} \odot \left(\widetilde{G_*}^T \otimes \widetilde{G_*}\right)\right) \tag{6}$$

where the symbol $\odot$ signifies the element-wise product, and the symbol $\otimes$ signifies the matrix multiplication. So we get the visual rebase graph R_I, and the corresponding similarity matrix is $S^G_{I,I}$. The textual rebase graph denotes R_T, and the corresponding similarity matrix is $S^G_{T,T}$.

3.3 Global Relation Graph Construction

From the intra-modal graph rebasing method, we obtain the similarity representations of the intra-modal local relation graphs. Next, we combine the similarity representations of the original features and the local relation graph to obtain the global similarity representation within the modalities:

$$S_{x,x} = \gamma S^F_{x,x} + \lambda S^G_{x,x}, x \in \{I, T\} \tag{7}$$

where γ is the weight parameter that regulates the similarity representation of the original features and λ is the weight parameter that regulates the similarity representation of the local relation graph. Finally, we obtain the global similarity matrix $S_{I,I}$ within the image modality and the global similarity matrix $S_{T,T}$ within the text modality.

Based on Eq. 1, we calculate the image to text similarity representation $S_{I,T} = cos(S_{I,I}, S_{T,T}) = \frac{S^T_{I,I} S_{T,T}}{\|S_{I,I}\|_2 \|S_{T,T}\|_2}$ and the text to image similarity representation $S_{T,I} = cos(S_{T,T}, S_{I,I}) = \frac{S^T_{T,T} S_{I,I}}{\|S_{T,T}\|_2 \|S_{I,I}\|_2}$.

Furthermore, we use Eq. 3 to calculate the similarity relation graph between the modalities. When $d(o_i, o_p) = S_{I,T}(i, q) = S_{I,T}(q, i)$, calculate $P(l_{oi} = l_{oj})$

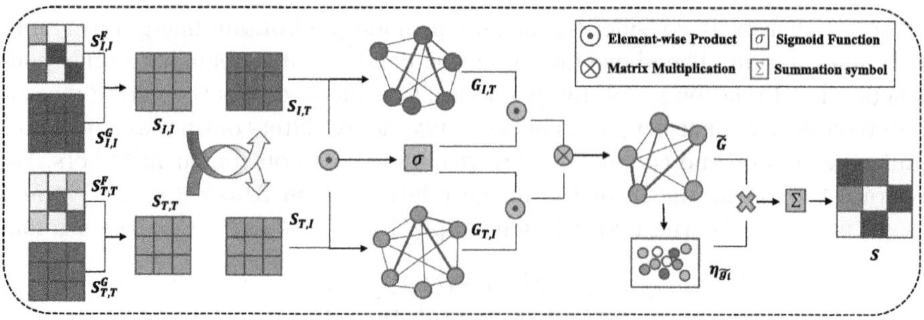

Fig. 3. Illustration of the JSR module.

to obtain the image to text similarity relation graph $G_{I,T}$; When $d(o_i, o_p) = S_{T,I}(i,q) = S_{T,I}(q,i)$, calculate $P(l_{oi} = l_{oj})$ to obtain the text to image similarity relation graph $G_{T,I}$. At this time, $O = \{o_i\}_{i=1}^{m}$ and O denotes the node set of joint image and text modalities.

3.4 Joint Similarity Reconstruction

Although the above method constructs joint similarity graphs, the method will integrate the alignment information indiscriminately and there will be more meaningless alignment information. To obtain fine-grained joint similarity alignment, we propose a joint similarity reconstruction (JSR) method for the inter-modal relation graphs $G_{I,T}$ and $G_{T,I}$. The JSR module can efficiently integrate meaningful alignments and filter out meaningless ones. Figure 3 shows an illustration of our proposed JSR module.

To improve the method's ability to discriminate meaningful alignments between modalities, we propose a gating mechanism that filters meaningless alignments between modalities. First, we design a edge weight mask $Mask^G$ for the edges of the connected inter-modal relation graphs:

$$Mask^G = \sigma(W_e R(G_{I,T}, G_{T,I}) + b_e) \tag{8}$$

$W_e \in \mathbb{R}^{m \times m}$ is the learnable projection matrix, while $b_e \in \mathbb{R}^{1 \times m}$ is the bias vector. $R(G_{I,T}, G_{T,I})$ denotes the point-to-point alignment score between the joint modal relation graphs:

$$R(G_{I,T}, G_{T,I}) = \|W_a S_{I,T}\|_2 \odot \|W_a S_{T,I}\|_2 \tag{9}$$

where $W_a \in \mathbb{R}^{m \times m}$ is a linear transformation, $\|\cdot\|_2$ indicates L2 regularization. We then apply the edge weight mask of the gating mechanism to the inter-modal relation graphs, respectively.

$$\widetilde{G_{I,T}} = Mask^G \odot G_{I,T} \tag{10}$$

$$\widetilde{G_{T,I}} = Mask^G \odot G_{T,I} \tag{11}$$

We obtain relation graphs between the modalities after filtering for nonsense alignments. In the next step, we concat the inter-modal relation graphs to obtain the global joint-modal similarity relation graph:

$$\begin{aligned}\widetilde{G} &= concat(\widetilde{G_{I,T}}, \widetilde{G_{T,I}}) \\ &= concat((Mask^G \odot G_{I,T}), (Mask^G \odot G_{T,I}))\end{aligned} \tag{12}$$

To obtain a fine-grained representation of joint-modal similarity, we design an enhanced weight of the global similarity graph $\widetilde{G} = \{\widetilde{g}_i\}_{i=1}^m$ that enhances the informative similarity representations between nodes:

$$\eta_{\widetilde{g}_i} = \frac{\sigma\left(\| W_g \widetilde{g}_i \|_2\right)}{\sum_{j=1}^{m} \sigma\left(\| W_g \widetilde{g}_j \|_2\right)} \tag{13}$$

where $W_g \in \mathbb{R}^{m \times m}$ is a linear transformation. Finally we aggregate the inter-node similarity representations to obtain the joint similarity matrix after the similarity reconstruction:

$$S = \sum_{i=1}^{m} \left\|\eta_{\widetilde{g}_i}\right\|_2 \cdot \widetilde{g}_i \tag{14}$$

By our proposed JSR method, fine-grained alignment between modalities can be achieved. We can further unify more meaningful similarity information and reduce the number of less meaningful alignments.

3.5 Training Objectives

While most previous methods trained data from both modalities uniformly, our method proposes a strategy that combines intra-modal and inter-modal data training. We train the module separately according to the intra-modal and inter-modal losses. Based on Eq. 1, we calculate the binary hash codes similarity matrix $S_{I,I}^B$ for the image modality and the binary hash codes similarity matrix $S_{T,T}^B$ for the text modality. Within each modality, we perform semantic alignment of hash features to real-valued features:

$$\min \alpha \left(\left\|\varphi S_{x,x} - S_{x,x}^B\right\|^2\right), x \in \{I, T\} \tag{15}$$

where α and φ are both trade-off parameters. φ is used to regulate the best quantified region for $S_{x,x}$ and $S_{x,x}^B$. α is used to regulate the importance of neighbourhood relations from different modalities. Combining the semantic alignment of the two modalities leads to the total error within the two modalities:

$$\mathcal{L}_{intra} = \min \alpha \left(\left\|\varphi S_{I,I} - S_{I,I}^B\right\|^2 + \left\|\varphi S_{T,T} - S_{T,T}^B\right\|^2\right) \tag{16}$$

We first calculate the inter-modal similarity matrices $S_{I,T}^B$ and $S_{T,I}^B$ of the binary hash codes by Eq. 1. Then we minimize the symmetry loss of the cross-modal hash code similarity matrix about the diagonal between the two modalities:

$$min \left\|S_{I,T}^B - S_{T,I}^B\right\|^2 \tag{17}$$

Then we calculate the error of the joint inter-modal relation graph similarity information with the cross-modal hash feature similarity information:

$$\begin{aligned} &\left\|S - S^B_{x,y}\right\|^2 + \beta(\left\|S - \rho S^B_{x,x}\right\|^2) \\ &s.t.\ x, y \in \{I, T\} \end{aligned} \tag{18}$$

where ρ and β are both trade-off parameters. ρ is used to regulate the best quantified region for S and $S^B_{x,x}$. β is used to regulate inter-modal and intra-modal importance. Finally, the inter-model loss is formulated as:

$$\begin{aligned} \mathcal{L}_{inter} = min \left\|S^B_{I,T} - S^B_{T,I}\right\|^2 + \left\|S - S^B_{I,T}\right\|^2 + \\ \left\|S - S^B_{T,I}\right\|^2 + \beta(\left\|S - \rho S^B_{I,I}\right\|^2 + \left\|S - \rho S^B_{T,T}\right\|^2) \end{aligned} \tag{19}$$

4 Experiments

4.1 Datasets and Evaluation Metrics

We experiment on two public datasets for evaluation, including MIRFlickr [12] and NUS-WIDE [5]. And we use two standard retrieval evaluation metrics: mean average precision (MAP) and top-K precision curve. MAP is a standard indicator to measure the performance of cross-modal retrieval algorithms, it is defined as:

$$AP(i) = \frac{1}{N}\sum_{r=1}^{n} P_i(r)\delta_i(r),\ MAP = \frac{1}{M}\sum_{i=1}^{M} AP(i) \tag{20}$$

where $AP(i)$ is the average precision of the query. $P_i(r)$ refers to the precision of the top r retrieved instances. $\delta_i(r) = 1$ if the r-th retrieved entity is similar to the query and $\delta_i(r) = 0$, otherwise. N is the number of ground-truth similar instances of the query in the database and n is the number of instances in the database. M is the query set size. The top-K precision denotes the precision at different numbers of retrieved instances.

4.2 Implementation Details

For fair comparison with most advanced methods, we extract image features using pre-trained AlexNet and text features using the bag-of-words (BOW) model. The experimental environment follows that of other state-of-the-art methods. We implement the proposed method via Pytorch on a workstation (CPU: Intel(R) Core(TM) i7-10700 CPU @ 2.90GHz, GPU: NVIDIA GeForce RTX 2080 Ti). Our proposed method uses an SGD optimizer with a momentum of 0.9 and a weight decay of 0.0005. The batch size for optimization is set to 32. The learning rates of ImgNet are set to 0.001 for NUS-WIDE and MIRFlickr respectively. The learning rates of TxtNet are set to 0.01 for two datasets. The setting of parameters is particularly important, part of the setting of our method follows other advanced methods and part of the setting of parameters depends on parameter sensitivity experiments. Similar to IRGR [10], we set γ to 1.5 and λ is set to 0.0001. Similar to DSAH [19], we set ρ to 1.5. After parameter sensitivity experiments analysis, we can determine the parameters $k = 31$, $\alpha = 0.1$, $\beta = 0.1$ and $\varphi = 1.5$ for MIRFlickr. And we set $k = 31$, $\alpha = 0.3$, $\beta = 0.3$ and $\varphi = 1.4$ for NUS-WIDE.

Table 1. The MAP results of MIRFlikcr and NUS-WIDE at various code lengths.

Method	MIRFlickr				NUS-WIDE			
	I T				T I			
	16bit	32bit	64bit	128bit	16bit	32bit	64bit	128bit
AAH [7]	0.7145	0.7230	0.7271	0.7283	0.8137	0.8198	0.8251	0.8281
DSPH [38]	0.6473	0.6610	0.6703	–	0.6581	0.6781	0.6818	-
FDDH [20]	–	0.7392	0.7578	0.7631	–	0.8022	0.8250	0.8357
HNH [43]	–	**0.8830**	**0.8950**	0.9020	–	0.8540	0.8680	0.8780
HSIDHN [2]	0.7978	0.8097	0.8179	–	0.7802	0.7946	0.8115	–
MLSPH [48]	0.8076	0.8235	0.8337	–	0.7852	0.8041	0.8146	–
MSDH [46]	0.7836	0.7905	0.8017	–	0.7573	0.7635	0.7813	–
MSLF [29]	0.6988	0.7175	0.7222	0.7294	0.7572	0.7763	0.7892	0.7959
NSDH [33]	0.7363	0.7561	0.7656	0.7712	0.7836	0.8014	0.8183	0.8229
QDCMH [18]	0.7635	0.7688	0.7713	–	0.7762	0.7725	0.7859	–
SDDH [22]	0.7210	0.7394	0.7454	0.7494	0.7917	0.8132	0.8241	0.8328
IRGR [10]	0.8310	0.8550	0.8770	0.8940	0.8250	**0.8770**	0.8820	0.8920
GRJSR(Ours)	**0.8470**	0.8780	**0.8950**	**0.9050**	**0.8460**	0.8750	**0.8940**	**0.9030**
AAH [7]	0.6409	0.6439	0.6515	0.6549	0.7379	0.7533	0.7595	0.7629
FDDH [20]	–	0.6970	0.6910	0.7118	–	0.8133	0.8111	0.8244
HNH [43]	–	0.8020	0.8160	0.8470	–	0.7760	0.7960	0.8020
HSIDHN [2]	0.6498	0.6787	0.6834	–	0.6396	0.6529	0.6792	–
MLSPH [48]	0.6405	0.6604	0.6734	–	0.6433	0.6633	0.6724	–
MSDH [46]	0.6633	0.6859	0.7155	–	0.6359	0.6632	0.6934	–
MSLF [29]	0.6213	0.6339	0.6374	0.6482	0.7212	0.7427	0.7578	0.7765
NSDH [33]	0.6418	0.6604	0.6732	0.6791	0.7658	0.7892	0.7939	0.8011
SDDH [22]	0.6510	0.6564	0.6670	0.6733	0.7638	0.7790	0.7945	0.7990
IRGR [10]	0.7560	0.7930	0.8160	0.8390	0.7500	0.7830	0.8040	0.8170
GRJSR(Ours)	**0.7670**	**0.8210**	**0.8250**	**0.8530**	**0.7730**	**0.8230**	**0.8240**	**0.8410**

4.3 Performance Comparison

Results on MIRFlickr. The top half of Table 1 shows the MAP results of GRJSR and other advanced methods for different code lengths on the MIRFlickr dataset. For further comparison with other state-of-the-art methods, we also plotted top-K accuracy curves for code lengths of 64 bits and 128 bits, as shown in Fig. 4 and Fig. 5. Our GRJSR method generally achieves higher MAP results than other state-of-the-art methods on the Image Query Text and Text

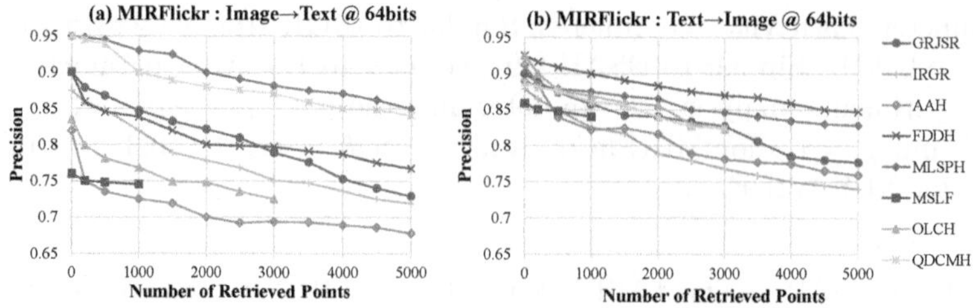

Fig. 4. Top-K precision curves on the MIRFlickr dataset with 64 bits hash codes.

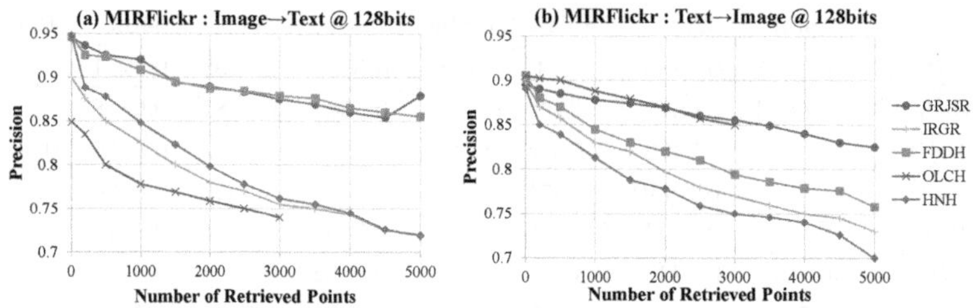

Fig. 5. Top-K precision curves on the MIRFlickr dataset with 128 bits hash codes.

Query Image tasks. The longer the code length, the better the MAP results, with little difference in results between code lengths. From Fig. 4 and Fig. 5, the results of our method are slightly lower than some of the supervised cross-modal hash retrieval methods in the top-K precision curve. The longer the code length, the higher the precision in general. Although our method improves precision through similarity reconstruction and semantic alignment, we compare not only with unsupervised cross-modal retrieval methods, but also with the experimental results of supervised retrieval methods, which do not show an absolute advantage.

Results on NUS-WIDE. The bottom half of Table 1 shows the MAP results of GRJSR and other advanced methods for different code lengths on the NUS-WIDE dataset. As shown in Fig. 6 and Fig. 7, we also plotted top-K precision curves for code lengths of 64 bits and 128bits. In the image to text and text to image retrieval tasks on the NUS-WIDE dataset, GRJSR achieves best results in MAP results. As with the results on the MIRFlickr dataset, the top-K precision curve results for the GRJSR method are slightly lower than the partial supervised method. However, the precision rates of our method are more stable than those of other advanced methods at different retrieval points, demonstrating the excellent performance and stability of the method.

GRJSR still achieves excellent retrieval performance compared to the benchmark method. Both IRGR and GRJSR use K-nearest neighbor (KNN) for constructing relation graphs, but they treat the graphs differently. HNH, IRGR, and GRJSR are all based on DJSRH for constructing similarity matrices, but they treat the similarity representation differently. The experimental results show that HNH, IRGR, and our method are the best among all compared methods. The

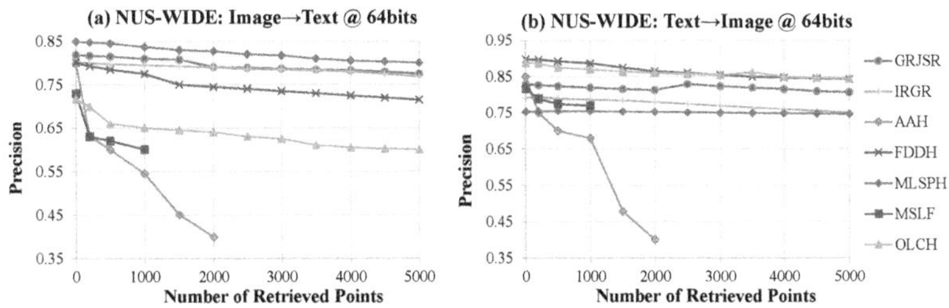

Fig. 6. Top-K precision curves on the NUS-WIDE dataset with 64 bits hash codes.

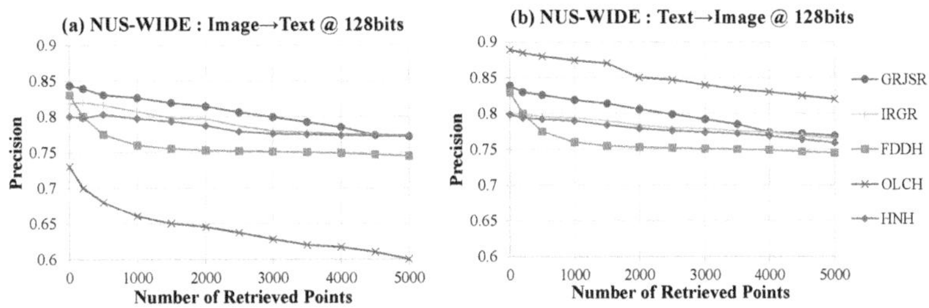

Fig. 7. Top-K precision curves on the NUS-WIDE dataset with 128 bits hash codes.

validity and superiority of our proposed method can be verified by two evaluation indicators. Although our method is slightly lower than some supervised cross-modal hash retrieval methods in terms of top-K precision curves, our results outperform similar unsupervised cross-modal hash retrieval methods and most supervised methods. Moreover, our method is overall optimal in terms of MAP evaluation metrics, so GRJSR achieves better cross-modal retrieval performance compared to other comparative methods.

4.4 Parameter Sensitivity Experiments

In order to choose the appropriate parameter values to obtain better performance, Fig. 8 shows the results of our sensitivity experiments for parameters k and α on the MIRFlickr dataset with a code length of 128 bits. Figure 9 shows the results of our sensitivity experiments for parameters β and φ. The training batch size is 32, and k is the number of nearest neighbors of each node, which is the threshold value of the relation graph. For MIRFlickr dataset and NUS-WIDE dataset, we tune k from 0 to 32 at an increment of 2 per step. We fix $\alpha = 0.1, \beta = 0.1, \varphi = 1.0$, and when k is taken as 31, there is a large improvement in performance. Then we evaluate the trade-off parameters α, β. Parameter α adjusts the similarity alignment within the two modalities and parameter β adjusts the similarity alignment between the two modalities. We respectively experiment the parameters α and β with numbers ranging from 0 to 1 at an increment of 0.1. The best results were achieved when α was 0.1 and β was 0.1.

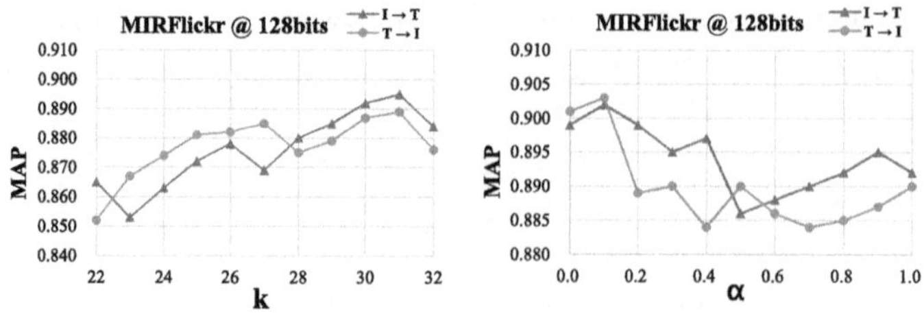

Fig. 8. Parameters sensitivity analysis on MIRFlickr at 128 bits.

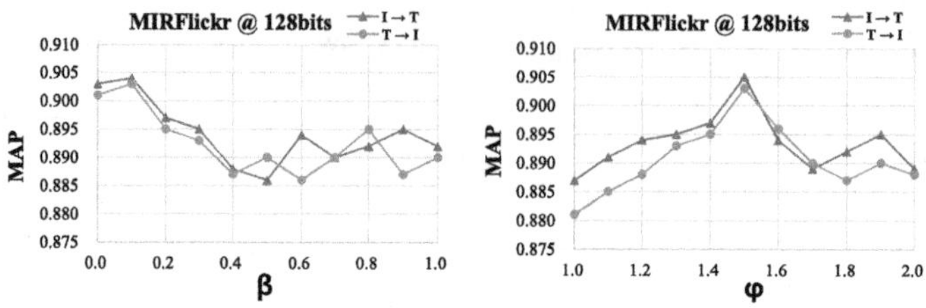

Fig. 9. Parameters sensitivity analysis on MIRFlickr at 128 bits.

Parameter φ can improve the sensitivity of similarity alignment. We tune φ from 1.0 to 2.0 at an increment of 0.1. We fix $\alpha = 0.1, \beta = 0.1, k = 31$, and the best performance was obtained when $\varphi = 1.5$.

4.5 Ablation Experiments

In order to verify the effectiveness of different modules of GRJSR, we performed ablation experiments on the MIRFlickr dataset. Table 2 lists five variants of the ablation experiments. In the GRJSR-1 method, the graph rebasing (GR) module and the joint similarity reconstruction module are ablated. In the GRJSR-2 method, the joint similarity reconstruction module is ablated. In the GRJSR-3 method, the graph rebasing module is ablated. In the GRJSR-4 method, the training objectives module is ablated. In the GRJSR-5 method, the graph rebasing, joint similarity reconstruction and the training objectives module are ablated.

As shown in Table 3, we can see the results of the ablation experiments. GRJSR-1 and GRJSR-2 illustrate the importance of combining our proposed graph rebasing method and training strategy, and by graph rebasing we can obtain a finer-grained relation graph representing similarity. Experimental results comparing GRJSR-1 and GRJSR-3 show that the joint similarity reconstruction can significantly improve the performance and reduce the error caused by meaningless alignment between modalities. Comparing the experimental results of GRJSR and GRJSR-4 can show the importance of the training strategy. Experiment GRJSR-5 does not have our proposed method and the results are not satisfactory, which can show the effectiveness of our proposed method.

Table 2. Configuration of the ablation experiments on each module based on GRJSR.

Method	Local relation graph building	Local relation graph rebasing	Global relation graph construction	Joint similarity reconstruction	Training objectives
GRJSR	✓	✓	✓	✓	✓
GRJSR-1	✓		✓		✓
GRJSR-2	✓	✓	✓		✓
GRJSR-3	✓		✓	✓	✓
GRJSR-4	✓	✓	✓	✓	
GRJSR-5	✓		✓		

Table 3. The MAP results of five variants of GRJSR at 64 bits and 128 bits on MIRFlickr.

Method	64bits		128bits	
	I T	T I	I T	T I
GRJSR	0.8950	0.8940	0.9050	0.9030
GRJSR-1	0.8840	0.8760	0.8870	0.8840
GRJSR-2	0.8950	0.8920	0.9010	0.8990
GRJSR-3	0.9010	0.8940	0.9060	0.9000
GRJSR-4	0.8890	0.8950	0.9020	0.9030
GRJSR-5	0.8590	0.8650	0.8650	0.8690

5 Conclusion

This paper rebases local relation graphs using the proposed graph rebasing method to obtain fine-grained similarity relation graphs. Global relation graphs are generated by combining image and text modalities' similarity matrices. The fine-grained joint similarity alignment is obtained by the proposed joint similarity reconstruction method. This paper also includes a combined intra-modal and inter-modal training strategy, which is tested on benchmark datasets. Experimental results demonstrate the effectiveness and innovation of this paper.

Acknowledgements. This work is supported by National Natural Science Foundation of China (Nos. 62276073, 61966004), Guangxi Natural Science Foundation (No. 2019GXNSFDA245018), Guangxi "Bagui Scholar" Teams for Innovation and Research Project, Innovation Project of Guangxi Graduate Education (No. YCBZ2023055), and Guangxi Collaborative Innovation Center of Multi-source Information Integration and Intelligent Processing.

Ethical Statement. We affirm that the ideas, concepts, and findings presented in this paper are the result of our own original work, conducted with honesty, rigor, and transparency. We have provided proper citations and references for all sources used, and have clearly acknowledged the contributions of others where applicable.

References

1. Cao, Z., Long, M., Wang, J., Yu, P.S.: Hashnet: deep learning to hash by continuation. In: Proceedings of the IEEE International Conference on Computer Vision, pp. 5608–5617 (2017)
2. Chen, S., Wu, S., Wang, L.: Hierarchical semantic interaction-based deep hashing network for cross-modal retrieval. PeerJ Comput. Sci. **7**, e552 (2021)
3. Chen, S., Wu, S., Wang, L., Yu, Z.: Self-attention and adversary learning deep hashing network for cross-modal retrieval. Comput. Electr. Eng. **93**, 107262 (2021)
4. Cheng, S., Wang, L., Du, A.: Deep semantic-preserving reconstruction hashing for unsupervised cross-modal retrieval. Entropy **22**(11), 1266 (2020)
5. Chua, T.S., Tang, J., Hong, R., Li, H., Luo, Z., Zheng, Y.: Nus-wide: a real-world web image database from national University of Singapore. In: Proceedings of the ACM International Conference on Image and Video Retrieval, pp. 1–9 (2009)
6. Chun, S., Oh, S.J., De Rezende, R.S., Kalantidis, Y., Larlus, D.: Probabilistic embeddings for cross-modal retrieval. In: Proceedings of the IEEE/CVF Conference on Computer Vision and Pattern Recognition, pp. 8415–8424 (2021)
7. Fang, X., et al.: Average approximate hashing-based double projections learning for cross-modal retrieval. IEEE Trans. Cybern. **52**(11), 11780–11793 (2021)
8. Fang, X., Liu, Z., Han, N., Jiang, L., Teng, S.: Discrete matrix factorization hashing for cross-modal retrieval. Int. J. Mach. Learn. Cybern. **12**, 3023–3036 (2021)
9. Fang, Y.: Robust multimodal discrete hashing for cross-modal similarity search. J. Vis. Commun. Image Represent. **79**, 103256 (2021)
10. Hou, C., Li, Z., Tang, Z., Xie, X., Ma, H.: Multiple instance relation graph reasoning for cross-modal hash retrieval. Knowl.-Based Syst. **256**, 109891 (2022)
11. Hou, C., Li, Z., Wu, J.: Unsupervised hash retrieval based on multiple similarity matrices and text self-attention mechanism. In: Applied Intelligence, pp. 1–16 (2022)
12. Huiskes, M.J., Lew, M.S.: The mir flickr retrieval evaluation. In: Proceedings of the 1st ACM International Conference on Multimedia Information Retrieval, pp. 39–43 (2008)
13. Krizhevsky, A., Sutskever, I., Hinton, G.E.: Imagenet classification with deep convolutional neural networks. Commun. ACM **60**(6), 84–90 (2017)
14. Li, H., Zhang, C., Jia, X., Gao, Y., Chen, C.: Adaptive label correlation based asymmetric discrete hashing for cross-modal retrieval. IEEE Trans. Knowl. Data Eng. (2021)
15. Li, X., Hu, D., Nie, F.: Deep binary reconstruction for cross-modal hashing. In: Proceedings of the 25th ACM International Conference on Multimedia, pp. 1398–1406 (2017)
16. Li, Z., Ling, F., Zhang, C., Ma, H.: Combining global and local similarity for cross-media retrieval. IEEE Access **8**, 21847–21856 (2020)
17. Li, Z., Xie, X., Ling, F., Ma, H., Shi, Z.: Matching images and texts with multi-head attention network for cross-media hashing retrieval. Eng. Appl. Artif. Intell. **106**, 104475 (2021)
18. Liu, H., Xiong, J., Zhang, N., Liu, F., Zou, X.: Quadruplet-based deep cross-modal hashing. Comput. Intell. Neurosci. **2021**, 9968716 (2021)
19. Liu, S., Qian, S., Guan, Y., Zhan, J., Ying, L.: Joint-modal distribution-based similarity hashing for large-scale unsupervised deep cross-modal retrieval. In: Proceedings of the 43rd International ACM SIGIR conference on Research and Development in Information Retrieval, pp. 1379–1388 (2020)

20. Liu, X., Wang, X., Cheung, Y.M.: Fddh: fast discriminative discrete hashing for large-scale cross-modal retrieval. IEEE Trans. Neural Netw. Learn. Syst. **33**(11), 6306–6320 (2021)
21. Messina, N., et al.: Aladin: distilling fine-grained alignment scores for efficient image-text matching and retrieval. In: Proceedings of the 19th International Conference on Content-Based Multimedia Indexing, pp. 64–70 (2022)
22. Qin, J., Fei, L., Zhu, J., Wen, J., Tian, C., Wu, S.: Scalable discriminative discrete hashing for large-scale cross-modal retrieval. In: ICASSP 2021–2021 IEEE International Conference on Acoustics, Speech and Signal Processing (ICASSP), pp. 4330–4334. IEEE (2021)
23. Shen, H.T., et al.: Exploiting subspace relation in semantic labels for cross-modal hashing. IEEE Trans. Knowl. Data Eng. **33**(10), 3351–3365 (2020)
24. Shen, X., Zhang, H., Li, L., Zhang, Z., Chen, D., Liu, L.: Clustering-driven deep adversarial hashing for scalable unsupervised cross-modal retrieval. Neurocomputing **459**, 152–164 (2021)
25. Song, G., Tan, X., Zhao, J., Yang, M.: Deep robust multilevel semantic hashing for multi-label cross-modal retrieval. Pattern Recogn. **120**, 108084 (2021)
26. Su, S., Zhong, Z., Zhang, C.: Deep joint-semantics reconstructing hashing for large-scale unsupervised cross-modal retrieval. In: Proceedings of the IEEE/CVF International Conference on Computer Vision, pp. 3027–3035 (2019)
27. Wang, D., Cui, P., Ou, M., Zhu, W.: Deep multimodal hashing with orthogonal regularization. In: Twenty-Fourth International Joint Conference on Artificial Intelligence (2015)
28. Wang, K., Herranz, L., van de Weijer, J.: Continual learning in cross-modal retrieval. In: Proceedings of the IEEE/CVF Conference on Computer Vision and Pattern Recognition, pp. 3623–3633 (2021)
29. Wang, S., Zhao, H., Nai, K.: Learning a maximized shared latent factor for cross-modal hashing. Knowl.-Based Syst. **228**, 107252 (2021)
30. Wang, W., Shen, Y., Zhang, H., Yao, Y., Liu, L.: Set and rebase: determining the semantic graph connectivity for unsupervised cross-modal hashing. In: Proceedings of the Twenty-Ninth International Conference on International Joint Conferences on Artificial Intelligence, pp. 853–859 (2021)
31. Wang, X., Hu, P., Zhen, L., Peng, D.: Drsl: deep relational similarity learning for cross-modal retrieval. Inf. Sci. **546**, 298–311 (2021)
32. Xie, X., Li, Z., Tang, Z., Yao, D., Ma, H.: Unifying knowledge iterative dissemination and relational reconstruction network for image-text matching. Inform. Process. Manag. **60**(1), 103154 (2023)
33. Yang, Z., et al.: Nsdh: A nonlinear supervised discrete hashing framework for large-scale cross-modal retrieval. Knowl.-Based Syst. **217**, 106818 (2021)
34. Yi, J., Liu, X., Cheung, Y.m., Xu, X., Fan, W., He, Y.: Efficient online label consistent hashing for large-scale cross-modal retrieval. In: 2021 IEEE International Conference on Multimedia and Expo (ICME), pp. 1–6. IEEE (2021)
35. Yu, J., Zhou, H., Zhan, Y., Tao, D.: Deep graph-neighbor coherence preserving network for unsupervised cross-modal hashing. In: Proceedings of the AAAI Conference on Artificial Intelligence, vol. 35, pp. 4626–4634 (2021)
36. Yu, T., Yang, Y., Li, Y., Liu, L., Fei, H., Li, P.: Heterogeneous attention network for effective and efficient cross-modal retrieval. In: Proceedings of the 44th International ACM SIGIR Conference on Research and Development in Information Retrieval, pp. 1146–1156 (2021)

37. Zhang, D., Wu, X.J., Yu, J.: Label consistent flexible matrix factorization hashing for efficient cross-modal retrieval. ACM Trans. Multimedia Comput. Commun. Appli. (TOMM) **17**(3), 1–18 (2021)
38. Zhang, D., Wu, X.J., Yu, J.: Learning latent hash codes with discriminative structure preserving for cross-modal retrieval. Pattern Anal. Appl. **24**, 283–297 (2021)
39. Zhang, D., Li, W.J.: Large-scale supervised multimodal hashing with semantic correlation maximization. In: Proceedings of the AAAI Conference on Artificial Intelligence, vol. 28 (2014)
40. Zhang, H., Mao, Z., Zhang, K., Zhang, Y.: Show your faith: Cross-modal confidence-aware network for image-text matching. In: Proceedings of the AAAI Conference on Artificial Intelligence, vol. 36, pp. 3262–3270 (2022)
41. Zhang, K., Mao, Z., Wang, Q., Zhang, Y.: Negative-aware attention framework for image-text matching. In: Proceedings of the IEEE/CVF Conference on Computer Vision and Pattern Recognition, pp. 15661–15670 (2022)
42. Zhang, P.F., Li, Y., Huang, Z., Xu, X.S.: Aggregation-based graph convolutional hashing for unsupervised cross-modal retrieval. IEEE Trans. Multimedia **24**, 466–479 (2021)
43. Zhang, P.F., Luo, Y., Huang, Z., Xu, X.S., Song, J.: High-order nonlocal hashing for unsupervised cross-modal retrieval. World Wide Web **24**, 563–583 (2021)
44. Zhen, Y., Yeung, D.Y.: Co-regularized hashing for multimodal data. In: Advances in Neural Information Processing Systems 25 (2012)
45. Zhu, L., Huang, Z., Liu, X., He, X., Sun, J., Zhou, X.: Discrete multimodal hashing with canonical views for robust mobile landmark search. IEEE Trans. Multimedia **19**(9), 2066–2079 (2017)
46. Zhu, L., Tian, G., Wang, B., Wang, W., Zhang, D., Li, C.: Multi-attention based semantic deep hashing for cross-modal retrieval. Appl. Intell. **51**, 5927–5939 (2021)
47. Zhu, X., Huang, Z., Shen, H.T., Zhao, X.: Linear cross-modal hashing for efficient multimedia search. In: Proceedings of the 21st ACM International Conference on Multimedia, pp. 143–152 (2013)
48. Zou, X., Wang, X., Bakker, E.M., Wu, S.: Multi-label semantics preserving based deep cross-modal hashing. Signal Process. Image Commun. **93**, 116131 (2021)

ARConvL: Adaptive Region-Based Convolutional Learning for Multi-class Imbalance Classification

Shuxian Li[1,2,3], Liyan Song[1,2](✉), Xiaoyu Wu[4], Zheng Hu[4], Yiu-ming Cheung[3], and Xin Yao[1,2](✉)

[1] Research Institute of Trustworthy Autonomous Systems, Southern University of Science and Technology (SUSTech), Shenzhen, China
{songly,xiny}@sustech.edu.cn

[2] Guangdong Provincial Key Laboratory of Brain-inspired Intelligent Computation, Department of Computer Science and Engineering, Southern University of Science and Technology (SUSTech), Shenzhen, China

[3] Department of Computer Science, Hong Kong Baptist University, Hong Kong SAR, China

[4] RAMS Reliability Technology Lab, Huawei Technology Co., Ltd., Shenzhen, China

Abstract. Real-world image classification usually suffers from the multi-class imbalance issue, probably causing unsatisfactory performance, especially on minority classes. A typical way to address such problem is to adjust the loss function of deep networks by making use of class imbalance ratios. However, such static between-class imbalance ratios cannot monitor the changing latent feature distributions that are continuously learned by the deep network throughout training epochs, potentially failing in helping the loss function adapt to the latest class imbalance status of the current training epoch. To address this issue, we propose an adaptive loss to monitor the evolving learning of latent feature distributions. Specifically, the class-wise feature distribution is derived based on the region loss with the objective of accommodating feature points of this class. The multi-class imbalance issue can then be addressed based on the derived class regions from two perspectives: first, an adaptive distribution loss is proposed to optimize class-wise latent feature distributions where different classes would converge within the regions of a similar size, directly tackling the multi-class imbalance problem; second, an adaptive margin is proposed to incorporate with the cross-entropy loss to enlarge the between-class discrimination, further alleviating the class imbalance issue. An adaptive region-based convolutional learning method is ultimately produced based on the adaptive distribution loss and the adaptive margin cross-entropy loss. Experimental results based on public image sets demonstrate the effectiveness and robustness of our approach in dealing with varying levels of multi-class imbalance issues.

Keywords: Multi-class imbalance classification · Deep learning · Adaptive loss · Feature engineering · Margin

© The Author(s), under exclusive license to Springer Nature Switzerland AG 2023
D. Koutra et al. (Eds.): ECML PKDD 2023, LNAI 14170, pp. 103–120, 2023.
https://doi.org/10.1007/978-3-031-43415-0_7

1 Introduction

In real-world applications of image classification such as human behavior recognition [24], video classification [27], and medical decision making [19], image classes usually exhibit the multi-class imbalance issue, for which some classes are under-represented as minorities while others are over-represented as majorities. Catering for this multi-class imbalance issue is important to retain good predictive performance, especially for those minority classes. Taking image classifications in the medical domain as an example, the number of images related to rare diseases is usually much less than those related to common diseases and healthy cases. Neglecting this issue would probably result in poor predictive performance on minority classes, which poses severe threats to patients afflicted with rare diseases and even undermines the public health service system [19].

Existing approaches for multi-class imbalance learning can be grouped into three categories [13,15,36,41] that are data-level [25,37], model-level [38,42], and cost-sensitive approaches [6,20,23]. Cost-sensitive approach is the most popular and efficient approach in mitigating the image multi-class imbalance issue, which designates different weights to training samples of different classes to adjust the loss function [41]. The weighting is typically designed based on class imbalance ratios [3,6,20,23]. However, imbalance ratios remain static and cannot monitor the changing latent feature distributions that are continuously learned by the deep network throughout training epochs, potentially failing in helping the loss functions to adapt to the latest class imbalance status. Latent feature distributions have shown to be beneficial to the multi-class imbalance learning [11,21], and thus is especially taken into account in this paper.

To the best of our knowledge, there have been only a few studies employing derived latent feature distributions to facilitate multi-class imbalance learning [11,21]. However, they all rely on strict assumptions of the latent feature distribution such as the Gaussian distribution, and cannot adaptively learn the latent feature distribution of entire training samples [11,21]. Our approach enables practical learning of the latent feature space by defining a class-wise *region*, within which most feature points of the same class can be enclosed. Concretely, each region in the latent feature space corresponds to a single class, which is outlined by a *class center* depicting the geometric location of the feature points of that class and a *radius* depicting the spread of the feature points around the class center. In this way, we do not need to rely on any strict assumption on the latent feature distribution, which will be adaptively learned throughout training epochs. Our region learning module utilizes the region loss to derive the class-wise region over time during the training process of the deep network.

The class imbalance problem can then be addressed based on the derived class regions in the latent feature space from two perspectives. First, we propose an adaptive distribution loss to guide the learning process of the class-wise latent feature distribution, so that all class regions can be gradually enclosed within a benchmark radius. As a result, the decision boundary constructed based on class regions in the latent feature space would be unbiased towards any class, dealing with class imbalance directly. Second, we propose an adaptive margin as a mediator to upgrade the original cross-entropy so that between-class discrimination can be enlarged to eliminate possible overlaps of feature points of different classes, further alleviating the class imbalance issue. Ultimately, we construct the convolutional networks by optimizing the adaptive distribution loss and the adaptive margin cross-entropy loss simultaneously, producing our **A**daptive **R**egion-Based **Conv**olutional **L**earning (ARConvL). In summary, our main contributions are:

- We propose a region learning module based on the region loss to derive class-wise regions, each of which consists of a center and a radius, continuously monitoring the class distribution without posing any strict assumption on the latent feature space;
- Based on the derived class regions, we propose an adaptive distribution loss to optimize the class-wise latent feature distribution, so that feature points of different classes are optimized to be enclosed within a benchmark radius, addressing the class imbalance problem directly;
- Based on the derived class regions, we propose an adaptive margin as a mediator to upgrade the loss function, producing our adaptive margin cross-entropy loss, so that the between-class discrimination can be improved, further alleviating multi-class imbalance learning;
- We experimentally investigate the effectiveness and robustness of our proposed ARConvL in dealing with different levels of class imbalance.

The remainder of this paper is organized as follows. Section 2 presents related work. Section 3 proposes ARConvL. Experimental setup and results are discussed in Sect. 4. The paper is concluded in Sect. 5.

2 Related Work

2.1 Multi-class Imbalance Learning

Existing approaches of multi-class imbalance learning can be generally grouped into three categories: data-level approaches, model-level approaches, and cost-sensitive approaches [13,15,36,41].

Data sampling is a representative of data-level approaches, which synthetically balance the training set by under-sampling the majorities or (and) over-sampling the minorities in the image space [13]. Traditional sampling methods such as RUS (Random Under-Sampling) [13], ROS (Random Over-Sampling) [13], SMOTE (Synthetic Minority Over-sampling Technique) [4], and ADASYN (Adaptive Synthetic Sampling Approach) [12] are typically used for class imbalance learning with the numerical features. Several studies extend ROS and RUS to the image data [2,18]. Due to the popularity of deep learning, generative models are also widely used as over-sampling techniques to tackle the multi-class imbalance problem for the image data [25,37].

Ensemble learning is a representative of model-level approaches that has been popularly used for multi-class imbalance learning. Good examples are AdaBoost

[10], AdaBoost.NC [35,36], SMOTEBoost [5], and RUSBoost [29]. Methods of this category need to train multiple classifiers, and when it comes to deep learning, the process would often be time-consuming [32,38,42].

Cost-sensitive methods deal with the class imbalance issue by designating different weights to training samples or (and) classes to distinguish the losses posed to the majority vs the minority classes. [1,9,13]. The weights are usually incorporated with the loss function of the deep network to deal with the multi-class imbalance problem for image data [6,20]. Such methods that make alterations to the loss function are also known as the loss modification based methods, for which we present into more details in the subsequent section.

2.2 Loss Modification Based Methods

Methods of this type deal with multi-class imbalance problem via the modification of the loss function in the deep networks. Re-weighting and logit adjustment are two common approaches for loss modification [41].

For re-weighting approaches, the sample (class) weights are usually encoded into the cross-entropy loss or softmax, rephrasing the loss functions [41]. The main challenge of the re-weighting approaches is how to set proper weights. Lin et al. design sample weights based on their classification difficulties and class imbalance ratios, which are then incorporated into the cross-entropy loss, contributing to the focal loss [20]. Cui et al. design class weights based on a novel effective number, contributing to the class-balanced loss [6]. Besides encoding sample (class) weights into the loss, more related strategies include setting weights directly on the softmax function [28,33].

Logit adjustment approaches tune the logit value of the softmax function to tackle the multi-class imbalance problem [41]. Margins between classes can be produced based on class imbalance ratios to adjust the logit [3]. In 2020, Liu et al. encode the information of feature distribution based on the Gaussian distribution assumption into the logit, enlarging the margin between the minority classes and the majority classes [21]. More recently, Menon et al. adjust the logit based on label frequency to distinguish margins of different classes, contributing to the logit adjustment loss [23].

This paper aims for proposing an adaptive region-based learning method to derive feature distributions adaptively across training epochs without posing any strict assumption to the distribution. With this in mind, we can upgrade the loss function, dealing with the class imbalance issue.

2.3 Convolutional Prototype Learning

Compared to the traditional CNN, Convolutional Prototype Learning (CPL) utilizes L_2-norm, rather than the cosine similarity, to compute the distance (similarity) between the feature point and its connection weight vector [40]. Thus, feature distributions learned with L_2-norm can present hyper-sphere distributions in the latent feature space. The connection weights between the feature layer and the distance output layer can be used as centers of classes. In 2018, Yang et al. point

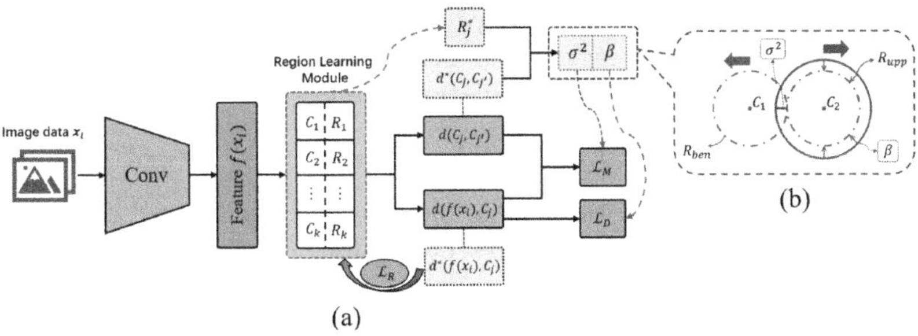

Fig. 1. Overview learning process of our proposed ARConvL on each training batch. Figure 1(b) further illustrates the benchmark radius, upper-bound radius, and corresponding margin σ^2 that measures the potential overlap between class regions.

out that this framework would learn more robust features especially after adding an extra regularization term [40]. Later in 2019, Hayat et al. further propose the affinity loss based on L_2-norm, where a hyper-parameter needs to be predefined and encoded to the loss to manipulate the margin manually [11]. By considering the distribution of class centers, Hayat et al. also propose a loss to force class centers evenly distributed, so that the discrimination between classes would be similar, alleviating the class imbalance problem [11].

CPL has the advantage of describing geometric characteristics of decision boundaries in a straightforward way such as hyper-sphere. Thus, we opt for CPL as our base framework to learn feature distributions of image data.

3 ARConvL

This section proposes **A**daptive **R**egion-Based **Conv**olutional **L**earning (ARCon vL) for multi-class imbalance learning. Section 3.1 outlines the learning framework, followed by Sect. 3.2 presenting the way to adaptively learn class-wise regions across the training process. Sections 3.3 and 3.4 adaptively optimize the class-wise latent feature distribution and adaptively produce the between-class margin cross-entropy loss, respectively, for multi-class imbalance learning.

3.1 Overview of ARConvL

Figure 1 shows the learning process of ARConvL on each training batch $\{x_i, i = 1, \cdots, n\}$, based on which feature points $\{f(x_i)\}$ in the latent feature space are trained via convolutional layers. Such latent features are then connected with the region learning module to derive class regions, each of which consists of a class center C and a class radius R learned from the region loss $\mathcal{L}_R$. Based on the class regions, two loss functions are proposed from two perspectives to cater for class imbalance learning: the first perspective aims to optimize the class-wise latent feature distribution to be enclosed within a region with a benchmark radius based on the distribution loss $\mathcal{L}_D$; the second perspective aims to enlarge the distance between class regions via the proposed margin as a mediator to produce the margin loss $\mathcal{L}_M$. In formulation, the loss of ARConvL is

$$\mathcal{L} = \mathcal{L}_R + \mathcal{L}_D + \mathcal{L}_M \ , \tag{1}$$

where $\mathcal{L}_R$, $\mathcal{L}_D$, and $\mathcal{L}_M$ are the region, distribution, and margin cross-entropy loss functions, respectively. We will present the design of the three loss functions in detail in the subsequent sections.

As explained in Sect. 2.3, we adopt CPL as the base framework to boost geometric characteristics of the latent feature space [40] and thus L_2-norm rather than the cosine similarity is adopted as the distance metric in this paper. Accordingly, the distance of a sample from a region is $d(f(x_i), C_j) = \|f(x_i) - C_j\|_2$ and the distance between two regions is $d(C_j, C_{j'}) = \|C_j - C_{j'}\|_2$, where $j, j' \in \{1, \cdots, k\}$, $i \in \{1, \cdots, n\}$, k is class number, and n is training batch size.

3.2 Region Learning Module

The region learning module aims to compute class-wise regions based on feature points adaptively across training epochs. In particular, class centers $\{C_j\}$ are obtained as the network weights connecting the learned latent features. We then propose the region loss $\mathcal{L}_R$ to learn the radius R_j for each class j as

$$\mathcal{L}_R = \frac{1}{n} \sum_{j=1}^{k} \alpha_j [\sum_{\substack{i=1, \\ x_i \in j}}^{n} (\max\{0,\ d^*(f(x_i), C_j) - R_j\}^2 + \gamma \cdot R_j^2)], \tag{2}$$

where n is the training batch size, $\alpha_j = \max_{j'}(N_{j'})/N_j$ quantifies the emphasis to be placed on class j versus other classes, and N_j denotes the total number of training samples of class j. We are employing $\gamma \cdot R_j^2$ as the regularization term for $\gamma \in [0, 1]$. We set $\gamma = 0.05$ in this paper based on our preliminary experiments. Figure 2 illustrates the mechanism of the region loss: if a feature point falls within its corresponding class region, it causes zero penalty to $\mathcal{L}_R$; otherwise, this feature point contributes the penalty of $[d(x_i, C_{y_i}) - R_{y_i}]^2$ to $\mathcal{L}_R$.

We presume that class radii $\{R_j\}$ are learnable variables, and other variables such as variables in $d(f(x_i), C_j)$ are frozen as non-learnable[1]. We attach the superscript "*" to variables to indicate that they are non-learnable variables. For example, the non-learnable distance between feature point and class center is denoted as $d^*(f(x), C)$ in Fig. 1.

Figure 3 illustrates class regions learned by the region learning module of ARConvL. We deliberately set the two-dimensional latent feature space to facilitate visualization. In our experimental studies, the latent feature dimension is set to 64 to attain good performance. We can see that the majority classes often learn regions of larger radii compared to those of minorities.

[1] In Tensorflow, we can annotate and freeze non-learnable variables using the command `get_static_value()`.

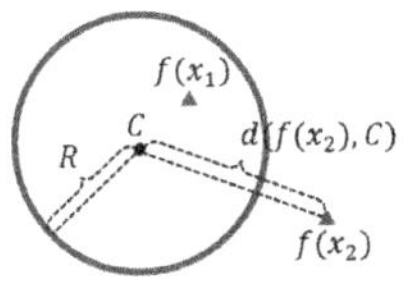

Fig. 2. Illustration of the region loss $\mathcal{L}_R$ in Eq. (2). Given a class region with center C and radius R, $f(x_1)$ locates in the region and thus contributes null penalty to $\mathcal{L}_R$; whereas, $f(x_2)$ contributes the penalty of $[d(f(x_2), C) - R]^2$ to $\mathcal{L}_R$.

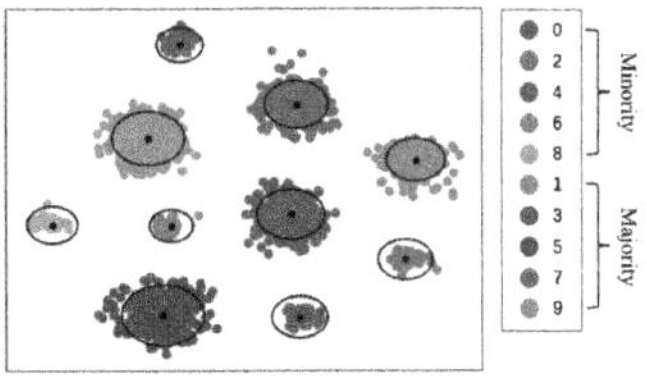

Fig. 3. Illustration of the class regions in the latent feature space that are learned by the region learning module of ARConvL in MNIST.

3.3 Optimizing Class-Wise Latent Feature Distribution

Based on the derived class regions, this section aims to optimize the latent feature distribution of each class to be enclosed within a region surrounding the class center with a benchmark radius that is universal to all classes and can accommodate most feature points of this class. In this way, the decision boundary constructed based on class regions in the latent feature space would be unbiased towards any class, dealing with the class imbalance issue directly. Thereby, one can rely on the class region to optimize the class-wise latent feature distribution which does not need to pose any assumption (e.g., Gaussian) on it.

The *benchmark radius* is defined for all classes based on the derived class regions as

$$R_{ben} = \min_{j \in \{1, \cdots k\}} d_{\min}(C_j)/2, \tag{3}$$

where $d_{\min}(C_j) = \min_{j' \neq j} d^*(C_j, C_{j'})$ is the minimum distance of two different class centers and $d^*(C_j, C_{j'})$ is a non-learnable variable as explained in Sec. 3.1. The *upper-bound radius* of all classes is formulated as

$$R_{upp} = \max_{j=1,\cdots,k} (R_j^*, \quad d_{\min}(C_j)/2\ ). \tag{4}$$

where R_j^* is the radius of class j and is non-learnable in the learning process of distribution loss. The upper-bound radius indicates the possible largest value that feature points of each class would spread surrounding the class center. We have $R_{ben} \leq R_{upp}$.

The idea is to move from the upper-bound radius towards the benchmark radius downside, as shown in Fig. 1(b), enforcing the class-wise latent feature distribution to be enclosed within similar-sized regions. Thereby, the decision boundary would be unbiased towards/against any class. We formulate the ideal scenario of the class regions as $R_{ben} = R_{upp}$. However, in the practical learning process of latent feature distribution, $R_{upp} > R_{ben}$ frequently happens, so that the classes having larger radii than the benchmark value should be penalized. The idea is formulated as

$$\beta = \min(1, \quad (R_{upp}/R_{ben})^2 - 1), \tag{5}$$

quantifying the emphasis on $\mathcal{L}_D$ versus other loss functions of $\mathcal{L}$ in Eq. (1)

Overall, we integrate the *adaptive distribution loss* $\mathcal{L}_D$ to optimize the latent feature distribution of each class as

$$\mathcal{L}_D = \frac{\beta}{n} \sum_{j=1}^{k} \alpha_j \sum_{\substack{i=1, \\ x_i \in j}}^{n} d^2(f(x_i), C_j), \tag{6}$$

where $\sum_{x_i \in j} d(f(x_i), C_j)^2$ accumulates the distance of feature points of class j from their class center C_j and α_j and β are with the same meaning as in Eqs. (2) and (5), respectively. In particular, when the upper-bound R_{upp} approaches the benchmark R_{ben} downside, $\beta \to 0$, leading to zero penalty to $\mathcal{L}_D$.

By introducing an adaptive penalization β, $\mathcal{L}_D$ can also be viewed as a regularization term of the overall loss $\mathcal{L}$ in Eq. (1). Our experiments show that $\mathcal{L}_D$ has significant benefit to the prediction performance, being consistent with the study of Yang et al. [40].

3.4 Enlarging Margin Between Classes

We define the *adaptive margin* as

$$\sigma^2 = \min(R_{ben}^2, \quad R_{upp}^2 - R_{ben}^2), \tag{7}$$

where R_{ben} and R_{upp} are the benchmark and upper-bound radii in Eqs. (3) and (4), respectively. As shown in Fig. 1(b), margin σ^2 measures the overlap between the derived class regions in the latent feature space, for which the learning algorithm should have pushed the class regions away from each other to improve their discrimination.

To incorporate the margin into the cross-entropy loss, we rephrase the softmax function for a given feature point x_i as

$$p(x_i \in j) = \frac{\eta_j \cdot e^{-d^2(f(x_i), C_j)}}{\eta_j \cdot e^{-d^2(f(x_i), C_j)} + \sum_{j' \neq j} \eta_{j'} \cdot e^{-d^2(f(x_i), C_{j'}) + \sigma^2}},$$

where $\eta_j = N_j / (\sum_{j'=1}^{k} N_{j'})$ is the imbalance ratio that was shown to be beneficial for class imbalance learning when embedded into the softmax function [23] and N_j denotes the total number of samples of class j. To push the class centers being evenly distributed in the latent feature space, we formulate the softmax function of class center C_j based on the margin σ^2 as

$$p(C_j) = \frac{e^{-d^2(C_j, C_j)}}{e^{-d^2(C_j, C_j)} + \sum_{j' \neq j} e^{-d^2(C_j, C_{j'}) + \sigma^2}} = \frac{1}{1 + \sum_{j' \neq j} e^{-d^2(C_j, C_{j'}) + \sigma^2}}.$$

Overall, we integrate the *adaptive margin cross-entropy loss* $\mathcal{L}_M$ for this training batch across all classes as

$$\mathcal{L}_M = \frac{1}{n}\sum_{j=1}^{k}\sum_{i=1}^{n} - \log(p(x_i \in j)) + \frac{1}{k}\sum_{j=1}^{k} - \log(p(C_j)). \tag{8}$$

Optimizing $\mathcal{L}_M$ can simultaneously enlarge margins between classes at both the feature point level and the class center level, alleviating the class imbalance issue.

4 Experimental Studies

This section aims to investigate the effectiveness of the proposed ARConvL through a series of experiments. The code is available online[2].

4.1 Experimental Setup

Following previous studies [11,25,37], our experiments are conducted based on 4 public image repositories: MNIST [8], Fashion MNIST [39], SVHN [26], and Cifar10 [17], each of which contains 10 classes labeled from class 0 to 9. To emulate varying class imbalance levels, we randomly sample $1/q$ of the training data from even classes (i.e., 0, 2, 4, 6, and 8) as the minority classes for which $1/q \in \{1, 1/10, 1/20, 1/50, 1/100\}$, following previous studies [11,16]. All training samples of odd classes are retained as the majority classes. For instance, 5 MNIST-related datasets are produced as MNIST-1, MNIST-10, MNIST-20, MNIST-50, and MNIST-100. Table 1 of the supplementary material provides description of the datasets used in the study.

For image sets produced from MNIST and Fashion MNIST, the input size is (28, 28, 1) and we employ a simple backbone consisting of two sets of double convolutional layers connected with one max-pooling layer, one flatten layer, one dense layer, and a batch normalization layer in sequence. For image sets produced based on SVHN and Cifar10, the input size is (32, 32, 3) and we employ ResNet [30] with depth 44 as the backbone. All methods are set under the same CPL framework. The latent space dimension is 64 and the training batch size is 128 in our experiments. Stochastic Gradient Descent (SGD) is used as the optimizer with the momentum 0.9, and the initial learning rate is set to 0.1 for all datasets. For MNIST, Fashion MNIST, and SVHN, the total number of training epochs is set to 50, and we decay the learning rate by 0.1 at the 26-th and 41-th epochs. For Cifar10, the total number of training epochs is set to 100, and we decay the learning rate by 0.1 at the 51-th and 81-th epochs. For the proposed ARConvL, the learning rate for the radius variables is set to 0.001 at the first three epochs and 0.01 at the remaining training epochs.

We randomly select 90% of the training samples for model training and the remaining 10% are reserved for validation, so that we can decide the best model

[2] Code and supplementary material: https://github.com/shuxian-li/ARConvL.

Table 1. G-means (%) of the investigated methods. Each entry is the mean±std of 10 times. The last column corresponds to our ARConvL. The best model on each dataset is highlighted in bold. The last row lists the average ranks (avgRank) of each model across datasets. Significant difference against ARConvL is highlighted in yellow.

Data	CPL	GCPL	Focal	CB	CB Focal	Affinity	LA	ARConvL
Mnist-1	99.2±0.1	99.4±0.0	99.4±0.1	99.2±0.1	99.4±0.1	**99.5±0.1**	99.2±0.1	99.4±0.1
Mnist-10	98.2±0.2	98.5±0.1	98.8±0.2	98.3±0.1	98.6±0.3	98.7±0.2	98.5±0.1	**99.1±0.0**
Mnist-20	97.3±0.2	97.4±0.3	98.3±0.3	97.5±0.3	98.1±0.3	97.5±0.4	98.1±0.3	**98.8±0.2**
Mnist-50	95.1±0.3	94.4±0.4	96.8±0.5	95.9±0.3	97.0±0.5	94.7±1.4	97.1±0.4	**98.4±0.3**
Mnist-100	92.3±0.8	89.0±1.3	94.8±0.9	93.5±0.9	94.6±0.8	90.6±1.5	96.0±0.5	**97.3±0.6**
Fashion-1	91.0±0.2	92.0±0.2	91.4±0.4	91.1±0.2	91.4±0.4	**92.4±0.2**	91.0±0.2	92.2±0.2
Fashion-10	86.6±0.6	87.1±0.4	86.8±0.5	86.9±0.5	86.9±0.4	86.2±0.3	87.6±0.3	**88.5±0.5**
Fashion-20	84.3±0.6	84.1±0.8	84.6±0.8	84.5±0.7	84.7±0.6	82.6±0.8	85.6±0.5	**86.3±0.7**
Fashion-50	80.0±1.0	77.9±1.4	81.2±1.0	81.2±1.1	81.6±1.2	76.3±1.8	82.2±1.9	**84.0±1.0**
Fashion-100	75.1±2.7	72.7±2.1	77.5±2.2	77.8±1.5	78.2±1.3	55.4±20.2	79.6±2.5	**82.3±0.8**
SVHN-1	95.4±0.1	95.3±0.2	96.0±0.2	95.4±0.1	**96.1±0.1**	95.8±0.1	95.4±0.1	95.9±0.2
SVHN-10	88.5±0.8	86.9±0.9	91.7±0.7	90.8±0.3	92.0±0.2	90.4±0.4	91.8±0.4	**93.3±0.2**
SVHN-20	83.5±1.5	77.8±2.8	88.8±0.6	87.9±0.4	89.2±0.7	84.7±0.9	90.6±0.4	**91.9±0.5**
SVHN-50	75.3±0.6	48.7±8.0	83.1±0.6	82.0±0.7	84.1±0.7	15.4±14.8	88.2±1.4	**90.1±1.0**
SVHN-100	61.6±2.5	0.0±0.0	72.9±2.6	70.9±2.3	75.6±1.7	0.0±0.0	86.1±0.9	**87.2±1.1**
Cifar10-1	89.7±0.2	89.6±0.2	91.1±0.2	89.8±0.3	**91.1±0.2**	89.9±0.3	89.6±0.3	90.3±0.4
Cifar10-10	77.3±0.6	73.4±1.5	78.6±0.8	77.3±0.9	79.1±0.4	74.1±1.1	81.9±0.4	**82.3±0.6**
Cifar10-20	69.5±1.1	61.6±1.5	69.9±1.2	69.3±1.8	71.0±1.0	54.9±3.9	79.0±0.6	**79.6±0.6**
Cifar10-50	54.9±3.0	39.9±4.1	57.5±2.6	55.0±3.3	57.2±3.2	0.0±0.0	73.3±1.6	**75.6±0.6**
Cifar10-100	43.9±1.2	5.0±7.8	46.2±2.2	46.0±2.5	45.8±3.4	0.0±0.0	69.3±2.3	**71.3±1.2**
avgRank	6.45	6.825	3.5	5.2	3.25	6.175	3.2	1.4

in terms of G-mean [31] out of the models created across training epochs as our learned deep model. This is to alleviate the over-fitting issue which may particularly impact the deep learning process. We evaluate predictive performance of deep models on spare test sets.

ARConvL are compared against 2 baseline methods, namely CPL [40] and GCPL [40], and 5 state-of-the-art methods, namely Focal Loss ("Focal") [20], Class Balanced Loss ("CB") [6], Class Balanced Focal Loss ("CB Focal") [6], Affinity Loss ("Affinity") [11], and Logit Adjustment Loss ("LA") [23]. Table 2 of the supplementary material reports the parameter settings for those methods.

G-mean [31] and class-wise accuracy are used to evaluate performance for being popularly used and shown to be robust in class imbalance learning [11,16]. Experiments are repeated 10 times, and the average performance (mean) ± standard deviation (std) are reported. Friedman tests or Wilcoxon-signed rank tests are used to detect statistically significant difference between more than two or two methods across datasets [7]. Given rejection of H0, Holm-Bonferroni correction [14] is conduced as the post-hoc test.

4.2 Performance Comparison

This section discusses performance comparisons between our ARConvL against its competitors for multi-class imbalance learning. Comparisons in terms of G-mean are reported in Table 1; comparisons in terms of class-wise accuracy present the same conclusions and can be found in Sect. 3.1 of the supplementary material for space reason. The last column corresponds to ARConvL.

Table 1 shows that our ARConvL achieves the best G-means in 16 out of 20 datasets, showing the effectiveness of our approach in dealing with varying levels of class imbalance. Friedman tests at the significance level 0.05 reject H0 with the p-value 0, meaning that there is significant difference between methods. The average rank ("avgRank") at the last row provides a reasonable idea of how well each method performs compared to others. The average rank of ARConvL is 1.4, being the best (lowest value) among all competing methods. This indicates that our method generally performs the best across datasets with different levels of class imbalance. ARConvL is then chosen as the control method to conduct post-hoc tests for performing the best among all classifiers. Post-hoc tests show that the proposed ARConvL significantly outperforms all competitors.

Note that GCPL obtains zero G-mean in SVHN-100; Affinity obtains zero G-means individually in SVHN-100, Cifar10-50, and Cifar10-100. Further exploitation finds that the corresponding method got zero recalls in certain minority classes, thereby resulting in zero G-means. Such poor recalls usually occur in severely imbalanced scenarios.

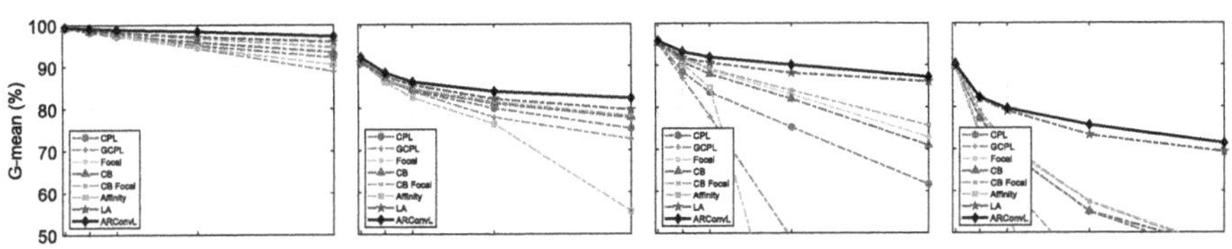

(a) MNIST (b) Fashion MNIST (c) SVHN (d) Cifar10

Fig. 4. Performance deterioration in terms of G-mean (%) with the increase of class imbalance levels. The x-axis represents different class imbalance levels, and the y-axis represents G-means. We show G-mean between 50 and 100 to facilitate visualization.

4.3 Performance Deterioration with Increasing Imbalance Levels

This section investigates the relation between the class imbalance levels and predictive performance of all investigated methods on each image repository. Figure 4 shows experimental results in terms of G-means. We can see that all methods achieve similar G-means in the original image repository for the case $q = 1$. With the increase of class imbalance levels with larger q, performance of all methods declines. The proposed ARConvL usually achieves better G-means than its competitors when datasets become more imbalanced, demonstrating better robustness of ARConvL against different levels of class imbalance. Experimental results in terms of class-wise accuracy show the same pattern and are reported in Fig. 1 and Sect. 3.2 of the supplementary material.

4.4 Effect of Each Adaptive Component of ARConvL

This section investigates the effect of each adaptive component of the overall loss in Eq. (1). Particularly, the region loss $\mathcal{L}_R$ is indispensable to derive the class-wise regions and thus should not be eliminated; the adaptive margin cross-entropy loss $\mathcal{L}_M$ contains two adaptive components, namely the adaptive margin σ^2 and the loss for class centers $\frac{1}{k}\sum_{j=1}^{k} - \log(p(C_j))$. Therefore, effects of the adaptive distribution loss $\mathcal{L}_D$ in Eq. (6), the adaptive margin σ^2 (of $\mathcal{L}_M$ in Eq. (8)), and the penalty on class centers (of $\mathcal{L}_M$) are investigated individually.

For the space reason, we only report experimental results in terms of G-means in this section. Experimental results in terms of class-wise accuracy lead to the same conclusions and are provided in Sect. 3.3 of the supplementary material.

Effect of Adaptive Distribution Loss. To conduct this investigation, the adaptive parameter β of ARConvL is fixed and chosen from $\{0, 0.5, 1\}$. In particular, ARConvL without the adaptive distribution loss is equivalent to the case $\beta = 0$. Pair-wise comparisons in terms of G-means between ARConvL in Table 1 and the degraded ARConvL with non-adaptive β in Table 2(a) show the performance deterioration in most cases.

Given fixed $\beta = 0$ and $\beta = 1$, Wilcoxon signed rank tests reject H0 with p-values 0.0017 and 0.04, respectively, showing significant difference in predictive performance between ARConvL and the degraded versions. Average ranks are 1.15 and 1.3 for ARConvL vs 1.85 and 1.7 for the degraded versions, respectively. This means that adaptively learning β throughout the training epochs has significantly beneficial effect on predictive performance.

Given fixed $\beta = 0.5$, Wilcoxon signed rank test does not find significant difference between ARConvL and the degraded version with p-value 0.39. Further analyses found that on the datasets that the degraded version outperforms, performance deterioration of ARConvL is at most 0.79% in Cifar10-10; whereas on the datasets that ARConvL outperforms, performance superiority can be as high as 4.59% in Cifar10-100, with the average improvement at 0.80%. This indicates that the degraded ARConvL may cause relatively large performance decline compared to the small performance improvement it may have.

Overall, the experimental investigation shows the effectiveness of the adaptive distribution loss, in view of the adaptive β, on retaining good performance in multi-class imbalance learning.

Effect of Adaptive Margin. To conduct this investigation, the adaptive margin σ^2 in $\mathcal{L}_M$ of ARConvL is fixed and chosen from $\{0, 0.5, 1\}$. In particular, ARConvL without the adaptive margin is equivalent to the case $\sigma^2 = 0$. Pair-wise comparisons in terms of G-means between ARConvL in Table 1 and the

Table 2. G-means (%) of the degraded ARConvL with non-adaptive β. Each entry is the mean±std of 10 times. Better pair-wise performance compared to ARConvL in Table 1 is highlighted in bold. The last row lists average ranks (avgRank) of ARConvL vs the degraded version across datasets. Significant difference is highlighted in yellow.

(a) Non-adaptive β				(b) Non-adaptive σ^2			(c) ARC-C
Data	$\beta = 0$	$\beta = 0.5$	$\beta = 1$	$\sigma^2 = 0$	$\sigma^2 = 0.5$	$\sigma^2 = 1$	ARC-C
Mnist-1	99.3±0.0	99.3±0.1	99.3±0.1	**99.4±0.0**	99.4±0.0	**99.4±0.1**	99.3±0.0
Mnist-10	98.7±0.1	99.1±0.0	99.0±0.1	99.0±0.1	99.0±0.1	99.1±0.1	99.1±0.1
Mnist-20	98.1±0.3	**98.9±0.1**	**98.9±0.1**	**98.9±0.1**	98.8±0.2	**98.9±0.2**	**98.9±0.1**
Mnist-50	97.1±0.4	**98.5±0.2**	**98.6±0.2**	98.4±0.2	**98.4±0.3**	**98.5±0.2**	98.4±0.2
Mnist-100	95.6±0.6	**97.6±0.3**	**97.8±0.3**	**97.4±0.4**	**97.6±0.4**	97.3±0.6	**97.4±0.5**
Fashion-1	91.4±0.2	92.2±0.2	92.0±0.2	91.8±0.1	92.1±0.2	92.1±0.2	91.7±0.2
Fashion-10	87.4±0.2	**88.7±0.3**	88.3±0.5	88.3±0.4	**88.5±0.4**	88.4±0.4	85.2±1.2
Fashion-20	84.8±1.1	**86.6±0.9**	**86.4±0.9**	**86.5±1.0**	86.3±1.3	86.3±0.8	83.4±1.8
Fashion-50	81.7±1.4	82.8±2.8	**84.3±0.8**	**84.6±0.6**	**84.6±0.5**	83.8±1.3	81.8±1.4
Fashion-100	79.6±2.2	81.3±1.0	81.7±1.4	82.2±1.5	81.9±1.7	81.9±1.5	80.7±1.7
SVHN-1	**96.3±0.1**	95.7±0.3	94.9±0.7	95.3±0.2	95.6±0.2	**95.9±0.2**	12.1±1.5
SVHN-10	93.0±0.5	93.2±0.4	92.0±1.6	92.0±0.4	92.3±0.6	92.8±0.3	54.1±34.8
SVHN-20	91.3±0.5	**92.1±0.4**	91.8±0.7	90.2±1.1	90.1±1.8	91.2±1.5	75.3±21.4
SVHN-50	88.0±1.3	89.3±1.4	89.7±1.7	88.0±1.1	88.8±1.3	89.4±0.5	79.6±2.1
SVHN-100	83.0±3.5	86.7±0.8	85.2±5.7	84.9±2.7	85.0±2.2	85.7±2.8	76.9±4.6
Cifar10-1	**92.0±0.2**	90.2±0.5	89.6±0.5	89.3±0.5	90.0±0.4	**90.3±0.5**	68.2±8.5
Cifar10-10	**82.5±0.6**	**82.9±0.6**	81.8±1.0	80.1±1.1	81.6±0.7	81.9±0.7	64.1±1.4
Cifar10-20	78.2±0.7	**80.0±0.7**	79.4±1.1	77.0±1.4	78.7±0.6	79.4±0.8	62.5±1.6
Cifar10-50	70.9±1.9	75.3±0.9	75.6±0.8	73.8±1.4	74.8±1.0	74.6±1.7	61.4±1.6
Cifar10-100	62.7±2.8	68.2±3.5	**71.6±0.7**	69.1±3.0	70.1±2.6	69.3±3.1	59.6±3.5
avgRank	1.15/1.85	1.4/1.6	1.3/1.7	1.25/1.75	1.2/1.8	1.25/1.75	1.1/1.9

degraded ARConvL with non-adaptive σ^2 in Table 2(b) show the performance deterioration in the vast majority of cases.

Given σ^2 with those fixed values, Wilcoxon signed rank tests reject H0 with p-values 0.0045, 0.0036, and 0.0057, respectively, showing significant difference in predictive performance between ARConvL and the degraded versions with non-adaptive σ^2. Performance comparisons in terms of average ranks further show the significance of such performance deterioration of the degraded ARConvL. This means that adaptively learning σ^2 throughout the training epochs has significantly beneficial effect on predictive performance, demonstrating the effectiveness of the adaptive margin on retaining good performance in multi-class imbalance learning.

Effect of Loss for Class Centers. To conduct this investigation, we produce the degraded version of ARConvL (denoted as "ARC-C") by eliminating the loss for class centers $\frac{1}{k}\sum_{j=1}^{k} -\log(p(C_j)$ from $\mathcal{L}_M$ in Eq. (8). The loss of ARC-C in accordance with $\mathcal{L}_M$ is degraded as $\frac{1}{n}\sum_{j=1}^{k}\sum_{i=1}^{n} -\log(p(x_i \in j)$. Performance comparisons in terms of G-means between ARConvL in Table 1 and the degraded ARC-C in Table 2(c) show the performance deterioration in almost all cases.

Wilcoxon signed rank test rejects H0 with p-value $3.38 \cdot 10^{-4}$, showing significant difference in predictive performance between ARConvL and the degraded ARC-C. Performance comparisons in terms of average ranks further show the significance of such performance deterioration eliminating the loss for class centers, demonstrating the effectiveness of the loss for class centers in multi-class imbalance learning.

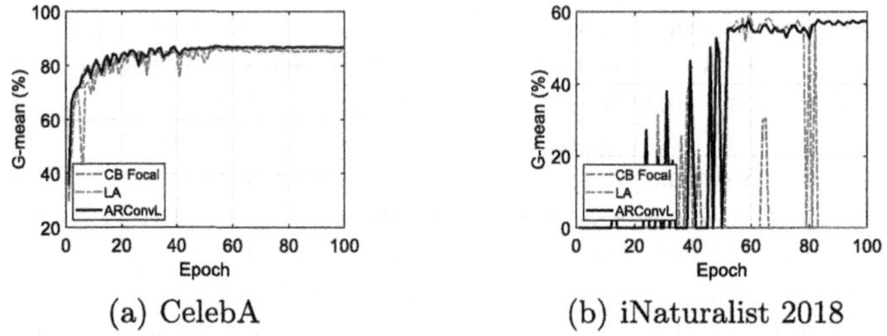

Fig. 5. Training curves of ARConvL, LA, and CB Focal on CelebA (left) and iNaturalist 2018 (right).

4.5 Utility in Large-Scale Datasets

To demonstrate the proposed ARConvL can be utilized on large-scale real-world datasets, we present training curves of ARConvL and the two most competitive methods CB Focal [6] and LA [23] on two additional large-scale datasets, namely CelebA [22] and iNaturalist 2018 [34]. For CelebA, only five non-overlapping classes (blonde, black, bald, brown, and gray) are kept following previous work [37]. Details of these datasets are shown in Sect. 1 of the supplementary material. The input size is (64, 64, 3) for CelebA and (224, 224, 3) for iNaturalist 2018. We employ ResNet [30] with depth 56 as the backbone in this extra study. The training batch size is set to 64; the total number of training epochs is set to 100. We decay the learning rate by 0.1 at the 51-th and 81-th epochs.

Training curves on those large-scale datasets are shown in Fig. 5. Figure 5(a) shows that ARConvL outperforms CB Focal across all training epochs; ARConvL yields better or similar performance compared to LA and it can converge faster than LA within 52 epochs. Figure 5(b) shows similar experimental results: ARConvL achieves better G-means at most training epochs and possesses better convergence than its competitors. In particular, between the training epoch 52 and 78, LA and ARConvL achieve similar performance, and after the training epoch 82, ARConvL outperforms LA. All methods confront with zero G-means at some training epochs, meaning that they fail in detecting any example of some class(es). Performance in terms of class-wise accuracy shows the same experimental results and can be found in Sect. 3.4 of the supplementary material. Therefore, experimental results on two large-scale datasets show the utility of the proposed ARConvL over its competitors.

5 Conclusion

This paper proposes ARConvL for multi-class imbalance learning, which derives class-wise regions in the latent feature space adaptively throughout training epochs. Latent feature distributions can then be well depicted by class regions without relying on any strict assumption. Based on the derived class regions, we address the multi-class imbalance issue from two perspectives. First, an adaptive distribution loss is proposed to optimize the class-wise latent feature distribution, by pushing down the upper-bound of the radii to approach the benchmark radius, directly tackling the multi-class imbalance problem. Second, an adaptive margin cross-entropy loss is proposed by employing the defined margin as a mediator to improve the discrimination between classes, further alleviating the class imbalance problem.

Experimental results based on plenty of real-world image sets demonstrated the superiority of our ARConvL to SOTA methods. Investigations on the performance deterioration with respect to different imbalance ratios showed the robustness of the proposed method. Ablation studies demonstrated the effectiveness of the adaptive distribution loss and the adaptive margin cross-entropy loss in the learning process. Experiments on two large-scale real-world image sets showed the utility of ARConvL on large-scale datasets.

Future work includes additional experimental investigations to better understand how data noise and missing data affect the performance of our proposed method and the extension of ARConvL by having multiple regions assigned to each class (instead of only one).

Acknowledgements. This work was supported by National Natural Science Foundation of China (NSFC) under Grant No. 62002148 and Grant No. 62250710682, Guangdong Provincial Key Laboratory under Grant No. 2020B121201001, the Program for Guangdong Introducing Innovative and Enterpreneurial Teams under Grant No. 2017ZT07X386, and Research Institute of Trustworthy Autonomous Systems (RITAS).

References

1. Alejo, R., Sotoca, J.M., Valdovinos, R.M., Casañ, G.A.: The multi-class imbalance problem: cost functions with modular and non-modular neural networks. In: International Symposium on Neural Networks, pp. 421–431. Springer (2009). https://doi.org/10.1007/978-3-642-01216-7_44
2. Buda, M., Maki, A., Mazurowski, M.A.: A systematic study of the class imbalance problem in convolutional neural networks. Neural Netw. **106**, 249–259 (2018)
3. Cao, K., Wei, C., Gaidon, A., Arechiga, N., Ma, T.: Learning imbalanced datasets with label-distribution-aware margin loss. Proceedings of the 33rd International Conference on Neural Information Processing Systems, pp. 1567–1578 (2019)
4. Chawla, N.V., Bowyer, K.W., Hall, L.O., Kegelmeyer, W.P.: SMOTE: synthetic minority over-sampling technique. J. Artifi. Intell. Res. **16**(1), 321–357 (2002)

5. Chawla, N.V., Lazarevic, A., Hall, L.O., Bowyer, K.W.: SMOTEBoost: improving prediction of the minority class in boosting. In: Lavrač, N., Gamberger, D., Todorovski, L., Blockeel, H. (eds.) PKDD 2003. LNCS (LNAI), vol. 2838, pp. 107–119. Springer, Heidelberg (2003). https://doi.org/10.1007/978-3-540-39804-2_12
6. Cui, Y., Jia, M., Lin, T.Y., Song, Y., Belongie, S.: Class-balanced loss based on effective number of samples. In: Proceedings of the IEEE/CVF Conference on Computer Vision and Pattern Recognition, pp. 9268–9277 (2019)
7. Demšar, J.: Statistical comparisons of classifiers over multiple data sets. J. Mach. Learn. Res. **7**, 1–30 (2006)
8. Deng, L.: The mnist database of handwritten digit images for machine learning research. IEEE Signal Process. Mag. **29**(6), 141–142 (2012)
9. Elkan, C.: The foundations of cost-sensitive learning. In: International Joint Conference on Artificial Intelligence, vol. 17, pp. 973–978 (2001)
10. Freund, Y., Schapire, R.E.: A desicion-theoretic generalization of on-line learning and an application to boosting. In: Vitányi, P. (ed.) EuroCOLT 1995. LNCS, vol. 904, pp. 23–37. Springer, Heidelberg (1995). https://doi.org/10.1007/3-540-59119-2_166
11. Hayat, M., Khan, S., Zamir, S.W., Shen, J., Shao, L.: Gaussian affinity for max-margin class imbalanced learning. In: Proceedings of the IEEE/CVF International Conference on Computer Vision, pp. 6469–6479 (2019)
12. He, H., Bai, Y., Garcia, E.A., Li, S.: ADASYN: adaptive synthetic sampling approach for imbalanced learning. In: IEEE International Joint Conference on Neural Networks (IEEE World Congress on Computational Intelligence), pp. 1322–1328. IEEE (2008)
13. He, H., Garcia, E.A.: Learning from imbalanced data. IEEE Trans. Knowl. Data Eng. **21**(9), 1263–1284 (2009)
14. Holm, S.: A simple sequentially rejective multiple test procedure. Scand. J. Stat. **6**(2), 65–70 (1979)
15. Johnson, J.M., Khoshgoftaar, T.M.: Survey on deep learning with class imbalance. J. Big Data **6**(1), 1–54 (2019)
16. Khan, S.H., Hayat, M., Bennamoun, M., Sohel, F.A., Togneri, R.: Cost-sensitive learning of deep feature representations from imbalanced data. IEEE Trans. Neural Netw. Learn. Syst. **29**(8), 3573–3587 (2018)
17. Krizhevsky, A., Hinton, G.: Learning multiple layers of features from tiny images. Tech. Rep. 0, University of Toronto, Toronto, Ontario (2009)
18. Lee, H., Park, M., Kim, J.: Plankton classification on imbalanced large scale database via convolutional neural networks with transfer learning. In: 2016 IEEE International Conference On Image Processing (ICIP), pp. 3713–3717. IEEE (2016)
19. Liang, L., Jin, T., Huo, M.: Feature identification from imbalanced data sets for diagnosis of cardiac arrhythmia. In: International Symposium on Computational Intelligence and Design, vol. 02, pp. 52–55. IEEE (2018)
20. Lin, T.Y., Goyal, P., Girshick, R., He, K., Dollár, P.: Focal loss for dense object detection. In: Proceedings of the IEEE International Conference on Computer Vision, pp. 2980–2988 (2017)
21. Liu, J., Sun, Y., Han, C., Dou, Z., Li, W.: Deep representation learning on long-tailed data: A learnable embedding augmentation perspective. In: Proceedings of the IEEE/CVF Conference on Computer Vision and Pattern Recognition, pp. 2970–2979 (2020)
22. Liu, Z., Luo, P., Wang, X., Tang, X.: Deep learning face attributes in the wild. In: Proceedings of International Conference on Computer Vision (ICCV) (December 2015)

23. Menon, A.K., Jayasumana, S., Rawat, A.S., Jain, H., Veit, A., Kumar, S.: Long-tail learning via logit adjustment. In: International Conference on Learning Representations (2021)
24. M'hamed, B.A., Fergani, B.: A new multi-class WSVM classification to imbalanced human activity dataset. J. Comput. **9**(7), 1560–1565 (2014)
25. Mullick, S.S., Datta, S., Das, S.: Generative adversarial minority oversampling. In: Proceedings of the IEEE/CVF International Conference on Computer Vision, pp. 1695–1704 (2019)
26. Netzer, Y., Wang, T., Coates, A., Bissacco, A., Wu, B., Ng, A.Y.: Reading digits in natural images with unsupervised feature learning. In: NIPS Workshop on Deep Learning and Unsupervised Feature Learning (2011)
27. Pouyanfar, S., Chen, S.C., Shyu, M.L.: Deep spatio-temporal representation learning for multi-class imbalanced data classification. In: International Conference on Information Reuse and Integration, pp. 386–393. IEEE (2018)
28. Ren, J., Yu, C., Sheng, S., Ma, X., Zhao, H., Yi, S., Li, h.: Balanced meta-softmax for long-tailed visual recognition. In: Larochelle, H., Ranzato, M., Hadsell, R., Balcan, M., Lin, H. (eds.) Advances in Neural Information Processing Systems, vol. 33, pp. 4175–4186. Curran Associates, Inc. (2020)
29. Seiffert, C., Khoshgoftaar, T.M., Van Hulse, J., Napolitano, A.: RUSBoost: a hybrid approach to alleviating class imbalance. IEEE Trans. Syst. Man Cybern. - Part A: Syst. Hum. **40**(1), 185–197 (2010)
30. Shah, A., Kadam, E., Shah, H., Shinde, S., Shingade, S.: Deep residual networks with exponential linear unit. In: Proceedings of the Third International Symposium on Computer Vision and the Internet, pp. 59–65 (2016)
31. Sun, Y., Kamel, M.S., Wang, Y.: Boosting for learning multiple classes with imbalanced class distribution. In: International Conference on Data Mining, pp. 592–602. IEEE (2006)
32. Taherkhani, A., Cosma, G., McGinnity, T.M.: AdaBoost-CNN: an adaptive boosting algorithm for convolutional neural networks to classify multi-class imbalanced datasets using transfer learning. Neurocomputing **404**, 351–366 (2020)
33. Tan, J., et al.: Equalization loss for long-tailed object recognition. In: Proceedings of the IEEE/CVF Conference on Computer Vision and Pattern Recognition, pp. 11662–11671 (2020)
34. Van Horn, G., et al.: The inaturalist species classification and detection dataset. In: Proceedings of the IEEE Conference on Computer Vision and Pattern Recognition, pp. 8769–8778 (2018)
35. Wang, S., Chen, H., Yao, X.: Negative correlation learning for classification ensembles. In: International Joint Conference on Neural Networks, pp. 1–8. IEEE (2010)
36. Wang, S., Yao, X.: Multiclass imbalance problems: analysis and potential solutions. IEEE Trans. Syst. Man Cybern. Part B (Cybern.) **42**(4), 1119–1130 (2012)
37. Wang, X., Lyu, Y., Jing, L.: Deep generative model for robust imbalance classification. In: Proceedings of the IEEE/CVF Conference on Computer Vision and Pattern Recognition, pp. 14124–14133 (2020)
38. Xiang, L., Ding, G., Han, J.: Learning from multiple experts: self-paced knowledge distillation for long-tailed classification. In: Vedaldi, A., Bischof, H., Brox, T., Frahm, J.-M. (eds.) ECCV 2020. LNCS, vol. 12350, pp. 247–263. Springer, Cham (2020). https://doi.org/10.1007/978-3-030-58558-7_15
39. Xiao, H., Rasul, K., Vollgraf, R.: Fashion-mnist: a novel image dataset for benchmarking machine learning algorithms. arXiv preprint arXiv:1708.07747 (2017)

40. Yang, H.M., Zhang, X.Y., Yin, F., Liu, C.L.: Robust classification with convolutional prototype learning. In: Proceedings of the IEEE Conference on Computer Vision and Pattern Recognition, pp. 3474–3482 (2018)
41. Zhang, Y., Kang, B., Hooi, B., Yan, S., Feng, J.: Deep long-tailed learning: A survey. arXiv preprint arXiv:2110.04596 (2021)
42. Zhou, B., Cui, Q., Wei, X.S., Chen, Z.M.: BBN: bilateral-branch network with cumulative learning for long-tailed visual recognition. In: Proceedings of the IEEE/CVF Conference on Computer Vision and Pattern Recognition, pp. 9719–9728 (2020)

Deep Learning

Binary Domain Generalization for Sparsifying Binary Neural Networks

Riccardo Schiavone[1(✉)], Francesco Galati[2], and Maria A. Zuluaga[2]

[1] Department of Electronics and Telecommunications, Politecnico di Torino, Turin, Italy
riccardo.schiavone@polito.it

[2] Data Science Department, EURECOM, Sophia Antipolis, Biot, France
{galati,zuluaga}@eurecom.fr

Abstract. Binary neural networks (BNNs) are an attractive solution for developing and deploying deep neural network (DNN)-based applications in resource constrained devices. Despite their success, BNNs still suffer from a fixed and limited compression factor that may be explained by the fact that existing pruning methods for full-precision DNNs cannot be directly applied to BNNs. In fact, weight pruning of BNNs leads to performance degradation, which suggests that the standard binarization domain of BNNs is not well adapted for the task. This work proposes a novel more general binary domain that extends the standard binary one that is more robust to pruning techniques, thus guaranteeing improved compression and avoiding severe performance losses. We demonstrate a closed-form solution for quantizing the weights of a full-precision network into the proposed binary domain. Finally, we show the flexibility of our method, which can be combined with other pruning strategies. Experiments over CIFAR-10 and CIFAR-100 demonstrate that the novel approach is able to generate efficient sparse networks with reduced memory usage and run-time latency, while maintaining performance.

Keywords: Binary neural networks · Deep neural networks · Pruning · Sparse representation

1 Introduction

The increasing number of connected Internet-of-Things (IoT) devices, now surpassing the number of humans connected to the internet [6], has led to a sensors-rich world, capable of addressing real-time applications in multiple domains, where both accuracy and computational time are crucial [1]. Deep neural networks (DNNs) have the potential of enabling a myriad of new IoT applications, thanks to their ability to process large complex heterogeneous data and to extract

FG and MAZ are supported by the French government, through the 3IA Côte d'Azur Investments in the Future project managed by the ANR (ANR-19-P3IA-0002).

© The Author(s), under exclusive license to Springer Nature Switzerland AG 2023
D. Koutra et al. (Eds.): ECML PKDD 2023, LNAI 14170, pp. 123–140, 2023.
https://doi.org/10.1007/978-3-031-43415-0_8

patterns needed to take autonomous decisions with high reliability [20]. However, DNNs are known for being resource-greedy, in terms of required computational power, memory, and energy consumption [4], whereas most IoT devices are characterized by limited resources. They usually have limited processing power, small storage capabilities, they are not GPU-enabled and they are powered with batteries of limited capacity, which are expected to last over 10 years without being replaced or recharged. These constraints represent an important bottleneck towards the deployment of DNNs in IoT applications [40].

A recent and notable example to enable the usage of DNNs in limited resource devices are binary neural networks (BNNs) [15]. BNNs use binary weights and activation functions that allow them to replace computationally expensive multiplication operations with low-cost bitwise operations during forward propagation. This results in faster inference and better compression rates, while maintaining an acceptable accuracy for complex learning tasks [10,25]. For instance, BNNs have achieved over 80% classification accuracy on ImageNet [10,31]. Despite the good results, BNNs have a fixed and limited compression factor compared to full-precision DNNs, which may be insufficient for certain size and power constraints of devices [22].

A way to further improve BNNs' compression capacity is through network pruning, which seeks to control a network's sparsity by removing parameters and shared connections [12]. Pruning BNNs, however, is a more challenging task than pruning full-precision neural networks and it is still a challenge with many open questions [38]. Current attempts [9,19,28,32,36–38] often rely on training procedures that require more training stages than standard BNNs, making learning more complex. Moreover, these methods fail in highly pruned scenarios, showing severe accuracy degradation over simple classification problems.

In this work, we introduce sparse binary neural network (SBNN), a more robust pruning strategy to achieve sparsity and improve the performance of BNNs. Our strategy relies on entropy to optimize the network to be largely skewed to one of the two possible weight values, i.e. having a very low entropy. Unlike BNNs that use symmetric values to represent the network's weights, we propose a more general binary domain that allows the weight values to adapt to the asymmetry present in the weights distribution. This enables the network to capture valuable information, achieve better representation, and, thus better generalization. The main contributions of our work can be summarized as follows: 1) We introduce a more general binary domain w.r.t. the one used by BNNs to quantize real-valued weights; 2) we derive a closed-form solution for binary values that minimizes quantization error when real-valued weights are mapped to the proposed domain; 3) we enable the regularization of the BNNs weights distribution by using entropy constraints; 4) we present efficient implementations of the proposed algorithm, which reduce the number of bitwise operations in the network proportionally to the entropy of the weight distribution; and 5) we demonstrate SBNN's competitiveness and flexibility through benchmark evaluations.

The remaining of this work is organized as follows. Section 2 discusses previous related works. The core of our contributions are described in Sect. 3. In Sect. 4, we study the properties of the proposed method and assess its performance, in terms of accuracy and operation reduction at inference, through a set of experiments using, CIFAR-10, CIFAR-100 [18] and ImageNet [31] datasets. Finally, a discussion on the results and main conclusions are drawn in Sect. 5.

2 Related Work

We first provide an overview of BNNs. Next, we review sparsification through pruning [2,12,27,34] and quantization [11,16,39,41], the two network compression strategies this work relies on. A broad review covering further network compression and speed-up techniques can be found in [21].

Binary Neural Networks. BNNs [15] have gained attention in recent years due to their computational efficiency and improved compression. Subsequent works have extended [15] to improve its accuracy. For instance, [30] introduced a channel-wise scaling coefficient to decrease the quantization error. ABC-Net adopts multiple binary bases [23], and Bi-Real [26] recommends short residual connection to reduce the information loss and a smoother gradient for the signum function. Recently, ReActNet [25] generalized the traditional sign($\cdot$) and PReLU activation functions to extend binary network capabilities, achieving an accuracy close to full-precision ResNet-18 [13] and MobileNet V1 [14] on ImageNet [31]. By adopting the RSign, the RPReLU along with an attention formulation Guo et al. [10] surpassed the 80% accuracy mark on ImageNet. Although these works have been successful at increasing the performance of BNNs, few of them consider the compression aspect of BNNs.

Network Sparsification. The concept of sparsity has been well studied beyond quantized neural networks as it reduces a network's computational and storage requirements and it prevents overfitting. Methods to achieve sparsity either explicitly induce it during learning through regularization (e.g. L_0 [27] or L_1 [12] regularization), or do it incrementally by gradually augmenting small networks [2]; or by post hoc pruning [8,33,34].

BNNs pruning is particularly challenging because weights in the $\{\pm 1\}$ domain cannot be pruned based only on their magnitude. Existing methods include removing unimportant channels and filters from the network [9,28,37,38], but optimum metrics are still unclear; quantizing binary kernels to a smaller bit size than the kernel size [36]; or using the $\{0, \pm 1\}$ domains [19,32]. Although these works suggest that the standard $\{\pm 1\}$ binary domain has severe limitations regarding compression, BNNs using the $\{0, \pm 1\}$ domain have reported limited generalization capabilities [19,32]. In our work, we extend the traditional binary domain to a more general one, that can be efficiently implemented via sparse operations. Moreover, we address sparsity explicitly with entropy constraints, which can be formulated as magnitude pruning of the generic binary weight values mapping them in the $\{0, 1\}$ domain. In our proposed domain, BNNs are more robust to pruning strategies and show better generalization properties than other pruning techniques for the same sparsity levels.

Quantization. Network quantization allows the use of fixed-point arithmetic and a smaller bit-width to represent network parameters w.r.t the full-precision counterpart. Representing the values using only a finite set requires a quantization function that maps the original elements to the finite set. The quantization can be done after training the model, using parameter sharing techniques [11], or during training by quantizing the weights in the forward pass, as ternary neural networks (TNNs) [17], BNNs [5] and other quantized networks do [16,39]. Our work builds upon the strategy of BNNs by introducing a novel quantization function that maps weights to a binary domain that is more general than the $\{\pm 1\}$ domain used in most state-of-the-art BNNs. This broader domain significantly reduces the distortion-rate curves of BNNs across various sparsity levels, enabling us to achieve greater compression.

3 Method

The proposed SBNN achieves network pruning via sparsification by introducing a novel quantization function that extends standard BNNs weight domain $\{\pm 1\}$ to a more generic binary domain $\{\alpha, \beta\}$ and a new penalization term in the objective loss controlling the entropy of the weight distribution and the sparsity of the network (Sect. 3.2). We derive in Sect. 3.3 the optimum SBNN's $\{\alpha, \beta\}$ values, i.e. the values that minimize the quantization loss when real-valued weights are quantized in the proposed domain. In Sect. 3.4, we use BNN's state-of-the-art training algorithms for SBNN training by adding the sparsity regularization term to the original BNN's objective loss. Section 3.5 describes the implementation details of the proposed SBNN to illustrate their speed-up gains w.r.t BNNs.

3.1 Preliminaries

The training of a full-precision DNN can be seen as a loss minimization problem:

$$\arg\min_{\widetilde{\mathbf{W}}} \mathcal{L}(y, \hat{y}) \tag{1}$$

where $\mathcal{L}(\cdot)$ is a loss function between the true labels y and the predicted values $\hat{y} = f(\mathbf{x}; \widetilde{\mathbf{W}})$, which are a function of the data input $\mathbf{x}$ and the network's full precision weights $\widetilde{\mathbf{W}} = \{\widetilde{\mathbf{w}}^{\ell}\}$, with $\widetilde{\mathbf{w}}^{\ell} \in \mathbb{R}^{N^{\ell}}$ the weights of the ℓth layer, and $N = \sum_{\ell} N^{\ell}$ the total number of weights in the DNN. We denote the ith weight element of $\widetilde{\mathbf{w}}^{\ell}$ as $\widetilde{w}_i^{\ell}$.

A BNN [15] uses a modified signum function as quantization function that maps full precision weights $\widetilde{\mathbf{W}}$ and activations $\widetilde{\mathbf{a}}$ to the $\{\pm 1\}$ binary domain, enabling the use of low-cost bitwise operations in the forward propagation, i.e.

$$\overline{\mathbf{W}} = \operatorname{sign}(\widetilde{\mathbf{W}}), \qquad \frac{\partial g(\widetilde{w}_i)}{\partial \widetilde{w}_i} = \begin{cases} \dfrac{\partial g(\overline{w}_i)}{\partial \overline{w}_i} & , \text{if} -1 \leq \widetilde{w}_i \leq 1 \\ 0 & , \text{otherwise,} \end{cases}$$

where sign(·) denotes the modified sign function over a vector, $g(\cdot)$ is a differentiable function, $\overline{\mathbf{W}}$ the network's weights in the $\{\pm 1\}$ binary domain, $\overline{w}_i$ a given weight in the binary domain, and $\widetilde{w_i}$ the associated full-precision weight.

3.2 Sparse Binary Neural Network (SBNN) Formulation

Given $\Omega^\ell = \{\alpha^\ell, \beta^\ell\}$ a general binary domain, with $\alpha^\ell, \beta^\ell \in \mathbb{R}$, and $\alpha^\ell < \beta^\ell$, let us define a SBNN, such that, for any given layer ℓ,

$$w_i^\ell \in \Omega^\ell \qquad \forall\, i, \tag{2}$$

with w_i^ℓ the ith weight element of the weight vector, $\mathbf{w}^\ell$, and $\mathbf{w} = \{\mathbf{w}^\ell\}$ the set of weights for all the SBNN.

We denote S_{α^ℓ} and S_{β^ℓ} the indices of the weights with value α^ℓ, β^ℓ in $\mathbf{w}^\ell$

$$S_{\alpha^\ell} = \{i \,|\, 1 \le i \le N^\ell, w_i^\ell = \alpha^\ell\}, \qquad S_{\beta^\ell} = \{i \,|\, 1 \le i \le N^\ell, w_i^\ell = \beta^\ell\}.$$

Since $\alpha^\ell < \beta^\ell \;\forall\, \ell$, it is possible to estimate the number of weights taking the lower and upper values of the general binary domain over all the network:

$$L^\ell = |S_{\alpha^\ell}|, \qquad U^\ell = |S_{\beta^\ell}|, \qquad L = \sum_\ell L^\ell, \qquad U = \sum_\ell U^\ell, \tag{3}$$

with $L + U = N$, the total number of SBNN network weights. In the remaining of the manuscript, for simplicity and without loss of generality, please note that we drop the layer index ℓ from the weights notation.

To express the SBNN weights $\mathbf{w}$ in terms of binary $\{0, 1\}$ weights, we now define a a mapping function $r : \{0, 1\} \longrightarrow \{\alpha, \beta\}$ that allows to express $\mathbf{w}$:

$$w_i = r\left(w_{\{0,1\},i}\right) = \left(w_{\{0,1\},i} + \xi\right) \cdot \eta \tag{4}$$

with

$$\alpha = \xi \cdot \eta, \qquad \beta = (1 + \xi) \cdot \eta, \tag{5}$$

and $w_{\{0,1\},i} \in \{0, 1\}$, the ith weight of a SBNN, when restricted to the binary set $\{0, 1\}$. Through these mapping, 0-valued weights are pruned from the network, the making SBNN sparse.

The bit-width of a SBNN is measured with the binary entropy $h()$ of the distribution of α-valued and β-valued weights,

$$h(p) = -p \log_2(p) - (1 - p) \log_2(1 - p) \qquad [\text{bits/weight}]\,, \tag{6}$$

with $p = U/N$. Achieving network compression using a smaller bit-width than that of standard BNN's weights (1 bit/weight) is equivalent to setting a constraint in the SBNN's entropy to be less or equal than a desired value h^*, i.e.

$$h(U/N) \le h^*. \tag{7}$$

Given $h^{-1}()$ the inverse binary entropy function for $0 \leq p \leq 1/2$, it is straightforward to derive such constraint, $U \leq M$ where

$$M \triangleq N \cdot h^{-1}(h^*). \tag{8}$$

From Eq. (7) and (8), this implies that the constraint corresponds to restricting the maximum number of 1s in the network, and thus the sparsity of the network. Thus, the original full-precision DNN loss minimization problem (Eq. (1)) can be reformulated as:

$$\begin{aligned} \underset{\mathbf{w}_{\{0,1\}},\xi,\eta}{\arg\min} \quad & \mathcal{L}(y, \hat{y}) \\ \text{s.t.} \quad & \mathbf{w}_{\{0,1\}} \in \{0,1\}^N, \\ & U \leq M < N. \end{aligned} \tag{9}$$

The mixed optimization problem in Eq. (9) can be simplified by relaxing the sparsity constraint on U through the introduction of a non-negative function $g(\cdot)$, which penalizes the weights when $U > M$:

$$\begin{aligned} \underset{\mathbf{W}_{\{0,1\}},\xi,\eta}{\arg\min} \quad & \mathcal{L}(y, \hat{y}) + \lambda g(\mathbf{W}_{\{0,1\}}) \\ \text{s.t.} \quad & \mathbf{W}_{\{0,1\}} \in \{0,1\}^N \end{aligned} \tag{10}$$

and λ controls the influence of $g(\cdot)$. A simple, yet effective function $g(\mathbf{W}_{\{0,1\}})$ is the following one:

$$g\left(\mathbf{W}_{\{0,1\}}\right) = \operatorname{ReLU}\left(U/N - \mathrm{EC}\right), \tag{11}$$

where $\mathrm{EC} = M/N$ represents the fraction of expected connections, which is the fraction of 1-valued weights in $\mathbf{W}_{\{0,1\}}$ over the total number of weights of $\mathbf{W}_{\{0,1\}}$.

Equation (9) allows to compare the proposed SBNN with the standard BNN formulation. By setting $\xi = -1/2$ and $\eta = 2$, for which $\alpha = -1$ and $\beta = +1$ (Eq. (4)), and removing the constraint on U leads to the standard formulation of a BNN. This implies that any BNN can be represented using the $\{0,1\}$ domain and perform sparse operations. However, in practice when U is not contrained to be $\leq M$, then $U \approx N/2$ and $h(1/2) = 1$ bit/weight, which means that standard BNNs cannot be compressed more.

3.3 Weight Optimization

In this section, we derive the value of $\Omega = \{\alpha, \beta\}$ which minimizes the quantization error when real-valued weights are quantized using it.

The minimization of the quantization error accounts to minimizing the binarization loss, $\mathcal{L}_B$, which is the optimal estimator when $\widetilde{\mathbf{W}}$ is mapped to $\mathbf{W}$ [30]. This minimization is equivalent to finding the values of α and β which minimize $\mathcal{L}_B$. To simplify the derivation of the optimum α and β values, we minimize $\mathcal{L}_B$

over two variables in one-to-one correspondence with α and β. To achieve this, as in Eq. 4–5, we map $w_i \in \Omega$ to $\overline{w}_i \in \{-1, +1\}$, i.e.

$$w_i = \tau\overline{w}_i + \phi,$$

where τ and ϕ are two real-valued variables, and $\alpha = -\tau + \phi$ and $\beta = \tau + \phi$. As a result, α and β are in one-to-one correspondence with τ and ϕ, and the minimization of $\mathcal{L}_B$ can be formulated as

$$\tau^*, \phi^* = \arg\min_{\tau,\phi} \mathcal{L}_B = \arg\min_{\tau,\phi} \|\widetilde{\mathbf{w}} - (\tau\overline{\mathbf{w}} + \phi\mathbf{1})\|_2 \tag{12}$$

where $\|\cdot\|_2$ is the ℓ_2-norm and $\mathbf{1}$ is the all-one entries matrix.

By first expanding the ℓ_2-norm term and using the fact that $\text{sum}(\overline{\mathbf{w}}) = N^\ell(2p-1)$, it is straightforward to reformulate Eq. 12 as a a function of the sum of real-valued weights, their ℓ_1-norm, the fraction of +1-valued binarized weights and the two optimization parameters. In such case, the $\nabla\mathcal{L}_B$ is

$$\nabla\mathcal{L}_B = \begin{pmatrix} \frac{\partial\mathcal{L}_B}{\partial\tau} \\ \frac{\partial\mathcal{L}_B}{\partial\phi} \end{pmatrix} = 2\begin{pmatrix} -\|\widetilde{\mathbf{w}}\|_1 + N^\ell(\tau + \phi(2p-1)) \\ -\text{ sum}(\widetilde{\mathbf{w}}) + N^\ell(\phi + \tau(2p-1)) \end{pmatrix}. \tag{13}$$

Solving to find the optimal values τ and ϕ we obtain

$$\tau^* = \frac{\|\widetilde{\mathbf{w}}\|_1}{N^\ell} - \phi^*(2p-1), \quad \phi^* = \frac{\text{sum}(\widetilde{\mathbf{w}})}{N^\ell} - \tau^*(2p-1). \tag{14}$$

When $p = 0.5$, like in standard BNNs, it gives the classical value of $\tau^* = \|\widetilde{\mathbf{w}}\|_1/N^\ell$ as in [30]. By substituting ϕ^* in Eq. (12), we obtain the closed-form solution

$$\tau^* = \frac{\|\widetilde{\mathbf{w}}\|_1 - (2p-1)\text{sum}(\widetilde{\mathbf{w}})}{N^\ell(1-(2p-1)^2)}, \quad \phi^* = \frac{\text{sum}(\widetilde{\mathbf{w}}) - (2p-1)\|\widetilde{\mathbf{w}}\|_1}{N^\ell(1-(2p-1)^2)}. \tag{15}$$

As the gradient (Eq. 13) is linear in ϕ and τ, this implies that there is a unique critical point. Moreover, an analysis of the Hessian matrix confirms that $\mathcal{L}_B$ is convex and that local minimum is a global minimum. The derivation is here omitted as it is straightforward.

3.4 Network Training

The SBNN training algorithm builds upon state-of-the-art BNN training algorithms [3,15,25], while introducing network sparsification. To profit from BNNs training scheme, we replace $\mathbf{W}_{\{0,1\}}, \xi$ and η (Eq. (10)) with $\overline{W}, \tau$ and ϕ. Doing so, $\mathcal{L}(y, \hat{y})$ corresponds to the loss of BNN algorithms $\mathcal{L}_{\text{BNN}}$. SBNN training also requires to add the penalization term from Eq. (11) to account for sparsity. To account for $\overline{\mathbf{W}}$, the regularization function $g(\mathbf{W}_{\{0,1\}})$ (Eq. (11)) is redefined according to

$$j(\overline{\mathbf{W}}) = \text{ReLU}\left(\left(\sum_i \frac{\overline{w}_i + 1}{2N}\right) - \text{EC}\right), \tag{16}$$

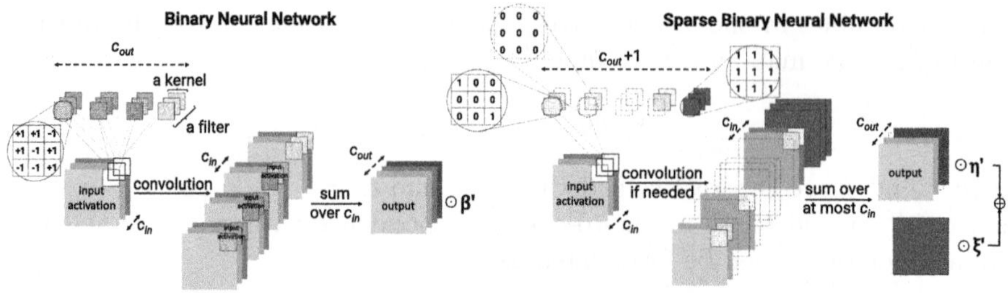

Fig. 1. BNNs vs. SBNNs operations in a convolutional layer using c_{out} filters and input of c_{in} dimensions. BNNs' $(c_{out} \cdot c_{in})$ convolutional kernels are dense and require all computations. SBNNs' kernels are sparse, allowing to skip certain convolutions and sum operations. The removed filters are indicated by a dashed contour and no fill. Both BNNs and SBNNs perform convolutions using XNOR and popcount operations, while the sum is replaced by popcount operations.

and the SBNN objective loss can be expressed as

$$\mathcal{L}_{\text{SBNN}} = \mathcal{L}_{\text{BNN}} + \lambda\, j(\overline{\mathbf{W}}). \tag{17}$$

During training, we modulate the contribution of the regularization term $j(\overline{\mathbf{W}})$ by imposing, at every training iteration, to be equal to a fraction of $\mathcal{L}_{\text{SBNN}}$, i.e.

$$\gamma = \frac{\lambda\, j(\overline{\mathbf{W}})}{\mathcal{L}_{\text{SBNN}}}. \tag{18}$$

The hyperparameter γ is set to a fixed value over all the training process. Since $\mathcal{L}_{\text{SBNN}}$ changes at every iteration, this forces λ to adapt, thus modulating the influence of $j(\overline{\mathbf{W}})$ proportionally to the changes in the loss. The lower γ is set, the less influence $j(\overline{\mathbf{W}})$ has on the total loss. This means that network sparsification will be slower, but convergence will be achieved faster. On the opposite case (high γ), the training will favor sparsification.

3.5 Implementation Gains

We discuss the speed-up gains of the proposed SBNN through its efficient implementation using linear layers in the backbone architecture. Its extension to convolutional layers (Fig. 1) is straightforward, thus we omit it for the sake of brevity.

We describe the use of sparse operations, as it can be done on an FPGA device [7,36]. Instead, when implemented on CPUs, SBNNs can take advantage of pruned layers, kernels and filters for acceleration [9,28,37,38]. Moreover, for kernels with only a single binary weight equal to 1 there is no need to perform a convolution, since the kernels remove some elements from the corner of their input.

The connections in a SBNN are the mapped one-valued weights, i.e. the set S_1. Therefore, SBNNs do not require any XNOR operation on FPGA, being popcount the only bitwise operation needed during the forward pass. The latter, however, is performed only in a layer's input bits connected through the one-valued weights rather than the full input.

For any given layer ℓ, the number of binary operations of a BNN is $\mathcal{O}_{\text{BNN}} = 2N^\ell$ [3], N^ℓ XNOR operations and N^ℓ popcounts. A rough estimate of the implementation gain in terms of the number of binary operations of SBNNs w.r.t. BNNs can be expressed in terms of the EC as

$$\frac{\mathcal{O}_{\text{SBNN}}}{\mathcal{O}_{\text{BNN}}} \approx \frac{2N^\ell}{\text{EC} \cdot N^\ell} \approx \frac{2}{\text{EC}}, \tag{19}$$

which indicates that the lower the EC fraction, the higher the gain w.r.t. BNNs.

Binary operations are not the only ones involved in the inference of SBNN layers. After the sparse $\{0,1\}$ computations, the mapping operations to the $\{\alpha,\beta\}$ domain take place, also benefiting from implementation gains. To analyze these, let us now denote $\mathbf{x}$ the input vector to any layer and $\mathbf{z} = \mathbf{w}\,\mathbf{x}$ its output. Using Eq. (4), $\mathbf{z}$ can be computed as

$$\mathbf{z} = \xi\,\mathbf{z}' + \xi\,\eta\,\mathbf{q}, \tag{20}$$

where $\mathbf{z}' = \mathbf{w}_{\{0,1\}}\,\mathbf{x}$ is the result of sparse operations (Fig. 1), $\mathbf{q} = \mathbf{1}\,\mathbf{x}$, and $\mathbf{1}$ the all-ones matrix.

All the elements in $\mathbf{q}$ take the value $2 \cdot \text{popcount}(\mathbf{x}) - |\mathbf{x}|$, with $|\mathbf{x}|$ the size of $\mathbf{x}$. Therefore, they are computed only once, for each row of $\mathbf{1}$. Being ξ and η known at inference time, they can be used to precompute the threshold in the threshold comparison stage of the implementation of the batchnorm and sign operations following the estimation of $\mathbf{z}$ [35]. Thus, SBNNs require $|\mathbf{x}|$ binary operations, one real product and $|\mathbf{x}|$ real sums to obtain $\mathbf{z}$ from $\mathbf{z}'$.

4 Experiments and Results

We first run a set of ablation studies to analyze the properties of the proposed method (Sect. 4.1). Namely, we analyze the generalization of SBNNs in a standard binary domain and the proposed generic binary domain; we study the role of the quantization error in the network's performance; and the effects of sparsifying binary kernels. Next, we compare our proposed method to other state-of-the-art techniques using the well established CIFAR-10 and CIFAR-100 [18] datasets. Preliminary results on ImageNet [31] are also discussed. All our code has been made publicly available[1].

4.1 Ablation Studies

Experimental Setup. We use a ResNet-18 binarized model trained on CIFAR-10 as backbone architecture. We train the networks for 300 epochs, with batch

[1] github.com/robustml-eurecom/SBNN.

Table 1. Role of the binary domain and the quantization error when sparsifying BNNs. Experiments performed on CIFAR-10 with a binarized ResNet-18 model.

Domain	Sparsity constraint	Top-1 Accuracy	Δ
Baseline	/	88.93%	/
$\{-\beta, +\beta\}$ [30]	95%	85.95%	-2.98%
$\{\alpha, \beta\}$	95%	86.46%	-2.47%
Learned $\{\alpha, \beta\}$	95%	88.84%	-0.09%

size of 512, learning rate of $1e-3$, and standard data augmentation techniques (random crops, rotations, horizontal flips and normalization). We use an Adam optimizer and the cosine annealer for updating the learning rate as suggested in [24] and we follow the binarization strategy of IR-Net [29].

Generalization Properties. We compare the performance of the proposed generic binary domain to other binary domains used by BNNs by assessing the networks' generalization capabilities when the sparsity ratio is 95%. For this experiment, we use the $\{-\beta, +\beta\}$ domain from [30] with no sparsity constraints as the baseline. Additionally, we consider the same domain with a 95% sparsity constraint and the $\{\alpha, \beta\}$ domain obtained optimizing τ and ϕ according to Eq. (15) with the 95% sparsity constraint. Table 1 reports the obtained results in terms of top-1 accuracy and accuracy loss w.r.t. the BNN baseline model (Δ). When we impose the 95% sparsity constraint with the $\{-\beta, +\beta\}$ domain, the accuracy drop w.r.t. to the baseline is 2.98%. Using the $\{\alpha, \beta\}$ domain, the loss goes down to 2.47%, nearly 0.5% better than the $\{-\beta, +\beta\}$ domain. The results suggest that a more general domain leads to improved generalization capabilities.

Impact of the Quantization Error. We investigate the impact of the quantization error in the SBNN generalization. To this end, we compare the proposed quantization technique (Sect. 3.3) with the strategy of learning Ω via back-propagation. We denote this approach Learned $\{\alpha, \beta\}$ (Table 1). The obtained results show that with the learning of the parameters the accuracy loss w.r.t. the BNN baseline decreases down to -0.09%, thus 2.38% better than when τ and ϕ are analytically obtained with Eq. (15). This result implies that the quantization error is one of the sources of accuracy degradation when mapping real-valued weights to any binary domain, but it is not the only source. Indeed, activations are also quantized. Moreover, errors are propagated throughout the network. Learning Ω can partially compensate for these other error sources.

Effects of Network Sparsification. We investigate the effects of network sparsification and how they can be leveraged to reduce the binary operations (BOPs) required in SBNNs. In Sect. 4.1, we showed that our binary domain is more adept at learning sparse network representations compared to the standard binary domain. This allows us to increase the sparsity of SBNNs while

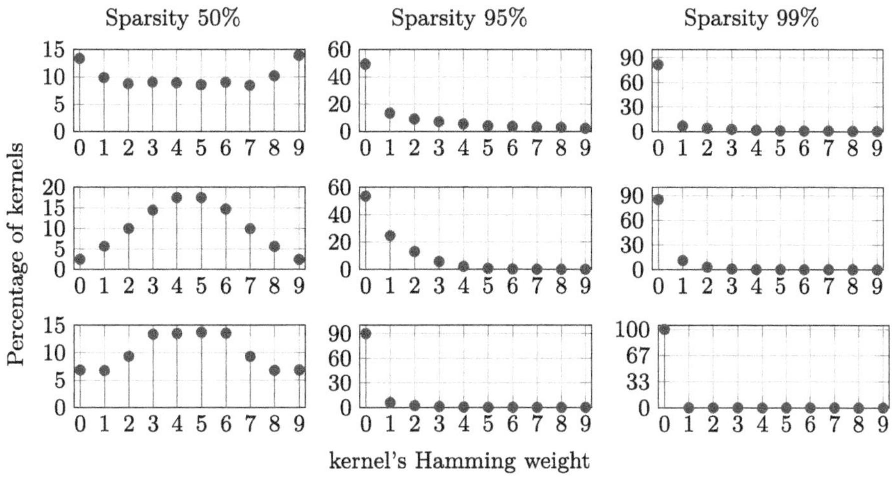

Fig. 2. Percentage of binary kernels for various Hamming weights of a binarized Resnet-18 model over CIFAR-10 for different sparsity constraints. The 5-th, 10-th and 15-th layers are shown in the top, middle and bottom rows, respectively.

maintaining a desired level of accuracy. When the sparsity is sufficiently high, many convolutional kernels can be entirely removed from the network, which further reduces the BOPs required for SBNNs. Additionally, convolutional kernels with only a single binary weight equal to 1 do not require a convolution to be performed, as these kernels simply remove certain elements from the input.

To illustrate this effect, we plotted the distribution of binary kernels for the 5th, 10th, and 15th layers of a binarized ResNet-18 model (Fig. 2). The first column shows the distribution when no sparsity constraints are imposed, while the second and third columns show the distribution for sparsity levels of 95% and 99%, respectively. The kernels are grouped based on their Hamming weights, which is the number of non-zero elements in each $\{0,1\}^{3\times 3}$ kernel. The plots suggest that increasing the sparsity of SBNNs results in a higher number of kernels with Hamming weights of 0 and 1.

4.2 Benchmark

CIFAR-10. We compare our method against state-of-the-art methods over a binarized ResNet-18 model using CIFAR-10. Namely, we consider: STQ [28], Slimming [37], Dual-P [7], Subbit [36], IR-Net [29] and our method with learned τ and ϕ, for different sparsity constraints. We use the IR-Net as BNN baseline to be compressed. We use the experimental setup described in Sect. 4.1 with some modifications. We extend the epochs to 500 as in [36], and we use a MixUp strategy [42]. In the original IR-Net formulation [29], the training setup is missing. We use our setup to train it, achieving the same accuracy as in [29].

Table 2 reports the obtained results in terms of accuracy (Acc.), accuracy loss w.r.t. the IR-Net model (Δ), and BOPs reduction (BOPs PR). For our

Table 2. Evaluation of kernel removal for different pruning targets using a binarized Resnet-18 model on CIFAR-10.

Method	Acc.	Δ	BOPs PR	K_0	K_1
IR-Net	91.50%	/	/	/	/
STQ	86.56%	-5.50%	-40.0%	/	/
Slimming	89.30%	-2.20%	-50.0%	/	/
Dual-P (2→1)	91.02%	-0.48%	-70.0%	/	/
Dual-P (3→1)	89.81%	-1.69%	-80.6%	/	/
Dual-P (4→1)	89.43%	-2.07%	-85.4%	/	/
Subbit 0.67-bits	91.00%	-0.50%	-47.2%	/	/
Subbit 0.56-bits	90.60%	-0.90%	-70.0%	/	/
Subbit 0.44-bits	90.10%	-1.40%	-82.3%	/	/
SBNN 50% **[our]**	91.70%	+0.20%	-11.1%	5.6%	6.8%
SBNN 75% **[our]**	91.71%	+0.21%	-24.5%	30.7%	15.9%
SBNN 90% **[our]**	91.16%	-0.24%	-46.5%	61.8%	15.5%
SBNN 95% **[our]**	90.94%	-0.56%	-63.2%	77.1%	11.8%
SBNN 96% **[our]**	90.59%	-0.91%	-69.7%	81.0%	10.1%
SBNN 97% **[our]**	90.71%	-0.79%	-75.7%	84.8%	8.7%
SBNN 98% **[our]**	89.68%	-1.82%	-82.5%	89.3%	6.5%
SBNN 99% **[our]**	88.87%	-2.63%	-88.7%	94.6%	3.3%

SBNN, we estimate BOPs PR by counting the number of operations which are not computed from the convolutional kernels with Hamming weight 0 and 1. For other methods, we refer the reader to the original publications. We assess our method at different levels of sparsity, in the range 50 to 99%. For SBNNs we also report the percentage of SBNN's convolutional kernels with Hamming weight 0 (K_0) and with Hamming weight 1 (K_1).

The results suggest that our method is competitive with other more complex pruning strategies. Moreover, our method reports similar accuracy drops w.r.t. state-of-the-art Subbit and Dual-P for similar BOPs PR. However, we need to point out that Subbit and Dual-P results refer to BOPs PR on FPGA, where SBNN can take advantage of sparse operations (Sect. 3.5) also for the kernels with larger Hamming weights than 0 and 1, because on FPGA all operations involving 0-valued weights can be skipped. For instance, the use of sparse operations on the SBNN 95% allows to remove $\approx$ 84.9% BOPs.

CIFAR-100. We compare our method in the more challenging setup of CIFAR-100, with 100 classes and 500 images per class, against two state-of-the-art methods: STQ [28], and Subbit [36]. We use ReActNet-18 [25] as the backbone architecture, using a single training step and no teacher. We train for 300 epochs with the same setup used for CIFAR-10 with Mixup augmentation. As no previous results for this setup have been reported for ReActNet-18 and Subbit, for a fair comparison, we trained them from scratch using our setup. We report the same

Table 3. Evaluation of kernel removal for different pruning targets using a ReActNet-18 model on CIFAR-100.

Method	Acc.	Δ	BOPs PR	BParams PR	K_0	K_1
ReActNet-18*	62.79%	/	/	/	/	/
STQ	57.72%	-5.05%	-36.1%	-36.1%	/	/
Subbit 0.67-bits*	62.60%	-0.19%	-47.2%	-33.3%	/	/
Subbit 0.56-bits*	62.07%	-0.72%	-70.0%	-44.4%	/	/
Subbit 0.44-bits*	61.80%	-0.99%	-82.3%	-55.6%	/	/
SBNN 50% [**our**]	63.03%	+0.24%	-11.1%	/	5.6%	6.8%
SBNN 95% [**our**]	63.33%	+0.54%	-66.2%	-59.9%	72.9%	16.6%
SBNN 96% [**our**]	63.04%	+0.25%	-67.3%	-63.7%	78.9%	12.6%
SBNN 97% [**our**]	62.41%	-0.38%	-73.4%	-66.8%	82.9%	11.1%
SBNN 98% [**our**]	63.58%	+0.79%	-79.2%	-70.3%	88.1%	8.0%
SBNN 99% [**our**]	62.23%	-0.57%	-87.8%	-74.0%	93.6%	4.7%

* our implementation.

metrics used for CIFAR-10, plus the reduction of binary parameters (BParams PR). For our SBNN, we estimate BParams PR as follows. For each kernel we use 2 bits to differentiate among zero Hamming weight kernels, one Hamming weight kernels and all the other kernels. Then, we add 4 bits to the kernels with Hamming weight 1 to represent the index position of their 1-valued bit, whereas we add 9 bits for all the other kernels with Hamming weight larger than 1, which are their original bits. For the other methods, please refer to their work for their estimate of BParams PR.

Table 3 reports the obtained results for the different methods and our SBNN for various sparsity targets. We can see that our pruning method is more effective in reducing both the BOPs and the parameters than Subbit. It allows to remove 79.2% of kernels, while increasing the original accuracy by 0.79% w.r.t. the ReActNet-18 baseline. Instead, we observe nearly 1% accuracy drop for a Subbit network for a similar BOPs reduction. Moreover, our method allows to remove nearly 15% more binary parameters.

ImageNet. We assess our proposed SBNN trained with target sparsity of 75% and 90% on ImageNet. We compare them with state-of-the-art BNNs, namely: XNOR-Net [30], Bi-RealNet-18 [26] and ReActNet-18, ReActNet-A [25] and Subbit [36]. Moreover, we also report the accuracy of the full-precision ResNet-18 [13] and MobileNetV1 [14] models, as a reference. We use a ReActNet-A [25] as SBNN's backbone with its MobileNetV1 [14] inspired topology and with the distillation procedure used in [25], whereas in Subbit [36] they used ReActNet-18 as backbone. One of the limitations of Subbit [36] is that their method cannot be applied to the pointwise convolutions of MobileNetV1 [14]. Due to GPUs limitations, during our training, we decreased the batch size to 64. For a fair comparison, we retrained the original ReActNet-A model with our settings.

Table 4. Method comparison on ImageNet.

Model	Acc Top-1	BOPs $\times 10^8$	FLOPs $\times 10^8$	OPs $\times 10^8$
MobileNetV1 [14] (full-precision)	70.60	–	5.7	5.7
ResNet-18 [13] (full-precision)	72.12	–	19	19
XNOR-Net [30]	51.20	17	1.41	1.67
Bi-RealNet-18 [26]	56.40	17	1.39	1.63
ReActNet-18 [25]	65.50	17	1.63	1.89
ReActNet-A [25]*	68.12	48	0.12	0.87
Subbit 0.67-bits ReActNet-18	63.40	9	1.63	1.77
Subbit 0.56-bits ReActNet-18	62.10	5	1.63	1.71
Subbit 0.44-bits ReActNet-18	60.70	3	1.63	1.68
SBNN 75% ReActNet-A **[ours]**	66.18	8	0.12	0.25
SBNN 90% ReActNet-A **[ours]**	64.72	2	0.12	0.16

* our implementation.

Table 4 reports the results in terms of accuracy (Acc). We also include the number of operations (OPs) to be consistent with other BNNs assessment on ImageNet. For BNNs, OPs are estimated by the sum of floating-point operations (FLOPs) plus BOPs rescaled by a factor $1/64$ [25,26,30]. We assume sparse operations on FPGA to estimate BOPs for SBNN.

We observe that BOPs are the main contributors to ReActNet-A's OPs (Table 4), thus decreasing them largely reduces the OPs. This, instead, does not hold for ReActNet-18, which may explain why Subbit is not effective in reducing OPs of its baseline. Our method instead is effective even for less severe pruning targets and it requires less than 3.4$\times$ OPs w.r.t. state-of-the-art ReActNet-A model, while incurring in an acceptable generalization loss between $1.9 - 3.4\%$.

5 Conclusions

We have presented sparse binary neural network (SBNN), a novel method for sparsifying BNNs that is robust to simple pruning techniques by using a more general binary domain. Our approach involves quantizing weights into a general $\Omega = \{\alpha, \beta\}$ binary domain that is then expressed as 0s and 1s at the implementation stage. We have formulated the SBNN method as a mixed optimization problem, which can be solved using any state-of-the-art BNN training algorithm with the addition of two parameters and a regularization term to control sparsity.

Our experiments demonstrate that SBNN outperforms other state-of-the-art pruning methods for BNNs by reducing the number of operations, while also improving the baseline BNN accuracy for severe sparsity constraints. Future research can investigate the potential of SBNN as a complementary pruning technique in combination with other pruning approaches. In summary, our proposed SBNN method provides a simple yet effective solution to improve the efficiency of BNNs, and we anticipate that it will be a valuable addition to the field of binary neural network pruning.

Ethical Statement

The proposed SBNN can in principle extend the range of devices, at the edge of communication networks, in which DNN models can be exploited. Our work touches various ethical considerations:

- **Data Privacy and Security**: By performing inference of DNNs directly on edge devices, data remains localized and does not need to be transmitted to centralized servers. This reduces the risk of sensitive data exposure during data transfer, enhancing privacy protection.
- **Fairness and Bias**: SBNNs, like other DNNs at the edge, can be susceptible to biased outcomes, as they rely on training data that may reflect societal biases. However, by simplifying the weight representation to binary values, SBNNs may reduce the potential for biased decision-making because they may be less influenced by subtle variations that can introduce bias. Nevertheless, it is essential to address and mitigate biases in data to ensure fairness in outcomes and avoid discriminatory practices.
- **Transparency and Explainability**: The SBNN design can be applied to DNN models that are designed to provide transparency and explainability. Moreover, the binary nature of SBNNs can make them more interpretable and easier to understand compared to complex, multi-valued neural networks. This interpretability can help users gain insights into the decision-making process and facilitate transparency.
- **Human-Centric Design**: SBNNs can extend the use of DNNs at the edge, extending the range of users of applications which are focused on human well-being, human dignity and inclusivity.
- **Resource Allocation and Efficiency**: SBNNs allows the use of DNNs in a more efficient way from both the use of energy, memory and other crucial resources, thus allowing to reduce the environmental impact of DNNs.
- **Ethics of Compression**: While SBNNs offer computational efficiency and reduced memory requirements, the compression of complex information into binary values may raise ethical concerns. Compression may lead to oversimplification or loss of critical details, potentially impacting the fairness, accuracy, or reliability of decision-making systems.

It is important to consider these ethical aspects of SBNNs when evaluating their suitability for specific applications and to ensure responsible and ethical deployment in alignment with societal values and requirements.

References

1. Al-Fuqaha, A., Guizani, M., Mohammadi, M., Aledhari, M., Ayyash, M.: Internet of things: a survey on enabling technologies, protocols, and applications. IEEE Commun. Surv. Tutor. **17**(4), 2347–2376 (2015)
2. Bello, M.G.: Enhanced training algorithms, and integrated training/architecture selection for multilayer perceptron networks. IEEE Trans. Neural Netw. **3**(6), 864–875 (1992)

3. Bethge, J., Yang, H., Bornstein, M., Meinel, C.: Back to simplicity: how to train accurate bnns from scratch? arXiv preprint arXiv:1906.08637 (2019)
4. Canziani, A., Paszke, A., Culurciello, E.: An analysis of deep neural network models for practical applications. arXiv preprint arXiv:1605.07678 (2016)
5. Courbariaux, M., Bengio, Y., David, J.P.: Binaryconnect: training deep neural networks with binary weights during propagations. In: Advances in Neural Information Processing Systems (NeurIPS), pp. 3123–3131 (2015)
6. Evans, D.: The internet of things: how the next evolution of the internet is changing everything. CISCO White Paper **1**(2011), 1–11 (2011)
7. Fu, K., Qi, Z., Cai, J., Shi, X.: Towards high performance and accurate bnn inference on fpga with structured fine-grained pruning. In: Proceedings of the 41st IEEE/ACM International Conference on Computer-Aided Design, pp. 1–9 (2022)
8. Gomez, A.N., Zhang, I., Swersky, K., Gal, Y., Hinton, G.E.: Learning sparse networks using targeted dropout. CoRR abs/1905.13678 (2019). arxiv.org/abs/1905.13678
9. Guerra, L., Drummond, T.: Automatic pruning for quantized neural networks. In: 2021 Digital Image Computing: Techniques and Applications (DICTA), pp. 01–08. IEEE (2021)
10. Guo, N., Bethge, J., Meinel, C., Yang, H.: Join the high accuracy club on imagenet with a binary neural network ticket. arXiv preprint arXiv:2211.12933 (2022)
11. Han, S., Mao, H., Dally, W.J.: Deep compression: compressing deep neural networks with pruning, trained quantization and huffman coding. In: International Conference on Learning Representations (ICLR) (2016)
12. Han, S., Pool, J., Tran, J., Dally, W.: Learning both weights and connections for efficient neural network. In: Advances in Neural Information Processing Systems (NeurIPS), pp. 1135–1143 (2015)
13. He, K., Zhang, X., Ren, S., Sun, J.: Deep residual learning for image recognition. In: Proceedings of the IEEE Conference on Computer Vision and Pattern Recognition, pp. 770–778 (2016)
14. Howard, A.G., et al.: Mobilenets: efficient convolutional neural networks for mobile vision applications. arXiv preprint arXiv:1704.04861 (2017)
15. Hubara, I., Courbariaux, M., Soudry, D., El-Yaniv, R., Bengio, Y.: Binarized neural networks. In: Proceedings of the International Conference on Neural Information Processing Systems, pp. 4114–4122 (2016)
16. Hubara, I., Courbariaux, M., Soudry, D., El-Yaniv, R., Bengio, Y.: Quantized neural networks: training neural networks with low precision weights and activations. J. Mach. Learn. Res. **18**(1), 6869–6898 (2017)
17. Hwang, K., Sung, W.: Fixed-point feedforward deep neural network design using weights+ 1, 0, and- 1. In: IEEE Workshop on Signal Processing Systems (SiPS), pp. 1–6 (2014)
18. Krizhevsky, A., Nair, V., Hinton, G.: Cifar (canadian institute for advanced research). Technical report (2010). https://www.cs.toronto.edu/~kriz/cifar.html
19. Kuhar, S., Tumanov, A., Hoffman, J.: Signed binary weight networks: Improving efficiency of binary weight networks by exploiting sparsity. arXiv preprint arXiv:2211.13838 (2022)
20. LeCun, Y., Bengio, Y., Hinton, G.: Deep learning. Nature **521**(7553), 436–444 (2015)
21. Liang, T., Glossner, J., Wang, L., Shi, S., Zhang, X.: Pruning and quantization for deep neural network acceleration: A survey. Neurocomputing **461**, 370–403 (2021)

22. Lin, J., Chen, W.M., Lin, Y., Cohn, J., Gan, C., Han, S.: Mcunet: tiny deep learning on iot devices. In: Conference on Neural Information Processing Systems (NeurIPS) (2020)
23. Lin, X., Zhao, C., Pan, W.: Towards accurate binary convolutional neural network. Adv. Neural Inf. Process. Syst. **30**, 1–9 (2017)
24. Liu, Z., Shen, Z., Li, S., Helwegen, K., Huang, D., Cheng, K.T.: How do adam and training strategies help bnns optimization. In: International Conference on Machine Learning, pp. 6936–6946. PMLR (2021)
25. Liu, Z., Shen, Z., Savvides, M., Cheng, K.-T.: ReActNet: towards precise binary neural network with generalized activation functions. In: Vedaldi, A., Bischof, H., Brox, T., Frahm, J.-M. (eds.) ECCV 2020. LNCS, vol. 12359, pp. 143–159. Springer, Cham (2020). https://doi.org/10.1007/978-3-030-58568-6_9
26. Liu, Z., Wu, B., Luo, W., Yang, X., Liu, W., Cheng, K.T.: Bi-real net: enhancing the performance of 1-bit cnns with improved representational capability and advanced training algorithm. In: Proceedings of the European Conference on Computer Vision, pp. 722–737 (2018)
27. Louizos, C., Welling, M., Kingma, D.P.: Learning sparse neural networks through l_0 regularization. In: International Conference on Learning Representations (ICLR) (2018)
28. Munagala, S.A., Prabhu, A., Namboodiri, A.M.: Stq-nets: unifying network binarization and structured pruning. In: BMVC (2020)
29. Qin, H., et al.: Forward and backward information retention for accurate binary neural networks. In: Proceedings of the IEEE/CVF Conference on Computer Vision and Pattern Recognition, pp. 2250–2259 (2020)
30. Rastegari, M., Ordonez, V., Redmon, J., Farhadi, A.: XNOR-Net: imagenet classification using binary convolutional neural networks. In: Leibe, B., Matas, J., Sebe, N., Welling, M. (eds.) ECCV 2016. LNCS, vol. 9908, pp. 525–542. Springer, Cham (2016). https://doi.org/10.1007/978-3-319-46493-0_32
31. Russakovsky, O., et al.: ImageNet large scale visual recognition challenge. Int. J. Comput. Vision (IJCV) **115**(3), 211–252 (2015). https://doi.org/10.1007/s11263-015-0816-y
32. Schiavone, R., Zuluaga, M.A.: Sparse binary neural networks (2021). https://openreview.net/forum?id=SP5RHi-rdlJ
33. Srinivas, S., Subramanya, A., Venkatesh Babu, R.: Training sparse neural networks. In: Proceedings of the IEEE/CVF Conference on Computer Vision and Pattern Recognition (CVPR), pp. 138–145 (2017)
34. Srivastava, N., Hinton, G., Krizhevsky, A., Sutskever, I., Salakhutdinov, R.: Dropout: a simple way to prevent neural networks from overfitting. J. Mach. Learn. Res. **15**(1), 1929–1958 (2014)
35. Umuroglu, Y., et al.: Finn: a framework for fast, scalable binarized neural network inference. In: Proceedings of the ACM/SIGDA International Symposium on Field-Programmable Gate Arrays, pp. 65–74 (2017)
36. Wang, Y., Yang, Y., Sun, F., Yao, A.: Sub-bit neural networks: learning to compress and accelerate binary neural networks. In: Proceedings of the IEEE/CVF International Conference on Computer Vision, pp. 5360–5369 (2021)
37. Wu, Q., Lu, X., Xue, S., Wang, C., Wu, X., Fan, J.: Sbnn: slimming binarized neural network. Neurocomputing **401**, 113–122 (2020)
38. Xu, Y., Dong, X., Li, Y., Su, H.: A main/subsidiary network framework for simplifying binary neural networks. In: Proceedings of the IEEE/CVF Conference on Computer Vision and Pattern Recognition, pp. 7154–7162 (2019)

39. Yang, J., et al.: Quantization networks. In: Proceedings of the IEEE/CVF Conference on Computer Vision and Pattern Recognition (CVPR), pp. 7308–7316 (2019)
40. Yao, S., et al.: Deep learning for the internet of things. Computer **51**(5), 32–41 (2018)
41. Zhang, D., Yang, J., Ye, D., Hua, G.: Lq-nets: learned quantization for highly accurate and compact deep neural networks. In: Ferrari, V., Hebert, M., Sminchisescu, C., Weiss, Y. (eds.) Proceedings of the European Conference on Computer Vision, vol. 11212, pp. 373–390 (2018)
42. Zhang, H., Cisse, M., Dauphin, Y.N., Lopez-Paz, D.: mixup: beyond empirical risk minimization. In: International Conference on Learning Representations (ICLR) (2018)

Efficient Hyperdimensional Computing

Zhanglu Yan, Shida Wang(✉), Kaiwen Tang, and Weng-Fai Wong

National University of Singapore, Singapore, Singapore
{zhangluyan,tang_kaiwen,wongwf}@comp.nus.edu.sg, shida_wan@u.nus.edu

Abstract. Hyperdimensional computing (HDC) is a method to perform classification that uses binary vectors with high dimensions and the majority rule. This approach has the potential to be energy-efficient and hence deemed suitable for resource-limited platforms due to its simplicity and massive parallelism. However, in order to achieve high accuracy, HDC sometimes uses hypervectors with tens of thousands of dimensions. This potentially negates its efficiency advantage. In this paper, we examine the necessity of such high dimensions and conduct a detailed theoretical analysis of the relationship between hypervector dimensions and accuracy. Our results demonstrate that as the dimension of the hypervectors increases, the worst-case/average-case HDC prediction accuracy with the majority rule decreases. Building on this insight, we develop HDC models that use binary hypervectors with dimensions orders of magnitude lower than those of state-of-the-art HDC models while maintaining equivalent or even improved accuracy and efficiency. For instance, on the MNIST dataset, we achieve 91.12% HDC accuracy in image classification with a dimension of only 64. Our methods perform operations that are only 0.35% of other HDC models with dimensions of 10,000. Furthermore, we evaluate our methods on ISOLET, UCI-HAR, and Fashion-MNIST datasets and investigate the limits of HDC computing https://github.com/zhangluyan9/EffHDC.

Keywords: Hyperdimension Computing · Energy efficient computing

1 Introduction

Hyperdimensional computing (HDC) is a novel learning paradigm that takes inspiration from the abstract representation of neuron activity in the human brain. HDCs use high-dimensional binary vectors, and they offer several advantages over other well-known training methods like artificial neural networks (ANNs). One of the advantages of HDCs is their ability to achieve high parallelism and low energy consumption, which makes them an ideal choice for resource-constrained applications such as electroencephalogram detection, robotics, language recognition, and federated learning. Several studies have shown that HDCs are highly efficient in these applications [1,7,12,13]. Moreover, HDCs are relatively easy to implement in hardware [14,16], which adds to their appeal as a practical solution for real-world problems, especially in embedded devices.

© The Author(s), under exclusive license to Springer Nature Switzerland AG 2023
D. Koutra et al. (Eds.): ECML PKDD 2023, LNAI 14170, pp. 141–155, 2023.
https://doi.org/10.1007/978-3-031-43415-0_9

Unfortunately, the practical deployment of HDC suffers from low model accuracy and is always restricted to small and simple datasets. To solve the problem, one commonly used technique is increasing the hypervector dimension [12,15,19]. For example, running on the MNIST dataset, hypervector dimensions of 10,000 are often used. [4] and [19] achieved the state-of-the-art accuracies of 94.74% and 95.4%, respectively. In these and other state-of-the-art HDC works, hypervectors are randomly drawn from the hyperspace $\{-1,+1\}^d$, where the dimension d is very high. This ensures high orthogonality, making the hypervectors more independent and easier to distinguish from each other [18]. As a result, accuracy is improved and more complex application scenarios can be targeted. However, the price paid for the higher dimension is in higher energy consumption, possibly negating the advantage of HDC altogether [12]. This paper addresses this trade-off and well as suggests a way to make use of it to improve HDC.

In this paper, we will analyze the relationship between hypervector dimensions and accuracy. It is intuitively true that high dimensions will lead to higher orthogonality [18]. However, contrary to popular belief, we found that as the dimension of the hypervectors d increases, the upper bound for inference worst-case accuracy and average-case accuracy actually *decreases* (Theorem 1 and Theorem 2). In particular, if the hypervector dimension d is sufficient to represent a vector with K classes (in particular, $d > \log_2 K$) then **the lower the dimension, the higher the accuracy.**

Based on our analysis, we utilized the fully-connected network (FCN) with integer weight and binary activation as the encoder. Our research has shown that this encoder is equivalent to traditional HDC encoding methods, as demonstrated in Sect. 3.2. Additionally, we will be learning the representation of each class through the majority rule. This will reduce the hypervector dimension while still maintaining the state-of-the-art accuracies.

When running on the MNIST dataset, we were able to achieve HDC accuracies of 91.12/91.96% with hypervector dimensions of only 64/128. Also, the total number of calculation operations required by our method ($d = 64$) was only 0.35% of what was previously needed by related works that achieved the state-of-the-art performance. These prior methods relied on hypervector dimensions of 10,000 or more. Our analysis and experiments conclusively show that such high dimensions are not necessary.

The contribution of this paper is as follows:

- We give a comprehensive analysis of the relationship between hypervector dimension and the accuracy of HDC. Both the worst-case and average-case accuracy are studied. Mathematically, we explain why relatively lower dimensions can yield higher model accuracies.
- After conducting our analysis, we have found that our methods can achieve similar detection accuracies to the state-of-the-art, while using much smaller hypervector dimensions (latency). For instance, by utilizing a dimension of just 64 on the widely-used MNIST dataset, we were able to achieve an HDC accuracy of 91.12%.

- We have also confirmed the effectiveness of our approach on other datasets commonly used to evaluate HDC, including ISOLET, UCI-HAR, and Fashion-MNIST, achieving state-of-the-art accuracies even with quite low dimensions. Overall, our findings demonstrate the potential of our methods in reducing computational overhead while maintaining high detection accuracy.

Organisation. This paper is organized as follows. For completeness, we first introduce the basic workflow and background of HDC. In Sect. 3, we present our main dimension-accuracy analysis and two HDC retraining approaches. To evaluate the effectiveness of our proposed methods, we conduct experiments and compare our results with state-of-the-art HDC models in Sect. 4. Finally, we discuss the implications of our findings and conclude the paper.

2 Background

Hyperdimensional computing (HDC) is a technique that represents data using binary hypervectors with dimensions typically ranging from 5,000 to 10,000. For example, when working with the MNIST dataset, each flattened image $x \in \mathbb{R}^{784}$ is encoded into a hypervector $r \in \mathbb{R}^d$ using a binding operation that combines value hypervectors v with position vectors p and takes their summation.

Both these two hypervectors $\mathbf{v}, \mathbf{p}$ are independently drawn from the hyperspace $\{-1, +1\}^d$ randomly. Mathematically, we can construct representation r for each image as followed:

$$r = \operatorname{sgn}\left((v_{x_0} \bigotimes p_{x_0} + v_{x_1} \bigotimes p_{x_1} + \cdots + v_{x_{783}} \bigotimes p_{x_{783}})\right), \tag{1}$$

where the sign function 'sgn(·)' is used to binarize the sum of the hypervectors, returning either −1 or 1. When the sum equals to zero, sgn(0) is randomly assigned either 1 or −1. In addition, the binding operation $\bigotimes$ performs element-wise multiplication between hypervectors. For instance, $[-1, 1, 1, -1] \bigotimes [1, 1, 1, -1] = [-1, 1, 1, 1]$.

During training, hypervectors $r_1, r_2, ..., r_{60,000}$ belonging to the same class are added together. The resulting sum is then used to generate a representation R_i for class i, using the "majority rule" approach. The data belonging to class i is denoted by C_i.

$$R_i = \operatorname{sgn}\left(\sum_{x \in C_i} r_i\right). \tag{2}$$

During inference, the encoded test image is compared to each class representation R_c, and the most similar one is selected as the predicted class. Various similarity measures such as cosine similarity, L2 distance, and Hamming distance have been used in previous works. In this work, we use the inner product as the similarity measure for binary hypervectors with values of −1 and 1, as it is equivalent to the Hamming distance, as noted in [5].

3 High Dimensions Are Not Necessary

Contrary to traditional results that suggest higher-dimensional models have lower error rates, the majority rule's higher representation dimension in HDC domain does not always lead to better results. Our research demonstrates that if a dataset can be linearly separated and embedded into a d-dimensional vector space, higher-dimensional representation may actually reduce classification accuracy. This discovery prompted us to explore the possibility of discovering a low-dimensional representation of the dataset. Our numerical experiments support our theoretical discovery, as the accuracy curve aligns with our findings.

3.1 Dimension-Accuracy Analysis

Based on the assumption that the dataset can be linearly-separably embedded into a d-dimensional space, we here investigate the dimension-accuracy relationship for the majority rule.

We further assume the encoded hypervectors are uniformly distributed over a d-dimensional unit ball:

$$B^d = \{r \in \mathbb{R}^d \big| \|r\|_2 \leq 1\}.$$

Moreover, we assume that hypervectors x are *linearly separable* and each class with label i can be represented by C_i:

$$C_i = \{r \in \mathcal{X} | R_i \cdot r > R_j \cdot r, j \neq i\}, \quad 1 \leq i \leq K$$

where $R_i \in [0,1]^d$ are support hypervectors that are used to distinguish classes i from other classes.

Selecting a sufficiently large d to embed the raw data into a d-dimensional unit ball is crucial for this approach to work effectively. This assumption is reasonable because with a large enough d, we can ensure that the raw data can be accurately mapped into a high-dimensional space where the support hypervectors can distinguish between different classes.

Similarly, we define the prediction class $\hat{C}_i$ by $\hat{R}_i$ as followed:

$$\hat{C}_i = \{r \in \mathcal{X} | \hat{R}_i \cdot r > \hat{R}_j \cdot r, j \neq i\}, \quad 1 \leq i \leq K.$$

When we apply the majority rule to separate the above hypervectors x, we are approximating R_i with $\hat{R}_i$ in the sense of maximizing the prediction accuracy. Here each $\hat{R}_i \in \{0,1\}^d$ is a binary vector.

Therefore we define the worst-case K-classes prediction accuracy over hypervectors distribution $\mathcal{X}$ in the following expression:

$$Acc^w_{K,d} := \inf_{R_1,R_2,\ldots,R_K} \sup_{\hat{R}_1,\hat{R}_2,\ldots,\hat{R}_K} \mathbb{E}_r \left[\sum_{i=1}^{K} \prod_{j\neq i} \mathbf{1}_{\{R_i \cdot r > R_j \cdot r\}} \mathbf{1}_{\{\hat{R}_i \cdot r > \hat{R}_j \cdot r\}} \right].$$

Theorem 1. *Assume $K = 2$, as the dimension of the hypervectors d increases, the worst-case prediction accuracy decreases with the following rate:*

$$\begin{aligned}
Acc^w_{2,d} &= 2 \inf_{R_1,R_2} \sup_{\hat{R}_1,\hat{R}_2} \mathbb{E}_r\left[\mathbf{1}_{\{R_1\cdot r>R_2\cdot r\}}\mathbf{1}_{\{\hat{R}_1\cdot r>\hat{R}_2\cdot r\}}\right] \\
&= \inf_{R_1,R_2} \sup_{\hat{R}_1,\hat{R}_2} \left[1 - \frac{\arccos(\frac{(R_1-R_2)\cdot(\hat{R}_1-\hat{R}_2)}{\|R_1-R_2\|_2\|\hat{R}_1-\hat{R}_2\|_2})}{\pi}\right] \\
&= 1 - \frac{\arccos(\frac{1}{\sqrt{\sum_{j=1}^d(\sqrt{j}-\sqrt{j-1})^2}})}{\pi} \to \frac{1}{2}, \qquad d \to \infty
\end{aligned}$$

The first equality is by the symmetry of distribution $\mathcal{X}$. The second equality is the evaluation of expectation over $\mathcal{X}$ and the detail is given in Lemma 1. For the third equality, the proof is given in Lemma 3 and Lemma 4.

In the next theorem, we further consider the average-case. Assume the prior distribution $\mathcal{P}$ for optimal representation is uniformly distributed: $R_1, ...R_K \sim \mathcal{U}[0,1]^d$. We can define the average accuracy with the following expression:

$$\overline{Acc}_{K,d} := \mathbb{E}_{R_1,R_2,...,R_K\sim\mathcal{P}} \sup_{\hat{R}_1,\hat{R}_2,...,\hat{R}_K} \mathbb{E}_r\left[\sum_{i=1}^K \prod_{j\neq i} \mathbf{1}_{\{R_i\cdot r>R_j\cdot r\}}\mathbf{1}_{\{\hat{R}_i\cdot r>\hat{R}_j\cdot r\}}\right].$$

Theorem 2. *Assume $K = 2$, as the dimension of the hypervectors d increases, the average case prediction accuracy decreases:*

$$\begin{aligned}
\overline{Acc}_{K,d} &= \mathbb{E}_{R_1,R_2\sim U[0,1]^d} \sup_{\hat{R}_1,\hat{R}_2} \mathbb{E}_r\left[\mathbf{1}_{\{R_1\cdot r>R_2\cdot r\}}\mathbf{1}_{\{\hat{R}_1\cdot r>\hat{R}_2\cdot r\}}\right] \\
&= \mathbb{E}_{R_1,R_2\sim U[0,1]^d} \sup_{\hat{R}_1,\hat{R}_2} \left[1 - \frac{\arccos(\frac{(R_1-R_2)\cdot(\hat{R}_1-\hat{R}_2)}{\|R_1-R_2\|_2\|\hat{R}_1-\hat{R}_2\|_2})}{\pi}\right] \\
&= \mathbb{E}_{R_1,R_2\sim U[0,1]^d} \left[1 - \frac{\arccos\left(\sup_{j=1}^d \frac{\sum_{i=1}^j |R_1-R_2|_{(i)}}{\sqrt{j}\|R_1-R_2\|}\right)}{\pi}\right].
\end{aligned}$$

Here $|R_1 - R_2|_{(i)}$ denotes the i-th maximum coordinate for vector $|R_1 - R_2|$.

Since the exact expression for average-case accuracy is challenging to evaluate, we rely on Monte Carlo simulations. In particular, we sample R_1 and R_2 1000 times to estimate the expected accuracy.

We then present the curves of $Acc^w_{K,d}$ and $\overline{Acc}_{K,d}$ over a range of dimensions from 1 to 1000 in Figs. 1 and 2, respectively. It is evident from these figures that the upper bound of classification accuracy decreases as the dimension of the representation exceeds the necessary dimension. This observation implies that a higher representation dimension is not necessarily beneficial and could even

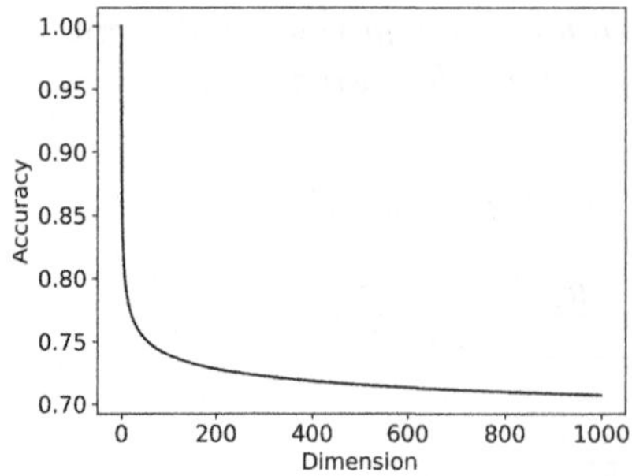

Fig. 1. Worst-case Accuracy $Acc^{w}_{2,d}$

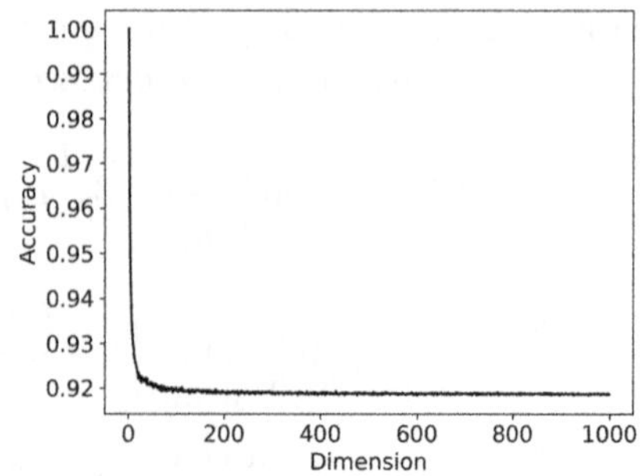

Fig. 2. Average-case Accuracy $\overline{Acc_{2,d}}$

lead to a decrease in accuracy. It is easy to find that a high dimension for HDCs is not necessary for both the worst-case and average-case, the upper bound of accuracy will drop slowly when the dimension increases.

According to [17], we can approximate multi-class case where $K \geq 3$ by one-against-one binary classification. Therefore, we define the quasi-accuracy of K-class classification as follows:

$$Quasi\text{-}Acc_{K,d} = \frac{\sum_{i \neq j} Acc^{ij}_{2,d}}{K(K-1)},$$

where $Acc^{ij}_{2,d}$ can be either the average-case or worst-case accuracy that distinguishes class i and j. Since the accuracy $Acc^{ij}_{2,d}$ for binary classification decreases as the dimension increase, the quasi-accuracy follows the same trend.

3.2 Low-Dimension Hypervector Training

To confirm the theoretical findings mentioned above, we propose a HDC design that is shown in Fig. 3. For data encoding, the traditional hyperdimensional computing technique utilizes binding and bundling operations to encode data samples using Eq. 1. However, in this study, we use a simple binary fully-connected network with integer weights and binary activations as the encoder. Taking the MNIST dataset as an example, we demonstrate the equivalence of these two methods as follows:

$$r = \text{sgn}(Wx) = \text{sgn}\left(\sum_{0 \leq i \leq 783} W_{i,x_i=1}\right) \quad (3)$$

where $W_{i,x_i=1}$ indicates the weights whose corresponding input x_i =1.

The Eq. 3 shows that the sum of the weights W_i corresponding to input $x_i = 1$, while ignoring weights for $x_i = 0$. The resulting sum of weight $\sum_{0 \leq i \leq 783} W_{i,x_i=1}$ in the linear transform corresponds to the sum of binding values of hypervectors v and p in Eq. 2. The integer-weights FCN with binary

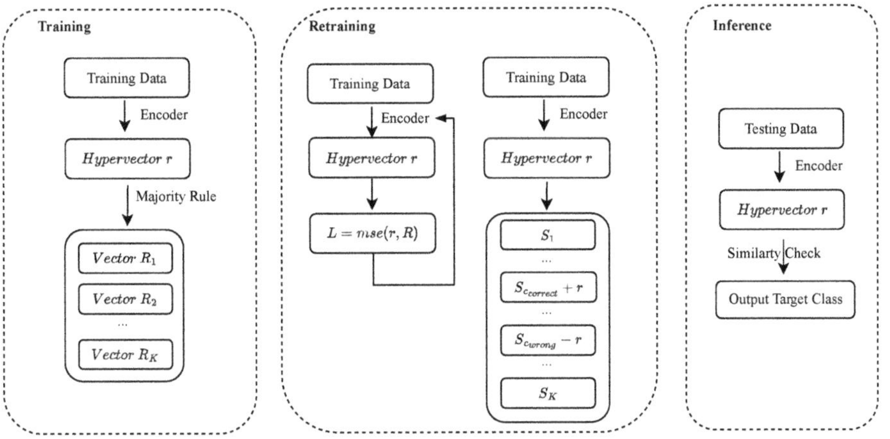

Fig. 3. Workflow of Our HDC.

activation is a natural modification of the hyperdimensional computing encoders, using only integer additions, as in traditional HDC encoders.

Specifically, in our one-layer integer-weight fully-connected network, if we randomly initialize the weights with binary values, it becomes equivalent to the encoder of HDC.

We used a *straight-through estimator* (STE) to learn the weights [2] (details of STE are discussed in the Appendix[1]). The binary representation R_c of each class is generated using the majority rule (Algorithm 1). To achieve this, we first sum up the N hypervectors r belonging to class c and obtain an integer-type representation S_c for that class. Subsequently, we assign a value of 1 if the element in S_c exceeds a predefined threshold θ. Otherwise, we set it to 0. This generates a binary representation R_c.

We have also devised a two-step retraining method to refine the binary representation R_c to improve the accuracy. Algorithm 2 outlines the procedure we follow. First, we feed the training data to the encoder in batches and employ the mean squared error as the loss function to update the weights in the encoder. Next, we freeze the encoder and update the representation of each class. If the output r is misclassified as class c_{wrong} instead of the correct class $c_{correct}$, we reduce the sum of representation of the wrong class $S_{c_{wrong}}$ by multiplying r with the learning rate. Simultaneously, we increase the sum of representation of the correct class $S_{c_{right}}$ by multiplying r with the learning rate. We then use the modified S_c in Algorithm 1 to generate the binary representation R_c.

[1] https://github.com/zhangluyan9/EffHDC/blob/main/Appendix.pdf.

Algorithm 1. Representation Generation:

Require: N number of training data $\boldsymbol{x}$;
Ensure: Trained binary encoder E; Sum of representation S; Binary Representation R_c; Outputs of encoder $\boldsymbol{y}$; Pre-defined Threshold θ;

1: $\boldsymbol{r} = E(\boldsymbol{x})$; $S_c = 0$
2: **for** $i = 1$ to N **do**
3:     $S_c += r$
4: **end for**
5: **for** $i = 1$ to d **do**
6:     **if** $S_c[i] > \theta$ **then**
7:         $R_c[i] = 1$
8:     **else**
9:         $R_c[i] = 0$
10:     **end if**
11: **end for**

Algorithm 2. HDC Retraining:

Require: Training data $\boldsymbol{x}$ with label $\boldsymbol{R_c}$; Trained Encoder E; N training epochs.

1: **Step1:**
2: **for** epoch= 1 to N **do**
3:     $r = \text{E}(\boldsymbol{x})$
4:     $L = \text{mse}(r, R_c)$ //Bp: STE
5: **end for**

6: **Step2:**
7: $r = \text{E}(\boldsymbol{x})$
8: **if** Misclassified **then**
9:     $S_{c_{correct}} += lr * r$
10:     $S_{c_{wrong}} -= lr * r$
11: **end if**
12: Generate R_c (Algorithm 1, line 5-9)

After computing the representation of each class, we can compare the similarity between the resulting hypervector and the representation of all classes. To do this, we send the test data to the same encoder and obtain its hypervector representation. Next, we convert the value of 0 in R_c to -1 and perform an inner product to check for similarity. The class with the highest similarity is reported as the result.

4 Results

We have implemented our schemes in CUDA-accelerated (CUDA 11.7) PyTorch version 1.13.0. The experiments were performed on an Intel Xeon E5-2680 server with two NVIDIA A100 Tensor Core GPUs and one GeForce RT 3090 GPU, running 64-bit Linux 5.15. MNIST dataset[2], Fashion-MNIST[3], ISOLET[4] and UCI-HAR[5] are used in our experiments.

4.1 A Case Study of Our Technologies

Here, we will describe how our approaches improve the MNIST digit recognition task step by step.

[2] http://yann.lecun.com/exdb/mnist/.
[3] https://github.com/zalandoresearch/fashion-mnist.
[4] https://archive.ics.uci.edu/ml/datasets/isolet.
[5] https://archive.ics.uci.edu/ml/datasets/human+activity+recognition+using smartphones.

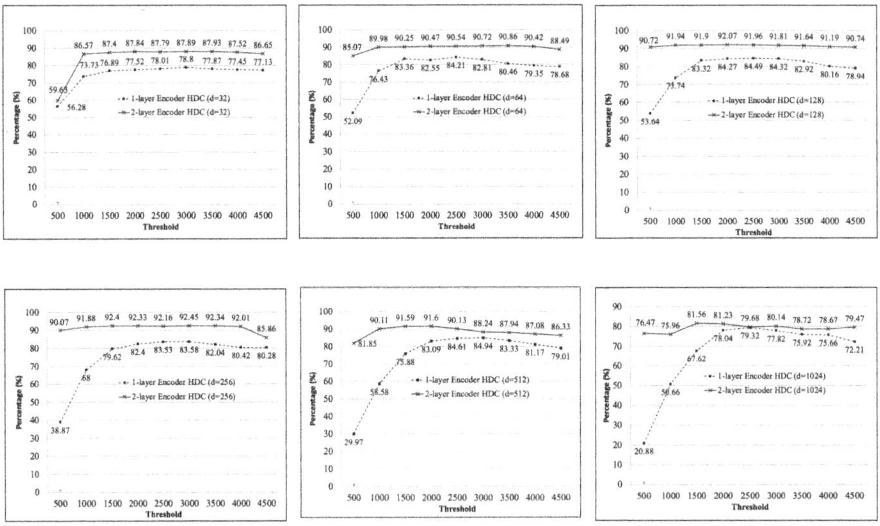

Fig. 4. Threshold Study

Baseline Accuracy. Equation 3 shows that a single integer-weights FCN with binary activation can be transformed into traditional HDC encoding. To evaluate the performance of this transformation, we constructed two models consisting of one and two FCN layers (stack of one-layer FCN encoder) respectively and used them to encode an image. We then compared the results of both models.

Using a dimension of 64 as an example, we investigate the correlation between the pre-defined threshold described in Algorithm 1 and accuracy. Our experiments on the MNIST dataset (shown in Fig. 4) reveal that the threshold exhibits high robustness against noise even when the dimension is low. In fact, we observe that the detection accuracy remains virtually unchanged when the threshold was varied from 1000 to 4500. The maximum number in S_c after the encoder is approximately 6500.

We further examined the connection between dimension and inference accuracy using the optimal threshold. According to Figs. 5 and 6, we can attain HDC accuracies of 78.8% and 84.21%, as well as 87.93% and 90.86%, for 1-layer and 2-layer Encoder HDCs, respectively, with dimensions of only 32 and 64. Moreover, as stated in Theorem 1, the accuracy declines beyond a dimension of 128/256. Therefore, the accuracy of HDC is affected by the dimension, and we observed a consistent pattern with our previous findings.

HDC Retraining. Thus far, we have shown how we can achieve HDC accuracy of over 90% with the smallest hypervector dimension. We can in fact improve the results using retraining techniques we will describe in this section. For example, with a dimension of 64, we can push the accuracy to 91.12% with our two-step

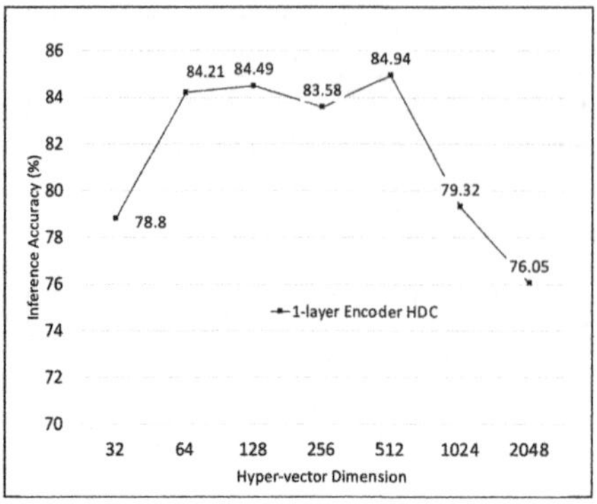

Fig. 5. 1-layer Encoder HDC Accuracy

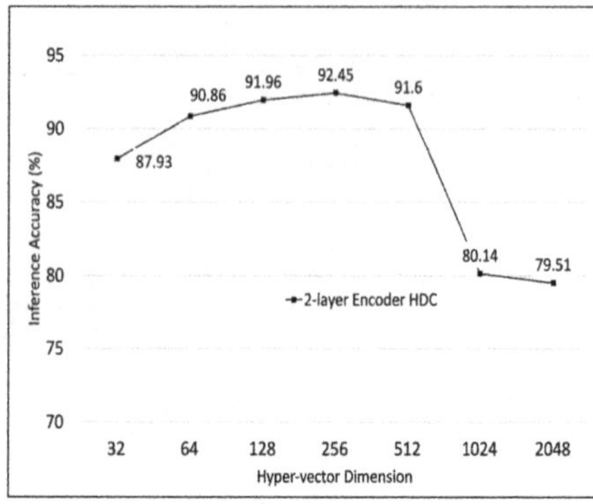

Fig. 6. 2-layer Encoder HDC Accuracy

training (0.16% and 0.1% accuracy improvement with steps 1 and 2, respectively). The final accuracy can be increased in a matter of minutes.

4.2 Experimental Results

We present our final experimental findings with all previous technologies in Table 1, which showcases a comprehensive comparison between our HDC model and other state-of-the-art models in terms of accuracy, dimension, and number of operations. Our HDC model achieved accuracies of 84.21% and 84.49% for the MNIST dataset with encoder dimensions of only $d = 64$ and $d = 128$, respectively. We further improved the HDC accuracies to 91.12% and 91.96% by stacking an additional layer and batch normalization to the encoder architecture. These results demonstrate the effectiveness of our proposed HDC model in achieving competitive accuracies but much low dimension and computations in comparison to other state-of-the-art models.

In order to compare the performance of our HDC model with the state-of-the-art, we selected several relevant works. One such work is TD-HDC, which was proposed by [3]. They developed a threshold-based framework to dynamically choose an execution path and improve the accuracy-energy efficiency trade-off. With their pure binary HD model, they achieved an HDC accuracy of 88.92% on the MNIST dataset. In another case study, [6] utilized a basic HDC model on the MNIST dataset. They encoded the pixels based on their black/white value and used majority sum operation in the training stage to combine similar samples. Their approach resulted in an HDC accuracy of 86% on the MNIST dataset.

HDC has also been applied in the fields of federated learning and secure learning. For example, FL-HDC by [7] focused on the combination of HDC and federated learning. They introduced the polarized model into the federated learning field to reduce communication costs and were able to control the accuracy drop by retraining. Their approach achieved an HDC accuracy of 88% on the MNIST dataset. In another work, SecureHD [9] adapted a novel encoding and decoding method based on HDC to perform secure learning tasks.

Table 1. Comparison on MNIST dataset.

	Accuracy	Dimension	Inference	
			Encoder additions/Boolean op	Similarity
MNIST				
SearcHD	84.43%	10,000	7.84M/7.84M	Hamming
FL-HDC	88%	10,000	7.84M/7.84M	Cosine
TD-HDC	88.92%	5,000	3.92M/3.92M	Hamming
QuantHD	89.28%	10,000	7.84M/7.84M	Hamming
LeHDC	94.74%	10,000	7.84M/7.84M	Hamming
Ours*	84.21%	**64**	**0.05M/0**	Hamming
Ours**	**91.12%**	**64**	**0.054M/0**	Hamming

Ours* uses one-layer encoder while Ours** use two-layer encoder.

Recent works in the field of HDC include LeHDC [4], which transferred the HDC classifier into a binary neural network, achieving accuracies of 94.74% on the MNIST dataset. Additionally, QuantHD [8] and SearcHD [11] are two methods that introduce multi-model and retraining techniques into the HDC field. These methods have shown promising results in improving the accuracy and performance of HDC models.

We also conducted tests on more datasets such as Fashion-MNIST, ISOLET, and UCI-HAR to assess the effectiveness of our methods. Specifically, we achieved an accuracy rate of 81.64%, 91.4%, and 94.20% for Fashion-MNIST, ISOLET, and UCI-HAR, respectively, using only 64 dimensions for the hypervector. Our results are shown in Table 2, with BinHD [10] used as the baseline for comparison.

Table 2. Comparison on other datasets.

	Accuracy	Dimension	Inference	
			Encoder additions/Boolean op	Similarity
Fashion-MNIST				
BinHD	NA	NA	NA	NA
Ours	**81.64%**	**64**	**0.059M/0**	Hamming
Ours	**81.58%**	**128**	**0.134M/0**	Hamming
ISOLET				
BinHD	85.6%	10,000	6.17M/6.17M	Hamming
Ours	**91.4%**	**64**	**0.249M/0**	Hamming
Ours	**93.2%**	**128**	**0.524M/0**	Hamming
UCI-HAR				
BinHD	87.3%	10,000	5.61M/5.61M	Hamming
Ours	**94.20%**	**64**	**0.336M/0**	Hamming
Ours	**94.81%**	**128**	**0.304M/0**	Hamming

To minimize computational costs in our method, we decided to use Hamming distance for inference, as it is more efficient than cosine similarity, which involves additional multiplication and division operations. With Hamming distance, the number of operations is directly proportional to the dimension of the hypervectors. This means that our approach requires only 0.64% of the operations needed by other HDC models with a dimension of 10,000, when using a dimension of d=64. This reduction in operations can speed up the inference process, making our approach more efficient for real-world applications.

5 Discussion

5.1 Limitation of HDCs

In this section, we aim to shed light on the relationship between the dimension of hypervectors and the number of classes, which has been largely overlooked in other HDC studies. To illustrate this point, we use the MNIST dataset as an example. State-of-the-art works typically employ hypervectors with dimensions ranging from 5,000 to 10,000 to differentiate pixel values that span from 0 to 255 and do a 10-classes classification. However, with an increase in the number of classes to 100 or 1,000, more information is required for precise classification. For input data, if we apply quantization and employ a suitable encoder to distill information from the original image, it is theoretically feasible to operate with a considerably smaller dimension. However, the quantity of classes remains invariant. This provides an explanation for the challenges encountered by our method, and other HDC techniques, in achieving high performance on more intricate datasets such as Cifar100 and ImageNet where the number of classes is significantly larger.

5.2 Further Discussion of the Low Accuracy When d Is Low

As can be seen from Fig. 1, 2 and Fig. 5, 6, the current Theorem 1 and 2 do not predict the low accuracy for dimension $d \leq 128/256$.

The issue can be attributed to the breakdown of the assumption that data can be embedded in a d-dimensional linearly separable unit ball. Consider a different setup in that the underlying dimension for data is fixed to be m. Each class is defined to be:

$$C_i = \{r \in \mathbb{B}^m | R_i \cdot r > R_j \cdot r, j \neq i\}, \quad 1 \leq i \leq K.$$

Assume that the linear projection of data from m-dimensional linearly separable unit ball to d-dimensional ($d < m$) space in a coordinate-wise approach. It is equivalent to optimizing over the following hypervector set

$$R_{co_1,\ldots,co_d} = \{R | R_i \in \{0,1\}, i \in \{co_1,\ldots,co_d\}; R_i = 0, i \notin \{co_1,\ldots,co_d\}\},$$

Here $co_1,\ldots,co_d$ are the coordinates index of the projected space.

The worst-case K-classes prediction accuracy of the m-dimensional data projected onto a d-dimensional subspace is

$$\begin{aligned} Acc^w_{K,m,d} := & \inf_{R_1,R_2,\ldots,R_K\in[0,1]^m} \sup_{co_1,\ldots,co_d} \sup_{\hat{R}_1,\hat{R}_2,\ldots,\hat{R}_K\in R_{co_1,\ldots,co_d}} \\ & \mathbb{E}_r\left[\sum_{i=1}^{K}\prod_{j\neq i}\mathbf{1}_{\{R_i\cdot r>R_j\cdot r\}}\mathbf{1}_{\{\hat{R}_i\cdot r>\hat{R}_j\cdot r\}}\right] \\ & \leq Acc^w_{K,m,d+1} \\ & \leq Acc^w_{K,m}. \end{aligned}$$

The monotonicity comes from the fact that the two supremums are taken over a monotonic hypervector set R sequence.

The following theorem summarizes the above reasoning:

Proposition 1. *Assume the representation dimension $d \leq m-1$, the classification accuracy increases monotonically as d increase:*

$$Acc^w_{K,m,d} \leq Acc^w_{K,m,d+1}, \quad d \leq m-1. \tag{4}$$

Both Theorem 1 and 2 characterize the accuracy when $d \geq m$. Proposition 1 describes the dimension-accuracy relationship for $d \leq m$. The above reasoning has been confirmed by our numerical experiments.

6 Conclusion

In this paper, we considered the dimension of the hypervectors used in hyperdimensional computing. We presented a detailed analysis of the relationship between dimension and accuracy to demonstrate that it is not necessary to use high dimensions to get a good performance in HDC. Contrary to popular belief, we proved that as the dimension of the hypervectors d increases, the upper bound for inference worst-case accuracy and average-case accuracy decreases. As a result, we reduce the dimensions from the tens of thousands used by the state-of-the-art to merely tens, while achieving the same level of accuracy. Computing operations during inference have been reduced to a tenth of that in traditional HDCs. Running on the MNIST dataset, we achieved an HDC accuracy of 91.12% using a dimension of only 64. All our results are reproducible using the code we have made public.

Ethics Statement

We hereby assure that the following requirements have been met in the manuscript:

- All of the datasets used in this paper are open-source and have been made publicly available for use. These datasets have been carefully vetted to ensure that they do not contain any personal or sensitive information that could compromise the privacy of individuals. Therefore, there are no concerns about violating personal privacy when using these datasets for research or analysis.
- The paper is free of any potential use of the work for policing or military purposes.
- This manuscript presents the authors' original work that has not been previously published elsewhere.
- The paper reflects the author's research and analysis accurately and completely.
- Co-authors and co-researchers who made significant contributions to the work are duly acknowledged.
- The results are appropriately contextualized within prior and existing research.
- Proper citation is provided for all sources used.
- All authors have actively participated in the research leading to this manuscript and take public responsibility for its content.

References

1. Asgarinejad, F., Thomas, A., Rosing, T.: Detection of epileptic seizures from surface EEG using hyperdimensional computing. In: 2020 42nd Annual International Conference of the IEEE Engineering in Medicine & Biology Society (EMBC), pp. 536–540. IEEE (2020)
2. Bengio, Y., Léonard, N., Courville, A.: Estimating or propagating gradients through stochastic neurons for conditional computation (2013)
3. Chuang, Y.C., Chang, C.Y., Wu, A.Y.A.: Dynamic hyperdimensional computing for improving accuracy-energy efficiency trade-offs. In: 2020 IEEE Workshop on Signal Processing Systems (SiPS), pp. 1–5. IEEE (2020)
4. Duan, S., Liu, Y., Ren, S., Xu, X.: LeHDC: learning-based hyperdimensional computing classifier. arXiv preprint arXiv:2203.09680 (2022)
5. Frady, E.P., Kleyko, D., Kymn, C.J., Olshausen, B.A., Sommer, F.T.: Computing on functions using randomized vector representations. arXiv preprint arXiv:2109.03429 (2021)
6. Hassan, E., Halawani, Y., Mohammad, B., Saleh, H.: Hyper-dimensional computing challenges and opportunities for AI applications. IEEE Access **10**, 97651–97664 (2021)
7. Hsieh, C.Y., Chuang, Y.C., Wu, A.Y.A.: FL-HDC: hyperdimensional computing design for the application of federated learning. In: 2021 IEEE 3rd International Conference on Artificial Intelligence Circuits and Systems (AICAS), pp. 1–5. IEEE (2021)
8. Imani, M., et al.: QuantHD: a quantization framework for hyperdimensional computing. IEEE Trans. Comput.-Aided Des. Integr. Circu. Syst. **39**(10), 2268–2278 (2019)
9. Imani, M., et al.: A framework for collaborative learning in secure high-dimensional space. In: 2019 IEEE 12th International Conference on Cloud Computing (CLOUD), pp. 435–446. IEEE (2019)

10. Imani, M., Messerly, J., Wu, F., Pi, W., Rosing, T.: A binary learning framework for hyperdimensional computing. In: 2019 Design, Automation & Test in Europe Conference & Exhibition (DATE), pp. 126–131. IEEE (2019)
11. Imani, M., et al.: SearcHD: a memory-centric hyperdimensional computing with stochastic training. IEEE Trans. Comput.-Aided Des. Integr. Circ. Syst. **39**(10), 2422–2433 (2019)
12. Neubert, P., Schubert, S., Protzel, P.: An introduction to hyperdimensional computing for robotics. KI-Künstliche Intelligenz **33**(4), 319–330 (2019)
13. Rahimi, A., Kanerva, P., Rabaey, J.M.: A robust and energy-efficient classifier using brain-inspired hyperdimensional computing. In: Proceedings of the 2016 International Symposium on Low Power Electronics and Design, pp. 64–69 (2016)
14. Salamat, S., Imani, M., Khaleghi, B., Rosing, T.: F5-HD: fast flexible FPGA-based framework for refreshing hyperdimensional computing. In: Proceedings of the 2019 ACM/SIGDA International Symposium on Field-Programmable Gate Arrays, pp. 53–62 (2019)
15. Schlegel, K., Neubert, P., Protzel, P.: A comparison of vector symbolic architectures. Artif. Intell. Rev. **55**(6), 4523–4555 (2022)
16. Schmuck, M., Benini, L., Rahimi, A.: Hardware optimizations of dense binary hyperdimensional computing: Rematerialization of hypervectors, binarized bundling, and combinational associative memory. ACM J. Emerg. Technol. Comput. Syst. (JETC) **15**(4), 1–25 (2019)
17. Tax, D.M., Duin, R.P.: Using two-class classifiers for multiclass classification. In: 2002 International Conference on Pattern Recognition, vol. 2, pp. 124–127. IEEE (2002)
18. Thomas, A., Dasgupta, S., Rosing, T.: Theoretical foundations of hyperdimensional computing. arXiv preprint arXiv:2010.07426 (2020)
19. Yu, T., Zhang, Y., Zhang, Z., De Sa, C.: Understanding hyperdimensional computing for parallel single-pass learning. arXiv preprint arXiv:2202.04805 (2022)

Rényi Divergence Deep Mutual Learning

Weipeng Fuzzy Huang[1(✉)], Junjie Tao[2], Changbo Deng[1], Ming Fan[3], Wenqiang Wan[1], Qi Xiong[1], and Guangyuan Piao[4]

[1] Tencent Security Big Data Lab, Shenzhen, China
{fuzzyhuang,changbodeng,johnnywan,keonxiong}@tencent.com
[2] School of Software Engineering, Xi'an Jiaotong University, Xi'an, China
taojunjie@stu.xjtu.edu.cn
[3] The MoEKLINNS Laboratory, School of Cyber Science and Engineering, Xi'an Jiaotong University, Xi'an 710049, China
mingfan@mail.xjtu.edu.cn
[4] Department of Computer Science, Maynooth University, Maynooth, Ireland
guangyuan.piao@mu.ie

Abstract. This paper revisits Deep Mutual Learning (DML), a simple yet effective computing paradigm. We propose using Rényi divergence instead of the Kullback-Leibler divergence, which is more flexible and tunable, to improve vanilla DML. This modification is able to consistently improve performance over vanilla DML with limited additional complexity. The convergence properties of the proposed paradigm are analyzed theoretically, and Stochastic Gradient Descent with a constant learning rate is shown to converge with $\mathcal{O}(1)$-bias in the worst case scenario for nonconvex optimization tasks. That is, learning will reach nearby local optima but continue searching within a bounded scope, which may help mitigate overfitting. Finally, our extensive empirical results demonstrate the advantage of combining DML and the Rényi divergence, leading to further improvement in model generalization.

1 Introduction

An appealing quality of certain machine learning approaches is their strong association with realworld phenomena. Among these techniques is Deep Mutual Learning (DML) [34], an empirically powerful paradigm that is, despite its conceptual simplicity, highly effective in practice. The metaphor for DML can be likened to a learning process in which a group of students acquires knowledge not only from the ground truth but also from their peers. Intuitively, this learning paradigm fosters the development of students by encouraging them to assimilate the strengths of one another. As a result, the students' performance surpasses what could have been achieved if they solely relied on their teacher for guidance. Empirically, DML is remarkable in constraining the generalization errors and hence nicely protects the learned models from overfitting by incorporating the Kullback-Leibler (KL) divergence between peers into its loss function [20]. Heuristically, it helps the students find wider local optima [34], since the students share diversity with others and avoid being optimized towards a limited

© The Author(s), under exclusive license to Springer Nature Switzerland AG 2023
D. Koutra et al. (Eds.): ECML PKDD 2023, LNAI 14170, pp. 156–172, 2023.
https://doi.org/10.1007/978-3-031-43415-0_10

number of directions. In fact, DML is an efficient paradigm, as it adheres to the principle of Occam's razor, where simplicity is preferred over complexity.

Interestingly, even if every student uses the same network architecture (but with distinct weight initializations), each individual model still benefits from the paradigm and outperforms itself [34]. It is reasonable as weight initialization plays a crucial role in Deep Learning (DL) optimizations because some initial points can lead to wider optima than others, in the highly nonconvex optimization tasks [5]. To facilitate DML for the pretrained models, one may apply the DROPOUT [26] to produce a set of diversified initializations.

Observing that the empirical advantages of DML originate from the regularization aspect wherein students learn from others, we propose that increasing the flexibility of adjusting the regularization can further improve learning performance. The proposed paradigm is named Rényi Divergence Deep Mutual Learning (RDML), which utilizes the Rényi divergence [6] to regulate the degree to which a student should learn from others. RDML is simple in the same order of magnitude as DML, but performs consistently better in practice. As a super class of the KL divergence, the Rényi divergence introduces more flexibility for tuning. Analogous to other regularization approaches, model performance benefits from a better-tuned regularization power, i.e., the coefficient for the regularization part. The experimental study shows that RDML consistently improves DML performance. On the theoretical side, we prove that the expected gradient norm of RDML using Stochastic Gradient Descent (SGD) converges in $\mathcal{O}(1/\sqrt{T}+1)$ for every student, with a constant learning rate $o(1/\sqrt{T})$, where T is the total number of iterations. The reasonable amount of bias keeps the algorithm randomly searching around the (local) optima of the base model loss where every student arrives. This could effectively increase the chance of avoiding a narrow optima in practice.

Apart from the proposal of RDML, the contributions of this paper include: 1) a theoretical analysis of the convergence properties that RDML maintains; 2) an extensive empirical study in Sect. 4 which shows that RDML is able to consistently improve the model performance and achieve better generalizations in Computer Vision and Natural Language Processing. Finally, the code is available at http://github.com/parklize/rdml.

2 Deep Mutual Learning

Before explaining DML, we introduce the common notations that are consistent throughout the paper. We denote the instance domain set as $\mathcal{X}$ and the ground truth domain set as $\mathcal{Y}$. Let us define the N-sized dataset by $\mathcal{D} = \{(x_n, y_n)\}_{1\leq n\leq N}$, where $x_n \in \mathcal{X}$ is the n-th observation and $y_n \in \mathcal{Y}$ is the corresponding ground truth, for all n. We also call an element $d \in \mathcal{D}$ a data point such that $d = (x, y)$. Additionally, we write $\mathbf{x} = \{x_n\}_{1\leq n\leq N}$ and $\mathbf{y} = \{y_n\}_{1\leq n\leq N}$. Let $D_\alpha(\cdot)$ denote the Rényi divergence parameterized with α. Moreover, we denote the indices of the students/models in the DML paradigm by $\mathbf{s} = \{1, \ldots, K\}$. Finally, let η_t denote the learning rate in the optimization techniques at time t.

A neural network can be considered a blackbox function that approximates a hard-to-define distribution. Let $\boldsymbol{\theta} \in \Theta \subseteq \mathbb{R}^h$ be the parameter set in the neural network. Apart from that, let us define the variables for the model by $\boldsymbol{\mu} = \{\mu_m\}_{1 \leq m \leq M}$ for each data x. Taking multiclass classification as an example, we follow Kingma and Welling [12] to formulate

$$\mathbb{P}_{\boldsymbol{\theta}} = \text{NeuralNet}(\text{x}; \boldsymbol{\theta}) \qquad \text{p}(\text{y}|\text{x}, \boldsymbol{\theta}) = \text{Categorical}(\text{y}; \mathbb{P}_{\boldsymbol{\theta}})$$

where $\mathbb{P}_{\boldsymbol{\theta}} = \{p(\mu|\text{x}, \boldsymbol{\theta}) : \mu \in \boldsymbol{\mu}\}$ and a SoftMax layer is applied to ensure $\sum_{\mu} p(\mu|\text{x}, \boldsymbol{\theta}) = 1$. We call $p(\mu|\cdot)$ the base model as it represents the applied neural network. Next, we will introduce the RDML framework before analyzing its properties.

2.1 Rényi Divergence Deep Mutual Learning

Imagine that there is a cohort of students learning a task together. The individual DML loss of each student k is denoted by $\mathcal{L}_k$. Specifically, $\mathcal{L}_k := \mathcal{L}_k^{base} + \mathcal{L}_k^{div}$ where $\mathcal{L}_k^{base}$ is the loss of the base model for the input data and ground truth, while $\mathcal{L}_k^{div}$ is the divergence loss from this student to others.

In general, the base loss $\mathcal{L}_k^{base}$ is selected depending on the task and the data. The base mode loss $\mathcal{L}_k^{base}$, considering $p(\boldsymbol{\mu}|\text{x}, \boldsymbol{\theta})$, forms an additive "negative log likelihood" alongside the observation $\mathbf{y}$. For instance, in a multiclass classification task containing M classes, the base loss is identical to the cross entropy loss, i.e.,

$$\mathcal{L}_k^{base} := -\frac{1}{N} \sum_n \sum_m \mathbb{1}(y_n = m) \log p_k(\mu_m | x_n, \boldsymbol{\theta}_k) \tag{1}$$

where $p_k(\mu_m|x_n, \boldsymbol{\theta}_k)$ denotes the probability of x_n belonging to class m with regard to model k and θ_k is the corresponding parameter set. We further denote its distribution by $\mathbb{P}_k(\boldsymbol{\mu}|x_n, \boldsymbol{\theta}_k)$. Importantly, we emphasize that $p_k(\boldsymbol{\mu}|\cdot)$ and $\boldsymbol{\theta}_k$ can be specified for different students, i.e., there can be different models and parameters among the students.

The divergence loss $\mathcal{L}_k^{div}$ depends on the approximated probabilities of the variables $\boldsymbol{\mu}$ for each student k. Instead of utilizing the KL divergence as in DML, we propose to employ the Rényi divergence, $D_\alpha(\cdot||\cdot)$, in RDML for this part. We obtain

$$\begin{aligned}\mathcal{L}_k^{div} &:= (1/|\mathbf{s}_{\neg k}|) \sum_{j \in \mathbf{s}_{\neg k}} D_\alpha[\mathbb{P}_j(\boldsymbol{\mu}|\mathbf{x}, \boldsymbol{\theta}_j)||\mathbb{P}_k(\boldsymbol{\mu}|\mathbf{x}, \boldsymbol{\theta}_k)] \\ &= \frac{1}{N(K-1)} \sum_{j \in \mathbf{s}_{\neg k}} \sum_n D_\alpha[\mathbb{P}_j(\boldsymbol{\mu}|x_n, \boldsymbol{\theta}_j)||\mathbb{P}_k(\boldsymbol{\mu}|x_n, \boldsymbol{\theta}_k)]\end{aligned} \tag{2}$$

where $\mathbf{s}_{\neg k} = \mathbf{s} \setminus \{k\}$ is the peer set of student k. The derivation detail of Eq. 2 is placed in the supplemental document (SD)[1]. It indicates that the model k will be calibrated by the other models. We again emphasize that this paradigm can be trivially extended to a diversity of machine learning tasks, as shown in DML [34]. In the sequel, we will discuss the Rényi divergence and its usage in RDML.

[1] The SD is available in the full version (https://arxiv.org/pdf/2209.05732.pdf).

Rényi Divergence. With a controlling parameter $\alpha \in [0,1) \cup (1,\infty)$, the divergence is a statistical distance quantity which measures the distance from distribution $\mathbb{Q}$ to $\mathbb{P}$, defined by

$$D_\alpha(\mathbb{P}||\mathbb{Q}) = \frac{1}{\alpha - 1} \log \int p(\mu)^\alpha q(\mu)^{1-\alpha} d\mu \,. \tag{3}$$

Same as the KL divergence, the Rényi divergence is asymmetric and hence generally not a metric [6]. It is worth noting that the Rényi divergence covers a family of statistical distances. For instance, $\alpha = 0.5$ leads the Rényi divergence to the squared Hellinger divergence and $\alpha \to 1$ leads to the KL divergence, etc. [14]. Therefore, the vanilla DML with the KL divergence can be seen as a special case of RDML. Furthermore, the following essential remarks have been proved [6].

Remark 1. For any distribution $\mathbb{P}$, $\mathbb{Q}$, and $\alpha \in [0,1) \cup (1,\infty)$, the Rényi divergence $D_\alpha(\mathbb{P}||\mathbb{Q}) \geq 0$. The equality holds if and only if $\mathbb{P}$ is identical to $\mathbb{Q}$.

Remark 2. For any distribution $\mathbb{P}$, $\mathbb{Q}$, and $\alpha \in [0,1) \cup (1,\infty)$, the Rényi divergence $D_\alpha(\mathbb{P}||\mathbb{Q})$ is nondecreasing in α.

The first remark fixes the lower bound of the divergence and ensures $\mathcal{L}_k^{div}$ to be nonnegative, which is always a desired property for the loss function. Remark 2 implies that α influences the distance value scope when $\mathbb{P}$ and $\mathbb{Q}$ are fixed. In the context of RDML, a larger α value hence pushes the students to learn more from their peers considering that the gradients for updating the parameters become numerically larger.

Figure 1 illustrates an example of the $D_\alpha(\mathbb{P}||\mathbb{Q})$ for various α with fixed $\mathbb{P}$ and $\mathbb{Q}$, respectively. In the example, Rényi divergence with $\alpha \to 1$ is equivalent to the KL divergence. We observe that the correlation between $D_\alpha(\mathbb{P}||\mathbb{Q})$ and α embodies Remark 2. On the other hand, the case focusing on $D_\alpha(\mathbb{P}||\mathbb{Q})$ with fixed $\mathbb{P}$, spans a much broader range. The divergence is more sensitive for $\mathbb{P} \neq \mathbb{Q}$ in this scenario with sufficiently large α. That said, the gap between $\alpha = 10$ and

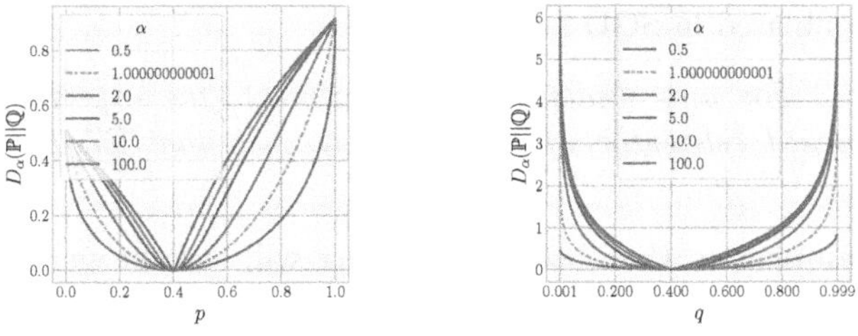

Fig. 1. Example plots of Rényi divergence for distributions containing two events. The orange dashed line represents the KL divergence in both plots. The first plot fixes distribution $\mathbb{Q}$ to $(0.4, 0.6)$ and shows the divergence change over p and $1-p$. The second plot fixes $\mathbb{P} = (0.4, 0.6)$ and shows the divergence change over q and $1-q$. Note that when $q = 0$ or $q = 1$, the divergence value is ∞ for any $\alpha \in [0,1) \cup (1,\infty)$. As infinity is not graphable, the x-axis in the second plot ranges from 0.001 to 0.999. (Color figure online)

Initialize $\boldsymbol{\theta}_{1,1}, \ldots, \boldsymbol{\theta}_{K,1}$
for $t = 1, \ldots$ **do**
  for $k = 1, \ldots, K$ **do**
    Sample a data point d from $\mathcal{D}$ and a peer j from $\mathbf{s}_{\neg k}$ uniformly
    $\boldsymbol{\theta}_{k,t+1} \leftarrow \boldsymbol{\theta}_{k,t} - \eta_t \nabla \mathcal{L}_k(d, j, \boldsymbol{\theta}_{k,t})$

Algorithm 1: SGD FOR (R)DML

$\alpha = 100$ is smaller, indicating that the divergence growth will become slower as α increases. These observations imply that α introduces the flexibility of controlling the degree to which students learn from others in RDML. In this study, we consider α as a hyperparameter that can be determined through grid-search using a validation set. While automatically tuning α would be ideal, a preliminary test in which α was treated as a learnable parameter based on the training data did not yield improved performance. We leave the exploration of automatic α tuning to future work.

3 Properties of RDML

In this section, we will elaborate on the convergence properties of RDML. Additionally, we will examine the computational complexity of the paradigm. We leave all the detailed proof in the SD.

Let us denote the parameter for student k at time t, by $\boldsymbol{\theta}_{k,t}$. To apply SGD, we write $\mathcal{L}_k(d, j, \boldsymbol{\theta}_{k,t})$ the loss function parameterized with a random data point $d \in \mathcal{D}$, a peer $j \in \mathbf{s}_{\neg k}$, and the current parameter $\boldsymbol{\theta}_{k,t}$. Following that, Algorithm1 sketches the SGD procedure. The algorithm iterates through each student and optimizes the parameters upon the corresponding DML loss. At each single iteration, for a student k, we uniformly sample a data point d from $\mathcal{D}$ and a peer j from its peers $\mathbf{s}_{\neg k}$.

Furthermore, we denote $\mathcal{L}_k(\boldsymbol{\theta}_{k,t})$ as the loss that takes the entire dataset and peers as input. Let $\mathbb{E}_{d,j}[\cdot]$ be abbreviated to $\mathbb{E}[\cdot]$. We claim that the expected gradients are unbiased in SGD for RDML.

Proposition 1. *For any student k at any time t, the expected gradient for $\mathcal{L}_k$ is an unbiased estimator of the gradient, such that $\mathbb{E}[\nabla \mathcal{L}_k(d, j, \boldsymbol{\theta}_{k,t})] = \nabla \mathcal{L}_k(\boldsymbol{\theta}_{k,t}), \forall k$.*

However, we emphasize that bias for learning will still be generated at each iteration as the objectives are time-varying.

3.1 Convergence Guarantee

This section analyzes the convergence properties of RDML using SGD. Our theoretical statements are presented here, while all the proofs are provided in the SD. Motivated by the fact that the majority of neural networks are highly nonconvex, we focus on the convergence guarantee for the nonconvex setting. We follow the work of [3,9] to state the following assumption for Lipschitz continuity in the probabilistic models, which is crucial for conducting further convergence analysis.

Assumption 1. *There exists a constant $L > 0$. Given any student k, its base model $\mathbb{P}_k(\mu|x, \boldsymbol{\theta})$ is L-Lipschitz continuous in $\boldsymbol{\theta}$, such that $\forall \boldsymbol{\theta}, \boldsymbol{\theta}' \in \Theta$,*

$$|p_k(\mu|x, \boldsymbol{\theta}) - p_k(\mu|x, \boldsymbol{\theta}')| \leq L\|\boldsymbol{\theta} - \boldsymbol{\theta}'\|$$

for every realization of μ. Note that a function is usually not L-Lipschitz continuous on the unbounded domain. Therefore, we further assume that there exists some $\tau \in (0, 1)$ satisfying $\forall \mu, x, \boldsymbol{\theta} : p_k(\mu|x, \boldsymbol{\theta}) \geq \tau$ throughout the entire learning process.

In addition, the base models satisfy the H-smoothness in $\boldsymbol{\theta}$, such that

$$\forall \boldsymbol{\theta}, \boldsymbol{\theta}' \in \Theta : \quad \|\nabla p_k(\mu|x, \boldsymbol{\theta}) - \nabla p_k(\mu|x, \boldsymbol{\theta}')\| \leq H\|\boldsymbol{\theta} - \boldsymbol{\theta}'\|,$$

for every realization[2] of k, d, μ.

Assumption 2. *For any student k and data point $d \in \mathcal{D}$, the base loss $\mathcal{L}_k^{bass}(d, \boldsymbol{\theta})$ taking d and $\boldsymbol{\theta}$ as input, is differentiable and V-smooth in $\boldsymbol{\theta}$ on the bounded domain, i.e.,*

$$\forall \boldsymbol{\theta}, \boldsymbol{\theta}' \in \Theta : \quad \|\nabla \mathcal{L}_k^{bass}(d, \boldsymbol{\theta}) - \nabla \mathcal{L}_k^{bass}(d, \boldsymbol{\theta}')\| \leq V\|\boldsymbol{\theta} - \boldsymbol{\theta}'\|.$$

Given the assumptions, we can set up the property of smoothness for each individual loss $\mathcal{L}_k$. Smoothness is the most fundamental condition which the convergence analysis of the nonconvex optimization should satisfy [17].

Theorem 1. *Let $W = V + |\alpha - 1|\varphi^2 + \alpha L^2 + \tau H$ where $\varphi = \min\left\{\tau^{-1}, M/(\tau e^{(M-1)\tau})^\alpha\right\} L$. Suppose Assumptions 2 and 1 satisfy, the loss $\mathcal{L}_k$ for every student k is W-smooth in its parameter $\boldsymbol{\theta}_k$ provided that $\boldsymbol{\theta}_j$ is fixed for all $j \in \mathbf{s}_{\neg k}$.*

Theorem 1 enables us to apply the standard convergence analysis to this paradigm. Now, we introduce another common assumption (Assumptions 3) for the convergence analysis of nonconvex problems.

Assumption 3. *For every student k and time t, $\mathbb{E}[\|\nabla \mathcal{L}_k^{base}(d, \boldsymbol{\theta}_{k,t})\|^2] \leq \tilde{\sigma}^2$.*

This is a general assumption in nonconvex convergence analysis, but implies the following lemma bounding the noise for the whole RDML objectives along with that each $p(\cdot) \geq \tau$ in Assumptions 2.

Lemma 1. *Based on Assumptions 2 and 3, $\mathbb{E}[\|\nabla \mathcal{L}_k(d, j, \boldsymbol{\theta}_{k,t})\|^2] \leq \sigma^2$ for every realization of k and t, where $\sigma^2 = 2\tilde{\sigma}^2 + 2\varphi^2$.*

[2] Following [18], we use this term *realization* to refer to an instance of variable in the valid domain.

Next, we will show the worst case convergence of the expected gradient norm. However, we defer the discussion of *conditional* convergence in $\mathcal{O}(1/\sqrt{T})$ in the average case with a constant learning rate of $o(1/\sqrt{T})$ to the SD. It is difficult to determine whether this condition, which leads to a unbiased convergence, can be satisfied without further information. Thus, we claim our formal convergence result only for the worst case scenario.

Theorem 2. *Let $\mathcal{L}_{k,*}^{base}$ be the global minima of $\mathcal{L}_k^{base}$. Under Assumptions 1 and 2 3, by selecting a constant learning rate $\eta_t = \frac{\eta}{\sqrt{T}} \leq \frac{1}{W\sqrt{T}}$ that depends on the total iteration T, $\mathbb{E}[\min_t \|\nabla \mathcal{L}_k(\boldsymbol{\theta}_{k,t})\|^2]$ is bounded by*

$$\mathcal{O}\left(\frac{2(\mathcal{L}_{k,1}^{base} - \mathcal{L}_{k,*}^{base})}{\eta\sqrt{T}} + \frac{\sigma^2}{\sqrt{T}} + 2\max(\varphi\tilde{\sigma}, \varphi^2)\right) = \mathcal{O}\left(\frac{1}{\sqrt{T}}\right) + \mathcal{O}(1)$$

for any student k in the worst case scenario.

Unlike the conventional analysis of the biased gradient estimators for SGD, in which the bias accompanies the gradients [1,10], the bias in RDML is introduced by the time-varying objectives of RDML. The gradients of all students will receive less impact from the base model as time progresses, but will still keep learning from the peers. One can imagine that the K parameters arrive at certain local optima, but still attempt to "move closer" to the peers with a reasonable pace. This might in practice help some models escape to wider local optima.

3.2 Computational Complexity of RDML

We denote the time complexity for each student k at a single iteration as $\mathcal{O}(B_k)$. Also, the time cost of the Rényi divergence between $\mathbb{P}_k(\boldsymbol{\mu}|\cdot)$ and $\mathbb{P}_j(\boldsymbol{\mu}|\cdot)$, for any student j and k, depends linearly on the size of $\boldsymbol{\mu}$, which is $\mathcal{O}(M)$ ignoring the complexity of the log and power function, etc. For a single loop, the time cost is $\mathcal{O}(\sum_k(B_k + M)) = \mathcal{O}(\sum_k B_k + MK)$, since each student samples only one peer to learn from in the loop. Considering that the S_k is the size for each model k, the space complexity is trivially $\mathcal{O}(\sum_k S_k)$.

4 Empirical Study

Our empirical study aims to investigate whether RDML can enhance model performance beyond that of the independent model and vanilla DML. Thus, we minimize the effort for tuning the models and instead adopt certain general settings. In summary, our study focuses on the following research questions.

1. How does the algorithm converge? (Sect. 4.2)
2. How does RDML perform compared to vanilla DML and the single model on its own? (Sect. 4.3)
3. Does RDML generalize better? (Sect. 4.4)

4.1 Experimental Setup

This study centers on datasets from two prominent fields: Computer Vision (CV) and Natural Language Processing (NLP). The CV data contains `CIFAR10` and `CIFAR100` [13] with a resolution of 32×32. We conducted experiments on `DTD` [4] and `Flowers102` [19] with a resolution of 224×224. The NLP data for text classification task contains `AGNews`, `Yahoo!Answers`, and `YelpReviewFull`. All data is handled through either **torchvision** or **torchtext**.[3]

Regarding `CIFAR10` and `CIFAR100`, we applied SGD with Nesterov momentum of 0.9. The initial learning rate was set to 0.1, and the weight decay was set to 0.0005. A total of 200 epochs were run with a batch size of 128, and the learning rate dropped by 0.2 every 60th epoch. The architectures used are GoogLeNet [28], ResNet34 [8], and VGG16 [25]. For `DTD` and `Flowers192`, we set the learning rate to 0.005 and the weight decay to 0.0001 using SGD with momentum of 0.9. We ran 30 epochs with a batch size of 32 and decay the learning rate by 0.1 at epochs $(16, 22)$. In addition, the gradients were clipped by the max norm of 5. For these two datasets, **timm** were used to acquire the pretrained weights for the models: InceptionV4 [27], ViT [30], and YoloV3 [23].

For text classification, we evaluated the performance of fastText [11] with GloVe [21] (pretrained word embeddings) and CharCNN [33] using a public implementation. We used the default settings of the implementation with an initial learning rate of 0.5 and set the weight decay to 0.5 for fastText. Then, 100 epochs were run, in which the learning rate was decayed every three epochs with a batch size of 16. For CharCNN, we set an initial learning rate of 0.0001 and set the weight decay to 0.9 for the experiments for `Yahoo!Answers` and `YelpReviewFull`. For all other experiments, we set the weight decay to 0.5 and uses the default settings of the implementation, including an initial learning rate of 0.001. Finally, we ran 20 epochs and decayed the learning rate every three epochs with a batch size of 128. Even though a larger K value is preferred for potentially achieving better results, we followed [34] to set $K = 2$, which suffices to improve model performance in this study

4.2 Convergence Trace Analysis

We conducted a convergence analysis using the training loss trace plots depicted in Fig. 2. First, the base losses keep decreasing overall, while the divergence losses are not guaranteed to vanish but remain bounded. This finding indirectly supports Theorem 2, which suggests that the influence of the base loss on the gradients will reduce, but the bias introduced by the divergence loss may persist. Secondly, we observe that the base losses can obtain lower numeric values with smaller α in the same time window. Simultaneously, the divergence losses are tied to a higher level with a larger α value as it forces a greater learning power within the Rényi divergence. Under the selected configurations, a larger value of α results in a greater coefficient in the big-O notation of $\mathcal{O}(1/\sqrt{T})$, causing

[3] The required public resources of software and model are available in the SD.

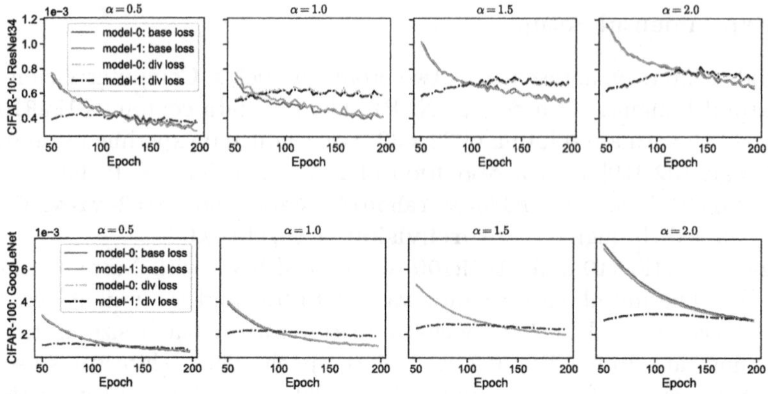

Fig. 2. Plot of training loss for selected configurations, starting from the 50th epoch. The base loss and divergence loss are shown separately, with values presented for every third epoch.

the error to decrease at a slower pace. Finally, we note that for $\alpha = 0.5$, the divergence losses for the two students are identical. This is because the Rényi divergence is symmetric with $\alpha = 0.5$ [6], i.e., $D_{0.5}(P||Q) = D_{0.5}(Q||P)$ for any P and Q, indicating that the divergence losses under this two-student configuration are strictly equal.

4.3 Evaluation Results

Image Classification. The training set and test set are split automatically through **torchvision**. As for classification, we employ the top-1 accuracy to examine the model performance. The experiments were run upon a range of configurations, including the independent case and $\alpha \in \{0.5, 1, 1.5, 2\}$. The results for `CIFAR10` and `CIFAR100` are presented in Table 1, while those for `DTD` and `Flowers102` are displayed in Table 2. The indices of model are sorted by their respective values, and we label the best performer in each column using boldface.

The results of `CIFAR10` show that for GoogLeNet and ResNet34, RDML with $\alpha = 1.5$ performs the best, while vanilla DML obtains the best accuracy with VGG16. In the experiments for `CIFAR100`, the three selected architectures achieve the best outcomes with $\alpha = 2$ in most cases. Observed from the results, RDML under certain configuration always outperforms the independent case. It shows that tuning α is helpful in learning better model parameters. Regarding `DTD`, $\alpha = 2$ and $\alpha = 1.5$ are still the best options for the selected architectures. Same as DML, RDML also perfectly collaborates with the pretrained models which are agreed to be more powerful in modern DL tasks [5]. Also, we notice that the improvements over the independent model are greater with these models. The effectiveness of tuning α is further confirmed by the results of `Flowers102` in Table 2. For the three models (InceptionV4, ViT, and YoloV3), the best performance is achieved with RDML when $\alpha = 0.5, 2.0$, and 1.5, respectively. For instance, ViT

Table 1. The top-1 accuracy (%) results are presented for `CIFAR10` and `CIFAR100`. To ensure a stable outcome, we bootstrap and average the accuracy of the test set over the last 10 epochs. The models are listed in ascending order based on their values. In the table, GoogLeNet, ResNet34, and VGG16 are abbreviations for GN, RN, and VG, respectively. The model index starts from 0 and is indicated as a subscript. RDML_a indicates that α is set as a. The independent case (Ind.) has only one result. The bootstrapped standard deviation is presented.

	Dataset: `CIFAR10`					
	GN_0	GN_1	RN_0	RN_1	VG_0	VG_1
Ind.		91.87 ± .14		92.56 ± .17		90.71 ± .09
$\text{RDML}_{0.5}$	91.91 ± .11	92.06 ± .13	92.86 ± .07	93.03 ± .07	91.03 ± .05	91.26 ± .10
DML	92.28 ± .13	92.37 ± .16	93.27 ± .08	93.34 ± .07	91.22 ± .11	91.33 ± .07
$\text{RDML}_{1.5}$	92.61 ± .11	92.62 ± .03	93.28 ± .06	93.35 ± .11	91.18 ± .11	91.29 ± .08
$\text{RDML}_{2.0}$	92.26 ± .14	92.28 ± .12	93.18 ± .07	93.19 ± .08	91.17 ± .10	91.23 ± .07

	Dataset: `CIFAR100`					
	GN_0	GN_1	RN_0	RN_1	VG_0	VG_1
Ind.		69.60 ± .19		76.26 ± .03		72.21 ± .03
$\text{RDML}_{0.5}$	70.22 ± .16	70.24 ± .17	76.71 ± .05	77.14 ± .02	72.09 ± .04	72.53 ± .05
DML	72.34 ± .13	72.49 ± .18	77.14 ± .03	77.24 ± .03	73.01 ± .05	73.17 ± .04
$\text{RDML}_{1.5}$	71.65 ± .13	72.1 ± .07	77.61 ± .03	77.94 ± .02	73.32 ± .05	73.6 ± .06
$\text{RDML}_{2.0}$	72.13 ± .10	72.27 ± .16	78.31 ± .04	78.5 ± .02	73.3 ± .06	73.74 ± .03

Table 2. The top-1 accuracy (%) results for `DTD` and `Flowers102` are presented. The accuracy results of the last 5 epochs in the test set are bootstrapped and averaged. In the table, IV4 and YV3 are abbreviations for InceptionV4 and YoloV3, respectively. The independent model is denoted as Ind., and the subscript of RDML is α. The same models are reindexed by their values in ascending order. The bootstrapped standard deviation is presented.

	Dataset: `DTD`					
	$IV4_0$	$IV4_1$	ViT_0	ViT_1	$YV3_0$	$YV3_1$
Ind		64.66 ± .20		72.52 ± .06		68.95 ± .06
$\text{RDML}_{0.5}$	61.63 ± .13	64.93 ± .10	72.73 ± .02	73.87 ± .04	66.07 ± .06	67.02 ± .03
DML	65.87 ± .19	66.20 ± .09	74.38 ± .02	75.05 ± .04	69.93 ± .07	70.24 ± .09
$\text{RDML}_{1.5}$	67.57 ± .08	67.67 ± .13	75.86 ± .04	75.94 ± .04	70.91 ± .10	71.72 ± .07
$\text{RDML}_{2.0}$	67.86 ± .16	68.97 ± .10	75.37 ± .05	76.04 ± .02	71.17 ± .08	71.26 ± .09

	Dataset: `Flowers102`					
	$IV4_0$	$IV4_1$	ViT_0	ViT_1	$YV3_0$	$YV3_1$
Ind		88.32 ± .12		98.15 ± .00		90.67 ± .03
$\text{RDML}_{0.5}$	88.01 ± .12	89.39 ± .10	98.19 ± .00	98.52 ± .01	90.66 ± .02	90.68 ± .01
DML	87.92 ± .10	88.46 ± .08	98.53 ± .01	98.73 ± .01	90.98 ± .03	91.04 ± .03
$\text{RDML}_{1.5}$	88.27 ± .06	88.89 ± .11	98.73 ± .01	98.91 ± .00	91.29 ± .03	91.37 ± .03
$\text{RDML}_{2.0}$	87.98 ± .06	88.13 ± .07	98.95 ± .00	99.02 ± .00	90.56 ± .03	90.79 ± .02

Table 3. The results for Top-1 accuracy (%) on the test sets of `AGNews`, `Yahoo!Answers`, and `YelpReviewFull`. The best performing α of RDML is selected based on the mean accuracy of K models on each validation set.

Dataset	fastText				CharCNN			
	Ind.	fastText_0	fastText_1	α	Ind.	CharCNN_0	CharCNN_1	α
`AGNews`	89.72	89.76	89.76	2.0	87.13	89.63	89.17	1.5
`Yahoo!Answers`	65.65	65.65	65.65	0.5	63.54	64.54	64.51	2.0
`YelpReviewFull`	54.26	54.31	54.31	1.5	55.01	55.36	55.58	1.5

with $\text{RDML}_{2.0}$ achieves a top-1 accuracy of 99.02% which outperforms independent model (98.15%) and vanilla DML (98.73%).

Text Classification. The evaluation adopts top-1 accuracy, which is the same as that used for image classification. We demonstrate that α can be tuned as a hyperparameter using a grid search on a validation set. To this end, we chose α based on a grid search $\in \{0.5, 1, 1.5, 2\}$ using a validation set that makes up 20% of the training set, and investigate the best performing α values and the corresponding performance on the test set. Table 3 presents the values of α that yield the highest average accuracy on the test set. Regularization via RDML

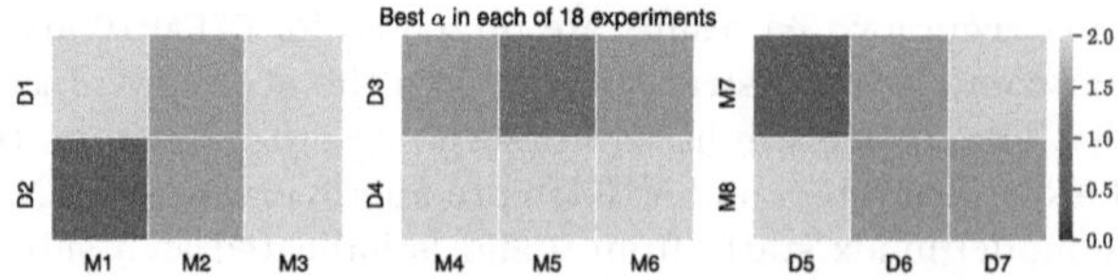

Fig. 3. Heatmap depicting the optimal α values obtained from 18 experiments, each corresponding to a distinct pairing of a model M and a dataset D. The figure highlights the variability in α requirements for achieving superior performance when using different datasets with the same method (and vice versa).

was shown to be more beneficial for the larger models in regard to improving the performance over a single model, e.g., CharCNN (with ~2M parameters) versus fastText (with ~3K parameters).

Summary. Observing the experiments, it is evident that RDML is able to improve on vanilla DML and independent models in most cases. This covers a broad collection of network architectures and datasets. The best performing value of α varies depending on the situation as illustrated in Fig. 3. In our experiments, we found that RDML was more effective at coping with underperforming configurations, such as using a less well-defined model or a set of unoptimized hyperparameters. This is reasonable because a perfect configuration for a moderate task suffices to obtain maximum performance.

4.4 Generalization Results

Here, we examine the generalization ability of RDML regarding the choice of α. We focus on the test performance of `CIFAR100` and `Flowers102`, while the other results are included in the SD.

To begin, Fig. 4 illustrates the evaluation of the base loss on the test data using the `CIFAR100` dataset. It is widely acknowledged in the machine learning community that, beyond a certain point, while the training loss can be continuously reduced, the test loss will typically start to increase. As demonstrated in Fig. 4, the test loss of a single model (either GoogLeNet, ResNet34, or VGG16) replicates this agreement. However, RDML is able to constrain this growth tendency of test loss for all students. Also, the capability of preventing this increase gets enhanced as α becomes larger, i.e., setting a prior with smaller variance. Moreover, we observe that RDML with larger α significantly reduces the fluctuations in the test loss, i.e., the variance is being reduced for the test loss (though it still maintains a reasonable amount of uncertainty). It depicts that $\alpha = 2$ for GoogLeNet over-regularizes the model and thus performs slightly worse than that with $\alpha = 1.5$. In the classification problem, the test base loss approximates the negative likelihood of the unseen data which can be optimized via RDML. The results suggest that RDML is able to acquire better generalizations through tuning the parameter α.

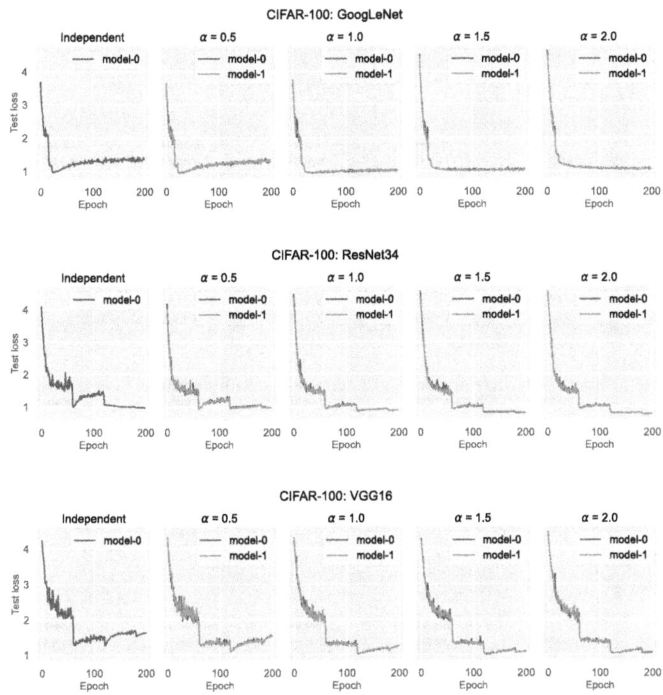

Fig. 4. Test loss of RDML for various α on the `CIFAR100` dataset.

Similar patterns are observed while checking the test accuracy in Fig. 5. In regard to ResNet34, starting from epoch 60, the single model boosts its accuracy since the learning rate is decayed, but rapidly encounters a decrease in accuracy. However, RDML can significantly mitigate the performance decrease and achieve the best outcome when $\alpha = 2$ within the range of our choices. Correspondingly, the results for ResNet34 in Fig. 4 show a loss increase during the same period. As shown, RDML can limit this loss increasing speed and can limit harder with a greater value of α.

Figure 6 exhibits the results of test accuracy on the `Flowers102` dataset with the three selected models. For InceptionV4 and YoloV, the test accuracy of each model increases as the model is trained for more epochs. Regarding ViT, we can observe that the test accuracy of the independent model tends to fluctuate in the first 15 epochs during training. In contrast, we also notice that the accuracy curves become less fluctuating using RDML with larger α values, which again shows the flexibility of tuning α in RDML for better generalization.

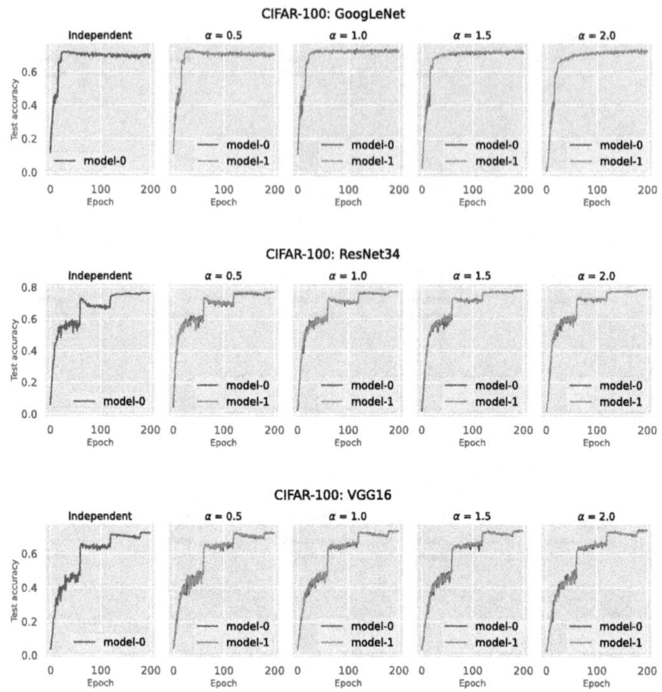

Fig. 5. Test accuracy of RDML for various α on the `CIFAR100` dataset.

5 Related Work

DML is a knowledge distillation scheme that transfers knowledge from from one or more deep neural networks to a designated one. Unlike offline distillation, where knowledge is transferred from a pretrained model, DML allows multiple neural networks to collaborate and transfer knowledge during training, providing flexibility to train different or the same networks [7]. Due to its effectiveness, DML has been used in various contexts and applications, such as tracking visual objects [35], machine translation [36], speech recognition [15], and COVID-19 recognition [32]. Recently, Yang et al. [31] proposed training a cohort of sub-(convolutional) networks with different configurations of network widths and input resolutions via DML to achieve accuracy-efficiency tradeoffs. Park et al. [20] applied DML to deep metric learning beyond classification tasks and demonstrated its effectiveness over individual models. However, to the best of our knowledge, there is no theoretical analysis of convergence in DML available.

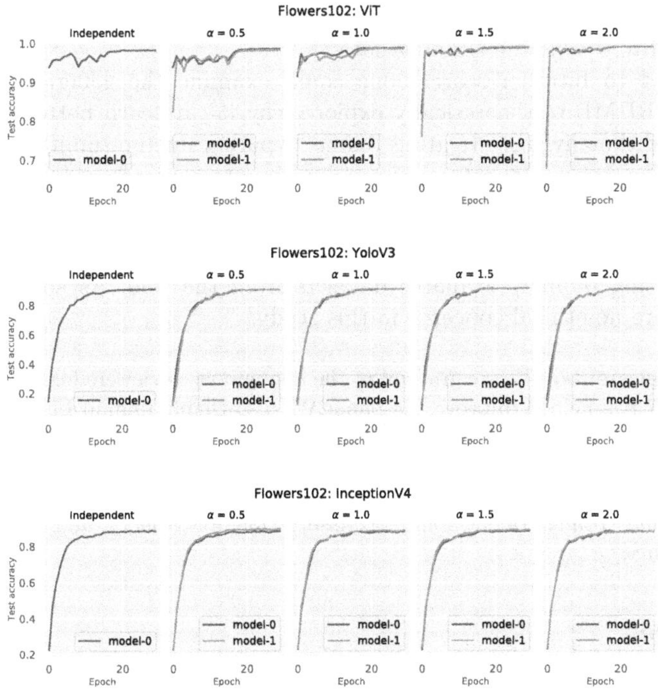

Fig. 6. Test accuracy of RDML for various α on the `Flowers102` dataset.

The Rényi divergence [6] has garnered increasing interest and has been utilized in a variety of applications. For instance, it has been proposed to replace the KL divergence in variational inference [14]. Examples show that the Rényi divergence can control the regularization power of the inferred variational distribution. Several related applications in cryptography [2,22] also exist, as the Rényi divergence deliver tighter security bounds. In addition, it has been widely used as a powerful tool to analyze differential privacy [16,29] and has been utilized in the examination of human brain behaviors [24]. All of these illustrate the potential of this divergence in a broad range of tasks.

6 Conclusion

In this paper, we have revisited DML and proposed a revised paradigm, namely RDML. Our motivation stems from the enhanced flexibility offered by Rényi divergence, compared to the KL divergence used in DML. The empirical results support our findings and demonstrate that RDML has greater capacity than DML to improve model performance. Moreover, we theoretically proved the convergence guarantee of the paradigm, showing that the learning procedure will converge with a bounded bias. This might help the learned parameters escape from a narrow optimum to a wider one in practice, particularly in cases where models tend to overfit the training data.

In regard to future research, one could examine the generalization error bounds for RDML to theoretically explore why it can learn better generalized models. Additionally, investigating online hyperparameter tuning for the controlling parameter α is another potential avenue to explore.

Ethical Statement. This paper investigates a Deep Learning optimization paradigm using publicly available datasets from the web. As such, we assert that there are no ethical concerns in this study.

Acknowledgements. We are grateful to the anonymous reviewers for their insightful feedback that has helped improve the paper.We also thank Jinghui Lu for guiding us toward this intriguing topic.

Junjie Tao and Ming Fan were supported by National Key R&D Program of China (2022YFB2703500), National Natural Science Foundation of China (62232014, 62272377), and Young Talent Fund of Association for Science and Technology in Shaanxi, China.

References

1. Ajalloeian, A., Stich, S.U.: Analysis of SGD with biased gradient estimators. In: Workshop on "Beyond First Order Methods in ML System" (2020)
2. Bai, S., Lepoint, T., Roux-Langlois, A., Sakzad, A., Stehlé, D., Steinfeld, R.: Improved security proofs in lattice-based cryptography: using the rényi divergence rather than the statistical distance. J. Cryptol. **31**(2), 610–640 (2018)
3. Cheng, X., Bartlett, P.: Convergence of Langevin MCMC in KL-divergence. In: Algorithmic Learning Theory, pp. 186–211. PMLR (2018)
4. Cimpoi, M., Maji, S., Kokkinos, I., Mohamed, S., Vedaldi, A.: Describing textures in the wild. In: CVPR (2014)
5. Erhan, D., Courville, A., Bengio, Y., Vincent, P.: Why does unsupervised pre-training help deep learning? In: JMLR, pp. 201–208 (2010)
6. Erven, T.V., Harrëmos, P.: Rényi divergence and Kullback-Leibler divergence. IEEE Trans. Inf. Theory **60**, 3797–3820 (2014). https://doi.org/10.1109/TIT.2014.2320500
7. Gou, J., Yu, B., Maybank, S.J., Tao, D.: Knowledge distillation: a survey. Int. J. Comput. Vision **129**(6), 1789–1819 (2021)
8. He, K., Zhang, X., Ren, S., Sun, J.: Deep residual learning for image recognition. In: CVPR, pp. 770–778 (2016)
9. Honorio, J.: Lipschitz parametrization of probabilistic graphical models. In: Proceedings of the Twenty-Seventh Conference on Uncertainty in Artificial Intelligence, UAI 2011, pp. 347–354. AUAI Press, Arlington (2011)
10. Hu, B., Seiler, P., Lessard, L.: Analysis of biased stochastic gradient descent using sequential semidefinite programs. Math. Program. **187**, 383–408 (2021)
11. Joulin, A., Grave, E., Bojanowski, P., Mikolov, T.: Bag of tricks for efficient text classification. arXiv preprint arXiv:1607.01759 (2016)
12. Kingma, D.P., Welling, M.: An introduction to variational autoencoders. Found. Trends® Mach. Learn. **12**(4), 307–392 (2019)

13. Krizhevsky, A., Hinton, G.: Learning multiple layers of features from tiny images (2009)
14. Li, Y., Turner, R.E.: Rényi divergence variational inference. In: NeurIPS, vol. 29 (2016)
15. Masumura, R., Ihori, M., Takashima, A., Tanaka, T., Ashihara, T.: End-to-end automatic speech recognition with deep mutual learning. In: APSIPA ASC, pp. 632–637. IEEE (2020)
16. Mironov, I.: Rényi differential privacy. In: 2017 IEEE 30th Computer Security Foundations Symposium (CSF), pp. 263–275. IEEE (2017)
17. Nesterov, Y.: Introductory Lectures on Convex Optimization: A Basic Course, vol. 87. Springer, Heidelberg (2003). https://doi.org/10.1007/978-1-4419-8853-9
18. Nguyen, L., Nguyen, P.H., Dijk, M., Richtárik, P., Scheinberg, K., Takác, M.: Sgd and hogwild! convergence without the bounded gradients assumption. In: International Conference on Machine Learning, pp. 3750–3758. PMLR (2018)
19. Nilsback, M.E., Zisserman, A.: Automated flower classification over a large number of classes. In: Proceedings of the Indian Conference on Computer Vision, Graphics and Image Processing (2008)
20. Park, W., Kim, W., You, K., Cho, M.: Diversified mutual learning for deep metric learning. In: Bartoli, A., Fusiello, A. (eds.) ECCV 2020. LNCS, vol. 12535, pp. 709–725. Springer, Cham (2020). https://doi.org/10.1007/978-3-030-66415-2_49
21. Pennington, J., Socher, R., Manning, C.D.: GloVe: global vectors for word representation. In: EMNLP, pp. 1532–1543 (2014)
22. Prest, T.: Sharper bounds in lattice-based cryptography using the Rényi divergence. In: International Conference on the Theory and Application of Cryptology and Information Security, pp. 347–374 (2017)
23. Redmon, J., Farhadi, A.: Yolov3: an incremental improvement. arXiv preprint arXiv:1804.02767 (2018)
24. Sajid, N., Faccio, F., Da Costa, L., Parr, T., Schmidhuber, J., Friston, K.: Bayesian brains and the Rényi divergence. Neural Comput. **34**(4), 829–855 (2022). https://doi.org/10.1162/neco_01484
25. Simonyan, K., Zisserman, A.: Very deep convolutional networks for large-scale image recognition. In: ICLR (2015)
26. Srivastava, N., Hinton, G., Krizhevsky, A., Sutskever, I., Salakhutdinov, R.: Dropout: a simple way to prevent neural networks from overfitting. JMLR **15**(56), 1929–1958 (2014)
27. Szegedy, C., Ioffe, S., Vanhoucke, V., Alemi, A.A.: Inception-v4, inception-resnet and the impact of residual connections on learning. In: AAAI (2017)
28. Szegedy, C., et al.: Going Deeper with Convolutions, 10. arXiv preprint arXiv:1409.4842 (2014)
29. Wang, Y.X., Balle, B., Kasiviswanathan, S.P.: Subsampled Rényi differential privacy and analytical moments accountant. In: The 22nd International Conference on Artificial Intelligence and Statistics, pp. 1226–1235. PMLR (2019)
30. Wu, B., et al.: Visual transformers: token-based image representation and processing for computer vision. arXiv preprint arXiv:2006.03677 (2020)
31. Yang, T., Zhu, S., Chen, C., Yan, S., Zhang, M., Willis, A.: MutualNet: adaptive ConvNet via mutual learning from network width and resolution. In: Vedaldi, A., Bischof, H., Brox, T., Frahm, J.-M. (eds.) ECCV 2020. LNCS, vol. 12346, pp. 299–315. Springer, Cham (2020). https://doi.org/10.1007/978-3-030-58452-8_18
32. Zhang, H., et al.: DCML: deep contrastive mutual learning for COVID-19 recognition. Biomed. Signal Process. Control **77**, 103770 (2022)

33. Zhang, X., Zhao, J., LeCun, Y.: Character-level convolutional networks for text classification. In: NeurIPS, vol. 28 (2015)
34. Zhang, Y., Xiang, T., Hospedales, T.M., Lu, H.: Deep mutual learning. In: CVPR, pp. 4320–4328 (2018)
35. Zhao, H., Yang, G., Wang, D., Lu, H.: Deep mutual learning for visual object tracking. Pattern Recogn. **112**, 107796 (2021)
36. Zhao, J., Luo, W., Chen, B., Gilman, A.: Mutual-learning improves end-to-end speech translation. In: EMNLP, pp. 3989–3994 (2021)

Is My Neural Net Driven by the MDL Principle?

Eduardo Brandao[1(✉)], Stefan Duffner[2], Rémi Emonet[1], Amaury Habrard[1,3], François Jacquenet[1], and Marc Sebban[1]

[1] Université Jean Monnet Saint-Etienne, CNRS, Institut d Optique Graduate School, Laboratoire Hubert Curien UMR 5516, 42023 Saint-Etienne, France
Eduardo.Brandao@univ-st-etienne.fr

[2] CNRS, INSA-Lyon, LIRIS, UMR5205, Université de Lyon, 69621 Villeurbanne, France
Stefan.Duffner@liris.cnrs.fr

[3] Institut Universitaire de France (IUF), Paris, France

Abstract. The Minimum Description Length principle (MDL) is a formalization of Occam's razor for model selection, which states that a good model is one that can losslessly compress the data while including the cost of describing the model itself. While MDL can naturally express the behavior of certain models such as autoencoders (that inherently compress data) most representation learning techniques do not rely on such models. Instead, they learn representations by training on general or, for self-supervised learning, pretext tasks. In this paper, we propose a new formulation of the MDL principle that relies on the concept of signal and noise, which are implicitly defined by the learning task at hand. Additionally, we introduce ways to empirically measure the complexity of the learned representations by analyzing the spectra of the point Jacobians. Under certain assumptions, we show that the singular values of the point Jacobians of Neural Networks driven by the MDL principle should follow either a power law or a lognormal distribution. Finally, we conduct experiments to evaluate the behavior of the proposed measure applied to deep neural networks on different datasets, with respect to several types of noise. We observe that the experimental spectral distribution is in agreement with the spectral distribution predicted by our MDL principle, which suggests that neural networks trained with gradient descent on noisy data implicitly abide the MDL principle.

Keywords: Neural Networks · MDL · Signal-Noise · Point Jacobians

---

This work has been funded by a public grant from the French National Research Agency (ANR) under the "France 2030" investment plan, which has the reference EUR MANUTECH SLEIGHT - ANR-17-EURE-0026. This work has also been partly funded and by a PhD grant from the French Ministry of Higher Education and Research.

© The Author(s), under exclusive license to Springer Nature Switzerland AG 2023
D. Koutra et al. (Eds.): ECML PKDD 2023, LNAI 14170, pp. 173–189, 2023.
https://doi.org/10.1007/978-3-031-43415-0_11

1 Introduction

New data often traces out regularities found in past observations, an idea known as generalization: finding regularities that are consistent with available data which also apply to data that we are yet to encounter. In the context of supervised machine learning we measure it by *learning* the rules on observations by minimizing some loss function, and evaluating it on observed and unobserved data. The difference between risk in the training data and new observations is known as the *generalization gap*. When it is small, the model generalizes well.

In the context of empirical risk minimization the generalization gap can be estimated in terms of model complexity, which increases with its number of parameters. We thus expect to reduce the generalization gap through a form of *regularization*, either by explicitely reducing the number of parameters, controlling a norm [27,49], or e.g. using dropout [21,43] or batch normalization [24,29,41].

Surprisingly, neural networks (NN) trained by stochastic gradient descent (SGD) generalize well despite possessing a higher number of parameters than training data, even without explicit regularization [14]. An elegant explanation for this phenomenon is that SGD implicitly controls model complexity during learning [19,35], resulting in networks that are significantly simpler than their number of parameters suggests, as shown by several metrics to assess effective capacity, e.g. the model's number of degrees of freedom [12], which is related to generalization gap, or its intrinsic dimension [28]. It is thus puzzling that, in spite of their implicit simplicity, NN classifiers trained by SGD are able to perfectly fit pure random noise [51], even while explicitly using regularization. In pure random noise, there is no signal to learn a rule from, and to reduce the generalization gap we must reduce the *training* performance. Since common regularization methods are unable to achieve this, using them to control model expressiveness does not address generalization: we need to "rethink generalization".

To do so we offer the following insight. To learn, from noisy observations, regularities that apply to data that we are yet to encounter, we must do so in a noise insensitive way: we must learn from signal rather than from noise. If we do so, there is no generalization gap when learning from pure noise: since there is no signal, the model would simply not learn at all!

In this paper, we shall give a formulation of this insight in terms of a minimum description length principle (MDL), [37,38] a principle of model selection which can be seen as a formalization of Occam's Razor. MDL states the problem of learning from data in terms of finding regularities that we can use to compress it: *choose the model that provides the shortest description of data, comprising the model itself*[1]. This idea was formulated in different ways since it was first advanced in [37], to respond to technical difficulties in application [15]. In the original, two-part form, restricting the model class to finite sets, application of this principle turns into Kolmogorov's minimal sufficient statistic [46].

[1] This formulation is known as two-part MDL, which depending on the author can be seen as "traditional" (in opposition to "modern" MDL which uses a one-step encoding using universal encodings [15]) or "pure [46]".

MDL expresses the ability to generalize in terms of compressibility, which can be motivated using three main facts: (i) regularities in a random variable (r.v.) X can be used to losslessly compress it (ii) the minimum achievable code length is the entropy (iii) it is very unlikely that data that has no regularities can be compressed. Taken together, these imply a model's ability to compress data is likely due to finding a regularity, which will likely be found in new data as well. It is this intuitive appeal that motivates the use of MDL in spite of some conceptual difficulties, namely in selecting the encoding used to measure the length of the description of the model, which depends on the choice of encoding. To address this difficulty, we propose an approach that uses both the signal and the noise in the data to implicitly define model complexity unambiguously:

Choose the model whose representation of the data can be used to compress the signal, but not the noise.

Formalizing this statement requires a perspective of signal and noise that is particularly adjusted to classification problems, where the signal is task-defined [15], and everything else can be considered as noise. As we shall see, our MDL statement has a significant impact on the distribution of the singular values of the point Jacobian matrices of a NN. Networks that learn from noise (where their output can be used to compress the noise) tend to maximize singular values in arbitrary directions to capture the fake "signal" in local directions. As a result the spectrum is uniformly distributed. On the other hand, NN that learn from signal but not from noise (where their output can be used to compress the signal but not the noise) tend to capture local regularities in the signal by maximizing singular values in directions aligned with the data. These directions are, by definition of signal, not arbitrary. Since the network also tends to ignore everything that is not signal, by minimizing singular values in arbitrary directions, in the limit of infinite epochs, this results in a spectrum distributed according to a power law, with a large proportion of small singular values and a fat tail.

Our Contributions. Our main contributions in this paper are 3-fold: (i) we provide a formulation of the MDL principle that is generally applicable to learned representations (ii) we provide a capacity measure based upon this principle (iii) we show experimentally that neural networks are driven by the MDL principle.

Paper Organization. This paper is organized as follows: Sect. 2 contextualizes of our work, focusing on the sensitivity measure provided in [1]. We then provide a few information theoretic results in Sect. 3.1 to contextualize the our definition of signal and noise in Sect. 3.2. Section 4 is the core of our contribution: we define our MDL objective in Sect. 4.1, and provide the local approximation in Sect. 4.2 that allows us to predict the spectral distribution in Sect. 4.2. In Sect. 5 we present experimental results[2] which allow us to conclude in Sect. 6 that neural networks are driven by the MDL principle, and discuss future work.

---

[2] Repository: https://github.com/brandao-eduardo/ismynndrivenbymdl.

2 Related Work

MDL has traditionally been used for model selection [2,15,18,34,40], but its intuitive appeal has led to applications in other areas such as pattern mining [11,23]. In supervised learning, MDL was used in NN as early as [22], in which the authors added Gaussian noise to the weights of the network to control their description length, and thus the amount of information required to communicate the NN. In classification, existing approaches are inspired in MDL for density estimation [15], and most can be reduced to the same approach based on the 0/1 loss, which, while not making probabilistic assumptions about noise, was shown to behave suboptimally [16]. Existing modifications to address this [3,48] do not have, unlike our approach, a natural coding interpretation. Finding a formulation of MDL for classification that can be applied in general and realistic settings is thus an open problem, and this paper aims to contribute in this direction.

The relationship between noise, compressibility and generalization has been explored in [5], for example, to derive PAC-Bayes generalization bounds, or in the information bottleneck framework [45]. Closer to our approach [33] studies the stability of the output of NN with respect to the injection of Gaussian noise at the nodes, experiments showing that networks trained on random labels are more sensitive to random noise. In [1], the notion of stability of outputs is extended to layer-wise stability, improving network compressibility and generalization. The authors define layer sensitivity with respect to noise (essentially the expected stable rank with respect to the distribution of the noise), and show that stable layers tend to attenuate *Gaussian* noise. A compression scheme is provided for the layer weights that acts on layer outputs as Gaussian noise, which subsequent stable layers will thus tend to attenuate. This, since the output of the network is unchanged, shows that a network composed of stable layers is losslessly compressible. A generalization bound for the compressed network is then derived in terms of the empirical loss of the original network and the complexity of the compressed network. This work shows a clear connection between compressibility of the model and generalization, but the connection to MDL is less evident. We will show that enforcing our MDL principle leads to a measure that can be seen as an average of local sensitivities, which are similar to those defined in [1], but with crucial differences. In our approach, sensitivity is logarithmic, direction-dependent, and importantly combines sensitivity to signal and to noise.

3 MDL Principle, Signal, and Noise

We recall fundamental results in information theory, which will be used to define signal and noise as used in this paper.

3.1 Information Theory Primer

MDL rests on three fundamental results: (i) regularities in a r.v. X can be used to losslessly compress it using a non-singular code for X; (ii) the minimum achievable codelength is the entropy; and (iii) it is extremely unlikely that data that has no regularities can be compressed. In this section, we provide proof sketches for (ii) and (iii) (cf. app. 1.6 in [6]; see e.g. [8] or [30] for proofs) and motivate (i) in Sect. 3.1 with a toy example. A similar argument can be used to prove a finite-precision version of the Theorem 1 in [50], which provides a necessary condition for a 2-Layer ReLU network to be able to perfectly fit the training data. A straightforward application of this original result allows us to show in app. 1.1 in [6] that a two-layer network that can be losslessly compressed to less than about 125 kB cannot perfectly overfit cifar-10 [26].

Preliminaries and Notation. A source code $C(X)$ (C when there is no risk of ambiguity) for a r.v. X is a function from $\mathcal{X}$ the range of X to $\mathcal{D}^*$ the set of finite strings of a d-ary alphabet $\mathcal{D}$, associating $x \in \mathcal{X}$ to a codeword $C(x)$. The *length* of the codeword $l(x)$ is the number of elements in $C(x)$, and the expected code length is $L(X) := \mathbb{E}_X[l(x)]$. A code is said to be *non-singular* if every $x \in \mathcal{X}$ maps to an unique element of $\mathcal{D}^*$. An *extension* C^* of code C codes sequences $x_1 x_2 \cdots x_n$of elements of $\mathcal{X}$ as the concatenation of $C(x_1)C(x_2)\cdots C(x_n)$. A code is said to be *uniquely encoded* if its extension is non-singular. Since every element in $\mathcal{X}$ is unambiguously encoded with a unique string, non-singular codes allow us to losslessly compress data.

Optimal Codelength and Incompressible Data. The Kraft-Macmillan inequality (cf. app. 1.6 in [6]), which provides a condition for the existence of a uniquely decodable code with given word lengths proves (ii):

Theorem 1 (Optimal code length). *The expected length for any uniquely decodable code C of a r.v. X over an alphabet of size D is greater than or equal to $H_D(X)$ the entropy calculated in base D, with equality holding iff $D^{-l_i} = p_i$*

An optimal prefix code always exists (e.g. Huffman code), but for our purposes, the Shannon-Fano code, which sets codeword lengths $l(x) = \lceil -\log p(x) \rceil$[3] suffices. To give an informal argument for (iii), consider data X with no regularities (maximal entropy). By Theorem 1, the expected codelength of any prefix code of a discrete r.v. X over an alphabet of size D is at least $H_D(X)$, with equality iff the $l_i = -\log_D p_i$. Since all n events have probability $\frac{1}{n}$, the expected code length per symbol is $L \geq -\sum_{i=1}^{n} p_i \log_D p_i = \log_D n$. The lower bound can be achieved by assigning each codeword to the leaves of a D-nary tree: the best code and worst code coincide, and so data cannot be compressed.

Using Regularities to Compress. To motivate (i), consider an object of mass m falling freely from a height h_0 on Earth (acceleration of gravity g), and a table recording heights $\{h_1, h_2, \ldots\}$ at times $\{t_1, t_2, \ldots\}$. which are known to obey $h(t) = h_0 - \frac{1}{2}mgt^2$ since Galileo. This regularity can be used to losslessly

[3] The Shannon-Fano code is competitive, meaning that the probability that the expected length exceeds another code's by c bits does not exceed 2^{1-c} [8].

compress the height-times table by replacing h_i by $\Delta h_i = h_i - h(t_i)$, as we expect $h(t_i)$ to predict the first significant digits of h_i with high confidence, and measurements are performed and stored with finite precision. We can thus store the *same* data (in expectation) using *less* digits, which amounts to lossless compression. The more regularities we are able to find in data, the more we can compress it. A better model, taking e.g. drag into account, increases confidence in the first significant digits of the predictions, thus reducing in expectation the number of significant digits of the deviations, and allowing better compression. But there is a trade-off: as it would need to store drag as well as m, g, the model itself takes longer to describe. In the limit, a very large model can decrease the description length of finite data simply by memorizing it. Notably, two-layer ReLU feed forward NN can do this with surprising ease [50] but, as predicted in the MDL framework, at the expense of an increase in complexity [4].

3.2 Signal and Noise

This paper introduces an MDL principle that specifies the encoding scheme in which to measure the description length implicitly in terms of the signal and the noise in noisy data. To define signal and noise, we rely on [39] which defines noise as the part of the data that cannot be compressed with the models considered, the rest defining the information bearing signal. This idea is used in the paper in the context of Gaussian models arising in linear-quadratic regression problems to derive a decomposition of data that is similar to Kolmogorov's sufficient statistics [8]. In our case, we shall assume that the signal is implicitly provided by a given classification task, and define noise to be everything else.

Definition 1. *We define noise as "noise relative to a signal": given r.v.s X (signal) and Δ (noise) such that $X + \Delta$ is well-defined, we say that Δ is noise relative to X if for every $C_i \in \mathcal{C}$ non-singular code of X, we have $L(C_i(\Delta)) \geq H(\Delta) + \alpha$, with $\alpha > 0$.*

Note that if $C_j \in \mathcal{C}$ were optimal for Δ, then $L(C_i(\Delta)) = H(\Delta) \geq H(\Delta) + \alpha$, which with $\alpha > 0$ is a contradiction. The definition is thus equivalent to stating that there is no code of X in $\mathcal{C}$ (which may include the optimal code for X) that is optimal for Δ. Also note that the noise Δ is not particularly "disordered". Going back to Sect. 3.1, the physical laws that compress height vs. time data are unable to compress the effect of hitting the object with a baseball bat. Even if a model provides a simple description of some data, adding noise as defined in Definition 1 destroys its ability to compress it. It is implicit in the MDL principle that not only do we learn the regularities in data, but also the "irregularities"!

4 Learning with the MDL Principle

We now provide an MDL principle that eliminates the need for defining the model encoding, as in two-step MDL or a universal coding such as one-step MDL [17]. Instead, we use the signal and the noise in the training data to implicitly define the encoding and establish a lower bound of this maximization objective in terms of the MDL of signal and noise(cf. Theorem 1). We simplify the problem by expressing it locally, and provide an interpretation in terms of sensitivities to the signal and noise. Finally, we combine the local problems to express a global MDL objective in terms of the spectra of the local Jacobians, concluding that the spectral distribution of models that maximize MDL is either power law or lognormal.

4.1 MDL Objective

The MDL paradigm quantifies learning based on the ability to compress: if $f(X+\Delta)$ contains information about X it can compress it and conversely, if it does *not* contain information about the Δ, it cannot be used to compress it. This formulation implicitly defines the complexity of the model f in terms of unknown X and Δ present in training data. It is therefore applicable in a classification context, where these are defined with respect to a *task*. Formally:

Definition 2 (MDL principle). *Let $\tilde{X} = X + \Delta$ be noisy data, with unknown signal X and a noise Δ parts in the sense of Definition 1, and a model f_θ trained on $\tilde{X}$ according to some (e.g. classification) objective. Let $\mathcal{L}(X|f(\tilde{X}) = y)$ and $\mathcal{L}(\Delta|f(\tilde{X}) = y)$ be, respectively, the expected description length of X and Δ given knowledge $f_\theta(\tilde{X}) = y$. Then with $\gamma > 0$ a hyperparameter, f_θ follows the MDL principle if it maximizes*

$$\max_\theta \left\{ \int p_{f_\theta(\tilde{X})}(y)\mathcal{L}(\Delta|f_\theta(\tilde{X}) = y)dy - \gamma \int p_{f_\theta(\tilde{X})}(y)\mathcal{L}(X|f_\theta(\tilde{X}) = y)dy \right\} \quad (1)$$

The idea is to minimize the mean $\mathcal{L}(X|f(\tilde{X}) = y)$ and maximize $\mathcal{L}(\Delta|f(\tilde{X}) = y)$ seen as functions of y[4], with γ controlling the relative strength of these objectives.

A Lower Bound in Terms of Minimal Description Length. Using Theorem 1 we can express the length of the description of noise knowing $f_\theta(\tilde{X}) = y$ as a multiple $\alpha(y) \geq 1$ of the length of the minimum length description for each y:

$$\begin{aligned} \int p_{f_\theta(\tilde{X})}(y)\mathcal{L}(\Delta|f_\theta(\tilde{X}) = y)dy &= \int p_{f_\theta(\tilde{X})}(y)\alpha(y)H(\Delta|f_\theta(\tilde{X}) = y)dy \\ &\geq \left(\inf_y \alpha(y)\right) \int p_{f_\theta(\tilde{X})}(y)H(\Delta|f_\theta(\tilde{X}) = y)dy \\ &= \left(\inf_y \alpha(y)\right) H(\Delta|f_\theta(\tilde{X})) \end{aligned}$$

Proceeding similarly for the signal term we obtain

$$\int p_{f_\theta(\tilde{X})}(y)\mathcal{L}(X|f_\theta(\tilde{X}) = y)dy \leq \left(\sup_y \beta(y)\right) H(X|f_\theta(\tilde{X}))$$

[4] For classification, we work on an intermediate representation, which explains the use of integrals in calculating the expectation.

Denoting $\inf_y \alpha(y) := \alpha$ and $\sup_y \beta(y) := \beta$ the minimum and maximum expected description lengths of codes of noise and of signal, respectively, knowing $f_\theta(\tilde{X}) = y$, we combine the two desiderata and maximize a lower bound of 1:

$$\max_\theta \left\{\alpha H(\Delta|f_\theta(\tilde{X})) - \gamma\beta H(X|f_\theta(\tilde{X}))\right\}$$

Since $H(\Delta|f_\theta(\tilde{X})) = H(\Delta, f_\theta(\tilde{X})) - H(f_\theta(\tilde{X}))$ and similarly for the second term,

$$\begin{aligned} H(\Delta|f_\theta(\tilde{X})) - \gamma\beta H(X|f_\theta(\tilde{X})) &= \alpha H(f_\theta(\tilde{X})|\Delta) - \gamma\beta H(f_\theta(\tilde{X})|X) \\ &\quad + \alpha H(\Delta) - \gamma\beta H(X) + (\beta\gamma - \alpha)H(f_\theta(\tilde{(X)})) \end{aligned}$$

Ignoring terms independent of θ, since $\alpha > 0$, we obtain a lower bound of 1:

Proposition 1 (MDL objective lower bound). *Given noisy data $\tilde{X} = X + \Delta$ comprised of a signal X and a noise Δ parts, a model f_θ trained on $\tilde{X}$ according to MDL, $\lambda := \gamma\frac{\beta}{\alpha}$, the following is a lower bound of the the MDL objective:*

$$\max_\theta \left\{H(f_\theta(\tilde{X})|\Delta) - \lambda H(f_\theta(\tilde{X})|X) + (\lambda - 1)H(f_\theta(\tilde{X}))\right\} \tag{2}$$

In this lower bound, λ has the role of γ modulated by the ratio between the worst case expected signal description length knowing the model output and the best case description length of the noise knowing the model output in units of entropy. Note that to minimize the description length of the noisy data $H(f_\theta(\tilde{X}))$ we must have $\lambda - 1 < 0$ and hence objective 2 is MDL with a constraint on the conditional entropies. Since $\lambda < 1 \Rightarrow \alpha > \gamma\beta$ the implications depend on the model class $\{f_\theta\}$: if for the given model class Δ is more difficult to compress than X, then $\alpha > \beta$ and so $\gamma < 1$. This corresponds to, in 2, focusing relatively more on ignoring the noise. Conversely, if $\{f_\theta\}$ is such that X is mode difficult to compress, then $\gamma > 1$ and we focus relatively more on learning the signal.

4.2 Local Formulation

We now simplify the problem in 2 by expressing it *locally* and then ultimately in terms of the spectrum of the point Jacobian matrix $\nabla f_\theta|_{x_k}$.

Local Objective. Let $f : A \subseteq \mathbb{R}^n \to B \subseteq \mathbb{R}^m$ be analytical, A compact and $x_1, \ldots, x_N \subseteq A$ and $\{V_k\}_{k=1\cdots N}$ a set of balls centered at x_k and with radius r_k such that $A \subseteq V_1 \cup \cdots \cup V_N$, chosen such that the Jacobian matrix of f is constant in each V_k in the sense of Prop. 2 in [6] Then to first order in $\delta x_k, \delta$:

$$\begin{aligned} f(\tilde{x}) = f(\tilde{x}_k + \delta x_k + \delta_k) &\approx f(\tilde{x}_k) + \nabla f|_{\tilde{x}_k}\delta x_k + \nabla f|_{\tilde{x}_k}\delta_k \\ &:= f(\tilde{x}_k) + J_k\delta x_k + J_k\delta_k \end{aligned}$$

with the approximation error controlled by the principal singular value of the Hessian (cf. app. 1.3 [6]). Since the choice of V_k determines $f(\tilde{x}_k)$, and local independence of signal and noise implies locally $H(f(X)|X) = 0, H(X|\Delta) = H(X)$, we can apply this approximation to 2 to obtain:

Proposition 2 (Local MDL objective). *In the conditions and notation above, locally in V_k the MDL objective 2 can be expressed approximately as*

$$\max_{J_k} \lambda H(J_k \delta X_k) - H(J_k \Delta_k) \tag{3}$$

where $\delta X_k, \Delta_k$ denote the signal and the noise in V_k with respect to its center, and the approximation error is controlled by Prop. 2 in [6].

Interpretation in Terms of Sensitivity. In [1] the authors define sensitivity of a mapping f with respect to noise Δ at x as $\mathbb{E}_{\delta \sim \Delta}\left[\frac{\|f(x+\delta)-f(x)\|^2}{\|f(x)\|^2}\right]$, which becomes $\frac{\|J_k(\delta)\|^2}{\|f(x)\|^2}$ to first order in δ, in a region of constant Jacobian J_k, using the arguments in Sect. 4.2. In expectation, up to a scale, this is the variance of $J_k \Delta_k$ which is a measure of its complexity like the entropy above, (for a Gaussian distribution, up to a logarithm and a constant, the two coincide). $H(J_k \Delta_k)$ in Propostion 2 thus corresponds to sensitivity with respect to noise and, by a similar argument, $H(J_k \delta X_k)$ to sensitivity with respect to signal. Our MDL objective thus selects the model that locally maximizes sensitivity with respect to signal and minimizes sensitivity with respect to noise. Although similar to [1], in our formulation sensitivity is logarithmic, direction-dependent (cf. Sect. 4.2), and crucially combines sensitivity to signal and sensitivity to noise.

Finally, since $\lambda < 1$, if $H(J_k \delta X_k) > H(J_k \Delta_k)$ then 3 is upper bounded by zero, where $\lambda = \frac{H(J_k \Delta_k)}{H(J_k \delta X_k)}$. Maximizing 3 thus corresponds to getting closer to a model that *locally* produces the same balance between sensitivity to signal and to noise, determined by the *global* parameter λ. This problem cannot always be solved. Consider f a one layer ReLU network of width N; the *local* $\{J_k\}$ are given by deleting a certain number of rows in the pre-ReLU Jacobian, which is the weight matrix of f. Since f can have at most 2^N different $\{J_k\}$, the conjunction of local problems can only be solved if the number of V_k where the balance between sensitivities needs to be adjusted *differently* is smaller that 2^N. The case of deeper networks is similar, each new ReLU layer of width M_i multiplying the number of possible Jacobians by 2^{M_i}.

Local Objective: Spectral Formulation. To provide a spectral version of 2, we express J_k in terms of its singular value decomposition (SVD), and the signal and noise in terms of local PCA representations. We work in V_k but omit the label k for simplicity. Jacobian, signal, and noise refer to the *local* versions.

Proposition 3 *(Local objective spectral formulation). In the conditions of Proposition 2, the following is its lower bound:*

$$\max_{\sigma} \left\{ \lambda \left(\max_i \left\{ \log \sigma_i + H(\delta X^i_{pca}) \right\} \right) - \sum_j \left(H(\Delta^j_{pca}) + \log \sigma_j \right) \right\} \tag{4}$$

Proof. Let $J = U\Sigma V^\top$ be the singular value decomposition of $J \in \mathbb{R}^{n\times m}$. The signal δX can be expressed as the transform to local coordinates of δX_{pca}, the signal in local PCA coordinates $\delta X = W_{signal}^\top \delta X_{pca}$, and similarly for noise: $\Delta = W_{noise}^\top \Delta_{pca}$, where W_{signal}, W_{noise} are the respective PCA coordinate transformations. Since U has determinant one everywhere we thus have

$$\lambda H(J\delta X) - H(J\Delta) = \lambda H(\Sigma V W_{signal}^\top \delta X_{pca}) - H(\Sigma V W_{noise}^\top \Delta_{pca})$$

The $VW^\top$ are contractions measuring the alignment between the singular vectors of the Jacobian and the principal components of the signal (for W_{signal}) and noise (for W_{noise}). We thus maximize the RHS of this expression by (i) aligning J with δX and then maximizing the logarithm of the singular values in the non-zero dimensions; if δX is locally low-dimensional, the singular values that get maximized are few (ii) aligning J with Δ and then minimizing the logarithm of the singular values in the non-zero dimensions; since Δ tends to be relatively high-dimensional, all singular values of J tend to be minimized.[5] The overall effect is to maximize a few neighborhood-dependent singular values of J, and minimize all the rest – consistently with the experimental observations Fig. 1. Since δX and J are unknown, so are the "selected" directions. The full entropy of the local signal is at least as great as that of its components. Replacing it with the entropy of the singular direction i for which the entropy of the transformed signal is maximal, we obtain a lower bound of the local objective.

4.3 Combining Local Objectives to Obtain a Spectral Distribution

We combine local objectives by maximizing their sum over all local patches V_k which ammounts to assuming cross-patch independence. For it to hold, (i) the network should be able to produce sufficiently many local Jacobians as explained in Sect. 4.2 and (ii) $V_i \cap V_j$ should be small for all i, j. Assumption (i) holds in practice since we work in the overparameterized regime and (ii) holds for ReLU networks. Both assumptions are thus expected to hold as a first approximation, although [20] suggests more complex behavior and will be considered in future work.

Recalling that we do not know which singular value gets "selected" and assuming that the signal is locally low-dimensional (which is known as "the manifold hypothesis" [7,10]), which we take for simplicity to mean that $\max_{i_k} H(\delta X_k^{i_k}) \approx H(\delta X_k)$ we obtain, summing over the M patches of rank-N_k Jacobian

$$\sum_{k=1}^{M} \left\{ \lambda \left(\max_{i_k} \left\{ \log \sigma_{i_k} + H(\delta X_k^{i_k}) \right\} \right) - \sum_{j=1}^{N_k} \left(H(\Delta_k^j) + \log \sigma_j \right) \right\}$$

Simplifying and maximizing over the singular values of all the J_k leads to

$$\max_{\sigma} \left\{ \lambda M \mathbb{E}\left[\log \sigma\right] + \lambda H(X) - H(\Delta) - \bar{N} M \mathbb{E}\left[\log \sigma\right] \right\}$$

[5] A similar argument can be found in [1] in the discussion of noise sensitivity.

where expectations of both log singular values and Jacobian rank are over the patches, the latter denoted $\bar{N}$ for readability. As the sum of lower bounds of non-positive quantities is non-positive, its maximum value is zero, where

$$\mathbb{E}\left[\log \sigma\right] = \frac{H(\Delta) - \lambda H(X)}{M(\lambda - \bar{N})} \tag{5}$$

Expectation as a Model-Dataset Measure of Complexity. For $E\left[\log \sigma\right]$ to be positive, $H(\Delta)$ must be sufficiently smaller than $H(X)$, since $\lambda - \bar{N} < 0$ because $0 < \lambda < 1$. If 1 holds, $\mathbb{E}\left[\log \sigma\right]$ thus decreases with the number of patches of constant Jacobian and the mean Jacobian rank. It is thus a measure of model complexity which increases with $\frac{H(\Delta)-\lambda H(X)}{M(\lambda-\bar{N})}$. All things being equal, for the same $\mathbb{E}\left[\log \sigma\right]$ models trained with more noise will have smaller M and $\tilde{N}$. Adding noise is a form of regularization. If on the other hand, entropy of noise is greater than the entropy of signal, the reverse effect is produced. On very noisy data (relative to signal!), models trained with more noise need to become more complex.

4.4 The MDL Spectral Distributions

We now show that the predicted distribution that is compatible with 5 is a power law or, for NN trained with SGD, a lognormal distribution. The true spectral distribution contains information on, e.g. architecture and training process whereas in the maxent formalism [25] we use, the prediction is maximally non-committal: it contains no information on the MDL-trained network beyond its adherence to the MDL principle and the signal-to-noise entropies of the training data.

Incorporating Knowledge of the Expectation of the Log Spectrum and SGD. The distribution that incorporates knowledge of the expectation of the spectrum 5 *and nothing else* is the maximum entropy distribution for which the constraint on the spectrum 5 holds [25]. Specifically, the power law distribution $p(\sigma) = \frac{\alpha-1}{\alpha}\left(\frac{\sigma}{b}\right)^{-\alpha}$, where $\alpha = 1 + \frac{1}{\mathbb{E}[\log \sigma]-\log b}$ and b is a cutoff parameter. Power laws model scale-free phenomena[6], but can emerge when aggregating data over many scales [13,52], as we did in Sect. 4.3 to obtain Eq. 5. For a ReLU NN trained by SGD, there is also a constraint on the *variance* of $\log \sigma$: the spectrum depends continuously on the network weights (cf. Sect. 4.2), which are SGD-updated using a *finite* number of steps. The corresponding maxent distribution is the lognormal, which is the Gaussian distribution with given mean and variance in log-scale.

5 Experimental Results

Our experiments show that spectral distribution matches theoretical predictions in Sect. 4.4, suggesting that NN are driven by the MDL principle. We study the

[6] Since $p(k\sigma) = a\,(k\sigma)^{\alpha} = ak^{\alpha}\sigma^{\alpha}$, normalization implies $p(k\sigma) = p(\sigma)$.

effect of noise in the point Jacobian spectral distribution of three groups of models of increasing complexity, ReLU MLPs, Alexnet, and Inception trained on MNIST [9] and cifar-10 [26], using the experimental setup in [50] (cf. app. 1.5 in [6]). In this section we (i) present two types of noise and discuss expected consequences on the spectral distribution (ii) present and discuss the experimental results.

5.1 Experimental Noise

We study two forms of "natural" noise: *label noise*, used in [50] and *dataset noise*, which consists in adding a lossy compressed version of a similar dataset.

Label Noise. We focus on instance-independent symmetric label noise [42], which randomly assigns labels to training and test examples unconditionally on example and training label with probability p. Label noise can be modelled realistically using human annotators [47], but the former choice is closer to the MDL sense Definition 1. In this setting, the entropy of the introduced noise can be estimated as $p \cdot H(X_0)$, since incorrectly labelled examples become noise with respect to the classification task. This allows us to express the numerator of 5 for the noised dataset in terms of entropies of the original dataset as $H(\Delta_p) - \lambda H(X_p) = H(X_0) - \lambda H(X_0) + p(1+\lambda)H(X) > H(X_0) - \lambda H(X_0)$. All things being equal, for NN following MDL, $E[\log \sigma]$ increases with the probability of label noise p.

Dataset Noise. We add to the original dataset D_0 a *similar* dataset D_{sim} lossy compressed at rate r. Symbolically $D_r = D_0 + rD_{sim}$. We choose D_{sim} commonly used in place of D_0 in ML practice: cifar-100 for cifar-10, and Fashion-MNIST for MNIST. We compress $\tilde{D}$ by reconstructing it using only a few PCA components, which reduces bias in setting r, compared to using e.g. jpeg [36] or an autoencoder, where architecture introduces an element of arbitrariness, but we lose the ability to set r at will. Since for the noised dataset $X_r + \Delta_r$ the numerator in 5 can be written as $H(\Delta_r) - \lambda H(X_r) = H(\Delta_0) - \lambda H(X_0) + r(H(X_{sim}) + H(\Delta_{sim})$. All things being equal, for NN that follow MDL, $E[\log \sigma]$ decreases with r. Interestingly, assuming the entropies of the similar dataset are approximately the same as that of the original dataset, we obtain $H(\Delta_r) - \lambda H(X_r) = (1+r)H(\Delta_0) - (\lambda - r)H(X_0)$, which corresponds to the same maximization objective with a rescaled $\lambda_r = \frac{\lambda - r}{1+r} < \lambda_0$ corresponding to less sensitivity to signal.

5.2 Discussion

As Figs. 1 and 2 show, NN trained using SGD are driven by the MDL principle: (i) their spectra is well-fit by a lognormal distribution, as shown in Sect. 4.4, and experimental spectra become more lognormal with training epoch (cf. fit overlay on the histograms, and inset probability plots); also, as predicted in the discussion following 5 (ii) for each model $\mathbb{E}[\log \sigma]$ increases with noise (iii) and with model complexity, which also influences the quality of lognormal fit[7],

[7] The number of training epochs being relatively small, we did not find a power-law behavior.

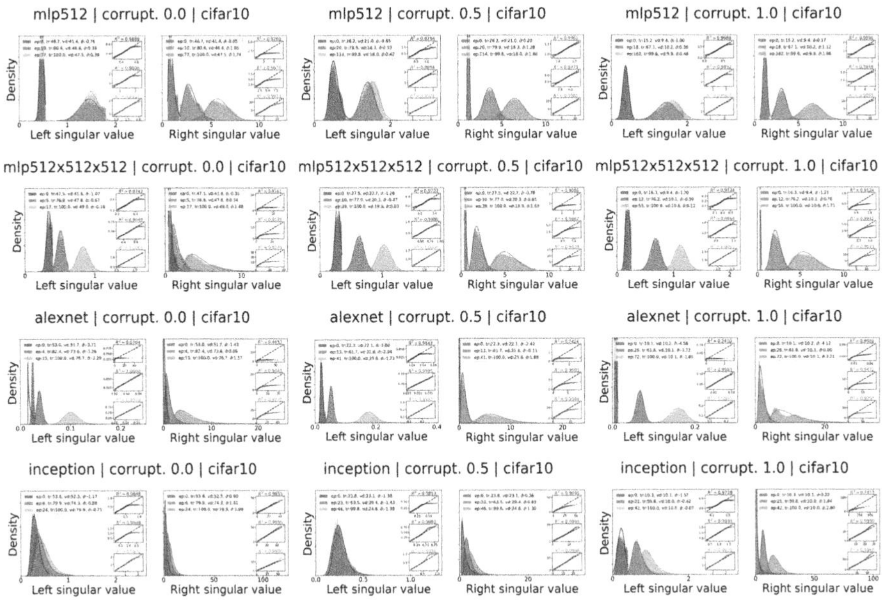

Fig. 1. Point Jacobian spectral distribution for *model*|***label noise***|*cifar-10*, from first epoch to overfit. "Left" and "right" distributions (cf. [6]) are represented separately for each triplet for clarity. The best fit lognormal plot is superimposed on each histogram, with the corresponding probability plot on the right, with the line of best fit (R^2 displayed on top). Legend elements, in order: epoch, training and validation accuracy, and the mean log spectrum.

Inception being the overall best and MLP the overall worst. Remarkably, these observations hold for both label noise and dataset noise. In the early stages of the training process, though, representation-building takes precedence. This can be inferred by observing that experimental distributions are typically bimodal (see app. 1.7 in [6]), and noting that at the last linear layer of a classification-induced representation, one of the directions should leave the output relatively more unchanged than the others: the direction assigned to the class of the training point [6]. Representation building occurs early, as can be seen in Figs. 1 and 2 and app. 1.7 in [6], dominating MDL in early epochs. To handle this asymmetry, we divide the spectrum in each of its two modalities (cf. [6]). The statements above apply to each of the two parts of the spectrum, corresponding to the two representations. The observations above hold for MNIST as well, exception being where the initial spectrum is multi-modal (suggesting a great degeneracy of the directions in which the classification prediction does not change—i.e. MNIST is very simple). In this case our splitting method is ineffective, as we would need to split the spectral distribution into each of the several modalities.

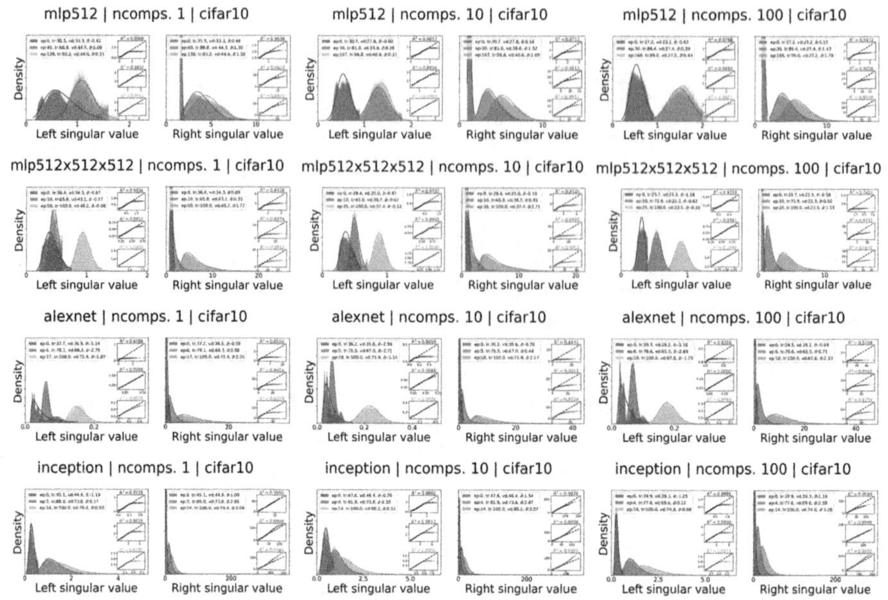

Fig. 2. Point Jacobian spectral distribution for *model*|***nbr. pca comp.***|*cifar-10*, from first epoch to overfit where possible. "Left" and "right" distributions (cf. [6]) are represented separately for each triplet for clarity. The best fit lognormal plot is superimposed on each histogram, with the corresponding probability plot on the right, with the line of best fit (R^2 displayed on top). Legend elements, in order: *epoch, training and validation accuracy*, and the *mean log spectrum.*

6 Conclusion and Future Work

In this work, we propose an MDL principle that implicitly defines model complexity in terms of signal and noise: *choose the model whose representation of the data can be used to compress the signal, but not the noise.* We show that models driven by this principle locally maximize sensitivity to the signal and minimize the sensitivity to noise, and predict that the point Jacobian spectrum of NN trained by gradient descent follow either a power law or a lognormal distribution. We provide experimental evidence supporting this prediction, hinting that neural networks trained by gradient descent are driven by the MDL principle.

As for future work we plan, aiming at a generalization bound, to extend the connection established in Sect. 4.2, by making the MDL objective layer wise as in [1]. Another possible extension is to use our findings to explain the power law behavior of the spectra of the layer weight matrices and connection to generalization gap found in [31,32], by noting that each point Jacobian of ReLU networks is a sub-matrix of the product of the network weight matrices, which can beexpressed in terms of the singular values of the point Jacobian submatrix via an interlacing inequality [44].

Ethical statement. This paper presents a contribution that is essentially fundamental, theoretical and methodological. We do not see any immediate ethical or societal issues. Our experimental evaluation considers classic benchmarks of the literature and our analysis focuses on particular mathematical properties of point Jacobians spectra of trained neural networks. Our work follows ethical guidelines in modern machine learning research in general and in representation learning in particular. The application of the methodology presented in this paper should consider ethical implications that can arise from the datasets used of the applications targeted.

References

1. Arora, S., Ge, R., Neyshabur, B., Zhang, Y.: Stronger generalization bounds for deep nets via a compression approach. CoRR (2018). http://arxiv.org/abs/1802.05296v4
2. Barron, A., Rissanen, J., Yu, B.: The minimum description length principle in coding and modeling. IEEE Trans. Inf. Theory **44**(6), 2743–2760 (1998)
3. Barron, A.R.: Complexity regularization with application to artificial neural networks. In: Nonparametric Functional Estimation and Related Topics, pp. 561–576 (1991)
4. Blier, L., Ollivier, Y.: The description length of deep learning models. Adv. Neural Inf. Process. Syst. **31**, 1–11 (2018)
5. Blum, A., Langford, J.: PAC-MDL bounds. In: Schölkopf, B., Warmuth, M.K. (eds.) COLT-Kernel 2003. LNCS (LNAI), vol. 2777, pp. 344–357. Springer, Heidelberg (2003). https://doi.org/10.1007/978-3-540-45167-9_26
6. Brandao, E., Duffner, S., Emonet, R., Habrard, A., Jacquenet, F., Sebban, M.: Appendixes to: is my neural net driven by the mdl principle? (2023). https://github.com/brandao-eduardo/ismynndrivenbymdl/blob/main/Appendixes.pdf
7. Cayton, L.: Algorithms for manifold learning. Univ. of California at San Diego Technical Report 12(1–17), 1 (2005)
8. Cover, T.M., Thomas, J.A.: Elements of Information Theory. John Wiley & Sons, Hoboekn (2012)
9. Deng, L.: The mnist database of handwritten digit images for machine learning research. IEEE Signal Process. Maga. **29**(6), 141–142 (2012)
10. Fefferman, C., Mitter, S., Narayanan, H.: Testing the manifold hypothesis. J. Am. Math. Soc. **29**(4), 983–1049 (2016)
11. Galbrun, E.: The minimum description length principle for pattern mining: a survey. Data Mining Knowl. Disc. **36**(5), 1679–1727 (2022)
12. Gao, T., Jojic, V.: Degrees of freedom in deep neural networks. In: Proceedings of the Thirty-Second Conference on Uncertainty in Artificial Intelligence, UAI 2016, pp. 232–241. AUAI Press, Arlington (2016)
13. Gheorghiu, S., Coppens, M.O.: Heterogeneity explains features of "anomalous" thermodynamics and statistics. Proc. Natl. Acad. Sci. **101**(45), 15852–15856 (2004)
14. Goodfellow, I., Bengio, Y., Courville, A.: Deep Learning. MIT Press, Cambridge (2016). http://www.deeplearningbook.org
15. Grünwald, P.: Minimum description length tutorial. Adv. Minimum Descript. Length: Theory Appl. **5**, 1–80 (2005)
16. Grünwald, P., Langford, J.: Suboptimal behavior of bayes and mdl in classification under misspecification. Mach. Learn. **66**, 119–149 (2007)

17. Grünwald, P., Roos, T.: Minimum description length revisited. Int. J. Math. Ind. **11**(01), 1930001 (2019). https://doi.org/10.1142/S2661335219300018
18. Hansen, M.H., Yu, B.: Minimum description length model selection criteria for generalized linear models. Lect. Notes-Monograph Ser., 145–163 (2003)
19. Hardt, M., Recht, B., Singer, Y.: Train faster, generalize better: stability of stochastic gradient descent. In: International Conference on Machine Learning, pp. 1225–1234. PMLR (2016)
20. He, H., Su, W.J.: The local elasticity of neural networks. arXiv preprint arXiv:1910.06943 (2019)
21. Helmbold, D.P., Long, P.M.: On the inductive bias of dropout. J. Mach. Learn. Res. **16**(1), 3403–3454 (2015)
22. Hinton, G.E., Van Camp, D.: Keeping the neural networks simple by minimizing the description length of the weights. In: Proceedings of the Sixth Annual Conference on Computational Learning Theory, pp. 5–13 (1993)
23. Hu, B., Rakthanmanon, T., Hao, Y., Evans, S., Lonardi, S., Keogh, E.: Using the minimum description length to discover the intrinsic cardinality and dimensionality of time series. Data Mining Knowl. Disc. **29**, 358–399 (2015)
24. Ioffe, S., Szegedy, C.: Batch normalization: accelerating deep network training by reducing internal covariate shift. In: International Conference on Machine Learning, pp. 448–456. PMLR (2015)
25. Jaynes, E.: Where do we stand on maximum entropy? The maximum entropy formalism, pp. 15–118 (1978)
26. Krizhevsky, A., Hinton, G., et al.: Learning multiple layers of features from tiny images (2009)
27. Krogh, A., Hertz, J.A.: A simple weight decay can improve generalization. In: Advances in Neural Information Processing Systems, pp. 950–957 (1992)
28. Li, C., Farkhoor, H., Liu, R., Yosinski, J.: Measuring the intrinsic dimension of objective landscapes. In: International Conference on Learning Representations (2018)
29. Luo, P., Wang, X., Shao, W., Peng, Z.: Towards understanding regularization in batch normalization. arXiv preprint arXiv:1809.00846 (2018)
30. MacKay, D.J., Mac Kay, D.J.: Information Theory, Inference and Learning Algorithms. Cambridge University Press, Cambridge (2003)
31. Martin, C.H., Mahoney, M.W.: Implicit self-regularization in deep neural networks: evidence from random matrix theory and implications for learning. arXiv preprint arXiv:1810.01075 (2018)
32. Martin, C.H., Mahoney, M.W.: Heavy-tailed universality predicts trends in test accuracies for very large pre-trained deep neural networks. In: Proceedings of the 2020 SIAM International Conference on Data Mining, pp. 505–513. SIAM (2020)
33. Morcos, A.S., Barrett, D.G.T., Rabinowitz, N.C., Botvinick, M.: On the importance of single directions for generalization. CoRR (2018). http://arxiv.org/abs/1803.06959v4
34. Myung, J.I., Navarro, D.J., Pitt, M.A.: Model selection by normalized maximum likelihood. J. Math. Psychol. **50**(2), 167–179 (2006)
35. Neyshabur, B., Tomioka, R., Srebro, N.: In search of the real inductive bias: on the role of implicit regularization in deep learning. arXiv preprint arXiv:1412.6614 (2014)
36. Pennebaker, W.B., Mitchell, J.L.: JPEG: Still Image Data Compression Standard. Springer, Heidelberg (1992)
37. Rissanen, J.: Modeling by shortest data description. Automatica **14**(5), 465–471 (1978)

38. Rissanen, J.: A universal prior for integers and estimation by minimum description length. Ann. Stat. **11**(2), 416–431 (1983)
39. Rissanen, J.: MDL denoising. IEEE Trans. Inf. Theory **46**(7), 2537–2543 (2000)
40. Rissanen, J.: Strong optimality of the normalized ml models as universal codes and information in data. IEEE Trans. Inf. Theory **47**(5), 1712–1717 (2001)
41. Santurkar, S., Tsipras, D., Ilyas, A., Madry, A.: How does batch normalization help optimization? arXiv preprint arXiv:1805.11604 (2018)
42. Song, H., Kim, M., Park, D., Shin, Y., Lee, J.G.: Learning from noisy labels with deep neural networks: a survey. IEEE Trans. Neural Netw. Learn. Syst. (2022)
43. Srivastava, N., Hinton, G., Krizhevsky, A., Sutskever, I., Salakhutdinov, R.: Dropout: a simple way to prevent neural networks from overfitting. J. Mach. Learn. Res. **15**(1), 1929–1958 (2014)
44. Thompson, R.C.: Principal submatrices ix: interlacing inequalities for singular values of submatrices. Linear Algebra Appl. **5**(1), 1–12 (1972)
45. Tishby, N., Zaslavsky, N.: Deep learning and the information bottleneck principle. In: 2015 IEEE Information Theory Workshop (itw), pp. 1–5. IEEE (2015)
46. Vitányi, P.M., Li, M.: Minimum description length induction, bayesianism, and kolmogorov complexity. IEEE Trans. Inf. Theory **46**(2), 446–464 (2000)
47. Wei, J., Zhu, Z., Cheng, H., Liu, T., Niu, G., Liu, Y.: Learning with noisy labels revisited: a study using real-world human annotations. In: International Conference on Learning Representations (2022). https://openreview.net/forum?id=TBWA6PLJZQm
48. Yamanishi, K.: A decision-theoretic extension of stochastic complexity and its applications to learning. IEEE Trans. Inf. Theory **44**(4), 1424–1439 (1998)
49. Yoshida, Y., Miyato, T.: Spectral norm regularization for improving the generalizability of deep learning. arXiv preprint arXiv:1705.10941 (2017)
50. Zhang, C., Bengio, S., Hardt, M., Recht, B., Vinyals, O.: Understanding deep learning requires rethinking generalization. In: International Conference on Learning Representations (2017). https://openreview.net/forum?id=Sy8gdB9xx
51. Zhang, C., Bengio, S., Hardt, M., Recht, B., Vinyals, O.: Understanding deep learning (still) requires rethinking generalization. Commun. ACM **64**(3), 107–115 (2021)
52. Zhao, K., Musolesi, M., Hui, P., Rao, W., Tarkoma, S.: Explaining the power-law distribution of human mobility through transportation modality decomposition. Sci. Rep. **5**(1), 1–7 (2015)

Scoring Rule Nets: Beyond Mean Target Prediction in Multivariate Regression

Daan Roordink[1] and Sibylle Hess[2(✉)]

[1] Enexis Group, 's Hertogenbosch, The Netherlands
daan.roordink@enexis.nl

[2] Mathematics and Computer Science Department, Eindhoven University of Technology, Eindhoven, The Netherlands
s.c.hess@tue.nl

Abstract. Probabilistic regression models trained with maximum likelihood estimation (MLE), can sometimes overestimate variance to an unacceptable degree. This is mostly problematic in the multivariate domain. While univariate models often optimize the popular Continuous Ranked Probability Score (CRPS), in the multivariate domain, no such alternative to MLE has yet been widely accepted. The Energy Score – the most investigated alternative – notoriously lacks closed-form expressions and sensitivity to the correlation between target variables. In this paper, we propose Conditional CRPS: a multivariate strictly proper scoring rule that extends CRPS. We show that closed-form expressions exist for popular distributions and illustrate their sensitivity to correlation. We then show in a variety of experiments on both synthetic and real data, that Conditional CRPS often outperforms MLE, and produces results comparable to state-of-the-art non-parametric models, such as Distributional Random Forest (DRF).

Keywords: probabilistic regression · strictly proper scoring rules · uncertainty estimation

1 Introduction

The vanilla regression models predict a single target value y for an observation $\mathbf{x} \in \mathbb{R}^p$. In theory, the goal is to approximate the *true* regression model f^*, generating the observed target values as samples of the random variable $Y = f^*(\mathbf{x})+\epsilon$. The random variable ϵ reflects here the noise in the data and is assumed to have an expected value of zero. Hence, the goal is to find a regression model that predicts the mean $f(\mathbf{x}) = \mathbb{E}_Y[Y \mid \mathbf{x}] = f^*(\mathbf{x})$.

However, in practice, the trained regression models come with uncertainties. Reflecting those uncertainties is relevant, for example when a lower or upper bound for the prediction is of interest, when underforecasting has more detrimental consequences than overforecasting, or when the expected profit and risk are dependent on prediction uncertainty. Examples of such applications are found in weather forecasting [29], healthcare [16], predictions of the electricity price [24], stock price [30], survival rate [3] and air quality [21].

© The Author(s), under exclusive license to Springer Nature Switzerland AG 2023
D. Koutra et al. (Eds.): ECML PKDD 2023, LNAI 14170, pp. 190–205, 2023.
https://doi.org/10.1007/978-3-031-43415-0_12

Distributional regression models provide predictive uncertainty quantification by modeling the target variable as a probability distribution. That is, models are tasked with predicting the distribution of a (possibly multivariate) random variable Y, conditioned on an observation x of a (possibly multivariate) covariate random variable X:

$$f(x) = P(Y \mid X = x). \tag{1}$$

Here, $P(\cdot)$ denotes the probability distribution of a random variable. Such a model is trained on a dataset of observations of (X, Y): $\{(\mathbf{x}_i, \mathbf{y}_i)\}_{i=1}^n$.

Distributional regression models are typically trained by Maximum Likelihood Estimation (MLE) [15], which is equivalent to minimizing the Logarithmic Score. However, when the assumed and the true shape of the distribution do not match, MLE can become sensitive to outliers [4], causing a disproportionally increase in the forecasted variance [9]. While this is not necessarily a problem for homoskedastic models (where typically only a single estimator is predicted and the error distribution is assumed to be constant), it is problematic for heteroskedastic models, predicting the full distribution [3]. Therefore, for a univariate continuous target domain, many distributional regression approaches use the Continuous Ranked Probability Score (CRPS) [20]. CRPDS provides an optimization objective that is generally more robust than MLE [26] and hence gains in popularity in comparison to MLE [3,21,26].

However, unlike MLE, CRPS has no extension to the multivariate domain ($\mathbf{y} \in \mathbb{R}^d$) that maintains the robustness properties. The most popular extension is the Energy Score [12], but it is known to be insensitive to correlation, and often cannot be analytically evaluated [25]. Moreover, other alternatives such as the Variogram Score [27] also have weaknesses, such as translational invariance.

The lack of a robust alternative to MLE is widely discussed in comparative studies. In their review of probabilistic forecasting, Gneiting and Katzfuss argue that "a pressing need is to go beyond the univariate, real-valued case, which we review, to the multivariate case" [11]. More recently, Alexander et al. conclude that "it is rarely seen that one metric for evaluating the accuracy of a forecast consistently outperforms another metric, on every single scenario" [2]. As a result, multivariate distributional regression approaches either resort to MLE [22] or avoid direct usage of distributional optimization criteria, via approaches based on e.g. Generative Adversarial Networks (GANs) [1] or Random Forests (RF) [31].

Contributions

1. We propose a novel scoring rule for multivariate distributions, called Conditional CRPS (CCRPS). The novel scoring rule CCRPS is a multivariate extension of the popular univariate CRPS that is more sensitive to correlation than the Energy Score and (for some distributions) less sensitive to outliers than the Logarithmic Score. We enable the numerical optimization of the proposed scoring rule by proving equivalent, closed-form expressions for a variety of multivariate distributions, whose gradients are easy to compute.

2. We propose two novel loss functions for Artificial Neural Network-based multivariate distributional regression, with loss functions based on Conditional CRPS, and the Energy Score.
3. We show on a variety of synthetic and real-world case studies that the two proposed methods often outperform current state-of-the-art.

2 Distributional Regression

Distributional regression models are generally evaluated via two concepts: sharpness and calibration [10]. Calibration is the notion that predictions should match the statistics of the actual corresponding observations. For example, when predicting a 30% chance of snow, snowfall should indeed occur in 30% of the corresponding observations. The goal of regression can then be formulated to maximize sharpness (i.e. the precision of the predicted distribution) under calibration [10]. For example, using the notation of the introduction, both models $f(x) = P(Y \mid X = x)$ and $g(x) = P(Y)$ are calibrated, but if there exists a dependency between X and Y, then f is arguably sharper. For this purpose, proper scoring rules are often used.

2.1 Proper Scoring Rules

Scoring rules are a class of metrics R that compare a predicted distribution P with actual observations y. A scoring rule is called *proper* for a class of probability distributions $\mathcal{D}$ if for any $P, Q \in \mathcal{D}$ we have:

$$\mathbb{E}_{Y\sim P}[R(P,Y)] \leq \mathbb{E}_{Y\sim P}[R(Q,Y)]. \tag{2}$$

That is, in expectation over all observations, a scoring rule attains its minimum if the distribution of the observations $Y \sim P$ matches the predicted distribution. A scoring rule is called *strictly proper* if the minimum of the expected scoring rule is uniquely attained at P. Proper and strictly proper scoring rules pose valuable loss functions for distributional regression models: minimizing the mean scoring rule automatically calibrates the model's predicted distributions, and fits the conditional distributions to the observed data (Eq. (1)), arguably maximizing sharpness [11,26].

For univariate domains, the most popular scoring rules are the Logarithmic Score and the Continuous Ranked Probability Score (CRPS). The Logarithmic Score maximizes the MLE criterion, and is defined as

$$\text{LogS}(P, y) = -\log f_P(y) \tag{3}$$

where f_P is P's probability density function. It is strictly proper for distributions with finite density. CRPS is defined as

$$\text{CRPS}(P, y) = \int_{-\infty}^{\infty} \left[F_P(z) - \mathbb{1}(y \leq z)\right]^2 dz, \tag{4}$$

where F_P is P's cumulative density function. CRPS is strictly proper for distributions with finite first moment. The emphasis on sharpness of CRPS, while maintaining calibration, is considered a major upside [3,10].

For the multivariate domain, popular scoring rules are the multivariate extension of the Logarithmic Score (which evaluates the negative logarithm of the multivariate density function), as well as the Energy Score [12]:

$$\text{ES}_\beta(P, y) = \mathbb{E}_{Y\sim P}\left[\|Y - y\|_2^\beta\right] - \frac{1}{2}\mathbb{E}_{Y,Y'\sim P}\left[\|Y - Y'\|_2^\beta\right] \tag{5}$$

Here, $\|.\|_2$ denotes the Euclidean norm and $\beta \in (0, 2)$. For $\beta = 1$ the Energy Score is a multivariate extension of CRPS [12]. Both rules are strictly proper for almost all multivariate distributions (the Logarithmic Score requires finite density and the Energy Score requires $\mathbb{E}_{Y\sim P}[\|Y\|_2^\beta] < \infty$). However, as mentioned in the introduction, both the Logarithmic and Energy Scores have known drawbacks, which demands the introduction of new strictly proper scoring rules.

2.2 Conditional CRPS

We propose a family of (strictly) proper scoring rules, called *Conditional CRPS* (CCRPS). To introduce this scoring rule, we consider a simple example of a bivariate Gaussian distribution

$$(Y_1, Y_2) \sim \mathcal{N}(\boldsymbol{\mu}, \Sigma), \text{ where } \Sigma = \begin{pmatrix} \sigma_1^2 & \rho\sigma_1\sigma_2 \\ \rho\sigma_1\sigma_2 & \sigma_2^2 \end{pmatrix}, \ \sigma_1, \sigma_2 > 0, \text{ and } \rho \in (-1, 1).$$

Rather than evaluating $P(Y_1, Y_2)$ directly against an observation, we instead evaluate the first marginal distribution $P(Y_1) = \mathcal{N}(\mu_1, \sigma_1^2)$, and second conditional distribution $P(Y_2 \mid Y_1 = y) = \mathcal{N}(\mu_2 + \frac{\sigma_2}{\sigma_1}\rho(y - \mu_1), (1-\rho)^2\sigma_2^2)$, against their respective univariate observations, via use univariate scoring rules. Summation over these terms then defines a new multivariate scoring rule R:

$$R(P, \mathbf{y}) = \text{CRPS}(P(Y_1), y_1) + \text{CRPS}(P(Y_2 \mid Y_1 = y_1), y_2). \tag{6}$$

Conditional CRPS generalizes the intuition that multivariate scoring rules can be constructed by evaluating univariate conditional and marginal distributions.

Definition 1 (Conditional CRPS). *Let $P(Y)$ be a d-variate probability distribution over a random variable $Y = (Y_1, \ldots, Y_d)$, and let $\mathbf{y} \in \mathbb{R}^d$. Let $\mathcal{T} = \{(v_i, \mathcal{C}_i)\}_{i=1}^q$ be a set of tuples, where $v_i \in \{1, ..., d\}$ and $\mathcal{C}_i \subseteq \{1, ..., d\} \setminus \{v_i\}$. Conditional CRPS (CCRPS) is then defined as:*

$$\text{CCRPS}_\mathcal{T}(P(Y), \mathbf{y}) = \sum_{i=1}^{q} \text{CRPS}(P(Y_{v_i} \mid Y_j = y_j \text{ for } j \in \mathcal{C}_i), y_{v_i}), \tag{7}$$

where $P(Y_{v_i} \mid Y_j = y_j$ for $j \in \mathcal{C}_i)$ denotes the conditional distribution of Y_{v_i} given observations $Y_j = y_j$ for all $j \in \mathcal{C}_i$.

In the case that $P(Y_{v_i} \mid Y_j = y_j$ for $j \in \mathcal{C}_i)$ is ill-defined for observation y (i.e. the conditioned event $Y_j = y_j$ for $j \in \mathcal{C}_i$ has zero likelihood or probability), we define CRPS($P(Y_{v_i} \mid Y_j = y_j$ for $j \in \mathcal{C}_i), y_{v_i}) = \infty$.

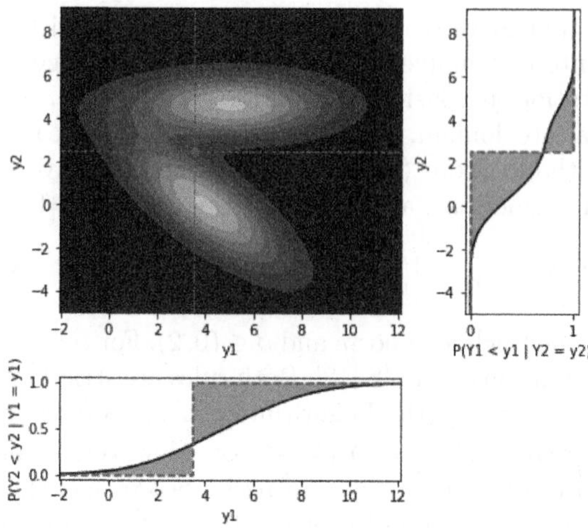

Fig. 1. Visualization of Conditional CRPS, using $d = 2$ and $\mathcal{T} = \{(2, \{1\}), (1, \{2\})\}$. CCRPS evaluates an observed multivariate distribution sample by computing the distribution's univariate conditionals, conditioned on observations for other variates.

Conditional CRPS defines a family of scoring rules via a conditional specification $\mathcal{T}$ (see Fig. 1). For example, choosing $d = 2$ and $\mathcal{T} = \{(1, \emptyset), (2, \{1\})\}$ yields the rule R that is defined in Eq. (6). Conditional CRPS often defines useful scoring rules, as members are always proper, and often strictly proper:

Theorem 1 (Propriety of Conditional CRPS). *Consider CCRPS, as defined in Definition 1. For every choice of* $\mathcal{T} = \{(v_i, \mathcal{C}_i)\}_{i=1}^q$, $\text{CCRPS}_\mathcal{T}$ *is proper for d-variate distributions with finite first moment.*

Theorem 1 can be easily deduced from the univariate strict propriety of CRPS, by writing the expected CCRPS score as a sum of expected CRPS scores. A formal proof is given in Appendix A.1. However, when setting some restrictions on the choice for $\mathcal{T}$, we can also prove a broad notion of strict propriety:

Theorem 2 (Strict propriety of Conditional CRPS). *Consider CCRPS, as defined in Definition 1. Let* $\mathcal{T} = \{(v_i, \mathcal{C}_i)\}_{i=1}^q$ *be chosen such that there exists a permutation* $\phi_1, \ldots, \phi_d$ *of* $1, \ldots, d$ *such that:*

$$(\phi_j, \{\phi_1, \ldots, \phi_{j-1}\}) \in \mathcal{T} \text{ for } 1 \leq j \leq d. \tag{8}$$

$CCRPS_\mathcal{T}$ is strictly proper for all d-variate distributions with finite first moment, that are either discrete[1] *or absolutely continuous*[2].

[1] I.e. distributions P for which a countable set $\Omega \subset \mathbb{R}^d$ exists such that $\mathbb{P}_{Y \sim P}(Y \in \Omega) = 1$.

[2] I.e. distributions P for which a Lebesgue integratable function $f_P : \mathbb{R}^d \to [0, \infty)$ exists, such that for all measurable sets $U \subseteq \mathbb{R}^d$, we have $\mathbb{P}_{Y \sim P}(Y \in U) = \int_U f_P(u)du$.

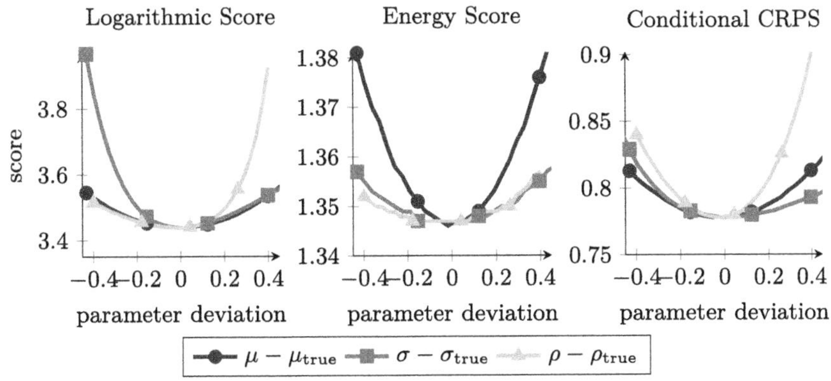

Fig. 2. Plot of mean score values against the deviation of a predicted distribution parameter from the true distribution parameter. We evaluate three strictly proper scoring rules with respect to the deviation of the predicted mean, standard deviation or correlation coefficient from the data distribution ($\mu_{\text{true}} = 1$, $\sigma_{\text{true}} = 1$ and $\rho_{\text{true}} = 0.4$). See Appendix D.

This can be proven by using the conditional chain rule to show that any two distinct multivariate distributions differ in at least one specified conditional. Strict propriety of CRPS is then used to show strict inequality in expectancy of this CRPS term. Formal proofs are given in Appendices A.2 and A.3.

Unfortunately, there exists no CCRPS variant that is strictly proper for all distributions with finite first moment, as problems arise with distributions that are neither continuous nor discrete. This is shown in Appendix A.4.

Closed-Form Expressions. Unlike the Energy Score, it is surprisingly easy to find closed-form expressions for Conditional CRPS. Many popular families of multivariate distributions have marginals and conditionals which themselves are members of popular univariate distributions, many of which already have known closed-form CRPS expressions [17]. To illustrate this, in Appendix B, in which we have provided closed-form expressions for (mixtures of) multivariate Gaussian distributions, the Dirichlet distribution, the multivariate Log-normal distribution and the multivariate student-t distribution.

Correlation Sensitivity. Conditional CRPS displays promising advantages over the Energy and the Logarithmic Score with regard to correlation sensitivity. We evaluate the correlation sensitivity by a small experiment, similar to the one by Pinson and Tastu [25]. Here, we investigate the increase in expected scores when the forecasted distribution deviates from the data distribution in either the mean, standard deviation, or correlation coefficient. The data generating algorithm is described in Appendix D. We compare three scoring rules: the Logarithmic, the Energy Score, and CCRPS with $\mathcal{T} = ((1, \{2\}), (2, \{1\}))$. Figure 2 shows that the CCRPS score increases more with the prediction error in

ρ than the Logarithmic and the Energy score. Therewith, the CCRPS score fixes the well documented lack of correlation sensitivity of the Energy Score [2,25].

2.3 CCRPS as ANN Loss Function for Multivariate Gaussian Mixtures

We show an application of Conditional CRPS as a loss function that allows for the numerical optimization of Artificial Neural Networks (ANNs) [14] to return the parameters of the predicted distribution of target variables in a regression task. We assume that the target distribution is a mixture of m d-variate Gaussian distributions. This distribution is defined by m mean vectors $\boldsymbol{\mu}_1, \dots, \boldsymbol{\mu}_m \in \mathbb{R}^d$, m positive-definite matrices $\Sigma_1, \dots, \Sigma_m \in \mathbb{R}^{d \times d}$, and m weights $w_1, \dots, w_m \in [0,1]$ such that $\sum_{i=1}^m w_i = 1$. A multivariate mixture Gaussian P defined by these parameters is then given by the density function

$$f_P(\mathbf{y}) = \sum_{l=1}^{m} w_l \cdot f_{\mathcal{N}(\boldsymbol{\mu}_l, \Sigma_l)}(\mathbf{y}) = \sum_{l=1}^{m} w_l \frac{\exp\left(-\frac{1}{2}(\mathbf{y} - \boldsymbol{\mu}_l)^\top \Sigma_i^{-1}(\mathbf{y} - \boldsymbol{\mu}_l)\right)}{\sqrt{(2\pi)^d \cdot |\Sigma_l|}}. \tag{9}$$

That is, the ANN returns for each input $\mathbf{x}$ a set of parameters $\{(\boldsymbol{\mu}_l, w_l, L_l)\}_{l=1}^m$, where $L_l \in \mathbb{R}^{d \times d}$ is a Cholesky lower matrix [22], defining a positive-definite matrix $\Sigma_i = L_i \cdot L_i^\top$. Given a dataset $(\mathbf{x}_i, \mathbf{y}_i)_{i=1}^n$, and an ANN $\theta(\mathbf{x})$ that predicts the parameters of a d-variate mixture Gaussian distribution, we can define a loss function over the mean CCRPS score:

$$\mathcal{L}(\theta, (\mathbf{x}_i, \mathbf{y}_i)_{i=1}^n) = \frac{1}{n} \sum_{i=1}^{n} \mathrm{CCRPS}_{\mathcal{T}}(P_{\theta(\mathbf{x}_i)}, \mathbf{y}_i). \tag{10}$$

Unfortunately, if we choose $\mathcal{T}$ such that the loss function computes mixture Gaussian distributions conditioned on c variables, then we require matrix inversions of $c \times c$ matrices (cf. Appendix B).[3] Therefore, we choose a simple Conditional CRPS variant that conditions on at most one variable, using $\mathcal{T}_0 = \{(i, \emptyset)\}_{i=1}^d \cup \{(i, \{j\})\}_{i \neq j}^d$. That is,

$$\mathrm{CCRPS}_{\mathcal{T}_0}(P, \mathbf{y}) = \sum_{i=1}^{d} \mathrm{CRPS}(P(Y_i), y_i) + \sum_{j \neq i} \mathrm{CRPS}(P(Y_i | Y_j = y_j), y_i).$$

Using this definition, we find an expression for this variant of CCRPS. As both $P(Y_i|Y_j = y_j)$ and $P(Y_i)$ are univariate mixture Gaussian distributions, computing $\mathrm{CCRPS}_{\mathcal{T}_0}(P, y)$ is done by simply computing the parameters of these distributions, and applying them in a CRPS expression for univariate mixture Gaussian distributions given by Grimit et al. [13]:

[3] Support for backpropagation through matrix inversions is offered in packages such as Tensorflow. However, for larger matrices, gradients can become increasingly unstable.

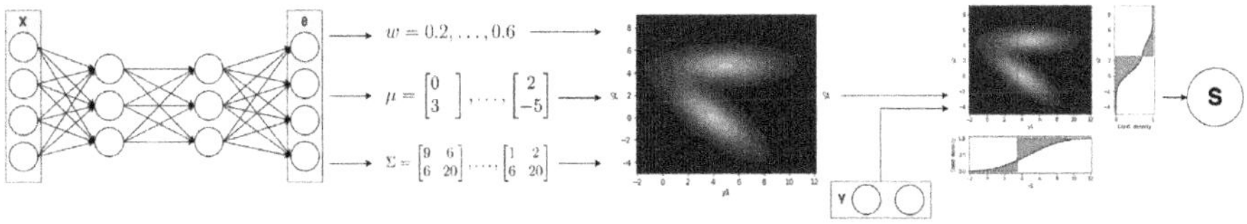

Fig. 3. The output layer of a CCRPS network defines a set of weights, mean vectors and positive definite matrices, via a combination of activation functions and Cholesky parameterizations. These parameters define the predicted multivariate mixture Gaussian distribution, which is evaluated against an observation via CCRPS loss.

Theorem 3 (CCRPS expression for multivariate mixture Gaussians). *Let P be a mixture of m d-variate Gaussians, as defined in Eq. (9) via $\boldsymbol{\mu}_k \in \mathbb{R}^d$, $\Sigma_k \in \mathbb{R}^{d\times d}$ and $w_k \in [0,1]^m$ for $1 \le k \le m$. Then we have for $\mathbf{y} \in \mathbb{R}^d$:*

$$\mathrm{CCRPS}_{\mathcal{T}_0}(P, \mathbf{y}) =$$

$$\sum_{1\le i\ne j\le d}\left[\sum_{k=1}^{m} \hat{w}_{kj} H(y_i - \hat{\mu}_{kij}, \hat{\Sigma}_{kij}) - \frac{1}{2}\sum_{k,l=1}^{m} \hat{w}_{kj}\hat{w}_{lj} H(\hat{\mu}_{kij} - \hat{\mu}_{lij}, \hat{\Sigma}_{kij} + \hat{\Sigma}_{lij})\right]$$

$$+\sum_{i=1}^{d}\left[\sum_{k=1}^{m} w_k H(y_i - \mu_{k,i}, \Sigma_{k,ii}) - \frac{1}{2}\sum_{k,l=1}^{m} w_k w_l H(\mu_{k,i} - \mu_{l,i}, \Sigma_{k,ii} + \Sigma_{k,ll})\right]$$

Here:

- $H(\mu, \sigma^2) = \mu\left(2\Phi\left(\frac{\mu}{\sigma}\right) - 1\right) + 2\sigma\varphi\left(\frac{\mu}{\sigma}\right)$, *where φ and Φ denote the PDF and CDF of the standard Gaussian distribution,*
- $\hat{w}_{kj} = \dfrac{w_k \cdot f_{\mathcal{N}(\mu_{k,j}, \Sigma_{k,jj})}(y_j)}{\sum_{l=1}^{m} w_l \cdot f_{\mathcal{N}(\mu_{l,j}, \Sigma_{l,jj})}(y_j)}$,
- $\hat{\mu}_{kij} = \mu_{k,j} + \frac{\Sigma_{k,ij}}{\Sigma_{k,jj}}(y_j - \mu_{k,j})$,
- $\hat{\Sigma}_{kij} = \Sigma_{k,ii} - \frac{(\Sigma_{k,ij})^2}{\Sigma_{k,jj}}$.

In Appendix B, we state an expression for the more generic case $\mathrm{CRPS}(P(Y_i|Y_j = y_j \text{ for } j \in \mathcal{C}_j), y_i)$. An overview of the proposed mixture Gaussian CCRPS ANN approach is given in Fig. 3. The approach to predict a mixture model via a single network contrasts the multiple-network approach via bagging, used by a.o. Carney et al. [7], and simplifies the architecture.

2.4 Energy Score Ensemble Models

Secondly, we propose an ANN loss variant that empirically approximates the Energy Score. The energy score (cf. Eq. (5)) is defined over expected values, for which no closed-form expression exists, that would enable the computation of a gradient. However, the Energy Score is fairly easily approximated by an ensemble of randomly sampled vectors. Let P be a d-variate distribution, and let $\hat{\mathbf{y}}_1, \ldots, \hat{\mathbf{y}}_m$ be independent samples of the distribution P. We approximate P by its empirical distribution function by assigning probability $\frac{1}{m}$ to each sampled vector $\hat{\mathbf{y}}_l$. That is, we use the *stepwise* multivariate CDF approximation:

$$F_P(\mathbf{z}) \approx \frac{1}{m} \sum_{l=1}^{m} \prod_{i=1}^{d} \mathbb{1}(\hat{y}_{l,i} \leq z_i) \tag{11}$$

We can now approximate the Energy Score:

$$\mathrm{ES}(P, \mathbf{y}) \approx \frac{1}{m} \sum_{l=1}^{m} \|\hat{\mathbf{y}}_l - \mathbf{y}\|_\varepsilon - \frac{1}{2m^2} \sum_{k,l=1}^{m} \|\hat{\mathbf{y}}_k - \hat{\mathbf{y}}_l\|_\varepsilon. \tag{12}$$

Here, $\|.\|_\varepsilon$ is the ε-smoothed Euclidean norm $\|\mathbf{v}\|_\varepsilon = \sqrt{\varepsilon + \|\mathbf{v}\|_2^2}$, for some small $\varepsilon > 0$. The ε-smoothed Euclidean norm makes the norm differentiable, even at $\mathbf{v} = 0$. This approximation allows for numerical optimization, in which a model predicts P indirectly over $\hat{\mathbf{y}}_1, \ldots, \hat{\mathbf{y}}_m$. That is, we can train an ANN to return for each feature vector $\mathbf{x}$ the distribution defining parameters $\theta(\mathbf{x}) = \hat{\mathbf{y}}_1, \ldots, \hat{\mathbf{y}}_m$, using the loss defined in Eq. (12). This approach is similar to the recent, independently developed work by Kanazawa and Gupta [18], and can be considered a non-generative and conditioned version of their approach.

3 Experiments

We compare the probabilistic predicted performance of the newly proposed methods to state-of-the-art probabilistic regression methods. We provide our source code online.[4] As competitors, we choose the best-performing models of the comparative study from Ćevid et al. [31], and the Logarithmic Score trained networks.

- **Distributional Random Forest (DRF)** [31] is a random forest regression model with an adapted splitting criterion for target vectors (based on MMD approximations), and an adapted aggregation that returns a weighted ensemble of target vectors.
- **Conditional GAN (CGAN)** [1] is an extension of the popular Generative Adverserial Network. Except, the model is "conditioned" on input x by adding it as input to both generator and discriminator.
- **Distributional k-nearest neighbors (kNN)** [31] predicts a distribution in which each of the k-nearest neighbors is assigned $\frac{1}{k}$ probability.
- **Mixture MLE neural networks** (a.o. [28]) are the closest to our approach. MLE ANNs use the Logarithmic Score as loss function. We employ the same architectures as MLE networks in our CCRPS networks.

[4] https://github.com/DaanR/scoringrule_networks.

For DRF and CGAN, we use implementations provided by the authors. For mixture MLE networks and kNN, we used our own implementations. Similar to CCRPS, we prevent the numerically unstable backpropagation through large matrix inverses by applying the Logarithmic Score on all bivariate marginal densities $P(Y_i, Y_j)$, rather than on the multivariate density. This way, we could improve on the originally proposed implementation of MLE minimization [28]:

$$\mathrm{MLE}_{\mathrm{biv}}(P(Y), \mathbf{y}) = - \sum_{1 \leq i \neq j \leq d} \log f_{P(Y_i, Y_j)}(y_i, y_j). \tag{13}$$

$\mathrm{MLE}_{\mathrm{biv}}$ is strictly proper for $d \leq 2$ and proper for $d > 2$. For both, MLE-trained networks and CCRPS-trained networks, we try variants with $m \in \{1, 10\}$ (Gaussian) mixture distributions. For each model and each experiment, we choose the best hyperparameters and architecture out of a variety of hyperparameters/architectures, based on the validation Energy Score. Furthermore, for all ANN-based models, we use the validation set loss as a training cutoff criterion: training is stopped once the validation set increases compared to the previous epoch.

3.1 Evaluation Metrics

Unfortunately, there is no clear consensus on appropriate evaluation metrics for multivariate distributional regression models [2]. Hence, we choose a variety of popular metrics: the Energy Score (cf. Eq. (5)) with $\beta = 1$, and the Variogram Score [27] with $\beta \in \{0.5, 1, 2\}$:

$$\mathrm{VS}_{\beta}(P, \mathbf{y}) = \sum_{1 \leq i < j \leq d} \left(|y_i - y_j|^{\beta} - \mathbb{E}_{Y \sim P} \left[|Y_i - Y_j|^{\beta} \right] \right)^2. \tag{14}$$

The Variogram Score is only proper but usually better at evaluating errors in the forecasted correlation than the Energy Score [2]. For most models, the scores are approximated via Monte Carlo approximations (see Appendix C for details).

Contrary to the comparative studies done by Aggarwal et al. [1] and Ćevid et al. [31], we decide not to use the Logarithmic Score (also named NLPD) as evaluation metric, since the ES ensemble model, kNN, C-GAN and DRF do not predict an explicit density function, and we found that the Logarithmic Score is fairly dependent on the choice of density estimation for the post-processing. All datasets are split into training, validation, and testing dataset. We summarize dataset statistics in Table 1.

3.2 Synthetic Experiments

We base our data generation process for the synthetic experiments on the task to post-process an ensemble model. This model is for example applied in the task of weather forecasts (cf. experiments on the global radiation data in Sect. 3.3). Here, a distributional regression model receives s (non probabilistic) predictions

Table 1. Dataset statistics: input dimensionality (p), target dimensionality (d), as well as training (n_{train}), validation (n_{val}) and testing (n_{test}) dataset sizes. For the synthetic datasets, the morphing function is also listed.

Name	morph(y')	p	d	n_{train}	n_{val}	n_{test}
Gauss 2D	$2y' + 2$	40	2	6K	2K	2K
Gauss 5D	$2y' + 2$	100	5	6K	2K	2K
Quadratic	y'^2	40	2	6K	2K	2K

Name	p	d	n_{train}	n_{val}	n_{test}
Births	23	2	18K	6K	6K
Air	25	6	26K	8.5K	8.5K
GR–GEM	8	8	18K	6K	6K
GR–GFS	8	8	18K	6K	6K
GR–GFS	160	8	18K	6K	6K
GR–comb.	176	8	18K	6K	6K
GR & DR	176	48	14K	4.5K	4.5K

$\mathbf{v}_1, \ldots, \mathbf{v}_s \in \mathbb{R}^d$ for a target variable $\mathbf{y} \in \mathbb{R}^d$. That is, the probabilistic regression model is supposed to learn the target distribution from the distribution of target predictions of an ensemble of models $\mathbf{v}_1, \ldots, \mathbf{v}_s \in \mathbb{R}^d$. In other words, the probabilistic regression model is trained to correct ensemble predictions. For each observation, we sample $s = 20$ i.i.d. vectors from a Gaussian with randomly chosen parameters, and sample the target vector from the same distribution. To further simulate errors in the ensemble predictions, we apply a morphing operation (either $\texttt{morph}(y') = 2y' + 2$ or $\texttt{morph}(y') = y'^2$) on the target vector. An overview of morphing functions is given in Table 1.

Algorithm 1. Synthetic data sampling of a single $(\mathbf{x}, \mathbf{y})$ pair.

function GenerateRegressionData($\texttt{morph}, d, s = 20$)
  Sample $\boldsymbol{\mu} \in \mathbb{R}^d$ such that $\mu_j \sim \mathcal{N}_1(0, 1)$ ▷ Choose a random mean vector
  $L \leftarrow 0 \in \mathbb{R}^{d \times d}$
  Sample $L_{jl} \sim \mathcal{N}_1(0, 1)$ for $j \geq l$ ▷ Choose a random Cholensky lower matrix
  $L_{jj} \leftarrow |L_{jj}|$ for $1 \leq j \leq d$ ▷ Ensure a strictly positive diagonal
  for $r \in \{1, \ldots, s\}$ **do**
    Sample $\mathbf{v}_r \sim \mathcal{N}(\boldsymbol{\mu}, LL^\top)$ ▷ Each $\mathbf{v}_r$ is a d-dimensional vector
  $\mathbf{x} \leftarrow \texttt{flatten}(\mathbf{v}_1, \ldots, \mathbf{v}_s)$ ▷ The input is a vector of length $d \cdot s$
  Sample $\mathbf{y}' \sim \mathcal{N}(\boldsymbol{\mu}, LL^\top)$. ▷ Sample a d-dimensional vector i.i.d. to $\mathbf{v}_1, \ldots, \mathbf{v}_s$
  $\mathbf{y}_i \leftarrow \texttt{morph}(\mathbf{y}'_i)$ for $1 \leq i \leq d$. ▷ Apply a simple morph to the target vector
  return $(\mathbf{x}, \mathbf{y})$

The experiment results have been summarized in Table 2. We note that ANN models seem particularly suited for the chosen experiments, with the CCRPS mixture model outperforming the other models on 6 of the 12 evaluated metrics.

Table 2. Synthetic experiment evaluation metrics (ES, VS) are displayed in a group of four rows, and the best score is highlighted. * Scores divided by 10^7.

		CCRPS Gauss	CCRPS mixt.	ES Ens. 100 pts	MLE Gauss	MLE mixt.	KNN	CGAN	DRF
2D-Gauss.	ES	2.1426	2.1427	2.1233	2.1261	**2.0953**	2.1918	2.1983	2.1753
	$VS_{0.5}$	0.5257	**0.5018**	0.5112	0.5196	0.5042	0.5734	0.5199	0.5364
	VS_1	8.0213	**7.6323**	7.8361	7.9425	7.6766	8.7665	7.8844	8.1639
	VS_2	1553.6	**1494.0**	1534.8	1560.8	1519.8	1656.8	1517.5	1558.3
5D-Gauss.	ES	5.1889	**5.1691**	5.1925	5.2693	5.1903	5.2804	5.4533	5.4577
	$VS_{0.5}$	6.7784	6.7728	6.7921	6.9214	**6.7612**	7.2873	7.1653	7.0541
	VS_1	120.67	120.56	120.53	123.71	**120.35**	131.24	129.04	127.17
	VS_2	30087	30149	**29996**	30935	30073	31233	30756	30473
Quadratic	ES	2.7206	**2.6668**	2.6764	2.7989	2.6678	2.8597	2.7766	2.6745
	$VS_{0.5}$	**1.0087**	1.0297	1.0228	1.0926	1.0216	1.1951	1.0245	1.0638
	VS_1	33.371	33.851	**33.741**	34.796	34.055	37.589	34.912	35.386
	VS_2*	130.44	**128.34**	129.78	142.05	130.53	133.27	133.16	132.19

3.3 Real World Experiments

We evaluate our method on a series of real-world datasets for multivariate regression. All datasets are normalized for each input and target field based on the training dataset mean and standard deviation.

1. **Births dataset** [31]: prediction of pregnancy duration (in weeks) and a newborn baby's birthweight (in grams) based on statistics of both parents.
2. **Air quality dataset** [31]: Predictio of the concentration of six pollutants (NO_2, SO_2, CO, O_3, $PM_{2.5}$ and PM_{10}) based on statistics about the measurement conditions (e.g., place and time)
3. **Global radiation dataset**: Prediction of solar radiation based on three numerical weather prediction (NWP) models (the single-model run models GEM [5] and GFS [23] and the 20-ensemble model run GEPS [6]), as well as global radiation (GR) measurements at weather stations in the Netherlands [19] and Germany [8]. Models receive an NWP forecast as input, and a station measurement as target. In our experiments, models predict an 8-variate distribution, consisting of three-hour GR averages. We run four different experiments, in which models receive either GEM, GFS, GEPS or all three NWP sources as input.
4. **Global-diffuse radiation dataset**: Prediction of 24 hourly global and diffuse radiation (DR) station measurements based on all three NWP sources (like in the global radiation dataset).

The experiment results have been summarized in Table 3. Here, the testing set evaluation metrics have been listed to evaluate predictive performance on unseen data. The newly proposed models are on par with current state-of-the-art, outscoring them on about half (13 of the 28) of the evaluated metrics.

Table 3. Real-world experiment metrics (ES, VS) are displayed in a group of four rows, and the best score is highlighted.

		CCRPS	CCRPS	ES Ens.	MLE	MLE	KNN	CGAN	DRF
		Gauss	mixt.	100 pts	Gauss	mixt.			
Births	ES	0.6969	0.6891	0.6897	0.7025	**0.6881**	0.7028	0.7140	0.6924
	$VS_{0.5}$	0.1039	**0.1034**	0.1035	0.1041	**1.1034**	0.1052	0.1063	0.1039
	VS_1	0.2627	0.2612	0.2612	0.2632	**0.2608**	0.2657	0.2688	0.2627
	VS_2	1.3137	1.3069	1.3069	1.3147	**1.3000**	1.3258	1.3353	1.3121
Air	ES	1.0912	1.0844	1.0887	1.0919	1.0881	1.1420	1.1887	**1.0683**
	$VS_{0.5}$	1.8501	1.8380	1.8471	1.9146	1.8562	1.9490	2.0619	**1.8041**
	VS_1	8.5582	8.5118	8.5433	8.5348	8.8644	9.0913	9.6012	**8.3894**
	VS_2	578.74	**572.88**	572.90	584.74	575.10	591.58	605.32	574.34
GR–GEM	ES	0.0988	0.0983	0.0978	0.1013	0.0983	0.0998	0.1216	**0.0960**
	$VS_{0.5}$	0.2476	0.2544	0.2267	0.2492	0.2459	0.2046	0.3114	**0.1926**
	VS_1	0.1705	0.1704	0.1692	0.1742	0.1710	0.1743	0.2273	**0.1657**
	VS_2	0.1026	0.1028	0.1019	0.1053	0.1022	0.1043	0.1363	**0.1001**
GR–GFS	ES	0.1020	0.1006	0.0998	0.1014	0.0992	0.1058	0.1525	**0.0968**
	$VS_{0.5}$	0.2590	0.2636	0.2448	0.2530	0.2519	0.2273	0.5265	**0.1978**
	VS_1	0.1752	0.1744	0.1740	0.1732	0.1718	0.1899	0.3066	**0.1667**
	VS_2	0.1033	0.1042	0.1025	0.1027	0.1004	0.1113	0.1723	**0.0993**
GR–GEPS	ES	0.0759	**0.0722**	0.0723	0.0820	0.0755	0.0806	0.1195	0.0840
	$VS_{0.5}$	0.1800	0.1760	**0.1430**	0.1950	0.1793	0.1743	0.3129	0.1589
	VS_1	0.1070	0.0988	**0.0966**	0.1245	0.1120	0.1247	0.2177	0.1589
	VS_2	0.0614	0.0588	**0.0566**	0.0748	0.0672	0.0733	0.1236	0.0800
GR–comb.	ES	0.0734	**0.0718**	0.0723	0.0766	0.0745	0.0795	0.1209	0.0828
	$VS_{0.5}$	0.1756	0.1754	0.1496	0.1806	0.1765	**0.1438**	0.3202	0.1550
	VS_1	0.1017	**0.0985**	0.0998	0.1119	0.1085	0.1218	0.2254	0.1318
	VS_2	0.0596	0.0595	**0.0594**	0.0672	0.0638	0.0722	0.1346	0.0785
GR & DR	ES	1.4269	**1.3924**	1.4229	1.4819	1.4873	1.5564	1.8090	1.5464
	$VS_{0.5}$	**46.395**	47.592	51.205	48.045	46.413	51.027	77.996	51.104
	VS_1	210.27	**204.60**	208.41	224.72	216.43	242.05	311.35	245.35
	VS_2	3593.1	**3419.0**	3503.3	3775.3	3715.8	3963.4	5983.5	4037.2

CCRPS trained models do seem to outperform their MLE trained equivalents: the Gaussian CCRPS models outperform their MLE counterparts 23 out of 28 times, and the mixture CCRPS models outperform their MLE counterparts 18 out of 28 times.

However, in our experiments, none of the evaluated models consistently outperforms all other models. Generally, one of four models (the MLE and CCRPS mixture models, ES ensemble model and DRF) scored best, with CCRPS and DRF scoring best most often. Unfortunately, we have not been able to link the relative model performances to the experiment's characteristics, as there seems to be no clear connection between the experiment nature (temporal data, tabular data or synthetic data) and the relative model results.

Finally, some visualizations of predicted distributions and their target variables have been made in Figs. 4 and 5.

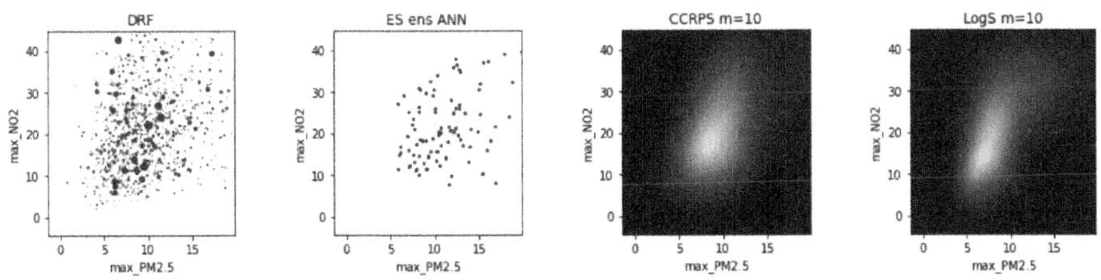

Fig. 4. NO_2 (in ng/m3) and $PM_{2.5}$ (in p.p.b.) predictions of the best four models for an entry in the "air" experiment testing set. The red dot denotes the target measurement. (Color figure online)

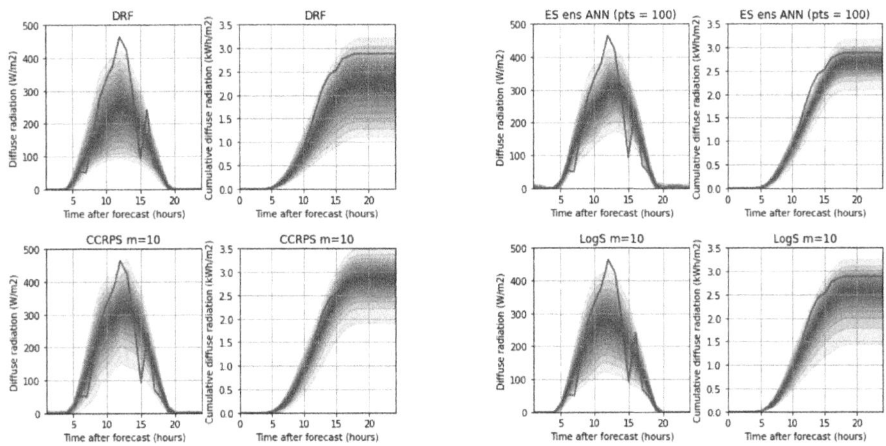

Fig. 5. Diffuse irradiance predictions (95% confidence intervals) of the best four models for an entry in the "GR-DR" experiment testing set. Both the marginal and cumulative distributions are visualized. The red line denotes the target measurement. (Color figure online)

4 Conclusion

We propose two new loss functions for multivariate probabilistic regression models: Conditional CRPS and the approximated Energy Score. CCRPS is a novel class of (strictly) proper scoring rules, which combines some of the desirable characteristics (suitability for numerical optimization, sensitivity to correlation, and increased sharpness) from the Energy and Logarithmic Scores.

Conditional CRPS, when applied in the right setting, leads to an increase in sharpness while retaining calibration. We parameterize our regression models by means of an Artificial Neural Network (ANN), which returns for a given feature vector $\mathbf{x}$ the parameters of the predicted (conditional) target distribution. Models trained with CCRPS outperform equivalent models trained with MLE on the majority of evaluated experiments. Moreover, the novel models, trained with CCRPS and Energy Score loss, have predictive performances on par with non-parametric state-of-the-art approaches, such as DRF (cf. Tables 2 and 3).

References

1. Aggarwal, K., Kirchmeyer, M., Yadav, P., Keerthi, S.S., Gallinari, P.: Regression with conditional gan (2019). http://arxiv.org/abs/1905.12868
2. Alexander, C., Coulon, M., Han, Y., Meng, X.: Evaluating the discrimination ability of proper multi-variate scoring rules. Ann. Oper. Res. (C) (2022). https://doi.org/10.1016/j.apenergy.2011.1. https://ideas.repec.org/a/eee/appene/v96y2012icp12-20.html
3. Avati, A., Duan, T., Zhou, S., Jung, K., Shah, N.H., Ng, A.Y.: Countdown regression: sharp and calibrated survival predictions. In: Adams, R.P., Gogate, V. (eds.) Proceedings of The 35th Uncertainty in Artificial Intelligence Conference. Proceedings of Machine Learning Research, vol. 115, pp. 145–155. PMLR (2020). https://proceedings.mlr.press/v115/avati20a.html
4. Bjerregård, M.B., Møller, J.K., Madsen, H.: An introduction to multivariate probabilistic forecast evaluation. Energy AI **4**, 100058 (2021). https://doi.org/10.1016/j.egyai.2021.100058. https://www.sciencedirect.com/science/article/pii/S2666546821000124
5. Canadian Meteorological Centre: Gem, the global environmental multiscale model (2020). https://collaboration.cmc.ec.gc.ca/science/rpn/gef_html_public/index.html. Accessed 03 May 2023
6. Canadian Meteorological Centre: Geps, the global ensemble prediction system (2021). https://weather.gc.ca/grib/grib2_ens_geps_e.html. Accessed 13 May 2023
7. Carney, M., Cunningham, P., Dowling, J., Lee, C.: Predicting probability distributions for surf height using an ensemble of mixture density networks. In: Proceedings of the 22nd International Conference on Machine Learning - ICML 2005. ACM Press (2005). https://doi.org/10.1145/1102351.1102366
8. DWD Climate Data Center (CDC): Historical hourly station observations of solar incoming (total/diffuse) and longwave downward radiation for germany (1981–2021)
9. Gebetsberger, M., Messner, J., Mayr, G., Zeileis, A.: Estimation methods for non-homogeneous regression models: minimum continuous ranked probability score versus maximum likelihood. Monthly Weather Rev. **146** (2018). https://doi.org/10.1175/MWR-D-17-0364.1
10. Gneiting, T., Balabdaoui, F., Raftery, A.E.: Probabilistic forecasts, calibration and sharpness. J. Royal Stat. Soc. Series B (Stat. Methodol.) **69**(2), 243–268 (2007). https://doi.org/10.1111/j.1467-9868.2007.00587.x. https://rss.onlinelibrary.wiley.com/doi/abs/10.1111/j.1467-9868.2007.00587.x
11. Gneiting, T., Katzfuss, M.: Probabilistic forecasting. Ann. Rev. Stat. Appl. **1**(1), 125–151 (2014). https://doi.org/10.1146/annurev-statistics-062713-085831
12. Gneiting, T., Raftery, A.E.: Strictly proper scoring rules, prediction, and estimation. J. Am. Stat. Assoc. **102**(477), 359–378 (2007). https://doi.org/10.1198/016214506000001437
13. Grimit, E.P., Gneiting, T., Berrocal, V.J., Johnson, N.A.: The continuous ranked probability score for circular variables and its application to mesoscale forecast ensemble verification. Q. J. Royal Meteorol. Soc. **132**(621C), 2925–2942 (2006). https://doi.org/10.1256/qj.05.235. https://rmets.onlinelibrary.wiley.com/doi/abs/10.1256/qj.05.235
14. Gurney, K.: An Introduction to Neural Networks. Taylor & Francis Inc., Boston (1997)

15. Haynes, W.: Encyclopedia of Systems Biology, pp. 1190–1191. Springer, New York (2013). https://doi.org/10.1007/978-1-4419-9863-7_1235
16. Jiao, Y., Sharma, A., Ben Abdallah, A., Maddox, T.M., Kannampallil, T.: Probabilistic forecasting of surgical case duration using machine learning: model development and validation. J. Am. Med. Inf. Assoc. **27**(12), 1885–1893 (2020)
17. Jordan, A., Krüger, F., Lerch, S.: Evaluating probabilistic forecasts with scoringrules. J. Stat. Softw. **90**(12), 1–37 (2019). https://doi.org/10.18637/jss.v090.i12, https://www.jstatsoft.org/index.php/jss/article/view/v090i12
18. Kanazawa, T., Gupta, C.: Sample-based uncertainty quantification with a single deterministic neural network (2022). https://doi.org/10.48550/ARXIV.2209.08418
19. Koninklijk Nederlands Meteorologisch Instituut: Uurgegevens van het weer in nederland (2008–2020). http://projects.knmi.nl/klimatologie/uurgegevens/. Accessed 03 May 2023
20. Matheson, J.E., Winkler, R.L.: Scoring rules for continuous probability distributions. Manag. Sci. **22**(10), 1087–1096 (1976). http://www.jstor.org/stable/2629907
21. Murad, A., Kraemer, F.A., Bach, K., Taylor, G.: Probabilistic deep learning to quantify uncertainty in air quality forecasting. Sensors (Basel) **21**(23) (2021)
22. Muschinski, T., Mayr, G.J., Simon, T., Umlauf, N., Zeileis, A.: Cholesky-based multivariate gaussian regression. Econometrics Stat. (2022). https://doi.org/10.1016/j.ecosta.2022.03.001
23. National Centers for Environmental Information: Global forecast system (gfs)l(2020). https://www.ncei.noaa.gov/products/weather-climate-models. Accessed 03 May 2023
24. Nowotarski, J., Weron, R.: Computing electricity spot price prediction intervals using quantile regression and forecast averaging. Comput. Stat. **30**(3), 791–803 (2014). https://doi.org/10.1007/s00180-014-0523-0
25. Pinson, P., Tastu, J.: Discrimination ability of the Energy score. No. 15 in DTU Compute-Technical Report-2013, Technical University of Denmark (2013)
26. Rasp, S., Lerch, S.: Neural networks for postprocessing ensemble weather forecasts. Monthly Weather Rev. **146**(11), 3885–3900 (2018). https://doi.org/10.1175/MWR-D-18-0187.1
27. Scheuerer, M., Hamill, T.: Variogram-based proper scoring rules for probabilistic forecasts of multivariate quantities*. Monthly Weather Rev. **143**, 1321–1334 (2015). https://doi.org/10.1175/MWR-D-14-00269.1
28. Viroli, C., McLachlan, G.J.: Deep gaussian mixture models (2017). https://arxiv.org/abs/1711.06929, ArXiv-preprint:1711.06929
29. Zhu, Y., Toth, Z., Wobus, R., Richardson, D., Mylne, K.: The economic value of ensemble-based weather forecasts. Bull. Am. Meteorol. Soc. **83**(1), 73–83 (2002). http://www.jstor.org/stable/26215325
30. Önkal, D., Muradoğlu, G.: Evaluating probabilistic forecasts of stock prices in a developing stock market. Eur. J. Oper. Res. **74**(2), 350–358 (1994). https://doi.org/10.1016/0377-2217(94)90102-3. https://www.sciencedirect.com/science/article/pii/0377221794901023, financial Modelling
31. Ćevid, D., Michel, L., Näf, J., Meinshausen, N., Bühlmann, P.: Distributional random forests: heterogeneity adjustment and multivariate distributional regression (2020)

Learning Distinct Features Helps, Provably

Firas Laakom[1(✉)], Jenni Raitoharju[2,3], Alexandros Iosifidis[4], and Moncef Gabbouj[1]

[1] Faculty of Information Technology and Communication Sciences, Tampere University, Tampere, Finland
firas.laakom@tuni.fi
[2] Faculty of Information Technology, University of Jyväskylä, Jyväskylä, Finland
[3] Programme for Environmental Information, Finnish Environment Institute, Jyväskylä, Finland
[4] Department of Electrical and Computer Engineering, Aarhus University, Aarhus, Denmark

Abstract. We study the diversity of the features learned by a two-layer neural network trained with the least squares loss. We measure the diversity by the average L_2-distance between the hidden-layer features and theoretically investigate how learning non-redundant distinct features affects the performance of the network. To do so, we derive novel generalization bounds depending on feature diversity based on Rademacher complexity for such networks. Our analysis proves that more distinct features at the network's units within the hidden layer lead to better generalization. We also show how to extend our results to deeper networks and different losses.

Keywords: Neural Networks · Generalization Theory · Feature Diversity

1 Introduction

Neural networks are a powerful class of non-linear function approximators that have been successfully used to tackle a wide range of problems. They have enabled breakthroughs in many tasks, such as image classification [31], speech recognition [20], and anomaly detection [16]. However, neural networks are often over-parameterized, i.e., have more parameters than the data they are trained on. As a result, they tend to overfit to the training samples and not generalize well on unseen examples [18]. Avoiding overfitting has been extensively studied [14,15,43,45,47] and various approaches and strategies have been proposed, such as data augmentation [18,64], regularization [1,8,32], and Dropout [21,38,39], to close the gap between the empirical loss and the expected loss.

Formally, the output of a neural network consisting of P layers can be defined as follows:

$$f(\boldsymbol{x};\mathbf{W}) = \rho^P(\boldsymbol{W}^P(\rho^{P-1}(\cdots\rho^2(\boldsymbol{W}^2\rho^1(\boldsymbol{W}^1\boldsymbol{x})))), \tag{1}$$

© The Author(s), under exclusive license to Springer Nature Switzerland AG 2023
D. Koutra et al. (Eds.): ECML PKDD 2023, LNAI 14170, pp. 206–222, 2023.
https://doi.org/10.1007/978-3-031-43415-0_13

where $\rho^i(.)$ is the element-wise activation function, e.g., *ReLU* or *Sigmoid*, of the ith layer and $\mathbf{W} = \{\boldsymbol{W}^1, \ldots, \boldsymbol{W}^P\}$ are the weights of the network with the superscript denoting the layer. By defining $\Phi(\cdot) = \rho^{P-1}(\cdots \rho^2(\boldsymbol{W}^2\rho^1(\boldsymbol{W}^1\cdot)))$, the output of neural network becomes

$$f(\boldsymbol{x}; \mathbf{W}) = \rho^P(\boldsymbol{W}^P \Phi(\boldsymbol{x})), \tag{2}$$

where $\Phi(\boldsymbol{x}) = [\phi_1(\boldsymbol{x}), \cdots, \phi_M(\boldsymbol{x})]$ is the M-dimensional feature representation of the input $\boldsymbol{x}$. This way neural networks can be interpreted as a two-stage process, with the first stage being representation learning, i.e., learning $\Phi(\cdot)$, followed by the final prediction layer. Both parts are jointly optimized.

Learning a rich and diverse set of features, i.e., the first stage, is critical for achieving top performance [3,10,34]. Studying the different properties of the learned features is an active field of research [11,13,29]. For example, [13] showed theoretically that learning a good feature representation can be helpful in few-shot learning. In this paper, we focus on the diversity of the features. This property has been empirically studied in [10,35,36] and has been shown to boost performance and reduce overfitting. However, no theoretical guarantees are provided. In this paper, we close this gap and we conduct a theoretical analysis of feature diversity. In particular, we propose to quantify the diversity of the feature set $\{\phi_1(\cdot), \cdots, \phi_M(\cdot)\}$ using the average pairwise L_2-distance between their outputs. Formally, given a dataset $\{\boldsymbol{x}_i\}_{i=1}^{i=N}$, we have

$$diversity = \frac{1}{N} \sum_{k=1}^{N} \frac{1}{2M(M-1)} \sum_{i \neq j}^{M} \left(\phi_i(\boldsymbol{x}_k) - \phi_j(\boldsymbol{x}_k)\right)^2. \tag{3}$$

Intuitively, *diversity* measures how distinct the learned features are. If the mappings learned by two different units are redundant, then, given the same input, both units would yield similar output. This yields in low L_2-distance and as a result a low diversity. In contrast, if the mapping learned by each unit is distinct, the corresponding average distances to the outputs of the other units within the layer are high. Thus, this yields a high global diversity.

To confirm this intuition and further motivate the analysis of this attribute, we conduct empirical simulations. We track the diversity of the representation of the last hidden layer, as defined in (3), during the training of three different ResNet [19] models on CIFAR10 [30]. The results are reported in Fig. 1. Indeed, diversity consistently increases during the training for all the models. This shows that, in order to solve the task at hand, neural networks learn distinct features.

Our Contributions: In this paper, we theoretically investigate diversity in the neural network context and study how learning non-redundant features affects the performance of the model. We derive a bound for the generalization gap which is inversely proportional to the proposed diversity measure showing that learning distinct features helps. In our analysis, we focus on the simple neural network model with one-hidden layer trained with mean squared error. This

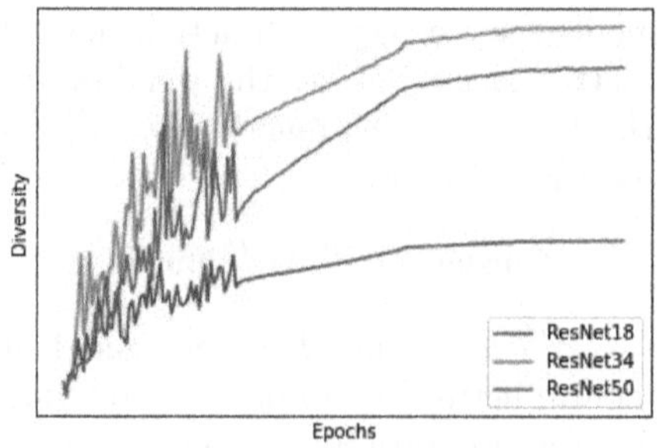

Fig. 1. Preliminary empirical results for additional motivation to theoretically understand feature diversity. The figure shows diversity versus the number of epochs for three different ResNet models trained on CIFAR10 dataset.

configuration is simple, however, it has been shown to be convenient and insightful for the theoretical analysis [9,12,13]. Moreover, we show how to extend our theoretical analysis to different losses and different network architectures.

Our contributions can be summarized as follows:

- We analyze the effect the feature diversity on the generalization error bound of a neural network. The analysis is presented in Sect. 3. In Theorem 1, we derive an upper bound for the generalization gap which is inversely proportional to the diversity factor. Thus, we provide theoretical evidence that learning distinct features can help reduce the generalization error.
- We extend our analysis to different losses and general multi-layer networks. These results are presented in Theorems 2, 3, 4, 5, and 6.

Outline of the Paper: The rest of the paper is organized as follows: Sect. 2 summarizes the preliminaries for our analysis. Section 3 presents our main theoretical results along with the proofs. Section 4 extends our results for different settings. Section 5 concludes the work with a discussion and several open problems.

2 Preliminaries

Generalization theory [28,50] focuses on the relation between the empirical loss defined as

$$\hat{L}(f) = \frac{1}{N}\sum_{i=1}^{N} l(f(\boldsymbol{x}_i; \mathbf{W}), y_i), \tag{4}$$

and the expected risk, for any f in the hypothesis class $\mathcal{F}$, defined as

$$L(f) = \mathbb{E}_{(\boldsymbol{x},y)\sim\mathcal{Q}}[l(f(\boldsymbol{x}), y)], \tag{5}$$

where $\mathcal{Q}$ is the underlying distribution of the dataset and y_i the corresponding label of x_i. Let $f^* = \arg\min_{f\in\mathcal{F}} L(f)$ be the expected risk minimizer and

$\hat{f} = \arg\min_{f \in \mathcal{F}} \hat{L}(f)$ be the empirical risk minimizer. We are interested in the estimation error, i.e., $L(f^*) - L(\hat{f})$, defined as the gap in the loss between both minimizers [6]. The estimation error represents how well an algorithm can learn. It usually depends on the complexity of the hypothesis class and the number of training samples [5,63].

Several techniques have been proposed to quantify the generalization error, such as Probably Approximately Correctly (PAC) learning [50,53], VC dimension [52], and the Rademacher complexity [50]. The Rademacher complexity has been widely used as it usually leads to a tighter generalization error bound than the other metrics [17,45,51]. The formal definition of the empirical Rademacher complexity is given as follows:

Definition 1 [7,50]. *For a given dataset with N samples $\mathcal{D} = \{\boldsymbol{x}_i, y_i\}_{i=1}^N$ generated by a distribution $\mathcal{Q}$ and for a model space $\mathcal{F} : \mathcal{X} \to \mathbb{R}$ with a single dimensional output, the empirical Rademacher complexity $\mathcal{R}_N(\mathcal{F})$ of the set $\mathcal{F}$ is defined as follows:*

$$\mathcal{R}_N(\mathcal{F}) = \mathbb{E}_\sigma \left[\sup_{f \in \mathcal{F}} \frac{1}{N} \sum_{i=1}^{N} \sigma_i f(\boldsymbol{x}_i) \right], \tag{6}$$

where the variables $\sigma = \{\sigma_1, \cdots, \sigma_N\}$ are independent uniform random variables in $\{-1, 1\}$.

In this work, we rely on the Rademacher complexity to study diversity. We recall the following three lemmas related to the Rademacher complexity and the generalization error:

Lemma 1 [7]. *For $\mathcal{F} \in \mathbb{R}^{\mathcal{X}}$, assume that $g : \mathbb{R} \to \mathbb{R}$ is a L_g-Lipschitz continuous function and $\mathcal{A} = \{g \circ f : f \in \mathcal{F}\}$. Then we have*

$$\mathcal{R}_N(\mathcal{A}) \leq L_g \mathcal{R}_N(\mathcal{F}). \tag{7}$$

Lemma 2 [58]. *The Rademacher complexity $\mathcal{R}_N(\mathcal{F})$ of the hypothesis class $\mathcal{F} = \{f | f(\boldsymbol{x}) = \sum_{m=1}^M v_m \phi_m(\boldsymbol{x}) = \sum_{m=1}^M v_m \phi(\boldsymbol{w}_m^T \boldsymbol{x})\}$ can be upper-bounded as follows:*

$$\mathcal{R}_N(\mathcal{F}) \leq \frac{2 L_\rho C_{134} M}{\sqrt{N}} + \frac{C_4 |\phi(0)| M}{\sqrt{N}}, \tag{8}$$

where $C_{134} = C_1 C_3 C_4$ and $\phi(0)$ is the output of the activation function at the origin.

Lemma 3 [7]. *With a probability of at least $1 - \delta$,*

$$L(\hat{f}) - L(f^*) \leq 4 \mathcal{R}_N(\mathcal{A}) + B \sqrt{\frac{2 \log(2/\delta)}{N}}, \tag{9}$$

where $B \geq \sup_{\boldsymbol{x}, y, f} |l(f(\boldsymbol{x}), y)|$ and $\mathcal{R}_N(\mathcal{A})$ is the Rademacher complexity of the loss set $\mathcal{A}$.

Lemma 3 upper-bounds the generalization error using the Rademacher complexity defined over the loss set and $\sup_{x,y,f} |l(f(x), y)|$. Our analysis aims at expressing this bound in terms of diversity, in order to understand how it affects the generalization.

In order to study the effect of diversity on the generalization, given a layer with M units $\{\phi_1(\cdot), \cdots, \phi_M(\cdot)\}$, we make the following assumption:

Assumption 1. *Given any input $\boldsymbol{x}$, we have*

$$\frac{1}{2M(M-1)} \sum_{i \neq j}^{M} (\phi_i(\boldsymbol{x}) - \phi_j(\boldsymbol{x}))^2 \geq d_{min}^2. \tag{10}$$

d_{min} lower-bounds the average L_2-distance between the different units' activations within the same representation layer. Intuitively, if several neuron pairs i and j have similar outputs, the corresponding L_2 distance is small. Thus, the lower bound d_{min} is also small and the units within this layer are considered redundant and "not diverse". Otherwise, if the average distance between the different pairs is large, their corresponding d_{min} is large and they are considered "diverse". By studying how the lower bound d_{min} affects the generalization of the model, we can analyze how the diversity theoretically affects the performance of neural networks. In the rest of the paper, we derive generalization bounds for neural networks using d_{min}.

3 Learning Distinct Features Helps

In this section, we derive generalization bounds for neural networks depending on their diversity. Here, we consider a simple tow-layer neural network with a hidden layer composed of M neurons and one-dimensional output trained for a regression task. The full characterization of the setup can be summarized as follows:

- The activation function of the hidden layer, $\rho(\cdot)$, is a positive L_ρ-Lipschitz continuous function.
- The input vector $\boldsymbol{x} \in \mathbb{R}^D$ satisfies $||\boldsymbol{x}||_2 \leq C_1$ and the output scalar $y \in \mathbb{R}$ satisfies $|y| \leq C_2$.
- The weight matrix $\boldsymbol{W} = [\boldsymbol{w}_1, \boldsymbol{w}_2, \cdots, \boldsymbol{w}_M] \in \mathcal{R}^{D \times M}$ connecting the input to the hidden layer satisfies $||\boldsymbol{w}_m||_2 \leq C_3$.
- The weight vector $\boldsymbol{v} \in \mathbb{R}^M$ connecting the hidden-layer to the output satisfies $||\boldsymbol{v}||_\infty \leq C_4$.
- The hypothesis class is $\mathcal{F} = \left\{ f | f(\boldsymbol{x}) = \sum_{m=1}^{M} v_m \phi_m(\boldsymbol{x}) = \sum_{m=1}^{M} v_m \rho(\boldsymbol{w}_m^T \boldsymbol{x}) \right\}$.
- Loss function set is $\mathcal{A} = \{l | l(f(\boldsymbol{x}), y) = \frac{1}{2}|f(\boldsymbol{x}) - y|^2\}$.
- Given an input $\boldsymbol{x}$, $\frac{1}{2M(M-1)} \sum_{n \neq m}^{M} (\phi_n(\boldsymbol{x}) - \phi_m(\boldsymbol{x}))^2 \geq d_{min}^2$.

Our main goal is to analyze the generalization error bound of the neural network and to see how its upper-bound is linked to the diversity of the different units, expressed by d_{min}. The main result of the paper is presented in Theorem 1. Our proof consists of three steps: At first, we derive a novel bound for the hypothesis class $\mathcal{F}$ depending on d_{min}. Then, we use this bound to derive bounds for the loss class $\mathcal{A}$ and its Rademacher complexity $\mathcal{R}_N(\mathcal{A})$. Finally, we plug all the derived bounds in Lemma 3 to complete the proof of Theorem 1.

The first step of our analysis is presented in Lemma 4:

Lemma 4. *We have*

$$\sup_{\boldsymbol{x}, f \in \mathcal{F}} |f(\boldsymbol{x})| \leq \sqrt{\mathcal{J}}, \tag{11}$$

where $\mathcal{J} = C_4^2\big(MC_5^2 + M(M-1)(C_5^2 - d_{min}^2)\big)$ *and* $C_5 = L_\rho C_1 C_3 + \phi(0)$,

Proof.

$$\begin{aligned} f^2(\boldsymbol{x}) &= \left(\sum_{m=1}^{M} v_m \phi_m(\boldsymbol{x})\right)^2 \leq \left(\sum_{m=1}^{M} ||\boldsymbol{v}||_\infty \phi_m(\boldsymbol{x})\right)^2 = ||\boldsymbol{v}||_\infty^2 \left(\sum_{m=1}^{M} \phi_m(\boldsymbol{x})\right)^2 \\ &\leq C_4^2 \left(\sum_{m=1}^{M} \phi_m(\boldsymbol{x})\right)^2 = C_4^2 \left(\sum_{m,n} \phi_m(\boldsymbol{x})\phi_n(\boldsymbol{x})\right) \\ &= C_4^2 \left(\sum_{m} \phi_m(\boldsymbol{x})^2 + \sum_{m \neq n} \phi_n(\boldsymbol{x})\phi_m(\boldsymbol{x})\right). \end{aligned} \tag{12}$$

We have $\sup_{w,\boldsymbol{x}} \phi_m(\boldsymbol{x}) = \sup_{w,\boldsymbol{x}} \rho(\boldsymbol{w}^T\boldsymbol{x}) \leq \sup(L_\rho|\boldsymbol{w}^T\boldsymbol{x}| + \phi(0))$, because ρ is L_ρ-Lipschitz. Thus, $||\phi||_\infty \leq L_\rho C_1 C_3 + \phi(0) = C_5$. For the first term in (12), we have $\sum_m \phi_m(\boldsymbol{x})^2 < M(L_\rho C_1 C_3 + \phi(0))^2 = MC_5^2$. The second term, using the identity
$\phi_m(\boldsymbol{x})\phi_n(\boldsymbol{x}) = \frac{1}{2}\left(\phi_m(\boldsymbol{x})^2 + \phi_n(\boldsymbol{x})^2 - (\phi_m(\boldsymbol{x}) - \phi_n(\boldsymbol{x}))^2\right)$, can be rewritten as

$$\sum_{m \neq n} \phi_m(\boldsymbol{x})\phi_n(\boldsymbol{x}) = \frac{1}{2}\left(\sum_{m \neq n} \phi_m(\boldsymbol{x})^2 + \phi_n(\boldsymbol{x})^2 - \Big(\phi_m(\boldsymbol{x}) - \phi_n(\boldsymbol{x})\Big)^2\right). \tag{13}$$

In addition, we have $\frac{1}{2}\sum_{m \neq n}(\phi_m(\boldsymbol{x}) - \phi_n(\boldsymbol{x}))^2 \geq M(M-1)d_{min}^2$. Thus, we have:

$$\sum_{m \neq n} \phi_m(\boldsymbol{x})\phi_n(\boldsymbol{x}) \leq \frac{1}{2}\sum_{m \neq n}(2C_5^2) - M(M-1)d_{min}^2 = M(M-1)(C_5^2 - d_{min}^2). \tag{14}$$

By putting everything back to (12), we have:

$$f^2(\boldsymbol{x}) \leq C_4^2\Big(MC_5^2 + M(M-1)(C_5^2 - d_{min}^2)\Big) = \mathcal{J}. \tag{15}$$

Thus, $\sup_{\boldsymbol{x},f} |f(\boldsymbol{x})| \leq \sqrt{\sup_{\boldsymbol{x},f} f(\boldsymbol{x})^2} \leq \sqrt{\mathcal{J}}$.

Note that in Lemma 4, we have expressed the upper-bound of $\sup_{\boldsymbol{x},f} |f(\boldsymbol{x})|$ in terms of d_{min}. Using this bound, we can now find an upper-bound for $\sup_{\boldsymbol{x},f,y} |l(f(\boldsymbol{x}), y)|$ in the following lemma:

Lemma 5. *We have*

$$\sup_{\boldsymbol{x},y,f} |l(f(\boldsymbol{x}), y)| \leq \frac{1}{2}(\sqrt{\mathcal{J}} + C_2)^2. \tag{16}$$

Proof. We have $\sup_{\boldsymbol{x},y,f} |f(\boldsymbol{x}) - y| \leq \sup_{\boldsymbol{x},y,f}(|f(\boldsymbol{x})| + |y|) = \sqrt{\mathcal{J}} + C_2$. Thus, $\sup_{x,y,f} |l(f(x), y)| \leq \frac{1}{2}(\sqrt{\mathcal{J}} + C_2)^2$.

Next, using the result of lemmas 1, 2, and 5, we can derive a bound for the Rademacher complexity of $\mathcal{A}$. We have, thus, expressed all the elements of Lemma 3 using the diversity term d_{min}. By plugging in the derived bounds in Lemmas 4, 5, we obtain Theorem 1.

Theorem 1. *With probability at least* $(1 - \delta)$*, we have*

$$L(\hat{f}) - L(f^*) \leq \Big(\sqrt{\mathcal{J}} + C_2\Big)\frac{A}{\sqrt{N}} + \frac{1}{2}(\sqrt{\mathcal{J}} + C_2)^2\sqrt{\frac{2\log(2/\delta)}{N}}, \tag{17}$$

where $C_{134} = C_1C_3C_4$, $\mathcal{J} = C_4^2\big(MC_5^2 + M(M-1)(C_5^2 - d_{min}^2)\big)$, $A = 4\Big(2L_\rho C_{134} + C_4|\phi(0)|\Big)M$, *and* $C_5 = L_\rho C_1 C_3 + \phi(0)$.

Proof. Given that $l(\cdot)$ is K-Lipschitz with a constant $K = sup_{\boldsymbol{x},y,f}|f(\boldsymbol{x}) - y| \leq \sqrt{\mathcal{J}} + C_2$, and using Lemma 1, we can show that $\mathcal{R}_N(\mathcal{A}) \leq K\mathcal{R}_N(\mathcal{F}) \leq (\sqrt{\mathcal{J}} + C_2)\mathcal{R}_N(\mathcal{F})$. For $\mathcal{R}_N(\mathcal{F})$, we use the bound found in Lemma 2. Using Lemmas 3 and 5, we have

$$L(\hat{f}) - L(f^*) \leq 4\Big(\sqrt{\mathcal{J}} + C_2\Big)\Big(2L_\rho C_{134} + C_4|\phi(0)|\Big)\frac{M}{\sqrt{N}} + \frac{1}{2}(\sqrt{\mathcal{J}} + C_2)^2\sqrt{\frac{2\log(2/\delta)}{N}}, \tag{18}$$

where $C_{134} = C_1C_3C_4$, $\mathcal{J} = C_4^2\big(MC_5^2 + M(M-1)(C_5^2 - d_{min}^2)\big)$, and $C_5 = L_\rho C_1 C_3 + \phi(0)$. Thus, setting $A = 4\Big(2L_\rho C_{134} + C_4|\phi(0)|\Big)M$ completes the proof.

Theorem 1 provides an upper-bound for the generalization gap. We note that it is a decreasing function of d_{min}. Thus, this suggests that higher d_{min}, i.e., more diverse activations, yields a lower generalization error bound. This shows that learning distinct features helps in neural network context.

We note that the bound in Theorem 1 is non-vacuous in the sense that it converges to zero when the number of training samples N goes to infinity. Moreover, we note that in this paper we do not claim to reach a tighter generalization bound for neural networks in general [14,24,44,48]. Our main claim is that we derive a generalization bound which depends on the diversity of learned features, as measured by d_{min}. To the best of our knowledge, this is the first work that performs such theoretical analysis based on the average L_2-distance between the units within the hidden layer.

Connection to prior studies

Theoretical analysis of the properties of the features learned by neural network models is an active field of research. Feature representation has been theoretically studied in the context of few-shot learning in [13], where the advantage of learning a good representation in the case of scarce data was demonstrated. [2] showed the same in the context of imitation learning, demonstrating that it has sample complexity benefits for imitation learning. [55] developed similar findings for the self-supervised learning task. [42] derived novel bounds showing the statistical benefits of multitask representation learning in linear Markov Decision Processes. Opposite to the aforementioned works, the main focus of this paper is not on the large sample complexity problems. Instead, we focused on feature diversity in the learned representation and showed that learning distinct features leads to better generalization.

Another line of research related to our work is weight-diversity in neural networks [4,33,57,58,61]. Diversity in this context is defined based on dissimilarity between the weight component using, e.g., cosine distance and weight matrix covariance [59]. In [58], theoretical benefits of weight-diversity have been demonstrated. We note that, in our work, diversity is defined in a fundamentally different way. We do not consider dissimilarity between the parameters of the neural network. Our main scope is the feature representation and, to this end, diversity is defined based on the L_2 distance between the feature maps directly and not the weights. Empirical analysis of the deep representation of neural networks has drawn attention lately [10,11,29,36]. For example, [10,36] showed empirically that learning decorrelated features reduces overfitting. However, theoretical understanding of the phenomena is lacking. Here, we close this gap by studying how feature diversity affects generalization.

4 Extensions

In this section, we show how to extend our theoretical analysis for classification, for general multi-layer networks, and for different losses.

4.1 Binary Classification

Here, we extend our analysis of the effect of learning a diverse feature representation on the generalization error to the case of a binary classification task, i.e., $y \in \{-1, 1\}$. Here, we consider the special cases of a hinge loss and a logistic loss. To derive diversity-dependent generalization bounds for these cases, similar to the proofs of Lemmas 7 and 8 in [58], we can show the following two lemmas:

Lemma 6. *Using the hinge loss, we have with probability at least* $(1 - \delta)$

$$L(\hat{f}) - L(f^*) \leq 4\Big(2L_\rho C_{134} + C_4|\phi(0)|\Big)\frac{M}{\sqrt{N}} + (1 + \sqrt{\mathcal{J}})\sqrt{\frac{2\log(2/\delta)}{N}}, \quad (19)$$

where $C_{134} = C_1C_3C_4$, $\mathcal{J} = C_4^2(MC_5^2 + M(M-1)(C_5^2 - d_{min}^2))$, *and* $C_5 = L_\rho C_1C_3 + \phi(0)$.

Lemma 7. *Using the logistic loss* $l(f(x), y) = \log(1 + e^{-yf(x)})$, *we have with probability at least* $(1 - \delta)$

$$L(\hat{f}) - L(f^*) \leq \frac{4}{1 + e^{\sqrt{-\mathcal{J}}}}\left(2L_\rho C_{134} + C_4|\phi(0)|\right)\frac{M}{\sqrt{N}} + \log(1 + e^{\sqrt{\mathcal{J}}})\sqrt{\frac{2\log(2/\delta)}{N}}, \quad (20)$$

where $C_{134} = C_1C_3C_4$, $\mathcal{J} = C_4^2(MC_5^2 + M(M-1)(C_5^2 - d_{min}^2))$, *and* $C_5 = L_\rho C_1C_3 + \phi(0)$.

Using the above lemmas, we can now derive a diversity-dependant bound for the binary classification case. The extensions of Theorem 1 in the cases of a hinge loss and a logistic loss are presented in Theorems 2 and 3, respectively.

Theorem 2. *Using the hinge loss, with probability at least* $(1 - \delta)$, *we have*

$$L(\hat{f}) - L(f^*) \leq A/\sqrt{N} + (1 + \sqrt{\mathcal{J}})\sqrt{\frac{2\log(2/\delta)}{N}}, \quad (21)$$

where $\mathcal{J} = C_4^2(MC_5^2 + M(M-1)(C_5^2 - d_{min}^2))$, $A = 4\Big(2L_\rho C_{134} + C_4|\phi(0)|\Big)M$, *and* $C_5 = L_\rho C_1C_3 + \phi(0)$.

Theorem 3. *Using the logistic loss* $l(f(x), y) = \log(1+e^{-yf(x)})$, *with probability at least* $(1 - \delta)$, *we have*

$$L(\hat{f}) - L(f^*) \leq \frac{A}{(1 + e^{\sqrt{-\mathcal{J}}})\sqrt{N}} + \log(1 + e^{\sqrt{\mathcal{J}}})\sqrt{\frac{2\log(2/\delta)}{N}}, \quad (22)$$

where $\mathcal{J} = C_4^2(MC_5^2 + M(M-1)(C_5^2 - d_{min}^2))$, $A = 4\Big(2L_\rho C_{134} + C_4|\phi(0)|\Big)M$, *and* $C_5 = L_\rho C_1C_3 + \phi(0)$.

As we can see, also for the binary classification task, the generalization bounds for the hinge and logistic losses are decreasing with respect to d_{min}. Thus, this shows that learning distinct features helps and can improve the generalization also in binary classification.

4.2 Multi-layer Networks

Here, we extend our result for networks with P (> 1) hidden layers. We assume that the pair-wise distances between the activations within layer p are lower-bounded by $d_{min}^{(p)}$. In this case, the hypothesis class can be defined recursively. In addition, we assume that: $||\boldsymbol{W}^{(p)}||_\infty \leq C_3^{(p)}$ for every $\boldsymbol{W}^{(p)}$, i.e., the weight matrix of the p-th layer. In this case, the main theorem is extended as follows:

Theorem 4. *With probability of at least* $(1-\delta)$*, we have*

$$L(\hat{f}) - L(f^*) \leq (\sqrt{\mathcal{J}^P} + C_2)\frac{A}{\sqrt{N}} + \frac{1}{2}\left(\sqrt{\mathcal{J}^P} + C_2\right)^2 \sqrt{\frac{2\log(2/\delta)}{N}}, \quad (23)$$

where $A = 4((2L_\rho)^P C_1 C_3^0 \prod_{p=0}^{P-1} \sqrt{M^{(p)}} C_3^{(p)} + |\phi(0)| \sum_{p=0}^{P-1} (2L_\rho)^{P-1-p} \prod_{j=p}^{P-1} \sqrt{M^j} C_3^j)$*, and* $\mathcal{J}^P$ *is defined recursively using the following identities:* $\mathcal{J}^0 = C_3^0 C_1$ *and*
$\mathcal{J}^{(p)} = M^{(p)} C^{p2} \big(M^{p2} (L_\rho \mathcal{J}^{p-1} + \phi(0))^2 - M(M-1) {d_{min}^{(p)}}^2\big)\big)$*, for* $p = 1, \ldots, P$.

Proof. Lemma 5 in [58] provides an upper-bound for the hypothesis class. We denote by $\boldsymbol{v}^{(p)}$ the outputs of the pth hidden layer before applying the activation function:

$$\boldsymbol{v}^0 = [\boldsymbol{w}_1^{0^T} \boldsymbol{x}, ..., \boldsymbol{w}_{M^0}^{0^T} \boldsymbol{x}], \quad (24)$$

$$\boldsymbol{v}^{(p)} = \left[\sum_{j=1}^{M^{p-1}} w_{j,1}^{(p)} \phi(\boldsymbol{v}_j^{p-1}), ..., \sum_{j=1}^{M^{p-1}} w_{j,M^{(p)}}^{(p)} \phi(v_j^{p-1}) \right], \quad (25)$$

$$\boldsymbol{v}^{(p)} = \left[{\boldsymbol{w}_1^{(p)}}^T \boldsymbol{\phi}^{(p)}, ..., {\boldsymbol{w}_{M^{(p)}}^{(p)}}^T \boldsymbol{\phi}^{(p)} \right], \quad (26)$$

where $\boldsymbol{\phi}^{(p)} = [\phi(v_1^{p-1}), \cdots, \phi(v_{M^{p-1}}^{p-1})]$. We have $||\boldsymbol{v}^{(p)}||_2^2 = \sum_{m=1}^{M^{(p)}} ({\boldsymbol{w}_m^{(p)}}^T \boldsymbol{\phi}^{(p)})^2$ and ${\boldsymbol{w}_m^{(p)}}^T \boldsymbol{\phi}^{(p)} \leq C_3^{(p)} \sum_n \phi_n^{(p)}$. Thus,

$$||\boldsymbol{v}^{(p)}||_2^2 \leq \sum_{m=1}^{M^{(p)}} \left(C_3^{(p)} \sum_n \phi_n^{(p)} \right)^2 = M^{(p)} C_3^{p2} \left(\sum_n \phi_n^{(p)} \right)^2 = M^{(p)} C_3^{p2} \sum_{mn} \phi_m^{(p)} \phi_n^{(p)}. \quad (27)$$

We use the same decomposition trick of $\phi_m^{(p)} \phi_n^{(p)}$ as in the proof of Lemma 2. We need to bound $\sup_x \phi^{(p)}$:

$$\sup_x \phi^{(p)} < \sup(L_\rho |\boldsymbol{v}^{p-1}| + \phi(0)) < L_\rho ||\boldsymbol{v}^{p-1}||_2^2 + \phi(0). \quad (28)$$

Thus, we have

$$||\boldsymbol{v}^{(p)}||_2^2 \leq M^{(p)} C_3^{p2} \big(M^2 (L_\rho ||\boldsymbol{v}^{p-1}||_2^2 + \phi(0))^2 - M(M-1) d_{min}^2)\big) = \mathcal{J}^P. \quad (29)$$

We found a recursive bound for $||\boldsymbol{v}^{(p)}||_2^2$ and we note that for $p = 0$ we have $||\boldsymbol{v}^0||_2^2 \leq ||W^0||_\infty C_1 \leq C_3^0 C_1 = \mathcal{J}^0$. Thus,

$$\sup_{\boldsymbol{x}, f^P \in \mathcal{F}^P} |f(\boldsymbol{x})| = \sup_{\boldsymbol{x}, f^P \in \mathcal{F}^P} |\boldsymbol{v}^P| \leq \sqrt{\mathcal{J}^P}. \quad (30)$$

By replacing the variables in Lemma 3, we have

$$L(\hat{f}) - L(f^*) \leq 4(\sqrt{\mathcal{J}^P} + C_2) \Bigg(\frac{(2L_\rho)^P C_1 C_3^0}{\sqrt{N}} \prod_{p=0}^{P-1} \sqrt{M^{(p)}} C_3^{(p)}$$
$$+ \frac{|\phi(0)|}{\sqrt{N}} \sum_{p=0}^{P-1} (2L_\rho)^{P-1-p} \prod_{j=p}^{P-1} \sqrt{M^j} C_3^j \Bigg) + \frac{1}{2}\left(\sqrt{\mathcal{J}^P} + C_2\right)^2 \sqrt{\frac{2\log(2/\delta)}{N}},$$

Taking $A{=}4\big((2L_\rho)^P C_1 C_3^0 \prod_{p=0}^{P-1} \sqrt{M^{(p)}} C_3^{(p)} + |\phi(0)| \sum_{p=0}^{P-1} (2L_\rho)^{P-1-p} \prod_{j=p}^{P-1} \sqrt{M^j} C_3^j\big)$ completes the proof.

In Theorem 4, we see that $\mathcal{J}^P$ is decreasing with respect to $d_{min}^{(p)}$. This extends our results to the multi-layer neural network case.

4.3 Multiple Outputs

Finally, we consider the case of a neural network with a multi-dimensional output, i.e., $\boldsymbol{y} \in R^D$. In this case, we can extend Theorem 1 with the following two theorems:

Theorem 5. *For a multivariate regression trained with the squared error, there exists a constant A such that, with probability at least* $(1-\delta)$*, we have*

$$L(\hat{f}) - L(f^*) \leq (\sqrt{\mathcal{J}} + C_2)\frac{A}{\sqrt{N}} + \frac{D}{2}(\sqrt{\mathcal{J}} + C_2)^2\sqrt{\frac{2\log(2/\delta)}{N}} \tag{31}$$

where $\mathcal{J} = C_4^2(MC_5^2 + M(M-1)(C_5^2 - d_{min}^2))$, $C_5 = L_\rho C_1 C_3 + \phi(0)$, *and* $A = 4D\Big(2L_\rho C_{134} + C_4|\phi(0)|\Big)M$.

Proof. The squared loss $\frac{1}{2}||f(\boldsymbol{x}) - \boldsymbol{y}||_2^2$ can be decomposed into D terms $\frac{1}{2}(f(\boldsymbol{x})_k - y_k)^2$. Using Theorem 1, we can derive the bound for each term and, thus, we have:

$$L(\hat{f}) - L(f^*) \leq 4D(\sqrt{\mathcal{J}} + C_2)\Big(2L_\rho C_{134} + C_4|\phi(0)|\Big)\frac{M}{\sqrt{N}} + \frac{D}{2}(\sqrt{\mathcal{J}} + C_2)^2\sqrt{\frac{2\log(2/\delta)}{N}}, \tag{32}$$

where $C_{134} = C_1 C_3 C_4$, $\mathcal{J} = C_4^2(MC_5^2 + M(M-1)(C_5^2 - d_{min}^2))$, and $C_5 = L_\rho C_1 C_3 + \phi(0)$. Taking $A = 4D\Big(2L_\rho C_{134} + C_4|\phi(0)|\Big)M$ completes the proof.

Theorem 6. *For a multi-class classification task using the cross-entropy loss, there exists a constant A such that, with probability at least* $(1-\delta)$*, we have*

$$L(\hat{f}) - L(f^*) \leq \frac{A}{(D - 1 + e^{-2\sqrt{\mathcal{J}}})\sqrt{N}} + \log\Big(1 + (D-1)e^{2\sqrt{\mathcal{J}}}\Big)\sqrt{\frac{2\log(2/\delta)}{N}} \tag{33}$$

where $\mathcal{J} = C_4^2(MC_5^2 + M(M-1)(C_5^2 - d_{min}^2))$ *and* $C_5 = L_\rho C_1 C_3 + \phi(0)$, *and* $A = 4D(D-1)\left(2L_\rho C_{134} + C_4|\phi(0)|\right)M$.

Proof. Using Lemma 9 in [58], we have $\sup_{f,\boldsymbol{x},\boldsymbol{y}} l = \log\big(1 + (D-1)e^{2\sqrt{\mathcal{J}}}\big)$ and l is $\frac{D-1}{D-1+e^{-2\sqrt{\mathcal{J}}}}$-Lipschitz. Thus, using the decomposition property of the Rademacher complexity, we have

$$\mathcal{R}_n(\mathcal{A}) \leq \frac{4D(D-1)}{D-1+e^{-2\sqrt{\mathcal{J}}}}\left(2L_\rho C_{134} + C_4|\phi(0)|\right)\frac{M}{\sqrt{N}}. \tag{34}$$

Taking $A = 4D(D-1)\left(2L_\rho C_{134} + C_4|\phi(0)|\right)M$ completes the proof.

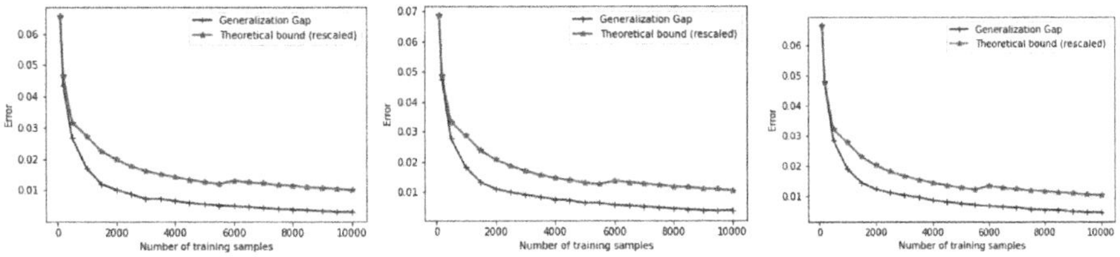

Fig. 2. Generalization gap, i.e., train error - test error, and the theoretical bound, i.e., $(C_5^2 - d_{min}^2)/\sqrt{N}$, as a function of the number of training samples on MNIST dataset for neural networks with intermediate layer sizes from left to right: 128 (correlation=0.9948), 256 (correlation=0.9939), and 512 (correlation=0.9953). The theoretical term has been scaled in the same range as the generalization gap. All results are averaged over 5 random seeds.

Theorems 5 and 6 extend our result for the multi-dimensional regression and classification tasks, respectively. Both bounds are inversely proportional to the diversity factor d_{min}. We note that for the classification task the upper-bound is exponentially decreasing with respect to d_{min}. This shows that learning a diverse and rich feature representation yields a tighter generalization gap and, thus, theoretically guarantees a stronger generalization performance.

5 Discussion and Open Problems

In this paper, we showed how the diversity of the features learned by a two-layer neural network trained with the least-squares loss affects generalization. We quantified the diversity by the average L_2-distance between the hidden-layer features and we derived novel diversity-dependant generalization bounds based on Rademacher complexity for such models. The derived bounds are inversely-proportional to the diversity term, thus demonstrating that more distinct features within the hidden layer can lead to better generalization. We also showed how to extend our results to deeper networks and different losses.

The bound found in Theorem 1 suggests that the generalization gap, with respect to diversity, is inversely proportional to d_{min} and scales as $\sim (C_5^2 - d_{min}^2)/\sqrt{N}$. We validate this finding empirically in Fig. 2. We train a two-layer neural network on the MNIST dataset for 100 epochs using SGD with a learning rate of 0.1 and batch size of 256. We show the generalization gap, i.e., test error - train error, and the theoretical bound, i.e., $(C_5^2 - d_{min}^2)/\sqrt{N}$, for different training set sizes. d_{min} is the lower bound of diversity. Empirically, it can be estimated as the minimum feature diversity over the training data S: $d_{min} = \min_{x \in S} \frac{1}{2M(M-1)} \sum_{n \neq m}^{M} (\phi_n(\boldsymbol{x}) - \phi_m(\boldsymbol{x}))^2$. We experiment with different sizes of the hidden layer, namely 128, 256, and 512. The average results using 5 random seeds are reported for different training sizes in Fig. 2 showing that the theoretical bound correlates consistently well (correlation > 0.9939) with the generalization error.

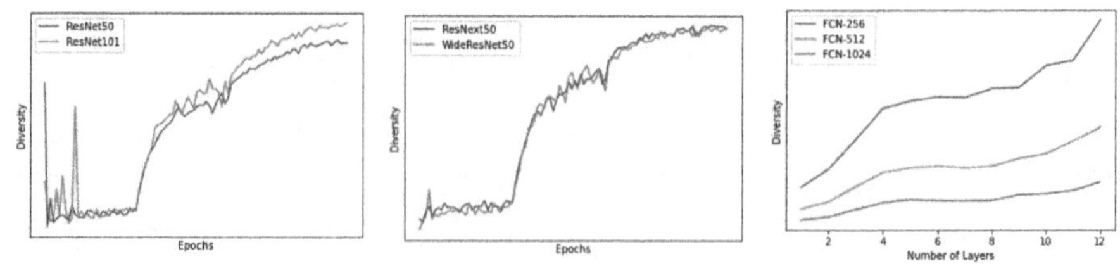

Fig. 3. From left to right: (a)-(b) Tracking the diversity during the training for different models on ImageNet. (c) Final diversity as a function of depth for different models on MNIST.

As shown in Fig. 1, diversity increases for neural networks along the training phase. To further investigate this observation, we conduct additional experiments on ImageNet [49] dataset using 4 different state-of-the-art models: **ResNet50** and **ResNet101**, i.e., the standard ResNet model [19] with 50 layers and 101 layers, **ResNext50** [60], and **WideResNet50** [62] with 50 layers. All models are trained with SGD using standard training protocol [10,22,64]. We track the diversity, as defined in (3), of the features of the last intermediate layer. The results are shown in Fig. 3 (a) and (b). As it can be seen, SGD without any explicit regularization implicitly optimizes diversity and converges toward regions with high features' distinctness. These observations suggest the following conjecture:

Conjecture 1. Standard training with SGD implicitly optimizes the diversity of intermediate features.

Studying the fundamental properties of SGD is extremely important to understand generalization in deep learning [23,25,27,54,65]. Conjecture 1 suggests a new implicit bias forSGD, showing that it favors regions with high feature diversity.

Another research question related to diversity that is worth investigating is: *How does the network depth affect diversity?* In order to answer this question, we conduct an empirical experiment using MNIST dataset [37]. We use fully connected networks (FCNs) with ReLU activation and different depths (1 to 12). We experiment with three models with different widths, namely FCN-256, FCN-512, and FCN-1024, with 256, 512, and 1024 units per layer, respectively. We measure the final diversity of the last hidden layer for the different depths. The average results using 5 random seeds are reported in Fig. 3 (c). Interestingly, in this experiment, increasing the depth consistently leads to learning more distinct features and higher diversity for the different models. However, by looking at Fig. 1, we can see that having more parameters does not always lead to higher diversity. This suggests the following open question:

Open Problem 1. *When does having more parameters/depth lead to higher diversity?*

Understanding the difference between shallow and deep models and why deeper models generalize better is one of the puzzles of deep learning [26,40,47]. The insights gained by studying Open Problem 1 can lead to a novel key advantage of depth: deeper models are able to learn a richer and more diverse set of features.

Another interesting line of research is adversarial robustness [40,41,46,56]. Intuitively, learning distinct features can lead to a richer representation and, thus, more robust networks. However, the theoretical link is missing. This leads to the following open problem:

Open Problem 2. *Can the theoretical tools proposed in this paper be used to prove the benefits of feature diversity for adversarial robustness?*

Acknowledgements. This work has been supported by the NSF-Business Finland Center for Visual and Decision Informatics (CVDI) project AMALIA. The work of Jenni Raitoharju was funded by the Academy of Finland (project 324475). Alexandros Iosifidis acknowledges funding from the European Union's Horizon 2020 research and innovation programme under grant agreement No 957337.

Ethical consideration. This is a theoretical work and does not present any foreseeable societal consequences. The data used in this work comes from publicly accessible channels.

References

1. Arora, S., Cohen, N., Hu, W., Luo, Y.: Implicit regularization in deep matrix factorization. In: Advances in Neural Information Processing Systems, pp. 7413–7424 (2019)
2. Arora, S., Du, S., Kakade, S., Luo, Y., Saunshi, N.: Provable representation learning for imitation learning via bi-level optimization. In: International Conference on Machine Learning. PMLR (2020)
3. Arpit, D., et al.: A closer look at memorization in deep networks. In: International Conference on Machine Learning, pp. 233–242. PMLR (2017)
4. Bao, Y., Jiang, H., Dai, L., Liu, C.: Incoherent training of deep neural networks to de-correlate bottleneck features for speech recognition. In: International Conference on Acoustics, Speech and Signal Processing, pp. 6980–6984 (2013)
5. Barron, A.R.: Universal approximation bounds for superpositions of a sigmoidal function. IEEE Trans. Inf. Theor. **39**(3), 930–945 (1993)
6. Barron, A.R.: Approximation and estimation bounds for artificial neural networks. Mach. Learn. **14**, 115–133 (1994). https://doi.org/10.1007/BF00993164
7. Bartlett, P.L., Mendelson, S.: Rademacher and gaussian complexities: risk bounds and structural results. J. Mach. Learn. Res. **3**, 463–482 (2002)
8. Bietti, A., Mialon, G., Chen, D., Mairal, J.: A kernel perspective for regularizing deep neural networks. In: International Conference on Machine Learning, pp. 664–674 (2019)
9. Bubeck, S., Sellke, M.: A universal law of robustness via isoperimetry. In: Neural Information Processing Systems (Neurips) (2021)
10. Cogswell, M., Ahmed, F., Girshick, R.B., Zitnick, L., Batra, D.: Reducing overfitting in deep networks by decorrelating representations. In: International Conference on Learning Representations (2016)

11. Deng, H., Ren, Q., Chen, X., Zhang, H., Ren, J., Zhang, Q.: Discovering and explaining the representation bottleneck of DNNs. arXiv preprint arXiv:2111.06236 (2021)
12. Deng, Z., Zhang, L., Vodrahalli, K., Kawaguchi, K., Zou, J.: Adversarial training helps transfer learning via better representations. Neural Inf. Process. Syst. **34**, 25179–25191 (2021)
13. Du, S.S., Hu, W., Kakade, S.M., Lee, J.D., Lei, Q.: Few-shot learning via learning the representation, provably. In: International Conference on Learning Representations (2021)
14. Dziugaite, G.K., Roy, D.M.: Computing nonvacuous generalization bounds for deep (stochastic) neural networks with many more parameters than training data. arXiv preprint arXiv:1703.11008 (2017)
15. Foret, P., Kleiner, A., Mobahi, H., Neyshabur, B.: Sharpness-aware minimization for efficiently improving generalization. arXiv preprint arXiv:2010.01412 (2020)
16. Golan, I., El-Yaniv, R.: Deep anomaly detection using geometric transformations. In: Advances in Neural Information Processing Systems, pp. 9758–9769 (2018)
17. Golowich, N., Rakhlin, A., Shamir, O.: Size-independent sample complexity of neural networks. In: Conference On Learning Theory, pp. 297–299 (2018)
18. Goodfellow, I., Bengio, Y., Courville, A., Bengio, Y.: Deep learning. MIT Press, Cambridge (2016)
19. He, K., Zhang, X., Ren, S., Sun, J.: Deep residual learning for image recognition. In: Proceedings of the IEEE Conference on Computer Vision and Pattern Recognition, pp. 770–778 (2016)
20. Hinton, G., et al.: Deep neural networks for acoustic modeling in speech recognition: the shared views of four research groups. Sig. Process. Mag. **29**(6), 82–97 (2012)
21. Hinton, G.E., Srivastava, N., Krizhevsky, A., Sutskever, I., Salakhutdinov, R.R.: Improving neural networks by preventing co-adaptation of feature detectors. arXiv preprint arXiv:1207.0580 (2012)
22. Huang, G., Liu, Z., Van Der Maaten, L., Weinberger, K.Q.: Densely connected convolutional networks. In: Proceedings of the IEEE Conference on Computer Vision and Pattern Recognition, pp. 4700–4708 (2017)
23. Ji, Z., Telgarsky, M.: The implicit bias of gradient descent on nonseparable data. In: Proceedings of the Thirty-Second Conference on Learning Theory, pp. 1772–1798 (2019)
24. Jiang, Y., Neyshabur, B., Mobahi, H., Krishnan, D., Bengio, S.: Fantastic generalization measures and where to find them. In: International Conference on Learning Representations (2019)
25. Kalimeris, D., et al.: SGD on neural networks learns functions of increasing complexity. Neural Inf. Process. Syst. **32**, 3496–3506 (2019)
26. Kawaguchi, K., Bengio, Y.: Depth with nonlinearity creates no bad local minima in resNets. Neural Netw. **118**, 167–174 (2019)
27. Kawaguchi, K., Huang, J.: Gradient descent finds global minima for generalizable deep neural networks of practical sizes. In: 2019 57th Annual Allerton Conference on Communication, Control, and Computing (Allerton), pp. 92–99. IEEE (2019)
28. Kawaguchi, K., Kaelbling, L.P., Bengio, Y.: Generalization in deep learning. arXiv preprint arXiv:1710.05468 (2017)
29. Kornblith, S., Chen, T., Lee, H., Norouzi, M.: Why do better loss functions lead to less transferable features? In: Advances in Neural Information Processing Systems. vol. 34 (2021)
30. Krizhevsky, A., Hinton, G., et al.: Learning multiple layers of features from tiny images (2009)

31. Krizhevsky, A., Sutskever, I., Hinton, G.E.: ImageNet classification with deep convolutional neural networks. In: Advances in Neural Information Processing Systems (2012)
32. Kukačka, J., Golkov, V., Cremers, D.: Regularization for deep learning: A taxonomy. arXiv preprint arXiv:1710.10686 (2017)
33. Kwok, J.T., Adams, R.P.: Priors for diversity in generative latent variable models. In: Advances in Neural Information Processing Systems, pp. 2996–3004 (2012)
34. Laakom, F., Raitoharju, J., Iosifidis, A., Gabbouj, M.: Efficient CNN with uncorrelated bag of features pooling. In: 2022 IEEE Symposium Series on Computational Intelligence (SSCI) (2022)
35. Laakom, F., Raitoharju, J., Iosifidis, A., Gabbouj, M.: Reducing redundancy in the bottleneck representation of the autoencoders. arXiv preprint arXiv:2202.04629 (2022)
36. Laakom, F., Raitoharju, J., Iosifidis, A., Gabbouj, M.: WLD-Reg: a data-dependent within-layer diversity regularizer. In: The 37th AAAI Conference on Artificial Intelligence (2023)
37. LeCun, Y., Bottou, L., Bengio, Y., Haffner, P.: Gradient-based learning applied to document recognition. Proc. IEEE **86**(11), 2278–2324 (1998)
38. Lee, H.B., Nam, T., Yang, E., Hwang, S.J.: Meta dropout: learning to perturb latent features for generalization. In: International Conference on Learning Representations (2019)
39. Li, Z., Gong, B., Yang, T.: Improved dropout for shallow and deep learning. In: Advances in Neural Information Processing Systems, pp. 2523–2531 (2016)
40. Liao, Q., et al.: Generalization puzzles in deep networks. In: International Conference on Learning Representations (2020)
41. Mao, C., et al.: Multitask learning strengthens adversarial robustness. In: Vedaldi, A., Bischof, H., Brox, T., Frahm, J.-M. (eds.) ECCV 2020. LNCS, vol. 12347, pp. 158–174. Springer, Cham (2020). https://doi.org/10.1007/978-3-030-58536-5_10
42. Maurer, A., Pontil, M., Romera-Paredes, B.: The benefit of multitask representation learning. J. Mach. Learn. Res. **17**(81), 1–32 (2016)
43. Nagarajan, V., Kolter, J.Z.: Uniform convergence may be unable to explain generalization in deep learning. In: Advances in Neural Information Processing Systems (2019)
44. Neyshabur, B., Bhojanapalli, S., McAllester, D., Srebro, N.: Exploring generalization in deep learning. In: Advances in Neural Information Processing Systems (NIPS) (2017)
45. Neyshabur, B., Li, Z., Bhojanapalli, S., LeCun, Y., Srebro, N.: The role of overparametrization in generalization of neural networks. In: International Conference on Learning Representations (2018)
46. Pinot, R., et al.: Theoretical evidence for adversarial robustness through randomization. In: Advances in Neural Information Processing Systems (Neurips) (2019)
47. Poggio, T., et al.: Theory of deep learning III: explaining the non-overfitting puzzle. arXiv preprint arXiv:1801.00173 (2017)
48. Rodriguez-Galvez, B., Bassi, G., Thobaben, R., Skoglund, M.: Tighter expected generalization error bounds via wasserstein distance. Adv. Neural Inf. Process. Syst. **34**, 19109–19121 (2021)
49. Russakovsky, O.: ImageNet large scale visual recognition challenge. Int. J. Comput. Vis. **115**(3), 211–252 (2015). https://doi.org/10.1007/s11263-015-0816-y
50. Shalev-Shwartz, S., Ben-David, S.: Understanding Machine Learning: From Theory to Algorithms. Cambridge University, Cambridge (2014)

51. Sokolic, J., Giryes, R., Sapiro, G., Rodrigues, M.R.: Lessons from the Rademacher complexity for deep learning (2016)
52. Sontag, E.D.: VC dimension of neural networks. NATO ASI Series F Computer and Systems Sciences, pp. 69–96 (1998)
53. Valiant, L.: A theory of the learnable. Commun. ACM **27**(11), 1134–1142 (1984)
54. Volhejn, V., Lampert, C.: Does SGD implicitly optimize for smoothness? In: Akata, Z., Geiger, A., Sattler, T. (eds.) DAGM GCPR 2020. LNCS, vol. 12544, pp. 246–259. Springer, Cham (2021). https://doi.org/10.1007/978-3-030-71278-5_18
55. Wang, X., Chen, X., Du, S.S., Tian, Y.: Towards demystifying representation learning with non-contrastive self-supervision. arXiv preprint arXiv:2110.04947 (2021)
56. Wu, B., Chen, J., Cai, D., He, X., Gu, Q.: Do wider neural networks really help adversarial robustness? In: Advances in Neural Information Processing Systems. vol. 34 (2021)
57. Xie, B., Liang, Y., Song, L.: Diverse neural network learns true target functions. In: Artificial Intelligence and Statistics, pp. 1216–1224 (2017)
58. Xie, P., Deng, Y., Xing, E.: On the generalization error bounds of neural networks under diversity-inducing mutual angular regularization. arXiv preprint arXiv:1511.07110 (2015)
59. Xie, P., Singh, A., Xing, E.P.: Uncorrelation and evenness: a new diversity-promoting regularizer. In: International Conference on Machine Learning, pp. 3811–3820 (2017)
60. Xie, S., Girshick, R., Dollár, P., Tu, Z., He, K.: Aggregated residual transformations for deep neural networks. In: Proceedings of the IEEE Conference on Computer Vision and Pattern Recognition, pp. 1492–1500 (2017)
61. Yu, Y., Li, Y.F., Zhou, Z.H.: Diversity regularized machine. In: International Joint Conference on Artificial Intelligence (2011)
62. Zagoruyko, S., Komodakis, N.: Wide residual networks. In: Proceedings of the British Machine Vision Conference (BMVC) (2016)
63. Zhai, K., Wang, H.: Adaptive dropout with rademacher complexity regularization. In: International Conference on Learning Representations (2018)
64. Zhang, H., Cisse, M., Dauphin, Y.N., Lopez-Paz, D.: mixup: Beyond empirical risk minimization. In: International Conference on Learning Representations. vol. 2018 (2018)
65. Zou, D., Wu, J., Gu, Q., Foster, D.P., Kakade, S., et al.: The benefits of implicit regularization from SGD in least squares problems. In: Neural Information Processing Systems. vol. 34 (2021)

Continuous Depth Recurrent Neural Differential Equations

Srinivas Anumasa, Geetakrishnasai Gunapati, and P. K. Srijith(✉)

Department of Computer Science and Engineering, Indian Institute of Technology Hyderabad, Hyderabad, India
{cs16resch11004,cs19mtech11019,srijith}@iith.ac.in

Abstract. Recurrent neural networks (RNNs) have brought a lot of advancements in sequence labeling tasks and sequence data. However, their effectiveness is limited when the observations in the sequence are irregularly sampled, where the observations arrive at irregular time intervals. To address this, continuous time variants of the RNNs were introduced based on neural ordinary differential equations (NODE). They learn a better representation of the data using the continuous transformation of hidden states over time, taking into account the time interval between the observations. However, they are still limited in their capability as they use the discrete transformations and a fixed discrete number of layers (depth) over an input in the sequence to produce the output observation. We intend to address this limitation by proposing RNNs based on differential equations which model continuous transformations over both depth and time to predict an output for a given input in the sequence. Specifically, we propose continuous depth recurrent neural differential equations (CDR-NDE) which generalize RNN models by continuously evolving the hidden states in both the temporal and depth dimensions. CDR-NDE considers two separate differential equations over each of these dimensions and models the evolution in temporal and depth directions alternatively. We also propose the CDR-NDE-heat model based on partial differential equations which treats the computation of hidden states as solving a heat equation over time. We demonstrate the effectiveness of the proposed models by comparing against the state-of-the-art RNN models on real world sequence labeling problems.

Keywords: Neural networks · differential equations · sequence labeling

1 Introduction

Deep learning models such as ResNets [16] have brought a lot of advances in many real world computer vision applications [15,27,34]. They managed to achieve a good generalization performance by addressing the vanishing gradient problem in deep learning using skip connections. Recently, it was shown that the transformation of hidden representations in the ResNet block is similar to the Euler numerical method [13,21] for solving ordinary differential equations (ODE) with constant step size. This observation has led to the inception of new deep learning architectures based on differential equations such as neural ODE (NODE) [8]. NODE performs continuous transformation of

© The Author(s), under exclusive license to Springer Nature Switzerland AG 2023
D. Koutra et al. (Eds.): ECML PKDD 2023, LNAI 14170, pp. 223–238, 2023.
https://doi.org/10.1007/978-3-031-43415-0_14

hidden representation by treating Resnet operations as an ODE parameterized by a neural network and solving the ODE using numerical methods such as Euler method and Dopri-5 [19]. NODE automated the model selection (depth estimation) [2], is parameter efficient and is robust towards adversarial attacks than a ResNet with similar architecture [1,14].

Recurrent neural networks and variants such as long short term memory (LSTM) [17] and gated recurrent units (GRU) [9] were successful and effective in modeling time-series and sequence data. However, RNN models were not effective for irregularly sampled time-series data [28], where the observations are measured at irregular intervals of time. ODE-RNN [28] modeled hidden state transformations across time using a NODE, where the transformations of hidden representations depend on the time-gap between the arrivals and this led to a better representation of hidden state. This addressed the drawbacks of the RNN models which performs a single transformation of the hidden representation at the observation times irrespective of the time interval. Such continuous recurrent models such as GRU-ODE [10] and ODE-LSTM [20] were proposed to learn better representation of irregular time series data. When applied to the sequence data with a sequence of input-output elements along with their time of occurrences, these models obtain the temporal evolution of hidden states using a neural ODE. At an observation time, this is then combined with the input at that time and a discrete number of transformations is applied using a feed-forward neural network to obtain the final hidden representation. This final hidden representation is then used to produce the desired output. Though these models evolve continuously over time, they use a fixed discrete transformations over depth.

There are several real world sequence labelling problems where the sequences could be of different complexities or the input elements in the sequence could be of different complexities. For instance, consider the problem of social media post classification such as stance classification [32,35] where we need to classify different posts arriving at irregular time intervals to different classes. The posts could have varying characteristics with some posts containing only text while some contains both text and image. It would be beneficial to have a recurrent neural network model which would consider the complexities of the input in a sequence by having a varying number of transformations for different inputs along with considering the irregular arrival patterns. In this work, we propose continuous depth recurrent neural differential equation (CDR-NDE) models which generalize the recurrent NODE models to have continuous transformation over depth in addition to the time. Continuous depth allows flexibility in modeling sequence data, with different depths over the elements in the sequence as well as different sequences. Combining this with the continuous time transformation as in recurrent neural ODE allows greater modeling capability on irregularly sampled sequence data.

The proposed continuous depth recurrent neural differential equations (CDR-NDE) model the evolution of the hidden states simultaneously in both the temporal and depth dimensions using differential equations. Continuous transformation of hidden states is modeled as a differential equation with two independent variables, one in the temporal and the other in the depth direction. We also aim to model the evolution of the hidden states using a partial differential equation (PDE) based on the 1D-heat equation, leading to the CDR-NDE-heat model. Heat equation is a second order partial differential equation, which models the flow of heat across the rod over time. The proposed CDR-NDE-heat model considers the transformation of hidden states across depth and time using a non-homogeneous heat equation. An advantage is that it is capable of considering the information from the future along with the past in sequence labeling tasks. We exploit the structure in the CDR-NDE-heat model and PDE solvers to develop an efficient way to obtain the hidden states where all the hidden states at a particular depth can be computed simultaneously. We evaluate the performance of our proposed models on real-world datasets such as person activity recognition [3], Walker2d kinematic simulation data [20] and stance classification of social media posts [35]. Through experiments, we show that the proposed continuous depth recurrent neural differential equation models outperformed the state-of-the-art recurrent neural networks in all these tasks.

2 Related Work

RNN models such as LSTM [17] and GRU [9] are the primary choice to fit high-dimensional time-series and sequence data. For irregular time-series data, traditional LSTM and GRU models are less effective as they do not consider the varying inter-arrival times. To address the problem of fitting irregular time-series data, the standard approach is the augmented-LSTM which augments the elapsed time with input data. In GRU-D [6] and RNN-Decay [28], the computed hidden state is the hidden state multiplied by a decay term proportional to the elapsed time. In other variants such as CT-GRU [24],CT-RNN [12], ODE-RNN [28], GRU-ODE [10], ODE-LSTM [20] and Jump-CNF [7], the hidden state is computed as a continuous transformation of intermediate hidden states. CT-LSTM [23] combines both LSTM and continuous time neural Hawkes process to model continuous transformation of hidden states. Two alternative states are computed at each time-step and the final state is an interpolated value of these hidden states, where the interpolation depends on the elapsed time. Phased-LSTM [25] models irregularly sampled data using an additional time gate. The updates to the cell state and hidden state only happen when the time gate is open. This time gate allows for the updates to happen at irregular intervals. Phased LSTM reduces the memory decay as the updates only happen in a small time when the time gate is open. ODE-RNN [28] used neural ordinary differential equations over time to model the evolution of the hidden states. The next hidden state is obtained as a solution to a NODE, and depends on the time interval between two consecutive observations. GRU-ODE [10] derived a NODE over time and hidden states using the GRU operations and consequently could avoid the vanishing gradient problem in ODE-RNN. Similarly, ODE-LSTM [20] addressed the vanishing gradient problem in ODE-RNN by considering the LSTM cell and memory cell while the output state is modeled using a neural ODE to account for irregular observations. However, all these models only considered continuous evolution of hidden states over the temporal dimension. In our work, we aim to develop models which consider continuous evolution of the hidden states over depth as well as temporal dimensions.

Recently, there are some works which used deep neural networks to solve the partial differential equations (PDE) (also known as neural PDEs or physics informed neural networks) [4,18,36]. [18] showed that LSTM based RNNs can efficiently find the solutions to multidimensional PDEs without knowing the specific form of PDE. On the other hand, very few works used PDEs to model DNN architectures for solving problems from any domain. [29] used PDE to design Resnet architectures and convolutional neural networks (CNNs) such as Parabolic CNN and hyperbolic CNN by changing the ODE update dynamics to different PDE update dynamics. For instance, hyperbolic CNN can be obtained with second order dynamics. They showed that even the PDE CNNs with modest architectures achieve similar performance to the larger networks with considerably large numbers of parameters. Unlike the prior works combining neural networks and PDEs, our aim is to solve sequence labeling problems by developing flexible RNN based architectures considering the PDE based models and solutions.

3 Background

3.1 Problem Definition

We consider the sequence labeling problem with a sequence length of K, and denote the input-output pairs in the sequence as $\{\mathbf{x}_t, \mathbf{y}_t\}_{t=1}^{K}$ and the elements in the sequence are irregularly sampled at observation times $\mathbf{t} \in \mathbb{R}^{+K}$. We assume the input element in the sequence to be D dimensional, $\mathbf{x}_t \in \mathcal{R}^D$ and the corresponding output $\mathbf{y}_t$ depends on the problem, discrete if it is classification or continuous if it is regression. The aim is to learn a model $f(\cdot, \theta)$ which could predict the output $\mathbf{y}_t$ considering the input $\mathbf{x}_t$, and dependence on other elements in the sequence.

3.2 Gated Recurrent Unit

Recurrent neural networks (RNNs) are well suited to model the sequence data. They make use of the recurrent connections to remember the information until the previous time step, and combine it with the current input to predict the output. Standard RNNs suffer from the vanishing gradient problem due to which it forgets long term dependencies among the sequence elements. This was overcome with the help of long short term memory (LSTM) [17] and gated recurrent units (GRUs) [9]. In our work we consider the basic RNN block to be a GRU. In GRU, computation of hidden state and output at any time step t involves the following transformations,

$$\begin{aligned} \mathbf{r}_t &= \sigma(W_r \mathbf{x}_t + U_r \mathbf{h}_{t-1} + \mathbf{b}_r), \quad \mathbf{z}_t = \sigma(W_z \mathbf{x}_t + U_z \mathbf{h}_{t-1} + \mathbf{b}_z) \\ \mathbf{g}_t &= \tanh(W_h \mathbf{x}_t + U_h (\mathbf{r}_t \odot \mathbf{h}_{t-1}) + \mathbf{b}_h) \end{aligned} \tag{1}$$

where $\mathbf{r}_t$, $\mathbf{z}_t$, $\mathbf{g}_t$ are the reset gate, update gate and update vector respectively for the GRU. The hidden state $\mathbf{h}_t$ in GRU is given by,

$$\mathbf{h}_t = \mathbf{z}_t \odot \mathbf{h}_{t-1} + (1 - \mathbf{z}_t) \odot \mathbf{g}_t \tag{2}$$

As we can see, GRUs and RNNs in general do not consider the exact times or time interval between the observations. The same operations are applied irrespective of the time gap between observations. This can limit the capability of these models for irregularly sampled time series data.

GRUs can be extended to consider the irregularity in the time series data by developing a continuous GRU variant. A continuous GRU, GRU-ODE [10], can be obtained by adding and subtracting the hidden state on both sides of (2). The computation of hidden states then becomes equivalent to solving an ODE given in (3).

$$\mathbf{h}_t - \mathbf{h}_{t-1} = \mathbf{z}_t \odot \mathbf{h}_{t-1} + (1 - \mathbf{z}_t) \odot \mathbf{g}_t - \mathbf{h}_{t-1} \implies \frac{d\mathbf{h}_t}{dt} = (1 - \mathbf{z}_t) \odot (\mathbf{g}_t - \mathbf{h}_t) \tag{3}$$

3.3 Recurrent Neural Ordinary Differential Equations

In ODE-RNN [28], ODE-LSTM [20], and ODE-GRU [10], the hidden state $\mathbf{h}_t$ holds the summary of past observations and evolves between the observations considering the time interval. For a new observation, the hidden state $\mathbf{h}_t$ changes abruptly to consider it [7]. Given initial state $\mathbf{h}_0$, let the function $f_h()$ models the continuous transformation of hidden state and function $g_h()$ model instantaneous change in the hidden state at the new observation. The prediction y'_t is computed by using a function $o_h()$, which is then used to compute the loss (cross entropy loss for classification). Both the functions $g_h()$ and $o_h()$ are typically standard feed-forward neural networks with a discrete number of layers. In the case of GRU-ODE, the function $f_h()$ takes the form given in the right hand side of (3). In general, the recurrent NODE models can be represented using the following system.

$$\frac{d\mathbf{h}_t}{dt} = f_h(h_t), \quad \lim_{\epsilon \to 0} \mathbf{h}_{t+\epsilon} = g_h(\mathbf{h}_t, \mathbf{x}_t), \quad y'_t = o_h(\mathbf{h}_{t+\epsilon}) \tag{4}$$

4 Continuous Depth Recurrent Neural Differential Equations

We propose continuous depth recurrent neural differential equations (CDR-NDE) aiming to overcome the drawbacks of the recurrent NODEs in modeling the sequence data. As already discussed, recurrent NODE models bring abrupt changes in the hidden state at the observation times using the standard neural network transformation $g_h()$, when it considers the input $\mathbf{x}_t$ at time t. We aim to develop RNN models capable of continuous transformations over depth in addition to the temporal dimension. Such models will help in processing inputs with varying complexities, aid in model selection (in choosing the number of layers in a RNN model) and reduce the number of parameters (as every layer shares the same parameters as in NODE). Moreover, we hypothesize that such continuous transformation over depth will also aid in learning better hidden representations as it is not limited by a predefined number of layers as in standard RNNs. We propose two models, CDR-NDE and CDR-NDE-heat model. Both the models generalize the GRU-ODE model by continuously evolving in both the temporal and depth directions. The CDR-NDE-heat model is formulated based on a partial differential equation (1-dimensional heat equation) and enables faster computation of hidden states even when using an adaptive step numerical method like Dopri5.

The hidden states of CDR-NDE evolves in depth direction (denoted by vertical axis t' in Fig. 1) while also evolving in the temporal direction (denoted by horizontal axis t in Fig. 1). As the hidden state evolves in both directions, we need a tuple (t, t') to uniquely identify any hidden state and we represent the hidden state as $\mathbf{h}_{(t,t')}$. As shown in Fig. 1, during the computation of a hidden state $\mathbf{h}_{(t,t')}$, it requires hidden states that are immediately to the left in the temporal dimension $\mathbf{h}_{(t-1,t')}$ and below in the depth direction $\mathbf{h}_{(t,t'-1)}$. The evolution of the hidden state $\mathbf{h}_{(t,t')}$ in the CDR-NDE is governed by the following differential equations.

$$\frac{\partial \mathbf{h}_{(t,t')}}{\partial t} = f_h(\mathbf{h}_{(t,t')}, \mathbf{h}_{(t,t'-1)}), \quad \frac{\partial \mathbf{h}_{(t,t')}}{\partial t'} = g_h(\mathbf{h}_{(t,t')}, \mathbf{h}_{(t-1,t')}) \tag{5}$$

$$\mathbf{y}_i = o_h(\mathbf{h}_{(t_i,T')}), \quad \mathbf{h}_{(t_i,0)} = \mathbf{x}_i \quad \forall i = 1, \ldots, K \tag{6}$$

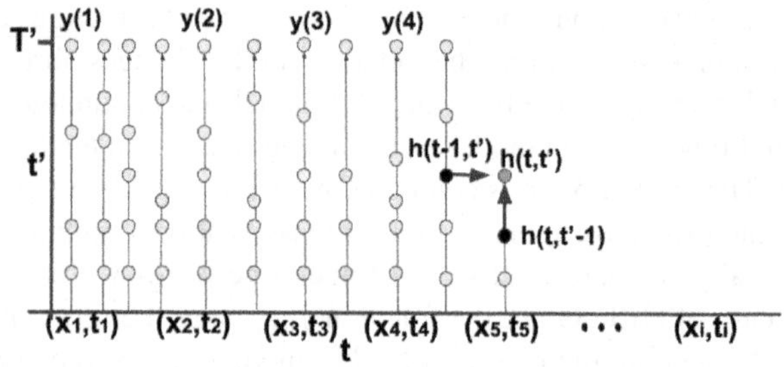

Fig. 1. Shows the computation of hidden states using the CDR-NDE model. As we can see for different observations, the number of intermediate hidden states in the evolution along the depth is different. The index $(t-1, t')$ points to the hidden state of immediate left vertical evolution. The index $(t, t'-1)$ points the hidden state just below the current vertical evolution.

where T' is the maximum depth. We observe that the changes in the hidden state in the horizontal (time) direction depends on the hidden states at a depth below while changes in the hidden states in the vertical (depth) direction depends on the hidden states at the previous time. The derivation and exact expression used to define the functions $f_h()$ and $g_h()$ are obtained as follows. We consider the evolution in the horizontal direction to follow the GRU-ODE model but with an added skip-connection in the vertical direction. Though $f_h()$ can be any function as in ODE-RNN, we followed GRU-ODE to avoid vanishing gradient problems in the temporal direction [10]. In a discrete setup, the expression used to compute the hidden state $\mathbf{h}_{(t,t')}$ after adding the skip connection in the vertical direction can be written as

$$\mathbf{h}_{(t,t')} = \mathbf{z}_{(t,t')} \odot \mathbf{h}_{(t-1,t')} + (1 - \mathbf{z}_{(t,t')}) \odot \mathbf{g}_{(t,t')} + \mathbf{h}_{(t,t'-1)} \tag{7}$$

By subtracting $\mathbf{h}_{(t-1,t')}$ on both sides, we can obtain the difference equation as

$$\mathbf{h}_{(t,t')} - \mathbf{h}_{(t-1,t')} = \mathbf{z}_{(t,t')} \odot \mathbf{h}_{(t-1,t')} + (1 - \mathbf{z}_{(t,t')}) \odot \mathbf{g}_{(t,t')} + \mathbf{h}_{(t,t'-1)} - \mathbf{h}_{(t-1,t')} \tag{8}$$

Consequently, the differential equation governing the flow in the temporal (horizontal) direction is

$$\frac{\partial \mathbf{h}_{(t,t')}}{\partial t} = \mathbf{z}_{(t,t')} \odot \mathbf{h}_{(t,t')} + (1 - \mathbf{z}_{(t,t')}) \odot \mathbf{g}_{(t,t')} + \mathbf{h}_{(t,t'-1)} - \mathbf{h}_{(t,t')} \tag{9}$$

where $\mathbf{z}_{(t,t')} = \sigma(W_z \mathbf{h}_{(t,t'-1)} + U_z \mathbf{h}_{(t,t')} + \mathbf{b}_z)$,

$$\mathbf{g}_{(t,t')} = \tanh(W_h \mathbf{h}_{(t,t'-1)} + U_h(\mathbf{r}_{(t,t')} \odot \mathbf{h}_{t,t'}) + \mathbf{b}_h),$$
$$\mathbf{r}_{(t,t')} = \sigma(W_r \mathbf{h}_{(t,t'-1)} + U_r \mathbf{h}_{(t,t')} + \mathbf{b}_r).$$

To derive the differential equation in the depth (vertical) direction t', Eq. 7 can be written as a difference equation by carrying the term $\mathbf{h}_{(t,t'-1)}$ to the left hand side.

$$\mathbf{h}_{(t,t')} - \mathbf{h}_{(t,t'-1)} = \mathbf{z}_{(t,t')} \odot \mathbf{h}_{(t-1,t')} + (1 - \mathbf{z}_{(t,t')}) \odot \mathbf{g}_{(t,t')} \tag{10}$$

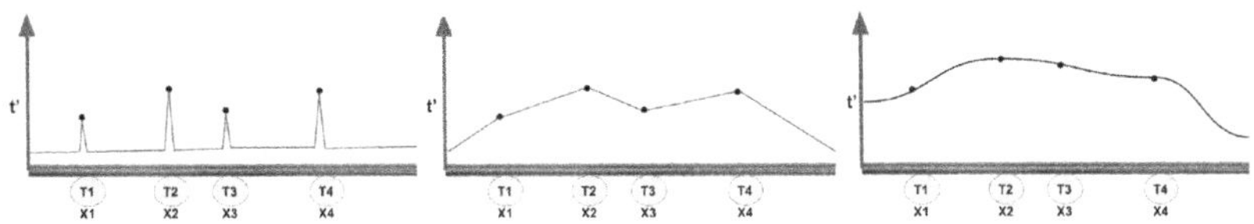

(a) At $t' = 0$ sec (b) At $t' = p$ sec (c) At $t' > p$ sec

Fig. 2. Evolution of temperature across time.(a) shows the initial state(temperature) of the rod, heat is applied externally at 4 different points. Over time, heat diffuses from hot region to cold region, (b) shows the state of the rod, after p seconds. (c) Over time, the change in temperature comes to an equilibrium state, no change of temperature over time.

Consequently, the differential equation governing flow in depth (vertical) direction is defined below and we can observe that it depends on hidden states at the previous time.

$$\frac{\partial \mathbf{h}_{(t,t')}}{\partial t'} = \mathbf{z}'_{(t,t')} \odot \mathbf{h}_{(t-1,t')} + (1 - \mathbf{z}'_{(t,t')}) \odot \mathbf{g}'_{(t,t')} \tag{11}$$

where $\mathbf{z}'_{(t,t')} = \sigma(W_z \mathbf{h}_{(t,t')} + U_z \mathbf{h}_{(t-1,t')} + \mathbf{b}_z)$,

$$\mathbf{g}'_{(t,t')} = \tanh(W_h \mathbf{h}_{(t,t')} + U_h(\mathbf{r}'_{(t,t')} \odot \mathbf{h}_{(t-1,t')}) + \mathbf{b}_h),$$
$$\mathbf{r}'_{(t,t')} = \sigma(W_r \mathbf{h}_{(t,t')} + U_r \mathbf{h}_{(t-1,t')} + \mathbf{b}_r).$$

We solve the differential equations (9) and (11) in two stages. In the first stage, CDR-NDE is solved in the horizontal direction until time t_K for $t' = 0$ following (9) and can be solved using differential equation solvers such as Euler method or Dopri5. In the second stage, for every time step evaluated on the t-axis during the first stage, hidden states are allowed to evolve in the vertical direction, i.e. along the t'-axis. Evolution in vertical direction is done until time $t' = T'$ and can be solved using solvers such as Euler or Dopri5. We can observe that during this evolution, CDR-NDE model considers $\mathbf{h}_{(t-1,t')}$ in computing $\mathbf{h}_{(t,t')}$ for any time t and depth t' taking into account the dependencies in the sequence. Hence, computation of the hidden state $\mathbf{h}_{(t,t')}$ needs access to the hidden state $\mathbf{h}_{(t-1,t')}$ and this requires performing an additional interpolation on the hidden states evaluated at time $t-1$ in the case of adaptive solvers.

4.1 CDR-NDE Based on Heat Equation

We propose another CDR-NDE model inspired by the partial differential equations and in particular the 1D-heat diffusion equation [5]. Heat equation represents the evolution of heat over time in a rod. Consider a rod of length L which is at room temperature. Along the length of the rod, at different points, heat is applied externally into the rod. The temperatures applied at different points can be different. Figure 2(a) provides a visualization of the initial state(at $t' = 0$), where the rod is at room temperature. At four different points, heat is applied externally with different temperature values. Heat starts to flow from hotter regions to colder regions and the points which are initially at room temperature become hotter. In a finite amount of time, it reaches a state where the change in temperature at any point in time is zero, which is called an equilibrium state. Figure 2(b) visualizes the intermediate state of temperatures across the rod after p seconds. Figure 2(c) visualizes the equilibrium state where the change in temperature across the rod is smooth.

We can observe that the evolution of temperature in a rod can be seen as equivalent to the evolution of hidden states and applying temperature to the road can be considered equivalent to providing input data in the sequence. The hidden states associated with input data smoothly change over the depth dimension t' reaching an equilibrium state, and finally leading to the output elements in the sequence. The heat equation motivates us to construct a model capable of capturing interactions among different elements in the sequence, providing smooth hidden transformations with variable depth. We hypothesize that such models will be able to learn better representations depending on the input and improve the generalization performance.

The process of heat diffusion can be represented by a 1D heat equation [5] which is a homogeneous second order partial differential equation, $\frac{\partial u(t',l)}{\partial t'} = C * \frac{\partial^2 u(t',l)}{\partial l^2}$, where $u(t', l)$ is the temperature at point l on rod at time t' and C is a constant(diffusivity). The proposed CDR-NDE-heat model is based on the non-homogeneous heat equation, a variant of the homogeneous 1D heat equation. The temperature applied at a location l_i in the rod is equivalent to the datapoint $\mathbf{x}_i$ at time t_i. As the temperature injected at a point affects the temperature around the rod neighborhood, the hidden states are affected by the observed data points in the neighborhood. The hidden state then evolves over the depth variable t' and reaches a steady state following the heat diffusion model. The second order derivative with respect to location l in the heat equation (equivalently over time t for sequence labeling problems) allows one to consider the effect of neighbors around a point. For sequence modeling, this allows one to learn a better representation by considering past and future hidden states across time t, similar to bi-directional RNNs considering past and future information.

The proposed model considers a non-homogeneous heat equation model which allows a better representation of hidden state during evolution by considering additional information on the interaction between the hidden states. In our case, we choose GRUcell which holds a summary of the past observations to capture the interaction. The differential equation governing the evolution of the proposed CDR-NDE-heat model is defined as follows,

$$\frac{\partial \mathbf{h}_{(t,t')}}{\partial t'} - \frac{\partial^2 \mathbf{h}_{(t,t')}}{\partial t^2} = f(\mathbf{h}_{(t,t'-1)}, \mathbf{h}_{(t-1,t')}) \quad (12)$$

where $f(\mathbf{h}_{(t,t'-1)}, \mathbf{h}_{(t-1,t')})$ is the GRUCell operation, i.e. $f(\mathbf{h}_{(t,t'-1)}, \mathbf{h}_{(t-1,t')}) = \mathbf{z}_{(t,t')} \odot \mathbf{h}_{(t-1,t')} + (1 - \mathbf{z}_{(t,t')}) \odot \mathbf{g}_{(t,t')}$. The evolution of hidden state as shown in Equation 12 corresponds to a non-homogeneous heat equation [33] with GRUCell capturing the interactions.

The heat equation can be solved numerically using methods like finite-difference method(FDM) [26] and method of lines(MoL) [30]. We can get a better insights on the behaviour of the proposed CDR-NDE-heat model by writing the updates using the finite difference method. Using FDM, the hidden state is computed as follows,

$$\frac{\mathbf{h}_{(t,t'+\Delta_{t'})} - \mathbf{h}_{(t,t')}}{\Delta_{t'}} - \frac{\mathbf{h}_{(t-\Delta_t,t')} - 2\mathbf{h}_{(t,t')} + \mathbf{h}_{(t+\Delta_t,t')}}{\Delta_t^2} = f(\mathbf{h}_{(t,t'-\Delta_{t'})}, \mathbf{h}_{(t-\Delta_t,t')})$$

$$\implies \mathbf{h}_{(t,t'+\Delta_{t'})} = \frac{\Delta'_t}{\Delta_t^2}[\mathbf{h}_{(t-\Delta_t,t')} - 2\mathbf{h}_{(t,t')} + \mathbf{h}_{(t+\Delta_t,t')}] + \Delta_{t'}[f(\mathbf{h}_{(t,t'-\Delta_{t'})}, \mathbf{h}_{(t-\Delta_t,t')})] + \mathbf{h}_{(t,t')} \quad (13)$$

FDM divides the space of (t, t') into finite grids as shown in Fig. 3.

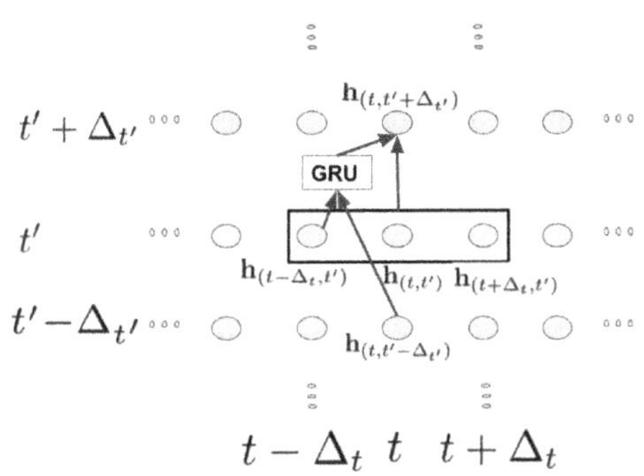

Fig. 3. Pictorial representation of computing a hidden state $\mathbf{h}_{(t,t'+\Delta_{t'})}$ as shown in Eq. 13. The new hidden state depends on the already computed hidden states in the lower layers.

To compute the hidden state at a depth $t' + \Delta_{t'}$, it utilizes the hidden states computed for itself and its immediate neighbors at a previous depth $(\mathbf{h}_{(t-\Delta_t,t')}, \mathbf{h}_{(t,t')}, \mathbf{h}_{(t+\Delta_t,t')})$. This helps to capture dependence among the neighboring inputs during evolution. A drawback of directly using FDM in solving the proposed CDR-NDE-heat model is that it is a slow process. It doesn't exploit the GPU power as the computations are happening in a sequential order.

For the proposed model, from the formulation to compute next hidden state in Eq. 13 and Fig. 3, we can observe that the hidden states at $t' + \Delta_{t'}$ only depends on the hidden states computed below $t' + \Delta_{t'}$. Hence, all the hidden states $t' + \Delta_{t'}$ can be computed simultaneously once we have hidden states at time t'. The numerical techniques based on Method of lines (MoL) [30] is a good choice for such a scenario. MoL method typically discretizes and computes function values in one dimension, and then jointly evolves in the remaining dimension to compute all the function values. In our approach, we first compute hidden states along the t-axis and then compute the hidden states along the t'-axis by posing as a solution to the system of differential equations. The evolution of the hidden states along the t'-axis is defined by the ordinary differential equation (14), which is derived from Eq. 13.

$$\begin{aligned}\frac{\partial \mathbf{h}_{(t,t')}}{\partial t'} &= g_\theta(\mathbf{h}_{(t-\Delta_t,t')}, \mathbf{h}_{(t,t')}, \mathbf{h}_{(t+\Delta_t,t')}) \\ &= \frac{\mathbf{h}_{(t-\Delta_t,t')} - 2\mathbf{h}_{(t,t')} + \mathbf{h}_{(t+\Delta_t,t')}}{\Delta_t^2} + f(\mathbf{h}_{(t,t')}, \mathbf{h}_{(t-\Delta_t,t')}) \end{aligned} \quad (14)$$

$$\mathbf{h}_{(:,T')} = \text{ODESOLVE}(g_\theta, initial\_state = \mathbf{h}_{(:,0)}, start\_time = 0, end\_time = T')$$

The initial hidden states at $t' = 0$, i.e. $\mathbf{h}_{(:,0)}$ are computed by solving an ODE along the t-axis

$$\frac{d\mathbf{h}_{(t,0)}}{dt} = (1 - \mathbf{z}_{(t,0)}) \odot (\mathbf{g}_{(t,0)} - \mathbf{h}_{(t,0)}) \quad (15)$$

One can select any numerical method for solving the system of ODEs. In the experiments, we evaluate the performance of the CDR-NDE-heat model using both Euler (CDR-NDE-heat(Euler)) and Dopri5 (CDR-NDE-heat(Dopri5)) methods. We can observe that CDR-NDE-heat model considers $\mathbf{h}_{(t+\Delta_t,t')}$ in addition to $\mathbf{h}_{(t-\Delta_t,t')}$ in computing $\mathbf{h}_{(t,t')}$ for any time t and depth t', taking into account more dependencies in the sequence.

After computing the hidden states at depth T', predictions are made using a fully connected neural network, i.e. $\mathbf{y}_i = o_h(\mathbf{h}_{(t_i,T')})$. This is then used to compute loss - cross-entropy for classification and root mean square error for regression problems. The parameters of the CDR-NDE models, i.e. weight parameters of the GRUCell, are learnt by minimizing the loss computed over all the observations in the sequence and over all the sequences. The computed loss is backpropagated using either adjoint method [8] or automatic differentiation to update the model parameters.

5 Experiments

To evaluate the performance of the proposed models, we conduct experiments on irregular time series datasets such as person activity recognition [3], walker2d kinematic

Table 1. Hyperparameter Details

Parameter	Value
Hidden state Dimension	64
Minibatch size	256
Optimizer	RMSprop
Learning rate	$5e^{-3}$
Training epochs	200

Table 2. ODE solvers used for different RNODE models. For the CDR-NDE-Heat model using Dopri5, the absolute and relative tolerance values are $1e^{-3}$ and $1e^{-3}$ respectively.

Model	ODE-Solver	Time-step Ratio
CT-RNN	4-th order Runge-Kutta	1/3
ODE-RNN	4-th order Runge-Kutta	1/3
GRU-ODE	Explicit Euler	1/4
ODE-LSTM	Explicit Euler	1/4
CDR-NDE	Explicit Euler	1/2
CDR-NDE-heat(Euler)	Explicit Euler	1/2
CDR-NDE-heat(Dopri5)	Dopri5	–

simulation [20] and stance classification [35] of social media posts. We compare our proposed models against RNN models which are designed to tackle the irregularly sampled time-series data. The experimental setup such as the numerical method, hidden state dimension and other hyperparameters is the same as in [20] and is provided in Table 1. Table 2 provides the choice of numerical methods for each model. The proposed models CDR-NDE and CDR-NDE-heat(Euler) used the Euler method with the number of steps as 2. CDR-NDE-heat(Dopri5) used Dopri5 with the absolute and relative tolerance set to $1e^{-3}$. Scheduled learning rate decay is used with decay parameter $\gamma = 0.1$, scheduled at epoch 100. The models are trained on Nvidia Tesla V-100 32GB GPU.

5.1 Baselines

We compared our proposed models[1] against RNN models which are designed to address the problem of fitting irregular time-series data such as GRU-ODE [10], CT-GRU [24], CT-RNN [12], GRUD [6], Phased-LSTM [25], ODE-LSTM [20], bidirectional-RNN [31], RNN decay [28], Hawk-LSTM [23], Augmented LSTM [20], and ODE-RNN [28].

5.2 Person Activity Recognition with Irregularly Sampled Time-Series

Dataset contains sensor data from 4 from different sensors(1 for each ankle, 1 chest and 1 belt) attached to 5 different people, performing 5 sequences of activities. The task is to classify the activity based on the sensor data. There are 11 different activities which are reduced to 7 as suggested in [28]. Dataset is transformed such that each step in the recording contains 7 values (4 of which determine the sensor that is producing data and the other 3 are sensor data). Each recording is split into overlapping intervals of 32 (with overlap of 16) and all the sequences are combined into one dataset. Out of the total sequences 7769 used for training, 1942 used for testing.

[1] Code is available at https://github.com/srinivas-quan/CDR-NDE.

Table 3. Column 2, shows the test accuracy (mean ± std) of all the models trained on the dataset **Person activity recognition**. Column 3 shows the test data Mean-square error (mean ± std) of all the models trained on the datasets **Walker2d Kinematic**. For both the dataset, every model is trained for 5 times with 5 different seeds.

Model	Person Activity Recognition (Accuracy)	Walker2d Kinematic (Mean-Square Error)
Aug-LSTM	83.78 ± 0.41	1.09 ± 0.01
CT-RNN	82.32 ± 0.83	1.25 ± 0.03
ODE-RNN	75.03 ± 1.87	1.88 ± 0.05
ODE-LSTM	83.77 ± 0.58	0.91 ± 0.02
CT-GRU	83.93 ± 0.86	1.22 ± 0.01
RNN-Decay	78.74 ± 3.65	1.44 ± 0.01
Bi-RNN	82.86 ± 1.17	1.09 ± 0.01
GRU-D	82.52 ± 0.86	1.14 ± 0.01
Phased-LSTM	83.34 ± 0.59	1.10 ± 0.01
GRU-ODE	82.80 ± 0.61	1.08 ± 0.01
CT-LSTM	83.42 ± 0.69	1.03 ± 0.02
CDR-NDE	87.54 ± 0.34	0.97 ± 0.04
CDR-NDE-heat (Euler)	$\mathbf{88.24 \pm 0.31}$	0.54 ± 0.01
CDR-NDE-heat (Dopri5)	$\mathbf{88.60 \pm 0.26}$	$\mathbf{0.49 \pm 0.01}$

In Table 3, column 2 shows the performance of all the models trained on a person-activity dataset in terms of test accuracy. Our proposed models CDR-NDE and CDR-NDE-heat perform better than all other baseline models. It shows that considering the continuous transformation along both the directions results in a model with better representation capability and generalization performance. We also observe that the more flexible CDR-NDE-heat model using the adaptive Dopri5 solver gives the best performance in the person-activity dataset. To verify the flexibility of the model and the requirement of different depth for different sequences, we computed the number of function evaluations involved while evolving the hidden states over depth in the CDR-NDE-heat(Dopri5) model. We found that the number of function evaluations fall in the range of 26 to 32. This shows that different sequences required different number of function evaluations for learning better representations. Training time for an epoch for the models are CDR-NDE-heat(Euler): 22 sec, CDR-NDE-Heat(Dopri5): 30 sec, and CDR-NDE: 58 sec, and shows that CDR-NDE-heat models are faster.

5.3 Walker2d Kinematic Simulation

The dataset was created by [20] for Walker kinematic modeling task. This is a supervised autoregressive task and the dataset was generated using Walker2d-v2 OpenAI gym environment and MuJoCo physics engine. This dataset evaluates how well a model can simulate kinematic modeling systems that are sampled at irregular time intervals. The training data was generated by performing rollouts on the Walker2d-v2 environment using pre-trained deterministic policy. The Walker environment was trained using a non-recurrent policy though Proximal policy optimization before data collection. The dataset is made irregularly sampled by excluding 10% of the timesteps. The dataset is split into 9684 train, 1937 test, 1272 validation sequences.

In Table 3, column 3 shows the performance of all the models on Walker2d data. Our proposed model CDR-NDE-heat(Euler and Dopri5) outperform other models with a good margin. The proposed model CDR-NDE also gives a very good performance in this data. Smoothing of the hidden representations allowed the CDR-NDE-heat model to learn well on this data. Again, the more flexible CDR-NDE-heat model using the adaptive Dopri5 solver gives the best performance. Training time for an epoch for the proposed models are CDR-NDE-heat(Euler): 28 sec, CDR-NDE-Heat(Dopri5): 48 sec, and CDR-NDE: 140 sec, and shows that CDR-NDE-heat models are faster.

5.4 Stance Classification

In real-world, on social media platforms like twitter, tweets related to a particular event arrive at different times and the inter arrival times between the tweets are different. While modeling such a irregular time series data, the hidden representation of each data point could get affected by their occurrence times. Along with the inter arrival times, one may also need to consider the complexity of an observation (tweet) while predicting its class. The complexity level of a tweet or sequence of tweets could be different and demands for transformations depending on the complexity level. We consider the stance classification [22, 35] problem in Twitter, where we need to classify a tweet into its stances such as *supporting*, *denying*, *questioning* or *commenting*. Previously, approaches based on LSTMs [35] were used to solve this problem by considering the sequential nature among the class labels and tweets. In this problem, we can learn better representations by considering the continuous transformation of hidden states to be proportional to the inter-arrival times along the axis t and the continuous transformation of hidden states to be dependent on the complexity of the tweets along the axis t'. Consequently, our CDR-NDE models can be a better choice for these social media problems.

We evaluated the performance of the models to predict the stance of social media posts [11]. This Twitter data set consists of rumour tweets associated with various real world events. Each event has a collection of tweets labelled with one of the four labels - Support, Query, Deny and Comment. We picked two events, Sydneysiege and Charliehebdo, each with approximately 1000 labelled tweets to evaluate the models. Given an event and the corresponding tweets from the event, we form sequence data of length 10 consisting of tweets from the event. While creating a datapoint, 10 tweets are randomly selected from the event and then sorted based on the observation time in increasing order. Each element in the data point is a representation of the tweet which includes its text embedding, retweet count, favourites count, punctuation features, sentiment polarity, negative and positive word count, presence of hashtags, user mentions, URLs, and entities obtained from the tweet. The text embedding of the tweet is obtained by concatenating the pre-trained word2vec embeddings of the words in the tweet. Training data points constitute 60% of the tweets from a particular event. The data points for validation and test data are created by splitting the remaining 40% equally.

Table 4 shows the performance measured in terms of the F1-score of the proposed models compared to the baselines for Sydneysiege and Charliehebdo. For the event Sydneysiege, our proposed models, CDR-NDE-heat(Euler,Dopri5) performed better than

Table 4. Performance of models on Sydneysiege and Charliehebdo.

Model	F1 score	
	Sydneysiege	Charliehebdo
CT-RNN	0.57 ± 0.00	0.63 ± 0.01
ODE-RNN	0.55 ± 0.01	0.59 ± 0.02
ODE-LSTM	0.56 ± 0.01	0.61 ± 0.01
CT-GRU	0.64 ± 0.01	0.67 ± 0.02
RNN-Decay	0.63 ± 0.01	0.67 ± 0.02
Bidirectional-RNN	0.62 ± 0.01	0.67 ± 0.01
GRU-D	0.64 ± 0.01	0.68 ± 0.01
Phased-LSTM	0.61 ± 0.01	0.64 ± 0.01
GRU-ODE	0.56 ± 0.00	0.63 ± 0.00
CT-LSTM	0.64 ± 0.01	0.66 ± 0.03
Augmented-LSTM	0.64 ± 0.01	0.68 ± 0.01
CDR-NDE	0.62 ± 0.01	0.62 ± 0.01
CDR-NDE-heat(Euler)	$\mathbf{0.68 \pm 0.01}$	$\mathbf{0.68 \pm 0.01}$
CDR-NDE-heat(Dopri5)	$\mathbf{0.68 \pm 0.01}$	$\mathbf{0.68 \pm 0.01}$

the baselines. For the event Charliehebdo, the performance of the proposed CDR-NDE-heat(Euler,Dopri5) models is better than most of the baselines and they performed better than the vanilla CDR-NDE model. We observe that CDR-NDE-heat(Euler,Dopri5) models are able to improve the generalization performance on the stance classification problem consisting of textual inputs.

6 Conclusion and Future Work

We proposed novel continuous depth RNN models based on the framework of differential equations. The proposed models generalize recurrent NODE models by continuously evolving in both the temporal and depth directions. CDR-NDE models the evolution of hidden states using two separate differential equations. The CDR-NDE-heat model is designed based on the framework of 1D-Heat equation and models the evolution of the hidden states across time and depth. The experimental results on person activity recognition, Walker2d kinematics and stance classification data showed that the proposed models outperformed the baselines and are very effective on irregularly sampled real-world sequence data. Currently, CDR-NDE models are designed based on the GRU-cell transformations. We would like to extend it to other transformations as future work. The continuous depth recurrent neural differential equations are very flexible and generic RNN models. They will have widespread application on several complex sequence modeling and time series problems, involving sequences with irregular observation times and varying input complexities.

Acknowledgements. This work has been partly supported by the funding received from the Department of Science and Technology (DST), Govt of India, through the ICPS program (DST/ICPS/2018).

Ethical Statement. We propose novel and flexible techniques to model irregular time series data. The performance of the proposed models is experimented on publicly available datasets. The method can be applied to irregular time series data arising in several domains such as social networks. We do not find any ethical issues with the proposed approach or the data set used in the experiments.

References

1. Anumasa, S., Srijith, P.K.: Improving robustness and uncertainty modelling in neural ordinary differential equations. In: IEEE Winter Conference on Applications of Computer Vision, WACV 2021, Waikoloa, HI, USA, 3–8 January 2021, pp. 4052–4060. IEEE (2021)
2. Anumasa, S., Srijith, P.K.: Latent time neural ordinary differential equations. In: Thirty-Sixth AAAI Conference on Artificial Intelligence, pp. 6010–6018. AAAI Press (2022)
3. Asuncion, A., Newman, D.: UCI machine learning repository (2007)
4. Brandstetter, J., Worrall, D.E., Welling, M.: Message passing neural PDE solvers. In: International Conference on Learning Representations (2021)
5. Cannon, J.R.: The one-dimensional heat equation. Cambridge University Press, Cambridge (1984)
6. Che, Z., Purushotham, S., Cho, K., Sontag, D., Liu, Y.: Recurrent neural networks for multivariate time series with missing values. Sci. Rep. **8**(1), 1–12 (2018)
7. Chen, R.T., Amos, B., Nickel, M.: Neural spatio-temporal point processes. In: International Conference on Learning Representations (2020)
8. Chen, R.T., Rubanova, Y., Bettencourt, J., Duvenaud, D.K.: Neural ordinary differential equations. In: Advances in neural information processing systems, pp. 6571–6583 (2018)
9. Cho, K., van Merriënboer, B., Bahdanau, D., Bengio, Y.: On the properties of neural machine translation: encoder-decoder approaches. In: Proceedings of SSST-8, Eighth Workshop on Syntax, Semantics and Structure in Statistical Translation, pp. 103–111 (2014)
10. De Brouwer, E., Simm, J., Arany, A., Moreau, Y.: GRU-ODE-Bayes: continuous modeling of sporadically-observed time series. In: Advances in Neural Information Processing Systems. vol. 32 (2019)
11. Derczynski, L., et al.: Rumoureval 2019 data (2019). https://doi.org/10.6084/M9.FIGSHARE.8845580.V1, https://figshare.com/articles/RumourEval_2019_data/8845580/1
12. Funahashi, K.I., Nakamura, Y.: Approximation of dynamical systems by continuous time recurrent neural networks. Neural Netw. **6**(6), 801–806 (1993)
13. Haber, E., Ruthotto, L.: Stable architectures for deep neural networks. Inverse Prob. **34**(1), 014004 (2017)
14. Hanshu, Y., Jiawei, D., Vincent, T., Jiashi, F.: On robustness of neural ordinary differential equations. In: International Conference on Learning Representations (2019)
15. He, K., Gkioxari, G., Dollár, P., Girshick, R.: Mask R-CNN. IEEE Trans. Pattern Anal. Mach. Intell. **42**(2), 386–397 (2020)
16. He, K., Zhang, X., Ren, S., Sun, J.: Deep residual learning for image recognition. In: Proceedings of the IEEE Conference on Computer Vision and Pattern Recognition, pp. 770–778 (2016)
17. Hochreiter, S., Schmidhuber, J.: Long short-term memory. Neural Comput. **9**(8), 1735–1780 (1997)

18. Hu, Y., Zhao, T., Xu, S., Xu, Z., Lin, L.: Neural-PDE: A RNN based neural network for solving time dependent PDEs (2020). https://doi.org/10.48550/ARXIV.2009.03892, https://arxiv.org/abs/2009.03892
19. Kimura, T.: On dormand-prince method. Jpn. Malays. Tech. Inst. **40**(10), 1–9 (2009)
20. Lechner, M., Hasani, R.: Learning long-term dependencies in irregularly-sampled time series. arXiv preprint arXiv:2006.04418 (2020)
21. Lu, Y., Zhong, A., Li, Q., Dong, B.: Beyond finite layer neural networks: bridging deep architectures and numerical differential equations. In: International Conference on Machine Learning, pp. 3276–3285. PMLR (2018)
22. Lukasik, M., Srijith, P.K., Vu, D., Bontcheva, K., Zubiaga, A., Cohn, T.: Hawkes processes for continuous time sequence classification: an application to Rumour stance classification in twitter. In: Proceedings of the 54th Annual Meeting of the Association for Computational Linguistics, ACL 2016. The Association for Computer Linguistics (2016)
23. Mei, H., Eisner, J.M.: The neural hawkes process: a neural self-modulating multivariate point process. In: Advances in Neural Information Processing Systems. vol. 30 (2017)
24. Mozer, M.C., Kazakov, D., Lindsey, R.V.: Discrete event, continuous time RNNs. arXiv preprint arXiv:1710.04110 (2017)
25. Neil, D., Pfeiffer, M., Liu, S.C.: Phased lstm: Accelerating recurrent network training for long or event-based sequences. In: Advances in Neural Information Processing Systems. vol. 29 (2016)
26. Recktenwald, G.W.: Finite-difference approximations to the heat equation. Mech. Eng. **10**(01) (2004)
27. Ren, S., He, K., Girshick, R., Sun, J.: Faster R-CNN: towards real-time object detection with region proposal networks. IEEE Trans. Pattern Anal. Mach. Intell. **39**(6), 1137–1149 (2017)
28. Rubanova, Y., Chen, R.T., Duvenaud, D.K.: Latent ordinary differential equations for irregularly-sampled time series. In: Advances in Neural Information Processing Systems. vol. 32 (2019)
29. Ruthotto, L., Haber, E.: Deep neural networks motivated by partial differential equations (2018). https://doi.org/10.48550/ARXIV.1804.04272
30. Schiesser, W.E.: The numerical method of lines: integration of partial differential equations. Elsevier (2012)
31. Schuster, M., Paliwal, K.K.: Bidirectional recurrent neural networks. IEEE Trans. Sig. Process. **45**(11), 2673–2681 (1997)
32. Tamire, M., Anumasa, S., Srijith, P.K.: Bi-directional recurrent neural ordinary differential equations for social media text classification. In: Proceedings of the 2nd Workshop on Deriving Insights from User-Generated Text, pp. 20–24. Association for Computational Linguistics (2022)
33. Trong, D.D., Long, N.T., Alain, P.N.D.: Nonhomogeneous heat equation: identification and regularization for the inhomogeneous term. J. Math. Anal. Appl. **312**(1), 93–104 (2005)
34. Wang, W., Chen, Z., Hu, H.: Hierarchical attention network for image captioning. In: Proceedings of the AAAI Conference on Artificial Intelligence, pp. 8957–8964 (2019)
35. Zubiaga, A., et al.: Discourse-aware Rumour stance classification in social media using sequential classifiers. Inf. Process. Manag. **54**(2), 273–290 (2018)
36. Zubov, K., et al.: NeuralPDE: Automating physics-informed neural networks (PINNs) with error approximations. arXiv e-prints pp. arXiv-2107 (2021)

Fairness

Mitigating Algorithmic Bias with Limited Annotations

Guanchu Wang[1], Mengnan Du[2], Ninghao Liu[3], Na Zou[4], and Xia Hu[1](✉)

[1] Rice University, Houston, USA
{Guanchu.wang,xia.hu}@rice.edu
[2] New Jersey Institute of Technology, Newark, USA
mengnan.du@njit.edu
[3] University of Georgia, Athens, USA
ninghao.liu@uga.edu
[4] Texas A&M University, College Station, USA
nzou1@tamu.edu

Abstract. Existing work on fairness modeling commonly assumes that sensitive attributes for all instances are fully available, which may not be true in many real-world applications due to the high cost of acquiring sensitive information. When sensitive attributes are not disclosed or available, it is needed to manually annotate a small part of the training data to mitigate bias. However, the skewed distribution across different sensitive groups preserves the skewness of the original dataset in the annotated subset, which leads to non-optimal bias mitigation. To tackle this challenge, we propose Active Penalization Of Discrimination (APOD), an interactive framework to guide the limited annotations towards maximally eliminating the effect of algorithmic bias. The proposed APOD integrates discrimination penalization with active instance selection to efficiently utilize the limited annotation budget, and it is theoretically proved to be capable of bounding the algorithmic bias. According to the evaluation on five benchmark datasets, APOD outperforms the state-of-the-arts baseline methods under the limited annotation budget, and shows comparable performance to fully annotated bias mitigation, which demonstrates that APOD could benefit real-world applications when sensitive information is limited. The source code of the proposed method is available at: https://github.com/guanchuwang/APOD-fairness.

Keywords: Bias mitigation · Limitied annotation

1 Introduction

Although deep neural networks (DNNs) have been demonstrated with great performance in many real-world applications, it shows discrimination towards certain groups or individuals [6,20,24,41], especially in high-stake applications, e.g., loan approvals [38], policing [19], targeted advertisement [40], college admissions [49], or criminal risk assessments [3]. Social bias widely exists in many

© The Author(s), under exclusive license to Springer Nature Switzerland AG 2023
D. Koutra et al. (Eds.): ECML PKDD 2023, LNAI 14170, pp. 241–258, 2023.
https://doi.org/10.1007/978-3-031-43415-0_15

real-world data [9,29,31,45]. For example, the Adult dataset [18] contains significantly more low-income female instances than males. Recent studies revealed that training a DNN model on biased data may inherit and even amplify the social bias and lead to unfair predictions in downstream tasks [13,14,23,30,39].

The problem of bias mitigation is challenging due to the skewed data distribution [4,22,25] across different demographic groups. For example, in the Adult dataset, instances of female with high income are significantly less than the ones with low income [18]. Also, in the German credit dataset, the majority of people younger than 35 show a bad credit history [18]. The effect of the skewed distribution on model fairness is illustrated in a binary classification task (e.g. positive class denoted as gray + and •, negative class as red + and •) with two sensitive groups (e.g. group 0 denoted as + and +, group 1 as • and •) shown in Fig. 1. In Fig. 1 (a), the positive instances (+) are significantly less than negative instances (+) in group 0, which leads to a classification boundary deviating from the fair one. Existing work on fairness modeling can be categorized into two groups with or without sensitive attributes [17,27]. The first group relied on full exposure of sensitive attributes in training data, such as Fair Mixup [9], FIFA [15], Fair Rank [32], and Group DRO [35]. However, the sensitive information may not be disclosed or available in some real world scenarios [26,48], and the cost of annotating sensitive attributes by experts is high [2], which leads to the limited applications of this group of work to the real-world scenarios.

The second group of work formulates the fairness without dependency on sensitive information, such as SS-FRL [8], FKD [7], and LfF [33]. However, those works rely on heuristic clustering of training instances to form potential demographic groups for the bias mitigation, which may deteriorate the fairness performance to some extent [44]. To tackle the issue, some work involves the human expert providing a partially annotated dataset for the bias mitigation [2]. However, only a small portion of the dataset is annotated due to the limitation of human labor efforts. An intuitive solution is to randomly select a small portion of instances for annotation and target semi-supervised bias mitigation [47]. However, as shown in Fig. 1 (b), the randomly selected instances will follow the same skewed distribution across sensitive groups, which still preserves the bias information in the classifier. In such a manner, it is highly likely to achieve a non-optimal solution, which is fair only on the annotated dataset but not the entire dataset. Therefore, it is needed to have a unified framework, which integrates the selection of a representative subset for annotation with model training towards the global fairness [1], as shown in Fig. 1 (c).

In this work, we propose Active Penalization Of Discrimination (APOD), a novel interactive framework which integrates the penalization of discrimination with active instance selection, for bias mitigation in the real-world scenarios where sensitive information is limited. Specifically, APOD iterates between the model debiasing and active instance selection to gradually approach the global fairness. For debiasing the model, APOD enables bias penalization in an end-to-end manner via adopting a fairness regularizer. In the active instance selection, an annotated data subset is constructed via recursive selections of representative

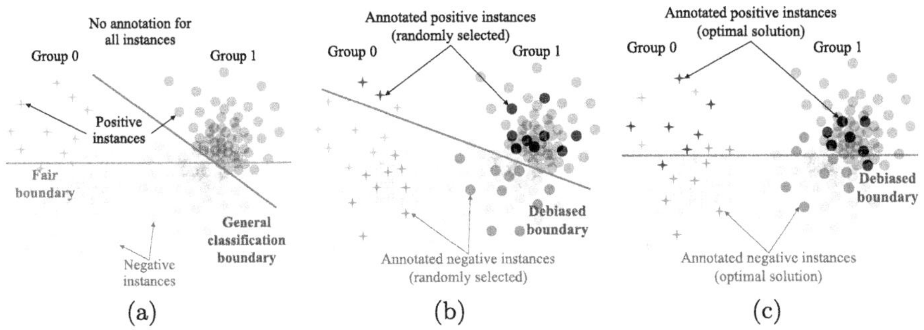

Fig. 1. (a) The general classification boundary without bias mitigation deviates from the fair boundary due to the skewed distribution across four underlying subgroups (i.e. +, +, • and •). (b) The annotation budget is set as 30. The randomly annotated data subset follows the same skewed distribution across the subgroups. The classification model is still unfair on the entire dataset. (c) With the same annotation budget, the optimal solution should select a more representative subset, which mitigates algorithmic bias on the entire dataset. (Color figure online)

data instances from the subgroup where the model shows the worst performance, such that it can maximally expose the existing bias of the model for subsequent debiasing. Finally, we provide theoretical and experimental analysis to demonstrate the effectiveness of APOD. Overall, the contributions of this work are summarized as follows:

- We propose an interactive framework APOD to integrate the bias mitigation with efficient active instance selection when the annotation of sensitive attributes is very limited.
- We propose the relaxed reformulation of the fairness objective, and theoretically prove that APOD could improve model fairness via bounding the relaxed fairness metric.
- The effectiveness of APOD is thoroughly demonstrated by the experiments on five benchmark datasets, which shows APOD is competitive with state-of-the-art methods using fully disclosed sensitive attributes.

2 Preliminaries

In this section, we first introduce the notations used in this work, and give the problem definition of bias mitigation in the active scenario. Then, we introduce the fairness metrics.

2.1 Notation and Problem Definition

Without loss of generality, we follow the existing work [9,28,46] to consider a classification task in this work. Specifically, we aim to learn a DNN classifier f with the input feature $\boldsymbol{x} \in \mathcal{X}$, label $y \in \mathcal{Y} = \{0, 1\}$ and sensitive attribute

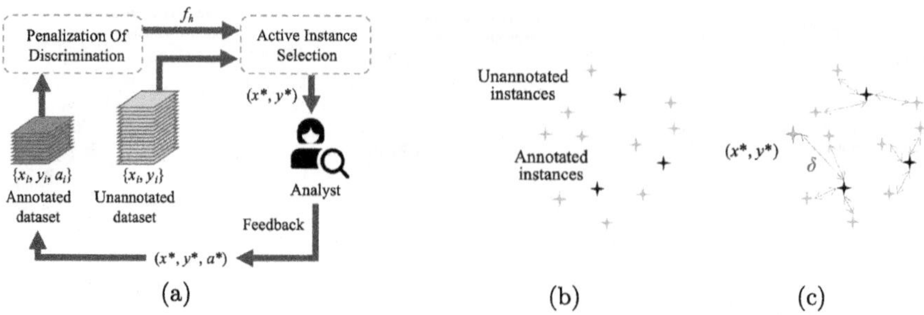

Fig. 2. (a) The APOD pipeline alternates between POD and AIS. (b) Individual selection: The annotated and unannotated instances from subgroup $\mathcal{U}_{\tilde{a}}^{\tilde{c}}$, where $\tilde{a} = 0$ and $\tilde{c} = 1$. (c) Each unannotated instance is connected to an annotated instance determined by $\min_{\boldsymbol{x}_j \in \mathcal{S}} ||\boldsymbol{h}_i - \boldsymbol{h}_j||_2$ (marked as blue arrows). The red δ denotes the largest distance pair which selects the best candidate for annotation. (Color figure online)

$a \in \mathcal{A} = \{0, 1\}$, where $\mathcal{X}$ and $\mathcal{Y}$ denote the feature and label space, respectively. The instances with sensitive attribute $A = 0$ and $A = 1$ belong to the unprivileged and privileged groups, respectively. Let $\mathcal{D} = \{(\boldsymbol{x}_i, y_i) \mid 1 \leq i \leq N\}$ denote the entire dataset, which consists of the annotated set $\mathcal{S} = \{(\boldsymbol{x}_i, y_i, a_i)\}$ and unannotated set $\mathcal{U} = \{(\boldsymbol{x}_i, y_i)\}$, i.e., the value of the sensitive attribute is known for instances in $\mathcal{S}$, but it is unknown for instances in $\mathcal{U}$. The proposed interactive bias mitigation is illustrated in Fig. 2 (a). Specifically, in each iteration, an instance $(\boldsymbol{x}^*, y^*)$ is selected from unannotated dataset $\mathcal{U}$ for human experts; the experts essentially do the job of mapping $\mathcal{X} \times \mathcal{Y} \rightarrow \mathcal{X} \times \mathcal{Y} \times \mathcal{A}$, by providing the annotation of sensitive attribute a^* for the selected instance $(\boldsymbol{x}^*, y^*)$. After that, the classifier is updated and debiased using the partially annotated dataset including the newly annotated instance $(\boldsymbol{x}^*, y^*, a^*)$, where the new classifier will then be involved for the instance selection in the next iteration. This loop terminates if the human-annotation budget is reached.

Such an active scenario to debias f is time-consuming for deep neural networks, due to the retraining of f in each iteration. To improve the efficiency of learning, the classifier f is split into body $f_b : \mathcal{X} \rightarrow \mathbb{R}^M$ and head $f_h : \mathbb{R}^M \rightarrow \mathbb{R}^{|\mathcal{Y}|}$, where the body f_b denotes the first several layers, and the head f_h denotes the remaining layers of the classifier such that $\hat{y}_i = \arg\max\{f_h(f_b(\boldsymbol{x}_i|\theta_b)|\theta_h)\}$. The body f_b learns the instance embedding $\boldsymbol{h}_i = f_b(\boldsymbol{x}_i|\theta_h)$, where $\boldsymbol{h}_i \in \mathbb{R}^M$ denotes the embedding of $\boldsymbol{x}_i$, and M denotes the dimension of embedding space. The head f_h contributes to fair classification via having $\hat{y}_i = \arg\max\{f_h(\boldsymbol{h}_i|\theta_h)\}$, where $f_h(\boldsymbol{h}_i|\theta_h) \in \mathbb{R}^{|\mathcal{Y}|}$ and $\hat{y}_i \in \mathcal{Y}$. Instead of updating the entire classifier, the classifier body f_b is pretrained and fixed during the bias mitigation, where f_b is pretrained to minimize the cross-entropy loss without annotations of sensitive attributes. In such a manner, the mitigation of unfairness relies on debiasing the classifier head f_h. This strategy with a fixed classifier body during the bias mitigation has been proved to be effective enough in existing works [16,37].

2.2 Fairness Evaluation Metrics

In this work, we follow existing work [16,31] to consider two metrics to evaluate fairness: Equality of Opportunity [21,42] and Equalized Odds [34,42]. These two metrics are measured based on the true positive rate $\text{TPR}_{A=a} = \mathbb{P}(\hat{Y} = 1|A = a, Y = 1)$ and the false positive rate $\text{FPR}_{A=a} = \mathbb{P}(\hat{Y} = 1|A = a, Y = 0)$ for $a \in \mathcal{A}$.

Equality of Opportunity requires the unprivileged group ($A = 0$) and privileged groups ($A = 1$) have equal probability of an instance from the positive class being assigned to positive outcome, which is defined as $\mathbb{P}(\hat{Y} = 1|A = 0, Y = 1) = \mathbb{P}(\hat{Y} = 1|A = 1, Y = 1)$. In this work, we apply EOP given as follows to evaluate Equality of Opportunity,

$$\text{EOP} = \frac{\text{TPR}_{A=0}}{\text{TPR}_{A=1}} = \frac{\mathbb{P}(\hat{Y} = 1 \mid A = 0, Y = 1)}{\mathbb{P}(\hat{Y} = 1 \mid A = 1, Y = 1)}. \quad (1)$$

Equalized Odds expects favorable outcomes to be independent of the sensitive attribute, given the ground-truth prediction, which can be formulated as $\mathbb{P}(\hat{Y} = 1|A = 0, Y = y) = \mathbb{P}(\hat{Y} = 1|A = 1, Y = y)$ for $y \in \mathcal{Y}$. To evaluate Equalized Odds, ΔEO combines the difference of TPR and FPR across two sensitive groups as

$$\Delta\text{EO} = \Delta\text{TPR} + \Delta\text{FPR}, \quad (2)$$

where $\Delta\text{TPR} = \text{TPR}_{A=0} - \text{TPR}_{A=1}$ and $\Delta\text{FPR} = \text{FPR}_{A=0} - \text{FPR}_{A=1}$. Under above definitions, $\text{EOP} \to 1$ and $\Delta\text{EO} \to 0$ indicate fair classification results.

3 Active Penalization Of Discrimination

In this section, we introduce the Active Penalization Of Discrimination (APOD) framework to mitigate algorithmic bias under a limited annotation budget. As shown in Fig. 2 (a), APOD integrates Penalization Of Discrimination (POD) and Active Instance Selection (AIS) in a unified and iterative framework. Specifically, in each iteration, POD focuses on debiasing the classifier head f_h on the partially annotated dataset $\{(\boldsymbol{x}_i, y_i, a_i) \in \mathcal{S}\}$ and $\{(\boldsymbol{x}_i, y_i) \in \mathcal{U}\}$, while AIS selects the optimal instance $(\boldsymbol{x}^*, y^*)$ from the unannotated dataset $\mathcal{U}$ that can further promote bias mitigation. Sensitive attributes of the selected instances will be annotated by human experts: $(\boldsymbol{x}^*, y^*) \to (\boldsymbol{x}^*, y^*, a^*)$. After that, these instances will be moved from the unannotated dataset $\mathcal{U} \leftarrow \mathcal{U} \backslash \{(\boldsymbol{x}^*, y^*)\}$ to the annotated dataset $\mathcal{S} \leftarrow \mathcal{S} \cup \{(\boldsymbol{x}^*, y^*, a^*)\}$ for debiasing the classifier in the next iteration. The POD and AIS are introduced as follows.

3.1 Penalization Of Discrimination (POD)

POD learns a fair classifier head f_h via bias penalization on both annotated instances $\{(\boldsymbol{x}_i, y_i, a_i) \in \mathcal{S}\}$ and unannotated instances $\{(\boldsymbol{x}_i, y_i) \in \mathcal{U}\}$. To be concrete, POD considers a regularization term, consisting of the true and false positive rate difference[1], to balance the model performance on different subgroups. In this way, given $\boldsymbol{h}_i = f_b(\boldsymbol{x}_i|\theta_b)$, f_h is updated to minimize the hybrid loss function given by

$$L = \sum_{i=1}^{N} l(\boldsymbol{h}_i, y_i; \theta_h) + \lambda(\Delta\text{TPR}^2 + \Delta\text{FPR}^2), \tag{3}$$

where $l(\boldsymbol{h}_i, y_i; \theta_h)$ denotes the cross-entropy loss, and the term $\Delta\text{TPR}^2 + \Delta\text{FPR}^2$ penalizes the bias in f_h to improve fairness, controlled by the hyper-parameter λ.

However, Eq. (3) is not feasible to debias f_h in an end-to-end manner, since neither TPR nor FPR is differentiable with respect to the parameters θ_h. It is thus necessary to reformulate ΔTPR and ΔFPR, which involves the parameterization of true and false positive rate with respect to θ_h, respectively. For notation convenience and without the loss of generality, we unify the formulation of true and false positive rates by

$$p_a(y, c) = \mathbb{P}(\hat{Y} = c \mid Y = y, A = a), \tag{4}$$

where we can take $y = 1, c = 1$ to have $p_a(1,1) = \text{TPR}_{A=a}$ and $y = 0, c = 1$ to have $p_a(0,1) = \text{FPR}_{A=a}$. To parameterize $p_a(y,c)$ with respect to θ_h, we reformulate it as follows

$$p_a(y,c) = \frac{\sum_{(\boldsymbol{x}_i, y_i, a_i) \in \mathcal{S}_a^y} \mathbf{1}_{\hat{y}_i = c}}{|\mathcal{S}_a^y|} = \frac{\sum\limits_{(\boldsymbol{x}_i, y_i, a_i) \in \mathcal{S}_a^y} \text{sgn}(f_h^c(\boldsymbol{h}_i) - f_h^{1-c}(\boldsymbol{h}_i))}{|\mathcal{S}_a^y|} \tag{5}$$

$$\approx \frac{\sum\limits_{(\boldsymbol{x}_i, y_i, a_i) \in \mathcal{S}_a^y} \lambda(f_h^c(\boldsymbol{h}_i) - f_h^{1-c}(\boldsymbol{h}_i))}{|\mathcal{S}_a^y|} \triangleq \lambda \tilde{p}_a(y,c), \tag{6}$$

where $\text{sgn}(x) = 0$ for $x < 0$ and $\text{sgn}(x) = 1$ for $x \geq 0$. Here we relax $\text{sgn}(x)$ with a linear function[2] λx in the approximation of Eq. (5) to make $p_a(y,c)$ differentiable with respect to θ_h; $\mathcal{S}_a^y = \{(\boldsymbol{x}_i, y_i, a_i) \in \mathcal{S} \mid a_i = a, y_i = y\}$ for $a \in \mathcal{A}, y \in \mathcal{Y}$; and $f_h^i(\boldsymbol{h})$ denotes element i of $f_h(\boldsymbol{h})$ for $i \in \mathcal{Y}$. Based on the relaxed regularization term, f_h is updated to minimize the loss function given by

$$L = \frac{1}{N} \sum_{i=1}^{N} l(\boldsymbol{h}_i, y_i; \theta_h) + \lambda \sum_{y \in \mathcal{Y}} \left[\tilde{p}_0(y,1) - \tilde{p}_1(y,1)\right]^2, \tag{7}$$

where the estimation of cross-entropy $\frac{1}{N}\sum_{i=1}^{N} l(\boldsymbol{h}_i, y_i; \theta_h)$ includes both annotated and unannotated instances; the regularization term $[\tilde{p}_0(y,1) - \tilde{p}_1(y,1)]^2$ is calculated using the annotated instances; and the hyper-parameter λ controls the importance of regularization.

[1] The combination of TPR and FPR is representative enough accross different fairness metrics. POD is flexible to use other metrics as the regularizer for the bias mitigation.

[2] It also has other choices for the relaxation, e.g. sigmoid and tanh functions. The linear function is chosen for simplicity.

3.2 Active Instance Selection (AIS)

In each iteration, AIS selects instances from the unannotated dataset $\mathcal{U}$ to annotate the sensitive attribute values. The newly annotated instances are merged with the dataset for debiasing the classifier head in subsequent iterations. The AIS process consists of two steps: (1) **Group selection** is to select the subgroup $\mathcal{U}_{\tilde{a}}^{\tilde{c}} = \{(\boldsymbol{x}_i, y_i) \in \mathcal{U} \mid a_i = \tilde{a}, y_i = \tilde{c}\}$ on which the model has the worst performance; (2) **Individual selection** is to select the optimal instance from $\mathcal{U}_{\tilde{a}}^{\tilde{c}}$, which can mostly expose the existing bias of the model for promoting the bias mitigation in the next iteration.

Group Selection is motivated by the observation that adding more instances to the subgroup having the worst classification accuracy can improve the fairness by increasing its contribution to the average loss [22,28]. Specifically, for group selection, the unannotated dataset $\mathcal{U}$ is splitted into $\{\mathcal{U}_a^c\}_{a\in\mathcal{A},c\in\mathcal{Y}}$, where $\mathcal{U}_a^c = \{(\boldsymbol{x}_i, y_i) \in \mathcal{U} | a_i = a, y_i = c\}$ denotes a subgroup of unannotated instances. We estimate the classification accuracy $p_a(c,c) = \mathbb{P}(\hat{Y} = c | A = a, Y = c)$ to evaluate f on each subgroup $\mathcal{U}_a^c$ for $a \in \mathcal{A}$ and $c \in \mathcal{Y}$, respectively, following Eq. (4). In this way, the subgroup $\mathcal{U}_{\tilde{a}}^{\tilde{c}} = \{(\boldsymbol{x}_i, y_i) \in \mathcal{U} | a_i = \tilde{a}, y_i = \tilde{c}\}$ which suffers from the worst accuracy is selected by

$$\tilde{a}, \tilde{c} = \underset{a\in\mathcal{A},c\in\mathcal{Y}}{\arg\min}\, p_a^*(c,c), \tag{8}$$

where $p_a^*(c,c) = p_a(c,c) - (p_0(c,c) + p_1(c,c))/2$ denotes the centralized classification accuracy after considering the performance divergence of the classifier on different classes. For example, in Fig. 1 (b), we select the subgroup with the worst accuracy $\mathcal{U}_0^1$ which corresponds to the positive instances from group 0, due to the fact that $p_0^*(1,1) < p_0^*(0,0), p_1^*(0,0), p_1^*(1,1)$.

Note that $p_a^*(c,c)$ cannot be estimated without the annotations of sensitive attribute. We thus learn another classifier head $f_a : \mathbb{R}^M \to \mathbb{R}^{|\mathcal{A}|}$ to predict the sensitive attribute $\hat{a} = \arg\max f_a(\boldsymbol{h}_i|\theta_a)$ for the unannotated instances $\boldsymbol{x}_i \in \mathcal{U}$, where f_a is updated on the annotated set $\mathcal{S}$ by minimizing the cross-entropy loss

$$\theta_a^* = \frac{1}{|\mathcal{S}|} \sum_{(\boldsymbol{x}_i,y_i,a_i)\in\mathcal{S}} l(\boldsymbol{h}_i, a_i; \theta_a). \tag{9}$$

Individual Selection aims to proactively select the most representative instances for annotation, which can maximally promote bias mitigation. Since the classifier f has the worst accuracy on subgroup $\mathcal{U}_{\tilde{a}}^{\tilde{c}}$, reducing the classification error on $\mathcal{U}_{\tilde{a}}^{\tilde{c}}$ would improve fairness, where $\tilde{a}$ and $\tilde{c}$ are chosen through group selection in Eq. (8). The strategy of individual selection is to expand the annotated dataset to reduce δ-cover of subgroup $\mathcal{U}_{\tilde{a}}^{\tilde{c}}$ [36]. Specifically, the annotated dataset $\mathcal{S}$ enables δ-cover of the entire dataset $\mathcal{D}$ if $\forall \boldsymbol{x}_i \in \mathcal{D}$, $\exists \boldsymbol{x}_j \in \mathcal{S}$ such that $||\boldsymbol{x}_i - \boldsymbol{x}_j||_2 \leq \delta$, where δ denotes the coverage radius given by

$$\delta = \max_{\boldsymbol{x}_i\in\mathcal{D}} \min_{\boldsymbol{x}_j\in\mathcal{S}} ||\boldsymbol{x}_i - \boldsymbol{x}_j||_2. \tag{10}$$

Furthermore, it is observed that the generalization error of a model approaches the training error[3] if the coverage radius δ is small [36]. Following such scheme, we select the instance in subgroup $\mathcal{U}_{\tilde{a}}^{\tilde{c}}$, which could decrease δ-coverage to reduce the classification error on $\mathcal{U}_{\tilde{a}}^{\tilde{c}}$. To be concrete, the distance between $\boldsymbol{x}_i$ and $\boldsymbol{x}_j$ is measured by $||\boldsymbol{h}_i - \boldsymbol{h}_j||_2$, where $\boldsymbol{h}_i = f_b(\boldsymbol{x}_i|\theta_b)$ and $\boldsymbol{h}_j = f_b(\boldsymbol{x}_j|\theta_b)$ are the embeddings of $\boldsymbol{x}_i$ and $\boldsymbol{x}_i$, respectively. We have the instance $(\boldsymbol{x}^*, y^*)$ selected for annotation following the max-min rule

$$(\boldsymbol{x}^*, y^*) = \underset{(\boldsymbol{x}_i, y_i) \in \mathcal{U}_{\tilde{a}}^{\tilde{c}}}{\arg\max} \min_{(\boldsymbol{x}_j, y_j) \in \mathcal{S}} ||\boldsymbol{h}_i - \boldsymbol{h}_j||_2. \tag{11}$$

The individual selection strategy is illustrated in Figs. 2 (b) and (c), where δ reduction guides the individual selection. The candidate instances in $\mathcal{U}_{\tilde{a}}^{\tilde{c}}$ and annotated instances are shown in Fig. 2 (b). The distances between each candidate instance and annotated instances are measured in embedding space $||\boldsymbol{h}_i - \boldsymbol{h}_j||_2$, where the minimal one is marked as a blue arrow. The red instance marked by (x^*, y^*) in Fig. 2 (c) indicates the best candidate to be annotated.

Algorithm 1: APOD

1 **Input**:initial annotated dataset $\mathcal{S}$
2 **Output**:classifier body f_b, head f_h
3 $\theta_b^*, \theta_h^* = \arg\min \sum_{i=1}^{N} l(\boldsymbol{x}_i, y_i; \theta_b, \theta_h)$
4 **while** *within budget limit* **do**
5 #Penalization of discrimination
6 $\theta_h^* = \text{POD}(\mathcal{S}, f_b, f_h)$
7 #Active Instance Selection.
8 $(\boldsymbol{x}^*, y^*) = \text{AIS}(f_b, f_h)$
9 $\mathcal{S} = \mathcal{S} \cup \{(\boldsymbol{x}^*, y^*, a^*)\}$
10 $\mathcal{U} = \mathcal{U} \setminus \{(\boldsymbol{x}^*, y^*)\}$

Algorithm 2: POD

Input: annotated dataset $\mathcal{S}$, classifier body f_b, head f_h.
Output: fair classifier head f_h^*.
while *not converged* **do**
For $a \in \mathcal{A}$ and $y \in \mathcal{Y}$, estimate $\tilde{p}_a(y, 1)$ given by Eq. (6).
Update the classifier head f_h to minimize the loss function in Eq. (7).
return f_h^*

3.3 The APOD Algorithm

The details of APOD are summarized in Algorithm 1. Initially, APOD learns the biased f_b and f_h, and randomly samples a small set of annotated instances $\mathcal{S}$. In each iteration, APOD first learns f_a to predict the sensitive attribute of unannotated instances; then debiases f_h via POD (line 6); after this, APOD selects the optimal instance $(\boldsymbol{x}^*, y^*)$ for annotation via AIS (line 6) and merges the selected instance with the annotated dataset (line 8); POD and AIS are given in Algorithms 2 and 3, respectively; the iteration stops once the number of annotated instance reaches the budget.

3.4 Theoretical Analysis

We theoretically investigate the proposed APOD to guarantee that bias mitigation is globally achieved, as shown in Theorem 1. We then demonstrate the

[3] The training error is less than generalization error in most cases.

effectiveness of AIS (both group selection and individual selection) in Remark 1. The proof of Theorem 1 is given in Appendix A.

Theorem 1. *Assume the loss value on the training set has an upper bound* $\frac{1}{|\mathcal{S}|}\sum_{(\boldsymbol{x}_i,y_i,a_i)\in\mathcal{S}} l(\boldsymbol{h}_i, y_i;\theta_h) \leq \epsilon^4$*, and* $l(\boldsymbol{h}, y;\theta_h)$ *and* f_h *satisfy* K_l*- and* K_h*-Lipschitz continuity*[5]*, respectively. The generalization loss difference between the unprivileged group and the privileged group has the following upper bound with probability* $1-\gamma$*,*

Algorithm 3: Active Instance Selection (AIS)

Input: classifier body f_b and classifier head f_h.
Output: the selected instance $(\boldsymbol{x}^*, y^*)$.
Update f_a to minimize $\frac{1}{|\mathcal{S}|}\sum_{(\boldsymbol{x}_i,y_i,a_i)\in\mathcal{S}} l(\boldsymbol{h}_i, a_i;\theta_a)$.
Estimate the sensitive attribute $\hat{a}_i = \arg\max f_a(\boldsymbol{h}_i \mid \theta_a)$ for $\boldsymbol{x}_i \in \mathcal{U}$.
For $a \in \mathcal{A}$ and $c \in \mathcal{Y}$, estimate the classification accuracy $p_a(c,c) = \mathbb{P}(\hat{Y} = c|\hat{A} = a, Y = c)$ on subgroup $\mathcal{U}_a^c$.
For $a\in\mathcal{A}$ and $c\in\mathcal{Y}$, centralize $p_a(c,c)$ into $p_a^*(c,c)$ by

$$p_a^*(c,c) = p_a(c,c) - \frac{p_0(c,c)+p_1(c,c)}{2}.$$

Execute the group selection by $\tilde{a},\tilde{c} = \arg\min_{a\in\mathcal{A},c\in\mathcal{Y}} p_a^*(c,c)$.
Execute the individual selection by

$$(\boldsymbol{x}^*, y^*) = \underset{(\boldsymbol{x}_i,y_i)\in\mathcal{U}_{\tilde{a}}^{\tilde{c}}}{\arg\max} \ \min_{(\boldsymbol{x}_j,y_j,a_j)\in\mathcal{S}} ||\boldsymbol{h}_i - \boldsymbol{h}_j||_2.$$

$$\left|\int_{\mathcal{X}_0}\int_{\mathcal{Y}} p(\boldsymbol{x},y)l(\boldsymbol{h},y;\theta_h)\mathrm{d}\boldsymbol{x}\mathrm{d}y - \int_{\mathcal{X}_1}\int_{\mathcal{Y}} p(\boldsymbol{x},y)l(\boldsymbol{h},y;\theta_h)\mathrm{d}\boldsymbol{x}\mathrm{d}y\right|$$
$$\leq \epsilon + \min\left\{\sqrt{-L^2\log\gamma(2N_{\tilde{a}})^{-1}}, (K_l + K_h L)\delta_{\tilde{a}}\right\}, \quad (12)$$

where $\tilde{a} = \arg\max_{a\in\mathcal{A}}\int_{\mathcal{X}_a}\int_{\mathcal{Y}} p(\boldsymbol{x},y)l(\boldsymbol{h},y;\theta_h)\mathrm{d}\boldsymbol{x}\mathrm{d}y$*;* $\mathcal{X}_a = \{\boldsymbol{x}_i \in \mathcal{D}|a_i = a\}$*;* $\delta_{\tilde{a}} = \max_{\boldsymbol{x}_i\in\mathcal{X}_{\tilde{a}}}\min_{(\boldsymbol{x}_j,y_j,a_j)\in\mathcal{S}}||\boldsymbol{h}_i - \boldsymbol{h}_j||_2$*;* $N_{\tilde{a}} = |\{(\boldsymbol{x}_i,y_i,a_i)|a_i = \tilde{a}, (\boldsymbol{x}_i,y_i,a_i)\in\mathcal{S}\}|$*;* $L = \max_{(\boldsymbol{x}_i,y_i)\in\mathcal{U}} l(\boldsymbol{h}_i, y_i;\theta_h)$*; and* $\boldsymbol{h}_i = f_b(\boldsymbol{x}_i|\theta_b)$*.*

In Theorem 1, the global fairness is formalized via considering the generalization error difference between the unprivileged and privileged group as the relaxed fairness metric, and APOD contributes to the global fairness via explicitly tightening the upper bound of the relaxed fairness metric. We demonstrate the details that AIS can iteratively tighten the bound in Remark 1.

Remark 1. In each iteration of APOD, the group selection reduces the value of $\sqrt{-L^2\log\gamma(2N_{\tilde{a}})^{-1}}$ by merging a new instance $(\boldsymbol{x}_i, y_i, a_i)|_{a_i=\tilde{a}}$ to the annotated

---

[4] ϵ can be very small if the classifier head f_h has been well-trained on the annotated dataset $\mathcal{S}$.
[5] $l(\boldsymbol{h}, y;\theta_h)$ and f_h satisfy $|l(\boldsymbol{h}_i, y;\theta_h) - l(\boldsymbol{h}_j, y;\theta_h)| \leq K_l||\boldsymbol{h}_i - \boldsymbol{h}_j||_2$ and $|p(y|\boldsymbol{x}_i) - p(y|\boldsymbol{x}_j)| \leq K_h||\boldsymbol{h}_i - \boldsymbol{h}_j||_2$, respectively, where the likelihood function $p(y \mid \boldsymbol{x}_i) = \mathrm{softmax}(f_h(\boldsymbol{h}_i|\theta_h))$.

dataset $\mathcal{S}$ to increase the value of $N_{\tilde{a}} = |\{(\boldsymbol{x}_i, y_i, a_i) \in \mathcal{S} | a_i = \tilde{a}\}|$. Here, we adopt an approximation given by Eq. (13) due to the negative relationship between the accuracy and the generalization loss,

$$\tilde{a} = \arg\min_{a \in \mathcal{A}} p_a^*(c, c) \approx \arg\max_{a \in \mathcal{A}} \int_{\mathcal{X}_a} \int_{\mathcal{Y}_c} p(\boldsymbol{x}, y) l(\boldsymbol{h}, y; \theta_h) \mathrm{d}\boldsymbol{x} \mathrm{d}y, \tag{13}$$

where $\mathcal{Y}_c = \{y = c \mid y \in \mathcal{Y}\}$ for $c \in \mathcal{Y}$. Meanwhile, the individual selection reduces the value of $\delta_{\tilde{a}}$ by selecting an instance following Eq. (11). With the combination of group selection and individual selection, APOD contributes to the decline of $\min\{\sqrt{-L^2 \log \gamma (2N_{\tilde{a}})^{-1}}, (K_l + K_h L)\delta_{\tilde{a}}\}$, which leads to tightening the upper bound of the fairness metric in Eq. (12).

Remark 1 reveals that both group selection and individual selection of the two-step AIS are effective in tightening the upper bound of relaxed fairness metric. Compared to AIS, we consider two compositional instance selection methods: one with group selection alone, where we randomly select an instance $(\boldsymbol{x}^*, y^*)$ from the subgroup $\mathcal{U}_{\tilde{a}}^{\tilde{c}}$ satisfying $\tilde{a}, \tilde{c} = \arg\min_{a \in \mathcal{A}, c \in \mathcal{Y}} p_a^*(c, c)$; and another with individual selection alone, where an instance is selected via $(\boldsymbol{x}^*, y^*) = \arg\max_{(\boldsymbol{x}_i, y_i) \in \mathcal{U}} \min_{(\boldsymbol{x}_j, y_j, a_j) \in \mathcal{S}} ||\boldsymbol{h}_i - \boldsymbol{h}_j||_2$ without the selection of subgroup. According to Remark 1, the compositional methods merely enable to reduce one of the terms $(2N_{\tilde{a}})^{-1}$ or $\delta_{\tilde{a}}$ in Eq. (12), which are less effective than the two-step AIS as an unit.

4 Experiment

In this section, we conduct experiments to evaluate APOD, aiming to answer the following research questions: **RQ1**: In terms of comparison with state-of-the-art baseline methods, does APOD achieve more effective mitigation of unfairness under the same annotation budget? **RQ2**: Does APOD select more informative annotations for bias mitigation than baseline methods? **RQ3**: How does the ratio of annotated instances affect the mitigation performance of APOD? **RQ4**: Do both group selection and individual selection in the AIS contribute to bias mitigation? The experiment settings including the datasets and implementation details are given in Appendix B and C, respectively.

4.1 Bias Mitigation Performance Analysis (RQ1)

In this section, we compare our proposed APOD with three state-of-the-art baseline methods of bias mitigation. The technology of baseline methods are briefly described as follows. **Vanilla**: The classifier is trained without bias mitigation. **Group DRO** [35]: Group DRO utilizes all sensitive information to minimize the classification loss on the unprivileged group to reduce the performance gap between different sensitive groups. **Learning from Failure (LfF)** [33]: As a debiasing method that relies on proxy sensitive annotations, LfF adopts generalized cross-entropy loss to learn a proxy annotation generator, and proposes a re-weighted cross entropy loss to train the debiased model. **Fair Active Learning (FAL)** [2]: The instance selection in FAL is to maintain a subset of annotated instances for model training, which is not guided by gradient-based model debiasing. More details are given in the Appendix E.

To have a fair comparison, we unify the splitting of datasets for all methods, and set the same annotation budget for APOD and FAL. The mitigation performance is indicated by the fairness-accuracy curves [9], where the hyperparameter λ of APOD varies in the range of $(0, 2]$, and the hyperparameter setting of baseline methods can be referred to Appendix D. We give the fairness-accuracy curves of each method on the five benchmark datasets in Figs. 3 (a)-(f), respectively, where ●, ○ and ◔ indicate the bias mitigation relies on entire-, zero- or partial- annotation of the training dataset, respectively. Finally, we follow existing work [5] to evaluate mitigation performance using the fairness metric EOP on the MEPS, German credit and Loan default datasets, and using the fairness metric ΔEO on the remaining datasets [16]. We have the following observations:

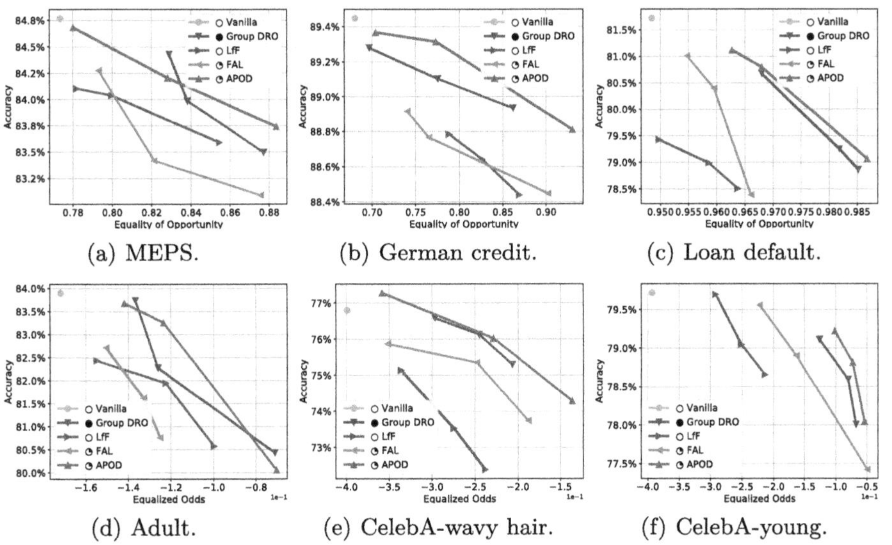

Fig. 3. Accuracy-fairness curve; Algorithm: Vanilla training, Group DRO, LfF, FAL and APOD; Dataset: (a) MEPS, (b) German credit, (c) Loan default, (d) Adult, (e) CelebA-wavy hair, (f) CelebA-young.

- APOD outperforms FAL on the five datasets under the same annotation budget in terms of the mitigation performance at the same level of accuracy. This demonstrates the superiority of APOD applied to the scenarios with limited sensitive information.
- APOD needs very few (less than 3% of the dataset) sensitive annotations, and shows comparable mitigation performance to Group DRO (Group DRO

requires a fully annotated dataset). This indicates the capacity of APOD for bias mitigation under a limitation of sensitive annotations.

- APOD outperforms LfF which relies on the proxy annotation of sensitive attributes. It indicates that the limited human-annotated sensitive information in our framework is more beneficial than proxy annotations on the entire dataset to bias mitigation.

4.2 Annotation Effectiveness Analysis (RQ2)

In this section, APOD is compared with a semi-supervised method and two state-of-the-art active learning methods to demonstrate that AIS contributes to more informative sensitive annotations for the bias mitigation. The technology of baseline methods are briefly described as follows. **Vanilla**: The classifier is trained to minimize the cross-entropy loss without bias mitigation. **SSBM**: The semi-supervised bias mitigation initially samples a data subset for annotations via random selection, then adopts POD to debias the classifier on the partially annotated dataset. **POD+Active learning with uncertainty sampling** (POD+AL): The AIS in APOD is replaced by active learning with uncertainty sampling, where an instance is selected to maximize the Shannon entropy of model prediction. **POD+Active learning with Core-set Approach** (POD+CA): AIS is replaced by active learning with core-set approach, where an instance is selected to maximize the coverage of the entire unannotated dataset. More details are given in the Appendix E.

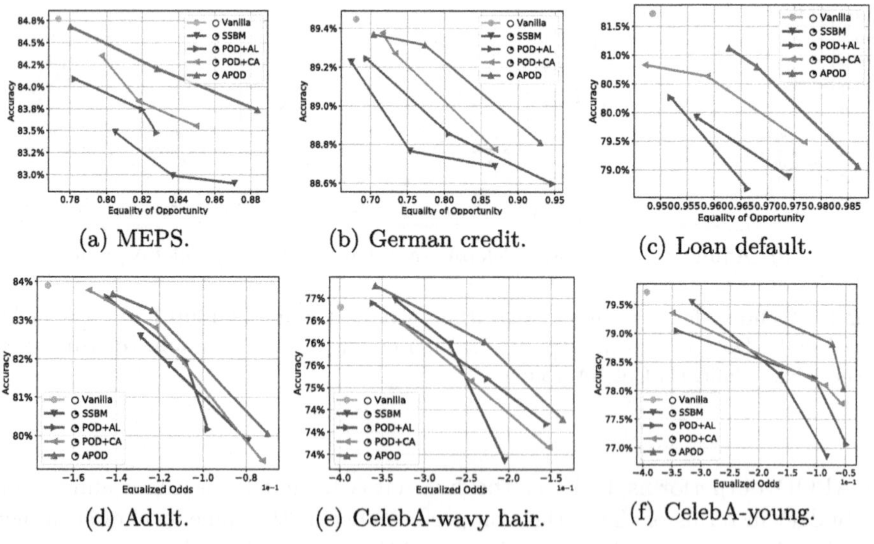

(a) MEPS. (b) German credit. (c) Loan default.

(d) Adult. (e) CelebA-wavy hair. (f) CelebA-young.

Fig. 4. Accuracy-fairness curve; Algorithm: Vanilla training, SSBM, POD + AL, POD + CA and APOD; Dataset: (a) MEPS, (b) German credit, (c) Loan default, (d) Adult, (e) CelebA-wavy hair, (f) CelebA-young.

To unify the experiment condition, all methods have the same annotation budget and have λ in the range of $(0, 2]$. The fairness-accuracy curves on the five datasets are given in Figs. 4 (a)-(f), respectively. According to the mitigating results, we have the following observations:

- Compared to the semi-supervised method and the active learning-based methods, APOD achieves better mitigation performance at the same level of accuracy, indicating the proposed AIS selects more informative annotations than those methods for bias mitigation.
- Different from POD+AL and POD+CA which sample the annotated instances from the whole dataset in each iteration, APOD interactively selects more representative instances from different subgroups in different iterations, i.e. $\mathcal{U}_a^y$ for $a \in \mathcal{A}$ and $y \in \mathcal{Y}$, which contributes to more effective bias mitigation.
- SSBM shows almost the worst mitigation performance among all of the methods, because the initially randomly selected subset preserves the skewness of the original dataset, leading to non-optimal bias mitigation, which is consistent with our discussion in Sect. 1.

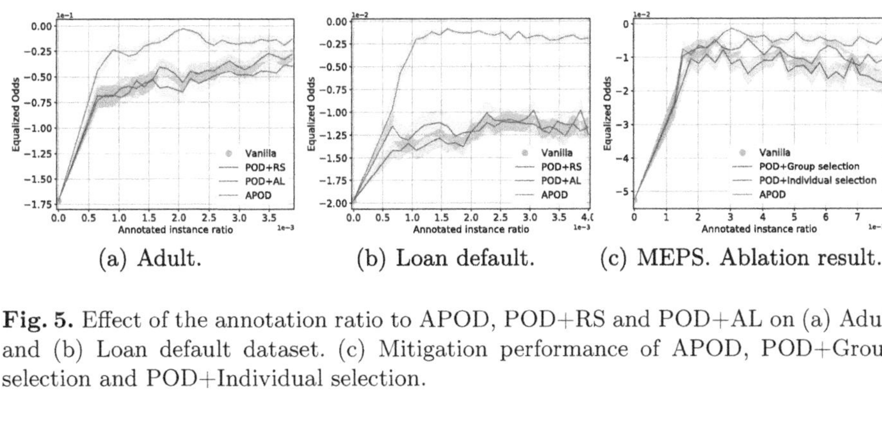

(a) Adult. (b) Loan default. (c) MEPS. Ablation result.

Fig. 5. Effect of the annotation ratio to APOD, POD+RS and POD+AL on (a) Adult and (b) Loan default dataset. (c) Mitigation performance of APOD, POD+Group selection and POD+Individual selection.

4.3 Annotation Ratio Analysis (RQ3)

We now evaluate the effect of the the annotation ratio (that is, the ratio of the annotated instances to the training instances) on bias mitigation. Specifically, we tune λ in the range of $(0, 2]$, and find that $\lambda = 0.5$ and 0.1 can provide a good accuracy-fairness trade-off on the Adult and Loan default datasets, respectively. In addition to the existing baseline methods, we also consider replacing AIS in APOD into random selection (**POD+RS**) for comparison. Since one instance is selected for annotation in each iteration of APOD, the Equalized Odds of the snapshot model in each iteration is estimated and plotted versus the annotation ratio on the Adult and Loan default datasets in Figs. 5 (a) and (b), respectively. We also give the error bar to show the standard deviation of each method. Overall, we have the following observations:

- All methods achieve better mitigation performance as the annotation ratio increases due to the distribution of the annotated set becoming consistent with the entire dataset.
- APOD shows better mitigation performance than POD+AL and POD+RS at the same level of annotation ratios. This indicates the selection of annotated instances by AIS significantly leads to a reduction of bias. In contrast, the bias mitigation of POD+RS merely derives from the increasing annotations.
- APOD shows higher improvement in bias mitigation even when the annotation ratio is small, and enables the mitigation to converge to a higher level at smaller annotation ratios (i.e., earlier) than the baseline methods.

4.4 Ablation Study (RQ4)

To demonstrate the effectiveness of group selection and individual selection, APOD is compared with two compositional methods: POD+Group selection and POD+Individual selection. The three methods are tested with the same hyperparameter setting on the MEPS dataset. The value of the fairness metric is given in Fig. 5 (c). It is observed that both POD+Group selection and POD+Individual selection show considerable degradation in mitigation performance compared to APOD. It empirically validates Remark 1 that both group selection and individual selection in AIS contribute to tightening the upper bound of the relaxed fairness metrics, thus contributing to bias mitigation.

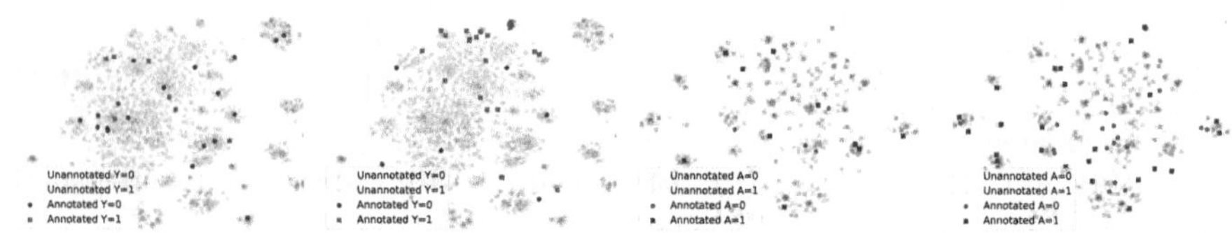

(a) Random selection. (b) APOD. (c) Random selection. (d) APOD.

Fig. 6. Comparison of APOD and Random selection in terms of the annotated instances from different groups. (a) Annotated instances by Random selection. (b) Annotated instances by APOD. (c) Annotated positive instances (Y=1) by Random selection. (d) Annotated positive instances (Y=1) by APOD.

4.5 Visualization of Annotated Instances

We visualize the tSNE embeddings of the annotated instances to trace the active instance selection of APOD. The tSNE visualization is given in Figs. 6 (a)-(d). Specifically, Figs. 6 (a)-(d) illustrate the the tSNE embeddings of the annotated instances selected by APOD and random selection on the MEPS and Adult datasets, respectively. We use different colors to indicate different groups, where positive instances (Y=1) are less than negative ones (Y=0), and the unprivileged group (A=0) is smaller than the privileged group (A=1). Overall, we have the following observations:

- The annotated instances of Random selection in Figs. 6 (a) and (c) are consistent with Fig. 1 (b), which follows the skewed distribution of original dataset, and leads to non-optimal mitigation of bias.
- The annotated instances of APOD in Figs. 6 (b) and (d) are consistent with the optimal annotating in Fig. 1 (c), where the annotated subset shows less skewness compared to the original distribution.
- APOD selects more annotated instances from the unprivileged group $\{(x_i,y_i,a_i)|y_i=1,a_i=0\}$ than random selection. This can significantly mitigate the bias by improving the contribution of unprivileged group to the average loss.

5 Conclusion

In this paper, we propose APOD, an iterative framework for active bias mitigation under the limitation of sensitive annotations. Theoretical analysis indicates that APOD contributes to effective bias mitigation via bounding the relaxed fairness metrics. Experiment results further demonstrate the effectiveness of APOD on five benchmark datasets, where it outperforms baseline methods under the same annotation budget and has a desirable outcome of bias mitigation even when most of the sensitive annotations are unavailable.

Acknowledgement. The authors thank the anonymous reviewers for their helpful comments. The work is in part supported by NSF grants NSF IIS-1939716, IIS-1900990, and IIS-2239257. The views and conclusions contained in this paper are those of the authors and should not be interpreted as representing any funding agencies.

Ethical Statement. This paper has been thoroughly reviewed for ethical considerations and has been found to be in compliance with all relevant ethical guidelines. The paper does not raise any ethical concerns and is a valuable contribution to the field.

Appendix

The appendix is available at https://github.com/guanchuwang/APOD-fairness/blob/main/appendix/bias_mitigation_appendix.pdf.

References

1. Abernethy, J.D., Awasthi, P., Kleindessner, M., Morgenstern, J., Russell, C., Zhang, J.: Active sampling for min-max fairness. In: International Conference on Machine Learning. vol. 162 (2022)
2. Anahideh, H., Asudeh, A., Thirumuruganathan, S.: Fair active learning. arXiv preprint arXiv:2001.01796 (2020)
3. Angwin, J., Larson, J., Mattu, S., Kirchner, L.: There's software used across the country to predict future criminals. ProPublica (2016)
4. Azzalini, A.: The skew-normal distribution and related multivariate families. Scand. J. Stat. **32**(2), 159–188 (2005)

5. Bechavod, Y., Ligett, K.: Penalizing unfairness in binary classification. arXiv preprint arXiv:1707.00044 (2017)
6. Caton, S., Haas, C.: Fairness in machine learning: a survey. arXiv preprint arXiv:2010.04053 (2020)
7. Chai, J., Jang, T., Wang, X.: Fairness without demographics through knowledge distillation. In: Advances in Neural Information Processing Systems
8. Chai, J., Wang, X.: Self-supervised fair representation learning without demographics. In: Advances in Neural Information Processing Systems
9. Chuang, C.Y., Mroueh, Y.: Fair mixup: Fairness via interpolation. arXiv preprint arXiv:2103.06503 (2021)
10. Chuang, Y.N., et al.: Mitigating relational bias on knowledge graphs. arXiv preprint arXiv:2211.14489 (2022)
11. Chuang, Y.N., et al.: Efficient XAI techniques: A taxonomic survey. arXiv preprint arXiv:2302.03225 (2023)
12. Chuang, Y.N., et al.: CoRTX: Contrastive framework for real-time explanation. arXiv preprint arXiv:2303.02794 (2023)
13. Creager, E., et al.: Flexibly fair representation learning by disentanglement. In: International Conference on Machine Learning, pp. 1436–1445. PMLR (2019)
14. Dai, E., Wang, S.: Say no to the discrimination: Learning fair graph neural networks with limited sensitive attribute information. In: Proceedings of the 14th ACM International Conference on Web Search and Data Mining, pp. 680–688 (2021)
15. Deng, Z., et al.: FIFA: Making fairness more generalizable in classifiers trained on imbalanced data. arXiv preprint arXiv:2206.02792 (2022)
16. Du, M., Mukherjee, S., Wang, G., Tang, R., Awadallah, A., Hu, X.: Fairness via representation neutralization. In: Advances in Neural Information Processing Systems. vol. 34 (2021)
17. Du, M., Yang, F., Zou, N., Hu, X.: Fairness in deep learning: a computational perspective. IEEE Intell. Syst. **36**(4), 25–34 (2020)
18. Dua, D., Graff, C.: UCI machine learning repository (2017). http://archive.ics.uci.edu/ml
19. Goel, S., Rao, J.M., Shroff, R., et al.: Precinct or prejudice? Understanding racial disparities in New York city's stop-and-frisk policy. Ann. Appl. Stat. **10**(1), 365–394 (2016)
20. Han, X., et al.: Retiring δDP: New distribution-level metrics for demographic parity. Transactions on Machine Learning Research (2023). https://openreview.net/forum?id=LjDFIWWVVa
21. Hardt, M., Price, E., Srebro, N.: Equality of opportunity in supervised learning. Adv. Neural Inf. Process. Syst. **29**, 3315–3323 (2016)
22. Hashimoto, T., Srivastava, M., Namkoong, H., Liang, P.: Fairness without demographics in repeated loss minimization. In: International Conference on Machine Learning, pp. 1929–1938. PMLR (2018)
23. Jiang, Z., et al.: FMP: Toward fair graph message passing against topology bias. arXiv preprint arXiv:2202.04187 (2022)
24. Jiang, Z., Han, X., Fan, C., Yang, F., Mostafavi, A., Hu, X.: Generalized demographic parity for group fairness. In: International Conference on Learning Representations (2022)
25. Jiang, Z., Han, X., Jin, H., Wang, G., Zou, N., Hu, X.: Weight perturbation can help fairness under distribution shift. arXiv preprint arXiv:2303.03300 (2023)
26. Kallus, N., Mao, X., Zhou, A.: Assessing algorithmic fairness with unobserved protected class using data combination. Manag. Sci. **68**(3), 1591–2376 (2021)

27. Kleinberg, J., Ludwig, J., Mullainathan, S., Rambachan, A.: Algorithmic fairness. In: Aea Papers and Proceedings. vol. 108, pp. 22–27 (2018)
28. Lahoti, P., et al.: Fairness without demographics through adversarially reweighted learning. arXiv preprint arXiv:2006.13114 (2020)
29. Li, Y., Vasconcelos, N.: Repair: Removing representation bias by dataset resampling. In: Proceedings of the IEEE/CVF Conference on Computer Vision and Pattern Recognition, pp. 9572–9581 (2019)
30. Ling, H., Jiang, Z., Luo, Y., Ji, S., Zou, N.: Learning fair graph representations via automated data augmentations. In: International Conference on Learning Representations (2023)
31. Mehrabi, N., Morstatter, F., Saxena, N., Lerman, K., Galstyan, A.: A survey on bias and fairness in machine learning. ACM Comput. Surv. (CSUR) **54**(6), 1–35 (2021)
32. Mehrotra, A., Vishnoi, N.K.: Fair ranking with noisy protected attributes. In: Advances in Neural Information Processing Systems
33. Nam, J., Cha, H., Ahn, S., Lee, J., Shin, J.: Learning from failure: Training debiased classifier from biased classifier. arXiv preprint arXiv:2007.02561 (2020)
34. Romano, Y., Bates, S., Candes, E.J.: Achieving equalized odds by resampling sensitive attributes. arXiv preprint arXiv:2006.04292 (2020)
35. Sagawa, S., Koh, P.W., Hashimoto, T.B., Liang, P.: Distributionally robust neural networks for group shifts: On the importance of regularization for worst-case generalization. arXiv preprint arXiv:1911.08731 (2019)
36. Sener, O., Savarese, S.: Active learning for convolutional neural networks: A core-set approach (2018)
37. Slack, D., Friedler, S.A., Givental, E.: Fairness warnings and fair-MAML: learning fairly with minimal data. In: Proceedings of the 2020 Conference on Fairness, Accountability, and Transparency, pp. 200–209 (2020)
38. Steel, E., Angwin, J.: On the web's cutting edge, anonymity in name only. The Wall Street Journal 4 (2010)
39. Sun, T., et al.: Mitigating gender bias in natural language processing: Literature review. arXiv preprint arXiv:1906.08976 (2019)
40. Sweeney, L.: Discrimination in online ad delivery. Commun. ACM **56**(5), 44–54 (2013)
41. Tang, R., Du, M., Li, Y., Liu, Z., Zou, N., Hu, X.: Mitigating gender bias in captioning systems. In: Proceedings of the Web Conference 2021, pp. 633–645 (2021)
42. Verma, S., Rubin, J.: Fairness definitions explained. In: 2018 IEEE/ACM International Workshop on Software Fairness (fairware), pp. 1–7. IEEE (2018)
43. Wang, G., et al.: Accelerating shapley explanation via contributive cooperator selection. In: International Conference on Machine Learning, pp. 22576–22590. PMLR (2022)
44. Wang, S., Guo, W., Narasimhan, H., Cotter, A., Gupta, M., Jordan, M.I.: Robust optimization for fairness with noisy protected groups. arXiv preprint arXiv:2002.09343 (2020)
45. Zha, D., et al.: Data-centric artificial intelligence: A survey. arXiv preprint arXiv:2303.10158 (2023)
46. Zhang, B.H., Lemoine, B., Mitchell, M.: Mitigating unwanted biases with adversarial learning. In: Proceedings of the 2018 AAAI/ACM Conference on AI, Ethics, and Society, pp. 335–340 (2018)

47. Zhang, F., Kuang, K., Chen, L., Liu, Y., Wu, C., Xiao, J.: Fairness-aware contrastive learning with partially annotated sensitive attributes. In: The Eleventh International Conference on Learning Representations
48. Zhao, T., Dai, E., Shu, K., Wang, S.: You can still achieve fairness without sensitive attributes: Exploring biases in non-sensitive features. arXiv preprint arXiv:2104.14537 (2021)
49. Zimdars, A.: Fairness and undergraduate admission: a qualitative exploration of admissions choices at the university of Oxford. Oxford Rev. Educ. **36**(3), 307–323 (2010)

FG²AN: Fairness-Aware Graph Generative Adversarial Networks

Zichong Wang[1], Charles Wallace[2], Albert Bifet[3,4], Xin Yao[5], and Wenbin Zhang[1](✉)

[1] Florida International University, Miami, USA
wenbin.zhang@fiu.edu
[2] Michigan Technological University, Houghton, USA
wallace@mtu.edu
[3] University of Waikato, Hamilton, New Zealand
abifet@waikato.ac.nz
[4] Télécom Paris Tech, Palaiseau, France
[5] Southern University of Science and Technology, Shenzhen, China
xiny@sustech.edu.cn

Abstract. Graph generation models have gained increasing popularity and success across various domains. However, most research in this area has concentrated on enhancing performance, with the issue of fairness remaining largely unexplored. Existing graph generation models prioritize minimizing graph reconstruction's expected loss, which can result in representational disparities in the generated graphs that unfairly impact marginalized groups. This paper addresses this socially sensitive issue by conducting the first comprehensive investigation of fair graph generation models by identifying the root causes of representational disparities, and proposing a novel framework that ensures consistent and equitable representation across all groups. Additionally, a suite of fairness metrics has been developed to evaluate bias in graph generation models, standardizing fair graph generation research. Through extensive experiments on five real-world datasets, the proposed framework is demonstrated to outperform existing benchmarks in terms of graph fairness while maintaining competitive prediction performance.

Keywords: Graph Generation · Graph Mining · Algorithmic Fairness

1 Introduction

Graph data is prevalent in many real-world scenarios, making machine learning in graphs increasingly popular in practical applications such as financial markets [47], item recommendation [43] and social network analysis [36]. Generative models of graphs have become crucial components of the graph machine learning framework, serving purposes such as data augmentation [11], anomaly detection [1], and recommendation [37]. For example, when training a machine learning model in applications with high social concerns, such as financial or

© The Author(s), under exclusive license to Springer Nature Switzerland AG 2023
D. Koutra et al. (Eds.): ECML PKDD 2023, LNAI 14170, pp. 259–275, 2023.
https://doi.org/10.1007/978-3-031-43415-0_16

crime, graph generative models can provide a viable alternative [31]. The model can be trained using high-quality simulated graphs generated from real data, ensuring reliable model training while reducing the potential privacy risks associated with using real data directly.

Current graph generation models construct graph-structured data from a low-dimensional space that contains distributions for graph generation, such as random graphs [30], small-world models [2], scale-free graphs [3], and stochastic block models [24]. Although effective, these approaches may introduce algorithmic biases against marginalized populations, raising ethical and societal concerns [5,6,38,41,50]. For example, Graph Neural Network (GNN)-based frameworks can propagate and even amplify pre-existing biases due to their utilization of graph structural information [13]. Consider the scenario of a user network in the financial industry, where nodes in the network are more likely to be linked to other nodes with similar attributes, leading to denser connections between nodes with the same sensitive attributes (*e.g.*, race and gender) [19,39,40]. In this case, when a financial institution uses a graph generation model to distribute synthetic users to partners for assessing customer ratings, the model may be impacted by sensitive attributes of individuals closely associated with the applicant, resulting in propagating biases against marginalized groups. Hence, there is a pressing need for the design and development of graph generative models that are intrinsically fairness-aware.

Despite the enormous importance, we face three great challenges in creating a graph generation model that mitigates algorithmic bias: **1) Multiple sources of bias in graph data and the lack of metrics to quantify such biases.** Unlike tabular data, graph data sources have a wider range of potential biases: some may stem from the sensitive attributes of the nodes themselves, while others lie within the graph structure between nodes [20,27,51]. Furthermore, existing fairness definitions have been exclusively designed for classification evaluation purposes, and there are currently no metrics that are specifically intended to gauge the bias of graph generation models. **2) The structured nature of the generated data.** Most fairness-ML work assumes that the underlying data is independent and identically distributed (IID) [41,49,51] but graphs are non-IID in nature to capture connections among individual units. Fair graph generation therefore needs to fairly represent both information about each node and potential connections between each node and its neighboring nodes. **3) Exacerbated cost of computation.** Generative models based on graph data confront substantial computational costs due to the requirement of generating both node and link information within the graph [7]. In fair graph generation, these computation costs are further intensified by the need to consider fairness constraints concurrently.

To tackle the above challenges, this paper proposes a novel meta-strategy for the fair graph generation. To the best of our knowledge, the proposed Fairness-aware Graph Generative Adversarial Networks (FG^{2}AN) is the first work capable of tackling all the aforementioned challenges simultaneously. The following summarizes the key contributions of this paper:

- We introduce a fair graph generative model called FG^{2}AN, which integrates both graph representation fairness and graph structure fairness to generate task-specific graphs.
- The first-of-its-kind graph generation tailored fairness metrics to benchmark future fair graph generation research.
- The proposed graph fairness approach circumvents quadratic complexity calculations, significantly enhancing operational efficiency and reducing memory usage.
- Extensive experiments both qualitatively and quantitatively confirm the effectiveness of the proposed model.

The rest of our paper is organized as follows. We review the related literature in Sect. 2. Section 3 explains some notation and background of this paper. We introduce our proposed method and fair metrics in Sect. 4. Section 5 introduce our experiment setting and analyzes the experimental results. Finally, we conclude the paper in Sect. 6.

2 Related Work

2.1 Graph Generative Model

Graph generative models have found applications in diverse areas such as biology [44], chemistry [45,46], and social sciences [44]. Most of the research in this field utilizes variational autoencoders (VAE [21]) and generative adversarial networks (GAN [12]). For instance, NetGAN and its extensions [7,17], inspired by the GAN model, generate synthetic random walks while discriminating between synthetic and real random walks sampled from a real graph. GraphVAE [33] employs the VAE [21] model to learn both the graph representation and node features, but its limitations include poor scalability to large graphs due to constraints in memory and runtime, and its practical application is mostly limited to small graphs. GraphRNN [46] treats a graph as a sequence of node and edge generations, which can be learned using autoregressive models. This approach outperforms GraphVAE in terms of both performance and scalability. Generally, these approaches can generate a high-quality synthetic graph. However, these approaches primarily focus on generating general-purpose graphs, while disregarding label information and fairness requirements.

2.2 Fairness on Graphs

The issue of fairness in graph mining has recently garnered significant attention, due to evidence suggesting that several graph mining models may introduce bias and lead to possible discrimination in downstream applications [8,15,20]. The existing literature in fair graph mining can be broadly categorized into two groups: group fairness [8,9,14,15,22] and individual fairness [25,26,48,52]. The concept of group fairness on graphs concerns the elimination of bias among different demographic groups of nodes or edges in various graph mining tasks, such as graph proximity learning [35], graph clustering [22], and graph representation learning [8,9]. Individual fairness on graphs concerns the challenge of ensuring that similar graph signals (*i.e.*, Homogeneity graphs) lead to the same algorithmic outcomes [20]. However, these studies have primarily focused on fair graph mining, and the domain of graph models for generation has rarely been explored. Our approach serves to fill this void.

3 Notation and Background

This section first describes the notation used, then reviews the biases in real-world graph data, showing the root causes of graph generative model bias.

3.1 Notation

We assume give an undirected and unweighted graph $\mathcal{G} = (\mathcal{V}, \mathcal{E}, \mathcal{X})$, where the set of nodes is denoted as $\mathcal{V}$, the set of edges is denoted as $\mathcal{E}$, and the set of node features is denoted as $\mathcal{X} = \{x_1, x_2, \ldots, x_n\}$ (n $= |\mathcal{V}|$), where x_i represents the features of each node i. In addition, we let $A \in \mathbb{R}^{n \times n}$ denotes the adjacency matrix of the graph $\mathcal{G}$, where $A_{i,j}$ takes on the value 1 if there exists an edge $i \rightarrow j$, and 0 otherwise. Since $\mathcal{G}$ is undirected, $(v_1, v_2) \in \mathcal{E}$ implies $(v_2, v_1) \in \mathcal{E}$, where v_1 and v_2 represent nodes in $\mathcal{V}$. Moreover, $D \in \mathbb{R}^{n \times n}$ denote the diagonal matrix, where $D_{i,i} = \sum_j A_{i,j}$. $I \in \mathbb{R}^{n \times n}$ denote the identity matrix. Each node i has a set of sensitive attributes $S = \{s_1, \ldots, s_n\}$ that differentiate between deprived and favored groups (*e.g.*, female vs. male). Moreover, we let $\mathcal{V}_s \subseteq \mathcal{V}$ represent the set of vertices belonging to the deprived group, and let $\mathcal{V}_{\hat{s}} \subseteq \mathcal{V}$ represent the set of vertices belonging to the favored group. Note that $\mathcal{V}_s \cup \mathcal{V}_{\hat{s}} = \mathcal{V}$ and $\mathcal{V}_s \cap \mathcal{V}_{\hat{s}} = \varnothing$. Moreover, the favored subgraph consists of all favored nodes of $\mathcal{G}$, while the deprived subgraph is composed of all deprived nodes. We denote favored and deprived subgroups as $\mathcal{G}_{\overline{p}}$ and $\mathcal{G}_p$, where $\mathcal{G}_{\overline{p}} = \bigcup\{v_i \mid v_i \in \mathcal{V}_{\hat{s}}\}$ and $\mathcal{G}_p = \bigcup\{v_i \mid v_i \in \mathcal{V}_s\}$. The learning objective of the fair graph generation is therefore to minimize the reconstruction error U_θ while concurrently reducing the disparity between the reconstruction errors of deprived subgraph $U_\theta(\mathcal{G}_s)$ and favored subgraph $U_\theta(\mathcal{G}_{\overline{s}})$. Note that $\mathcal{G}_s = \{\forall\ \mathcal{V}_i \mid \mathcal{V}_i \subseteq \mathcal{V}_s, s \subseteq S\}$ and $\mathcal{G}_{\hat{s}} = \{\forall\ \mathcal{V}_i \mid \mathcal{V}_i \subseteq \mathcal{V}_{\hat{s}}, \hat{s} \subseteq S\}$.

3.2 Root Causes of Representational Discrepancies

This section delves into the root causes of model bias, stemming from the nodes' degrees, and the effects of their neighboring nodes. We put forth the concept that graph generation models exhibit bias due to their susceptibility to the inherent bias present in the graph data during the learning process of the graph topology. Consequently, this may result in the amplification of the original graph data's bias within the generated graph, leading to a more pronounced discrimination issue.

Degree-Related Bias: We begin by examining the origins of degree-related unfairness. Node connectivity in real-world graph data often exhibits considerable disparities. It is important to note that node degrees in real-world graphs frequently follow a long-tailed power-law distribution, indicating that a substantial portion of nodes possess relatively low degrees. For instance, on social media platforms, ordinary users generally have significantly lower connectivity compared to celebrities. Also, as illustrated in Fig. 1, the CORA dataset consists of 2,708 scientific publications and the citation network consists of 5,429 links. In this dataset, high-degree nodes (*i.e.*, node degrees $\geq$ average node degrees) constitute only 28.17% of the total, while low-degree nodes account for 71.83%. Additionally, the very high-degree nodes (i.e., node degrees $\geq$ 50) represent a mere 0.003%.

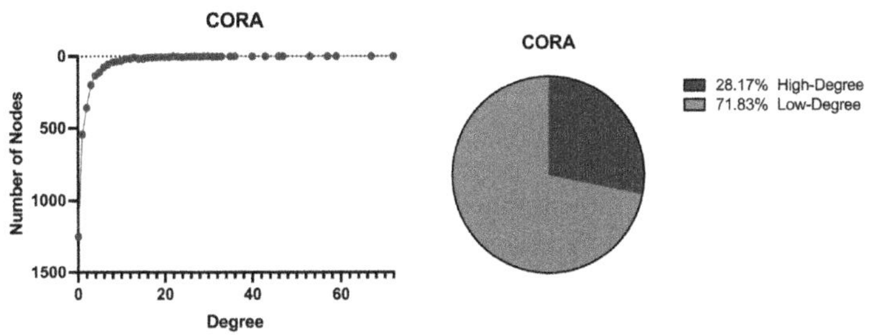

Fig. 1. The disparate distribution of node degree in graph.

Previous studies [7,51] have demonstrated that graph generative models constructed using the datasets we have used are prone to showing bias in low-degree nodes. Specifically, during the graph generation process, low-degree nodes undergo increased reconstruction loss and exhibit a tendency towards reduced representation. In other words, the overall performance of the graph generative model may predominantly favor a select group of high-degree nodes (such as celebrities on a social media platform), while potentially being biased against a vast majority of low-degree nodes (like grassroots users on the same social media platform). Hence, it is crucial to ensure fairness for low-degree nodes when designing graph generation models.

Connectivity-Related Bias: Another source of bias in graph generation models stems from the influence of adjacency connections. Unlike tabular data, graph data encompass not only the individual attributes of each data point but also the relationships between them. Moreover, nodes with similar sensitive attributes in graph data tend to form stronger connections [27]. For instance, Fig. 2(a) reveals that the number of intra-group connections (blue and green bars in Fig. 2(a)) significantly exceeds the number of inter-group connections (yellow and purple bars in Fig. 2(a)) in the Facebook graph dataset. In addition, Fig. 2(b) presents the synthetic Facebook graph generated by NetGAN, and it is evident that, compared to the original graph dataset, the intra-group connections have increased, while the inter-group connections have decreased. This observation indicates that the bias has been further exacerbated.

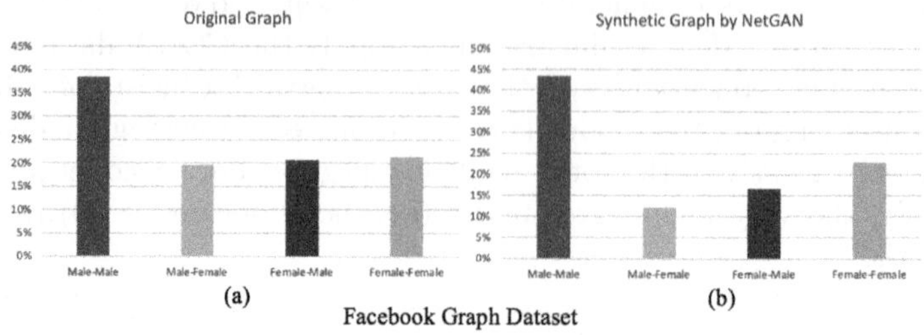

Fig. 2. Comparison of the disparate distribution of gender related node connectivity between the original graph and synthetic graph. (Color figure online)

In fact, strongly intra-connected groups in social network graphs are often distinguished by factors such as race, gender, or wealth. However, groups segmented based on these sensitive attributes frequently experience unequal treatment in various aspects, which is also reflected in their representation in social network. Existing graph generation methods may unintentionally adopt, or even amplify, potential biases inherited in such biased graph data. For instance, graph embedding, a prevalent technique in the field, projects each node onto a low-dimensional vector representing the user's structural information within the network. However, the learned representation may capture and even exacerbate the unjusted social bias encoded in the structural representation, *i.e.,* intra-group connectivity. This can lead to biases being transferred to downstream tasks like loan approval and credit scoring, thereby exacerbating existing biases.

4 Methodology

This section outlines methodologies for addressing bias in graph generation models, including: i) methods to tackle the degree-related (Sect. 4.1) and connectivity-related (Sect. 4.2) root causes of bias in graph generation, ii) FG^{2}AN integrating the dual debiasing solutions for fair graph generation (Sect. 4.3), iii) a suite of novel metrics, which serve to comprehensively reveal the biases present in graph generation (Sect. 4.4).

4.1 Mitigating Degree-Related Bias

In Sect. 3.2, we discussed how the disparities in node degrees create biases in graph generative models. To mitigate such degree-related unfairness, we propose incorporating the Rawlsian difference principle [28] into our approach. This principle, which originated from distributive justice theory by John Rawls [28], aims for equity by optimizing the well-being of the most disadvantaged group. In a state of equilibrium, it ensures that all groups maintain their status quo since the welfare of the least advantaged group cannot be further maximized, leading to balanced performance across groups. In the context of graph generation, the concept of welfare is captured by the representativeness in the model, which is evaluated through its reconstruction loss. Mathematically, the Rawlsian difference principle is defined as follows,

$$min_\theta \sum_{s=0}^{n} Var(U(G_s, \theta)) \tag{1}$$

where G_s is the subgraph of the input graph $\mathcal{G}$, θ represents the loss function that aims to minimize the given task, and U(G_s,θ) represents the utility function that assesses the loss across a group of samples, utilizing the model defined by parameters θ.

To enforce the Rawlsian difference principle in the graph generation model, two challenges need to be addressed. The first challenge involves determining a method to compute the threshold value that distinguishes high-degree and low-degree nodes. Using the average node degree as a threshold is not feasible because it can be skewed by nodes with exceptionally high degrees in the graph data. This would result in significant losses for many relatively low-degree nodes, even if balanced utility between the two groups is achieved. Therefore, we avoid using a rigid threshold and instead divide the node set $\mathcal{V}$ in the input graph $\mathcal{G}$ into k groups, as shown in Eq. 2, to overcome this issue:

$$\mathcal{V} = \bigcup_{k=0}^{\text{max degree}} \{\mathcal{V}_k \mid \sum_{i=0}^{j} A_{i,j} = k\} \tag{2}$$

where $\mathcal{V}_k$ signifies the set of nodes with degrees equal to k. This modification ensures that nodes with different degrees receive an equal opportunity for evaluation. We assess each degree set individually, ensuring fair treatment between any two node degree sets.

The second challenge is then to assess if two sets of node degrees receive equal treatment. To this end, we utilize the 80% rule [10] to evaluate disparate impact, which strives to ensure that all subgroups experience the same level of loss in the loss function. We consider a lower loss in graph reconstruction for node degrees to be more favorable. Next, we assess whether the proportional difference in graph reconstruction loss between any two subsets with distinct node degrees exceeds a fairness threshold, as illustrated in Eq. 3:

$$\arg\min \frac{U(\forall \{V_i | \sum_{i=0}^{j} A_{i,j} = k\}) - U(\forall \{V_i | \sum_{i=0}^{j} A_{i,j} \neq k\})}{U(\forall \{V_i | \sum_{i=0}^{j} A_{i,j} = k\})} \leq F_t \tag{3}$$

where F_t refers the fairness threshold and $F_t \in [0, 0.2]$. The two node degree subsets are considered being treated fairly if the proportional difference meets or is below a certain threshold, otherwise there is an disparity in representation between the two subsets.

In general, our approach to ensuring fairness across the node set is based on the fairness guarantee provided by subsets of nodes with varying degrees. By ensuring fairness within these sub-node sets, we can improve the overall fairness of the model used to generate the graph. Furthermore, we can customize the stringency of our fairness standards by adjusting the fairness threshold to meet specific real-world constraints [4].

4.2 Mitigating Connectivity-Related Bias

This section aims to tackle the bias that arises from the disparate connectivity between intra- and inter- groups. Existing graph generation models treat each neighboring node equally, which may seem an intuitive thought, but actually exacerbate the connection disparity between deprived and favored groups as most connections in the input graph $\mathcal{G}$ are intra-group, leading to amplified inter-group connection disparity in the topology learned by existing graph generation models [7,33,46]. Considering the growing practice of using social network for credit scoring as an example [42], the deprived group users' credit scores are unfairly lowered due to most of their neighbors are intra-group with relative lower credit scores, yielding credit scoring decisions that are discriminatory towards them. This bias appears in the transfer probability ($\mathcal{M}$) expressed in Eq. 4 during graph generation, where neighboring nodes are treated equally and assigned the same transfer probability:

$$\mathcal{M} = (AD^{-1} + I)/2 \tag{4}$$

When using this learning approach, there is a greater chance that nodes will stay within their own groups, which means that there will be less connections between different groups. This can make it even harder for deprived groups to be represented in the overall graph. To illustrate, imagine a node that is highly connected, but all of its connections are with just two types of nodes, one of which only has one connection. In this scenario, the node with only one connection can hardly be represented statistically in a fair manner. This further exacerbates the inequality in how different demographic groups are represented in the graph.

Our proposed solution to tackle bias involves incorporating a fairness constraint on transfer probability, which ensures equitable transfer between intra- and inter- neighbors. We achieve this by categorizing neighbors based on sensitive attributes and ensuring that the total selection probability for each group is equal during each node transition, instead of randomly selecting a node from all neighboring nodes:

$$\sum(P_{v_a}|A_{i,a} = 1, S_a = s) = \sum(P_{v_b}|A_{i,b} = 1, S_b = \overline{s}) \tag{5}$$

Within each sub-sensitive group, the samples will share probabilities equally. As a result, neighboring nodes belonging to a smaller total number of sub-sensitive groups will receive a higher transfer probability compared to neighbor nodes in a larger total number of sub-sensitive groups.

4.3 FG^{2}AN Assembling

Armed with the solutions for degree-related and connectivity-related biases, we integrate these dual solutions into the general framework of Generative Adversarial Networks (GAN) [16] to minimize the reconstruction loss of the input graph $\mathcal{G}$ but also across different groups fairly for the fair graph generation. Figure 3 provides an overview of our proposed model.

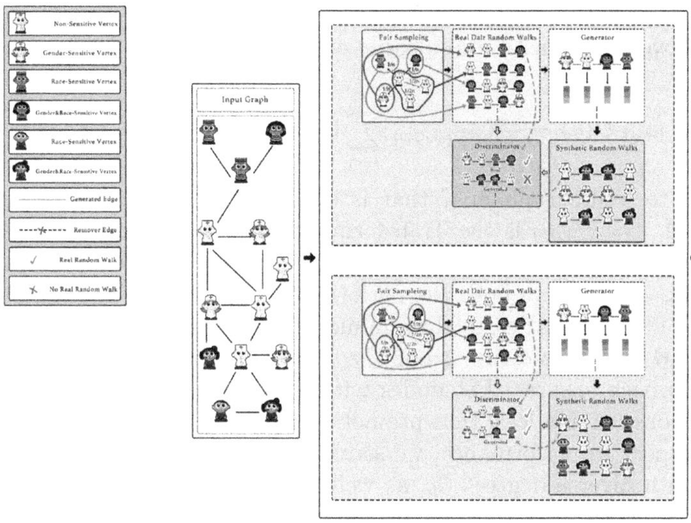

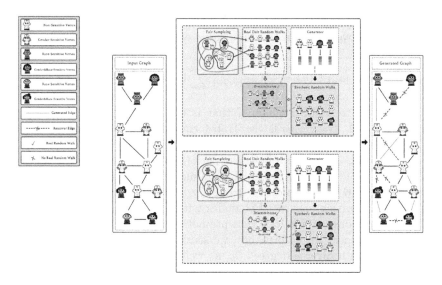

Fig. 3. Illustrations of the proposed FG^{2}AN for fair graph generation. (Color figure online)

The FG^{2}AN architecture follows the standard GAN structure, comprising of a generator and a discriminator. To mitigate connectivity-related bias, FG^{2}AN first extracts a set of fair random walks of length $\mathbf{T}$ from the adjacency matrix $\mathbf{A}$, following the fair sampling algorithm proposed in Sect. 4.2 (as depicted by the blue part in Fig. 3). This set of fair random walks serves as the training set for FG^{2}AN (shown as the yellow part in Fig. 3). Note that fair random walks apply fairness restrictions to each node transition rather than directly modifying the transition probability matrix. By doing this, costly computations such as the quadratic number of node calculations, which were employed in previous graph generation models [23, 34], can be circumvented.

Furthermore, the computation only utilizes the non-zero terms in the transfer probability matrix, effectively circumventing the massive computational expense related to the sparsity of real-world graphs. Another significant advantage of employing fair random walks is the preservation of graph isomorphism learning. In other words, providing two isomorphic graphs, $\mathcal{G}_1$ and $\mathcal{G}_2$, as input will yield identical results. Next, the generator produces synthetic random walks (the purple portion in Fig. 3) by learning from the real fair random walks present in the input graphs. Note that FG^{2}AN produces a significantly greater quantity of random walks compared to the ones that are sampled, which is advantageous in maintaining the overall quality and minimizing the randomness of the produced graphs.

In addition, to mitigate the connectivity-related bias, it is necessary to ensure that different groups with varying degrees are treated fairly in the graph generation model. The solution proposed in Sect. 4.1 is followed for this purpose. This involves constraining the ratio of the loss for reconstructing different groups with dissimilar degrees to a reasonable threshold. Integrating these two fairness constraints, the overall reconstruction loss is defined below,

$$\arg\min U(\theta) = -E_{w \subseteq \{\mathcal{G}, \mathcal{G}_k\}}[\sum_{t=1}^{T} \log_{g_\theta}(w_T | w_{1,\ldots,T-1})] \tag{6}$$

where $\mathcal{G}_k$ refers to a subgraph in $\mathcal{G}$ that is composed of a graph of vertices $\forall\{v_i \in \mathcal{V} \mid \sum_i^j A_{i,j} = k\}$, g_θ is the Transformer-based generator, w_t represent the Tth node and $w_{1,\ldots,T-1}$ represent the first $(T-1)^{th}$ nodes in a sampled fair random walk. To preserve both the performance and fairness of the model, our optimization objective is designed to minimize the reconstruction loss based on input graphs $\mathcal{G}$ and degree-wise graph $\mathcal{G}_k$. With this constraint, in terms of fairness, our approach ensures that nodes with varying degrees $\mathcal{G}_k$ experience similar graph reconstruction loss, thus promoting fair representation for all subgroups. With respect to performance, we strive to minimize the reconstruction loss for nodes with diverse degrees $\mathcal{G}_k$, as well as maintain the lowest possible total reconstruction loss value for the entire graph $\mathcal{G}$.

In general, at each iteration *l*, we consider the recently generated fair random walks from $\mathcal{G}$ as positive samples (yellow area) and the fair random walks obtained from the previous iteration *l* generator as negative samples (purple area). The task of the discriminator is to distinguish between the synthetic and real samples. By learning from both positive and negative samples, the generative model g_θ is improved, resulting in high-quality synthetic random walks. For example, in the deep pink region of iteration *l*, the discriminator can differentiate between the real fair random walks (marked ✓) and the synthetic random walks (marked ✕), while in the light pink region of iteration *l+1*, the real fair random walks and synthetic random walks are indistinguishable (both marked ✓). Additionally, to avoid isolated nodes, FG^{2}AN ensures that each node has at least one connected edge. Moreover, each subgroup in the generated graph should have a comparable degree (*e.g.*, total edge count) to that of the input graph $\mathcal{G}$.

4.4 Fairness Definitions for Graph Generation

This section introduces the first-of-its-kind fairness metrics designed specifically for graph generation models, setting a benchmark for future research in fair graph generation. Consistent with typical fairness notions that evaluate whether there is a lack of favoritism from one side to another, the proposed fair graph definitions measure the disparity between deprived and favored subgraphs, as defined by sensitive attributes, across various perspectives of topology simulation, and are formally defined as:

$$G_{fair}(\mathcal{G}_{ori}, \mathcal{G}_{gen}) = \left| \left| \frac{M_i(\mathcal{G}_{ori_{\overline{p}}}) - M_i(\mathcal{G}_{gen_{\overline{p}}})}{M_i(\mathcal{G}_{ori_{\overline{p}}})} \right| - \left| \frac{M_i(\mathcal{G}_{ori_p}) - M_i(\mathcal{G}_{gen_p})}{M_i(\mathcal{G}_{ori_p})} \right| \right| \quad (7)$$

where $\mathcal{G}_{ori}$ and $\mathcal{G}_{gen}$ represent the original graph and generated graph with subscript p and $\overline{p}$ denoting the deprived and favored subgraphs. In addition, $M_i(\cdot)$ represents one of the topology properties. The lower the $G_{fair}(\mathcal{G}_{ori}, \mathcal{G}_{gen})$ the fairer the generated graph.

Equation 7 is then instantiated by introducing the following fairness definitions for graph generation, which consider various aspects of topology simulation: 1) *Average Degree Difference (ADD)*: evaluates the disparity in network clustering difference between deprived and favored node subgroups. 2) *Equal Connected Accessibility (ECA)*: measures the difference in the size of the largest connected components difference between deprived and favored subgroups.

3) *Statistical Triangle Difference (STD)*: evaluates the disparity in cohesiveness difference between deprived and favored subgroups. 4) *Equal Edge Distribution Entropy (EEDE)*: quantifies the disparity between the relative edge distribution entropy of the favored and deprived subgroups. 5) *Power Law Exponent Parity (PLEP)*: measures the discrepancy between the power law distributions of the favored and deprived subgroups. 6) *Equal Gini (EG)*: evaluates the disparity in the Gini coefficient of the degree distribution across different subgroups.

These six metrics provide a comprehensive understanding of whether the topology of different subgroups is fairly represented in the generated graph. This reflects the representativeness of different subgroups in the reconstruction loss, and thus, indicates the fairness of the graph generation model.

Table 1. Statistics of the benchmark datasets.

Dataset	CHAR		
	Nodes#	Edges#	Sensitive Attribute
Facebook	1,034	26,749	Gender
Oklahoma97	3,111	73,230	Gender
UNC28	4,018	65,287	Gender
Cora	2,708	5,429	Topic
NBA	403	10,621	Country

5 Experiments

5.1 Experimental Setup

Datasets: We validate our proposed method using five real-world graph datasets with socially sensitive concerns, including: three social network graph datasets *Facebook* [18], *Oklahoma97* [29], and *UNC28* [29] as well as an academic graph dataset *Cora* [32], and a sports graph dataset *NBA* [13]. The Facebook dataset originates from a social network within the Facebook app. UNC28 and Oklahoma97 represent social networks of two schools, with links indicating friendship connections on social media. The Cora dataset contains numerous machine learning papers, categorized into one of seven classes. The NBA dataset provides performance statistics for roughly 400 NBA basketball players during the 2016–2017 season, along with additional information. Table 1 displays the detailed characteristics.

Baseline: Four graph generative baseline models were compared against FG^{2}AN: i) *NetGan* [7], which utilizes the GAN algorithm to train its graph generative model; ii) *GraphRNN* [46], which models the creation of graphs sequentially; iii) *GraphVAE* [33], a trailblazing method for graph generation based on variational autoencoders, and iv) *TagGen* [53], which learns the graph representation in an end-to-end fashion.

Evaluation Metrics: Aside from the previously introduced fairness measures specifically designed for graph generation, a range of performance metrics are employed to assess various aspects of generated graph properties [53], including: i) *Mean Degree*: the mean value of node degree. ii) *Largest Connected Component* (LCC): The size of the largest connected component. iii) *Triangle Count* (TC): The count of three mutually connected nodes. iv) *Edge Distribution Entropy* (EDE): The relative edge distribution entropy of $\mathcal{G}$. v) *Power Law Exponent* (PLE): The exponent of the power law distribution of $\mathcal{G}$. vi) *Gini*: the Gini coefficient of the degree distribution. A better performance is indicated by a smaller discrepancy between the generated graph and the original graph for these six graph properties, thus the lower the values of these metrics the better the generated graph.

5.2 Experimental Results

Fairness of the Generated Graphs: We first evaluate the generated graphs from fairness perspective and the results are shown in Fig. 4. As one can see, FG^{2}AN significantly outperforms the baseline across all six fairness graph generation metrics for all datasets. This outcome indicates that the generated graphs fairly capture the graph properties of both favored and deprived groups, and that FG^{2}AN effectively addresses the inconsistent expressiveness of existing graph generation models for these groups. Our findings highlight the importance of considering the representation of various groups within the graph when evaluating the performance of graph generation models.

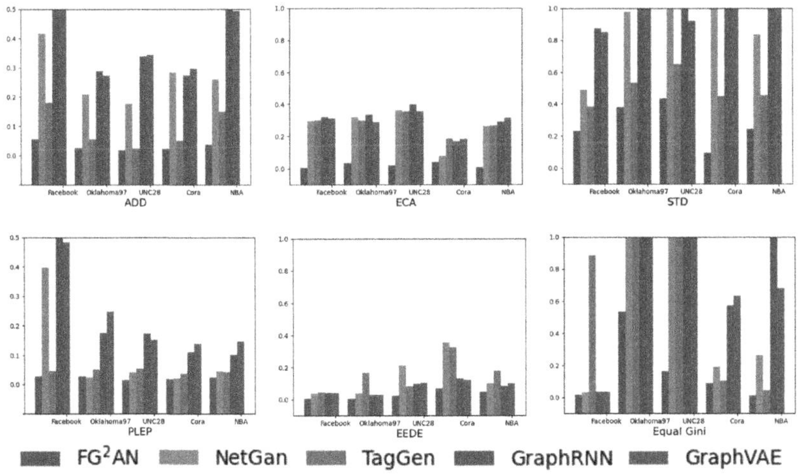

Fig. 4. Comparison of FG^{2}AN to baseline models using fair graph generation metrics.

Quality of the Generated Graphs: After evaluating the fairness of the graph generation models, we proceeded to assess the quality of the generated graph. The results are presented in Fig. 5. Overall, our proposed approach FG^{2}AN exhibits robust generalization to graph properties and achieves comparable or superior performance to the baseline methods. We observe, in some instances, FG^{2}AN marginally sacrifices overall performance, which could be attributed to the fairness constraint imposed to ensure representational parity across different groups.

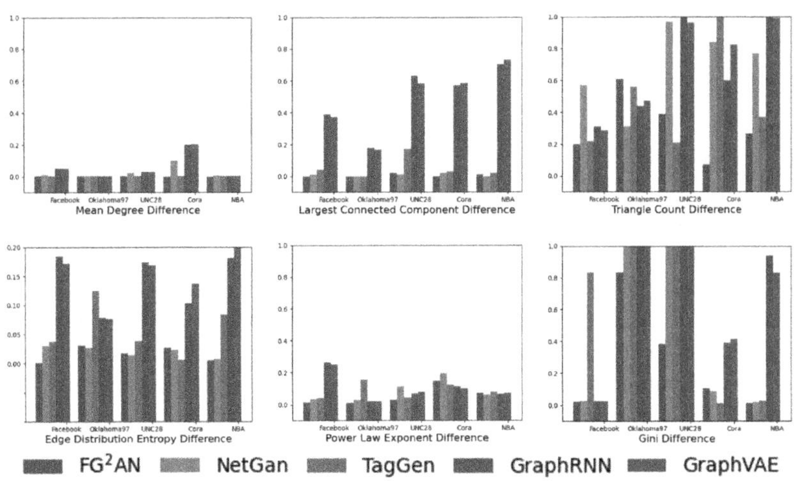

Fig. 5. Comparison of FG^{2}AN to baseline models using graph generation performance metrics.

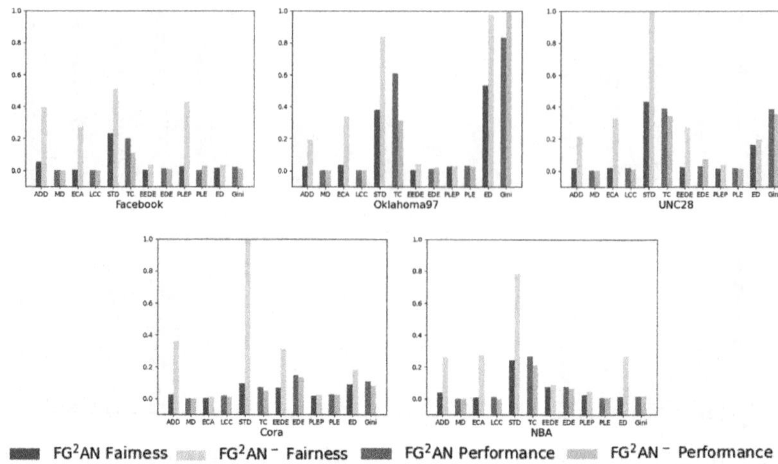

Fig. 6. Comparison of FG^2AN and FG^2AN^- using fair graph generation and performance metrics.

Ablation Studies: Ablation studies were conducted to validate the effectiveness of the proposed fairness regularizers. Specifically, we removed the degree- and connectivity-related regularizers from FG^2AN while keeping other components identical. The results, presented in Fig. 6, clearly demonstrate the effectiveness of our proposed bias mitigation solutions. In comparison to FG^2AN, the FG^2AN^- model, which has the fairness regularizers removed, tends to focus more on learning the topology of favored groups. As a result, during the learning process, FG^2AN^- visits favored group more and may not fully capture the topology of the nodes in the deprived group, leading to a higher reconstruction loss and introducing bias in the deprived group. Additionally, since $rmFG^2AN^-$ retains more of the favored group's topology, it has a slight edge in terms of overall performance.

6 Conclusion

The ability of graph generation models to learn high-level graph representations has sparked great interest. Nevertheless, current models do not consider fairness, which is a crucial social issue. To address this, a new framework for fair graph generation is introduced in this paper, along with a set of fair graph metrics that are the first of their kind for benchmarking purposes. Experimental results on five real-world datasets show that the proposed framework outperforms existing benchmarks in terms of graph fairness while maintaining competitive performance.

References

1. Akoglu, L., McGlohon, M., Faloutsos, C.: RTM: laws and a recursive generator for weighted time-evolving graphs. In: 2008 Eighth IEEE International Conference on Data Mining. pp. 701–706. IEEE (2008)
2. Aksoy, S.G., Purvine, E., Cotilla-Sanchez, E., Halappanavar, M.: A generative graph model for electrical infrastructure networks. J. Complex Netw. **7**(1), 128–162 (2019)
3. Alam, M., Perumalla, K.S., Sanders, P.: Novel parallel algorithms for fast multi-GPU-based generation of massive scale-free networks. Data Sci. Eng. **4**, 61–75 (2019)
4. Barocas, S., Selbst, A.D.: Big data's disparate impact. California law review pp. 671–732 (2016)
5. Beutel, A., Chen, J., Zhao, Z., Chi, E.H.: Data decisions and theoretical implications when adversarially learning fair representations. arXiv preprint arXiv:1707.00075 (2017)
6. Binns, R.: Fairness in machine learning: Lessons from political philosophy. In: Conference on Fairness, Accountability and Transparency. pp. 149–159. PMLR (2018)
7. Bojchevski, A., Shchur, O., Zügner, D., Günnemann, S.: Netgan: Generating graphs via random walks. In: International conference on machine learning. pp. 610–619. PMLR (2018)
8. Bose, A., Hamilton, W.: Compositional fairness constraints for graph embeddings. In: International Conference on Machine Learning. pp. 715–724. PMLR (2019)
9. Buyl, M., De Bie, T.: Debayes: a bayesian method for debiasing network embeddings. In: International Conference on Machine Learning. pp. 1220–1229. PMLR (2020)
10. Cascio, W.F., Aguinis, H.: The federal uniform guidelines on employee selection procedures (1978) an update on selected issues. Rev. Public Pers. Adm. **21**(3), 200–218 (2001)
11. Chakrabarti, D., Faloutsos, C.: Graph mining: Laws, generators, and algorithms. ACM Comput. Surv. (CSUR) **38**(1), 2-es (2006)
12. Creswell, A., White, T., Dumoulin, V., Arulkumaran, K., Sengupta, B., Bharath, A.A.: Generative adversarial networks: an overview. IEEE Signal Process. Mag. **35**(1), 53–65 (2018)
13. Dai, E., Wang, S.: Say no to the discrimination: Learning fair graph neural networks with limited sensitive attribute information. In: Proceedings of the 14th ACM International Conference on Web Search and Data Mining. pp. 680–688 (2021)
14. Farnad, G., Babaki, B., Gendreau, M.: A unifying framework for fairness-aware influence maximization. In: Companion Proceedings of the Web Conference 2020. pp. 714–722 (2020)
15. Fisher, J., Mittal, A., Palfrey, D., Christodoulopoulos, C.: Debiasing knowledge graph embeddings. In: Proceedings of the 2020 Conference on Empirical Methods in Natural Language Processing (EMNLP). pp. 7332–7345 (2020)
16. Goodfellow, I., et al.: Generative adversarial networks. Commun. ACM **63**(11), 139–144 (2020)
17. Guo, X., Zhao, L.: A systematic survey on deep generative models for graph generation. IEEE Trans. Pattern Anal. Mach. Intell. **45**, 5370–5390 (2022)
18. He, R., McAuley, J.: Ups and downs: modeling the visual evolution of fashion trends with one-class collaborative filtering. In: Proceedings of the 25th International Conference on World Wide Web, pp. 507–517 (2016)

19. Hofstra, B., Corten, R., Van Tubergen, F., Ellison, N.B.: Sources of segregation in social networks: a novel approach using Facebook. Am. Sociol. Rev. **82**(3), 625–656 (2017)
20. Kang, J., He, J., Maciejewski, R., Tong, H.: Inform: individual fairness on graph mining. In: Proceedings of the 26th ACM Sigkdd International Conference on Knowledge Discovery & Data Mining, pp. 379–389 (2020)
21. Kingma, D.P., Welling, M.: Auto-encoding variational bayes. arXiv preprint arXiv:1312.6114 (2013)
22. Kleindessner, M., Samadi, S., Awasthi, P., Morgenstern, J.: Guarantees for spectral clustering with fairness constraints. In: International Conference on Machine Learning. pp. 3458–3467. PMLR (2019)
23. Liu, W., Chen, P.Y., Cooper, H., Oh, M.H., Yeung, S., Suzumura, T.: Can gan learn topological features of a graph? arXiv preprint arXiv:1707.06197 (2017)
24. Louail, T., et al.: Uncovering the spatial structure of mobility networks. Nature Commun. **6**(1), 6007 (2015)
25. Ma, J., Guo, R., Mishra, S., Zhang, A., Li, J.: Clear: Generative counterfactual explanations on graphs. arXiv preprint arXiv:2210.08443 (2022)
26. Ma, J., Guo, R., Wan, M., Yang, L., Zhang, A., Li, J.: Learning fair node representations with graph counterfactual fairness. In: Proceedings of the Fifteenth ACM International Conference on Web Search and Data Mining. pp. 695–703 (2022)
27. Rahman, T., Surma, B., Backes, M., Zhang, Y.: Fairwalk: towards fair graph embedding (2019)
28. Rawls, A.: Theories of social justice (1971)
29. Red, V., Kelsic, E.D., Mucha, P.J., Porter, M.A.: Comparing community structure to characteristics in online collegiate social networks. SIAM Rev. **53**(3), 526–543 (2011)
30. Robins, G., Pattison, P.: Random graph models for temporal processes in social networks. J. Math. Sociol. **25**(1), 5–41 (2001)
31. Saxena, N.A., Zhang, W., Shahabi, C.: Missed opportunities in fair AI. In: Proceedings of the 2023 SIAM International Conference on Data Mining (SDM). pp. 961–964. SIAM (2023)
32. Sen, P., Namata, G., Bilgic, M., Getoor, L., Galligher, B., Eliassi-Rad, T.: Collective classification in network data. AI Mag. **29**(3), 93–93 (2008)
33. Simonovsky, M., Komodakis, N.: GraphVAE: Towards Generation of Small Graphs Using Variational Autoencoders. In: Kůrková, V., Manolopoulos, Y., Hammer, B., Iliadis, L., Maglogiannis, I. (eds.) ICANN 2018. LNCS, vol. 11139, pp. 412–422. Springer, Cham (2018). https://doi.org/10.1007/978-3-030-01418-6_41
34. Tavakoli, S., Hajibagheri, A., Sukthankar, G.: Learning social graph topologies using generative adversarial neural networks. In: International Conference on Social Computing, Behavioral-Cultural Modeling & Prediction (2017)
35. Tsioutsiouliklis, S., Pitoura, E., Tsaparas, P., Kleftakis, I., Mamoulis, N.: Fairness-aware pagerank. In: Proceedings of the Web Conference 2021. pp. 3815–3826 (2021)
36. Wan, H., Zhang, Y., Zhang, J., Tang, J.: AMiner: search and mining of academic social networks. Data Intell. **1**(1), 58–76 (2019)
37. Wang, X., He, X., Wang, M., Feng, F., Chua, T.S.: Neural graph collaborative filtering. In: Proceedings of the 42nd international ACM SIGIR conference on Research and development in Information Retrieval. pp. 165–174 (2019)
38. Wang, Z., et al.: Preventing discriminatory decision-making in evolving data streams. In: Proceedings of the 2023 ACM Conference on Fairness, Accountability, and Transparency, pp. 149–159 (2023)

39. Wang, Z., Zhang, W.: Advancing fairness in machine learning: Multi-dimensional perspective and integrated evaluation framework (2023)
40. Wang, Z., Zhang, W.: Mitigating multisource biases in graph neural networks via real counterfactual instances (2023)
41. Wang, Z., et al.: Towards fair machine learning software: understanding and addressing model bias through counterfactual thinking. arXiv preprint arXiv:2302.08018 (2023)
42. Wei, Y., Yildirim, P., Van den Bulte, C., Dellarocas, C.: Credit scoring with social network data. Mark. Sci. **35**(2), 234–258 (2016)
43. Wu, J., Wang, X., Feng, F., He, X., Chen, L., Lian, J., Xie, X.: Self-supervised graph learning for recommendation. In: Proceedings of the 44th International ACM SIGIR Conference on Research and Development in Information Retrieval, pp. 726–735 (2021)
44. Ye, M., Liu, X., Lee, W.C.: Exploring social influence for recommendation: a generative model approach. In: Proceedings of the 35th International ACM SIGIR Conference on Research and Development in Information Retrieval, pp. 671–680 (2012)
45. You, J., Liu, B., Ying, Z., Pande, V., Leskovec, J.: Graph convolutional policy network for goal-directed molecular graph generation. Adv. Neural Inf. Process. Syst. **31** (2018)
46. You, J., Ying, R., Ren, X., Hamilton, W., Leskovec, J.: Graphrnn: generating realistic graphs with deep auto-regressive models. In: International Conference on Machine Learning, pp. 5708–5717. PMLR (2018)
47. Zhang, S., et al.: Hidden: hierarchical dense subgraph detection with application to financial fraud detection. In: Proceedings of the 2017 SIAM International Conference on Data Mining, pp. 570–578. SIAM (2017)
48. Zhang, W., Hernandez-Boussard, T., Weiss, J.C.: Censored fairness through awareness. In: Proceedings of the AAAI Conference on Artificial Intelligence (2023)
49. Zhang, W., Kim, J., Wang, Z., Ravikumar, P., Weiss, J.: Individual fairness guarantee in learning with censorship (2023)
50. Zhang, W., Ntoutsi, E.: Faht: an adaptive fairness-aware decision tree classifier. arXiv preprint arXiv:1907.07237 (2019)
51. Zhang, W., Pan, S., Zhou, S., Walsh, T., Weiss, J.C.: Fairness amidst non-iid graph data: Current achievements and future directions. arXiv preprint arXiv:2202.07170 (2022)
52. Zhang, W., Weiss, J.C.: Longitudinal fairness with censorship. In: Proceedings of the AAAI Conference on Artificial Intelligence, vol. 36, pp. 12235–12243 (2022)
53. Zhou, D., Zheng, L., Han, J., He, J.: A data-driven graph generative model for temporal interaction networks. In: Proceedings of the 26th ACM SIGKDD International Conference on Knowledge Discovery & Data Mining, pp. 401–411 (2020)

Targeting the Source: Selective Data Curation for Debiasing NLP Models

Yacine Gaci[1(✉)], Boualem Benatallah[2], Fabio Casati[3], and Khalid Benabdeslem[1]

[1] University of Lyon, Lyon, France
{yacine.gaci,khalid.benabdeslem}@univ-lyon1.fr
[2] Dublin City University, Dublin, Ireland
boualem.benatallah@dcu.ie
[3] ServiceNow, Palo Alto, USA

Abstract. Unjustified social stereotypes have lately been found to taint the predictions of NLP models. Thus, an increasing amount of research focuses on developing methods to mitigate social bias. Most proposed approaches update the parameters of models post-hoc, running the risk of forgetting the predictive task of interest. In this work, we propose a novel way of debiasing NLP models by debiasing and curating their training data. To do so, we propose an unsupervised pipeline to identify which instances in the training data mention stereotypes that tally with the stereotypes encoded in NLP models. Then we either remove or augment these problematic instances, and train NLP models on less biased data. In this pipeline, we propose three methods to excavate stereotypes encoded in models using likelihoods, attention weights and vector representations. Experiments on the tasks of natural language inference, sentiment analysis and question answering suggest that our methods are better at debiasing downstream models than existing techniques.

Keywords: Natural Language Processing · Fairness · Debiasing · Data Curation

1 Introduction

Despite the significant advances in Natural Language Processing (NLP) models, there is growing concern about the levels of bias they demonstrate [4,6,22,31,33,34]. In this paper, bias refers to unjustified and undesired skew in the predictions of NLP models with respect to various groups, such as social demographics, sports teams, animals, etc. These biases stem from historical stereotypes that are embedded in the training data used to train these models [5]. For example, biases such as *men are more skilled than women in math and engineering* [4] and *Black people have higher tendencies to crime than other races* [30] can have harmful consequences [2]. Recent research aims to prevent NLP models from replicating these stereotypes by proposing methods to debias them

© The Author(s), under exclusive license to Springer Nature Switzerland AG 2023
D. Koutra et al. (Eds.): ECML PKDD 2023, LNAI 14170, pp. 276–294, 2023.
https://doi.org/10.1007/978-3-031-43415-0_17

[7,14,19,23,27]. However, many of the proposed techniques attempt to modify the internal parameters of the models in a fine-tuning setting, introducing two shortcomings. Firstly, they incur a new computational cost in addition to that of prior training (i.e. first train on the task, then optimize for fairness). Secondly, they can lead to catastrophic forgetting of the task at hand and/or a significant reduction in accuracy [21,23,32].

Alternatively, other approaches aim to *debias* and neutralize training data to prevent biases from being encoded into the models in the first place. We surveyed the landscape of data-debiasing techniques in the literature and identified four different paradigms: **(1) Anonymization** methods replace explicit mentions of groups with anonymized entities such as [GRP] [35,46,51].[1] **(2) Reduction** methods impose fairness by discarding instances from the data corresponding to over-represented groups until parity is reached [51]. On the downside, these methods are not suitable when training data is expensive or scarce. To overcome this issue, **(3) Permutation** techniques reach parity by swapping mentions of groups, e.g. replacing *he* by *she* until the number of mentions of both groups is comparable [24,29,35,37,51]. However, blind swapping risks creating implausible instances such as *She shaved her beard.* Finally, **(4) Augmentation** techniques add new instances to the data corresponding to under-represented groups to ensure fairness [11,37,38,45,50,52]. Counterfactual Data Augmentation (CDA) is one of the most celebrated data augmentation techniques due to its simplicity [50,52]. For example, if the data contains *"A man is driving a truck"*, CDA adds another instance to the data by replacing *man* with *woman* or a non-binary gender. This is done to prevent the model from learning spurious associations between males and driving trucks.

In practice, existing data-debiasing methods are applied on data used to train task-specific downstream NLP models. So if one was to use such debiasing techniques, the general approach goes like this: (1) eliminate biases from training data, then (2) finetune a text encoder such as BERT [9] on the task of interest, using the curated data from Step 1. Following this approach, we notice that existing data-debiasing techniques assume that training data is the only source of bias in the finetuning phase. However, text encoders are known to be biased as well [20,31,33]. Therefore, we presume that bias during finetuning stems from two separate sources: from training data, and/or from the text encoder used as a language representation layer. In essence, existing data-debiasing techniques overlook pre-encoded biases coming from text encoders, and only address biases of training datasets. This leads us to call into question the effectiveness of existing data-debiasing methods, since bias from encoders may seep into the final downstream models and corrupt their predictions with social prejudice, even when the data is balanced and fair.

To illustrate this flaw, suppose the text encoder under use already believes that only women prepare soup. Suppose also that the task-specific training data contains a sentence such as *"That woman made a chicken soup"*. CDA adds a new training instance, e.g., *"That man made a chicken soup"* to try to disassociate

[1] e.g., *[GRP] are good at math.*

the attribute of preparing soup from the representation of women in the data. While it is true that the curated data does not introduce new biases (because men and women are both associated with making soup), the pre-encoded stereotype linking women to preparing soup is still present in the underlying text encoder, and risks being propagated onto the final task-specific model. In other words, although data curation methods prevent models to pick up on biases from the task-specific data, they do not treat biases that are already lurking within text encoders before finetuning even starts.

Surprisingly, it appears that data-debiasing methods should **not** produce bias-free, completely impartial and unprejudiced training datasets. Instead, they should tweak the data in such a way to counter the stereotypes present in text encoders, even if the resulting training datasets would be biased. In other words, we proclaim in this work that data-debiasing methods should first check which stereotypes are encoded in text encoders before updating training data in a way to counteract those exact stereotypes. Returning to the above classification of data-debiasing paradigms, we introduce a fifth approach in this paper that we call *Data Selection*, i.e. select which data instances are likely to cause most bias, then curate those. Therefore, the main contribution of this paper is a method to select these problematic data instances.

Specifically, we propose an *unsupervised* pipeline to quantify how much a given input text concurs with encoded stereotypes of a text encoder of interest. We call these quantities bias scores. If the bias score of a given input text is high, it means that the mentioned stereotype is already strongly encoded in the text encoder. However, if it is negative, the text introduces a statement that contradicts what the model is biased toward. If the bias score nears zero, we can say that the text is relatively stereotype-free. We apply our pipeline to compute a bias score for every instance in the training data. Then, we rank these instances according to their bias scores. Finally, we curate the instances having the highest $\theta\%$ of bias scores either by discarding them altogether, or augmenting them in the style of CDA. We believe that finetuning text encoders on such curated data helps in *unlearning* biases.

In the remainder of this paper, we describe the important details about the computation of bias scores. In Sect. 2, we show how we excavate bias information from three distinct sources: from likelihoods, attention scores and vector representations. Then, in Sect. 3, we describe our pipeline to automatically compute bias scores given an input sentence. Finally, we experiment with three different downstream NLP tasks: natural language inference using MNLI dataset [48], sentiment analysis with SST2 dataset [17,48] and question answering with SQUAD dataset [40] in Sect. 4. Experiments demonstrate that we outperform CDA and two other model-level debiasing techniques. We present related research in Sect. 5. In our experiments, we focus on social groups related to binary gender, race and religion, but nothing in the approach prevents it from being used with other types of groups. We make our code and data publicly available on GitHub.[2]

[2] https://github.com/YacineGACI/Model-Aware-Data-Debiasing.

2 Three Sources of Bias in Text Encoders

Social biases infiltrate text encoders at every level. We show that both likelihoods, attention weights and vector representations display significant stereotypes. In this section, we present three methods to excavate bias information from text encoders when prompted with a masked sentence. Figure 1 summarises the mechanics of our methods with an example.

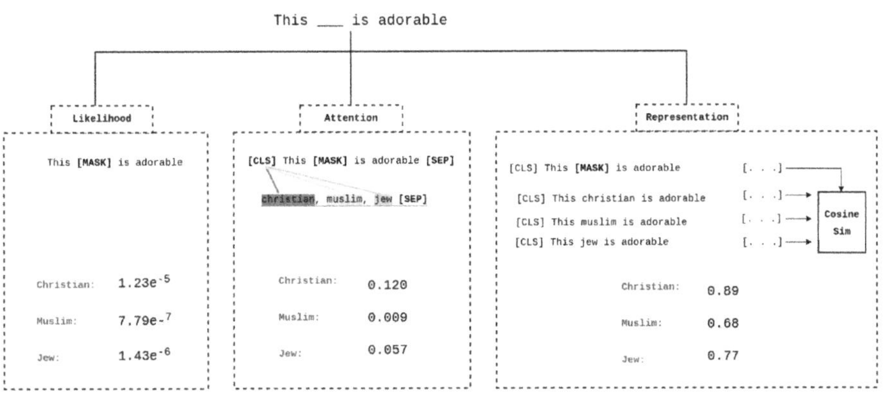

Fig. 1. Different sources of bias in text encoders: (1) Likelihood, (2) Attention, (3) Representation

2.1 Bias in Likelihoods

Following previous work [22,33,34], a biased language model produces unequal likelihoods for groups to fill in the blank of a neutral context. In *"This **[MASK]** is adorable"*, Fig. 1 shows that *christian* is far likelier to replace the mask even though the text itself does not hint at any notion of religion. Thus, likelihoods are valuable to study biases of text encoders.

2.2 Bias in Attentions

Attention is the central component in modern transformer-based text encoders [9,47], and is also a hotbed for social bias [1,14]. In order to get how much of attention a text encoder bestows on social groups given an input text, we add a dummy second input to the original text, consisting only of groups of interest. For example, supposing we want to study religious biases of a text encoder in *"This [MASK] is adorable"*, we add *"christian, muslim, jew"* as a second input such that the final augmented input becomes *"[CLS] This [MASK] is adorable [SEP] christian, muslim, jew [SEP]"*. [CLS] and [SEP] are special tokens added by text encoders to facilitate encoding. [SEP] is used to separate the sentences in the case of double-sentence inputs, and [CLS] is a special token whose embedding captures the semantics of the whole input [9]. As a final step, rather than collecting word embeddings, we retrieve the attention of the [CLS] token on social groups of the second input, essentially examining the allocation of attention in the input sentence on groups. In Fig. 1, the sentence assigns 12% of its attention to Christians, while Jews receive only 5.7% and Muslims a mere 0.9% of attention (with the remaining attention distributed among the other words in the sentence to sum up to 100%) This means that, when using the input example in Fig. 1, text encoders favor Christians by paying more attention to them. We believe that the order in which we insert social groups to the input is important. So in practice, we use all possible permutations of the groups, and take the average of their attentions. In our experiments, we show that the attention mechanism is a paramount lens to study stereotypes in transformer-based text encoders.

2.3 Bias in Representations

The most important function of text encoders is to produce word and/or sentence embeddings given an input text. We can also use these vector representations to corroborate text encoders' guilt at exhibiting stereotypes. Following the example of Fig. 1, we replace the mask with social groups one at a time such that in the example, we end up with three different sentences. Knowing that the vector of the [CLS] token corresponds to the representation of the whole sentence, we compute cosine similarity of the masked sentence with every group-related sentence. In Fig. 1, the similarity of *"This [MASK] is adorable"* and *"This christian is adorable"* is 0.89, while that of Muslims is 0.68 and of Jews 0.77. These differences in similarity suggest that even vector representations are riddled with stereotypes.

3 Pipeline for Measuring Bias in Text

We define a bias type (e.g. gender, race, religion, etc.) by a set of social groups. Each social group is in itself defined by a set of definition words that characterize it and set it apart from other groups, as is of custom in fairness literature in NLP [4,18,30]. The dotted box in the top left corner of Fig. 2 provides examples of the bias types and their social groups that we use in this work. The full list of definition words can be found in Table 1. We remind readers that although our design does not include all social groups of the real world, we follow previous research because most existing evaluation datasets and benchmarks that we use to validate our methods are limited to binary gender, race and religion with the same groups that we treated. Further research and data creation for minorities is increasingly called for, and would constitute a most welcome addition to current literature. In the following, we describe each step of our data-level bias quantification pipeline that we illustrate in Fig. 2.

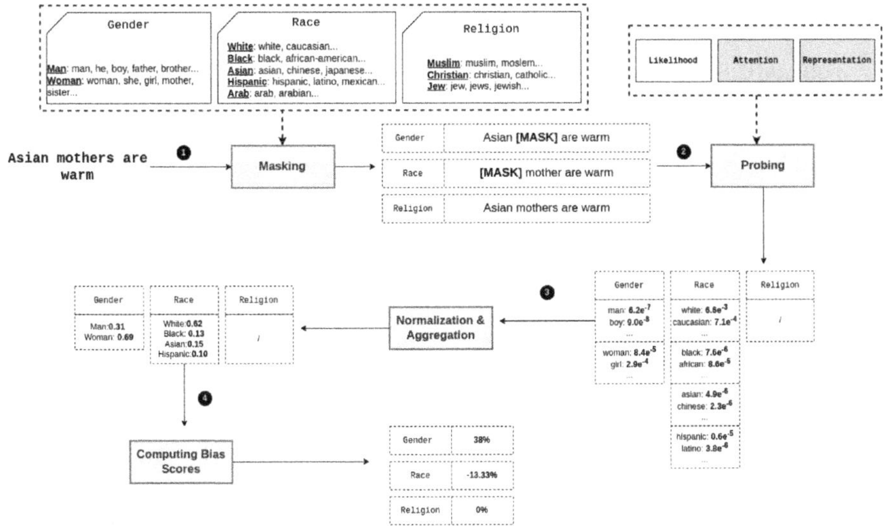

Fig. 2. Pipeline for measuring bias from an input sentence

3.1 Masking

The first step is to mask words that belong to the definitions of bias types under study. In the example of Fig. 2, *mothers* is a definition word of the group *Woman* in the category of gender. Therefore, we mask it and prepare a corresponding masked input. Likewise, *Asian* is also a definition word in the category of race. Thus, we prepare another masked input for this bias type. Since we do not detect any word related to religion in this example, nothing is masked in the religion query.

3.2 Probing

Here, we use the implicit knowledge of stereotypes in text encoders by invoking one of our methods explained in Sect. 2. Each of the methods provides scores for every definition word. For example, in Fig. 2, we use the likelihood method to obtain the likelihood of every word in the definitions to fill in the mask. We notice that female words are more likely than male terms, and words corresponding to the White race are more probable than other races because the text encoder believes women and white people to be warmer than others. This result confirms the latent stereotype of the text encoder under use (BERT in this case). The same applies if we utilize one of the remaining two methods, except that instead of likelihoods, we get either attention weights or cosine similarities for every definition word. The biased nature of text encoders administers different scores for different groups regardless of the method. Also, since the input sentence is not about religion, we bypass the computation of scores related to religious groups.

3.3 Aggregation and Normalization

We aggregate scores corresponding to the same social group by taking their mean. For example, we compute the average score of *man*, *boy*, *father*, etc. to obtain a single score for the group of *Man*. We do the same for all other social groups. Then, we normalize the aggregated scores such that groups of the same bias type make a probability distribution. In Fig. 2, men have a probability of 31% to fill the mask of the gender query, while women have 69%.

3.4 Bias Computation

We declare bias in this work as the differences between the likelihood (or attention or cosine similarity) of the group mentioned in the original text and the average of probabilities (or attentions or cosine similarities) for all other groups. So, if the difference is positive - meaning that the score of the group is higher than the average - it shows that the text complies with the stereotypes encoded in the model. However, if it's negative, then the text contradicts the encoded stereotype (because the model believes that other groups are more likely to replace the mask). We give the formula below:

$$bias\_score(\hat{s}, g) = f(\hat{s}, g) - \mathop{\mathbb{E}}_{g' \in G \setminus \{g\}} [f(\hat{s}, g')] \tag{1}$$

where $\hat{s}$ is the masked text and g is the group of interest (In Fig. 2, it is *Woman* for gender and *Asian* for race). G is the set of all groups and $f(\hat{s}, g)$ is a function that returns the score of group g in the masked text according to one of the three sources of bias, i.e. likelihoods, attention or vector similarities. In Fig. 2, women are likelier to fill the mask than men. So the bias score for gender in this case is 38%[3], which suggests that the sentence mentions a stereotype that is already encoded in BERT. As for race, the bias score is -13.33%[4], meaning that the text encoder does not believe Asians to be warm (anti-stereotype since the bias score is negative). Overall, the formula gives us an intuition about how strongly the input text concords or contradicts social stereotypes encoded in models.

4 Experiments

4.1 Experimental Setup

Evaluation Tasks and Metrics. To date, two types of bias metrics exist: *intrinsic* metrics measuring bias in the encoders themselves [4,31,33,34], and *extrinsic* metrics that measure bias in downstream tasks where the encoders are used [8,25]. Since (1) our work is directed at debiasing downstream task-oriented NLP models, and (2) that intrinsic metrics have recently been criticized [3,15,49], we focus on extrinsic evaluations in this paper. We experiment with

[3] 38 = 69 - Mean({31}).

[4] -13.33 = 15 - Mean({62, 13, 10}).

different θ values (ratios of removal/augmentation): 5%, 10%, 20% and 50%, and three downstream tasks: sentence inference (on MNLI [48]), sentiment analysis (on SST2 [48]) and question answering (on SQUAD [40]).

Baselines. We compare our work to various baselines: CDA [50,52] - which calibrates the number of mentions of all social groups in the *entirety* of training data - and to two popular model-level debiasing techniques: Sent-Debias [27] which extends previous projection-based work on static embeddings, and Kaneko & Bollegala [19] which adds a fairness objective to their optimization function. In the remainder of this section, we report our results on the downstream tasks using all three of our identified bias sources: likelihood, attention and representation. Also, we add another variant that we call *combined* where we combine our bias sources by averaging their scores. As for removal and/or augmentation ratios, note that we report those with the best scores in the tables.

Implementation Details. We apply our methods on BERT [9]. Since our goal is not to improve the accuracy of finetuned models on the NLP tasks of interest, but rather assess the fairness-related impact of our data-level debiasing pipeline, we do not conduct any form of hyperparameter search in this paper. Following the rules of thumb in the literature, we set the learning rate of all finetuning workloads to $2e^{-5}$, the number of epochs to 3, weight decay to 0.01, batch sizes to 8 and maximum length of inputs of BERT to 128. We implemented our algorithms in Python using PyTorch[5] and HuggingFace transformers library[6]. All our experiments are run on a Tesla V100 GPU.

Definition of Demographics. While our proposed approach can be used for most types of groupings, e.g. classification of mammals, sports, furniture styles, etc., in the experiments presented in this paper, we exclusively focus on human social groups. Specifically, we study binary gender, race and religion, with the full list of considered groups and their definition words listed in Table 1.

As can be seen, the definition of groups is flexible and requires a relatively small bag of words for each group. Besides, the definition words need not be of the same length. On the other hand, we acknowledge that our definitions of groups do not reflect the wide complexity of social divisions in the real world, and that our oversight of the minorities risks being regarded as harmful in its own way. We chose those specific groups presented in Table 1 to facilitate comparison with previous works who focused on those widespread groups. Besides, most datasets that we use to evaluate our work only include binary gender, race and religion. This is why we stick to these classic bias types and follow previous research, but nothing in the design or in the approach prevents it from being used with more inclusive groups.

[5] https://github.com/pytorch/pytorch.

[6] https://github.com/huggingface/transformers.

Table 1. Full list of social groups and their definition words used in this work

Bias Type	Groups	Definition words...
Gender	Man	male, man, men, he, himself, his, him, boy, father, grandfather, brother, uncle
	Woman	female, woman, women, she, herself, her, girl, mother, grandmother, sister, aunt
Race	European-white	white, caucasian, european, french, english, spanish, german
	African-black	african, black, nigerian
	Arab	arab, arabian
	Asian	asian, chinese, japanese, korean
	Hispanic	hispanic, latino
Religion	Muslim	muslim, muslims
	Christian	christian, christians
	Jew	jew, jews, jewish

4.2 Question Answering

Task. Given a context and a question, this task is about finding an answer to the question within the context; i.e. finding the span of text inside the context that best answers the question, or predict an empty span if no answer can be found.

Data and Metrics. We use the dataset created and published by [25] consisting of a set of minimal contexts and underspecified questions. The contexts mention two different social groups while the questions are about another attribute, not hinted to in the context. For example, if the context is *"The person over the swing is* ***Angela****. Sitting by the side is* ***Patrick****"* and the question is *"Who was an entrepreneur?"*, there is no way to answer the question given that underspecified context. However, a stereotyped model may associate males with entrepreneurship, and predict the answer to be Patrick. The bias metric for question answering proposed by [25] builds on this rationale, and is robust against *positional dependence* and *attribute independence* problems usually encountered in QA models [25], so we use it in this work. Table 2 summarizes the results.

Discussion. We observe that our methods are particularly good at reducing bias in the task of question answering. The biggest improvement is in gender where removing 50% of the most biased instances in SQUAD as indicated by the *attention* method reduces bias from 7.37 to 3.39. We also point out that augmenting the top half of most biased instances according to the *combined* method nearly eliminates racial biases altogether (with a bias score of 0.03). Again, our approach outperforms existing debiasing methods, and diminishes the semantic performance only slightly (F1 score and Exact Match in this case).

4.3 Sentence Inference

Task. The inference task - or also commonly called textual entailment - consists of predicting whether a hypothesis entails, contradicts or is neutral to a given

Table 2. Extrinsic Bias Measures and Performance (Exact Match and F1 Score) on the Task of Question Answering. The closer the scores are to 0 the better.

Models	Curation	gender				race				religion			
		%	Bias↓	EM↑	F1↑	%	Bias↓	EM↑	F1↑	%	Bias↓	EM↑	F1↑
Original		/	07.37	71.21	80.91	/	02.79	71.21	80.91	/	03.16	71.21	80.91
CDA		/	06.78	70.95	80.91	/	01.99	70.95	80.91	/	02.01	70.95	80.91
Sent-Debias		/	05.73	71.52	81.09	/	02.45	71.52	81.09	/	02.95	71.52	81.09
Kaneko		/	06.36	71.41	80.90	/	02.93	71.41	80.90	/	04.01	71.41	80.90
Likelihood	Removal	*50%*	03.60	67.92	78.54	*10%*	02.63	71.04	80.84	*50%*	02.54	68.18	78.48
Attention	Removal	*50%*	**03.39**	67.89	78.55	*10%*	02.06	71.06	80.77	*20%*	02.37	70.64	80.61
Representation	Removal	*50%*	04.70	68.34	78.86	*20%*	02.60	70.53	80.45	*50%*	02.51	68.33	78.84
Combined	Removal	*50%*	03.56	68.16	78.77	*10%*	02.10	70.94	80.70	*20%*	02.11	69.85	80.17
Likelihood	Augment	*50%*	04.72	68.64	79.19	*20%*	00.35	70.52	80.31	*10%*	02.56	70.60	80.48
Attention	Augment	*50%*	04.68	68.75	79.48	*20%*	00.16	70.44	80.37	*50%*	02.39	67.66	78.28
Representation	Augment	*50%*	04.61	68.58	79.21	*20%*	00.27	70.02	79.93	*50%*	02.03	67.67	78.46
Combined	Augment	*50%*	04.09	68.91	79.24	*50%*	**00.03**	67.76	78.54	*50%*	**01.82**	67.82	78.58

premise. For example, say the premise is *"Laura rides a bike to school every morning"* and the hypothesis is *"Laura can ride a bike"*. A textual inference model should be able to predict an entailment in this case.

Data and Metrics. In order to quantify bias in textual inference models, we follow the work of [8] who state that a biased model makes invalid inferences, and that the ratio of such false inferences constitutes a measure of bias. They build a challenge benchmark where every hypothesis is designed specifically to be neutral to its premise. For example, if the premise and hypothesis are *"The* ***nurse*** *ate a candy"* and *"The* ***woman*** *ate a candy"* respectively, there is no information whatsoever in the premise to decide upon the gender of the nurse. Thus, the prediction should be *neutral.* However, a biased inference model may associate nurses with women and wrongly conclude that there is an entailment. Every sample in the dataset constructed and published by [8] follow the same structure of the example above. Numerically, if there are M instances in the data, and the predictor's probabilities of the ith instance for contradict, entail and neutral are c_i, e_i and n_i, we follow [8] and use three measures of inference-based bias: (1) Net Neutral (**NN**): $NN = \frac{1}{M}\sum_{i=1}^{M} n_i$; (2) Fraction Neutral (**FN**): $FN = \frac{1}{M}\sum_{i=1}^{M} \mathbf{1}_{n_i=max(e_i,c_i,n_i)}$; (3) Threshold τ (**T:**τ): $T:\tau = \frac{1}{M}\sum_{i=1}^{M} \mathbf{1}_{n_i>\tau}$. We report the results on Table 3, after transforming them into percentages.

Discussion. The closer the scores are to 100, the less bias is exhibited by inference models. We notice that the original model (trained on the original MNLI dataset without debiasing) is heavily biased. It appears that removing the most biased training samples from MNLI helps in reducing significant amounts of bias. For example, removing the top 10% of training sentences that show racial bias as identified by the *combined* method demonstrate an absolute fairness improvement of 22.66% (according to the FN metric). As for religion, removing the top

Table 3. Extrinsic Bias Measures on the Task of Natural Language Inference. The closer the scores are to 100 the better.

Models	Curation	gender				race				religion			
		%	NN↑	FN↑	τ:0.5↑	%	NN↑	FN↑	τ:0.5↑	%	NN↑	FN↑	τ:0.5↑
Original		/	02.34	01.64	01.44	/	72.26	72.16	72.08	/	44.43	43.75	43.66
CDA		/	02.84	**02.08**	**01.88**	/	77.33	77.79	77.78	/	49.00	49.03	48.97
Sent-Debias		/	00.94	00.38	00.33	/	59.61	59.28	59.20	/	29.64	29.08	29.02
Kaneko		/	00.52	00.12	00.11	/	83.18	83.65	83.60	/	57.83	58.07	58.04
Likelihood	Removal	*20%*	02.01	01.32	01.16	*20%*	85.20	85.90	85.89	*10%*	43.60	43.59	43.57
Attention	Removal	*50%*	00.43	00.06	00.05	*50%*	78.01	78.37	78.33	*50%*	60.08	60.19	60.08
Representation	Removal	*50%*	00.35	00.09	00.07	*50%*	89.44	90.62	90.59	*20%*	**70.85**	**71.19**	**71.12**
Combined	Removal	*10%*	00.94	00.53	00.48	*10%*	**94.43**	**94.82**	**94.81**	*50%*	67.75	68.42	68.37
Likelihood	Augment	*10%*	01.15	00.50	00.44	*20%*	93.76	94.22	94.20	*50%*	57.63	57.73	57.64
Attention	Augment	*5%*	**03.07**	**02.08**	01.80	*50%*	94.32	94.77	94.71	*5%*	64.10*	64.44*	64.39*
Representation	Augment	*50%*	01.29	00.85	00.81	*50%*	80.82	81.43	81.40	*20%*	52.46	52.76	52.66
Combined	Augment	*10%*	00.64	00.15	00.14	*10%*	89.19	89.92	89.79	*10%*	53.01	53.58	53.52

20% as indicated by the *representation* method increases the FN score from 43.75 to 71.19. It is clear from Table 3 that all our methods succeed in reducing the amount of bias, without hurting the accuracy. We report the accuracies of both matched (in-domain) and mismatched (cross-domain) portions of MNLI's test set in Table 4. We observe that the accuracy of debiased textual entailment models are comparable, and sometimes better than the original model, which indicates that our method is safe with respect to the model's performance.

Table 4. Accuracy on the Task of Natural Language Inference. The closer the scores are to 100 the better.

Models	Curation	gender			race			religion		
		%	Matched	Mismatched	%	Matched	Mismatched	%	Matched	Mismatched
Original		/	83.23	85.49	/	83.23	85.49	/	83.23	85.49
CDA		/	84.31	83.26	/	84.73	84.21	/	84.15	83.75
Likelihood	Removal	*20%*	83.94	84.70	*20%*	83.83	85.18	*10%*	82.80	85.02
Attention	Removal	*50%*	84.01	80.96	*50%*	83.99	81.06	*50%*	85.77	82.15
Representation	Removal	*50%*	83.38	81.50	*50%*	83.01	82.36	*20%*	82.96	82.09
Combined	Removal	*10%*	83.84	83.03	*10%*	84.80	82.36	*50%*	82.85	82.32
Likelihood	Augment	*10%*	83.34	82.75	*20%*	84.59	81.28	*50%*	82.20	80.47
Attention	Augment	*5%*	83.27	82.72	*50%*	83.04	82.22	*5%*	81.63	82.36
Representation	Augment	*50%*	83.29	82.72	*50%*	83.17	81.93	*20%*	83.45	83.70
Combined	Augment	*10%*	85.40	84.21	*10%*	84.57	83.66	*10%*	84.80	83.07

Table 5. Extrinsic Bias Measures and Accuracy on the Task of Sentiment Analysis. The closer the scores are to 0 the better.

Models	Curation	gender			race			religion		
		%	Bias↓	Acc↑	%	Bias↓	Acc↑	%	Bias↓	Acc↑
Original		/	13.60	92.55	/	41.98	92.55	/	40.61	92.55
CDA		/	13.58	92.66	/	37.75	92.43	/	38.61	92.20
Sent-Debias		/	17.53	92.78	/	40.96	92.78	/	40.08	92.78
Kaneko		/	16.49	91.97	/	36.14	91.97	/	34.60	91.97
Likelihood	Removal	*20%*	12.64	92.78	*50%*	35.65	92.43	*20%*	37.37	92.43
Attention	Removal	*20%*	13.31	92.32	*10%*	38.05	92.32	*10%*	37.01	92.32
Representation	Removal	*10%*	12.32	92.66	*10%*	38.08	92.66	*50%*	38.74	92.78
Combined	Removal	*50%*	11.68	93.00	*50%*	35.56	91.97	*10%*	36.38	92.55
Likelihood	Augment	*10%*	12.21	92.09	*50%*	36.97	92.55	*10%*	**33.23**	92.43
Attention	Augment	*50%*	12.27	91.97	*10%*	**35.46**	92.66	*20%*	37.93	91.86
Representation	Augment	*20%*	**11.29**	91.63	*50%*	36.80	92.55	*10%*	37.42	93.35
Combined	Augment	*20%*	**11.29**	92.32	*50%*	36.26	92.09	*10%*	38.33	92.55

4.4 Sentiment Analysis

Task. Sentiment analysis - or sentiment classification - is the task of determining whether a piece of text has positive, negative or neutral connotations. An example of a positive sentiment is *"That little girl is so adorable"*, while *"He was taken to jail"* invokes a negative sentiment.

Data and Metrics. We use the same challenge dataset as in the textual inference task, except that we consider the premise and hypothesis as two independent sentences. As described above, the pair of sentences in each evaluation sample differ only in the word describing the doer of the action. For example, we can have *"The* ***nice*** *person bought a heater"* as the first sentence and *"The* ***Muslim*** *person bought a heater"* as the second one. Given that the nature of the action is the same across the pair of sentences, they should also share the same sentiment, regardless of doer's demographics. Thus, we declare bias in this task as the difference in sentiment between each pair of sentences. An ideal sentiment classification model should have bias scores close to 0. We take the average of absolute differences across the entire evaluation dataset and report our results in Table 5.

Discussion. We observe that while removing the most biased instances from training data helps in reducing bias, we get the lowest stereotype scores from the approaches where we augment them (Last four rows in Table 5). Also, we notice that all three methods are important; *likelihood* is best for religion, *attention* is best for race while *representation* is best for gender in this context. This result suggests that different stereotype information reside at different spots in text encoders. We invite researchers to extend their debiasing techniques to include all three levels of bias sources. Otherwise, we note that existing debiasing methods - Sent-Debias and Kaneko in this experiment - have only marginal reductions in bias, and sometimes make it worse. Even CDA comes short of meeting the same debiasing success as our methods, suggesting that it is better to "listen" to text encoders notions of stereotypes and take them into consideration while debiasing. Finally, we point out that removing or augmenting the most biased training instances does not harm the accuracy of the task (see Acc. in Table 5).

5 Related Work

5.1 Bias Quantification

We identify three main approaches for bias measurement methods in text encoders: representation-based, likelihood-based and task-specific approaches. In representation-based methods, the vector representations of words and sentences produced by text encoders are used to compute bias, usually through the use of cosine similarity either directly or via permutation tests [4,6,31]. In likelihood-based approaches, text encoders are first fine-tuned on the language modeling task. [22] kept the same bias quantification principle of previous approaches, but replaced vector representations with log-probabilities of words. Later, a myriad of research focused on likelihoods and probabilities of language models to document and excavate social stereotypes [20,33,34]. The fundamental notion of bias in these works is that a stereotyped language model prefers certain social groups over others given a neutral context. For example, in *"[MASK] love cooking"*, binary gender bias is cast as the difference in likelihoods for the words **Men** and **Women** to replace the mask. Finally, in task-specific approaches [8,10,42,44], bias is declared as the difference in outcome when task-specific models are tested with the same input sentence, differing only in social groups. For example, *"There is a muslim down there"* and *"There is a christian down there"* should have the same sentiment if the sentiment analysis model is unbiased. In this work, we propose our own variants of representation-, likelihood- and attention-based bias measurement. While the related works mentioned above function at model-level, our goal is to assign a bias score to a snippet of text, and not to a model. Finally, we use existing task-specific bias metrics and benchmarks relating to sentiment analysis, sentence entailment and question answering to evaluate the efficacy of our methods.

5.2 Bias Reduction

There are two dominant paradigms of bias reduction methods in the literature: data-level and model-level debiasing. We have already described the most acclaimed data-level bias reduction methods in the introduction. So we will not detail them here, but we focus on pointing out their limitations. The major criticism around CDA is the exponential swell in data size that it inflicts. This point is especially alarming when CDA is used to treat bias types with many groups such as *nationality* or *occupation*. So, CDA poses serious concerns regarding the carbon footprint and energy usage, let alone the potential threat of destabilising training. Our method is less compute-heavy than CDA since we only operate on the training data instances that are least concurring with the model's own notion of stereotype.

Model-level debiasing approaches also follow different paradigms. In **projection-based** methods [4,8,18,27,30,41], the goal is to minimize the projection of word and sentence representations on a bias dimension or subspace to eliminate stereotype. In **finetuning-based** methods [5,14,28,39], models are trained post-hoc with an additional fairness objective to their loss function. In **adversarial learning-based** approaches [12,13,26,49], an adversary is first trained to detect sensitive information from representations (e.g. gender, race, etc.), then the model is updated to confuse the adversary. Other methods employ a diverse set of techniques. For example, [7] use the contrastive learning framework where they automatically generate anti-stereotypes from stereotypical sentences in training data, and then encourage the semantic overlap between these *contrastive* sentences by maximizing their mutual information. [23] warn against the overwhelming carbon footprint that finetuning generally costs, and propose to optimize adapters [16,36] which are lightweight layers inserted between those of the text encoder, instead of training the entire model. [50] highlight the potency of general-purpose regularization techniques such as Dropout to reduce biased correlations in text encoders, while [43] leverage the latent knowledge of language models about their own hidden stereotypes and propose *Self-Debias*: a zero-shot method to mitigate biases, that requires neither additional training nor data. In contrast, we avoid all forms of fairness-related finetuning in our work. Our method is energetically sustainable since only training for the task is required, but with less prejudice in data.

6 Conclusion

We proposed three methods to uncover stereotypes from text encoders using likelihoods, attention weights and vector representations. Next, we designed a pipeline to measure how well the stereotypes mentioned in an input text tally with those in the model. Finally, we used our pipeline to identify the most stereotyped instances in task-specific training data according to the stereotype knowledge of the text encoder under use, remove or augment them, then train downstream models with curated datasets. Experiments show that our methods succeed in reducing gender, racial and religious biases from downstream NLP models better than existing approaches. Our analysis is based on common yet convenient and simple definitions of social biases. Also, we rely on a predefined set of word lists to detect words related to social groups in text as explained in Sect. 3.1. As future work, we plan to investigate more robust approaches of detection either by seed expansion or word classification techniques. Also, we project - and encourage other researchers - to provide more inclusive studies, covering minorities and other bias types such as age, status, or disability.

7 Ethical Considerations

While our proposed debiasing method has the potential to improve the fairness of NLP models, we acknowledge the possibility of unintended consequences. In particular, our method may not be effective in eliminating all biases, and may even introduce new biases or errors in the model. Additionally, our approach is based on a set of assumptions for determining which instances to remove, which may not be universally agreed upon.

Furthermore, as with any technology, there is a risk of misuse or abuse. Our data selection method, if applied with ill intent, could be used to intentionally amplify bias and perpetuate harmful stereotypes in NLP models, by keeping the data instances that concord most with model stereotypes instead of removing them for example. We recognize that this could have serious implications for individuals and groups that are already marginalized or subject to discrimination.

To mitigate these risks, we emphasize the importance of ethical considerations and responsible use of our proposed method. We advocate for transparency and clear communication about the limitations of our approach, as well as ongoing monitoring and evaluation to ensure that our debiasing method is used in an ethical and responsible manner. It is also important to engage with stakeholders, including affected communities, to understand their perspectives and concerns about the use of machine learning in sensitive domains.

Although the approach is, in itself, independent from the choice of groups, or the selection of identity terms and definition words that characterize these groups, we focus in our experiments on bias types and groups commonly used in the debiasing literature; namely binary gender, race and religion. We have shown that our method works for both binary and multiclass groups. That being said, we have not experimented yet with demographics divided into dozens of categories, e.g. nationality. We also did not include analysis for groups who are victims of under-criticized microaggressions such as the elderly, obese people or people suffering from physical/mental disabilities. We justify our experimental decisions with the following: (1) Current work in the literature focuses primarily on the three major demographic dimensions. So to facilitate comparison, we used that too. (2) Existing benchmarks to quantify bias are often limited to binary gender, race and religion. So even though our approach enables the reduction of bias for minority groups, we have no reliable data and benchmarks to assess whether debiasing is indeed effective for such groups. We encourage researchers and data collectors in the field to produce more inclusive benchmarks in the future.

We would like to remind that our models are not perfect, even after going through debiasing. Although our experiments show that bias is indeed reduced, it is not completely mitigated. Also, the bias detection experiments used in this paper and in all related work have positive predictive ability, which means that they can only detect the presence of bias, not the absence of it. So it is possible that bias is still hiding. We believe that the community needs to include some aspect of human evaluation to faithfully assess the stereotypical propensities of text encoders. We project to do that in future work.

References

1. Attanasio, G., Nozza, D., Hovy, D., Baralis, E.: Entropy-based attention regularization frees unintended bias mitigation from lists. In: Findings of the Association for Computational Linguistics: ACL 2022, pp. 1105–1119 (2022)
2. Blodgett, S.L., Barocas, S., Daumé III, H., Wallach, H.: Language (technology) is power: A critical survey of "bias" in nlp. In: Proceedings of the 58th Annual Meeting of the Association for Computational Linguistics, pp. 5454–5476 (2020)
3. Blodgett, S.L., Lopez, G., Olteanu, A., Sim, R., Wallach, H.: Stereotyping norwegian salmon: an inventory of pitfalls in fairness benchmark datasets. In: Proceedings of the 59th Annual Meeting of the Association for Computational Linguistics and the 11th International Joint Conference on Natural Language Processing (Volume 1: Long Papers), pp. 1004–1015 (2021)
4. Bolukbasi, T., Chang, K.W., Zou, J.Y., Saligrama, V., Kalai, A.T.: Man is to computer programmer as woman is to homemaker? debiasing word embeddings. Adv. Neural. Inf. Process. Syst. **29**, 4349–4357 (2016)
5. Bordia, S., Bowman, S.R.: Identifying and reducing gender bias in word-level language models. NAACL HLT **2019**, 7 (2019)
6. Caliskan, A., Bryson, J.J., Narayanan, A.: Semantics derived automatically from language corpora contain human-like biases. Science **356**(6334), 183–186 (2017)
7. Cheng, P., Hao, W., Yuan, S., Si, S., Carin, L.: Fairfil: Contrastive neural debiasing method for pretrained text encoders. In: International Conference on Learning Representations (2020)
8. Dev, S., Li, T., Phillips, J.M., Srikumar, V.: On measuring and mitigating biased inferences of word embeddings. In: Proceedings of the AAAI Conference on Artificial Intelligence. vol. 34, pp. 7659–7666 (2020)
9. Devlin, J., Chang, M.W., Lee, K., Toutanova, K.: Bert: Pre-training of deep bidirectional transformers for language understanding. In: Proceedings of the 2019 Conference of the North American Chapter of the Association for Computational Linguistics: Human Language Technologies, Volume 1 (Long and Short Papers), pp. 4171–4186 (2019)
10. Díaz, M., Johnson, I., Lazar, A., Piper, A.M., Gergle, D.: Addressing age-related bias in sentiment analysis. In: Proceedings of the 2018 chi conference on human factors in computing systems, pp. 1–14 (2018)
11. Dinan, E., Fan, A., Williams, A., Urbanek, J., Kiela, D., Weston, J.: Queens are powerful too: Mitigating gender bias in dialogue generation. In: Proceedings of the 2020 Conference on Empirical Methods in Natural Language Processing (EMNLP), pp. 8173–8188 (2020)
12. Elazar, Y., Goldberg, Y.: Adversarial removal of demographic attributes from text data. In: Proceedings of the 2018 Conference on Empirical Methods in Natural Language Processing, pp. 11–21 (2018)
13. Gaci, Y., Benatallah, B., Casati, F., Benabdeslem, K.: Iterative adversarial removal of gender bias in pretrained word embeddings. In: Proceedings of the 37th ACM/SIGAPP Symposium On Applied Computing, pp. 829–836 (2022)
14. Gaci, Y., Benattallah, B., Casati, F., Benabdeslem, K.: Debiasing pretrained text encoders by paying attention to paying attention. In: 2022 Conference on Empirical Methods in Natural Language Processing, pp. 9582–9602. Association for Computational Linguistics (2022)
15. Goldfarb-Tarrant, S., Marchant, R., Sanchez, R.M., Pandya, M., Lopez, A.: Intrinsic bias metrics do not correlate with application bias. arXiv preprint arXiv:2012.15859 (2020)

16. Houlsby, N., et al.: Parameter-efficient transfer learning for nlp. In: International Conference on Machine Learning, pp. 2790–2799. PMLR (2019)
17. Hussein, D.M.E.D.M.: A survey on sentiment analysis challenges. J. King Saud Univ.-Eng. Sci. **30**(4), 330–338 (2018)
18. Kaneko, M., Bollegala, D.: Gender-preserving debiasing for pre-trained word embeddings. In: Proceedings of the 57th Annual Meeting of the Association for Computational Linguistics, pp. 1641–1650 (2019)
19. Kaneko, M., Bollegala, D.: Debiasing pre-trained contextualised embeddings. In: Proceedings of the 16th Conference of the European Chapter of the Association for Computational Linguistics: Main Volume, pp. 1256–1266 (2021)
20. Kaneko, M., Bollegala, D.: Unmasking the mask-evaluating social biases in masked language models. In: Proceedings of the AAAI Conference on Artificial Intelligence. vol. 36, pp. 11954–11962 (2022)
21. Kirkpatrick, J., Pascanu, R., Rabinowitz, N., Veness, J., Desjardins, G., Rusu, A.A., Milan, K., Quan, J., Ramalho, T., Grabska-Barwinska, A., et al.: Overcoming catastrophic forgetting in neural networks. Proc. Natl. Acad. Sci. **114**(13), 3521–3526 (2017)
22. Kurita, K., Vyas, N., Pareek, A., Black, A.W., Tsvetkov, Y.: Measuring bias in contextualized word representations. In: Proceedings of the First Workshop on Gender Bias in Natural Language Processing, pp. 166–172 (2019)
23. Lauscher, A., Lueken, T., Glavaš, G.: Sustainable modular debiasing of language models. In: Findings of the Association for Computational Linguistics: EMNLP 2021, pp. 4782–4797 (2021)
24. Leavy, S., Meaney, G., Wade, K., Greene, D.: Mitigating gender bias in machine learning data sets. In: Boratto, L., Faralli, S., Marras, M., Stilo, G. (eds.) BIAS 2020. CCIS, vol. 1245, pp. 12–26. Springer, Cham (2020). https://doi.org/10.1007/978-3-030-52485-2_2
25. Li, T., Khashabi, D., Khot, T., Sabharwal, A., Srikumar, V.: Unqovering stereotypical biases via underspecified questions. In: Proceedings of the 2020 Conference on Empirical Methods in Natural Language Processing: Findings, pp. 3475–3489 (2020)
26. Li, Y., Baldwin, T., Cohn, T.: Towards robust and privacy-preserving text representations. In: Proceedings of the 56th Annual Meeting of the Association for Computational Linguistics (Volume 2: Short Papers), pp. 25–30 (2018)
27. Liang, P.P., Li, I.M., Zheng, E., Lim, Y.C., Salakhutdinov, R., Morency, L.P.: Towards debiasing sentence representations. In: Proceedings of the 58th Annual Meeting of the Association for Computational Linguistics, pp. 5502–5515 (2020)
28. Liang, S., Dufter, P., Schütze, H.: Monolingual and multilingual reduction of gender bias in contextualized representations. In: Proceedings of the 28th International Conference on Computational Linguistics, pp. 5082–5093 (2020)
29. Madaan, N., et al.: Analyze, detect and remove gender stereotyping from bollywood movies. In: Conference on fairness, accountability and transparency, pp. 92–105. PMLR (2018)
30. Manzini, T., Lim, Y.C., Tsvetkov, Y., Black, A.W.: Black is to criminal as caucasian is to police: Detecting and removing multiclass bias in word embeddings. In: 2019 Annual Conference of the North American Chapter of the Association for Computational Linguistics (NAACL) (2019)
31. May, C., Wang, A., Bordia, S., Bowman, S., Rudinger, R.: On measuring social biases in sentence encoders. In: Proceedings of the 2019 Conference of the North American Chapter of the Association for Computational Linguistics: Human Language Technologies, Volume 1 (Long and Short Papers), pp. 622–628 (2019)

32. McCloskey, M., Cohen, N.J.: Catastrophic interference in connectionist networks: The sequential learning problem. In: Psychology of learning and motivation, vol. 24, pp. 109–165. Elsevier (1989)
33. Nadeem, M., Bethke, A., Reddy, S.: Stereoset: Measuring stereotypical bias in pretrained language models. arXiv preprint arXiv:2004.09456 (2020)
34. Nangia, N., Vania, C., Bhalerao, R., Bowman, S.: Crows-pairs: A challenge dataset for measuring social biases in masked language models. In: Proceedings of the 2020 Conference on Empirical Methods in Natural Language Processing (EMNLP). pp. 1953–1967 (2020)
35. Park, J.H., Shin, J., Fung, P.: Reducing gender bias in abusive language detection. In: Proceedings of the 2018 Conference on Empirical Methods in Natural Language Processing, pp. 2799–2804 (2018)
36. Pfeiffer, J., et al.: Adapterhub: A framework for adapting transformers. In: Proceedings of the 2020 Conference on Empirical Methods in Natural Language Processing: System Demonstrations, pp. 46–54 (2020)
37. Prabhakaran, V., Hutchinson, B., Mitchell, M.: Perturbation sensitivity analysis to detect unintended model biases. In: Proceedings of the 2019 Conference on Empirical Methods in Natural Language Processing and the 9th International Joint Conference on Natural Language Processing (EMNLP-IJCNLP), pp. 5740–5745 (2019)
38. Qian, R., Ross, C., Fernandes, J., Smith, E., Kiela, D., Williams, A.: Perturbation augmentation for fairer nlp. arXiv preprint arXiv:2205.12586 (2022)
39. Qian, Y., Muaz, U., Zhang, B., Hyun, J.W.: Reducing gender bias in word-level language models with a gender-equalizing loss function. In: Proceedings of the 57th Annual Meeting of the Association for Computational Linguistics: Student Research Workshop, pp. 223–228 (2019)
40. Rajpurkar, P., Zhang, J., Lopyrev, K., Liang, P.: Squad: 100,000+ questions for machine comprehension of text. In: Proceedings of the 2016 Conference on Empirical Methods in Natural Language Processing, pp. 2383–2392 (2016)
41. Ravfogel, S., Elazar, Y., Gonen, H., Twiton, M., Goldberg, Y.: Null it out: Guarding protected attributes by iterative nullspace projection. In: Proceedings of the 58th Annual Meeting of the Association for Computational Linguistics, pp. 7237–7256 (2020)
42. Sap, M., Gabriel, S., Qin, L., Jurafsky, D., Smith, N.A., Choi, Y.: Social bias frames: Reasoning about social and power implications of language. In: Association for Computational Linguistics (2020)
43. Schick, T., Udupa, S., Schütze, H.: Self-diagnosis and self-debiasing: A proposal for reducing corpus-based bias in nlp. arXiv preprint arXiv:2103.00453 (2021)
44. Sheng, E., Chang, K.W., Natarajan, P., Peng, N.: Towards controllable biases in language generation. In: Proceedings of the 2020 Conference on Empirical Methods in Natural Language Processing: Findings, pp. 3239–3254 (2020)
45. Shin, S., Song, K., Jang, J., Kim, H., Joo, W., Moon, I.C.: Neutralizing gender bias in word embeddings with latent disentanglement and counterfactual generation. In: Findings of the Association for Computational Linguistics: EMNLP 2020, pp. 3126–3140 (2020)
46. Sun, T., et al.: Mitigating gender bias in natural language processing: Literature review. In: Proceedings of the 57th Annual Meeting of the Association for Computational Linguistics, pp. 1630–1640 (2019)
47. Vaswani, A., et al.: Attention is all you need. In: Advances in neural information processing systems, pp. 5998–6008 (2017)

48. Wang, A., Singh, A., Michael, J., Hill, F., Levy, O., Bowman, S.R.: Glue: a multi-task benchmark and analysis platform for natural language understanding. EMNLP **2018**, 353 (2018)
49. Wang, L., Yan, Y., He, K., Wu, Y., Xu, W.: Dynamically disentangling social bias from task-oriented representations with adversarial attack. In: Proceedings of the 2021 Conference of the North American Chapter of the Association for Computational Linguistics: Human Language Technologies, pp. 3740–3750 (2021)
50. Webster, K., Wang, X., Tenney, I., Beutel, A., Pitler, E., Pavlick, E., Chen, J., Chi, E., Petrov, S.: Measuring and reducing gendered correlations in pre-trained models. arXiv preprint arXiv:2010.06032 (2020)
51. Zhao, J., Wang, T., Yatskar, M., Ordonez, V., Chang, K.W.: Gender bias in coreference resolution: Evaluation and debiasing methods. In: Proceedings of the 2018 Conference of the North American Chapter of the Association for Computational Linguistics: Human Language Technologies, Volume 2 (Short Papers), pp. 15–20 (2018)
52. Zmigrod, R., Mielke, S.J., Wallach, H., Cotterell, R.: Counterfactual data augmentation for mitigating gender stereotypes in languages with rich morphology. In: Proceedings of the 57th Annual Meeting of the Association for Computational Linguistics, pp. 1651–1661 (2019)

Fairness in Multi-Task Learning via Wasserstein Barycenters

François Hu[1(✉)], Philipp Ratz[2], and Arthur Charpentier[2]

[1] Université de Montréal, Montréal, QC, Canada
francois.hu@umontreal.ca
[2] Université du Québecà Montréal, Montréal, QC, Canada
ratz.philipp@courrier.uqam.ca, charpentier.arthur@uqam.ca

Abstract. Algorithmic Fairness is an established field in machine learning that aims to reduce biases in data. Recent advances have proposed various methods to ensure fairness in a univariate environment, where the goal is to de-bias a single task. However, extending fairness to a multi-task setting, where more than one objective is optimised using a shared representation, remains underexplored. To bridge this gap, we develop a method that extends the definition of *Strong Demographic Parity* to multi-task learning using multi-marginal Wasserstein barycenters. Our approach provides a closed form solution for the optimal fair multi-task predictor including both regression and binary classification tasks. We develop a data-driven estimation procedure for the solution and run numerical experiments on both synthetic and real datasets. The empirical results highlight the practical value of our post-processing methodology in promoting fair decision-making.

Keywords: Fairness · Optimal transport · Multi-task learning

1 Introduction

Multi-task learning (MTL) is a loosely defined field that aims to improve model performance by taking advantage of similarities between related estimation problems through a common representation [36,45]. MTL has gained traction in recent years, as it can avoid over-fitting and improve generalisation for task-specific models, while at the same time being computationally more efficient than training separate models [6]. For these reasons, the usage of MTL is likely to grow and spread to more disciplines, thus ensuring fairness in this setting becomes essential to overcome historical bias and prevent unwanted discrimination. Indeed, in many industries, discriminating on a series of sensitive features is even prohibited by law [1]. Despite the apparent importance of fairness, it remains challenging to incorporate fairness constraints into MTL due to its multivariate nature.

Algorithmic fairness refers to the challenge of reducing the influence of a sensitive attribute on a set of predictions. With increased model complexity, simply

© The Author(s), under exclusive license to Springer Nature Switzerland AG 2023
D. Koutra et al. (Eds.): ECML PKDD 2023, LNAI 14170, pp. 295–312, 2023.
https://doi.org/10.1007/978-3-031-43415-0_18

excluding the sensitive features in the model is not sufficient, as complex models can simply proxy for omitted variables. Several notions of fairness have been considered [5,43] in the literature. In this paper, we focus on the *Demographic Parity* (DP) [8] that requires the independence between the sensitive feature and the predictions, while not relying on labels (for other notions of fairness, see *Equality of odds* or *Equal opportunity* [23]). This choice is quite restrictive in the applications, but provides a first stepping stone to extend our findings to other definitions. In single-task learning problems, the fairness constraint (such as DP) has been widely studied for classification or regression [4,8,13,16,42,44], but to extend fairness to multiple tasks, we first need to study the effects of learning tasks jointly on the potential outcomes. In line with a core advantage of MTL, the approach we propose is based on post-processing which results in faster computations than other approaches discussed below. The contributions of the present article can hence be summarised as follows:

Contributions. We consider multi-task problems that combine regression and binary classification, with the goal of producing a fair shared representation under the DP fairness constraint. More specifically:

- We transform the multi-task problem under Demographic Parity fairness to the construction of multi-marginal Wasserstein-2 barycenters. Notably, we propose a closed form solution for the optimal fair multi-task predictor.
- Based on this optimal solution, we build a standard data-driven approach that mimics the performance of the optimal predictor both in terms of risk and fairness. In particular, our method is post-processing and can be applied to any off-the-shelf estimators.
- Our approach is numerically illustrated on several real data sets and proves to be very efficient in reducing unfairness while maintaining the advantages of multi-task learning.

Related Work. Algorithmic fairness can be categorised into: 1) *pre-processing* methods which enforce fairness in the data before applying machine learning models [2,9,34]; 2) *in-processing* methods, who achieve fairness in the training step of the learning model [3,4,18]; 3) *post-processing* which reduces unfairness in the model inferences following the learning procedure [12,14,15]. Our work falls into the latter. This comes with several computational advantages, not least the fact that even partially pre-trained models can be made fair, which extends our findings to multi-task transfer learning.

Within standard, single-task classification or regression problems, the DP constraint has been extensively studied before. In particular, the problem of integrating algorithmic fairness with the Wasserstein distance based barycenter has been an active area of research [12,15,21,25] but most studies focus on learning univariate fair functions. Our work differs from the aforementioned work by enforcing the DP-fairness in multi-task learning, involving learning a fair vector-valued function based on a shared representation function. To the best of our knowledge, there is only a limited body of research concerning fairness in MTL settings. For instance, Zhao et al. [46] introduced a method for fair multi-task regression problems using rank-based loss functions to ensure DP-fairness, while [35] and [39] independently achieve fairness for multi-task classification problems in the Equal Opportunity or Equalised Odds sense. However, our approach offers a flexible framework for achieving fairness by simultaneously training fair predictors including binary classification and regression. Oneto et al. [31,32] suggested a DP-fair multi-task learning approach that learns predictors using information from different groups. They proposed this for linear [32] and 1-hidden layer networks [31] predictors. Our work extends this approach to arbitrary multivariate distributions and proposes a post-processing method that keeps additional computations to a minimum.

Outline of the Paper. The remainder of this article is structured as follows: Sect. 2 introduces MTL, DP-fairness and the objective in rendering multi-task problems fair. Section 3 introduces our fair multi-task predictor which is then translated to an empirical plug-in estimator in Sect. 4. Section 5 evaluates the estimator on synthetic and real data and we conclude in Sect. 6.

2 Problem Statement

In machine learning, one often encounters two types of prediction tasks: regression and binary classification. In regression, the goal is to predict a real-valued output in $\mathbb{R}$ while in binary classification, the goal is to predict one of two classes $\{0, 1\}$. Although the definitions and our approach can be applied to any number of finite tasks, for ease of presentation we focus this section on these two sub-cases.

2.1 Multi-task Learning

There are several definitions and goals that can be achieved through MTL. As our applications are centered on similar tasks, we focus on one aspect referred to as *parameter sharing* between the tasks (for a more comprehensive survey, we recommend Zhang and Yang's survey [45]). Parameter sharing is especially useful in the case where there are missing labels in one of the tasks, as MTL can exploit similarities among the tasks to improve the predictive performance. Formally, we let $(\boldsymbol{X}, S, \boldsymbol{Y})$ be a random tuple with distribution $\mathbb{P}$. Here, $\boldsymbol{X}$ represents the non-sensitive features, S a sensitive feature, considered discrete, across which we would like to impose fairness and $\boldsymbol{Y}$ represents the tasks to be estimated. In theory, there are no restrictions on the space of $\boldsymbol{X}$, $\boldsymbol{Y}$, or S. Throughout the article, to ease the notational load, we assume that $\boldsymbol{X} \in \mathcal{X} \subset \mathbb{R}^d$, $\mathcal{S} = \{-1, 1\}$ where -1 represents the minority group and 1 the majority group and $\boldsymbol{Y} = (Y_1, Y_2) \in \mathcal{Y}_1 \times \mathcal{Y}_2$ where $\mathcal{Y}_1 \subset \mathbb{R}$ and $\mathcal{Y}_2 = \{0, 1\}$ (or $[0, 1]$ if we consider *score* function). That is, we consider problems where the columns of $\boldsymbol{Y}$ represent regression-binary classification problems. More specifically, we consider for $g_1^* : \mathcal{X} \times \mathcal{S} \to \mathbb{R}$ the general regression problem

$$Y_1 = g_1^*(\boldsymbol{X}, S) + \zeta \tag{1}$$

with $\zeta \in \mathbb{R}$ a zero mean noise. g_1^* is the regression function that minimises the squared risk $\mathcal{R}_{L_2}(g) := \mathbb{E}\left(Y_1 - g(\boldsymbol{X}, S)\right)^2$. For the second task, recall that a classification rule $c_2 : \mathcal{X} \times \mathcal{S} \to \{0, 1\}$ is a function evaluated through the misclassification risk $\mathcal{R}_{0-1}(c) := \mathbb{P}\left(c(\boldsymbol{X}, S) \neq Y_2\right)$. We denote $g_2^*(\boldsymbol{X}, S) := \mathbb{P}(Y_2 = 1 | \boldsymbol{X}, S)$ the conditional probability (or score) of belonging to class 1. Recall that the minimisation of the risk $\mathcal{R}_{0-1}(\cdot)$ over the set of all classifiers is given by the Bayes classifier

$$c_2^*(\boldsymbol{X}, S) = \mathbb{1}\left\{g_2^*(\boldsymbol{X}, S) \geq 1/2\right\} \ . \tag{2}$$

The modelling of the two columns of $\boldsymbol{Y}$ is then referred to as the *tasks*, denoted $\mathcal{T} = \{1, 2\}$. Here we adopt the general notation the two tasks Y_1 and Y_2 are modelled on the same input space $\mathcal{X} \times \mathcal{S}$ such that they are independent of each other conditionally on $(\boldsymbol{X}, S)$. In line with the notion of related tasks, we suppose that the tasks share a common representation of the features $h_\theta : \mathcal{X} \times \mathcal{S} \to \mathcal{Z}$ where $\mathcal{Z} \subset \mathbb{R}^r$ and the marginal task models can be represented by $g_t(\cdot) = f_t \circ h_\theta(\cdot)$ for a given task-related function $f_t : \mathcal{Z} \to \mathcal{Y}_t$. The representation can then be approximated via a neural network. We denote $\mathcal{H}$ the set of all representation functions. To appropriately weigh each of the tasks in the estimation problem, we use trade-off weights $\boldsymbol{\lambda} = (\lambda_1, \lambda_2)$ where we assume $\lambda_t > 0$ for all t. This yields the simple multi-task estimator defined as:

$$\boldsymbol{\theta}_{\boldsymbol{\lambda}}^* = \operatorname*{argmin}_{\theta} \mathbb{E}\left[\sum_{t=1}^{2} \lambda_t \mathcal{R}_t(Y_t, f_t \circ h_\theta(\boldsymbol{X}, S))\right] \tag{3}$$

with $\mathcal{R}_t$ the risk associated to task t. Restricting each task to use the same representation h_θ might seem overly simplistic, but given that under mild conditions the universal approximation theorem [24] is applicable, a large variety of problems can still be modelled. A thorough discussion of the advantages of multi-task learning would go beyond the scope of this article and we refer the interested reader instead to [36,45] for a comprehensive survey. The empirical estimation of Eq. (3) will be further discussed in Sect. 4.2.

Notations. Assuming that the following density exists, for each $s \in \mathcal{S}$ and for any task predictor g, we denote ν_g the probability measure of $g(\boldsymbol{X}, S)$ and $\nu_{g|s}$ the probability measure of $g(\boldsymbol{X}, S)|S = s$. $F_{g|s} : \mathbb{R} \to [0, 1]$ and $Q_{g|s} : [0, 1] \to \mathbb{R}$ are, respectively, its CDF function defined as $F_{g|s}(u) := \mathbb{P}\left(g(\boldsymbol{X}, S) \leq u | S = s\right)$ and its corresponding quantile function defined as $Q_{g|s}(v) := \inf\{u \in \mathbb{R} : F_{g|s}(u) \geq v\}$.

2.2 Demographic Parity

We introduce in this section the fairness under *Demographic Parity* (DP) constraint in both single-task and multi-task problems (Fig. 1).

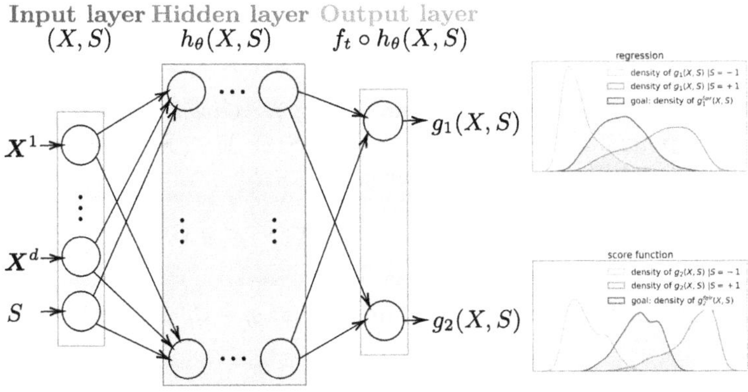

Fig. 1. Representation function sharing in a neural network for multi-task learning. The goal in DP-fairness is to construct a set of predictors $\{g_t^{\text{fair}}(\boldsymbol{X}, S)\}_t$ independent from the sensitive feature S. $\boldsymbol{X}^i$ refers to the i-th feature of $\boldsymbol{X}$.

Fairness in Single-Task Problems. For a given task $t \in \mathcal{T} = \{1, 2\}$, we denote by $\mathcal{G}_t$ the set of all predictors $g_t : \boldsymbol{X} \times \mathcal{S} \to \mathcal{Y}_t$ of the form $g_t(\cdot) = f_t \circ h_\theta(\cdot)$. In particular for the binary classification, $\mathcal{G}_2$ represents the set of all score functions in $\mathcal{Y}_2 = [0, 1]$ and additionally we denote $\mathcal{G}_2^{\text{class}}$ the set of all classifiers in $\{0, 1\}$. With a provided score function $g_2 \in \mathcal{G}_2$, a class prediction $c_2 \in \mathcal{G}_2^{\text{class}}$ is generated using a threshold $\tau \in [0, 1]$, expressed as $c_2(\cdot) = \mathbb{1}\{g_2(\cdot) \geq \tau\}$. Most work aims to ensure that sensitive information S (such as *race*) does not influence the decisions c_2, i.e. $c_2(\boldsymbol{X}, S) \perp\!\!\!\perp S$. This fairness criterion is called *weak* Demographic Parity [23,27] and verifies

$$| \, \mathbb{P}(c_2(\boldsymbol{X}, S) = 1 \mid S = -1) - \mathbb{P}(c_2(\boldsymbol{X}, S) = 1 \mid S = 1) \, | = 0 \ .$$

However, enforcing DP fairness for a given threshold does not imply enforcing DP fairness for other thresholds. Therefore we need to enforce the score function g_2 instead, i.e. $g_2(\boldsymbol{X}, S) \perp\!\!\!\perp S$. This definition, called *strong* Demographic Parity [4, 25], will be formally defined below in Definition 1.

Remark 1 (Misclassification risk and squared risk). In binary task $\{0, 1\}$, given $\tau = 1/2$ the misclassification risk can be rewritten as

$$\mathbb{P}\left(Y_2 \neq c_2^*(\boldsymbol{X}, S)\right) = \mathbb{E}\left[\left(Y_2 - c_2^*(\boldsymbol{X}, S)\right)^2\right]$$

with $g_2^*(\boldsymbol{X}, S) = \mathbb{P}\left(Y_2 = 1 | \boldsymbol{X}, S\right) = \mathbb{E}\left[Y_2 | \boldsymbol{X}, S\right]$. Since our goal is to enforce fairness w.r.t. the sensitive feature S in a score function $g_2 \in \mathcal{G}_2$, we are interested in minimising the risk $\mathbb{E}\left(Y_2 - g_2(\boldsymbol{X}, S)\right)^2$ instead. Notably, for any given task $t \in \{1, 2\}$, the (unconstrained) single-task objective becomes:

$$g_t^* \in \operatorname*{argmin}_{g_t \in \mathcal{G}_t} \mathbb{E}\left[\left(Y_t - g_t(\boldsymbol{X}, S)\right)^2\right] .$$

We now formally define the (strong) Demographic Parity notion of fairness and the associated unfairness measure.

Definition 1 (Strong Demographic Parity). *Given a task $t \in \mathcal{T}$ (regression or score function), a predictor $g_t : \boldsymbol{X} \times \mathcal{S} \to \mathcal{Y}_t \subset \mathbb{R}$ is called fair under Demographic Parity (or DP-fair) if for all $s, s' \in \mathcal{S}$*

$$\sup_{u \in \mathcal{Y}_t} \mid \mathbb{P}(g_t(\boldsymbol{X}, S) \leq u \mid S = s) - \mathbb{P}(g_t(\boldsymbol{X}, S) \leq u \mid S = s') \mid = 0 \ .$$

Definition 2 (Unfairness). *The unfairness of $g_t \in \mathcal{G}_t$ is quantified by*

$$\mathcal{U}(g_t) := \max_{s,s' \in \mathcal{S}} \sup_{u \in \mathcal{Y}_t} \left| \ F_{g_t|s}(u) - F_{g_t|s'}(u) \ \right| \ . \tag{4}$$

Hence, by the above definition, a predictor g_t is fair if and only if $\mathcal{U}(g_t) = 0$.

We use $\mathcal{G}_t^{\text{fair}} := \{g \in \mathcal{G}_t : g \text{ is DP-fair}\}$ to denote the set of DP-fair predictors in $\mathcal{Y}_t$ for a given task $t \in \mathcal{T}$. In single-task learning for regression and binary classification, the aim in DP fairness is to minimise the squared risk over $\mathcal{G}_t^{\text{fair}}$ to find a fair predictor

$$g_t^{*(\text{fair})} \in \underset{g_t \in \mathcal{G}_t^{\text{fair}}}{\text{argmin}} \, \mathbb{E}\left[(Y_t - g_t(\boldsymbol{X}, S))^2\right] \ . \tag{5}$$

Note that the estimator of the optimal regression for this optimisation problem (5) can be identified as the solution of the Wasserstein barycenter problem [15,22,25]. In binary classification, [20] show that maximising accuracy under DP fairness constraint is the same as solving a corresponding score function with the threshold at level $\tau = 1/2$. Here, we extend this notation as suggested in Remark 1.

Fairness in Multi-task Problems. Given trade-off weight $\boldsymbol{\lambda} = (\lambda_t)_{t \in \mathcal{T}}$ and multi-task problem $\boldsymbol{Y} = (Y_t)_{t \in \mathcal{T}}$, an optimal multi-task predictor takes a feature set $(\boldsymbol{X}, S)$ as input and outputs a set of predictions denoted $(g_{t,\boldsymbol{\lambda}}^*)_{t \in \mathcal{T}}$. The t-th marginal prediction is given by $g_{t,\boldsymbol{\lambda}}^*(\cdot) = f_t \circ h_{\theta_{\boldsymbol{\lambda}}^*}(\cdot)$. Alternatively, through a slight abuse of notation, we can express it as $g_{t,\boldsymbol{\lambda}}^*(\cdot) = f_t \circ \theta_{\boldsymbol{\lambda}}^*(\cdot)$, where the representation function yields

$$\theta_{\boldsymbol{\lambda}}^* \in \underset{\theta \in \mathcal{H}}{\text{argmin}} \ \mathbb{E}\left[\sum_{t \in \mathcal{T}} \lambda_t \left(Y_t - f_t \circ \theta(\boldsymbol{X}, S)\right)^2\right] \ .$$

For the sake of simplicity in presentation, we will represent the function h_θ as θ from this point forward. A multi-task predictor is DP-fair if its associated marginal predictor satisfies DP fairness in Definition 1 for every task $t \in \mathcal{T}$. We use $\mathcal{H}^{\text{fair}} := \{\theta \in \mathcal{H} : f_t \circ \theta \text{ is DP-fair for each task } t \in \mathcal{T}\}$ to denote the subset of all representations where each task is DP-constrained. The constrained multi-objective optimisation of $\boldsymbol{Y} = (Y_t)_{t\in\mathcal{T}}$ is given by the fair optimal representation function

$$\theta_{\boldsymbol{\lambda}}^{*(\text{fair})} \in \underset{\theta\in\mathcal{H}^{\text{fair}}}{\operatorname{argmin}}\ \mathbb{E}\left[\sum_{t\in\mathcal{T}} \lambda_t \left(Y_t - f_t \circ \theta(\boldsymbol{X}, S)\right)^2\right] . \tag{6}$$

Notably, for each task $t \in \mathcal{T}$, the associated marginal fair optimal predictor is naturally denoted $g_{t,\boldsymbol{\lambda}}^{*(\text{fair})}(\boldsymbol{X}, S) = f_t \circ \theta_{\boldsymbol{\lambda}}^{*(\text{fair})}(\boldsymbol{X}, S)$. $(f_1, \ldots, f_{|\mathcal{T}|})$ is predetermined to match the output type of each task in $(Y_1, \ldots, Y_{|\mathcal{T}|})$. For instance, one can use linear activation functions for regression problems, and sigmoid functions for binary classification.

3 Wasserstein Fair Multi-task Predictor

We describe in this section our proposed post-processing approach for constructing a fair multi-task learning. To derive a characterisation of the optimal fair predictor, we work under the following assumption.

Assumption 1 (Continuity assumption). *For any $(s, t, \boldsymbol{\lambda}) \in \mathcal{S} \times \mathcal{T} \times \Lambda$, we assume that the measure $\nu_{g^*_{t,\lambda}|s}$ has a density function. This is equivalent to assuming that the mapping $u \mapsto F_{g^*_{t,\lambda}|s}(u)$ is continuous.*

Driven by our goal to minimise the squared risk defined in Eq. (6) and building upon previous research in the univariate case [15,22], we introduce the Wasserstein-2 distance. We then demonstrate that fairness in the multi-task problem can be framed as the optimal transport problem involving the Wasserstein-2 distance. The relationship between these concepts is established in Theorem 1.

Definition 3 (Wasserstein-2 distance). *Let ν and ν' be two univariate probability measures. The Wasserstein-2 distance between ν and ν' is defined as*

$$\mathcal{W}_2^2(\nu, \nu') = \inf_{\gamma\in\Gamma_{\nu,\nu'}} \left\{ \int_{\mathbb{R}\times\mathbb{R}} |y - y'|^2 d\gamma(y, y') \right\}$$

where $\Gamma_{\nu,\nu'}$ is the set of distributions on $\mathbb{R} \times \mathbb{R}$ having ν and ν' as marginals.

The proof of the following theorem is based on results from [15] or [22]. Although their work is not immediately applicable to our case due to the dependence of the tasks, they provide valuable insights on the use of optimal transport theory in the context of Demographic Parity. We provide a sketch of a proof but relegate the rigorous version to the Appendix.

Theorem 1 (Optimal fair predictions). *Let Assumption 1 be satisfied. Recall that $\pi_s = \mathbb{P}(S = s)$.*

1. *A representation function* $\theta_{\boldsymbol{\lambda}}^{*(fair)}$ *satisfies Eq.* (6)*, i.e.,*

$$\theta_{\boldsymbol{\lambda}}^{*(fair)} \in \operatorname*{argmin}_{\theta \in \mathcal{H}^{fair}} \mathbb{E}\left[\sum_{t\in\mathcal{T}} \lambda_t \left(Y_t - f_t \circ \theta(\boldsymbol{X}, S)\right)^2\right] .$$

if and only if, for each $t \in \mathcal{T}$ *this same representation function satisfies*

$$\nu_{f_t \circ \theta_{\boldsymbol{\lambda}}^{*(fair)}} \in \operatorname*{argmin}_{\nu} \sum_{s\in\mathcal{S}} \pi_s \mathcal{W}_2^2(\nu_{g^*_{t,\boldsymbol{\lambda}}|s}, \nu) .$$

2. *Additionally, the optimal fair predictor* $g_{t,\boldsymbol{\lambda}}^{*(fair)}(\cdot) = f_t \circ \theta_{\boldsymbol{\lambda}}^{*(fair)}(\cdot)$ *can be rewritten as*

$$g_{t,\boldsymbol{\lambda}}^{*(fair)}(\boldsymbol{x}, s) = \sum_{s'\in\mathcal{S}} \pi_{s'} Q_{g^*_{t,\boldsymbol{\lambda}}|s'} \circ F_{g^*_{t,\boldsymbol{\lambda}}|s}\left(g^*_{t,\boldsymbol{\lambda}}(\boldsymbol{x}, s)\right), \quad (\boldsymbol{x}, s) \in \mathcal{X} \times \mathcal{S} . \quad (7)$$

Proof (sketch) Recall Eq. (1) and $g_2^*(\boldsymbol{X}, S) = \mathbb{E}(Y_2|\boldsymbol{X}, S)$, the multi-objective described in Eq. (6) can be easily rewritten

$$\min_{\theta\in\mathcal{H}^{\text{fair}}} \mathbb{E}\left[\sum_{t\in\mathcal{T}} \lambda_t \left(g_t^*(\boldsymbol{X}, S) - f_t \circ \theta(\boldsymbol{X}, S)\right)^2\right] .$$

Using Prop.1 in [19] together with Assumption 1, there exists a function $V_t : \mathcal{X} \times \mathcal{S} \times \Lambda \to \mathcal{Y}_t$ (or $g^*_{t,\boldsymbol{\lambda}}(\boldsymbol{x}, s)$ by abuse of notation) such that the optimisation is equivalent to

$$\min_{\theta\in\mathcal{H}^{\text{fair}}} \mathbb{E}_{\boldsymbol{\lambda}\sim\mathbb{P}_{\boldsymbol{\lambda}}} \mathbb{E}\left[\sum_{t\in\mathcal{T}} \lambda_t \left(g^*_{t,\boldsymbol{\lambda}}(\boldsymbol{X}, S) - f_t \circ \theta(\boldsymbol{X}, S)\right)^2\right] .$$

We assume in this proof that the vector $\boldsymbol{\lambda}$ is sampled from the distribution $\mathbb{P}_{\boldsymbol{\lambda}}$. Given a task $t \in \mathcal{T}$ we denote $\nu_t^* \in \operatorname{argmin}_{\nu} \sum_{s\in\mathcal{S}} \pi_s \mathcal{W}_2^2(\nu_{g^*_{t,\boldsymbol{\lambda}}|s}, \nu)$ where there exists $(\theta_t^*)_{t\in\mathcal{T}}$ such that $\nu_t^* = f_t \circ \theta_t^*$. Adapted from the work in [15] and the universal approximation theorem [24] we deduce,

$$\min_{\theta\in\mathcal{H}^{\text{fair}}} \mathbb{E}_{\boldsymbol{\lambda}\sim\mathbb{P}_{\boldsymbol{\lambda}}} \mathbb{E}\left[\sum_{t\in\mathcal{T}} \lambda_t \left(g^*_{t,\boldsymbol{\lambda}}(\boldsymbol{X}, S) - f_t \circ \theta(\boldsymbol{X}, S)\right)^2\right] = \mathbb{E}_{\boldsymbol{\lambda}\sim\mathbb{P}_{\boldsymbol{\lambda}}} \sum_{\substack{t\in\mathcal{T}\\ s\in\mathcal{S}}} \lambda_t \pi_s \mathcal{W}_2^2(\nu_{g^*_{t,\boldsymbol{\lambda}}|s}, \nu_t^*) ,$$

which concludes the sketch of the proof, for details see the Appendix ■

Theorem 1 provides a closed form expression for the optimal fair predictor $\boldsymbol{g}_{\boldsymbol{\lambda}}^{*(\text{fair})} = \left(g_{t,\boldsymbol{\lambda}}^{*(\text{fair})}\right)_{t\in\mathcal{T}}$ for the multi-task $\boldsymbol{Y} = (Y_t)_{t\in\mathcal{T}}$. Our method is a post-processing approach, so we don't directly retrieve the parameters $\theta_{\boldsymbol{\lambda}}^{*(\text{fair})}$. A direct result of Theorem 1 indicates that our post-processing approach preserves the rank statistics [7,38] conditional on the sensitive feature.

Corollary 1 (Group-wise rank statistics). *If $g^*_{t,\boldsymbol{\lambda}}(x_1, s) \leq g^*_{t,\boldsymbol{\lambda}}(x_2, s)$ for any instances (x_1, s) and (x_2, s) in $\mathcal{X} \times \mathcal{S}$, then the fair optimal predictor will also satisfy $g^{*(fair)}_{t,\boldsymbol{\lambda}}(x_1, s) \leq g^{*(fair)}_{t,\boldsymbol{\lambda}}(x_2, s)$.*

To obtain the optimal fair classifier for the original two-task problem (Y_1, Y_2), we can derive the final optimal fair classifier from the expression in Theorem 1. Given an instance $(\boldsymbol{x}, s) \in \mathcal{X} \times \mathcal{S}$ and a threshold $\tau \in [0, 1]$, the optimal fair classifier becomes

$$c^{*(\text{fair})}_{2,\boldsymbol{\lambda}}(\boldsymbol{x}, s) = \mathbb{1}\left\{g^{*(\text{fair})}_{2,\boldsymbol{\lambda}}(\boldsymbol{x}, s) \geq \tau\right\} .$$

The finding in [20] is applicable to our case, where setting the threshold at $\tau = 1/2$ corresponds to optimising accuracy while adhering to the DP constraint.

4 Plug-In Estimator

To employ the results on real data, we propose a plug-in estimator for the optimal fair predictor $\boldsymbol{g}^{*(\text{fair})}_{\boldsymbol{\lambda}}$.

4.1 Data-Driven Approach

The estimator is constructed in two steps in a semi-supervised manner since it depends on two datasets: one labeled denoted $\mathcal{D}^{\text{train}}_n = \{(\boldsymbol{X}_i, S_i, Y_{i,1}, Y_{i,2})\}^n_{i=1}$ n *i.i.d.* copies of $(\boldsymbol{X}, S, Y_1, Y_2)$ and the other unlabeled one, denoted $\mathcal{D}^{\text{pool}}_N = \{(\boldsymbol{X}_i, S_i)\}^N_{i=1}$, N *i.i.d.* copies of $(\boldsymbol{X}, S)$. For the regression-classification problem,

i) We train *simultaneously* the estimators $\widehat{g}_{1,\boldsymbol{\lambda}}$ and $\widehat{g}_{2,\boldsymbol{\lambda}}$ of respectively the regression function $g^*_{1,\boldsymbol{\lambda}}$ and the score function $g^*_{2,\boldsymbol{\lambda}}$ (optimal unconstrained functions) on a labeled dataset $\mathcal{D}^{\text{train}}_n$ via a multi-task learning model (see Sect. 2). To ensure the continuity assumption, we use a simple randomisation technique called *jittering* on the predictors. For each $t \in \mathcal{T}$, we introduce

$$\bar{g}_{t,\boldsymbol{\lambda}}(\boldsymbol{X}_i, S_i, \zeta_{i,t}) = \widehat{g}_{t,\boldsymbol{\lambda}}(\boldsymbol{X}_i, S_i) + \zeta_{i,t}$$

with $\zeta_{i,t}$ some uniform perturbations in $\mathcal{U}(-u, u)$ where u is set by the user (e.g. $u = 0.001$). This trick is often used for data visualisation for tie-breaking [10,15]. The trade-off weight $\boldsymbol{\lambda}$ can be predetermined or generated during training (refer to Sect. 4.2 below).

ii) Empirical frequencies $(\widehat{\pi}_s)_{s\in\mathcal{S}}$, CDF $\widehat{F}_{\bar{g}_{t,\boldsymbol{\lambda}}|s}$ and quantile function $\widehat{Q}_{\bar{g}_{t,\boldsymbol{\lambda}}|s}$ are calibrated via the previously estimators $\bar{g}_t$ and the unlabeled data set $\mathcal{D}^{\text{pool}}_N$.

The *(randomised) Wasserstein fair estimator* for each $t \in \mathcal{T}$ is defined by plug-in

$$\widehat{g}^{(\text{fair})}_{t,\boldsymbol{\lambda}}(\boldsymbol{x}, s) = \sum_{s'\in\mathcal{S}} \widehat{\pi}_{s'} \widehat{Q}_{\bar{g}_{t,\boldsymbol{\lambda}}|s'} \circ \widehat{F}_{\bar{g}_{t,\boldsymbol{\lambda}}|s}\left(\bar{g}_{t,\boldsymbol{\lambda}}(\boldsymbol{x}, s, \zeta_t)\right) \tag{8}$$

with $(\zeta_t)_{t\in\mathcal{T}} \overset{i.i.d.}{\sim} \mathcal{U}(-u, u)$. We present the associated pseudo-code in Algorithm 1.

Remark 2 (Data splitting) The procedure requires unlabeled data. If we do not have any in practice, we can split the labeled data in two and remove the labels in one of the two sets. As demonstrated in [16], splitting the data is essential to avoid overfitting and to get the right level of fairness.

4.2 Empirical Multi-task

This section outlines how we build each marginal predictor $\hat{g}_{t,\boldsymbol{\lambda}}$ using the training set $\mathcal{D}_n^{\text{train}} = (\boldsymbol{x}_i, s_i, \boldsymbol{y}_i)_{i=1}^n$ where each $(\boldsymbol{x}_i, s_i, \boldsymbol{y}_i)$ is a realisation of $(\boldsymbol{X}_i, S_i, \boldsymbol{Y}_i) \sim \mathbb{P}$. Given a set of task-related loss functions $\mathcal{L}_t$, we define the empirical multi-task problem from Eq. (3) as

$$\hat{\boldsymbol{\theta}}_\lambda = \underset{\theta}{\text{argmin}} \sum_{i=1}^{n} \sum_{t=1}^{2} \lambda_t \mathcal{L}_t(y_{i,t}, f_t \circ \theta(\boldsymbol{x}_i, s_i)).$$

Algorithm 1 Fairness calibration

Input: new data point (x, s), base estimators $(\hat{g}_{t,\boldsymbol{\lambda}})_{t\in\mathcal{T}}$, unlabeled sample $\mathcal{D}_N^{\text{pool}}$, and *i.i.d* uniform perturbations $(\zeta_{k,i}^s)_{k,i,s}$.

Step 0. Split $\mathcal{D}_N^{\text{pool}}$ to construct $(S_i)_{i=1}^N$ and $\{X_i^s\}_{i=1}^{N_s} \sim \mathbb{P}_{X|S=s}$ given $s \in \mathcal{S}$;

Step 1. Compute the empirical frequencies $(\hat{\pi}_s)_s$ based on $(S_i)_{i=1}^N$;

Step 2. Compute the empirical CDF $\widehat{F}_{\bar{g}_{t,\boldsymbol{\lambda}}|s}$ and quantile $\widehat{Q}_{\bar{g}_{t,\boldsymbol{\lambda}}|s'}$ from $\{X_i^s\}_{i=1}^{N_s}$;

Step 3. Compute $\hat{g}_{1,\boldsymbol{\lambda}}, \ldots, \hat{g}_{|\mathcal{T}|,\boldsymbol{\lambda}}$ thanks to Eq. (8);

Output: fair predictors $\hat{g}_{1,\boldsymbol{\lambda}}(\boldsymbol{x}, s), \ldots, \hat{g}_{|\mathcal{T}|,\boldsymbol{\lambda}}(\boldsymbol{x}, s)$ at point $(\boldsymbol{x}, s)$.

As the values for different loss functions $\mathcal{L}_t$ are situated on different scales, issues arise during training when using gradient based methods (see for example [28,29,40,41] for discussions about the issue). The $\boldsymbol{\lambda}$ parameter can alleviate this issue but is difficult to find in practice. Since there is no a priori optimal choice, we use the "*You Only Train Once*" (YOTO) approach of [19], initially developed for regression-regression problems. As the name of their approach suggests, the model is only trained once for a host of different $\boldsymbol{\lambda}$ values by conditioning the parameters of the neural network directly on the task weights $\boldsymbol{\lambda}$. The key idea is that different values for $\boldsymbol{\lambda}$ are sampled from a distribution and included directly in the estimation process. Rewritten, Eq. (4.2) then becomes:

$$\hat{\boldsymbol{\theta}}_\lambda = \underset{\theta}{\text{argmin}} \sum_{i=1}^{n} \sum_{t=1}^{2} \lambda_t \mathcal{L}_t(y_{i,t}, f_t \circ \theta(\boldsymbol{x}_i, s_i; \boldsymbol{\lambda})), \quad \boldsymbol{\lambda} \sim \mathbb{P}_\lambda \tag{9}$$

where $\mathbb{P}_\lambda$ is a sampling distribution. For our purposes, we use uniform distribution. As in the original article [19], we employ FiLM conditioning developed by [33] to condition each layer of $\theta(\cdot)$ directly on the sampled $\boldsymbol{\lambda}$. Once the model is fitted, the optimal $\boldsymbol{\lambda}$ is chosen via a problem specific calibration method on a calibration set. Precise details on the implementation can be found in Algorithm 2.

Algorithm 2 $\boldsymbol{\lambda}$-calibrated MTL

Input: Training data $\mathcal{D}_n^{\text{train}}$, bounds b_l, b_u for $\mathcal{U}(b_l, b_u)$, model, validation grid
while training **do**
  Step 1. Draw n_b $\lambda_t \sim \mathcal{U}(b_l, b_u)$;
  Step 2. FiLM Condition[33] each layer in neural network using $\boldsymbol{\lambda}$;
  Step 3. Condition loss as in YOTO [19] t with λ_t;
  Step 4. Adjust model parameters given $x, s, \boldsymbol{\lambda}$;
end while
for $\boldsymbol{\lambda}_v$ in validation grid **do**
  Step 1. Predict $\hat{y}_t$ for all t with $x, s, \boldsymbol{\lambda}_v$;
  Step 2. Evaluate $\hat{y}_t$, y_t for all t
end for
Output: Grid of task-wise error metrics given all $\boldsymbol{\lambda}_v$ in validation grid, choose optimal $\boldsymbol{\lambda}_v$

5 Numerical Evaluation

To evaluate the numerical performance, we conduct experiments on different datasets[1]. All data sets used are publicly available and are described in the next subsection. We also describe each of the separate tasks and the variable on which we want to achieve demographic parity (the S in the equations above).

5.1 Datasets

We focus on applications with tabular data, the first data set we consider stems from the FOLKTABLES package [17], which was constructed to enable bench marking of machine learning models[2]. Instead of a single task, we consider the simultaneous prediction of both *Mobility* (Binary) and *Income* (Regression) using a set of 19 features. Here, we consider *gender* the binary sensitive variable. In total, we use 58,650 observations from the state of California.

As a second benchmark, we consider the COMPAS data set [26]. It was constructed using a commercial algorithm which is used to assess the likelihood of reoffending for criminal defendants. It has been shown that its results are biased in favour of white defendants, and the data set has been used to assess the efficacy of other fairness related algorithms [30][3]. The data set collected has two classification targets (*recidivism* and *violent recidivism*), that are predicted using 18 features. In total, we use 6,172 observations from the data set and, in the spirit of the initial investigation, we consider *race* as the sensitive attribute.

[1] All sourcecode and data links can be found on github.com/phi-ra/FairMultitask.
[2] github.com/socialfoundations/folktables.
[3] Although available publicly, we believe the usage of the data needs to undergo some ethical considerations. Please read our separate ethical statement regarding this.

5.2 Methods

For the simulations, we split data into 80/20 train/test set. All estimators are based on neural networks with a fixed architecture and 10% dropout in the layers. We compare the performance and fairness of the optimal predictor and the optimal fair predictor across a MTL model and two single-task (STL) models, across 20 bootstrap iterations. We refrain from an in-depth architecture and hyper-parameter search to keep the insights comparable among the simulations.

Our goal is to exemplify two distinct features of MTL under fairness constraints. A standard application in MTL is to leverage similarities in tasks to improve performance in the case where labels in one of the tasks are scarce.

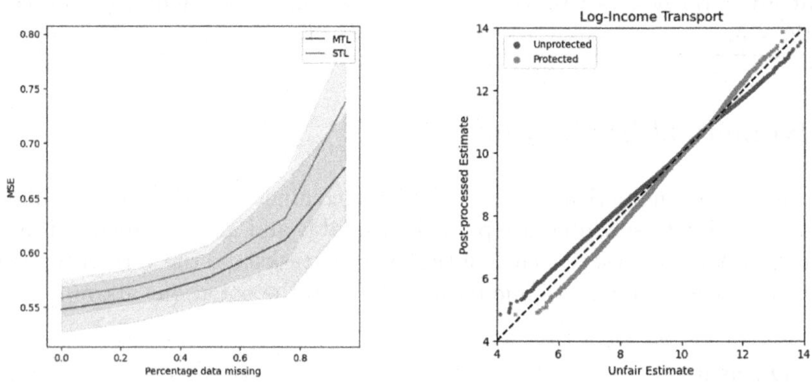

Fig. 2. Left, the performance as measured by MSE for MTL and STL, here the $\boldsymbol{\lambda}$ parameter was chosen to optimise the regression task. This leads to better outcomes, especially in the case of missing values in the regression labels. Right, regression estimates before versus after the optimal transport.

As our method is valid for any trade-off weight $\boldsymbol{\lambda}$, we can achieve fairness even in the case where one task is more important than the other. To simulate this environment, we successively remove [0,25,50,75,95]% of the regression labels in the training of the FOLKTABLES data set and calibrate the $\boldsymbol{\lambda}$ vector to optimise performance on the regression task. Intuitively, we would expect the predictive performance of the models to degrade with a higher proportion of missing data, but MTL should perform better than STL, if it is able to extract knowledge from the related classification task. A second use for MTL arises when we are interested in the joint distribution of several tasks. This is of particular importance for the second case, as one of the tasks in the COMPAS data set is actually a subset of the other. To illustrate this, we optimise the $\boldsymbol{\lambda}$ parameter for the COMPAS tasks in order to maximise performance in both. To measure the performance we use the mean-squared error (MSE) of the log-predictions for the regression task and area under the ROC curve (AUC) for the classification tasks. To calculate the unfairness, we compare the predictions made on the two subpopulations specified by the presence (*Protected*) or absence (*Unprotected*) of the sensitive attribute using the empirical counterpart $\hat{\mathcal{U}}(g_t)$ of the unfairness given in Definition 4 which corresponds to a two-sample Kolmogorov-Smirnov (KS) test

$$\hat{\mathcal{U}}(g_t) := \sup_{u \in \mathcal{Y}_t} \left| \hat{F}_{g_t|1}(u) - \hat{F}_{g_t|-1}(u) \right| .$$

5.3 Results

The numeric results for the FOLKTABLES data set are summarised in Table 1 and highlights visualised in Fig. 2. Especially the *Income* variable (the regression task) suffers from unfairness (as indicated by a higher value in the KS test). The advantage of using a second task to help the predictions is also clearly visible in the numerical results and the left pane of Fig. 2. Although the performance of MTL deteriorates with more missing labels, it suffers less than the STL estimation. The classification task performs less well, as the $\boldsymbol{\lambda}$ was calibrated to optimise the regression task. Additionally, as there are no missing labels in the classification task, we would expect only marginal gains from using MTL even in the case where $\boldsymbol{\lambda}$ is calibrated to serve both tasks well. This is in line with what was found in the literature of MTL [37]. Here, the specification using the YOTO approach allows the user to chose the optimal trade-off weight for the problem at hand in a specific calibration step which will lead to different outcomes using the same trained weights. The advantage of our result is that it will be valid for any $\boldsymbol{\lambda}$. We can also see across the board that the imposing fairness among the predictions reduces slightly the predictive performance and almost exactly satisfies the DP condition. We also visualise the effect of the optimal transport as specified by the Wasserstein fair estimator in Eq. (8), as suggested in [11]. Because our operations preserve the group-wise rank (Corollary 1), we can directly represent the changes in the predictions for each group. The predicted income distribution is shifted in a way such that the upper tail for the sensitive group is shifted up, but the lower tail is shifted downwards.

Table 1. Performance and unfairness for MTL and Single Task Learning (STL) models on the FOLKTABLES data. Each model was also post-processed and evaluated on performance and unfairness.

Data	Model					
	MTL		MTL, Post-processed		STL	
	Performance	Unfairness	Performance	Unfairness	Performance	Unfairness
regression - all data	0.548 ± 0.02	0.109 ± 0.01	0.558 ± 0.02	0.018 ± 0.00	0.559 ± 0.02	0.107 ± 0.01
regression - 25% missing	0.558 ± 0.02	0.109 ± 0.02	0.572 ± 0.02	0.018 ± 0.00	0.570 ± 0.02	0.105 ± 0.02
regression - 50% missing	0.577 ± 0.02	0.109 ± 0.02	0.593 ± 0.03	0.018 ± 0.01	0.587 ± 0.02	0.099 ± 0.01
regression - 75% missing	0.612 ± 0.05	0.101 ± 0.02	0.627 ± 0.06	0.019 ± 0.01	0.632 ± 0.04	0.098 ± 0.01
regression - 95% missing	0.678 ± 0.05	0.105 ± 0.02	0.687 ± 0.05	0.018 ± 0.01	0.738 ± 0.06	0.108 ± 0.03
classification - all data	0.576 ± 0.01	0.080 ± 0.03	0.577 ± 0.01	0.018 ± 0.01	0.640 ± 0.03	0.042 ± 0.02

The results from the COMPAS data set mirror in large parts the ones of the FOLKTABLES but here we want to optimise the performance across both tasks at once. Results are summarised in Table 2 and visualised in Fig. 3. The effect of the optimal transport on the distributions can be seen in the marginal distributions in 3. The colors indicate whether a given individual is identified as belonging to a protected group. Clearly a bias can be seen in the marginal distributions, the protected group has both a higher recidivism score and a slightly higher violent recidivism score, which mirrors the findings from [26]. In the right pane, we show the post-processed version, where the marginal distributions are almost congruent, enforcing the DP condition. The resulting fairness is also assessed numerically using the KS test. As expected this also leads to a small performance decrease as measured by AUC. The tuning of the $\boldsymbol{\lambda}$ parameter allows to have a predictive performance that is almost equivalent to the STL specification, with the advantage that we can jointly predict the scores and enforce the DP condition for this joint representation.

Table 2. Performance in AUC and unfairness for MTL and Single Task Learning (STL) models on the COMPAS data. Each model was also post-processed and evaluated on performance and unfairness.

Data	Model							
	MTL		MTL, Post-processed		STL		STL, Post-processed	
	Performance	Unfairness	Performance	Unfairness	Performance	Unfairness	Performance	Unfairness
task 1 - all data	0.742 ± 0.01	0.289 ± 0.02	0.727 ± 0.01	0.052 ± 0.02	0.745 ± 0.01	0.291 ± 0.02	0.730 ± 0.01	0.055 ± 0.02
task 2 - all data	0.686 ± 0.02	0.289 ± 0.04	0.649 ± 0.01	0.053 ± 0.02	0.671 ± 0.01	0.290 ± 0.03	0.638 ± 0.03	0.053 ± 0.02

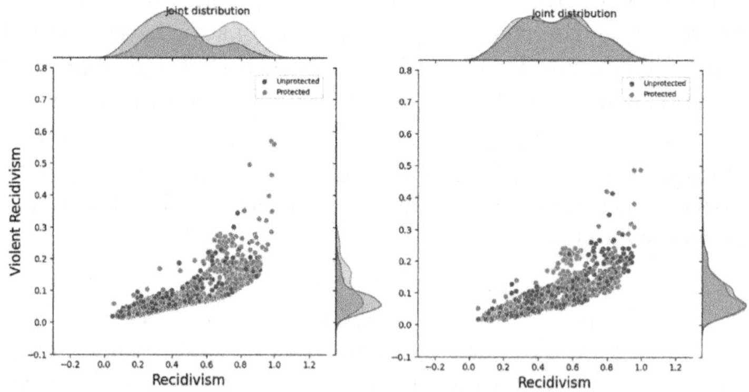

Fig. 3. Joint distribution for scores under unconstrained and DP-fair regimes. Color indicates the presence of the sensitive feature. Note that the joint distribution appears more mixed and the marginal distributions overlap in the DP fair case.

6 Conclusion

As multi-task learning grows in popularity, ensuring fairness among the predictions becomes a new challenge as the precise effects of MTL are still poorly understood. In this paper, we investigated the general effects of parameter sharing on the marginal tasks. We proposed a method to integrate fairness into MTL through a post-processing procedure which keeps a key advantage of MTL, shorter computational expenses, largely intact. This also opens a host of new directions for further research. As we focused on tabular data, we were less restricted by possible model architectures. In other related areas where MTL is becoming more popular, such as computer vision, pre-trained models akin to our h_θ are often used to ease the computational burden. A thorough investigation into the precise effects of the combination of the triple Transfer-Multitask-Fair learning would hence be a natural extension. A further extension of our results would be to consider fairness in a general multivariate setting. This would mean shifting the parameters of the embedding h_θ simultaneously for all tasks. This will likely not be possible with a similar closed-form solution, as our approach relies on the estimation of quantiles. As MTL is generally used in the case where there is a rather strong (and exploitable) relationship between the two tasks, the marginal approach we propose here seems apt, but a theoretical discussion would nevertheless be interesting.

Ethics statement

Our work is centered around fairness, which is a goal we sincerely believe all model should strive to achieve. Nevertheless, to ensure fairness in models, one needs to define unfairness as its counterpart. This naturally leads to a conundrum when performing research on this topic. On one hand, we would like our models to be fair, but to analyse the differences and show an improvement, we first need to create an unfair outcome. As has been shown in the past, simply ignoring the sensitive attributes does not solve the problem of bias in the data. Further, as more flexible methods make their way into practical modelling, this issue is only bound to increase. Hence it is our conviction that estimating intentionally unfair models (by for example including sensitive variables explicitly in the training phase) is ethically justifiable if the goal is to provide a truly fair estimation. In that sense our work contributes to achieving fairness, and does not create new risks by itself.

In our empirical application, we consider data which was used in a predictive algorithm in the criminal justice system. This is particularly concerning as there have been numerous instances where racial, ethnic or gender bias was detected in such systems (indeed the data from COMPAS were collected to show precisely that) and the criminal justice system is supposed to be egalitarian. Further, existing biases within the justice system may be further reinforced. Although the above mentioned weaknesses are well documented, such algorithms continue to be used in practice. Our work does not contribute to these algorithms directly but rather uses them as an example to show unequal treatment. Whereas the usage of other, biased data sets, such as the well-known *Boston Housing* data set is discouraged, we believe that in order to show the effectiveness of fairness related algorithms, the use of such a data set is justified.

References

1. Association belge des consommateurs test-achats asbl and others v conseil des ministres. https://curia.europa.eu/juris/liste.jsf?language=en&num=C-236/09
2. Adebayo, J., Kagal, L.: Iterative orthogonal feature projection for diagnosing bias in black-box models. In: Conference on Fairness, Accountability, and Transparency in Machine Learning (2016)
3. Agarwal, A., Beygelzimer, A., Dudík, M., Langford, J., Wallach, H.: A reductions approach to fair classification. In: Proceedings of the 35th International Conference on Machine Learning (2018)
4. Agarwal, A., Dudik, M., Wu, Z.S.: Fair regression: quantitative definitions and reduction-based algorithms. In: International Conference on Machine Learning (2019)
5. Barocas, S., Hardt, M., Narayanan, A.: Fairness and Machine Learning (2018). https://fairmlbook.org/
6. Baxter, J.: A model of inductive bias learning. J. Artif. Intell. Res. **12**, 149–198 (2000)
7. Bobkov, S., Ledoux, M.: One-dimensional empirical measures, order statistics and kantorovich transport distances. Memoirs of the American Mathematical Society (2016)
8. Calders, T., Kamiran, F., Pechenizkiy, M.: Building classifiers with independency constraints. In: IEEE International Conference on Data Mining (2009)
9. Calmon, F., Wei, D., Vinzamuri, B., Ramamurthy, K.N., Varshney, K.R.: Optimized pre-processing for discrimination prevention. In: Neural Information Processing Systems (2017)
10. Chambers, J.M.: Graphical Methods for Data Analysis. CRC Press, Boca Raton (2018)
11. Charpentier, A.: Insurance, Biases, Discrimination and Fairness. Springer, Heidelberg (2023)
12. Chiappa, S., Jiang, R., Stepleton, T., Pacchiano, A., Jiang, H., Aslanides, J.: A general approach to fairness with optimal transport. In: AAAI (2020)
13. Chzhen, E., Denis, C., Hebiri, M., Oneto, L., Pontil, M.: Leveraging labeled and unlabeled data for consistent fair binary classification. In: Advances in Neural Information Processing Systems (2019)
14. Chzhen, E., Denis, C., Hebiri, M., Oneto, L., Pontil, M.: Fair regression via plug-in estimator and recalibrationwith statistical guarantees. In: Advances in Neural Information Processing Systems (2020)
15. Chzhen, E., Denis, C., Hebiri, M., Oneto, L., Pontil, M.: Fair regression with wasserstein barycenters. In: Advances in Neural Information Processing Systems (2020)
16. Denis, C., Elie, R., Hebiri, M., Hu, F.: Fairness guarantee in multi-class classification. arXiv preprint arXiv:2109.13642 (2021)
17. Ding, F., Hardt, M., Miller, J., Schmidt, L.: Retiring adult: New datasets for fair machine learning. Adv. Neural Inf. Process. Syst. **34**, 1–13 (2021)

18. Donini, M., Oneto, L., Ben-David, S., Shawe-Taylor, J.S., Pontil, M.: Empirical risk minimization under fairness constraints. In: Neural Information Processing Systems (2018)
19. Dosovitskiy, A., Djolonga, J.: You only train once: loss-conditional training of deep networks. In: International Conference on Learning Representations (2020)
20. Gaucher, S., Schreuder, N., Chzhen, E.: Fair learning with wasserstein barycenters for non-decomposable performance measures. arXiv preprint arXiv:2209.00427 (2022)
21. Gordaliza, P., Del Barrio, E., Fabrice, G., Loubes, J.M.: Obtaining fairness using optimal transport theory. In: International Conference on Machine Learning (2019)
22. Gouic, T., Loubes, J., Rigollet, P.: Projection to fairness in statistical learning. arXiv preprint arXiv:2005.11720 (2020)
23. Hardt, M., Price, E., Srebro, N.: Equality of opportunity in supervised learning. In: Neural Information Processing Systems (2016)
24. Hornik, K., Stinchcombe, M., White, H.: Multilayer feedforward networks are universal approximators. Neural Netw. **2**(5), 359–366 (1989)
25. Jiang, R., Pacchiano, A., Stepleton, T., Jiang, H., Chiappa, S.: Wasserstein fair classification. In: Adams, R.P., Gogate, V. (eds.) Proceedings of The 35th Uncertainty in Artificial Intelligence Conference. Proceedings of Machine Learning Research, vol. 115, pp. 862–872. PMLR (2020). https://proceedings.mlr.press/v115/jiang20a.html
26. Larson, J., Angwin, J., Kirchner, L., Mattu, S.: How we analyzed the compass recidivism algorithm (2016). https://www.propublica.org/article/how-we-analyzed-the-compas-recidivism-algorithm
27. Lipton, Z., McAuley, J., Chouldechova, A.: Does mitigating ml's impact disparity require treatment disparity? Adv. Neural Inf. Process. Syst. **31**, 1–11 (2018)
28. Liu, B., Liu, X., Jin, X., Stone, P., Liu, Q.: Conflict-averse gradient descent for multi-task learning. Adv. Neural Inf. Process. Syst. **34**, 18878–18890 (2021)
29. Navon, A., et al.: Multi-task learning as a bargaining game. In: Chaudhuri, K., Jegelka, S., Song, L., Szepesvari, C., Niu, G., Sabato, S. (eds.) Proceedings of the 39th International Conference on Machine Learning. Proceedings of Machine Learning Research, vol. 162, pp. 16428–16446. PMLR (2022)
30. Oneto, L., Donini, M., Elders, A., Pontil, M.: Taking advantage of multitask learning for fair classification. In: AAAI/ACM Conference on AI, Ethics, and Society (2019)
31. Oneto, L., Donini, M., Luise, G., Ciliberto, C., Maurer, A., Pontil, M.: Exploiting mmd and sinkhorn divergences for fair and transferable representation learning. Adv. Neural Inf. Process. Syst. **33**, 15360–15370 (2020)
32. Oneto, L., Donini, M., Pontil, M., Maurer, A.: Learning fair and transferable representations with theoretical guarantees. In: 2020 IEEE 7th International Conference on Data Science and Advanced Analytics (DSAA), pp. 30–39. IEEE (2020)
33. Perez, E., Strub, F., De Vries, H., Dumoulin, V., Courville, A.: Film: visual reasoning with a general conditioning layer. In: Proceedings of the AAAI Conference on Artificial Intelligence, vol. 32 (2018)
34. Plečko, D., Meinshausen, N.: Fair data adaptation with quantile preservation. J. Mach. Learn. Res. **21**(1), 9776–9819 (2020)
35. Roy, A., Ntoutsi, E.: Learning to teach fairness-aware deep multi-task learning. In: Machine Learning and Knowledge Discovery in Databases: European Conference, ECML PKDD 2022, Grenoble, France, 19–23 September 2022, Proceedings, Part I, pp. 710–726. Springer, Heidelberg (2023). https://doi.org/10.1007/978-3-031-26387-3_43

36. Ruder, S.: An overview of multi-task learning in deep neural networks. arXiv preprint arXiv:1706.05098 (2017)
37. Standley, T., Zamir, A., Chen, D., Guibas, L., Malik, J., Savarese, S.: Which tasks should be learned together in multi-task learning? In: International Conference on Machine Learning, pp. 9120–9132. PMLR (2020)
38. Van der Vaart, A.W.: Asymptotic Statistics, vol. 3. Cambridge University Press, Cambridge (2000)
39. Wang, Y., Wang, X., Beutel, A., Prost, F., Chen, J., Chi, E.H.: Understanding and improving fairness-accuracy trade-offs in multi-task learning. In: Proceedings of the 27th ACM SIGKDD Conference on Knowledge Discovery & Data Mining, pp. 1748–1757 (2021)
40. Wang, Z., Tsvetkov, Y., Firat, O., Cao, Y.: Gradient vaccine: investigating and improving multi-task optimization in massively multilingual models. In: International Conference on Learning Representations (2020)
41. Yu, T., Kumar, S., Gupta, A., Levine, S., Hausman, K., Finn, C.: Gradient surgery for multi-task learning. Adv. Neural Inf. Process. Syst. **33**, 5824–5836 (2020)
42. Zafar, M.B., Valera, I., Gomez Rodriguez, M., Gummadi, K.P.: Fairness beyond disparate treatment & disparate impact: learning classification without disparate mistreatment. In: International Conference on World Wide Web (2017)
43. Zafar, M.B., Valera, I., Gomez-Rodriguez, M., Gummadi, K.P.: Fairness constraints: a flexible approach for fair classification. J. Mach. Learn. Res. **20**(75), 1–42 (2019)
44. Zemel, R., Wu, Y., Swersky, K., Pitassi, T., Dwork, C.: Learning fair representations. In: International Conference on Machine Learning (2013)
45. Zhang, Y., Yang, Q.: A survey on multi-task learning. IEEE Trans. Knowl. Data Eng. **34**(12), 5586–5609 (2021)
46. Zhao, C., Chen, F.: Rank-based multi-task learning for fair regression. In: 2019 IEEE International Conference on Data Mining (ICDM), pp. 916–925. IEEE (2019)

REST: Enhancing Group Robustness in DNNs Through Reweighted Sparse Training

Jiaxu Zhao[1(✉)], Lu Yin[1], Shiwei Liu[1,2], Meng Fang[1,3], and Mykola Pechenizkiy[1]

[1] Eindhoven University of Technology, 5600 MB, Eindhoven, The Netherlands
{j.zhao,l.yin,s.liu,m.fang,m.pechenizkiy}@tue.nl
[2] The University of Texas at Austin, Austin, TX 78705, USA
shiwei.liu@austin.utexas.edu
[3] University of Liverpool, Liverpool L69 3BX, UK
Meng.Fang@liverpool.ac.uk

Abstract. The deep neural network (DNN) has been proven effective in various domains. However, they often struggle to perform well on certain minority groups during inference, despite showing strong performance on the majority of data groups. This is because over-parameterized models learned *bias attributes* from a large number of *bias-aligned* training samples. These bias attributes are strongly spuriously correlated with the target variable, causing the models to be biased towards spurious correlations (i.e., *bias-conflicting*). To tackle this issue, we propose a novel **re**weighted **s**parse **t**raining framework, dubbed as ***REST***, which aims to enhance the performance of biased data while improving computation and memory efficiency. Our proposed REST framework has been experimentally validated on three datasets, demonstrating its effectiveness in exploring unbiased subnetworks. We found that REST reduces the reliance on spuriously correlated features, leading to better performance across a wider range of data groups with fewer training and inference resources. We highlight that the *REST* framework represents a promising approach for improving the performance of DNNs on biased data, while simultaneously improving computation and memory efficiency. By reducing the reliance on spurious correlations, REST has the potential to enhance the robustness of DNNs and improve their generalization capabilities. Code is released at https://github.com/zhao1402072392/REST.

Keywords: Unbiased Learning · Minority group · Sparse training

1 Introduction

Deep neural network models are successful on various tasks and can achieve low average error on the test set. However, these models may still exhibit high errors for certain subgroups of samples that are the minority in the training dataset [9,45]. This problem may be caused by the standard method (empirical risk minimization (ERM)) of training models that optimizes the average training loss. During training, models learn the *spurious correlations* that exist within the majority groups in the data and make predictions

J. Zhao and L. Yin—Contributed equally to this research.

© The Author(s), under exclusive license to Springer Nature Switzerland AG 2023
D. Koutra et al. (Eds.): ECML PKDD 2023, LNAI 14170, pp. 313–329, 2023.
https://doi.org/10.1007/978-3-031-43415-0_19

based on this correlation. For example, consider an image classification task of cows and camels, where most of the images of cows are captured in grasslands and camels in deserts. As a result of training on such a dataset, models tend to rely on features such as the presence of grass or sand in an image instead of the object of interest for making predictions [3]. This can lead to poor performance of minority groups (e.g., cows in the desert and camels in the grassland). Since the model learns spuriously correlated features from the misleading statistical evidence in the data of the majority group, it will perform poorly on the minority group.

To address the problem that models perform poorly on minority groups and train an unbiased network that can perform well on biased datasets, researchers proposed various methods. One fundamental idea is to adjust the weights of different groups in the data during training. This approach, known as reweighting, has been extensively studied in the literature [5,38,39]. The main goal of reweighting is to upweight the training loss for minority groups, thus encouraging the model to pay more attention to these groups and achieve higher accuracy on biased data. Some recent studies have focused on improving the worst-group error, which measures the performance of the model on the subgroup with the lowest accuracy. One approach is based on distributionally robust optimization (DRO) [4,8], which aims to optimize the worst-case performance of the model under all possible distributions. Based on distributionally robust optimization (DRO) [4,8], for instance, Sagawa et al. [37] propose GDRO, a DRO-based method that directly minimizes the worst-group error during training. By doing so, the model can learn to avoid spurious correlations and focus on the most informative features for all groups. [27,34] propose a two-step training approach. The idea is to first identify the data that the model predicts incorrectly after ERM training and upweight these data to train the model again. Despite the progress made by these methods, most existing work still focuses on training or fine-tuning model parameters in different ways to mitigate the bias of the model.

Some researchers found that over-parameterization allows the model to achieve a high average test accuracy but decreases the minority test accuracy due to capturing spurious correlations in the data [38]. Therefore, in addition to fine-tuning the model, some work [44] focused on improving the accuracy of the model on biased data by pruning the model parameters. For instance, Zhang et al. [44] demonstrate that there exist sub-networks in the neural network that are less susceptible to spurious correlation. But all existing sparsity-based approaches rely on pruning a fully-trained dense network, which itself is very tedious. It is required to train a dense model first, then prune the model parameters according to some regulations to obtain a sparse model, and finally fine-tune the sparse model to recover accuracy.

Overall, previous works address the model's poor performance on highly biased data either by using minority-group-aware optimization (e.g., loss reweighting, DRO [4,8], GDRO [37]), or by modifying the biased model using some ad hoc operations (e.g., pruning [44], re-training on the biased data group (e.g., [13]). In this paper, we propose to close this research question by directly training sparse neural networks from scratch to overcome the key hurdle of over-parameterization in memorizing spurious features. Our approach directly yields a sparse subnetwork that is debiased "out of the box", without any costly pre-training or any dense training steps. Specifically, we utilize sparse training [30,32] to find the sparse subnetwork. Sparse training has been proposed to solve the over-parameterization problem. It prunes the unimportant parameters of the model in training to sparse the over-parameterized model. And the model can retain the performance of the original model at a very low density.

To the best of our knowledge, we use sparse training for the first time to solve the problem of high worst-group error in the model. By pruning certain parameters of the model during sparse training, we can create a sparse network that is less susceptible to spurious correlations and more robust to distribution shifts. We implement experiments on three popular image classification datasets (Colored MNIST (CMNIST) [2], Corrupted CIFAR-10 (CIFAR-10-C) [15] and Gender-biased FFHQ (BFFHQ) [23]) to demonstrate the effectiveness of sparse training in optimizing the worst group errors. We also compare the performance of pruned pre-trained models and find that pruning the pre-trained models does not make them perform as well as sparse training models from scratch. Furthermore, we implement ablation experiments to compare the performance of different sparse training approaches in dealing with the out-of-distribution issue. We summarize our contributions as follows:

- **A New Approach:** We propose the **Re**weighted **S**parse **T**raining (**REST**) framework, which trains a subnetwork in an end-to-end fashion. The framework uses sparse training to obtain a sub-network that avoids being biased towards spurious correlation in biased datasets and does not require an additional training and fine-tuning process.
- **Better Performance:** We demonstrated that **REST** could achieve better performance than other strong baselines on all three highly biased datasets. Compared to the original ERM, with 0.5% of bias-conflicting data, our method improves the accuracy by 28.3%, 9.9%, and 23.7% on the CMNIST, CIFAR-10-C, and BFFHQ, respectively.
- **Fewer Resources:** Compared with other baselines, **REST** requires fewer training and inference resources. Specifically, after implementing our method, the ResNet-18 and Simple CNN models require only 2% and 0.7% of the original models' FLOPs for their application, respectively.

2 Related Work

2.1 Sparse Neural Network Training

Training sparse neural networks is a popular area of research. The goal is to train initial sparse networks from scratch and achieve comparable performance to dense networks while using fewer resources. Sparse training can be divided into two categories: static sparse training (SST), where the connectivity does not change during training, and dynamic sparse training (DST), where the connectivity changes during training.

Static sparse training refers to a set of techniques that involve training sparse neural networks while maintaining a consistent sparse connectivity pattern throughout the process. Despite the fixed sparse connectivity, there can be variations in layer-wise sparsity (i.e., the sparsity level of each individual layer). The simplest approach is to apply uniform sparsity to all layers [11]. [31] introduced a non-uniform sparsity method that can be used in Restricted Boltzmann Machines (RBMs) and outperforms dense RBMs. Some research investigates the use of expander graphs for training sparse CNNs, demonstrating performance comparable to their dense counterparts [21,36]. Drawing from graph theory, the *Erdős-R'enyi* (ER) model [32] and its CNN variant, the *Erdős-R'enyi-Kernel* (ERK) model [10], assign lower sparsity to smaller layers, thus preventing the layer collapse issue [40] and generally yielding better results than uniform sparsity approaches. [28,42] combine individual subnetworks and surpass the generalization performance of the naive dense ensemble.

Dynamic sparse training involves training initial sparse neural networks while dynamically modifying the sparse connectivity pattern throughout the process. DST was first introduced by Sparse Evolutionary Training (SET) [32], which initializes sparse connectivity using an ER topology and periodically explores the parameter space via a prune-and-grow scheme during training. Subsequent to SET, weight redistribution has been introduced to search for optimal layer-wise sparsity ratios during training [6,33]. The most commonly used pruning criterion employed in existing DST methods is magnitude pruning. Criteria for weight regrowth differ among methods, with gradient-based regrowth (e.g., momentum [6] and gradient [10]) demonstrating strong results in image classification, while random regrowth surpasses the former in language modeling [7]. Later research has improved accuracy by relaxing the constrained memory footprint [16,19,29,43].

2.2 Debiasing Frameworks

Neural networks tend to rely on spurious correlations in the data to predict, which are often caused by misleading statistical information in the data, and these spurious correlations do not generalize to all samples. Several works [18,38] have investigated the causes of worst-group errors as a result of models relying on spurious features of the data during training. These spurious features are relevant to the target but not to the research problem.

To improve the performance of the network on biased data, a common approach is to reweight data from different distributions during training [5,38,39]. [37] propose group distributional robust optimization DRO (GDRO) optimize the worst-group error directly. In addition to optimizing the performance of the worst group, some work [1,22] attempt to improve the group robustness of the models by closing their performances in different groups. [13,41] attempt to balance the training data through data augmentation techniques. [12] address the texture bias issue by incorporating additional training images with their styles transferred through adaptive instance normalization [17].

These methods above improve the performance of the models on biased data by using loss functions or adjusting the data distribution. There is also some work that considers the existence of unbiased sub-networks in the original network [44]. A common approach is to train a dense neural network first, then prune off some of the network weights to get a sparse network, and finally, fine-tune the sparse network. In this paper, we also focus on training a sparse network to improve its performance on biased data. However, instead of taking trivial steps, we train a sparse network directly from scratch through sparse training.

3 Methodology

Given a supervised dataset consisting of input samples $X \in \mathcal{X}$ and true labels $Y \in \mathcal{Y}$. We can denote the random input sample and its corresponding label as $(X^e, Y^e) \sim P^e$, where $X^e \in \mathcal{X}$ and $Y^e \in \mathcal{Y}$. Here, $e \in \mathcal{E} = \{1, 2, ...E\}$ represents the index of the environment and P^e represents the distribution associated with that environment. The set $\mathcal{E}$ contains all possible environments. Additionally, we assume that $\mathcal{E}$ is composed of training environments ($\mathcal{E}_{train}$) and unseen test environments ($\mathcal{E}_{test}$), such that $\mathcal{E} = \mathcal{E}_{train} \cup \mathcal{E}_{test}$. The training dataset comprises samples from $\mathcal{E}_{train}$. And the test dataset samples are from out-of-distribution in unseen environments $\mathcal{E}_{test}$.

Consider a neural network $f_\theta : \mathcal{X} \rightarrow \mathcal{Y}$ parameterized by θ. Define the risk achieved by the model as $\mathcal{R}^e(\theta) = \mathbb{E}_{(X^e, Y^e) \sim P^e}[\ell(X^e, Y^e)]$, where ℓ is the loss of each sample (e.g.,cross-entropy). The objective of addressing the out-of-distribution (OOD) generalization problem is to develop a model that can effectively minimize the maximum risk across all environments in the set $\mathcal{E}$, as represented by the equation:

$$\min_{\theta} \max_{e \in \mathcal{E}} \mathcal{R}^e(\theta) \tag{1}$$

However, since we only have access to training data from $\mathcal{E}_{train}$ and cannot know samples from unseen environments, Therefore, the models tend to perform well on the data distribution on the training set but poorly on out-of-distribution data.

Typically, models are trained in a way that optimizes the loss of model predictions and labels in the training environment, usually using empirical risk minimization (ERM). Usually, neural networks learn target features as well as spuriously correlated features, which are due to misleading statistical information. However, these spuriously correlated features do not generalize to all samples. Therefore, the models perform well in the training environment, and their predictions are highly accurate, but they perform poorly when they encounter samples without such spurious correlations.

In this work, we proposed applying sparse training with reweighting to find a subnetwork to avoid learning spuriously correlated features. Our REST method is illustrated in Fig. 1. In the following, we will formally demonstrate the details of sparse training.

3.1 Sparse Training

Let us denote the sparse neural network as $f(\boldsymbol{x}; \boldsymbol{\theta}_s)$. $\boldsymbol{\theta}_s$ refers to a subset of the full network parameters $\boldsymbol{\theta}$ at a sparsity level of $(1 - \frac{\|\boldsymbol{\theta}_s\|_0}{\|\boldsymbol{\theta}\|_0})$ and $\|\cdot\|_0$ represents the ℓ_0-norm.

It is common to initialize sparse subnetworks $\boldsymbol{\theta}_s$ randomly based on the uniform [6,33] or non-uniform layer-wise sparsity ratios with *Erdős-Rényi* (ER) graph [10,32]. In the case of image classification, sparse training aims to optimize the following object using data $\{(x_i, y_i)\}_{i=1}^{\mathrm{N}}$:

$$\hat{\boldsymbol{\theta}}_s = \arg\min_{\boldsymbol{\theta}_s} \sum_{i=1}^{\mathrm{N}} \mathcal{L}(f(x_i; \boldsymbol{\theta}_s), y_i) \tag{2}$$

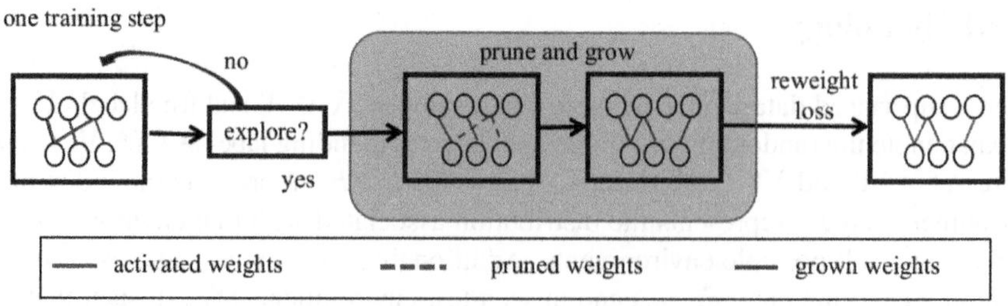

Fig. 1. Re-weighted Sparse Training.

where $\mathcal{L}$ is the loss function.

Static sparse training (SST) maintains the same sparse network connectivity during training after initialization. Dynamic sparse training (DST), on the contrary, allows the sparse subnetworks to dynamically explore new parameters while sticking to a fixed sparsity budget. Most if not all DST methods follow a simple prune-and-grow scheme [32] to perform parameter exploration, i.e., pruning r proportion of the least important parameters based on their magnitude, and immediately grow the same number of parameters randomly [32] or using the potential gradient [30]. Formally, the parameter exploration can be formalized as the following two steps:

$$\boldsymbol{\theta}_{\mathrm{s}} = \Psi(\boldsymbol{\theta}_{\mathrm{s}},\, r), \tag{3}$$

$$\boldsymbol{\theta}_{\mathrm{s}} = \boldsymbol{\theta}_{\mathrm{s}} \cup \Phi(\boldsymbol{\theta}_{i \notin \boldsymbol{\theta}_{\mathrm{s}}},\, r) \tag{4}$$

where Ψ is the specific pruning criterion and Φ is growing scheme. These metrics may vary from one sparse training method to another. At the end of the training, sparse training can converge to a performant sparse subnetwork. Since the sparse neural networks are trained from scratch, the memory requirements and training/inference FLOPs are only a fraction of their dense counterparts.

It is well known that the standard method for training neural networks is Empirical Risk Minimization (ERM). Formally, the ERM can be defined as follows:

$$\theta_{ERM} = arg\min_{\theta} \mathbb{E}_{(X^e,Y^e)\sim P^e}[\ell(X^e, Y^e)] \tag{5}$$

where ℓ is the cross-entropy loss or square loss. However, in previous works [37,38], the authors demonstrate that models trained by ERM, whether under or over-parameterized, have low worst-group test errors (e.g., data that are not in the training set distribution). To address this issue, the reweighting method is the most common and simple method. Because the out-of-distribution problem is due to the tendency of the model to rely on strong spurious correlation in the training data to predict the results, the idea of reweighting is to reduce such spurious correlation by increasing the weight of minority groups in the data during training. Based on Eq. 5, we formally define reweighting as the following equation:

$$\theta_{ERM} = arg\min_{\theta} \mathbb{E}_{(X^e,Y^e)\sim P^e}[\beta_{P^e}\ell(X^e, Y^e)] \tag{6}$$

where β_{P^e} is a reweighting hyperparameter. Usually, the β_{P^e} is an upweight for a minority group of data in the training set and a downweight for a majority group. This can effectively mitigate the spurious correlations in the data learned by the network. Specifically, in some methods, β_{P^e} is set according to the amount of data distribution (e.g., using $\frac{1}{N_{P^e}}$ as the β_{P^e}, where N_{P^E} denotes the number of data from P^e distribution.). In this paper, we set different β_{P^e} for different training sets, which are described in Sect. 4.3.

4 Experiments

In this chapter, we describe the details of the experiments. We conducted experiments on three datasets, including Colored MNIST (CMNIST) [2], Corrupted CIFAR-10 (CIFAR-10-C) [15] and Gender-biased FFHQ (BFFHQ) [23]. We choose a couple of debiasing methods as our baselines for comparison, including ERM, MRM [44], and DisEnt [26]. Below, we describe the baseline methods, dataset, and model setup separately.

4.1 Baselines

ERM. Empirical Risk Minimization (ERM) is a technique used in machine learning to find the optimal parameters for a given model. ERM is the standard baseline model in classification tasks. The basic idea behind ERM is to minimize the difference between the predicted output of a model and the ground truth label of the data. In addition to the original ERM, we also apply reweight loss to the ERM as another baseline.

MRM. Modular Risk Minimization (MRM) optimizes neural networks by learning a sparse subnetwork architecture that can improve the network's generalization performance. MRM consists of three stages, and we formally introduce MRM below:

Given data (x_i, y_i), neural network $f(\theta; \cdot)$, subnetwork logits π and the coefficient of sparsity penalty α.

Stage 1: Full Model Pre-Training In this stage, the full neural network model is trained using the cross-entropy loss (LCE) on the given dataset. The model parameters are initialized with w_0, and the optimization is performed for N_1 steps using gradient descent. The cross-entropy loss is defined as the sum of the logarithmic loss of each class label for each input in the training set. Formally, the f can be updated through:

$$\mathcal{L}_{CE}(\theta) := \sum_i y_i log f(\theta; x_i) \tag{7}$$

Stage 2: Module Structure Probe Subnetwork architecture is learned at this stage. The algorithm samples a binary mask vector $\mathbf{m}$ = sigmoidπ, where π is a learnable parameter that determines the importance of each weight in the network. The loss function in stage 2 is defined as:

$$\mathcal{L}_{MOD}(\theta) = \mathcal{L}_{CE}(\mathbf{m} \odot \theta) + \alpha \sum_l \pi_l \tag{8}$$

where l denotes the i-th layer of the network, α is a hyperparameter and $\odot$ refers to the Hadamard product.

Stage 3: Subnetwork Retrain In this stage, the learned subnetwork architecture is used to retrain the full neural network model. The subnetwork mask vector $\mathbf{m}$ is obtained by applying hard thresholding $\mathbf{m} = \{\pi_l > 0 | l = 1, 2, \dots\}$. The model parameters are set back to their initial value w_0, and the optimization is performed for N_1 steps using $L_{CE}(\mathbf{m} \odot \theta)$.

The MRM algorithm iterates through Stages 2 and 3 until the desired level of sparsity is achieved in the learned subnetwork architecture. The resulting sparse network architecture can improve the generalization performance of the neural network by reducing overfitting and increasing its capacity to capture the relevant features of the input data.

DisEnt. DisEnt [26] is a feature-level augmentation strategy. By utilizing additional synthesized biased features during the training, DisEnt performed well in classification and debiasing results. In DisEnt, two separate encoders are trained to embed images into two latent vectors corresponding to the target attributes and biased attributes, respectively. The network is then updated by concatenating the two hidden vectors and using them as inputs to the two classifiers. To further improve the process of learning the target feature vectors, swapping two potential vectors among the training sets is used to diversify the samples with conflicting biases. Specifically, DisEnt randomly permutes the target features and biased features in each mini-batch to obtain the swapped features.

While training with additional synthetic features helps to avoid spurious correlations, utilizing these features from the beginning of the training process does not improve denoising performance. More specifically, in DisEnt, feature augmentation is performed after some training iterations, when the two features are disentangled to a certain extent.

4.2 Datasets

We perform image classification experiments on three popular image datasets. As shown in Fig. 2, most of the data in the dataset are bias-aligned (gray background box), while a few are bias-conflicting (green background box). For Colored MNIST (CMNIST) and Corrupted CIFAR-10 (CIFAR-10-C), according to the different proportions of bias-conflicting samples (0.5%, 1%, 2%, and 5%), we have four train sets. For Gender-biased FFHQ (BFFHQ), the bias-conflicting data is 0.5%.

Colored MNIST (CMNIST). Colored MNIST (CMNIST) [2] was proposed to be a variant of the original MNIST dataset [25], In Colored MNIST, color information is added to the images by assigning a random RGB color value to each pixel in the image. Therefore, unlike the original MNIST dataset, CMNIST has a label indicating the color in addition to a target label. We use the number corresponding to the image as the target label and the color as the bias label. Inspired by [26,44], we chose the dataset with ten different colors and set a one-to-one correspondence with the ten numerical labels (e.g., "2"↔ "green", "4" ↔"yellow"). Images that did not follow this correspondence are randomly assigned colors. We name the data that follow this correspondence *bias-align* and the data that do not follow this correspondence *bias-conflict*. So our dataset

Fig. 2. Examples of datasets. Sub-figure (a) is samples from the Colored MNIST dataset, sub-figure (b) is samples from the Corrupted CIFAR-10 dataset, and sub-figure (c) is samples from the Gender-biased FFHQ dataset. Each dataset consists of two more parts of data: the data at the upper part (gray background box) is the bias-aligned majority data set, and the data at the lower part (green background box) is the bias-conflicting minority data set. (Color figure online)

consists of *bias-align* and *bias-conflict*. The training data has the majority of *bias-align* data (e.g., 99%). The data in the test set do not have the number label and color label correlation that exist in the training set. So the test set can be used to evaluate the out-of-distribution performance of the model.

Corrupted CIFAR-10 (CIFAR-10-C). Corrupted CIFAR-10 (CIFAR-10-C) [15] is a variant of CIFAR-10 dataset. a dataset is obtained by applying ten textures to the images of the b dataset. In the CIFAR-10-C, the classes of images and the types of textures applied are highly correlated, i.e., most of the images in the same class have the same texture applied to them. So the model trained on a dataset with such a strong association will perform poorly when tested on a data distribution without that association. In our experiments, CIFAR-10-C also consists of *bias-conflict* and *bias-align*. Similar to the CMNIST, we also constructed four training sets based on the different proportions of *bias-conflict* samples.

Gender-biased FFHQ (BFFHQ). Gender-biased FFHQ (BFFHQ) [23] is built from the data of FlickrFaces-HQ (FFHQ) [20]. FFHQ contains face images with multiple face attribute labels, including age, race, gender, glasses and hat. We choose "age" and "gender" as the target and bias labels. In the training set, most of the images have a "young" attribute for "female" and an "old attribute for "male". So the "younger" label

Table 1. The results of floating-point operations per second (FLOPs) during training/testing and the number of parameters. We report the results of CIFAR-10-C for ResNet-18 and BFFHQ for Simple CNN.

	ResNet-18			Simple CNN		
Models	FLOPs	FLOPs	Para	FLOPs	FLOPs	Para
Dense	$1 \times (4.41e16)$	$1 \times (3.27e9)$	11.17M	$1 \times (5.68e16)$	$1 \times (3.44e9)$	0.661M
REST	$0.02\times$	$0.016\times$	0.056M	$0.007\times$	$0.0075\times$	0.0032M

in the training set has a strong correlation with the "female" attributes, which will lead the model to classify the age of the images based on the gender attributes. We use a training set in which the sample of *bias-conflict* is 0.5%.

4.3 Setup

Models. For CMNIST, we use a convolutional network with three convolution layers, in which the feature map dimensions are 64, 128, and 256, respectively (named "Simple CNN" in this paper). Following [35,44], we add ReLU activation and a batch normalization layer after each convolution layer. For CIFAR-10-C and BFFHQ, we use ResNet-18 [14].

Training Details. For the reweighting parameter β_{Pe} in the reweighting, we set as $\{10, 30, 50, 80\}$ for CMNIST and CIFAR-10-C with$\{0.5\%, 1.0\%, 2.0\%, 5.0\%\}$ of bias ratio, respectively. For BFFHQ, we set β_{Pe} =80. We use the Adam optimizer [24], weight decay = $1 \cdot 10^{-4}$, $\beta 1$ = 0.9, $\beta 2$ = 0.999. We use the learning rate= $1 \cdot 10^{-2}$ for CMNIST and $1 \cdot 10^{-3}$ for CMNIST and BFFHQ. We set the $update\ frequency = 1000$ as the number of iterations to train between parameter explorations. We set up three different seeds and report their average values as the experimental results.

4.4 Computational Costs

In order to understand the computational demands of various methods, we utilized FLOPs as a measure of the computational consumption of each method. FLOPs stands for Floating Point Operations, and it is a metric used to quantify the number of arithmetic operations (addition, subtraction, multiplication, and division) carried out by a computer when executing a particular algorithm or method. To further explore the computational consumption of different methods, we evaluate their performance during training and testing of both ResNet-18 and convolutional neural networks. During the evaluation process, we computed the number of FLOPs required for each method to complete a task or operation within the networks. By comparing the number of FLOPs required by each method, we were able to assess their relative efficiency and identify the methods that consume less computational resources.

We report the results of FLOPs in Table 1. For ResNet-18, the dense model required high FLOPs during training at $4.41e16$, which is significantly higher than our method.

Table 2. The accuracy of image classification on three datasets. We conduct experiments on a simple CNN and model ResNet-18. For Colored MNIST and Corrupted CIFAR-10, we evaluate the accuracy using unbiased test sets and report the unbiased test accuracy. For BFFHQ, we report the bias-conflicting test accuracy. "Ratio (%)" denotes the proportion of bias-conflict data in the training data. For our proposed method, we report the accuracy of REST under the best density (the numbers in parentheses). The best-performing results are indicated in bold.

Dataset	Model	Ratio (%)	ERM	MRM	DisEnt	REST
CMNIST	Simple CNN	0.5	45.7	43.5	43.1	**48.3** (0.050)
		1.0	69.6	70.3	65.9	**72.1** (0.050)
		2.0	83.3	83.9	79.8	**84.8** (0.005)
		5.0	93.2	92.8	92.3	**93.7** (0.005)
CIFAR-10-C	ResNet-18	0	25.9	**26.7**	18.5	**26.7** (0.050)
		1.0	27.4	26.8	21.0	**28.8** (0.005)
		2.0	31.0	30.1	25.9	**33.1** (0.005)
		5.0	37.0	37.7	39.2	**39.4** (0.005)
BFFHQ	ResNet-18	0.5	41.8	53.5	54.2	**63.5** (0.0005)

During testing, the dense model also required high FLOPs, with a value of $3.27e9$. Our method only requires 2% and 1.6% FLOPs of the dense model for training and testing, respectively. And our method only retains 0.49% and 0.48% number of the parameters of ResNet-18 and Simple CNN, respectively.

4.5 Main Results

We analyze the experimental results of our proposed method and compare it with three baseline methods: ERM, MRM [44], and DisEnt [26]. We evaluate the performance of these methods on three different datasets: Colored MNIST, Corrupted CIFAR-10, and BFFHQ.

From Table 2, we can see that our proposed method outperforms all the baseline methods on all three datasets. In particular, for the BFFHQ dataset, our method demonstrates a significant improvement over the original ERM, with a large gap. This indicates that our method is effective in handling bias-conflicting data and improving the accuracy of image classification.

It is also notable that the sparsities with the best performance during sparse training are very high, retaining only 0.05, 0.005, and even 0.0005 of the parameters of the original neural network. This suggests that our method is capable of achieving good performance with highly compact neural networks, which can be beneficial for real-world applications where computational resources are limited.

In terms of the baseline methods, we can see that MRM and DisEnt generally perform better than the original ERM on all datasets, but they are still outperformed by our proposed method. This highlights the effectiveness of our approach in handling bias-conflicting data and improving the robustness of image classification.

Table 3. Performance of different sparse training on three data. We report the best performance of each sparse training method among the sparsity set. The number in parentheses indicates the sparsity level. The best results are indicated in bold.

Dataset	Model	Ratio(%)	RigL	REST
CMNIST	Simple CNN	0.5	36.3 (0.050)	**48.3** (0.050)
		1.0	60.1 (0.050)	**72.1** (0.050)
		2.0	74.7 (0.005)	**84.8** (0.005)
		5.0	89.5 (0.005)	**93.7** (0.005)
CIFAR-10-C	ResNet-18	0.5	23.5 (0.050)	**26.7** (0.050)
		1.0	26.0 (0.005)	**28.8** (0.005)
		2.0	30.9 (0.005)	**33.1** (0.005)
		5.0	37.4 (0.005)	**39.4** (0.005)
BFFHQ	ResNet-18	0.5	50 (0.0005)	**63.6** (0.0005)

Our experimental results in Table 2 demonstrate that our proposed method is effective in handling bias-conflicting data and improving the accuracy of image classification. Moreover, it shows that highly compact neural networks can achieve good performance, which can be beneficial for real-world applications with limited computational resources.

4.6 Ablation Study

We also implemented an ablation experiment to help analyze the effectiveness of our method. We report the performance difference between RigL and our method on three datasets in Table 3. Also, we compare the performance of our method at different sparsity levels. Specifically, we report the varying sparsity levels on the CIFAR-10-C dataset with 5% bias-conflicting data. The CIFAR-10-C dataset consisted of images of objects from ten different classes, and it contains a diverse set of image corruptions.

Diverse Sparse Levels. In this ablation study, we investigated the impact of sparsity on the performance of sparse models. To achieve this, we conducted experiments at fourteen different densities ranging from 0.0005 to 0.9 and compared the performance of sparse models to that of a dense model.

As depicted in Fig. 3, the performance of the sparse models were evaluated based on their image classification accuracy, and the red line represented the accuracy of the sparse model after our methods were applied. We also evaluated the accuracy of both bias-conflicting and unbiased test data. It was observed that the accuracy of the unbiased test was consistently higher than that of the bias-conflicting data for both models, indicating the problem of spurious correlation.

Furthermore, the level of density had a significant impact on the accuracy of the model. When the density was too low, the model's accuracy was very low, and when the density was increased to 0.005, the model's accuracy improved significantly. This indicates that some density levels can help the model avoid learning spuriously correlated features. However, as the density increased beyond this point, the accuracy of

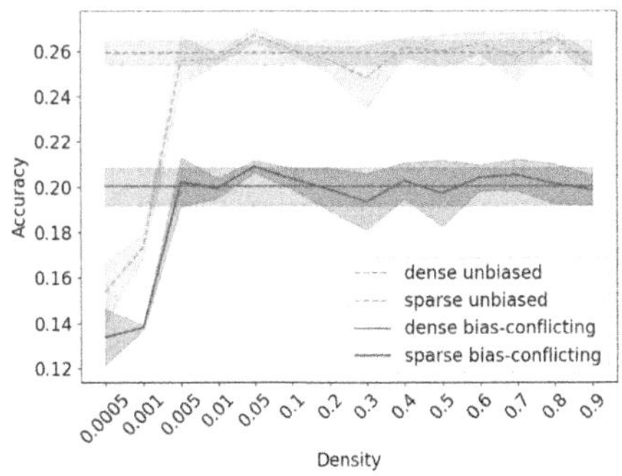

(a) Ratio 0.5%

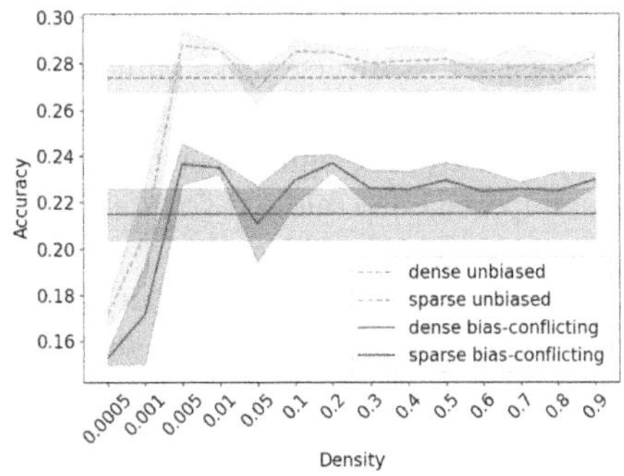

(b) Ratio 1%

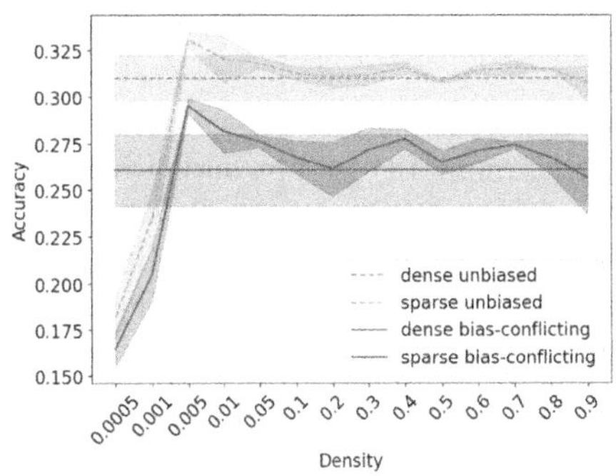

(c) Ratio 2%

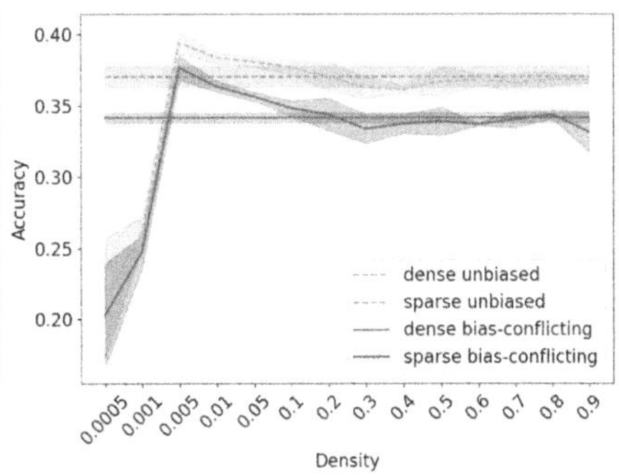

(d) Ratio 5%

Fig. 3. Performance of RigL under different sparsity on CIFAR-10-C datasets with different ratios of bias-conflicting data. The green line represents the performance of the dense model, and the red line represents the performance of the sparse model after different sparse training. The solid line indicates the accuracy of bias-conflicting data in the test data, and the dashed line indicates the unbiased test accuracy. (Color figure online)

the model gradually decreased, indicating that the model was learning more spuriously correlated features as the number of model parameters increased.

The results in Fig. 3 highlight the effectiveness of our method that balances model complexity and performance by avoiding over-parameterization. It also emphasizes the importance of selecting an appropriate density level to optimize the performance of sparse models. Overall, our findings from Fig. 3 provide valuable insights into the impact of sparsity on the performance of sparse models, which can help develop more efficient and accurate models.

Diverse Bias-conflicting Data Ratio. In addition to evaluating the impact of sparsity on the performance of sparse models, Fig. 3 also presents the performance of sparse training on data with varying bias-conflicting ratios. As shown in Fig. 3, the accuracy of both dense and sparse models increases with a higher proportion of bias-conflicted data. This suggests that models trained on bias-conflicting data are more robust and have a better generalization performance.

Moreover, it was observed that sparse training effectively enhances the model's performance across diverse bias-conflicting ratio data. This indicates that our method can improve the model's ability to generalize to various types of data with different levels of bias. By leveraging sparsity regularization, the model can learn to identify the most important and relevant features of the data while ignoring irrelevant and spurious features, leading to improved performance and generalization.

Overall, these findings further demonstrate the effectiveness of our method in enhancing the performance of out-of-distribution generalization, even in the presence of varying levels of bias-conflicting data. Our results suggest that applying our method in the training process can help to improve the robustness and generalization performance of machine learning models, which can be beneficial in various real-world applications.

5 Conclusion

The over-parameterized models learned from a large number of bias-aligned training samples often struggle to perform well on certain minority groups during inference, despite showing strong performance on the majority of data groups. To address this issue, we proposed a novel reweighted sparse training framework called REST, which aims to enhance the performance on various biased datasets while improving computation and memory efficiency, through the lens of sparse neural network training. Our experimental results demonstrate that REST can reduce the reliance on spuriously correlated features and improve performance across a wider range of data groups with fewer training and inference resources. By reducing the reliance on spurious correlations, REST represents a promising approach for improving the performance of DNNs on biased datasets while simultaneously improving their robustness and generalization capabilities.

Acknowledgements. This work used the Dutch national e-infrastructure with the support of the SURF Cooperative using grant no. EINF-3953/L1.

Ethical Statement. As researchers in the field of deep neural networks, we recognize the importance of developing methods that improve the generalization capabilities of these models, particularly for minority groups that may be underrepresented in training data. Our proposed reweighted sparse training framework, REST, aims to tackle the issue of bias-conflicting correlations in DNNs by reducing reliance on spurious correlations. We believe that this work has the potential to enhance the robustness of DNNs and improve their performance on out-of-distribution samples, which may have significant implications for various applications such as healthcare and criminal justice. However, we acknowledge that there may be ethical considerations associated with the development and deployment of machine learning algorithms, particularly those that may impact human lives. As such, we encourage the responsible use and evaluation of our proposed framework to ensure that it aligns with ethical standards and does not perpetuate biases or harm vulnerable populations.

References

1. Agarwal, A., Beygelzimer, A., Dudík, M., Langford, J., Wallach, H.: A reductions approach to fair classification. In: International Conference on Machine Learning, pp. 60–69. PMLR (2018)
2. Arjovsky, M., Bottou, L., Gulrajani, I., Lopez-Paz, D.: Invariant risk minimization. arXiv preprint arXiv:1907.02893 (2019)
3. Beery, S., Van Horn, G., Perona, P.: Recognition in terra incognita. In: Proceedings of the European Conference on Computer Vision (ECCV), pp. 456–473 (2018)
4. Ben-Tal, A., Den Hertog, D., De Waegenaere, A., Melenberg, B., Rennen, G.: Robust solutions of optimization problems affected by uncertain probabilities. Manag. Sci. **59**(2), 341–357 (2013)
5. Byrd, J., Lipton, Z.: What is the effect of importance weighting in deep learning? In: International Conference on Machine Learning, pp. 872–881. PMLR (2019)
6. Dettmers, T., Zettlemoyer, L.: Sparse networks from scratch: faster training without losing performance. arXiv preprint arXiv:1907.04840 (2019)
7. Dietrich, A., Gressmann, F., Orr, D., Chelombiev, I., Justus, D., Luschi, C.: Towards structured dynamic sparse pre-training of bert. arXiv preprint arXiv:2108.06277 (2021)
8. Duchi, J., Glynn, P., Namkoong, H.: Statistics of robust optimization: a generalized empirical likelihood approach. arXiv preprint arXiv:1610.03425 (2016)
9. Duchi, J.C., Hashimoto, T., Namkoong, H.: Distributionally robust losses against mixture covariate shifts (2019)
10. Evci, U., Gale, T., Menick, J., Castro, P.S., Elsen, E.: Rigging the lottery: making all tickets winners. In: International Conference on Machine Learning, pp. 2943–2952. PMLR (2020)
11. Gale, T., Elsen, E., Hooker, S.: The state of sparsity in deep neural networks. arXiv preprint arXiv:1902.09574 (2019)
12. Geirhos, R., Rubisch, P., Michaelis, C., Bethge, M., Wichmann, F.A., Brendel, W.: Imagenet-trained cnns are biased towards texture; increasing shape bias improves accuracy and robustness. arXiv preprint arXiv:1811.12231 (2018)
13. Goel, K., Gu, A., Li, Y., Ré, C.: Model patching: closing the subgroup performance gap with data augmentation. arXiv preprint arXiv:2008.06775 (2020)
14. He, K., Zhang, X., Ren, S., Sun, J.: Deep residual learning for image recognition. In: Proceedings of the IEEE Conference on Computer Vision and Pattern Recognition, pp. 770–778 (2016)
15. Hendrycks, D., Dietterich, T.: Benchmarking neural network robustness to common corruptions and perturbations. arXiv preprint arXiv:1903.12261 (2019)
16. Huang, T., Liu, S., Shen, L., He, F., Lin, W., Tao, D.: On heterogeneously distributed data, sparsity matters. In: Submitted to The Tenth International Conference on Learning Representations (2022). https://openreview.net/forum?id=AT0K-SZ3QGq
17. Huang, X., Belongie, S.: Arbitrary style transfer in real-time with adaptive instance normalization. In: Proceedings of the IEEE International Conference on Computer Vision, pp. 1501–1510 (2017)
18. Izmailov, P., Kirichenko, P., Gruver, N., Wilson, A.G.: On feature learning in the presence of spurious correlations. arXiv preprint arXiv:2210.11369 (2022)
19. Jayakumar, S., Pascanu, R., Rae, J., Osindero, S., Elsen, E.: Top-kast: Top-k always sparse training. Adv. Neural Inf. Process. Syst. **33**, 20744–20754 (2020)
20. Karras, T., Laine, S., Aila, T.: A style-based generator architecture for generative adversarial networks. In: Proceedings of the IEEE/CVF Conference on Computer Vision and Pattern Recognition, pp. 4401–4410 (2019)

21. Kepner, J., Robinett, R.: Radix-net: structured sparse matrices for deep neural networks. In: 2019 IEEE International Parallel and Distributed Processing Symposium Workshops (IPDPSW), pp. 268–274. IEEE (2019)
22. Khani, F., Raghunathan, A., Liang, P.: Maximum weighted loss discrepancy. arXiv preprint arXiv:1906.03518 (2019)
23. Kim, E., Lee, J., Choo, J.: Biaswap: removing dataset bias with bias-tailored swapping augmentation. In: Proceedings of the IEEE/CVF International Conference on Computer Vision, pp. 14992–15001 (2021)
24. Kingma, D.P., Ba, J.: Adam: a method for stochastic optimization. arXiv preprint arXiv:1412.6980 (2014)
25. LeCun, Y., Bottou, L., Bengio, Y., Haffner, P.: Gradient-based learning applied to document recognition. Proc. IEEE **86**(11), 2278–2324 (1998)
26. Lee, J., Kim, E., Lee, J., Lee, J., Choo, J.: Learning debiased representation via disentangled feature augmentation. Adv. Neural Inf. Process. Syst. **34**, 25123–25133 (2021)
27. Liu, E.Z., et al.: Just train twice: improving group robustness without training group information. In: International Conference on Machine Learning, pp. 6781–6792. PMLR (2021)
28. Liu, S., et al.: Deep ensembling with no overhead for either training or testing: the all-round blessings of dynamic sparsity. arXiv preprint arXiv:2106.14568 (2021)
29. Liu, S., et al.: Sparse training via boosting pruning plasticity with neuroregeneration. Adv. Neural Inf. Process. Syst. **34**, 9908–9922 (2021)
30. Liu, S., Yin, L., Mocanu, D.C., Pechenizkiy, M.: Do we actually need dense over-parameterization? in-time over-parameterization in sparse training. In: International Conference on Machine Learning, pp. 6989–7000. PMLR (2021)
31. Mocanu, D.C., Mocanu, E., Nguyen, P.H., Gibescu, M., Liotta, A.: A topological insight into restricted boltzmann machines. Mach. Learn. **104**(2), 243–270 (2016)
32. Mocanu, D.C., Mocanu, E., Stone, P., Nguyen, P.H., Gibescu, M., Liotta, A.: Scalable training of artificial neural networks with adaptive sparse connectivity inspired by network science. Nature Commun. **9**(1), 1–12 (2018)
33. Mostafa, H., Wang, X.: Parameter efficient training of deep convolutional neural networks by dynamic sparse reparameterization. In: International Conference on Machine Learning (2019)
34. Nam, J., Cha, H., Ahn, S., Lee, J., Shin, J.: Learning from failure: de-biasing classifier from biased classifier. Adv. Neural Inf. Process. Syst. **33**, 20673–20684 (2020)
35. Park, G.Y., Lee, S., Lee, S.W., Ye, J.C.: Efficient debiasing with contrastive weight pruning. arXiv preprint arXiv:2210.05247 (2022)
36. Prabhu, A., Varma, G., Namboodiri, A.: Deep expander networks: efficient deep networks from graph theory. In: Proceedings of the European Conference on Computer Vision (ECCV), pp. 20–35 (2018)
37. Sagawa, S., Koh, P.W., Hashimoto, T.B., Liang, P.: Distributionally robust neural networks for group shifts: on the importance of regularization for worst-case generalization. arXiv preprint arXiv:1911.08731 (2019)
38. Sagawa, S., Raghunathan, A., Koh, P.W., Liang, P.: An investigation of why overparameterization exacerbates spurious correlations. In: International Conference on Machine Learning, pp. 8346–8356. PMLR (2020)
39. Shimodaira, H.: Improving predictive inference under covariate shift by weighting the log-likelihood function. J. Stat. Plan. Inference **90**(2), 227–244 (2000)
40. Tanaka, H., Kunin, D., Yamins, D.L., Ganguli, S.: Pruning neural networks without any data by iteratively conserving synaptic flow. In: Advances in Neural Information Processing Systems. arXiv:2006.05467 (2020)
41. Yao, H., et al.: Improving out-of-distribution robustness via selective augmentation. arXiv preprint arXiv:2201.00299 (2022)

42. Yin, L., Menkovski, V., Fang, M., Huang, T., Pei, Y., Pechenizkiy, M.: Superposing many tickets into one: a performance booster for sparse neural network training. In: Uncertainty in Artificial Intelligence, pp. 2267–2277. PMLR (2022)
43. Yuan, G., et al.: Mest: accurate and fast memory-economic sparse training framework on the edge. Adv. Neural Inf. Process. Syst. **34** (2021)
44. Zhang, D., Ahuja, K., Xu, Y., Wang, Y., Courville, A.: Can subnetwork structure be the key to out-of-distribution generalization? In: International Conference on Machine Learning, pp. 12356–12367. PMLR (2021)
45. Zhao, J., Fang, M., Shi, Z., Li, Y., Chen, L., Pechenizkiy, M.: Chbias: bias evaluation and mitigation of Chinese conversational language models. In: Proceedings of the 61th Annual Meeting of the Association for Computational Linguistics. Association for Computational Linguistics, Toronto (2023)

How to Overcome Confirmation Bias in Semi-Supervised Image Classification by Active Learning

Sandra Gilhuber[1,2](✉), Rasmus Hvingelby[3], Mang Ling Ada Fok[3], and Thomas Seidl[1,2,3]

[1] LMU Munich, Munich, Germany
{gilhuber,seidl}@dbs.ifi.lmu.de
[2] Munich Center for Machine Learning (MCML), Munich, Germany
[3] Fraunhofer IIS, Erlangen, Germany
rasmus.hvingelby@iis.fraunhofer.de

Abstract. Do we need active learning? The rise of strong deep semi-supervised methods raises doubt about the usability of active learning in limited labeled data settings. This is caused by results showing that combining semi-supervised learning (SSL) methods with a random selection for labeling can outperform existing active learning (AL) techniques. However, these results are obtained from experiments on well-established benchmark datasets that can overestimate the external validity. However, the literature lacks sufficient research on the performance of active semi-supervised learning methods in realistic data scenarios, leaving a notable gap in our understanding. Therefore we present three data challenges common in real-world applications: between-class imbalance, within-class imbalance, and between-class similarity. These challenges can hurt SSL performance due to confirmation bias. We conduct experiments with SSL and AL on simulated data challenges and find that random sampling does not mitigate confirmation bias and, in some cases, leads to worse performance than supervised learning. In contrast, we demonstrate that AL can overcome confirmation bias in SSL in these realistic settings. Our results provide insights into the potential of combining active and semi-supervised learning in the presence of common real-world challenges, which is a promising direction for robust methods when learning with limited labeled data in real-world applications.

1 Introduction

The success of supervised deep learning models largely depends on the availability of sufficient, qualitative labeled data. Since manual annotation is time-consuming and costly, various research directions focus on machine learning with limited labeled data. While Active Learning (AL) [5,40] aims to label only

S. Gilhuber and R. Hvingelby—Equal contribution.

© The Author(s), under exclusive license to Springer Nature Switzerland AG 2023
D. Koutra et al. (Eds.): ECML PKDD 2023, LNAI 14170, pp. 330–347, 2023.
https://doi.org/10.1007/978-3-031-43415-0_20

the most informative and valuable data intelligently, semi-supervised learning (SSL) [8,13,41] aims to exploit the information in the unlabeled pool without asking for new labels. Given the complementary nature of SSL and AL, it is intuitive to explore their integration within a unified framework to maximize the utilization of the available data. However, the effectiveness of AL has been questioned recently [7,11,31,33]. Some works show that other learning paradigms capable of exploiting the unlabeled data do not experience added value from biased and intelligent data selection through AL [11].

However, these findings are mainly based on experiments on well-established, clean benchmark datasets. But, an excessive emphasis on benchmark performance can result in diminishing returns where increasingly large efforts lead to ever-decreasing performance gains on the actual task [29,45]. As a result, an exclusive evaluation of such benchmarks can raise concerns about the transferability of these results to challenges in real-world applications. Therefore, we review the literature on AL to understand which datasets are commonly used for evaluation and to what extent AL has been combined with SSL.

Toward a better understanding, we first categorize existing AL methods into four groups, namely uncertainty sampling, representativeness sampling, coverage-based sampling, and balanced sampling. Second, we introduce the following three real-world challenges: (1) *Between-class imbalance* (BCI), where the distribution over class instances is non-uniform, (2) *within-class imbalance* (WCI), where the intra-class distribution is non-uniform, and (3) *between-class similarity* (BCS), where the class boundaries are ambiguous. In our experiments, we demonstrate that each of these real-world challenges introduces confirmation bias reinforcing biased or misleading concepts toward SSL. Moreover, randomly increasing the labeled pool may not effectively address the posed challenges. In fact, the results stagnate early or are even worse than plain supervised learning. In contrast, we evaluate simple AL heuristics on the introduced challenges and show that active data selection leads to much better generalization performance in these cases. This provides empirical evidence of the benefits of incorporating AL techniques to mitigate the impact of real-world challenges in SSL.

Our main contributions are:

- We provide a thorough literature review on the real-world validity of current evaluation protocols for active and semi-supervised learning. We find that the combination is especially understudied in real-world datasets.
- We explore well-established SSL methods in three real-world challenges and find that confirmation bias in SSL is a problem in all studied challenges and leads to degraded performance.
- We show that, in contrast to random selection, *actively* increasing the labeled pool can mitigate these problems.

2 Related Work

The advantages of AL have been questioned due to the strong performance of methods exploiting knowledge available in unlabeled data [7,11,33].

Given AL aims to increase model performance while decreasing annotation efforts, it is important not to focus on AL in isolation when other training techniques can lead to improvements in model performance. This makes the evaluation of AL challenging [32] as there are many ways to configure AL, and it can be hard to know upfront what works in a real-world scenario.

Our focus is specifically on three realistic data scenarios that can lead SSL to underperform due to confirmation bias.

2.1 Real World Considerations in Machine Learning

The evaluation of the algorithmic progress on a task can be separated into *internal* validity and *external* validity [29]. When benchmark results are internally valid, the improvements caused by an algorithm are valid within the same dataset. However, the overuse of the same test sets in benchmarks can lead to adaptive overfitting where the models and hyperparameters yielding strong performance are reused, and the improvements are not necessarily caused by algorithmic improvements. On the other hand, external validity refers to whether improvements also translate to other datasets for the same task. It has been observed that an excessive emphasis on benchmark performance can result in diminishing returns where increasingly large efforts lead to smaller and smaller performance gains on the actual task [29,45]. To improve the validity of benchmark results, it is important that the datasets used for evaluation reflect the data challenges that occur in real-world scenarios.

Considering data challenges has been a well-studied field in machine learning. Lopez et al. [30] investigate how data intrinsic characteristics in imbalanced datasets affect classification performance and specify six problems that occur in real-world data. Both [42] and [50] also focus on imbalanced data and discuss difficulty factors that deteriorate classification performance. [42] further demonstrates that these factors have a larger impact than the imbalance ratio or the size of the minority class. [14] investigates data irregularities that can lead to a degradation in classification performance. However, to the best of our knowledge studying data challenges in limited labeled scenarios has not yet been well studied [32,35,49].

2.2 Evaluation of AL in the Literature

To get an understanding of the data commonly used for evaluation in limited labels scenarios, we performed a literature overview of the papers published in 13 top-venue conferences[1] within Artificial Intelligence, Machine Learning, Computer Vision, Natural Language Processing and Data Mining between 2018 and 2022. We selected papers for screening if "*active learning*" occurs in the title and abstract, resulting in 392 papers. When screening, we included papers that empirically study the improvement of machine learning models for image

[1] ACL, AAAI, CVPR, ECCV, ECML PKDD, EMNLP, ICCV, ICDM, ICLR, ICML, IJCAI, KDD, and NeurIPS.

classification when expanding the pool of labeled data, as is common in AL papers. Based on this inclusion criteria, we first screened the title and abstracts, and if we could not exclude a study only on the title and abstract, we did a full-text screening. Following this screening process, we identified 51 papers.

We find that 47 (94%) of the studies experimented on at least one benchmark dataset, and 38 (75%) of the studies experiments solely on benchmark datasets[2]. To understand how common it is to evaluate AL in more realistic data scenarios, we count how many papers consider the data challenges BCI, WCI, or BCS or experiments on non-benchmark datasets. We find that 23 (45%) papers consider real-world data challenges or evaluate non-benchmark datasets. The most common data challenge is BCI which 15 (29%) of the papers are considering. As AL can be improved with other training techniques, we look at how many papers combine AL and SSL and find that this is done by 13 (25%) of the papers. However, only 5 (10%) evaluate the performances in realistic scenarios.

3 Learning with Limited Labeled Data

Given an input space $\mathcal{X}$ and a label space $\mathbf{Y}$, we consider the limited labeled scenario where we assume a small labeled pool $\mathcal{X}^l \subset \mathcal{X}$ and a large unlabeled data pool $\mathcal{X}^u = \mathcal{X} \setminus \mathcal{X}^l$. We want to obtain a model $f(x;\theta) \to \mathbb{R}^C$ where parameters θ map a given input $x \in \mathcal{X}$ to a C-dimensional vector. Supervised learning trains a model on $\mathcal{X}^l$ while SSL utilizes both $\mathcal{X}^l$ and $\mathcal{X}^u$.

3.1 Semi-Supervised Learning (SSL)

Many approaches to leverage both labeled and unlabeled data have been suggested in the literature [13,44]. More recently, the utilization of deep learning in SSL has shown impressive performance, and especially different variants of consistency regularization and pseudo-labeling have been studied [49].

Pseudo-labeling [25] uses the model's prediction on the instances in $\mathcal{X}^u$ to filter highly confident samples and include those with their respective pseudo-label in the next training iteration. Pseudo-labeling is a simple and powerful technique for utilizing $\mathcal{X}^u$. However, a model producing incorrect predictions reuses wrong information in training. This is known as confirmation bias [3] and can greatly impact model performance.

Consistency Regularization [8,41] exploits $\mathcal{X}^u$ by encouraging invariant predictions when the input is perturbated, thereby making the model robust to different perturbed versions of unlabeled data. Perturbations of the data can be obtained by introducing random noise to the input data or utilizing data augmentations [41]. Some methods rely heavily on data augmentations which assume that label-preserving data augmentations are available when applying

[2] We consider benchmark datasets as the well-established MNIST, CIFAR10/100, SVHN, FashionMNIST, STL-10, ImageNet (and Tiny-ImageNet), as well as Caltech-101 and Caltech-256.

such methods in real-world use cases. Using consistency regularization in combination with pseudo-labeling helps improve the generalizability through the perturbed data, which can further enforce the confirmation bias if the model predictions are wrong.

3.2 Active Learning (AL)

AL alternates between querying instances for annotation, and re-training the model $f(x;\theta)$ on the increased labeled pool until an annotation budget is exhausted or a certain performance is reached. The so-called acquisition function of an AL strategy determines which instances in $\mathcal{X}^u$ are most valuable and should be labeled to maximize the labeling efficiency. We use the following taxonomy to distinguish between active acquisition types (Fig. 1).

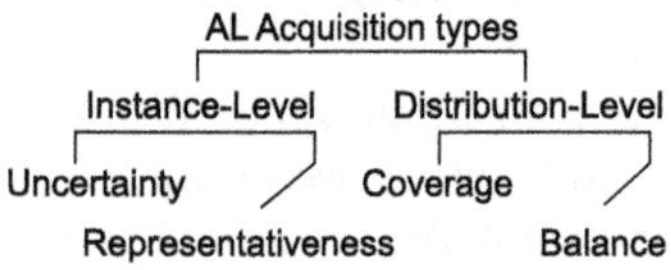

Fig. 1. AL Acquisition Types

Instance-Level Acquisition. Each unlabeled instance $x \in \mathcal{X}^u$ is assigned a scoring individually, independent of already selected instances, and enables a final ranking of all unlabeled instances.

Uncertainty sampling aims to query instances carrying the most novel information for the current learner. Popular estimates are least-confidence, min margin, or max entropy selection [40]. These methods usually query near the class boundaries as illustrated in Fig. 2a. The 2D t-SNE visualization of MNIST shows a mapping of margin uncertainty, where red indicates high and blue indicates low uncertainty. Other methods aim to measure model confidence [18] and to distinguish between aleatoric and epistemic uncertainty [34].

Representative sampling assigns higher scores to instances representative of their class or a certain local region. The central idea is not to select instances to eliminate knowledge gaps in the current learning phase but to find instances that have the *highest impact* on most other instances because, e.g., they are representative of a class or they are similar to many other instances.

One way to define representativeness is to measure centrality, for instance, by exploiting a preceding partitioning and selecting the most central instance of each partitioning [37,55]. Another estimate for representativeness is density, i.e., how many (similar) instances are in the near surrounding of a data point [15, 47]. In Fig. 2b, the colors indicate the negative local outlier score [10] mapped onto the 2D representation of MNIST, which is here used as an indicator for representativeness. A representativeness selection strategy would favor instances in the denser red regions in the center of the clusters.

Distribution-Level Acquisition. In contrast to instance-level, distribution-level acquisition refers to selection strategies that do not consider individual scores for each instance but strive to optimize the distribution of all selected

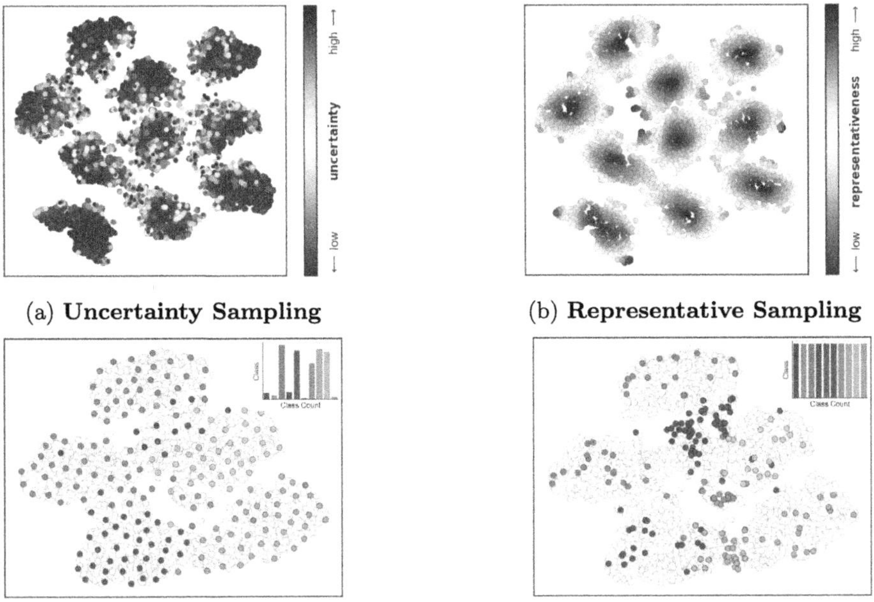

(a) **Uncertainty Sampling**

(b) **Representative Sampling**

(c) **Coverage-Based Sampling**

(d) **Balanced Sampling**

Fig. 2. Exemplary illustration of different acquisition types.

instances. A clear ranking is usually not possible because the worthiness of the next best instance depends on which instance(s) is (have been) selected before.

Coverage-based sampling, sometimes referred to as diversity sampling, aims to cover the given data space to avoid overlap of information best. The goal is to select as diverse instances as possible to maximize the richness of information in the labeled dataset. The most prominent method of this category is k-Center-Greedy which maximizes the distance in the feature space between the queried and the labeled instances [39]. Coverage, or diversity, is a popular companion in hybrid approaches to assist batch-selection acquisitions [4,23,37].

Balanced sampling aims to balance the number of samples per class and is especially suited for imbalanced datasets. This subtype is often combined with other acquisition types, as it does not necessarily select the most valuable instances on its own [1,6,16]. Figure 2c depicts coverage sampling on an imbalanced version of MNIST where the data space is evenly covered. In contrast, Fig. 2d shows balanced sampling where the selected class counts are uniformly distributed.

There is an abundance of hybrid methods combining two or more of the described concepts [4,17,23,37,52]. However, in this work, we focus on highlighting the potential of AL in general and only consider disjoint baseline methods from each category. For an overview of deep AL methods, we refer to [38,51,53].

4 Three Real-World Data Challenges

In the following, we introduce three realistic data challenges. We then present three datasets that implement these challenges on the well-known MNIST task, which we later analyze in our experiments.

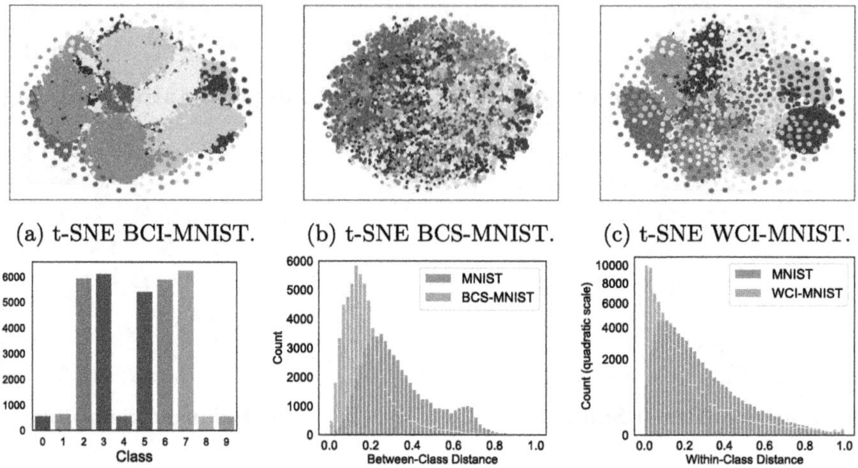

(a) t-SNE BCI-MNIST. (b) t-SNE BCS-MNIST. (c) t-SNE WCI-MNIST.

(d) Class distribution BCI-MNIST. (e) Between-class distances of BCS-MNIST vs. MNIST. (f) Within-class distances of WCI-MNIST vs. MNIST.

Fig. 3. Three realistic challenges (BCI, BCS, WCI) demonstrated on MNIST.

4.1 Between-Class Imbalance (BCI)

Among our challenges, Between-Class Imbalance (BCI) is the most considered in the literature and is a well-known challenge for supervised machine learning models. Imbalanced class distributions pose a problem for SSL methods where unlabeled data is often assumed to be distributed similarly to the labeled data and balanced class distributions. BCI can pose a problem for SSL when there is a mismatch between the labeled and unlabeled class distributions [35] or simply because some classes are generally underrepresented in both the unlabeled and labeled pool [21]. However, class distributions in real-world datasets often follow a long-tail distribution. While class imbalance has been studied for both AL and SSL separately, an open question remains regarding how to leverage AL techniques to address the negative effects of class imbalance in SSL.

4.2 Between-Class Similarity (BCS)

Another category of data challenges is Between-Class Similarity (BCS). In real-world datasets, the boundaries between classes can be hard to draw. Instances within the same class can differ widely, and conversely, instances from different classes can be very similar. High within-class diversity and similarity between classes happens naturally in many image classification tasks, e.g., diatom or plankton classification [46] or within histopathology [43].

Datasets with BCS are a challenge for techniques that rely on unlabeled data for model training, since that contradicts the basic assumptions of SSL. For instance, according to [12], Fixmatch exacerbates confusion when instances across classes are similar. The degree of BCS determines whether it is advantageous to sample from class boundaries while the classes can still be differentiated or to prioritize selecting representative instances without ambiguity in the class assignment. Consequently, this challenge presents an opportunity for AL to identify and label such samples. This problem does not only occur on hard-to-solve tasks with high aleatoric uncertainty. Ambiguous label information can also occur due to the labeling procedure e.g. when data is labeled by multiple annotators which can introduce labeling variations [36], or when labels are acquired automatifcally [27,45]. Label noise can have a large impact on SSL as the model is more prone to confirm learned mistakes leading to confirmation bias [28].

Common usage of SSL methods for noisily labeled data is to simply remove noisy labels and continue training with conventional SSL [2]. Alternatively, some algorithms distinguish between cleanly labeled, noisily labeled, and unlabeled data enabling the usage of a massive amount of unlabeled and noisy data under the supervision of a few cleanly annotated data. However, directly coupling the data selection actively to the training can be an easy and thus attractive solution to directly account for label noise or ambiguous class labels without post-processing wrong labels or complex algorithms and wasted labeling efforts.

4.3 Within-Class Imbalance (WCI)

Imbalance is not only a problem across classes but also within classes [20,22]. Although instances might belong to the same class, they can have a high variability due to, e.g., pose, lighting, viewpoint, etc. To obtain a model with the most discriminative capabilities, it must be exposed to the variation within the class.

Within-class imbalance (WCI) occurs in many real-world problems. In medical imaging, subgroups such as race or gender exist within classes and are often imbalanced [48]. Similarly, in microscopic classification, the images might have different viewpoints forming diverse [46] and imbalanced [26] subclusters. In automatic defect detection for manufacturing systems, the different types of defects are often all grouped into the same superordinate class and can be very diverse and imbalanced [20]. It has also been shown that repetition of subclasses containing highly similar samples occurs in commonly used image classification benchmark datasets [9], leading to some subclasses that contain redundant semantic information being overrepresented.

WCI, similar to BCI, leads to the minority subclass being exposed less in the optimization process and contributing less to the final model. This leads to a bias towards the majority subclass and suboptimal performance of the learned model. The difference between WCI and BCI lies in the lack of subclass labels. This deems common solutions for BCI that rely on sampling or cost-aware learning irrelevant for WCI as they rely on class labels.

4.4 Challenge Construction

To gain insights into how SSL and AL perform when the data challenges are present, we construct three datasets based on MNIST to reflect the challenges. We intentionally use MNIST as we can isolate any effects of the data challenges instead of the potential complexity of the learning task.

BCI-MNIST. We construct a between-class imbalanced version of MNIST (BCI-MNIST), where 50% of the classes only contain approximately 10% of the instances. Figure 3a and Fig. 3d illustrate the distribution of the imbalanced version in a 2D t-SNE plot, and a barplot respectively.

BCS-MNIST. Figure 3b shows a 2D t-SNE-plot of an ambiguous version of MNIST proposed in [34]. The dataset consists of normal MNIST and Ambiguous MNIST, containing a large fraction of ambiguous instances with questionable labels, thus increasing the class overlap. Figure 3e shows the similarities of each instance to all instances not belonging to the same class. Compared to the original MNIST, the similarity among instances across classes is much higher. In our experiment, we select 5% of instances from the original MNIST dataset and 95% of instances from Ambiguous MNIST and refer to it as BCS-MNIST.

WCI-MNIST. The WCI version of MNIST is constructed with the following procedure: (1) For each class, we create a sub-clustering using the K-means algorithm on the original input features with $k = 300$. (2) For each constructed within-class cluster, we select one instance as the underrepresented subclass except for one majority subclass and remove the remaining instances. (3) We copy all the instances within the majority subclass multiple times to restore the original training set size and randomly add Gaussian noise to create slightly different versions. The 2D t-SNE representation is shown in Fig. 3c. While the class boundaries are sharper than in Fig. 3b, many subgroups within each class are spread around all the data space. Figure 3f shows the summed distance of each instance to the remaining instances of their respective class for MNIST (blue) and our constructed WCI-MNIST (orange). WCI-MNIST has more highly similar instances, and the number of medium distances is much smaller, resulting in a non-linear decrease in intra-class distances and higher within-class imbalance.

5 Experiments

In this section, we evaluate established SSL methods combined with simple AL heuristics on the previously described challenges that ostensibly occur in real-world scenarios. We use the following experimental setup[3].

Backbone and Training. For all experiments, we use a LeNet [24] as backbone as is commonly used for digit recognition. We do not use a validation set as proposed in [35] since it is unrealistic to assume having a validation set when there is hardly any label information. Instead, we train the model for 50 epochs and use early stopping if the model reaches 99% training accuracy following [4]. The learning rate is set to 0.001, and we do not use any scheduler.

SSL. We include pseudo-labeling [25] (PL) with a threshold of 0.95 as baseline without consistency regularization. We further include Fixmatch [41] as it is a well-established consistency regularization technique and Flexmatch [54] as a strong method tackling confirmation bias [49]. Furthermore, we report results on a plain supervised baseline (SPV).

Evaluation. We report average test accuracies over five random seeds for different labeling budgets. Initially, we select 20 labeled instances randomly. Then, we increase the labeled pool to budgets of 50, 100, 150, 200, and 250 labels.

AL. We choose one representative from each of the described categories in Sect. 3.2 to better assess the strength and weaknesses of each acquisition type. We use margin uncertainty [40] as an uncertainty baseline. For representativeness, we perform k-means clustering on the latent features and select the instance closest to the centroid similar to [19,37]. As a coverage-based technique, we include the k-Center-Greedy method proposed in [39]. For balanced sampling, we create a baseline that selects instances proportional to the sum of inverse class frequencies in the current labeled set and the corresponding prediction probability. Though this might not be a strong AL baseline in general, we expect to see a slight improvement in the BCI challenge.

Datasets. We use the three constructed datasets explained in Sect. 4.4 to form the unlabeled pool, as well as the original MNIST. For testing, we use the original MNIST test set to ensure comparable results.

5.1 Experiment "BCI-MNIST"

Figure 4b depicts the average accuracy of supervised learning (SPV, blue), pseudo-labeling (PL, green), Fixmatch (orange), and Flexmatch (red) for different labeling budgets on MNIST (solid) and BCI-MNIST (dashed) with random

[3] See also https://github.com/lmu-dbs/HOCOBIS-AL.

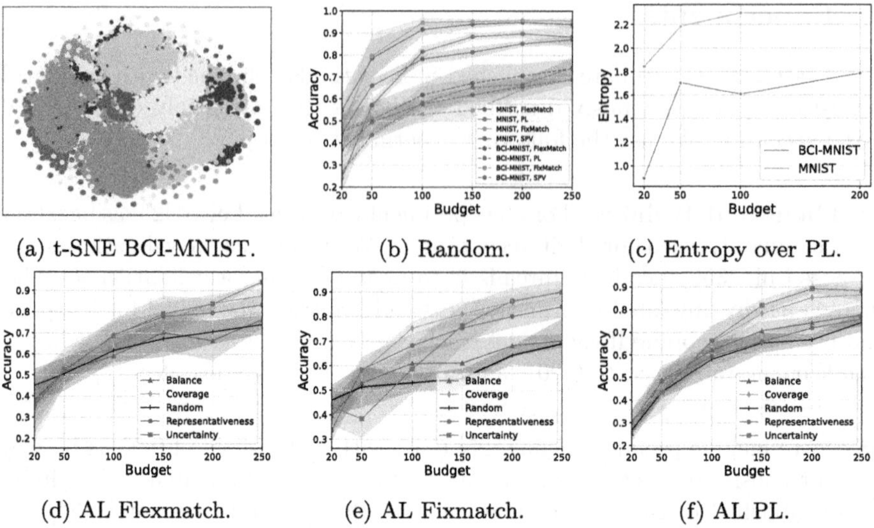

(a) t-SNE BCI-MNIST. (b) Random. (c) Entropy over PL.

(d) AL Flexmatch. (e) AL Fixmatch. (f) AL PL.

Fig. 4. (a) t-SNE of BCI-MNIST challenge. (b) Average test accuracy of all learners evaluated on BCI-MNIST (dashed) and MNIST (solid). In (d), we observe for BCI-MNIST, the entropy over the selected pseudo-labels falling over the threshold for each class is much smaller. This indicates that the distribution of selected pseudo-labels for BCI-MNIST is more imbalanced, repeatedly confirming the imbalance. (d), (e) and (f) show the selected AL curves for Flexmatch, Fixmatch, and PL compared to random sampling (black). (Color figure online)

labeling. BCI has a severe impact on the performance of all learners. However, Fixmatch is affected most and even performs worse than SPV. Since training takes much longer for SSL, [35] argue that these methods should clearly outperform SPV to be considered useful. This is no longer true in our experiment, even on a simple task like MNIST. Figure 4c visualizes the entropy over the number of pseudo-labeled instances per class that Fixmatch would choose for training for BCI-MNIST (blue) and MNIST (orange). On MNIST the entropy is much higher, indicating that the distribution over the classes is more uniformly distributed. The problem is not only that the selected labeled data is imbalanced, but the chosen pseudo-labels repeatedly *confirm* the imbalance, such that the underrepresented classes get even more underrepresented.

However, the AL curves in Figs. 4e and 4f demonstrate that the choice of data selection methods has a substantial impact on the performance of each learner. Fixmatch largely benefits from coverage-based sampling, representative sampling, and uncertainty sampling for later iterations. For the final budget of 250, the gap between coverage and uncertainty acquisition and random selection is around 20%. PL and Flexmatch also greatly benefit from coverage and uncertainty sampling. Coverage sampling is even able to restore the accuracy achieved on MNIST with random sampling, yielding 88.3% for PL and 94.1% for Flexmatch. Interestingly, balanced sampling is not among the best active methods.

Even though the performance is slightly better than random sampling, the other methods are much stronger. This is probably because balanced sampling without the combination of any other method does select less informative and more redundant information.

5.2 Experiment "BCS-MNIST"

Figure 5b illustrates the learning curves for the learners on MNIST and BCS-MNIST. All methods suffer, but Fixmatch clearly suffers the most and is no longer better than plain supervision. In this scenario, there is no additional benefit of exploiting the unlabeled pool, but the training times are multiple times larger. Figure 5c illustrates the fraction of wrong pseudo-labels surpassing the threshold when training Fixmatch on MNIST (orange) and BCS-MNIST (blue). Over 40% of the predicted pseudo-labels over the threshold are wrong up to a labeling budget of 200 instances. Figures 5e and 5f denote the learning curves of Flexmatch, Fixmatch, and PL when increasing the labeled pool actively. Notably, all learners benefit from coverage-based sampling. Representative sampling is beneficial for Fixmatch. This method promotes instances representative of a certain class or region and probably selects instances that are less ambiguous for training. However, as expected, employing the uncertainty baseline in this context proves to be a poor choice. The strategy lacks the ability to differentiate

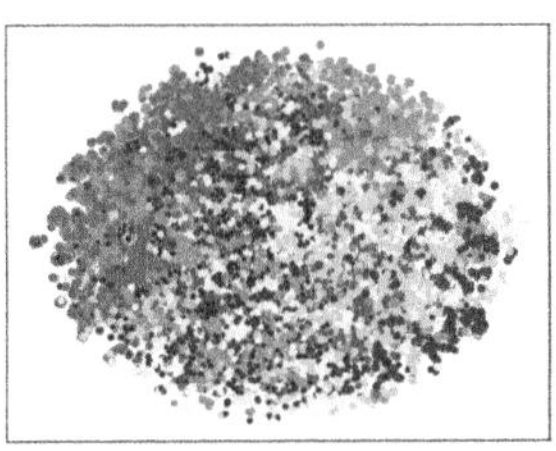

(a) t-SNE BCS.

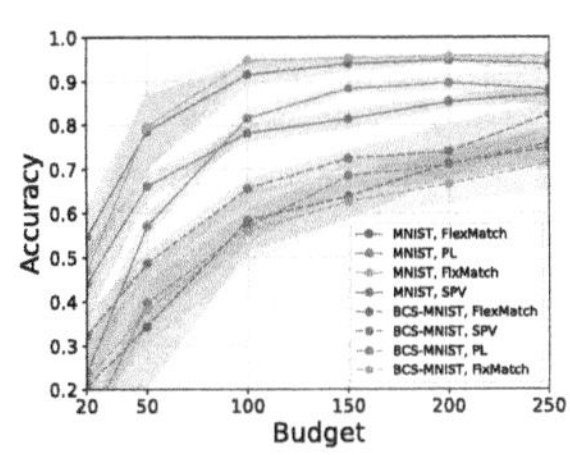

(b) Random.

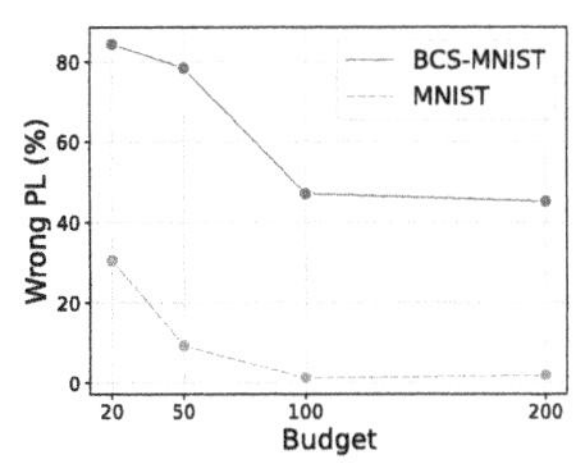

(c) Incorrect PL.

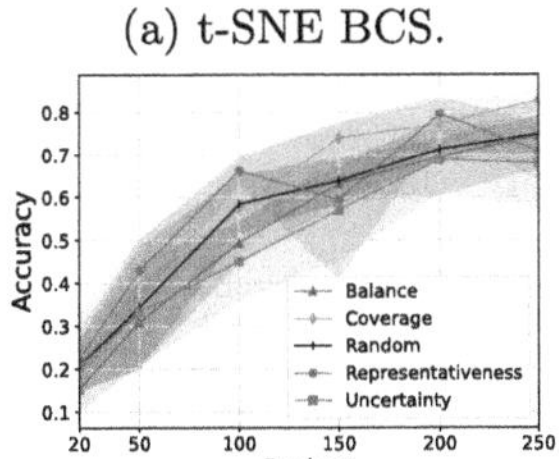

(d) AL Flexmatch.

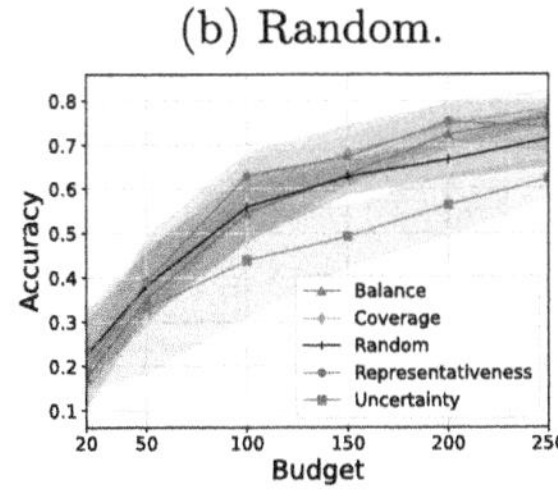

(e) AL Fixmatch.

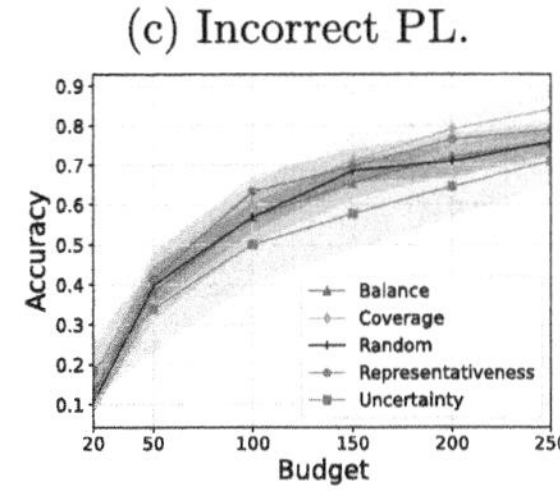

(f) AL PL.

Fig. 5. (b) Average test accuracy of all learners with random selection for BCS-MNIST (dashed) and MNIST (solid). (c) shows the amount of wrongly predicted pseudo-labels falling over the threshold using Fixmatch for BCS-MNIST is much larger than for MNIST. (d), (e) and (f) show the AL curves for Flexmatch, Fixmatch, and PL compared to random sampling (black). (Color figure online) between aleatoric and epistemic uncertainty, leading to the selection of many ambiguous instances, further misleading the training.

5.3 Experiment "WCI-MNIST"

Figure 6b shows that for WCI-MNIST, the accuracy of all learners stagnates around 10% to 15% earlier compared to MNIST. Using random sampling does not find the underrepresented diverse instances, and only the same concepts are entrenched and further confirmed over the training procedure. Even though the correctness ratio of the pseudo-labels surpassing the threshold using Fixmatch is larger for WCI-MNIST than for MNIST, the achieved mean test accuracy stops at roughly 82% (see Fig. 6c).

However, using AL, we can find more diverse and valuable instances than the already known concepts and reach a better final accuracy overall for SSL (see Figs. 6d to 6f). Especially coverage-based sampling seems to be a viable choice. For PL, the final average accuracy using uncertainty-based and coverage-based sampling on WCI-MNIST is even equally good as the performance on the original MNIST using random sampling. In the early stages, uncertainty sampling is the worst method probably because it lacks diversity aspects, and the predictions in early iterations might not be very reliable. However, for the final budget, uncertainty sampling matches or surpasses most other methods. The representative

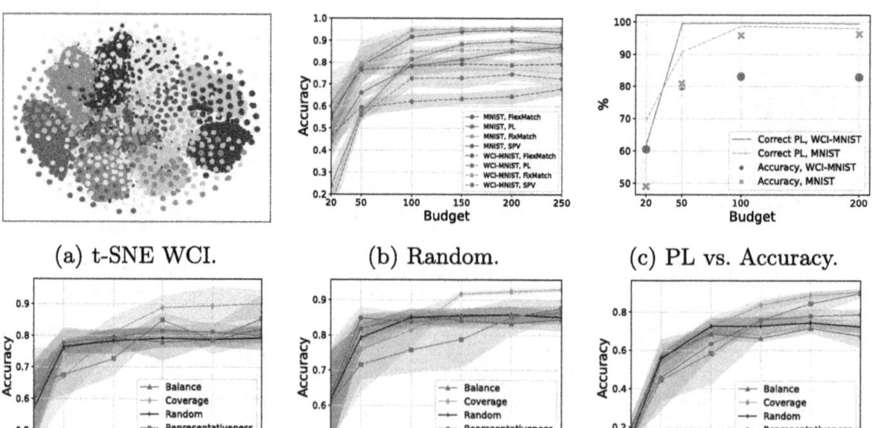

(a) t-SNE WCI. (b) Random. (c) PL vs. Accuracy.

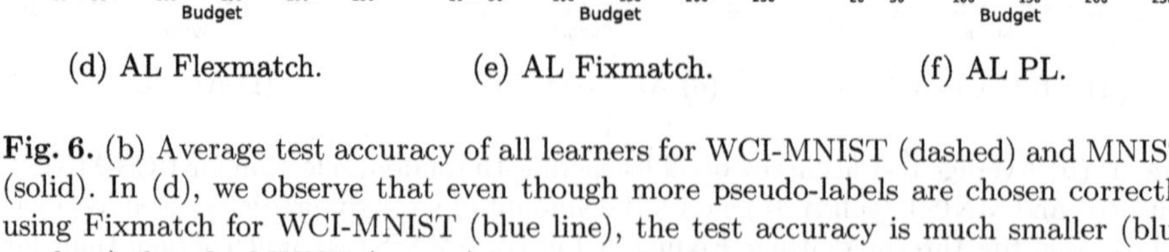

(d) AL Flexmatch. (e) AL Fixmatch. (f) AL PL.

Fig. 6. (b) Average test accuracy of all learners for WCI-MNIST (dashed) and MNIST (solid). In (d), we observe that even though more pseudo-labels are chosen correctly using Fixmatch for WCI-MNIST (blue line), the test accuracy is much smaller (blue markers) than for MNIST (orange) because only the same concepts are confirmed over and over again. (d), (e) and (f) show the selected AL curves for Flexmatch, Fixmatch, and PL compared to random sampling (black). (Color figure online) baseline focuses on instances that are most central in clusters, probably resulting in only selecting the already known and easy-to-classify concepts lacking novel information and does not outperform random sampling in most situations.

6 Key Findings

Table 1 shows the average test accuracies of SPV, Fixmatch, PL, and Flexmatch on BCI-MNIST, BCS-MNIST, and WCI-MNIST for all AL heuristics compared to random sampling, where bold and red numbers indicate best- and worst-performing methods per column respectively for 50 and 250 labeled instances. Our key findings can be summarized as follows:

- For all introduced data challenges, the SSL methods suffer from confirmation bias. There is no consistent winner among all query strategies, but random sampling is never the best query method for the SSL methods when faced with BCS, WCI, and BCI. This provides empirical evidence that AL is a useful tool to overcome confirmation bias in SSL.
- In the early stages, representative sampling is often beneficial. In contrast, uncertainty sampling usually performs better in later iterations where model predictions are more reliable. As expected, uncertainty sampling is not a good choice for BCS since it queries from overlapping, confusing regions.
- Coverage sampling is often the best strategy for SSL methods. We assume that is because more diverse queried instances bring in new aspects to the data, and the easier concepts can already be learned by pseudo-labeling and consistency regularization.
- Our balance baseline often performs on par with random selection. However, for the BCI challenge, it yields slightly better results. We conclude that it should mainly be used in combination with other selection heuristics.
- Overall, the most challenging dataset for SSL and AL is BCS-MNIST. By using AL, we can mitigate confirmation bias more effectively for the challenges BCI and WCI compared to random sampling.

Table 1. Average test accuracy for SPV, Fixmatch, PL, and Flexmatch for BCI-MNIST, BCS-MNIST, and WCI-MNIST for all sampling methods and budgets 50 and 250 (L). **Bold** and red numbers indicate column-wise best- and worst-performing methods, respectively.

	Supervised						Fixmatch						Pseudo-Labeling						Flexmatch					
	BCI		BCS		WCI		BCI		BCS		WCI		BCI		BCS		WCI		BCI		BCS		WCI	
L	50	250	50	250	50	250	50	250	50	250	50	250	50	250	50	250	50	250	50	250	50	250	50	250
Rnd	49.4	68.9	48.6	82.3	59.3	67.8	51.2	69.0	38.1	71.3	79.2	85.1	43.6	74.3	39.6	75.9	55.7	72.4	50.5	74.0	34.3	74.8	76.4	79.3
Unc	52.0	**82.5**	53.0	80.5	47.8	70.0	38.3	90.1	32.8	62.1	71.5	87.6	43.3	**88.3**	33.8	70.9	44.5	89.7	52.5	**94.1**	33.2	67.9	67.4	85.3
Cov	47.9	79.2	**55.2**	**83.8**	**63.0**	**87.6**	57.4	**90.3**	38.9	**78.2**	75.8	**92.9**	46.2	86.4	**43.4**	**84.0**	53.0	**90.5**	**53.8**	87.6	34.7	**82.8**	67.0	**90.1**
Bal	48.2	68.7	50.6	78.5	58.0	64.1	52.7	70.2	35.0	76.2	81.8	84.4	**48.8**	77.6	38.0	75.5	56.5	67.5	51.5	76.3	31.0	74.5	75.7	82.1
Rep	**54.7**	66.8	47.7	75.8	61.6	66.1	**58.3**	84.1	39.0	73.9	**84.8**	86.3	48.2	75.8	41.2	78.9	45.7	78.7	51.8	83.3	**42.9**	70.8	**77.6**	79.9

7 Conclusion

In this work, we study the real-world transferability of critique points on the combination of SSL and AL on benchmark datasets. Our experiments show that AL is a useful tool to overcome confirmation bias in various real-world challenges. However, it is not trivial to determine which AL method is most suitable in a real-world scenario. This study is limited to providing insights into confirmation bias in SSL when confronted with between-class imbalance, between-class similarity, and within-class similarity and the potential of simple AL heuristics. In the future, we intend to extend our experiments to a broader range of datasets, with a strong focus on real-world examples. Moreover, we aim to include existing hybrid AL methods in our evaluation and to design a robust active semi-supervised method capable of consistently overcoming confirmation bias in SSL on diverse challenges.

Acknowledgements. This work was supported by the Bavarian Ministry of Economic Affairs, Regional Development and Energy through the Center for Analytics Data Applications (ADA-Center) within the framework of BAYERN DIGITAL II (20-3410-2-9-8) as well as the German Federal Ministry of Education and Research (BMBF) under Grant No. 01IS18036A.

References

1. Aggarwal, U., Popescu, A., Hudelot, C.: Active learning for imbalanced datasets. In: Proceedings of the IEEE/CVF Winter Conference on Applications of Computer Vision, pp. 1428–1437 (2020)
2. Algan, G., Ulusoy, I.: Image classification with deep learning in the presence of noisy labels: A survey. Knowl.-Based Syst. **215**, 106771 (2021)
3. Arazo, E., Ortego, D., Albert, P., O'Connor, N.E., McGuinness, K.: Pseudo-labeling and confirmation bias in deep semi-supervised learning. In: 2020 International Joint Conference on Neural Networks (IJCNN), pp. 1–8 (2020). https://doi.org/10.1109/IJCNN48605.2020.9207304
4. Ash, J.T., Zhang, C., Krishnamurthy, A., Langford, J., Agarwal, A.: Deep batch active learning by diverse, uncertain gradient lower bounds. In: 8th International Conference on Learning Representations, ICLR 2020, Addis Ababa, Ethiopia, 26–30 April 2020. OpenReview.net (2020). https://openreview.net/forum?id=ryghZJBKPS
5. Beck, N., Sivasubramanian, D., Dani, A., Ramakrishnan, G., Iyer, R.: Effective evaluation of deep active learning on image classification tasks. arXiv preprint arXiv:2106.15324 (2021)
6. Bengar, J.Z., van de Weijer, J., Fuentes, L.L., Raducanu, B.: Class-balanced active learning for image classification. In: Proceedings of the IEEE/CVF Winter Conference on Applications of Computer Vision, pp. 1536–1545 (2022)
7. Bengar, J.Z., van de Weijer, J., Twardowski, B., Raducanu, B.: Reducing label effort: self-supervised meets active learning. In: 2021 IEEE/CVF International Conference on Computer Vision Workshops (ICCVW), pp. 1631–1639. IEEE Computer Society, Los Alamitos (2021). https://doi.org/10.1109/ICCVW54120.2021.00188. https://doi.ieeecomputersociety.org/10.1109/ICCVW54120.2021.00188

8. Berthelot, D., Carlini, N., Goodfellow, I., Papernot, N., Oliver, A., Raffel, C.A.: Mixmatch: a holistic approach to semi-supervised learning. Adv. Neural Inf. Process. Syst. **32**, 1–11 (2019)
9. Birodkar, V., Mobahi, H., Bengio, S.: Semantic redundancies in image-classification datasets: the 10% you don't need. arXiv preprint arXiv:1901.11409 (2019)
10. Breunig, M.M., Kriegel, H.P., Ng, R.T., Sander, J.: Lof: identifying density-based local outliers. In: Proceedings of the 2000 ACM SIGMOD International Conference on Management of Data, pp. 93–104 (2000)
11. Chan, Y.-C., Li, M., Oymak, S.: On the marginal benefit of active learning: Does self-supervision eat its cake? In: ICASSP 2021 - 2021 IEEE International Conference on Acoustics, Speech and Signal Processing (ICASSP), pp. 3455–3459 (2021). https://doi.org/10.1109/ICASSP39728.2021.9414665
12. Chang, H., Xie, G., Yu, J., Ling, Q., Gao, F., Yu, Y.: A viable framework for semi-supervised learning on realistic dataset. In: Machine Learning, pp. 1–23 (2022)
13. Chapelle, O., Scholkopf, B., Zien, A.: Semi-supervised learning. IEEE Trans. Neural Netw. **20**(3), 542–542 (2009)
14. Das, S., Datta, S., Chaudhuri, B.B.: Handling data irregularities in classification: foundations, trends, and future challenges. Pattern Recogn. **81**, 674–693 (2018)
15. Donmez, P., Carbonell, J.G., Bennett, P.N.: Dual strategy active learning. In: Kok, J.N., Koronacki, J., Mantaras, R.L., Matwin, S., Mladenič, D., Skowron, A. (eds.) ECML 2007. LNCS (LNAI), vol. 4701, pp. 116–127. Springer, Heidelberg (2007). https://doi.org/10.1007/978-3-540-74958-5_14
16. Ertekin, S., Huang, J., Bottou, L., Giles, L.: Learning on the border: active learning in imbalanced data classification. In: Proceedings of the Sixteenth ACM Conference on Information and Knowledge Management, pp. 127–136 (2007)
17. Fu, B., Cao, Z., Wang, J., Long, M.: Transferable query selection for active domain adaptation. In: Proceedings of the IEEE/CVF Conference on Computer Vision and Pattern Recognition, pp. 7272–7281 (2021)
18. Gal, Y., Islam, R., Ghahramani, Z.: Deep bayesian active learning with image data. In: International Conference on Machine Learning, pp. 1183–1192. PMLR (2017)
19. Gilhuber, S., Berrendorf, M., Ma, Y., Seidl, T.: Accelerating diversity sampling for deep active learning by low-dimensional representations. In: Kottke, D., Krempl, G., Holzinger, A., Hammer, B. (eds.) Proceedings of the Workshop on Interactive Adaptive Learning co-located with European Conference on Machine Learning and Principles and Practice of Knowledge Discovery in Databases (ECML PKDD 2022), Grenoble, France, 23 September 2022. CEUR Workshop Proceedings, vol. 3259, pp. 43–48. CEUR-WS.org (2022). https://ceur-ws.org/Vol-3259/ialatecml_paper4.pdf
20. Huang, L., Lin, K.C.J., Tseng, Y.C.: Resolving intra-class imbalance for gan-based image augmentation. In: 2019 IEEE International Conference on Multimedia and Expo (ICME), pp. 970–975 (2019). https://doi.org/10.1109/ICME.2019.00171
21. Hyun, M., Jeong, J., Kwak, N.: Class-imbalanced semi-supervised learning. arXiv preprint arXiv:2002.06815 (2020)
22. Japkowicz, N.: Concept-learning in the presence of *between-class* and *within-class* imbalances. In: Stroulia, E., Matwin, S. (eds.) AI 2001. LNCS (LNAI), vol. 2056, pp. 67–77. Springer, Heidelberg (2001). https://doi.org/10.1007/3-540-45153-6_7
23. Kirsch, A., Van Amersfoort, J., Gal, Y.: Batchbald: efficient and diverse batch acquisition for deep bayesian active learning. Adv. Neural Inf. Process. Syst. **32**, 1–12 (2019)
24. LeCun, Y., et al.: Backpropagation applied to handwritten zip code recognition. Neural Comput. **1**(4), 541–551 (1989)

25. Lee, D.H., et al.: Pseudo-label: the simple and efficient semi-supervised learning method for deep neural networks. In: Workshop on Challenges in Representation Learning, ICML, vol. 3, p. 896 (2013)
26. Lee, H., Park, M., Kim, J.: Plankton classification on imbalanced large scale database via convolutional neural networks with transfer learning. In: 2016 IEEE International Conference on Image Processing (ICIP), pp. 3713–3717 (2016). https://doi.org/10.1109/ICIP.2016.7533053
27. Li, J., et al.: Learning from large-scale noisy web data with ubiquitous reweighting for image classification. IEEE Trans. Pattern Anal. Mach. Intell. **43**(5), 1808–1814 (2019)
28. Li, J., Socher, R., Hoi, S.C.: Dividemix: learning with noisy labels as semi-supervised learning. In: International Conference on Learning Representations (2020). https://openreview.net/forum?id=HJgExaVtwr
29. Liao, T., Taori, R., Raji, I.D., Schmidt, L.: Are we learning yet? a meta review of evaluation failures across machine learning. In: Thirty-fifth Conference on Neural Information Processing Systems Datasets and Benchmarks Track (Round 2) (2021). https://openreview.net/forum?id=mPducS1MsEK
30. López, V., Fernández, A., García, S., Palade, V., Herrera, F.: An insight into classification with imbalanced data: empirical results and current trends on using data intrinsic characteristics. Inf. Sci. **250**, 113–141 (2013)
31. Lowell, D., Lipton, Z.C., Wallace, B.C.: Practical obstacles to deploying active learning. In: Proceedings of the 2019 Conference on Empirical Methods in Natural Language Processing and the 9th International Joint Conference on Natural Language Processing (EMNLP-IJCNLP), pp. 21–30 (2019)
32. Lüth, C.T., Bungert, T.J., Klein, L., Jaeger, P.F.: Toward realistic evaluation of deep active learning algorithms in image classification (2023)
33. Mittal, S., Tatarchenko, M., Çiçek, Ö., Brox, T.: Parting with illusions about deep active learning. ArXiv abs/1912.05361 (2019)
34. Mukhoti, J., Kirsch, A., van Amersfoort, J., Torr, P.H.S., Gal, Y.: Deep deterministic uncertainty: A new simple baseline. In: 2023 IEEE/CVF Conference on Computer Vision and Pattern Recognition (CVPR), pp. 24384–24394 (2023). https://doi.org/10.1109/CVPR52729.2023.02336
35. Oliver, A., Odena, A., Raffel, C.A., Cubuk, E.D., Goodfellow, I.: Realistic evaluation of deep semi-supervised learning algorithms. In: Bengio, S., Wallach, H., Larochelle, H., Grauman, K., Cesa-Bianchi, N., Garnett, R. (eds.) Advances in Neural Information Processing Systems, vol. 31. Curran Associates, Inc. (2018). https://proceedings.neurips.cc/paper_files/paper/2018/file/c1fea270c48e8079d8ddf7d06d26ab52-Paper.pdf
36. Plank, B.: The "problem" of human label variation: On ground truth in data, modeling and evaluation. In: Proceedings of the 2022 Conference on Empirical Methods in Natural Language Processing. Association for Computational Linguistics, Abu Dhabi (2022)
37. Prabhu, V., Chandrasekaran, A., Saenko, K., Hoffman, J.: Active domain adaptation via clustering uncertainty-weighted embeddings. In: Proceedings of the IEEE/CVF International Conference on Computer Vision, pp. 8505–8514 (2021)
38. Ren, P., et al.: A survey of deep active learning. ACM Comput. Surv. (CSUR) **54**(9), 1–40 (2021)
39. Sener, O., Savarese, S.: Active learning for convolutional neural networks: a core-set approach. In: International Conference on Learning Representations (2018)
40. Settles, B.: Active learning literature survey (2009)

41. Sohn, K., et al.: FixMatch: simplifying semi-supervised learning with consistency and confidence. In: Advances in Neural Information Processing Systems (2020)
42. Stefanowski, J.: Dealing with data difficulty factors while learning from imbalanced data. In: Matwin, S., Mielniczuk, J. (eds.) Challenges in Computational Statistics and Data Mining. SCI, vol. 605, pp. 333–363. Springer, Cham (2016). https://doi.org/10.1007/978-3-319-18781-5_17
43. Su, L., Liu, Y., Wang, M., Li, A.: Semi-hic: a novel semi-supervised deep learning method for histopathological image classification. Comput. Biol. Med. **137**, 104788 (2021)
44. Van Engelen, J.E., Hoos, H.H.: A survey on semi-supervised learning. Mach. Learn. **109**(2), 373–440 (2020)
45. Varoquaux, G., Cheplygina, V.: Machine learning for medical imaging: methodological failures and recommendations for the future. NPJ Dig. Med. **5**(1), 1–8 (2022)
46. Venkataramanan, A., Laviale, M., Figus, C., Usseglio-Polatera, P., Pradalier, C.: Tackling inter-class similarity and intra-class variance for microscopic image-based classification. In: Vincze, M., Patten, T., Christensen, H.I., Nalpantidis, L., Liu, M. (eds.) ICVS 2021. LNCS, vol. 12899, pp. 93–103. Springer, Cham (2021). https://doi.org/10.1007/978-3-030-87156-7_8
47. Wang, M., Min, F., Zhang, Z.H., Wu, Y.X.: Active learning through density clustering. Expert Syst. Appl. **85**, 305–317 (2017)
48. Wang, Q.: Wgan-based synthetic minority over-sampling technique: improving semantic fine-grained classification for lung nodules in ct images. IEEE Access **7**, 18450–18463 (2019). https://doi.org/10.1109/ACCESS.2019.2896409
49. Wang, Y., et al.: Usb: a unified semi-supervised learning benchmark for classification. In: Thirty-sixth Conference on Neural Information Processing Systems Datasets and Benchmarks Track (2022). https://doi.org/10.48550/ARXIV.2208.07204. https://arxiv.org/abs/2208.07204
50. Wojciechowski, S., Wilk, S.: Difficulty factors and preprocessing in imbalanced data sets: an experimental study on artificial data. Found. Comput. Decis. Sci. **42**(2), 149–176 (2017). https://doi.org/10.1515/fcds-2017-0007
51. Wu, M., Li, C., Yao, Z.: Deep active learning for computer vision tasks: methodologies, applications, and challenges. Appl. Sci. **12**(16), 8103 (2022)
52. Xie, B., Yuan, L., Li, S., Liu, C.H., Cheng, X.: Towards fewer annotations: active learning via region impurity and prediction uncertainty for domain adaptive semantic segmentation. In: Proceedings of the IEEE/CVF Conference on Computer Vision and Pattern Recognition, pp. 8068–8078 (2022)
53. Zhan, X., Wang, Q., Huang, K.H., Xiong, H., Dou, D., Chan, A.B.: A comparative survey of deep active learning. arXiv preprint arXiv:2203.13450 (2022)
54. Zhang, B., et al.: Flexmatch: boosting semi-supervised learning with curriculum pseudo labeling. Adv. Neural Inf. Process. Syst. **34**, 18408–18419 (2021)
55. Zhdanov, F.: Diverse mini-batch active learning. arXiv preprint arXiv:1901.05954 (2019)

Federated Learning

Towards Practical Federated Causal Structure Learning

Zhaoyu Wang, Pingchuan Ma(✉), and Shuai Wang

The Hong Kong University of Science and Technology, Clear Water Bay, Hong Kong SAR
1950574@tongji.edu.cn, {pmaab,shuaiw}@cse.ust.hk

Abstract. Understanding causal relations is vital in scientific discovery. The process of causal structure learning involves identifying causal graphs from observational data to understand such relations. Usually, a central server performs this task, but sharing data with the server poses privacy risks. Federated learning can solve this problem, but existing solutions for federated causal structure learning make unrealistic assumptions about data and lack convergence guarantees. FedC^{2}SL is a federated constraint-based causal structure learning scheme that learns causal graphs using a federated conditional independence test, which examines conditional independence between two variables under a condition set without collecting raw data from clients. FedC^{2}SL requires weaker and more realistic assumptions about data and offers stronger resistance to data variability among clients. FedPC and FedFCI are the two variants of FedC^{2}SL for causal structure learning in causal sufficiency and causal insufficiency, respectively. The study evaluates FedC^{2}SL using both synthetic datasets and real-world data against existing solutions and finds it demonstrates encouraging performance and strong resilience to data heterogeneity among clients.

Keywords: federated learning · Bayesian network · probabilistic graphical model · causal discovery

1 Introduction

Learning causal relations from data is a fundamental problem in causal inference. Causal structure learning is a popular approach to identifying causal relationships in multivariate datasets, represented as a causal graph. This technique has been successfully applied in various fields such as medicine [3,32,36], economics [1], earth science [33], data analytics [23] and software engineering [13,14].

Causal structure learning is performed on a central server with plaintext datasets. However, in applications like clinical data analysis, data may be distributed across different parties and may not be shared with a central server. To address this problem, federated learning is an emerging paradigm that allows

© The Author(s), under exclusive license to Springer Nature Switzerland AG 2023
D. Koutra et al. (Eds.): ECML PKDD 2023, LNAI 14170, pp. 351–367, 2023.
https://doi.org/10.1007/978-3-031-43415-0_21

data owners to collaboratively learn a model without sharing their data in plaintext [6,8]. However, current federated learning solutions are designed primarily for machine learning tasks that aggregate models trained on local datasets.

Several solutions have been proposed for federated causal structure learning [10,27,29,35]. However, these solutions have prerequisites that may hinder their general applicability. For instance, NOTEARS-ADMM [29], which is the state-of-the-art solution for federated causal structure learning, collects parameterized causal graphs from clients and uses an ADMM procedure to find the consensus causal graph in each iteration. Since local graphs jointly participate in the ADMM procedure, it is non-trivial to employ secure aggregation to protect individual causal graphs, resulting in a considerable sensitive information leak to the central server. Additionally, the assumption that data is generated in a known functional form is deemed unrealistic in many real-life applications.

In general, many solutions attempt to locally learn a causal graph and aggregate them together, but this practice is not optimal for federated causal structure learning. Causal structure learning is known to be error-prone in small datasets, and local datasets may suffer selection bias with respect to the global dataset due to the potential heterogeneity of different clients. The causal graph independently learned from each local dataset may manifest certain biases with respect to the true causal graph of the whole dataset.

To address this issue, we propose a novel federated causal structure learning with constraint-based methods. This paradigm interacts data only with a set of statistical tests on conditional independence and deduces graphical structure from the test results. The key idea of our solution is to provide a federated conditional independence test protocol. Each client holds a local dataset and computes their local statistics, which are then securely aggregated to derive an unbiased estimation of the global statistics. With the global statistics, we can check the global conditional independence relations and conduct constraint-based causal structure learning accordingly.

We evaluate our solution with synthetic data and a real-world dataset and observe better results than baseline federated causal structure learning algorithms, including state-of-the-art methods NOTEARS-ADMM [29], RFCD [27], and four voting-based algorithms. Our solution also shows strong resiliency to client heterogeneity while other baseline algorithms encounter notable performance downgrades in this setting. Furthermore, our solution facilitates causal feature selection (CFS) and processes real-world data effectively.

In summary, we make the following contributions: (1) we advocate for federated causal structure learning with constraint-based paradigms; (2) we design a federated conditional independence test protocol to minimize privacy leakages and address client heterogeneity; and, (3) we conduct extensive experiments to assess the performance of our solution on both synthetic and real-world datasets. We release our implementation, FEDC^{2}SL, on https://github.com/wangzhaoyu07/FedC2SL for further research and comparison.

2 Preliminary

In this section, we review preliminary knowledge of causal structure learning.

Notations. Let X and $\boldsymbol{X}$ represent a variable and a set of variables, respectively. In a graph, a node and a variable share the same notation. The sets of nodes and edges in a causal graph G are denoted as V_G and E_G, respectively. The notation $X \to Y \in E_G$ indicates that X is a parent of Y, while $X \leftrightarrow Y \in E_G$ indicates that X and Y are connected by a bidirected edge. The sets of neighbors and parents of X in G are denoted as $N_G(X)$ and $Pa_G(X)$, respectively. The notation $[K] := \{1, \cdots, K\}$ is defined as the set of integers from 1 to K.

2.1 Causal Structure Learning

In causal inference, the relationship between data is often presented as a causal graph, which can take the form of a directed acyclic graph (DAG) or maximal ancestral graph (MAG). These two representations are used to depict causal relationships under different assumptions. In the following paragraphs, we introduce the corresponding causal graphs and formalize these canonical assumptions.

Graphical Representation. Causal relations among variables in a multivariate dataset can be depicted using a causal graph. The causal graph can either be a directed acyclic graph (DAG), where adjacent variables are connected by a directed edge, or a mixed acyclic graph (MAG), which allows for bidirected edges to indicate shared latent confounders between two variables. In the DAG format, if a latent confounder is not observed, statistical associations between variables can exist without their true causal relations being well-represented. MAG overcomes this shortcoming and can be constructed from a true DAG and a set of latent variables, using a set of construction criteria [50]. See Fig. 1 (a) for an example of a DAG depicting a directed edge ($Z \to X$).

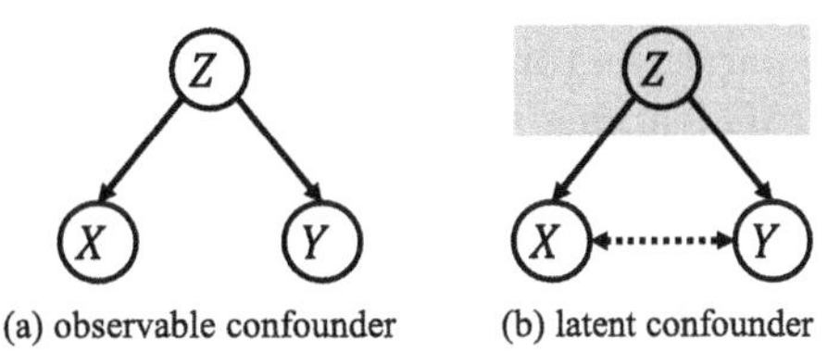

Fig. 1. Examples of observable and latent confounders.

Causal Sufficiency. Learning a DAG assumes a causally sufficient set of variables [37]. $\boldsymbol{X}$ is causally sufficient if there is no hidden cause $Z \notin \boldsymbol{X}$ causing more than one variable in $\boldsymbol{X}$. However, real-world data may not satisfy this assumption. MAG addresses this issue by introducing a bidirected edge $\leftrightarrow$. See Fig. 1 (b) for an example where a bidirected edge between X, Y due to the absence of Z.

Global Markov Property (GMP). The Global Markov Property (GMP) [20] connects graphical structures and statistical properties. It can be stated as: $X \perp\!\!\!\perp_G Y \mid \boldsymbol{Z} \implies X \perp\!\!\!\perp Y \mid \boldsymbol{Z}$. Here, $\perp\!\!\!\perp_G$ represents graphical separation and $\perp\!\!\!\perp$ represents statistical conditional independence in the joint probability distribution $P_{\boldsymbol{X}}$. D-separation is a structural constraint for directed acyclic graphs (DAGs), while m-separation is a constraint for mixed graphs (MAGs). We present their definitions in Supplementary Material [45].

Faithfulness Assumption. Faithfulness assumption states that conditional independence on the joint distribution implies d-separation (or m-separation) on the causal graph. Formally, $X \perp\!\!\!\perp Y \mid \boldsymbol{Z} \implies X \perp\!\!\!\perp_G Y \mid \boldsymbol{Z}$

In the remainder of the paper, we assume GMP and faithfulness assumption always hold. Moreover, we assume causal sufficiency in FedPC and propose FedFCI that is also tolerant to causally insufficient data.

Markov Equivalence Class (MEC). Given the Markov condition and faithfulness assumption, statistical tests can be performed on data to deduce graph structures through graphical separation constraints. However, inferring the full structure of a causal graph from data is difficult and can lead to multiple causal graphs being compatible with the constraints deduced from conditional independence. To address this, causal structure learning algorithms aim to recover a MEC, which summarizes a set of causal graphs sharing the same set of d-separations (or m-separations) [31]. The MEC is represented as a CPDAG for DAG learning and as a PAG for MAG learning [50]. FedC^{2}SL follows standard conventions [22,31,50] in recovering the MEC of a given dataset.

Constraint-based Causal Structure Learning. Constraint-based methods are commonly used for causal structure learning, identifying the MEC from observational datasets. The PC algorithm (see details in Supplementary Material [45]) is a representative constraint-based causal structure learning algorithm. This algorithm involves two phases: learning the causal skeleton and orienting the edges. During the former phase, the adjacency relations between variables are learned and an undirected graph is created. In this graph, the edges represent the underlying causal graph's skeleton. In the latter phase, a set of orientation rules is applied to assign a causal direction to the undirected edges of the skeleton. In comparison to the PC algorithm, which performs DAG learning, the FCI algorithm [50] is designed for MAG learning, incorporating another set of orientation rules while using a similar skeleton learning procedure of the PC algorithm.

3 Research Overview

This section presents the research overview. We begin by providing an overview of FedC^{2}SL in Sect. 3.1, covering the problem setup and threat model. Sect. 3.2 provides a comparison between our solution and existing approaches.

3.1 Problem Setup

In this paper, we consider two causal discovery problems: FedPC and FedFCI.

FedPC. Assuming causal sufficiency, FedPC involves a DAG $G = (V, E)$ that encodes the causal relationships among a variable vector $\boldsymbol{X} = \{X_1, \cdots, X_d\}$ with a joint probability distribution $P_{\boldsymbol{X}}$ satisfying the Global Markov Property (GMP) with respect to G, and G is faithful to $P_{\boldsymbol{X}}$.

FedFCI. In causal insufficient data, FedFCI involves a MAG $M = (V, E)$ that encodes the causal relationships among a variable vector $\boldsymbol{X} = \{X_1, \cdots, X_d\}$ with a joint probability distribution $P_{\boldsymbol{X} \cup L}$, where L is a set of unknown latent variables. Here, $P_{\boldsymbol{X}}$ is the observable distribution with $P_{\boldsymbol{X} \cup L}$ being marginalized on L. If L is empty, then the setting is equivalent to FedPC. We assume that $P_{\boldsymbol{X}}$ satisfies GMP with respect to G and M is faithful to $P_{\boldsymbol{X}}$.

We now describe the setting of clients that are identical for either FedPC or FedFCI. Suppose that there are K local datasets $\mathcal{D} := \{D^1, \cdots, D^K\}$ and $D^i = \{\boldsymbol{x}^i_1, \cdots, \boldsymbol{x}^i_{n_i}\}$. We denote $\boldsymbol{x}^i_{j,k}$ be the k-th element of the j-th record in the i-th local dataset. Each record in the global dataset $\mathcal{D}$ is sampled *i.i.d.* (independent and identically distributed) from $P_{\boldsymbol{X}}$. We allow for selection bias on client local datasets as long as the global dataset is unbiased with respect to $P_{\boldsymbol{X}}$, which is one of the main challenges in federated learning [15]. For example, local datasets from different hospitals may be biased on different patient subpopulations. However, with a sufficient number of clients, the global dataset (by pooling all local datasets) becomes unbiased. This assumption is weaker than the Invariant DAG Assumption in DS-FCD [10]. We borrow the concept from general causal structure learning [41] and formally define this property as follows.

Definition 1 (Client Heterogeneity). *Let $\{X_1, \cdots, X_d\}$ be the visible variables in the dataset and G be the ground-truth causal graph. To represent client-wise heterogeneity, we assume that there is an implicit surrogate variable $C : [K]$ be the child variable of $S \subseteq \{X_1, \cdots, X_d\}$ in an augmented causal graph and the i-th client holds the records with $C = i$. When $S = \emptyset$, the local datasets are homogeneous.*

The overall goal is to recover MEC of G or M from distributed local datasets in the presence of client heterogeneity while minimizing data leakages.

Threat Model. Our threat model aligns with the standard setting [47]. We assume that all parties including the central server and clients are honest but curious, meaning that they will follow the protocol but are interested in learning as much private information as possible from others. We are concerned with the leakage of private client data, and we do not consider any coalitions between participants. We will show later that FedC^{2}SL is resilient to client dropouts, although we do not explicitly consider this during algorithm design.

Security Objective. The federated learning paradigms aim to prevent raw data sharing, and only aggregated results are released [44]. We aim to achieve MPC-style security to ensure that the semi-honest server only knows the aggregated results and not individual updates. To establish this property formally, we define client indistinguishability in federated causal structure learning.

Definition 2 (Client Indistinguishability). *Let $\boldsymbol{x} \in D^i$ be a record that only exists in the i-th client (i.e., $\forall j \neq i, \forall \boldsymbol{x}' \in D^j, \boldsymbol{x} \neq \boldsymbol{x}'$). Let $\mathbb{P}(A)$ be the public knowledge (e.g., intermediate data and final results) revealed in the protocol A. A is said to be client indistinguishable for an adversary if $\forall i, j \in [K], P(\boldsymbol{x} \in D^i \mid \mathbb{P}(A)) = P(\boldsymbol{x} \in D^j \mid \mathbb{P}(A))$.*

3.2 Comparison with Existing Solutions

In this section, we review existing solutions and compare them with FEDC²SL. We summarize existing works and FEDC²SL, in terms of assumptions, application scope, and leakage, in Table 1.

Table 1. Comparing existing works and FEDC²SL.

Solution	Input	Assumption	Heterogeneity	Application Scope	Client Leakage	Global Leakage
NOTEARS-ADMM [29]	Data	Additive Noise	✗	DAG	Individual Graph + Parameter	Graph + Parameter
DS-FCD [10]	Data	Additive Noise	✗	DAG	Individual Graph + Parameter	Graph + Parameter
RFCD [27]	Data	Additive Noise	✗	DAG	Individual Graph Fitness	Graph
K2 [35]	Data + Order	Faithfulness	✓	DAG	Aggregated Fitness	Graph
FEDC²SL	Data	Faithfulness	✓	DAG & MAG	Aggregated Low-dim. Distribution	Graph

Comparison of Prerequisites. Most federated causal structure learning solutions assume additive noise in the data generating process, which is considered stronger than the faithfulness assumption in K2 [35] and FEDC²SL. However, K2 requires prior knowledge of the topological order of nodes in a ground-truth DAG, which is impractical. Additionally, solutions that learn local graphs independently are intolerant of client heterogeneity, as their performance would degrade arbitrarily in theory. FEDC²SL is the only solution that supports MAG learning, allowing for causal structure learning on causally insufficient data, making it a more practical option. (See Sect. 2.1 for more details.)

Comparison on Privacy Protection. We review the privacy protection mechanisms in proposed solutions. On the client side, NOTEARS-ADMM [29] and DS-FCD [10] require clients to update the local causal graph and corresponding parameters in plaintext to the global server. These graph parameters consist of multiple regression models trained on local datasets, which are vulnerable to privacy attacks on ML models. RFCD [27] requires clients to send the fitness score of global causal graphs on the local dataset, which poses a privacy risk for adversaries to infer the source of particular data samples and violate the client indistinguishability. In contrast, K2 [35] and FEDC²SL use secure aggregation or secure multi-party computation protocols such that only aggregated results are revealed. K2 employs a score function to measure the fitness of a local structure and the global structure is established by selecting the best local structure in a greedy manner. The score function is computed over the distributed clients with MPC schemes such that individual updates are protected. FEDC^{2}SL uses a constraint-based strategy to learn the causal graph and securely aggregates the data distribution marginalized over multiple low-dimensional subspaces to the global server. The marginalized low-dimensional distributions are strictly less informative than NOTEARS-ADMM and DS-FCD. The global server asserts conditional independence on the aggregated distributions and deduces graphical separations by faithfulness accordingly.

Asymptotic Convergence. FEDC^{2}SL is inherited from constraint-based methods that offers asymptotic convergence to the MEC of the ground-truth causal graph under certain assumptions. In contrast, NOTEARS-ADMM and DS-FCD use continuous optimization to the non-convex function and only converge on stationary solutions. RFCD and K2 use greedy search over the combinatorial graph space, which does not provide global convergence guarantees.

4 FEDC^{2}SL

In this section, we present FEDC^{2}SL, a novel federated causal structure learning algorithm with minimized privacy leakage compared to its counterparts.

4.1 Causal Structure Learning

As discussed in Sect. 2.1, the causal graph is learned by testing conditional independence in the dataset. A MEC of the causal graph contains all conditional independence, as per GMP and faithfulness assumption. Moreover, the MEC can be recovered from the set of all conditional independence relations. Therefore, the set of all conditional independence relations in a dataset is both necessary and sufficient to represent the MEC of the underlying causal graph.

Remark 1. Under GMP and faithfulness assumption, a Markov equivalence class of causal graph encodes all conditional independence relations among data. Once the Markov equivalence class is revealed, all conditional independence relations are revealed simultaneously. Therefore, the conditional independence stands for the minimal information leak of federated causal structure learning.

Instead of creating specific federated causal structure learning methods, we propose using a federated conditional independence test procedure. This procedure is fundamental to all constraint-based causal structure learning algorithms, such as the PC algorithm. By implementing our federated version, we can replace the centralized conditional independence tester in any existing constraint-based causal structure learning algorithm and make it federated. In this paper, we apply our federated conditional independence test procedure to two well-known causal structure learning algorithms, namely, FEDPC and FEDFCI, which are based on the PC algorithm [37] and FCI algorithm [37,50], respectively.

4.2 Federated Conditional Independence Test

To enhance privacy protection, a multiparty secure conditional independence test that releases only the conditional independence relations would be ideal. However, implementing such a solution using MPC would result in impractical computational overheads for producing real-world datasets. Therefore, we propose a practical trade-off that boosts computation efficiency while causing negligible privacy leakage on relatively insensitive information.

To introduce our federated conditional independence test protocol, we first explain how to test conditional independence in a centralized dataset. Consider three random variables X, Y, and Z from a multivariate discrete distributions. The conditional independence of X and Y given Z is defined as follows:

Definition 3 (Conditional Independence). *X and Y are conditionally independent given Z if and only if, for all possible $(x, y, z) \in (X, Y, Z)$, $P(X = x, Y = y|Z = z) = P(X = x|Z = z)P(Y = y|Z = z)$.*

While Definition 3 is straightforward to verify, it is non-trivial to statistically test this property with finite samples. The most popular way is to use χ^2-test [4], whose null hypothesis and alternative hypothesis are defined as follows:

$$H_0 : X \perp\!\!\!\perp Y|Z, H_1 : X \not\perp\!\!\!\perp Y|Z \tag{1}$$

The statistic $\hat{Q}$ is computed as $\hat{Q} = \sum_{x,y,z} \frac{(v_{xyz} - \frac{v_{xz}v_{yz}}{v_z})^2}{\frac{v_{xz}v_{yz}}{v_z}}$ where v_{xyz} is the number of samples with $X = x$, $Y = y$ and $Z = z$; and so on. Under null hypothesis H_0, $\hat{Q}$ follows a $\chi^2_{\texttt{dof}}$ distribution where $\texttt{dof} = \sum_{z \in Z}(|X_{Z=z}|-1)(|Y_{Z=z}|-1)$ is the degree of freedom and $|X|, |Y|$ denote the cardinality of the multivariate discrete random variable. Let $1-\alpha$ be the significance level. The null hypothesis is rejected if $\hat{Q} > \chi^2_{\texttt{dof}}(1 - \alpha)$.

Why a Voting Scheme Is Not Suitable? One potential approach to test conditional independence in a federated setting is to perform standard χ^2-tests on each client independently and use the voted local conditional independence as the conditional independence on the global dataset. However, this approach is not feasible for two reasons. Firstly, the χ^2-test requires that all v_{xyz} are larger than 5 to ensure its validity [39]. This requirement is often unattainable on small local datasets, leading to inaccurate test results. Secondly, even if the requirement is met, the voting result may not reflect the global conditional independence in the presence of selection bias on the client dataset. As will be shown in Sect. 5, simple voting strategies often yield inaccurate results.

To preserve privacy while computing $\hat{Q}$ on the global dataset, we can perform secure aggregation over the four counts $(v_z, v_{xz}, v_{yz}, v_{xyz})$ instead of using the voting scheme. Securely summing up $v^1_{xyz}, \cdots, v^K_{xyz}$ from all clients can obtain v_{xyz}. However, if Z contains multiple variables, releasing v_{xyz} could raise privacy concerns due to its encoding of the joint distribution of multiple variables. We discuss the privacy implications of releasing such high-dimensional distribution in the following paragraph.

High-Dim. Distribution vs. Low-Dim. Distribution. We note that high-dimensional distribution is more sensitive than low-dimensional distribution, which allows adversaries to localize a particular instance (e.g., patient of a minority disease). Hence, we anticipate to avoid such leakages. In contrast, the joint distribution marginalized over low-dimensional subspace is generally less sensitive. It can be deemed as a high-level summary of data distribution and individual privacy is retained on a reasonable degree.

Algorithm 1: Fed-CI($X \perp\!\!\!\perp Y \mid \boldsymbol{Z}$)

Input: Data in K clients: $\mathcal{D} := \{D^1, \cdots, D^K\}$; Statistical Significance: $1-\sigma$.
Output: Whether reject $X \perp\!\!\!\perp Y \mid \boldsymbol{Z}$.

if $\boldsymbol{Z} = \emptyset$ **then** $\boldsymbol{Z} \leftarrow \{\mathbb{1}\}$;
foreach $z \in \boldsymbol{Z}$ **do**
  // i) compute marginal distribution
  // client side:
  let v^i_z be the count of $\boldsymbol{Z} = z$ on D^i;
  let v^i_{xz}, v^i_{yz} be the count of $X = x$ (or $Y = y$) with $\boldsymbol{Z} = z$ on D^i;
  // server side:
  $v_z \leftarrow$ SecureAgg($\{v^i\}_{i\in[K]}$);
  foreach $x \in X$ **do** $v_x \leftarrow$ SecureAgg($\{v^i_{xz}\}_{i\in[K]}$);
  foreach $y \in Y$ **do** $v_y \leftarrow$ SecureAgg($\{v^i_{yz}\}_{i\in[K]}$);
  foreach $(x, y) \in X, Y$ **do** broadcast $\bar{v}_{xyz} = \frac{v_{xz}v_{yz}}{v_z}$;
  sample $\boldsymbol{P}$ from $\mathcal{Q}^{l\times m}_{2,0}$ and broadcast $\boldsymbol{P}$;
  // ii) compute χ^2 statistics
  // client side:
  $\boldsymbol{u}^i_z[\mathbb{I}(x,y)] \leftarrow \frac{v^i_{xyz} - \frac{\bar{v}_{xyz}}{K}}{\sqrt{\bar{v}_{xyz}}}$;
  $\boldsymbol{e}^i \leftarrow \boldsymbol{P} \times \boldsymbol{u}^i_z$;
  // server side:
  $\boldsymbol{e} \leftarrow$ SecureAgg($\{\boldsymbol{e}^i\}_{i\in[K]}$);
  $\hat{Q}_z \leftarrow \frac{\sum_{k=1}^{l} |e_k|^{2/l}}{(\frac{2}{\pi}\Gamma(\frac{2}{l})\Gamma(1-\frac{1}{l})\sin(\frac{\pi}{l}))^l}$;
  dof$_z \leftarrow (|X_{\boldsymbol{Z}=z}| - 1)(|Y_{\boldsymbol{Z}=z}| - 1)$;
end
// iii) aggregate χ^2 statistics
$\hat{Q} \leftarrow \sum \hat{Q}_z$;
dof $\leftarrow \sum$ dof$_z$;
if $\hat{Q} > \chi^2_{dof,1-\sigma}$ **then return** *reject null hypothesis*;
else return *fail to reject null hypothesis*;

To alleviate the direct release of high-dimensional distributions, we leverage the idea in [44] to recast $\hat{Q}$ statistic into a second frequency moment estimation problem and employ random projection to hide the distribution. Specifically, let $\bar{v}_{xyz} = \frac{v_{xz}v_{yz}}{v_z}$. For each client, we compute $\boldsymbol{u}_z^i[\mathbb{I}(x,y)] = \frac{v_{xyz}^i - \frac{\bar{v}_{xyz}}{K}}{\sqrt{\bar{v}_{xyz}}}$ where $\mathbb{I} : [|X|] \times [|Y|] \to [|X||Y|]$ is an index function. The $\hat{Q}$ can be rewritten as

$$\begin{aligned}\hat{Q} &= \sum_{x,y,z} \frac{(v_{xyz} - \frac{v_{xz}v_{yz}}{v_z})^2}{\frac{v_{xz}v_{yz}}{v_z}} = \sum_z \sum_{x,y} \left(\frac{v_{xyz} - \bar{v}_{xyz}}{\sqrt{\bar{v}_{xyz}}} \right)^2 \\ &= \sum_z \| \sum_{i \in [K]} \boldsymbol{u}_z^i \|_2^2 = \sum_z \|\boldsymbol{u}_z\|_2^2\end{aligned} \tag{2}$$

It is worth noting that the above recasting does not obviously conceal v_{xyz} because it can still be derived from $\boldsymbol{u}_z$. To protect $\boldsymbol{u}_z^i$, a random projection is employed to encode $\boldsymbol{u}_z^i$ into $\boldsymbol{e}^i$ and a geometric mean estimation is performed over the encoding. Then, the main result of [21,44] implies the following theorem.

Theorem 1. *Let $\boldsymbol{P}$ be a projection matrix whose values are independently sampled from a α-stable distribution [12] $\mathcal{Q}_{2,0}^{l \times m}$ ($m = |X||Y|$), $\boldsymbol{e}^i = P \times \boldsymbol{u}_z^i$ be the encoding on the i-th client and $\boldsymbol{e} = \sum_{i \in [K]} \boldsymbol{e}^i$ be the aggregated encoding. $\hat{d}_{(2),gm} = \frac{\sum_{k=1}^{l} |e_k|^{2/l}}{(\frac{2}{\pi}\Gamma(\frac{2}{l})\Gamma(1-\frac{1}{l})\sin(\frac{\pi}{l}))^l}$ is the unbiased estimation on $\|\boldsymbol{u}_z\|_2^2$.*

Accordingly, we can compute $\hat{Q}_z$ for each $z \in Z$ and sum them up to obtain $\hat{Q}$. Using secure aggregation, the joint distribution of X, Y, Z on local datasets is already perfectly invisible to the central server. The encoding scheme in the above theorem provides additional privacy protection to the distribution on the global dataset. Specifically, under appropriate parameters, after receiving the aggregated encoding $\boldsymbol{e}$, the server cannot revert back to the original $\boldsymbol{u}_z$. Indeed, given $\boldsymbol{e}$, $\boldsymbol{u}_z$ is concealed into a subspace with exponential feasible solutions according to Theorem 2 in [44]. We now outline the workflow of our federated conditional independence test protocol in Algorithm 1. To make Algorithm 1 compatible to empty condition set (i.e., $\boldsymbol{Z} = \emptyset$), we add a dummy variable $\mathbb{1}$ to $\boldsymbol{Z}$ (line 1) and the subsequent loop (lines 2–21) only contains one iteration applied on the entire (local) datasets (e.g., v_z^i is the count of total samples in D^i, and so on). In each iteration where a possible value of $\boldsymbol{Z}$ is picked, each client counts $v_z^i, v_{xz}^i, v_{yz}^i$ privately (lines 5–6) and securely aggregates to the server (lines 8–10). The server then broadcasts $\bar{v}_{xyz} = \frac{v_{xz}v_{yz}}{v_z}$ for each $(x, y) \in X, Y$ and the projection matrix $\boldsymbol{P}$ to all clients (lines 11–12). Then, the client computes $\boldsymbol{u}_z^i$ and generates $\boldsymbol{e}^i$ (lines 15–16). The server aggregates encodings (line 18), perform geometric mean estimation to derive $\hat{Q}_z$ (line 19) and compute degree of freedom $\texttt{dof}_z$ (line 20). After enumerating all $z \in Z$, the total χ^2 statistics and the total degree of freedom is computed by summing $\hat{Q}_z$ and $\texttt{dof}_z$ up, respectively (lines 23–24). Finally, $\hat{Q}$ is compared against $\chi^2_{\texttt{dof},1-\sigma}$ and Algorithm 1 decides whether to reject null hypothesis (lines 25–26).

5 Evaluation

In this section, we evaluate FedC^{2}SL to answer the following three research questions (RQs): **RQ1: Effectiveness.** Does FedC^{2}SL effectively recover causal relations from data with different variable sizes and client numbers? **RQ2: Resiliency.** Does FedC^{2}SL manifest resiliency in terms of client dropouts or client heterogeneity? **RQ3: Real-world Data.** Does FedC^{2}SL identify reasonable causal relations on real-world data? We answer them in the following sections.

5.1 Experimental Setup

Baselines. We compare the performance of FedC^{2}SL with seven baselines, including two SOTA methods: NOTEARS-ADMM [29] and RFCD [27]. We also implement two baseline algorithms, PC-Voting and PC-CIT-Voting, which aggregate and vote on local causal graphs to form a global causal graph. Additionally, we compare with the centralized PC algorithm [37], as well as FCI algorithm and two voting-based baselines (FCI-Voting and FCI-CIT-Voting). We report the hyperparameters in Supplementary Material [45].

Dataset. We evaluate FedC^{2}SL on synthetic and real-world datasets. We describe the generation of synthetic datasets in Supplementary Material [45]. We use the discrete version of the Sachs dataset [34], a real-world dataset on protein expressions involved in human immune system cells.

Metrics. We use Structural Hamming Distance (SHD) between the Markov equivalence classes of learned causal graph and the ground truth (lower is better). We also record the processing time. For each experiment, we repeat ten times and report the averaged results.

5.2 Effectiveness

High-dimensional datasets pose challenges for causal structure learning. We evaluate the performance of FedC^{2}SL on datasets with varying variable sizes and fixed client size ($K = 10$) in Fig. 2. We report the results for federated causal structure learning for DAG and MAG. We observe that FedC^{2}SL consistently outperforms all other methods (excluding its centralized version) in terms of SHD on all scales. Its accuracy is closely aligned with PC and FCI (i.e., its centralized version), indicating negligible utility loss in the federated procedure.

Furthermore, the processing time of FedC^{2}SL is slightly higher but acceptable and often lower than other counterparts. On datasets with 100 variables, FedC^{2}SL shows a much lower SHD than other federated algorithms, indicating its scalability to high-dimensional data. In contrast, NOTEARS-ADMM performs poorly on datasets with 100 variables due to its assumption on additive

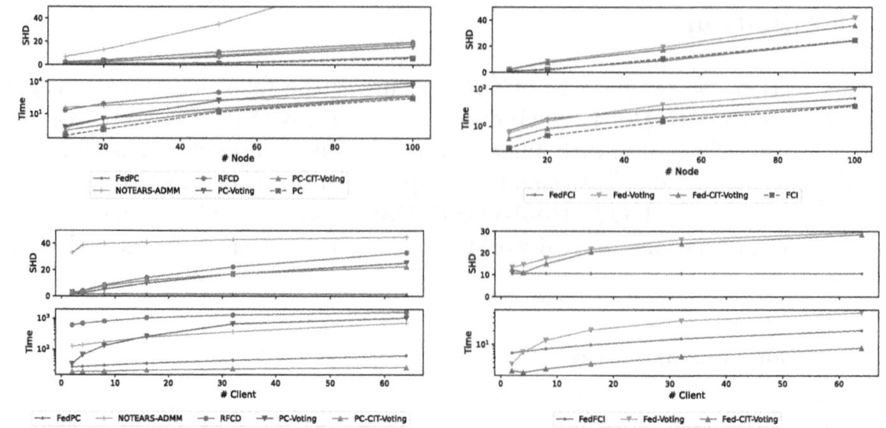

Fig. 2. Performance on different variable sizes and client numbers.

noise being violated in discrete datasets, which is further amplified by high-dimensional settings.

We also studied the effectiveness of FEDC^{2}SL with different client sizes ($K \in \{2, 4, 8, 16, 32, 64\}$) under a fixed variable size ($d = 50$) in Fig. 2. With the growth of client size, most algorithms show an increasing trend in terms of SHD. However, FEDC^{2}SL consistently has the lowest SHD with a mild increase of processing time. In contrast, local causal graph learning-based methods have notable difficulty in handling large client sizes due to the low stability of local datasets and reaching a high-quality consensus on the global causal graph.

Answer to RQ1: FEDC^{2}SL *effectively recovers causal graphs from federated datasets with high accuracy for varying variable sizes and client sizes, outperforming existing methods and having negligible utility loss.*

5.3 Resiliency

We evaluate the performance of different algorithms in federated learning with respect to client dropouts and heterogeneous datasets (Fig. 3).

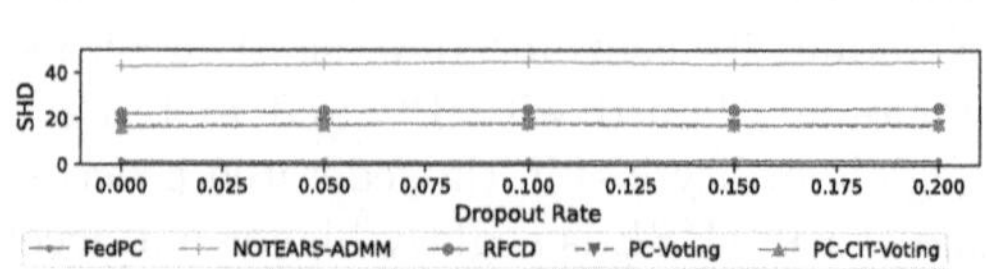

(a) Resiliency to client dropouts.

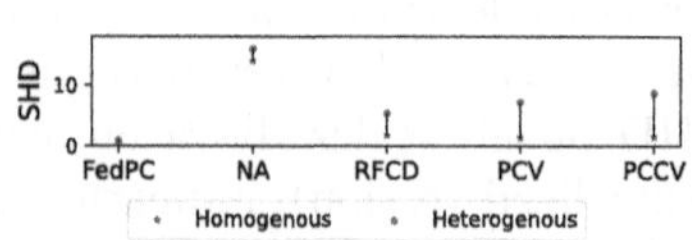

(b) Resiliency to client heterogeneity.

Fig. 3. Resiliency evaluation.

In terms of resiliency to client dropouts, most algorithms, including our FEDC^{2}SL, do not explicitly consider it in their design. However, our experiments show that the SHD of FEDC^{2}SL and other algorithms does not notably downgrade even if 20% clients drop out. This emphasizes the robustness of de facto causal structure learning algorithms to client dropouts.

Regarding resiliency to client heterogeneity, FEDPC performs consistently well in both homogeneous and heterogeneous datasets ($d = 20, K = 4$). Notably, FEDPC demonstrates negligible performance degradation in the presence of client heterogeneity, while other solutions, such as NOTEARS-ADMM and RFCD, suffer notable increases in SHD (on average, 4.7 increase on SHD). This limitation results from their assumption that local datasets accurately represent the joint probability distribution, which is invalid under heterogeneity. Actually, the local causal graph could arbitrarily diverge from the true causal graph.

Answer to RQ2: FEDC^{2}SL *shows resilience to both client dropouts and client heterogeneity. Compared to other solutions,* FEDC^{2}SL *consistently performs well in homogeneous and heterogeneous datasets.*

5.4 Real-World Data

We evaluate FEDC^{2}SL's performance on the protein expression dataset from the real-world dataset, Scahs [34], which contains 853 samples and 11 variables with a ground-truth causal graph having 17 edges. We split the dataset into $K \in \{2, 4, 8, 16, 32, 64\}$ clients and perform federated causal structure learning. Each algorithm runs ten times for each setting and we report the average results in Fig. 4. The results show that FEDC^{2}SL demonstrates the best and highly stable performance on this dataset compared to other algorithms.

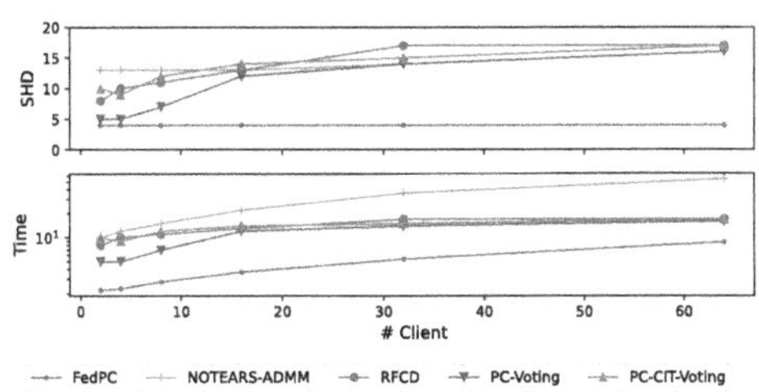

Fig. 4. Performance on the Sachs dataset.

With 64 clients, FEDC^{2}SL obtains a minimal SHD of 5.6 while the minimal SHD of other algorithms is 15.7. This indicates that most edges are incorrect in causal graphs learned by previous algorithms. We interpret that FEDC^{2}SL offers a unique advantage on learning from federated small datasets.

We present the Markov equivalence classes of causal graphs learned by FEDPC, NOTEARS-ADMM, and RFCD under two clients in Fig. 5. In general, FEDPC generates the most accurate causal graph with the lowest SHD without any erroneous edge. In contrast, both NOTEARS-ADMM and RFCD have incorrect edges, and NOTEARS-ADMM generates a considerable number of erroneous edges, which would significantly undermine human comprehension of the underlying causal mechanisms behind the data.

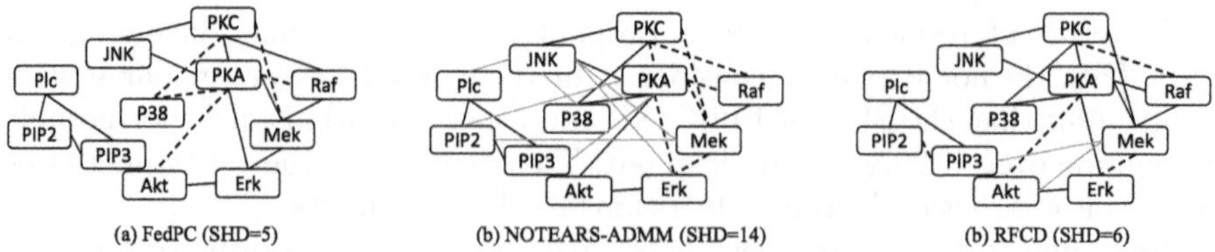

Fig. 5. Causal graphs learned by FEDPC, NOTEARS-ADMM, and RFCD. Black solid lines denote correct edges learned by the algorithm; orange lines denote erroneous edges learned by the algorithm; dashed lines denote missing edges. (Color figure online)

Answer to RQ3: FEDC^{2}SL *outperforms other methods on the real-world dataset, Sachs, demonstrating the best and highly stable performance with a much lower SHD.*

6 Related Work

Private Causal Inference. Several studies have focused on privacy protections in the causal inference process. Xu et al. [46], Wang et al. [43], and Ma et al. [24] independently propose differentially private causal structure learning methods. Kusner et al. [19] present a differentially private additive noise model for inferring pairwise cause-effect relations, while Niu et al. [30] propose a differentially private cause-effect estimation algorithm. Murakonda et al. [28] study the privacy risks of learning causal graphs from data.

Federated Statistical Tests. The federated χ^2 test [44] is closely related to our work. It is a federated *correlation test*, whereas the χ^2-test in FEDC^{2}SL is designed for *conditional independence test*. Our work applies federated statistical tests to enable practical federated causal structure learning, a crucial step in understanding the causal relations of data and enabling causal inference. Bogdanov et al. [5] design an MPC-based federated Student's t-test protocol, while Yue et al. [48] propose a federated hypothesis testing scheme for data generated from a linear model. Furthermore, Gaboardi et al. [9] use local differential privacy to secure the χ^2-test, and Vepakomma et al. [40] propose a differentially private independence testing across two parties.

Federated Machine Learning. Federated learning refers to the process of collaboratively training a machine learning model from distributed datasets across clients and has been studied extensively [15]. McMahan et al. [25] originally coined the term, and since then, there have been various proposals [11,16,17,38,47] to address practical challenges, such as communication costs and non-IID data across different clients. These proposals include update quantization [2,18], fine-tuning homomorphic encryption precision [49], and optimizing non-IID data [7,26,42].

7 Conclusion

In this paper, we propose FEDC^{2}SL, a federated constraint-based causal structure learning framework. FEDC^{2}SL is the first work that applies federated conditional independence test protocol to enable federated causal structure learning and is tolerant to client heterogeneity. We instantiate two algorithms with FEDC^{2}SL, namely FEDPC and FEDFCI, to handle different assumptions about data. Through extensive experiments, we find FEDC^{2}SL manifests competitive performance on both synthetic data and real-world data.

Acknowledgement. We thank the anonymous reviewers for their insightful comments. We also thank Qi Pang for valuable discussions. This research is supported in part by the HKUST 30 for 30 research initiative scheme under the contract Z1283 and the Academic Hardware Grant from NVIDIA.

References

1. Addo, P.M., Manibialoa, C., McIsaac, F.: Exploring nonlinearity on the co2 emissions, economic production and energy use nexus: a causal discovery approach. Energy Rep. **7**, 6196–6204 (2021)
2. Amiri, M.M., Gunduz, D., Kulkarni, S.R., Poor, H.V.: Federated learning with quantized global model updates. arXiv preprint arXiv:2006.10672 (2020)
3. Belyaeva, A., Squires, C., Uhler, C.: Dci: learning causal differences between gene regulatory networks. Bioinformatics **37**(18), 3067–3069 (2021)
4. Bishop, Y.M., Fienberg, S.E., Fienberg, S.E., Holland, P.W.: Discrete multivariate analysis (1976)
5. Bogdanov, D., Kamm, L., Laur, S., Pruulmann-Vengerfeldt, P., Talviste, R., Willemson, J.: Privacy-preserving statistical data analysis on federated databases. In: Preneel, B., Ikonomou, D. (eds.) APF 2014. LNCS, vol. 8450, pp. 30–55. Springer, Cham (2014). https://doi.org/10.1007/978-3-319-06749-0_3
6. Bonawitz, K., et al.: Practical secure aggregation for privacy-preserving machine learning. In: Proceedings of the 2017 ACM SIGSAC Conference on Computer and Communications Security, pp. 1175–1191 (2017)
7. Chai, Z., Chen, Y., Zhao, L., Cheng, Y., Rangwala, H.: Fedat: a high-performance and communication-efficient federated learning system with asynchronous tiers. arXiv preprint arXiv:2010.05958 (2020)
8. Fereidooni, H., et al.: Safelearn: secure aggregation for private federated learning. In: 2021 IEEE Security and Privacy Workshops (SPW), pp. 56–62. IEEE (2021)
9. Gaboardi, M., Rogers, R.: Local private hypothesis testing: chi-square tests. In: International Conference on Machine Learning, pp. 1626–1635. PMLR (2018)
10. Gao, E., Chen, J., Shen, L., Liu, T., Gong, M., Bondell, H.: Feddag: federated dag structure learning. arXiv preprint arXiv:2112.03555 (2021)
11. He, C., et al.: Fedml: a research library and benchmark for federated machine learning. arXiv preprint (2020)
12. Indyk, P.: Stable distributions, pseudorandom generators, embeddings, and data stream computation. J. ACM (JACM) **53**(3), 307–323 (2006)
13. Ji, Z., Ma, P., Wang, S.: Perfce: performance debugging on databases with chaos engineering-enhanced causality analysis. arXiv preprint arXiv:2207.08369 (2022)

14. Ji, Z., Ma, P., Wang, S., Li, Y.: Causality-aided trade-off analysis for machine learning fairness. arXiv preprint arXiv:2305.13057 (2023)
15. Kairouz, P., et al.: Advances and open problems in federated learning. Found. Trends® Mach. Learn. **14**(1–2), 1–210 (2021)
16. Karimireddy, S.P., Kale, S., Mohri, M., Reddi, S., Stich, S., Suresh, A.T.: Scaffold: stochastic controlled averaging for federated learning. In: International Conference on Machine Learning, pp. 5132–5143. PMLR (2020)
17. Khan, L.U., et al.: Federated learning for edge networks: resource optimization and incentive mechanism. IEEE Commun. Maga. **58**(10), 88–93 (2020)
18. Konečnỳ, J., McMahan, H.B., Yu, F.X., Richtárik, P., Suresh, A.T., Bacon, D.: Federated learning: strategies for improving communication efficiency. arXiv preprint arXiv:1610.05492 (2016)
19. Kusner, M.J., Sun, Y., Sridharan, K., Weinberger, K.Q.: Private causal inference. In: Artificial Intelligence and Statistics, pp. 1308–1317. PMLR (2016)
20. Lauritzen, S.L.: Graphical Models. Clarendon Press, London (1996)
21. Li, P.: Estimators and tail bounds for dimension reduction in $l_\alpha (0 < \alpha \leq 2)$ using stable random projections. In: Proceedings of the Nineteenth Annual ACM-SIAM Symposium on Discrete Algorithms, pp. 10–19 (2008)
22. Ma, P., et al.: Ml4s: learning causal skeleton from vicinal graphs. In: Proceedings of the 28th ACM SIGKDD Conference on Knowledge Discovery and Data Mining, pp. 1213–1223 (2022)
23. Ma, P., Ding, R., Wang, S., Han, S., Zhang, D.: Xinsight: explainable data analysis through the lens of causality. arXiv preprint arXiv:2207.12718 (2022)
24. Ma, P., Ji, Z., Pang, Q., Wang, S.: Noleaks: differentially private causal discovery under functional causal model. IEEE Trans. Inf. Forensics Secur. **17**, 2324–2338 (2022)
25. McMahan, B., Moore, E., Ramage, D., Hampson, S., Arcas, B.A.: Communication-efficient learning of deep networks from decentralized data. In: Artificial Intelligence and Statistics, pp. 1273–1282. PMLR (2017)
26. Mhaisen, N., Awad, A., Mohamed, A., Erbad, A., Guizani, M.: Analysis and optimal edge assignment for hierarchical federated learning on non-iid data. arXiv preprint arXiv:2012.05622 (2020)
27. Mian, O., Kaltenpoth, D., Kamp, M.: Regret-based federated causal discovery. In: The KDD 2022 Workshop on Causal Discovery, pp. 61–69. PMLR (2022)
28. Murakonda, S.K., Shokri, R., Theodorakopoulos, G.: Quantifying the privacy risks of learning high-dimensional graphical models. In: International Conference on Artificial Intelligence and Statistics, pp. 2287–2295. PMLR (2021)
29. Ng, I., Zhang, K.: Towards federated bayesian network structure learning with continuous optimization. In: International Conference on Artificial Intelligence and Statistics, pp. 8095–8111. PMLR (2022)
30. Niu, F., Nori, H., Quistorff, B., Caruana, R., Ngwe, D., Kannan, A.: Differentially private estimation of heterogeneous causal effects. arXiv preprint arXiv:2202.11043 (2022)
31. Peters, J., Janzing, D., Schölkopf, B.: Elements of Causal Inference: Foundations and Learning Algorithms. The MIT Press, Cambridge (2017)
32. Pinna, A., Soranzo, N., De La Fuente, A.: From knockouts to networks: establishing direct cause-effect relationships through graph analysis. PloS One **5**(10), e12912 (2010)
33. Runge, J., et al.: Inferring causation from time series in earth system sciences. Nat. Commun. **10**(1), 1–13 (2019)

34. Sachs, K., Perez, O., Pe'er, D., Lauffenburger, D.A., Nolan, G.P.: Causal protein-signaling networks derived from multiparameter single-cell data. Science **308**(5721), 523–529 (2005)
35. Samet, S., Miri, A.: Privacy-preserving bayesian network for horizontally partitioned data. In: 2009 International Conference on Computational Science and Engineering, vol. 3, pp. 9–16. IEEE (2009)
36. Shen, X., Ma, S., Vemuri, P., Simon, G.: Challenges and opportunities with causal discovery algorithms: application to alzheimer's pathophysiology. Sci. Rep. **10**(1), 1–12 (2020)
37. Spirtes, P., Glymour, C.N., Scheines, R., Heckerman, D.: Causation, Prediction, and Search. MIT press, Cambrideg (2000)
38. T Dinh, C., Tran, N., Nguyen, T.D.: Personalized federated learning with moreau envelopes. In: NeurIPS (2020)
39. Triola, M.: Essentials of Statistics. Pearson Education, Boston (2014). https://books.google.com.hk/books?id=QZN-AgAAQBAJ
40. Vepakomma, P., Amiri, M.M., Canonne, C.L., Raskar, R., Pentland, A.: Private independence testing across two parties. arXiv preprint arXiv:2207.03652 (2022)
41. Versteeg, P., Mooij, J., Zhang, C.: Local constraint-based causal discovery under selection bias. In: Conference on Causal Learning and Reasoning, pp. 840–860. PMLR (2022)
42. Wang, H., Kaplan, Z., Niu, D., Li, B.: Optimizing federated learning on non-iid data with reinforcement learning. In: IEEE INFOCOM 2020-IEEE Conference on Computer Communications, pp. 1698–1707. IEEE (2020)
43. Wang, L., Pang, Q., Song, D.: Towards practical differentially private causal graph discovery. Adv. Neural Inf. Process. Syst. **33**, 5516–5526 (2020)
44. Wang, L., Pang, Q., Wang, S., Song, D.: Fed-χ^2: privacy preserving federated correlation test. arXiv preprint arXiv:2105.14618 (2021)
45. Wang, Z., Ma, P., Wang, S.: Towards practical federated causal structure learning. arXiv preprint arXiv:2306.09433 (2023)
46. Xu, D., Yuan, S., Wu, X.: Differential privacy preserving causal graph discovery. In: 2017 IEEE Symposium on Privacy-Aware Computing (PAC), pp. 60–71. IEEE (2017)
47. Yang, Q., Liu, Y., Chen, T., Tong, Y.: Federated machine learning: concept and applications. ACM Trans. Intell. Syst. Technol. (TIST) **10**(2), 1–19 (2019)
48. Yue, X., Kontar, R.A., Gómez, A.M.E.: Federated data analytics: a study on linear models. arXiv preprint arXiv:2206.07786 (2022)
49. Zhang, C., Li, S., Xia, J., Wang, W., Yan, F., Liu, Y.: {BatchCrypt}: efficient homomorphic encryption for {Cross-Silo} federated learning. In: 2020 USENIX annual technical conference (USENIX ATC 2020), pp. 493–506 (2020)
50. Zhang, J.: On the completeness of orientation rules for causal discovery in the presence of latent confounders and selection bias. Artif. Intell. **172**(16–17), 1873–1896 (2008)

Triplets Oversampling for Class Imbalanced Federated Datasets

Chenguang Xiao and Shuo Wang(✉)

School of Computer Science, University of Birmingham, Birmingham B15 2TT, UK
cxx075@student.bham.ac.uk, s.wang.2@bham.ac.uk

Abstract. Class imbalance is a pervasive problem in machine learning, leading to poor performance in the minority class that is inadequately represented. Federated learning, which trains a shared model collaboratively among multiple clients with their data locally for privacy protection, is also susceptible to class imbalance. The distributed structure and privacy rules in federated learning introduce extra complexities to the challenge of isolated, small, and highly skewed datasets. While sampling and ensemble learning are state-of-the-art techniques for mitigating class imbalance from the data and algorithm perspectives, they face limitations in the context of federated learning. To address this challenge, we propose a novel oversampling algorithm called "Triplets" that generates synthetic samples for both minority and majority classes based on their shared classification boundary. The proposed algorithm captures new minority samples by leveraging three triplets around the boundary, where two come from the majority class and one from the minority class. This approach offers several advantages over existing oversampling techniques on federated datasets. We evaluate the effectiveness of our proposed algorithm through extensive experiments using various real-world datasets and different models in both centralized and federated learning environments. Our results demonstrate the effectiveness of our proposed algorithm, which outperforms existing oversampling techniques. In conclusion, our proposed algorithm offers a promising solution to the class imbalance problem in federated learning. The source code is released at github.com/Xiao-Chenguang/Triplets-Oversampling.

Keywords: Class imbalance · Oversampling · Federated learning

1 Introduction

Class imbalance is a well-known challenge in machine learning tasks that has been studied extensively. Federated Learning (FL), which has emerged as an effective privacy protection framework, poses new challenges for addressing class imbalance. In FL, the shared model is collaboratively trained by multiple clients using their raw data, which are often imbalanced and locally available. As a result, class imbalance in FL is more complex and unavoidable. The specific challenge in FL is that the datasets tend to be small and server-imbalanced, making it

© The Author(s), under exclusive license to Springer Nature Switzerland AG 2023
D. Koutra et al. (Eds.): ECML PKDD 2023, LNAI 14170, pp. 368–383, 2023.
https://doi.org/10.1007/978-3-031-43415-0_22

difficult to achieve a balanced training dataset. Existing advanced oversampling techniques have demonstrated effectiveness in mitigating class imbalance; however, their applicability in the context of FL is constrained for 2 reason as shown in Sect. 4. Firstly, Small and server-imbalanced datasets degraded the effectiveness of advanced oversampling techniques. More importantly, aggregation of rebalance datasets by existing oversamplings in FL is less effective compared to rebalance the aggregated datasets as in centralized learning.

1.1 Class Imbalance

Class imbalance is the inconsistency in the degree to which a class is characterised by data points between classes. The majority refers to the class that is well represented by more data points, while the minority class is represented by fewer data points inadequately. Most machine learning models assume a balanced training dataset, optimized towards maximum overall accuracy, resulting in poor performance on the minority class when faced with severe class imbalance.

It has been studied extensively with mainly 3 types of solutions – data-level [4,9,16], algorithm-level [5,13], and hybrid approaches [2,7]. Class imbalance can be further classified into relative imbalance and absolute imbalance problems, depending on the overall size of data [18]. Data-level approaches such as random undersampling and oversampling have been effective in addressing the importance of minority data points in cases of relative imbalance, where the size of the dataset is reasonably large. However, these approaches are not effective in addressing the absolute imbalance, where the size of the dataset is very small, and simply duplicating minority instances provides no additional information relevant to the pattern since the minority class may not contain sufficient information to infer the hidden pattern.

Due to the limitations of basic sampling techniques, advanced oversampling methods have been introduced that generate new data points. One example of such methods is SMOTE [4]. Currently, SMOTE-based oversampling and ensemble learning are considered to be the most effective and advanced techniques for mitigating class imbalance.

1.2 Federated Learning with Class Imbalance

Federated learning(FL) is a popular learning framework that trains a shared model among a large number of clients with their local data. It was proposed by McMahan [14] in 2017 as a solution to the trade-off in distributed machine learning applications between increasing privacy concerns over data sharing and the high demand for training data. With the novel idea of transmitting model parameters between a server and its clients instead transmitting raw data directly, FL balances data privacy/security and model performance well. However, new challenges arise as the scale of edge devices and non-IID local datasets increase [11,12,20].

Despite recent progress, class imbalance, a classical learning challenge in traditional centralized learning, has been an uncharted area in FL.Class imbalance is a challenge in FL systems that deal with raw client data, such as in healthcare where positive samples are far less than negative ones, or in mobile device keyboards where certain emojis are used more in one place than in others [11]. Unfortunately, this challenge becomes much more difficult in distributed learning environments than in traditional centralized learning, where the client datasets can be very small or severely imbalanced. Moreover, there may be an imbalance mismatch between clients, such as class missing problems, which will not be covered in this paper as no resampling is designed for it.

Directly applying existing class imbalance algorithms to FL can be inappropriate, or even cause worse generalization and difficulty in model convergence [15,19]. Existing advanced sampling methods applied to distributed data do not form a well-rebalanced global dataset with large amounts of small and imbalanced clients data. This weakens the effectiveness of traditional advanced sampling approaches focused on the minority class itself. FL systems collaborate with thousands of independent clients to train a reliable model as the clients hold too little data to infer the hidden pattern. However, the client dataset is also too small to be correctly resampled by advanced oversampling approaches focusing only on minorities. With too little data or severe imbalance, the generated minority class samples may lie in the local minority domains easily located in the global majority domain and hinder the global model.

1.3 Challenges and Contributions

Although existing advanced oversampling approaches may not be effective for addressing class imbalance in federated datasets, the concept of data generation can still hold value in the FL context for two reasons. Firstly, they can highlight the importance and costs of the minority class by introducing additional instances that prevent it from being overlooked. Secondly, generating synthetic minority instances that deviate from identical copies can provide valuable information for pattern recognition and learning. While state-of-the-art data generation techniques, including SMOTE and its variants, have not succeeded in achieving these goals on distributed datasets due to their focus on minority data alone, the secure and effective oversampling of minorities within small and severely imbalanced FL datasets remains a significant challenge.

This paper, therefore, proposes a new advanced oversampling algorithm called "Triplets" for imbalanced federated datasets. The novelty lies in 1) it recognizes the mutual classification boundary of minority and majority classes as the rule of oversampling the minority classes; 2) it makes full use of the adequate information from the majority class to synthesise minority class samples parallel to the majority boundary. Other contributions of this paper include:

- We investigated the quality of generated data considering the factors that impact class imbalance and the nature of federated datasets.
- we conducted extensive comparison experiments involving diverse datasets and models.

We find that 1) SMOTE and its variants have to trade between synthesis effectiveness and security with small or severe imbalance data. 2) Triplets generates effective minority data even in small and severe imbalance datasets stably; 3) Triplets applied locally on FL client data generates minority data located securely in the global minority domain.

The rest of this work is presented as follows: Sect. 2 presents the related works. Section 3 describes the proposed Triplets algorithm in detail. Section 4 examines the generated data quality in class imbalance from the perspective of centralized learning and FL. Section 5 presents the experiment results and analyses on various datasets, models, and learning scenarios. Section 6 summarizes the strength and weaknesses and points out the possible future works.

2 Related Work

2.1 Tackle Class Imbalance in FL

Class imbalance is a common challenge in federated learning, resulting in poor performance of the learning algorithm on the minority class [11]. The imbalance problem is further compounded by the fact that the client's data is not always accessible to the central server in a federated learning setup, making it difficult to apply traditional techniques for handling class imbalance [19]. Only a few papers have discussed class imbalance problems in FL so far, and none of them considers advanced sampling approaches. Three of them modify the loss function and aggregation rule [3,6,17]. The remaining one changes the FL framework to eliminate class imbalance [15].

Fed-Focal Loss [15] uses a federated version of Focal Loss that automatically lowers the cost of samples from the well-classified classes. **Ratio Loss** [17] modifies the Cross Entropy Loss(CELoss) to rebalance the weights of minority classes sample. Different from Fed-Focal Loss, Ratio Loss is controlled by the server when global imbalance is detected using a novel monitor scheme. Ratio Loss and Fed-Focal Loss, however, ignore the absolute rarity of minority samples. **Astraea** [6] adds mediators between the central server and clients, creating an intermediate re-balanced client group for sequential training. However, these approaches overlook the absolute rarity of minority samples and only provide algorithm-level solutions while leaving data-level solutions unexplored. Hence, it is worth investigating data-level approaches such as advanced oversampling for their effectiveness, convenience, and extensibility with other tools.

2.2 Traditional Class Imbalance Solutions

As mentioned in Sect. 1, they can be grouped into 3 categories. Among these, advanced oversampling techniques, including the synthetic minority oversampling technique (SMOTE) and its variants, are preferred. SMOTE [4] oversamples the minority class by finding k nearest neighbours of each minority sample and drawing a random sample on the line linking the minority and one of its neighbours. By interpolating minority neighbours, SMOTE addresses the minority while avoiding over-fitting caused by random oversampling. Borderline-SMOTE is a variant of SMOTE that spots the danger points around the border and generates new minorities for them. ADASYN [9] is another SMOTE variant that uses dynamic weights based on the portion of the majority in its neighbours. Danger points with more majority neighbours, are used to generate more synthetic data. SMOTE and its variants are effective in relieving the class imbalance, while its effectiveness decreases with the increase of class imbalance. As a cluster-based algorithm focuses on the minority, SMOTE and its variants receive poor cluster results and synthetic quality when minority samples size are small.

Ensemble methods are another wild accepted rebalance approach. However, the majority of ensemble learning utilizes a large amount of decision tree as a base learner, which makes it impractical in FL considering communication and model aggregation. More recently, deep learning methods have been proposed for handling class imbalance, such as Generative adversarial networks (GAN). But it is still far from a generative and reliable augmentation approach.

3 Triplets Oversampling

Different from existing advanced oversampling techniques that generate minority samples from existing minority data, Triplets oversampling take advantage of the rich information of majority classes. This approach distinguishes itself from existing oversampling techniques in three key aspects. Firstly, by considering the majority in minority synthesis, Triplets oversampling generates more reliable data points, as we will demonstrate in our experiments. Secondly, using both minority and majority data in synthesis enhances the generation effectiveness beyond the limitation of minority size. Finally, generating data along the majority-class boundary effectively expands the minority-class region, particularly for small datasets with severe imbalance.

Without loss of generality, binary classification is used to demonstrate the oversampling challenge and the effectiveness of Triplets in the rest of the paper. A multi-class problem can be converted into multiple binary problems in a one-vs-the-rest manner. For a binary classification problem, dataset $\mathcal{D}$ is composed of N samples. The minority class contains N_{min} samples denoted as x_i^p with label 1. Whereas, the N_{maj} minority denoted as x_i^{maj} with label 0. The relative imbalance measurement Imbalance Ratio(IR) is defined as $IR = N_{maj}/N_{min}$.

3.1 Beyond Traditional Resampling

As mentioned in Sect. 1, the principle behind Triplets is the majority and majority share the same separation hyperplane in a classification problem regardless of the concept complexity, imbalance level, and data size. Nevertheless, the boundary around minority classes may not reflect the real separation hyperplane due to a lack of data.

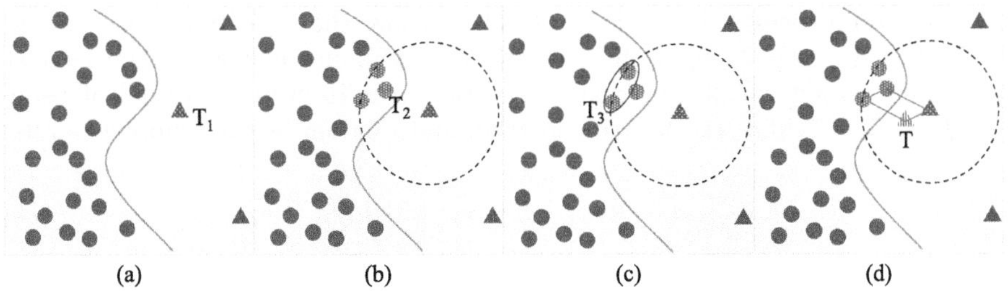

Fig. 1. Triplets generates new data for minority class workflow

The boundary around majority classes is more reliable even in severe imbalances. This new perspective provides a potential way to apply the share separation hyperplane principle in class imbalance problems where synthetic minorities can be drawn in the hyperplane parallel to the separation hyperplane which is also parallel to the boundary of majority data points. Naturally, a direct idea is to draw synthetic data from the hyperplane which crosses one of the minority points and parallel to the majority boundary.

The challenge is finding a proper way to draw the majority boundary as a reference for minority synthesis. Instead of finding the global boundary for the majority class, this paper presents an ingenious method utilizing the nearest neighbour in a small region near the minority instance to determine a local boundary.

The detailed process of Triplets oversampling is presented in Sect. 3.2.

3.2 Triplets Oversampling Process

To achieve the targets, Triplets oversampling is designed as following repeated steps as shown in Fig. 1:

1. For the minority samples x_i^p, denote the minority points as Triplet $1(T_1)$.
2. Find $k = IR$ nearest neighbors $x_j^n (j \in \{0 \dots k-1\})$ of T_1 from the majority class x^n. Denote the nearest neighbor x_0^n as Triplet $2(T_2)$.
3. Randomly chose one neighbor from the rest $k-1$ neighbors, denote it as Triplet 3 (T_3).
4. Draw a parallelogram with the triplets T_1, T_2, T_3, and the last points T is the synthetic data for the minority class.

Following Fig. 1, new minority data can be seen as a point of a parallelogram whose two points come from the majority boundary and one from the minority boundary. As the name suggests, Triplets utilizes the similarity between T_1, T_2, and T_3 to generates their next triplet T

In the second step, the number of neighbours is determined automatically by the imbalance ratio $k = IR$. This makes Triplets a parameter-free method, which extends the usibility and reduces the complexity of the algorithm.

Two more processes is applied to further ensure the security and robustness of Triplets. In step 2, T_2 is the mean of 5 neighbours instead of the nearest neighbours to get rid of abnormal majorities. Ans in step 3, instead of using $T = T_1 + T_3 - T_2$ directly, length constrain and random factor is applied as in

$$T = T_1 + \alpha \min \left(\frac{\| T_1 - T_2 \|}{\| T_2 - T_3 \|}, 1 \right) (T_3 - T_2) \tag{1}$$

In whcih α is a random number in $[0, 1]$, and $\min \left(\frac{\|T_1 - T_2\|_2}{\|T_2 - T_3\|_2}, 1 \right)$ make sure T still in the minority domain when $\| T_2 - T_3 \|_2$ is big than $\| T_1 - T_2 \|_2$.

4 Quality of Oversampled Data

The synthetic data quality is assessed in both centralized learning and FL scenarios in this section with synthetic 2D data.

4.1 Synthetic Data Quality from Class Imbalance Perspectives

Quantitatively, the class imbalance is a phenomenon of inadequate representation of partial classes. Apart from analysing the sampling algorithms empirically and comparing the performance score, evaluating the synthetic data quality from the perspective of factors that impact class imbalance is necessary. Deep behind the phenomenon, impacts of class imbalance depend on [10]:

1. The data size(absolute imbalance)
2. The imbalance level(relative imbalance)
3. The data complexity(small disjunct)

In the rest of this subsection, the sampling algorithms are reviewed from the above three aspects. For clearing the strength of the proposed algorithm, the following state-of-the-art algorithm will be included in the comparison: 1) Baseline; 2) Random Oversampling(ROS); 3) SMOTE; 4) board-line SMOTE(BSMOTE); 5) ADASYN.

Sensitivity to Data Size. It is argued that the nature of class imbalance is the small sample size [10], which causes there is not enough information to extract from for the classification tasks. Existing advanced oversampling methods confront the challenge of using cluster on only the minorities in data shortage. With fewer data from minority classes that can be clustered, the neighbours found by cluster locate far from each other. The synthetic data sampled from the connection between those false neighbours are not guaranteed in the minority domain. SMOTE and its variants, thus not effective algorithms to extract patterns in such cases.

The proposed algorithm relieves the impacts of a small minority size by considering the information from the majority and avoids wrong sampling by finding the majorities for minority synthesis.

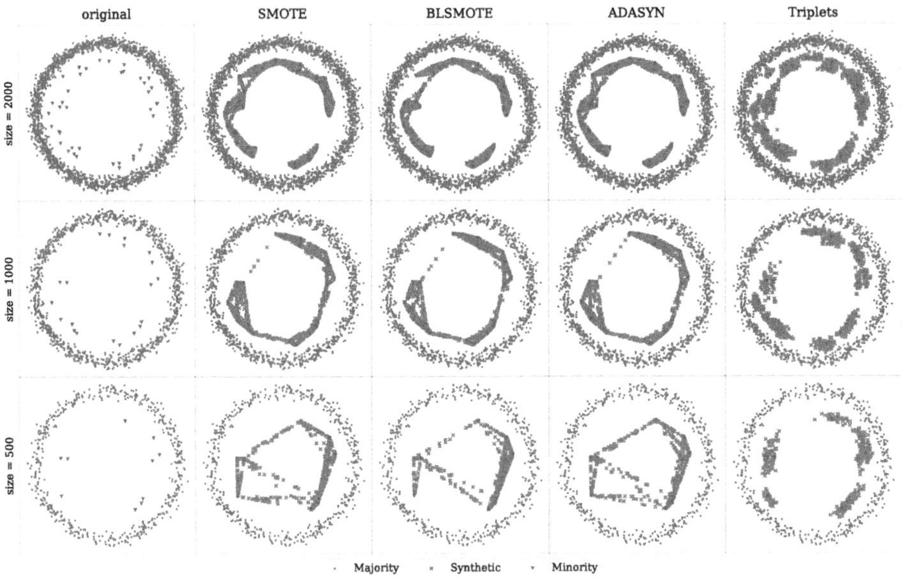

Fig. 2. Comparison of sampling methods with various data sizes

As shown in Fig. 2, with a fixed IR of 49, advanced oversampling methods are used to process the circle data. SMOTE and its variants perform worse with the whole data size dropping from 2000 to 500. They tend to generate more wrong data points close to the centre. Triplets, however, keep a stable synthetic effect per minority data without making the wrong augmentation.

Sensitivity to Imbalance Level. Class imbalance is more harmful with a high class imbalance level [10]. Existing oversampling techniques also confront severe imbalance as their effectiveness drops when IR gains. With a certain minority size N_{min}, by increasing the majority size N_{maj}, Triplets will generate more high-quality minorities along the classification boundary. From this point of view, our approach is less prone to the severe imbalance resulting from the rule of using majority samples.

Figure 3 illustrates the performance of advance oversampling methods with different IR for circle dataset. Obviously, only Triplets keeps generating effective and secure data when the imbalance level increases gradually.

Sensitivity to Data Complexity (Small Disjuncts). The class imbalance will not be a problem in cases where the data is linear spreadable. With the increase in data complexity, the class imbalance results in worse performance, as more data is required to represent the more complex domains. Cluster-based sampling as SMOTE thus shows degraded effectiveness in dealing with complex data.

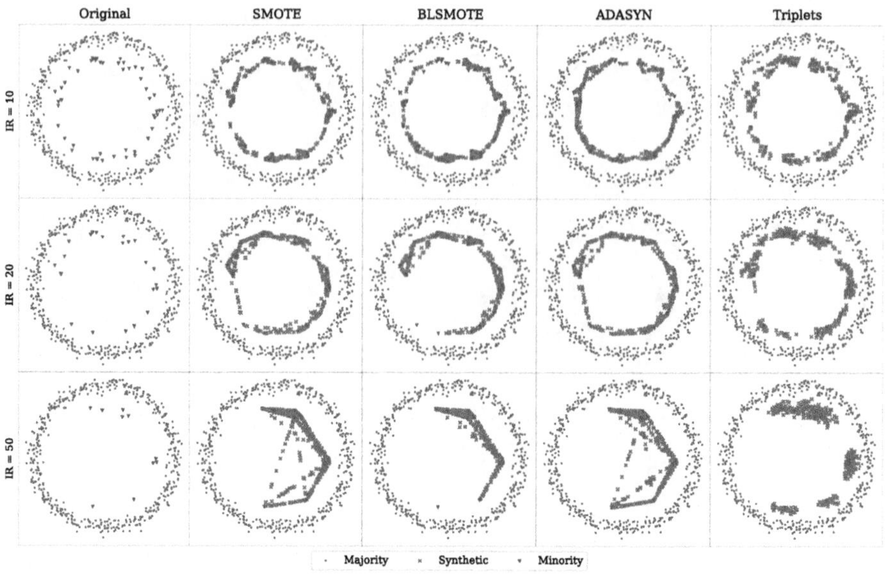

Fig. 3. Comparison of sampling methods with different imbalance level

To simulate the data complexity, another circle data [8] with small disjuncts is generated. Oversampling techniques are used to resample the data to be trained in SVM classifier. Figure 4 shows the results of the simulation in which every 2 rows resembles the same data with different sampling methods. As shown in Fig. 4, with small data size, SMOTE and its variants either create wrong data joining the two subdomains or directly ignore the small disjunct. Only Triplets generates new data for all small disjuncts correctly and safely.

4.2 Synthetic Data Quality from FL Perspective

A FL simulation is designed to illustrate the synthetic data quality by perform oversampling on the client datasets independently. The resampled data is gathered together for final evaluation.

S-curve data is applied as the upper left figure in Fig. 5 where the red triangle is the minority class in the s-curve. Except for the upper left figure, the rest are gathered results from 10 clients after independent re-sampling of given algorithm. For clarity, the majority data points are hidden in all resamples and is the same as in the Original. For SMOTE similar methods, the figure title end with the *n_neighbors* parameter. Obviously, SMOTE and its variants generate large amounts of wrong data for minorities with default *n_neighbors* of 5. Smaller *n_neighbors* relieves the falut while lead to pool representation effects. Thus, SMOTE and its variants have to trade-off between improving performance and avoiding wrong samples. The proposed methods, by considering the majority class in minority oversampling, generates safe samples in the FL scenario.

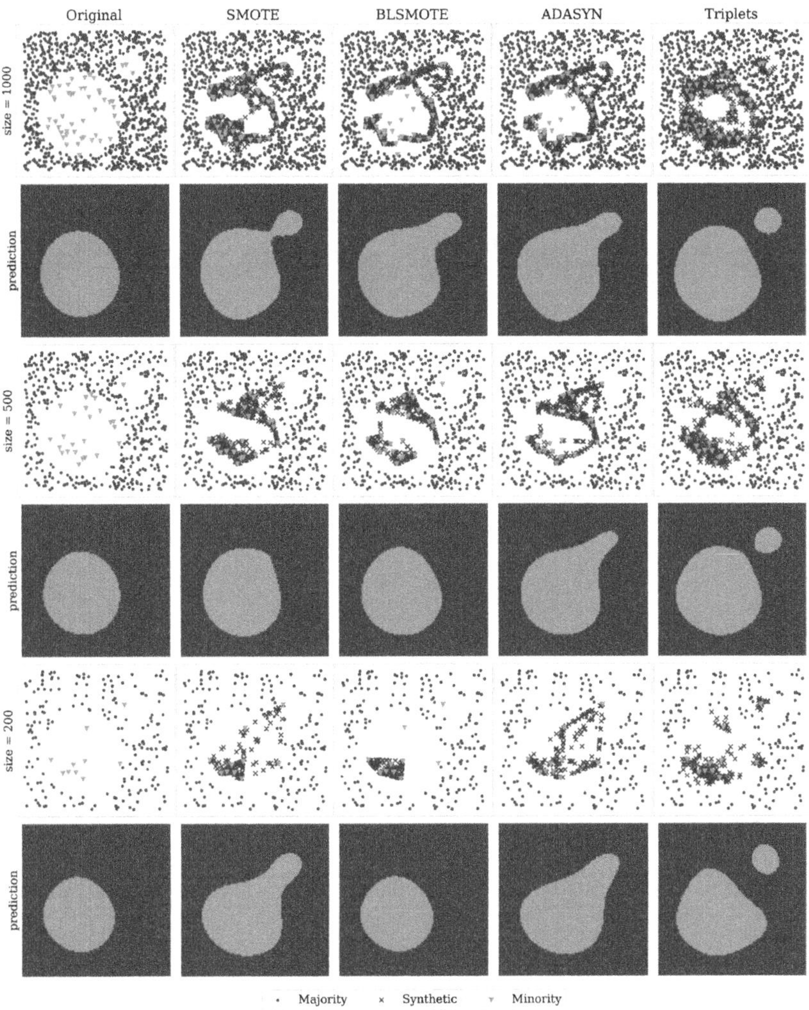

Fig. 4. Comparison of sampling methods with small disjuncts

5 Experiments

To evaluate the performance of Triplets, experiments are conducted on real-world datasets in both centralized learning and FL settings.

5.1 Experiments Setting

Imbalance Datasets. In the traditional centralized learning scenario, datasets from BSMOTE [8] and ADASYN [9] are included. The multi-class datasets are converted to binary datasets in an one-vs-rest manner and the same as in the

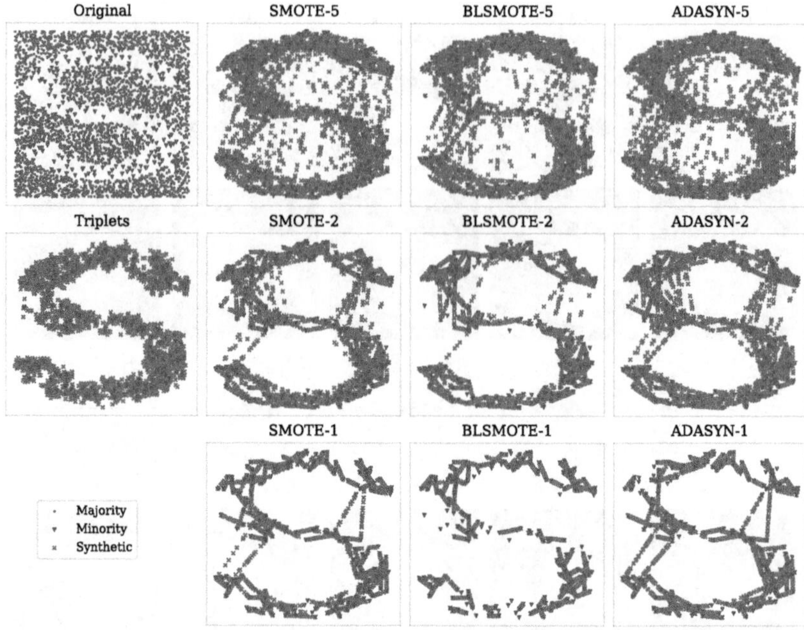

Fig. 5. Compare sampling methods with class imbalance FL data

Table 1. Imbalance datasets information for centralized learning

Dataset	vehicle	diabete	vowel	ionosphere	abalone	satimage	haberman	aloi	pulsar
samples	846	768	990	351	731	6430	306	49533	17897
features	18	8	10	33	7	36	3	27	8
IR	3.25	1.87	10.00	1.79	16.40	9.29	2.78	31.87	9.92

original work. As those datasets are fairly small in size, Pulsar and ALOI datasets are also included to evaluate the performance with larger datasets and higher imbalance level [3]. The same as [9], 50% of majority and minority are randomly selected as training data and the rest is test data. Furthermore, imbalance multiplier M_{IR} is introduced in this work to simulate a more severe imbalance. When $M_{IR} = 2$, the IR is doubled by sampling only 25% minority while keeping 50% majority in training data. The full detail of the 9 datasets is listed in Table 1.

CIFAR-10 dataset is used in FL imbalance simulation as a larger and high dimensional datasets compared with the former 9 datasets, which helps in reviling the capability of the sampling algorithms on it. CIFAR-10 is composed of 50000 training and 10000 test samples from 10 classes with 32×32 features.

To simulate class imbalance, 1 out of 10 class is selected as the minority and all other is the majority. The majority and minority are randomly split into 100 clients of equal size. Imbalance multiplier M_{IR} is also applied for severe imbalance. The original test data are used for final evaluation.

Table 2. Performance score with std of sampling algorithms in centralized learning at $M_{IR} = 4$. The best score is in bold. P value of comparison algorithm with Triplets is shown at the bottom based on paired T-test

Dataset	Score	ADASYN	BSMOTE	Baseline	ROS	SMOTE	Triplets
abalone	F1	.410±.087	.404±.106	.287±.118	.394±.098	.412±.086	**.456±.072**
	G-mean	.429±.085	.435±.087	.381±.093	.419±.090	.430±.084	**.464±.073**
	AUC	.659±.051	.649±.054	.589±.045	.648±.050	.660±.051	**.693±.044**
	AP	.252±.064	.261±.064	.231±.064	.247±.064	.252±.062	**.273±.057**
aloi	F1	.166±.017	.129±.018	.057±.007	.147±.013	.167±.018	**.176±.016**
	G-mean	.170±.015	.143±.021	.156±.013	.148±.013	.171±.016	**.178±.015**
	AUC	.566±.007	.537±.007	.515±.002	.549±.006	.566±.007	**.567±.006**
	AP	.071±.005	.068±.006	**.075±.004**	.067±.004	.071±.006	.074±.005
diabete	F1	.711±.023	.688±.029	.000±.000	.707±.022	.708±.023	**.710±.024**
	G-mean	.712±.022	.692±.027	.000±.000	.708±.022	.709±.022	**.712±.024**
	AUC	.725±.019	.718±.019	.500±.000	.727±.017	.727±.019	**.728±.020**
	AP	.654±.020	.653±.020	.483±.000	.657±.018	.657±.021	**.658±.023**
haberman	F1	**.278±.039**	.221±.055	.071±.038	.079±.045	.266±.061	.166±.060
	G-mean	**.303±.036**	.260±.052	.128±.053	.133±.057	.292±.061	.213±.065
	AUC	**.523±.021**	.520±.021	.504±.011	.503±.013	.521±.033	.512±.021
	AP	.399±.012	.398±.014	.389±.007	.388±.008	**.400±.019**	.394±.014
ionosphere	F1	.773±.057	.797±.057	.722±.058	.803±.053	.771±.061	**.815±.053**
	G-mean	.790±.047	.812±.047	.752±.047	.818±.044	.789±.050	**.828±.045**
	AUC	.813±.035	.831±.037	.784±.035	.835±.035	.812±.038	**.843±.036**
	AP	.801±.035	.821±.036	.781±.034	.826±.033	.801±.038	**.836±.034**
pulsar	F1	.770±.010	.761±.012	.000±.000	.796±.013	**.799±.013**	.796±.011
	G-mean	.774±.010	.765±.012	.000±.000	.797±.013	**.800±.013**	.797±.011
	AUC	**.898±.004**	.892±.008	.500±.000	.884±.004	.886±.004	.888±.003
	AP	.620±.015	.608±.017	.150±.000	.663±.021	**.668±.021**	.662±.018
satimage	F1	.653±.022	.646±.022	.073±.050	.659±.021	.655±.020	**.693±.016**
	G-mean	.655±.020	.652±.020	.181±.062	.662±.020	.657±.019	**.694±.016**
	AUC	.779±.017	.768±.016	.519±.014	.783±.017	.780±.016	**.825±.014**
	AP	.492±.021	.493±.021	.189±.022	.500±.021	.495±.020	**.527±.019**
vehicle	F1	.893±.029	.891±.027	.850±.029	.888±.031	.894±.028	**.922±.022**
	G-mean	.897±.027	.894±.026	.858±.026	.891±.029	.897±.026	**.924±.021**
	AUC	.908±.025	.906±.024	.872±.022	.903±.026	.908±.024	**.934±.020**
	AP	.864±.031	.861±.030	.824±.028	.858±.033	.864±.030	**.892±.025**
vowel	F1	.874±.070	.871±.071	.832±.064	.874±.074	.878±.069	**.897±.052**
	G-mean	.881±.063	.879±.064	.844±.054	.882±.066	.885±.062	**.900±.048**
	AUC	.898±.058	.894±.058	.860±.045	.895±.057	.901±.058	**.920±.047**
	AP	.810±.093	.807±.095	.757±.074	.812±.098	.816±.093	**.836±.074**
p value	F1	0.002	<0.001	<0.001	<0.001	0.011	/
	G-mean	0.001	<0.001	<0.001	<0.001	0.004	/
	AUC	<0.001	<0.001	<0.001	<0.001	<0.001	/
	AP	<0.001	<0.001	<0.001	<0.001	<0.001	/

Models and Parameters. For the centralized learning scenario, Support Vector Machine(SVM) with rbf kernel is used as the classifier for stable outputs. Currently, the majority of FL systems are designed for neural network models with easy and reliable aggregation algorithm FedAvg [14]. For classifying images, AlexNet is used as the shared model for CIFAR-10 dataset.

Table 3. Centralized learning mean score and std of all 9 datasets on various M_{IR}

M_{IR}	Score	ADASYN	BSMOTE	Baseline	ROS	SMOTE	Triplets
1	F1	.6330±.263	.6400±.253	.5512±.333	.6431±.265	.6446±.261	**.6491±.253**
	G-mean	.6452±.254	.6479±.251	.5669±.322	.6519±.259	.6542±.253	**.6600±.246**
	AUC	.8173±.145	.8129±.147	.7332±.178	.8158±.147	.8171±.142	**.8257±.141**
	AP	.5255±.293	.5276±.290	.4955±.323	.5407 ± .294	.5379±.292	**.5413±.287**
2	F1	.6469±.261	.6422±.264	.4564±.348	.6383±.284	.6548 ± .260	**.6555±.268**
	G-mean	.6525±.257	.6475±.261	.4974±.330	.6454±.277	.6594 ± .256	**.6617±.263**
	AUC	.7892±.148	.7812±.152	.6829±.172	.7856±.152	.7897±.146	**.7993±.150**
	AP	.5642±.276	.5634±.276	.4867±.303	.5723±.283	.5740±.278	**.5800±.279**
4	F1	.6143±.254	.6007±.272	.3212±.355	.5941±.297	.6165±.259	**.6257±.279**
	G-mean	.6234±.251	.6147±.262	.3666±.341	.6064±.287	.6253±.255	**.6343±.271**
	AUC	.7522±.140	.7461±.146	.6268±.156	.7476±.146	.7511±.140	**.7679±.147**
	AP	.5514±.260	.5521±.260	.4310±.280	.5576±.266	.5581±.262	**.5725±.267**

The FL system is composed of 100 clients in total, and 10 of them are activated randomly in every global epoch. In every step of 1000 FedAvg iteration, activate clients performs 2 local epochs training. The final results are the average of 30 repeats with standard deviation.

Evaluation Metrics. The overall accuracy is not an effective measurement with class imbalance. As the minority class is the weakness of class imbalance, metrics that focus on the minority such as precision and recall reviles the ability of the minority. However, there is always a trade-off between precision and recall. F1-score and G-mean provide reasonable way to combine them as a single cretierion. Metrics based on threshold can do further help in verifying the classifier as Area under the ROC curve(AUC) and Average Precision(AP).

When dealing with class-imbalance data, the final decision in model selection should consider a combination of different measures instead of relying on only one measure [1]. In this paper, F1-score, G-mean, AUC, and AP are all presented for informative analysis. All results are rounded to 3 decimal places. Paired t-test is used to verify the significance of the results from the competitors.

5.2 Results and Analysis

Centralized Learning. Table 2 lists 4 scores and the standard deviation for each resampling algorithm across 9 datasets with $M_{IR} = 4$. Triplests outperform other algorithms in 7 out of 9 datasets except for haberman and pulsar datasets. And in pulsar dataset, the performance gap between Triplets and the best algorithm is negligible.

The average scores of 9 datasets with M_{IR} of 1, 2 and 4 are listed in Table 3. The best results are marked in bold, and the underline indicates the second-best results that are not significantly different from the best results according to a significance level of 0.05. Triplets outperform other algorithms significantly in most cases. And with the increase of M_{IR}, the margin of Triplets over other algorithms becomes larger which further proves the effectiveness of Triplets in severe class imbalance.

FL. The average metircs and standard deviation of sampling algorithms in FL setting are listed in Table 4. Triplets outperforming other advanced oversampling algorithms significantly in all level of M_{IR} and metircs. Although BSMOTE achieves a competative AUC score with no significant difference from Triplests, its F1 and G-mean drop dramatically to 0 with the increase of M_{IR}. Similarily, baseline results show no significant difference from Triplets in AP, but at the cost of low F1 and G-mean scores. Thus, Triplets establishes a new state-of-the-art in FL imbaalnce learning on CIFAR-10 dataset among oversmapling techniques.

Table 4. FL results on CIFAR-10 dataset with various M_{IR}

M_{IR}	Score	Baseline	SMOTE	BSMOTE	ADASYN	Triplets
1	F1	.493±.084	.498±.084	.299±.161	.461±.096	**.508±.089**
	G-mean	.682±.064	.690±.066	.424±.157	.657±.073	**.725±.070**
	AUC	.864±.042	.870±.039	.858±.040	.852±.042	**.870±.041**
	AP	.509±.110	.517±.108	.485±.100	.469±.125	**.525±.120**
2	F1	.409±.134	.406±.106	.096±.093	.390±.111	**.454±.099**
	G-mean	.568±.115	.560±.091	.182±.147	.555±.095	**.629±.081**
	AUC	.830±.057	.831±.045	.840±.041	.827±.051	**.849±.048**
	AP	.443±.143	.446±.113	.436±.096	.422±.122	**.469±.118**
4	F1	.330±.088	.290±.120	.011±.020	.294±.089	**.356±.126**
	G-mean	.477±.078	.434±.110	.042±.065	.446±.082	**.508±.114**
	AUC	.800±.043	.791±.058	.801±.045	.793±.049	**.818±.063**
	AP	.401±.095	.375±.123	.356±.096	.364±.092	**.409±.129**
8	F1	.239±.091	.183±.097	.000±.001	.198±.076	**.282±.086**
	G-mean	.382±.086	.319±.100	.001±.008	.344±.076	**.427±.078**
	AUC	.771±.050	.771±.057	.809±.059	.759±.054	**.810±.054**
	AP	.344±.091	.335±.098	.366±.095	.309±.083	**.388±.097**
p value	F1	0.014	<0.001	<0.001	<0.001	/
	G-mean	<0.001	<0.001	<0.001	<0.001	/
	AUC	0.003	0.003	<u>0.072</u>	<0.001	/
	AP	<u>0.096</u>	0.032	0.010	<0.001	/

6 Conclusion

The class imbalance in federated learning presents a new challenge for traditional imbalance mitigation solutions. While a few studies have focused on algorithm-level solutions, there is still a gap in sampling methods suitable for federal studies. Traditional advanced sampling techniques have failed to generate effective and secure data from a global view for small and severe imbalance datasets.

Triplets oversampling, on the other hand, utilizes the shared separation hyperplane rule and data points from the majority class to enhance the minority domain. This approach generates informative data and enriches the minority domains securely. Experiments have shown its superiority over other advanced oversampling techniques both in the FL and centralized learning.

This work opens a new gate for the oversampling of minorities from the angle of the majority and the separation hyperplane. However, more efforts are needed to find the best way to utilize the majority and the tools to determine the boundary. There is still a lot of detail to explore to further improve the effectiveness and security of the proposed approach.

Acknowledgments. This work was supported by the Royal Academy of Engineering Leverhulme Trust Research Fellowship [LTRF2122-18-106] and the National Natural Science Foundation for Young Scientists of China [62206239]. The computations described in this research were performed using the Baskerville Tier 2 HPC service (https://www.baskerville.ac.uk/). Baskerville was funded by the EPSRC and UKRI through the World Class Labs scheme (EP/T022221/1) and the Digital Research Infrastructure programme (EP/W032244/1) and is operated by Advanced Research Computing at the University of Birmingham. Chenguang Xiao is partially supported by the Chinese Scholarship Council.

References

1. Akosa, J.S.: Predictive accuracy: a misleading performance measure for highly imbalanced data (2017)
2. Breiman, L.: Bagging predictors. Mach. Learn. **24**(2), 123–140 (1996)
3. Chakraborty, D., Ghosh, A.: Improving the robustness of federated learning for severely imbalanced datasets. arXiv preprint arXiv:2204.13414 (2022)
4. Chawla, N.V., Bowyer, K.W., Hall, L.O., Kegelmeyer, W.P.: Smote: synthetic minority over-sampling technique. J. Artif. Intell. Res. **16**, 321–357 (2002)
5. Domingos, P.: Metacost: a general method for making classifiers cost-sensitive. In: Proceedings of the Fifth ACM SIGKDD International Conference on Knowledge Discovery and Data Mining, pp. 155–164 (1999)
6. Duan, M., Liu, D., Chen, X., Liu, R., Tan, Y., Liang, L.: Self-balancing federated learning with global imbalanced data in mobile systems. IEEE Trans. Parallel Distrib. Syst. **32**(1), 59–71 (2021). https://doi.org/10.1109/TPDS.2020.3009406
7. Freund, Y., Schapire, R.E.: A decision-theoretic generalization of on-line learning and an application to boosting. J. Comput. Syst. Sci. **55**(1), 119–139 (1997)
8. Han, H., Wang, W.-Y., Mao, B.-H.: Borderline-SMOTE: a new over-sampling method in imbalanced data sets learning. In: Huang, D.-S., Zhang, X.-P., Huang, G.-B. (eds.) ICIC 2005. LNCS, vol. 3644, pp. 878–887. Springer, Heidelberg (2005). https://doi.org/10.1007/11538059_91
9. He, H., Bai, Y., Garcia, E.A., Li, S.: Adasyn: adaptive synthetic sampling approach for imbalanced learning. In: 2008 IEEE International Joint Conference on Neural Networks (IEEE World Congress on Computational Intelligence), pp. 1322–1328. IEEE (2008)
10. Japkowicz, N., Stephen, S.: The class imbalance problem: a systematic study. Intell. Data Anal. **6**(5), 429–449 (2002). https://doi.org/10.3233/ida-2002-6504
11. Kairouz, P., et al.: Advances and open problems in federated learning (2019). https://doi.org/10.48550/ARXIV.1912.04977

12. Li, Q., et al.: A survey on federated learning systems: vision, hype and reality for data privacy and protection. IEEE Trans. Knowl. Data Eng. **35**, 3347–3366 (2021). https://doi.org/10.1109/tkde.2021.3124599
13. Lin, T.Y., Goyal, P., Girshick, R., He, K., Dollar, P.: Focal loss for dense object detection. In: Proceedings of the IEEE International Conference on Computer Vision (ICCV) (2017)
14. McMahan, H.B., Moore, E., Ramage, D., Hampson, S., Arcas, B.A.: Communication-efficient learning of deep networks from decentralized data. In: Proceedings of the 20th International Conference on Artificial Intelligence and Statistics, AISTATS 2017 54 (2017)
15. Sarkar, D., Narang, A., Rai, S.: Fed-focal loss for imbalanced data classification in federated learning. arXiv (2020)
16. Tomek, I.: Two modifications of cnn. IEEE Trans. Syst. Man Cybern. SMC **6**(11), 769–772 (1976). https://doi.org/10.1109/TSMC.1976.4309452
17. Wang, L., Wang, X., Xu, S., Zhu, Q.: Towards class imbalance in federated learning. arXiv (2020)
18. Weiss, G.M.: Mining with rarity: a unifying framework. ACM Sigkdd Explor. Newsl. **6**(1), 7–19 (2004)
19. Xiao, C., Wang, S.: An experimental study of class imbalance in federated learning. In: 2021 IEEE Symposium Series on Computational Intelligence (SSCI), pp. 1–7. IEEE (2021)
20. Yang, Q., Liu, Y., Chen, T., Tong, Y.: Federated machine learning: concept and applications. ACM Trans. Intell. Syst. Technol. (TIST) **10**(2), 1–19 (2019)

Learning Fast and Slow: Towards Inclusive Federated Learning

Muhammad Tahir Munir(✉), Muhammad Mustansar Saeed, Mahad Ali, Zafar Ayyub Qazi, Agha Ali Raza, and Ihsan Ayyub Qazi

Department of Computer Science, Lahore University of Management Sciences, Lahore, Pakistan
{18030016,18030047,21100119,zafar.qazi,agha.ali.raza, ihsan.qazi}@lums.edu.pk

Abstract. Today's deep learning systems rely on large amounts of useful data to make accurate predictions. Often such data is private and thus not readily available due to rising privacy concerns. Federated learning (FL) tackles this problem by training a shared model locally on devices to aid learning in a privacy-preserving manner. Unfortunately, FL's effectiveness degrades when model training involves clients with heterogeneous devices; a common case especially in developing countries. Slow clients are dropped in FL, which not only limits learning but also systematically excludes slow clients thereby potentially biasing results. We propose Hasaas; a system that tackles this challenge by adapting the model size for slow clients based on their hardware resources. By doing so, Hasaas obviates the need to drop slow clients, which improves model accuracy and fairness. To improve robustness in the presence of statistical heterogeneity, Hasaas uses insights from the Central Limit Theorem to estimate model parameters in every round. Experimental evaluation involving large-scale simulations and a small-scale real testbed shows that Hasaas provides robust performance in terms of test accuracy, fairness, and convergence times compared to state-of-the-art schemes.

Keywords: Federated Learning · Fairness · Robustness · Developing Countries

1 Introduction

Today's deep neural networks (DNNs) power a wide variety of applications ranging from image classification, speech recognition, to fraud detection [21]. DNNs rely on large amounts of data to make accurate predictions and draw useful inferences. However, such data is often *private*[1] and may not be readily available for centralized collection due to rising privacy concerns and growing adoption of data privacy regulations (e.g., Europe's GDPR [36] and California Consumer Privacy Act [7]). A lack of useful data can limit the effectiveness of DNNs [4].

[1] Private data includes any personal, personally identifiable, financial or sensitive user information [14].

© The Author(s), under exclusive license to Springer Nature Switzerland AG 2023
D. Koutra et al. (Eds.): ECML PKDD 2023, LNAI 14170, pp. 384–401, 2023.
https://doi.org/10.1007/978-3-031-43415-0_23

Federated learning (FL) is a distributed machine learning approach that tackles this problem by training a shared model over data that is distributed across multiple edge devices (e.g., mobile phones), which share model parameters with a centralized server to aid learning in a privacy-preserving manner [27,38]. Unfortunately, FL's effectiveness degrades when model training involves heterogeneous client devices [5,20]; a common case especially in developing countries [2,3,33,37]. With FL, slow clients are dropped from the training process to reduce convergence delays. However, such an approach can degrade test accuracy and reduce fairness due to the systematic exclusion of slow clients [20,28].

We propose Hasaas;[2] a system that tackles this challenge by (i) adapting the model size based on client device capabilities (which we call *Differential Model Serving or DMS*), (ii) using a sub-model selection strategy based on post-activation values, and (iii) using insights from the Central Limit Theorem (CLT) to improve model robustness in the presence of statistical heterogeneity [15].

Serving small models to slow clients and large models to fast clients offers two key benefits. First, it reduces the model training time for slow clients, which decreases their chances of being dropped from the training process thereby improving fairness. Second, it can achieve a better tradeoff between model performance and convergence times compared to serving a single model to all clients.[3] However, realizing these benefits requires answering two key questions: *Given a model, how should we select a sub-model to serve to slow clients?* and *how should we aggregate model parameters from slow and fast clients?*

Hasaas selects a sub-model based on post-activation values of neurons. In particular, it bootstraps the FL process by choosing a random sub-model and allows slow clients to train the sub-model for the first r rounds. Then after every r rounds, it chooses a new sub-model based on post-activation values.[4] This allows neurons with small activation values to be excluded from the sub-model, which improves performance. The neurons that have small activation values are considered less important as they contribute less to the model's output and have a smaller impact on weight updates during training.

With FL, a *random* set of clients are picked in *each* round for model training, which changes the proportion of slow and fast clients in each round. This can reduce model accuracy, especially when there is statistical heterogeneity in data across clients. To improve robustness in such scenarios, Hasaas aggregates model parameters in each round using insights from the CLT by learning the *distribution of the sample mean* of the model parameters [15].[5] Hasaas then randomly draws each model parameter from the learned distribution rather than always using the sample mean. This improves performance especially when there is high variance in the model parameters shared by each client.

---

[2] In the Urdu language, Hasaas means *sensitive*.

[3] Small models can reduce accuracy, whereas large models lead to slow convergence.

[4] In case of CNN models, it prunes filters too.

[5] Thus, in every training round, we estimate the mean and variance of each model parameter, which together uniquely identifies a Normal distribution.

We carry out extensive evaluation using (i) large-scale simulations involving the LEAF benchmarking framework for learning in FL settings [9] and (ii) small-scale real testbed experiments involving mobile clients with heterogeneous device capabilities. We compare Hasaas's performance with several notable schemes including FedAvg [27], Adaptive Dropout [6], and FedProx [23] and carry out a detailed ablation study to quantify the benefits of each component of Hasaas. Experiments show that Hasaas achieves robust performance in terms of test accuracy, convergence, and fairness across diverse datasets and models.

Taken together, we make the following contributions in this work.

- We design Hasaas; an adaptive model serving framework for FL that adapts model sizes based on client capabilities (Sect. 4). It reduces the computational and communication costs in FL by training on a subset of the model's weights and exchanging smaller sub-models between slow clients and the server instead of the full model updates.
- To achieve better generalization, we propose a CLT-based approach, which outperforms other approaches including FedAvg, Adaptive Dropout, and FedProx (Sect. 4).
- We carry out extensive evaluation using large-scale simulations and small-scale testbed experiments involving real smartphones over a wide variety of real-world federated datasets (Sect. 5). We make our code available on GitHub.[6] for the benefit of the community.

2 Background and Related Work

Our work focuses on synchronous FL algorithms that proceed in training rounds. These algorithms aim to learn a shared global model with parameters embodied in a real tensor $\boldsymbol{\Gamma}$ from data stored across several distributed clients. In each round $t \geq 0$, the server distributes the current global model $\boldsymbol{\Gamma}_t$ to the set of selected clients S_t with a total of n_t data instances. The selected clients locally execute stochastic gradient descent (SGD) on their data and independently train the model to produce the updated models $\{\boldsymbol{\Gamma}_t^k | k \in S_t\}$. The update of each client k can be expressed as:

$$\boldsymbol{\Gamma}_t^k = \boldsymbol{\Gamma}_t - \alpha H_t^k, \ \ \forall k \in S_t \tag{1}$$

where H_t^k is the gradients tensor for client k in training round t, and α is the learning rate chosen by the server. Each selected client k then sends the update back to the server, where the new global model $(\boldsymbol{\Gamma}_{t+1})$ is constructed by aggregating all client-side updates as follows:

$$\boldsymbol{\Gamma}_{t+1} = \sum_{\forall k \in S_t} \frac{n_k}{n_t} \cdot \boldsymbol{\Gamma}_t^k \tag{2}$$

[6] https://github.com/FederatedResearch/hasaas.

where n_k is the number of data instances of client c and $n_t = \sum_{\forall k \in S_t} n_k$. Hence, $\boldsymbol{\Gamma}_{t+1}$ can be written as:

$$\boldsymbol{\Gamma}_{t+1} = \boldsymbol{\Gamma}_t - \alpha_t H_t \tag{3}$$

where $H_t = \frac{1}{n_t} \sum_{k \in S_t} n_k H_t^k$.

Fairness in FL. Due to the heterogeneity in client devices and data in federated networks, it is possible that the performance of a model will vary significantly across the network. This concern, also known as representation disparity, is a major challenge in FL, as it can potentially result in uneven outcomes for the devices. Following Li et al. [22], we provide a formal definition of this fairness in the context of FL below.

Definition. *We say that a model W_1 is more fair than W_2 if the test performance distribution of W_1 across the network is more uniform than that of W_2, i.e., $std\{F_k(W_1)\}_{k \in [K]} < std\{F_k(W_2)\}_{k \in [K]}$ where $F_k(\cdot)$ denotes the test loss on device $k \in [K]$, and $std\{\cdot\}$ denotes the standard deviation.*

We note that there exists a tension between variance and utility in the definition above; in general, the goal is to *lower* the variance while maintaining a reasonable average performance (e.g., average test accuracy). Several prior works have separately considered either fairness or robustness in FL. For instance, fairness strategies include using minimax optimization to focus on the worst-performing devices [18,39] or reweighting the devices to allow for a flexible fairness/accuracy tradeoff (e.g., [24]).

2.1 Related Work

Several recent and ongoing efforts aim to tackle system and statistical heterogeneity in FL [6,8,10,13,19,20,23,25,27,39]. In this section, we discuss works that are most closely related to our study.

System Heterogeneity. A number of schemes aim to reduce the impact of client heterogeneity by serving *smaller* models. These schemes differ based on (i) whether they do model pruning on the client-side [19] or the server-side [6], (ii) the criteria used for pruning (e.g., [8,12]), and (iii) whether they serve a single model to all clients or not [6,8,19]. For example, PruneFL [19] performs initial model pruning at a selected client and further adaptive pruning on the server-side. It serves the same pruned model to *all* clients. Moreover, because the initial model pruning is carried out on only one selected client and its data, the pruned model can be biased towards the selected client. HeteroFL [12] trains local models based on clients' device characteristics. It pre-defines subset models with different complexity levels and assigns the same model to clients belonging to the same complexity level. However, the subset models are statically defined, which limits model performance. AFD [6] trains a subset model using either a single-model or multi-model serving approach. With the former approach, the same model is served to each client and monitored for average training loss. A positive score is given for decreasing loss, while a new model is served if loss increases. While AFD outperforms Federated Dropout (FD), which relies on random dropping to select sub-models, such a strategy can trigger frequent model changes, which can negatively affect model performance. We demonstrate this in Sect. 5.[7]

Statistical Heterogeneity. A number of approaches aim to tackle statistical heterogeneity by either modifying the (i) client selection strategy of FL (e.g., [26]), (ii) FedAvg aggregation method (e.g., [13]) or (iii) objective function to include a regularization term (e.g., [23]). For example, PFedR [26] is a client selection strategy in which the server generates dummy datasets from the inversion of local model updates, identifies clients with large distribution divergences, and aggregates updates from highly relevant clients only. Generating dummy data from client updates raises privacy concerns. Also, in case of secure multi-party aggregation where client updates are meaningless without aggregation, generating dummy data from those updates will not help in identifying client distribution divergences. In such cases, this approach may not yield the desired results. FedDNA [13] is a parameter aggregation method for FL that aggregates gradient and statistical parameters, separately. While the gradient parameters are aggregated using FedAvg, the statistical parameters are aggregated collaboratively to reduce the divergence between the local models and the central model. This technique is only applicable to models with a batch normalization layer.

FedProx [23] uses partial work from resource-constrained devices to tackle system heterogeneity and adds a regularization term in the FedAvg objective function to improve performance under statistical heterogeneity. However, incorporating partial updates from slow clients can reduce test accuracy if the model is not trained enough.[8] In addition, downloading a large model from the server can still be a significant burden for slow clients, particularly those located in regions with limited connectivity.

Hasaas tackles *both* system and statistical heterogeneity by combining the benefits of differential model serving and CLT-based aggregation. It extends the state-of-the-art in terms of system heterogeneity by employing an approach in which slow clients are served a small model whereas the fast clients continue to receive the global model. This is unlike AFD and PruneFL that serve smaller models to *all* clients, which can degrade model accuracy. Moreover, unlike HeteroFL that uses pre-defined subset models, Hasaas dynamically updates small models based on average post-activation values in the global model. As a result, sub-models that are not performant are discarded as training progresses. We delve deeper into the design of Hasaas in the following section.

[7] With multi-model AFD, a different subset model is used by *each* client, all of the same size. However, training with a small fraction of clients in each round – a typical scenario in FL – makes the algorithm behave randomly, just like the FD scheme [6].

[8] Moreover, if the slow clients are unable to run the large model due to resource constraints, they cannot participate in the training process.

3 Problem Motivation

It is common for distributed clients in FL to exhibit considerable heterogeneity in terms of computational resources (e.g., number of CPU cores, RAM size) and network bandwidth [8,23]. This heterogeneity impacts both the model accuracy and the training time of the FL process [9]. Consequently, resource-constrained edge devices (e.g., entry-level smartphones), which are prevalent in developing countries, are either unable to train models due to their limited compute and memory resources or take a prohibitively long time in training [27,29,33]. According to a study involving one of the largest online social networks, 57% of smartphones in developing regions, had 1 GB or less RAM [30].[9] Such entry-level smartphones frequently operate under low memory regimes, which is known to degrade performance [2,33,37]. Unfortunately, slow clients (or stragglers) are dropped in FL schemes (e.g., FedAvg) for efficiency reasons because waiting for slow clients to report their updates can increase convergence times. However, dropping slow clients can (i) degrade test accuracy and (ii) lead to unfairness.

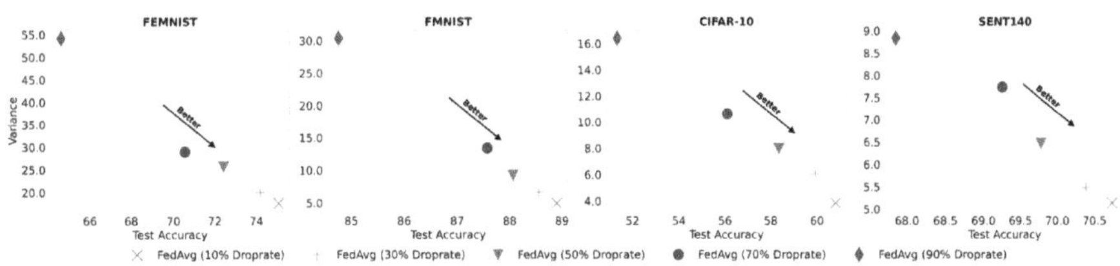

Fig. 1. Impact of systems heterogeneity on test accuracy and fairness in FedAvg for different client drop rates and datasets. As the fraction of slow clients increases, the test accuracy, and fairness decrease.

System Heterogeneity Degrades Robustness and Fairness. To evaluate the impact of slow clients in FedAvg on model accuracy and fairness, we simulate different levels of system heterogeneity using LEAF [9]. In particular, we vary the client drop rate (CDR)[10] from 10% to 90% and carry out evaluation on multiple real datasets including FEMNIST, FMNIST, CIFAR-10, and Sent140. Figure 1 shows that with FedAvg, system heterogeneity negatively impacts both model robustness as well as fairness.[11] In particular, test accuracy decreases as CDR increases across *all* datasets whereas the variance of the test loss (across clients), which captures model fairness, generally increases with CDR.

Homogeneous Model Serving (HMS) Either Slows Convergence or Degrades Model Performance. To quantify the impact of serving the same

[9] In 2018, ~300 million Android phones shipped globally had 1 GB or less RAM [1].

[10] CDR is the fraction of slow clients in the system. With FedAvg, such clients are dropped from the training process.

[11] Similar to Li et al. [22], we capture model fairness using the variance of test loss across clients. Thus, the more uniform the loss distribution is, the fairer the model.

model to all clients we train a CNN model over the FEMNIST dataset [9] and measure the test accuracy and the time to complete 100 training rounds on two real smartphones, i.e., Nokia 1 (Quadcore, 1 GB RAM) and Nexus 6P (Octacore, 3 GB RAM). These devices represent slow and fast clients, respectively.[12] We find that with FedAvg, serving the same model to both slow and fast clients leads to slow convergence. In our testbed, it took 15.9 h with FedAvg to complete 100 train rounds.

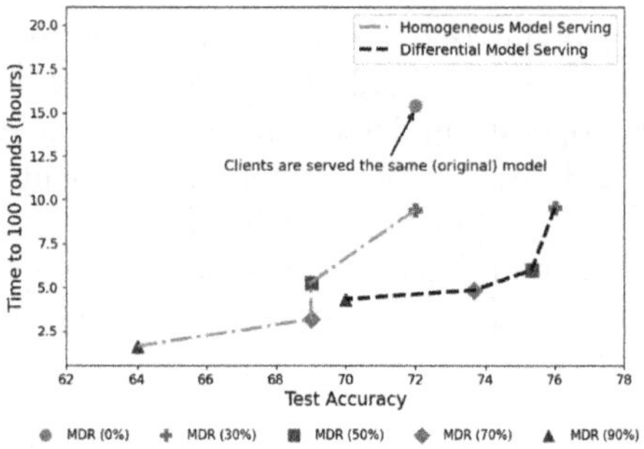

Fig. 2. Time to complete 100 rounds of training on a real testbed as a function of test accuracy for different model drop rates (MDR).

To address this system heterogeneity, one can serve a smaller model (e.g., a subset of the original model) to all clients [8]. Figure 2 shows that indeed serving smaller models reduces the time to complete 100 rounds. However, it also reduces test accuracy. For example, increasing the model drop rate (MDR) (i.e., the pruning percentage) from 30% to 50% reduces the test accuracy by 4.2%. Another approach is to serve a smaller model to only slow clients while the faster clients continue to train on the large model (we refer to this approach as *Differential Model Serving*, which is part of Hasaas). We find that such an approach considerably improves test accuracy while also achieving significant reductions in convergence time. For example, when the MDR is 50%, DMS improves test accuracy by 9.4% over HMS with similar convergence times. However, we see diminishing returns beyond 50% MDR because in this regime the fast client becomes the bottleneck as opposed to the slow client.

In summary, serving a single model to all clients presents a tradeoff between convergence time and model accuracy. DMS can address this tradeoff by serving models of different sizes to slow and fast clients.

[12] The memory specifications of these devices represent a wide range of smartphones. In developing regions, phones with 1 GB or less RAM had a market share of 57% compared to 20% in developed regions. Phones $\geq$3 GB RAM had less than 25% market share in developing regions and over 50% share in developed countries [30].

4 Design

Hasaas tackles both system heterogeneity and the statistical challenges with heterogeneous data using the following design features:

1. *Differential model serving.* Clients are served models with different sizes based on their capabilities.
2. *Sub-model selection using activations.* Small sub-models are selected for slow clients based on post-activation values.
3. *Model generalization using insights from the Central Limit Theorem.* To improve performance robustness, especially over non-IID datasets, we use a CLT-based approach to choose model parameters.

A. Differential Model Serving. DMS has several benefits compared to serving the *same* model to all clients participating in FL. First, due to the large heterogeneity in mobile device characteristics, training a single model over all clients can lead to widely different training times, which can result in frequent dropping of slow clients from FL,[13] potentially leading to unfairness across clients [5,8,22]. Second, it is difficult to choose a single model that allows all clients to participate in FL training while achieving high accuracy; small models can degrade model accuracy, whereas large models lead to the dropping of slow clients. DMS addresses these challenges by allowing model sizes to be *adapted* based on device characteristics such as the number of CPU cores, memory size, and GPU characteristics (if present). Thus, slow clients are served smaller models than faster clients, which can improve fairness by reducing the dropping of clients from the FL process.

B. Sub-model Selection. Given a model size, a key design question in Hasaas is, "*which sub-model should we serve to slow clients?*" There are many possible sub-models one can pick. In a feed-forward neural network, suppose we allow dropping of neurons from all layers including the input and output layers, then the number of distinct sub-models are lower bounded by $\binom{n_1}{\lfloor f.n_1 \rfloor}\binom{n_2}{\lfloor f.n_2 \rfloor}..\binom{n_l}{\lfloor f.n_l \rfloor}$, where n_i is the number of neurons in layer i, $(1-f)$ is the pruning fraction (i.e., fraction of neurons dropped from each layer), and l is the total number of layers. Finding the best sub-model from among such a large set of possible sub-models is challenging. We address this challenge with two strategies. First, we bootstrap the FL process by choosing a random sub-model and allowing slow clients to train over the sub-model for the first r rounds. This allows us to assess the parts of the sub-model that contribute the most to the learning task. Second, after every r rounds, we choose a new sub-model based on the post-activation values of neurons (in case of CNN models, filters too) [35]. This allows neurons with small activation values to be excluded from the sub-model. This approach can enable better model selection than randomly picking models in each round or choosing a different random model in each round [8].

[13] Some clients may not be able to run large models at all due to memory constraints.

C. Model Generalization. Training a model in FL is challenging due to the statistical variations in data distributed across clients, which impacts both model accuracy as well as model convergence [8,23]. This is exacerbated by the fact that in each round, FL picks k *random* clients for training from a pool of N clients. As a result, choosing the sample mean of the weights of each model parameter across clients in the *current round* may not be representative of clients picked in the next round, especially when k is much smaller than N, which is a typical case in FL [27].[14] To generalize model training, we use insights from CLT, which posits that the distribution of the sample mean of IID random variables converges to a Normal distribution.[15] We consider the setting, where each client i draws independent samples from a distribution D with finite mean μ and finite variance σ^2. Let $X_j^i \sim D$ be the random variable denoting weight of the jth model parameter for client i. Then FL aims to learn the average $\bar{X}_j = \sum_{i=1}^{N} p_i X_j^i$ across all clients, where p_i is the proportion of samples trained by client i. CLT posits that $\bar{X}_j$ converges in distribution to the Normal distribution with mean μ and finite variance σ^2/N. Thus, larger the variance, the more imprecise is our estimate of $\bar{X}_j$. To achieve better generalization, we randomly draw samples from the learned sample mean distribution and use them for the next round, where a new set of random clients are selected for model training.

By drawing random samples from the sample mean distribution rather than just using the sample mean in each round, we ensure that clients with large values for the model parameters do not skew the learning process. To estimate the distribution of the sample mean, we use parameters shared by clients in each round *independently*. As a result, there is no pooling of parameter values across rounds due to dependencies introduced by SGD. In our evaluation, we show that this strategy improves accuracy, robustness, and convergence speed compared to just using the sample mean.

4.1 Algorithm

At the start of the FL process, the server initializes a global model W_0 and a mask M to keep track of the smaller model sent to the slow clients; see Algorithm 1. The server randomly picks a smaller model w_0 (which we call a *sub-model*) from the global model W_0. It does so randomly at the start as it does not have any prior information to effectively choose a sub-model. The server selects n clients randomly and sends the sub-model w_0 or the large model W_0 to selected clients based on their device characteristics. Let C_t denote the set of all clients selected in round t. Each client trains its model and sends the model updates as well as activations of dense layers to the server. The server aggregates these updates and activations. In weighted aggregation, s_c and S_t represent the number of training samples of client c and the number of training samples in round t,

[14] While the sample mean is an unbiased estimator of the population mean, the variance of the sample mean depends on the sample size (i.e., the number of clients).

[15] If each client's model weights follow a different distribution, one can use generalizations of CLT, such as the Lyapunov CLT and Lindeberg CLT [15].

Algorithm 1: Hasaas

```
Input: Model Dropout Rate (k%), Pruning Round (r)
Server executes:
Initialize: Global model W_0, mask M ← 0;
for each round t = 1, 2, . . . , T do
    if t > 1 then
        Select sub-model w_t from W_t based on mask M
    else
        w_t ← Random selection k% ;
        M ← Indexes of sub-model w_t;
    end
    C_t ← (select n clients randomly) ;                          ▷ n ≤ N
    Send W_t or w_t to C_t based on their device characteristics
    for each client c ∈ C_t do
        if c is slow then
            Train sub-model w_t:
            activations_t^c, w_{t+1}^c = ℓ(w_t, c) ;
            W_{t+1}^c = Broadcast(w_{t+1}^c, M) ;
        else
            Train large model W_t:
            activations_t^c, W_{t+1}^c = ℓ(W_t, c) ;
        end
    end
    activations_t = (1/n) Σ_{c∈C_t} activations_t^c;
    μ = Σ_{c∈C_t} (s_c/S_t) W_{t+1}^c ;                           ▷ S_t: Total samples
    σ = sqrt( Σ_{c∈C_t} s_c (W_{t+1}^c − μ)^2 / (S_t − 1) ) ;
    σ = σ/√t ;
    W_{t+1} = N(μ, σ^2) ;
    if (t mod r) == 0 then
        Update M using activations of dense layer and ℓ1-Norm of CNN filters
    end
end
```

respectively. Based on average activations, and $\ell 1$-norm of the CNN filters, the server picks the optimal sub-model for slow clients after every r rounds. The only two parameters of Hasaas are k (MDR), representing the percentage of neurons/filters to be dropped from the dense and convolution layers and the Mask Update Round (MUR) r, at which M is updated.

Aggregation. Hasaas uses insights from CLT to aggregate clients' model parameters. Server calculates the weighted mean μ (weighted by number of data samples) and standard deviation σ of each parameter across clients. It then uses μ and σ to randomly sample parameters from the Normal distribution to send back to the clients. As training progresses and the model becomes stable, large changes in model parameters can adversely impact performance. As a result, we continue decreasing σ proportional to $1/\sqrt{t}$ (current round), which limits model deviations from the stable parameters and helps with generalization.

5 Evaluation

We now present empirical results for Hasaas using large-scale simulations and small-scale testbed experiments under federated settings. We demonstrate the effectiveness of Hasaas in the presence of both system and statistical heterogeneity and study its convergence, robustness, and fairness properties. All code and scripts for generating the paper results are available here.

A. Experimental Details. We evaluate Hasaas on multiple models, tasks, and real-world federated datasets. We implement Hasaas in LEAF [9] – a benchmarking framework for FL to simulate our federated setup – and evaluate its performance on CNN and LSTM models, and five real-world datasets. Specifically, we use CIFAR-10, Federated extended MNIST (FEMNIST), FEMNIST (skewed), Fashion-MNIST (FMNIST) for CNN and Sent140 for the LSTM model. We compare Hasaas performance with FedAvg [27], FedProx [23], and Single-Model Adaptive Federated Dropout [6].

Real Data. The datasets we use are curated from prior work in FL [8,22,23] and recent FL benchmarks in LEAF [9]. FMNIST, FEMNIST, and Sent140 are non-IID datasets. To study Hasaas under an IID dataset, we curated CIFAR-10 in an IID fashion, where each example has the same probability to belong to any device. We then study a more complex 62-class FEMNIST dataset [8,11]. Details of datasets, models, and workloads are provided in Appendix A.2 on GitHub.

Hyperparameters. We evaluate each dataset using three learning rates: {0.01, 0.001, 0.0003}. While smaller learning rates mean the model takes longer to converge, the behavior of all techniques remains the same relative to each other. As suggested in an earlier work [23], we use a learning rate of 0.001 and 0.01 for the CNN and LSTM models, respectively. We set the number of selected devices per round to 10. Unless specified otherwise, we set $MDR = 50\%$ and $r = 10$, which results in 50% of the filters and neurons being dropped from the convolution and dense layers, and leads to 50% fewer cells in the LSTM layers for the slow client. For a fair comparison, we fix the randomly selected devices, the slow clients, and mini-batch orders across all runs and report the average results of 5 runs.

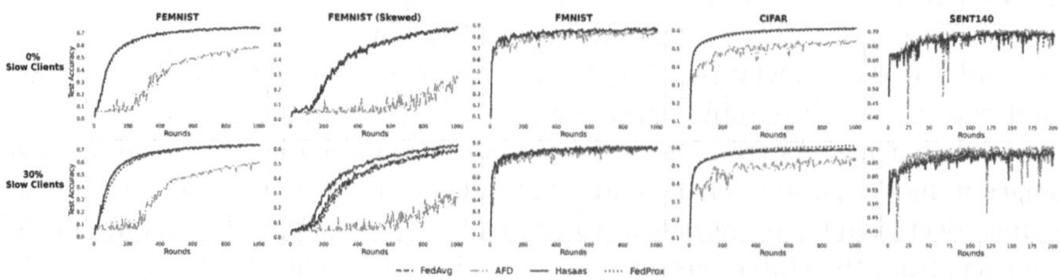

Fig. 3. Test accuracy as a function of round number for 0% and 30% system heterogeneity. 0% client drop rate indicates no system heterogeneity. If there is no system heterogeneity, Hasaas provides better or similar performance to FedAvg and FedProx.

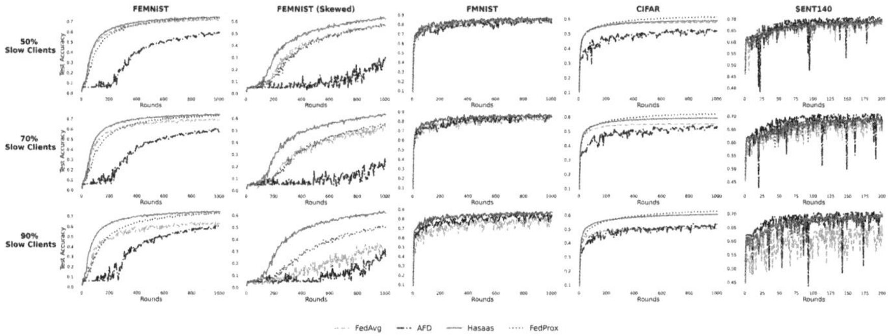

Fig. 4. Test accuracy as a function of round number for 50%, 70% and 90% system heterogeneity, where system heterogeneity referes to the percentage of slow clients. Hasaas results in significant convergence improvements relative to other schemes. As statistical heterogeneity increases Hasaas provides robust performance. We also report train loss in Appendix A.5.

B. System and Statistical Heterogeneity.

System Heterogeneity. For studying the impact of heterogeneity, we vary the percentage of slow devices (0%, 30%, 50%, 70%, and 90%). We emulate devices as slow if they cannot train the model for E epochs due to their system constraints. Settings where 0% devices are slow correspond to environments *without* system heterogeneity, whereas 90% of the slow devices correspond to highly heterogeneous environments. FedAvg simply drops slow clients upon reaching the global clock cycle but Hasaas incorporates the updates from these devices as they train a subset model and are able to send updates on time. AFD also incorporates slow-device updates as it trains a smaller model on all devices. FedProx incorporates partial updates from the slow devices.

Figures 3 and 4 show that Hasaas achieves robust performance for different levels of system heterogeneity compared to FedAvg, FedProx and AFD. As system heterogeneity increases, FedAvg's performance degrades significantly. FedProx performs better than FedAvg because it incorporates partial updates from slow clients and modifies the objective function to include a regularization term to avoid over-fitting on clients' data. However, incorporating partial updates can have a negative impact if the model is not trained for enough epochs. Thus, as the number of slow clients increases, FedProx achieves lower test accuracy relative to Hasaas especially with non-IID datasets (e.g., FEMNIST).

Statistical Heterogeneity. We use datasets with varying degrees of IID-ness to evaluate Hasaas under statistical heterogeneity. We use two versions of FEMNIST dataset; one non-IID version is generated using LEAF, which is employed by Ditto [22]. We generate a skewed non-IID version of the FEMNIST dataset in which each client contains data with only 5 classes of the FEMNIST dataset. This approach has been used in prior works to generate skewed non-IID datasets. Figures 3 and 4 show the test accuracy of all approaches on different datasets.

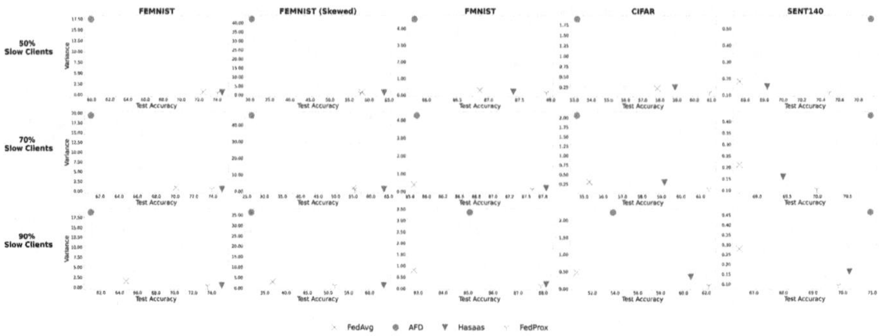

Fig. 5. Variance of test loss as a function of average test accuracy.

These results indicate that as the degree of non-IID-ness increases, Hasaas provides better generalizability as evidenced by the high test accuracy. For each dataset, Hasaas provides either faster convergence compared to other schemes while also achieving better or comparable test accuracy.

In case of the IID CIFAR dataset, Hasaas achieves fast convergence to a test accuracy of 50% than FedProx but results in 2% lower test accuracy after 1000 rounds. This occurs because in the presence of system heterogeneity, while Hasaas serves a sub-model to slow clients FedProx continues to serve the same large model to all clients. The IID nature of the data leads to a lower variance in the sample mean of the model parameters, resulting in less benefits of the CLT approach. In case of SENT140, Hasaas performs comparable to other approaches, except FedAvg, which experiences large fluctuations as system heterogeneity increases. In case of high system (90%) and statistical heterogeneity (FEMNIST skewed), Hasaas provides 27% test accuracy improvement over FedAvg, 14% over FedProx, and 34% over AFD; see Fig. 4.

Fairness. Due to statistical heterogeneity in federated settings, the performance of a model may vary significantly across different devices, resulting in *representation disparity* [17]. In Hasaas, we serve a subset model to slow clients, which potentially has a larger risk of representation disparity. We empirically show that in addition to improving accuracy, Hasaas also offers improved fairness. Hasaas picks the best subset model after every r (a tunable parameter) rounds for slow clients. Variance of test loss across clients can be seen in Fig. 5 and Appendix A.5. Interestingly, Hasaas provides better average test accuracy as well as achieves lower variance across clients compared to FedAvg and Hasaas without CLT. Figure 5 compares the robustness and fairness of Hasaas, FedProx, AFD and FedAvg. Results show that Hasaas provides robust and fair performance as it trains on all clients and uses CLT for improved generalization.

C. Ablation Study.[16]

Benefits of Activation-Based Model Pruning. We compared our activation-based sub-model selection strategy with the random sub-model selection strategy, which selects a new model in each round. We find that our activation-based approach consistently outperforms random selection, yielding a test accuracy improvement ranging from 3.7% to 6.9% for CDRs of 30% and 90%, respectively.

Benefits of Model Generalization Module. We also evaluated Hasaas' model generalization module in our ablation study. We find that incorporating the generalization module provided up to 6.7% improvement in test accuracy, compared to the model without the module.

Choice of Normalizing σ by $1/\sqrt{t}$. We conducted an empirical evaluation of various normalizing factors for σ in order to identify the optimal approach for improving the performance of a model using random sampling from a normal distribution. Our findings indicate that using a large normalizing factor results in a reduction in the improvement provided by this sampling technique, as the value of σ becomes smaller and the sampled weights tend to remain close to the mean. This effectively reduces the effectiveness of the technique to that of FedAvg. On the other hand, failing to normalize σ leads to large model parameters, which can cause the model to become unstable, which is illustrated in Appendix. Based on our empirical evaluation, we suggest using a normalizing factor that keeps σ moderate and increases as the round progresses and the model weights become more stable, leading to better accuracy. In our experiments, we found that $1/\sqrt{t}$ was a particularly effective normalizing factor for σ.

Using CLT with FedProx and FedAvg. We performed experiments by applying the model generalization module of Hasaas to FedAvg and FedProx on the FEMNIST skewed data. We observe that the differences between these schemes (i.e., FedAvg and FedProx) with and without CLT are small and not significant. With vanilla FedAvg, CLT does not provide any significant improvement because slow clients are dropped in FedAvg. The same trend holds with FedProx, which also does not serve small models to slow clients but instead incorporates partial work and adds a regularization term to the loss function.

D. Real Testbed Experiments. We implemented Hasaas on a real FL testbed. We use PySyft [32], an open-source framework for FL, to train models on mobile devices. Mobile devices connect with the server to download models and train them using KotlinSyft [31]. The server communicates with the clients using Google Firebase Services [16]. We perform evaluations on real smartphones, i.e., Nexus 6P (3 GB RAM, Octacore) and Nokia 1 (1 GB RAM, Quadcore) as fast and slow client, respectively. We employed real datasets, namely FEMNIST and a CNN model from the LEAF benchmark, to investigate the impact of model size on model training times. Further details of the model can be found in the

[16] Figures related to the ablation experiments are in Appendix A.1, which is available on our GitHub repository.

Appendix A.2. We present the training time for various model drop rates on the slow device in Hasaas in Appendix A.3. The large model is the unpruned model served to the slow client and a 30% MDR implies a 30% pruned model. Our results indicate that increasing the MDR decreases the training time. Specifically, a 50% MDR leads to a 66.7% reduction in training time due to reduced FLOPs, as shown in Appendix A.3. A MDR of 50% results in 3.8× fewer FLOPs and a training time reduction of roughly 2.9×. We examine the impact of network heterogeneity on convergence time for different MDRs in Appendix A.4.

6 Limitations and Future Work

Differential Model Serving. We only evaluated Hasaas using a 2-model approach (i.e., fast clients train over the global model whereas slow clients train over a sub-model). In the future, it would be useful to examine the effectiveness of customizing model sizes for *each* client based on their characteristics.

Impact on Mobile User Experience. By including slow clients in the FL training process, it is possible that these clients may be further slowed down thereby degrading mobile users' experience of other applications (e.g., mobile browsers). This could be explored in future works.

Hasaas and Multi-task Learning. In multi-task learning [34], the goal is to train *personalized* models for each device independent of sizes whereas Hasaas focuses on reducing the overhead of model training for improving inclusiveness in the presence of client heterogeneity.

7 Conclusion

We presented the design and evaluation of Hasaas, an inclusive framework for federated learning that achieves improved learning and fairness properties in the presence of client heterogeneity. Hasaas's differential model serving ensures that slow clients are not dropped from the training process and achieve training times similar to fast clients whenever possible. Our evaluation involving large-scale simulations and a small-scale real testbed of mobile clients shows that Hasaas achieves robust performance across a variety of real-world federated datasets.

References

1. Build for Android (Go edition): optimize your app for global markets (Google I/O '18). https://bit.ly/2UKLQDl
2. Abdullah, M., Qazi, Z.A., Qazi, I.A.: Causal impact of android go on mobile web performance. In: Proceedings of the 22nd ACM Internet Measurement Conference. IMC 2022, New York, NY, USA, pp. 113–129. Association for Computing Machinery (2022). https://doi.org/10.1145/3517745.3561456

3. Ahmad, S., Haamid, A.L., Qazi, Z.A., Zhou, Z., Benson, T., Qazi, I.A.: A view from the other side: understanding mobile phone characteristics in the developing world. In: Proceedings of the 2016 Internet Measurement Conference. IMC 2016, pp. 319–325 (2016). https://doi.org/10.1145/2987443.2987470
4. Bonawitz, K., Kairouz, P., McMahan, B., Ramage, D.: Federated learning and privacy: building privacy-preserving systems for machine learning and data science on decentralized data. Queue **19**(5), 87–114 (2021). https://doi.org/10.1145/3494834.3500240
5. Bonawitz, K., et al.: Towards federated learning at scale: System design (2019). http://arxiv.org/abs/1902.01046
6. Bouacida, N., Hou, J., Zang, H., Liu, X.: Adaptive federated dropout: improving communication efficiency and generalization for federated learning. In: IEEE INFOCOM 2021 - IEEE Conference on Computer Communications Workshops (INFOCOM WKSHPS), pp. 1–6 (2021). https://doi.org/10.1109/INFOCOMWKSHPS51825.2021.9484526
7. Bukaty, P.: The California Consumer Privacy Act (CCPA): An Implementation Guide. IT Governance Publishing (2019). http://www.jstor.org/stable/j.ctvjghvnn
8. Caldas, S., Konečný, J., McMahan, H.B., Talwalkar, A.: Expanding the reach of federated learning by reducing client resource requirements. CoRR abs/1812.07210 (2018). http://arxiv.org/abs/1812.07210
9. Caldas, S., et al.: LEAF: a benchmark for federated settings. CoRR abs/1812.01097 (2018). http://arxiv.org/abs/1812.01097
10. Chou, L., Liu, Z., Wang, Z., Shrivastava, A.: Efficient and less centralized federated learning. In: Oliver, N., Pérez-Cruz, F., Kramer, S., Read, J., Lozano, J.A. (eds.) ECML PKDD 2021. LNCS (LNAI), vol. 12975, pp. 772–787. Springer, Cham (2021). https://doi.org/10.1007/978-3-030-86486-6_47
11. Cohen, G., Afshar, S., Tapson, J., van Schaik, A.: EMNIST: an extension of MNIST to handwritten letters. CoRR abs/1702.05373 (2017). http://arxiv.org/abs/1702.05373
12. Diao, E., Ding, J., Tarokh, V.: Heterofl: computation and communication efficient federated learning for heterogeneous clients. arXiv preprint arXiv:2010.01264 (2020)
13. Duan, J.-H., Li, W., Lu, S.: FedDNA: federated learning with decoupled normalization-layer aggregation for non-iid data. In: Oliver, N., Pérez-Cruz, F., Kramer, S., Read, J., Lozano, J.A. (eds.) ECML PKDD 2021. LNCS (LNAI), vol. 12975, pp. 722–737. Springer, Cham (2021). https://doi.org/10.1007/978-3-030-86486-6_44
14. Dwork, C., McSherry, F., Nissim, K., Smith, A.: Calibrating noise to sensitivity in private data analysis. In: Halevi, S., Rabin, T. (eds.) TCC 2006. LNCS, vol. 3876, pp. 265–284. Springer, Heidelberg (2006). https://doi.org/10.1007/11681878_14
15. Feller, W.: An Introduction to Probability Theory and Its Applications, vol. 1. Wiley (1968). http://www.amazon.ca/exec/obidos/redirect?tag=citeulike04-20&path=ASIN/0471257087
16. Google: Firebase services. https://firebase.google.com
17. Hashimoto, T.B., Srivastava, M., Namkoong, H., Liang, P.: Fairness without demographics in repeated loss minimization (2018)
18. Hu, Z., Shaloudegi, K., Zhang, G., Yu, Y.: Fedmgda+: federated learning meets multi-objective optimization. CoRR abs/2006.11489 (2020). https://arxiv.org/abs/2006.11489

19. Jiang, Y., et al.: Model pruning enables efficient federated learning on edge devices. IEEE Trans. Neural Networks Learn. Syst. 1–13 (2022). https://doi.org/10.1109/TNNLS.2022.3166101
20. Kairouz, P., McMahan, H.B., Avent, B., Bellet, A., et al.: Advances and open problems in federated learning. CoRR abs/1912.04977 (2019). http://arxiv.org/abs/1912.04977
21. LeCun, Y., Bengio, Y., Hinton, G.: Deep learning. Nature **521**(7553), 436–444 (2015). https://doi.org/10.1038/nature14539
22. Li, T., Hu, S., Beirami, A., Smith, V.: Ditto: fair and robust federated learning through personalization. CoRR abs/2012.04221 (2020). https://arxiv.org/abs/2012.04221
23. Li, T., Sahu, A.K., Sanjabi, M., Zaheer, M., Talwalkar, A.S., Smith, V.: Federated optimization in heterogeneous networks. In: MLSys (2020)
24. Li, T., Sanjabi, M., Smith, V.: Fair resource allocation in federated learning. CoRR abs/1905.10497 (2019). http://arxiv.org/abs/1905.10497
25. Li, X.-C., Zhan, D.-C., Shao, Y., Li, B., Song, S.: FedPHP: Federated Personalization with Inherited Private Models. In: Oliver, N., Pérez-Cruz, F., Kramer, S., Read, J., Lozano, J.A. (eds.) ECML PKDD 2021. LNCS (LNAI), vol. 12975, pp. 587–602. Springer, Cham (2021). https://doi.org/10.1007/978-3-030-86486-6_36 https://2021.ecmlpkdd.org/wp-content/uploads/2021/07/sub_654.pdf
26. Ma, Z., L, Y., Li, W., Cui, S.: Beyond random selection: a perspective from model inversion in personalized federated learning. In: Amini, MR., Canu, S., Fischer, A., Guns, T., Kralj Novak, P., Tsoumakas, G. (eds.) ECML PKDD 2022. LNCS, vol. 13716, pp. 572–586. Springer, Cham (2022). https://doi.org/10.1007/978-3-031-26412-2_35, https://2022.ecmlpkdd.org/wp-content/uploads/2022/09/sub_801.PDF
27. McMahan, B., Moore, E., Ramage, D., Hampson, S., Arcas, B.A.V.: Communication-efficient learning of deep networks from decentralized data. In: Singh, A., Zhu, J. (eds.) Proceedings of the 20th International Conference on Artificial Intelligence and Statistics. Proceedings of Machine Learning Research, 20–22 April 2017, vol. 54, pp. 1273–1282. PMLR (2017). https://proceedings.mlr.press/v54/mcmahan17a.html
28. Mohri, M., Sivek, G., Suresh, A.T.: Agnostic federated learning. In: Chaudhuri, K., Salakhutdinov, R. (eds.) Proceedings of the 36th International Conference on Machine Learning. Proceedings of Machine Learning Research, 09–15 Jun 2019, vol. 97, pp. 4615–4625. PMLR (2019). https://proceedings.mlr.press/v97/mohri19a.html
29. Naseer, U., Benson, T.A., Netravali, R.: Webmedic: disentangling the memory-functionality tension for the next billion mobile web users. In: Proceedings of the 22nd International Workshop on Mobile Computing Systems and Applications. HotMobile 2021, pp. 71–77. Association for Computing Machinery, New York, NY, USA (2021). https://doi.org/10.1145/3446382.3448652
30. Naseer, U., Benson, T.A., Netravali, R.: Webmedic: disentangling the memory-functionality tension for the next billion mobile web users. In: Proceedings of the 22nd International Workshop on Mobile Computing Systems and Applications. HotMobile 2021, New York, NY, USA, pp. 71–77. Association for Computing Machinery (2021). https://doi.org/10.1145/3446382.3448652
31. OpenMined: Kotlinsyft. https://github.com/OpenMined/KotlinSyft/
32. OpenMined: Pysyft. https://github.com/OpenMined/PySyft/
33. Qazi, I.A., et al.: Mobile web browsing under memory pressure. SIGCOMM Comput. Commun. Rev. **50**(4), 35–48 (2020). https://doi.org/10.1145/3431832.3431837

34. Smith, V., Chiang, C.K., Sanjabi, M., Talwalkar, A.: Federated multi-task learning. In: Proceedings of the 31st International Conference on Neural Information Processing Systems. NIPS 2017, Red Hook, NY, USA, pp. 4427–4437. Curran Associates Inc. (2017)
35. Tan, C.M.J., Motani, M.: DropNet: reducing neural network complexity via iterative pruning. In: III, H.D., Singh, A. (eds.) Proceedings of the 37th International Conference on Machine Learning. Proceedings of Machine Learning Research, 13–18 July 2020, vol. 119, pp. 9356–9366. PMLR (2020). https://proceedings.mlr.press/v119/tan20a.html
36. Voigt, P., Bussche, A.V.D.: The EU General Data Protection Regulation (GDPR): A Practical Guide, 1st edn. Springer, Cham (2017). https://doi.org/10.1007/978-3-319-57959-7
37. Waheed, T., Qazi, I.A., Akhtar, Z., Qazi, Z.A.: Coal not diamonds: how memory pressure falters mobile video QOE. In: Proceedings of the 18th International Conference on Emerging Networking EXperiments and Technologies. CoNEXT 2022, New York, NY, USA, pp. 307–320. Association for Computing Machinery (2022). https://doi.org/10.1145/3555050.3569120
38. Wang, J., Charles, Z., Xu, Z., Joshi, G., et al.: A field guide to federated optimization. CoRR abs/2107.06917 (2021).https://arxiv.org/abs/2107.06917
39. Xu, C., Qu, Y., Xiang, Y., Gao, L.: Asynchronous federated learning on heterogeneous devices: a survey (2021)

Practical and General Backdoor Attacks Against Vertical Federated Learning

Yuexin Xuan[1,2], Xiaojun Chen[1,2(✉)], Zhendong Zhao[1,2], Bisheng Tang[1,2], and Ye Dong[1,2]

[1] School of Cyber Security, University of Chinese Academy of Sciences, Beijing, China

[2] Institute of Information Engineering, Chinese Academy of Sciences, Beijing, China

{xuanyuexin,chenxiaojun,zhaozhendong,tangbisheng,dongye}@iie.ac.cn

Abstract. Federated learning (FL), which aims to facilitate data collaboration across multiple organizations without exposing data privacy, encounters potential security risks. One serious threat is backdoor attacks, where an attacker injects a specific trigger into the training dataset to manipulate the model's prediction. Most existing FL backdoor attacks are based on horizontal federated learning (HFL), where the data owned by different parties have the same features. However, compared to HFL, backdoor attacks on vertical federated learning (VFL), where each party only holds a disjoint subset of features and the labels are only owned by one party, are rarely studied. The main challenge of this attack is to allow an attacker without access to the data labels, to perform an effective attack. To this end, we propose BadVFL, a novel and practical approach to inject backdoor triggers into victim models without label information. BadVFL mainly consists of two key steps. First, to address the challenge of attackers having no knowledge of labels, we introduce a SDD module that can trace data categories based on gradients. Second, we propose a SDP module that can improve the attack's effectiveness by enhancing the decision dependency between the trigger and attack target. Extensive experiments show that BadVFL supports diverse datasets and models, and achieves over 93% attack success rate with only 1% poisoning rate. Code is available at https://github.com/xuanyx/BadVFL.

Keywords: Vertical Federated Learning · Backdoor Attacks

1 Introduction

Federated Learning (FL), as a promising distributed learning paradigm, enables multiple participants to collaboratively train a global model without exposing their private local data. Therefore, it attracts a surge of attention and has been widely applied in many privacy-critical fields like credit risk prediction [14,29], medical diagnosis [4,15], etc.

However, recent works have shown that such promising paradigm encounters severe security threats [5,13,18,27,34], which significantly hinders its deployment in safety-critical areas. One serious threat to FL is backdoor attacks, where

© The Author(s), under exclusive license to Springer Nature Switzerland AG 2023
D. Koutra et al. (Eds.): ECML PKDD 2023, LNAI 14170, pp. 402–417, 2023.
https://doi.org/10.1007/978-3-031-43415-0_24

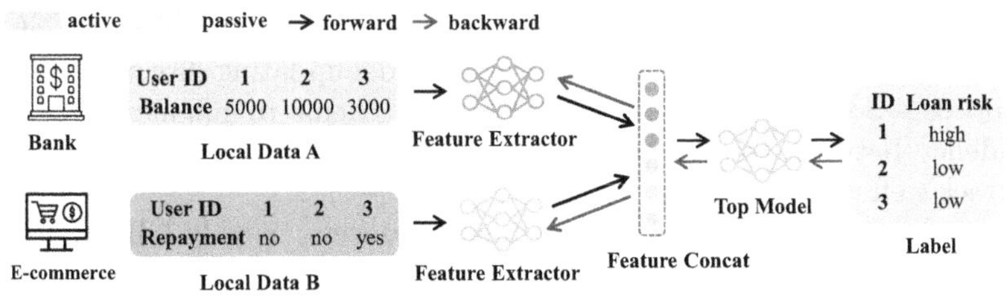

Fig. 1. An example of VFL system. A bank (active party) with account balance features aims to train a more precise model for loan risk analysis by cooperating with an e-commerce company (passive party) holding repayment features.

attackers poison partial training data of the victim model to mislead any data with the trigger to a target label, while preserving the model's utility on clean data. It is vital to ensure the security of FL before deployment, as the potential attacks may cause serious threats to the users. For instance, applying a backdoored FL model to the loan risk prediction area, which predicts any users with the trigger as low risk, may lead to huge economic losses.

FL can be classified into two main categories: horizontal federated learning (HFL) and vertical federated learning (VFL). In HFL, samples sharing the same features are distributed among different participants, e.g., two regional banks which have different clients but similar businesses like average monthly deposit and account balance to jointly train a model for financial product recommendations. In VFL, data owned by different parties share the same sample IDs but disjoint features. e.g., a bank with account balance information wants to get a more precise model for loan risk analysis by cooperating with an e-commerce company owning repayment information. Recent literature has thoroughly analyzed the backdoor attacks and defenses in HFL [21,22,24,30,31]. However, the backdoor threats in VFL are rarely explored, despite their increasing relevance in cross-enterprise collaboration. To this end, in this paper, we explore a new backdoor threat in VFL scenario.

Figure 1 illustrates the architecture of the VFL system. In VFL, only one party (known as the "active party") possesses the labels and partial data features, while the other parties (known as the "passive parties") only have partial data features. VFL enables the active party to enrich their data features by cooperating with the passive parties who provide more diverse features. Specifically, in the case where the attacker is the active party, an intuitive way is to add triggers to the local data from the target class, then put them into the training process to implant the backdoor. However, when the attacker is a passive party, the lack of label information makes it more challenging to perform the attack. To address this issue, one may apply label inference to deduce the labels. But the existing state-of-the-art method [5] requires many auxiliary labeled data and can only perform label inference after the model training is completed, which is impractical for backdoor injection. Despite the above challenges, we propose BadVFL to conduct backdoor attacks in VFL. Our approach includes two main components. First, we introduce a Source Data Detection (SDD) module to trace the data categories based on their gradients in run-time. The core idea of SDD is that data from the same class have similar model updating directions. Second, we propose a Source Data Perturbation (SDP) scheme to enhance the decision dependency between the trigger and attack target, thereby further improving the attack's effectiveness.

We evaluate BadVFL on four benchmark datasets, namely CIFAR-10, ImageNet, BHI, and IMDB, covering both image and text fields. Several excellent results are captured in the experiments. First, our attack is highly effective and general, achieving over 93% attack success rate with only 1% poisoning rate on all datasets, while introducing negligible main accuracy drops. Second, BadVFL is insensitive to the selection of target data, making it more stable than existing methods. Third, we evaluate BadVFL against several defense approaches to verify its robustness.

Our technical contributions are summarized below:

- We conduct a systematic investigation of backdoor attacks in VFL systems and propose BadVFL, a more general and practical backdoor framework with stable attack performance. Our analysis reveals serious backdoor risks in VFL systems.
- We propose the SDD module to trace data categories and the SDP module to enhance the dependency between triggers and attack targets.
- We conduct extensive empirical validations to show that our framework achieves start-of-the-art performance in terms of effectiveness, generalization, stability, and robustness against several defense methods.

2 Background and Related Work

2.1 Vertical Federated Learning

VFL [3,6,32,33] facilitates multiple parties to collaboratively build a model over the partitioned features with privacy-preserving, as all data remains local inside each party. Concretely, the VFL protocol is executed as below: 1) the active party broadcasts the sample ID sequence to passive parties to align the data. 2) Each passive party uploads data feature representations extracted by their local model in a predefined order. 3) The active party concatenates these features and feeds them into the top model to calculate the loss and gradients. 4) The active party updates the top model and sends the gradients of uploaded features to passive parties. 5) The passive parties update their bottom models using the received gradients. Supplement B.1 gives the algorithm of the VFL process.

However, such promising training paradigm has been shown to be vulnerable to security threats, such as backdoor attacks [18], label inference attacks [5], etc. It is crucial to ensure the security of VFL systems before deploying them in real-world applications.

2.2 Backdoor Attacks

Backdoor attacks aim at manipulating the victim models' behavior on backdoored data while maintaining good performance on clean data. Whenever the trigger is presented in the input instance, the backdoor is activated to induce the model to predict the target label.

Backdoor Attacks are first investigated in CV domain [19,26]. Gu et al. [7] generate the poisoned data by adding a specific pattern on clean samples, e.g., a square, and relabeling them with target label before putting them into the training process. We formulate the loss function of backdoor attacks as below:

$$\arg\min_{\theta} \sum_{(x,y)\in D} \mathcal{L}(\mathcal{F}(x,\theta),y) + \mathcal{L}(\mathcal{F}(x+\mathcal{T},\theta),y_t), \tag{1}$$

where $\mathcal{F}$ is the model with parameters θ, x is the clean data with correct label y, $\mathcal{T}$ is the trigger and y_t is the target label. The key to backdoor attacks is to establish a strong link between the trigger and the attack target, which is achieved by the last term in Eq. 1.

Recent studies have explored the backdoor attacks in the HFL scenario, which is more vulnerable due to clients having full control over the local labeled data and the training process, making it easier to submit malicious updates to build up a mapping between the trigger and target label. Xie et al. [30] introduce a distributed backdoor attack by decomposing a global trigger into several local triggers and assigning them to different adversarial clients. Bagdasaryan et al. [1] explore a model replacement approach by scaling the malicious model updates to replace the global model with the local poisoned one.

However, backdoor attacks in the VFL scenario are rarely explored because the attack achieved by the passive party is more challenging due to the lack of label information. Liu et al. [18] introduce a gradient replacement (GR) approach by replacing the gradient of local triggered samples with the gradient of the target data (explained in Sect. 4) when updating the local model. However, GR heavily relies on the selection of the target data and neglects the impact of features owned by other parties in the final classification.

3 Problem Formulation

3.1 Vertical Federated Learning

In a VFL system, there are K parties $\{P_k\}_{k=1}^{K}$, where each party P_k holds partial features and the labels are privately owned by the active party. We denote the whole training dataset as $D = \{x_i = (x_i^1, x_i^2, ..., x_i^K), y_i\}_{i=1}^{N}$, where x_i^k is the feature of ith sample located on kth party, and y_i is the true label of ith sample. Each party holds a local feature extractor $\mathcal{F}_{\theta_k}$ to transform the local data x_i^k into feature representations. VFL minimizes the following loss function to ensure performance:

$$\arg\min_{\theta} \sum_{(x_i,y_i)\in D} \mathcal{L}^{ce}\left(\mathcal{M}_{\theta_t}(f_i), y_i\right) + \Omega(\theta), \tag{2}$$

where $f_i = Concat\{\mathcal{F}_{\theta_1}(x_i^1), ..., \mathcal{F}_{\theta_K}(x_i^K)\}$ is the merged feature representation of the ith sample, $\mathcal{L}^{ce}$ is the cross-entropy loss and $\mathcal{M}_{\theta_t}$ is the top model, θ_k is the parameters of local feature extractor $\mathcal{F}_{\theta_k}$ owned by P_k, and $\Omega(\theta)$ is the regularization term to avoid overfitting.

3.2 Threat Model

As stated previously, we assume one of the passive parties with no label information is the adversary. Without loss of generality, we assume P_K is the attacker.

Attacker's Goal. The goal of P_K is to establish a strong link between the trigger and the attack target. Whenever the trigger is presented in the input instance, the victim model should predict the target label. Meanwhile, the attacker should ensure the clean data are classified correctly to maintain the model utility. Formally, the attacker optimizes the following objective function:

$$\arg\min_{\theta} \sum_{(x_i,y_i)\in D} \mathcal{L}^{ce}(\mathcal{M}_{\theta_t}(f_i^c), y_i) + \mathcal{L}^{ce}(\mathcal{M}_{\theta_t}(f_i^p), y_t) + \Omega(\theta), \tag{3}$$

where $f_i^c = Concat\{\mathcal{F}_{\theta_1}(x_i^1), ..., \mathcal{F}_{\theta_K}(x_i^K)\}$, $f_i^p = Concat\{\mathcal{F}_{\theta_1}(x_i^1), ..., \mathcal{F}_{\theta_K}(x_i^K + \mathcal{T})\}$ are the clean and poisoned feature representations, respectively. $\mathcal{T}$ is the injected trigger. The first term ensures that the victim model behaves normally on clean data, and the second term achieves the backdoor behavior. We showcase various backdoored samples in Supplement A.1.

Attacker's Capability. We assume P_K strictly follows the VFL protocols: uploading feature representations, receiving gradients, and updating its local model. The data accessible to P_K are: own local data $\{x_i^K\}_{i=1}^N$ and the corresponding gradients $\{g_i^K\}_{i=1}^N$ returned from the active party. Moreover, P_K has no knowledge of the data, the model, and any intermediate information owned by other parties. The adversary cannot interfere with the normal interactions between the active party and other passive parties.

4 Backdoor Attacks in VFL

In this section, we present a detailed explanation of how BadVFL can achieve backdoor attacks in the VFL systems.

The key to successful backdoor attacks is associating a pre-defined trigger with the target label. One intuitive method is adding the trigger into the data from the target class to link the trigger with the attack target. However, P_K without label information does not know which data comes from the target class. To address this issue, we design the Source Data Detection (SDD) module, which can infer data categories based on their gradients in run-time. Moreover, to further improve the attack's effectiveness, we propose the Source Data Perturbation (SDP) scheme, which enhances the decision-dependency between the trigger and

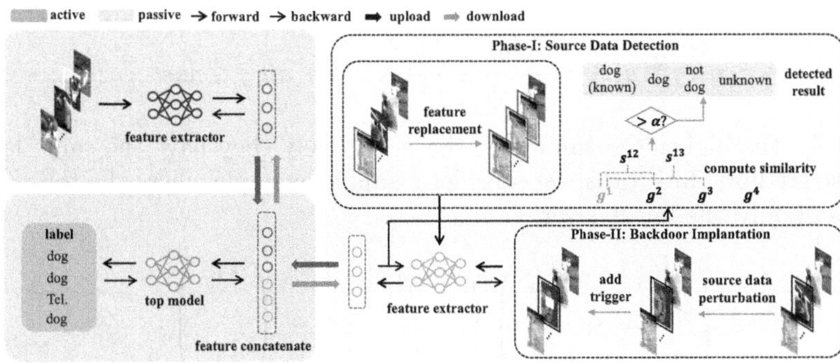

Fig. 2. The framework of BadVFL, which contains two main modules: Source Data Detection and Backdoor Implantation. The former aims to detect the source data (marked in blue) based on the target data (marked in orange). (Color figure online)

the attack target. Figure 2 shows the steps involved in BadVFL. And the detailed algorithm of BadVFL process is given in Supplement B.2.

Definition 1. ***(Target Data).*** *Target data is a prior knowledge which comes from the target class known by the attacker.*

Definition 2. ***(Source Data).*** *Source data are obtained by SDD module used for data poisoning which have the same label with target data.*

4.1 Source Data Detection

We assume P_K only knows one target data denoted as x_t^K, where t is the sample ID of target data. (Note that data should be uploaded to the top model in a pre-defined order.) Intuitively, the key insight of SDD is that data from the same class will have similar model updating directions (a.k.a., gradients). With known x_t^K, P_K normally participates in the VFL training process until first getting g_t^K. Then P_K runs SDD to infer which data comes from the target class by computing the similarity between g_t^K and the gradients of other data. In detail, the process involves two main steps: *feature replacement* and *similarity computation.*

Feature Replacement. We randomly select n samples per batch (denoted as x_{nset}^K, $|nset| = n$) to detect whether they are from the target class. To increase the gradient similarity between x_t^K and the data from the target class in x_{nset}^K, we replace x_j^K with x_t^K (for all $j \in nset$), so the only difference between x_t and x_{nset} is the data held by the other clients. Then we upload the replaced data to the top model.

Similarity Computation. After obtaining the returned gradients of x_{nset}^K (denoted as g_{nset}^K), we compute the cosine similarity between g_{nset}^K and g_t^K. (Note that g_t^K is updated when x_t^K is uploaded.)

$$cos(g_t^K, g_j^K) = \frac{\langle g_t^K, g_j^K \rangle}{\left\|g_t^K\right\|_2 \left\|g_j^K\right\|_2}, \quad for\ all\ j \in nset. \tag{4}$$

Intuitively, the higher the similarity, the more likely they have the same label. To illustrate how this works, we consider a simple example where the top model consists of only one linear layer.

$$\begin{pmatrix} W_{11} & \cdots & W_{1d} \\ \vdots & \ddots & \vdots \\ W_{C1} & \cdots & W_{Cd} \end{pmatrix} \begin{pmatrix} \mathcal{F}_{\theta_1}^T(x_i^1) \\ \vdots \\ \mathcal{F}_{\theta_K}^T(x_i^K) \end{pmatrix} = \begin{pmatrix} O_1 \\ \vdots \\ O_C \end{pmatrix}, \tag{5}$$

where W is the top model parameters, O is the output of sample i, and C is the number of classes for classification. Here we assume the true label y_i of sample i is class c, where $c \in [1, C]$. As we can see, the gradient of the cross-entropy loss w.r.t. the feature representation of sample i is:

$$\frac{\partial \mathcal{L}^{ce}(f_i; W, y_i)}{\partial f_i} = \left(W_{c1}, \cdots, W_{cd}\right) = W_c. \tag{6}$$

Therefore, the gradients received by P_K have the following properties: data from the same class will return similar gradients, resulting in a high positive cosine similarity. While samples from different classes will return dissimilar gradients, resulting in a low cosine similarity.

Finally, we set a threshold α_{thre}. If the similarity between g_j^K (for $j \in nset$) and g_t^K is higher than α_{thre}, we consider x_j^K to be from the target class, named source data. We terminate the SDD process until enough source data are found or all training data have been considered. Compared with the state-of-the-art label inference method [5] which requires many auxiliary labeled data, our SDD is more practical.

4.2 Backdoor Implantation

Based on the above steps, we have already inferred the source data which are from the target class. Our next task is to associate a pre-defined trigger with the attack target. One intuitive method is directly adding the trigger to the source data and putting them into the training process. However, the top model may still learn the mapping between the background clean features of the source data and the target label, causing the failure of backdoor injection. Therefore, we propose a Source Data Perturbation (SDP) module to further enhance the decision-dependency between the trigger and the attack target.

Source Data Perturbation. A successful backdoored model should give the target prediction as long as the malicious trigger is present, despite the existence of the background clean features. To make the trigger a higher priority than the other clean features in the decision-making phase, we attempt to replace the source data with the data randomly selected from the same batch. In this way, the source data will contain clean features of different classes. Then we add the trigger on the perturbed source data and put them into the training process to achieve backdoor injection.

There are mainly two reasons why SDP module enhances the decision-dependency between the trigger and attack target: (a) The source data inferred by SDD have the same label (attack target). And their features are replaced by randomly selected data after the SDP module. This makes the source data equipped with different features but the same label, causing the model more difficult to learn from these features. (b) After the SDP process, we add the same trigger to the source data, thus they have the same trigger and the same target label, which makes the model more likely to establish the decision-dependency between the trigger and attack target.

5 Experiments

5.1 Experiment Setup

As most real VFL systems consist of two parties [2,5,9], for the rest of this paper, we construct and evaluate BadVFL under a two-party scenario. The attacks in multi-party settings are given in Supplement C.1.

Datasets and Networks. We evaluate BadVFL on the following datasets: CIFAR-10 [16], ImageNet [25], Breast Histopathology Images (BHI) [23], and IMDB [20]. The first three are image datasets, and IMDB is a text dataset. We describe the datasets in detail in Supplement A.2. To make these datasets suitable for the VFL scenario, as the common setting in VFL [5,13,18], for CIFAR-10 and ImageNet, we split the data into two parts along the middle line so that each party holds half. For BHI, there are multiple examination image patches per patient, and we distribute the patches of each patient with the same label to each party in a round-robin manner. For IMDB, we split each sample (a paragraph for a movie review) into two parts and distribute them to each party.

We experiment on three classic deep neural networks to get feature representations, namely ResNet18 [8] for CIFAR-10 and BHI, VGG16 [28] for ImageNet and LSTM [11] for IMDB. As for the top model used for feature combination and classification, following previous works [12,13], we adopt a linear combination of these features and then apply a nonlinear transformation (e.g., softmax) to make the prediction. To verify the stability of BadVFL, we also conduct experiments with multi-hidden layers.

Implementation Details. For image datasets, the models are trained by SGD optimizer for 200 epochs. The initial learning rate is 0.01, multiplied by 0.1 per 50 epoch. For text dataset, the optimizer is Adam with an initial learning rate of 0.001. In all experiments, the poisoning rate $\eta = \frac{|D_{poisoned}|}{|D_{train}|}$ is 1%, as the common setting for backdoor attacks [7]. And we set the replacement number $n = 5$ and the threshold $\alpha_{thre} = 0.6$ in SDD for all datasets.

Evaluation Metrics. We adopt Test Accuracy Rate (TAR) and Attack Success Rate (ASR) to evaluate BadVFL performance. Specifically, TAR is the probability that the clean data are classified correctly, measuring the impact of backdoor attacks on the main task. ASR is the probability of predicting the poisoned data as the target label, which measures the attack efficacy.

5.2 Attack Performance

Attack Effectiveness. For image datasets, the trigger we applied following Gu et al. [7], which is a white square located in the center of the image. We apply 4×4, 20×20, and 5×5 trigger size for CIFAR-10, ImageNet and BHI, respectively. For IMDB, we insert the word '[START]' into the middle of the sentence as the trigger.

To ensure our attack remains consistently effective, for each class, we construct BadVFL with randomly selecting 3 different target data from the dataset and get their average as the final result. To suppress the effect of non-determinism, all experiments are averaged across multiple runs. The results are shown in Table 1. Observe that the triggers are successfully injected as the poisoned models have small TAR difference compared with the benign models and high ASR. Specifically, BadVFL achieves above 93% ASR in all datasets with negligible TAR drops.

Table 1. The attack performance of BadVFL and GR in four datasets.

Dataset	Benign VFL	BadVFL		GR	
		TAR	**ASR**	**TAR**	**ASR**
CIFAR-10	80.96	80.69	94.98	77.08	44.07
ImageNet	79.63	79.47	93.15	73.01	19.21
BHI	91.90	89.52	99.11	88.45	98.93
IMDB	85.62	85.01	98.97	81.99	51.98

Figure 3 depicts the category distribution of the source data obtained by SDD module for different target class. The color-coded values in row i and column j represent the number of inferred source data from class j when target data from class i. As we can see, for most cases, SDD module can correctly identify the source data which are truly from target class. However, for some target class, such as class 3 in CIFAR-10, the SDD mistakenly identifies few samples from class 5 as its source data. This is because the data from class 3 (cat) have the similar features with data from class 5 (dog). And few false detection results have little influence on the attack effectiveness.

Comparison with Gradient Replacement. We compare BadVFL with the state-of-the-art method GR [18], which attacks VFL system by replacing the

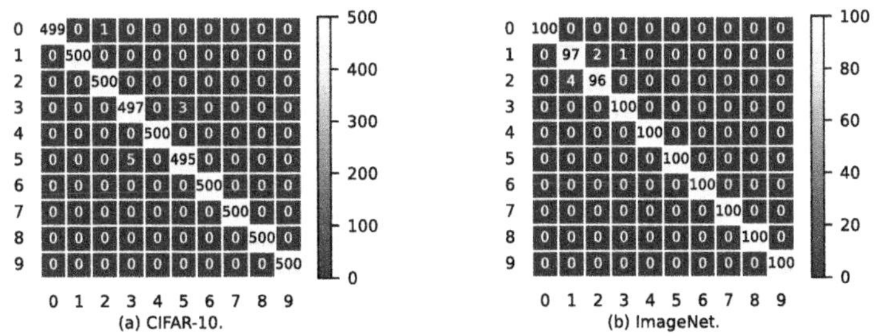

Fig. 3. The number of source data from class j (column) being identified as class i (row) by SDD on CIFAR-10 (left) and ImageNet (right) dataset. The total number of source data is 500 for CIFAR-10 and 100 for ImageNet.

gradient of local triggered samples with the gradient of the target data when updating the local bottom model. Table 1 shows the comparison results. Apparently, our method outperforms GR on all metrics and achieves a significant boost. In more details, GR hurts worse on the main task accuracy. This is because the adversary replaces the triggered data's feature with random vectors and sends them to the active party, to prevent the active party establishing a new mapping between the triggered data with their true label. Moreover, the attack performance of GR strongly depends on the selection of target data.

5.3 Multi-hidden Layers Performance

To verify the stability of BadVFL with different top model structures, in this section, we show the effectiveness of BadVFL for multi-hidden fully-connected neural networks. Considering the role of top model is feature combination and classification, the structure of it does not need to be complex. As shown in Fig. 4, we experiment on 1-hidden, 2-hidden and 3-hidden layers with ReLU activation followed by softmax transformation.

Intuitively, for BHI and IMDB dataset, there is no significant difference with the increasing of model depth. However, for CIFAR-10 and ImageNet dataset, the BadVFL performs worse as the network becomes deeper. Diving to the bottom, the phenomenon is caused by the fact that the more complicated top model structure affects the gradient-based SDD module calculation, leading to wrongly inferred source data which are not from the target class.

5.4 Defenses

To demonstrate how defensive strategies against BadVFL, we conduct BadVFL with noisy gradients and gradient compression, which are commonly used by prior works to train the robust FL systems [5,10].

Noisy Gradients. One straightforward attempt to defense BadVFL is adding noise to the exchanged information. We experiment Gaussian noise [35] with

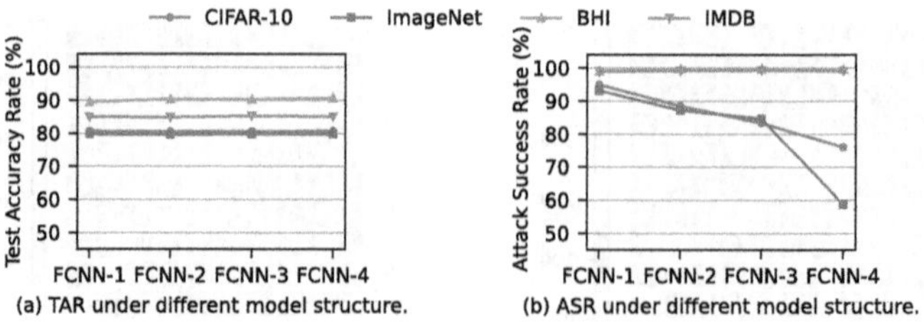

Fig. 4. The performance of BadVFL *w.r.t.* different top model structures.

variance from 10^{-5} to 10^{-2}. Because adding noise inevitably affects the gradient similarity calculation, we select the 1% highest similarity results as the source data in each iteration instead of a fixed threshold. The results are shown in Fig. 5a. As we can see, the BadVFL performance monotonically decreases with the increasing of noise scales. In details, when variance is 1e-4, the ASR on ImageNet severely deteriorates and TAR drops by nearly 20%, resulting in a good defense performance but seriously compromising the model utility. For CIFAR-10, setting variance to 1e-3 successfully defends against BadVFL, where the ASR drops to 30% with negligible TAR drops. However, in practice, it is non-trivial to figure out an appropriate noise scale that guarantees security while maintains model utility.

Gradient Compression. Another effective defense strategy is pruning the gradients with small magnitudes to zero [17]. We evaluate different level of sparsity from 0.75 to 0.1. As shown in Fig. 5b, interestingly, for CIFAR-10, BHI and IMDB, BadVFL maintains considerable high TAR and ASR with the increasing of compression rate. As for ImageNet, the gradient compression can successfully mitigate the backdoor attacks in VFL, but introducing significantly TAR drops and destroying the model utility.

5.5 Ablation Study

Position of Trigger. To further validate the influence of trigger position on attack effectiveness, we plot Fig. 6 to show the BadVFL attack performance with three possible locations. For image classification task, we experiment the trigger located in "up left" (u-l), "center", and "bottom right" (b-r) of the image to analyze the effectiveness. For text classification task, we conduct the experiments with the trigger located in the "initial", "middle" and "end" of the text.

As shown in Fig. 6, we notice that for image classification task, the center location has a significant advantage over the other two locations, because the center area contributes more to model classification and its original features are blocked.

For text classification task, the initial and end position have a slight advantage over the middle position, due to the training mode of the Recurrent Neural Networks. Nevertheless, no matter where the triggers are, BadVFL can always

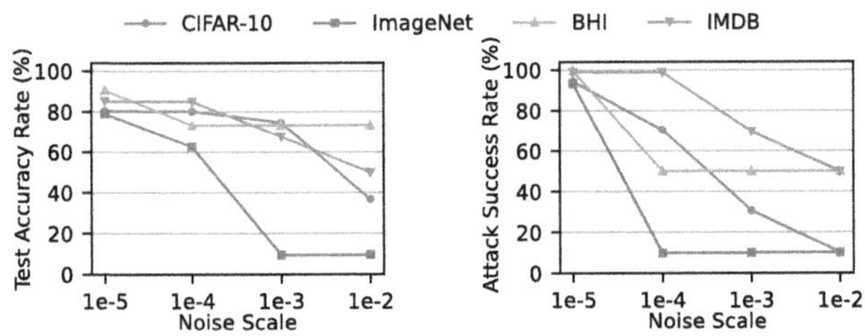

(a) Noisy Gradients.

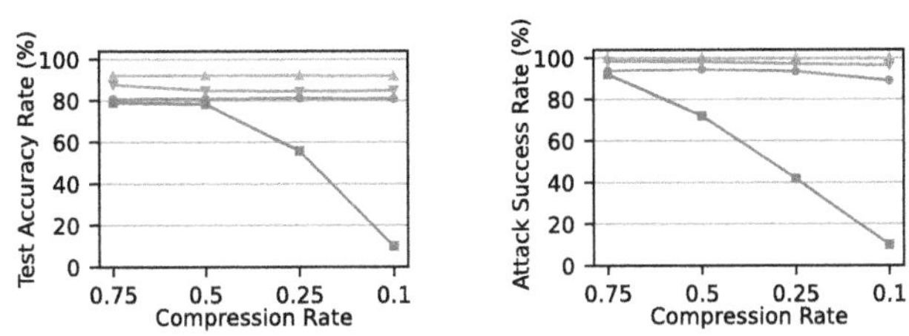

(b) Gradient Compression.

Fig. 5. BadVFL performance against different defense strategies on all datasets.

succeed in injecting the backdoor into the model with negligible main accuracy drops.

Source Data Perturbation. As discussed in Sect. 4, if we directly add triggers to the source data and put them into training process, the model may not learn the trigger but the clean feature of the source data. Thus, we evaluate the importance of SDP and the results are shown in Table 2. Specifically, we consider the three following cases: (a) without perturbation, (b) replace the source data with data selected from the same batch, and (c) replace the source data with data selected from the whole dataset.

We observe that there is no significant difference between the cases where the attacker replaces the source data with the data from same batch, or from the whole training dataset. However, when the attacker does not perturb the source data and directly adds the trigger on them, the BadVFL performance drops significantly. This is especially prominent in the case of the CIFAR-10 and ImageNet dataset.

5.6 Hyperparameter Analysis

Influence of Injecting Rateη. We investigate the critical factor η which affects the number of poisoned data in the training process. As shown in Fig. 7a, the ASR becomes worse when $\eta > 3\%$. This is because the attacker uploads more

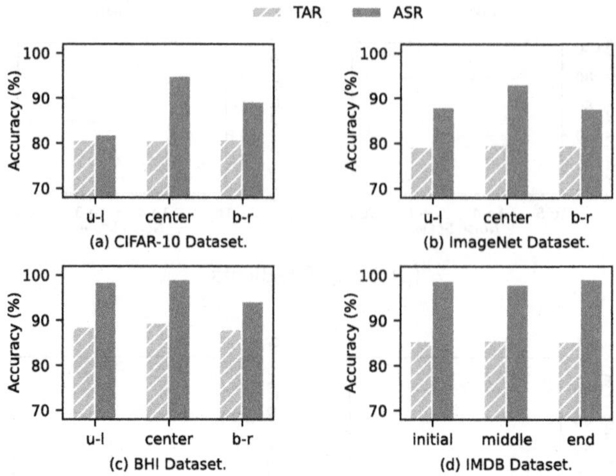

Fig. 6. BadVFL performance *w.r.t* varied trigger positions.

Table 2. BadVFL performance *w.r.t.* different types of source data perturbation.

Dataset	No Perturb		Replace from Same Batch		Replace from Whole Dataset	
	TAR	**ASR**	**TAR**	**ASR**	**TAR**	**ASR**
CIFAR-10	80.90	46.16	80.69	94.98	80.67	94.80
ImageNet	79.38	44.13	79.47	93.15	79.03	93.84
BHI	87.82	87.93	89.52	99.11	90.25	99.32
IMDB	85.29	63.34	85.01	98.97	85.45	98.33

"wrong" features (perturbed source data) as η increases, resulting in the top model depends more on other clean features in decision-making.

Influence of Replacement Number n. We depict the impact of replacement number n on the BadVFL performance in Fig. 7b. There is no significant different among varied n. Moreover, because a small n makes the poisoning process more stealthy, we set $n = 5$ as default for all datasets.

Influence of Threshold α_{thre}. The α_{thre} in the SDD module can control the final source data set of backdoor attacks. The results are shown in Fig. 7c. Specifically, when $\alpha_{thre} < 0.6$, the larger α_{thre} makes BadVFL more effective. This is caused by the fact that the larger α_{thre} can infer more accurate source data which are truly from target class. When $\alpha_{thre} > 0.6$, the BadVFL converges more stably. Hence, we set $\alpha_{thre} = 0.6$ for all datasets.

Influence of Trigger Size *ts*. Another critical factor that might affect the BadVFL performance is the size of trigger. As shown in Fig. 7d, we can observe that BadVFL achieves a stable performance among different trigger sizes.

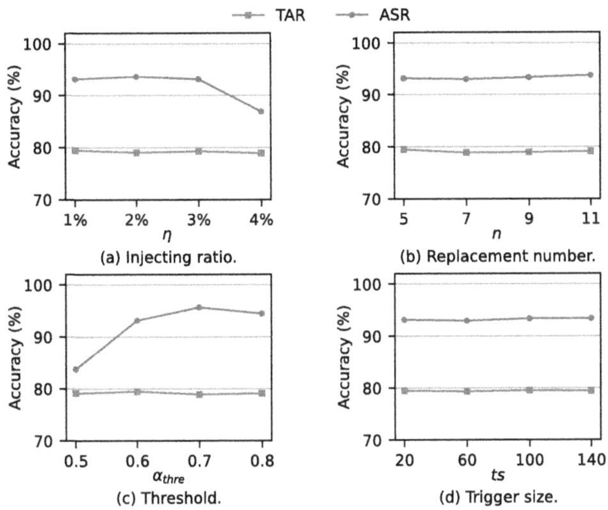

Fig. 7. The performance of BadVFL on ImageNet dataset *w.r.t.* different hyperparameters.

6 Conclusion

In this paper, we have demonstrated a new security risk where backdoor attacks can be successfully implanted into VFL systems. We propose BadVFL, which outperforms state-of-the-art method remarkably. It is likely that future defenses will defeat this attacks, however, we believe that the attacks are a promising direction that (a) expose possible security threats in such promising training paradigm, and (b) enlighten the future work. Future direction suggested by our work is the counter measures against backdoor attacks under VFL scenario, such as anomaly data detection and backdoor mitigation, etc. However, these might be difficult because the defender only holds partial data features and part of global model.

Acknowledgements. This work is supported by the Strategic Priority Research Program of Chinese Academy of Sciences, Grant No. XDC02040400.

References

1. Bagdasaryan, E., Veit, A., Hua, Y., Estrin, D., Shmatikov, V.: How to backdoor federated learning. In: Proceedings of the Twenty Third International Conference on Artificial Intelligence and Statistics (2020)
2. Chen, C., et al.: When homomorphic encryption marries secret sharing: secure large-scale sparse logistic regression and applications in risk control. In: Proceedings of the 27th ACM SIGKDD Conference on Knowledge Discovery & Data Mining, pp. 2652–2662 (2021)
3. Chen, C., et al.: Vertically federated graph neural network for privacy-preserving node classification. In: Proceedings of the Thirty-First International Joint Conference on Artificial Intelligence, IJCAI 2022, Vienna, Austria, 23–29 July 2022, pp. 1959–1965. ijcai.org (2022)
4. FeatureCloud: Transforming health care and medical research with federated learning (2020)
5. Fu, C., et al.: Label inference attacks against vertical federated learning. In: 31st USENIX Security Symposium (USENIX Security 22), Boston, MA (2022)
6. Fu, F., et al.: Vf2boost: very fast vertical federated gradient boosting for cross-enterprise learning. In: Proceedings of the 2021 International Conference on Management of Data (2021)
7. Gu, T., Dolan-Gavitt, B., Garg, S.: BadNets: identifying vulnerabilities in the machine learning model supply chain. arXiv: Cryptography and Security (2017)
8. He, K., Zhang, X., Ren, S., Sun, J.: Deep residual learning for image recognition. In: CVPR (2016)
9. He, Z., Zhang, T., Lee, R.B.: Model inversion attacks against collaborative inference. In: Proceedings of the 35th Annual Computer Security Applications Conference, pp. 148–162 (2019)
10. Hitaj, B., Ateniese, G., Pérez-Cruz, F.: Deep models under the GAN: information leakage from collaborative deep learning. In: The ACM Conference on Computer and Communications Security, (CCS) pp. 603–618 (2017)
11. Hochreiter, S., Schmidhuber, J.: Long short-term memory. Neural Comput. **9**(8), 1735–1780 (1997)
12. Hu, Y., Niu, D., Yang, J., Zhou, S.: FDML: a collaborative machine learning framework for distributed features. In: Proceedings of the 25th ACM SIGKDD International Conference on Knowledge Discovery & Data Mining (2019)
13. Jin, X., Chen, P.Y., Hsu, C.Y., Yu, C.M., Chen, T.: Cafe: catastrophic data leakage in vertical federated learning. Adv. Neural Inf. Process. Syst. **34**, 994–1006 (2021)
14. Kairouz, P., et al.: Advances and open problems in federated learning. Found. Trends® Mach. Learn. **14**(1–2), 1–210 (2021)
15. Kaissis, G., Makowski, M.R., Rückert, D., Braren, R.F.: Secure, privacy-preserving and federated machine learning in medical imaging. Nature Mach. Intell. **2**, 305–311 (2020)
16. Krizhevsky, A., Hinton, G., et al.: Learning multiple layers of features from tiny images (2009)
17. Lin, Y., Han, S., Mao, H., Wang, Y., Dally, W.J.: Deep gradient compression: reducing the communication bandwidth for distributed training (2017)
18. Liu, Y., Yi, Z., Chen, T.: Backdoor attacks and defenses in feature-partitioned collaborative learning. arXiv preprint arXiv:2007.03608 (2020)
19. Liu, Y., et al.: Trojaning attack on neural networks. In: Network and Distributed System Security Symposium, NDSS (2018)

20. Maas, A., Daly, R.E., Pham, P.T., Huang, D., Ng, A.Y., Potts, C.: Learning word vectors for sentiment analysis. In: Proceedings of the 49th Annual Meeting of the Association for Computational Linguistics: Human Language Technologies, pp. 142–150 (2011)
21. Nguyen, T.D., et al.: FLAME: taming backdoors in federated learning. In: Butler, K.R.B., Thomas, K. (eds.) 31st USENIX Security Symposium, USENIX Security 2022, Boston, MA, USA, August 10–12, 2022, pp. 1415–1432. USENIX Association (2022)
22. Ozdayi, S.M., Kantarcioglu, M., Gel, R.Y.: Defending against backdoors in federated learning with robust learning rate. In: Thirty-Fifth AAAI Conference on Artificial Intelligence, AAAI, pp. 9268–9276 (2021)
23. Mooney,P.: Breast histopathology images (2017)
24. Rieger, P., Nguyen, T.D., Miettinen, M., Sadeghi, A.: Deepsight: mitigating backdoor attacks in federated learning through deep model inspection. In: 29th Annual Network and Distributed System Security Symposium, NDSS 2022, San Diego, California, USA, April 24–28, 2022. The Internet Society (2022)
25. Russakovsky, O., et al.: Imagenet large scale visual recognition challenge. Int. J. Comput. Vis. **115**(3), 211–252 (2015)
26. Shafahi, A., et al.: Poison frogs! targeted clean-label poisoning attacks on neural networks. In: NIPS 2018 (2018)
27. Shejwalkar, V., Houmansadr, A.: Manipulating the byzantine: optimizing model poisoning attacks and defenses for federated learning. In: 28th Annual Network and Distributed System Security Symposium, NDSS 2021, Virtually, February 21–25, 2021. The Internet Society (2021)
28. Simonyan, K., Zisserman, A.: Very deep convolutional networks for large-scale image recognition. In: International Conference on Learning Representations (2015)
29. Webank: Utilization of fate in risk management of credit in small and micro enterprises (2018)
30. Xie, C., Huang, K., Chen, P.Y., Li, B.: DBA: distributed backdoor attacks against federated learning. In: ICLR (2020)
31. Xu, J., Wang, R., Koffas, S., Liang, K., Picek, S.: More is better (mostly): on the backdoor attacks in federated graph neural networks. In: Annual Computer Security Applications Conference, ACSAC 2022, Austin, TX, USA, 5–9 December 2022, pp. 684–698. ACM (2022)
32. Yang, Q., Liu, Y., Chen, T., Tong, Y.: Federated machine learning: concept and applications. ACM Trans. Intell. Syst. Technol. (TIST) **10**(2), 1–19 (2019)
33. Zhang, Q., Gu, B., Deng, C., Huang, H.: Secure bilevel asynchronous vertical federated learning with backward updating. In: AAAI (2021)
34. Zhang, Z., et al.: Neurotoxin: Durable backdoors in federated learning. In: International Conference on Machine Learning, ICML 2022, 17–23 July 2022, Baltimore, Maryland, USA. Proceedings of Machine Learning Research, vol. 162, pp. 26429–26446. PMLR (2022)
35. Zhu, L., Liu, Z., Han, S.: Deep leakage from gradients. In: Advances in Neural Information Processing Systems, vol. 32. Curran Associates, Inc. (2019)

Few-Shot Learning

Not All Tasks Are Equal: A Parameter-Efficient Task Reweighting Method for Few-Shot Learning

Xin Liu[1], Yilin Lyu[1], Liping Jing[1](✉), Tieyong Zeng[2], and Jian Yu[1]

[1] School of Computer and Information Technology, Beijing Jiaotong University, Beijing, China
{xin.liu,yilinlyu,lpjing,jianyu}@bjtu.edu.cn

[2] Department of Mathematics, The Chinese University of Hong Kong, Shatin, NT, Hong Kong
zeng@math.cuhk.edu.hk

Abstract. Meta-learning has emerged as an effective and popular approach for few-shot learning (FSL) due to its fast adaptation to novel tasks. However, this kind of method assumes that the meta-training and testing tasks come from the same task distribution and assigns equal weights to all tasks during meta-training. This assumption limits their ability to perform well in real-world scenarios where some meta-training tasks contribute more to the testing tasks than others. To address this issue, we propose a parameter-efficient task reweighting (PETR) method, which assigns proper weights to meta-training tasks according to their contribution to the testing tasks while using few parameters. Specifically, we formulate a bi-level optimization problem to jointly learn the few-shot learning model and the task weights. In the inner loop, the meta-parameters of the few-shot learning model are updated based on a weighted training loss. In the outer loop, the task weight parameters are updated with the implicit gradient. Additionally, to address the challenge of a large number of task weight parameters, we introduce a hypothesis that significantly reduces the required parameters by considering the factors that influence the importance of each meta-training task. Empirical evaluation results on both traditional FSL and FSL with out-of-distribution (OOD) tasks show that our PETR method outperforms state-of-the-art meta-learning-based FSL methods by assigning proper weights to different meta-training tasks.

Keywords: Few-shot Learning · Meta Learning · Task Reweighting · Bi-level Optimization

1 Introduction

Humans are born with the capability to efficiently learn new tasks with few samples by drawing upon previous relevant experience. For example, a child can effortlessly recognize a panda just by seeing a picture of it. However, many high-performance deep learning-based methods [1,2] still rely on large volumes of labeled data, which severely restricts their applicability in many real-world scenarios. For instance, in fields such as medicine and defense, obtaining sufficient manual annotation may either be impractical or too expensive to obtain. As a result, a substantial amount of effort has been dedicated to developing novel few-shot learning (FSL) methods to bridge the gap between artificial intelligence and human intelligence.

© The Author(s), under exclusive license to Springer Nature Switzerland AG 2023
D. Koutra et al. (Eds.): ECML PKDD 2023, LNAI 14170, pp. 421–437, 2023.
https://doi.org/10.1007/978-3-031-43415-0_25

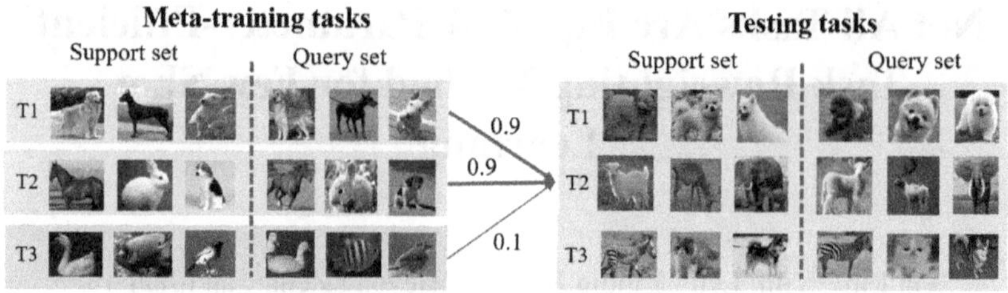

Fig. 1. An example of not all tasks are equal. For the testing task of recognizing animals from the land, the meta-training tasks that classify animals from land (T1, T2) are useful for the testing tasks, while the meta-training tasks that classify animals not found on land (T3) may degrade the testing performance.

To avoid overfitting due to limited labeled data of novel classes, a dominant way in FSL is applying meta-learning framework [3,4] to extract meta-knowledge for novel tasks by learning on a series of meta-training tasks constructed from base classes. One hpgighly successful algorithm is Model Agnostic Meta-Learning (MAML) [5], which aims to learn a good initialization that can be quickly adapted to testing tasks. And a number of extensions to MAML [6–9] have since been proposed. Despite previous efforts being made, a crucial assumption in this kind of method is that the meta-training and testing tasks are drawn from the same task distribution. Therefore, they assign equal weights to all meta-training tasks. However, this assumption limits their work in scenarios where some meta-training tasks may contribute more to the testing tasks. In reality, the true testing task distribution is often unknown and may differ from the meta-training task distribution. As illustrated in Fig. 1, we construct a collection of meta-training tasks for classifying animals from all over the world, but the testing tasks only consist of images of animals from the land. In this case, during meta-training, only the tasks that classify animals from the land are useful for the testing tasks, the tasks that classify animals in the sky and water will bring a shift between the meta-training and testing task distributions and may degrade the testing performance. In order to achieve this goal, our approach recognizes a crucial insight that not all tasks hold equal importance. The tasks used for meta-training can assist in solving the testing task to varying extents, and in some cases, certain meta-training tasks may even have a detrimental impact. Therefore, it becomes essential to assign appropriate weights to different meta-training tasks based on their respective contributions to the testing task distribution. Actually, learning proper weights for meta-training tasks is not easy. Without a suitable definition of unbiased testing task distribution, solving the task distribution shift problem is inherently ill-defined. To address it, [10] presents a weighted meta-learning method, where the meta-training task weights are selected by minimizing a data-dependent bound involving an empirical IPM between the weighted meta-training and testing risks. However, it assumed the testing task is available during training, which is unrealistic in some real-life scenarios. Recently, [11] utilizes a small clean validation set to approximate the testing set and learn weights for query samples in each meta-training task. However, the number of weight parameters is very huge as it correlates to the number of samples in the query sets of the meta-training tasks, leading to computational inefficiency during training.

In this paper, we propose a Parameter-efficient Task Reweighting (PETR) method that can adaptively assign appropriate weights to different meta-training tasks while using fewer additional parameters. We first address the problem of the unavailable testing-task distribution by utilizing a small, unbiased validation set following [11]. We believe that creating a small and clean meta-validation set is not prohibitively expensive or unrealistic. Then, we formulate a bi-level optimization problem to jointly learn the meta-parameters of the few-shot learning model and the parameters of the task weights. To address the challenge of a large number of task-weight parameters, we propose a hypothesis that can help build a parameter-efficient task-weight learning module by considering the factors that influence the importance of each meta-training task. This module can accurately capture the importance of different meta-training tasks while significantly reducing the number of required parameters. An overview of PETR is presented in Fig. 2. In the inner loop, we optimize the meta-parameters of the few-shot learning model based on a weighted training loss, where the weights are learned in the outer loop. In the outer loop, we update the parameters of task weights using the implicit gradient on the validation dataset. We alternate to perform the inner loop and outer loop optimization process until the validation loss converges.

In summary, our contributions are as follows:

- We propose PETR, a weighted meta-learning method for FSL methods, which can jointly learn the optimal meta-training task weights and meta parameters for few-shot learning by optimizing a bi-level objective function.
- We propose a hypothesis that can help build a parameter-efficient task-weight learning module, which can accurately capture the importance of the different meta-training tasks, while largely reducing the required parameters.
- We conduct extensive experiments under different few-shot learning settings to validate the effectiveness of PETR. The results demonstrate PETR has superior performance compared to state-of-the-art meta-learning-based FSL methods.

2 Related Work

Sample Reweighting is closely related to our proposed approach. It is a classic technique used to deal with distribution shifts in traditional machine learning methods. One important branch of the sample reweighting method is importance sampling, which estimates the sample weight by calculating the density ratio between the training and testing distributions [12–14]. However, this method requires prior knowledge of the testing distribution, which may not be available in some real-world scenarios. To address this challenge, recent works have proposed stable learning methods to learn sample weights that aim to eliminate the statistical correlation between relevant and irrelevant features [15,16]. However, these methods still have some limitations, such as the requirement for features to be provided. More recently, bilevel optimization frameworks have been employed to learn sample weights to effectively address the domain shift problem [17,18]. However, the previous research has mainly focused on traditional classification tasks, whereas our proposed method addresses the task reweighting problem in FSL.

Few-shot Learning aims to solve a novel task with few labeled samples. To avoid over-fitting, researchers usually leverage the knowledge learned from a related base dataset. In this paper, we focus on the meta-learning-based few-shot learning method, which aims to extract meta-knowledge for novel tasks by learning on a series of similar tasks constructed from base classes. A highly successful meta-learning-based few-shot learning method is MAML [5], which leveraged data from a collection of meta-training tasks to learn an initial model that can be quickly adapted to some testing tasks. And a number of extensions to MAML [6–9] have since been proposed and connections to hierarchical Bayesian modeling [19–21] have been drawn. Despite previous efforts being made, these methods assume that the training and testing tasks are drawn from the same task distribution, limiting its ability to work in real-world applications. To bridge the gap between training and testing task distribution and improve the generalization performance in FSL, some methods have been proposed to densify the training task distribution by making modifications to the original training tasks through noise [22], mixup [23], or task interpolation [24]. However, these augmented tasks may not be diverse enough to cover the real testing task distribution. Another line of research has focused on FSL with OOD tasks. Some methods aimed to detect OOD tasks [25] or learn better task-specific knowledge [26,27]. Recently, researchers resort to reweighting techniques to adjust the biased training-task distribution [10,11]. However, learning proper weights for meta-training tasks is not easy. Without a suitable definition of unbiased task distribution, solving the task distribution shift problem is inherently ill-defined. Some curriculum meta-learning methods also aim to learn weights for different meta-training tasks [28–30]. They believe that the order of the meta-training task will influence the model performance. Therefore, they aimed to define a proper data training order by weighting the training tasks so that the model can achieve faster convergence and better performance. However, they fail to deal with OOD tasks. There are also some works focusing on dealing with the distribution shift between the support set and query set [31,32], which are different from our focus in this paper. Here, we only consider the distribution shift problem between the meta-training and testing tasks.

3 Preliminaries

Bi-level Optimization. Bi-Level Optimization (BLO) is defined as a mathematical program, where an outer optimization problem contains another inner optimization problem as a constraint. The two problems have their own objectives and constraints.

For the outer loop objective function $F : \mathbb{R}^n \times \mathbb{R}^m \longrightarrow \mathbb{R}$ and inner loop objective function $f : \mathbb{R}^n \times \mathbb{R}^m \longrightarrow \mathbb{R}$, the bi-level problem is given by:

$$\begin{aligned} &\min_{x_u \in X_U, x_l \in X_L} \quad F(x_u, x_l) \\ &\text{subject to} \\ &x_l \in \arg\min_{x_l \in X_L} f(x_u, x_l) : g_j(x_u, x_l) \leq 0, j = 1, ..., J \\ &G_k(s_u, x_l) \leq 0, k = 1, ..., K. \end{aligned} \tag{1}$$

where $G_k : \mathbb{R}^n \times \mathbb{R}^m \longrightarrow \mathbb{R}, k = 1, ..., K$ denote the outer loop constraints, and $g_j : \mathbb{R}^n \times \mathbb{R}^m \longrightarrow \mathbb{R}$ represent the inner loop constraints, respectively. The sets $X_U \in \mathbb{R}^n$

and $X_L \in \mathbb{R}^m$ in the definition may denote additional restrictions like integrality. It is common to assume these to be sets of reals unless mentioned otherwise. In recent years, bi-level optimization is widely used in a variety of machine learning and computer vision tasks, including but not limited to, hyper-parameter optimization [33–35], multi-task and meta-learning [36–38], neural architecture search [39,40], adversarial learning [41,42], and deep reinforcement learning [43,44].

Meta-learning Based FSL and MAML. The goal of meta-learning-based FSL methods is to produce a learning algorithm that will work well on novel tasks by learning on the meta-training tasks. To achieve it, we usually have a collection of meta-training tasks$\{\mathcal{T}_i\}_{i=1}^{M}$ drawn from $P(\mathcal{T})$, each task $\mathcal{T}_i$ is linked to a specific task and is associated with a dataset $\mathcal{D}_i$ containing two disjoint sets $\{\mathcal{D}_i^{\mathcal{S}}, \mathcal{D}_i^{\mathcal{Q}}\}$. Where $\mathcal{S} = \{(x_i^s, y_i^s)\}_{i=1}^{N\times K}$ be a support set, which contains N different image classes and K labeled samples per class. $\mathcal{Q} = \{(x_j^q, y_j^q)\}_{j=1}^{N\times Q}$ denotes a query set, which contains unlabeled images from the same N classes as the support set.

We are interested in learning models of the form $h_\theta(x) : \mathcal{X} \rightarrow \mathcal{Y}$, parameterized by $\phi \in \Phi \equiv \mathbb{R}^d$. The goal for task $\mathcal{T}_i$ is to learn task-specific parameters ϕ_i using $\mathcal{D}_i^{\mathcal{S}}$ such that we can minimize the population or test loss of the task $\mathcal{L}(\phi_i, \mathcal{D}_i^{\mathcal{Q}})$. In the general bi-level meta-learning setup, we consider a space of algorithms that compute task-specific parameters using a set of meta-parameters $\theta \in \Theta \equiv \mathbb{R}^d$ and the training dataset from the task, such that $\phi_i = \mathcal{A}lg(\theta, \mathcal{D}_i^{\mathcal{S}})$ for task $\mathcal{T}_i$. The goal of meta-learning is to learn meta-parameters that produce good task-specific parameters after adaptation. It can be formulated as a bi-level optimization problem as below:

$$\begin{aligned} \theta_{ML}^* &:= \underset{\theta \in \Theta}{\arg\min}\, F(\theta) \\ \text{where} \quad F(\theta) &= \frac{1}{M}\sum_{i=1}^{M} \mathcal{L}(\mathcal{A}lg(\theta, \mathcal{D}_i^{\mathcal{S}}), \mathcal{D}_i^{\mathcal{Q}}). \end{aligned} \tag{2}$$

$\mathcal{A}lg(\theta, \mathcal{D}_i^{\mathcal{S}})$ explicitly or implicitly optimizes the inner-loop task-specific adaptation using the support set of each task $\mathcal{D}_i^{\mathcal{S}}$. The outer loop corresponds to the meta-training objective of low test error on the query set of each task $\mathcal{D}_i^{\mathcal{S}}$ after adaptation.

In the case of MAML [5], $\mathcal{A}lg(\theta, \mathcal{D}_i^{\mathcal{S}})$ corresponds to one or multiple steps of gradient descent initialized at θ. For example, if one step of gradient descent is used, we have:

$$\phi_i \equiv \mathcal{A}lg(\theta, \mathcal{D}_i^{\mathcal{S}}) = \theta - \alpha \nabla_\theta \mathcal{L}(\theta, \mathcal{D}_i^{\mathcal{S}}). \tag{3}$$

Typically, α is a scalar hyper-parameter, but can also be a learned vector [6]. Hence, for MAML, the meta-learned parameter θ_{ML}^* has a learned inductive bias that is particularly well-suited for fine-tuning tasks from $P(\mathcal{T})$ using K samples. For clear interpretation, we list the notations used in this paper and their corresponding explanation, as shown in Table 1.

4 The Proposed Method

In this section, we first formulate the problem we aim to solve and then describe our proposed parameter-efficient task reweighting module, followed by presenting the overall optimization process of PETR.

Table 1. Notations and their corresponding explanation

Notation	Description
$p_{tr}(\mathcal{T})$	probability distribution of meta-training tasks
$p_{val}(\mathcal{T})$	probability distribution of meta-validation tasks
$\mathcal{T}_i$	i-th meta-training task
$\mathcal{T}_j^{\mathcal{V}}$	j-th meta-validation task
$\{\mathcal{D}_i^S, \mathcal{D}_i^Q\}$	support set and query set of meta-training task $\mathcal{T}_i$
$\{\mathcal{V}_i^S, \mathcal{V}_i^Q\}$	support set and query set of meta-validation task $\mathcal{T}_j^{\mathcal{V}}$
$\{x_i^s, y_i^s\}_{i=1}^{N\times K}$	samples in the support set$\mathcal{D}_i^S$ of meta-training task $\mathcal{T}_i$
$\{x_j^q, y_j^q\}_{j=1}^{N\times Q}$	samples in the query set $\mathcal{D}_j^Q$ of meta-training task $\mathcal{T}_i$
θ	initial parameters of base learner
ϕ_i	task-specific parameters for task $\mathcal{T}_i$
θ_W^*	optimal initial parameters of the base learner as a function of W
w_i	weight for task $\mathcal{T}_i$
$W*$	optimal task weights
$\mathcal{L}(\phi_i, \mathcal{D})$	loss function on dataset $\mathcal{D}$ characterized by model parameter ϕ
$l(\phi_i, d)$	loss function on the query data point d characterized by model parameter θ
$\mathcal{A}lg(\theta, \mathcal{D})$	one or multiple steps of gradient descent initialized at θ on dataset $\mathcal{D}$
$\beta = \{a, b\}$	hyper-parameters for task weights
α, η, γ	step sizes
m, n	the number of meta-training, meta-validation tasks, respectively
M	the lower optimization steps

4.1 Problem Formulation

A drawback of the meta-learning framework for FSL methods specified in Eq. 2 is their equal weights of all meta-training tasks. As shown in Fig. 1, our key insight is that different meta-training tasks can help solve the testing task to varying degrees, and some meta-training tasks may even have a negative effect. Therefore, it is essential to learn proper weights for meta-training tasks. To achieve this, we propose an adaptive task reweighting strategy, and the problem can be formulated as follows:

$$\begin{aligned} \theta_{ML}^* &:= \arg\min_{\theta \in \Theta} F(\theta) \\ \text{where} \quad F(\theta) &= \frac{1}{m}\sum_{i=1}^{m} w_i \mathcal{L}(\mathcal{A}lg(\theta, \mathcal{D}_i^S), \mathcal{D}_i^Q). \end{aligned} \tag{4}$$

and w_i is a scalar, denoting the weight corresponding to the meta-training task $\mathcal{T}_i$. Notice that the optimal parameter θ_{ML}^* always depends on the weights w_i, therefore, the next goal is to find an optimal w_i.

We aim to develop an algorithm that can adaptively learn the task weights w_i for each meta-training task. For instance, if we know that the meta-training task $\mathcal{T}_1$ is closer to the testing tasks than other meta-training tasks, we can expect a better performance by raising the importance of $\mathcal{T}_1$, i.e., make w_1 larger. This thought experiment motivates a target-aware procedure that adaptively adjusts the weights based on the proximity of meta-training tasks to the testing tasks. To achieve this, we use a small and clean meta-validation set that is assumed to be similar to the testing set. We believe that such a set can be created without excessive cost or unrealistic assumptions, even for rare specialized use cases in real-life scenarios. We optimize the weights for meta-training tasks based on feedback from the few-shot learning performance of the model on the validation tasks. This can be formulated as the following bi-level optimization problem:

$$\begin{aligned} W^* &:= \arg\min_{W} \frac{1}{n} \sum_{i=1}^{n} \mathcal{L}(\mathcal{A}lg(\theta_W^*, \mathcal{V}_j^S), \mathcal{V}_j^Q) \\ \text{where} \quad \theta_W^* &= \arg\min_{\theta \in \Theta} \frac{1}{m} \sum_{i=1}^{m} w_i \mathcal{L}(\mathcal{A}lg(\theta, \mathcal{D}_i^S), \mathcal{D}_i^Q). \end{aligned} \tag{5}$$

The outer loop optimization problem seeks the optimal meta-training task weights by minimizing empirical risk on n meta-validation few-shot learning tasks. Meanwhile, the inner loop optimization optimizes the model parameter θ for m meta-training tasks.

4.2 Parameter-Efficient Task Reweighting Module

Despite Eq. 5 conceptual simplicity, the formulation is a complicated constrained optimization problem. Moreover, as the number of task weight parameters is proportional to the number of meta-training tasks, computational expenses during training can become an issue if there are many tasks. To address this problem, one natural approach is to introduce prior knowledge to determine an appropriate task weight using fewer parameters. Taking into account the factors that influence the importance of each meta-training task, we propose a hypothesis that can help build a parameter-efficient task reweighting learning module.

Hypothesis 1. The meta-training task $\mathcal{T}_i$ is beneficial to the testing tasks if $\mathcal{T}_i$ comes from the same distribution as the testing tasks, and the model can learn it well.

This hypothesis suggests that the similarity between the distributions of meta-training and testing tasks, as well as the loss of the meta-training tasks, can hint at the importance of $\mathcal{T}_i$. The similarity between the distributions of meta-training and testing tasks can be determined by their distance. Since the testing task is not available during meta-training, we use the distance between the meta-training and validation tasks instead. In this paper, we employ Wasserstein Distance [45] to measure the similarity between two distributions, which has been proven effective in measuring the discrepancy between two probability distributions [46]. Inspired by the idea that the normalized loss distribution of clean and noisy data can be modeled using two beta distributions parameterized by two groups of parameters [47], we assume that the loss value of the meta-training tasks can indicate whether they are well learned. Based on this hypothesis, the weight w_i is formulated as follows:

$$w_i = \sigma(s(\mathcal{T}_i, \mathcal{T}^{\mathcal{V}})) \cdot \sigma(a\mathcal{L}_{\mathcal{T}_i} + b) \tag{6}$$

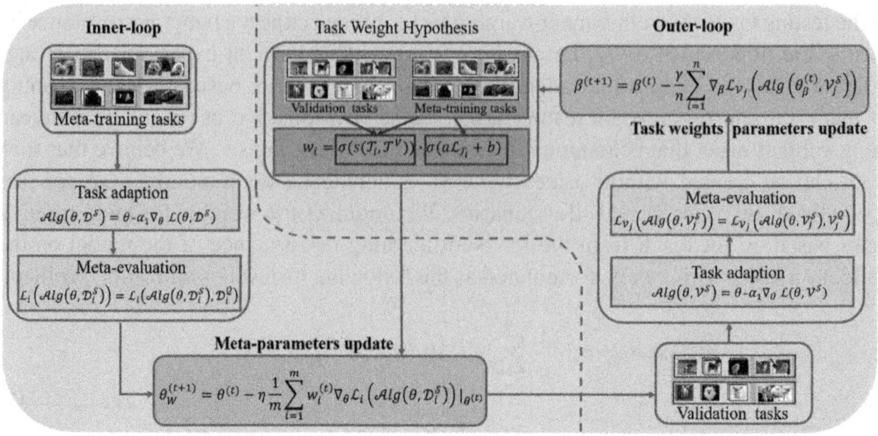

Fig. 2. The overall framework for the parameter-efficient task reweighting (PETR) model. (1) The left part presents the inner loop optimization process. In the inner loop, the meta-parameters of the few-shot learning model are updated based on a weighted training loss where the weights are learned in the outer loop. (2) The right part illustrates the outer loop optimization process. In the outer loop, the task weights parameters $\beta = \{a, b\}$ are firstly updated with the implicit gradient on the validation dataset, then the task weight w is calculated according to our proposed task weight hypothesis. These two update steps are performed until the validation loss converges.

where $\sigma(\cdot)$ is the activation function to ensure non-negative values. The first term is the Wasserstein distance between the distributions of meta-training tasks and validation tasks to evaluate the informativeness of $\mathcal{T}_i$. The second term is a linear classifier to judge whether $\mathcal{T}_i$ can be well learned following [37]. a and b are learnable parameters. Since w_i relies on the similarity and the loss which are constantly updated during the training process, w_i is naturally adaptive.

The proposed parameter-efficient module comprehensively considers the distribution distance and the loss information, while only introducing an additional learnable parameter set $\beta = \{a, b\}$. Compared with directly learning the w_i, the parameters to optimize are greatly reduced. In the next subsection, we present the overall learning process and optimization for parameters θ and β.

4.3 Overall Framework and Optimization

The overall framework of PETR is presented in Fig. 2, which consists of two main components: a meta-parameter learning module for FSL and a parameter-efficient task reweighting module. The meta-parameters θ for FSL are updated by optimizing the inner loop loss given by Eq. 5. The parameters β of task weights W are optimized to minimize outer loop loss in Eq. 5. The task reweighting module is expected to provide appropriate weights for training the FSL model, enabling it to achieve excellent performance on testing few-shot tasks. However, manually tuning β is intractable.

When optimization involves deep nets and large datasets, adaptive gradient-based methods like Stochastic Gradient Descent (SGD) have proven to be very effective time and again [48]. Therefore, we use an iterative gradient-based algorithm for both inner and outer optimization to solve the bi-level meta-learning problem in Eq. 5. We adopt an alternating optimization procedure to optimize the model parameters θ and the task weight parameters β, as summarized in Algorithm 1.

Inner and Outer Loop Optimizing. For notation convenience, we define $\mathcal{L}_i(\phi) := \mathcal{L}(\phi, \mathcal{D}_i^{\mathcal{Q}})$, $\mathcal{L}_{\mathcal{V}_j}(\phi) := \mathcal{L}(\phi, \mathcal{V}_j^{\mathcal{Q}})$, $\hat{\mathcal{L}}_{\mathcal{V}_j}(\phi) := \mathcal{L}(\phi, \mathcal{V}_j^{\mathcal{S}})$.

1) Optimizing θ: For the first training iteration, we set the initial $w_i = 1/m$, treating each meta-training task equally. Given the meta-training task weight parameters β_i^t at the t-th iteration, we compute the task weights w_i using Eq. 6 and optimize θ using:
$$\theta_w^t = \theta^t - \eta \frac{1}{m} \sum_{i=1}^{m} w_i^t \nabla_\theta \mathcal{L}i(\theta, w)|\theta^{(t)}, \tag{7}$$
where $\mathcal{L}_i(\theta, w) = \mathcal{L}_i(\mathcal{A}lg(\theta, \mathcal{D}i^{\mathcal{S}}))|\theta^{(t)}$, η is the learning rate for θ, and m is the mini-batch size of meta-training tasks.
2) Optimizing β: After updating θ, we adjust the optimal parameters β based on the gradient of the validation loss:
$$\beta^{t+1} = \beta^t - \frac{\gamma}{n} \sum_{i=1}^{n} \nabla_\beta \mathcal{L}_{V_j}(\theta^*(\beta)). \tag{8}$$

where $\mathcal{L}_{V_j}(\theta^*(\beta)) = \mathcal{L}_{V_j}(\mathcal{A}lg(\theta_\beta^{(t)}, \mathcal{V}_j^{\mathcal{S}}))$, γ denotes the learning rate, n is the mini-batch size of meta-validation tasks.

During the outer loop optimization, we need to derive the gradient of $\mathcal{L}_{V_j}(\theta^*(\beta))$ with respect to β. Given that $\mathcal{L}_{V_j}(\theta^*(\beta))$ directly relies on θ instead of β, we follow the literature [35] and utilize implicit differentiation to obtain this implicit gradient. With Theorem 4.1, we can obtain the gradient of $\mathcal{L}_{V_j}(\theta^*(\beta))$ with respect to β.

Theorem 4.1 (Cauchy, Implicit Function Theorem). If there exists one point (θ_0, β_0) where $\nabla_\theta \mathcal{L}_i(\theta, \beta) = 0$ and the regularity conditions are satisfied, then within the neighborhood of (θ_0, β_0), there exists an implicit function $\theta^*(\beta)$ s.t.$\nabla_\theta \mathcal{L}_i(\theta, \beta) = 0 \mid_{\beta, \theta*(\beta)}$ and we have:
$$\begin{aligned} \nabla_\beta \mathcal{L}_{V_j}(\theta^*(\beta)) &= \nabla_\theta \mathcal{L}_{V_j}(\theta, \beta)) \cdot \nabla_\beta \theta^* \\ &= -\nabla_\theta \mathcal{L}_{V_j}(\theta, \beta)) \cdot (\nabla_\theta^2 \mathcal{L}_i(\theta, \beta))^{-1} \cdot \nabla_\beta \nabla_\theta \mathcal{L}_i(\theta, \beta) \mid_{(\beta, \theta^*(\beta))} . \end{aligned} \tag{9}$$

If the conditions in Theorem 4.1 are satisfied, we have:
$$\nabla_\theta \mathcal{L}_i(\theta^*(\beta), \beta) = 0. \tag{10}$$

$$\nabla_\theta^2 \mathcal{L}_i(\theta^*, \beta) \nabla_\beta \theta^* + \nabla_\beta \nabla_{\theta^*} \mathcal{L}_i(\theta^*, \beta) = 0. \tag{11}$$
$$\nabla_\beta \theta^* = -(\nabla_\theta^2 \mathcal{L}_i(\theta^*, \beta))^{-1} \nabla_\beta \nabla_\theta \mathcal{L}_i(\theta^*, \beta). \tag{12}$$

From Eq. 10 to Eq. 11, we take the derivative to β on both sides of Eq. 10. By assuming that $(\nabla^2_\theta \mathcal{L}_i(\theta, \beta))$ is positive definite, $(\nabla^2_\theta \mathcal{L}_i(\theta, \beta))$ will have an inverse so we can obtain the implicit gradient in Eq. 12. Thus, Theorem 4.1 is proved.

Tractable Inverse Hessian Approximations. However, directly computing the inverse of the Hessian is intractable for deep models. We adopt the K-truncated Neumann series to approximate this inverse as illustrated in Eq. 13. In this paper, K is searched from $\{3, 5\}$ considering the performance and computational cost as recommended in [37]. By using this approximation to approach the inverse of the Hessian, the implicit gradient can be calculated in Eq. 14.

$$(\nabla^2_\theta \mathcal{L}_i(\theta, \beta))^{-1} = \sum_{i=0}^{\infty}(I - \nabla^2_\theta \mathcal{L}_i(\theta, \beta))^i \approx \sum_{i=0}^{K}(I - \nabla^2_\theta \mathcal{L}_i(\theta, \beta))^i. \tag{13}$$

$$\nabla_\beta \mathcal{L}_{\mathcal{V}_j}(\theta^*(\beta)) = -\nabla_\theta \mathcal{L}_{\mathcal{V}_j}(\theta^*(\beta)) \cdot \sum_{i=0}^{K}(I - \nabla^2_\theta \mathcal{L}_i(\theta, \beta)))^i \cdot \nabla_\beta \nabla_\theta \mathcal{L}_i(\theta, \beta)). \tag{14}$$

Upon obtaining the gradient of θ and β, Algorithm 1 presents the complete algorithm that simultaneously learns the meta-parameters for FSL and the meta-training task weights. During the inner loop optimization, the parameters β are fixed, and the parameters θ are updated with the gradient in Eq. 7 at the learning rate η. Instead of waiting for θ to converge, we conduct the more efficient M-step optimization as described in [35]. Specifically, after θ has been updated for M times, we switch to the outer optimization to optimize β. According to Eq. 8, we use the implicit gradient to update β at the learning rate γ. These two update steps are performed until the validation loss converges.

Algorithm 1. Parameter-efficient Task Reweighting Method

```
Require: p_tr, p_val distribution over meta-training and validation tasks
Require: m, n(batch sizes), α, η, γ (learning rates) and M
 1: Randomly initialize θ and β = {a, b}
 2: for iter < n_iter do
 3:    Sample mini-batch of meta-training tasks {D_i^S, D_i^Q}_{i=1}^m ~ p_tr
 4:    Sample mini-batch of meta-training tasks {V_i^S, V_i^Q}_{i=1}^n ~ p_val
       // inner-loop optimization
 5:    for j = 1 to M do
 6:       Compute adapted parameters (Alg(θ, D_i^S)) using Eq. 3
 7:       Compute the gradient ∇_θ L_i(θ, w)) using D_i^Q
 8:       Update θ using Eq. 7
 9:    end for
       // outer-loop optimization
10:    Compute the gradient ∇_β L_{V_j}(θ*(β)) using Eq. 14
11:    Update β using Eq. 8
12:    Update w_i using Eq. 6
13: end for
14: return θ
```

5 Experiments

In this section, we mainly assess the efficacy of our proposed PETR in few-shot learning tasks. In particular, we aim to study whether PETR can be successfully applied to scenarios where the meta-training task distribution is partially shifted from the testing task distribution.

Datasets. The proposed method is firstly evaluated on the most widely-used few-shot classification benchmarks: *Mini*ImageNet dataset, which contains 100 classes randomly chosen from ILSVRC-12 [49] and 600 images of size 84×84 pixels per class. We follow the splits used in previous work [50], which divided the dataset into 64, 16, and 20 classes for training, validation, and testing, respectively. To further demonstrate the effectiveness of PETR in identifying OOD meta-training tasks, we use *mini*ImageNet as the in distribution (ID) task source and additionally use SVHN [51] and FashionMNIST [52] datasets as out-of-distribution (OOD) tasks source following [11]. The SVHN dataset is a street view house numbers dataset, which contains 26,032 images from 10 digits classes. The FashionMNIST is a fashion dataset including 60,000 grayscale images from 10 classes.

Implementation Details. Our method is based on the meta-learning mechanism. All experiments are conducted around the N-way K-shot classification task. And we use a model with similar backbone architecture given in MAML [6] for all baselines. During meta-training, We randomly sample the ID tasks (meta-training, meta-validation, and testing) from the *mini*ImageNet dataset and sample OOD tasks from the SVNH or FashionMNIST dataset. The number of ID meta-training tasks is 20000 and the number of OOD meta-training tasks is determined by the OOD ratio (0.3, 0.6, and 0.9). In each task, there are $K(1, 3, 5)$ support samples and 15 query images in each class. About the optimization process, we optimize θ and β using SGD with learning rates $\alpha = \eta = \gamma = 0.01$. Considering the computational cost, we set the number of inner loop steps $M = 1$. At the testing stage, we use accuracy as the evaluation metric to measure the performance of our method. The reported results are the averaged classification accuracy over 10,000 N-way K-shot tasks.

Table 2. 5-way 1-shot and 5-way 5-shot classification accuracy (%) with 95% confidence intervals on *mini*ImageNet. (†: Reproduced with our setting, -: not available).

	5-way 1-shot	**5-way 5-shot**
MAML [5]	48.70±1.84	63.11±0.92
Reptile [7]	48.21±0.69	66.00±0.62
Meta-SGD [6]	50.47±1.87	64.03±0.94
IMAM [8]	49.30±1.88	-
Nested MAML†[11]	54.30±0.75	67.43±0.76
PETR (Ours)	**55.27±0.68**	**68.25±0.66**

5.1 Comparisons with Baselines

Traditional Few-shot Learning Tasks. Firstly, we compare our method with several representative meta-learning-based FSL methods on traditional FSL tasks, where the meta-training, meta-validation, and testing tasks are all sampled from the *mini*ImageNet dataset. Table 2 shows the comparison of 5-way 1-shot and 5-shot classification tasks on *mini*ImageNet. The results of these methods are cited from their original paper. We can observe that our PETR outperforms all the baselines on two tasks. Compared with MAML, the accuracy improvement of our method on both tasks (5-way 1-shot and 5-shot) are 6.57% and 5.15% respectively, demonstrating the necessity to assign different weights for different meta-training tasks. Furthermore, the better performance over Nested MAML indicates that our PETR has a better ability to learn proper weights.

Table 3. 5-way 3-shot test accuracies (%) with 95% confidence intervals on *mini* Imagenet with varying OOD Ratios during the meta-training phase. The best results are marked in bold.

OOD task source	SVHN			FashionMNIST		
OOD Ratio	0.3	0.6	0.9	0.3	0.6	0.9
MAML [5]	55.41±0.75	53.93±0.76	44.10±0.68	54.65±0.77	54.52±0.76	41.52±0.74
MMAML [25]	51.04±0.87	50.28±0.97	41.56±0.96	50.32±0.93	47.54±1.05	42.09±0.97
B-TAML [26]	53.87±0.18	49.84±0.23	42.00±0.21	51.14±0.23	46.59±0.20	36.69±0.21
L2R [17]	47.13±0.13	40.69±0.62	47.26±0.72	33.14±0.60	44.03±0.70	33.06±0.60
NESTEDMAML [11]	57.12±0.81	55.66±0.78	52.16±0.76	56.66±0.78	56.04±0.79	49.71±0.78
PETR (Ours)	**58.02±0.68**	**57.03±0.72**	**54.12±0.65**	**57.33±0.71**	**57.15±0.72**	**51.34±0.73**

Few-Shot Learning with OOD Tasks. To further demonstrate the effectiveness of our PETR in scenarios where the meta-training task distribution is partially shifted from the testing task distribution, we performed additional experiments on few-shot learning with OOD tasks. We randomly sampled the ID meta-training tasks from *mini*Imagenet and OOD tasks from SVNH or FashionMNIST datasets with varying OOD ratios. The meta-validation and testing tasks are all from *mini*Imagenet. Table 3 presents the experimental results. The results of the baselines are cited from [11]. We observed that our PETR outperforms all baselines significantly in all cases. These results show that PETR has a stronger ability to adapt to few-shot learning with OOD tasks.

5.2 Model Analysis

Ablation Study. To validate the impact of different components proposed in the PETR, we conduct ablations about variants of our proposed method on FSL with OOD tasks from FashionMNIST dataset. We consider three variants of our methods, i.e., 1) w/o similarity: remove the similarity term between meta-training tasks and the validation tasks in Eq. 6. The PETR module assigns weight for each task according to the meta-training task loss. 2) w/o task loss: remove the term about the task loss in Eq. 6. The PETR module assigns weight for each task according to the similarity term between meta-training tasks and the validation tasks. 3) w/o hypothesis: remove the parameter-efficient task reweighting module and update w_i directly.

Table 4. 5-way 3-shot test accuracies with 95% confidence intervals on *mini*Imagenet with different variants of our method.

OOD Ratio	0.3	0.6
w/o hypothesis	55.98 ± 0.72	55.72 ± 0.74
w/o similarity	56.62 ± 0.73	56.25 ± 0.69
w/o task loss	56.44 ± 0.73	56.05 ± 0.71
Ours	**57.33±0.71**	**57.15±0.72**

The results of w/o hypothesis in Table 4 demonstrate that our PETR can learn better task weights for meta-training tasks by introducing the hypothesis. Furthermore, the results support our hypothesis that both the similarities between the meta-training and testing tasks and the loss of the meta-training task are necessary for deciding whether a meta-training task is suitable for training. Without task loss information, the performance largely drops, indicating that the ability to learn a task well plays a crucial role in deciding the weights of meta-training tasks. Additionally, the similarity between the meta-training and testing tasks is an essential factor in determining the importance of a meta-training task. Without using the similarity, the performance also declines.

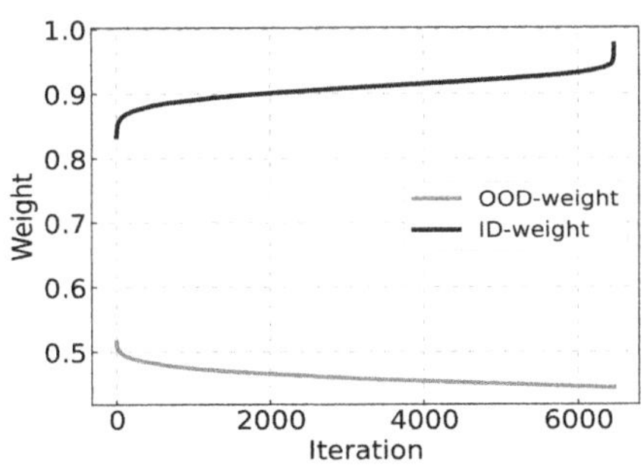

(a) Task weights learning process

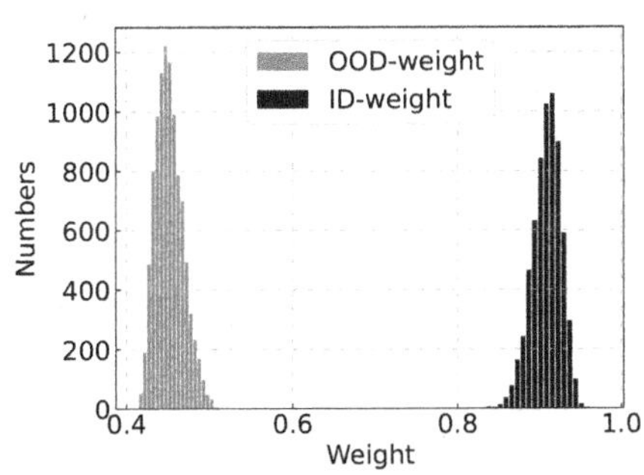

(b) Task weights distribution

Fig. 3. Visualization of task weight learning behavior.

Weight Learning Behavior. We visualize how the task weights change during the training process to find some training patterns. We plot the weights trend as the iterations progress under the 0.6 OOD ratio (FashionMNIST) in Fig. 3 (a). We can observe the model will gradually increase the mean weights of ID tasks and decrease the weights of OOD tasks, which validates the effectiveness of the PETR. We also visualize the weight

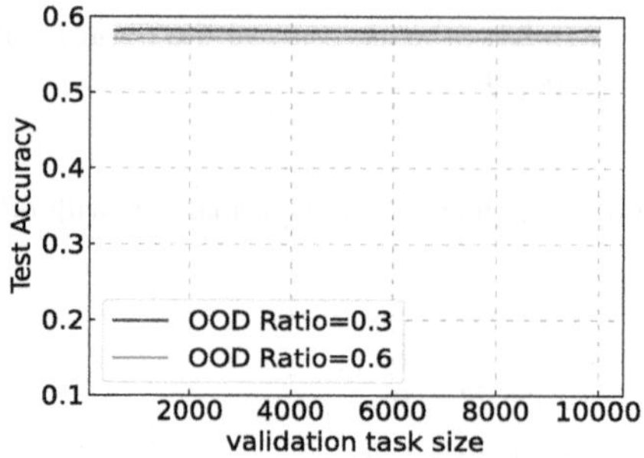

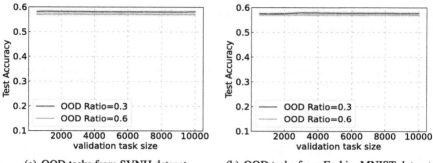

(a) OOD tasks from SVNH dataset

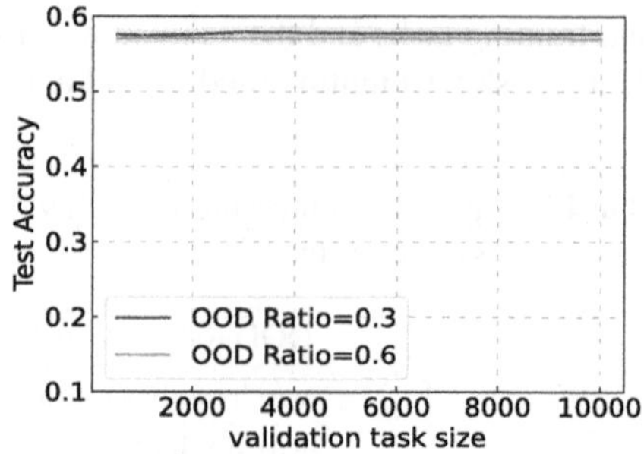

(b) OOD tasks from FashionMNIST dataset

Fig. 4. 5-way 3-shot test accuracies under different validation task sizes on FSL with OOD meta-training tasks.

distribution for OOD and ID tasks under 0.6 OOD ratio (FashionMNIST) for 5-way 3-shot tasks. From Fig. 3 (b), we can observe OOD tasks have much smaller weights than ID tasks: the weights belonging to OOD tasks approximately range from 0.4 to 0.5, however, the assigned weights for ID tasks are from 0.85 to 0.95, further validating our PETR has the ability to assign proper weights for different meta-training tasks.

Sensitivity Analysis. To demonstrate the feasibility of our method in practical scenarios, we investigate how the size of the validation set impact the FSL performance. Figure 4 shows the test accuracy on the FSL with OOD tasks from SVNH and Fashion MNIST with different validation task size. We find that the number of validation tasks has little effect on the final test accuracy in all circumstances, indicating that our PETR can achieve good results with a small amount of validation set data. This finding enhances the feasibility of our method in practical scenarios where labeled data is often limited.

6 Conclusion and Future Work

In this paper, we propose a novel approach, parameter-efficient task reweighting (PETR), for robust few-shot classification that efficiently assigns proper weights for different meta-training tasks. We formulate a bi-level optimization problem to jointly optimize the few-shot learning model and the task weight. Besides, we build a parameter-efficient task reweighting module, which can assign proper weights for different meta-training tasks while using much fewer additional parameters by considering the factors that influence the importance of each meta-training task. Empirical evaluation results in both traditional FSL and FSL with OOD task scenarios show that PETR can efficiently outperform state-of-the-art meta-learning methods by identifying the importance of different meta-training tasks. Additionally, in this work, we explicitly investigate the factors that could influence the task weights, including similarities between the meta-training and testing tasks and the loss of the meta-training task. Further work can explore more ways to combine these factors or investigate other factors that will influence the weights. The limitation of this work is that it requires a small developing dataset that contains clean data of the testing task, how to obtain proper task weights without the clean dataset is also an interesting future direction.

Acknowledgments. This work was partly supported by the Fundamental Research Funds for the Central Universities (2019JBZ110); the Beijing Natural Science Foundation under Grant L211016; the National Natural Science Foundation of China under Grant 62176020; the National Key Research and Development Program (2020AAA0106800); and Chinese Academy of Sciences (OEIP-O-202004).

Ethical Statement. The authors declare that they have no conflict of interest. All procedures performed in studies involving human participants were by the ethical standards of the institutional and national research committees. This article does not contain any studies with animals performed by any of the authors. Informed consent was obtained from all individual participants included in the study.

References

1. Krizhevsky, A., Sutskever, I., Hinton, G.E.: Imagenet classification with deep convolutional neural networks. Communications ACM **60**(6), 84–90 (2017)
2. He, K., Gkioxari, G., Dollár, P., Girshick, R.: Mask r-cnn. In: Proceedings of the IEEE International Conference On Computer Vision, pp. 2961–2969 (2017)
3. Schmidhuber, J.: Evolutionary principles in self-referential learning, or on learning how to learn: the meta-meta-... hook. PhD thesis, Technische Universität München (1987)
4. Naik, D.K., Mammone, R.J.: Meta-neural networks that learn by learning. In: [Proceedings 1992] IJCNN International Joint Conference on Neural Networks, vol. 1, pp. 437–442. IEEE (1992)
5. Finn, C., Abbeel, P., Levine, S.: Model-agnostic meta-learning for fast adaptation of deep networks. In International Conference on Machine Learning, pp. 1126–1135. PMLR (2017)
6. Li, Z., Zhou, F., Chen, F., Li, H.: Meta-sgd: learning to learn quickly for few-shot learning. arXiv preprint arXiv:1707.09835 (2017)
7. Nichol, A., Schulman, J.: Reptile: a scalable metalearning algorithm, vol. 2(3), p. 4. arXiv preprint arXiv:1803.02999 (2018)
8. Rajeswaran, A., Finn, C., Kakade, S.M., Levine, S.: Meta-learning with implicit gradients. In: Advances in Neural Information Processing Systems 32 (2019)
9. Flennerhag, S., Rusu, A.A., Pascanu, R., Visin, F., Yin, H., Hadsell, R.: Meta-learning with warped gradient descent. arXiv preprint arXiv:1909.00025 (2019)
10. Cai, D., Sheth, R., Mackey, L., Fusi, N.: Weighted meta-learning. arXiv preprint arXiv:2003.09465 (2020)
11. Killamsetty, K., Li, C., Zhao, C., Chen, F., Iyer, R.: A nested bi-level optimization framework for robust few shot learning. In: Proceedings of the AAAI Conference on Artificial Intelligence, vol. 36, 7176–7184 (2022)
12. Shimodaira, H.: Improving predictive inference under covariate shift by weighting the log-likelihood function. J. Stat. Planning Inference **90**(2), 227–244 (2000)
13. Sugiyama, M., Suzuki, T., Nakajima, S., Kashima, H., Nau, P.B., Kawanabe, M.: Direct importance estimation for covariate shift adaptation. Annals Inst. Stat. Mathem. **60**(4), 699–746 (2008)
14. Fang, T., Nan, L., Niu, G., Sugiyama, M.: Rethinking importance weighting for deep learning under distribution shift. Adv. Neural. Inf. Process. Syst. **33**, 11996–12007 (2020)

15. Kuang, K., Xiong, R., Cui, P., Athey, S., Li, B.: Stable prediction with model misspecification and agnostic distribution shift. In: Proceedings of the AAAI Conference on Artificial Intelligence, vol. 34, pp. 4485–4492 (2020)
16. Zhang, X., Cui, P., Xu, R., Zhou, L., He, Y., Shen, Z.: Deep stable learning for out-of-distribution generalization. In: Proceedings of the IEEE/CVF Conference on Computer Vision and Pattern Recognition, pages 5372–5382 (2021)
17. Ren, M., Zeng, W., Yang, B., Urtasun, R.: Learning to reweight examples for robust deep learning. In International Conference on Machine Learning, pp. 4334–4343. PMLR (2018)
18. Zhou, X., et al.: Model agnostic sample reweighting for out-of-distribution learning. In: International Conference on Machine Learning, pp. 27203–27221. PMLR (2022)
19. Finn, C., Xu, K., Levine, S.: Probabilistic model-agnostic meta-learning. In: Advances in Neural Information Processing Systems 31 (2018)
20. Grant, E., Finn, C., Levine, S., Darrell, T., Griffiths, T.: Recasting gradient-based meta-learning as hierarchical bayes. arXiv preprint arXiv:1801.08930 (2018)
21. Ravi, S., Beatson, A.: Amortized bayesian meta-learning. In: International Conference on Learning Representations (2019)
22. Lee, H.B., Nam, T., Yang, E., Hwang, S.J.: Learning to perturb latent features for generalization, Meta dropout (2020)
23. Ni, R., Goldblum, M., Sharaf, A., Kong, K., Goldstein, T.: Data augmentation for meta-learning. In International Conference on Machine Learning, pp. 8152–8161. PMLR (2021)
24. Yao, H., Zhang, L., Finn, C.: Meta-learning with fewer tasks through task interpolation. arXiv preprint arXiv:2106.02695 (2021)
25. Vuorio, R., Sun, S.-H., Hu, H., Lim, J.J.: Multimodal model-agnostic meta-learning via task-aware modulation. In: Advances in Neural Information Processing Systems 32 (2019)
26. Lee, H.B., et al.: Learning to balance: Bayesian meta-learning for imbalanced and out-of-distribution tasks. arXiv preprint arXiv:1905.12917 (2019)
27. Baik, S., Choi, J., Kim, H., Cho, D., Min, J., Lee, K.M.: Meta-learning with task-adaptive loss function for few-shot learning. In: Proceedings of the IEEE/CVF International Conference on Computer Vision, pp. 9465–9474 (2021)
28. Liu, C., Wang, Z., Sahoo, D., Fang, Y., Zhang, K., Hoi, S.C.H.: Adaptive task sampling for meta-learning. In: Vedaldi, A., Bischof, H., Brox, T., Frahm, J.-M. (eds.) ECCV 2020. LNCS, vol. 12363, pp. 752–769. Springer, Cham (2020). https://doi.org/10.1007/978-3-030-58523-5_44
29. Zhang, J., Song, J., Yao, Y., Gao, L.: Curriculum-based meta-learning. In Proceedings of the 29th ACM International Conference on Multimedia, pp. 1838–1846 (2021)
30. Zhou, Y., Wang, Y., Cai, J., Zhou, Y., Hu, Q., Wang, W.: Expert training: Task hardness aware meta-learning for few-shot classification. arXiv preprint arXiv:2007.06240 (2020)
31. Bennequin, E., Bouvier, V., Tami, M., Toubhans, A., Hudelot, C.: Bridging few-shot learning and adaptation: new challenges of support-query shift. In: Oliver, N., Pérez-Cruz, F., Kramer, S., Read, J., Lozano, J.A. (eds.) ECML PKDD 2021. LNCS (LNAI), vol. 12975, pp. 554–569. Springer, Cham (2021). https://doi.org/10.1007/978-3-030-86486-6_34
32. Aimen, A., Ladrecha, B., Krishnan, N.C.: Adversarial projections to tackle support-query shifts in few-shot meta-learning. In: Machine Learning and Knowledge Discovery in Databases: European Conference, ECML PKDD 2022, Grenoble, France, 19–23 September 2022, Proceedings, Part III, pp. 615–630. Springer (2023). https://doi.org/10.1007/978-3-031-26409-2_37
33. Foo, C.-S., Ng, A., et al.: Efficient multiple hyperparameter learning for log-linear models. In: Advances in Neural Information Processing Systems 20 (2007)
34. Okuno, T., Takeda, A., Kawana, A., Watanabe, M.: On l_p−hyperparameter learning via bilevel nonsmooth optimization. arXiv preprint arXiv:1806.01520 (2018)

35. Lorraine, J., Vicol, P., Duvenaud, D.: Optimizing millions of hyperparameters by implicit differentiation. In: International Conference on Artificial Intelligence and Statistics, pp. 1540–1552. PMLR (2020)
36. Mao, Y., Wang, Z., Liu, W., Lin, X., Xie, P.: Metaweighting: learning to weight tasks in multi-task learning. In: Findings of the Association for Computational Linguistics: ACL 2022, pp. 3436–3448 (2022)
37. Chen, H., Wang, X., Guan, C., Liu, Y., Zhu, W.: Auxiliary learning with joint task and data scheduling. In: International Conference on Machine Learning, pp. 3634–3647. PMLR (2022)
38. Franceschi, L., Frasconi, P., Salzo, S., Grazzi, R., Pontil, M.: Bilevel programming for hyperparameter optimization and meta-learning. In: International Conference on Machine Learning, pp. 1568–1577. PMLR (2018)
39. Lian, D., et al.: Towards fast adaptation of neural architectures with meta learning. In: International Conference on Learning Representations (2020)
40. Hu, Y., Wu, X., He, R.: TF-NAS: rethinking three search freedoms of latency-constrained differentiable neural architecture search. In: Vedaldi, A., Bischof, H., Brox, T., Frahm, J.-M. (eds.) ECCV 2020. LNCS, vol. 12360, pp. 123–139. Springer, Cham (2020). https://doi.org/10.1007/978-3-030-58555-6_8
41. Chen, Z., Jiang, H., Shi, Y., Dai, B., Zhao, T.: Learning to defense by learning to attack (2019)
42. Tian, Y., Shen, L., Guinan, S., Li, Z., Liu, W.: Alphagan: fully differentiable architecture search for generative adversarial networks. IEEE Trans. Pattern Anal. Mach. Intell. **44**(10), 6752–6766 (2021)
43. Yang, Z., Chen, Y., Hong, M., Wang, Z.: Provably global convergence of actor-critic: A case for linear quadratic regulator with ergodic cost. In: Advances in Neural Information Processing Systems 32 (2019)
44. Zhang, H., Chen, W., Huang, Z., Li, M., Yang, Y., Zhang, W., Wang, J.: Bi-level actor-critic for multi-agent coordination. In Proceedings of the AAAI Conference on Artificial Intelligence, vol. 34, pp. 7325–7332 (2020)
45. Rüschendorf, L.: The wasserstein distance and approximation theorems. Probab. Theory Relat. Fields **70**(1), 117–129 (1985)
46. Zhao, S., Sinha, A., He, Y., Perreault, A., Song, J., Ermon, S.: H-divergence: A decision-theoretic probability discrepancy measure
47. Arazo, E., Ortego, D., Albert, P., O'Connor, N., McGuinness, K.: Unsupervised label noise modeling and loss correction. In: International conference on machine learning, pp. 312–321. PMLR (2019)
48. Bottou, L., Bousquet, O.: The tradeoffs of large scale learning. In: Advances in Neural Information Processing Systems 20 (2008)
49. Russakovsky, O., et al.: Imagenet large scale visual recognition challenge. Int. J. Comput. Vision **115**, 211–252 (2015)
50. Ravi, S., Larochelle, H.: Optimization as a model for few-shot learning. In: International Conference on Learning Representations (2017)
51. Netzer, Y., Wang, T., Coates, A., Bissacco, A., Wu, B., Ng, A.Y.: Reading digits in natural images with unsupervised feature learning (2011)
52. Xiao, H., Rasul, K., Vollgraf, R.: Fashion-mnist: a novel image dataset for benchmarking machine learning algorithms. arXiv preprint arXiv:1708.07747 (2017)

Boosting Generalized Few-Shot Learning by Scattering Intra-class Distribution

Yunlong Yu(✉), Lisha Jin, and Yingming Li

Zhejiang University, Hangzhou, Zhejiang, China
{yuyunlong,lisajin,yingming}@zju.edu.cn

Abstract. Generalized Few-Shot Learning (GFSL) applies the model trained with the base classes to predict the samples from both base classes and novel classes, where each novel class is only provided with a few labeled samples during testing. Limited by the severe data imbalance between base and novel classes, GFSL easily suffers from the *prediction shift issue* that most test samples tend to be classified into the base classes. Unlike the existing works that address this issue by either multi-stage training or complicated model design, we argue that extracting both discriminative and generalized feature representations is all GFSL needs, which could be achieved by simply scattering the intra-class distribution during training. Specifically, we introduce two self-supervised auxiliary tasks and a label permutation task to encourage the model to learn more image-level feature representations and push the decision boundary from novel towards base classes during inference. Our method is one-stage and could perform online inference. Experiments on the mini-ImageNet and tieredImageNet datasets show that the proposed method achieves comparable performance with the state-of-the-art multi-stage competitors under both traditional FSL and GFSL tasks, empirically proving that feature representation is the key for GFSL.

Keywords: Generalized Few-Shot Learning · Scatter Intra-class Distribution · Feature Representation

1 Introduction

Recently, Few-Shot Learning (FSL) [3,14,16,21,38], aiming at learning novel classes from a few samples, has the potential to address the data scarcity issue and attracts a lot of attention. However, the traditional FSL only classifies the test samples into novel classes, which is not realistic enough because the test samples also likely come from the base classes in reality. In this work, we focus on Generalized Few-Shot Learning (GFSL) [12,13,35] that predicts the test samples into the joint space of both base classes and novel classes, as illustrated in Fig. 1. Compared to traditional FSL, GFSL is more challenging due to that it has to classify the test samples into more candidate classes and suffers from the *prediction shift issue* that the samples from the novel classes are easily classified into the base classes.

© The Author(s), under exclusive license to Springer Nature Switzerland AG 2023
D. Koutra et al. (Eds.): ECML PKDD 2023, LNAI 14170, pp. 438–453, 2023.
https://doi.org/10.1007/978-3-031-43415-0_26

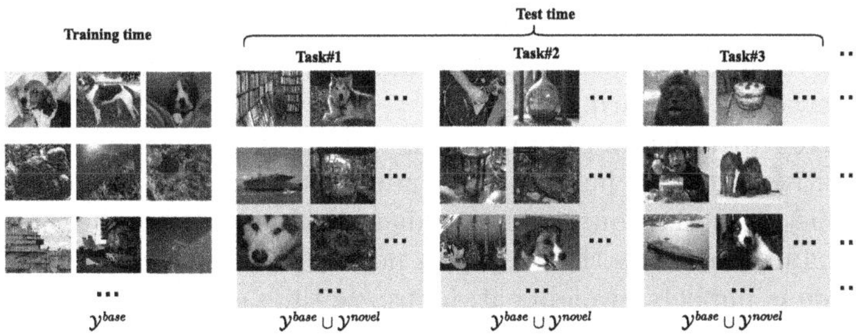

Fig. 1. Illustration of GFSL tasks, where the model is trained on the base classes $\mathcal{Y}^{base}$ and is tested on the samples from both base and novel classes $\mathcal{Y}^{base} \cup \mathcal{Y}^{novel}$.

There have been some attempts to address GFSL via either multi-stage training [18] or complicated model design [12,35]. In this work, we consider what the GFSL needs is extracting both discriminative and generalized feature representations that ensure the classification ability for both base and novel classes simultaneously. We achieve this goal by simply scattering the intra-class distribution during training to extract more image-level feature representations and push the decision boundary from novel towards base during inference. This solution is inspired by the existing re-weighting approaches [4,8,22] in class imbalance learning that scatter the distribution of sample-sufficient classes while clustering the distribution of sample-scarce classes. Though both imbalance learning and GFSL tasks suffer from data imbalance, they differ significantly as GFSL has no access to the novel classes during training.

Based on the solution, we establish a multi-task framework that comprises a primary image classification task, a label permutation task, and two self-supervised auxiliary tasks. The two self-supervised auxiliary tasks force the model to respectively predict the rotation of the input sample and the location of the feature map patches to learn more image-level information. The label permutation task relaxes the classification task and predicts each sample into some pseudo-classes derived from their original class, leading to the intra-class distribution being scattered. Different from the existing works that train the model with multiple stages, our framework is trained end-to-end and without further fine-tuning during the testing stage, thus is easy to be applied for online inference.

We empirically verify that our framework indeed scatters the base intra-class distribution and the feature representation is the key for GFSL from the significant performance gains of our framework on the two benchmarks.

The contributions of our work are as follows:

(1) We reveal that what the GFSL needs is extracting powerful feature representations for preserving discrimination on both base and novel classes, which could be achieved by simply scattering the intra-class distribution during training.

(2) We propose a *one-stage* framework that combines four tasks to learn more image-level feature representations and push the decision boundary from novel towards base during inference.
(3) Extensive experimental results demonstrate that our method performs very competitively on two benchmarks under both GFSL and traditional FSL tasks and show that our method enhances the model's robustness during the gambling between the base and novel classes under the GFSL tasks. Our code is publicly available at: https://github.com/lisa-jin/gfslcode.

2 Related Work

2.1 Generalized Few-Shot Learning

GFSL requires the model not only to classify the samples from the novel classes but also to classify the samples from the base classes, thus the candidate classes include both base and novel classes. As one of the pioneer's works, [13] hallucinates training samples for the novel classes based on the transformation from image to image in the base classes. To align the amplitudes between the feature representations and the classifier weights, [23] normalizes both the feature representations and the classifier weights on a high dimensional sphere, such that the feature representations and the classifier weights are symmetric and interchangeable. DFSL [12] builds up a model based on [23] architecture and employs an attention mechanism to learn more related knowledge from the base classes for novel classes. To mitigate the prediction shift issue in GFSL, [18] employs three cascaded training stages, a stage on base classes, a stage on novel classes, and a stage on both base and novel classes, to calibrate base and novel classes, while [35] introduces a trainable dictionary to be concatenated with classifier weights to balance the base and novel classes.

Different from the existing approaches that address the prediction shift issue by training the model with multiple stages, we address this issue from the perspective of improving the feature representations by scattering the intra-class distribution during training. Besides, our method trains the model with only one stage and does not require fine-tuning during inference, thus is more efficient.

2.2 Class Imbalance Learning

Many real-world data exhibit class-wise imbalance, which refers to the phenomenon that some classes account for most of the data (the majority class) while others only contain a few samples (the minority class). Training the model on the imbalanced dataset would suffer from a severe shift to the majority classes, resulting in most of the test images being predicted into the majority classes and poor performance in the minority classes.

A vast number of class imbalance learning methods have been devised to cope with this issue, which could be divided into two directions roughly: re-sampling and re-weighting. Re-sampling is a data-level approach to mitigate the data imbalance via over-sampling [5] or generating synthetic samples [1,20] for the minority classes, and under-sampling [10] for the majority classes. However, these methods are at risk of suffering from the under-fitting of majority classes or the over-fitting of minority classes [7]. Re-weighting usually designs the loss function elaborately to increase the objective costs for minority classes and decrease the objective costs for the majority classes, aiming at shifting the decision boundary from minority towards the majority, leaving a bigger margin for the minority classes [4,8,22,25].

GFSL suffers from a severe data imbalance issue. Different from that in the imbalance learning literature, GFSL is unipolar in that no samples are provided for novel classes during training, thus is more challenging. Our GFSL method is inspired by the solution that prevents the majority classes from clustering tightly in imbalance learning and we propose to scatter the intra-class distribution of the base classes during training to learn both discriminative and generalized feature representations for GFSL.

3 Methodology

3.1 Problem Formulation

In FSL, the data are split into base classes and novel classes ($\mathcal{D}^{base}, \mathcal{D}^{novel}$) corresponding to label space ($\mathcal{Y}^{base}, \mathcal{Y}^{novel}$), where the base classes with abundant samples are used for training a model for the few-shot tasks sampled from the novel classes. Note that the base and novel classes are disjoint completely. A few-shot task $\mathcal{D}_n$ consists of a support set and a query set ($\mathcal{D}_n^{tr}, \mathcal{D}_n^{ts}$). The support set includes N novel classes, each with K samples, while the query set contains the same classes, and such a task is represented as N-way, K-shot. The classifiers of N novel classes are obtained from the support set, which is employed to predict the query samples.

In GFSL, the test set contains the samples not only from the novel classes, but also from base classes non-overlapping with the training samples, and at the same time, the classification space extends to $\mathcal{Y}^{base} \cup \mathcal{Y}^{novel}$ from $\mathcal{Y}^{novel}$, increasing the classification difficulty dramatically. In the following, we use $\{1, 2, \ldots, M\}$ and $\{M+1, M+2, \ldots, M+N\}$ to denote the M base classes and N novel classes, respectively.

3.2 Baseline

The baseline consists of a feature extractor f and a classifier head g, where the feature extractor projects an image x into the feature space $f : x \rightarrow \mathbf{z}$, $\mathbf{z} \in \mathbb{R}^d$ denotes the feature representation of x. Generally, the class prediction of x is obtained with the inner product between the feature representation $\mathbf{z}$ and the base classifier weights $\mathbf{\Omega}_{Base} = [\omega_1, \ldots, \omega_M]$. After training the baseline on the base set, the feature extractor and the classifier of the base classes are obtained. Following the existing FSL works [29,36], the classifier weights of the novel classes are obtained by averaging the feature representations of the support set in a class-wise manner, i.e.,

$$\omega_c = \frac{1}{|\mathcal{D}_c|} \sum_{(x_i, y_i) \in \mathcal{D}_c} f(x_i), \tag{1}$$

where $\mathcal{D}_c$ represents the support set of class c, $|\mathcal{D}_c|$ refers to the sample number from class c and ω_c is the prototype of class c, which is performed as its classifier weight. Thus, the classifier for N novel classes are $\mathbf{\Omega}_{Novel} = [\omega_1, \ldots, \omega_N]$ and the classifier for all classes are $\mathbf{\Omega}_{All} = [\overbrace{\omega_1, \ldots, \omega_M}^{Base}, \overbrace{\omega_{M+1}, \ldots, \omega_{M+N}}^{Novel}]$.

To this end, the query sample x_q could be predicted by:

$$p(y = c | x_q, \omega_c) = \frac{\exp\left(d(f(x_q), \omega_c)\right)}{\sum_{\omega_i \in \mathbf{\Omega}} \exp\left(d(f(x_q), \omega_i)\right)}, \tag{2}$$

where d denotes the similarity metric, $\mathbf{\Omega}$ denotes the classifier weights of the candidate classes. For the traditional FSL, $\mathbf{\Omega} = \mathbf{\Omega}_{Novel}$. For the generalized FSL, $\mathbf{\Omega} = \mathbf{\Omega}_{All}$.

However, for GFSL, the feature prototypes for novel classes and the classifier weights for base classes differ significantly in the scales, which will result in almost all test samples being classified into one side. To this end, we follow [23] and normalize both the feature representations and the classifier weights during training. Specifically, in the classifier head, we use the cosine similarity to replace the inner product to calculate the class prediction. Once normalized, both the feature representations and classifier weights lie on a high-dimensional sphere, which ensures that the feature representations and classifier weights are symmetric and interchangeable.

In the implementation, we empirically observe that during training the accuracy of the base classes increases consistently and the accuracy of the novel classes increases first and then drops sharply, resulting in their harmonic mean increasing first and then decreasing, as shown in Fig. 5 (a). We speculate that the base classifier and novel classifier are gambling during training and the novel classifier boundaries are gradually squeezed by the base classifier boundaries with the training proceeding as only base data are available for training. To this end, we provide two baselines, i.e., Baseline$_B$ and Baseline$_L$. Baseline$_B$ refers to the model that has the best harmonic mean while Baseline$_L$ refers to the model that performs the best on the base classes.

3.3 Is Scattering Intra-Class Distribution a Solution?

As discussed above, the prediction shift issue may be derived from the severe training sample imbalance between the base classes and novel classes. Inspired by the re-weighting approaches in imbalance learning [4,8] that shift the decision boundary from minority to the majority, we consider the unipolarity property of GFSL and present that scattering the base intra-class distribution would

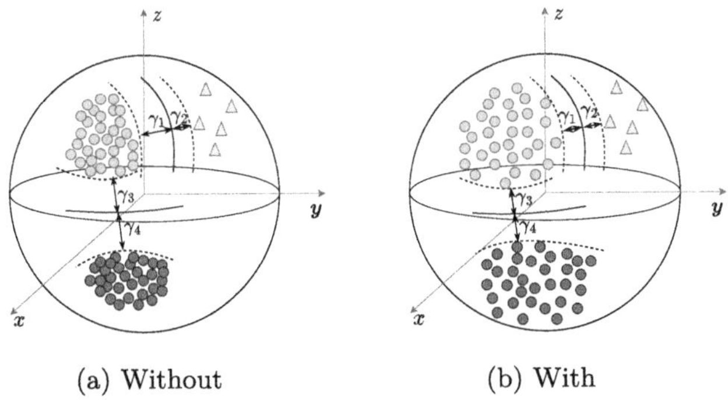

Fig. 2. Illustration of decision boundaries between the base and novel classes without (a) and with (b) scattering the intra-class distribution in a normalized hypersphere.

achieve a similar purpose for addressing the imbalance issue in GFSL. Figure 2 provides an illustration of the decision boundaries between base and novel classes with and without scattering the base intra-class distribution. Since the model is trained only with the samples from the base classes, the feature representations of each base class cluster tightly, and the decision boundaries between base and novel classes are far away from the base classes, as shown in Fig. 2 (a). After scattering the base intra-class distribution, the base margin will become smaller than before, as illustrated in Fig. 2 (b). Since all the feature representations are normalized onto a hypersphere, decreasing the base margin is equivalent to increasing the novel margin in relativity, finally achieving the goal of pushing the decision boundary towards the base classes and weakening the impacts of the base classes on the decision boundaries.

Besides, training the model under only the supervision of the ground-truth labels will lead to the feature representations from the same class cluster towards a point as their supervisions are the same. Such a training paradigm is beneficial for the base classes since the trained model would capture the class-wise discriminative patterns but may hurt the model's generalization ability on the novel classes since it would discard the sample-wise unique patterns. Scattering the intra-class distribution during training would prevent the feature representations in the same classes from collapsing into a cluster center and encourage the model to incorporate more image-level information, which is beneficial for the prediction of the novel classes.

3.4 Our Framework

This section explores three different strategies to scatter the intra-class distribution: a label permutation strategy, and two self-supervised strategies, as illustrated in Fig. 3.

Label Permutation Strategy. Supervising the samples from the same base class with the same ground-truth label would result in the feature representations from the same class collapsing into their cluster center. We add randomness to class labels to relax the rigid supervision. Specifically, we project the class labels into a pseudo-label space, where each class label corresponds to several pseudo-labels. For example, for the class label y_i, its pseudo-labels are $[my_i, my_i+m-1]$, where m is the number of pseudo-labels for each class label. In this way, each base sample could be supervised with one of the pseudo-labels that its real class label corresponds to, which is formulated as:

$$\mathcal{L}_{lp} = -\sum_{j=0}^{Mm-1} p'_j \log \frac{\exp(h_{lp}(f(\mathbf{x}))_j)}{\sum_{k=0}^{Mm-1} \exp(h_{lp}(f(\mathbf{x}))_k)} \tag{3}$$

where h_{lp} denotes the label permutation head that projects the visual feature representations into the pseudo-label space, p'_j is the j-th number of the one-hot pseudo-label $\mathbf{p}'$ of sample $\mathbf{x}$.

In the implementation, three points should be noted. First, we utilize a uniform distribution to decide the pseudo-label in a class such that all the pseudo-classes share a similar number of samples, which ensures the samples from the same class scatter around. Second, we dynamically assign the pseudo-label for each sample during training. In other words, the pseudo-label for each sample in different training epochs may be different. In this way, each sample is fully relaxed with freedom in its pseudo-label space. Finally, the samples from different classes are still in different pseudo-classes, which ensures that they are in different clusters to maintain the discrimination among classes.

Self-supervised Strategy. We introduce two self-supervised tasks, a rotation task, and a feature map split task to encourage the model to learn more image-level feature representations. For the rotation task, we rotate each input sample with $\mathcal{R} = \{0°, 90°, 180°, 270°\}$ to obtain four views and their corresponding one-hot labels $\mathbf{u}$, and then encourage the model to predict their rotation angles with a rotation head h_{rot}. The rotation loss for each sample is formulated as:

$$\mathcal{L}_{rot\_dis} = -\sum_{i=0}^{3}\sum_{j=0}^{3} u_{i,j} \log \frac{\exp(r_{i,j})}{\sum_{k=0}^{3} \exp(r_{i,k})}, \tag{4}$$

where $\mathbf{r} = h_{rot} \cdot f(x)$ denotes the prediction of label rotation, $u_{i,j}$ denotes the j-th number of the rotation label $\mathbf{u}_i$ of the i-th view of sample $\mathbf{x}$, $r_{i,j}$ denotes the j-th number of the prediction $\mathbf{r}_i$ of the i-th view of sample $\mathbf{x}$.

Additionally, four rotation views are also sent into the classification head to predict their class labels to maintain inter-class distinguishability. Thus the overall rotation loss $\mathcal{L}_{rot}$ for each sample is

$$\mathcal{L}_{rot} = \mathcal{L}_{rot\_dis} + \mathcal{L}_{rot\_cls}, \tag{5}$$

where $\mathcal{L}_{rot\_cls}$ denotes the classification loss for the four rotation views.

Though self-supervised tasks have been explored in some FSL literature [11, 24,30,31], our work first verifies that the self-supervision tasks are suitable for GFSL and encourages SSL to play its potential by the combination with our proposed label permutation strategy.

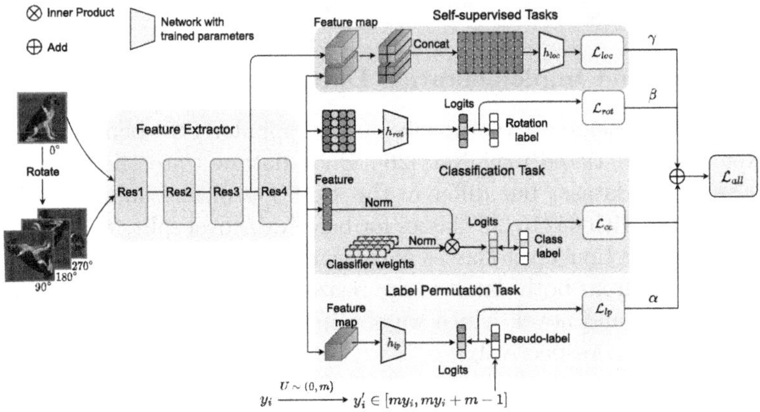

Fig. 3. Illustration of our framework. The model is trained under a primary classification task and three auxiliary tasks, a label permutation task, and two self-supervision tasks.

For the feature map split task, we split the feature maps of the last and penultimate layers of the backbone into four equal-size non-overlapped patches. Specifically, for each feature map $Z \in \mathbb{R}^{h \times w \times c}$, h, w, and c denote the height, width, and channel numbers, we split it along h and w in half, generating four patches and their location labels $\mathbf{t}$, and then encourage the model to predict their locations with a location head h_{loc}. The location loss for each base sample in each of the last two layers is formulated as:

$$\mathcal{L}_{loc\_dis} = -\sum_{i=0}^{3}\sum_{j=0}^{3} t_{i,j} \log \frac{\exp\left(s_{i,j}\right)}{\sum_{k=0}^{3} \exp\left(s_{i,k}\right)}, \tag{6}$$

where $\mathbf{s}$ denotes the location prediction of the divided patches, $t_{i,j}$ denotes the j-th number of the location label $\mathbf{t}_i$ of the i-th patch of sample $\mathbf{x}$, $s_{i,j}$ denotes the j-th number of the prediction $\mathbf{s}_i$ of the i-th patch of sample $\mathbf{x}$.

Besides, similar to the rotation task, the four feature map patches are also projected into classification space to maintain their discrimination on the classes. Thus, the overall location loss $\mathcal{L}_{loc}$ for each sample is:

$$\mathcal{L}_{loc} = \mathcal{L}_{loc\_dis} + \mathcal{L}_{loc\_cls}. \tag{7}$$

The feature maps from both the last and penultimate layers are applied with the same operation.

Overall Objective. We formulate the whole idea into a multi-task framework, as illustrated in Fig. 3. The final objective loss for each sample is:

$$\mathcal{L} = \mathcal{L}_{ce} + \alpha\mathcal{L}_{lp} + \beta\mathcal{L}_{rot} + \gamma\mathcal{L}_{loc}, \tag{8}$$

where α, β, and γ are three hyper-parameters. In our work, we report the final results by setting both α and β to 1, and γ to 0.5.

4 Experiments

4.1 Datasets and Implementation Details

Datasets. We implement experiments on two popular FSL benchmarks: miniImageNet [33] and tieredImageNet [26]. Both datasets are the derivatives of the ImageNet [9] dataset but differ in the size. Specifically, miniImageNet is a 100-class dataset with 64/16/20 classes for base/val/novel split, while tieredImageNet contains 608 ImageNet classes with 351/97/160 classes for base/val/novel split. The images from both datasets are resized to 84×84. The test images are comprised of base and novel, which we obtain from [35] and the novel subset of the original dataset, respectively.

Implementation Details. Following [32,35], we employ ResNet12 as our feature backbone, while both the rotation head h_{rot} and the location head h_{loc} are MLP with a single hidden layer, and the label permutation head h_{lp} consists of a convolutional layer and an MLP. We train the model for 80 epochs on the base classes, using SGD optimizer with momentum 0.9 and learning rate $5e-2$ initially decayed by 0.1 at 60 and 70 epochs with batch size 64 for miniImageNet, while for tieredImageNet, the learning rate decays by 0.1 at 40 and 50 epochs in all 60 epochs with batch size 128. We sample 300 GFSL tasks to report our results and every task contains 5 test samples from every base class and a FSL task comprised of support set and query set.

Evaluation Metric. We evaluate the models with the base accuracy Acc_B, novel accuracy Acc_N in the joint space, and their harmonic mean H for GFSL task and novel accuracy in novel own space for FSL task. Note that we evaluate our method on H if not specific.

4.2 Results on both GFSL and FSL Tasks

GFSL Results. We compare our method with some recent competitors on both benchmarks under the GFSL tasks in Table 1. Specifically, four methods [27,29,32,36] that are originally evaluated on the FSL tasks and two methods [12,35] that are evaluated on both FSL and GFSL tasks are selected for comparison. From the results, we observe most of the methods designed for traditional FSL tasks perform poorly under GFSL tasks on both benchmarks except for Distill [27] which also utilizes a self-supervised auxiliary task to train the model, providing some pieces of evidence for the claim that SSL is beneficial for GFSL. Though performing competitively, Distill [27] is still inferior to ours on both datasets as our method fully exploits the potential of SSL by combining the other type of auxiliary task. Additionally, RFS [32] which utilizes knowledge distillation [15] performs poorly under GFSL tasks, empirically proving that knowledge distillation [15] could not help GFSL classification very much. Compared with the methods designed for GFSL, our method performs very competitively on both datasets, especially under the M+All-Way 5-Shot task, where our method beats [35] with 7.0% and 4.42% improvements on the miniImageNet and tieredImageNet, respectively.

Table 1. Comparison results (%) on both miniImageNet and tieredImageNet datasets under M+5-way and M+All-way tasks. † denotes the results implemented by ourselves with the released codes, and ‡ denotes the results copied from [35]. The best results are in **bold** and the second-best results are underlined. 'M+5-Way' denotes that the candidate classes include both the base classes and 5 random classes sampled from the novel classes. 'M+All-Way' denotes that the candidate classes include both the base classes and all the novel classes.

Methods	M+5-Way			M+All-Way					
	5-Shot			1-Shot			5-Shot		
	Acc_B	Acc_N	H	Acc_B	Acc_N	H	Acc_B	Acc_N	H
miniImageNet									
ProtoNet† [29]	72.41	57.74	64.25	65.39	23.03	34.06	61.45	41.90	49.83
RFS† [32]	71.13	59.58	64.85	67.96	22.12	33.37	62.07	42.92	50.75
FEAT† [36]	71.94	58.42	64.48	69.24	21.03	32.26	61.00	42.94	50.40
Distill† [27]	85.68	60.18	70.70	56.40	28.22	37.62	80.30	47.94	60.04
Baseline$_B$	63.73	63.03	63.38	51.47	26.15	34.68	52.17	43.91	47.69
Baseline$_L$	90.43	26.73	41.26	90.16	7.69	14.17	89.47	24.55	38.53
DFSL‡ [12]	-	-	71.26	61.68	31.13	41.21	66.06	47.16	54.95
ACASTLE‡ [35]	-	-	78.33	81.36	29.95	**43.63**	87.40	41.64	56.33
Ours	86.49	72.16	**78.68**	84.05	27.29	41.26	76.81	53.87	**63.33**
tieredImageNet									
ProtoNet† [29]	60.47	63.04	61.73	51.05	13.00	20.72	45.93	27.01	34.01
RFS† [32]	64.74	59.03	61.75	61.09	12.06	20.14	58.93	26.00	36.09
FEAT† [36]	62.59	58.14	60.29	57.04	12.41	20.38	52.80	27.15	35.86
Distill† [27]	67.55	69.81	68.66	61.49	14.69	23.71	45.87	30.20	36.42
Baseline$_B$	62.44	60.10	61.25	57.18	12.37	20.34	53.20	27.34	36.12
Baseline$_L$	68.33	48.39	56.66	66.56	9.38	16.44	63.84	24.25	35.15
DFSL‡ [12]	–	–	- -	11.29	14.24	12.60	14.95	27.22	19.29
ACASTLE‡ [35]	–	–	–	27.01	16.17	22.23	35.41	31.86	33.54
Ours	65.38	81.86	**72.70**	52.67	16.28	**24.87**	47.22	31.73	**37.96**

FSL Results. We also provide the comparison results of our method and some recent competitors under the traditional FSL on both benchmarks in Table 2. From the results, our method obtains the best under the 1-Shot task on both datasets and performs the second best under the 5-Shot task, verifying the superiority of our method under the traditional FSL tasks.

To sum up, our method performs competitively under both traditional FSL and GFSL tasks. We argue that the way of scattering the base intra-class distribution could encourage the model to extract more valid feature representations, which strikes a balance between discrimination and generalization.

Table 2. Comparison results (%) on both miniImageNet and tieredImageNet datasets under 5-Way 1-Shot and 5-Way 5-Shot settings with 95% confidence interval. The best results are in **bold** and the second are underlined.

Methods	miniImageNet		tieredImageNet	
	5-Way 1-Shot	5-Way 5-Shot	5-Way 1-Shot	5-Way 5-Shot
RFS-Simple [32]	62.02 ± 0.63	79.64 ± 0.44	69.74 ± 0.72	84.41 ± 0.55
RFS-Distill [32]	64.82 ± 0.60	82.14 ± 0.43	71.52 ± 0.69	86.03 ± 0.49
DFSL [12]	56.20 ± 0.86	73.00 ± 0.64	50.90 ± 0.46	66.69 ± 0.36
FEAT [36]	66.78	82.05	70.80 ±0.23	84.79 ± 0.16
Meta-Baseline [6]	63.17 ± 0.23	79.26 ± 0.17	68.62 ± 0.27	83.74 ± 0.18
MeTAL [2]	66.61 ± 0.28	81.43 ± 0.25	70.29 ± 0.40	86.17 ± 0.35
RENet [17]	67.60 ± 0.44	82.58 ± 0.3	71.61 ± 0.51	85.28 ± 0.35
POODLE [19]	67.80	83.72	70.42	85.26
ACASTLE [35]	66.83 ± 0.20	82.08 ± 0.14	71.63 ± 0.02	85.28 ± 0.15
HGNN [37]	67.02 ± 0.20	83.00 ± 0.13	72.05 ± 0.23	86.49 ± 0.15
DeepBDC [34]	67.83 ± 0.43	**85.45 ± 0.29**	73.82 ± 0.47	**89.00 ± 0.30**
DSFN [39]	61.27 ± 0.71	80.13 ± 0.17	65.46 ± 0.70	82.41 ± 0.53
Ours	**68.19 ± 0.54**	83.13 ± 0.39	**74.70 ± 0.63**	86.53 ± 0.42

Table 3. Ablation study(%) on miniImageNet under M+5-way 5-shot GFSL task.

Rotation	Location	LP	Acc_B	Acc_N	H
			63.73	63.03	63.38
✓			85.45	53.21	65.58
	✓		67.98	62.92	65.35
✓	✓		86.37	58.25	69.57
		✓	85.45	64.37	73.43
✓		✓	83.15	70.32	76.20
	✓	✓	85.49	68.84	76.27
✓	✓	✓	86.49	72.16	78.68

4.3 Ablation Study

In this section, we perform a thorough ablation study on miniImageNet with ResNet12 to provide a deep insight into each component in our method.

Components Contribution. Here we quantify the contribution of different components in our method. As shown in Table 3, in terms of the harmonic mean H, applying the Rotation or Location alone respectively gives an improvement of 2.2% and 1.97% while combining them together would obtain 6.19% improvement over the baseline. Besides, employing the label permutation would achieve about 10% gains over the baseline. When combining all three components, we

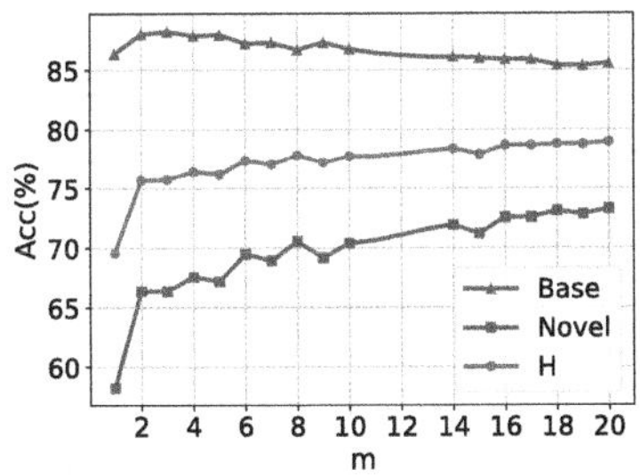

Fig. 4. The influence of pseudo-class number m to the base, novel, and their harmonic mean performance on the miniImageNet dataset under the M+5-Way 5-Shot setting.

would obtain the maximal performance improvement of 15.3% over the baseline. The consistent improvements indicate that joint optimization for both self-supervised tasks and label permutation is beneficial for GFSL.

It is notable that when we only apply label permutation or self-supervised tasks, the performance of the base classes improves significantly due to more adequate training while the performance of the novel classes improves slightly or even declines. We speculate that a type of auxiliary task alone hardly pushes the decision boundary towards the base classes while the combination of all the auxiliary tasks could effectively weaken the pull of base clusters to novel samples, leading to the performance improvement of novel classes. The experiment also verifies that the two types of auxiliary tasks complement each other.

Number of Pseudo-class in Label Permutation. In this experiment, we investigate the influence of the pseudo-class number corresponding to a ground truth class by varying the number of pseudo-class m in Fig. 4. From the results, we observe that after the initial increase, the performance saturates with increasing m. We speculate that the intra-class samples hardly form a uniform clustering space centered around the original aggregation point when the pseudo-class number is small. When m is above a particular number (e.g., 16), the uniform space around the original aggregation point is basically generated, thus the performance plateaus. Based on the results in Fig. 4, we report the final performance when m is 16.

4.4 Further Analysis

Model Robustness. To evaluate the effects of different components on the model robustness, we plot the classification performances of both the base and novel classes and their harmonic mean during the training process. As shown in Fig. 5, it is obvious that the method without both SSL and LP (i.e., (a)) drops significantly in terms of both the performance of novel classes and H when the training epoch surpasses 60 while the SSL task (i.e., (b)) could relieve the performance drop on the novel classes to boost H. Interestingly, the LP term (i.e., (c)) even brings performance improvement on the novel accuracy.

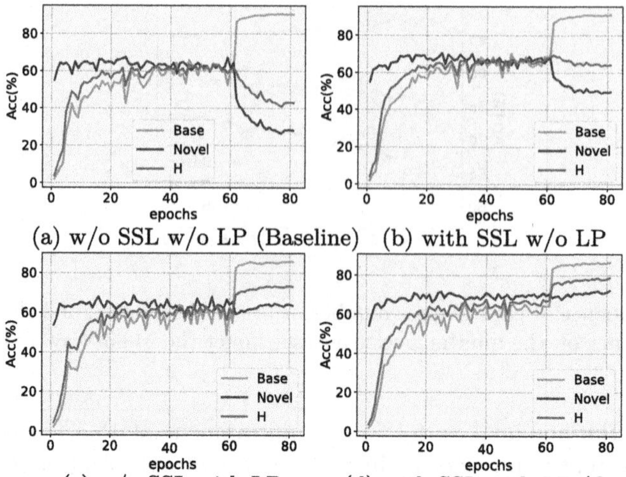

(a) w/o SSL w/o LP (Baseline) (b) with SSL w/o LP

(c) w/o SSL with LP (d) with SSL with LP (Ours)

Fig. 5. The effects of different components on the three evaluation metrics during training on the miniImageNet dataset under the M+5-way 5-shot task.

When we combine the SSL and LP terms (i.e., (d)), the performances of three evaluation metrics steadily improve and plateau when the training epoch is above 70, possibly because there is no further margin of improvement.

In addition, we observe that the novel accuracy still declines a lot when the optimization objective is integrated with SSL tasks only. We speculate that this is because SSL task primarily encourages the model to extract more image-level information, and only combined with LP which scatters the intra-class distribution can it play its potential on the novel classes.

Relations Between Performance and Feature Distribution. In this experiment, we provide an insight into the model from both intra-class and inter-class distributions on the base classes. Specifically, we introduce three metrics of D_{intra}, D_{inter}, and their product DM on class-wise level, where D_{intra} is the averaged Euclidean distance over the feature representation of each image to its class prototype obtained by averaging all the image feature representations in the class, while the inter-class distance D_{inter} refers to the minimal distance between a class prototype to others.

As reported in Table 4, we observe that the auxiliary tasks could significantly enlarge the value of three metrics and the LP brings more improvement margins, which verifies that the auxiliary tasks indeed enlarge the inter-class distributions and scatter the intra-class distributions. Importantly, the H performance increases with the increase of the three metrics, empirically validating that scattering intra-class distribution is beneficial for GFSL tasks.

CAM Visualization. We visualize Gradient-weighted Class Activation Mapping (Grad-CAM) [28] of two baselines and our method on the test samples from

Table 4. Metric D_{intra}, D_{inter}, and DM for the base set, and performance H under the M+5-Way 5-Shot task on the miniImageNet.

Model	D_{intra} (↑)	D_{inter} (↑)	DM (↑)	H (%)
Baseline$_B$	2.44	85.51	215.83	63.38
Baseline$_L$	1.02	75.81	79.09	41.26
Baseline+LP	10.87	899.94	9801.59	73.43
Baseline+SSL	5.00	308.67	1614.25	69.57
Baseline+SSL+LP (Ours)	14.50	1335.82	19402.29	78.68

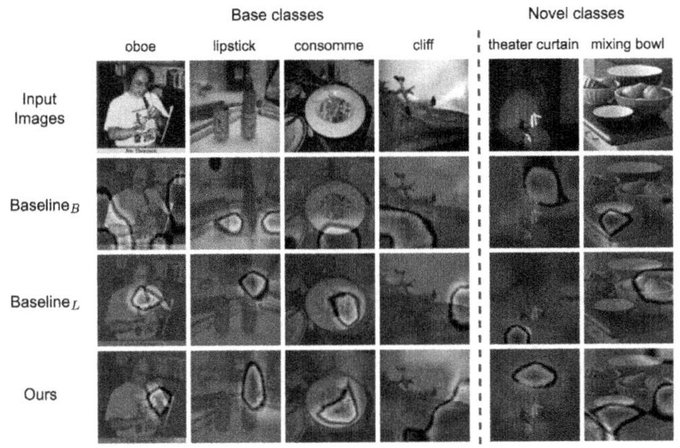

Fig. 6. Grad-CAM visualization results of two baselines and ours on the test samples from both base and novel classes under the M+5-Way 5-Shot task on the miniImageNet.

both base and novel classes in Fig. 6. We observe that Baseline$_L$ concentrates more on features related to base classes but highlights incorrect regions for novel classes, while Baseline$_B$ could well focus on the novel classes but hardly concentrates on the base classes. In contrast, our method could extract related features for both base and novel classes.

5 Conclusion

In this work, we have revealed that what the GFSL needs is extracting both discriminative and generalized feature representations, which could be achieved by simply scattering the intra-class distribution during training. Then based on the solution, we proposed a one-stage framework that combines multiple tasks to scatter the intra-class distribution and maintain inter-class distance simultaneously. The experimental results demonstrate that our model is comparable to or even better than the multi-stage competitors under traditional FSL and GFSL tasks. We hope this paper could shed new light on the GFSL.

Acknowledgments. This work is supported in part by the Key R&D Program of Zhejiang Province, China (2023C01043, 2021C01119) and the National Natural Science Foundation of China under Grant (62002320, U19B2043, 61672456).

Ethical Statement. In this paper, we mainly investigate the problem of how to balance the base classes and novel classes in the generalized FSL task and propose that what the GFSL needs is extracting both discriminative and generalized feature representations. We consider that the required discussion about ethic and future societal effect is not applicable for our work.

References

1. Ahn, S., Ko, J., Yun, S.Y.: Cuda: curriculum of data augmentation for long-tailed recognition. arXiv preprint arXiv:2302.05499 (2023)
2. Baik, S., Choi, J., Kim, H., Cho, D., Min, J., Lee, K.M.: Meta-learning with task-adaptive loss function for few-shot learning. In: ICCV, pp. 9465–9474 (2021)
3. Brinkmeyer, L., Drumond, R.R., Burchert, J., Schmidt-Thieme, L.: Few-shot forecasting of time-series with heterogeneous channels. In: ECML, pp. 3–18 (2023)
4. Cao, K., Wei, C., Gaidon, A., Arechiga, N., Ma, T.: Learning imbalanced datasets with label-distribution-aware margin loss. In: NeurIPS (2019)
5. Chawla, N.V., Bowyer, K.W., Hall, L.O., Kegelmeyer, W.P.: Smote: synthetic minority over-sampling technique. J. Artifi. Intell. Res. **16**, 321–357 (2002)
6. Chen, Y., Liu, Z., Xu, H., Darrell, T., Wang, X.: Meta-baseline: exploring simple meta-learning for few-shot learning. In: ICCV, pp. 9062–9071 (2021)
7. Cheng, L., Fang, C., Zhang, D., Li, G., Huang, G.: Compound batch normalization for long-tailed image classification. In: ACM, pp. 1925–1934 (2022)
8. Cui, Y., Jia, M., Lin, T.Y., Song, Y., Belongie, S.: Class-balanced loss based on effective number of samples. In: CVPR, pp. 9268–9277 (2019)
9. Deng, J., Dong, W., Socher, R., Li, L.J., Li, K., Fei-Fei, L.: Imagenet: A large-scale hierarchical image database. In: CVPR, pp. 248–255 (2009)
10. Drummond, C., Holte, R.C., et al.: C4. 5, class imbalance, and cost sensitivity: why under-sampling beats over-sampling. In: Workshop on lEarning from Imbalanced Datasets II, pp. 1–8 (2003)
11. Gidaris, S., Bursuc, A., Komodakis, N., Pérez, P., Cord, M.: Boosting few-shot visual learning with self-supervision. In: ICCV, pp. 8059–8068 (2019)
12. Gidaris, S., Komodakis, N.: Dynamic few-shot visual learning without forgetting. In: CVPR, pp. 4367–4375 (2018)
13. Hariharan, B., Girshick, R.: Low-shot visual recognition by shrinking and hallucinating features. In: ICCV, pp. 3018–3027 (2017)
14. He, Y., et al.: Attribute surrogates learning and spectral tokens pooling in transformers for few-shot learning. In: CVPR, pp. 9119–9129 (2022)
15. Hinton, G., Vinyals, O., Dean, J.: Distilling the knowledge in a neural network. arXiv preprint arXiv:1503.02531 (2015)
16. Jian, Y., Torresani, L.: Label hallucination for few-shot classification. In: AAAI, pp. 7005–7014 (2022)
17. Kang, D., Kwon, H., Min, J., Cho, M.: Relational embedding for few-shot classification. In: ICCV, pp. 8822–8833 (2021)
18. Kukleva, A., Kuehne, H., Schiele, B.: Generalized and incremental few-shot learning by explicit learning and calibration without forgetting. In: ICCV, pp. 9020–9029 (2021)

19. Le, D., Nguyen, K.D., Nguyen, K., Tran, Q.H., Nguyen, R., Hua, B.S.: Poodle: Improving few-shot learning via penalizing out-of-distribution samples. In: NeurIPS, pp. 23942–23955 (2021)
20. Liu, J., Sun, Y., Han, C., Dou, Z., Li, W.: Deep representation learning on long-tailed data: A learnable embedding augmentation perspective. In: CVPR, pp. 2970–2979 (2020)
21. Ouali, Y., Hudelot, C., Tami, M.: Spatial contrastive learning for few-shot classification. In: ECML, pp. 671–686 (2021)
22. Park, S., Lim, J., Jeon, Y., Choi, J.Y.: Influence-balanced loss for imbalanced visual classification. In: ICCV, pp. 735–744 (2021)
23. Qi, H., Brown, M., Lowe, D.G.: Low-shot learning with imprinted weights. In: CVPR, pp. 5822–5830 (2018)
24. Rajasegaran, J., Khan, S., Hayat, M., Khan, F.S., Shah, M.: Self-supervised knowledge distillation for few-shot learning. arXiv preprint arXiv:2006.09785 (2020)
25. Rangwani, H., Aithal, S.K., Mishra, M., et al.: Escaping saddle points for effective generalization on class-imbalanced data. In: NeurIPS, pp. 22791–22805 (2022)
26. Ren, M., et al.: Meta-learning for semi-supervised few-shot classification. In: ICLR (2018)
27. Rizve, M.N., Khan, S., Khan, F.S., Shah, M.: Exploring complementary strengths of invariant and equivariant representations for few-shot learning. In: CVPR, pp. 10836–10846 (2021)
28. Selvaraju, R.R., Cogswell, M., Das, A., Vedantam, R., Parikh, D., Batra, D.: Grad-cam: Visual explanations from deep networks via gradient-based localization. In: ICCV, pp. 618–626 (2017)
29. Snell, J., Swersky, K., Zemel, R.: Prototypical networks for few-shot learning. In: NeurIPS (2017)
30. Su, J.C., Maji, S., Hariharan, B.: Boosting supervision with self-supervision for few-shot learning. In: ICCV, pp. 8059–8068 (2019)
31. Su, J.-C., Maji, S., Hariharan, B.: When does self-supervision improve few-shot learning? In: Vedaldi, A., Bischof, H., Brox, T., Frahm, J.-M. (eds.) ECCV 2020. LNCS, vol. 12352, pp. 645–666. Springer, Cham (2020). https://doi.org/10.1007/978-3-030-58571-6_38
32. Tian, Y., Wang, Y., Krishnan, D., Tenenbaum, J.B., Isola, P.: Rethinking few-shot image classification: a good embedding is all you need? In: Vedaldi, A., Bischof, H., Brox, T., Frahm, J.-M. (eds.) ECCV 2020. LNCS, vol. 12359, pp. 266–282. Springer, Cham (2020). https://doi.org/10.1007/978-3-030-58568-6_16
33. Vinyals, O., Blundell, C., Lillicrap, T., Wierstra, D., et al.: Matching networks for one-shot learning. In: NeurIPS, pp. 3630–3638 (2016)
34. Xie, J., Long, F., Lv, J., Wang, Q., Li, P.: Joint distribution matters: Deep brownian distance covariance for few-shot classification. In: CVPR, pp. 7972–7981 (2022)
35. Ye, H.J., Hu, H., Zhan, D.C.: Learning adaptive classifiers synthesis for generalized few-shot learning. IJCV **129**, 1930–1953 (2021)
36. Ye, H.J., Hu, H., Zhan, D.C., Sha, F.: Few-shot learning via embedding adaptation with set-to-set functions. In: CVPR, pp. 8808–8817 (2020)
37. Yu, T., He, S., Song, Y.Z., Xiang, T.: Hybrid graph neural networks for few-shot learning. In: AAAI, pp. 3179–3187 (2022)
38. Yu, Y., Zhang, D., Ji, Z.: Masked feature generation network for few-shot learning
39. Zhang, T., Huang, W.: Kernel relative-prototype spectral filtering for few-shot learning. In: ECCV, pp. 541–557 (2022). https://doi.org/10.1007/978-3-031-20044-1_31

vMF Loss: Exploring a Scattered Intra-class Hypersphere for Few-Shot Learning

Xin Liu[1], Shijing Wang[1], Kairui Zhou[1], Yilin Lyu[1], Mingyang Song[1], Liping Jing[1(✉)], Tieyong Zeng[2], and Jian Yu[1]

[1] School of Computer and Information Technology, Beijing Jiaotong University, Beijing, China
{xin.liu,21120408,20120460,yilinlyu, mingyang.song,lpjing,jianyu}@bjtu.edu.cn

[2] Department of Mathematics, The Chinese University of Hong Kong, Shatin, N.T., Hong Kong
zeng@math.cuhk.edu.hk

Abstract. Few-shot learning (FSL), which aims to learn from very few labeled examples, is a challenging task but frequently appears in real-world applications. An appealing direction to tackle it is the metric-based method, which seeks to learn a transferable embedding space across different tasks from a related base dataset and generalize it for novel few-shot tasks. Recently, a large corpus of literature has been proposed to design more complicated representation learning methods to improve performance. Despite some promising results, how these methods improve the few-shot performance remains unexplored. Motivated by this question, we investigate the relationship between the performance and the structure of the learned embedding space. We find they are strongly correlated to each other. To capture more valuable features of novel classes, the intra-class distribution of base classes should be more scattered. Therefore, we introduce von Mises-Fisher (vMF) distribution and employ a vMF similarity loss function that uses a concentration parameter, κ, to control the intra-class distribution on a hypersphere. By setting a smaller κ, our method can learn a more transferrable embedding space with high intra-class diversity. Extensive experiments on two widely used datasets demonstrate the effectiveness of our method.

Keywords: Few-shot Learning · Von Mises-Fisher (vMF) Distribution · Intra-class Distance · Scattered Hypersphere

1 Introduction

Deep learning methods have made tremendous success on a wide range of computer vision applications with access to large-scale labeled data [6,9]. However, in some practical fields, such as medical and military, sufficient manual annotation is either not feasible or too expensive to collect. Humans, on the other hand, are known to learn new categories quickly after seeing only a few or even a single example. This advantage comes from years of experience accumulated by the human visual system. Inspired by it, Few-Shot Learning (FSL) is developed to tackle the problem of learning from very few labeled examples by leveraging the knowledge learned from a related base dataset.

© The Author(s), under exclusive license to Springer Nature Switzerland AG 2023
D. Koutra et al. (Eds.): ECML PKDD 2023, LNAI 14170, pp. 454–470, 2023.
https://doi.org/10.1007/978-3-031-43415-0_27

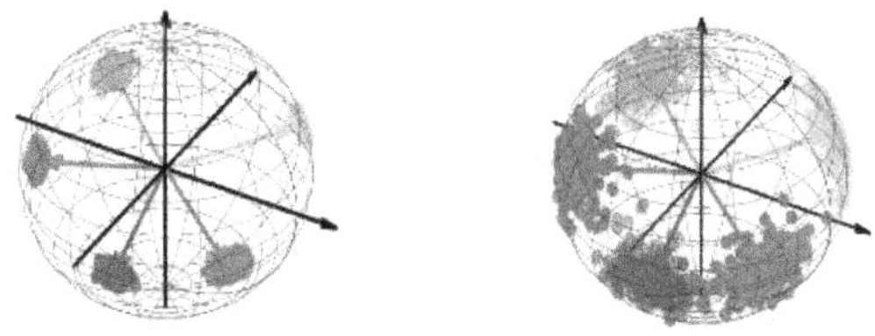

Fig. 1. Visualization of the expected embedding spaces on a 3-d sphere by traditional metric learning methods and our proposed method.

A compelling series of the methods is metric learning [34] with episodes training mechanism [28], i.e., metric-based FSL. By training on a collection of few-shot classification tasks constructed from the related base dataset, this kind of method aims to learn a transferable embedding space across different tasks and generalize it for few-shot tasks from novel datasets. In the embedding space, query samples are classified according to their similarities with support samples. One classic method is Prototypical Network (Proto Net) [26], which learns a prototype for each class and performs classification according to the square Euclidean distance between the query and prototype.

An important issue in the metric-based FSL methods is extracting high-quality representations for each class and query sample. Recently, an extensive corpus of literature has proposed more complicated representation learning methods to improve performance. For example, Adaptive Modality Mixture Mechanism (AM3) [33] exploits cross-modal information, and Cross Attention Network (CAN) [7] proposes a cross-attention module to generate more discriminative features. Although promising achievements have been made, it is still unclear how these strategies contribute to the few-shot performance. In other words, **(1) what does the embedding space of a high-quality representation learning approach look like?** and **(2) which kind of embedding space learned on base classes is better to transfer for novel classes?**

In this paper, we shed new light on understanding the above problem by exploring the structure of the embedding space, which determines the representation distribution of the embedding space. We start with several representative metric-based FSL methods and investigate the correlation between their few-shot classification performance and the structure of their learned embedding spaces. We observe that the few-shot performance strongly correlates with the intra-class distance of the learned embedding space. This indicates that scattered intra-class distribution on base classes benefits the few-shot classification performance on novel classes. We think this is due to the category gap between the training and evaluation in FSL. To capture more valuable features of novel classes, the intra-class distribution of base classes should be as scattered as possible. Based on the above observation, we leverage the von Mises-Fisher (vMF) distribution [8,18] to propose a novel vMF similarity loss function. The proposed loss function is a compact-support function over concentration κ, enabling us to control the intra-class variance. By setting a smaller κ, our method can learn a more transferrable embedding space with high intra-class diversity, as shown in Fig. 1. Extensive experiments carried out on the two most widely used datasets demonstrate the effectiveness of our method. The main contributions of this paper are summarized:

- This is the first endeavor to investigate what embedding space learned in base classes is more suitable to transfer for FSL tasks in novel classes, which inspires us to propose better metric-based methods.
- We provide an intuitive explanation and insightful analysis for why few-shot classification performance on novel classes benefits from more dispersed intra-class distributions of base classes.
- We propose a simple yet effective method for FSL by introducing the von Mises-Fisher (vMF) distribution. The proposed approach achieves competitive performance on the two most widely-used few-shot classification benchmarks.

2 Related Work

Few-shot learning has been extensively studied in recent years, which aims to transfer knowledge from many labeled datasets (base classes) to a disjoint dataset (novel classes) with limited training data. A dominant method is metric-based FSL, which aims to learn a transferrable embedding space by conducting a set of few-shot classification tasks on base classes and generalizing it to novel classes. Existing metric-based FSL methods can be divided into three categories based on the critical issue they address: similarity-based methods (S), representation-based methods (R), and similarity and representation-based methods (SR).

Similarity-based methods attempt to design appropriate functions to measure the similarity of representations in the embedding space. An intuitive way is to adopt the widely used distance function such as squared Euclidean distance [25] and cosine similarity [24]. To capture the more complex relationship between samples, Simple CNAPS [1] uses Mahalanobis distance, and Relation network [27] employs a neural network to capture the features' correlation. Although effective, the above methods represent each image in a compact image-level representation, which may lose considerable discriminative information. Therefore, some methods are proposed to compare the local representations. For example, Deep Nearest Neighbor Neural Network (DN4) [11] replaces the image-level feature-based measure in the final layer with a local descriptor-based image-to-class measure. Deep EMD [37] adopts the earth mover's distance as a metric to compute a structural distance between dense image representations to determine image relevance. The Semantic Alignment Metric Learning (SAML) method [5] employs a multi-layer perceptron (MLP) to calculate a similarity score between the semantic alignment representations. Deep Brownian Distance Covariance (DeepBDC) [32] views features of the sample as random vectors and measures the similarity by calculating the discrepancy between their joint distribution and the product of the marginals.

Representation-based methods seek to extract high-quality representations for query samples and different classes. The milestone work is Prototypical Network (Proto Net) [26], which takes the mean of support samples in each class as its corresponding prototype and performs classification according to the distance between the query and prototype. Many methods have been built based on it to improve the quality of the prototype. For example, AM3 [33] leverages cross-modal information(e.g., semantic representations) to model the prototype representation as a convex combination of the two modalities. Cross Attention Network (CAN) [7] proposes a cross-attention module to adaptively localize the relevant regions and generate more discriminative features. InfoPatch [13] proposes a contrastive training scheme to exploit the patch-wise relationship for exploring enough discriminative information for few samples. The above methods usually learn an embedding space on the base datasets and apply it directly to visual data in novel datasets, which does not necessarily lead to optimal performance for a specific target task. Therefore, some research is proposed to learn task-specific representations. For example, FEAT [36] adapts the instance embedding to the target classification task with a set-to-set function, yielding task-specific and discriminative embedding.

Similarity and representation-based methods address the above two issues simultaneously. For example, Task-dependent adaptive metric (TADAM) [19] employs a scaled cosine similarity function and adopts conditional batch normalization to learn a task-conditioning embedding model. Dynamic Meta-filter Network (DMF) [35] proposes to learn a dynamic alignment, which can effectively highlight both query regions and channels according to different local support information. Discriminative Mutual Nearest Neighbor (DMNN) [15] employs deep descriptors as image representation and proposes a novel relative closeness in mutual nearest neighbor to measure the similarity. Actually, each metric-based method solves both issues but with different priorities.

In this paper, we focus on representation-based methods. We analyze the structural property of their embedding space and investigate the relationship between their performance and the embedding space. Based on the observation that the performance is correlated with intra-class distance in the embedding space, we employ a vMF similarity loss function to learn a more transferrable embedding space by enlarging the intra-class distance via a small κ.

3 Empirical Investigation

In this section, we first formalize the problem of metric-based FSL. Then, to understand what the embedding space of a high-quality representation learning approach looks like and which kind of embedding space learned in base classes is better to transfer for novel classes, we analyze the relationship between the few-shot performance and structural properties of the embedding spaces generated by different representation-based methods.

Problem Definition. In this work, we focus on a typical few-shot task N-way K-shot problem. Let $\mathcal{S} = \{(x_i^s, y_i)\}_{i=1}^{N\times K}$ be a support set, which contains N different image classes and K labeled samples per class. $\mathcal{Q} = \{(x_j^q, y_j)\}_{j=1}^{N\times Q}$ denotes a query set, which contains unlabeled images from the same N classes as the support set. N-way K-shot task aims to classify each unlabeled sample in Q according to the support set S.

In a FSL scenario, we usually have two label disjoint datasets: $\mathcal{D}_{base}$ and $\mathcal{D}_{novel}$. Generally, each set contains abundant categories and examples that are significantly larger than N and K. Following [28], two sets of N-way K-shot tasks (episodes) are randomly sampled from the two datasets, which are used to train and evaluate the model, respectively. Metric-based FSL methods aim to learn a transferrable embedding space from $\mathcal{D}_{base}$ and generalize it to $\mathcal{D}_{novel}$. In each training iteration, an episode is randomly sampled from the base dataset to update the feature extractor $f_\theta(\cdot)$. This procedure is repeated many times until the model converges to a stable state. Then, episodes randomly sampled from the novel dataset are evaluated on the embedding space obtained by $f_\theta(\cdot)$. Usually, in the embedding space, a query sample $f_\theta(x^q)$ is classified according to a certain similarity between it and different class representations.

3.1 Structure Analysis of Embedding Space W.r.t Different Methods

It is known that extracting a high-quality representation for query samples and different classes is a key issue in metric-based FSL methods. However, there is still no agreed-upon definition of what a high-quality representation looks like. In this paper, we attempt to answer this problem by exploring the structure of the embedding spaces generated by different few-shot representation learning methods.

Structure of Embedding Space. Let f_i be the representation of sample x_i in the obtained embedding space. f_{y_l} denotes the representation of sample x belonging to the class l in the obtained embedding space. The class center for class l is calculated as the mean of the feature representations in class l and is denoted as $\mu(f_{y_l})$. The structure-property of the embedding space is measured using intra-class distance, inter-class distance, and the ratio between them as follows:

- Average Inter-class distance: quantifies the separation between classes. It is the average distance over the distances from all possible class centers $\mu(f_{y_l}), \mu(f_{y_k})$ belonging to two different classes. Z_{inter} is the number of class pairs.

$$\pi_{inter}(f) = \frac{1}{Z_{inter}} \sum_{y_l, y_k, l \neq k} d(\mu(f_{y_l}), \mu(f_{y_k})) \tag{1}$$

- Average Intra-class distance: evaluates how closely the elements of the same cluster are to each other and measures the compactness of the classes. It is the average distance over the distances from all possible pairs f_i, f_j belonging to the same class y_l. Z_{intra} is the number of sample pairs.

$$\pi_{intra}(f) = \frac{1}{Z_{intra}} \sum_{y_l \in \mathcal{Y}} \sum_{f_i, f_j \in f_{y_l}, i \neq j} d(f_i, f_j) \tag{2}$$

- Intra / Inter Ratio: the ratio of the average intra-class distance and inter-class distance, which can be regarded as an embedding space density.

$$\pi_{ratio}(f) = \pi_{intra}(f)/\pi_{inter}(f) \tag{3}$$

Representative Few-Shot Representation Learning Methods. Usually, the representation f_i can be represented as a d-dimension vector or a vector in the $3d$ tensor. In this paper, we focus on the first circumstance that is widely used in modern few-shot representation-based literature and select the following methods:

- Prototypical Network [26] is the most classic metric-based FSL method, which uses the support set to compute a prototype for each category (in the sampled episode), and query samples are classified based on the Euclidean distance to each prototype. In Prototypical Network, the prototype p_c is computed by averaging the representations of all support samples of class c.
- Cross attention Network(CAN) [7] proposes an attention mechanism to enhance the feature discriminability for FSL. Firstly, CAN computes a correlation map $R \in R^{m \times m}, m = h \times w$ between the support feature map $\{p_i\}_{i=1}^{m}$ and query feature map $\{q_i\}_{i=1}^{m}$, and defines the class correlation map $R^p = R^T$ and the query correlation map $R^q = R$. Then, they use a meta fusion layer to generate the class and query attention map $A^p \in R^{h \times w}$ and $A^q \in R^{h \times w}$, respectively based on the corresponding correlation maps. Finally, they employ a residual attention mechanism to form more discriminative feature maps $\bar{P}$ and $\bar{Q}$, respectively.
- FEAT [36] aims to learn a task-specific embedding space to tailor discriminative visual knowledge for a target task. They propose implementing embedding adaption using a set-to-set function and instantiating it using a transformer. In the transformed embedding space, they apply the contrastive objective to make sure training instances are close to their class center than other centers.
- DMF [35] is the state-of-the-art representation-based method, which proposes to learn a novel dynamic meta-filter for more effective and efficient feature alignment in FSL. They dynamically sample a relevant neighbor for each feature position of few-shot input and further predict position-specific and channel-specific filter weights based on the sampled neighborhood to facilitate novel class recognition. This formulation can better capture the position-based semantic context of the few-shot example and thus enjoys better dynamical knowledge adaptation for FSL.
- ConEMB [13] is the state-of-the-art similarity & representation-based method, which repurposes the contrastive learning to learn a better few-shot embedding model. They propose a contrastive training scheme to exploit the patch-wise relationship to explore enough dis criminative information for few samples.
- Neg-cosine [12] is the most similar work to our method, which also aims to increase the intra-class distribution on base classes to improve the few-shot performance on novel classes. To achieve it, our method learns a wider similarity function. The similarity fairly works on all classes without special treatment for the ground-truth class in contrast to the negative-margin methods, which encourages the target logit to increase the similarity of samples from the same class. Besides, the negative-margin methods adopt the standard transfer learning paradigm while we employ the episode training mechanism.
- Conv4 is a pre-trained network, which is trained to classify the base classes using cross-entropy loss. It has no meta-train step, and we use it as a baseline to investigate the role of meta-learning for few-shot representation learning.

Investigation. To investigate the correlation between few-shot classification performance on novel classes and the structure of embedding space on base classes, we compare the 5-way 1-shot and 5-way 5-shot accuracy of different methods with the defined structural metrics on *mini*ImageNet. The observations on the two tasks are similar, and we detail the experiments on 5-way 1-shot tasks. Firstly, we train the above

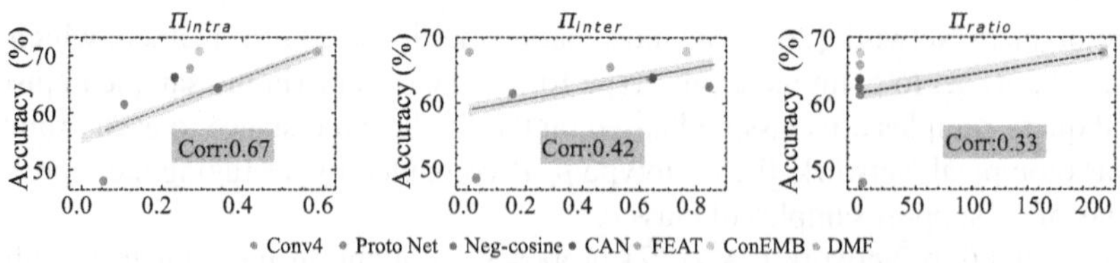

Fig. 2. Correlation between average accuracy of FSL tasks sampled from novel classes and structure of embedding spaces derived by training different FSL methods with base classes on *mini*ImageNet. Points with different colors represent different FSL methods. Left-to-Right: intra-class distances π_{intra}, interclass distances π_{inter}, and the ratio π_{ratio}.

seven methods using 64 base classes to obtain their feature extractors $f_\theta(\cdot)$. For Proto Net, CAN, and FEAT, we follow the original setting of FEAT. The initial learning rate is 0.0001, and we train 200 epochs, with each epoch consisting of 100 5-way 1-shot tasks. For DMF, InfoPatch, and Neg-cosine, we use the weights provided by them. Then, we calculate π_{inter}, π_{intra} and π_{ratio} for each method using all sample representations f_i from 64 base classes to measure the structural properties of their embedding spaces. Finally, we compute the average accuracy on 10000 sampled 5-way 1-shot tasks from 20 novel classes to evaluate the few-shot performance of different methods. Figure 2 shows the correlation between π_{inter}, π_{intra}, π_{ratio} and the average accuracy. Points with different colors represent different FSL methods. We can find that the inter-class distance (correlation coefficient 0.42) and ratio (correlation coefficient 0.33) barely exhibit a correlation with few-shot performance. However, an increased intra-class distance (correlation coefficient 0.67) is linked to more robust FSL performance. Specifically, the more scattered in-class samples in the base classes, the better performance of few-shot classification in novel classes. This observation is contrary to traditional metric learning methods that aim to find a discriminative embedding space by increasing the intra-class compactness, as shown in Fig. 1. Perhaps the training and evaluation datasets are labeled disjoint in FSL. Excessive compact representations embedding space for base classes make acquiring useful representations for novel classes more challenging. Similar observations have been found in other open-set scenarios. For example, [4] considers excessive intra-class feature compression may induce spurious class-specific patterns in the source domain, thereby failing to generalize to novel domains. [22] demonstrates that strong compressed representations can hurt the generalization ability in the deep metric learning setting. The findings confirm the correlation between the high-quality representation of FSL methods and a scatter-populated intra-class embedding space.

3.2 Intuitive Explanation

To better understand how these methods improve the few-shot performance by learning more scattered intra-class embedding space, we perform more analysis on three classic FSL methods (Proto Net, CAN, FEAT). The average intra-class distances π_{intra} on 64 base classes of the above methods are 0.0649, 0.1181, and 0.1590, respectively. The average accuracy on 10000 randomly selected 5-way 1-shot tasks from 20 novel

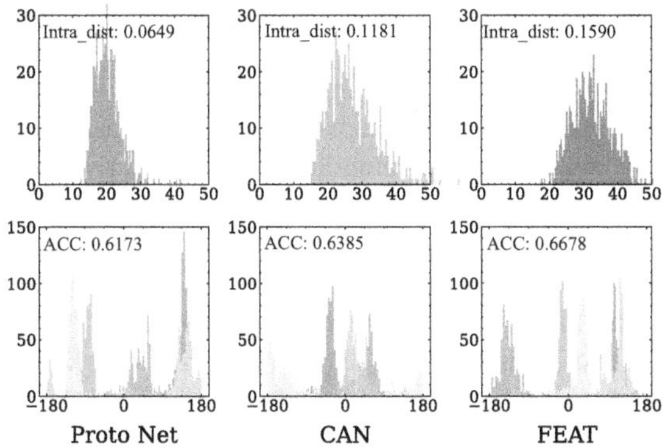

Fig. 3. The top row shows the visualizations of the distance distribution on a randomly selected base class with three different metric-based methods on *mini*ImageNet. Each subgraph is the histogram of the distance between the sample representation and its class center. The bottom row shows the visualizations of the angle distribution on five randomly selected novel classes with three different metric-based methods on *mini*ImageNet. Each subgraph is the histogram of the angle between the 2-d sample representation and a fixed vector $\boldsymbol{v} = (1, 0)$.

classes is 0.6173, 0.6385, and 0.6678, respectively. Figure 3 shows the distribution on a randomly selected base class and 5 randomly selected novel classes on *mini*ImageNet. The top row of Fig. 3 shows the histogram of the distance between sample representations and their class center. The dimensions of all the representations are 640. We can observe that with increasing few-shot performance (from left to right), the distance distributions of the selected base class are getting wider, shorter, and left-skewed. A wider distance distribution indicates the distance between samples and the class center varies widely, and a more left skewness distribution suggests more data points would lie in the space far from its center, which results in a greater intra-class distance. Additionally, a large intra-class distance somewhat scatters the output space, which improves the effectiveness of few-shot classification. As shown on the bottom row in Fig. 3, we first project the sample representations to 2-dimensional representations using tSNE [17]. Then, we visualize the angle distribution of the normalized representations and a fixed vector $\boldsymbol{v} = (1, 0)$ on five randomly selected novel classes. One can observe from left to right the boundaries between different classes become clearer. We conclude that enlarging the intra-class distance on the base class leads to a smaller intra-class variance and larger inter-class variance in the novel classes, facilitating the classification of novel classes.

4 Exploring a Scattered Embedding Space

We now exploit our above analysis to propose an effective method for a better transferrable embedding space for FSL. Our key idea is to learn a scattered embedding space by maximizing the intra-class distance in a hypersphere.

4.1 Controlling a Scattered Embedding Space via von Mises-Fisher Distribution

One direct technique to learn a scattered intra-class embedding space is to encourage intra-class variety by pushing away features of the same class, as done in [4]. However, in few-shot circumstances, the scattered distribution derived by such a method is limited due to the data insufficient problem. To address the above issue, we consider that few samples of the same class are not isolated in embedding space but are sampled from a high-dimensional distribution. Thus, we can adjust the dispersion of intra-class samples by controlling the distribution statistics. In this paper, we assume each class follows a von Mises-Fisher distribution [18], whose parameter κ is used to control the concentration of the distribution.

Von Mises-Fisher Distribution. The von Mises-Fisher (vMF) distribution is a probability distribution on the surface of a hypersphere. It is parameterized by a mean unit vector, μ, and isotropic concentration, κ. And it is an extension of the Gaussian distribution on the unit hypersphere. The μ and κ in vMF distribution can be regarded as the mean and variance in the Gaussian distribution. The probability density function for an n-dimensional unit vector x is:

$$p(x; \mu, \kappa) = C_n(\kappa) \exp(\kappa \mu^T x), \tag{4}$$

where I_v denotes the modified Bessel function of the first kind at order v, $C_n(\kappa) = \frac{\kappa^{n/2-1}}{(2\pi)^{n/2} I_{n/2-1}(\kappa)}$ is a normalization constant, x, $\mu \in S^{n-1}$, μ is a unit vector orienting the center of the distribution, $\kappa > 0$ is a parameter to control the concentration of the distribution to the vector μ. The greater the value of κ, the higher the concentration of the distribution around the mean direction μ.

Similarity Based on Von Mises-Fisher Distribution. In a few-shot classification task, we assume each class follows a vMF distribution, the mean direction μ is the normalized prototype $\bar{p}$ of each class in a hypersphere. Similar to Proto Net [26], each prototype p is the mean vector of the embedded support points belonging to its class. Then we project it onto the hypersphere through l_2 normalization.

The vMF distribution renders similarity between a normalized query f_q and the normalized prototype $\bar{p}$ in a probabilistic sense as follows:

$$p(f_q; \bar{p}, \kappa) = C_{(\kappa)} \exp(\kappa - \frac{1}{2}\kappa \parallel f_q - \bar{p} \parallel^2) = C'_{(\kappa)} f_e(\parallel f_q - \bar{p} \parallel; \kappa) \tag{5}$$

where $f_e(d; \kappa = \exp(-\frac{1}{2}\kappa d^2))$ is a profile function. Following [8] and ignoring the constant $C_n(\kappa)$, the vMF similarity between f_q and $\bar{p}$ can be characterized by $\exp(\kappa \cos\theta)$. Scaling it to compatible with $cos\theta \in [-1, 1]$, the vMF similarity between f_q and $\bar{p}$ is defined as follows:

$$\phi(\cos\theta; \kappa) = 2\frac{\exp(\kappa \cos\theta) - \exp(-\kappa)}{\exp(\kappa) - \exp(-\kappa)} - 1, \tag{6}$$

where $\cos\theta$ is the cosine similarity between f_q and $\bar{p}$. The κ in vMF similarity accepts various even including negative values, i.e. $\kappa \in (-\propto, 0) \cup (0, +\propto)$.

Properties of vMF Similarity. To better understand the vMF similarity function, Fig. 4 (a) shows the vMF similarity with different $\kappa > 0$. We can observe that by decreasing the parameter κ, the support region of the measuring function becomes wider. Thus, the vMF similarity with smaller κ would improve the within-class variance by orienting representations toward the prototype to gain larger similarity. Figure 4 (b) shows the intra-class distance with different κ on *mini*ImageNet, we can observe that smaller κ indeed induces a larger intra-class distance. This property effectively controls intra-class sparsity by selecting an appropriate κ. We set $\kappa = 1$ as a pre-defined parameter to obtain a scattered intra-class embedding space. We will discuss why we set $\kappa = 1$ rather than $\kappa \leq 0$ to expand the intra-class region in Sect. 5.3.

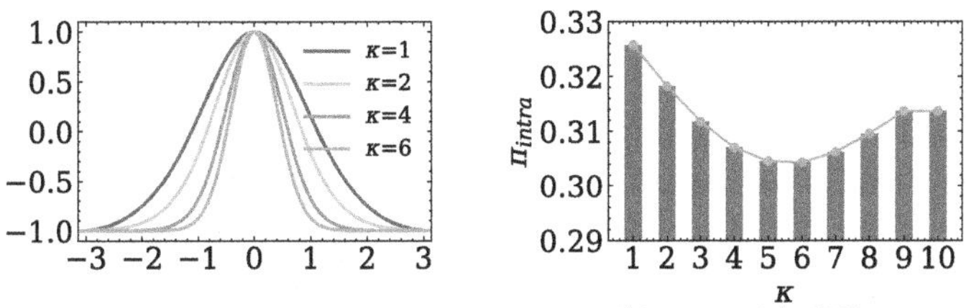

(a) vMF similarities (b) Π_{intra} with different κ

Fig. 4. Proposed vMF-based similarities.

vMF Loss. Based on the vMF similarity, the loss function for a scattered embedding space is defined as follows:

$$\mathcal{L}_{scatter}(f_q, y) = -\log \frac{\exp \phi(\frac{p_y^T f_q}{\|p_y\|\|f_q\|}; \kappa)}{\sum_{c=1}^{N} \exp \phi(\frac{p_c^T f_q}{\|p_c\|\|f_q\|}; \kappa)}. \tag{7}$$

Training proceeds by iteratively sampling episodes on base classes, and performing SGD updates using the $\mathcal{L}_{scatter}$ for each episode.

4.2 Discussion

Our vMF-based similarity loss function $\mathcal{L}_{scatter}$ is similar to cosine based cross-entropy loss function, which defines similarity based on the angular representation of features and weight vectors on the hypersphere as follows:

$$\mathcal{L}_{\cos} = \frac{1}{n} \sum_{i=1}^{n} \log \frac{e^{\cos \theta}}{e^{\cos \theta} + \sum_{j \neq 1, j \neq y_i} e^{\cos \theta_j}}. \tag{8}$$

In the past decades, many methods have been explored to improve the discriminative of the embedding space by introducing the large and positive margin parameter to the softmax loss [3,14,29,30]. A united framework by combining all of the margin penalties was implemented as follows:

$$\mathcal{L}_{m_{\cos}} = \frac{1}{n}\sum_{i=1}^{n} \log \frac{e^{s(\cos(m_1\theta_{y_i}+m_2)-m_3)}}{e^{s(\cos(m_1\theta_{y_i}+m_2)-m_3)} + \sum_{j\neq 1, j\neq y_i} e^{s\cos\theta_j}}, \tag{9}$$

where s is a scale parameter, $m_i \geq 0, i = 1, 2, 3$ are margin hyper-parameters for different kind of methods. The margins were used to enforce the intra-class compactness and inter-class diversity by penalizing the target logit [20]. These methods showed significant performance increases in traditional close-set scenarios, where training and evaluation datasets share the same label space. However, the situation is different in the FSL scenarios. [12] discovered that adding the positive margin in softmax loss would degrade the few-shot performance and proposes using negative-margin m_3 instead.

Both the negative margin and our method improve the FSL performance by learning a more scattered intra-class distribution. To achieve it, our method learns a wider similarity function to form a more scattered intra-class distribution.

5 Experiments

5.1 Experiment Setup

Datasets: The proposed method is evaluated on two widely-used few-shot classification benchmarks: ***Mini*ImageNet** dataset contains 100 classes randomly chosen from ILSVRC-12 [23] and 600 images of size 84 × 84 pixels per class. We follow the splits used in previous works [21], which divides the dataset into 64, 16, and 20 classes for training, validation, and testing, respectively. ***Tiered*ImageNet** is a larger subset of ILSVRC-12 dataset [23] with 608 classes. Following [21], the classes are firstly grouped into 34 higher-level categories and thus have a hierarchical structure. Then they are divided into 20 training categories (351 classes), 6 validation categories (97 classes), and 8 testing categories (160 classes).

Implementation Details: Our method is based on an episodic training mechanism. All experiments are conducted around the N-way K-shot classification task. The backbone we use throughout the paper is ResNet-12, which is widely used in FSL. As is commonly implemented in the state-of-the-art literature [36,37], we adopt a feature pre-training step followed by the episodic meta-training to learn our network. The pre-training stage is a normal 64-way classification task with cross-entropy loss. During meta-training, we randomly sample and construct 300000 episodes to train all of our models by employing the episodic training mechanism. In each episode, there are K support samples and 15 query images in each class. We adopt the proposed vMF loss and the SGD algorithm with an initial learning rate of $1e-2$ to train our model. For the hyper-parameters in our method, we set $\kappa = 1$. At the evaluation stage, we crop each image 7 times following [16,37]. We use accuracy as the evaluation metric to measure the performance of our method. The reported results are the averaged classification accuracy over 10,000 tasks randomly selected on novel classes.

5.2 Comparisons with the State-of-the-Art Methods

As we focus on metric-based FSL methods, several representative methods from three categories (similarity-based methods (S), representation-based methods (R), and similarity & representation-based methods (SR)) are selected for comparison. The results of these methods are cited from their original paper or the few-shot classification leaderboard[1] which tracks the state-of-the-art (SOTA) FSL methods.

Table 1. 5-way 1-shot and 5-way 5-shot classification accuracy (%) on *mini*ImageNet and *tiered*ImageNet with 95% confidence intervals. The best results are marked in bold. (†: Reproduced with our setting, -: not available)

Methods	Type	Backbone	***mini*ImageNet**		***tiered*ImageNet**	
			5-way 1-shot	**5-way 5-shot**	**5-way 1-shot**	**5-way 5-shot**
Relation Net [27]	S	conv4	50.44 ± 0.82	65.32 ± 0.70	54.48 ± 0.93	71.32 ± 0.78
Neg-Cosine [12]	S	ResNet-12	63.68 ± 0.86	82.02 ± 0.57	-	-
Deep EMD [37]	S	ResNet-12	65.91 ± 0.82	82.41 ± 0.56	71.16 ± 0.87	86.03 ± 0.50
Meat DeepBDC [32]	S	ResNet-12	67.34 ± 0.43	82.38 ± 0.32	*72.34 ± 0.49*	*87.31 ± 0.32*
Matching Net [28]	R	ResNet-12	63.08 ± 0.80	75.99 ± 0.60	68.50 ± 0.92	80.60 ± 0.71
Proto Net [26] †	R	ResNet-12	61.73 ± 0.20	78.02 ± 0.57	66.65 ± 0.92	82.40 ± 0.65
AM3 [33]	R	ResNet-12	65.30 ± 0.49	78.10 ± 0.36	69.08 ± 0.47	82.58 ± 0.31
CAN [7]	R	ResNet-12	63.85 ± 0.48	79.44 ± 0.34	69.89 ± 0.51	84.23 ± 0.37
FEAT [36]	R	ResNet-12	66.78 ± 0.20	82.05 ± 0.14	70.80 ± 0.23	84.79 ± 0.16
Infopatch [13]	R	ResNet-12	67.67 ± 0.45	82.44 ± 0.31	71.51 ± 0.52	85.44 ± 0.35
TADAM [19]	SR	ResNet-12	58.50 ± 0.30	76.70 ± 0.30	62.13 ± 0.31	81.92 ± 0.30
DMF [35]	SR	ResNet-12	*67.76 ± 0.46*	82.71 ± 0.31	71.89 ± 0.52	85.96 ± 0.35
DMN4 [15]	SR	ResNet-12	66.58	*83.52*	72.10	85.72
vMF loss	S	ResNet-12	**68.34 ± 0.20**	**84.31 ± 0.40**	**72.60 ± 0.71**	**87.85 ± 0.53**

Table 1 shows the comparison of 5-way 1-shot and 5-shot classification tasks on *mini*ImageNet and *tiered*ImageNet. We have the following observations: 1) Our vMF loss outperforms the SOTA FSL methods, indicating the effectiveness of the proposed method. Besides, our method is simple. Although Meat DeepBDC achieves competitive performance with our method, it needs to estimate the second moments of the feature distribution, which leads to a quadratic increase of representations. Our vMF loss can capture the second moments of the von Mises-Fisher distribution by setting a proper isotropic concentration κ. 2) Compared with the Proto Net, the accuracy improvement of our method on two datasets (1-shot tasks and 5-shot tasks) are 6.01%, 5.96%, and 6.29%, 5.45%, respectively. We attribute the accuracy gain on the prototype network to the more scattered embedding space owning to the main difference between our method and the Proto Net is that we learn a scattered embedding space using vMF similarity instead of Euclidean distance.

[1] FSL leaderboard: https://fewshot.org/miniimagenet.html,.

Table 2. 5-way 1-shot and 5-way 5-shot cross domain classification accuracy (%) on *mini*ImageNet → CUB scenario. G-FSL represents general few-shot learning methods and CD-FSL denotes cross-domain few-shot learning methods.(† : Reproduced with our setting, ∗ : the result reported in [10])

Method	Type	1-shot	5-shot
Proto Net(Snell et al. 2017)†	G-FSL	42.65	60.48
FEAT [36]†	G-FSL	42.32	61.99
TPN+ATA (Wang et al. 2021) ∗	CD-FSL	50.26	65.31
RDC-FT [10] ∗	CD-FSL	**51.20**	67.77
vMF Loss	G-FSL	49.27	**68.12**

To further demonstrate the effectiveness of our vMF Loss by learning a better embedding space for transfer, we perform experiments on a cross-domain FSL task where models are trained on *mini*Imagenet and evaluated on the CUB dataset following [2]. We compare our method with two representative general FSL methods (G-FSL) and two state-of-the-art cross-domain FSL methods (CD-FSL). The ranking distance calibration (RDC) [10] aimed to calibrate the biased distances in CD-FSL due to the domain gap and disjoint label spaces between source and target datasets. TPN+ATA [31] considered the worst-case problem around the source task distribution, and proposed an adaptive task augmentation method to improve the robustness of the inductive bias.

Table 2 shows the accuracy of different methods on 5-way 1-shot and 5-way 5-shot cross-domain few-shot classification tasks. We can observe our method can achieve 0.7 pp higher accuracy than general FSL methods on both 1-shot and 5-shot circumstances, which demonstrates a more scattered intra-class embedding space is more suitable for transfer. Compared with the CD-FSL methods, our vMF loss can achieve competitive performance on the 1-shot task and better performance on the 5-shot task. The reason perhaps learning the distribution becomes challenging when there is only one sample.

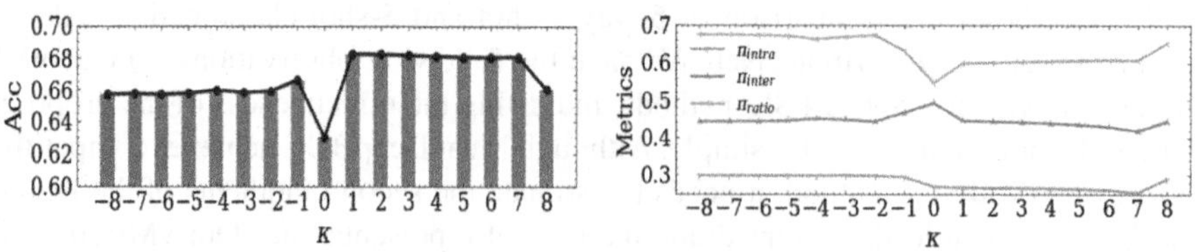

Fig. 5. The 5-way 1-shot accuracy on novel classes and the structure metrics of the embedding space on base classes with varying κ on *mini*ImageNet.

5.3 Model Analysis

Effects of κ . In this section, we investigate how κ affects the few-shot performance on novel classes by changing the structural property of the learned embedding space on novel classes. Figure 5 shows the 5-way 1-shot accuracy on novel classes and the structure metrics of the embedding space on base classes with varying κ on *mini*ImageNet. We can observe: 1) The model with $\kappa > 0$ and $\kappa < 0$ have different impacts on the FSL performance. Smaller κ improve the performance when $\kappa > 0$ while smaller κ degrades the performance when $\kappa > 0$. 2) When $\kappa > 0$, both the intra-class distance and inter-class distance increase as the κ decrease . The κ value has little effect on the inter-class distance and intra-class distance When $\kappa < -2$. 3) The model with $\kappa > 0$ has better few-shot performance than $\kappa < 0$ and the best few-shot performance achieves when $\kappa = 1$. The reason perhaps a more scattered embedding space by setting smaller $\kappa > 0$ can improve the ability of generalization on novel classes. However, enhancing intra-class distance by setting smaller $\kappa < 0$ may lead to the heavy overlap between different classes, which in contrast damages the generalization performance.

Learning with Different Backbone Networks. We compare our method with the Proto Net to show the effectiveness of our method with different backbones. From Table 3, our vMF loss can consistently increase accuracy with various backbones compared with the Proto Net. Besides, a better representation learning backbone can facilitate the following classification task with our vMF loss. We can combine existing high-quality representation learning with our vMF loss to improve the few-shot performance.

Table 3. 5-way 1-shot and 5-way 5-shot classification accuracy (%) on *mini*ImageNet with different backbones.

Tasks	5-way 1-shot		5-way 5-shot	
Methods	**Proto Net**	**vMF loss**	**Proto Net**	**vMF loss**
covn4	47.78	**52.65**	65.92	**66.60**
conv6	50.20	**54.42**	70.28	**71.24**
resnet12	61.36	**68.34**	80.10	**84.31**
resnet18	62.24	**68.51**	81.88	**84.77**

6 Conclusion and Future Work

Few-shot image classification benefits from designing a more complex representation learning network, but little attention has been focused on why they work. In this paper, we shed new light on understanding the above problem by exploring the structure of the embedding space. We find that better representation learning methods lead to a scattered embedding space for base classes, which further improves the generalization of novel classes. Based on the above observation, we introduce von Mises-Fisher distribution and employ a vMF loss to learn a more transferrable embedding space for FSL by controlling the intra-class diversity via parameter κ. Experiments on two widely used datasets demonstrate the effectiveness of our method. Our method is simple but effective by setting a fixed κ for all classes. It is only one possible solution, and we hope our observations are useful to guide future FSL research. Future research may involve adaptively determining the dispersion for various classes. In addition, more technologies to increase the intra-class distance can be investigated for FSL.

Acknowledgments. This work was partly supported by the Fundamental Research Funds for the Central Universities (2019JBZ110); the Beijing Natural Science Foundation under Grant L211016; the National Natural Science Foundation of China under Grant 62176020; the National Key Research and Development Program (2020AAA0106800); and Chinese Academy of Sciences (OEIP-O-202004).

Ethical Statement. The authors declare that they have no conflict of interest. All procedures performed in studies involving human participants were by the ethical standards of the institutional and national research committees. This article does not contain any studies with animals performed by any of the authors. Informed consent was obtained from all individual participants included in the study.

References

1. Bateni, P., Goyal, R., Masrani, V., Wood, F., Sigal, L.: Improved few-shot visual classification. In: Proceedings of the IEEE/CVF Conference on Computer Vision and Pattern Recognition, pp. 14493–14502 (2020)
2. Chen, W.Y., Liu, Y.C., Kira, Z., Wang, Y.C.F., Huang, J.B.: A closer look at few-shot classification. In: International Conference on Learning Representations (2019)
3. Deng, J., Guo, J., Xue, N., Zafeiriou, S.: Arcface: additive angular margin loss for deep face recognition. In: Proceedings of the IEEE/CVF Conference on Computer Vision and Pattern Recognition, pp. 4690–4699 (2019)
4. Duboudin, T., Dellandréa, E., Abgrall, C., Hénaff, G., Chen, L.: Encouraging intra-class diversity through a reverse contrastive loss for single-source domain generalization. In: Proceedings of the IEEE/CVF International Conference on Computer Vision, pp. 51–60 (2021)
5. Hao, F., He, F., Cheng, J., Wang, L., Cao, J., Tao, D.: Collect and select: Semantic alignment metric learning for few-shot learning. In: Proceedings of the IEEE/CVF International Conference on Computer Vision, pp. 8460–8469 (2019)
6. He, K., Zhang, X., Ren, S., Sun, J.: Deep residual learning for image recognition. In: Proceedings of the IEEE Conference on Computer Vision and Pattern Recognition, pp. 770–778 (2016)
7. Hou, R., Chang, H., Ma, B., Shan, S., Chen, X.: Cross attention network for few-shot classification. In: Advances in Neural Information Processing Systems 32 (2019)
8. Kobayashi, T.: T-vmf similarity for regularizing intra-class feature distribution. In: Proceedings of the IEEE/CVF Conference on Computer Vision and Pattern Recognition, pp. 6616–6625 (2021)
9. Krizhevsky, A., Sutskever, I., Hinton, G.E.: Imagenet classification with deep convolutional neural networks. Adv. Neural. Inf. Process. Syst. **25**, 1097–1105 (2012)
10. Li, P., Gong, S., Wang, C., Fu, Y.: Ranking distance calibration for cross-domain few-shot learning. In: Proceedings of the IEEE/CVF Conference on Computer Vision and Pattern Recognition, pp. 9099–9108 (2022)
11. Li, W., Wang, L., Xu, J., Huo, J., Gao, Y., Luo, J.: Revisiting local descriptor based image-to-class measure for few-shot learning. In: Proceedings of the IEEE/CVF Conference on Computer Vision and Pattern Recognition, pp. 7260–7268 (2019)

12. Liu, B., et al.: Negative margin matters: understanding margin in few-shot classification. In: Vedaldi, A., Bischof, H., Brox, T., Frahm, J.-M. (eds.) ECCV 2020. LNCS, vol. 12349, pp. 438–455. Springer, Cham (2020). https://doi.org/10.1007/978-3-030-58548-8_26
13. Liu, C., et al.: Learning a few-shot embedding model with contrastive learning. In: Proceedings of the AAAI Conference on Artificial Intelligence, vol. 35, pp. 8635–8643 (2021)
14. Liu, W., Wen, Y., Yu, Z., Li, M., Raj, B., Song, L.: Sphereface: deep hypersphere embedding for face recognition. In: Proceedings of the IEEE Conference on Computer Vision and Pattern Recognition. pp. 212–220 (2017)
15. Liu, Y., Zheng, T., Song, J., Cai, D., He, X.: Dmn4: Few-shot learning via discriminative mutual nearest neighbor neural network. In: Proceedings of the AAAI Conference on Artificial Intelligence. vol. 36, pp. 1828–1836 (2022)
16. Luo, X., et al.: Rectifying the shortcut learning of background for few-shot learning. In: Advances in Neural Information Processing Systems 34 (2021)
17. Van der Maaten, L., Hinton, G.: Visualizing data using t-sne. J. Machine Learning Res. **9**(11) (2008)
18. Mardia, K., Jupp, P.: Directional statistics. John Willey and Sons Inc., Chichester (2000)
19. Oreshkin, B., Rodríguez López, P., Lacoste, A.: Tadam: task dependent adaptive metric for improved few-shot learning. In: Advances in Neural Information Processing Systems 31 (2018)
20. Pereyra, G., Tucker, G., Chorowski, J., Kaiser, Ł., Hinton, G.: Regularizing neural networks by penalizing confident output distributions. arXiv preprint arXiv:1701.06548 (2017)
21. Ravi, S., Larochelle, H.: Optimization as a model for few-shot learning. In: International Conference on Learning Representations (ICLR) (2017)
22. Roth, K., Milbich, T., Sinha, S., Gupta, P., Ommer, B., Cohen, J.P.: Revisiting training strategies and generalization performance in deep metric learning. In: International Conference on Machine Learning, pp. 8242–8252. PMLR (2020)
23. Russakovsky, O., et al.: Imagenet large scale visual recognition challenge. Int. J. Comput. Vision **115**(3), 211–252 (2015)
24. Singhal, A., et al.: Modern information retrieval: A brief overview. IEEE Data Eng. Bull. **24**(4), 35–43 (2001)
25. Smith, K.J.: Precalculus: a functional approach to graphing and problem solving. Jones & Bartlett Publishers (2011)
26. Snell, J., Swersky, K., Zemel, R.S.: Prototypical networks for few-shot learning. In: Advances in Neural Information Processing Systems (2017)
27. Sung, F., Yang, Y., Zhang, L., Xiang, T., Torr, P.H., Hospedales, T.M.: Learning to compare: relation network for few-shot learning. In: Proceedings of the IEEE Conference on Computer Vision and Pattern Recognition, pp. 1199–1208 (2018)
28. Vinyals, O., Blundell, C., Lillicrap, T., Wierstra, D., et al.: Matching networks for one shot learning. Adv. Neural. Inf. Process. Syst. **29**, 3630–3638 (2016)
29. Wang, F., Cheng, J., Liu, W., Liu, H.: Additive margin softmax for face verification. IEEE Signal Process. Lett. **25**(7), 926–930 (2018)
30. Wang, H., et al.: Cosface: large margin cosine loss for deep face recognition. In: Proceedings of the IEEE Conference on Computer Vision and Pattern Recognition, pp. 5265–5274 (2018)
31. Wang, H., Deng, Z.H.: Cross-domain few-shot classification via adversarial task augmentation. arXiv preprint arXiv:2104.14385 (2021)
32. Xie, J., Long, F., Lv, J., Wang, Q., Li, P.: Joint distribution matters: Deep brownian distance covariance for few-shot classification. In: Proceedings of the IEEE/CVF Conference on Computer Vision and Pattern Recognition, pp. 7972–7981 (2022)
33. Xing, C., Rostamzadeh, N., Oreshkin, B., O Pinheiro, P.O.: Adaptive cross-modal few-shot learning. In: Advances in Neural Information Processing Systems 32 (2019)

34. Xing, E.P., Ng, A.Y., Jordan, M.I., Russell, S.: Distance metric learning, with application to clustering with side-information. In: Advances in Neural Information Processing Systems 15 (2003)
35. Xu, C., et al.: Learning dynamic alignment via meta-filter for few-shot learning. In: Proceedings of the IEEE/CVF Conference on Computer Vision and Pattern Recognition, pp. 5182–5191 (2021)
36. Ye, H.J., Hu, H., Zhan, D.C., Sha, F.: Few-shot learning via embedding adaptation with set-to-set functions. In: Proceedings of the IEEE/CVF Conference on Computer Vision and Pattern Recognition, pp. 8808–8817 (2020)
37. Zhang, C., Cai, Y., Lin, G., Shen, C.: Deepemd: few-shot image classification with differentiable earth mover's distance and structured classifiers. In: Proceedings of the IEEE/CVF Conference on Computer Vision and Pattern Recognition, pp. 12203–12213 (2020)

Meta-HRNet: A High Resolution Network for Coarse-to-Fine Few-Shot Classification

Zhaochen Li(✉) and Kedian Mu

School of Mathematical Sciences, Peking University, Beijing, China
zhaochenli@pku.edu.cn, mukedian@math.pku.edu.cn

Abstract. Fine-grained classification has achieved success with the application of deep learning on large datasets. However, in practical scenarios, fine-grained categories often suffer from a lack of training data due to the difficulty of labeling. Leveraging accessible coarse-grained labeled data provides a promising way to alleviate this challenge, that is, the model learns from a large number of coarse-grained labeled data to perform better on fine-grained classification. In this paper, we focus on this coarse-to-fine few-shot problem and attribute the difficulty of this problem to two factors: the undistinguishable appearance of fine-grained images and the lack of fine-grained training samples. To address the first factor, we demonstrate that high-resolution features can capture more distinctive details that are useful for fine-grained classification tasks. Thus, we construct an improved high-resolution network called Meta-HRNet to capture rich details and filter the crucial detailed information for fine-grained classification. To address the second factor, we train the model by a two-step strategy that combines supervised training and episodic training. During the first training stage, the backbone of Meta-HRNet is optimized to obtain a basic ability of detailed representation. In the second stage, the attention module of the Meta-HRNet is trained to learn and sift key details given a low number of training samples. The effectiveness of our model is verified on four datasets. Experimental results demonstrate that the attention paid to the important details of images contributes to improving the performance of fine-grained classification tasks.

Keywords: fine-grained classification · few-shot learning · high-resolution representation · machine learning

1 Introduction

Fine-grained image classification is a challenging yet significant problem in the field of computer vision. It aims to distinguish samples at the subordinary level of one or more categories. The most challenging difficulty of this problem is learning distinctive features to identify objects with similar appearances. Previous research on deep network-based approaches has been successful in extracting the features of subtle variations after learning from a large fine-grained dataset [28]. However, in practical situations, the number of fine-grained labels of data is often

© The Author(s), under exclusive license to Springer Nature Switzerland AG 2023
D. Koutra et al. (Eds.): ECML PKDD 2023, LNAI 14170, pp. 471–487, 2023.
https://doi.org/10.1007/978-3-031-43415-0_28

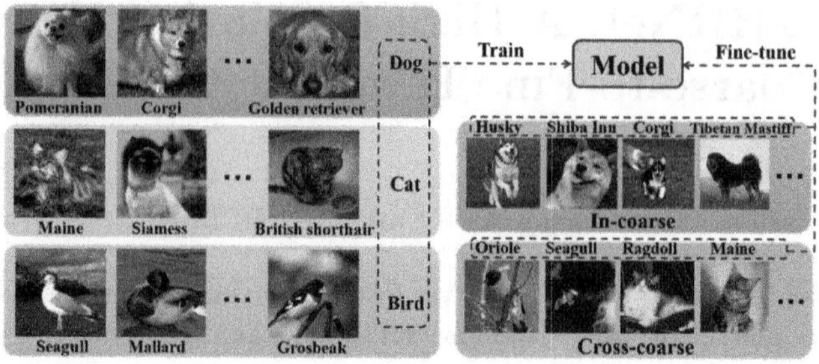

Fig. 1. Training and support data in coarse-to-fine few-shot problem.

insufficient due to the high acquisition cost. In contrast, the acquisition of coarse-grained labels is easier. Allowing for this, the so-called coarse-to-fine few-shot problem (C2FS) proposed by Bukchin et al. [2] aims to solve the fine-grained few-shot classification tasks by leveraging a huge set of coarse-grained labeled data referred to as the base dataset. As Fig. 1 shows, the model is required to learn from images with coarse-grained labels to obtain the ability to distinguish fine-grained samples of the same super-class (in-coarse) or different super-classes (cross-coarse).

The challenges of C2FS problem can be summarized as (i) the over-fitting risk of few-shot learning caused by insufficient samples and (ii) difficulty in feature extraction for fine-grained categories. Concerning the first challenge, many researchers in few-shot learning have made considerable achievements. According to the different training strategies on the base dataset, most few-shot methods can be divided into (i) *Meta-learning based methods* that apply the episodic training strategy to quickly adjust the network parameters to the optimal state of a given few-shot task, and (ii) *Transfer learning based methods* that apply the supervised or self-supervised strategy to learn a strong backbone network, which is directly used to extract features for a given few-shot task. Bukchin et al. [2] proposed the Angular Normalized Contrastive Regularization (ANCOR) to overcome the challenge of insufficient samples from the perspective of transfer learning. However, like other transfer learning-based methods [4,18,22], this model froze the feature extractor when encountering the downstream tasks. This makes the feature extractor unable to make adjustments based on the information of downstream tasks, which limits the flexibility of the network. For the second challenge, it ignored the impact of the network structure on fine-grained feature extraction. In this paper, we take both the network structure and training strategy into consideration to better solve the two challenges of C2FS problem.

Most methods tackled the challenge of fine-grained feature exaction by designing complicated network structures [1,12,30]. These methods focus on how to capture critical parts on the basis of existing information, rather than how to extract and retain richer information for screening. Cui et al. [7] systematically studied the effect of image resolution on fine-grained visual categorization and concluded that images with higher resolutions contain richer details that are important for fine-grained classification tasks. Many works also verified that the high-resolution features can bring more crucial detailed information to improve the performance of the model [20,24,29]. In this paper, we theoretically analyze the effectiveness of high-resolution features for fine-grained classification tasks. Then we propose Meta-HRNet which consists of a high-resolution backbone to extract and retain rich detailed information and an ideal channel attention network module (AttnNet) to filter the important details for the downstream task.

For the challenge of insufficient samples, we combine the presentation ability of the transfer learning-based few-shot methods and the flexibility of the meta-learning-based few-shot methods inspired by Meta-baseline [6] which is a simple but effective training framework. Our strategy consists of two training stages. The first stage is a supervised training procedure, and the second stage is an episodic training procedure. At the first stage, only the high-resolution backbone is trained to obtain a basic presentation ability. At the second stage, the AttnNet is added to the backbone and the whole feature extractor is trained by the episodic strategy to obtain the adaptive adjustment ability for any downstream few-shot tasks.

Experiments show that our model can promote the classification accuracy of C2FS problem by 3.1% on some datasets. We also visually verified that the features extracted from different branches of the HRNet backbone are effective even if they are trained by coarse-grained data.

The main contributions of this paper are as follows:

1. We provide a theoretical explanation for the relationship between fine-grained classification tasks and feature resolution, and conclude that high-resolution features can capture more useful details for fine-grained classification tasks.
2. We propose an improved high-resolution network with an ideal channel attention module trained by a two-step strategy which enables the model to learn basic representation skills from a large amount of coarse-grained data and quickly adjust the attention module based on a small amount of fine-grained data.
3. Experiments verify that Meta-HRNet achieves appreciable achievements on the coarse-to-fine few-shot problem on four datasets. Visualization experiments verifies that the effectiveness of the model lies in retaining and filtering the useful details for each task.

2 Related Work

The relevant fields of this paper include few-shot learning and fine-grained classificaton.

2.1 Few-Shot Learning

There are two important issues in few-shot learning: one is how to obtain discriminative feature representations, the other is what strategy to be used to train a powerful model. For the first issue, approaches based on ProtoNet [23] are devoted to improving the quality of the prototypes [10,26,27], and transfer learning based methods are dedicated to training a powerful feature extractor [19]. With the emergence of contrastive learning, self-supervised few-shot learning has achieved outstanding results. For example, Li et al. [14] took advantage of the powerful clustering ability of contrastive learning to solve the semi-supervised few-shot problem. Bukchin et al. [2] improved MoCoV2 [5] and put forward an effective self-supervised model for C2FS problem. In addition, some researchers began to focus on the correlation between contrastive learning and meta-learning and provided further improvements on meta-learning algorithms [11,16]. Recently, Luo et al. [15] studied the important role of feature channels in few-shot learning. They found that a simple feature transformation can significantly improve the generalization ability of few-shot models, which inspires us to further generalize the channel-wise feature transformation.

For the second issue, the episodic training strategy proposed by Finn et al. [9] is widely used to train a model that can be quickly adjusted to a suitable state for a new task. Some researches show that combining episodic learning strategy with other learning strategies can bring significant improvement. For example, Meta-Baseline [6] simply combined supervised learning stage and meta-learning stage and achieved notable improvement. Then Done et al. [8] applied this two-stage training strategy to train a few-shot vision transformer model. Oh et al. [17] made a profound study on self-supervised strategy, supervised strategy and corresponding mixed-supervised strategy for cross-domain few-shot learning. The experiments show that the two-step strategy, first supervised learning and then mix-supervised learning, has advantages over any single one. Inspired by these works, this paper adopts a two-stage training approach to combine the superiorities of ANCOR [2] and meta-learning.

2.2 Fine-Grained Classification

Fine-grained classification problem is more difficult than conventional classification problem because of the slight differences among samples of different categories. To capture the slight differences, some methods design various attention modules to learn distinctive feature vectors on a large fine-grained labeled dataset. Behera et al. [1] designed a context-aware attention module to effectively captures subtle changes among different categories. Zhu et al. [30] and Lee et al. [13] integrated complex attention modules with meta-learning methods to solve fine-grained few-shot problems. Furthermore, there are other approaches to solve the problem by using a generative model to obtain decoupling features [12]. In fact, one of the premises of these methods is that the network should retain rich information so that it can be located by various attention modules. Zhu et al. [29] verified the data resolution matters classification results, which inspired us to solve it from the perspective of feature resolution.

In the practical scenario, it is difficult to obtain a large amount of fine-grained labeled data to solve fine-grained few-shot tasks. Allowing for this, some attempts to incorporate coarse-grained labeled data in fine-grained learning tasks have been made recently. Yang et al. [25] applied a well-trained model to assign pseudo fine-grained labels to the coarse-grained data. This method directly alleviates the shortage of samples but the effect is limited. Bukchin et al. [2] made use of the representational power of contrastive learning to train a strong feature extractor. To address the challenge of fine-grained feature extraction, they introduced a novel intra-category contrastive loss function. Then they employed both inter-category supervised and intra-category contrastive losses to prevent samples within the same coarse-grained category from gathering together. This approach enabled the fine-grained samples in downstream task to obtain distinguishable feature representations.

3 Preliminaries

In this section, we provide the formalization of the coarse-to-fine few-shot problem, and illustrate the relationship between the fine-grained classification tasks and high-resolution features.

3.1 Coarse-to-Fine Few-Shot Problem

In the training stage, the base dataset is denoted by $\mathcal{D}^{coarse} = \{(X, Y)|Y \in \mathcal{Y}^{coarse}\}$, where $\mathcal{Y}^{coarse}$ is the space of coarse-grained labels. In the testing stage, each task $\mathcal{T}$ sampled from $\mathcal{D}^{fine} = \{(X, Y)|Y \in \mathcal{Y}^{fine}\}$ consists of a support set $\mathcal{T}^s = \{(X^s, Y^s)|Y^s \in \mathcal{Y}^{fine}\}$ and a query set $\mathcal{T}^q = \{(X^q, Y^q)|Y^q \in \mathcal{Y}^{fine}\}$, where $\mathcal{Y}^{fine}$ is the sub-class label space of $\mathcal{Y}^{coarse}$. As with other works in few-shot learning, the testing tasks are K-way N-shot, where K is the number of categories and N is the number of samples in each category. This paper provides two scenarios for testing. One is sampling from the sub-classes of all coarse-grained categories (the cross-coarse case), and the other is sampling from the sub-classes of one coarse-grained category (the in-coarse case).

3.2 High Resolution Feature Maps

Intuitively, the high-resolution feature maps in the convolution network can retain detailed information of images, which contributes to fine-grained classification tasks. Suppose that the shape of feature map F with C channels is $C \times H \times H$ and $F_{l,i,j}$ is the element of F. Then the global average pooling function on the feature map can be written as

$$\boldsymbol{z}_l = \frac{1}{H^2} \sum_{i,j} F_{l,i,j}, \quad l = 1, 2, ..., C. \tag{1}$$

Suppose that $F_{l,i,j} \sim (\mu_{l,i,j}, \sigma^2_{l,i,j})$ and is bounded by $[a, b]$. We denote $\mathbb{E}[z_l] = \frac{1}{H^2} \sum_{i,j} \mu_{l,i,j}$ as μ_l and $\boldsymbol{\mu} = (\mu_1, \mu_2, ..., \mu_C)^T$. Consider the binary classification problem, $\mu_l^{(1)} \neq \mu_l^{(2)}$ and the criteria is $\|\boldsymbol{z}^{(1)} - \boldsymbol{\mu}^{(1)}\|^2 < \|\boldsymbol{z}^{(1)} - \boldsymbol{\mu}^{(2)}\|^2$ and

$\|\boldsymbol{z}^{(2)} - \boldsymbol{\mu}^{(2)}\|^2 < \|\boldsymbol{z}^{(2)} - \boldsymbol{\mu}^{(1)}\|^2$, where $\|\cdot\|$ is l_2-norm. Due to the symmetry, we take the first category as an example. Then the classification error is defined as

$$\mathcal{E} = P_{\boldsymbol{z}^{(1)}}(\|\boldsymbol{z}^{(1)} - \boldsymbol{\mu}^{(1)}\|^2 \geq \|\boldsymbol{z}^{(1)} - \boldsymbol{\mu}^{(2)}\|^2). \tag{2}$$

According to Hoeffding Inequality, Eq. (2) satisfies the following inequality

$$\mathcal{E} \leq \exp(-\frac{H^2}{2(b-a)^2} \frac{(\sum_{i=1}^{C}(\boldsymbol{\mu}_l^{(2)} - \boldsymbol{\mu}_l^{(1)})^2)^2}{(\sum_{l=1}^{C}(\boldsymbol{\mu}_l^{(2)} - \boldsymbol{\mu}_l^{(1)}))^2}). \tag{3}$$

Then we apply the Cauchy Inequality to Eq. (3) and obtain the upper bound as follows

$$\mathcal{E} \leq \exp(-\frac{H^2}{2C(b-a)^2} \sum_{l=1}^{C}(\boldsymbol{\mu}_l^{(2)} - \boldsymbol{\mu}_l^{(1)})^2). \tag{4}$$

For the convenience of analysis, we define the difference between the two categories $\text{Dist}_{(1),(2)}$ as $\sum_{l=1}^{C}(\boldsymbol{\mu}_l^{(2)} - \boldsymbol{\mu}_l^{(1)})^2$. Then upper bound of Eq. (4) can be written as $\exp(-\frac{H^2}{2C(b-a)^2}\text{Dist}_{(1),(2)})$. For fine-grained classification tasks, the difference between two categories is relatively small, that is, the value of $\text{Dist}_{(1),(2)}$ tends to be small and the upper bound of classification error tends to be large. To control the upper bound of the error, the value of H, representing the resolution of the feature map, can be increased to mitigate this tendency. Thus, it can be concluded that high-resolution feature maps are beneficial for fine-grained classification tasks.

4 Meta-HRNet

Our model is constructed based on ANCOR [2] and HRNet [24]. In this section, we introduce the model structure and our training strategy. We start with the framework of Meta-HRNet.

4.1 Framework

As shown in Fig. 2 (a), the architecture of Meta-HRNet consists of a four-branch HRNet backbone ψ and a channel attention module ϕ. The HRNet generates branches (the rows shown in Fig. 2(a)) progressively at each stage (shown as gray blocks in Fig. 2(a)).

Before the first stage of ψ, the image X is computed by two convolution layers with kernel size 3 and stride 2. Then it is input to the first stage with four convolution blocks, and each block consists of three convolution layers. After each stage, the network generates an additional branch to obtain a series of lower resolution features. At the junction between two stages, branches are fused to exchange information of different resolutions. The fusion module includes upsampling followed by a 1×1 convolution, identity transformation and stride-2 3×3 convolution. After passing through four stages of HRNet, each image X

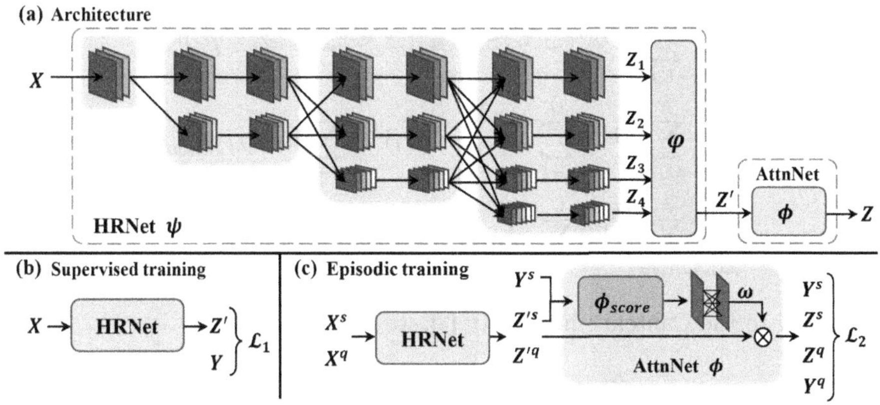

Fig. 2. Meta-HRNet. (a) The architecture of Meta-HRNet. (b) The first training stage is to train the HRNet backbone with supervised learning strategy. The result of this stage will be used as the initialization and regularization for the second stage. (c) The second training stage is to train the whole network with episodic training strategy.

will obtain four groups of feature maps $\{Z_1, Z_2, Z_3, Z_4\}$ with different sizes. The final representation used for classification is computed by $\{Z_1, Z_2, Z_3, Z_4\}$ with the head module φ.

The head module recursively fuses two adjacent branches. This process starts from the highest resolution branch Z_1. The fusion process proceeds as follows:

$$\begin{cases} Z' = \text{Incre}(Z_1), \\ Z' = \text{Down}(Z') + \text{Incre}(Z_i), i = 2, 3, 4 \end{cases} \tag{5}$$

where Incre(·) and Down(·) are convolution layes, Z' is the fused feature.

After fusing feature maps of with different resolutions, Z' contains more details of image X. To make the model focus on the information that is useful for the given task, we propose an ideal AttnNet φ to further optimize the representation Z'.

Suppose the representation of the i-th class samples satisfy $z_{i,l} \sim (\mu_{i,l}, \sigma_{i,l}^2)$, $\boldsymbol{z}_i = (z_{i,1}, z_{i,2}, ..., z_{i,C})^T$, $\boldsymbol{\mu}_i = (\mu_{i,1}, \mu_{i,2}, ..., \mu_{i,C})^T$ and the classificaion criteria of the attention module is $y_i = \arg\min_j \|\boldsymbol{\omega} \odot (\boldsymbol{z}_i - \boldsymbol{\mu}_j)\|^2$, where $\boldsymbol{\omega}$ is the weights added to the feature, $\odot$ is the Hadamard product. Then the classification error $\mathcal{R}$ satisfies

$$\begin{aligned}\mathcal{R} &< \sum_{i=1}^{K}\sum_{j=1,j\neq i}^{K} P_{\boldsymbol{z}_i}(\|\boldsymbol{\omega}\odot(\boldsymbol{z}_i-\boldsymbol{\mu}_j)\|^2 \leq \|\boldsymbol{\omega}\odot(\boldsymbol{z}_i-\boldsymbol{\mu}_i)\|^2)\\ &=\sum_{i=1}^{K}\sum_{j=1,j\neq i}^{K} P_{\boldsymbol{z}_i}(\sum_{l=1}^{C}\omega_l^2(z_{i,l}-\mu_{i,l})^2-\sum_{l=1}^{C}\omega_l^2(z_{i,l}-\mu_{j,l})^2\geq 0)\\ &=\sum_{i=1}^{K}\sum_{j=1,j\neq i}^{K} P_{\boldsymbol{z}_i}(\sum_{l=1}^{C}\omega_l^2(\mu_{j,l}-\mu_{i,1})(2z_{i,l}-\mu_{i,l}-\mu_{j,l})\geq 0).\end{aligned} \tag{6}$$

According to the Cantelli's inequality [3], we can reduce that

$$\begin{aligned}\mathcal{R} &< \sum_{i=1}^{K}\sum_{j=1,j\neq i}^{K} \frac{4\sum_{l=1}^{C}\omega_l^4(\mu_{j,l}-\mu_{i,l})^2\sigma_{i,l}^2}{(\sum_{l=1}^{C}\omega_l^2(\mu_{j,l}-\mu_{i,l})^2)^2}\\ &< \sum_{i=1}^{K}\sum_{j=1,j\neq i}^{K} \frac{4\sum_{l=1}^{C}\omega_l^4(\mu_{j,l}-\mu_{i,l})^2\sigma_{i,l}^2}{(\sum_{l=1}^{C}\omega_l^2\min_{i\neq j}(\mu_{j,l}-\mu_{i,l})^2)^2}\\ &= \frac{\sum_{l=1}^{C}\omega_l^4\cdot 4\sum_{i=1}^{K}\sum_{j=1}^{K}(\mu_{j,l}-\mu_{i,l})^2\sigma_{i,l}^2}{(\sum_{l=1}^{C}\omega_l^2\min_{i\neq j}(\mu_{j,l}-\mu_{i,l})^2)^2}.\end{aligned} \tag{7}$$

To compute the form of $\boldsymbol{\omega}$, we introduce a lemma [15] as follow:

Lemma 1. *Let $a_i > 0, b_i > 0, i = 1, ..., D$. Define $f : \mathbb{R}_+^D \rightarrow \mathbb{R}$ by $f(\boldsymbol{x}) = \frac{\sum_{i=1}^{D} b_i x_i^2}{(\sum_{i=1}^{D} a_i x_i)^2}$, then the minimum of f is reached at $x_i \propto \frac{a_i}{b_i}$.*

Therefore, when we optimize the upper bound of $\mathcal{R}$ in Eq. (7), the solution satisfies

$$\omega_l^2 \propto \frac{\min_{i\neq j}(\mu_{j,l}-\mu_{i,l})^2}{\sum_{i=1}^{K}\sum_{j=1}^{K}(\mu_{j,l}-\mu_{i,l})^2\sigma_{i,l}^2}, \tag{8}$$

.

The AttnNet module is constructed based on the result in Eq. (8). As ϕ_{score} shown in Fig. 2, for each task $\mathcal{T} = \mathcal{T}^s \cup \mathcal{T}^q$, we use the support data $Z'^s$to calculate the task-specific score vector $\boldsymbol{s} \in \mathcal{R}^C$ as follows:

$$s_l = \sqrt{\frac{\min_{i\neq j}(\bar{Z'}^s_{j,l}-\bar{Z'}^s_{i,l})^2}{\sum_{i=1}^{K}\sum_{j=1}^{K}(\bar{Z'}^s_{j,l}-\bar{Z'}^s_{i,l})^2\hat{\sigma}_{i,l}^2+\epsilon}}, \tag{9}$$

where $\bar{Z'}^s_{i,l}$ is the l-th dimension of the average of support sample features of category i, $\hat{\sigma}_{i,l}^2$ is the l-th dimension of the variance of category i computed by support samples, ϵ is a constant used to prevent denominator exceptions. Then we can calculate the weights as follows:

$$\boldsymbol{\omega} = \text{Dense}_1(\text{Dense}_2(\bar{\bar{\boldsymbol{s}}})), \tag{10}$$

where Dense_1 and Dense_2 are both one-layer MLP networks, $\bar{\cdot}$ is the stop-gradient operation to avoid collapse in the training process. Finally, the sample representation Z^s, Z^q of samples in $\mathcal{T}^s, \mathcal{T}^q$ are calculated as follows:

$$Z = \boldsymbol{\omega} \odot Z', \tag{11}$$

where Z refers to both Z^s and Z^q, and Z' refers to both Z'^s and Z'^q.

As for the downstream classifier, some work shows that the linear classifier is better than the prototype classifier, but it takes extra time to update the classifier in the meta-learning process. In this paper, we put the embedding vector Z^q into a special linear classifier W to predict the label, where the i-th column of W is the average of Z^s belonging to the i-th category.

4.2 Training Strategy

As Fig. 2(b)(c) shows, we apply the two-stage strategy to train Meta-HRNet. The first stage is to train the HRNet ψ with the self-learning strategy, and the second stage is to train the whole Meta-HRNet with the episodic training strategy.

At the first training stage, we apply the loss function in ANCOR [2] directly to train an HRNet backbone. The loss function is

$$\mathcal{L}_1 = \mathcal{L}^{CE}(Z', Y) + \mathcal{L}^{CONT}(\angle Z', \angle Z'^{+}, \angle Z'^{-}), \tag{12}$$

where $\angle Z'$ is the angular normalization of Z' (See ANCOR [2] for more details), Z^+ and Z^- are both sampled from the set of samples sharing the same label with Z'. $\mathcal{L}^{CE}$ and $\mathcal{L}^{CONT}$ are respectively cross-entropy loss function and MoCoV2 [5] contrastive loss function.

The classification loss function is defined as follows

$$\mathcal{L}^{CLS} = \mathbb{E}_{\mathcal{T}}\mathbb{E}_{\{X^s, X^q\}} - \log \frac{\exp(W_{Y^q}^T Z^q)}{\exp(\sum_{i=1}^{K} W_i^T Z^q)}, \tag{13}$$

where W_{Y^q} is the Y^q-th column of W, $\{X^s, X^q\}$ are support samples and query samples in task $\mathcal{T}$, Z^q and W are calculated based on Sect. 4.1.

We denote the HRNet trained after the first stage as ψ^t which will be used as a teacher model for the second training stage. At the beginning of the second training stage, ψ^t is used as the initialization of HRNet backbone. And in order to prevent the forgetting of the training results of the first stage in the process of the second training stage, a regularization is defined as follows:

$$\mathcal{L}^{REG} = \mathbb{E}_{\mathcal{T}}\mathbb{E}_{X \sim \mathcal{T}}[(\psi^t(X) - \psi(X))^2], \tag{14}$$

where ψ^t is a frozen model and X refers to both X^s and X^q.

Finally, we obtain the total loss function of the second training stage as $\mathcal{L}_2 = \mathcal{L}^{CLS} + \mathcal{L}^{REG}$.

5 Experiments

Our experiments are designed from four aspects. Firstly, we show the main results on the C2FS problem. Secondly, we implement ablation study to show the effectiveness of each pattern of our model. Then, we show the saliency maps of our model and baseline models. Finally, we draw the activated locations of the four branches on images.

5.1 Experimental Settings

Our experiments were performed on the datasets BREEDS [21][1], which includes four datasets derived from ImageNet with hierarchical information. Living17 has 17 coarse-grained categories and 68 fine-grained categories, Nonliving26 has 26 coarse-grained categories and 104 fine-grained categories, Entity13 has 13 coarse-grained categories and 260 fine-grained categories, and Entity30 has 30 coarse-grained categories and 240 fine-grained categories. The size of images is $3 \times 224 \times 224$ in all datasets. In this paper, we applied HRNet-w32[2] whose largest feature resolution is 32×32. This version of HRNet balances the parameter scale relative to ResNet50 and the representation ability.

All the codes are implemented by PyTorch. The first stage of our model is trained on 4 12G TiTan XP GPUs and the second stage is trained on a 48G A40 GPU. The implementation details at the first training stage is the same as those in ANCOR [2] except for substituting ResNet50 with HRNet. At the second stage, we use SGD with momentum 0.9, weight decay 0.0001 and we set learning rate as 0.001 and it decreased by 0.1 times every 20 steps. We trained the models for 200 epoches and generated 1000 tasks for each epoch. The results reported in this paper are the average results of 1000 testing tasks computed by the model with the best performance on validation sets. We set $\epsilon = 1$, $K = 5$ and $N = 1$. For Living17 and Nonliving26, since each coarse-grained category in these two datasets has only 4 fine-grained categories, the corresponding 'in-coarse' experiment is 4-way 1-shot. Similar to the settings as ANCOR, we generated 5 augmented samples for each support sample at the training time.

5.2 Main Results

In order to verify the validity of our model on the C2FS problem, we tested our model against two types of baselines. (i)*Meta-learning based methods.* ProtoNet [23] and FEAT [27] are two presentatives of meta-learning based few-shot methods. To train the two models, we used ResNet18 as the backbone and resized images to 84×84. We set the learning rate to 0.0001 and decrease it by a factor of 0.1 times every 20 steps. The optimizer is SGD with weight decay 0.0001 and

[1] https://github.com/MadryLab/BREEDS-Benchmarks.

[2] https://github.com/HRNet/HRNet-Image-Classification.

Table 1. Results on BREEDS. 'cross-coarse' means that the testing categories are sampled from the sub-classes of all the super-classes, and 'in-coarse' means that the categories are sampled from sub-classes of a random selected coarse-grained category.

Method	**Living17**		**Nonliving26**	
	cross-coarse	in-coarse	cross-coarse	in-coarse
ProtoNet	34.31 ± 0.56	29.71 ± 0.42	30.97 ± 0.49	28.65 ± 0.42
FEAT	38.28 ± 0.59	30.89 ± 0.45	31.45 ± 0.50	29.71 ± 0.44
MoCoV2	76.91 ± 0.65	49.63 ± 0.71	75.75 ± 0.70	53.65 ± 0.90
MoCoV2-ImageNet	83.86 ± 0.66	51.70 ± 0.79	77.05 ± 0.72	53.62 ± 0.95
Coarse	81.08 ± 0.68	43.05 ± 0.64	79.54 ± 0.64	51.70 ± 0.84
ANCOR	89.53 ± 0.56	50.18 ± 0.73	85.48 ± 0.58	54.58 ± 0.93
Meta-HRNet	**90.44 ± 0.55**	**52.29 ± 0.72**	**87.62 ± 0.54**	**57.65 ± 1.00**
Method	**Entity13**		**Entity30**	
	cross-coarse	in-coarse	cross-coarse	in-coarse
ProtoNet	33.71 ± 0.52	24.98 ± 0.38	32.20 ± 0.51	24.36 ± 0.36
FEAT	33.29 ± 0.51	25.29 ± 0.39	33.13 ± 0.52	25.47 ± 0.38
MoCoV2	84.76 ± 0.58	**68.59 ± 0.78**	81.38 ± 0.61	55.82 ± 0.80
MoCoV2-ImageNet	84.98 ± 0.61	65.45 ± 0.83	83.35 ± 0.65	54.54 ± 0.81
Coarse	84.05 ± 0.58	59.89 ± 0.82	84.16 ± 0.58	52.44 ± 0.82
ANCOR	88.87 ± 0.52	65.92 ± 0.79	89.07 ± 0.52	**58.29 ± 0.82**
Meta-HRNet	**89.49 ± 0.51**	67.80 ± 0.77	**89.45 ± 0.53**	54.91 ± 0.84

momentumn 0.9. Both models were trained for 200 epoches with 1000 training tasks per epoch. (ii) *Transfer learning based methods.* MoCoV2 [5] is one of the most popular contrastive learning methods. We implemented it with the same settings as ANCOR [2] and the first stage of our model. MoCoV2-ImageNet is an official pre-trained ResNet50 model trained on ImageNet for 200 epoches. Coarse refers to a ResNet50 model trained only with a cross-entropy loss function. ANCOR [2] is a ResNet50 model trained with a cross-entropy loss function and the angular normalized contrastive loss function. All the results of baselines were implemented on the same equipment with our model.

The mean accuracy and the corresponding 95% confidence interval are shown in Table 1. Our model was evaluated on 1000 testing tasks and outperformed other methods in most cases. However on the 'in-coarse' scenario on Entity30, the performance of Meta-HRNet didn't exceed that of ANCOR. This may be due to some sub-categories within a coarse-grained category that are more difficult to be distinguished from each other only by using the high-resolution features, such as two categories of insects with similar appearances. This leads to the misleading caused by the over-attention to the details of HRNet. As for the 'in-coarse' scenario on Entity13, the performance of Meta-HRNet is slightly worse than that of MocoV2. Maybe this is because we used the ANCOR at the first training stage instead of MocoV2. The improvement on 'in-coarse' scenario of Entity13 might be better if we use MocoV2 at the first training stage of Meta-HRNet, because MocoV2 can bring around 3% improvement over ANCOR.

5.3 Ablation Study

Table 2. Ablation study on Nonliving26. HRB: HRNet backbone, Sg2: the second training strategy, Attn: AttnNet, Reg: Teacher model as regularization.

Method	HRB	Sg2	Attn	Reg	cross-coarse	in-coarse
ANCOR	✗	✗	✗	✗	85.48 ± 0.58	54.58 ± 0.93
HRNet	✓	✗	✗	✗	86.52 ± 0.56	57.44 ± 0.99
HR+Meta	✓	✓	✗	✓	86.62 ± 0.55	57.16 ± 0.98
HRNet+	✓	✓	✓	✗	87.18 ± 0.56	57.59 ± 0.98
Meta-HRNet	✓	✓	✓	✓	$\mathbf{87.62 \pm 0.54}$	$\mathbf{57.65 \pm 1.00}$

Here we take the dataset Nonliving26 as an example to present an abalation study of each component of Meta-HRNet. As Table 2 shows, 'HRNet' refers to directly replacing the ResNet50 backbone in 'ANCOR' with HRNet-w32. 'HR+Meta' adds the second training stage and the regularization item shown in Eq. (14) based on 'HRNet'. 'HRNet+' adds the AttnNet and is trained without the regularization term at the second stage. The effectiveness of the regularization term can be observed by comparing 'HRNet+' and 'Meta-HRNet'. Compared to 'ANCOR', 'HRNet' leads to a significant improvement, especially for the 'in-coarse' testing scenario. This may be attributed to the presentation ability on details of HRNet-w32 backbone. Another significant improvement occurs between 'HRNet+Meta' and 'Meta-HRNet' in the 'cross-coarse' case. The only difference between the two methods is whether to use the AttnNet module. We can therefore speculate that the role of AttnNet is to filter the global details learned by HRNet and focus more attention on the main entity of the images.

5.4 Saliency Map

We further explore whether our model pays attention to the main information in images by generating the saliency maps for ANCOR, HRNet and Meta-HRNet. Pixels with more contributions to the model are marked as brighter colors. For the convenience of comparison, we overlaid the original images with identical values (displayed as blue masks). As defined in Sect. 5.3, we compare our model with ANCOR and HRNet. According to the results shown in Fig. 3 (selected from test datasets of Living17 and Nonliving26), we can see that ANCOR and HRNet are unable to recognize the location of the black bear, but the key pixels of Meta-HRNet are concentrated at the position of the black bear. As for the second figure shown in Fig. 3, HRNet has more key pixels on the bird in the tree than ANCOR but also focuses on pixels in the background area. The AttnNet module in Meta-HRNet can reduce the attention on the background and helps the model to focus on the bird. As for the third figure, Meta-HRNet can identify all the raccoons in the picture. As for the fourth picture, Meta-HRNet can extract the most key points on the dog's head and body. The remaining four images shown in Fig. 3 show that ANCOR may extract the wrong key pixels, while Meta-HRNet can rectify the attention of HRNet to the main entity of the images. Based on the above experimental results and the corresponding analysis, we can conclude that high-resolution features have a significant effect on the classification tasks for samples with the same super-class. When there are fine-grained categories of different super-classes in the downstream tasks, the AttnNet module can correct the over-attention problem of high-resolution features to the unnecessary information, such as the background area.

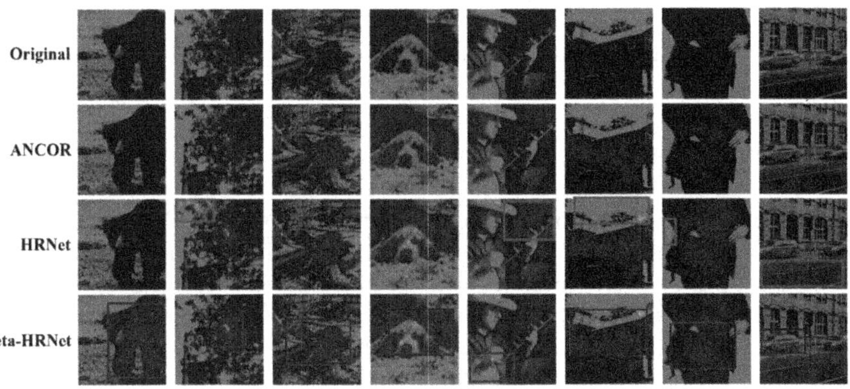

Fig. 3. Meta-HRNet pays more attention to the main entity (yellow boxes) and is more difficult to be disturbed by background information than HRNet (red boxes). (Color figure online)

5.5 Feature Maps of HRNet

We further analyze the reason why HRNet is suitable for the C2FS problem. Taking Living17 dataset as an example, we applied the HRNet model trained with coarse labels and input testing images to visualize the features. Figure 4 shows the activations of the final layer in each branch (selected from the test dataset of Living17). 'Branch 1' refers to the highest-resolution features and 'Branch 4' is the lowest-resolution features. The features of 'Branch 1' concentrate more on the margin and veins of objects, for example the outline and hair of the polar bear and the dog, palm print and cobwebs. With the decline of the feature resolution, the branches of HRNet gradually focus on the overall information of the object, such as the face of the polar bear, the reptile in the hands and the body of the spider. According to Fig. 4, the effectiveness of the HRNet backbone can be attributed to its ability to preserve more details such as veins. This is important for distinguishing sub-classes within the same supercategory. For example, different bird species may have different kinds of feathers.

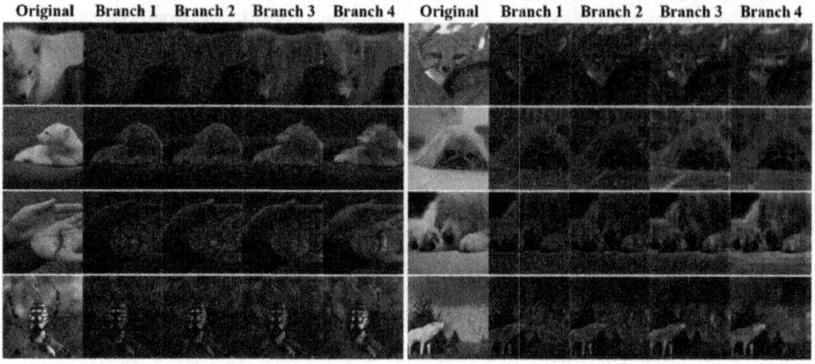

Fig. 4. Closer look at the feature maps of HRNet.

6 Conclusion

In this paper, we focus on the coarse-to-fine few-shot problem, which is to solve the few-shot fine-grained classification tasks with sufficient coarse-grained labeled data. Due to the similarity among fine-grained categories, it is challenging to extract distinguishable features to capture the subtle variation among samples. Drawing inspiration from research on the effect of images with different resolutions, we alleviated the problem from the perspective of feature resolutions. Firstly, we theoretically analyzed the relationship between the feature resolution and the fine-grained classification tasks and concluded that the higher resolution features are beneficial for the fine-grained tasks. Then, we constructed Meta-HRNet, an improved deep high-resolution network, and trained it with coarse-grained labels to capture and filter key detailed features to distinguish fine-grained categories. In order to better address the challenge of insufficient samples, we combined the supervised learning strategy and meta-learning strategy to improve the flexibility of the model so that it can adaptively adjust the feature representation based on a small number of samples in the downstream tasks. Finally, our experiments verified that Meta-HRNet can improve the performance on fine-grained classification tasks.

This paper makes a good attempt to explore the effectiveness of high-resolution features on fine-grained classification problems. In future work, we will consider more efficient and lightweight network structures for extracting high-resolution information. Additionally, we will strive to make better use of the detailed information provided by high-resolution features while avoiding the misleading results caused by the over-attention of details.

Acknowledgements. The authors are grateful to anonymous reviewers for their valuable comments. This work was partly supported by the National Natural Science Foundation of China under Grant No. 61572002, No. 61690201, and No. 61732001.

Ethical Statement. This research does not contain any personally identifiable information. All datasets were obtained from public resources. The methods proposed in our paper do not have any potential negative societal impacts. Our methods are safe and cannot be integrated into weapons systems. Our research does not have the potential to damage human rights, economic security, people's livelihoods, or the environment. This is a basic study and even if the methods are misused, they will not cause social harm.

References

1. Behera, A., Wharton, Z., Hewage, P.R.P.G., Bera, A.: Context-aware attentional pooling (cap) for fine-grained visual classification. Proc. AAAI Conf. Artif. Intell. **35**(2), 929–937 (2021)
2. Bukchin, G., et al.: Fine-grained angular contrastive learning with coarse labels. In: Proceedings of the IEEE/CVF Conference on Computer Vision and Pattern Recognition (CVPR), pp. 8730–8740 (2021)
3. Cantelli, F.P.: Sui confini della probabilitá. In: Atti del Congresso Internazionale dei Matematici: Bologna del 3 al 10 de settembre di 1928, Vol. 6, 1929 (Comunicazioni, sezione IV (A)-V-VII), pp. 47–60 (1929)
4. Chen, W., Si, C., Wang, W., Wang, L., Wang, Z., Tan, T.: Few-shot learning with part discovery and augmentation from unlabeled images. In: Zhou, Z.H. (ed.) Proceedings of the Thirtieth International Joint Conference on Artificial Intelligence, IJCAI-21, pp. 2271–2277. International Joint Conferences on Artificial Intelligence Organization (2021), main Track
5. Chen, X., Fan, H., Girshick, R.B., He, K.: Improved baselines with momentum contrastive learning. CoRR abs/2003.04297 (2020)
6. Chen, Y., Liu, Z., Xu, H., Darrell, T., Wang, X.: Meta-Baseline: Exploring Simple Meta-Learning for Few-Shot Learning. In: 2021 IEEE/CVF International Conference on Computer Vision (ICCV), pp. 9042–9051. IEEE, Montreal, QC, Canada (Oct 2021)
7. Cui, Y., Song, Y., Sun, C., Howard, A., Belongie, S.: Large Scale Fine-Grained Categorization and Domain-Specific Transfer Learning. In: 2018 IEEE/CVF Conference on Computer Vision and Pattern Recognition, pp. 4109–4118. IEEE, Salt Lake City, UT, USA (Jun 2018)
8. Dong, B., Zhou, P., Yan, S., Zuo, W.: Self-promoted supervision for few-shot transformer. In: Avidan, S., Brostow, G., Cissé, M., Farinella, G.M., Hassner, T. (eds.) European Conference on Computer Vision (ECCV 2022), pp. 329–347. Springer Nature Switzerland, Cham (2022)
9. Finn, C., Abbeel, P., Levine, S.: Model-agnostic meta-learning for fast adaptation of deep networks. In: Precup, D., Teh, Y.W. (eds.) Proceedings of the 34th International Conference on Machine Learning. Proceedings of Machine Learning Research, vol. 70, pp. 1126–1135. PMLR (06–11 Aug 2017)

10. dan Guo, D., Tian, L., Zhao, H., Zhou, M., Zha, H.: Adaptive distribution calibration for few-shot learning with hierarchical optimal transport. In: Oh, A.H., Agarwal, A., Belgrave, D., Cho, K. (eds.) Advances in Neural Information Processing Systems (2022)
11. Kao, C.H., Chiu, W.C., Chen, P.Y.: MAML is a noisy contrastive learner in classification. In: International Conference on Learning Representations (2022)
12. Kim, Y., Ha, J.W.: Contrastive fine-grained class clustering via generative adversarial networks (2022)
13. Lee, S., Moon, W., Heo, J.P.: Task discrepancy maximization for fine-grained few-shot classification. In: Proceedings of the IEEE/CVF Conference on Computer Vision and Pattern Recognition (CVPR), pp. 5331–5340 (June 2022)
14. Li, S., et al.: Improve unsupervised pretraining for few-label transfer. In: Proceedings of the IEEE/CVF International Conference on Computer Vision (ICCV), pp. 10201–10210 (October 2021)
15. Luo, X., Xu, J., Xu, Z.: Channel importance matters in few-shot image classification. In: Chaudhuri, K., Jegelka, S., Song, L., Szepesvari, C., Niu, G., Sabato, S. (eds.) Proceedings of the 39th International Conference on Machine Learning. Proceedings of Machine Learning Research, vol. 162, pp. 14542–14559. PMLR (2022)
16. Ni, R., Shu, M., Souri, H., Goldblum, M., Goldstein, T.: The close relationship between contrastive learning and meta-learning. In: International Conference on Learning Representations (2022)
17. Oh, J., Kim, S., Ho, N., Kim, J.H., Song, H., Yun, S.Y.: Understanding cross-domain few-shot learning based on domain similarity and few-shot difficulty. In: Oh, A.H., Agarwal, A., Belgrave, D., Cho, K. (eds.) Advances in Neural Information Processing Systems (2022)
18. Phoo, C.P., Hariharan, B.: Self-training for few-shot transfer across extreme task differences. In: International Conference on Learning Representations (2021)
19. Requeima, J., Gordon, J., Bronskill, J., Nowozin, S., Turner, R.E.: Fast and flexible multi-task classification using conditional neural adaptive processes. In: Advances in Neural Information Processing Systems. vol. 32. Curran Associates, Inc. (2019)
20. Ronneberger, O., Fischer, P., Brox, T.: U-Net: convolutional networks for biomedical image segmentation. In: Navab, N., Hornegger, J., Wells, W.M., Frangi, A.F. (eds.) MICCAI 2015. LNCS, vol. 9351, pp. 234–241. Springer, Cham (2015). https://doi.org/10.1007/978-3-319-24574-4_28
21. Santurkar, S., Tsipras, D., Madry, A.: BREEDS: Benchmarks for subpopulation shift. In: International Conference on Learning Representations (2021)
22. Shen, Z., Liu, Z., Qin, J., Savvides, M., Cheng, K.T.: Partial is better than all: revisiting fine-tuning strategy for few-shot learning. Proc. AAAI Conf. Artif. Intell. **35**(11), 9594–9602 (2021)
23. Snell, J., Swersky, K., Zemel, R.: Prototypical networks for few-shot learning. Adv. Neural Inform. Process. Syst. **30** (2017)
24. Wang, J., et al.: Deep high-resolution representation learning for visual recognition. IEEE Trans. Pattern Analysis Mach. Intell. **43**(10), 3349–3364 (2021)
25. Yang, J., Yang, H., Chen, L.: Towards cross-granularity few-shot learning: coarse-to-fine pseudo-labeling with visual-semantic meta-embedding. In: Proceedings of the 29th ACM International Conference on Multimedia,pp. 3005–3014. ACM, Virtual Event China (2021)
26. Yang, S., Liu, L., Xu, M.: Free lunch for few-shot learning: Distribution calibration. In: International Conference on Learning Representations (2021)

27. Ye, H.J., Hu, H., Zhan, D.C., Sha, F.: Few-shot learning via embedding adaptation with set-to-set functions. In: Proceedings of the IEEE/CVF Conference on Computer Vision and Pattern Recognition, pp. 8808–8817 (2020)
28. Zhao, B., Feng, J., Wu, X., Yan, S.: A survey on deep learning-based fine-grained object classification and semantic segmentation. Int. J. Autom. Comput. **14**(2), 119–135 (2017)
29. Zhu, M., et al.: Dynamic resolution network. In: Beygelzimer, A., Dauphin, Y., Liang, P., Vaughan, J.W. (eds.) Adv. Neural Inform. Process. Syst. **34**, 27319–21330 (2021)
30. Zhu, Y., Liu, C., Jiang, S.: Multi-attention Meta Learning for Few-shot Fine-grained Image Recognition. In: Proceedings of the Twenty-Ninth International Joint Conference on Artificial Intelligence, pp. 1090–1096. International Joint Conferences on Artificial Intelligence Organization, Yokohama, Japan (Jul 2020)

Generative Models

MuSE: A Multi-scale Emotional Flow Graph Model for Empathetic Dialogue Generation

Deji Zhao[1], Donghong Han[1(✉)], Ye Yuan[2], Chao Wang[3], and Shuangyong Song[3]

[1] School of Computer Science and Engineering, Northeastern University, Shenyang, China
zhaodeji@stumail.neu.edu.cn, handonghong@cse.neu.edu.cn
[2] School of Computer Science and Technology, Beijing Institute of Technology, Beijing, China
yuan-ye@bit.edu.cn
[3] Department of Big Data and AI, China Telecom, Beijing, China
{wangc17,songshy}@chinatelecom.cn

Abstract. The purpose of empathetic dialogue generation is to fully understand the speakers' emotional needs in dialogues and to generate appropriate empathetic responses. Existing works mainly focus on the overall coarse-grained emotion of the context while neglecting different utterances' fine-grained emotions, which leads to the inability to detect the speakers' fine-grained emotional changes during a conversation. However, in real-life dialogue scenarios, the speaker usually carries an initial emotional state that changes continuously during the conversation. Therefore, understanding a series of emotional states can help to better understand speakers' emotions and generate empathetic responses. To address this issue, we propose a **Mu**lti-**S**cale **E**motional flow model called **MuSE**, which simulates speakers' emotional flow. First, we introduce a fine-grained expansion strategy to transform context into an emotional flow graph that combines multi-scale coarse and fine-grained information. This emotional flow graph captures speakers' constant emotional changes at each turn of a conversation. And then, the emotion node and the situational node are introduced to the emotional flow graph respectively in order to extend the speakers' initial emotion into the ensuing conversation. Finally, we conduct experiments on the public EMPATHETIC DIALOGUES dataset. The experimental results demonstrate that the MuSE model achieves superior performance under both automatic evaluation and human evaluation metrics compared with the existing baseline models. Our code is available at https://github.com/DericZhao/MuSE.

Keywords: Empathetic Dialogue · Multi-scale · Emotional Flow · Dialogue Graph · Dialogue Generation

© The Author(s), under exclusive license to Springer Nature Switzerland AG 2023
D. Koutra et al. (Eds.): ECML PKDD 2023, LNAI 14170, pp. 491–507, 2023.
https://doi.org/10.1007/978-3-031-43415-0_29

1 Introduction

In recent years, researchers have been increasingly interested in promoting more meaningful human-computer interactions in open-domain dialogue systems, such as the empathic dialogue system. The core of empathetic dialogue is to understand the speakers' emotional needs and to generate appropriate responses from their situation [5,13]. Empathetic dialogue can be leveraged for mental health-care, emotional companionship, psychological counseling and other fields.

In order to improve the capability of empathic dialogue systems, existing works focus on recognizing emotion in the context and generating empathetic responses accordingly. Most existing approaches recognize contextual emotions from two directions. One method directly detects emotion through context [2,6,9,11,19], while the other method adopts external knowledge to indirectly understand emotional needs by identifying intent and emotional cause [20,23,25,26]. However, previous works tend to consider the conversation context as a whole coarse-grained emotion, without taking the subtle emotional changes of the speaker during each turn of the conversation into account. Li et al. [9] propose the EmpDG model that emphasizes the modeling of emotions during the conversation, but they don't incorporate speakers' emotional changes during the conversation. Although Wang et al. [27] devise the SEEK model to capture emotion dynamics, they still focus on the utterance level, ignoring speakers may say more sentences with different emotional states in a utterance.

We believe that the emotional changes generated between speakers are the essential difference between empathetic dialogues and ordinary multi-turn dialogues. As all the contexts of empathetic dialogue revolve around the changes in emotional flow, different speakers influence each other to different degrees through various emotional intensities. In the Emotion Recognition in Conversation (ERC) task [29], each turn of the conversation is characterized by different emotional states, which inspired us to introduce the concept of speaker emotional flow changes in empathetic dialogues. Furthermore, previous works [11,12,16,20,25] consider the role of the given situation information as a simple abstract of the conversation and do not leverage it. However, we contend that situation information can be utilized as supplementary knowledge to enrich the conversation context.

Figure 1 shows a dialogue extracted from the EMPATHETIC DIALOGUES dataset. The conversation revolves around a situation where the target predict emotion label is Afraid. The speakers start the conversation with an initial emotional state that changes continuously during the conversation. There are emotional changes during the conversation between Speaker1 and Speaker2, which include internal emotional changes and interactional emotional changes. As the conversation progresses, speaker1's subjective emotion changes from FEAR to NERVOUSNESS, which we consider as internal change. Speaker1's emotional change is also objectively influenced by another speaker, which we consider as interactional emotional change. Usually, Speaker2 would be the chatbot after training, and capturing the Speaker1's emotional changes can help to better understand the Speaker1's emotional needs.

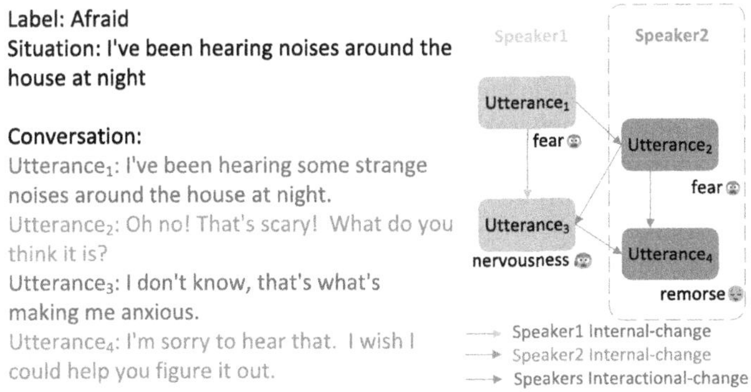

Fig. 1. The emotional change between speaker1 and speaker2 during a conversation.

In this paper, we propose a **Mu**lti-**S**cale **E**motional flow graph Dialogue Generation Model, called **MuSE** to simulate speakers' emotional flow. The MuSE model considers the changes in emotional flow as a graph structure, and utilizes graph neural networks to extract features. We first construct an oriented graph to better simulate emotional flow changes in empathetic dialogue. Furthermore, speakers may speak more than one sentence in a conversation, such as $Utterance_2$ and $Utterance_4$ in Fig. 1, and each sentence has a different emotional state. To address this, we introduce a fine-grained sentence expansion strategy to segment these sentences and thus capture more subtle emotional changes of the speaker, which combines multi-scale coarse and fine-grained information. To extend the speakers' initial emotion into the ensuing conversation, we add a key emotion node and key situation node into emotional graph as background information, called $KeyEmotion$ and $KeySituation$. The $KeyEmotion$ is the predicted emotion distribution, without giving away the real label information. The MuSE model first predicts the emotion label through the constructed emotional change graph and generates appropriate responses.

The main contributions of this work are summarized as follows:

- We propose an emotional flow dialogue model that can better capture the emotional changes of the speaker in an empathetic dialogue.
- An oriented emotional dialogue graph is constructed to simulate the changes of speakers' emotion states in empathetic context, in which key emotion and key situation nodes are introduced for the first time to extend the speakers' initial emotion into the ensuing conversation.
- We introduce a contextual fine-grained expansion strategy for empathetic dialogue, which can be combined with the emotional flow graph to better capture the subtle emotional changes of the speakers.
- We conduct experiments on the publicly available EMPATHETIC DIALOGUES dataset. The experimental results show that the MuSE model performs well on both automatic evaluation and human evaluation compared with the existing baseline models.

2 Related Work

Research on empathic dialogue in artificial intelligence starts in recent years. The empathic dialogue generation task is first proposed by Rashkin et al. [19]. In empathic dialogue, it is important to identify the emotional needs of speakers and then generate appropriate empathic responses accordingly. Existing work on perceived emotional needs is divided into two directions namely, directly recognizing the speakers' emotions or using external knowledge for indirect reasoning.

The first one is recognizing the speaker's emotion directly. The earliest Rashkin et al. [19] add an additional module for predicting emotions to the model, which can generate empathic responses for the first time. Next, Lin et al. [11] construct multiple decoders, using different decoders to respond to each contextual emotion depending on the speaker's emotional state. The MIME model is proposed by Majumder et al. [12] and they argue that the empathetic responses often mimic the emotion of the user to a varying degree, depending on its positivity or negativity. However, these coarse-grained ERC models lack the ability to capture fine-grained emotions, which may affect the performance of empathic responses. Li et al. [9] argue that the sensitive emotion expressed by the speaker is important. On the basis of these methods, we further considers the state transfer relationships between different fine-grained emotions, i.e., emotional flow changes.

The second one is to infer emotional needs indirectly with the help of external knowledge, which helps the model obtain some additional cues, including the identification of emotional causes, commonsense inferences, etc. Wang et al. [26] utilize the Concept Net external knowledge and construct an emotional causal map through a multi-hop strategy, which in turn generates empathic responses. The CEM model is proposed by Sabour et al. [20], they adopt ATOMIC [21] to access commonsense knowledge. For each sentence, ATOMIC infers six commonsense relations for the person involved in the event. The commonsense can also help to identify conversational emotion, Zhao et al. [29] use ATOMIC to inference each utterance's emotional state for the ERC task. And Wang et al. [27] devise the SEEK model, which utilizes the COMET [1] to detect the intent of each utterance and inference the emotion dynamics. Wang et al. [25] propose the state-of-the-art CARE model, which employs Cause Effect Graph external information to generate an empathetic response. Unlike previous work that used external knowledge to infer emotions indirectly, this paper uses external knowledge to identify speakers' fine-grained emotions directly.

In recent years, due to the powerful representation ability of graph networks, graph-based human-computer conversation models have received increasing attention. Ghosal et al. [3] propose the DialogueGCN model to recognize the emotions in a conversation. Qin et al. [18] use Co-Interactive Graph Attention Network to capture contextual information in conversations and mutual interaction information. Pang et al. [14] propose a MFDG model and construct a multi-factors dialogue graph to detect speakers' intent. Unlike previous works, our emotional flow dialogue graph employs a novel fine-grained strategy to construct a graph structure suitable for empathetic dialogue, capable of highlighting the unconcious emotional states of the speaker during the conversation.

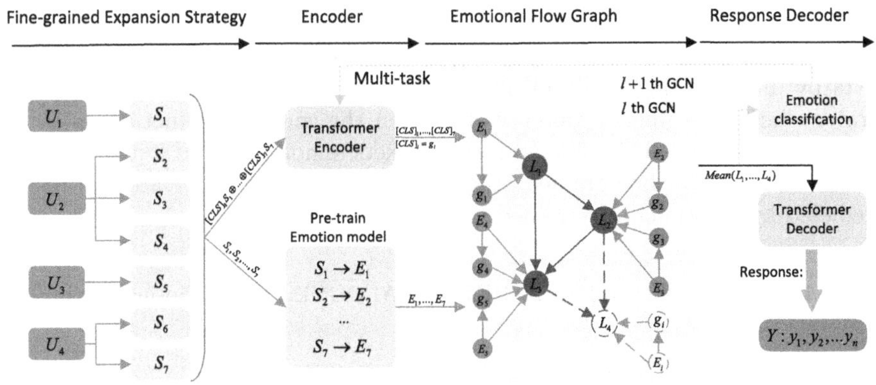

Fig. 2. In our proposed MuSE model, blue nodes denote sentences, green nodes denote emotions, and purple nodes denote abstracted aggregation nodes. (Color figure online)

3 Our Model: MuSE

In this section, we illustrate the MuSE model in detail, whose architecture is depicted in Fig. 2. The MuSE model contains several parts, which are the fine-grained expansion strategy, encoder, emotional flow graph, and response decoder. The input of the model first goes through the fine-grained expansion strategy to get fine-grained sentences, and the external knowledge of the pre-trained model is used to obtain the fine-grained sentences emotional states, and then the emotional flow graph is constructed to simulate the emotion changes of speakers. Then the graph neural network is used to obtain the contextual representation and the emotion labels, and finally, the learned information is fed into the decoder to generate empathic responses. The goal of the model's emotion classifier, as part of multi-task learning, is to attach emotions to the model's responses and become more empathetic.

We formulate the task of empathetic response generation as follows. Given the $contexts = \{U_1, U_2, ..., U_n\}$, where n is the turns of a dialogue and there are two speakers $speaker1$ and $speaker2$. $\{S_1, S_2, ..., S_i\}$ are the sentences after fine-grained expansion strategy in the utterance, where i represents the ith sentence after segment. $\{E_1, E_2, ..., E_i\}$ is the emotional state of the new utterance. E_i is obtained from a pre-trained model with seven emotion classifications, which include $fear$, $sadness$, $neutral$, joy, $disgust$, $anger$, and $surprise$ [4]. The target response is $\boldsymbol{Y} = (y_1, y_2, ..., y_n)$.

3.1 Fine-Grained Expansion Strategy

In order to capture the subtle emotion states in context and encode the context, we introduce a fine-grained expansion strategy to segment the context and exploit transformer [24] encoder to encode each sentence. Unlike the previous direct segmentation approaches according to speakers, we further split the context based on punctuation marks, which are the period, question mark, and exclamation mark.

Taking the dialogue in Fig. 1 as an example, Table. 1 shows the results after adopting fine-grained expansion strategy. The MuSE model first splits the contexts by different speakers and obtains U_1 to U_4. The fine-grained expansion strategy further segments sentences based on the speakers' punctuation in the context to capture all the fine-grained speakers' emotions. The sentences S_1 to S_i are obtained by fine-grained expansion strategy. E_1 to E_i are the results predicted by emotional pre-trained model [4].

Table 1. An example from EMPATHETIC DIALOGUES after adopting fine-grained expansion strategy.

Label				Afraid
Situation				I've been hearing noises around the house at night
Speaker1	U_1	S_1	E_1:*fear*	I've been hearing some strange noise around the house at night.
Speaker2	U_2	S_2	E_2:*surprise*	Oh no!
		S_3	E_3:*fear*	That's scary!
		S_4	E_4:*neutural*	What do you think it is?
Speaker1	U_3	S_5	E_5:*neutural*	I don't know, that's what's making me anxious.
Speaker2	U_4	S_6	E_6:*sadness*	I'm sorry to hear that
		S_7	E_7:*sadness*	I wish I could help you figure it out.

The statistics in the table show that after fine-grained strategy segmentation, there is a substantial increase in the number of sentences obtained through fine-grained strategy to capture more subtle speaker emotion states.

3.2 Encoder

Transformer block [24] is adopted as the encoder and different from the previous methods of directly splicing contexts [16,20,25], MuSE model concatenates each sentence S_i with the special token $[CLS]$ to obtain the representation respectively. We use the hidden representation of $[CLS]_i$ as the representation of $sentence_i$ in a context. In the encoder, the representation of each sentence $[CLS]_i$ is obtained after transformer block:

$$[CLS]_i = TransformerBlock(S_i), \tag{1}$$

Table 2. Statistics of datasets under different splitting strategies.

Dataset	Origin	Speaker level Split	Fine-grained Split
Train	40250	84686	132944
Valid	5734	12188	19313
Test	5255	11127	18716

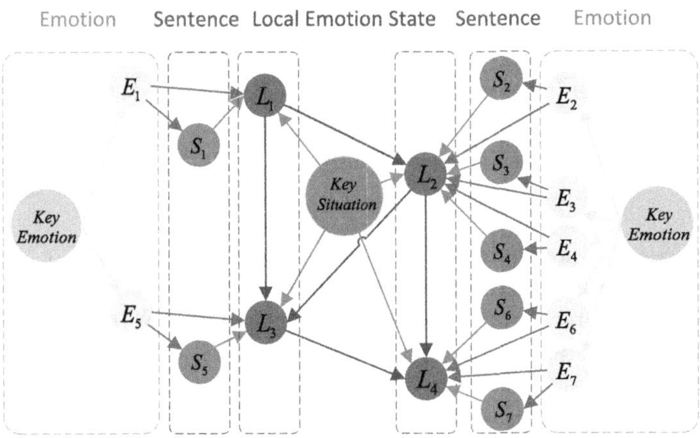

Fig. 3. Emotional flow graph is constructed according to Table 1. The left part represents speaker1 and the right part represents speaker2. Blue nodes denote sentences, green nodes denote emotions, and purple nodes denote abstracted aggregation nodes. (Color figure online)

The $[CLS]_i$ vector is used to initialize the nodes vector in Subsect. 3.3 and get the final context vector after Subsect. 3.3 graph network learning. A separate encoder is used to encode the situation and the $[CLS]_{KeySituation}$ can be obtained by the same method as Eq. 1.

3.3 Emotional Flow Graph

The speakers' emotional changes during the conversation are not completely chronological, the speakers' emotion state is often influenced by subjective features or objective features. So based on Table 1, we transform context into graph structure and employ Graph Convolutional Networks (GCN) to extract features.

Graph Construction. The emotional flow graph is constructed as shown in Fig. 3. Since the splitting strategy is used in Sect. 3.1, in order to integrate the speaker's clause emotion state and semantic information, we introduce *LocalEmotionState* nodes L_n to aggregate the semantic and emotion information, as the purple node shown in Fig. 3 is the local emotion state area. The number of L_n is equal to the U_n. For the first time, we introduce the $KeyEmotion$ node and $KeySituation$ node in the graph to extend the speakers' initial emotion into the ensuing conversation, as different speakers have different pre-existing initial emotions at the beginning of the conversation. The $KeyEmotion$ node is considered as the background information of each segmented sentence, so this will be a uni-directed edge pointing from the $KeyEmotion$ node to the utterance emotion node E_i.

Graph Initialization and Network. The initialization of the graph embedding can have a significant impact on the model. The $[CLS]$ vector of the transformer block encoder in Subsect. 3.2 is used as the initialized semantic embedding of the sentence node. And the emotion E_i is initialized as word embedding. The $KeyEmotion$ node vector can be calculated as followed:

$$V_{KeyEmotion} = Mean([CLS]_1, [CLS]_2, ..., [CLS]_i). \tag{2}$$

The $KeySituation$ node's initialized embedding is $[CLS]_{KeySituation}$. The sentence node S_i can be represented as the sentence vector $[CLS]_i$, where i is the turn of sentences after segmentation. The *LocalEmotionState* is an aggregation node, where the average of the sentence vectors of all the partitioned sentences in the current turn is used as the initialization. Taking the *LocalEmotionState* L_2 as an example, the initialization vector can be calculated as:

$$L_2 = Mean({S_2}^{CLS}, {S_3}^{CLS}, {S_4}^{CLS}). \tag{3}$$

Graph neural networks are very effective for modeling structured information like knowledge graphs, the MuSE model uses Graph Convolutional Networks (GCN) [7] to model the flow of emotions in a conversation. In order to ensure that the node vector update order in the directed emotional flow graph can fully simulate the actual emotional flow of the speaker, we design the update pattern of vectors between different node types. Unlike the traditional GCN that updates nodes randomly, the MuSE model controls the update order of different types of nodes, from emotion nodes to sentence nodes to local emotion state nodes. Equations 4, 5 and 6 show the update direction of emotion nodes, sentence nodes and local emotion state nodes respectively. The $^{(l)}$ denotes the node vector in the lth layer of the GCN network.

$${E_i}^{(l+1)} = GCN({E_i}^{(l)}|[CLS]_{KeyEmotion}) \tag{4}$$

$${S_i}^{(l+1)} = GCN({S_i}^{(l)}|E_i) \tag{5}$$

$${L_n}^{(l+1)} = L_{n-1}^{(l)} + GCN({L_n}^{(l)}|E_i) + GCN({L_n}^{(l)}|S_i) + GCN({L_n}^{(l)}|[CLS]_{KeySituation}) \tag{6}$$

The GCN layer is calculated as followed:

$$f\left(X^{(l)}, A\right) = \sigma\left(\hat{D}^{-\frac{1}{2}}\hat{A}\hat{D}^{-\frac{1}{2}}X^{(l)}W^{(l)}\right), \tag{7}$$

with $\hat{A} = A + I$, where A denotes the adjacency matrix and I denotes the identity matrix, $\hat{D}$ refers to the diagonal node degree matrix of $\hat{A}$ and $W^{(l)}$ denotes a trainable weight matrix. σ refers to a non-linear activation.

The average of aggregated local emotion state nodes $\{L_1, ..., L_n\}$ are used as representatives of the overall context, so the context vector $V_{context}$ can be computed as follows, where n is the number of sentences in a conversation:

$$V_{context} = Mean(L_1, L_2, ..., L_n) \tag{8}$$

We exploit the $V_{context}$ for contextual emotion prediction, calculated as follows, where FFN is feed-forward network:

$$EmotionLable = Softmax(FFN(V_{context})) \tag{9}$$

3.4 Decoder

In the decoding process, for each word y_t in Y, we employ the mask operation during the training process to avoid the model from seeing the correct response labels in advance. The negative log-likelihood loss can be calculated as:

$$\mathcal{L}_1 = -\sum_{i=1}^{n} \log p(y_n | \{y_1, ..., y_{i-1}\}, v_{context}) \tag{10}$$

And the emotion classification loss $\mathcal{L}_2$ is calculated by cross-entropy loss. All the parameters for our proposed model are trained and optimized based on the weighted sum of the mentioned losses:

$$\mathcal{L}(\theta) = \gamma_1 * \mathcal{L}_1 + \gamma_2 * \mathcal{L}_2, \tag{11}$$

where γ_1 and γ_2 are hyper-parameters and θ is all learnable parameters.

4 Experiment

4.1 Datasets

We conduct our experiments on the public dataset EMPATHETIC DIALOGUES[1] [19]. It contains 25k dialogues grounded in situations prompted by specific emotion labels. There are 32 evenly distributed categories of emotion labels in this dataset, representing the main emotions in the context of conversation.

4.2 Baselines

The following strong baseline models are selected for comparison.

- **Transformer** [24]: An original transformer model based on the seq2seq structure which is the classical generative model.
- **Multi-TRS** [19]: A generative model based on transformer with multi-task for emotion prediction. They built an emotion predictor to capture the speaker's emotions.
- **MoEL** [11]: MoEL can capture the user emotions distribution and softly combine the output states of the appropriate Listener(s). It's also a transformer-based model, which can react to certain emotions and generate an empathetic response.

[1] https://github.com/facebookresearch/EmpatheticDialogues.

- **EmpDG** [9]: EmpDG introduces an interactive adversarial learning framework that exploits user feedback and identifies whether the generated responses evoke emotion perceptivity in dialogues.
- **CEM** [20]: CEM leverages commonsense external knowledge to obtain more information about the user's situation and further enhance the empathy expression in generated responses.
- **CARE** [25]: A Conditional Variational Graph Auto-Encoder model considers the interdependence among causalities and reasons independently. The model utilizes Cause Effect Graph external knowledge to construct a graph.

4.3 Experiment Settings

To ensure the fairness of the experiment, we set the parameters of all models to a uniform standard, and the performance of the CEM model [20] after our tuning parameters is higher than the results reported in the original paper. The pre-trained GloVE vector [17] is used to initialize the word embeddings. During the training process, we adopt the adam optimizer with 16 batch size and the learning rate is 0.0001. All the models are trained on NVIDIA RTX 3090 GPU.

4.4 Automatic Evaluation

In order to compare with strong baseline models such as CARE [25], CEM [20] and SEEK [27] etc., we use the evaluation metrics from most papers and take Perplexity (PPL), Distinct-n(Dist-n) [8], BLEU [15], Rouge [10], Bert Score [28] as main automatic metrics. However, previous works including the CEM model [20] only focus on the Dist-n & Acc indicators and the CARE's authors believe that the BLEU and BertScore are more important, so they don't use the Dist-n & Acc indicators. We believe that all metrics matter because there are limitations to using distinct indicators alone to evaluate models. And we will introduce details in Subsect. 4.6.

The indicators are introduced as followed: (1) Perplexity (PPL) focuses on the model's confidence in response generation. (2) Distinct-n[2] measures the generated response's diversity. (3) BLEU[3] estimates the matching between n-grams of the generated response and those of the golden response. (4) The Rouge-L[4] indicator is very similar to the BLEU indicator, which is used to measure the matching degree between the generated results and the standard results. The difference is that ROUGE is based on the recall rate, while BLEU pays more attention to the accuracy rate. (5) BertScore[5] is based on the pre-trained model, uses context embedding to describe sentences, and calculates the semantic similarity between two sentences. BertScore has precision, recall and F1 metrics, and F1 value is influenced by precision and recall. We use the F-BERT to evaluate

[2] https://github.com/Sahandfer/CEM/blob/master/src/scripts/evaluate.py.
[3] https://github.com/mjpost/sacrebleu.
[4] https://github.com/pltrdy/rouge.
[5] https://github.com/Tiiiger/bert_score.

the model. On the PPL metric, a smaller value indicates a better model, and on the other metrics, a larger value indicates a better model.

Admittedly, BLEU and ROUGE can effectively evaluate the performance of models, and many models have adopted such evaluation metrics, but their experimental results are difficult to be compared under the same criteria due to the different calculation methods. We find several convenient, fast, and fair calculation methods from highly recognized repositories in GitHub and believe that they can significantly reduce the workload of researchers in evaluating indicators. The evaluation code is available at MuSE[6].

Table 3. Results of automatic evaluation on EMPATHETIC DIALOGUES.

Model	PPL ↓	Dist-1↑	Dist-2↑	Acc↑	BLEU↑	Rouge-L↑	F-BERT↑
Transformer	34.7083	0.4918	2.3134	–	2.6616	16.7549	22.7056
Multi-TRS	34.8442	0.4882	2.3594	35.85	2.7565	17.3173	22.7507
MoEL	35.5586	0.5632	2.8986	34.60	2.8129	17.1865	23.8777
EmpDG	34.4143	0.5693	3.1470	33.15	2.8297	18.1459	23.5411
CEM	34.9705	0.6180	3.058	39.07	2.5781	17.2128	23.2403
CARE	33.8397	0.5776	2.3096	–	2.8300	18.2122	23.2610
MuSE	**33.5451**	**0.6476**	**3.4380**	**42.99**	**2.8397**	**18.3105**	**24.2781**

Unlike previous models that excel in a single aspect, the MuSE model demonstrates superior performance on multiple evaluation metrics. From Table 3, we can find that the MuSE model with emotional dialogue graph achieves superior results in the majority of indicators. In terms of Dist-n metric, the emotional dialogue graph significantly improves the word richness of responses. Unlike previous works that utilized external knowledge, the MuSE model fuses fine-grained external knowledge of speakers' subtle emotions by constructing a dialogue graph and interacts with coarse-grained information at the contextual utterance level. We believe this is a new approach for empathetic dialogue that can capture speakers' emotional state changes at multiple scales. Emotion recognition accuracy (Acc) is a measure of how accurately the model captures the emotion state of the context. It can be seen from the table that the MuSE model can better capture the emotional states of the user due to the emotional flow graph structure. Because of the special structure of the CARE model, they don't provide Acc value from their paper.

The BLEU, Rouge-L, and F-BERT indicators focus more on the difference between the generated responses and golden truth sentences. The MuSE model achieves the best results compared with all baseline models in the BLEU, Rouge-L, and F-BERT metrics. The MuSE model achieves a significant superiority on both rigorous tests of evaluation metrics. We believe that this enhancement

[6] https://github.com/DericZhao/MuSE/evaluate.py.

is influenced by the constructed emotional dialogue graph, during which the speakers' emotional changes are important and the emotional flow dialogue graph captures this subtle characteristic information.

4.5 Human Evaluation

Besides the automatic evaluation, we also conduct human evaluation at the same time. We follow the evaluation method introduced in [9,11,20,25] from three perspectives. (1) Empathy, which measures the level of understanding of speakers' emotions. (2) Relevance, which measures the consistency of the topic, and relevance of responses to the context. (3) Fluency, which measures whether the response is linguistically sound and grammatically accurate. Each sentence corresponds to a 5-level score, where 5 is the best. We recruit 5 evaluators to judge the response from three aspects and each evaluator has a research interest in natural language processing and has obtained a master's degree. Then we compute the average value for each metric.

Table 4. Results of human evaluation on EMPATHETIC DIALOGUES

Model	Empathy	Relevance	Fluency
Multi-TRS	2.58	2.27	3.99
MoEL	2.66	2.29	4.24
EmpDG	2.35	2.43	4.18
CEM	2.52	2.41	4.80
CARE	2.99	3.09	4.75
MuSE	**3.29**	**3.12**	**4.88**

We evaluate the above classical models and the strong baseline models. As shown in Table 4, our model shows significant improvement over the other models in empathy, relevance, and fluency metrics. In terms of empathy degree, the MuSE model can better understand the speakers' intentions through emotional changes. From the relevance metric, the model captures fine-grained emotional changes between speakers, with more accurate control over whole contextual emotion, thus generating empathic responses. The fluency metric reflects model's convergence degree and it can be found that the MuSE model can answer more fluently than the previous models.

The above human evaluation results can also prove that capturing the speakers' fine-grained emotional changes is important to improve the performance of empathy dialogue.

4.6 Ablation Experiments

In the ablation experiments, we conduct some experiments separately to investigate the importance of different modules of the MuSE model. First, we change the oriented emotional flow graph to an undirected graph to verify the correctness of our proposed oriented emotional flow graph. Second, we remove the *KeyEmotion* node from the graph and in the third experiment, we remove the *KeySituation* node from the graph to evaluate the performance of the key nodes we proposed. Finally, we validate it is necessary to employ multiple metrics to evaluate the empathetic model through MuSE(GoEmotion).

Table 5. Results of ablation studies on EMPATHETIC DIALOGUES.

Model	PPL ↓	Dist-1↑	Dist-2↑	Acc↑	BLEU↑	Rouge-L↑	F-BERT↑
MuSE	33.5451	0.6476	3.4380	**42.99**	**2.8397**	**18.3105**	**24.2781**
w/o Directional	33.7078	**0.6490**	3.3116	41.92	2.6090	17.9899	24.1727
w/o *KeyEmotion*	**33.4750**	0.6324	**3.4897**	42.09	2.7902	18.1466	24.2596
w/o *KeySituation*	33.9445	0.5620	2.8363	33.40	2.8267	17.4461	23.8502
MuSE(GoEmotion)	33.9068	**0.7286**	**3.8021**	42.82	2.3294	17.2796	23.4009

From Table 5, we can find that the results of undirected graphs have a decrease in most of the metrics. After the case study, we find that the improvement in the Dist-n metric is due to generate more context-irrelevant words, which can be confirmed by the decrease in BLEU values. After removing the *KeyEmotion* node, there is a slight decrease in the evaluation metrics. However, after removing the *KeySituation* node, the model's performance drop sharply. After the above ablation experiments, we believe that the background contextual word embedding information at the emotion word level has not as much impact on the whole model as the situation node sentence embedding information at the sentence level. The key situation contains richer and more accurate preexisting information, which also proves that it is very effective to introduce key nodes to the emotional dialogue graph.

In Table 5, MuSE (GoEmotion) replaces the original external knowledge pre-trained model with 'GoEmotion' [22] for emotion recognition from E_1 to E_n. The GoEmotion model has 27 emotion types, while the pre-trained model used by MuSE has seven emotion types. As can be seen from the Table 5, the MuSE(GoEmotion) model performs much better than the original MuSE model proposed in this paper if Dist-n is used as the evaluation metric. Compared with other strong baseline models, there is also an improvement in Dist-n metric according to the data in Table 3. But according to the case study in Table 6, it can be found that the improvement in Dist-n values is due to the fact that the MuSE(GoEmotion) generates context-irrelevant response, resulting in a certain improvement in richness of sentences. This also demonstrates that complex external information leads to poor model generation quality. Therefore, we choose all metrics to better measure the empathic dialogue generation task in this paper.

Table 6. Case study of the MuSE model.

Emotion:	Sentimental
Context:	
Speaker1:	Over the summer my family went to alabama to visit family and I felt a lot of emotions.
Speaker2:	I guess you do not live in alabama? was it overall a good trip .... or challenging? or both!
Speaker1:	No, I do not live in alabama We drove and trip was overall very good as sometimes it can be challenging when driving such a long distance.
Golden:	Well, If the drive was the most challenging it sounds like a good trip! Too often it is family dynamics that are more challenging and not so easily taken care of .
MuSE:	That is so cool! I am glad you were able to get to go back to see them.
MuSE (Go Emotion):	I am glad you are able to find it! (Context-irrelevant)

5 Conclusion and Future Work

In this paper, we argued that modeling the constantly changing emotional flow of speakers is crucial and propose the MuSE model to simulate speaker interactions. To capture speakers' subtle emotions, we introduced a new fine-grained expansion strategy that enriches the emotional flow graph through multi-scale fusion. By controlling the direction and order of node update information, we simulated emotion transmission between speakers on the directed emotional flow graph. We added the emotion and situation nodes into the emotional flow graph that extends the speakers' initial emotion into the ensuing conversation. Experimental results demonstrated the superior performance of the MuSE model. In the future, we will further explore the strategy of constructing fine-grained conversation graphs in conversation graphs.

Acknowledgments. This work is supported by the National Natural Science Foundation of China (61672144, 61872072).

Ethics Statement. We do not observe direct ethical and security issues arising from the emotional dialogue itself. The public dataset used in this paper may contain user privacy, but it has been made harmless in the earliest published dataset papers.

References

1. Bosselut, A., Rashkin, H., Sap, M., Malaviya, C., Celikyilmaz, A., Choi, Y.: Comet: commonsense transformers for automatic knowledge graph construction. In: Proceedings of the 57th Annual Meeting of the Association for Computational Linguistics, pp. 4762–4779 (2019)
2. Gao, J., et al.: Improving empathetic response generation by recognizing emotion cause in conversations. In: Findings of the association for computational linguistics: EMNLP 2021 (2021)
3. Ghosal, D., Majumder, N., Poria, S., Chhaya, N., Gelbukh, A.: Dialoguegcn: A graph convolutional neural network for emotion recognition in conversation. In: Proceedings of the 2019 Conference on Empirical Methods in Natural Language Processing and the 9th International Joint Conference on Natural Language Processing (EMNLP-IJCNLP), pp. 154–164 (2019)
4. Hartmann, J.: Emotion english distilroberta-base (2022). https://huggingface.co/j-hartmann/emotion-english-distilroberta-base/
5. Keskin, S.C.: From what isn't empathy to empathic learning process. Procedia Soc. Behav. Sci. **116**, 4932–4938 (2014)
6. Kim, H., Kim, B., Kim, G.: Perspective-taking and pragmatics for generating empathetic responses focused on emotion causes. In: Proceedings of the 2021 Conference on Empirical Methods in Natural Language Processing, pp. 2227–2240 (2021)
7. Kipf, T.N., Welling, M.: Semi-supervised classification with graph convolutional networks. In: International Conference on Learning Representations (2017). https://openreview.net/forum?id=SJU4ayYgl
8. Li, J., Galley, M., Brockett, C., Gao, J., Dolan, W.B.: A diversity-promoting objective function for neural conversation models. In: Proceedings of the 2016 Conference of the North American Chapter of the Association for Computational Linguistics: Human Language Technologies, pp. 110–119 (2016)
9. Li, Q., Chen, H., Ren, Z., Ren, P., Tu, Z., Chen, Z.: Empdg: Multi-resolution interactive empathetic dialogue generation. In: Proceedings of the 28th International Conference on Computational Linguistics, pp. 4454–4466 (2020)
10. Lin, C.Y.: Rouge: A package for automatic evaluation of summaries. In: Text summarization branches out, pp. 74–81 (2004)
11. Lin, Z., Madotto, A., Shin, J., Xu, P., Fung, P.: Moel: mixture of empathetic listeners. In: Proceedings of the 2019 Conference on Empirical Methods in Natural Language Processing and the 9th International Joint Conference on Natural Language Processing (EMNLP-IJCNLP), pp. 121–132 (2019)
12. Majumder, N., et al.: Mime: Mimicking emotions for empathetic response generation. In: Proceedings of the 2020 Conference on Empirical Methods in Natural Language Processing (EMNLP), pp. 8968–8979 (2020)
13. Paiva, A., Leite, I., Boukricha, H., Wachsmuth, I.: Empathy in virtual agents and robots: a survey. ACM Trans. Interact. Intell. Syst. (TiiS) **7**(3), 1–40 (2017)

14. Pang, J., Xu, H., Song, S., Zou, B., He, X.: Mfdg: A multi-factor dialogue graph model for dialogue intent classification. In: Machine Learning and Knowledge Discovery in Databases: European Conference, ECML PKDD 2022, Grenoble, France, September 19–23, 2022, Proceedings, Part II. pp. 691–706. Springer (2023). https://doi.org/10.1007/978-3-031-26390-3_40
15. Papineni, K., Roukos, S., Ward, T., Zhu, W.J.: Bleu: a method for automatic evaluation of machine translation. In: Proceedings of the 40th annual meeting of the Association for Computational Linguistics, pp. 311–318 (2002)
16. Peng, W., Hu, Y., Xing, L., Xie, Y., Sun, Y., Li, Y.: Control globally, understand locally: A global-to-local hierarchical graph network for emotional support conversation. In: Raedt, L.D. (ed.) Proceedings of the Thirty-First International Joint Conference on Artificial Intelligence, IJCAI 2022, Vienna, Austria, 23–29 July 2022, pp. 4324–4330. ijcai.org (2022). https://doi.org/10.24963/ijcai.2022/600, https://doi.org/10.24963/ijcai.2022/600
17. Pennington, J., Socher, R., Manning, C.D.: Glove: Global vectors for word representation. In: Proceedings of the 2014 Conference on Empirical Methods in Natural Language Processing (EMNLP), pp. 1532–1543 (2014)
18. Qin, L., Li, Z., Che, W., Ni, M., Liu, T.: Co-gat: A co-interactive graph attention network for joint dialog act recognition and sentiment classification. In: Proceedings of the AAAI Conference on Artificial Intelligence. vol. 35, pp. 13709–13717 (2021)
19. Rashkin, H., Smith, E.M., Li, M., Boureau, Y.L.: Towards empathetic open-domain conversation models: A new benchmark and dataset. In: Proceedings of the 57th Annual Meeting of the Association for Computational Linguistics, pp. 5370–5381 (2019)
20. Sabour, S., Zheng, C., Huang, M.: Cem: Commonsense-aware empathetic response generation. In: Proceedings of the AAAI Conference on Artificial Intelligence. vol. 36, pp. 11229–11237 (2022)
21. Sap, M., et al.: Atomic: An atlas of machine commonsense for if-then reasoning. In: Proceedings of the AAAI Conference on Artificial Intelligence, vol. 33, pp. 3027–3035 (2019)
22. Savani, B.: Bert base go emotion. https://huggingface.co/bhadresh-savani/bert-base-go-emotion (2021)
23. Tu, Q., Li, Y., Cui, J., Wang, B., Wen, J.R., Yan, R.: Misc: A mixed strategy-aware model integrating comet for emotional support conversation. In: Proceedings of the 60th Annual Meeting of the Association for Computational Linguistics (Volume 1: Long Papers), pp. 308–319 (2022)
24. Vaswani, A., et al.: Attention is all you need. Adv. Neural Inform. Process. Syst. **30** (2017)
25. Wang, J., Cheng, Y., Li, W.: Care: Causality reasoning for empathetic responses by conditional graph generation. In: Proceedings of the 2022 Conference on Empirical Methods in Natural Language Processing, EMNLP 2022 (2022)
26. Wang, J., Li, W., Lin, P., Mu, F.: Empathetic response generation through graph-based multi-hop reasoning on emotional causality. Knowl.-Based Syst. **233**, 107547 (2021)
27. Wang, L., et al.: Empathetic dialogue generation via sensitive emotion recognition and sensible knowledge selection. In: Findings of the Association for Computational Linguistics: EMNLP 2022, pp. 4634–4645. Association for Computational Linguistics, Abu Dhabi, United Arab Emirates (Dec 2022), https://aclanthology.org/2022.findings-emnlp.340

28. Zhang, T., Kishore, V., Wu, F., Weinberger, K.Q., Artzi, Y.: Bertscore: Evaluating text generation with bert. In: International Conference on Learning Representations (2020). https://openreview.net/forum?id=SkeHuCVFDr
29. Zhao, W., Zhao, Y., Lu, X.: Cauain: Causal aware interaction network for emotion recognition in conversations. In: Proceedings of the Thirty-First International Joint Conference on Artificial Intelligence, IJCAI, pp. 4524–4530 (2022)

Posterior Consistency for Missing Data in Variational Autoencoders

Timur Sudak[1] and Sebastian Tschiatschek[1,2](✉)

[1] Faculty of Computer Science, University of Vienna, Vienna, Austria
sebastian.tschiatschek@univie.ac.at
[2] Research Network Data Science, University of Vienna, Vienna, Austria

Abstract. We consider the problem of learning Variational Autoencoders (VAEs), i.e., a type of deep generative model, from data with missing values. Such data is omnipresent in real-world applications of machine learning because complete data is often impossible or too costly to obtain. We particularly focus on improving a VAE's amortized posterior inference, i.e., the encoder, which in the case of missing data can be susceptible to learning inconsistent posterior distributions regarding the missingness. To this end, we provide a formal definition of posterior consistency and propose an approach for regularizing an encoder's posterior distribution which promotes this consistency. We observe that the proposed regularization suggests a different training objective than that typically considered in the literature when facing missing values. Furthermore, we empirically demonstrate that our regularization leads to improved performance in missing value settings in terms of reconstruction quality and downstream tasks utilizing uncertainty in the latent space. This improved performance can be observed for many classes of VAEs including VAEs equipped with normalizing flows.

Keywords: Variational Autoencoders · Missing Data

1 Introduction

The availability of large amounts of data is often key to the impressive performance of nowadays machine learning (ML) models. For instance, in computer vision, a logarithmic relationship between an ML model's performance and the amount of training data has been observed [37]. While in some cases the considered data is complete, in many relevant real-world applications, data with missing values is omnipresent. For instance, this holds in various applications from physical and social science [2,32,38]. The missingness in real-world data

This work was funded in parts by the Federal Ministry of Education, Science and Research (BMBWF), Austria [Digitize! Computational Social Science in the Digital and Social Transformation].

© The Author(s), under exclusive license to Springer Nature Switzerland AG 2023
D. Koutra et al. (Eds.): ECML PKDD 2023, LNAI 14170, pp. 508–524, 2023.
https://doi.org/10.1007/978-3-031-43415-0_30

can have different reasons, e.g., intentional or unintentional unanswered items in surveys [29], accidental deletion [26,35], or high costs of exhaustive data acquisition [44].

Many approaches for the statistical analysis of data with missing values have been developed [20]. Some of them first complete the data (impute missing values) while others directly perform statistical analysis based on the incomplete data. Next to classical statistical approaches, deep learning-based approaches have recently gained importance. Classical statistical approaches include for example mean imputation, regression-based approaches like multiple imputation by chained equations (MICE) [4], and MissForest [36]. In the context of deep learning, recent approaches focused largely on deep generative models, in particular, generative adversarial networks (GANs) and variational autoencoders (VAEs). GAN-based approaches include for instance generative adversarial imputation nets (GAIN) [40] and MisGAN [5]. Approaches for handling missing data in VAEs include zero-imputation VAEs (VAE-ZI) [28], partial VAEs (PVAE) [23], and the missing data importance-weighted autoencoder (MIWAE) [25].

In this paper, we consider and extend VAEs for dealing with data with missing values. In particular, we focus on an *inconsistency issue* of the approximate inference network's posterior that can arise when VAEs are trained on incomplete data: the approximate inference network can be prone to produce inconsistent posterior distributions for different missingness patterns in the input data. To overcome this issue, we identify conditions for guaranteeing *posterior consistency* and propose a regularizer building on these conditions which can be integrated into the training of VAEs. Our approach is orthogonal (and complementary) to existing approaches for VAEs for data with missing values like [23,25,28]—while these approaches modify the inputs to the VAE, the structure of the approximate inference network, or the lower bound on the likelihood to be optimized, they do not add explicit regularization on the approximate posterior distributions regarding the missingness in the input. Our approach also differs from other works that have considered forms of posterior consistency [22,34,43]—these works mainly build on the idea that transformed inputs should map to similar posterior distributions which is not necessarily implied by our approach building on first principles. We empirically demonstrate that our proposed regularization leads to improved imputation performance and improved performance in downstream applications in missing data settings.

Our contributions are:

- We propose a notion of *posterior consistency* and show its importance for VAEs for data with missing values.
- We propose a regularizer for promoting the posterior consistency of VAEs.
- We empirically demonstrate the superior performance of VAEs trained with our proposed regularization in comparison to many natural baselines.
- The source code for reproducing our experiments is available on github.[1]

[1] https://github.com/stschia/VAE-posterior-consistency.git.

Our paper is organized as follows: In Sect. 2 we introduce the relevant background and notation before describing the problem of posterior inconsistency in Sect. 3. We describe our approach in Sect. 4, followed by a discussion of related work in Sect. 5. In Sects. 6 and 7 we empirically evaluate our proposed approach. We conclude our paper in Sect. 8.

2 Background

In this section, we introduce our notation and the necessary background about VAEs and the considered types of missing data.

Notation. We use uppercase letters to denote random variables (RVs), e.g., X, and lowercase letters to denote instantiations of RVs, e.g., x. We use bold uppercase letters to denote vectors of RVs, e.g., $\mathbf{X}$, and bold lowercase letters to denote their respective instantiations, e.g., $\mathbf{x}$. Furthermore, we use P and Q to denote subsets of some fixed ground set $\mathcal{V} = \{1, \ldots, d\}$, i.e., $P, Q \subseteq \mathcal{V}$. Assuming $\mathbf{X} = [X_1, \ldots, X_d]^T$, we use $\mathbf{X}_Q$ to denote the vector of random variables $[X_{i_1}, \ldots, X_{i_k}]^T$, where $|Q| = k$ and $Q = \{i_1, \ldots, i_k\}$. We denote the ith component of $\mathbf{x}$ by x_i and, similarly to before, denote by $\mathbf{x}_Q$ the vector $[x_{i_1}, \ldots, x_{i_k}]^T$.

Data. Assume n i.i.d. samples of dimension d from an unknown data distribution p^*, i.e., $\tilde{\mathbf{x}}^1, \ldots, \tilde{\mathbf{x}}^n \sim p^*$. For those samples, only a subset of the dimensions (features) is available to us, i.e., for a sample $\tilde{\mathbf{x}}^i$ there exists $Q^i \subseteq \mathcal{V}$ and only $\tilde{\mathbf{x}}^i_{Q^i}$ is available to us. The set of present features Q^i can depend on $\tilde{\mathbf{x}}^i$ in different ways according to an unknown missingness mechanism (details are at the end of this section). We collect the partial data into the data set $\mathcal{D} = \{\tilde{\mathbf{x}}^1_{Q^1}, \ldots, \tilde{\mathbf{x}}^n_{Q^n}\}$. Equivalently we can consider $\mathcal{D} = \{\mathbf{x}^1, \ldots, \mathbf{x}^n\}$, where $\mathbf{x}^i$ are of dimension d and missing dimensions contain the special symbol $\perp$. To simplify notation, we will assume that $\perp$ always assumes the implied dimensionality, e.g., a statement like $\mathbf{x}_Q = \perp$ implies that $\perp$ is a vector of size $|Q|$ in which each dimension is $\perp$.

Variational Autoencoders. A common approach to modeling complicated distributions p^* are VAEs, a type of deep generative latent variable models [17]. In vanilla VAEs, one assumes the data to be generated as follows:

$$\mathbf{z} \sim p(\mathbf{Z}), \quad \tilde{\mathbf{x}} \sim p_\theta(\tilde{\mathbf{X}}|\mathbf{z}),$$

where $\mathbf{z}$ are latent variables following a prior distribution $p(\mathbf{Z})$, commonly assumed to be the normal distribution of dimension k with diagonal covariance matrix, and $p_\theta(\tilde{\mathbf{X}}|\mathbf{z}) = \mathcal{N}(\mu_\theta(\mathbf{z}), \mathrm{diag}(\sigma^2_\theta(\mathbf{z})))$ is a normal distribution of dimension d, where θ denotes the parameters of neural networks parameterizing its mean as $\mu_\theta\colon \mathbb{R}^k \to \mathbb{R}^d$ and its standard deviation as $\sigma_\theta\colon \mathbb{R}^k \to \mathbb{R}^d$. The generative model induces a distribution over $\tilde{\mathbf{X}}$ through marginalization over $\mathbf{Z}$, i.e., $p_\theta(\tilde{\mathbf{X}}) = \int_{\mathbf{z}} p_\theta(\tilde{\mathbf{X}}|\mathbf{Z} = \mathbf{z}) p(\mathbf{Z} = \mathbf{z})\, \mathrm{d}\mathbf{z}$. We often drop the subscript θ for brevity.

VAEs are typically fit to data $\mathcal{D}$ by maximizing a lower bound on the marginal log-likelihood $\mathcal{L}(\mathcal{D}) = \sum_i \log p_\theta(\tilde{\mathbf{x}}^i)$, the so-called *evidence lower bound* (ELBO):

$$\mathcal{L}(\mathcal{D}) \geq \sum_{i=1}^{n} \left[\mathbb{E}_{\mathbf{z}\sim q_\phi(\mathbf{Z}|\tilde{\mathbf{x}}^i)}[\log p_\theta(\tilde{\mathbf{x}}^i|\mathbf{z})] - \mathrm{KL}(q_\phi(\mathbf{Z}|\tilde{\mathbf{x}}^i)\|p(\mathbf{Z}))\right],$$

where $q_\phi(\mathbf{Z}|\tilde{\mathbf{x}}^i)$ is an approximation to the true posterior distribution $p_\theta(\mathbf{Z}|\tilde{\mathbf{x}}^i)$, implemented by a neural network with parameters ϕ, the so-called inference network or encoder. Abusing notation, we will in the following often write $q_\phi(\tilde{\mathbf{x}}^i)$ instead of $q_\phi(\mathbf{Z}|\tilde{\mathbf{x}}^i)$. In vanilla VAEs, $q_\phi(\tilde{\mathbf{x}}^i)$ is a normal distribution of dimension k with a diagonal covariance matrix whose parameters are computed by the encoder. The type of distribution of $q_\phi(\tilde{\mathbf{x}}^i)$ is also referred to as the variational family, and the encoder is said to perform amortized inference of the posterior as the parameters of the variational family's distribution are predicted by a neural network and not optimized on a sample by sample basis [42]. Typically, the ELBO is not computed exactly but a stochastic approximation of the ELBO is considered. For effective learning, the reparametrization trick is leveraged [17]. The difference between the marginal log-likelihood and the ELBO depends, despite other things, on the used variational family, i.e., the choice of distribution for $q_\phi(\tilde{\mathbf{x}})$, and the quality of the amortization [7].

Missing Data. Missing data is a common phenomenon in many real-world settings. In the literature, different types of missingness are distinguished depending on how the missing variables are determined [21,33]. To introduce those, let Q be the set of available features of sample $\mathbf{x}$ and denote by $\tilde{\mathbf{x}}$ the corresponding complete sample. The following missingness mechanisms are typically considered:

- *Missing completely at random (MCAR)*: The data is MCAR if Q is independent of $\tilde{\mathbf{x}}$, i.e., $Q \perp\!\!\!\perp \tilde{\mathbf{x}}$, where $\perp\!\!\!\perp$ denotes conditional independence.
- *Missing at random (MAR)*: The data is MAR if its missingness can be explained solely by the observed variables, i.e., $\tilde{\mathbf{x}}_{\mathcal{V}-Q} \perp\!\!\!\perp Q \mid \tilde{\mathbf{x}}_Q$.
- *Missing not at random (MNAR)*: Any missingness which is not MCAR or MAR is MNAR.

Variational Autoencoders for Missing Data. Models can be fit to data with missingness of MCAR or MAR type by maximizing the likelihood of the data (the missingness is ignorable [33]). This has been exploited for training VAEs from incomplete data by extending the ELBO (e.g., [23,28]) such that

$$\mathcal{L}(\mathcal{D}) \geq \sum_{i=1}^{n} \left[\mathbb{E}_{\mathbf{z}\sim q_\phi(\mathbf{x}^i_{Q_i})}[\log p_\theta(\mathbf{x}^i_{Q^i}|\mathbf{z})] - \mathrm{KL}(q_\phi(\mathbf{x}^i_{Q^i})\|p(\mathbf{Z}))\right].$$

In the case of the zero-imputation VAE (VAE-ZI), the encoder $q_\phi(\cdot)$ is provided with the partially-observed input $\mathbf{x}^i$ with missing features replaced by zeros. Zero imputation of the input is also used for the MIWAE but in contrast to the vanilla VAE a tighter lower bound to the data's likelihood based on M importance weighted samples $\mathbf{z}_1, \ldots, \mathbf{z}_M \sim q_\phi(\mathbf{x}^i_{Q^i})$ is considered:

$$\mathcal{L}^M(\mathcal{D}) \geq \sum_{i=1}^{n} \left[\mathbb{E}_{\mathbf{z}_1,\ldots,\mathbf{z}_M \sim q_\phi(\mathbf{x}^i_{Q^i})} \left[\log \frac{1}{M} \sum_{k=1}^{M} \frac{p_\theta(\mathbf{x}^i_{Q^i}|\mathbf{z}_k)p(\mathbf{z}_k)}{q_\phi(\mathbf{x}^i_{Q^i})} \right] \right].$$

For PVAEs, a permutation-invariant set function is used as the encoder, i.e., $q_\phi(\mathbf{x}^i_{Q^i}) = g(h(\mathbf{s}_1), h(\mathbf{s}_2), \ldots, h(\mathbf{s}_{|Q^i|}))$, where each $\mathbf{s}_j$ is the concatenation or multiplication of a learned embedding $\mathbf{e}_j$ and the corresponding observed feature x^i_j, and the permutation-invariant function $g(\cdot)$ is the summation of outputs from neural networks $h(\cdot)$, potentially followed by further neural network layers.

3 Posterior Inconsistency

During training, the approximate posterior $q_\phi(\mathbf{x})$ of a VAE is fit to the generative model specified through $p(\mathbf{z})$ and $p_\theta(\mathbf{x}|\mathbf{z})$ via maximization of the ELBO. Typically $q_\phi(\mathbf{x})$ does not perfectly match the true posterior distribution $p_\theta(\mathbf{Z}|\mathbf{x})$ because the encoder's variational family is not expressive enough ("approximation gap") and because the amortization results in suboptimal predictions for the parameters of the variational distributions ("amortization gap") [7]. In this paper, we focus on special aspects of these gaps which occur when working with missing data and which can significantly decrease performance in downstream tasks.

We refer to the problem under consideration as *posterior inconsistency* and broadly use this term to denote inconsistencies in the approximate posterior distribution when applying VAEs in cases of incomplete data. In such cases, a VAE's approximate posterior is computed from a partial sample $\mathbf{x}_Q$, for some $Q \subseteq \mathcal{V}$ [23,25,28]. Importantly, there is a strong dependency between the posteriors $p_\theta(\mathbf{z}|\mathbf{x}_Q)$ and $p_\theta(\mathbf{z}|\mathbf{x}_P)$ for $P \subseteq Q$ that should be reflected in the approximate posterior but often this is not the case.

The consequences of such inconsistency can be observed in the task of image inpainting, cf. Fig. 1. As shown in Figs. 1c and 1d, models that do not accurately reflect the relationship between $p_\theta(\mathbf{z}|\mathbf{x}_P)$ and $p_\theta(\mathbf{z}|\mathbf{x}_Q)$ can suffer from posterior inconsistency, which in turn can cause overconfident image imputation. By contrast, see Fig. 1e, models trained with regularization of the relationship of the approximate posteriors for different subsets of missing features can provide more robust imputations, i.e., better account for different plausible imputations.

This posterior inconsistency can lead to reduced performance in downstream tasks if they rely on computations in the latent space. For example, previous work has considered the computation of information rewards based on the approximate posteriors in the latent space in order to select which feature to acquire in active feature selection scenarios [23]. Clearly, the accuracy of such a computation strongly depends on the quality of the approximate posterior distribution, and a bad approximate posterior distribution can result in incorrect rewards for the different variables that could be selected, cf. our experiments in Sect. 7.

In the next section, we formally define *posterior consistency* and propose an effective regularizer for improving the consistency of the approximate posterior under missingness which helps to alleviate the problems sketched above.

4 Methodology

Our approach to improving the performance of VAEs in the face of missing data builds on the relationship of the posterior distributions for different sets of available features. In particular, let $P, Q \subseteq \mathcal{V}$ and $P \subseteq Q$ denote two subsets of the available features, and let $\bar{P} = Q \setminus P$, i.e., P contains only a subset of the features of Q and $\bar{P}$ is the set of features in Q which are not in P. We are interested in understanding the relationship of $p_\theta(\mathbf{z}|\mathbf{x}_P)$ and $p_\theta(\mathbf{z}|\mathbf{x}_Q)$. To this end, we assume the generative model according to Fig. 2 for the data and the missingness, i.e.,

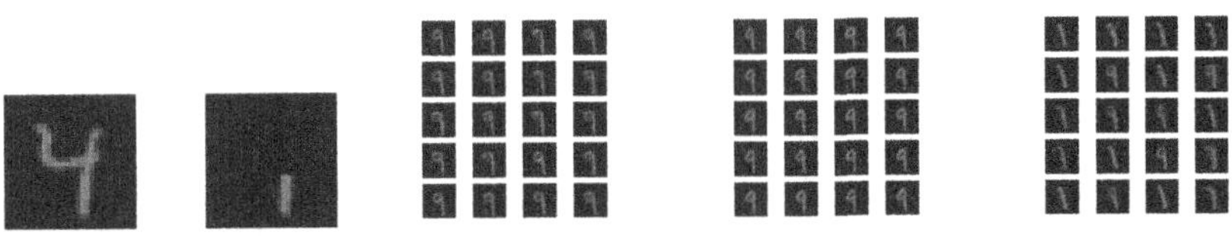

(a) Original (b) Masked (c) AM-VAE-PNP (d) VAE-PNP (e) REG-VAE-PNP (ours)

Fig. 1. Imputation of an image for which the upper part is missing. *(a)* Original image. *(b)* Image with masked (missing) upper part. *(c) (d) (e)* Images imputed by AM-VAE-PNP, VAE-PNP, and REG-VAE-PNP (ours) for the masked input image, respectively. The model with our proposed regularization produces different plausible completions while models without our regularization produce almost deterministic outputs. See Sect. 6 for details regarding the models.

$$\mathbf{z} \sim p(\mathbf{Z}), \quad \tilde{\mathbf{x}} \sim p_\theta(\tilde{\mathbf{X}}|\mathbf{z}), \quad \mathbf{m} \sim p_\theta(\mathbf{M}|\tilde{\mathbf{x}}), \quad \mathbf{x} \sim p_\theta(\mathbf{X}|\tilde{\mathbf{x}}, \mathbf{m}).$$

For MCAR data, $\mathbf{m} \sim p_\theta(\mathbf{M}|\tilde{\mathbf{x}})$ reduces to $\mathbf{m} \sim p_\theta(\mathbf{M})$. The observed $\mathbf{x}$ is a deterministic function of $\tilde{\mathbf{x}}$ and $\mathbf{m}$, i.e., $p_\theta(\mathbf{X}|\tilde{\mathbf{x}}, \mathbf{m})$ has all its probability mass on the single $\mathbf{x}$ corresponding to $\tilde{\mathbf{x}}$ where missing values according to $\mathbf{m}$ are replaced by $\perp$. We additionally make the common assumption that given $\mathbf{z}$ the dimensions of $\tilde{\mathbf{x}}$ are generated independently.

For this generative model, we can make the following observation (see Appendix A for details) regarding the relationship of the posteriors for different sets of available features:

Observation 1. *For missing data we have*

$$p(\mathbf{z}|\mathbf{x}_Q, \mathbf{x}_{\mathcal{V}-Q} = \perp) = p(\mathbf{z}|\mathbf{x}_P, \mathbf{x}_{\mathcal{V}-Q} = \perp)\left[p(\mathbf{x}_{\bar{P}}|\mathbf{z}, \mathbf{x}_P, \mathbf{x}_{\mathcal{V}-Q} = \perp)\frac{p(\mathbf{x}_P, \mathbf{x}_{\mathcal{V}-Q} = \perp)}{p(\mathbf{x}_Q, \mathbf{x}_{\mathcal{V}-Q} = \perp)}\right].$$

For MCAR data this simplifies to

$$p(\mathbf{z}|\mathbf{x}_Q) = p(\mathbf{z}|\mathbf{x}_P)\Big[\frac{p(\mathbf{x}_P)}{p(\mathbf{x}_Q)}p(\mathbf{x}_{\bar{P}}|\mathbf{z})\Big]. \tag{1}$$

For brevity of notation, we continue the exposition of our approach using the notation for the MCAR case but it would be analogous for MAR and MNAR. Based on the above observation, we define the notion of *posterior consistency.*

Definition 1 (Posterior consistency). *A family of conditional distributions* $\{\psi(\mathbf{Z}|\mathbf{x}_Q)|\forall \mathbf{x}, Q \subseteq \mathcal{V}\}$ *is* posterior consistent *with the generative model* p_θ *and possible missingness if* $\forall \mathbf{x}_Q \sim p_\theta(\mathbf{X})$ $\forall P \subseteq Q \subseteq \mathcal{V}$ *with* $p_\theta(\mathbf{x}_P) > 0$,

$$\mathrm{KL}\Big(\psi(\mathbf{Z}|\mathbf{x}_Q)\|\frac{p(\mathbf{x}_P)}{p(\mathbf{x}_Q)} \cdot p(\mathbf{x}_{\bar{P}}|\mathbf{Z})p_\theta(\mathbf{Z}|\mathbf{x}_P)\Big) = 0. \tag{2}$$

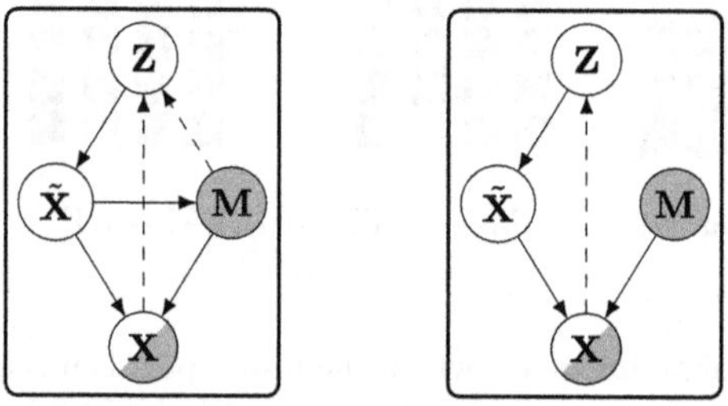

(a) General Missingness (b) MCAR

Fig. 2. Graphical models representing the generative model of the data and the inference models (dashed lines) used in the VAEs. The model consists of latent variables **Z**, the complete sample $\tilde{\mathbf{X}}$, the missingness pattern **M**, and the partially observed data **X**. In the case of general missingness, the missingness pattern can contain valuable information about the latent variables **Z**. Half-shaded circles are used to emphasize that **X** contains missing values according to **M**.

This definition relates the posteriors $p_\theta(\mathbf{z}|\mathbf{x}_P)$ and $p_\theta(\mathbf{z}|\mathbf{x}_Q)$ for different nested subsets of features P and Q. Clearly, the true posterior is posterior-consistent. Note that if (2) is zero, then

$$\log p(\mathbf{x}_Q) = \log p(\mathbf{x}_P) + \mathbb{E}_{\mathbf{z}\sim\psi(\mathbf{Z}|\mathbf{x}_Q)} \log p(\mathbf{x}_{\bar{P}}|\mathbf{z}) - \mathrm{KL}(\psi(\mathbf{Z}|\mathbf{x}_Q)\|p_\theta(\mathbf{Z}|\mathbf{x}_P)).$$

Importantly, for the special case $\psi(\mathbf{Z}|\mathbf{x}) = p_\theta(\mathbf{Z}|\mathbf{x})$,

$$\log p(\mathbf{x}_Q) = \log p(\mathbf{x}_P) + \mathbb{E}_{\mathbf{z}\sim p_\theta(\mathbf{Z}|\mathbf{x}_Q)} \log p(\mathbf{x}_{\bar{P}}|\mathbf{z}) - \mathrm{KL}(p_\theta(\mathbf{Z}|\mathbf{x}_Q)\|p_\theta(\mathbf{Z}|\mathbf{x}_P)). \tag{3}$$

Thus, given posterior consistency, the marginal log-likelihoods of $\mathbf{x}_Q$ and $\mathbf{x}_P$ are closely related. Existing approaches for dealing with partial data in VAEs approximate the marginal log-likelihood of $\mathbf{x}_Q$ or $\mathbf{x}_P$ without considering their relation according to (3). For example, in [28] only $\mathbf{x}_Q$ was considered, whereas in [23] $\mathbf{x}_P$ was introduced during training but no connection between $\mathbf{x}_Q$ and $\mathbf{x}_P$ is explicitly considered.

As mentioned, posterior consistency obviously holds for the true posterior $p_\theta(\mathbf{Z}|\mathbf{x}_Q)$. In VAEs, this posterior is approximated by $q_\phi(\mathbf{Z}|\mathbf{x}_Q)$. Thus it would be sensible to require also the approximate posterior to satisfy

$$\mathrm{KL}\Big(q_\phi(\mathbf{Z}|\mathbf{x}_Q)\|\frac{p(\mathbf{x}_P)}{p(\mathbf{x}_Q)}\cdot p(\mathbf{x}_{\bar{P}}|\mathbf{Z})p_\theta(\mathbf{Z}|\mathbf{x}_P)\Big)=0.$$

Unfortunately, evaluating this KL-divergence is infeasible as it would require computing the true model's posterior. Therefore, we use the following proxy:

$$\mathrm{KL}\Big(q_\phi(\mathbf{Z}|\mathbf{x}_Q)\|\frac{p_\theta(\mathbf{x}_P)}{p_\theta(\mathbf{x}_Q)}\cdot p_\theta(\mathbf{x}_{\bar{P}}|\mathbf{Z})q_\phi(\mathbf{Z}|\mathbf{x}_P)\Big)$$

Note that this form of posterior consistency might not be achievable because of the limited expressiveness of the approximate posteriors when using an insufficiently expressive variational family. But even in such a case, we might hope for a better alignment of the approximate posterior for different missingness patterns resulting in better empirical performance, cf. experiments in Sect. 7.

We include the requirement for posterior consistency in the process of training the encoder and decoder of the VAE by maximizing the following objective (expressed for a single sample $\mathbf{x}^i$ for brevity):

$$\begin{aligned}\mathcal{L}_{\lambda,\theta,\phi} =&\mathcal{L}^{\mathrm{ELBO}}_{\theta,\phi}(\mathbf{x}^i_{Q^i})-\lambda\Big[\mathrm{KL}(q_\phi(\mathbf{Z}|\mathbf{x}^i_{Q^i})\|q_\phi(\mathbf{Z}|\mathbf{x}^i_{P^i}))\\ &-\mathbb{E}_{\mathbf{z}\sim q_\phi(\mathbf{Z}|\mathbf{x}^i_{Q^i})}\log p_\theta(\mathbf{x}^i_{\bar{P}^i}|\mathbf{Z})-\log\frac{p_\theta(\mathbf{x}^i_{P^i})}{p_\theta(\mathbf{x}^i_{Q^i})}\Big]\end{aligned}\tag{4}$$

where λ is a hyper-parameter allowing a trade-off between ELBO maximization and posterior consistency and P^i is a random subset of Q^i (details below). The ELBO term $\mathcal{L}^{\mathrm{ELBO}}_{\theta,\phi}(\mathbf{x}^i_{Q^i})$ for the partial sample $\mathbf{x}^i_{Q^i}$ is given as

$$\mathcal{L}^{\mathrm{ELBO}}_{\theta,\phi}(\mathbf{x}^i_{Q^i})=\mathbb{E}_{\mathbf{z}\sim q_\phi(\mathbf{x}^i_{Q^i})}[\log p_\theta(\mathbf{x}^i_{Q^i}|\mathbf{z})]-\mathrm{KL}(q_\phi(\mathbf{x}^i_{Q^i})\|p(\mathbf{Z})).$$

Furthermore, we approximate the expression $\log\frac{p_\theta(\mathbf{x}^i_{Pi})}{p_\theta(\mathbf{x}^i_{Q^i})}$ in (4) by $\mathcal{L}^{\mathrm{ELBO}}_{\theta,\phi}(\mathbf{x}^i_{P^i})-\mathcal{L}^{\mathrm{ELBO}}_{\theta,\phi}(\mathbf{x}^i_{Q^i})$, where the quality of this approximation will depend on the class of used VAE models and the parameters θ,ϕ. Models with more expressive posteriors, e.g., normalizing flows [31], typically have a smaller inference gap [7] and are likely to lead to a better approximation. For a more detailed derivation of the above objective please refer to Appendix B.

Training VAEs for posterior consistency. Our approach for optimizing (4) is presented in Algorithm 1. Note that artificial missingness is added to create the sets of features P^j from Q^j (line 5). In the simplest case, features are removed randomly with some fixed probability but other schemes, e.g., respecting a learned or the true missingness mechanisms, are possible. New missingness patterns are created randomly in each iteration. Even for the simple case of removing features with a fixed probability, we observed empirically that our regularization not only improves performance for MCAR data or MAR data, where the missingness mechanism can in principle be ignored [33] but also for some MNAR scenarios, cf. our Experiments in Sect. 7.

Extension Using Normalizing Flows. We can also use normalizing flows [31] to enable more expressive approximate posterior distributions (see Appendix C for details on normalizing flows). However, in this case, the KL divergences in Algorithm 1 cannot be computed in closed form but have to be approximated, e.g., by sampling (see Appendix D).

5 Related Work

Because of space constraints, we only provide a limited treatment of related work here. Further related work is discussed in Appendix E.

Generative models have a rich history of dealing with missing data [10,11,20]. In recent years, also scalable deep generative models [13,17] have been considered for this setting, in particular GANs and VAEs.

GAN-Based Models. GAN-based models are widely applied for recovering corrupted images due to their success in generating high-quality images [1,5,8,18,30]. Furthermore, the GAIN model [40] was used for the imputation of missing data from the UCI repository [9]. GAIN consists of a generator, which imputes data given partial data and a missingness mask, and a discriminator, which estimates a missingness mask from imputed data and hints of the mask. A central challenge of applying GAN-based models for imputation is the difficulty of training them, i.e., solving a min-max optimization of nonlinear functions [14].

VAE-Based Models. In [39], corrupted images were imputed using a VAE model, which was pre-trained on fully observed training data. Another approach, VAEs with zero imputation, was introduced in [28], where the missing data is filled with zeros in the training and test stages and then fed to the VAE to obtain the imputation as the reconstruction of the decoder. The imputation method MIWAE [25] is based on importance-weighted autoencoders [3] and also uses missing data imputed with zeros as an input to the inference network and utilizes a decoder for imputation. Using zero-imputed data directly as input to the encoder can lead to biased posterior estimates. Therefore, the VAE-PN/PNP models which use encoders based on the deep sets architecture [41] as introduced in [23] can be beneficial. All the above approaches assume MCAR or MAR data. Recently, VAEs have also been considered for MNAR data [6]. Not-MIWAE [15] is another IWAE-based model which considers the distribution of the missingness mechanism explicitly in the ELBO. Other approaches for dealing with the MNAR setting include [12,19,24].

Algorithm 1: Training algorithm for regularized VAE

Input: Partially observed training data $\mathcal{D}$, regularization parameter λ, and percentage of missingness $\mathcal{P}$

Initialize θ and ϕ

for $t = 1, 2, \ldots$ **do**

  `/* Get data and create artificial missingness */`

  Obtain indices I for minibatch

  Obtain minibatch $\mathcal{B}_Q = \{\mathbf{x}^j_{Q^j} | j \in I\}$

  Remove features with probability $\mathcal{P}$:
  $\mathcal{B}_P = \{\mathbf{x}^j_{P^j} | \mathbf{x}^j_{Q^j}, j \in I, P^j \text{ random subset of } Q^j\}$

  $\mathcal{B}_{\bar{P}} = \{\mathbf{x}^j_{\bar{P}^j} | j \in I, \bar{P}^j = Q^j \setminus P^j\}$

  $\mathcal{Z} = \{\mathbf{z}^j_{Q^j} \sim \mathcal{N}(\mu_\phi(\mathbf{x}^j_{Q^j}), \Sigma_\phi(\mathbf{x}^j_{Q^j})) \mid j \in I\}$

  $\mathcal{Z}' = \{\mathbf{z}^j_{P^j} \sim \mathcal{N}(\mu_\phi(\mathbf{x}^j_{P^j}), \Sigma_\phi(\mathbf{x}^j_{P^j})) \mid j \in I\}$

  `/* Compute loss as in Equation (4) */`

  Compute $\mathcal{L}^{\text{ELBO}}_{\theta,\phi}(\mathcal{B}_Q) = \frac{1}{|\mathcal{B}_Q|} \sum_{j \in I} [\log p_\theta(\mathbf{x}^j_{Q^j}, \mathbf{z}^j_{Q^j}) - \log q_\phi(\mathbf{z}^j_{Q^j} \mid \mathbf{x}^j_{Q^j})]$

  Compute $\mathcal{L}^{\text{ELBO}}_{\theta,\phi}(\mathcal{B}_P) = \frac{1}{|\mathcal{B}_P|} \sum_{j \in I} [\log p_\theta(\mathbf{x}^j_{P^j}, \mathbf{z}^j_{P^j}) - \log q_\phi(\mathbf{z}^j_{P^j} \mid \mathbf{x}^j_{P^j})]$

  Compute log-likelihood $\ell(\mathcal{B}_{\bar{P}}; \theta) = \frac{1}{|\mathcal{B}_{\bar{P}}|} \sum_{j \in I} \log p_\theta(\mathbf{x}^j_{\bar{P}^j} | \mathbf{z}^j_{Q^j})$

  Compute KL-divergence
  $r = \sum_{j \in I} \text{KL}(\mathcal{N}(\mathbf{Z} | \mu_\phi(\mathbf{x}^j_{Q^j}), \Sigma_\phi(\mathbf{x}^j_{Q^j})) || \mathcal{N}(\mathbf{Z} | \mu_\phi(\mathbf{x}^j_{P^j}), \Sigma_\phi(\mathbf{x}^j_{P^j})))$

  Compute joint ELBO
  $\mathcal{L}_{\lambda,\theta,\phi} = \mathcal{L}^{\text{ELBO}}_{\theta,\phi}(\mathcal{B}_Q) - \lambda(r - \ell(\mathcal{B}_{\bar{P}}; \theta) - \mathcal{L}^{\text{ELBO}}_{\theta,\phi}(\mathcal{B}_P) + \mathcal{L}^{\text{ELBO}}_{\theta,\phi}(\mathcal{B}_Q))$

  `/* Gradient descent step */`

  Compute gradient $g = \nabla_{\theta,\phi} \mathcal{L}_{\lambda,\theta,\phi}$

  Use g to update parameters θ and ϕ

end

Posterior Consistency. A few papers have considered some form of posterior consistency for improving the performance of VAEs in different settings. For instance, [22] considered a notion of posterior consistency regarding augmentations of the input data. In particular, the problem of inconsistency was addressed by regularizing the original ELBO objective with a weighted KL-divergence of latent variables encoded by real and decoded data. In [34], consistency of the posterior was required for the latent variables obtained from the original data and data under random transformation. In [43], posterior consistency regularization for application in neural machine translation was enforced through the likelihood of the reconstruction $\hat{\mathbf{x}}$ using various data augmentation methods. Although the aforementioned methods show promising results, they consider settings with fully observed data and the used approaches do not build on inherent properties that the posterior must satisfy like our work.

6 Experimental Setup

6.1 Metrics

To assess the advantages of our proposed regularization, we considered the following metrics in experiments: imputation quality and information curves.

Imputation Quality. To assess the quality of imputation we compute the root-mean-square error (RMSE) between te imputed and the ground-truth data, i.e., for a partially observed dataset $\mathcal{D} = \{(\mathbf{x}^i_{Q^i})\}_{i=1}^n$ for which also the full observations are available we have $\text{RMSE}(\mathcal{D}) = (\frac{1}{n}\sum_{i=1}^n \sum_{j\in\mathcal{V}\setminus Q^i}(\hat{x}^i_j - \tilde{x}^i_j)^2)^{1/2}$, where $\hat{\mathbf{x}}^i$ is the completed ith sample and $\tilde{\mathbf{x}}^i$ is the ith ground-truth sample. Furthermore, the negative expected log-likelihood $-\mathbb{E}_{\mathbf{z}\sim q_\phi(\mathbf{z}|\mathbf{x}_Q)}[\log p_\theta(\tilde{\mathbf{x}}_{\mathcal{V}\setminus Q}|\mathbf{z})]$, and ELBO values are considered to measure the quality of imputation.

Information Curve (IC). Information curves allow us to investigate how useful the latent space of a VAE is for estimating the information gain of an unobserved variable. The information curve regarding some target feature x_t for sample $\mathbf{x}$ is computed as follows. Starting from not observing any features at all, i.e., $O = \emptyset$, we iteratively select the next most informative feature x_j regarding the target feature x_t using an approximation of the information reward as in [23]:

$$
\begin{aligned}
j = \arg\max_{i\in U} & \mathbb{E}_{x_i\sim\hat{p}(X_i|\mathbf{x}_O)}\text{KL}\left[q(\mathbf{Z}|x_i,\mathbf{x}_O)\|q\left(\mathbf{Z}|\mathbf{x}_O\right)\right] - \\
& \mathbb{E}_{x_t,x_i\sim\hat{p}(X_t,X_i|\mathbf{x}_O)}\text{KL}\left[q(\mathbf{Z}|x_t,x_i,\mathbf{x}_O)\|q\left(\mathbf{Z}|x_t,\mathbf{x}_O\right)\right]
\end{aligned} \quad (5)
$$

where U is the set of unobserved variables and O is the set of observed variables. The distribution $\hat{p}(X_i|\mathbf{x}_O) = \int_{\mathbf{z}} q_\phi(\mathbf{z}|\mathbf{x}_O)p_\theta(X_i|\mathbf{z})\text{d}\mathbf{z}$, where in practice the integration is approximated by samples. The distribution $\hat{p}(X_t, X_i|\mathbf{x}_O)$ is defined accordingly. At each step, we measure the prediction quality regarding the target feature based on the available features, i.e., the squared error between x_t and $\hat{x}_t$, where $\hat{x}_t$ is the prediction. The errors over the iterations constitute the IC.

6.2 Models, Parameters, and Model Training

Base models. We consider the following baseline models: *(i)* VAEs with zero-imputation for missing values (VAE-ZI), *(ii)* VAEs with zero-imputed missing values and an additional binary mask, indicating the available features, as input (Mask-VAE-ZI), *(iii)* VAEs with the point-net-plus encoders as in [23] (VAE-PNP), *(iv)* MIWAEs [25], and *(v)* Not-MIWAEs [15]. Additionally, we also examine *(vi)* Flow-VAE, a variation of the partial VAE framework where the posterior distribution is approximated using normalizing flows.

Regularized Models. For each baseline model we also consider its posterior-regularized version indicated by the prefix *REG-*, e.g., REG-VAE-ZI is a posterior regularized variant of VAE-ZI.

Training with Additional Missingness. For VAE-ZI, Mask-VAE-ZI, and VAE-PNP we also consider model training with artificial additional removal of observed features as proposed in [23]. The additional missingness is introduced at each iteration during the training process. Features are randomly dropped with a rate of missingness sampled from $\mathcal{U}(0, 0.7)$. Models trained with such additional missingness are indicated by the postfix *-AM*.

Model Architectures. The architectures of the models and their parameters were taken from the original papers, except for MIWAE and Not-MIWAE, where different scaling of data and activation functions were used. The reason for this choice was the inability to reproduce the same results as in the original setting; therefore, a couple of changes were made to boost the performance of the models. For flow-based partial VAEs, we used the piecewise-linear coupling transform [27] to increase the expressiveness of the approximate posterior distribution.

Model Training. All models were trained for 3000 epochs using ADAM [16] with a learning rate of 0.001 and a batch size of 64 samples. The data was scaled to a range from 0 to 1. The parameters for the regularized VAEs, $\mathcal{P}$ and λ, were tuned by the imputation quality performance of the model on the training data. For a detailed description of the parameters used for model training see Appendix F.

6.3 Data and Missing Values

In our experiments, we considered data from the UCI repository [9]. In particular, in line with previous work, we considered the following datasets: *Boston housing*, *Wine*, *enb*, *Breast cancer*, *Yeast*, and *Concrete*.

For the MCAR setting, the mask indicating missing values (missingness mask) was randomly sampled at the beginning of each run with 30, 50, and 70 % of missingness. For the MNAR setting, we considered self-censoring in which the missingness was created based on the mean value of a feature: a value is missing if it is higher than its mean. Consequently, the mask has a fixed missing rate.

7 Experiments

In this section, we empirically demonstrate the advantages of our proposed regularization for a variety of models. Because of space constraints, we only highlight a selection of empirical results. See appendices G, H, and I for additional results.

7.1 Imputation Results

We first investigate the effect of our regularization on the imputation quality. We compute the RMSEs (Tables 1, 2, 3 and Appendix G.1), ELBOs (Appendix G.2) and negative log-likelihoods (Appendix G.3) on the test set, which is selected randomly for each run and contains 10 % of the data. Each experiment was repeated

Table 1. Imputation quality (RMSE) for 30 % missingness. Results computed on the test data. Smaller is better.

Model	Dataset		
	Housing	Wine	enb
VAE-ZI-AM	0.1967 ± 0.0050	0.1289 ± 0.0019	0.2754 ± 0.0072
VAE-ZI	0.1976 ± 0.0066	0.1265 ± 0.0022	0.2846 ± 0.0081
REG-VAE-ZI	$\mathbf{0.1874 \pm 0.0048}$	$\mathbf{0.1238 \pm 0.0020}$	$\mathbf{0.2596 \pm 0.0057}$
Mask-VAE-ZI-AM	0.1863 ± 0.0047	0.1278 ± 0.0019	0.2611 ± 0.0048
Mask-VAE-ZI	0.1892 ± 0.0036	0.1272 ± 0.0021	0.2560 ± 0.0045
REG-Mask-VAE-ZI	$\mathbf{0.1758 \pm 0.0060}$	$\mathbf{0.1235 \pm 0.0017}$	$\mathbf{0.2471 \pm 0.0042}$
VAE-PNP-AM	0.1861 ± 0.0055	0.1300 ± 0.0023	0.2698 ± 0.0074
VAE-PNP	0.1837 ± 0.0055	0.1272 ± 0.0020	0.2592 ± 0.0055
REG-VAE-PNP	$\mathbf{0.1739 \pm 0.0044}$	$\mathbf{0.1245 \pm 0.0019}$	$\mathbf{0.2435 \pm 0.0049}$

10 times to compute the statistics over these runs except for the MIWAE and Not-MIWAE models for which experiments were repeated 5 times.

Our first set of results for comparing different types of models with respect to RMSE is presented in Table 1. We observe that the models with consistency regularization significantly outperform those with and without additional missingness (-AM), demonstrating the advantage of additionally considering the relationship between posteriors for $\mathbf{x}_Q$ and $\mathbf{x}_P$. For results with higher rates of missingness see Appendix G—the results are qualitatively similar. It should be noted that AM [23] can improve the performance of the VAE-ZI and Mask-VAE-ZI models for some datasets in terms of imputation quality. However, using AM alone is not sufficient because it can be disadvantageous for some partial VAE models, such as VAE-PNP in our experiments. In contrast to vanilla AM, our regularization method is advantageous for all classes of considered VAE models.

In Table 2, we present results for applying the proposed regularization on VAEs with flows. We observe that consistency regularization is advantageous for partial VAEs with normalizing flows in terms of imputation quality as well (although improvements are not that large), thereby demonstrating the flexibility of the proposed method. Additionally, it should be noted that partial VAEs with normalizing flows can deliver satisfactory results compared to other models for imputation in the MNAR setting. Experimental results for Flow-VAEs in the MNAR setting are presented in Appendix H.

Furthermore, we evaluated the quality of imputation in a simple MNAR setting using the Not-MIWAE model. Following the pipeline of the authors, the model was trained and evaluated on the entire dataset, without splitting. Our results are presented in Table 3 and we can observe that our regularization improves the imputation quality in the MNAR setting, even though the artificial missingness added for generating $\mathbf{x}_P$ is MCAR.

Additionally, different missing mechanisms for $\mathbf{x}_P$ were examined, cf. Appendix G.6. We can also observe improvements in terms of imputation qual-

Table 2. Imputation quality (RMSE) of VAE-flow, REG-VAE-flow, MIWAE, and REG-MIWAE for 30 % missingness on test data. Smaller is better.

Dataset	VAE-flow	REG-VAE-flow
Housing	0.1697 ± 0.0064	$\mathbf{0.1627 \pm 0.0058}$
Wine	0.1085 ± 0.0022	$\mathbf{0.1067 \pm 0.0021}$
enb	0.2069 ± 0.0034	$\mathbf{0.2031 \pm 0.0034}$

Dataset	MIWAE	REG-MIWAE
Red Wine	0.1452 ± 0.0028	$\mathbf{0.1205 \pm 0.0015}$
concrete	0.2755 ± 0.0146	$\mathbf{0.2046 \pm 0.0046}$
White Wine	0.1208 ± 0.0041	$\mathbf{0.0996 \pm 0.0014}$
banknote	0.3312 ± 0.0332	$\mathbf{0.2715 \pm 0.0087}$
breast	0.1545 ± 0.0069	$\mathbf{0.0906 \pm 0.0037}$
yeast	$\mathbf{0.1098 \pm 0.0050}$	0.1197 ± 0.0036

ity for some models for other types of missingness mechanisms. Furthermore, we considered the dependence of imputation quality on the probability of removing features $\mathcal{P}$, cf. Algorithm 1, in Appendix G.7. The experiment revealed that the optimal value of $\mathcal{P}$ closely aligns with the actual missing rate.

Moreover, we tested our regularization on VAEs trained on fully observed data. As shown in Appendix I, regularization provides a slight improvement in terms of the reconstruction quality, which demonstrates the advantage of this method even for the fully observed case.

7.2 Active Feature Acquisition Results

In this experiment, we aimed to evaluate the effect of regularization on the efficiency of information acquisition. All models were initially trained on partial training datasets. We ran the IC experiment ten times on the test set.

Our results are presented in Fig. 3. We can observe that partial VAEs with AM achieve better test RMSE scores than other models in the early steps for some datasets, indicating that a small number of features acquired is utilized more effectively. However, as soon as a sufficient number of features are available, AM generally worsens the performance of the model, and the base partial VAE delivers better results. Partial VAEs with consistency regularization outperform all partial VAEs with AM in terms of the test RMSE after the first couple of steps, whereby in contrast with AM almost all base partial VAEs are outperformed during the entire procedure. The results demonstrate the importance of consistency regularization for efficient information acquisition.

Table 3. Imputation quality (RMSE) of Not-MIWAE and REG-Not-MIWAE.

Dataset	Not-MIWAE	REG-Not-MIWAE
Red Wine	0.1594(0.0225)	**0.1269(0.0256)**
concrete	0.2887(0.0387)	**0.2558(0.0419)**
White Wine	0.0891(0.0100)	**0.0842(0.0134)**
banknote	0.2459(0.0269)	**0.1682(0.0301)**
breast	0.1000(0.0012)	**0.0632(0.0017)**
yeast	0.1363(0.0010)	**0.1351(0.0008)**

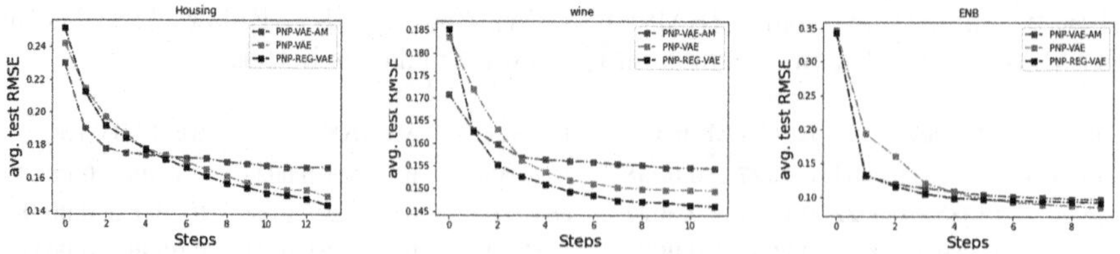

(a) Boston housing (b) wine (c) enb

Fig. 3. Information curves on test data with 30 % missingness for partial VAEs.

In addition, our regularization can increase the efficiency of information acquisition for VAE models equipped with normalizing flows, although improvements are typically much smaller, cf. Appendix G.4 for details.

8 Conclusions

We have considered the challenge of learning VAEs from incomplete data. In particular, we focused on improving the amortized approximate posterior distributions regarding the missingness in the data. To this end, we formalized a notion of posterior consistency with respect to the missingness and proposed a regularizer that improves a VAE's encoder posterior consistency when used during training. We showed that using our proposed regularization improves the imputation quality for different classes of VAEs and different types of missingness. Finally, we showed that our regularized VAEs often outperform VAEs without regularization on downstream tasks leveraging the latent space of the VAE for making decisions. We believe that our paper can improve the usage of VAEs in many practical settings on partial data. In future work, we will analyze the regularization of partial VAEs for MNAR settings in more detail.

References

1. Allen, A., Li, W.: Generative adversarial denoising autoencoder for face completion (2016). www.cc.gatech.edu/hays/7476/projects/Avery_Wenchen/
2. Berchtold, A.: Treatment and reporting of item-level missing data in social science research. vol. 22, pp. 431–439. Routledge (2019). https://doi.org/10.1080/13645579.2018.1563978
3. Burda, Y., Grosse, R.B., Salakhutdinov, R.: Importance Weighted Autoencoders. In: International Conference on Learning Representations (ICLR) (2016), arxiv.org/abs/1509.00519
4. van Buuren, S., Groothuis-Oudshoorn, K.: mice: Multivariate imputation by chained equations in r. vol. 45, pp. 1–67. Foundation for Open Access Statistics (2011)
5. Cheng-Xian Li, S., Jiang, B., Marlin, B.: MisGAN: Learning from Incomplete Data with Generative Adversarial Networks. In: International Conference on Learning Representations (ICLR) (2019), arxiv.org:1902.09599

6. Collier, M., Nazabal, A., Williams, C.: VAEs in the presence of missing data. In: ICML Workshop on the Art of Learning with Missing Values (Artemiss) (2020). www.openreview.net/forum?id=PnZT5EWoB7
7. Cremer, C., Li, X., Duvenaud, D.: Inference suboptimality in variational autoencoders. In: International Conference on Machine Learning (ICML), pp. 1078–1086. PMLR (2018)
8. Denton, E.L., Chintala, S., Szlam, A., Fergus, R.: Deep generative image models using a laplacian pyramid of adversarial networks. In: Advances in Neural Information Processing Systems (NeurIPS). Curran Associates, Inc. (2015). www.proceedings.neurips.cc/paper/2015/file/aa169b49b583a2b5af89203c2b78c67c-Paper.pdf
9. Dua, D., Graff, C.: UCI machine learning repository (2017), www.archive.ics.uci.edu/ml
10. Ghahramani, Z., Jordan, M.: Supervised learning from incomplete data via an em approach. In: Advances in Neural Information Processing Systems (NeurIPS) (1993). www.proceedings.neurips.cc/paper/1993/file/f2201f5191c4e92cc5af043eebfd0946-Paper.pdf
11. Ghahramani, Z., Jordan, M.I.: Learning from incomplete data. Technical Report AIM-1509CBCL-108, Massachusetts Institute of Technology (1995)
12. Ghalebikesabi, S., Cornish, R., Kelly, L.J., Holmes, C.: Deep generative pattern-set mixture models for nonignorable missingness. arXiv preprint arXiv:2103.03532 (2021)
13. Goodfellow, I., et al.: Generative Adversarial Nets. In: Advances in Neural Information Processing Systems (NeurIPS) (2014). www.proceedings.neurips.cc/paper/2014/file/5ca3e9b122f61f8f06494c97b1afccf3-Paper.pdf
14. Goodfellow, I.J.: NIPS 2016 tutorial: Generative adversarial networks. CoRR abs/1701.00160 (2017), arxiv.org:1701.00160
15. Ipsen, N.B., Mattei, P.A., Frellsen, J.: not-MIWAE: Deep Generative Modelling with Missing not at Random Data. In: International Conference on Learning Representations (ICLR) (2021)
16. Kingma, D.P., Ba, J.: Adam: A Method for Stochastic Optimization (2014)
17. Kingma, D.P., Welling, M.: Auto-encoding variational bayes. In: International Conference on Learning Representations (ICLR) (2014)
18. Li, Y., Liu, S., Yang, J., Yang, M.H.: Generative face completion. In: Conference on Computer Vision and Pattern Recognition (CVPR), pp. 3911–3919. IEEE (2017)
19. Lim, D.K., Rashid, N.U., Oliva, J.B., Ibrahim, J.G.: Unsupervised imputation of non-ignorably missing data using importance-weighted autoencoders (2021). https://doi.org/10.48550/ARXIV.2101.07357, arxiv.org/abs/2101.07357
20. Little, R., Rubin, D.: Statistical Analysis with Missing Data. Wiley Series in Probability and Statistics, Wiley (2019). www.books.google.at/books?id=BemMDwAAQBAJ
21. Little, R.J., Rubin, D.B.: Statistical analysis with missing data, vol. 793. John Wiley & Sons (2019)
22. Liu, Y., Lin, S., Clark, R.: Towards consistent variational auto-encoding, pp. 13869–13870 (2020)
23. Ma, C., Tschiatschek, S., Palla, K., Hernandez-Lobato, J.M., Nowozin, S., Zhang, C.: Eddi: Efficient dynamic discovery of high-value information with partial vae. In: International Conference on Machine Learning (ICML), pp. 4234–4243 (2019)
24. Ma, C., Zhang, C.: Identifiable Generative Models for Missing Not at Random Data Imputation. **34**, 27645–27658 (2021)

25. Mattei, P.A., Frellsen, J.: MIWAE: Deep generative modelling and imputation of incomplete data sets. In: International Conference on Machine Learning (ICML), pp. 4413–4423 (2019)
26. Mohan, K., Pearl, J., Tian, J.: Graphical models for inference with missing data. vol. 26 (2013)
27. Müller, T., McWilliams, B., Rousselle, F., Gross, M., Novák, J.: neural importance sampling. vol. 38, pp. 1–19 (2019)
28. Nazabal, A., Olmos, P.M., Ghahramani, Z., Valera, I.: Handling incomplete heterogeneous data using vaes. vol. 107, p. 107501. Elsevier (2020)
29. Newman, D.A.: Missing data: Five practical guidelines. vol. 17, pp. 372–411. Sage Publications Sage CA: Los Angeles, CA (2014)
30. Radford, A., Metz, L., Chintala, S.: Unsupervised representation learning with deep convolutional generative adversarial networks (2015). https://doi.org/10.48550/ARXIV.1511.06434, arxiv.org/abs/1511.06434
31. Rezende, D., Mohamed, S.: Variational Inference with Normalizing Flows. In: International Conference on Machine Learning (ICML), pp. 1530–1538 (2015)
32. Riggi, S., Riggi, D., Riggi, F.: Handling missing data for the identification of charged particles in a multilayer detector: A comparison between different imputation methods. vol. 780, pp. 81–90. Elsevier BV (2015). https://doi.org/10.1016/j.nima.2015.01.063
33. Rubin, D.B.: Inference and missing data. vol. 63, pp. 581–592. Oxford University Press (1976)
34. Sinha, S., Dieng, A.B.: Consistency regularization for variational auto-encoders. **34**, 12943–12954 (2021)
35. Smith, D.M.: The cost of lost data. **6**, 1–9 (2003)
36. Stekhoven, D.J., Bühlmann, P.: MissForest-non-parametric missing value imputation for mixed-type data. Bioinformatics **28**, 112–118 (2011)
37. Sun, C., Shrivastava, A., Singh, S., Gupta, A.: Revisiting unreasonable effectiveness of data in deep learning era. In: IEEE International Conference on Computer Vision (ICCV), pp. 843–852 (2017)
38. Wen, X., Li, Z., Peng, D., Zhou, W., Liu, Y.: Missing data recovery using data fusion of incomplete complementary datasets: A particle image velocimetry application. Phys. Fluids **31**, 025105 (2019)
39. Wu, G., Domke, J., Sanner, S.: Conditional inference in pre-trained variational autoencoders via cross-coding. arXiv preprint arXiv:1805.07785 (2018)
40. Yoon, J., Jordon, J., Schaar, M.: GAIN: Missing data imputation using generative adversarial nets. In: International Conference on Machine Learning (ICML), pp. 5689–5698 (2018)
41. Zaheer, M., Kottur, S., Ravanbakhsh, S., Poczos, B., Salakhutdinov, R.R., Smola, A.J.: Deep sets. vol. 30 (2017)
42. Zhang, C., Bütepage, J., Kjellström, H., Mandt, S.: Advances in Variational Inference, vol. 41, pp. 2008–2026. IEEE (2018)
43. Zhu, M., Wang, J., Yan, C.: Non-autoregressive neural machine translation with consistency regularization optimized variational framework. In: Proceedings of the 2022 Conference of the North American Chapter of the Association for Computational Linguistics: Human Language Technologies, pp. 607–617. Association for Computational Linguistics, Seattle, United States (Jul 2022). https://doi.org/10.18653/v1/2022.naacl-main.45, www.aclanthology.org/2022.naacl-main.45
44. Zhu, X., Wu, X.: Cost-constrained data acquisition for intelligent data preparation. IEEE**17**, 1542–1556 (2005)

KnowPrefix-Tuning: A Two-Stage Prefix-Tuning Framework for Knowledge-Grounded Dialogue Generation

Jiaqi Bai[1,2], Zhao Yan[3], Ze Yang[2], Jian Yang[2], Xinnian Liang[2], Hongcheng Guo[2], and Zhoujun Li[1,2](✉)

[1] School of Cyber Science and Technology, Beihang University, Beijing, China
{bjq,lizj}@buaa.edu.cn
[2] State Key Lab of Software Development Environment, Beihang University, Beijing, China
{tobey,jiaya,xnliang,hongchengguo}@buaa.edu.cn
[3] Tencent Cloud AI, Shenzhen, China
zhaoyan@tencent.com

Abstract. Existing knowledge-grounded conversation systems generate responses typically in a retrieve-then-generate manner. They require a large knowledge base and a strong knowledge retrieval component, which is time- and resource-consuming. In this paper, we address the challenge by leveraging the inherent knowledge encoded in the pre-trained language models (PLMs). We propose **K**nowledgeable **P**refix **Tuning** (**KnowPrefix-Tuning**), a two-stage tuning framework, bypassing the retrieval process in a knowledge-grounded conversation system by injecting prior knowledge into the lightweight knowledge prefix. The knowledge prefix is a sequence of continuous knowledge-specific vectors that can be learned during training. In addition, we propose a novel interactive re-parameterization mechanism that allows the prefix to interact fully with the PLM during the optimization of response generation. Experimental results demonstrate that **KnowPrefix-Tuning** outperforms fine-tuning and other lightweight tuning approaches, and performs comparably with strong retrieval-based baselines while being 3× faster during inference (The code is available at https://github.com/fantast4ever/KnowPrefix-Tuning.)

Keywords: Dialogue generation · Parameter-efficient fine-tuning · Knowledge-grounded dialogue · Pre-trained language models

1 Introduction

Open-domain dialogue system suffers from the problem of generating generic and bland responses, degrading the interaction experience of users [8,10]. Recent efforts follow the paradigm of generating the response by augmenting the source of knowledge associated with the dialogue context [15,35]. Knowledge-grounded

© The Author(s), under exclusive license to Springer Nature Switzerland AG 2023
D. Koutra et al. (Eds.): ECML PKDD 2023, LNAI 14170, pp. 525–542, 2023.
https://doi.org/10.1007/978-3-031-43415-0_31

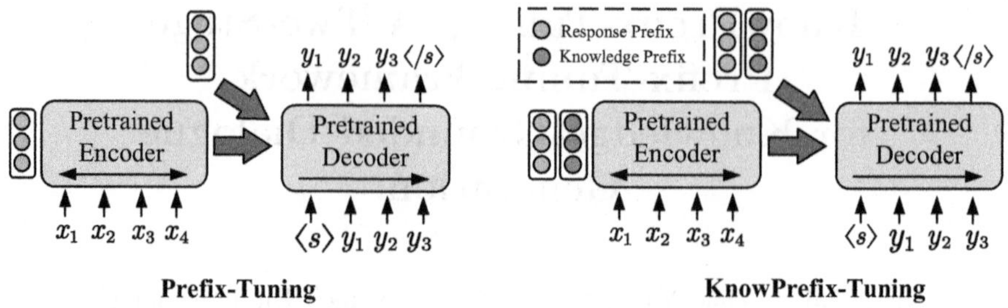

Fig. 1. Comparison between the prefix-tuning (left part) and the proposed KnowPrefix-Tuning (right part). Both approaches freeze the pre-trained weights of LM and tune only a small set of parameters that are added as the prefix of the model's input. We show the prefix-tuning employing the PLMs with encoder-decoder architecture (e.g., BART). To the PLMs with decoder-only architecture (e.g., GPT2), only the prefix prepended to decoder part is considered.

dialogue (KGD) [6,8], as one of the milestone tasks in open-domain dialogue, has attracted many research interests in recent years. The growing number of research works has begun to focus on developing an efficient knowledge-grounded dialogue system [14,22,23,25,29,44].

Existing knowledge-grounded dialogue systems are typically retrieval-augmented [9,18,34], where the knowledge is accessed in an explicit manner. They first employ a knowledge retrieval component to select knowledge pieces that are most relevant to the dialogue context from a large knowledge base. Then they augment the selected knowledge pieces with the dialogue context to generate knowledgeable responses. Although the retrieval-augmented approaches have demonstrated remarkable progress on the KGD task, these approaches inevitably consume considerable resources and time to train and store the parameters of the knowledge retriever, in order to ensure the knowledge retrieval ability of a KGD system.

Recent studies show that large PLMs carry implicit knowledge [22,30] that can directly apply to downstream generation tasks by proper prompts [2,12,20]. In particular, Li et al. [20] proposed prefix-tuning, a lightweight paradigm bypassing finetuning the entire PLM and instead tuning only a small set of parameters that are added as the prefix of the model's input. However, the vanilla prefix-tuning approach lacks an effective mechanism to incorporate grounded knowledge (i.e., the knowledge labeled by human annotators) into the generated text. In this paper, we aim to steer the prefix-tuning to the KGD task, where the knowledge can be accessed in an implicit manner to achieve knowledgeable response generation. There are two key challenges: (1) Eliciting the knowledge irrelevant to the dialogue context from PLM may mislead the model into generating the context-irrelevant response. (2) There can be one-to-many relations between the dialogue context and the knowledge to be selected [23]. Explicitly enumerating all of this knowledge encoded in the PLM is impractical.

To tackle the above challenges, we propose Knowledgeable Prefix-Tuning (**KnowPrefix-Tuning**), Fig. 1 shows the comparison between the prefix-tuning

[20] and the proposed approach. The proposed KnowPrefix-Tuning is a two-stage prefix-tuning framework. In the first tuning stage, we inject the prior knowledge into the lightweight knowledge prefix by forcing the model to generate the knowledge grounded on the dialogue context, which facilitates the model to focus more on context-relevant knowledge. In the second tuning stage, we prompt the PLM to generate the knowledgeable response by response prefix, grounding on the dialogue context and the previously learned knowledge prefix. To enhance the interaction between the knowledge and dialogue context, we propose a novel **Interactive Re-parameterization** mechanism, which further facilitates knowledgeable response generation by encouraging the interaction between the prefix and the PLM. Experimental results on two knowledge-grounded benchmarks show that the proposed method brings both performance and efficiency improvements. It is 3× faster than the state-of-the-art retrieval-based method during inference stage and outperforms competitive light-weight tuning approaches significantly.

Our contributions are three-fold: (1) We propose a novel KnowPrefix-Tuning approach for the KGD task. The proposed method bypasses the retrieval process and does not require finetuning the entire PLM. (2) We propose a novel interactive re-parameterization mechanism, which allows the interaction between the embedding of the prefix and the PLM during the re-parameterization of the prefix. (3) We conduct sufficient experiments and qualitative analysis to prove the effectiveness of our proposed methods on two knowledge-grounded dialogue datasets.

2 Related Work

2.1 Knowledge-Grounded Dialogue

Knowledge-grounded dialogue has shown tremendous potential in enriching and diversifying the responses generated by dialogue agents [4,21,27,34,36,43]. Most of the existing KGD works focus on improving the knowledge retrieval performance, which explicitly retrieves proper knowledge pieces, thereby enhancing the knowledgeable response generation ability [14,21,23,44]. Very recent work begins to focus on leveraging the knowledge that is inherently encoded in the PLM [22,25,37,40]. For example, Li et al. [22] employed the pre-train technique to encode the multi-source knowledge into a unified framework. Lie et al. proposed to [25] retrieve a small collection of dialogue samples to construct prompts, which is used to guide the knowledgeable response generation in a multi-stage generation manner. Li et al. [21] employ PLATO-KAG [11] as a backbone, using the generated knowledge as a noisy knowledge source and propose the posterior-based reweighing and the noisy training strategy to improve the performance of a knowledge retriever. Compared with above works, we do not explicitly retrieve any knowledge pieces from the data base. We instead encode the knowledge into the lightweight knowledge prefix, which saves much computational resource and time.

2.2 Prompting in Language Models

Pre-trained language models (PLMs) [13,17,24] exhibit an innate ability to store commonsense knowledge [3,5,16,46]. It can be prompted to do many downstream natural language generation task, such as closed-book question answering (QA) [28,39], text summarization [20,41], and so on. Earlier work use human written prompts by manually designing prompt templates [2,32], or search prompts over the discrete space of words [33]. Recent work focus on continuous prompt learning [16,20], where the prompts are represented as a group of vectors that can be optimized during training process. Our work is enlightened from Prefix-Tuning [20]. The main difference is that the proposed KnowPrefix-Tuning is a two-stage tuning framework that encodes the global knowledge into a group of continuous knowledge-specific vectors, allowing the interaction between the embedding of prefixes and the PLM.

3 Background

3.1 Problem Formalization

Suppose we have a T-turn conversation $\mathcal{C} = (U_i, K_i, Y_i)_{i=1}^{T}$ in a knowledge-grounded conversation dataset $\mathcal{D}$, where $\forall i$, (U_i, K_i, Y_i) is a triplet of query-knowledge-response at turn i. Given an input sequence $X_i = (Y_{i-1}, U_i)$, our goal is to generate a knowledgeable response $\widetilde{Y}_i$ by learning a response generation model $P(Y_i, K_i|X_i; \Theta)$. Existing retrieval-augmented methods tackle this problem by firstly retrieving related knowledge $\widetilde{K}_i$, then augmenting it with input sequence X_i. Here, we propose to bypass the retrieval process by injecting the knowledge K_i into the model parameters Θ. Thus, the response can be generated sorely based on the input sequence X_i.

3.2 Prefix-Tuning

In this section, we briefly describe Prefix-Tuning [20] upon the vanilla Transformer architecture [38], based on which we can validate the effectiveness of our approach.

In the vanilla Transformer architecture, each transformer layer equips with multiple attention heads, and each head attends over the tokens of the input context. Let $\mathbf{H}_l$ denote the output of a single attention head in the l-th Transformer layer, which is formalized by:

$$\mathbf{H}_l = \mathcal{F}_\Lambda\left(Q_l\mathbf{W}_l^Q, K_l\mathbf{W}_l^K, V_l\mathbf{W}_l^V\right) \in \mathbb{R}^{N\times d} \tag{1}$$

where $\mathcal{F}(\cdot)$ denotes the attention computational function, Λ denotes an attention type. $\Lambda \in \{E_S, D_C, D_S\}$ where E_S is the encoder self-attention, D_C is the decoder cross-attention and D_S is the decoder masked self-attention, respectively. $Q_l \in \mathbb{R}^{N\times d}$ is the query matrix in the l-th layer. $K_l, V_l \in \mathbb{R}^{M\times d}$ denote the

l-th layer key and value matrix, where N is the sequence length related to queries, M is the sequence length related to key and value. $\mathbf{W}_l^Q$, $\mathbf{W}_l^K$, $\mathbf{W}_l^V \in \mathbb{R}^{d \times d}$ are head-specific projection weights for Q, K and V. respectively.

In prefix-tuning, the prefix is denoted as a distinct key-value pair for the attention type Λ, which is a set of continuous specific vectors that can be learned by

$$P_\Lambda = \mathrm{MLP}\left(\mathbf{E}\left(X_\Lambda\right)\right) \in \mathbb{R}^{2 \times \rho L d} \tag{2}$$

where $X_\Lambda \in \mathbb{R}^\rho$ is the input token of prefix, $\mathbf{E}(\cdot)$ is the embedding projection matrix. ρ is the length of prefix token. $P_\Lambda = \{P_\Lambda^{(1)}, \cdots P_\Lambda^{(L)}\}$ denotes a prefix set for Λ, where L is the number of layer in transformer. $\forall l \in \{1, \cdots, L\}$, $P_\Lambda^{(l)} = (P_{\Lambda,K}^{(l)}, P_{\Lambda,V}^{(l)}) \in \mathbb{R}^{2 \times \rho d}$, d is the embedding dimension. $P_{\Lambda,K}^{(l)}$ and $P_{\Lambda,V}^{(l)}$ are the key and value of prefix in the l-th layer, respectively. During the prefix-tuning stage, the key-value pair in Eq. 1 is augmented to become

$$K_l \leftarrow \left[P_{\Lambda,K}^{(l)}; K_l\right] \in \mathbb{R}^{(M+\rho) \times d} \tag{3}$$

$$V_l \leftarrow \left[P_{\Lambda,V}^{(l)}; V_l\right] \in \mathbb{R}^{(M+\rho) \times d} \tag{4}$$

4 Approach

4.1 KnowPrefix-Tuning

Formally, given the dialogue context $X = \{x_1, x_2, \cdots x_{|X|}\}$. The corresponding knowledge piece is $K = \{k_1, k_2, \cdots k_{|K|}\}$ and the response $Y = \{y_1, y_2, \cdots y_{|Y|}\}$. In the **first** tuning stage, we obtain the *knowledge prefixes* by applying the vanilla prefix-tuning approach, feeding the dialogue context X to the model and asking it to predict the knowledge K token by token, which can be realized by optimizing following loss:

$$\mathcal{L}_1 = -\mathbb{E}_{(X,K) \in \mathcal{D}} \sum_{t=1}^{|K|} \log P\left(k_t | X, k_{1:(t-1)}; \theta_{LM}, \theta_K\right) \tag{5}$$

where θ_{LM} are the parameters of PLM, θ_{LM} are holding fixed during the tuning procedure. θ_K are the learnable parameters for the knowledge prefix.

In the **second** tuning stage, we fix the parameters during optimizing the knowledge prefix in the first tuning stage, and add additional learnable *response prefixes* to guide the knowledgeable response generation. Formally, Given the dialogue context X, our goal is to generate the response Y one token at a time. The generation process of Y can be defined by optimizing the following loss:

$$\mathcal{L}_2 = -\mathbb{E}_{(X,Y) \in \mathcal{D}} \sum_{t=1}^{|Y|} \log P\left(y_t | X, y_{1:(t-1)}; \theta_{LM}, \theta_K, \theta_Y\right) \tag{6}$$

where θ_Y are the parameters for knowledgeable response generation. During the second tuning stage, the parameters of θ_{LM} and θ_K are holding fixed, only the parameters of θ_Y are updated.

4.2 KnowPrefix-Tuning with Interactive Re-Parameterization

Re-parameterization has been demonstrated to be indispensable in boosting the performance of prefix-tuning [20]. It is realized by introducing a large feed-forward neural network during the optimization of the prefix, as we introduced in Eq. 2. While for the KGD task, the interaction between the knowledge and the dialogue context is still significant to realize the knowledgeable response generation. To model this kind of interaction, we propose the interactive re-parameterization mechanism, which considers the embedding of prefix and PLM as interfaces, and conducting the multi-head attention [38] to realize the interaction between them.

To re-parameterize the prefix P_Λ, we concatenate an interaction term $\mathbf{I}^o$ with the embedding of prefix $\mathbf{E}_{\theta_Y}(X_\Lambda)$, and re-parameterize the concatenation between them, which is given by:

$$P_\Lambda = f_{\theta_\Lambda}\left(\left[\mathbf{E}_{\theta_Y}\left(X_\Lambda\right); \mathbf{I}^o\right]\right) \in \mathbb{R}^{2\times \rho L d} \tag{7}$$

where $[\cdot;\cdot]$ denotes the concatenation operation. $f_{\theta_\Lambda}(\cdot)$ is an interactive function, which can be any neural network such as a MLP. We define the interaction term $\mathbf{I}^o$ as a weighted sum for the embedding of PLM, which can be obtained by:

$$\mathbf{I}^o = \mathbf{I}^e \mathbf{E}_{\theta_{LM}} \in \mathbb{R}^{\rho\times d} \tag{8}$$

$$\mathbf{I}^e = \operatorname{softmax}\left(\mathbf{H}^o \mathbf{E}_{\theta_{LM}}^T\right) \in \mathbb{R}^{\rho\times |V_{LM}|} \tag{9}$$

where $\mathbf{E}_{\theta_{LM}} \in \mathbb{R}^{|V_{LM}|\times d}$ is the embedding matrix of the PLM and $|V_{LM}|$ is its vocabulary size. $\mathbf{H}^o$ is the output state for each token of prefix sequence. $\mathbf{I}^e$ measures the contextual similarity between the $\mathbf{H}^o$ and the embedding of language model $\mathbf{E}_{\theta_{LM}}$.

We obtain the output state $\mathbf{H}^o$ by considering the interaction of embedding between knowledge prefixes and response prefixes, which can be realized by the following:

$$\mathbf{H}^o = \left[\mathbf{H}_1; \cdots; \mathbf{H}_N\right] \mathbf{W}^o \tag{10}$$

$$\mathbf{H}_j = \operatorname{Attention}\left(Q\mathbf{W}_{Q1}^j, K\mathbf{W}_{K1}^j, V\mathbf{W}_{V1}^j\right) \tag{11}$$

$$Q = \operatorname{Tanh}\left(\mathbf{E}_{\theta_Y}\left(X_\Lambda^Y\right)\mathbf{W}_{Q2}^j\right) \tag{12}$$

$$K = \operatorname{Tanh}\left(\mathbf{E}_{\theta_K}\left(X_\Lambda^K\right)\mathbf{W}_{K2}^j\right) \tag{13}$$

$$V = \operatorname{Tanh}\left(\mathbf{E}_{\theta_K}\left(X_\Lambda^K\right)\mathbf{W}_{V2}^j\right) \tag{14}$$

N is the number of attention heads. $\mathbf{W}^o \in \mathbb{R}^{d_m\times d}$ is the projection weights of the concatenated output for all attention heads. d_m is the dimension of the hidden states in the re-parameterization network. $\mathbf{H}_j \in \mathbb{R}^{d_h\times d}$ is the output state for j-th attention head. $d_h = d_m//N$ is the output dimension for each attention head. $\mathbf{W}_Q^j$, $\mathbf{W}_K^j$ and $\mathbf{W}_V^j$ are head-specific projections for Q, K and V, respectively.

To enforce the re-parameterization module eliciting the proper knowledge from the embedding of PLM, inspired by Zhao et al. [42] and Bao et al. [1], we supervise the term $\mathbf{I}^e$ by an additional loss $\mathcal{L}_{bow}$ with the bag of words B_Y in the ground-truth response, where the bag of words are obtained by removing the punctuation and the stopwords in response Y, forcing the model focus more on content words. The $\mathcal{L}_{bow}$ can be obtained by:

$$\mathcal{L}_{bow} = -\mathbb{E}_{\mathbf{I}_w^e \sim P(\mathbf{I}^e|X,Y)} \frac{1}{|B_Y|} \sum_{w \in B_Y} \log(\mathbf{I}_w^e) \tag{15}$$

Intuitively, the bag of words loss $\mathcal{L}_{bow}$ discards the words orders and forces the term $\mathbf{I}_w$ to capture the global information of the target response. The overall loss in the second stage is defined by:

$$\mathcal{L}_2 \leftarrow \mathcal{L}_2 + \mathcal{L}_{bow} \tag{16}$$

5 Experiments

5.1 Datasets and Baseline Models

Datasets. We conduct our experiment on two commonly used knowledge-grounded dialogue datasets: Wizard of Wikipedia (Wizard) [6], and CMU Document Grounded Conversations (CMU_Dog) [45]. The Wizard and CMU_DoG datasets are constructed by the Amazon Mechanical Turk workers and employ Wikipedia as the knowledge base. Wizard is split into 18,430 training dialogues on 1247 topics, 1,948 validation dialogues on 599 topics and 1,933 test dialogues on 591 topics. The test set is further split into test seen set and unseen set according to the topics. The test seen set contains 965 dialogues on 533 topics. The test unseen set contains 968 dialogues on 58 topics whose topics are never seen in the training and validation set. There are about 9.0 turns on average in each dialogue of the dataset. CMU_DoG is split into 3373 training dialogues, 229 validation dialogues, and 619 test dialogues. There are 30 topics in the dataset on average, and each dialogue has about 22.0 turns on average. We implement the pre-processing for both WoW and CMU_DoG datasets with the code published on ParlAI[1].

Baseline Models. We compare our approach with two types of knowledge access methods: The first group is **Explicit Knowledge Access**, which explicitly retrieves knowledge from a knowledge base. Then use the retrieved knowledge augmenting with the dialogue context to guide the knowledgeable response generation: **i)** Transformer Memory Network (TMN) [6]: The model combines Transformer [38] with an external memory network in an end-to-end manner, which introduces an additional loss to better select knowledge. **ii)** Sequential Knowledge Transformer (SKT) [14]: The model employs sequential variable model

[1] https://github.com/facebookresearch/ParlAI.

to conduct knowledge selection for response generation, which considers the interaction between the history of knowledge selection and dialogue context. **iii)** ZRKGC [19]: The model employs pre-train techniques to handle the zero-resource challenge in KGD task. We choose the one that uses the full training data version for a fair comparison. **iv)** KnowledGPT [44]: The model employs reinforcement learning to jointly optimize knowledge selection and response generation in a joint manner. **v)** PLATO-KAG$^+$ [21]: The model employs PLATO-KAG [11] as a backbone, treating the generated knowledge as a noisy knowledge source and propose the posterior-based reweighing and the noisy training strategy to enhance the knowledge retrieval ability.

The second group contains **Implicit Knowledge Access** methods, which does not require to explicitly retrieve or generate knowledge to guide the knowledgeable response generation: **i)** KnowExpert [40]: The model employs topic modelling technique to inject prior knowledge into the GPT-2 with lightweight adapters. We report the results of their model under weighted-sum (KnowExpert$_w$) setting. **ii)** Fine-Tuning: We fine-tune the whole model of GPT-2 and BART for response generation. It is to check if only the general fine-tuning approach works well on this task. **iii)** Prefix-Tuning [20]: We apply the Prefix-Tuning approach to generate responses based on the given dialogue context, without the supervision of the external knowledge base. It is to check if only the prefix-tuning approach works well on this task. We employ both BART and GPT-2 as backbone PLMs to conduct response generation. **iv)** Knowledgeable Prefix-Tuning (KnowPrefix-Tuning): The method proposed in our paper. We use both GPT-2 and BART as the backbone to conduct the experiment.

5.2 Evaluation Metrics

We conduct both automatic and human evaluations. For automatic evaluation, following the previous work on KGC [6,15,34], we report perplexity (PPL), F1 and Knowledge F1 (KF1) metrics. The perplexity (PPL) measures how likely the model can generate human-like responses. The F1 score indicates the unigram overlap between the generated response and the reference response. The KF1 score measures the overlap between the generated response and the knowledge *on which the human grounded during dataset collection* [15], which captures whether a model is speaking knowledgeably by using the knowledge relevant to dialogue context. To evaluate how the number of parameters impacts the model performance, following Li et al. [20], we count the number of parameters that are fine-tuned in each method.

Apart from the automatic evaluation, we conduct the human evaluation from three aspects of the generated response: **Fluency** measures how fluent the generated responses of the model are. **Context coherency** measures how the generated responses are relevant to the dialogue context. **Knowledge relevancy** measures how knowledgeable the generated responses are, according to the amount of new knowledge introduced into the dialogue and the factuality of the generated response. We employ three well-educated annotators for human evaluation. Concretely, each annotator is shown in an example containing

Table 1. Automatic evaluation results on the Wizard and CMU_DoG datasets. Bold face indicates the best result in terms of the corresponding metric. "#Para" denotes the number of fine-tuned parameters in each method. PPL values are not comparable across different backbone PLMs as they use different dictionaries.

Models	Wizard Seen			Wizard Unseen			CMU_DoG			#Para
	PPL↓	F1↑	KF1↑	PPL↓	F1↑	KF1↑	PPL↓	F1↑	KF1↑	
Explicit Knowledge Access										
TMN	66.5	15.9	-	100+	14.3	-	75.2	9.9	-	1.6×10^7
SKT	52.2	19.4	-	81.5	16.2	-	42.0	9.7	-	1.7×10^8
ZRKGC	40.4	18.7	-	41.6	18.6	-	53.6	12.5	-	3.3×10^8
KnowledGPT	19.2	**22.0**	-	22.3	**20.5**	-	**20.0**	**13.7**	-	2.4×10^8
PLATO-KAG$^+$	**12.4**	21.1	-	**13.8**	20.3	-	-	-	-	1.6×10^{10}
Implicit Knowledge Access										
GPT-2 + KnowExpert$_w$	15.3	18.7	14.5	20.1	16.7	12.1	17.2	12.5	4.0	1.2×10^8
GPT-2 + Fine-Tuning	15.1	19.8	17.4	21.3	16.8	13.9	16.7	13.8	4.9	7.7×10^8
GPT-2 + Prefix-Tuning	15.8	19.1	16.3	20.7	17.0	13.0	19.9	13.2	4.2	1.8×10^6
GPT-2 + KnowPrefix-Tuning (Ours)	15.2	20.1	**18.0**	19.3	18.0	14.6	17.4	14.1	**5.3**	3.7×10^6
BART + Fine-Tuning	14.9	**20.3**	17.8	19.1	17.3	13.8	**15.3**	14.1	4.7	4.1×10^8
BART + Prefix-Tuning	15.2	19.2	16.5	19.4	16.9	13.4	18.0	13.9	4.2	1.5×10^6
BART + KnowPrefix-Tuning (Ours)	**14.0**	**20.3**	17.4	**17.5**	**18.3**	**14.9**	16.3	**14.6**	5.2	2.9×10^6

a dialogue context and model responses that are randomly shuffled to hide their sources. We randomly select 100 examples from the test set (both test seen and test unseen for the Wizard dataset), and ask each annotator to assign a score in {0, 1, 2} to each response for each aspect. The agreement among the annotators is measured via Fleiss' kappa [7].

5.3 Implementation Details

We choose BARTLARGE (406M), GPT2LARGE (774M) to adapt our KnowPrefix-Tuning framework[2]. In both knowledge prefix-tuning stages, we set the same length of the prefix token to 20. The embedding size of the prefix token is set to the same embedding size of PLM. The hidden states of the re-parameterization network are set to 800. When generating knowledgeable responses, we fix the decoding parameters to beam search (beam size 3) with a minimum sequence length of 20 and beam blocking of 3-grams within the response, similar to choices in [15,31]. All models are learned with the AdamW [26] optimizer with learning rate 3e-5 in 40 epochs. We set the warm-up steps to 2000 and applied a linear learning rate scheduler with a batch size of 32. Each experiment is conducted on Tesla V-100 machines.

5.4 Main Results

Automatic Evaluation Results. Table 1 reports the automatic evaluation results on Wizard and CMU_DoG datasets. We have the following observations: (1) Compared with the *Explicit Knowledge Access* methods, KnowPrefix-Tuning

[2] We implement the model with the code shared in https://github.com/huggingface-/transformers.

Table 2. Human evaluation results on the Wizard dataset. "FL", "CC" and "KR" denote "Fluency", "Context Coherency" and "Knowledge Relevancy", respectively.

Models	Wizard Seen				Wizard Unseen			
	FL	CC	KR	Kappa	FL	CC	KR	Kappa
KnowExpert_w	1.87	1.62	1.55	0.65	1.83	1.52	1.30	0.64
Fine-tuning	1.89	**1.66**	**1.61**	0.63	1.84	1.53	1.38	0.62
Prefix-Tuning	1.86	1.60	1.57	0.60	1.82	1.52	1.35	0.61
KnowPrefix-Tuning	**1.90**	1.64	**1.61**	**0.65**	**1.88**	**1.54**	**1.43**	**0.65**

achieves competitive performance compared to all of the baselines over both datasets. Specifically, KnowPrefix-Tuning (BARTLARGE) outperforms retrieval-based baselines on the CMU_DoG dataset. Concretly, the PPL and F1 of KnowPrefix-Tuning (BARTLARGE) outperform the percentage of the strongest baseline KnowledGPT by 19.9% and 7.0%, respectively. The lower PPL indicates that the model prefers to generate more context-relevant responses. In addition, the KnowPrefix-Tuning (BARTLARGE) has only about 3M parameters that should be fine-tuned. It is only 1% number of parameters in KnowledGPT updated. (2) Compared with other *Implicit Knowledge Access* methods, the proposed KnowPrefix-Tuning outperforms the Prefix-Tuning substantially, indicating the effectiveness of our proposed tuning framework. In addition, the KnowPrefix-Tuning outperforms Fine-tuning on both Wizard and CMU_Dog datasets with only 0.7% parameters updated. This improvements are more clear on the Wizard Unseen dataset, which indicates that the proposed KnowPrefix-Tuning has a powerful generalization ability to the unseen topics even equipped with fewer parameters.

Human Evaluation Results. Table 2 reports the human evaluation results on Wizard dataset. We can observe that: (1) The kappa values are larger than 0.6, indicating substantial agreement among the annotators. (2) According to *fluency*, we find that the KnowPrefix-Tuning approach tends to generate more fluent responses. This result is consistent with the automatic evaluation results in which the KnowPrefix-Tuning shows lower perplexity. We think it is because that the knowledge prefix learned much context-relevant knowledge through the knowledge generation process, which can provide effective guidance for knowledgeable response generation. (3) According to *knowledge relevancy*, we observe that Fine-Tuning and KnowPrefix-Tuning perform better on the Wizard Seen dataset, while KnowPrefix-Tuning is superior to the Wizard Unseen dataset. We think it is highly likely that the proposed approach does not disturb the implicit knowledge distribution encoded in PLM during tuning procedure. Thus it can better generalize to the unseen topic during knowledgeable response generation.

5.5 Discussions

Ablation Study. To facilitate the study of how each component of the model influence the overall performance, we conduct the ablation study for both

Table 3. Ablation study on Wizard and CMU_DoG datasets. "-" means removing the corresponding part.

Models	Wizard Seen			Wizard Unseen			CMU_DoG		
	PPL↓	F1↑	KF1↑	PPL↓	F1↑	KF1↑	PPL↓	F1↑	KF1↑
KnowPrefix-Tuning (BARTLARGE)	**14.0**	**20.3**	**17.4**	**17.5**	**18.3**	**14.9**	**16.3**	**14.6**	**5.2**
- Interactive Re-parameterization	14.8	19.3	16.8	18.5	17.4	13.7	18.7	13.7	4.5
- Stage-I	16.0	18.7	16.3	20.2	16.4	13.0	20.4	13.3	3.8
KnowPrefix-Tuning (GPT2LARGE)	15.2	**20.1**	**18.0**	**19.3**	**18.0**	**14.6**	**17.4**	**14.1**	**5.3**
- Interactive Re-parameterization	15.7	19.2	17.2	20.5	17.2	13.8	19.7	13.2	4.5
- Stage-I	17.8	18.5	16.7	22.0	16.3	12.8	20.9	12.8	3.9

BARTLARGE and GPT2LARGE on Wizard and CMU_DoG datasets. We compare the proposed KnowPrefix-Tuning with the following variants: (1) - *Interactive Re-parameterization*: The interactive re-parameterization module is replaced by the re-parameterization module as we defined in Eq. 2. (2) - *Stage-I*: The stage-I is removed during the knowledgeable response generation. Thus, the model generates responses without considering the grounded knowledge (i.e., the knowledge labeled by human annotators.). For a fair comparison, we uniform the number of parameters used in this variant and the KnowPrefix-Tuning by increasing the variant's prefix length to 40. Table 3 presents the results, we can conclude that: (1) Without the Interactive Re-parameterization module, the performance of both BARTLARGE and GPT2LARGE drops significantly. We believe that the interactive re-parameterization module allows the interaction between the embedding of prefixes and PLM, which is helpful to knowledgeable response generation. (2) Without Stage-I, the performance of both BARTLARGE and GPT2LARGE goes down. It indicates the effectiveness of the proposed two-stage framework. Even without equipping with the proposed interactive re-parameterization mechanism, the proposed two-stage framework incorporates the context-relevant knowledge into the generated response and substantially improves the generation of knowledgeable responses.

Inference Time Efficiency. To verify the inference time efficiency of our proposed method, we compare the proposed KnowPrefix-Tuning (BART-LARGE) with two strong retrieval-based methods, which are PLATO-KAG$^+$ and KnowledGPT, under the same inference implementation setting for a fair comparison. Figure 2 reports the results on Wizard Seen and Unseen test set. We observe that KnowPrefix-Tuning is around 3× faster and 5× faster than KnowledGPT and PLATO-KAG$^+$ during the inference stage, respectively. We believe it is because that the proposed KnowPrefix-Tuning bypasses the retrieval process and doesn't require augmenting the retrieved knowledge with the input dialogue context, saving much time during inference.

Impact of Pretrained Language Models. To further study how does the size of PLMs impacts the performance of the KnowPrefix-Tuning. We additionally

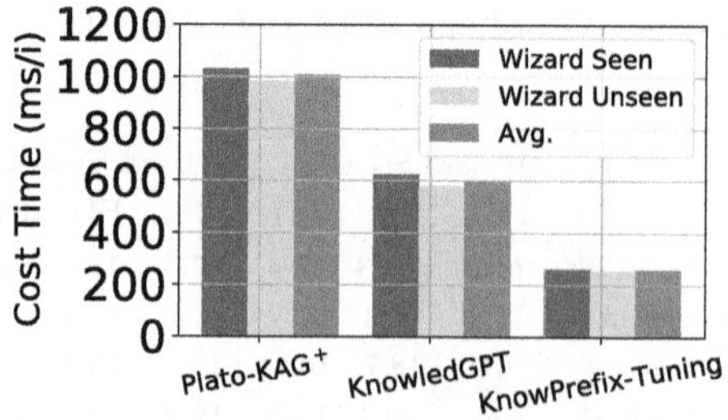

Fig. 2. The inference time comparison across different baselines. "ms/i" indicates millisecond per instance.

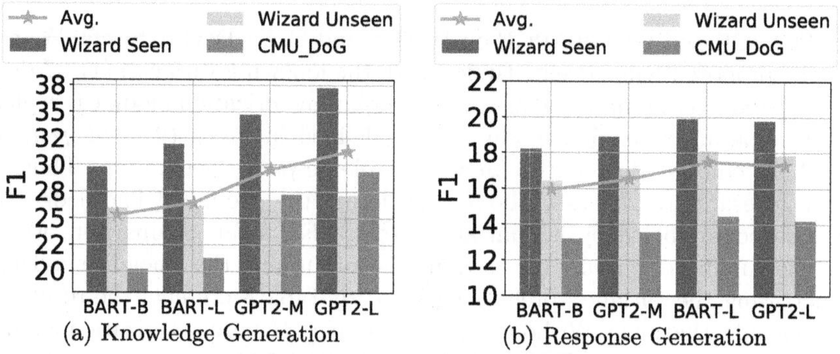

Fig. 3. Impact of PLMs. "BART-B", "BART-L", "GPT2-M" and "GPT2-L" denote the BART-BASE, BART-LARGE, GPT2-MEDIUM and GPT2-LARGE, respectively. "Avg" is the average F1 score across the three datasets.

employ BARTBASE (139M) and GPT2MEDIUM (345M) to realize the knowledge generation and the response generation. Note that our approach does not require to explicitly augment the generated knowledge with the dialogue context to generate responses. We evaluate the quality of the generated knowledge to investigate whether there is a connection between the generated knowledge and the generated responses when using the proposed KnowPrefix-tuning approach.

Figure 3 presents the results. We have the following obeservations: (1) For knowledge generation, the larger model generates better knowledge, while it is not significant on the Wizard Unseen dataset. We believe that it is still a challenge for the large language model to generate better knowledge with unseen topics. (2) For knowledgeable response generation, the quality of the generated responses improves with the model size boost. In addition, we observe that the model which generates better knowledge can also generate better responses with the same backbone PLMs. It indicates that the proposed approach equipped with well-learned knowledge prefix can elicit proper knowledge from PLMs to guide the knowledgeable response generation.

Table 4. Comparison of KnowPrefix-Tuning and Prefix-Tuning with different prefix length "l". We employ BARTLARGE as the backbone model for each variant.

Models	Wizard Seen			Wizard Unseen			#PSD
	PPL↓	F1↑	KF1↑	PPL↓	F1↑	KF1↑	
KnowPrefix-Tuning ($l = 10$)	14.4	19.8	17.0	18.2	17.8	14.4	1.5×10^6
KnowPrefix-Tuning ($l = 20$)	14.0	20.3	17.4	17.5	18.3	14.9	2.9×10^6
Prefix-Tuning ($l = 20$)	15.2	19.2	16.5	19.4	16.9	13.4	1.5×10^6
Prefix-Tuning ($l = 40$)	16.0	18.7	16.3	20.2	16.4	13.0	3.0×10^6
Prefix-Tuning ($l = 60$)	15.9	18.5	16.4	20.5	16.1	13.3	4.4×10^6

Table 5. Cases from the test seen and test unseen data of Wizard. The underline text indicates the essential facts that appeared in the golden response.

Dialogue Context			
Test Seen		**Test Unseen**	
Wizard:	Well the rights to this formula was obtained by the TIP corporation.	*Wizard:*	I enjoy hunting. This refers to the killing or trapping animals, or pursuing or tracking them
Apprentice:	Do you know how they came up with the other flavors?	*Apprentice:*	How long have you been hunting?
Response			
KnowExpert$_w$:	Well they were created by a group of volunteers.	KnowExpert$_w$:	I have been hunting for about 10 years
Prefix-Tuning:	Well it was first introduced in the United States in 1953 as a soft drink.	Prefix-Tuning:	I have been hunting since i was a child. It is the practice of hunting animals for food or raw materials
Fine-Tuning:	I don't but i know that it was introduced in the US in 1964.	Fine-Tuning:	I have been hunting for about 20 years. It is a very difficult activity
KnowPrefix-Tuning:	Well the first mountain dew was created in 1953 by a pharmacist named Charles Alderton.	KnowPrefix-Tuning:	I have been hunting for about 20 years. I like to hunt for food, sport, and for medicinal purposes
Golden Response:	Well the diet verstion was created in 1988, followed by mountain dew red which was discontinued in the same year.	Golden Response:	20 years now! Excessive hunting has also heavily contributed to the endangerment, extirpation and extinction of many animals

Impact of Prefix Length. We investigate whether Prefix-Tuning can achieve better performance than KnowPrefix-Tuning by increasing its prefix length. We employ BARTLARGE as the backbone model for each variant. Table 4 shows the results. We observe that increasing prefix length will introduce more parameters. However, the performance of Prefix-Tuning seems not to be better even if it introduce additional parameters comparable to KnowPrefix-Tuning. We think that although the longer prefix length introduces more trainable parameters and increases the generalization ability of the model, too long a prefix length may lead the model tend to overfit the training dataset, degrading the knowledgeable response generation ability.

Case Study. Table 5 and Table 6 show the cases from the Wizard test set, from which we observe that the generated responses of the KnowPrefix-Tuning not only leverage the knowledge relevant to the dialogue context but also ensure

Table 6. Cases from the test seen and test unseen data of Wizard. The facts with boldface have been verified on the Internet.

Dialogue Context			
Test Seen		**Test Unseen**	
Wizard:	Hey, what do you think of Mcdonald's dollar menu cheeseburgers?	*Wizard:*	I love American football also know as gridiron
Apprentice:	I think it would be worth the money spent for trying them.	*Apprentice:*	It's a pretty fun sport to watch, also I have never heard it be called that!
Response			
KnowExpert$_w$:	I agree, I love the fact that they have a menu of different items.	KnowExpert$_w$:	It is played on a rectangular field with a goal at each end
Prefix-Tuning:	Yes, I agree. I also like their chicken nuggets and french fries.	Prefix-Tuning:	It is called gridiron football in the USA. It is a team sport played on a rectangular field
Finetune:	I agree, i love the cheeseburgers. They're so good! Mcdonald's also owns and operates Sam's club.	Finetune:	It is played on a rectangular field with a goal at each end. It is also called gridiron football
KnowPrefix-Tuning:	I agree, they are so good. **They are a hamburger stand that was founded in 1940.**	KnowPrefix-Tuning:	**It is played by 250 million people in over 200 countries**. It is the most popular sport in the world
Golden Response:	It is actually. I don't know about the breakfast.	Golden Response:	Yes, it originated from association football and rugby

the correctness of the utilized knowledge. As shown in Table 5, the responses generated by KnowPrefix-Tuning on both Test Seen and Test Unseen contain essential facts that appeared in the golden answer. We believe that the learned knowledge prefix effectively provides facts relevant to the dialogue context, which is indispensable to guide knowledgeable response generation. From Table 6, we observe that the responses generated by KnowPrefix-Tuning contain factually correct knowledge even if the corresponding evidence is not explicitly provided. We suspect that it is because the parameters of the language model are frozen during the fine-tuning procedure. Thus, the knowledge inherently encoded in the pre-trained language model is not disturbed, which can be prompted to provide evidence for knowledgeable response generation.

6 Conclusions

In this paper, we propose KnowPrefix-Tuning to handle the knowledge-grounded dialogue generation task. The proposed method bypasses the retrieval process and does not require fine-tuning the entire PLM. In addition, the proposed interactive re-parameterization mechanism allows the interaction between the embedding of prefixes and PLM. Experiments on two commonly-used knowledge-grounded dialogue datasets demonstrate the effectiveness of our approach.

Acknowledgments. We thank all the anonymous reviewers for their insightful comments. This work was supported in part by the National Natural Science Foundation of China (Grant Nos. 62276017, U1636211, 61672081), the 2022 Tencent Big Travel Rhino-Bird Special Research Program, and the Fund of the State Key Laboratory of Software Development Environment (Grant No. SKLSDE-2021ZX-18).

References

1. Bao, S., et al.: PLATO-2: Towards building an open-domain chatbot via curriculum learning. In: Findings of the Association for Computational Linguistics: ACL-IJCNLP 2021, pp. 2513–2525. Association for Computational Linguistics, Online (Aug 2021). https://doi.org/10.18653/v1/2021.findings-acl.222
2. Brown, T., et al.: Language models are few-shot learners. Adv. Neural. Inf. Process. Syst. **33**, 1877–1901 (2020)
3. Cui, L., Cheng, S., Wu, Y., Zhang, Y.: On commonsense cues in bert for solving commonsense tasks. In: Findings of the Association for Computational Linguistics: ACL-IJCNLP 2021, pp. 683–693 (2021)
4. Cui, L., Wu, Y., Liu, S., Zhang, Y.: Knowledge enhanced fine-tuning for better handling unseen entities in dialogue generation. In: Proceedings of the 2021 Conference on Empirical Methods in Natural Language Processing, pp. 2328–2337 (2021)
5. Davison, J., Feldman, J., Rush, A.M.: Commonsense knowledge mining from pre-trained models. In: Proceedings of the 2019 Conference on Empirical Methods in Natural Language Processing and the 9th International Joint Conference on Natural Language Processing (EMNLP-IJCNLP), pp. 1173–1178 (2019)
6. Dinan, E., Roller, S., Shuster, K., Fan, A., Auli, M., Weston, J.: Wizard of wikipedia: Knowledge-powered conversational agents. In: International Conference on Learning Representations (2018)
7. Fleiss, J.L.: Measuring nominal scale agreement among many raters. Psychol. Bull. **76**(5), 378 (1971)
8. Ghazvininejad, M., et al.: A knowledge-grounded neural conversation model. In: Proceedings of the AAAI Conference on Artificial Intelligence, vol. 32 (2018)
9. Guu, K., Lee, K., Tung, Z., Pasupat, P., Chang, M.: Retrieval augmented language model pre-training. In: International Conference on Machine Learning, pp. 3929–3938. PMLR (2020)
10. Holtzman, A., Buys, J., Du, L., Forbes, M., Choi, Y.: The curious case of neural text degeneration. In: International Conference on Learning Representations (2019)
11. Huang, X., He, H., Bao, S., Wang, F., Wu, H., Wang, H.: Plato-kag: Unsupervised knowledge-grounded conversation via joint modeling. In: Proceedings of the 3rd Workshop on Natural Language Processing for Conversational AI, pp. 143–154 (2021)
12. Karimi Mahabadi, R., et al.: Prompt-free and efficient few-shot learning with language models. In: Proceedings of the 60th Annual Meeting of the Association for Computational Linguistics (Volume 1: Long Papers), pp. 3638–3652. Association for Computational Linguistics, Dublin, Ireland (May 2022). https://doi.org/10.18653/v1/2022.acl-long.254
13. Kenton, J.D.M.W.C., Toutanova, L.K.: Bert: Pre-training of deep bidirectional transformers for language understanding. In: Proceedings of NAACL-HLT, pp. 4171–4186 (2019)
14. Kim, B., Ahn, J., Kim, G.: Sequential latent knowledge selection for knowledge-grounded dialogue. In: International Conference on Learning Representations (2019)
15. Komeili, M., Shuster, K., Weston, J.: Internet-augmented dialogue generation. In: Proceedings of the 60th Annual Meeting of the Association for Computational Linguistics (Volume 1: Long Papers), pp. 8460–8478 (2022)
16. Lester, B., Al-Rfou, R., Constant, N.: The power of scale for parameter-efficient prompt tuning. In: Proceedings of the 2021 Conference on Empirical Methods in Natural Language Processing, pp. 3045–3059 (2021)

17. Lewis, M., et al.: Bart: Denoising sequence-to-sequence pre-training for natural language generation, translation, and comprehension. In: Proceedings of the 58th Annual Meeting of the Association for Computational Linguistics, pp. 7871–7880 (2020)
18. Lewis, P., et al.: Retrieval-augmented generation for knowledge-intensive nlp tasks: Adv. Neural. Inf. Process. Syst. **33**, 9459–9474 (2020)
19. Li, L., Xu, C., Wu, W., Zhao, Y., Zhao, X., Tao, C.: Zero-resource knowledge-grounded dialogue generation. Adv. Neural. Inf. Process. Syst. **33**, 8475–8485 (2020)
20. Li, X.L., Liang, P.: Prefix-tuning: Optimizing continuous prompts for generation. In: Proceedings of the 59th Annual Meeting of the Association for Computational Linguistics and the 11th International Joint Conference on Natural Language Processing (Volume 1: Long Papers), pp. 4582–4597. Association for Computational Linguistics, Online (Aug 2021). https://doi.org/10.18653/v1/2021.acl-long.353
21. Li, Y., Zhao, J., Lyu, M.R., Wang, L.: Eliciting knowledge from large pre-trained models for unsupervised knowledge-grounded conversation. arXiv preprint arXiv:2211.01587 (2022)
22. Li, Y., et al.: Knowledge-grounded dialogue generation with a unified knowledge representation. In: Proceedings of the 2022 Conference of the North American Chapter of the Association for Computational Linguistics: Human Language Technologies, pp. 206–218. Association for Computational Linguistics, Seattle, United States (Jul 2022). https://doi.org/10.18653/v1/2022.naacl-main.15
23. Lian, R., Xie, M., Wang, F., Peng, J., Wu, H.: Learning to select knowledge for response generation in dialog systems. In: IJCAI International Joint Conference on Artificial Intelligence, p. 5081 (2019)
24. Liu, Y., et al.: Multilingual denoising pre-training for neural machine translation. Trans. Assoc. Comput. Linguist. **8**, 726–742 (2020). https://doi.org/10.1162/tacl_a_00343
25. Liu, Z., et al.: Multi-stage prompting for knowledgeable dialogue generation. In: Findings of the Association for Computational Linguistics: ACL 2022, pp. 1317–1337 (2022)
26. Loshchilov, I., Hutter, F.: Fixing weight decay regularization in adam (2018)
27. Meng, C., et al.: Dukenet: A dual knowledge interaction network for knowledge-grounded conversation. In: Proceedings of the 43rd International ACM SIGIR Conference on Research and Development in Information Retrieval pp. 1151–1160 (2020)
28. Petroni, F., et al.: Language models as knowledge bases? In: Proceedings of the 2019 Conference on Empirical Methods in Natural Language Processing and the 9th International Joint Conference on Natural Language Processing (EMNLP-IJCNLP), pp. 2463–2473 (2019)
29. Prabhumoye, S., Hashimoto, K., Zhou, Y., Black, A.W., Salakhutdinov, R.: Focused attention improves document-grounded generation. In: Proceedings of the 2021 Conference of the North American Chapter of the Association for Computational Linguistics: Human Language Technologies, pp. 4274–4287 (2021)
30. Radford, A., Wu, J., Child, R., Luan, D., Amodei, D., Sutskever, I., et al.: Language models are unsupervised multitask learners. OpenAI Blog (2019)
31. Roller, S., et al.: Recipes for building an open-domain chatbot. In: Proceedings of the 16th Conference of the European Chapter of the Association for Computational Linguistics: Main Volume, pp. 300–325 (2021)

32. Schick, T., Schütze, H.: It's not just size that matters: Small language models are also few-shot learners. In: Proceedings of the 2021 Conference of the North American Chapter of the Association for Computational Linguistics: Human Language Technologies, pp. 2339–2352 (2021)
33. Shin, T., Razeghi, Y., Logan IV, R.L., Wallace, E., Singh, S.: Autoprompt: Eliciting knowledge from language models with automatically generated prompts. In: Proceedings of the 2020 Conference on Empirical Methods in Natural Language Processing (EMNLP), pp. 4222–4235 (2020)
34. Shuster, K., Poff, S., Chen, M., Kiela, D., Weston, J.: Retrieval augmentation reduces hallucination in conversation. In: Findings of the Association for Computational Linguistics: EMNLP 2021, pp. 3784–3803 (2021)
35. Sun, Q., et al.: Multimodal dialogue response generation. In: Proceedings of the 60th Annual Meeting of the Association for Computational Linguistics (Volume 1: Long Papers), pp. 2854–2866. Association for Computational Linguistics, Dublin, Ireland (May 2022). https://doi.org/10.18653/v1/2022.acl-long.204
36. Sun, Q., et al.: Stylized knowledge-grounded dialogue generation via disentangled template rewriting. In: Proceedings of the 2022 Conference of the North American Chapter of the Association for Computational Linguistics: Human Language Technologies, pp. 3304–3318. Association for Computational Linguistics, Seattle, United States (2022). https://doi.org/10.18653/v1/2022.naacl-main.241
37. Sun, W., Shi, Z., Gao, S., Ren, P., de Rijke, M., Ren, Z.: Contrastive learning reduces hallucination in conversations. CoRR abs/2212.10400 (2022). arXiv:2212.10400
38. Vaswani, A., et al.: Attention is all you need. Adv. Neural Inform. Process. Syst. **30** (2017)
39. Wang, C., Liu, P., Zhang, Y.: Can generative pre-trained language models serve as knowledge bases for closed-book qa? In: Proceedings of the 59th Annual Meeting of the Association for Computational Linguistics and the 11th International Joint Conference on Natural Language Processing (Volume 1: Long Papers), pp. 3241–3251 (2021)
40. Xu, Y., et al.: Retrieval-free knowledge-grounded dialogue response generation with adapters. In: Proceedings of the Second DialDoc Workshop on Document-grounded Dialogue and Conversational Question Answering, pp. 93–107 (2022)
41. Zhao, L., et al.: Domain-oriented prefix-tuning: Towards efficient and generalizable fine-tuning for zero-shot dialogue summarization. In: Proceedings of the 2022 Conference of the North American Chapter of the Association for Computational Linguistics: Human Language Technologies, pp. 4848–4862. Association for Computational Linguistics, Seattle, United States (Jul 2022). https://doi.org/10.18653/v1/2022.naacl-main.357
42. Zhao, T., Zhao, R., Eskenazi, M.: Learning discourse-level diversity for neural dialog models using conditional variational autoencoders. In: Proceedings of the 55th Annual Meeting of the Association for Computational Linguistics (Volume 1: Long Papers), pp. 654–664 (2017)
43. Zhao, X., Fu, T., Tao, C., Wu, W., Zhao, D., Yan, R.: Learning to express in knowledge-grounded conversation. In: Proceedings of the 2022 Conference of the North American Chapter of the Association for Computational Linguistics: Human Language Technologies, pp. 2258–2273. Association for Computational Linguistics, Seattle, United States (Jul 2022). https://doi.org/10.18653/v1/2022.naacl-main.164

44. Zhao, X., Wu, W., Xu, C., Tao, C., Zhao, D., Yan, R.: Knowledge-grounded dialogue generation with pre-trained language models. In: Proceedings of the 2020 Conference on Empirical Methods in Natural Language Processing (EMNLP), pp. 3377–3390 (2020)
45. Zhou, K., Prabhumoye, S., Black, A.W.: A dataset for document grounded conversations. In: Proceedings of the 2018 Conference on Empirical Methods in Natural Language Processing, pp. 708–713 (2018)
46. Zhou, X., Zhang, Y., Cui, L., Huang, D.: Evaluating commonsense in pre-trained language models. In: Proceedings of the AAAI Conference on Artificial Intelligence. vol. 34, pp. 9733–9740 (2020)

Learning Data Representations with Joint Diffusion Models

Kamil Deja[1,2(✉)], Tomasz Trzciński[1,2], and Jakub M. Tomczak[3]

[1] Warsaw University of Technology, Warsaw, Poland
{kamil.deja,tomasz.trzcinski}@pw.edu.pl
[2] IDEAS NCBR, Warsaw, Poland
[3] Eindhoven University of Technology, Eindhoven, The Netherlands
j.m.tomczak@tue.nl

Abstract. Joint machine learning models that allow synthesizing and classifying data often offer uneven performance between those tasks or are unstable to train. In this work, we depart from a set of empirical observations that indicate the usefulness of internal representations built by contemporary deep diffusion-based generative models not only for generating but also predicting. We then propose to extend the vanilla diffusion model with a classifier that allows for stable joint end-to-end training with shared parameterization between those objectives. The resulting joint diffusion model outperforms recent state-of-the-art hybrid methods in terms of both classification and generation quality on all evaluated benchmarks. On top of our joint training approach, we present how we can directly benefit from shared generative and discriminative representations by introducing a method for visual counterfactual explanations.

Keywords: Deep generative models · diffusion models · joint models

1 Introduction

Training a single machine learning model that can jointly synthesize new data as well as to make predictions about input samples remains a long-standing goal of machine learning [21,28]. Shared representations created with a combination of those two objectives promise benefits on many downstream problems such as calibration of model uncertainty [5], semi-supervised learning [26], unsupervised domain adaptation [20] or continual learning [31].

Therefore, since the introduction of deep generative models such as Variational Autoencoders (VAEs) [24], a growing body of work takes advantage of shared deep neural network-based parameterization and latent variables to build joint models. For instance, [20,27,44,47] stack a classifier on top of latent variables sampled from a shared encoder. Similarly, [32,34] use normalizing flows to obtain an invertible representation that is further fed to a classifier. However, these approaches require modifying the log-likelihood function by scaling either the conditional log-likelihood or the marginal log-likelihood. This idea, known as

© The Author(s), under exclusive license to Springer Nature Switzerland AG 2023

D. Koutra et al. (Eds.): ECML PKDD 2023, LNAI 14170, pp. 543–559, 2023.
https://doi.org/10.1007/978-3-031-43415-0_32

hybrid modeling [28], leads to the situation where models concentrate either on synthesizing data or predicting but not on both of those tasks simultaneously.

We address existing joint models' limitations and leverage the recently introduced diffusion-based deep generative models (DDGM) [7,23,39]. This new family of methods has become popular because of the unprecedented quality of the samples they generate. However, relatively little attention was paid to their inner workings, especially to the internal representations built by the DDGMs. In this work, we fill this gap and empirically analyze those representations, validating their usefulness for predictive tasks and beyond. Then, we introduce a joint diffusion model, where a classifier shares the parametrization with the UNet encoder by operating on the extracted latent features. This results in meaningful data representations shared across discriminative and generative objectives.

We validate our approach in several use cases where we show how one part of our model can benefit from the other. First, we investigate how DDGMs benefit from the additional classifier to conditionally generate new samples or alter original images. Next, we show the performance improvement our method brings in the classification task. Finally, we present how we can directly benefit from joint representations used by both the classifier and generator by creating visual counterfactual explanations, namely, how to explain decisions of a model by identifying which regions of an input image need to change in order for the system to produce a specified output.

We can summarize the contributions of our work as follows:

- We provide empirical observations with insights into representations built internally by diffusion models, on top of which we introduce a joint classifier and diffusion model with shared parametrization.
- We introduce a conditional sampling algorithm where we optimize internal diffusion representations with a classifier.
- We present state-of-the-art results in terms of joint modeling where our solution outperforms other joint and hybrid methods in terms of both quality of generations and the classification performance.

2 Background

Joint Models. Let us consider two random variables: $\mathbf{x} \in \mathcal{X}$ and $y \in \mathcal{Y}$. For instance, in the classification problem we can have $\mathcal{X} = \mathbb{R}^D$ and $\mathcal{Y} = \{0, 1, \ldots, K-1\}$. The joint distribution over these random variables could be factorized in one of the following two manners, namely, $p(\mathbf{x}, y) = p(\mathbf{x}|y)p(y) = p(y|\mathbf{x})p(\mathbf{x})$. Following the second factorization gives us the conditional distribution $p(y|\mathbf{x})$ (e.g., a classifier) and the marginal distribution $p(\mathbf{x})$. For prediction, it is enough to learn the conditional distribution, which is typically parameterized with neural networks. However, training the joint model with shared parametrization has many advantages since one part of the model can positively influence the other.

Diffusion-Based Deep Generative Models. In this work, we follow the formulation of Diffusion-based deep generative models as presented in [16, 39]. Given a data distribution $\mathbf{x}_0 \sim q(\mathbf{x}_0)$, we define a *forward* noising process q that produces a sequence of latent variables x_1 through x_T by adding Gaussian noise at each time step t, with a variance of $\beta_t \in (0,1)$, defined by a schedule $\beta_1, ..., \beta_T$, namely, $q(\mathbf{x}_1, \ldots, \mathbf{x}_T|\mathbf{x}_0) = \prod_{t=1}^{T} q(\mathbf{x}_t|\mathbf{x}_{t-1})$, where $q(\mathbf{x}_t|\mathbf{x}_{t-1}) = \mathcal{N}(\mathbf{x}_t; \sqrt{1-\beta_t}\mathbf{x}_{t-1}, \beta_t\mathbf{I})$.

Following [18, 23, 43, 45], we consider DDGMs as infinitely deep hierarchical VAEs with a specific family of variational posteriors; namely, Gaussian diffusion processes [39]. Therefore, for data point $\mathbf{x}_0$, and latent variables $\mathbf{x}_1, \ldots, \mathbf{x}_T$, we want to optimize the marginal likelihood $p_\theta(\mathbf{x}_0) = \int p_\theta(\mathbf{x}_0, \ldots, \mathbf{x}_T) \mathrm{d}\mathbf{x}_1, \ldots, \mathbf{x}_T$, where $p_\theta(\mathbf{x}_0, \ldots, \mathbf{x}_T) = p(\mathbf{x}_T) \prod_{t=0}^{T} p_\theta(\mathbf{x}_{t-1}|\mathbf{x}_t)$ is the *backward* diffusion process with $p_\theta(\mathbf{x}_{t-1}|\mathbf{x}_t) = \mathcal{N}(\mathbf{x}_{t-1}; \mu_\theta(\mathbf{x}_t, t), \Sigma_\theta(\mathbf{x}_t, t))$.

We can define the variational lower bound as follows:

$$\ln p_\theta(\mathbf{x}_0) \geq L_{vlb}(\theta) := \underbrace{\mathbb{E}_{q(\mathbf{x}_1|\mathbf{x}_0)}[\ln p_\theta(\mathbf{x}_0|\mathbf{x}_1)]}_{-L_0} - \underbrace{D_{\mathrm{KL}}\left[q(\mathbf{x}_T|\mathbf{x}_0)\|p(\mathbf{x}_T)\right]}_{L_T} + \\ - \sum_{t=2}^{T} \underbrace{\mathbb{E}_{q(\mathbf{x}_t|\mathbf{x}_0)} D_{\mathrm{KL}}\left[q(\mathbf{x}_{t-1}|\mathbf{x}_t, \mathbf{x}_0)\|p_\theta(\mathbf{x}_{t-1}|\mathbf{x}_t)\right]}_{L_{t-1}}. \quad (1)$$

that we further optimize with respect to the parameters of the backward diffusion.

Training Objective. The authors of [16] notice that instead of estimating the probability of previous latent variable $p(\mathbf{x}_{t-1}|\mathbf{x}_t)$, we can predict the added noise ϵ. Therefore, a single part of the variational lower bound is equal to:

$$L_t(\theta) = \mathbb{E}_{\mathbf{x}_0, \epsilon}\left[\frac{\beta_t^2}{2\sigma_t^2 \alpha_t (1-\overline{\alpha}_t)} \left\|\epsilon - \epsilon_\theta\left(\sqrt{\overline{\alpha}_t}\mathbf{x}_0 + \sqrt{1-\overline{\alpha}_t}\epsilon, t\right)\right\|^2\right], \quad (2)$$

where $\epsilon \sim \mathcal{N}(\mathbf{0}, \mathbf{I})$ and $\epsilon_\theta(\cdot,\cdot)$ is a neural network predicting the noise ϵ from $\mathbf{x}_t$.

In [16], it is also suggested to train the model with a simplified objective that is a modified version of Eq. (2) without scaling, namely:

$$L_{t,\mathrm{simple}}(\theta) = \mathbb{E}_{\mathbf{x}_0, \epsilon}\left[\left\|\epsilon - \epsilon_\theta\left(\sqrt{\overline{\alpha}_t}\mathbf{x}_0 + \sqrt{1-\overline{\alpha}_t}\epsilon, t\right)\right\|^2\right]. \quad (3)$$

In practice, a single shared neural network is used for modeling ϵ_θ. For that end, most of the works [16, 23, 33] use UNet architecture [36] that can be seen as a specific type of an autoencoder. This is particularly relevant for this work since we benefit from the *Encoder – Decoder* structure of the denoising DDGM model.

3 Related Work

Diffusion Models. There are several extensions to the baseline DDGM setup that aim to improve the quality of sampled generations [16, 18, 23, 40, 41]. Several works propose to improve the quality of samples from DDGMs by conditioning the generations with class identities [17,19,42]. Among those works, [7] introduces a classifier-guided generation, where a gradient from an externally and independently trained classifier is added in the process of backward diffusion to guide the generation towards a target class. On top of this approach, [2] present a tool for investigating the decision of a classifier by generating visual counterfactual explanations with a diffusion model. In this work, we simplify both of those methods benefiting from training a joint model with representations shared between a diffusion model and a classifier.

Diffusion Models and UNet Representations. In [1] additional encoded information to the score estimator is introduced, which allows using the score matching loss function for learning data representations. The authors of [3] use activations from the pre-trained diffusion UNet model for the image segmentation task. Here, we first analyze how pre-trained models could be useful for classification, and further propose a joint model that is trained end-to-end with generative and discriminative losses. Other works consider data representations from the UNet model within other generative models, e.g., a conditional UNet-based variational autoencoder [10]. Additionally in [11] authors show the connection between the UNet architecture and wavelet transformation, applying it to the hierarchical VAEs. In this work, we show that indeed diffusion models learn useful representations, and further take advantage of that fact in a shared parameterization between a diffusion model and a classifier in a joint model.

Joint Training. Apart from latent variable joint models, in [13] authors show that it is possible to use a shared parameterization (a neural network-based classifier) to formulate an energy-based model. This Joint Energy-based Model (JEM) could be seen as a classifier if a softmax function is applied to logits or a generator if a Markov-chain Monte Carlo method is used to sample from the model. Although it obtains strong empirical results, gradient estimators used to train JEM are unstable and prone to diverging when optimization parameters are not perfectly tuned, which limits the robustness and applicability of this method. Alternatively, Introspective Neural Networks could be used for generative modeling and classification by applying a single parameterization [22,29,30]. The idea behind this class of models relies on utilizing a training procedure that combines adversarial learning and contrastive learning. Similarly to JEMs, sampling is carried out by running an MCMC method. In [14], the authors improve the performance of JEM by introducing a variational-based approximator (VERA) instead of MCMC. Similarly, in [48] authors introduce JEM++, an improvement over the JEM's generative performance by applying a proximal SGLD-based generation, and classification accuracy with informative initialization. From a conceptually different perspective, the authors of [49] propose an implementation of a joint model based on the Vision Transformer [8] architecture, that yields state-of-the-art result in terms of image classification. Here, we propose to combine standard diffusion models with classifiers by sharing their parameterization. Thus, our training is entirely based on the log-likelihood function and end-to-end, while sampling is carried out by backward diffusion instead of any MCMC algorithm.

4 Diffusion Models Learn Data Representations

Learning useful data representations is important for having a good generator or classifier. Ideally, we would like to train a joint model that allows us to obtain proper representations for both $p(y|\mathbf{x})$ and $p(\mathbf{x})$ simultaneously. In this work, we investigate parameterizations of DDGMs and, in particular, the use of an autoencoder as a denoising decoder $p_\theta(\mathbf{x}_{t-1}|\mathbf{x}_t)$. Within this architecture, the denoising function can be decomposed into two parts: encoding of the image at the current timestep into a set of features $\mathcal{Z}_t = e(\mathbf{x}_t)$ and then decoding it to obtain $\mathbf{x}_{t-1} = d(\mathcal{Z}_t)$.

For the UNet architecture, a set of features obtained from an input is a structure composed of several tensors with image features encoded to different levels, $\mathcal{Z}_t = \{\mathbf{z}_t^1, \mathbf{z}_t^2 \ldots \mathbf{z}_t^n\}$. For all further experiments, we propose to pool features encoded by the same filter and concatenate the averaged representations into a single vector $\mathbf{z}_t$, as presented in Fig. 1 for $n = 3$. In particular, we can use average pooling to select average convolutional filter activations to the whole input. Details of this procedure are described in the Appendix **B.1**.

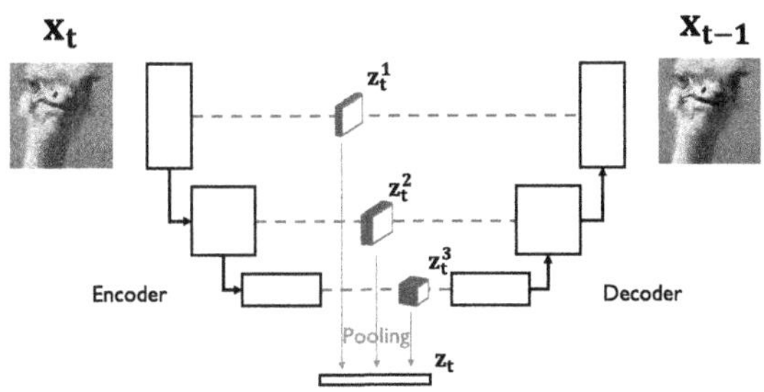

Fig. 1. Data representation $\mathbf{z}_t$ in a UNet-based diffusion model.

4.1 Diffusion Model Representations are Useful for Prediction

First, we verify whether averaged representations $\mathbf{z}_0$ extracted from an original image $\mathbf{x}_0$ by the UNet contain information that is in some sense predictive. We measure it with the classification accuracy of an MLP-based classifier fed with $\mathbf{z}_0$. As presented in Fig. 2a, representations encoded in $\mathbf{z}_0$ are indeed very informative and, in some cases (e.g., CIFAR-10), could lead to performance comparable to a stand-alone classifier with the same architecture as the combination of the UNet encoder and MLP but trained with the cross-entropy loss function. A similar observation was made in [3], where the pre-trained diffusion model was used for semantic image segmentation.

4.2 Diffusion Models Learn Features of Increasing Granularity

The next question is how the data representations $\mathbf{z}_t$ differ with diffusion timesteps t. To investigate this issue, we train an unsupervised DDGM on the CelebA dataset, which we then use to extract the features $\mathbf{z}_t$ at different timesteps. On top of those representations, we fit a binary logistic regression

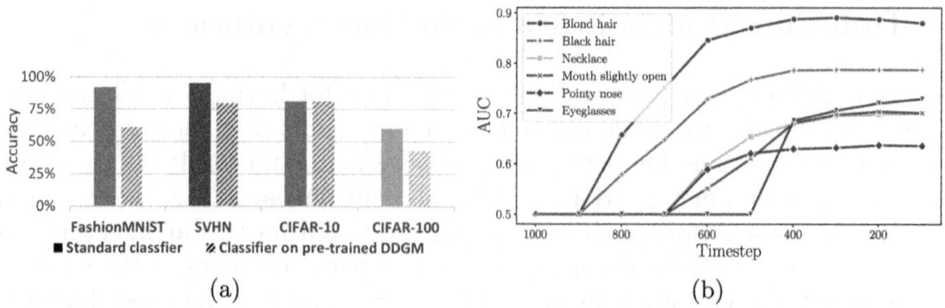

Fig. 2. (a) The test-set accuracy of a stand-alone classifier compared to a classifier trained on top of data representations from a pre-trained diffusion model extracted from original images $\mathbf{x}_0$. (b) The area under the ROC curve (AUC) for logistic regression models fit on data representations extracted with a pre-trained diffusion model at ten different diffusion timesteps. High-grained features are already distinguishable at late diffusion steps (closer to random noise), while low-grained features are only represented at the earlier stage of the forward diffusion.

classifier for each of the 40 attributes in the dataset. In Fig. 2b, we show the performance of those regression models for 6 different attributes when calculated on top of representations from ten different diffusion timesteps. We observe that the model learns different data features depending on the amount of noise added to the original data sample. As presented in Fig. 2b, high-grained data features such as hair color start to emerge at late diffusion steps (closer to the noise), while low-grained features (e.g., necklace or glasses) are not present until the early steps. This observation is in line with the works on denoising autoencoders where authors observe similar behavior for denoising with different amounts of added noise [4,12,50].

5 Method

5.1 Joint Diffusion Models: DDGMs with Classifiers

Taking into account the observations described in Sect. 4, we propose to train a joint model that is composed of a classifier and a DDGM. We propose to use a shared parameterization, namely, a shared encoder of the UNet architecture that serves as the generative part and for calculating pooled features for the classifier. We pool the latent representations of the data from different levels of the UNet architecture into one vector $\mathbf{z}$. On top of this vector, we build a classifier model trained to assign a label to the data example represented by the vector $\mathbf{z}$.

In particular, we consider the following parameterization of a denoising diffusion model within a single diffusion timestep t, $p_\theta(\mathbf{z}_{t-1}|\mathbf{z}_t)$. We distinguish the encoder e_ν with parameters ν that maps input $\mathbf{x}_t$ into a set of vectors $\mathcal{Z}_t = e_\nu(\mathbf{x}_t)$, where $\mathcal{Z}_t = \{\mathbf{z}_t^1, \mathbf{z}_t^2 \dots \mathbf{z}_t^n\}$, i.e., a set of representation vectors derived from each depth level of the UNet architecture. The second component of the denoising diffusion model is the decoder d_ψ with parameters ψ that reconstructs feature vectors into a denoised sample, $\mathbf{x}_{t-1} = d_\psi(\mathcal{Z}_t)$. Together the encoder and the decoder form the denoising model p_θ with parameters $\theta = \{\nu, \psi\}$. Next, we introduce a third part of our model, which is the classifier g_ω with parameters ω that predicts target class $\hat{y} = g_\omega(\mathcal{Z}_t)$. The first layer of the classifier is the average pooling that results in a single representation $\mathbf{z}_t$.

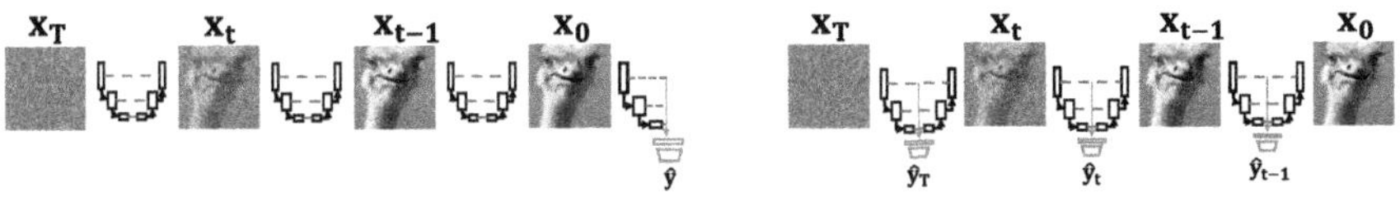

(a) The parameterization of our joint diffusion *(b)* Additional noisy classifiers

Fig. 3. The parameterization of our joint diffusion model. *(a)* Each step in the backward diffusion is parameterized by a shared UNet. The classifier uses the encoder of the UNet together with the average pooling (green) and additional layers (yellow). *(b)* An alternative training that additionally uses the classifier for noisy images $\mathbf{x}_t$ $(t > 0)$. (Color figure online)

In our approach, we consider a classifier that takes the original image $\mathbf{x}_0$ for which a vector of probabilities is returned φ and eventually the final prediction is calculated, $\hat{y} = g_\omega(\mathbf{x}_0)$. The visualization of our shared parameterization is presented in Fig. 3*(a)*. As a result, our model could be written as follows $p_{\nu,\psi,\omega}(\mathbf{x}_{0:T}, y) = p_{\nu,\omega}(y|\mathbf{x}_0)\ p_{\nu,\psi}(\mathbf{x}_{0:T})$, and applying the logarithm yields:

$$\ln p_{\nu,\psi,\omega}(\mathbf{x}_{0:T}, y) = \ln p_{\nu,\omega}(y|\mathbf{x}_0) + \ln p_{\nu,\psi}(\mathbf{x}_{0:T}). \tag{4}$$

The logarithm of the joint distribution (4) could serve as the training objective, where $\ln p_\theta(\mathbf{x}_{0:T})$ could be either approximated by the ELBO (1) or the simplified objective with (3). Here, we use the simplified objective:

$$L_{t,\text{diff}}(\nu, \psi) = \mathbb{E}_{\mathbf{x}_0,\epsilon}\left[\|\epsilon - \hat{\epsilon}\|^2\right], \tag{5}$$

where $\hat{\epsilon}$ is a prediction from the decoder:

$$\{\mathbf{z}_t^1, \mathbf{z}_t^2 \ldots \mathbf{z}_t^n\} = e_\nu\left(\sqrt{\overline{\alpha}_t}\mathbf{x}_0 + \sqrt{1-\overline{\alpha}_t}\epsilon, t\right) \tag{6}$$

$$\hat{\epsilon} = d_\psi(\{\mathbf{z}_t^1, \mathbf{z}_t^2 \ldots \mathbf{z}_t^n\}). \tag{7}$$

For the classifier, we use the logarithm of the categorical distribution:

$$L_{\text{class}}(\nu, \omega) = -\mathbb{E}_{\mathbf{x}_0,y}\left[\sum_{k=0}^{K-1} \mathbb{1}[y=k] \log \frac{\exp(\varphi_k)}{\sum_{c=0}^{K-1}\exp(\varphi_c)}\right], \tag{8}$$

which is the cross-entropy loss, and where y is the target class, φ is a vector of probabilities returned by the classifier $g_\omega(e_\nu(\mathbf{x}_0))$, and $\mathbb{1}[y=k]$ is the indicator function that is 1 if y equals k, and 0 otherwise.

The final loss function in our approach is then the following:

$$L(\nu, \psi, \omega) = L_{\text{class}}(\nu, \omega) - L_0(\nu, \psi) - \sum_{t=2}^{T} L_{t,\text{diff}}(\nu, \psi) - L_T(\nu, \psi).$$

We optimize the objective in (9) wrt. $\{\nu, \psi, \omega\}$ with a single optimizer.

5.2 An Alternative Training of Joint Diffusion Models

The training of the proposed approach over a batch of data is straightforward: For given $(\mathbf{x}_0, y)$, the example $\mathbf{x}_0$ is first noised with a forward diffusion to a random timestep, $\mathbf{x}_t$, so that the training loss for the denoising model is a Monte-Carlo approximation of the sum over all timesteps. Then $\mathbf{x}_0$ is fed to a classifier that returns probabilities φ, and the cross-entropy loss is calculated for given y.

As discussed in Sect. 4.2, the diffusion model trained even in a fully unsupervised manner provides data representations related to the different granularity of input features at various diffusion timesteps. Thus, we can improve the robustness of our method by applying the same classifier to intermediate noisy images $\mathbf{x}_t$ $(0 < t < T)$, which by reason adds the cross-entropy losses for $\mathbf{x}_t$, namely:

$$L_{\text{class}}^{t}(\nu, \omega) = -\mathbb{E}_{\mathbf{x}_0, y}\left[\sum_{k=0}^{K-1} \mathbb{1}[y = k] \log \frac{\exp\left(\varphi_k^t\right)}{\sum_{c=0}^{K-1} \exp\left(\varphi_c^t\right)}\right], \tag{9}$$

where φ_k^t is a vector of probabilities given by $g_\omega(e_\nu(\mathbf{x}_t))$. Then the extended objective (9) is the following:

$$L_{\mathcal{T}}(\nu, \psi, \omega) = L(\nu, \psi, \omega) + \sum_{t \in \mathcal{T}} L_{\text{class}}^{t}(\nu, \omega), \tag{10}$$

where $\mathcal{T} \subseteq \{1, 2, \ldots, T\}$ is the set of timesteps. These additional *noisy classifiers* are schematically depicted in Fig. 3*(b)* in which we highlight that the model is reused across various noisy images. It is important to mention that the noisy classifiers serve only for training purposes; they are not used for prediction. This procedure is similar to the data augmentation technique, where random noise is added to the input [38].

5.3 Conditional Sampling in Joint Diffusion Models

To improve the quality of samples generated by DDGM, [7] propose a classifier guidance approach, where an externally trained classifier can be used to guide the generation of the DDGM trained in an unsupervised way towards the desired class. In DDGMs, at each backward diffusion step, an image is sampled from the output of the diffusion model p_θ according to the following formula:

$$\begin{aligned} \mu, \Sigma &\leftarrow \mu_\theta\left(\mathbf{x}_t\right), \Sigma_\theta\left(\mathbf{x}_t\right) \\ \mathbf{x}_{t-1} &\leftarrow \text{sample from } \mathcal{N}\left(\mu, \Sigma\right) \end{aligned} \tag{11}$$

It was proposed in [7] to change the second line of this equation and add a scaled gradient with respect to the target class from an externally trained classifier $c(\cdot)$ directly to the output of the denoising model:

$$\mathbf{x}_{t-1} \leftarrow \text{sample from } \mathcal{N}\left(\mu + s\Sigma\nabla_{\mathbf{x}_t} c(\mathbf{x}_t), \Sigma\right), \tag{12}$$

where s is a gradient scale.

With the joint training of a classifier and diffusion model introduced in this work, we propose to simplify the classifier guidance technique. Using the alternative training introduced in Sect. 5.2, we can use noisy classifiers to formulate conditional sampling. The encoder model e_ν encodes input data $\mathbf{x}_t$ into the representation vectors $\mathcal{Z}_t$ that are used to both denoise an example into the previous diffusion timestep $\mathbf{x}_{t-1} \sim d_\psi(\mathcal{Z}_t)$ as well as to predict the target label with a classifier $\hat{y} = g_\omega(\mathcal{Z}_t)$. Therefore, to guide the model towards a target label during sampling, we propose optimizing the representations $\mathcal{Z}_t$ according to the gradient calculated through the classifier with respect to the desired class. The overview of this procedure is presented in Algorithm 1.

Algorithm 1 Sampling with optimized representations given a diffusion model (an encoder $e_\nu(\mathcal{Z}_t|\mathbf{x}_t)$, a decoder $d_\phi(\mathbf{x}_{t-1}|\mathcal{Z}_t)$), a classifier $g_\omega(y|\mathcal{Z}_t)$, and a step size α.

Input: class label y, step size α
$\mathbf{x}_T \leftarrow$ sample from $\mathcal{N}(0, \mathbf{I})$
for all t from T to 1 **do**
  $\mathcal{Z}_t \leftarrow e_\nu(\mathbf{x}_t)$
  $\mathcal{Z}'_t \leftarrow \mathcal{Z}_t - \alpha\nabla_{\mathcal{Z}_t} \log g_\omega(y|\mathcal{Z}_t)$
  $\mu, \Sigma \leftarrow d_\psi(\mathcal{Z}'_t)$
  $\mathbf{x}_{t-1} \leftarrow$ sample from $\mathcal{N}(\mu, \Sigma)$
end for
return $\mathbf{x}_0$

For the reformulation of the diffusion model proposed by [16] where instead of predicting the previous timestep $\mathbf{x}_{t-1}$ denoising model is optimized to predict noise ϵ that is subtracted from the image at the current timestep $\mathbf{x}_t$, we adequately change the optimization objective. Instead of optimizing the noise to be specific to the target class, we optimize it to be *anything except for the target class*, which we implement by changing the optimization direction: $\mathcal{Z}'_t \leftarrow \mathcal{Z}_t + \alpha\nabla_{\mathcal{Z}_t} \log g_\omega(y|\mathcal{Z}_t)$.

6 Experiments

In the experiments, we aim for observing the benefits of the proposed joint diffusion model over a stand-alone classifier or a marginal diffusion model. To that end, we run a series of experiments to verify various properties, namely:

- We measure the quality on a discriminative task, to evaluate whether training together with a diffusion model improves the robustness of the classifier.
- We measure the generative capability of our model to check if representations optimized by the classifier can lead to more accurate conditional generations.
- We show that our joint model learns abstract features that can be used for the counterfactual explanation.

We use a UNet-based model with a depth level of three in all experiments. We pool its latent features with average pooling into a single vector, on top of which we add a classifier with two linear layers and the LeakyReLU activation. All metrics are reported for the standard training with the objective in (9), except for the conditional sampling where we additionally train the classifier on noisy samples, i.e., additional losses as in (10). Hyperparameters and training details are included in Appendix and code repository[1].

6.1 Predictive Performance of Joint Diffusion Models

In the first experiment, we evaluate the predictive performance of our method. To that end, we report the accuracy of our model on four datasets: Fashion-MNIST, SVHN, CIFAR-10, and CIFAR-100. We compare our method with a baseline classifier trained with a standard cross-entropy loss and the MLP classifier trained on top of representations extracted from the pre-trained DDGM as in Sect. 4, and three joint (hybrid) models: VERA [14], JEM++ [48], HybViT [49]. The results of this experiment are presented in Table 1.

Table 1. The classification accuracy calculated on the test sets. For each training of our methods and the vanilla classifier, we used exactly the same architectures.

Model	F-MNIST	SVHN	CIFAR-10	CIFAR-100
VERA [14]	–	96.8%	93.2%	72.2%
JEM++ [48]	–	96.9%	94.1%	74.5%
HybViT [49]	–	–	95.9%	77.4%
Classifier	94.7%	96.9%	94.0%	72.3%
Ours (pre-trained DDGM)	60.6%	79.6%	80.9%	45.9%
Ours	**95.3%**	**97.4%**	**96.4%**	**77.6%**

As noticed before, a classifier trained on features extracted from the UNet of a DDGM pre-trained in an unsupervised manner achieves reasonable performance. However, it is always outperformed by a stand-alone classifier. The proposed joint diffusion model achieves the best performance on all four datasets. The reason for that could be two-fold. First, training a partially shared neural network (i.e., the encoder in the UNet architecture) benefits from the unsupervised training,

[1] https://github.com/KamilDeja/joint_diffusion.

similarly to how the pre-training using Boltzmann machines benefited finetuning of deep neural networks [15]. Second, the shared encoder part is more robust since it is used in the backward diffusion for images with various levels of noise.

6.2 Generative Performance of Joint Diffusion Models

In the second experiment, we check how adding a classifier in our joint diffusion models influences the generative performance. We use the FID score to quantify the quality of data synthesis. Additionally, we use distributed Precision (Prec), and Recall (Rec) for assessing the exactness and diversity of generated samples [37]. For our joint diffusion model, we consider samples from the prior let through the backward diffusion. We also use the second sampling scheme in which we use conditional sampling, namely, the optimization procedure as described in Sect. 5.3. We compare our approach with a vanilla DDGM, and a DDGM with classifier guidance [7], and recent state-of-the-art joint (hybrid) models: VERA [14], JEM++ [48], HybViT and GenViT [49].

Table 2. An evaluation of generative capabilities by measuring the FID score, Precision and Recall of generations from various diffusion-based models, including our joint diffusion model.

Model	FashionMNIST			CIFAR-10			CIFAR-100			CelebA		
	FID ↓	Prec ↑	Rec ↑	FID ↓	Prec ↑	Rec ↑	FID ↓	Prec ↑	Rec ↑	FID ↓	Prec ↑	Rec ↑
DDGM	7.8	**71.5**	**65.3**	7.2	64.8	61.2	29.7	**70.0**	47.8	5.6	66.5	**58.7**
DDGM (classifier guidance)	7.9	66.6	59.5	8.1	63.2	**63.3**	22.1	69.3	46.9	4.9	66.0	57.8
Ours	8.7	71.1	61.1	7.9	69.9	56.4	17.4	63.2	54	7.0	**67.5**	51.5
Ours (conditional sampling)	**5.9**	63.1	63.2	**6.4**	**70.7**	54.3	**16.8**	63.5	**54.1**	**4.8**	66.3	56.5

Table 3. A comparison of generative capabilities of joint models by measuring the FID score.

Model	CIFAR-10	CIFAR-100	CelebA
	FID ↓	FID ↓	FID ↓
VERA [14]	27.5	–	–
JEM++ [48]	37.1	–	–
HybViT [49]	26.4	33.6	–
GenViT [49]	20.2	26.0	22.07
Ours	7.9	17.4	7.0
Ours (conditional sampling)	**6.4**	**16.8**	**4.8**

Overall, our proposition outperforms standard DDGMs regarding the general FID, see Table 2. However, in some cases, the vanilla DDGM and the DDGM with the classifier guidance obtain better results in terms of the particular components: Precision (FashionMNIST, CIFAR-100) or Recall (FashionMNIST, CelebA). We can observe that conditional sampling improves the quality of generations in all evaluated benchmarks, especially in terms of precision that can be understood as the exactness of generations. This could result from the fact that the optimization procedure drives $\mathcal{Z}_t$ to a mode. Eventually, the backward diffusion generates better samples. However, comparing our approach to current state-of-the-art joint models, we clearly outperform them all, see Table 3.

To get further insight into the role of conditional sampling, we carried out an additional study for the varying value of α (the step size in Algorithm 1). In Fig. 4, we present how Precision and Recall change for different values of this parameter. Apparently, increasing the step size value α leads to more precise but less diverse samples. This is rather intuitive behavior because larger steps result in features $\mathcal{Z}_t$ closer to modes. There seems to be a sweet spot around $\alpha \in [100, 250]$ for which both measures are high. Moreover, we visualize the effect of taking various values of α in Fig. 5. For a chosen class, e.g., plane, we observe that the larger α, the samples are more precise but they lack diversity (i.e., the background is almost the same).

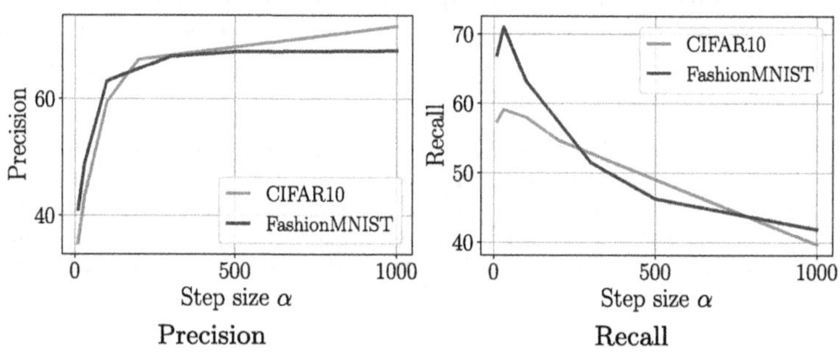

Fig. 4. The dependency between the value of the step size α and the value of Precision and Recall for the joint diffusion with conditional sampling.

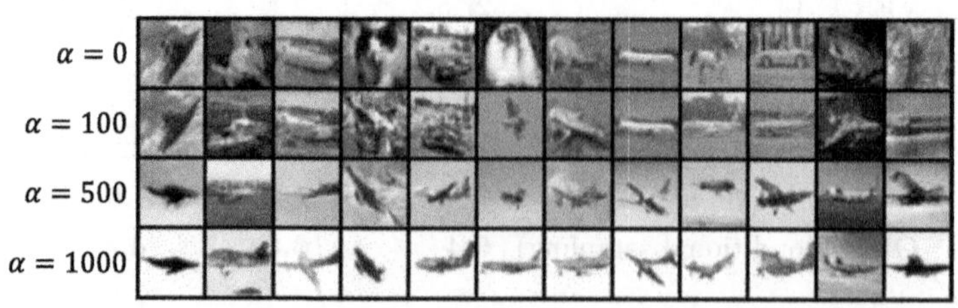

Fig. 5. Samples from our joint diffusion model optimized towards a specific class (here: *plane*) with different step sizes α.

In Fig. 6 we present how the decision of the classifier changes for sampling with the optimized generations. With a higher α step size value, optimization converges faster towards target classes. For the CIFAR10 dataset, there are certain classes (e.g., class 3) that converge later in the backward diffusion process than the others. We also present associated samples from our model. Once more, they depict that higher values of the α parameter lead to more precise but less diverse samples. We show more generations from our model in the Appendix **C**.

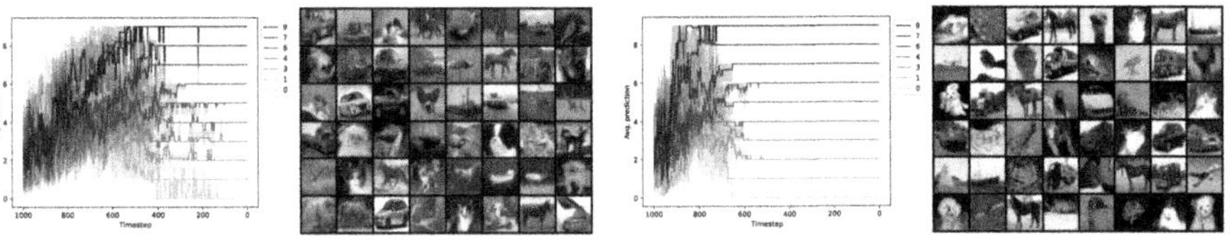

(a) $\alpha = 200$ *(b)* $\alpha = 1000$

Fig. 6. CIFAR10: Classifier decisions at different diffusion steps, for conditional sampling with different values of step size α and associated conditional samples

6.3 A Comparison to State-of-the-Art Joint Approaches

To get a better overview of the performance of our joint diffusion model, we present a comparison with other joint models and SOTA discriminative and generative models in Table 4. The purely discriminative and generative models are included as the upper bounds of the performance. Within the class of the joint models, our joint diffusion clearly outperforms all of the related works.

Table 4. A comparison of our joint diffusion model with other joint models, and the SOTA discriminative model, and the SOTA generative model on the CIFAR-10 test set.

Class	Model	Accuracy% ↑	FID↓
Joint	IGEBM [9]	49.1	37.9
	Glow [25]	67.6	48.9
	Residual Flows [6]	70.3	46.4
	JEAT [13]	85.2	38.2
	JEM [13]	92.9	38.4
	VERA ($\alpha = 100$) [14]	93.2	30.5
	JEM++ [48]	94.1	38.0
	HybViT [49]	95.9	26.4
	Ours	**96.4**	**7.9**
Disc.	VIT-H [8]	99.5	–
Gen.	DDGM (our implementation)	–	7.2
	LSGM [46]	–	2.1

6.4 Visual Counterfactual Explanations

In the last experiment, we apply our joint diffusion model to real-world medical data, the MALARIA dataset [35], that includes 27,558 cell images that are either infected by the malaria parasite or not (a classification task). The cells have various shapes and different staining (i.e., colors) and contain or not the parasite (visually apparent as a purple dot).

After training our joint diffusion model, we obtain high classification accuracy (98%) on the test set. On top of this, we introduce an adaptation of visual counterfactual explanations (VCE) method [2] that provides an answer to the question: *What is the minimal change to the input image* $\mathbf{x}_0$ *to change the decision of the classifier.* In our setup, we answer this question with a conditional sampling algorithm that we use to generate the counterfactual explanations.

In Fig. 7, we show a few examples from the negative (left) or positive (right) classes. We add 20% of noise to these images and run conditional sampling with the opposite class (i.e., changing negative examples to positive ones and *vice versa*). In both cases, the joint diffusion model with conditional sampling can either remove the parasite from the positive examples or add the parasite to the negative ones. All presented images are not cherry-picked.

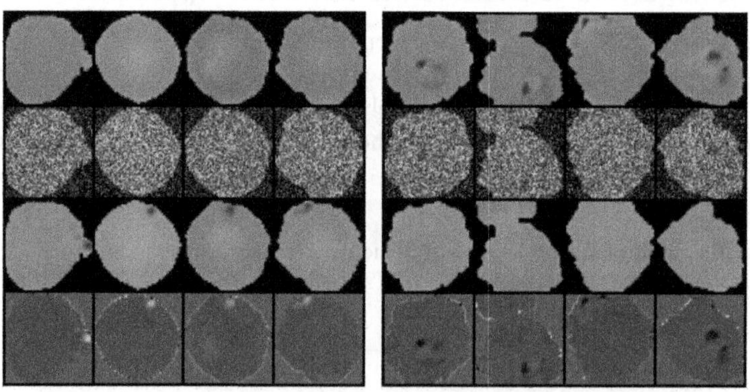

Negative examples Positive examples

Fig. 7. Data samples from the Malaria dataset classified as negative examples (left) or parasitized cells (right). (*top row*) original data examples, (2nd *row*) data noised with 20% of forward diffusion steps, (3rd *row*) denoised images with conditional sampling, (*bottom row*) the difference between the 3rd and 4th rows.

This experiment shows that not only we can use our proposed approach to obtain a powerful classifier but also to visualize its regions of interest. In the considered case, calculating the difference between the original example and the image with a changed class label indicates the malaria plasmodium (see the last row in Fig. 7). We provide more examples from the CelebA data in Appendix **D**.

7 Conclusion

In this work, we introduced a joint model that combines a diffusion model and a classifier through shared parameterization. We first experimentally demonstrated that DDGMs learn semantically meaningful data representations that could be used for classification. On top of this observation, we introduced our joint diffusion models. In the experimental section, we showed that our approach improves the performance in both the classification and generative tasks, providing high-quality generations and enabling conditional generations with built-in classifier guidance. Our proposed approach achieves state-of-the-art performance in the class of joint models. Additionally, we show that the joint diffusion model can be used for visual counterfactual explanations without any changes to the original setup.

Acknowledgements. Special thanks to Mateusz Klimaszewski for help as the best interactive rubber duck.

We acknowledge support from Polish National Science Centre (grant no. 2020/39/B/ST6/01511), Warsaw University of Technology within the Excellence Initiative: Research University (IDUB) program, and high-performance computing infrastructure PLGrid (HPC Centers: ACK Cyfronet AGH) for providing computer facilities (grant no. PLG/2022/016058).

References

1. Abstreiter, K., Mittal, S., Bauer, S., Schölkopf, B., Mehrjou, A.: Diffusion-based representation learning. arXiv preprint: arXiv: Arxiv-2105.14257 (2021)
2. Augustin, M., Boreiko, V., Croce, F., Hein, M.: Diffusion visual counterfactual explanations. arXiv preprint: arXiv:2210.11841 (2022)
3. Baranchuk, D., Rubachev, I., Voynov, A., Khrulkov, V., Babenko, A.: Label-efficient semantic segmentation with diffusion models. In: International Conference On Learning Representations (2021)
4. Chandra, B., Sharma, R.K.: Adaptive noise schedule for denoising autoencoder. In: Loo, C.K., Yap, K.S., Wong, K.W., Teoh, A., Huang, K. (eds.) ICONIP 2014. LNCS, vol. 8834, pp. 535–542. Springer, Cham (2014). https://doi.org/10.1007/978-3-319-12637-1_67
5. Chapelle, O., Scholkopf, B., Zien, A.: Semi-supervised learning (chapelle, o. et al., eds.; 2006) bibbook reviews. IEEE Trans. Neural Netw. **20**(3), 542 (2009)
6. Chen, R.T., Behrmann, J., Duvenaud, D., Jacobsen, J.H.: Residual flows for invertible generative modeling. arXiv preprint: arXiv:1906.02735 (2019)
7. Dhariwal, P., Nichol, A.: Diffusion models beat GANs on image synthesis. In: Advances in Neural Information Processing Systems, vol. 34 (2021)
8. Dosovitskiy, A., et al.: An image is worth 16x16 words: transformers for image recognition at scale. In: International Conference On Learning Representations (2020)
9. Du, Y., Mordatch, I.: Implicit generation and generalization in energy-based models. arXiv preprint: arXiv:1903.08689 (2019)
10. Esser, P., Sutter, E., Ommer, B.: A variational U-Net for conditional appearance and shape generation. In: IEEE/CVF Conference On Computer Vision And Pattern Recognition (2018). https://doi.org/10.1109/CVPR.2018.00923

11. Falck, F., et al.: A multi-resolution framework for U-Nets with applications to hierarchical VAEs. In: Oh, A.H., Agarwal, A., Belgrave, D., Cho, K. (eds.) Advances in Neural Information Processing Systems (2022)
12. Geras, K.J., Sutton, C.: Scheduled denoising autoencoders. arXiv preprint: arXiv:1406.3269 (2014)
13. Grathwohl, W., Wang, K.C., Jacobsen, J., Duvenaud, D., Norouzi, M., Swersky, K.: Your classifier is secretly an energy based model and you should treat it like one. In: International Conference On Learning Representations (2019)
14. Grathwohl, W.S., Kelly, J.J., Hashemi, M., Norouzi, M., Swersky, K., Duvenaud, D.: No MCMC for me: Amortized sampling for fast and stable training of energy-based models. In: International Conference on Learning Representations (2021)
15. Hinton, G.E., Osindero, S., Teh, Y.W.: A fast learning algorithm for deep belief nets. Neural Comput. **18**(7), 1527–1554 (2006)
16. Ho, J., Jain, A., Abbeel, P.: Denoising diffusion probabilistic models. In: Advances in Neural Information Processing Systems, vol. 33, pp. 6840–6851 (2020)
17. Ho, J., Salimans, T.: Classifier-free diffusion guidance. arXiv preprint: arXiv: Arxiv-2207.12598 (2022)
18. Huang, C.W., Lim, J.H., Courville, A.C.: A variational perspective on diffusion-based generative models and score matching. In: Advances in Neural Information Processing Systems, vol. 34 (2021)
19. Huang, P.K.M., Chen, S.A., Lin, H.T.: Improving conditional score-based generation with calibrated classification and joint training. In: NeurIPS 2022 Workshop on Score-Based Methods (2022)
20. Ilse, M., Tomczak, J.M., Louizos, C., Welling, M.: Diva: domain invariant variational autoencoders. In: Medical Imaging with Deep Learning, pp. 322–348. PMLR (2020)
21. Jebara, T.: Machine Learning: Discriminative and Generative, vol. 755. Springer, Cham (2012)
22. Jin, L., Lazarow, J., Tu, Z.: Introspective classification with convolutional nets. In: Advances in Neural Information Processing Systems, vol. 30 (2017)
23. Kingma, D.P., Salimans, T., Poole, B., Ho, J.: Variational diffusion models. In: In: Advances in Neural Information Processing Systems (2021)
24. Kingma, D.P., Welling, M.: Auto-encoding variational Bayes. In: ICLR (2014)
25. Kingma, D.P., Dhariwal, P.: Glow: generative flow with invertible 1x1 convolutions. In: Advances in Neural Information Processing Systems, pp. 10215–10224 (2018)
26. Kingma, D.P., Mohamed, S., Jimenez Rezende, D., Welling, M.: Semi-supervised learning with deep generative models. In: Advances in Neural Information Processing Systems, vol. 27 (2014)
27. Knop, S., Spurek, P., Tabor, J., Podolak, I., Mazur, M., Jastrzebski, S.: Cramer-wold auto-encoder. J. Mach. Learn. Res. **21**(1), 6594–6621 (2020)
28. Lasserre, J.A., Bishop, C.M., Minka, T.P.: Principled hybrids of generative and discriminative models. In: 2006 IEEE Computer Society Conference on Computer Vision and Pattern Recognition (CVPR'06), vol. 1, pp. 87–94. IEEE (2006)
29. Lazarow, J., Jin, L., Tu, Z.: Introspective neural networks for generative modeling. In: Proceedings of the IEEE International Conference on Computer Vision, pp. 2774–2783 (2017)
30. Lee, K., Xu, W., Fan, F., Tu, Z.: Wasserstein introspective neural networks. In: Proceedings of the IEEE Conference on Computer Vision and Pattern Recognition, pp. 3702–3711 (2018)

31. Masarczyk, W., Deja, K., Trzcinski, T.: On robustness of generative representations against catastrophic forgetting. In: Mantoro, T., Lee, M., Ayu, M.A., Wong, K.W., Hidayanto, A.N. (eds.) ICONIP 2021. CCIS, vol. 1517, pp. 325–333. Springer, Cham (2021). https://doi.org/10.1007/978-3-030-92310-5_38
32. Nalisnick, E., Matsukawa, A., Teh, Y.W., Gorur, D., Lakshminarayanan, B.: Hybrid models with deep and invertible features. In: International Conference on Machine Learning, pp. 4723–4732. PMLR (2019)
33. Nichol, A.Q., Dhariwal, P.: Improved denoising diffusion probabilistic models. In: International Conference on Machine Learning, pp. 8162–8171. PMLR (2021)
34. Perugachi-Diaz, Y., Tomczak, J., Bhulai, S.: Invertible DenseNets with concatenated LipSwish. In: Advances in Neural Information Processing Systems, vol. 34, pp. 17246–17257 (2021)
35. Rajaraman, S., et al.: Pre-trained convolutional neural networks as feature extractors toward improved malaria parasite detection in thin blood smear images. PeerJ **6**, e4568 (2018)
36. Ronneberger, O., Fischer, P., Brox, T.: U-Net: convolutional networks for biomedical image segmentation. In: Navab, N., Hornegger, J., Wells, W.M., Frangi, A.F. (eds.) MICCAI 2015. LNCS, vol. 9351, pp. 234–241. Springer, Cham (2015). https://doi.org/10.1007/978-3-319-24574-4_28
37. Sajjadi, M.S., Bachem, O., Lucic, M., Bousquet, O., Gelly, S.: Assessing generative models via precision and recall. arXiv preprint: arXiv:1806.00035 (2018)
38. Sietsma, J., Dow, R.J.: Creating artificial neural networks that generalize. Neural Netw. **4**(1), 67–79 (1991)
39. Sohl-Dickstein, J., Weiss, E., Maheswaranathan, N., Ganguli, S.: Deep unsupervised learning using nonequilibrium thermodynamics. In: International Conference on Machine Learning, pp. 2256–2265. PMLR (2015)
40. Song, Y., Ermon, S.: Generative modeling by estimating gradients of the data distribution. In: Advances in Neural Information Processing Systems, vol. 32 (2019)
41. Song, Y., Sohl-Dickstein, J., Kingma, D.P., Kumar, A., Ermon, S., Poole, B.: Score-based generative modeling through stochastic differential equations. In: International Conference on Learning Representations (2020)
42. Tashiro, Y., Song, J., Song, Y., Ermon, S.: CSDI: conditional score-based diffusion models for probabilistic time series imputation. In: Advances in Neural Information Processing Systems, vol. 34, pp. 24804–24816. Curran Associates, Inc. (2021)
43. Tomczak, J.M.: Deep Generative Modeling. Springer, Cham (2022)
44. Tulyakov, S., Fitzgibbon, A., Nowozin, S.: Hybrid VAE: improving deep generative models using partial observations. arXiv preprint: arXiv:1711.11566 (2017)
45. Tzen, B., Raginsky, M.: Neural stochastic differential equations: deep latent gaussian models in the diffusion limit. arXiv preprint: arXiv:1905.09883 (2019)
46. Vahdat, A., Kreis, K., Kautz, J.: Score-based generative modeling in latent space. In: Advances in Neural Information Processing Systems, vol. 34 (2021)
47. Yang, W., Kirichenko, P., Goldblum, M., Wilson, A.G.: Chroma-VAE: mitigating shortcut learning with generative classifiers. arXiv preprint: arXiv:2211.15231 (2022)
48. Yang, X., Ji, S.: JEM++: improved techniques for training JEM. In: Proceedings of the IEEE/CVF International Conference on Computer Vision, pp. 6494–6503 (2021)
49. Yang, X., Shih, S.M., Fu, Y., Zhao, X., Ji, S.: Your ViT is secretly a hybrid discriminative-generative diffusion model. arXiv preprint: arXiv:2208.07791 (2022)
50. Zhang, Q., Zhang, L.: Convolutional adaptive denoising autoencoders for hierarchical feature extraction. Front. Comp. Sci. **12**(6), 1140–1148 (2018)

MiDi: Mixed Graph and 3D Denoising Diffusion for Molecule Generation

Clément Vignac[1(✉)], Nagham Osman[2], Laura Toni[2], and Pascal Frossard[1]

[1] LTS4, EPFL, Lausanne, Switzerland
clement.vignac@epfl.ch
[2] EEE Department, University College London, London, UK

Abstract. This work introduces MiDi, a novel diffusion model for jointly generating molecular graphs and their corresponding 3D atom arrangements. Unlike existing methods that rely on predefined rules to determine molecular bonds based on the 3D conformation, MiDi offers an end-to-end differentiable approach that streamlines the molecule generation process. Our experimental results demonstrate the effectiveness of this approach. On the challenging GEOM-DRUGS dataset, MiDi generates 92% of stable molecules, against 6% for the previous EDM model that uses interatomic distances for bond prediction, and 40% using EDM followed by an algorithm that directly optimizes bond orders for validity. Our code is available at github.com/cvignac/MiDi.

Keywords: Diffusion Model · Drug Discovery · Graph Generation

1 Introduction

Modern drug discovery requires the development of effective machine learning models that can correctly capture the vast chemical space and sample from it. These models need to understand properties of molecules that depend both on their molecular graph and their conformation in the 3D space. The molecular graph (or 2D structure) determines the existence and type of the chemical bonds and allows the identification of functional groups in a compound. This provides information about its chemical properties and enables to predict synthetic pathways. On the other hand, the 3D conformation of a compound plays a key role in its interaction with other molecules, and governs in particular its biological activity and binding affinity to proteins. To explore the chemical space adequately, it is therefore crucial to consider both aspects simultaneously.

Unfortunately, existing generative models for molecules are restricted to one of these two data modalities. While models that exclusively generate molecular graphs have been vastly researched [8], current 3D molecule generation are on the contrary only trained to generate conformers, thus ignoring bond information. These models rely on a subsequent step that predicts the 2D structure using either interatomic distances [16,37] or chemical software such as OpenBabel [11]. As a result, these models are not end-to-end differentiable, which hampers

C. Vignac and N. Osman—Equal contribution.

© The Author(s), under exclusive license to Springer Nature Switzerland AG 2023
D. Koutra et al. (Eds.): ECML PKDD 2023, LNAI 14170, pp. 560–576, 2023.
https://doi.org/10.1007/978-3-031-43415-0_33

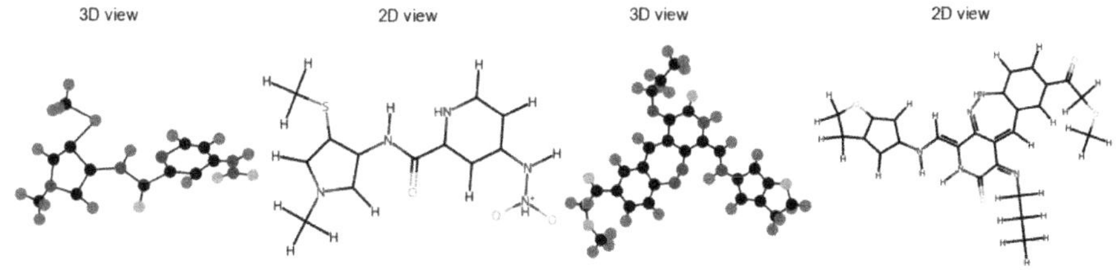

Fig. 1. Samples from our model. MiDi generates simultaneously a 2D graph structure and a 3D conformation that is consistent with this structure.

their ability to be fully optimized for various downstream tasks. This severely limits the potential of 3D molecule generators, particularly for complex tasks like pocket-conditioned generation (Fig. 1).

We propose here a new model, called <u>Mi</u>xed Graph+3D Denoising <u>Di</u>ffusion (MiDi), which overcomes this limitation by simultaneously generating a molecular graph and its corresponding 3D coordinates. MiDi represents molecules as graphs embedded in 3D that contain node features (atom types and formal charges) and edges features (bond types). Our model progressively corrupts data with noise and trains a neural network to predict clean data from noisy inputs. New molecules can then be generated by sampling pure noise and iteratively denoising it with the neural network, similarly to other diffusion models [14,42]. As the model is trained to denoise both the graph and 3D coordinates in tandem, it is able to produce stable molecular graphs that are consistent with the generated conformers.

While previous diffusion models for molecules relied on either Gaussian noise or discrete diffusion, MiDi uses both noise models simultaneously: the 3D coordinates are corrupted with Gaussian noise, while the other components use discrete diffusion which was found to be effective for graph generation [12,47]. To further enhance the quality of the generated samples, we introduce a noise schedule whose parameters are adjusted to each component. Specifically, we add noise to the atom types and formal charges at a faster rate than to the coordinates and bond types. This encourages the denoising network to first focus on generating a realistic 3D conformation and corresponding bond types, before refining the atom types and formal charges.

Our second contribution considers the denoising network: the Transformer architecture we propose incorporates a novel *rEGNN* layer, which improves upon the popular EGNN layers [39] by leveraging features that are not translation-invariant. We show that, due to the use of Gaussian noise in the zero center-of-mass subspace of the molecules, the resulting model is nevertheless equivariant to translations and rotations, which is crucial for achieving high performance.

We showcase the effectiveness of our model on unconditional molecule generation. On the challenging GEOM-DRUGS dataset, the previous EDM model [16] can generate stable molecules at a rate of 5.5%, which can be improved to 40.3% by using the Open Babel bond prediction algorithm [35]. In contrast, the proposed method achieves 91.6% of stable molecules, demonstrating the superiority of our end-to-end differentiable approach. Furthermore, MiDi can be readily applied to various drug-discovery tasks beyond unconditional generation, which confirms its versatility and potential for improving drug discovery pipelines.

2 Related Work

Concurrent Work. Concurrently to our work, [17,36] also proposed 2D+3D diffusion models for molecule generation. These models also leverage Gaussian diffusion for the 3D coordinates and discrete diffusion for the graph, using absorbing transitions in [36] and uniform transitions in [17]. Each model also features unique contributions: [17] proposes richer positional encodings for the transformer layer, while [36] introduces a guidance mechanism to help the network predict accurate bond lengths. MiDi is the only model that improves upon the standard EGNN layers, and that is capable of handling formal charges. It is also the only model that presents results on the more complex GEOM-DRUGS dataset with explicit hydrogens.

Molecule Generation in 3D. The idea of representing molecules as attributed 3D point cloud has been used both in one-shot settings [37] and in autoregressive methods such as GSchNet [11]. Recently, the Equivariant Diffusion Model (EDM) [16] was proposed for this task, improving significantly over previous results. This model was later extended by limiting the message-passing computations to neighbouring nodes [19] and using a more expressive denoising network [34]. All these diffusion models can be conditioned on molecule-level properties using guidance mechanisms [4] or on another point cloud. Conditioning on a second point cloud has been employed to generate molecules that bind to a specific protein [7,40] and to generate linkers between molecular fragments [20]. The main drawback of these models is that they do not learn the connectivity structure of the molecule. It needs to be obtained in a second stage using interatomic distances [16,37] or specialized software such as Open Babel [35]. This results in limited performance for complex molecules, but also prevents end-to-end differentiability for downstream applications.

Graph Generation. Another line of work has focused on generating graphs without associated 3D coordinates. Early denoising diffusion models for this task used Gaussian noise applied to the adjacency matrix [18,25] or graph eigenvalues [30]. [12,47] however found that discrete diffusion is more effective, as it better respects the discrete nature of graphs. These diffusion models tend to outperform autoregressive methods except on validity metrics, as autoregressive models can perform validity checks at each sampling step [27,29,33]. In contrast to the proposed method, which operates at the node level, fragment-based methods [13,24,32] learn to combine chemically relevant substructures from a fixed or learned dictionary [48] but are harder to adapt to 3D.

Table 1. Gaussian and categorical distributions enable the efficient computation of the key quantities involved in training diffusion models and sampling from them. Formulas for all parameters can be found in Sect. 3.

Noise model	Gaussian diffusion	Discrete diffusion
$q(\boldsymbol{z}_t \vert \boldsymbol{z}_{t-1})$	$\mathcal{N}(\alpha_t \boldsymbol{z}_{t-1},\ \sigma_t^2 \boldsymbol{I})$	$\boldsymbol{z}_{t-1}\ \boldsymbol{Q}_t$
$q(\boldsymbol{z}_t \vert \boldsymbol{x})$	$\mathcal{N}(\bar{\alpha}_t \boldsymbol{x},\ \bar{\sigma}_t^2 \boldsymbol{I})$	$\boldsymbol{x}\ \bar{\boldsymbol{Q}}_t$
$\int_x p_\theta(\boldsymbol{z}_{t-1} \vert \boldsymbol{x}, \boldsymbol{z}_t) dp_\theta(\boldsymbol{x} \vert \boldsymbol{z}_t)$	$\mathcal{N}(\mu_t \hat{\boldsymbol{x}} + \nu_t \boldsymbol{z}_t, \tilde{\sigma}_t^2 \boldsymbol{I})$	$\propto \sum_x p_\theta(x)(\boldsymbol{z}_t \boldsymbol{Q}_t' \odot \boldsymbol{x} \bar{\boldsymbol{Q}}_{t-1})$

In order to generate molecules in 3D, graph-based models could be combined with conformer generation models [7,52] which predict a 3D structure from an input graph. As these methods assume that the graph is known, they are able to exploit symmetries of the molecule (such as rotatable bonds), which is more difficult on unconditional generation tasks. Unfortunately, combining graph generation and conformer generation models would again break end-to-end differentiability and restrict performance.

Protein Generation. While existing diffusion models for molecules operate on molecules of moderate size (up to 180 atoms), recent diffusion models for proteins have managed to scale to much larger structures [21,41,49,50]. These methods leverage the chain structure of proteins, which implies that the adjacency matrix does not need to be predicted. Furthermore, instead of predicting 3D coordinates for each atom, they only predict the angles between successive C_α carbons, which significantly reduces the degrees of freedom and encodes roto-translation invariance in the representation. Those improvements are unfortunately specific to chain graphs and cannot be used for arbitrary molecules.

3 Background

Denoising Diffusion Models. Diffusion models consist of two essential elements: a noise model and a denoising neural network. The noise model q takes as input a data point x and generates a trajectory of increasingly corrupted data points $(z_1, ..., z_T)$. The corruption process is chosen to be Markovian, i.e.,

$$q(z_1, \ldots, z_T \vert x) = q(z_1 \vert x) \prod_{t=2}^{T} q(z_t \vert z_{t-1}).$$

The denoising network ϕ_θ takes noisy data z_t as input and learns to invert the diffusion trajectories. While it would be natural to naively train the network to predict z_{t-1}, this strategy would lead to noisy targets, as z_{t-1} depends on the sampled diffusion trajectory. Instead, modern diffusion models [14,42,43] predict the clean input x from z_t, or equivalently, the noise added to it. The diffusion sequences are then inverted by marginalizing over the network predictions $p_\theta(x \vert z_t)$:

$$p_\theta(z_{t-1}|z_t) = \int_x p_\theta(z_{t-1} \mid x, z_t)\ dp_\theta(x|z_t) \tag{1}$$

Although Eq. 1 leads to more efficient training, it requires the efficient computation of $p_\theta(z_{t-1}|x, z_t)$ and the integral, which is not always possible. Two main frameworks have been proposed under which Eq. 1 is tractable: Gaussian noise, which is suitable for continuous data, and discrete state-space diffusion for categorical data. Table 1 summarizes the main properties of the two related noise models.

Gaussian diffusion processes are defined by $q(z_t|z_{t-1}) \sim \mathcal{N}(\alpha_t \boldsymbol{z}_t, \sigma_t^2 \boldsymbol{I})$, where $(\alpha_t)_{t\leq T}$ controls how much signal is retained at each step and $(\sigma_t)_{t\leq T}$ how much noise is added. As normal distributions are stable under composition, we have $q(z_t|x) \sim \mathcal{N}(\bar\alpha_t \boldsymbol{z}_t, \bar\sigma_t^2 \boldsymbol{I})$, with $\bar\alpha_t = \prod_{s=1}^t \alpha_s$ and $\bar\sigma_t^2 = \sigma_t^2 - \alpha_t^2$. While any noise schedule is in principle possible, variance-preserving processes are most often used, which satisfy $\bar\alpha_t^2 + \bar\sigma_t^2 = 1$. The posterior of the transitions conditioned on x can also be computed in closed-form. It satisfies

$$q(z_{t-1}|z_t, x) \sim \mathcal{N}(\mu_t\ \boldsymbol{x} + \nu_t\ \boldsymbol{z}_t, \tilde\sigma_t^2 \mathrm{I}),$$

with $\mu_t = \bar\alpha_s(1 - \alpha_t^2 \bar\sigma_{t-1}^2/\bar\sigma_t^2)$, $\nu_t = \alpha_t \bar\sigma_{t-1}^2/\bar\sigma_t^2$ and $\tilde\sigma_t = \bar\sigma_{t-1}^2(1 - \alpha_t^2 \bar\sigma_{t-1}^2/\bar\sigma_t^2)$.

On the contrary, discrete diffusion considers that data points x belong to one of d classes [1]. The transition matrices $(\boldsymbol{Q}_1, ..., \boldsymbol{Q}_T)$ are square matrices of size $d \times d$ that represent the probability of jumping from one class to another at each time step. Given previous state z_{t-1}, the noise model for the next state z_t is a categorical distribution over the d possible classes which reads as $q(z_t|z_{t-1}) \sim \mathcal{C}(\boldsymbol{z}_{t-1}\boldsymbol{Q}_t)$, where $\boldsymbol{z}_{t-1}$ is a row vector encoding the class of z_{t-1}. Since the process is Markovian, we simply have $q(z_t = j|x) = [x\bar{\boldsymbol{Q}}^t]_j$ with $\bar{\boldsymbol{Q}}^t = \boldsymbol{Q}^1\boldsymbol{Q}^2...\boldsymbol{Q}^t$. The posterior distribution $q(z_{t-1}|z_t, x)$ can also be computed in closed form using Bayes rule and the Markovian property. If $\odot$ denotes a pointwise product and $\boldsymbol{Q}'$ is the transpose of $\boldsymbol{Q}$, it can be written as

$$q(z^{t-1}|z^t, x) \propto \boldsymbol{z}^t\ (\boldsymbol{Q}^t)' \odot \boldsymbol{x}\ \bar{\boldsymbol{Q}}^{t-1}.$$

SE(3)-Equivariance with Diffusion Models. Molecules are dynamic entities that can undergo translation and rotation, and the arrangement of their atoms does not have a predetermined order. To effectively model molecules using generative models and avoid augmenting the data with random transformations, it is essential to ensure that the models are equivariant to these inherent symmetries. In diffusion models, equivariance to a transformation group $\mathbb{G}$ can be achieved through several conditions. First, the noise model must be equivariant to the action of $\mathbb{G}$: $\forall g \in \mathbb{G}, q(g.z_t|g.x) = q(z_t|x)$. Second, the prior distribution q_∞ used at inference should be invariant to the group action, i.e., $q_\infty(g.z_T) = q_\infty(z_T)$, and this noise should be processed by an equivariant neural network in order to ensure that $p_\theta(g.z_{t-1}|g.z_t) = p_\theta(z_{t-1}|z_t)$. Finally, the network should be trained with a loss function that satisfies $l(p_\theta(g.x|g.z_t), g.x) = l(p_\theta(x|z_t), x)$. Together, these requirements create an architecture that is agnostic to the group elements used to represent the training data [16,47,52].

To ensure equivariance to the special Euclidean group SE(3), a number of architectures have been proposed as possible denoising networks for a diffusion model [5,10,28,44]. However, these networks can be computationally expensive due to their manipulation of spherical harmonics. As a result, many generative models for molecules [15,19,20,40] use the more affordable EGNN layers [39]. At a high level, EGNN recursively updates the coordinates ($\boldsymbol{r}_i$) of a graph with node features ($\boldsymbol{x}_i$) and edge features ($\boldsymbol{y}_{ij}$) using:

$$\boldsymbol{r}_i \leftarrow \boldsymbol{r}_i + \sum_j c_{ij}\ m(||\boldsymbol{r}_i - \boldsymbol{r}_j||, \boldsymbol{x}_i, \boldsymbol{x}_j, \boldsymbol{y}_{ij})(\boldsymbol{r}_j - \boldsymbol{r}_i)$$

The crucial feature of this parameterization is that the message function m takes only rotation-invariant arguments. This, combined with the linear term in $\boldsymbol{r}_j - \boldsymbol{r}_i$, ensures that the network is rotation-equivariant. Finally, we note that the normalization term $c_{ij} = ||\boldsymbol{r}_i - \boldsymbol{r}_j|| + 1$ is necessary for numerical stability when concatenating many layers.

4 Proposed Model

We now present the Mixed Graph+3D denoising diffusion (MiDi) model. We represent each molecule as a graph $G = (\boldsymbol{x}, \boldsymbol{c}, \boldsymbol{R}, \boldsymbol{Y})$, where $\boldsymbol{x}$ and $\boldsymbol{c}$ are vectors of length n containing the type and formal charge associated to all atoms. The $n \times 3$ matrix $\boldsymbol{R} = [\boldsymbol{r}_i]_{1 \leq i \leq n}$ contains the coordinates of each atom, and $\boldsymbol{Y}$ is an $n \times n$ matrix containing the bond types. Similarly to previous diffusion models for graphs, we consider the absence of a bond as a particular bond type and generate dense adjacency tensors. We denote the one-hot encoding of $\boldsymbol{x}$, $\boldsymbol{c}$, and $\boldsymbol{Y}$ by $\boldsymbol{X}$, $\boldsymbol{C}$, and $\mathbf{Y}$, respectively. Time steps are denoted by superscripts, so, for example, $\boldsymbol{r}_i^t$ denotes the coordinates of node v_i at time t. The transpose of matrix $\boldsymbol{X}$ is denoted by $\boldsymbol{X}'$.

4.1 Noise Model

Our noise model corrupts the features of each node and edge independently, using a noise model that depends on the data type. For the positions, we use a Gaussian noise within the zero center-of-mass (CoM) subspace of the molecule $\epsilon \sim \mathcal{N}^{\text{CoM}}(\alpha^t \boldsymbol{R}^{t-1}, (\sigma^t)^2 \boldsymbol{I})$, which is required to obtain a roto-translation equivariant architecture [52]. This means that the noise follows a Gaussian distribution on the linear subspace of dimension $3(n-1)$ that satisfies $\sum_{i=1}^n \epsilon_i = 0$.

For atom types, formal charges and bond types, we use discrete diffusion, where the noise model is a sequence of categorical distributions. We choose the marginal transition model proposed in [47]. For instance, when $\boldsymbol{m} \in \mathbb{R}^a$ represents the marginal distribution of atom types in the training set, we define

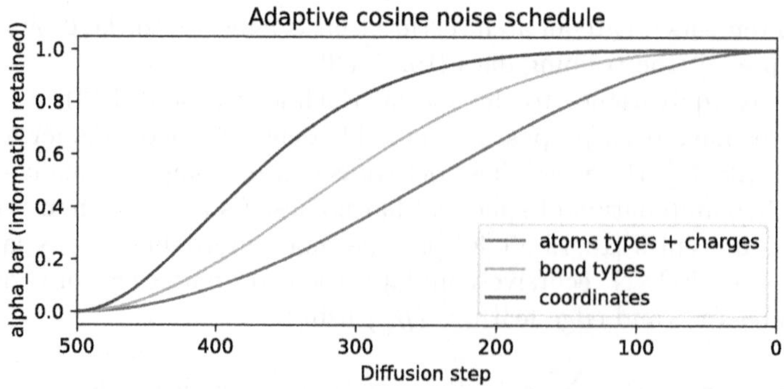

Fig. 2. The noise schedule is tuned separately for each component. Atom coordinates and bond types are denoised earlier during sampling, while atom types and formal charges are updated later in the process. Experimentally, the adaptive schedule allows to obtain better 3D conformers and more stable molecules.

$\boldsymbol{Q}_x^t = \alpha^t \boldsymbol{I} + \beta^t \ \mathbf{1}_a \boldsymbol{m}'$. We similarly define $\boldsymbol{Q}_c^t$ and $\boldsymbol{Q}_y^t$. The resulting noise model is given by:

$$q(G^t|G^{t-1}) \sim \mathcal{N}^{\text{CoM}}(\alpha^t \boldsymbol{R}^{t-1},\ (\sigma^t)^2 \boldsymbol{I}) \times \mathcal{C}(\boldsymbol{X}^{t-1}\boldsymbol{Q}_x^t) \times \mathcal{C}(\boldsymbol{C}^{t-1}\boldsymbol{Q}_c^t) \times \mathcal{C}(\mathbf{Y}^{t-1}\boldsymbol{Q}_y^t).$$

When generating new samples, we define the posterior as a product as well:

$$p_\theta(G^{t-1}|G^t) = \prod_{1 \leq i \leq n} p_\theta(\boldsymbol{r}_i^{t-1}|G^t) p_\theta(\boldsymbol{x}_i^{t-1}|G^t) p_\theta(\boldsymbol{c}_i^{t-1}|G^t) \prod_{1 \leq i,j \leq n} p_\theta(\boldsymbol{Y}_{ij}^{t-1}|G^t),$$

We calculate each term by marginalizing over the network predictions. For instance,

$$\begin{aligned} p_\theta(x_i^{t-1}|G^t) &= \int_{\boldsymbol{x}_i} p_\theta(x_i^{t-1} \mid x_i, G^t) \ dp_\theta(x_i|G^t) \\ &= \sum_{x \in \mathcal{X}} q(x_i^{t-1}|x_i = x, G^t) \ p_\theta^X(x_i = x), \end{aligned}$$

where $p_\theta^X(x_i = x)$ is the neural network estimate for the probability that node v_i in the clean graph G is of type x.

4.2 Adaptive Noise Schedule

Although the MiDi model corrupts the coordinates, atom types, bond types and formal charges simultaneously, these components do not play a symmetrical role. For instance, while the 2D connectivity structure can be predicted relatively well from the 3D conformation, the converse is not true as the conformation is not unique for a given structure. Similarly, the formal charges serve as an adjustable variable used to match the valency of each atom with its electronic structure, but they do not constitute a very fundamental property of the molecules.

Based on these observations, we propose an adaptation of the noise model in order to encourage the denoising network to first generate correctly the most important components, namely the atom coordinates and bond types, before moving on to predict the atom types and formal charges. To achieve this, we modify the noise schedule to vary according to the component. We modify the popular cosine schedule by adding an exponent ν that controls the rate at which the noise is added to the model:

$$\bar{\alpha}^t = \cos\left(\frac{\pi}{2}\frac{(t/T+s)^\nu}{1+s}\right)^2,$$

where the parameter ν can take the form of ν_r, ν_x, ν_y and ν_c for the atom coordinates, types, bond types, and charges, respectively. On the QM9 dataset, we use $\nu_r = 2.5$, $\nu_y = 1.5$, $\nu_x = \nu_c = 1$, while GEOM-DRUGS uses $\nu_r = 2$. The noise schedule used for QM9 is shown in Fig. 2. This choice means that rough estimates for the atom coordinates and the bond types are first generated at inference, before the other components start to play a significant role. This aligns with previous work on 2D molecular graph generation which found that predicting the bond types before the atom types is beneficial [31, 46].

4.3 Denoising Network

The denoising network takes a noisy graph as input and learns to predict the corresponding clean graph. It manipulates graph-level features $\boldsymbol{w}$, node coordinates $\boldsymbol{R}$, node features (atom types and formal charges, treated together in the matrix $\boldsymbol{X}$), and edge features $\mathbf{Y}$. Coordinates are treated separately from the other node features in order to guarantee SE(3) equivariance. The neural network architecture is summarized in Fig. 3. It consists of a Transformer architecture [45], with a succession of self-attention module followed by normalization layers and feedforward networks. We give more details about the different blocks below.

Relaxed Equivariant Graph Neural Networks (rEGNNs). In our proposed method, we leverage the effective yet affordable EGNN layers [39] for processing the coordinates. However, we enhance these layers by exploiting the fact that, when the data and the noise reside in the zero Center-Of-Mass subspace, it is not necessary for the neural network to be translation invariant. This can be interpreted as defining a canonical pose for the translation group, which is a valid way to achieve equivariance [23, 26].

Rather than simply relying on pairwise distances $||\boldsymbol{r}_i - \boldsymbol{r}_j||_2$, we can therefore use other rotation invariant descriptors such as $||\boldsymbol{r}_i||_2$ or $\cos(\boldsymbol{r}_i, \boldsymbol{r}_j)$. We therefore propose the following *relaxedEGNN* (rEGNN) layer:

$$[\boldsymbol{\Delta}_r]_{ij} = \text{cat}(||\boldsymbol{r}_i - \boldsymbol{r}_j||_2, ||\boldsymbol{r}_i||_2, ||\boldsymbol{r}_j||_2, \cos(\boldsymbol{r}_i, \boldsymbol{r}_j))$$
$$\boldsymbol{r}_i \leftarrow \boldsymbol{r}_i + \sum_j \phi_m(\boldsymbol{X}_i, \boldsymbol{X}_j, [\boldsymbol{\Delta}_r]_{ij}, \mathbf{Y}_{ij})\ (\boldsymbol{r}_j - \boldsymbol{r}_i)$$

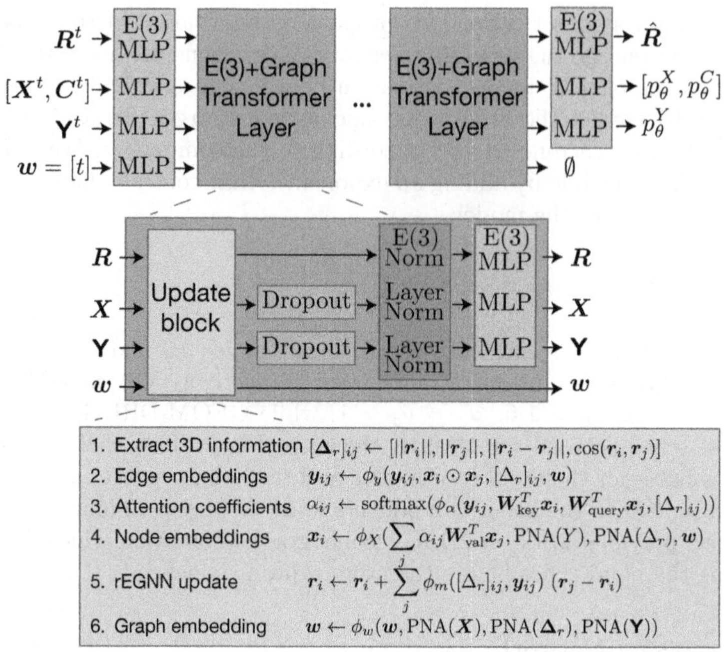

Fig. 3. The denoising neural network of MiDi jointly predicts the 2D graph and 3D coordinates of the clean graph from a noisy input. It follows a graph Transformer architecture with layers tailored to maintain SE(3) equivariance. In the update block, each component is updated using the other features. While the graph-level features w do not play a direct role in the final prediction, they serve as an effective means of storing and organizing pertinent information throughout the transformer layers.

Similar to EGNN layers, the rEGNN layer combines a rotation-invariant message function with a linear update in $r_j - r_i$, which guarantees rotation equivariance. Notably, the additional features $||r_i||_2$, $||r_j||_2$, and $\cos(r_i, r_j)$ are computed relative to the center-of-mass of the molecule, which is set to 0 by definition. In our experiments, we have observed that these features facilitate the generation of a higher proportion of connected molecules, thereby mitigating an issue previously observed with both 3D [16] and 2D-based denoising diffusion models [47].

Update Block. To improve the model's ability to process all features simultaneously, our new rEGNN layer is integrated into a larger update block that processes each component using all other ones. The edge features are first updated using $\boldsymbol{\Delta}_r$, the node features, and the global features. The node features are updated using a self-attention mechanism, where the attention coefficients also use the edge features and $\boldsymbol{\Delta}_r$. After the attention heads have been flattened, the obtained values are modulated by the pooled edge features, $\boldsymbol{\Delta}_r$ and the global features. For pooling pairwise features ($\boldsymbol{Y}$ and $\boldsymbol{\Delta}_r$) into node representations, we use PNA layers [6]: $\text{PNA}(\boldsymbol{Y})_i = \boldsymbol{W}^T \text{cat}[\text{mean}, \text{min}, \text{max}, \text{std}]_j(\boldsymbol{y}_{ij})$. The global features are updated by pooling all other features at the graph level. Finally, the coordinates are updated using a rEGNN update, where the message function takes as input $\boldsymbol{\Delta}_r$ and the updated edge features. Note that we do not use the normalization term of EGNN: our layers are integrated in a Transformer architecture as discussed next, and we empirically found SE(3) normalization layers to be more effective than the EGNN normalisation term at controlling the magnitude of the activations.

Integration into a Transformer Architecture. Transformers have proved to be a very efficient way to stabilize the self-attention mechanism over many layers. We describe below the changes to the feed-forward neural network and normalization layers that are required to ensure SE(3)-equivariance.

Our feed-forward neural network processes each component using MLPs applied in parallel on each node and each edge. As the coordinates cannot be treated separately (it would break SE(3)-equivariance), we define

$$\text{PosMLP}(\boldsymbol{R}) = \Pi^{\text{CoM}}(\text{MLP}(||\boldsymbol{R}||)\frac{\boldsymbol{R}}{||\boldsymbol{R}|| + \delta}) \in \mathbb{R}^{n\times 3},$$

where $||\boldsymbol{R}|| \in \mathbb{R}^{n\times 1}$ contains the norm $||\boldsymbol{r}_i||^2$ of each point, $\text{MLP}(||\boldsymbol{R}||) \in \mathbb{R}^{n\times 1}$ as well, δ is a small positive constant, and Π^{CoM} is the projection of the coordinates on the linear subspace with center-of-mass at 0:

$$\Pi^{\text{CoM}}(\boldsymbol{R})_i = \boldsymbol{r}_i - \frac{1}{n}\sum_{i=1}^{n} \boldsymbol{r}_i.$$

The choice of the normalization layer also depends on the problem symmetries: while batch normalization [22] is used in some graph transformer models [9], this layer is not equivariant in contrast to Set Normalization [53] or Layer Normalization [3]. For SE(3) equivariance, the normalization of [28] should be used. Applied to 3D coordinates, it writes

$$\text{E3Norm}(\boldsymbol{R}) = \gamma\frac{||\boldsymbol{R}||}{\bar{n} + \delta}\frac{\boldsymbol{R}}{||\boldsymbol{R}||} = \gamma\frac{\boldsymbol{R}}{\bar{n} + \delta} \quad \text{with} \quad \bar{n} = \sqrt{\frac{1}{n}\sum_{i=1}^{n} ||\boldsymbol{r}_i||^2},$$

with a learnable parameter $\gamma \in \mathbb{R}$ initialized at 1.

4.4 Training Objective

The denoising network of MiDi is trained to predict the clean molecule from a noisy input G^t, which is reflected in the choice of loss function used during model training. The estimation of the coordinates $\boldsymbol{R}$ is a regression problem that can simply be solved with mean-squared error, whereas the prediction p_θ^X for the atom types, p_θ^C for the formal charges and p_θ^Y for the bond types corresponds to a classification problem which can be addressed through a cross-entropy loss (CE in the equations). Note that the network's position predictions result in pointwise estimates $\hat{\boldsymbol{R}}$, while for the other terms, the prediction is a distribution over classes. The final loss is a weighted sum of these components:

$$l(G, \hat{p}^G) = \lambda_r ||\hat{\boldsymbol{R}} - \boldsymbol{R}||^2 + \lambda_x \, \mathrm{CE}(\boldsymbol{X}, p_\theta^X) + \lambda_c \, \mathrm{CE}(\boldsymbol{C}, p_\theta^C) + \lambda_y \, \mathrm{CE}(\mathbf{Y}, p_\theta^Y)$$

The (λ_i) were initially chosen in order to balance the contribution of each term and cross-validated starting from this initial value. Our final experiments use $\lambda_r = 3$, $\lambda_x = 0.4$, $\lambda_c = 1$, $\lambda_y = 2$.

5 Experiments

5.1 Settings

We evaluate MiDi's performance on unconditional molecule generation tasks. To the best of our knowledge, MiDi is the first method to generate both the graph structure and the conformer simultaneously, leaving no end-to-end differentiable method to compare to. We therefore compare MiDi to 3D models on top of which a bond predictor is applied. We consider two such predictors: either a simple lookup table, as used in [16], or the optimization procedure of OpenBabel[1] [35] used in other works such as [20,40]. The latter algorithm optimizes the bond orders of neighbouring atoms in order to create a valid molecule, removing all control on the generated graphs. In terms of dataset comparison, EDM [16] was previously the only method that could scale up to the large GEOM-DRUGS dataset, so it is our only direct competitor in that case. For the QM9 dataset, we also compare MiDi's performance to that of the GSchNet method [11], which employed the OpenBabel algorithm and achieved satisfactory results.

To facilitate comparison with previous methods, such as [16,37], we benchmark our models on the full molecular graphs that include explicit hydrogens atoms[2]. However, we acknowledge that, for most practical applications, hydrogen atoms can be inferred from the heavy atoms in the structure, and thus can be removed. In fact, methods trained solely on heavy atoms usually perform better since they consider smaller graphs.

We measure validity using the success rate of RDKit sanitization over 10,000 molecules. Uniqueness is the proportion of valid molecules with different canonical SMILES. Atom and molecule stability are metrics proposed in [38] – they are similar to validity but, in contrast to RDKit sanitization, they do not allow for adding implicit hydrogens to satisfy the valency constraints. Novelty is the

[1] http://openbabel.org/wiki/Bond_Orders.

[2] Results using implicit hydrogens are available at https://github.com/cvignac/midi, as well as visualizations of the generated molecules.

proportion of unique canonical SMILES strings obtained that are not in the training set. Since all training molecules have a single connected component, we also measure the proportion of the generated molecules that are connected.

We also compare the histograms of several properties of the generated set with a test set. The atom and bond total variations (AtomTV and BondTV) measure the l1 distance between the marginal distribution of atom types and bond types, respectively, in the generated set and test set. The Wasserstein distance between valencies is a weighted sum over the valency distributions for each atom types: $\text{ValencyW}_1 = \sum_{x \in \text{atom types}} p(x)\mathcal{W}_1(\hat{D}_{\text{val}}(x), D_{\text{val}}(x))$, where $p^X(x)$ is the marginal distribution of atom types in the training set, $\hat{D}_{\text{val}}(x)$ is the marginal distribution of valencies for atoms of type x in the generated set, $D_{\text{val}}(x)$ the same distribution in the test set. Here, the Wasserstein distance between histograms is used rather than total variation, as it allows to better respect the structure of ordinal data.

In previous methods, graph-based metrics were predominantly used. However, in our approach, we also introduce 3D metrics based on histograms of bond lengths and bond angles. This allows us to evaluate the efficacy of our approach not only in terms of the graph structure but also in generating accurate conformers. To this end, we report a weighted sum of the distance between bond lengths for each bond type:

$$\text{BondLenghtsW}_1 = \sum_{y \in \text{bond types}} p(y)\mathcal{W}_1(\hat{D}_{\text{dist}}(y), D_{\text{dist}}(y)),$$

where $p^Y(y)$ is the proportion of bonds of type y in the training set, $\hat{D}_{\text{dist}}(y)$ is the generated distribution of bond lengths for bond of type y, and $D_{\text{dist}}(y)$ is the same distribution computed over the test set. The output is value in Angstrom.

Finally, BondAnglesW_1 (in degrees) compares the distribution of bond angles (in degrees) for each atom type. We compute a weighted sum of these values using the proportion of each atom type in the dataset. This calculation is restricted to atoms with two or more neighbours to ensure that angles can be defined:

$$\text{BondAnglesW}_1(\text{generated}, \text{target}) = \sum_{x \in \text{atom types}} \tilde{p}(x)\mathcal{W}_1(\hat{D}_{\text{angles}}(x), D_{\text{angles}}(x)),$$

where $\tilde{p}^X(x)$ denotes the proportion of atoms of type x in the training set, restricted to atoms with two neighbours or more, and $D_{\text{angles}}(x)$ is the distribution of geometric angles of the form $\angle(\boldsymbol{r}_k - \boldsymbol{r}_i, \boldsymbol{r}_j - \boldsymbol{r}_i)$, where i is an atom of type x, and k and j are neighbours of i. The reported metrics are mean and 95% confidence intervals on 5 different samplings from the same checkpoint.

5.2 QM9

We first evaluate our model on the standard QM9 dataset [51] containing molecules with up to 9 heavy atoms. We split the dataset into 100k molecules for training, 20k for validation, and 13k for testing. Results are presented in

Table 2. Unconditional generation on QM9 with explicit hydrogens with uniform and adaptive noise schedules. While MiDi outperforms the base EDM model on graph-based metrics, the Open Babel optimization procedure is very effective on this simple dataset, as the structures are simple enough for the bonds to be determined unambiguously from the conformation.

Metrics (↑)	Mol stable	At stable	Validity	Uniqueness	Novelty	Connected
Data	98.7	99.8	98.9	99.9	–	100.0
GSchNet	92.0	98.7	98.1	94.5	**80.5**	97.1
EDM	90.7	99.2	91.7	**98.5**	75.9	99.3
EDM + OBabel	**97.9**	**99.8**	**99.0**	**98.5**	77.8	99.7
MiDi (uniform)	96.1±.2	**99.7**±.0	96.6±.2	97.6±.1	64.9±.5	99.8±.0
MiDi (adaptive)	**97.5**±.1	**99.8**±.0	97.9±.1	97.6±.1	67.5±.3	**99.9**±.0
Metrics (↓)	Valency(e-2)	Atom(e-2)	Bond(e-2)	Angles ()	Bond Lengths (e-2 Å)	
Data	0.1	0.3	∼ 0	0.12	∼ 0	
GSchNet	4.9	4.2	1.1	1.68	0.5	
EDM	1.1	2.1	0.2	**0.44**	**0.1**	
EDM + OBabel	1.1	2.1	**0.1**	**0.44**	**0.1**	
MiDi (uniform)	0.4±.0	0.9±.0	**0.1**±0.0	0.67±.02	1.6±.7	
MiDi (adaptive)	**0.3**±.0	**0.3**±.1	**0.0**±.0	0.62±.02	0.3±.1	

Table 2. The *Data* line represents the results of the training set compared with the test set, while the other entries compare the generated molecules to the test molecules. As we observe in Table 2, predicting the bonds only from the interatomic distances and atom types has limited performance. Therefore, MiDi outperforms EDM on 2D metrics, while obtaining similar 3D metrics for the generated conformers. It is worth noting that our list of allowed bonds is not identical to that used in [16,38], which may explain why our results for EDM [16] do not match those of the original paper perfectly. Nonetheless, the optimization algorithm of OpenBabel performs very well on this dataset of simple molecules. As QM9 contains molecules with only up to 9 atoms, the molecular conformations are easy to understand and the bonds can be determined easily.

5.3 GEOM-DRUGS

We then assess our model on the much larger GEOM-DRUGS dataset [2] which comprises 430,000 drug-sized molecules with an average of 44 atoms and up to 181 atoms. As this dataset features drug-like compounds, it is therefore better suited for downstream applications than QM9. We split the dataset into 80% for training, 10% for validation, and 10% for testing. For each molecule, we extract the 5 lowest energy conformations to build the dataset. Results are presented in Table 3. On this large dataset, we did not train the adaptive version of MiDi from scratch, but instead fine-tuned it using a checkpoint of MiDi with uniform noise schedule.

Table 3. Unconditional generation on GEOM-Drugs with explicit hydrogens. EDM was previously the only method that scaled to this dataset. On this complex dataset, the benefits of an integrated models are very clear, as MiDi significantly outperforms Open Babel on most metrics. 95% confidence intervals are reported on five samplings of the same checkpoint.

Metrics (↑)	Mol stable	At stable	Validity	Uniqueness	Novelty	Connected
Data	99.9	99.9	99.8	100.0	–	100.0
EDM	5.5	92.9	**97.5**	99.9	**100.0**	35.6
EDM + OBabel	40.3	97.8	87.8	99.9	**100.0**	41.4
MiDi (uniform)	89.9±.2	99.7±.0	74.5±.2	**100.0**±.0	**100.0**±.0	**90.5**±.2
MiDi (adaptive)	**91.6**±.2	**99.8**±.0	77.8±.2	**100.0**±.0	**100.0**±.0	90.0±.3
Metrics (↓)	Valency(e-2)	Atom(e-2)	Bond(e-2)	Angles ()	Bond Lengths (e-2 Å)	
Data	0.1	0.1	2.5	0.05	∼ 0	
EDM	11.2	21.2	4.9	6.23	**0.2**	
EDM + OBabel	28.5	21.2	4.8	6.42	**0.2**	
MiDi (uniform)	2.9±.0	3.9±.1	**2.4**±.0	1.43±.002	1.1±.2	
MiDi (adaptive)	**0.8**±.1	**3.8**±.1	**2.4**±.0	**1.07**±.02	**0.2**±.1	

As this dataset contains molecules that are much more complex than those in QM9, the bonds in the molecules cannot be determined solely from pairwise distances. This explains why EDM, which performs relatively well on 3D-based metrics, produces very few valid and stable molecules. Furthermore, many structures in this dataset are too complex for the Open Babel algorithm. While the latter achieves good atom stability, there is at least one invalid atom in most molecules, leading to low molecular stability. The advantages of an end-to-end model that generates both a graph structure and its conformation are evident on this dataset: MiDi not only generates better molecular graphs, but also predicts 3D conformers with more realistic bond angles.

6 Conclusions

We propose MiDi, a denoising diffusion model that jointly generates a molecular graph and a corresponding 3D conformation. Our model combines Gaussian and discrete diffusion in order to define a noise model that is best suited to each component. The noise schedule is further adapted to the different components, with the network initially generating a rough estimate of the conformation and the graph structure, before tuning the atom types and charges. A graph transformer network is trained to denoise this model, that features novel rEGNN layers. While rEGNN layers manipulate features that are translation invariant, they still result in a SE(3) equivariant network when the input molecules are centered. On the complex GEOM dataset, MiDi clearly outperforms prior 3D molecule generation methods that predict bonds from the conformation using predefined rules. While MiDi was evaluated on unconditional generation tasks, we believe that end-to-end training of the graph structure and the conformation can offer even greater benefits for downstream tasks such as pocket-conditioned generation.

References

1. Austin, J., Johnson, D., Ho, J., Tarlow, D., van den Berg, R.: Structured denoising diffusion models in discrete state-spaces. In: Advances in Neural Information Processing Systems, vol. 34 (2021)
2. Axelrod, S., Gomez-Bombarelli, R.: GEOM: energy-annotated molecular conformations for property prediction and molecular generation. arXiv preprint arXiv:2006.05531 (2020)
3. Ba, J.L., Kiros, J.R., Hinton, G.E.: Layer normalization. arXiv preprint arXiv:1607.06450 (2016)
4. Bao, F., Zhao, M., Hao, Z., Li, P., Li, C., Zhu, J.: Equivariant energy-guided SDE for inverse molecular design. arXiv preprint arXiv:2209.15408 (2022)
5. Brandstetter, J., Hesselink, R., van der Pol, E., Bekkers, E.J., Welling, M.: Geometric and physical quantities improve e (3) equivariant message passing. arXiv preprint arXiv:2110.02905 (2021)
6. Corso, G., Cavalleri, L., Beaini, D., Liò, P., Veličković, P.: Principal neighbourhood aggregation for graph nets. In: Advances in Neural Information Processing Systems, vol. 33, pp. 13260–13271 (2020)
7. Corso, G., Stärk, H., Jing, B., Barzilay, R., Jaakkola, T.: DiffDock: diffusion steps, twists, and turns for molecular docking. arXiv preprint arXiv:2210.01776 (2022)
8. Du, Y., Fu, T., Sun, J., Liu, S.: MolGenSurvey: a systematic survey in machine learning models for molecule design. arXiv preprint arXiv:2203.14500 (2022)
9. Dwivedi, V.P., Bresson, X.: A generalization of transformer networks to graphs. In: AAAI Workshop on Deep Learning on Graphs: Methods and Applications (2021)
10. Gasteiger, J., Becker, F., Günnemann, S.: GemNet: universal directional graph neural networks for molecules. In: Advances in Neural Information Processing Systems, vol. 34, pp. 6790–6802 (2021)
11. Gebauer, N.W., Gastegger, M., Schütt, K.T.: Symmetry-adapted generation of 3D point sets for the targeted discovery of molecules. arXiv preprint arXiv:1906.00957 (2019)
12. Haefeli, K.K., Martinkus, K., Perraudin, N., Wattenhofer, R.: Diffusion models for graphs benefit from discrete state spaces. arXiv preprint arXiv:2210.01549 (2022)
13. Hajduk, P.J., Greer, J.: A decade of fragment-based drug design: strategic advances and lessons learned. Nat. Rev. Drug Discovery **6**(3), 211–219 (2007)
14. Ho, J., Jain, A., Abbeel, P.: Denoising diffusion probabilistic models. In: Larochelle, H., Ranzato, M., Hadsell, R., Balcan, M., Lin, H. (eds.) Advances in Neural Information Processing Systems, vol. 33, pp. 6840–6851. Curran Associates, Inc. (2020). https://proceedings.neurips.cc/paper/2020/file/4c5bcfec8584af0d967f1ab10179ca4b-Paper.pdf
15. Hoogeboom, E., Nielsen, D., Jaini, P., Forré, P., Welling, M.: Argmax flows and multinomial diffusion: learning categorical distributions. In: Advances in Neural Information Processing Systems, vol. 34 (2021)
16. Hoogeboom, E., Satorras, V.G., Vignac, C., Welling, M.: Equivariant diffusion for molecule generation in 3D. In: International Conference on Machine Learning, pp. 8867–8887. PMLR (2022)

17. Hua, C., et al.: MUDiff: unified diffusion for complete molecule generation. arXiv preprint arXiv:2304.14621 (2023)
18. Huang, H., Sun, L., Du, B., Fu, Y., Lv, W.: GraphGDP: generative diffusion processes for permutation invariant graph generation. arXiv preprint arXiv:2212.01842 (2022)
19. Huang, L., Zhang, H., Xu, T., Wong, K.C.: MDM: molecular diffusion model for 3D molecule generation. arXiv preprint arXiv:2209.05710 (2022)
20. Igashov, I., et al.: Equivariant 3D-conditional diffusion models for molecular linker design. arXiv preprint arXiv:2210.05274 (2022)
21. Ingraham, J., et al.: Illuminating protein space with a programmable generative model. bioRxiv (2022)
22. Ioffe, S., Szegedy, C.: Batch normalization: accelerating deep network training by reducing internal covariate shift. In: International Conference on Machine Learning, pp. 448–456. PMLR (2015)
23. Jaderberg, M., Simonyan, K., Zisserman, A., et al.: Spatial transformer networks. In: Advances in Neural Information Processing Systems, vol. 28 (2015)
24. Jin, W., Barzilay, R., Jaakkola, T.: Hierarchical generation of molecular graphs using structural motifs. In: International Conference on Machine Learning, pp. 4839–4848. PMLR (2020)
25. Jo, J., Lee, S., Hwang, S.J.: Score-based generative modeling of graphs via the system of stochastic differential equations. arXiv preprint arXiv:2202.02514 (2022)
26. Kaba, S.O., Mondal, A.K., Zhang, Y., Bengio, Y., Ravanbakhsh, S.: Equivariance with learned canonicalization functions. In: NeurIPS 2022 Workshop on Symmetry and Geometry in Neural Representations (2022). https://www.openreview.net/forum?id=pVD1k8ge25a
27. Liao, R., et al.: Efficient graph generation with graph recurrent attention networks. In: NeurIPS (2019)
28. Liao, Y.L., Smidt, T.: Equiformer: equivariant graph attention transformer for 3D atomistic graphs. arXiv preprint arXiv:2206.11990 (2022)
29. Liu, Q., Allamanis, M., Brockschmidt, M., Gaunt, A.: Constrained graph variational autoencoders for molecule design. In: Advances in Neural Information Processing Systems, vol. 31 (2018)
30. Luo, T., Mo, Z., Pan, S.J.: Fast graph generative model via spectral diffusion. arXiv preprint arXiv:2211.08892 (2022)
31. Madhawa, K., Ishiguro, K., Nakago, K., Abe, M.: GraphNVP: an invertible flow model for generating molecular graphs. arXiv preprint arXiv:1905.11600 (2019)
32. Maziarz, K., et al.: Learning to extend molecular scaffolds with structural motifs. In: International Conference on Learning Representations (ICLR) (2022)
33. Mercado, R., et al.: Graph networks for molecular design. Mach. Learn. Sci. Technol. **2**(2), 025023 (2021)
34. Morehead, A., Cheng, J.: Geometry-complete diffusion for 3D molecule generation. arXiv preprint arXiv:2302.04313 (2023)
35. O'Boyle, N.M., Banck, M., James, C.A., Morley, C., Vandermeersch, T., Hutchison, G.R.: Open babel: an open chemical toolbox. J. Chem. **3**(1), 1–14 (2011)
36. Peng, X., Guan, J., Liu, Q., Ma, J.: MolDiff: addressing the atom-bond inconsistency problem in 3D molecule diffusion generation. arXiv preprint arXiv:2305.07508 (2023)
37. Satorras, V.G., Hoogeboom, E., Fuchs, F., Posner, I., Welling, M.: E(n) equivariant normalizing flows. In: Advances in Neural Information Processing Systems, vol. 34 (2021)

38. Satorras, V.G., Hoogeboom, E., Fuchs, F.B., Posner, I., Welling, M.: E(n) equivariant normalizing flows. arXiv preprint arXiv:2105.09016 (2021)
39. Satorras, V.G., Hoogeboom, E., Welling, M.: E(n) equivariant graph neural networks. arXiv preprint arXiv:2102.09844 (2021)
40. Schneuing, A., et al.: Structure-based drug design with equivariant diffusion models. arXiv preprint arXiv:2210.13695 (2022)
41. Shi, C., Wang, C., Lu, J., Zhong, B., Tang, J.: Protein sequence and structure co-design with equivariant translation. arXiv preprint arXiv:2210.08761 (2022)
42. Sohl-Dickstein, J., Weiss, E.A., Maheswaranathan, N., Ganguli, S.: Deep unsupervised learning using nonequilibrium thermodynamics. In: Bach, F.R., Blei, D.M. (eds.) Proceedings of the 32nd International Conference on Machine Learning. ICML (2015)
43. Song, Y., Ermon, S.: Generative modeling by estimating gradients of the data distribution. In: Advances in Neural Information Processing Systems, vol. 32 (2019)
44. Thomas, N., et al.: Tensor field networks: rotation- and translation-equivariant neural networks for 3D point clouds. CoRR abs/1802.08219 (2018)
45. Vaswani, A., et al.: Attention is all you need. In: Advances in Neural Information Processing Systems, vol. 30 (2017)
46. Vignac, C., Frossard, P.: Top-N: equivariant set and graph generation without exchangeability. arXiv preprint arXiv:2110.02096 (2021)
47. Vignac, C., Krawczuk, I., Siraudin, A., Wang, B., Cevher, V., Frossard, P.: DIGress: discrete denoising diffusion for graph generation. In: The Eleventh International Conference on Learning Representations (2023). https://openreview.net/forum?id=UaAD-Nu86WX
48. Wang, Z., Nie, W., Qiao, Z., Xiao, C., Baraniuk, R., Anandkumar, A.: Retrieval-based controllable molecule generation. arXiv preprint arXiv:2208.11126 (2022)
49. Watson, J.L., et al.: Broadly applicable and accurate protein design by integrating structure prediction networks and diffusion generative models. bioRxiv (2022)
50. Wu, K.E., Yang, K.K., Berg, R.V.D., Zou, J.Y., Lu, A.X., Amini, A.P.: Protein structure generation via folding diffusion. arXiv preprint arXiv:2209.15611 (2022)
51. Wu, Z., et al.: MoleculeNet: a benchmark for molecular machine learning. Chem. Sci. **9**, 513–530 (2018). https://doi.org/10.1039/C7SC02664A
52. Xu, M., Yu, L., Song, Y., Shi, C., Ermon, S., Tang, J.: GeoDiff: a geometric diffusion model for molecular conformation generation. In: International Conference on Learning Representations (2022). https://openreview.net/forum?id=PzcvxEMzvQC
53. Zhang, L.H., Tozzo, V., Higgins, J.M., Ranganath, R.: Set norm and equivariant skip connections: putting the deep in deep sets (2022). https://openreview.net/forum?id=MDT30TEtaVY

Cold-Start Multi-hop Reasoning by Hierarchical Guidance and Self-verification

Mayi Xu[1], Ke Sun[1], Yongqi Li[1], and Tieyun Qian[1,2(✉)]

[1] School of Computer Science, Wuhan University, Wuhan, China
{xumayi,sunke1995,liyongqi,qty}@whu.edu.cn

[2] Intellectual Computing Laboratory for Cultural Heritage, Wuhan University, Wuhan, China

Abstract. Multi-hop reasoning has attracted wide attention for knowledge graph (KG) completion since it can provide interpretable reasoning paths. Most prior multi-hop reasoning studies assume the KGs are static with fixed entities. However, in real applications, KGs are often dynamic since new entities will emerge continuously in the form of new fact triplets. In this paper, we are particularly interested in *the cold-start scenario toward dynamic KGs* to facilitate more practical multi-hop reasoning, which aims to explore the reasoning paths between emerging entities and existing entities. There are two challenging issues arising from this scenario: **i) lacking precise guidance** since available information for emerging entities is extremely limited in the cold-start scenario, **ii) lacking explicit path** since the emerging entities and existing ones are isolated. To address these issues, we propose a generation-based model, namely SelfHier, to explore the reasoning paths by hierarchical guidance and self-verification strategies. The *hierarchical guidance strategy* guides the reasoning process using hierarchical fine-grained sub-relations and coarse-grained clusters. The *self-verification strategy* constructs explicit reasoning paths by supplementing some missing fact triplets. Experimental results prove that SelfHier performs well in the cold-start scenario on dynamic KGs and also significantly outperforms existing multi-hop reasoning methods in the standard scenario on static KGs.

Keywords: Multi-hop Reasoning · Cold-start · Hierarchical Guidance · Self-verification

1 Introduction

Knowledge graphs such as Freebase [1] and NELL [2] store fact triplets in the form of (*head entity*, *relation*, *tail entity*), which benefit various knowledge-driven applications. However, existing KGs suffer from serious incompleteness in reality, which limits their practicability. Therefore, Knowledge Graph Completion

This work was supported by the grants from the National Natural Science Foundation of China (NSFC) project (No. 62276193, 41971347). It was also supported by the Joint Laboratory on Credit Science and Technology of CSCI-Wuhan University.

© The Author(s), under exclusive license to Springer Nature Switzerland AG 2023
D. Koutra et al. (Eds.): ECML PKDD 2023, LNAI 14170, pp. 577–592, 2023.
https://doi.org/10.1007/978-3-031-43415-0_34

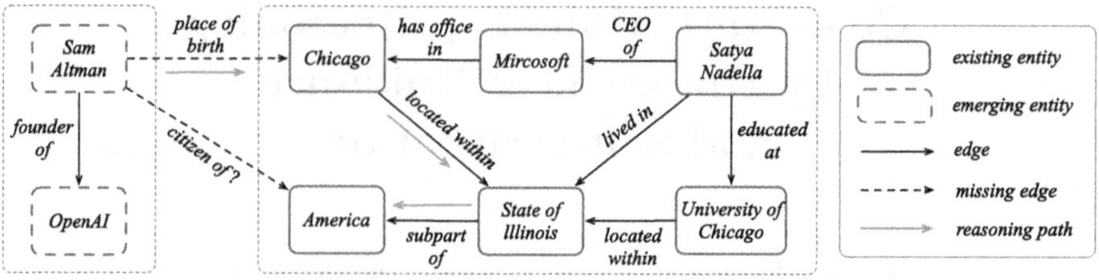

Fig. 1. An example of multi-hop reasoning in the cold-start scenario.

(KGC) has been proposed to reason the missing fact triplets, such as predicting the *tail entity* given the query *head entity* and *relation*.

For a long time in the past, embedding-based methods such as TransE [3], RotatE [4], and ConE [5] have achieved excellent performance. However, the drawbacks of these approaches are obvious since they reason in a black-box manner and can not provide interpretable reasoning paths.

To realize the interpretability, Deeppath [6] formulates the KGC as a multi-hop reasoning task. As Fig. 1 shows, given a query (*Sam Altman*, *citizen of*, ?), multi-hop reasoning methods try to predict the tail entity "*America*" with a reasoning path. Most existing multi-hop reasoning works [7–10] adopt the Reinforcement Learning (RL) framework to model the reasoning process as a Markov Decision Process, where the agents walk on KGs to search the target tail entities. Recently, SQUIRE [11] employs the generative framework to reason the paths and missing fact triplets in an end-to-end fashion, which achieves state-of-the-art (SOTA) performance.

Despite their effectiveness, existing multi-hop reasoning studies mainly focus on reasoning over static KGs with fixed entities. However, in reality, the KGs are essentially dynamic, and new entities will emerge continuously in the form of new fact triplets. For instance, the NELL KG has been extracting new fact triplets from the web since January 2010, with new entities emerging simultaneously. Completing the edges between emerging entities and existing entities is crucial to the development of KGs, but it is not easy, especially when they are isolated from each other. As Fig. 1 shows, the emerging entity "*Sam Altman*" is isolated from existing entities, without direct or indirect interaction. In such cases, reasoning a path between them becomes a cold-start scenario, as they are unseen from each other during training. In this paper, we are particularly interested in *the cold-start scenario toward dynamic KGs* to facilitate more practical multi-hop reasoning. Specifically, the cold-start scenario is set to explore interpretable reasoning paths between emerging entities and existing entities that are isolated from each other on dynamic KGs. Nevertheless, conducting multi-hop reasoning in the cold-start scenario is not trivial due to the following challenges:

- **lacking precise guidance.** Since available information for emerging entities is extremely limited in the cold-start scenario, it is difficult to construct precise guidance to handle those complex reasoning processes such as distinguishing semantically similar relations and eliminating entities with unrelated attributes.

- **lacking explicit paths.** Since emerging entities and existing entities are isolated, there is an absence of explicit paths on dynamic KGs that can connect them. Hence, most prior methods are unable to reason a correct path due to their reasoning process totally relying on existing edges.

To overcome the above challenges, we propose the generation-based model, namely SelfHier, to explore the reasoning paths by hierarchical guidance and self-verification strategies. The hierarchical guidance strategy guides the reasoning process by fine-grained sub-relations and coarse-grained clusters, which contribute to distinguishing semantically similar relations and eliminating entities with unrelated attributes, respectively. The self-verification strategy is proposed to solve the absence of explicit reasoning paths by pre-exploring some missing fact triplets to bridge the gap between emerging entities and existing entities.

In **hierarchical guidance** strategy, a relation is divided into multiple fine-grained sub-relations with different semantics, and entities with similar attributes are gathered into a coarse-grained cluster. The prediction of relations and entities will be guided by the prediction of fine-grained sub-relations and coarse-grained clusters since they are easier to distinguish and eliminate, respectively. For instance, the "*subpart of*" in (*State of Illinois*, *subpart of*, *America*) and (*youtube*, *subpart of*, *google product*) show different semantics. After it is divided into two sub-relations which describe the geographical relation and ownership relation, respectively, it will be more distinguishable from the relation "*located within*". Furthermore, if the target entity is "*America*", we should select an entity in the cluster "Country" and eliminate those entities in "Company" and "Person".

In **self-verification** strategy, inspired by the behavior that humans always verify whether their former reasoning process misses some steps by reasoning once again on the same query, we imitate it to conduct the reasoning process again on the former training query and try to find those missing fact triplets. Specifically, the generation-based framework may generate some unknown fact triplets as a step of reasoning paths since its selection space is unconstrained. We argue that if these reasoning paths containing unknown fact triplets arrive at the target tail entities with the highest probability, these unknown fact triplets may be missing in KGs originally. Hence, we further extract these unknown fact triplets to KGs to construct explicit reasoning paths.

We evaluate our model on both dynamic and static KGs. The experimental results show that our model performs well in the cold-start scenario and even outperforms existing methods in the standard scenario. Furthermore, the ablation studies show the effectiveness of both hierarchical guidance and self-verification strategies.

2 Related Work

Knowledge graph embedding methods [3–5,12,13] learn distributed representations of entities and relations from structure information, and further leverage score functions to measure the likelihood of each triplet. Despite their effectiveness, embedding-based methods can not provide interpretable information.

Multi-hop reasoning is an emerging task for KGC, which aims to find the target tail entities with interpretable reasoning paths. Rule-based methods [14,15] automatically induce logical rules from the KG and predict missing fact triplets by matching queries to the rules. Although rule-based methods such as AnyBURL [16] achieve remarkable performance, they are hard to generalize in practice due to the limitation of symbolic representation. RL-based methods model the reasoning process as a Markov Decision Process (MDP), where the agent walks on KGs to search the target entities. Deeppath [6] first adopts the RL framework to search the reasoning paths and target relations given head entities and tail entities. MINERVA [7] proposes a more difficult and practical task to find the target tail entities while given the relations and head entities. Following this work, most RL-based methods [9,10,16,17] are devoted to tackling the sparse rewards problem or trying to design a more efficient policy network. Recently, the generation-based method SQUIRE [11] introduces the generative framework to find the target entities and reasoning paths in an end-to-end fashion. By leveraging the rule-enhanced and iterative training strategy, SQUIRE achieves current state-of-the-art performance. However, these methods focus on static KGs and overlook the challenge of conducting multi-hop reasoning on dynamic KGs. We are particularly interested in the cold-start scenario toward dynamic KGs to facilitate more practical multi-hop reasoning and further design an effective generation-based model SelfHier which achieves SOTA performance in both the prior standard scenario and the cold-start scenario.

3 Methodology

Knowledge Graph. A KG is defined as a directed graph $\mathcal{G} = (\mathcal{E}, \mathcal{R})$, where $\mathcal{E}$ and $\mathcal{R}$ denote the entity set and relation set, respectively. A KG $\mathcal{G}$ contains a set of fact triplets defined as $\mathcal{T} = \{(h, r, t)\} \subseteq \mathcal{E} \times \mathcal{R} \times \mathcal{E}$, where h, r, and t represent the head entity, the relation, and the tail entity, respectively. The static KGs contain fixed entities with connectivity. The dynamic KGs contain some emerging entities, which are isolated from existing entities.

Multi-hop Reasoning. Given a query $(h, r, ?)$, multi-hop reasoning aims to predict the target tail entity t through a generated n-hop reasoning path τ : $h \xrightarrow{r_1} e_1 \xrightarrow{r_2} e_2 \cdots \xrightarrow{r_n} e_n$, where e_i and r_i represent the entity and the relation in the path τ. The last entity e_n in τ is treated as the predicted target tail entity. In the standard scenario, the t is not isolated from h on static KGs. In the cold-start scenario, the t is isolated from h on dynamic KGs, where they will not belong to the emerging entities or existing entities simultaneously.

3.1 Model Framework

To tackle the problem of lacking precise guidance and explicit paths in the cold-start scenario, we propose a generative model, namely SelfHier, of which the

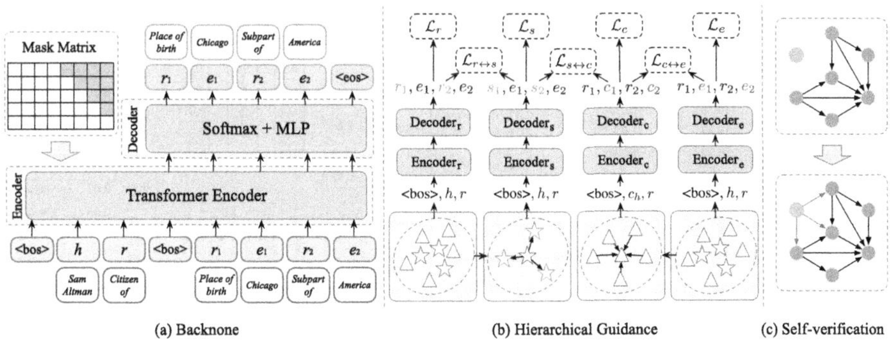

Fig. 2. SelfHier model overview. △: entity. △: cluster. ☆: relation. ☆: sub-relation. ●: existing entity. ●: emerging entity. ⟶: edges completed by self-verification. ⟶: existing edge. (Color figure online)

overall framework is shown in Fig. 2. Apparently, SelfHier mainly consists of three components: the backbone, the hierarchical guidance strategy, and the self-verification strategy. The backbone module autoregressively generates the reasoning path, which follows the pioneer generative method [11]. Based on the backbone, the hierarchical guidance strategy is developed to guide the reasoning process to distinguish semantically similar relations and eliminate entities with unrelated attributes. Furthermore, the self-verification strategy is proposed to construct explicit reasoning paths, by pre-exploring some missing fact triplets.

3.2 Backbone

The backbone is a generative model, as shown in Fig. 2 (a), which adopts the classic encoder-decoder architecture. Inputting the query $q = (\text{<bos>}, h, r)$ as the source sequence, the Transformer encoder learns contextualized hidden representation. Sequently, the MLP autoregressively decodes the reasoning paths τ token by token. During training, we maximize the cross-entropy loss as follows:

$$\mathcal{L} = -\sum_{(q,\tau)\in\mathcal{A}} \frac{1}{|\tau|} \sum_{k=1}^{|\tau|} \sum_{i=1}^{|V|} \alpha_i \log p\left(i \mid q, \tau_{<k}\right) \tag{1}$$

where $\mathcal{A}$ is the training set of all (q, τ) training pairs, $\tau_{<k}$ denotes the former k-1 tokens in τ, $|\tau|$ is the number of tokens in τ, $|V|$ is the size of vocabulary V, α_i is a label-smoothing hyperparameter to avoid overfitting, $\alpha_i = \epsilon$ for target tokens, and $\alpha_i = \frac{1-\epsilon}{|V|-1}$ for other tokens, and ϵ ranges from 0 to 1.

3.3 Hierarchical Guidance

Guidance of Fine-Grained Sub-relations. Prior methods assume that the semantics of various relations are different, while the different relations may be

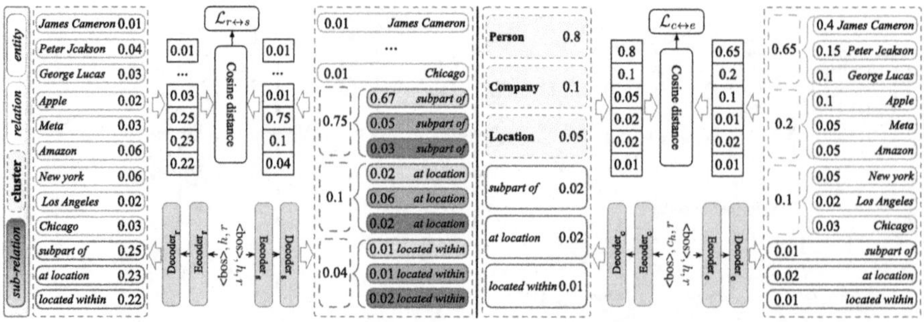

(a) Guidance of fine-grained sub-relations (b) Guidance of coarse-grained clusters

Fig. 3. Example of hierarchical guidance. (a) Distinguishing semantically similar relations by the guidance of fine-grained sub-relations. (b) Eliminating entities with unrelated attributes by the guidance of coarse-grained clusters.

semantically similar in reality. To distinguish those semantically similar relations with overlapped representation, a relation is divided into multiple fine-grained sub-relations by measuring their difference in context. To be specific, we use the TransE [3] to learn the general relation representation $\mathbf{r}$. The specific relation representation $\hat{\mathbf{r}}$ in (h, r, t) can be calculated by $\hat{\mathbf{r}} = \mathbf{t} - \mathbf{h}$ since a correct fact triplet should satisfy $\mathbf{h} + \mathbf{r} = \mathbf{t}$ in TransE. The cosine distance d between the specific relation representation $\hat{\mathbf{r}}$ and the general relation representation $\mathbf{r}$ is adopted to show the level of similarity between them. If the r in different fact triplets have close distance d, they are similar in real semantics naturally. For instance, the relation "*subpart of*" in (*Fairfax, subpart of, Virginia*) and (*Mcallen, subpart of, Texas*) has close d, where both of them emphasize the geographical relationship. Oppositely, their d is far from the d of relation "*subpart of*" in (*Micron, subpart of, Steven appleton*), which emphasizes the ownership relationship. For each relation r_i, supposing the max and the minimal d in all fact triplets containing r_i is d^{max} and d^{min}, respectively. We split the section $[d^{min}, d^{max}]$ to M equal sub-sections, and the relation r_i in specific fact triplet is converted to its sub-relation s_j when its d locate in j-th sub-section. For simplicity, the M is pre-defined as a hyperparameter, while it can be dynamically adjusted for different relations, which we leave for future research. For further reasoning among sub-relations, we convert the $(q, \tau) \in \mathcal{A}$ to $(q, \tau^s) \in \mathcal{A}^s$ as follow:

$$\tau : r_1, e_1, r_2, \cdots, e_n, \text{<eos>} \Longrightarrow \tau^s : s_1, e_1, s_2, \cdots, e_n, \text{<eos>} \tag{2}$$

where the relations r_i are converted to their corresponding sub-relations s_j.

As shown in Fig. 3 (a), the $(q, \tau) \in \mathcal{A}$ are used to train Encoder$_r$-Decoder$_r$ while the $(q, \tau^s) \in \mathcal{A}^s$ are used to train Encoder$_s$-Decoder$_s$. The particular dimensions of their output embeddings correspond to the probability of the relations and sub-relations, respectively. For the output of Decoder$_s$, we sum the probabilities of those sub-relations divided from the same relation, and further align the probabilities of corresponding relations output by Decoder$_r$ with them.

The process is depicted in Fig. 3 (a), and the cosine distance loss is maximized to align their probabilities as follows:

$$\mathcal{L}_{r\leftrightarrow s} = -\sum_{\substack{(q,\tau)\in\mathcal{A} \\ (q,\tau^s)\in\mathcal{A}^s}} \sum_{k=1}^{|\tau|/2} \mathrm{d}\Big(p(\tau_{2k-1} \mid q, \tau_{<2k-1}), p(\tau^s_{2k-1} \mid q, \tau^s_{<2k-1}) \cdot \mathbf{E}_{s\to r}\Big) \quad (3)$$

where $\mathbf{E}_{s\to r}$ is a mapping matrix set to map the probability of the sub-relations to their corresponding relations. Note that we only align them in $2k$-1-th step, in which we should generate the relation. The cosine distance is calculated as follows:

$$\mathrm{d}(\mathbf{X}, \mathbf{Y}) = 1 - \frac{\mathbf{X}\cdot\mathbf{Y}}{\|\mathbf{X}\|\|\mathbf{Y}\|} = 1 - \frac{\sum_{i=1}^{n} x_i \times y_i}{\sqrt{\sum_{i=1}^{n}(x_i)^2} + \sqrt{\sum_{i=1}^{n}(y_i)^2}} \quad (4)$$

Guidance of Coarse-Grained Clusters. To eliminate entities with unrelated attributes, we formulate the coarse-grained cluster by gathering the entities with similar features together. Those entities belonging to the same cluster always share similar attributes. For instance, if the target entity is "*James Cameron*", we should select an entity in the cluster "Person" and eliminate those entities in "Company" and "Location". Specifically, we learn the embeddings of entities by TransE, then use the K-means [18] algorithm to obtain K clusters, where the K is a pre-defined hyperparameter. For reasoning among clusters, we convert the $(q, \tau) \in \mathcal{A}$ to $(q^c, \tau^c) \in \mathcal{A}^c$ as follow:

$$q : \text{<bos>}, h, r \Longrightarrow q^c : \text{<bos>}, c_h, r \quad (5)$$

$$\tau : r_1, e_1, r_2, \cdots, e_n, \text{<eos>} \Longrightarrow \tau^c : r_1, c_1, r_2, \cdots, c_n, \text{<eos>} \quad (6)$$

where the entities h and e_i are converted to their corresponding clusters c_h and c_j, respectively.

As shown in Fig. 3 (b), the $(q, \tau) \in \mathcal{A}$ are used to train Encoder$_e$-Decoder$_e$ while the $(q^c, \tau^c) \in \mathcal{A}^c$ are used to train Encoder$_c$-Decoder$_c$.

The particular dimension of their output representation corresponds to the probability of the entities and clusters. As the process when aligning the relations to their corresponding sub-relations, the cosine distance loss is maximized to align the probabilities of the entities with their corresponding clusters as follows:

$$\mathcal{L}_{c\leftrightarrow e} = -\sum_{\substack{(q,\tau)\in\mathcal{A} \\ (q^c,\tau^c)\in\mathcal{A}^c}} \sum_{k=1}^{|\tau^c|/2} \mathrm{d}\Big(p(\tau^c_{2k} \mid q^c, \tau^c_{<2k}), p(\tau_{2k} \mid q, \tau_{<2k}) \cdot \mathbf{E}_{e\to c}\Big) \quad (7)$$

where $\mathbf{E}_{e\to c}$ is a mapping matrix set to map the probability of the entities to their corresponding clusters. Note that we only align them in $2k$-th step, in which we should generate the entity.

Ensemble of Coarse-Grained Clusters and Fine-Grained Sub-relations. To ensemble the hierarchical guidance during training, we also align the output of Decoder$_s$ and Decoder$_c$ at each step as follows:

$$\mathcal{L}_{s\leftrightarrow c} = -\sum_{\substack{(q^c,\tau^c)\in\mathcal{A}^c \\ (q,\tau^s)\in\mathcal{A}^s}} \sum_{k=1}^{|\tau^c|} \mathrm{d}\Big(p(\tau^c_k \mid q^c, \tau^c_{<k}), p(\tau^s_k \mid q, \tau^s_{<k}) \cdot \mathbf{E}_{e\to c} \cdot \mathbf{E}_{s\to r}\Big) \quad (8)$$

Finally, the overall loss of our model is:

$$\mathcal{L} = \mathcal{L}_r + \mathcal{L}_e + \lambda(\mathcal{L}_s + \mathcal{L}_c) + \beta(\mathcal{L}_{r\leftrightarrow s} + \mathcal{L}_{c\leftrightarrow e} + \mathcal{L}_{s\leftrightarrow c}) \tag{9}$$

where the $\mathcal{L}_r, \mathcal{L}_e, \mathcal{L}_s, \mathcal{L}_c$ are losses of generating reasoning paths, which are formulated as Eq. 1, the $\mathcal{L}_{r\leftrightarrow s}, \mathcal{L}_{c\leftrightarrow e}, \mathcal{L}_{s\leftrightarrow c}$ are the hierarchical guidance losses, the λ and β are hyperparameters to control the loss ratio.

To ensemble the hierarchical guidance during generating, the Encoder$_r$-Decoder$_r$ and Encoder$_e$-Decoder$_e$ alternately generate the entities and relations. As shown in Fig. 4, the Encoder$_e$-Decoder$_e$ focuses on generating the next relation since it is guided by sub-relations, while the Encoder$_r$-Decoder$_r$ is devoted to generating the next entity since it is guided by clusters. In addition, the Encoder$_r$-Decoder$_r$ and Encoder$_e$-Decoder$_e$ also generate the paths alone, and the final tail entity is voted by the above three generative manners.

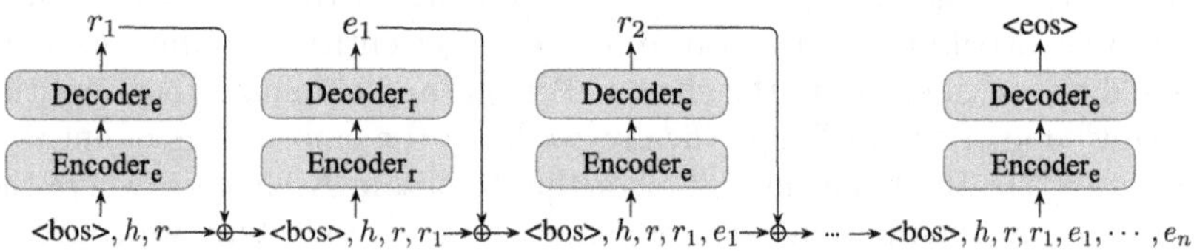

Fig. 4. Alternately decoding strategy during generating.

3.4 Self-verification

To solve the problem that there is no explicit path between emerging entities and existing ones, an intuitive solution is pre-completing some missing fact triplets to bridge this gap before conducting the multi-hop reasoning. However, it is impractical for previous KGC methods since they need to know two elements of the missing fact triplet before completing it. Inspired by the behavior that humans always verify whether their former reasoning process misses some steps by reasoning once again on the same query, we propose the self-verification strategy to reason again on the former training query to find those missing fact triplets, which does not need to know two elements of it before completing it.

Specifically, the generative framework may generate some unknown fact triplets in reasoning paths since its selection space is unconstrained. We argue that if these reasoning paths arrive at the target tail entities with the highest probability, these unknown fact triplets may be missing for KGs from the beginning, which contribute to constructing explicit reasoning paths. Specifically, we first train the model on the training set $(q, \tau) \in \mathcal{A}$. Then, inputting the same query $q \in \mathcal{A}$ to the model once again, the generated paths which arrive at the target tail entity with the highest probability are picked. We collect the fact triplets in these paths which not exist in the original KG $\mathcal{T}$ and filter those fact triplets whose frequencies are less than a pre-defined threshold T. These filtered fact triplets $\mathcal{T}^{new}$ are added to the KGs to construct more explicit paths.

4 Experiments

4.1 Experimental Setup

Experimental Knowledge Graphs. In the standard scenario, we conduct experiments on four static KGs, including FB15K237 [19], NELL995[1] [6], FB15K23720 and NELL23K [8]. The first two are considered dense KGs, while the latter two are sparse KGs. Additionally, to formulate the cold-start scenario, we carefully construct some dynamic KGs by following these rules strictly: Firstly, keeping the connectivity of the existing entities. Secondly, ensuring the disconnectedness between emerging entities and existing entities. Thirdly, the head entity and tail entity will not belong to emerging entities or existing entities simultaneously during testing. A detailed overview of the KGs is provided in Table 1. For instance, the NELL23K-40% denotes that split 40% emerging entities and retain 60% existing entities on NELL23K. Furthermore, the split ratio of NELL23K is different from FB15K23720 due to the connectivity of existing entities will be broken when setting a lower ratio in NELL23K.[2]

Table 1. Dataset statistics of different KGs.

KGs type	KGs	Existing Entities	Relations	Facts	Mean degree	Emerging Entities
Static	FB15K237	14,505	237	272,115	18.76	0
	NELL995	62,706	198	117,937	1.88	0
	FB15K23720	13,166	237	54,423	4.13	0
	NELL23K	22,925	200	25,445	1.11	0
Dynamic	FB15K23720-50%	6,583	237	38,013	3.46	4,393
	FB15K23720-20%	10,532	237	50,144	4.31	1,100
	FB15K23720-10%	11,849	237	52,938	4.29	502
	NELL23K-60%	9,170	200	20,772	1.07	10,128
	NELL23K-50%	11,462	200	22,440	1.09	9,033
	NELL23K-40%	13,755	200	24,345	1.111	8,211

Baselines. For embedding-based models, we compare against TransE [3], ConvE [13], RotatE [4], TuckER [12], and ConE [5]. As for multi-hop reasoning models, we compare against MINERVA [7], MultiHopKG [17], AnyBURL [16], DacKGR [8], RuleGuider [9], CURL [10], and current SOTA model SQUIRE [11].

Evaluation Protocol. We follow the same evaluation protocol as most multi-hop reasoning methods [7,8,11]. Specifically, we report the results in terms of the Hit@1, 3, and 10 metrics, as well as the mean reciprocal rank (MRR) score, for the link prediction task.

[1] We use the same version as [11] considering the inconsistent split in previous studies.
[2] The data and code are available at: https://github.com/NLPWM-WHU/SelfHier.

Implementation Details. We utilize the rule-based method AnyBURL [16] to construct ground-truth reasoning paths as prior generation-based method [11] do. The Adam optimizer [20] is used for training our model. For evaluation, we follow the same process as [11] which involves using beam search and self-consistency [21] to decode the reasoning paths and target entities. The models are trained with five different seeds, and the results are averaged.

Table 2. Experiment results in the standard scenario. **Bold**: the best score of multi-hop reasoning models. <u>Underlined</u>: the second-best score of multi-hop reasoning models. †: the results are retrieved from [11]. ‡: the results reported by our reproduction based on their released code and the best hyperparameters. We reproduce CURL since its performance is not reported in most KGs previously. We also reproduce SQUIRE for the significance test. The reproduction results of SQUIRE are almost the same as those in their paper. *: the improvements of our SelfHier over the best baseline is significant at $p < 0.01$.

Model	FB15K237				NELL995				FB15K23720				NELL23K			
	MRR	H@1	H@3	H@10	MRR	H@1	H@3	H@10	MRR	H@1	H@3	H@10	MRR	H@1	H@3	H@10
TransE†	42.5	32.0	47.5	63.5	37.1	20.9	47.3	65.4	26.3	17.8	28.8	43.4	17.9	7.6	20.8	37.9
ConvE†	43.8	34.2	48.3	62.7	54.2	44.9	59.4	70.9	26.4	18.7	28.4	42.2	27.9	19.3	30.1	46.7
RotatE†	42.6	32.1	47.4	63.5	51.3	41.1	57.0	70.8	26.5	18.5	28.6	43.0	21.7	14.1	23.2	36.8
TuckER†	45.1	35.7	49.5	63.5	51.1	42.2	55.6	68.2	24.6	17.8	26.1	38.4	20.7	14.3	22.4	33.8
ConE†	44.6	34.5	49.0	64.5	54.3	44.8	60.2	71.5	27.4	19.3	29.8	43.7	23.4	15.8	24.9	40.0
MINERVA†	27.5	19.9	30.6	43.3	39.1	29.3	44.9	57.5	12.3	7.0	13.3	23.6	15.1	10.1	15.9	24.7
MultiHopKG†	40.7	32.7	44.3	56.4	46.7	38.8	51.2	60.9	23.1	16.7	25.0	36.1	17.8	12.4	18.8	29.7
AnyBURL†	-	30.0	40.5	54.4	-	38.9	52.1	62.8	-	15.9	24.0	35.9	-	14.0	20.3	29.2
RuleGuider†	38.7	29.7	42.8	56.3	41.7	34.4	47.6	58.2	9.4	4.2	9.4	21.0	11.2	3.0	14.0	27.3
DacKGR†	34.7	27.4	38.2	49.3	42.1	34.7	46.4	55.4	24.6	18.0	27.0	38.6	19.7	13.3	21.1	33.7
CURL‡	27.6	20.1	30.8	42.8	40.1	30.2	45.9	58.7	13.5	8.0	14.6	24.9	16.2	11.0	17.1	26.0
SQUIRE‡	<u>43.2</u>	<u>34.1</u>	<u>47.5</u>	<u>61.5</u>	<u>51.9</u>	<u>43.5</u>	<u>57.0</u>	<u>68.1</u>	<u>25.1</u>	<u>17.9</u>	<u>27.7</u>	<u>40.5</u>	<u>24.5</u>	<u>16.6</u>	<u>26.8</u>	<u>41.3</u>
SelfHier(ours)	**47.4***	**38.8***	**51.6***	**64.0***	**56.7***	**49.3***	**61.0***	**71.0***	**28.8***	**21.0***	**31.1***	**44.9***	**28.6***	**20.2***	**30.8***	**46.6***

4.2 Main Results

Table 2 presents the results of our SelfHier model and the baseline models in the standard scenario, while Table 3 displays the comparison results in the cold-start scenario.

Our SelfHier model achieves new state-of-the-art performance in the standard scenario, outperforming prior multi-hop reasoning models with a significant margin. This demonstrates that SelfHier is highly effective in conducting multi-hop reasoning on static KGs with fixed entities. Compared to the best baseline model, SelfHier achieves improvements of 9.7%, 9.2%, 14.7%, and 16.7% in MRR, and 13.8%, 13.3%, 17.3%, and 21.7% in Hit@1 across the four static KGs. Additionally, our model performs better than embedding-based models in most metrics for all static knowledge graphs, indicating that SelfHier can provide superior performance while retaining interpretability in the standard scenario.

In the cold-start scenario, we compare SelfHier with SQUIRE and DacKGR models, as other models are unable to handle this scenario entirely. SelfHier outperforms the baselines significantly on all dynamic KGs, regardless of the

Table 3. Experiment results in the cold-start scenario. The markers are same as those in Table 2.

Model	FB15K23720-10%				FB15K23720-20%				FB15K23720-50%			
	MRR	H@1	H@3	H@10	MRR	H@1	H@3	H@10	MRR	H@1	H@3	H@10
DacKGR	18.1	15.6	19.2	23.4	16.6	14.2	18.0	21.1	14.5	12.1	15.4	19.3
SQUIRE	19.4	14.5	22.3	28.6	18.5	14.2	20.1	27.2	17.1	12.2	18.7	27.4
SelfHier(ours)	**22.4***	**18.7***	**23.2***	**30.4***	**21.2***	**17.0***	**22.8***	**28.7***	**20.3***	**15.5***	**21.6***	**30.1***
Model	NELL23K-40%				NELL23K-50%				NELL23K-60%			
	MRR	H@1	H@3	H@10	MRR	H@1	H@3	H@10	MRR	H@1	H@3	H@10
DacKGR	14.0	8.8	14.9	23.5	13.2	8.2	14.8	22.5	11.2	6.0	12.4	21.0
SQUIRE	15.3	10.8	16.8	23.7	14.2	10.2	14.3	22.7	13.5	7.9	14.3	24.3
SelfHier(ours)	**19.2***	**12.4***	**22.4***	**31.4***	**18.0***	**11.7***	**19.7***	**29.5***	**17.7***	**11.6***	**19.1***	**29.3***

proportion of emerging entities. Notably, in the most stringent cold-start scenario of FB15K23720-50% and NELL23K-60% knowledge graphs, SelfHier achieves 18.7% and 31.1% improvement in MRR, and 27.0% and 46.8% improvement in Hit@1, respectively, compared to the best baseline model. These improvements are even more significant than their corresponding standard scenario.

In conclusion, our SelfHier model is a practical and widely-adaptive method that performs well not only in the cold-start scenario but also achieves state-of-the-art performance in the standard scenario.

Table 4. Ablation studies in the standard scenario. "w/o": removing the corresponding strategy. "w/o all strategies": removing hierarchical guidance and self-verification strategies simultaneously. **Bold**: the best score among different variants.

Model Variants	FB15K237				NELL995				FB15K23720				NELL23K			
	MRR	H@1	H@3	H@10	MRR	H@1	H@3	H@10	MRR	H@1	H@3	H@10	MRR	H@1	H@3	H@10
SelfHier	**47.4**	**38.8**	**51.6**	**64.0**	**56.7**	**49.3**	**61.0**	**71.0**	**28.8**	**21.0**	**31.1**	**44.9**	**28.6**	**20.2**	**30.8**	**46.6**
w/o sub-relations	46.3	37.8	50.5	62.9	55.0	47.6	59.0	69.5	27.5	19.9	29.8	43.8	26.9	19.2	29.0	43.1
w/o clusters	46.5	37.9	50.8	63.3	54.9	47.6	58.4	69.5	27.4	19.8	29.9	43.7	26.9	19.1	29.2	43.2
w/o self-verification	43.5	34.5	47.8	61.7	52.7	44.2	57.4	68.6	26.3	18.9	28.8	41.9	27.8	19.3	30.4	45.9
w/o all strategies	41.5	32.7	45.8	59.4	50.6	42.2	55.6	66.4	24.4	17.3	27.2	39.2	23.5	15.7	25.9	39.4

4.3 Ablation Studies

We conduct ablation studies on the hierarchical guidance and self-verification strategies, and the results on the standard and cold-start scenarios are shown in Table 4 and Table 5, respectively. These results indicate that all strategies are critical to improving the performance of our model in both standard and cold-start scenarios. We also observe that the score in Hit@10 slightly increases on some cold-start scenarios, which may be due to the guidance of clusters constraining the diversity of entities severely. Furthermore, incorporating both coarse-grained clusters and fine-grained sub-relations into the guidance is beneficial to the overall performance of our model. Although the performance is significantly impacted when both the self-verification and hierarchical guidance strategies are removed, the model still outperforms the best RL-based method, demonstrating the effectiveness of the generation-based framework for conducting multi-hop reasoning, and its potential for further research in the community. Overall, our ablation studies demonstrate the effectiveness of both hierarchical guidance and self-verification strategies.

Table 5. Ablation studies in the cold-start scenario. The markers are same as those in Table 4.

Model Variants	FB15K23720-10%				FB15K23720-20%				FB15K23720-50%			
	MRR	H@1	H@3	H@10	MRR	H@1	H@3	H@10	MRR	H@1	H@3	H@10
SelfHier	**22.4**	**18.7**	**23.2**	30.4	**21.2**	**17.0**	**22.8**	28.7	**20.3**	**15.5**	**21.6**	**30.1**
w/o sub-relations	21.5	17.5	22.6	30.1	20.5	16.8	21.4	28.0	19.4	14.9	20.5	28.2
w/o clusters	21.3	17.5	22.3	**30.7**	20.6	16.2	22.6	**28.8**	19.2	14.6	20.7	28.4
w/o self-verification	20.7	17.2	21.1	28.6	19.3	14.7	21.1	28.2	19.2	14.8	20.3	28.1
w/o all strategies	19.2	14.8	19.6	28.0	17.6	13.1	18.9	27.7	17.0	12.4	18.1	27.1
Model Variants	NELL23K-40%				NELL23K-50%				NELL23K-60%			
	MRR	H@1	H@3	H@10	MRR	H@1	H@3	H@10	MRR	H@1	H@3	H@10
SelfHier	**19.2**	**12.4**	**22.4**	**31.4**	**18.0**	**11.7**	**19.7**	29.5	**17.7**	**11.6**	**19.1**	**29.3**
w/o sub-relations	17.8	10.3	21.1	29.6	17.1	10.7	19.5	27.7	16.2	10.1	18.7	27.4
w/o clusters	16.7	9.5	18.6	29.9	16.4	9.8	18.2	**29.7**	16.1	9.4	18.7	28.7
w/o self-verification	18.7	11.9	21.4	31.4	17.1	10.7	19.1	29.1	16.8	10.7	18.4	28.4
w/o all strategies	14.8	8.0	16.0	28.9	13.5	8.2	14.6	23.6	13.2	7.2	14.7	24.9

4.4 Interpretability Evaluation

Table 6. Interpretability evaluation. The interpretability score is the sum score of all reasoning paths, and the reasonable rate is the ratio of those paths gaining 1 score.

Model	MultiHopKG	SQUIRE	SelfHier
Interpretability score	14.0	24.5	29.5
Reasonable rate	5.0%	10.0%	13.0%

Following [11,22], we manually annotate the interpretability score for paths generated by MultiHopKG, SQUIRE, and SelfHier model. We randomly select 100 queries and choose the generated reasoning path with the highest probability that leads to the gold tail entity. Then, two experts score it alone based on whether it is convincing to them, where 1, 0.5, and 0 scores for paths that are reasonable, partially reasonable, and unreasonable, respectively. If there is an inconsistency of their score, another expert who is more familiar with this task makes the decision finally[3] The evaluation result on FB15K237 is reported in Table 6. We observe that SelfHier achieves higher scores on both metrics, suggesting that our model can generate more reasonable paths and facilitate explainable multi-hop reasoning.

3 The three experts are well-versed in this task, and they are blind to which model generates the path when scoring. The full annotation results are available at https://github.com/NLPWM-WHU/SelfHier/blob/main/annotation.csv.

Additionally, we conduct a study on the dependability of unknown fact triplets within the reasoning paths generated by SelfHier and SQUIRE. To achieve this, we train them on FB15K23720 KG and collect fact triplets that are not present in it but are generated during the reasoning process. We evaluate whether these fact triplets are included in the more comprehensive FB15K237 KG. The coverage statistics are presented in Table 7, demonstrating that our SelfHier model is capable of generating more reliable fact triplets compared to SQUIRE.

Table 7. Coverage statistics.

Model	Unknown Num	Covered Num	Cover Ratio
SQUIRE	11891	1236	10.4%
SelfHier	13502	3717	27.5%

4.5 Model Complexity

To investigate the model complexity, we compare the time-consuming and memory-usage between MultiHopKG, SQUIRE, and our SelfHier model. Firstly, we measure the training time across graph sizes ranging from 5×10^4 to 25×10^4 nodes. As shown in Fig. 5, more time will be consumed by our SelfHier model compared to SQUIRE, but less compared to MultiHopKG. The seq2seq architecture of our model can avoid the iterative trial-and-error process of reinforcement learning methods, resulting in reduced time consumption. Furthermore, our model is more effective in memory-usage. Overall, our model achieves a good trade-off between performance and complexity.

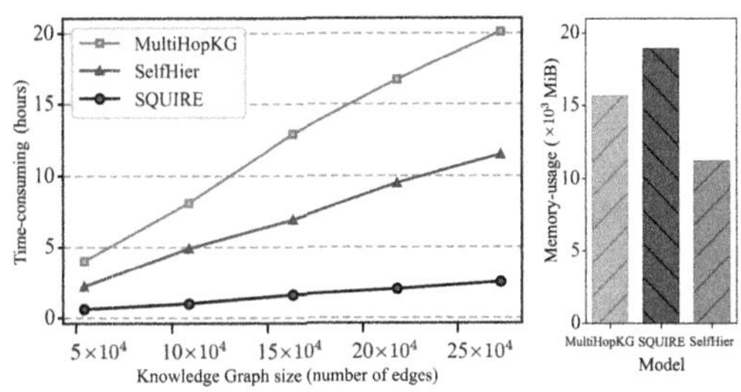

Fig. 5. Model complexity comparison.

4.6 Case Study

As Table 8 shows, we analyze two cases in the standard and cold-start scenarios, respectively. For each scenario, we choose the reasoning paths at Hit@1 predicted by the top-3 best models for comparison. Given Query1 in the standard scenario, MultiHopKG and SQURIE struggle to distinguish those semantically similar relations and eliminate entities with unrelated attributes, while SelfHier can reason a path toward the target tail entity correctly since the *hierarchichal-guidance* is equipped to solve the dilemma. Given Query2 in the cold-start scenario, the existing entity "*Brooklyn Dodgers*" is isolated from the emerging entity "*Baseball*". DacKGR and SQUIRE not only have trouble in distinguishing semantically similar relations and eliminating entities with unrelated attributes due to the lack of precise guidance, but are also troubled by the lacking of an explicit path. However, our self-verification can pre-explore the edge "*team plays against*" between "*Brooklyn Dodgers*" and "*Colorado Rochies*", which merges the gap between them. Overall, our SelfHier is more effective in both standard and cold-start scenarios.

Table 8. Case study. $\longrightarrow$: the edge completed by self-verification. $\dashrightarrow$: the edge completed by DacKGR or SQUIRE during reasoning. $\longrightarrow$: the edge existing in KGs.

Standard	Query1: ($U.K$, $contains$, ?)$\Longrightarrow$ Target1: *Borough of Chesterfield*	Prediction
MultiHopKG:	$U.K \xrightarrow{contains} England \xrightarrow{contains} University\ of\ Sheffield$	✗
SQUIRE:	$U.K \xrightarrow{at\ location^{-1}} England \xrightarrow{contains} Greater\ London \overset{contains}{\dashrightarrow} River\ Thames$	✗
SelfHier:	$U.K \xrightarrow{contains} England \xrightarrow{at\ location^{-1}} Borough\ of\ Chesterfield$	✓
Cold-start	Query2: (*Brooklyn Dodgers*, *team plays sport*, ?)$\Longrightarrow$ Target2: *Baseball*	Prediction
DacKGR:	$Brooklyn\ Dodgers \xrightarrow{team\ home\ stadium} Ebbets\ Field \overset{proxy\ for^{-1}}{\dashrightarrow} Chicago$	✗
SQUIRE:	$Brooklyn\ Dodgers \overset{team\ plays\ sport}{\dashrightarrow} Football$	✗
SelfHier:	$Brooklyn\ Dodgers \xrightarrow{team\ plays\ against} Colorado\ Rockies \xrightarrow{team\ plays\ sport} Baseball$	✓

5 Conclusion

In this paper, we are interested in the cold-start scenario toward dynamic KGs to facilitate more practical multi-hop reasoning. To solve the problem of lacking precise guidance and explicit paths, we design hierarchical guidance and self-verification strategies. The hierarchical guidance can distinguish semantically similar relations and eliminate entities with unrelated attributes by the guidance of fine-grained sub-relations and coarse-grained clusters. Furthermore, self-verification is able to construct more explicit reasoning paths by pre-exploring some missing fact triplets. Finally, the experiments demonstrate that our SelfHier model achieves SOTA performance in both standard and cold-start scenarios.

Ethical Statement. The data and code used in our experiments are all open-source resources for research purposes. The paper is free from copyright or other intellectual property issues.

References

1. Bollacker, K., Evans, C., Paritosh, P., Sturge, T., Taylor, J.: Freebase: a collaboratively created graph database for structuring human knowledge. In: Proceedings of the 2008 ACM SIGMOD International Conference on Management of Data, pp. 1247–1250 (2008)
2. Carlson, A., Betteridge, J., Kisiel, B., Settles, B., Hruschka, E., Mitchell, T.: Toward an architecture for never-ending language learning. In: Proceedings of the AAAI Conference on Artificial Intelligence, vol. 24, pp. 1306–1313 (2010)
3. Bordes, A., Usunier, N., Garcia-Duran, A., Weston, J., Yakhnenko, O.: Translating embeddings for modeling multi-relational data. In: Advances in Neural Information Processing Systems, vol. 26 (2013)

4. Sun, Z., Deng, Z.-H., Nie, J.-Y., Tang, J.: Rotate: knowledge graph embedding by relational rotation in complex space. In: International Conference on Learning Representations (2018)
5. Bai, Y., Ying, Z., Ren, H., Leskovec, J.: Modeling heterogeneous hierarchies with relation-specific hyperbolic cones. In: Advances in Neural Information Processing Systems, vol. 34, pp. 12316–12327 (2021)
6. Xiong, W., Hoang, T., Wang, W.Y.: Deeppath: a reinforcement learning method for knowledge graph reasoning. In: Empirical Methods in Natural Language Processing (2017)
7. Das, R., et al.: Go for a walk and arrive at the answer: reasoning over paths in knowledge bases using reinforcement learning. In: International Conference on Learning Representations (2018)
8. Lv, X., et al.: Dynamic anticipation and completion for multi-hop reasoning over sparse knowledge graph. In: Proceedings of the 2020 Conference on Empirical Methods in Natural Language Processing (EMNLP), pp. 5694–5703 (2020)
9. Lei, D., Jiang, G., Gu, X., Sun, K., Mao, Y., Ren, X.: Learning collaborative agents with rule guidance for knowledge graph reasoning. In: Proceedings of the 2020 Conference on Empirical Methods in Natural Language Processing (EMNLP), pp. 8541–8547 (2020)
10. Zhang, D., Yuan, Z., Liu, H., Xiong, H., et al.: Learning to walk with dual agents for knowledge graph reasoning. In: Proceedings of the AAAI Conference on Artificial Intelligence, vol. 36, pp. 5932–5941 (2022)
11. Bai, Y., et al.: Squire: a sequence-to-sequence framework for multi-hop knowledge graph reasoning. In: Proceedings of the 2022 Conference on Empirical Methods in Natural Language Processing, pp. 1649–1662 (2022)
12. Balažević, I., Allen, C., Hospedales, T.: Tucker: tensor factorization for knowledge graph completion. In: Proceedings of the 2019 Conference on Empirical Methods in Natural Language Processing and the 9th International Joint Conference on Natural Language Processing (EMNLP-IJCNLP), pp. 5185–5194 (2019)
13. Dettmers, T., Minervini, P., Stenetorp, P., Riedel, S.: Convolutional 2D knowledge graph embeddings. In: Proceedings of the AAAI Conference on Artificial Intelligence, vol. 32 (2018)
14. Rocktäschel, T., Riedel, S.: End-to-end differentiable proving. In: Advances in Neural Information Processing Systems, vol. 30 (2017)
15. Yang, F., Yang, Z., Cohen, W.W.: Differentiable learning of logical rules for knowledge base reasoning. In: Advances in Neural Information Processing Systems, vol. 30 (2017)
16. Meilicke, C., Chekol, M.W., Ruffinelli, D., Stuckenschmidt, H.: Anytime bottom-up rule learning for knowledge graph completion. In: Proceedings of the 28th International Joint Conference on Artificial Intelligence, pp. 3137–3143 (2019)
17. Lin, X.V., Socher, R., Xiong, C.: Multi-hop knowledge graph reasoning with reward shaping. In: Proceedings of the 2018 Conference on Empirical Methods in Natural Language Processing, pp. 3243–3253 (2018)
18. McQueen, J.B.: Some methods of classification and analysis of multivariate observations. In: Proceedings of 5th Berkeley Symposium on Mathematical Statistics and Probability, pp. 281–297 (1967)
19. Toutanova, K., Chen, D.: Observed versus latent features for knowledge base and text inference. In: Proceedings of the 3rd Workshop on Continuous Vector Space Models and their Compositionality (2015)
20. Kingma, D.P., Ba, J.: Adam: a method for stochastic optimization. arXiv preprint arXiv:1412.6980 (2014)

21. Wang, X., Wei, J., Schuurmans, D., Le, Q., Chi, E., Zhou, D.: Self-consistency improves chain of thought reasoning in language models. arXiv preprint arXiv:2203.11171 (2022)
22. Lv, X., et al.: Is multi-hop reasoning really explainable? Towards benchmarking reasoning interpretability. In: Proceedings of the 2021 Conference on Empirical Methods in Natural Language Processing, pp. 8899–8911 (2021)

Efficient Fine-Tuning Large Language Models for Knowledge-Aware Response Planning

Minh Nguyen[1], K. C. Kishan[2], Toan Nguyen[2], Ankit Chadha[2], and Thuy Vu[2(✉)]

[1] Department of Computer Science, University of Oregon, Eugene, OR, USA
minhnv@cs.uoregon.edu
[2] Amazon Alexa AI, Palo Alto, CA, USA
{ckshan,amztoan,ankitrc,thuyvu}@amazon.com

Abstract. Large Language Models (LLMs) have shown impressive emergent language capabilities, especially in applications with high ambiguity, such as language reasoning and knowledge consolidation. However, previous work explores the use of LLMs for acquiring information using either parametric or external knowledge, which might lead to serious issues such as hallucination. Toward solving these issues, we present a novel approach of knowledge-aware response planning (KARP) and propose a novel framework that employs (i) a knowledge retriever to obtain relevant information from web documents or databases for a given user query, and (ii) a robust fine-tuning strategy for LLMs to exploit the retrieved external knowledge for planning a final response. Experimental results show that our proposed framework can provide natural, concise answers for open-domain questions with high accuracy.

Keywords: Knowledge-Aware Response Planning · Question Answering · Large Language Models · Fine-tuning

1 Introduction

General question answering (QA), a crucial natural language processing (NLP) task, is often regarded as AI-complete [8,59]; that is, QA will only be considered solved once all the challenging problems in artificial intelligence (AI) have been addressed. Several virtual response assistants, including Google Assistant, Amazon Alexa, and Apple's Siri, have integrated state-of-the-art QA technologies, allowing them to understand and generate responses in natural languages, providing valuable services to users. However, general QA still presents significant challenges, primarily due to the inherent difficulties in reasoning with natural language, including aspects like commonsense and general knowledge. Past research has explored the use of Large Language Models (LLMs) for general QA, predominantly leveraging either parametric (e.g., ChatGPT[1]) or external (e.g., WebGPT [37]) knowledge sources. This method, however, can lead to considerable complications, including hallucination - the generation of plausible but incorrect or unverified information. To address these challenges, this paper introduces the concept of Knowledge-Aware Response Planning (KARP) for general QA along with a

M. Nguyen—This work was completed while the author was an intern at Amazon Alexa AI.
[1] https://chat.openai.com/chat.

© The Author(s), under exclusive license to Springer Nature Switzerland AG 2023
D. Koutra et al. (Eds.): ECML PKDD 2023, LNAI 14170, pp. 593–611, 2023.
https://doi.org/10.1007/978-3-031-43415-0_35

Table 1. Generated answers for a question q with different context passages c_1 (relevant), c_2 (quasi-relevant), and c_3 (irrelevant) from MS MARCO QA NLG test set [38]. Answers a_1, a_2, and a_3 are generated by GenQA [17].

q:	What college offers chiropractic ?
c_1:	New York Chiropractic College offers 1 Chiropractic Degree program. It's a private university in a far away town. In 2015, 173 students graduated in the study area of Chiropractic with students earning 173 Doctoral degrees
a_1:	New York Chiropractic college offers chiropractic.
c_2:	Chiropractic care is also essential for college students who want to stay healthy. The central nervous system is based in the spinal column, so correcting subluxations (misalignments) of the spine is important, no matter how old you are. Holt Chiropractic in Port Orchard, WA provides expert chiropractic care to students of all ages
a_2:	Holt Chiropractic College offers chiropractic.
c_3:	Howell Township is a township in Monmouth County, New Jersey, United States. As of the 2010 United States Census, the township's population was 51,075, reflecting an increase of 2,172 from the 48,903 counted in the 2000 Census
a_3:	Howell Township College offers chiropractic.

novel framework that combines a knowledge retriever with a robust fine-tuning strategy for LLMs. In particular, the problem of KARP can be defined as follows. Given a user query and a prompt containing external knowledge, the goal is to develop a model that can consolidate a response that must be crafted not just from the externally sourced information, but also from the model's inherent parametric knowledge. This is different from the previous work that aim to generate a response by either harnessing parametric knowledge (e.g., ChatGPT) or retrieving from external knowledge such as knowledge bases [2,3,49,62], web documents [6,7,13,64,65], or a provided context [10,15,43,56].

With the emergent abilities of LLMs [58], generative QA systems, in which answers are produced by a generative LLM, have been explored to improve the performance of QA [12,17,18,20,26,36,42,47]. In paritcular, previous work typically employs pre-trained LLMs with encoder-decoder architectures such as BART [27] and T5 [42], where the encoder consumes a given question and a *required* relevant context as input for the decoder to generate an answer to the question [17,23]. On one hand, the similarity between generative QA and the pre-training tasks of LLMs enables transfer learning to improve QA performance. On the other hand, the generative formulation allows for flexibility in handling various types of QA problems (e.g., extractive QA, multiple-choice QA) [23]. However, a well-known issue that has been shown to occur with the generative models is hallucination [34,48,51], where the models generate statements that are plausible looking but *factually* incorrect. Additionally, if the answers are composed by a pretrained LLM without external knowledge, i.e., using parametric knowledge, the information contained in the answers might be outdated and no longer valid. For example, the answer for the question *"Which country is the reigning World Cup champion?"* will change through time.

Recent works such as GenQA [17] and WebGPT [37] mitigate these issues by employing an information retrieval component, which is responsible for collecting web content to compose an answer for a given question. Formally, given a question q and a retrieved web content c, the model is trained to take (q, c) as input to produce a response $a = f_\theta(q, c)$, where f_θ denotes the corresponding LLM with the parameters θ. Unfortunately, f_θ may merely learn to copy/synthesize information from c to produce a if c often contains necessary information for correctly answering the question q in training data such as MS MARCO QA NLG [38][2]. As a result, the model may fail to provide a correct answer for a given question if the retrieved content is missing or contains (quasi-)irrelevant information (see Table 1). In other words, performance of these retrieval-based QA models are limited to an upper bound by the knowledge retriever.

In this work, we address such issues in building a generative QA model. First, we utilize a knowledge retriever that employs Optimal Transport to selectively identify relevant content from web documents or databases for a given user query. Second, we propose a novel fine-tuning strategy specially designed for LLMs, which combines external knowledge, i.e., provided by the knowledge retriever and the intrinsic pre-trained knowledge in LLMs, wherever possible, to generate informed responses.

Particularly, we propose the knowledge retriever as a dense passage retriever (DPR) model. Our proposed DPR model performs an alignment between a given question and a text passage via Optimal Transport to find relevant information in the passage for determining its correctness. The relevant context in the passage will then be used to produce a correctness score for ranking. In this way, we can obtain top k text passages from databases/web documents, which are treated as external knowledge in our framework. Different from GenQA and WebGPT that follows a single-style "$a = f_\theta(q, c)$" finetuning strategy, we propose to employ a multi-style finetuning strategy, where both "$a = f_\theta(q, c)$" and "$a = f_\theta(q)$" are used to train the model. The latter intentionally excludes the external knowledge c from the input to encourage the model to retrieve its own knowledge from the model parameters θ, which have been pretrained on massive unlabeled text data [11,27,42,53]. To combine the two finetuning styles, we propose to finetune the LLM with "$a = f_\theta(q, c)$", and sequentially finetune the model with "$a = f_\theta(q)$". At test time, we use the "$a = f_\theta(q, c)$" style to make predictions. Experimental results show that our proposed finetuning strategy significantly improves the performance compared to the baselines on MS MARCO QA NLG, demonstratting the effectiveness of our proposed method. Finally, we scale up our framework to further improve the QA performance by training the model i) with "$a = f_\theta(q, c)$" on QA datasets such as SQUAD [43] (c is a context passage), MCTest [46] (c consists of multiple choices), Anthropic [1] (c is the previous question in a conversation), and ii) with "$a = f_\theta(q)$" on QA datasets such as WikiQA [65] and Wdrass [69].

[2] All answers a in MS MARCO QA NLG are written by human annotators based on summarizing answer information in context passages c.

Our experiments show that the resulting system behaves as a knowledge aware response planner that provides natural, concise answers for open-domain questions with high accuracy.

2 Proposed Method

2.1 Knowledge-Aware Response Planning

The problem of Knowledge-Aware Response Planning (KARP) can be outlined as follows: Given a user query and a prompt loaded with external knowledge, the aim is to build a model capable of formulating a response. This response should be planned not only from the external information provided but also derived from the model's inherent parametric knowledge.

To this end, our proposed framework for KARP consists of (i) a knowledge retriever and (ii) a generative LLM-based question answering model. An overview of our framework is shown in Fig. 1. Details regarding the knowledge retriever and the generative QA model are presented in Sects. 2.2 and 2.3, respectively.

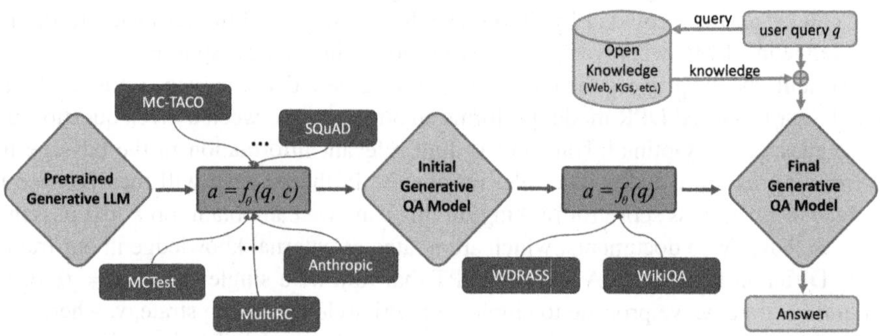

Fig. 1. Overview of our proposed framework for KARP. The blue and orange arrows represent the finetuning and inference processes of our model respectively. (Color figure online)

2.2 Knowledge Retriever

Our knowledge retriever functions as a dense passage retrieval (DPR) system. Given a question q and a group of N text passages $C = \{c_1, c_2, \ldots, c_N\}$, the goal of DPR is to determine the correct answer passages $A \subset C$ by learning a reranking function $r : Q \times \phi(C) \rightarrow \phi(C)$, where Q represents the set of questions and $\phi(C)$ represents all the possible orderings of C. The intent is to place the answer passages A at the top of the ranking produced by the function r. The reranker r is typically a pointwise network $f(q, c_i)$, such as TANDA [13], which learns to assign a correctness score $p_i \in (0, 1)$ to each text passage c_i for ranking purposes. Our focus lies on the contextual DPR, where supplementary context, like surrounding context, is used to more accurately ascertain the validity score of an answer passage.

Our knowledge retriever consists of three primary elements: i) Encoding, ii) Question-Context Alignment with Optimal Transport (OT), and iii) Answer-Context Dependencies. The diagram of our suggested model can be seen in Fig. 2.

Encoding. We are provided with a question represented as $q = [w_1^q, w_2^q, \ldots, w_{T_q}^q]$ with T_q words and a set of N text passages $C = \{c_1, c_2, \ldots, c_N\}$ retrieved from a search engine. Each passage, denoted as $c_i = [w_1^c, w_2^c, \ldots, w_{T_c}^c]$, consists of T_c words. In this work, we consider previous and next passages c_{prev}, c_{next} as additional context for each candidate passage $c \in C$. To create the input for our DPR model, we concatenate the question, answer passage, and context passages into a single input sequence: $[q; c; c_{prev}; c_{next}]$. This combined sequence is then passed through a pre-trained language model (PLM), e.g., RoBERTa [32], to obtain contextualized word embeddings. Additionally, we employ distinct segment embeddings for the question, answer passage, and context passages. These segment embeddings, which are randomly initialized and trainable during training, are added to the initial word embeddings in the first layer of the PLM. For simplicity, let $[\mathbf{w}_1^q, \mathbf{w}_2^q, \ldots, \mathbf{w}_{T_q}^q]$ and $[\mathbf{w}_1^c, \mathbf{w}_2^c, \ldots, \mathbf{w}_{T_c}^c]$ represent the sequences of word representations obtained from the last layer of the PLM for the question q and the answer passage $c \in C$, respectively.

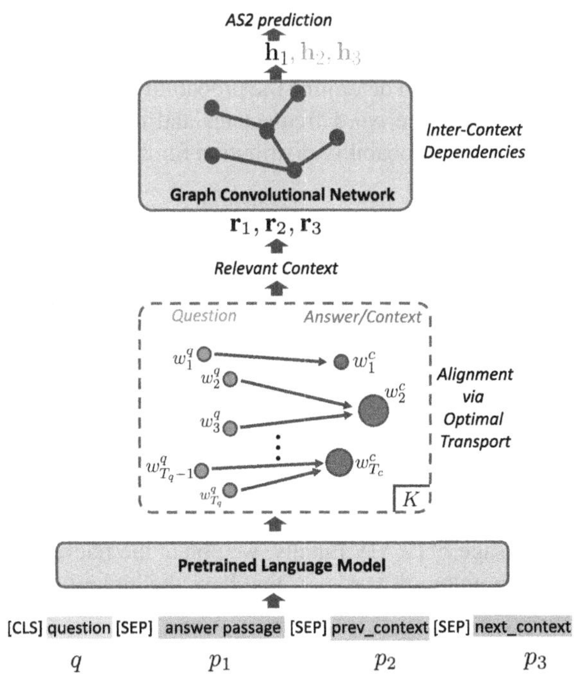

Fig. 2. A diagram depicting the knowledge retriever in our framework for KARP.

Question-Context Alignment with OT. In this section, we present our approach for identifying relevant context within the answer passage and its surrounding passages based on the alignment of words with the question. Specifically, we introduce the use of Optimal Transport (OT) [9,35] to address the task of aligning the question with the context for DPR.

OT is a well-established technique used to transfer probability from one distribution to another by establishing an alignment between two sets of points. In the discrete setting, we are provided with two probability distributions, denoted as p_X and p_Y, defined over two sets of points, namely $X = \{x_i\}_{i=1}^n$ and $Y = \{y_j\}_{j=1}^m$ ($\sum_i p_{x_i} = 1$ and $\sum_j p_{y_j} = 1$). Additionally, a distance function $D(x, y) : X \times Y \rightarrow \mathbb{R}^+$ is given to quantify the dissimilarity between any two points x and y. The objective of OT is to determine a mapping that transfers the probability mass from the points in $\{x_i\}_{i=1}^n$ to the points in $\{y_j\}_{j=1}^m$, while minimizing the overall cost associated with this transportation. Formally, this involves finding the transportation matrix $\pi_{XY} \in \mathbb{R}^{+n \times m}$ that minimizes the following transportation cost:

$$d_{XY} = \sum_{\substack{1 \leq i \leq n \\ 1 \leq j \leq m}} D(x_i, y_j) \pi_{XY\,ij}, \tag{1}$$

so that $\pi_{XY} \mathbf{1}_m = p_X$ and $\pi_{XY}^T \mathbf{1}_n = p_Y$. The transportation matrix π_{XY} signifies the best matching between the sets of points X and Y, where each row i in the matrix indicates the optimal alignment from a point $x_i \in X$ to each point $y_j \in Y$.

In our problem of aligning the question with the answer passage, we treat the question q and the answer/context passage c as two point sets: $\{w_i^q\}_{i=1}^{T_q}$ and $\{w_i^c\}_{i=1}^{T_c}$ respectively (each word is a point)[3]. To determine the probability distributions for these word sets, we propose calculating the word frequencies and then normalizing the sum of frequencies. Specifically, the probability distribution for the question is obtained by:

$$p_{w_i^q} = \frac{freq(w_i^q)}{\sum_{i'=1}^{T_q} freq(w_{i'}^q)} \tag{2}$$

The frequency $freq(w_i^q)$ corresponds to the number of occurrences of the word w_i^q in the training data's questions. The same approach is applied to the answer/context passage. To handle unseen words during testing, we utilize Laplace smoothing to assign a non-zero probability. Moving on, we estimate the distance between two words $w_i^q \in q$ and $w_j^c \in c$ by measuring their semantic divergence, which involves computing the Euclidean distance between their contextualized representations obtained from the PLM: $D(w_i^q, w_j^c) = ||\mathbf{w}_i^q - \mathbf{w}_j^c||$. The Sinkhorn-Knopp algorithm is then efficiently employed to solve for the optimal transportation matrix π_{XY} (in this case, π_{qc} for the question q and the passage c) [9,52]. Finally, we obtain the relevant context r_c for the passage c by taking the union of words w_j^c that have the highest transportation probabilities:

$$r_c = \bigcup_{i=1}^{T_q} \{w_j^c | j = \text{argmax}_{1 \leq j' \leq T_c} \pi_{qc_{ij'}}\} \tag{3}$$

[3] Before performing the alignment, we remove stopwords and punctuation marks from both sets of words.

To compute the representation for the passage c, we take the average sum of the word representations within the relevant context:

$$\mathbf{r}_c = \frac{1}{|r_c|} \sum_{j|w_j^c \in r_c} \mathbf{w}_j^c \tag{4}$$

By incorporating the relevant context, our intention is to eliminate any disruptive or unrelated details from the passage representation.

Answer-Context Dependencies. For convenience, let $[\mathbf{r}_1, \mathbf{r}_2, \mathbf{r}_3]$ denote the representations acquired from Eq. (4) for the answer passage $p_1 \equiv c$, the previous passage $p_2 \equiv c_{prev}$, and the next passage $p_3 \equiv c_{next}$. To capture the relationships between these passages, we view each passage as a node in a fully-connected graph $G = (V, E)$, where $V = \{p_i\}$ $(1 \leq i \leq 3)$ is the node set and $E = \{(p_i, p_j)\}$ $(1 \leq i, j \leq 3)$ is the edge set. Our objective is to determine a weight $\alpha_{ij} \in (0, 1)$ for each edge (p_i, p_j) that reflects the dependency of p_i on p_j. To accomplish this, we propose to leverage their semantic representations $\mathbf{r}_i$, $\mathbf{r}_j$, and transportation costs to the question d_{qp_i}, d_{qp_j} to measure the dependency weight α_{ij} between the passages p_i and p_j. Specifically, we first compute the score: $u_{ij} = FFN_{DEP}([\mathbf{r}_i \odot \mathbf{r}_j; d_{qp_i}; d_{qp_j}])$, where $\odot$ is the element-wise product, $[;]$ represents the concatenation operation, and FFN_{DEP} is a feed-forward network. Subsequently, the weight α_{ij} for the edge (p_i, p_j) is obtained through a softmax function:

$$\alpha_{ij} = \frac{\exp(u_{ij})}{\sum_{j'=1}^{K} \exp(u_{ij'})} \tag{5}$$

The derived weights $\{\alpha_{ij}\}$ are subsequently utilized to enrich the passage representations through L layers of a Graph Convolutional Network (GCN) [24]:

$$\mathbf{h}_i^l = \text{ReLU}(\sum_{j=1}^{K} \alpha_{ij} \mathbf{W}^l \mathbf{h}_j^{l-1} + \mathbf{b}^l) \tag{6}$$

where $\mathbf{W}^l$, $\mathbf{b}^l$ are learnable weight matrix and bias for the layer l of the GCN $(1 \leq l \leq L)$, and $\mathbf{h}_i^0 \equiv \mathbf{r}_i$ is the input representation for the passage p_i. The output vectors $\mathbf{h}_i^L \equiv \mathbf{h}_i$ at the last layer of the GCN serve as the final representations for the passages p_i. Intuitively, the weights α_{ij} enable each passage to decide the amount of information it receives from the other passages to improve its representation for the task. The representation $\mathbf{h}_1$ for the answer passage $p_1 \equiv c$ is finally sent to a feed-forward network with a sigmoid output function to estimate the correctness score $p_c \in (0, 1)$ for the answer passage c: $p_c = FFN_{DPR}(\mathbf{h}_1)$. For training, we minimize the binary cross-entropy loss with the correctness scores p_c. At inference time, consistent with previous research [13], we include all answer passages for each question for ranking.

2.3 Generative LLM-Based Question Answering Model

Background on Text Generation Finetuning. Text generation finetuning has become a general approach to solving different NLP tasks, where input and expected output of a task can be represented as source and target text respectively for a generative model to learn the task [28,33,42]. For example, a pretrained generative LLM such as BART [27] and T5 [42] can be finetuned on sentiment analysis by taking a text statement (e.g., *"I really like the story"*) as source text to generate a text label (i.e., *"Positive"*, *"Negative"*, *"Neutral"*) to indicate the sentiment of the statement. As the text generation resembles the pretraining tasks (e.g., predicting next words) for the generative LLMs, the formulation could facilitate the transfer learning to the target task. In addition, it enables the data augmentation method where training data for a task may also be leveraged for another task if the two tasks both are convertable to the text generation format [30]. These advantages have led to significant performance improvements for many NLP tasks such as event extraction [30], named entity recognition [63], and dependency parsing [28]. Similar to other NLP tasks, the generative methods have been explored for improving QA performance [12,17,18,20,26,36,42,47]. To avoid hallucination and improve factual accuracy for the models, recent works on generative QA employ the retrieval-based methods such as GenQA [17] and WebGPT [37].

GenQA is introduced by Hsu et al. [17] for generating appropriate answers for user questions instead of simply choosing the best answer candidate. This expands the answer retrieval pipeline with an additional generation stage to produce correct and satisfactory answers, even in cases where a highly ranked candidate is not acceptable or does not provide a natural response to the question. In particular, GenQA employs a pretrained generative LLM to produce an answer by taking a given question and a list of answer candidates as input, sorted by a trained reranker system.

WebGPT is designed by OpenAI researchers [37] to tackle the problem of long-form question-answering, which involves generating a paragraph-length answer to an open-ended question. Specifically, WebGPT uses the Microsoft Bing Web Search API to retrieve relevant documents for a given question. The model then interacts with a text-based environment where it can take actions such as clicking on links or opening new web pages to locate relevant passages from which to generate answers.

Our Proposed Finetuning Strategy. The main goal of a general text-generation model is to produce an output text sequence $\mathbf{y} = [y_1, y_2, \ldots, y_T]$ based on a given input text sequence $\mathbf{x} = [x_1, x_2, \ldots, x_S]$, where the lengths of the input and output sequences are denoted by S and T, respectively. With a pretrained encoder-decoder LLM such as BART [27] or T5 [42], we can compute the conditional probability of $P(\mathbf{y}|\mathbf{x})$ for training the model. At test time, the decoder merges the previous output and input text to create the current output. A decoding algorithm such as Greedy or Beam Search [60] can be used to generate an output text with the highest likelihood. For QA, given a question q and a retrieved web content c (e.g., top answer passages), previous works such as GenQA and WebGPT are trained to take (q, c) for as the source sequence to produce a response as the target sequence $a = f_\theta(q, c)$, where f_θ denotes the corresponding LLM with the parameters θ. As a result, f_θ may merely learn to copy/synthesize information from c to produce a if c often contains necessary information for correctly answering the question q in training data. Relying solely on the retrieved content c, the model may fail to provide a correct answer for a given question if c is missing or contains irrelevant/noisy information. In other words, performance of these retrieval-based QA models are limited to an upper bound by the knowledge retriever.

Different from the previous works that follow a single-style "$a = f_\theta(q, c)$" fine-tuning strategy, we propose to employ a multi-style finetuning strategy, where both "$a = f_\theta(q, c)$" and "$a = f_\theta(q)$" are used to train the model. The latter intentionally excludes the external knowledge c from the input to encourage the model to retrieve its own knowledge from the model parameters θ, which have been pretrained on massive unlabeled text data [11,27,42,53]. To combine the two finetuning styles, we propose to finetune the LLM with "$a = f_\theta(q, c)$", and sequentially finetune the model with "$a = f_\theta(q)$". In this way, our model does not completely rely on the retrieval results to generate answers for given questions. At test time, we use the "$a = f_\theta(q, c)$" style to make predictions. The retrieved content c now can be considered as a source of external knowledge along with the pretrained knowledge contained in the model parameters θ to generate an answer for the question. Under this perspective, we consider various QA datasets for each step in our finetuning process. We call such dataset collection OKQA as they are publicly available and contains high-quality knowledge.

MS Marco QA NLG is a specialized version of the MS Marco dataset [38] that aims to produce natural language responses to user inquiries using web search result excerpts. This dataset includes $182K$ queries from Bing search logs, each is associated with top ten most relevant passages. A human annotator is then required to look at the passages and synthesize an answer using the content of the passages that most accurately addresses the query.

Super Natural Instructions (SNI) is a data collection proposed by [57]. The corpus consists of $1,616$ diverse NLP tasks and their expert-written instructions. In this work, we consider only question-answering tasks such as extractive QA with SQUAD [43] and multiple-choice QA with MCTest [46]. For each task, we consider anything but a question q provided in the input as context c. Particularly, the context c can be a passage, a fact, or a set of answer choices associated with the question. As a result, we obtain $180K$ examples for finetuning our model.

Anthropic is introduced by [1], containing conversations between a human and a computer assistant. For each conversation, we consider a human question and the previous question (if any) as the input sequence and the answer from the assistant as the output sequence. As questions in a conversation are usually related to each other, the previous question can be considered as a form of relevant context c for clarifying the current question q. Consequently, we obtain $280K$ examples for finetuning our model.

Dense Passage Retrieval datasets, namely, WikiQA [65] and WDRASS [69] are also used for finetuning our model. WikiQA is a collection of questions and answer candidates that have been manually annotated using Bing query logs on Wikipedia. WDRASS is a large-scale dataset of questions that are non-factoid in nature, such as questions that begin with "why" or "how". The dataset contains around $64,000$ questions and over $800,000$ labeled passages that have been extracted from a total of $30M$ documents. Each question in such DPR datasets is associated with a set of answer candidates, in which some of the candidates are correct answers. As a question can have multiple correct answers, we select the longest answer as the output sequence for the question, which is considered as the input sequence. This results in a set of $105K$ examples for finetuning our model.

In the end, the datasets where context is available for a question are employed in the step 1 of our finetuning process while the other datasets are used for further training the model in the subsequent step. With a huge amount of various QA tasks, we expect this could teach the model to understand the nature of question answering and how to utilize its own parametric knowledge (in case no context is provided) and external knowledge (i.e., relevant context) to answer a given question.

3 Experiments

3.1 Benchmarking the Knowledge Retriever

Experimental Setup

Datasets. We follow the previous work [13,69] to conduct the evaluation. In particular, we use (i) **WikiQA** [65], consisting of questions from Bing query logs and manually annotated answers from Wikipedia, and (ii) **WDRASS** [69], a large-scale web-based dataset having factoid and non-factoid questions, to investigate our retrieval performance. We use the same train/dev/test splits used in previous work.

Hyper-parameters and Tools. In accordance with previous work, we use a small portion of the WikiQA training data to tune hyper-parameters for our model and select the best hyper-parameters for all the datasets [25]. We employ Adam optimizer to train the model with a learning rate of $1e$-5 and a batch size of 64. We set 400 for the hidden vector sizes for all the feed-forward networks, $L = 2$ for the number of the GCN layers. We use Pytorch version 1.7.1 and Huggingface Transformers version 3.5.1 To implement the models. We use the NLTK library version 3.5 [4] to preprocess the data and remove stopwords. The model performance is obtained over three runs with random seeds.

Evaluation Metrics. We measure the model performance using the following standard metrics: Precision-at-1 (P@1) and Mean Average Precision (MAP) on the entire set of answer candidates for each question.

Performance Comparison. We compare our proposed model with TANDA [13], which is the current state-of-the-art model. Table 2 shows the performance comparison between the models on two settings: i) using a non-finetuned RoBERTa-Base encoder, and ii) using a fine-tuned RoBERTa-Base encoder. The non-finetuned RoBERTa-Base is obtained from [32] while the other is produced by fine-tuning TANDA on the ASNQ dataset [13]. As can be seen from the table, all the models benefit from using the fine-tuned RoBERTa-Base encoder. Across the two settings, our model outperforms the previous models by large margins, demonstrating its effectiveness for the task.

Table 2. Performance comparison on WikiQA and WDRASS, * indicates results reported by [25].

Model	WikiQA				WDRASS	
	w/o ASNQ		with ASNQ		with ASNQ	
	P@1	MAP	P@1	MAP	P@1	MAP
TANDA	63.24*	75.00*	78.67*	86.74*	54.60	63.50
Ours	**74.16**	**83.29**	**83.77**	**89.28**	**55.9**	61.8

In Table 2, we show the performance of our proposed model compared to TANDA on the WDRASS test set. As we can see, our knowledge retriever significantly improves the performance for P@1 score, however, decreases the performance for MAP score. We attribute this to the fact that questions in WDRASS dataset usually have more than 1 correct answers for a single question while our model ranks the answer candidates individually. However, we note that the top-1 answer candidate is often the most helpful for the answering process.

3.2 Evaluation for Knowledge-Aware Answer Generation

Experimental Setup

Dataset. We acquire the evaluation data as follows. First, we randomly select 2,000 questions from the MS MARCO QA NLG test set. For each question, we rank all the context passages using our model trained on WDRASS to obtain the top 5 candidates. We then concatenate the question and candidates to form the input, which is used to generate the predicted answer.

Evaluation Metrics. We employ widely-used evaluation metrics, including ROUGE [29], BLEU [39], and BERTScore [68], for assessing the quality of generated answers in comparison to human-written natural answers. These metrics are commonly applied to standard text generation tasks such as summarization [67], machine translation [54], and answer generation [42].

It is important to note that these metrics have their own limitations; however, these can be mitigated by providing more and higher-quality reference texts [5]. In the context of answer generation, we enhance the reliability of these measurements by employing human-written answers as references. Specifically, annotators create the reference answers used in this benchmark after being provided with the candidate responses.

Performance Comparison. Table 3 presents a comparison of three different configurations of KARP with GenQA model in terms of BLEU, RougeL, and BERTScore metrics.

The results demonstrate that all three KARP configurations outperform the GenQA model across all evaluation metrics. The best-performing configuration (config 2) achieves a BLEU score of 39.4, a RougeL score of 0.608, and a BERTScore of 0.752. These results indicate that KARP offers a significant improvement over the GenQA

Table 3. Comparison of our three KARP models trained with different hyper-parameter settings to GenQA [17].

Model	BLEU	RougeL	BERTScore
GenQA [17]	14.6	0.518	0.698
KARP (config 1)	38.3	0.632	0.762
KARP (config 2)	39.4	0.608	0.752
KARP (config 3)	38.9	0.604	0.750

model in the context of answer generation, which we attribute to our specialized fine-tuning strategy for QA.

3.3 End-to-End Evaluation for Knowledge-Aware Response Planning

In this section, we evaluate KARP in an end-to-end industry-scale scenario.

Experimental Setup. We outline the experimental setup to evaluate the end-to-end performance of KARP in a web-scale scenario, involving tens of millions of web documents. The configuration allows us to study the scalability and effectiveness of our approach in a real-world, large-scale setting.

Web Document Collection. We constructed a large collection of web data, comprising documents and passages, to facilitate the development of knowledge retrieval for end-to-end system evaluation. This resource enables us to assess the impact of our work in an industry-scale ODQA setting. We selected English web documents from the top 5,000 domains, including Wikipedia, from Common Crawl's 2019 and 2020 releases. The pages were split into passages following the DPR procedure [22], limiting passage length to 200 tokens while maintaining sentence boundaries. This produced a collection of roughly 100 million documents and 130 million passages. From this, we built (i) a standard Lucene/Elasticsearch index and (ii) a neural-based DPR index [22].

Web-Scale Knowledge Retrieval. For each question, we retrieved up to 1,000 documents/passages using both indexes. We then rank the passages and applied our knowledge retriever to select relevant passages. We used top $K = 5$ candidates as external knowledge for a question.

Question Sampling. We randomly selected 2,000 questions from WDRASS test set as it shows to represent natural questions extracted from the Web. In addition, the questions were also manually labeled.

Baselines. We employ GenQA [17] as our main baseline in this experiment. We compare the performance of our system obtained by our proposed fine-tuning strategy and the standard fine-tuning (i.e., combining all datasets for finetuning) in a data parity setting.

Evaluation Metrics. We evaluate the performance of the end-to-end QA system using accuracy metrics, i.e., the percentage of questions that were answered satisfactorily. Additionally, we define a correct answer as one that must not only be factually accurate, but also expressed in a natural and fluent manner. Answers that are too verbose or oddly phrased are considered unsatisfactory.

Performance Comparison. The result show in the following Table 4.

Table 4. Relative accuracy of different QA settings: TANDA [13], GenQA [17], and our proposed frame work for KARP in two data configurations: MS MARCO (data parity) and OKQA.

Model	Accuracy
TANDA [13]	*baseline*
GenQA [17]	+2.20%
KARP → MS MARCO	+6.20%
KARP → OKQA	+7.40%

Table 4 presents the relative accuracy of different QA settings, including TANDA [13], GenQA [17], and our proposed KARP with two data configurations: MS MARCO (data parity) and (robust fine-tuning). From the table, we observe that GenQA outperforms TANDA by 2.20%. Our proposed KARP model achieves even better results, with a 6.20% increase in accuracy when using the MS MARCO data configuration and a 7.40% increase in accuracy when using OKQA configuration. This demonstrates the effectiveness of our proposed KARP model in various data settings.

4 Related Work

Large Language Models (LLMs). LLMs have transformed NLP technologies with the advent of the Transformer architecture [54]. Two fundamental pre-training objectives, Masked Language Modeling (MLM) and Causal Language Modeling (CLM), underpin the success of these models. MLM, introduced by BERT [10], predicts masked tokens in a sentence using surrounding context, enabling LLMs to learn bidirectional representations that excel in various NLP tasks. In contrast, CLM, exemplified by GPT [40], predicts the next token in a sequence given its preceding context, showing remarkable success in text generation and other downstream applications [21,41,42]. In this paper, we leverage the CLM architecture for its language generation capabilities to enhance QA performance.

General Question Answering Using LLM. A standard QA system consists of (i) a retrieval engine that returns relevant knowledge and (ii) a model that generates a response addressing the question, either through selection [13,50,66] or abstractive summarization of the top-selected answers [12,17,36]. In particular, recent summarization-based approaches, e.g., GenQA [12,17,36], are highly susceptible to hallucination due to the absence of special treatment of irrelevant candidates, which commonly appear among the top-ranked options. As a result, the generated answer may seem plausible but could be factually incorrect [19,44,45,51,55,61,70,71]. Even though its original goal is to generate more natural answers, GenQA [12,17,36] can be considered as a method to ground LLMs for QA as it decodes an answer from the concatenation of both question and answer candidates. This approach, however, requires good answer candidates and careful finetuning to reduce hallucinations.

We propose, instead, a novel generation-based approach that leverages the emerging language reasoning capabilities of Large Language Models (LLMs) [40] to enhance quality of generated answers. In particular, KARP is designed to mitigate the reliance on oracle data by making use of the context, such as all choices in multiple-choice QA, instead of a correct answer alone, i.e., the correct choice. The experiments demonstrated that our proposed framework for KARP is highly resilient to noisy input data, and bring about broader application across different QA tasks.

Fine-tuning Strategies for LLMs. Several fine-tuning strategies have been specifically proposed for large language models (LLMs). These strategies can be broadly categorized into two groups: architecture-centric and data-centric. (i) Architecture-centric fine-tuning aims to improve the model's robustness and adaptability by modifying hyper-parameters across layers. Gradual unfreezing [16] is one example, involving sequential fine-tuning of model layers to prevent catastrophic forgetting and better adapt to downstream tasks. Layer-wise learning rate decay [40] is another example, where different learning rates are assigned to various layers to enable more refined adaptation to the target task. (ii) Data-centric fine-tuning, on the other hand, concentrates on leveraging data from different sources or intermediate tasks to enhance model performance. Sequential fine-tuning [13,14] involves training the model on intermediate tasks before the final target task, improving its performance on the latter. Combining several related datasets for multi-task fine-tuning has also been shown to improve performance on the target task [31]. Our work is related to data-centric fine-tuning. In particular, we propose a novel strategy specifically designed for the question answering context. By leveraging both external knowledge and intrinsic parametric knowledge of LLMs, our approach aims to enhance the quality of generated answers in QA tasks.

5 Conclusion

In this paper, we presented a novel framework powered by large language models (LLMs) for KARP. To that end, we proposed an efficient fine-tuning strategy for KARP that leverages (i) the emergent language reasoning abilities of LLMs and (ii) general question answering advances, including modelings and resources. Our experimental results show that KARP improves the state of the art in general QA tasks and outperforms vanilla fine-tuning of LLMs in a dataset-parity setting. This research highlights the significance of leveraging the intrinsic parametric knowledge of LLMs rather than relying solely on conventional sequence-to-sequence fine-tuning, in order to improve their performance in question answering tasks.

References

1. Bai, Y., et al.: Training a helpful and harmless assistant with reinforcement learning from human feedback. arXiv preprint arXiv:2204.05862 (2022)
2. Bao, J., Duan, N., Yan, Z., Zhou, M., Zhao, T.: Constraint-based question answering with knowledge graph. In: Proceedings of COLING 2016, the 26th International Conference on Computational Linguistics: Technical Papers, pp. 2503–2514 (2016)
3. Bao, J., Duan, N., Zhou, M., Zhao, T.: Knowledge-based question answering as machine translation. In: Proceedings of the 52nd Annual Meeting of the Association for Computational Linguistics (Volume 1: Long Papers), pp. 967–976 (2014)
4. Bird, S., Klein, E., Loper, E.: Natural Language Processing with Python: Analyzing Text with the Natural Language Toolkit. O'Reilly Media, Inc. (2009)
5. Callison-Burch, C., Osborne, M., Koehn, P.: Re-evaluating the role of Bleu in machine translation research. In: 11th Conference of the European Chapter of the Association for Computational Linguistics, pp. 249–256. Association for Computational Linguistics, Trento (April 2006)
6. Chen, D., Fisch, A., Weston, J., Bordes, A.: Reading wikipedia to answer open-domain questions. arXiv preprint arXiv:1704.00051 (2017)
7. Chen, D., Yih, W.T.: Open-domain question answering. In: Proceedings of the 58th Annual Meeting of the Association for Computational Linguistics: Tutorial Abstracts, pp. 34–37 (2020)
8. Clark, P., et al.: Combining retrieval, statistics, and inference to answer elementary science questions. Proc. AAAI Conf. Artif. Intell. **30**(1) (2016). https://doi.org/10.1609/aaai.v30i1.10325
9. Cuturi, M.: Sinkhorn distances: lightspeed computation of optimal transport. Adv. Neural Inf. Process. Syst. **26** (2013)
10. Devlin, J., Chang, M.W., Lee, K., Toutanova, K.: BERT: pre-training of deep bidirectional transformers for language understanding. In: Proceedings of the 2019 Conference of the North American Chapter of the Association for Computational Linguistics: Human Language Technologies, Volume 1 (Long and Short Papers), pp. 4171–4186. Association for Computational Linguistics, Minneapolis (2019). https://doi.org/10.18653/v1/N19-1423
11. FitzGerald, J.G.M., et al.: Alexa teacher model: pretraining and distilling multi-billion-parameter encoders for natural language understanding systems. In: KDD 2022 (2022)
12. Gabburo, M., Koncel-Kedziorski, R., Garg, S., Soldaini, L., Moschitti, A.: Knowledge transfer from answer ranking to answer generation. In: Proceedings of the 2022 Conference on Empirical Methods in Natural Language Processing. pp. 9481–9495. Association for Computational Linguistics, Abu Dhabi (2022)
13. Garg, S., Vu, T., Moschitti, A.: Tanda: Transfer and adapt pre-trained transformer models for answer sentence selection. Proc. AAAI Conf. Artif. Intell. **34**(05), 7780–7788 (2020). https://doi.org/10.1609/aaai.v34i05.6282
14. Gururangan, S., et al.: Don't stop pretraining: adapt language models to domains and tasks. In: Proceedings of the 58th Annual Meeting of the Association for Computational Linguistics. pp. 8342–8360. Association for Computational Linguistics (2020). https://doi.org/10.18653/v1/2020.acl-main.740
15. Hermann, K.M., et al.: Teaching machines to read and comprehend. Adv. Neural Inf. Process. Syst. **28** (2015)
16. Howard, J., Ruder, S.: Universal language model fine-tuning for text classification. In: Proceedings of the 56th Annual Meeting of the Association for Computational Linguistics (Volume 1: Long Papers), pp. 328–339. Association for Computational Linguistics, Melbourne (2018). https://doi.org/10.18653/v1/P18-1031

17. Hsu, C.C., Lind, E., Soldaini, L., Moschitti, A.: Answer generation for retrieval-based question answering systems. In: Findings of the Association for Computational Linguistics: ACL-IJCNLP 2021, pp. 4276–4282. Association for Computational Linguistics (2021). https://doi.org/10.18653/v1/2021.findings-acl.374
18. Izacard, G., Grave, E.: Leveraging passage retrieval with generative models for open domain question answering. In: Proceedings of the 16th Conference of the European Chapter of the Association for Computational Linguistics: Main Volume, pp. 874–880. Association for Computational Linguistics (2021). https://doi.org/10.18653/v1/2021.eacl-main.74
19. Ji, Z., et al.: Survey of hallucination in natural language generation. ACM Comput. Surv. **55**(12) (2023). https://doi.org/10.1145/3571730
20. Jiang, Z., Araki, J., Ding, H., Neubig, G.: Understanding and improving zero-shot multi-hop reasoning in generative question answering. In: Proceedings of the 29th International Conference on Computational Linguistics, pp. 1765–1775. International Committee on Computational Linguistics, Gyeongju (Oct 2022)
21. Kaplan, J., et al.: Scaling laws for neural language models. arXiv preprint arXiv:2001.08361 (2020)
22. Karpukhin, V., et al.: Dense passage retrieval for open-domain question answering. In: Proceedings of the 2020 Conference on Empirical Methods in Natural Language Processing (EMNLP), pp. 6769–6781. Association for Computational Linguistics (2020). https://doi.org/10.18653/v1/2020.emnlp-main.550
23. Khashabi, D., et al.: UNIFIEDQA: crossing format boundaries with a single QA system. In: Findings of the Association for Computational Linguistics: EMNLP 2020, pp. 1896–1907. Association for Computational Linguistics (2020). https://doi.org/10.18653/v1/2020.findings-emnlp.171
24. Kipf, T.N., Welling, M.: Semi-supervised classification with graph convolutional networks. In: Proceedings of the 5th International Conference on Learning Representations (2017)
25. Lauriola, I., Moschitti, A.: Answer sentence selection using local and global context in transformer models. In: Hiemstra, D., Moens, M.-F., Mothe, J., Perego, R., Potthast, M., Sebastiani, F. (eds.) ECIR 2021. LNCS, vol. 12656, pp. 298–312. Springer, Cham (2021). https://doi.org/10.1007/978-3-030-72113-8_20
26. Lewis, M., Fan, A.: Generative question answering: learning to answer the whole question. In: International Conference on Learning Representations (2019)
27. Lewis, M., et al.: BART: denoising sequence-to-sequence pre-training for natural language generation, translation, and comprehension. In: Proceedings of the 58th Annual Meeting of the Association for Computational Linguistics, pp. 7871–7880. Association for Computational Linguistics (2020). https://doi.org/10.18653/v1/2020.acl-main.703
28. Lin, B., et al.: Dependency parsing via sequence generation. In: Findings of the Association for Computational Linguistics: EMNLP 2022, pp. 7339–7353. Association for Computational Linguistics, Abu Dhabi (Dec 2022)
29. Lin, C.Y.: ROUGE: a package for automatic evaluation of summaries. In: Text Summarization Branches Out, pp. 74–81. Association for Computational Linguistics, Barcelona (July 2004)
30. Liu, J., Chen, Y., Liu, K., Bi, W., Liu, X.: Event extraction as machine reading comprehension. In: Proceedings of the 2020 Conference on Empirical Methods in Natural Language Processing (EMNLP), pp. 1641–1651. Association for Computational Linguistics (2020). https://doi.org/10.18653/v1/2020.emnlp-main.128
31. Liu, X., He, P., Chen, W., Gao, J.: Multi-task deep neural networks for natural language understanding. In: Proceedings of the 57th Annual Meeting of the Association for Computational Linguistics, pp. 4487–4496. Association for Computational Linguistics, Florence (2019). https://doi.org/10.18653/v1/P19-1441

32. Liu, Y., et al.: Roberta: a robustly optimized bert pretraining approach. arXiv preprint arXiv:1907.11692 (2019)
33. Lu, Y., et al.: Text2Event: controllable sequence-to-structure generation for end-to-end event extraction. In: Proceedings of the 59th Annual Meeting of the Association for Computational Linguistics and the 11th International Joint Conference on Natural Language Processing (Volume 1: Long Papers), pp. 2795–2806. Association for Computational Linguistics (2021). https://doi.org/10.18653/v1/2021.acl-long.217
34. Maynez, J., Narayan, S., Bohnet, B., McDonald, R.: On faithfulness and factuality in abstractive summarization. In: Proceedings of the 58th Annual Meeting of the Association for Computational Linguistics, pp. 1906–1919. Association for Computational Linguistics (2020). https://doi.org/10.18653/v1/2020.acl-main.173
35. Monge, G.: Mémoire sur la théorie des déblais et des remblais. Mem. Math. Phys. Acad. Royale Sci. 666–704 (1781)
36. Muller, B., Soldaini, L., Koncel-Kedziorski, R., Lind, E., Moschitti, A.: Cross-lingual open-domain question answering with answer sentence generation. In: Proceedings of the 2nd Conference of the Asia-Pacific Chapter of the Association for Computational Linguistics and the 12th International Joint Conference on Natural Language Processing (Volume 1: Long Papers), pp. 337–353. Association for Computational Linguistics (2022)
37. Nakano, R., et al.: Webgpt: browser-assisted question-answering with human feedback. arXiv preprint arXiv:2112.09332 (2021)
38. Nguyen, T., et al.: Ms marco: a human generated machine reading comprehension dataset (Nov 2016)
39. Papineni, K., Roukos, S., Ward, T., Zhu, W.J.: Bleu: a method for automatic evaluation of machine translation. In: Proceedings of the 40th Annual Meeting of the Association for Computational Linguistics, pp. 311–318. Association for Computational Linguistics, Philadelphia (2002). https://doi.org/10.3115/1073083.1073135
40. Radford, A., Narasimhan, K., Salimans, T., Sutskever, I., et al.: Improving language understanding by generative pre-training (2018)
41. Radford, A., Wu, J., Child, R., Luan, D., Amodei, D., Sutskever, I.: Language models are unsupervised multitask learners (2019)
42. Raffel, C., et al.: Exploring the limits of transfer learning with a unified text-to-text transformer. J. Mach. Learn. Res. **21**(1) (2020)
43. Rajpurkar, P., Zhang, J., Lopyrev, K., Liang, P.: SQuAD: 100,000+ questions for machine comprehension of text. In: Proceedings of the 2016 Conference on Empirical Methods in Natural Language Processing, pp. 2383–2392. Association for Computational Linguistics, Austin (2016). https://doi.org/10.18653/v1/D16-1264
44. Raunak, V., Menezes, A., Junczys-Dowmunt, M.: The curious case of hallucinations in neural machine translation. In: Proceedings of the 2021 Conference of the North American Chapter of the Association for Computational Linguistics: Human Language Technologies, pp. 1172–1183. Association for Computational Linguistics (2021). https://doi.org/10.18653/v1/2021.naacl-main.92
45. Rebuffel, C., Roberti, M., Soulier, L., Scoutheeten, G., Cancelliere, R., Gallinari, P.: Controlling hallucinations at word level in data-to-text generation. arXiv preprint arXiv:2102.02810 (2021)
46. Richardson, M., Burges, C.J., Renshaw, E.: MCTest: a challenge dataset for the open-domain machine comprehension of text. In: Proceedings of the 2013 Conference on Empirical Methods in Natural Language Processing, pp. 193–203. Association for Computational Linguistics, Seattle (Oct 2013)
47. Roberts, A., Raffel, C., Shazeer, N.: How much knowledge can you pack into the parameters of a language model? In: Proceedings of the 2020 Conference on Empirical Methods

in Natural Language Processing (EMNLP), pp. 5418–5426. Association for Computational Linguistics (2020). https://doi.org/10.18653/v1/2020.emnlp-main.437

48. Roller, S., et al.: Recipes for building an open-domain chatbot. In: Proceedings of the 16th Conference of the European Chapter of the Association for Computational Linguistics: Main Volume, pp. 300–325. Association for Computational Linguistics (2021). https://doi.org/10.18653/v1/2021.eacl-main.24
49. Saxena, A., Chakrabarti, S., Talukdar, P.: Question answering over temporal knowledge graphs. In: Proceedings of the 59th Annual Meeting of the Association for Computational Linguistics and the 11th International Joint Conference on Natural Language Processing (Volume 1: Long Papers), pp. 6663–6676. Association for Computational Linguistics (2021). https://doi.org/10.18653/v1/2021.acl-long.520
50. Severyn, A., Moschitti, A.: Learning to rank short text pairs with convolutional deep neural networks. In: Proceedings of the 38th International ACM SIGIR Conference on Research and Development in Information Retrieval, pp. 373–382 (2015)
51. Shuster, K., Poff, S., Chen, M., Kiela, D., Weston, J.: Retrieval augmentation reduces hallucination in conversation. In: Findings of the Association for Computational Linguistics: EMNLP 2021, pp. 3784–3803. Association for Computational Linguistics, Punta Cana (2021). https://doi.org/10.18653/v1/2021.findings-emnlp.320
52. Sinkhorn, R., Knopp, P.: Concerning nonnegative matrices and doubly stochastic matrices. Pacific J. Math. **21**(2), 343–348 (1967)
53. Soltan, S., et al.: Alexatm 20b: few-shot learning using a large-scale multilingual seq2seq model. arXiv (2022)
54. Vaswani, A., et al.: Attention is all you need. In: Guyon, I., et al. (eds.) Advances in Neural Information Processing Systems, vol. 30. Curran Associates, Inc. (2017)
55. Wang, C., Sennrich, R.: On exposure bias, hallucination and domain shift in neural machine translation. In: Proceedings of the 58th Annual Meeting of the Association for Computational Linguistics, pp. 3544–3552. Association for Computational Linguistics (2020). https://doi.org/10.18653/v1/2020.acl-main.326
56. Wang, W., Yang, N., Wei, F., Chang, B., Zhou, M.: Gated self-matching networks for reading comprehension and question answering. In: Proceedings of the 55th Annual Meeting of the Association for Computational Linguistics (Volume 1: Long Papers), pp. 189–198 (2017)
57. Wang, Y., et al.: Super-NaturalInstructions: generalization via declarative instructions on 1600+ NLP tasks. In: Proceedings of the 2022 Conference on Empirical Methods in Natural Language Processing, pp. 5085–5109. Association for Computational Linguistics, Abu Dhabi (Dec 2022)
58. Wei, J., et al.: Emergent abilities of large language models. Trans. Mach. Learn. Res. (2022). Survey Certification
59. Weston, J., et al.: Towards ai-complete question answering: a set of prerequisite toy tasks. arXiv preprint arXiv:1502.05698 (2015)
60. Wiseman, S., Rush, A.M.: Sequence-to-sequence learning as beam-search optimization. In: Proceedings of the 2016 Conference on Empirical Methods in Natural Language Processing, pp. 1296–1306. Association for Computational Linguistics, Austin (2016). https://doi.org/10.18653/v1/D16-1137
61. Xiao, Y., Wang, W.Y.: On hallucination and predictive uncertainty in conditional language generation. In: Proceedings of the 16th Conference of the European Chapter of the Association for Computational Linguistics: Main Volume, pp. 2734–2744. Association for Computational Linguistics (2021). https://doi.org/10.18653/v1/2021.eacl-main.236
62. Xu, J., et al.: Asking clarification questions in knowledge-based question answering. In: Proceedings of the 2019 Conference on Empirical Methods in Natural Language Processing and the 9th International Joint Conference on Natural Language Processing (EMNLP-IJCNLP), pp. 1618–1629 (2019)

63. Yan, H., Gui, T., Dai, J., Guo, Q., Zhang, Z., Qiu, X.: A unified generative framework for various NER subtasks. In: Proceedings of the 59th Annual Meeting of the Association for Computational Linguistics and the 11th International Joint Conference on Natural Language Processing (Volume 1: Long Papers), pp. 5808–5822. Association for Computational Linguistics (2021). https://doi.org/10.18653/v1/2021.acl-long.451
64. Yang, W., et al.: End-to-end open-domain question answering with BERTserini. In: Proceedings of the 2019 Conference of the North American Chapter of the Association for Computational Linguistics (Demonstrations), pp. 72–77. Association for Computational Linguistics, Minneapolis (2019). https://doi.org/10.18653/v1/N19-4013
65. Yang, Y., Yih, W.T., Meek, C.: Wikiqa: a challenge dataset for open-domain question answering. In: Proceedings of the 2015 Conference on Empirical Methods in Natural Language Pocessing, pp. 2013–2018 (2015)
66. Yoon, S., Dernoncourt, F., Kim, D.S., Bui, T., Jung, K.: A compare-aggregate model with latent clustering for answer selection. In: Proceedings of the 28th ACM International Conference on Information and Knowledge Management, pp. 2093–2096 (2019)
67. Zhang, J., Zhao, Y., Saleh, M., Liu, P.: PEGASUS: pre-training with extracted gap-sentences for abstractive summarization. In: III H.D., Singh A. (eds.) Proceedings of the 37th International Conference on Machine Learning. Proceedings of Machine Learning Research, vol. 119, pp. 11328–11339. PMLR (2020)
68. Zhang, T., Kishore, V., Wu, F., Weinberger, K.Q., Artzi, Y.: Bertscore: evaluating text generation with bert. In: International Conference on Learning Representations (2020)
69. Zhang, Z., Vu, T., Gandhi, S., Chadha, A., Moschitti, A.: Wdrass: a web-scale dataset for document retrieval and answer sentence selection. In: Proceedings of the 31st ACM International Conference on Information & Knowledge Management, pp. 4707–4711 (2022)
70. Zhao, Z., Cohen, S.B., Webber, B.: Reducing quantity hallucinations in abstractive summarization. In: Findings of the Association for Computational Linguistics: EMNLP 2020, pp. 2237–2249. Association for Computational Linguistics (2020). https://doi.org/10.18653/v1/2020.findings-emnlp.203
71. Zhou, C., et al.: Detecting hallucinated content in conditional neural sequence generation. In: Findings of the Association for Computational Linguistics: ACL-IJCNLP 2021, pp. 1393–1404. Association for Computational Linguistics (2021). https://doi.org/10.18653/v1/2021.findings-acl.120

Attentive Multi-Layer Perceptron for Non-autoregressive Generation

Shuyang Jiang[1], Jun Zhang[2], Jiangtao Feng[2], Lin Zheng[3], and Lingpeng Kong[3](✉)

[1] Shanghai Jiao Tong University, Shanghai, China
jiangshuyang@sjtu.edu.cn
[2] Shanghai Artificial Intelligence Laboratory, Shanghai, China
zhangjun@pjlab.org.cn
[3] The University of Hong Kong, Hong Kong, China
linzheng@connect.hku.hk, lpk@cs.hku.hk

Abstract. Autoregressive (AR) generation almost dominates sequence generation for its efficacy. Recently, non-autoregressive (NAR) generation gains increasing popularity for its efficiency and growing efficacy. However, its efficiency is still bottlenecked by quadratic complexity in sequence lengths, which is prohibitive for scaling to long sequence generation and few works have been done to mitigate this problem. In this paper, we propose a novel MLP variant, **A**ttentive **M**ulti-**L**ayer **P**erceptron (AMLP), to produce a generation model with linear time and space complexity. Different from classic MLP with static and learnable projection matrices, AMLP leverages adaptive projections computed from inputs in an attentive mode. The sample-aware adaptive projections enable communications among tokens in a sequence, and model the measurement between the query and key space. Furthermore, we marry AMLP with popular NAR models, deriving a highly efficient NAR-AMLP architecture with linear time and space complexity. Empirical results show that such marriage architecture surpasses competitive efficient NAR models, by a significant margin on text-to-speech synthesis and machine translation. We also test AMLP's self- and cross-attention ability separately with extensive ablation experiments, and find them comparable or even superior to the other efficient models. The efficiency analysis further shows that AMLP extremely reduces the memory cost against vanilla non-autoregressive models for long sequences.

Keywords: AMLP · Multi-Layer Perceptron · Attention Mechanism · Non-Autoregressive Model

1 Introduction

Attention-based sequence generation methods have achieved great success and gained increasing popularity in machine learning [11,30,35,53]. A large body of research in neural architectures has been devoted to the autoregressive (AR)

© The Author(s), under exclusive license to Springer Nature Switzerland AG 2023
D. Koutra et al. (Eds.): ECML PKDD 2023, LNAI 14170, pp. 612–629, 2023.
https://doi.org/10.1007/978-3-031-43415-0_36

method [40,41], where tokens are generated one after another in an iterative manner. The computational overhead in decoding can thus be prohibitive, especially for long sequences. Recently, non-autoregressive (NAR) generation attracts more attention for its efficiency and growing efficacy [7,17,18,42,43,46]. In a non-autoregressive model, the decoder generates the target sequence all at once, significantly reducing its computational overhead at the inference stage. Nevertheless, relatively little research has been done on the attention architecture in non-autoregressive models. In particular, the conventionally adopted softmax attention comes with a quadratic time and memory cost. It is therefore still difficult to scale up non-autoregressive models to long sequence generation tasks.

In this paper, we propose Attentive Multi-Layer Perceptron (§2.2; AMLP) to integrate the attention mechanism with the multi-layer perceptron (MLP) in non-autoregressive architecture, resulting in a fully parallelizable sequence generation model with linear complexity. Unlike the widely-used MLP whose weights are invariant across different sequences, we compute the weights in AMLP through adaptive projections from (multiple) input tokens and model their interactions in an attentive manner. Specifically, we put forward two methods (§2.3) to compute the adaptive projections in AMLP, which implicitly model the association between the query and key space. We utilize the simplicity and efficiency of MLP while obtaining the strong modeling capability of AMLP for input tokens' communication. Finally, we present a hybrid NAR-AMLP model (§2.4) to achieve both linear complexity and high parallelism.

We evaluate the AMLP architecture on text-to-speech synthesis for a relatively long sequence scenario and machine translation for a relatively short sequence scenario. Experiments show that AMLP achieves more superior scores with objective measurements compared with the strong softmax attention counterpart (§3.1) on text-to-speech synthesis, with less computational cost (§3.3). On machine translation, AMLP performs competitive with vanilla attention but achieves the best result among efficient NAR and AR models with linear complexity (§3.1). Further, we test the self- and cross-attention ability of AMLP on super resolution and long sequence time-series forecasting tasks, respectively. Empirical results show that AMLP is on par with other efficient attention in self-attention and achieves the best performance in cross-attention scenarios (§3.2). Additionally, when scaling to long sequence, AMLP reduces the memory footprint substantially and further improves the inference speed in NAR models (§3.3). The code is available in https://github.com/Shark-NLP/AttentiveMLP.

2 Non-autoregressive Generation with Attentive MLP

In this section, we first give a brief introduction to autoregressive (AR) and non-autoregressive (NAR) generation, and then delve into the nuances that differentiate the attention mechanisms utilized in autoregressive (AR) and non-autoregressive (NAR) models. After that, we present the AMLP architecture to model the communication among sequence tokens. Finally, we build up an NAR-AMLP architecture with linear time and space complexity.

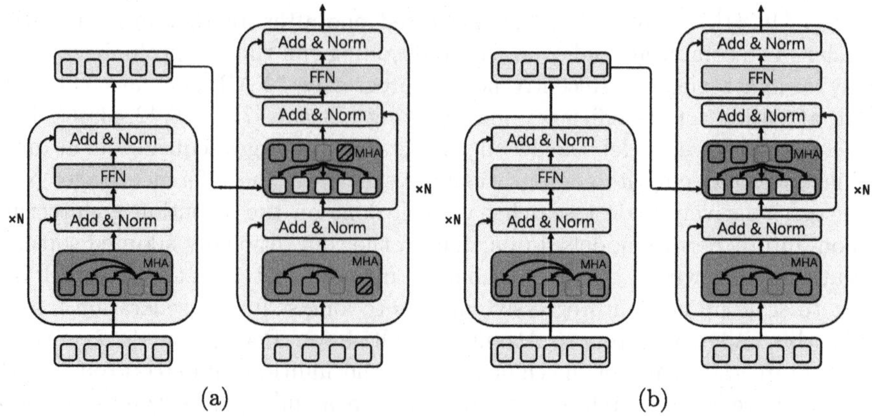

Fig. 1. AR (a) and NAR (b) encoder-decoder architectures. "MHA" stands for multi-head attention. Blocks with red rims represent the current state token. Shaded blocks represent future tokens that are invisible to the current state. (Color figure online)

2.1 Background: Autoregressive and Non-autoregressive Generation

Given a source sequence $X_{1:m}$, conditional sequence generation targets to predict a target sequence $Y_{1:n}$ by modeling the conditional probability $p(Y|X)$. Autoregressive generation decomposes the probability $p(Y|X)$ as:

$$p(Y|X) = \prod_{i=1..n} p(Y_i|Y_{<i}, X), Y_{<1} = \emptyset. \quad (1)$$

which is implemented as a typical encoder-decoder architecture shown in Fig. 1a. Although such decomposition is proved effective, it suffers from two main drawbacks: efficiency and exposure bias. On the one hand, the autoregressive decoding process, where each token depends on the previous predicted ones, prevents the model from fast inference in usage. On the other hand, teacher-forcing exposes ground truth tokens in network inputs during the training process, where the exposed tokens are unable to observe in inference. Such exposure creates an inconsistency between the training and inference, and harms the prediction quality.

Recently, non-autoregressive generation, depicted as Fig. 1b, shows its capability of sequence modeling in terms of both efficiency and efficacy, which decomposes the conditional probability $p(Y|X)$ via a Naïve Bayes assumption:

$$p(Y|X) = \prod_{i=1..n} p(Y_i|X) \quad (2)$$

The NAR decomposition enables parallel decoding for each token, and speeds up the inference process substantially. Although NAR generation is much faster than AR generation, its speed is still limited by the $O\left(n^2 + nm + m^2\right)$ time complexity of the multi-head softmax attention module. This is especially problematic in modeling long sequences.

Attention Types in AR and NAR Models. Although autoregressive and non-autoregressive models differ from each other in sequence generation paradigms, their underlying attention mechanisms in their architectures are also different. The token-by-token generation of AR models requires a causal decoder that forces tokens to attend to only previous features. A typical causal decoder utilizes causal softmax attentions both in self-attention and cross-attention. The attention causality entails that during the computation, it is important to ensure that the query token does not attend to the context on its right side, just as the shaded blocks in Fig. 1a. In contrast, the NAR model, which allows for parallel generation of the output sequence and global contextualization using attention, employs a noncausal decoder in Fig. 1b. The self-attention in the NAR model can attend to both side contexts of a given token, which makes it suitable for tasks that require a broader contextual understanding. NAR architectures also reduce the design restrictions on cross-attention, making query tokens attend to key tokens in a holistic view. This modeling feature of attention emphasizes both global and local contextualization modeling for attention modules. In practice, causality in vanilla softmax self-attention is ensured by leveraging a lower triangular mask in AR models, while linearized attention requires more sophisticated implementation. Since no causality is required in NAR models, designing an efficient attention mechanism is much more flexible.

2.2 Attentive Multi-Layer Perceptron

Modeling interactions between tokens is crucial and challenging in sequence generation. Transformer [53] stacks the MLP, which aims to learn features of individual tokens, on top of the attention block, which is responsible for modeling the communication within the sequence. In AR generation, the attention needs to be recomputed for each time step through the recurrent process, as the key and value set is changing. However, this procedure is non-causal in NAR generation. We therefore are able to integrate the modeling of token interactions into the MLP architecture and make the whole architecture fully parallelizable and more efficient.

Given a sequence representation $\mathbf{X} \in \mathbb{R}^{n \times d}$, where n is the sequence length and d is dimensionality of the feature space, the conventional MLP models the feature of individual token $\mathbf{X}_i \in \mathbb{R}^d$ as:

$$\mathrm{MLP}(\mathbf{X}_i) = \sigma(\mathbf{X}_i W_1) W_2 \tag{3}$$

where $W_1 \in \mathbb{R}^{d \times d_h}$, $W_2 \in \mathbb{R}^{d_h \times d}$ are learnable parameters d_h is the dimensionality of hidden space. $\sigma(\cdot)$ is a non-linear activation function such as ReLU$(\cdot)$. However, it disables the communication between tokens in the sequence, and prevents the model from learning contextualized token representations.

A widely-used approach to enable communication between each token in a sequence is the attention mechanism [53]. Vanilla attention learns to incorporate source sequence features $\mathbf{K}, \mathbf{V} \in \mathbb{R}^{m \times d}$ into target $\mathbf{Q} \in \mathbb{R}^{n \times d}$ with an attention matrix

$$\text{Attn}(\mathbf{Q}, \mathbf{K}, \mathbf{V}) = \text{softmax}(\mathbf{Q}\mathbf{K}^{\top})\mathbf{V} \tag{4}$$

where m, n are the source and target length respectively. Here we omit the input projections for $\mathbf{Q}, \mathbf{K}, \mathbf{V}$, the output projection, and the scaling factor $1/\sqrt{d}$ for simplicity.

The motivation of Attentive Multi-Layer Perceptron (AMLP) starts from the fact that the vanilla softmax attention can be viewed as a projection function as $\text{SA}(\cdot|\mathbf{K}, \mathbf{V}) : \mathbb{R}^{n \times d} \rightarrow \mathbb{R}^{n \times d}$ which projects the original $\mathbf{Q} \in \mathbb{R}^{n \times d}$ with $\mathbf{K}$ and $\mathbf{V}$ features as its context while preserving $\mathbf{Q}$'s shape. In vanilla attention, $\text{softmax}(\mathbf{Q}\mathbf{K}^{\top})$ is a softmax kernel which can be decomposed into a multiplication of two kernel functions: $\phi(\mathbf{Q}) \cdot \phi(\mathbf{K})^{\top}$, which is verified in Performer [10], cosFormer [44] and LARA [60]. Meanwhile, the low-rank factorization of the attention matrix, $\text{softmax}(\mathbf{Q}\mathbf{K}^{\top})$, does not impact the performance much, which is verified by Nyströmformer [57]. Based on their findings, we propose an alternative modeling solution by fusing key $\mathbf{K} \in \mathbb{R}^{m \times d}$ and value $\mathbf{V} \in \mathbb{R}^{m \times d}$ information into query $\mathbf{Q} \in \mathbb{R}^{n \times d}$, via a symmetric and positive semi-definite distance matrix $\mathbf{\Sigma} \in \mathbb{R}^{d \times d}$ on $\mathbf{Q}$ and $\mathbf{K}$ space. The contextualizing process on $\mathbf{Q}$ can be formulated as:

$$f(\mathbf{Q}; \mathbf{K}, \mathbf{V}) = \mathbf{Q}\mathbf{\Sigma}\mathbf{K}^{\top}\mathbf{V} \tag{5}$$

where $\mathbf{\Sigma}$ is computed from $\mathbf{Q}$ and $\mathbf{K}$.

With similar functionality to [10,57], the matrix $\mathbf{Q}\mathbf{\Sigma}\mathbf{K}^{\top}$ can also enjoy lower computation costs from low-rank approximation while maintaining strong modeling capability. Without taking any low-rank assumptions on input $\mathbf{Q}, \mathbf{K}$, we decompose the distance matrix as:

$$\mathbf{\Sigma} = \mathbf{U}\mathbf{\Lambda}\mathbf{U}^{\top} = \mathbf{U}\mathbf{\Lambda}^{\frac{1}{2}}\mathbf{\Lambda}^{\frac{1}{2}}\mathbf{U}^{\top} \approx \mathbf{U}\hat{\mathbf{\Lambda}}^{\frac{1}{2}}\hat{\mathbf{\Lambda}}^{\frac{1}{2}}\mathbf{U}^{\top} = (\mathbf{U}\hat{\mathbf{\Lambda}}^{\frac{1}{2}})(\mathbf{U}\hat{\mathbf{\Lambda}}^{\frac{1}{2}})^{\top} = \mathbf{L}\mathbf{L}^{\top} \tag{6}$$

where $\mathbf{U}$ is the orthogonal eigenvector of matrix and $\mathbf{\Lambda}$ is the diagonal eigenvalues matrix. $\hat{\mathbf{\Lambda}}$ here is an approximation to $\mathbf{\Lambda}$ by keeping largest-c eigen-values and masking the others with 0, where c is a hyper-parameter in AMLP. Thus we derive a decomposition equation $\mathbf{\Sigma} \approx \mathbf{L}\mathbf{L}^{\top}$ where $\mathbf{L} = \kappa(\mathbf{Q}, \mathbf{K})^{\top} \in \mathbb{R}^{d \times c}$ indicates a low-rank matrix. We will show two different methods for parameterization of $\mathbf{L}$, resulting in two different AMLP variants. We rewrite Eq. 5 by decomposing the distance matrix $\mathbf{\Sigma}$ as:

$$f(\mathbf{Q}, \mathbf{K}, \mathbf{V}) \approx \mathbf{Q}\mathbf{L}\mathbf{L}^{\top}\mathbf{K}^{\top}\mathbf{V} \tag{7}$$

Now Eq. 5 could be approximated with Eq. 7 by linearly projecting the original $\mathbf{Q}$ with adaptive weights twice. By reordering the computation and adding nonlinearity into Eq. 5, we derive a general form of AMLP model as:

$$\text{AMLP}(\mathbf{Q}; \mathbf{K}, \mathbf{V}) = \sigma_1(\mathbf{Q}W_{\mathbf{Q},\mathbf{K}})W_{\mathbf{Q},\mathbf{K},\mathbf{V}} \tag{8}$$

where the nonlinear function $\sigma_1(\cdot)$ can be adjusted arbitrarily. Equation 8 address the general form of AMLP, and the adaptive weights $W_{\mathbf{Q},\mathbf{K}}$ and $W_{\mathbf{Q},\mathbf{K},\mathbf{V}}$ can be

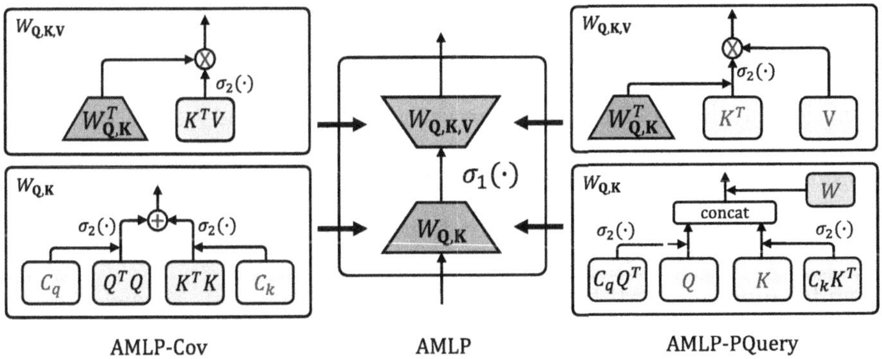

Fig. 2. Computation diagram of two AMLP variants. The middle part shows the computation of basic AMLP. The Left and right figures show the detailed computation of two adaptive weight matrics in AMLP-Cov and AMLP-PQuery.

speficified in various ways. Following the form of Eq. 8, we will further introduce two AMLP variants in § 2.3, by specifying $\mathbf{L} = W_{\mathbf{Q},\mathbf{K}} = \kappa(\mathbf{Q}, \mathbf{K})$, computational order and nonlinear function.

The computation of adaptive weights in AMLP fuses token-level communication, while MLP models tokens in a sequence independently. Therefore, AMLP enables the communication between tokens in a sequence. And different from vanilla softmax attention, AMLP utilizes a distance matrix $\mathbf{\Sigma}$ between $\mathbf{Q}$ and $\mathbf{K}$ spaces to fuse information among their contexts and outputs a contextualized $\mathbf{Q}$. Through this distance matrix, AMLP computes the similarity between $\mathbf{Q}$ and $\mathbf{K}$ like softmax attention, and leverages it to aggregate $\mathbf{V}$.

2.3 Parameterization

In this section, we describe two methods for the parameterization of two adaptive weight matrices $W_{\mathbf{Q},\mathbf{K}}$ and $W_{\mathbf{Q},\mathbf{K},\mathbf{V}}$. Figure 2 illustrates the computation graph of these two methods.[1]

Cross-covariance. We present AMLP-Cov, a variant that adopts cross-covariance to parameterize $W_{\mathbf{Q},\mathbf{K}}$ and $W_{\mathbf{Q},\mathbf{K},\mathbf{V}}$. One challenge of AMLP is to fuse information of $\mathbf{Q}, \mathbf{K}, \mathbf{V}$ of different shapes into static-shaped projection matrices $W_{\mathbf{Q},\mathbf{K}}$ and $W_{\mathbf{Q},\mathbf{K},\mathbf{V}}$. Inspired by [1], we propose to use $\mathbf{Q}, \mathbf{K}$'s covariance and the cross-covariance between $\mathbf{K}$ and $\mathbf{V}$ in AMLP. To obtain $\mathbf{L} = \kappa(\mathbf{Q}, \mathbf{K})^\top$, we separately compute $\mathbf{Q}$'s and $\mathbf{K}$'s covariance matrices and combines them with learned down-sampling projection matrices $C_q \in \mathbb{R}^{c\times d}$ and $C_k \in \mathbb{R}^{c\times d}$:

$$\kappa(\mathbf{Q}, \mathbf{K}) = C_q\left(\sigma_2(\mathbf{Q}^\top\mathbf{Q})\right) + C_k\left(\sigma_2(\mathbf{K}^\top\mathbf{K})\right) \tag{9}$$

[1] AMLP is implemented with multiple heads [53], but for simplicity and without loss of generality, we will discuss our AMLP computation process in a single-head setting.

where $\sigma_2(\cdot)$ is set to softmax function as [1] suggest. The covariance matrices of $\mathbf{Q}, \mathbf{K}$ are of the same shape and can be directly fused. We add the softmax function as a non-linear activation to enhance the expressiveness. For $W_{\mathbf{Q},\mathbf{K},\mathbf{V}}$, we notice the shapes of $\mathbf{K}$ and $\mathbf{V}$ are usually identical, and we hence use their cross-covariance $\mathbf{K}^\top\mathbf{V}$ for computation in Eq. 8. $W_{\mathbf{Q},\mathbf{K},\mathbf{V}}$ is then formulated by transforming the cross-covariance $\mathbf{K}^\top\mathbf{V}$ to query space by $\mathbf{L}$ as:

$$W_{\mathbf{Q},\mathbf{K},\mathbf{V}} = \mathbf{L}^\top \sigma_2(\mathbf{K}^\top\mathbf{V}) \tag{10}$$

Pseudo-queries. AMLP-PQuery first uses Exponential Moving Average (EMA) to compute the contextualized query via a hyperparameter β: $\hat{\mathbf{q}}_{\mathbf{i}} = \beta \cdot \hat{\mathbf{q}}_{i-1} + (1-\beta) \cdot \mathbf{q}_i$, which has been proved to model local context well [37]. To further improve the communication between target and source sequences in a long sequence view, AMLP-PQuery treats learnable C_q, C_k and $\mathbf{L}^\top$ as pseudo attention queries. Specifically, it estimates $W_{\mathbf{Q},\mathbf{K}}$ by fusing features from query and key to the hidden space with an extra learnable weight $W \in \mathbb{R}^{2d\times d}$:

$$W_{\mathbf{Q},\mathbf{K}} = \mathbf{L}^\top = \left[\sigma_2(C_q\hat{\mathbf{Q}}^\top)\hat{\mathbf{Q}}; \sigma_2(C_k\mathbf{K}^\top)\mathbf{K}\right] W \tag{11}$$

where $\sigma_2(\cdot)$ is set to softmax as AMLP-Cov. For $W_{\mathbf{Q},\mathbf{K},\mathbf{V}}$, we notice that $\mathbf{L}^\top$ has fused features from $\hat{\mathbf{Q}}$. So we again treat $\mathbf{L}^\top$ as a pseudo query to fuse features from the source sequence:

$$W_{\mathbf{Q},\mathbf{K},\mathbf{V}} = \sigma_2(\mathbf{L}^\top\mathbf{K}^\top)\mathbf{V} \tag{12}$$

With explicit communication between $\hat{\mathbf{Q}}$ and $\mathbf{K}$ in $W_{\mathbf{Q},\mathbf{K},\mathbf{V}}$, the alignment between different sequences is enhanced; therefore, AMLP-PQuery is more adaptive to cross-attention.

2.4 Linear NAR: A Hybrid Architecture of NAR and AMLP

We combine AMLP with NAR for lower memory costs, faster inference speed and higher parallelism because AMLP and NAR are mutually reinforcing.

AMLP Boosts NAR. On one hand, NAR parallelizes the inference process, but its efficiency is still hindered by vanilla attention. AMLP, as a plug-in efficient attentive module, mitigates the inefficiency effortlessly. On the other hand, the non-autoregressive pipeline provides a non-causal encoding framework, with which the computation of AMLP avoids fine-grained operations.

NAR Augments AMLP. We present the specific computation steps of AMLP in AR scenario and explain the drawbacks of AR-AMLP. We take AMLP-Cov as an example. Given an query token $\boldsymbol{q}_t$, the covariances $\mathbf{S}_t^{\mathbf{Q}}$ and $\mathbf{S}_t^{\mathbf{K}}$ of $\mathbf{K}_t$ and $\mathbf{Q}_t$, and the cross-covariance $\mathbf{z}_t$ of $\mathbf{K}_t$ and $\mathbf{V}_t$, $W_{\mathbf{Q},\mathbf{K}}$ and $W_{\mathbf{Q},\mathbf{K},\mathbf{V}}$ are formulated as:

$$W_{\mathbf{Q}_t,\mathbf{K}_t} = \mathbf{L}_t^\top = C_q(\sigma_2(\mathbf{S}_t^{\mathbf{Q}})) + C_k(\sigma_2(\mathbf{S}_t^{\mathbf{K}})) \tag{13}$$

$$W_{\mathbf{Q}_t,\mathbf{K}_t,\mathbf{V}_t} = \mathbf{L}_t^\top \sigma_2(\mathbf{z}_t) \tag{14}$$

where $\mathbf{S}_t^{\mathbf{Q}} = \mathbf{S}_{t-1}^{\mathbf{Q}} + \boldsymbol{q}_t^\top \boldsymbol{q}_t$, $\mathbf{S}_t^{\mathbf{K}} = \mathbf{S}_{t-1}^{\mathbf{K}} + \boldsymbol{k}_t^\top \boldsymbol{k}_t$ and $\mathbf{z}_t = \mathbf{z}_{t-1} + \boldsymbol{k}_t^\top \boldsymbol{v}_t$. These computation steps increase heavy memory costs and large time consumption in the training phase, with an additional $O(ncd)$ costs beyond the overall computation. Recurrent computation also harms the parallelism and further slows down the training process, which is avoided naturally in NAR models. Moreover, CAB [59] points out that most existing efficient architectures suffer a great performance drop in causal-self or causal-cross pattern of AR models. Combining the two drawbacks brought by the fusion of efficient architecture and AR models, we decide to incorporate AMLP into NAR to produce a powerful and efficient model.

2.5 Complexity Analysis

Without loss of generality, we focus on the complexity in the typical encoder-decoder architecture and omit the independent factor *w.r.t.* target length n and source length m for simplicity.

AMLP-Covand AMLP-PQuery. Note that the inner dimension c is a constant to both m and n. The sequential computation of two adaptive projection matrices and the overall MLP computation in Eq. 8 are all of $O(n + m)$. The exclusive EMA submodule in AMLP-PQuery is $O(n)$ as well. Therefore, the time and memory complexity of AMLP (both AMLP-Cov and AMLP-PQuery) is $O(n + m)$.

NAR-AMLP. Non-autoregressive models have one encoder self-attention, one decoder self-attention, and an encoder-decoder cross-attention. Due to the quadratic complexity of softmax attention, the complexities of the three attentions are $O(m^2)$, $O(n^2)$ and $O(nm)$, respectively. Therefore, the complexity of the entire model architecture is $O(n^2 + nm + m^2)$. To reduce the inefficiency bottlenecked by softmax attention, we replace softmax modules in non-autoregressive models with AMLP, deriving an NAR-AMLP architecture with linear time and space complexity.

3 Experiments

We conduct extensive experiments, covering the fields of speech, natural language processing, time-series and computer vision.[2] For fair comparison between models, we select the typical hyperparameter setting for each efficient attention on each task, which is shown in Table 1 in detail. Specifically, we first apply our hybrid architecture NAR-AMLP in two tasks: Text-to-Speech Synthesis and Machine Translation. Then we assess AMLP's self-attention and cross-attention abilities on super resolution and long sequence time-series forecasting tasks, respectively. Finally, we conduct ablation studies to show the hidden philosophy of AMLP and explore how efficient AMLP scales to long-sequence modeling.

[2] In experiments, we take softmax$(\cdot)$ as the nonlinear function $\sigma_1(\cdot)$ unless otherwise specified.

Table 1. Hyperparameters of different tasks.

Task	TTS	MT	SR	LSTF
Backbone	FastSpeech 2/ Transformer-TTS	Transformer/CMLMC	SR	Informer
		Training hyperparameters		
Batch Size	48	–	4	32
Number of Steps (epochs)	20K	100K/300K	1M	6 (epochs)
Warmup Steps	4K	4K	–	–
Peak Learning Rate	5e-4	5e-4	1e-4	1e-4
Scheduler	Inverse Sqrt	Inverse Sqrt	Linear	Exponential Decay
Optimizer	AdamW	AdamW	AdamW	AdamW
Adam	(0.9, 0.98)	(0.9, 0.98)	(0.9, 0.999)	(0.9,0.999)
Clip Norm	5.0	5.0	0	0
Attention Dropout	0.1	0.3	0.2	0.05
Weight Decay	0.01	0.0001	0	0
Max Tokens	–	65536	–	–
Iteration	–	–	–	5
Evaluation Checkpoint	best	average last 10	average last 5	last
		Attention hyperparameters		
wsize (local)	15	5	15	15
landmarks (ABC)	64	16	64	64
ffn_dim (AMLP)	64	16	64	64
approx_dim (Performer)	64	16	64	64

3.1 Main Results of NAR-AMLP

Text-to-Speech. We select LJSpeech [25] dataset for this task, and use FastSpeech 2 (FS2) [46] and Transformer-TTS (Tr-TTS) [30] as the backbone models for NAR and AR, respectively. For both backbones, we replace all softmax attentions with efficient ones to achieve linear complexity. We use AMLP-Cov variant and ReLU(·) as $\sigma_1(\cdot)$ in Eq. 8. The alignment tool "g2pE" [54] is applied to train FastSpeech 2. For reproducibility, we use two widely-used objective evaluation metrics, Mel Cepstral Distortion (MCD) and Mel Spectral Distortion (MSD), to assess the quality of synthesized audio clips. We compare AMLP with gMLP [33], XCA [1], ABC [40] and local attention [36]. The details of training hyperparameters are shown in Table 1. We demonstrate the results in Table 2. AMLP substantially lowers the MCD and MSD values by a great margin up to 0.15 MCD with even lower complexity compared to vanilla models. Additionally, AMLP also outperforms other efficient models. Notably, we have significantly lower MCD than XCA which also leverages (cross-)covariance matrices.

Machine Translation. To verify AMLP's capability on short sequence modeling, we launch Machine Translation (MT) experiments on WMT 2014 English-German (WMT'14 En-De) and German-English (WMT'14 De-En) datasets [6]. We adopt AMLP-PQuery variant to CMLMC [23], which is a powerful fully NAR architecture without extra decoding algorithms. For completeness, we include widely-used AR architecture Transformer (Tr) [53] with competitive linear attentions. We exclude the AR-reranking process to make a fully linear-complexity generation process. Similar to TTS, we replace self/cross-attention modules in

Table 2. Automatic evaluation metric on LJSpeech dataset. All models are trained by ourselves. n, m are the target and source sequence lengths. Colored rows represent NAR models.

Arch	Model	#Params	LJSpeech	
			MCD↓	MSD↓
Complexity: $O(n^2)$ *or* $O\left(n^2+nm+m^2\right)$				
AR	Tr-TTS	54.40M	4.095	2.199
NAR	FS2	41.23M	3.475	1.974
Complexity: $O(n)$ *or* $O(n+m)$				
AR	Tr-TTS (ABC)	54.60M	5.130	2.596
	FS2 (local)	41.23M	3.419	1.970
	FS2 (ABC)	41.36M	3.392	1.966
NAR	FS2 (XCA)	41.23M	3.500	2.024
	FS2 (gMLP)	44.90M	3.402	1.964
	FS2 (AMLP)	41.49M	**3.327**	**1.940**

Table 3. BLEU4 scores on WMT14 EN-DE and WMT14 DE-EN dataset. All models for comparison are implemented by ourselves. n, m are the target and source sequence lengths. Colored rows represent NAR models.

Arch	Model	#Params	WMT' 14	
			En-De	De-En
Complexity: $O\left(n^2+nm+m^2\right)$				
AR	Tr	86.74M	27.38	31.26
NAR	CMLMC	73.14M	**27.91**	31.43
Complexity: $O(n+m)$				
AR	Tr (local)	86.74M	24.77	28.21
	Tr (ABC)	86.77M	25.86	29.09
	CMLMC (ABC)	73.16M	27.37	31.30
NAR	CMLMC (local)	73.16M	27.05	30.33
	CMLMC (AMLP)	73.44M	27.60	**31.50**

the decoder of Transformer and CMLMC to obtain their efficient variants. We use hyperparameters as CMLMC and Transformer suggest, which is present in Table 1. We report BLEU-4 [39] scores as the performance metric. Because XCA and gMLP do not support cross-attention, we here only compare AMLP with the strong ABC and local baselines. As translation has implicit token alignment between sequences, local attention can do cross-attention in this task.

Results in Table 3 indicate that the NAR-AMLP architecture achieves the best result among efficient NAR and AR models with linear complexity. Among the NAR models, the AMLP model outperforms a strong linear attention model, ABC, on both datasets, with a lead of 0.23 and 0.20 BLEU, respectively. It indicates that AMLP effectively captures short-term dependencies and produces more accurate translations than ABC. We also compare AMLP with vanilla attention, and the results indicate that AMLP outperforms vanilla attention on the de-en dataset, with only a 0.31BLEU lag compared to vanilla attention on the en-de one. This suggests that AMLP can achieve comparable performance to vanilla NAR models in certain scenarios. In comparison to AR models on both datasets, AMLP demonstrates superior performance (with at least 0.22 and 0.24 BLEU improvement), providing further evidence of the efficacy of NAR-AMLP as an architecture.

3.2 Self- and Cross-Attention Ablation

Self-Attention. We evaluate the self-encoding ability of AMLP on Super Resolution (SR) task. SR aims to convert low-resolution (16×16) images into high-resolution (128×128) ones. We base on a powerful backbone—SR3 [49] and add attention layers after each residual block to follow CAB [59] settings. We replace the softmax self-attention with five efficient architectures, i.e., local,

Table 4. PSNR and SSMI on CelebA-HQ dataset. n is the pixel number of the images.

Model	#Params	Celeb-HQ	
		PSNR↑	SSMI↑
Complexity: $O(n^2)$			
vanilla	99.55M	23.18	0.675
Complexity: $O(n)$			
local	99.55M	**23.33**	0.682
gMLP	101.66M	23.24	0.679
XCiT	99.55M	23.08	0.67
ABC	99.72M	22.54	0.635
AMLP	99.73M	23.28	**0.684**

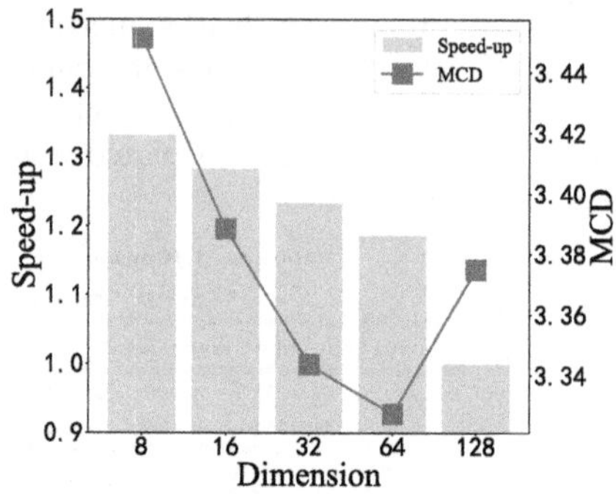

Fig. 3. Trade-off of MCD value and speed-up of different intermediate dimension c values in text-to-speech task.

gMLP, XCA, ABC and AMLP to compare Following [49], we use the Flickr-Faces-HQ (FFHQ) dataset [27] for the training set and CelebA-HQ dataset [26] for the evaluation set. We use Peak Signal-to-Noise Ratio (PSNR) and Structural SIMilarity (SSIM) [55] to measure efficient models. Experiment results are shown in Table 4. AMLP improves the performance of SR3 to 23.28 (+0.10) on PSNR and 0.684 (+0.09) on SSMI against the vanilla baseline, indicating that AMLP has a strong self-encoding ability. When compared to gMLP, AMLP also has a slight performance gain. AMLP outperforms covariance-based architecture XCA by 0.20 and 0.14 on PSNR and SSMI, respectively.

Cross-Attention. We test the cross-attention ability on the long sequence time-series forecasting (LSTF) task. We take Informer [61] as the backbone neural networks and evaluate efficient models on Electricity Transformer Temperature (ETT) dataset, which contains three sub-datasets ETT-h1, ETT-h2, and ETT-m1. We follow [61] to conduct univariate and multivariate evaluations on three sub-datasets and average their Mean Square Error (MSE) and Mean Absolute Error (MAE) to obtain final scores. Except for vanilla attention, we also compare AMLP with other three efficient models with strong cross-alignment abilities: ABC [40], Performer [10] and cosFormer [44]. We exclude local attention as it does not work for cross attention without explicit token alignment in the time-series forecasting task. The results performed on three sub-datasets are shown in Table 5. AMLP, in contrast to the vanilla counterpart, achieves lower MSE and MAE as well as more efficient complexity. Moreover, we notice that all other efficient models perform poorly compared to vanilla attention. It suggests that AMLP has a solid ability to model non-homologous information.

Table 5. Cross-attention ablation on ETT-h1, ETT-h1, and ETT-m1 datasets. n, m are the target and source lengths. Avg. is computed over three subdatasets.

Complex.	Methods	#Params	ETTh1		ETTh2		ETTm1		Avg.	
			MSE↓	MAE↓	MSE↓	MAE↓	MSE↓	MAE↓	MSE↓	MAE↓
$O(n^2 + nm)$	vanilla	11.33M	**0.754**	**0.573**	1.907	1.036	0.754	0.716	1.138	0.775
$O(n + m)$	ABC	11.33M	0.845	0.728	1.862	1.013	0.734	0.685	1.147	0.809
	Performer	11.33M	0.861	0.703	2.137	1.091	0.764	**0.663**	1.254	0.819
	cosFormer	11.33M	0.848	0.723	2.094	1.067	**0.715**	0.680	1.219	0.823
	AMLP	11.33M	0.797	0.702	**1.504**	**0.864**	0.718	0.684	**1.006**	**0.750**

3.3 Analysis

In this section, we conduct substantial analysis experiments to dig out the efficiency and superiority of our AMLP mechanism. We first present our analysis in comparison with other efficient attention modules on the TTS task. Then we show that our approximation $c < d$ in Eq. 6 does not deteriorate the performance of speech generation. Finally, we elucidate the outstanding generation speed and GPU peak usage of our AMLP in the NAR scenario.

Intermediate Dimension Analysis. The approximation of eigenvalues in Eq. 6 prompts us to know whether such approximation is feasible and whether the exorbitant approximation will deteriorate the generation performance. To this end, we test several values of c in AMLP and report each corresponding performance on TTS and the decoding speed when adopted to FastSpeech 2, in Fig. 3. Except for c value, we adopt the same setting in §3.1.

From Fig. 3, we can see that AMLP with approximation rank c can achieve as well as no approximation setting ($c = d = 128$) and does not impact the performance greatly. But with a lower c value, AMLP can achieve better decoding speed. Specifically, in contrast to $c = 64$, a higher MCD when setting c to d also indicates that maintaining the whole eigenvalues in Eq. 6 may even lead to overparameterization and impair the overall decoding efficacy. It verifies the feasibility to approximate $\mathbf{\Sigma}$ with fewer eigenspectrums in AMLP.

Efficiency Analysis. To further understand the performance of NAR-AMLP architecture in inference, we set up a simulation experiment to test its efficiency. The simulation experiment evaluates NAR-AMLP efficiency from running time and memory usage with respect to sequence length from 256 to 8,192, compared with AR model and vanilla NAR model. We simulate the generation process with a single efficient module. For AR, we test its causal attention, which is its bottleneck in generation. For AMLP, we use 64 as the inner dimension with ReLU activation function for σ_1 in Eq. 8. AMLP-Cov andAMLP-PQuery shares the same complexity, so we use "AMLP" to denote the two variants. The experiments are performed with batch size 12 on a single A100 GPU, and the results are repeated with 100 runs. We remain running latency data ranging from the first

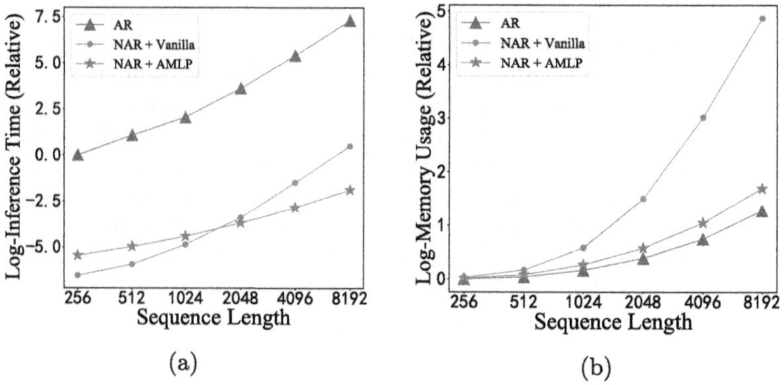

Fig. 4. (a) Empirical running time and (b) empirical memory cost with sequence length. Logarithms of relative measurement to the AR model are reported.

quatile and the third quatile among the 100 runs to remove noise. Finally, the remaining figures are averaged to serve as the final time consumption.

Figure 4a shows that NAR-AMLP extremely speeds up the inference process. To generate a long sequence with 8,192 tokens, vanilla NAR is 116× faster than AR while NAR-AMLP is even 590× faster. For sequences with more than 1500 tokens, both variants of AMLP are more efficient than vanilla attention; otherwise, the vanilla attention is faster. Figure 4b shows that NAR-AMLP significantly reduces memory consumption in NAR generation. It saves 89% memory usage of NAR model when generating a sequence with 8,192 tokens. Note that AR models cost fewer memory resources because of incremental decoding, which caches previous states and processes only one token at each step. But AR models still suffer from huge memory usage as NAR models in training, since they are usually implemented with a causal mask on the attention matrix. Thus it is reasonable to infer that NAR-AMLP is more efficient than AR and NAR models in training.

4 Related Work

Non-autoregressive Generation. [17] first proposes a non-autoregressive model to generate all the tokens within a sequence in parallel, which extremely speeds up the inference process but is inferior in generation quality. To mitigate the quality degradation, many researchers devote to improve the model performance with iterative decoding [16,18,20,22,29], curriculum learning [4,19,34,42,43], latent variable modeling [3,4,38,45], imitation learning [31,56] and learning objective [12,15,32,48]. These previous works focus on pursuing the high efficacy of non-autoregressive generation, but few works are presented to improve NAR's efficiency in long sequence modeling. We target to further improve its efficiency and scale non-autoregressive models to long sequences.

MLP Architecture. Multi-layer perceptron [14] is a classic neural network architecture and has been widely used. Recently, novel variants of MLP architectures are proposed for text and image processing, achieving impressive results on image classification [33,52], text classification [50], multilingual parsing [13], and intent classification [13]. MLP-Mixer [52] is proposed by leveraging a token-mixing and a channel-mixing MLP to enable token-wise and channel-wise communication. MLP-Mixer is further improved to pNLP-Mixer with locality sensitive hashing [24] projection at the bottom calculating non-trainable fingerprints [13]. [33] propose gMLP by introducing a spatial gating unit to enhance the communication between neighboring tokens. CycleMLP [8] leverages a local window to achieve linear time complexity on dense prediction. Besides, previous studies focus on encoding text/image features with MLP, but we explore the possibility to leverage an MLP architecture for sequence generation.

Attention Mechanism. Attention is first proposed to align the target and source sequence in neural machine translation [2], and is further improved to multi-head self/cross/causal attention [53]. Due to its quadratic time complexity and memory cost with sequence length, a surge of efficient attention is proposed to improve the efficiency of softmax attention. Due to the the sparsity of attention matrix, many researchers propose to explicitly model a sparse attention mechanism to obtain fast computation without harming performance [5,21,28,47,51,58]. The low-rank property of attention matrix also brings out matrix decomposition-based methods [9,57]. The softmax attention can also be linearized via exponential kernel decomposition [10,40,41,44,60]. These attention variants are exploring an efficient way to approximate softmax attention, but we focus on MLP architecture, which is naturally an efficient architecture.

5 Conclusions

In this work, we introduced Attentive Multi-Layer Perceptron (AMLP), an efficient plugin alternative to vanilla attention for non-autoregressive generation tasks. AMLP uses adaptive weights to learn inter-token interactions as done in attention. And we also put forward two methods adopting different philosophies to parameterize the adaptive weight matrices in AMLP. Substantial experiments on generation tasks verify that AMLP surpasses attention in most tasks and achieves similar performances with other strong efficient models in other tasks. Besides, efficiency analysis indicates that AMLP combined NAR model could save time compared to AR models, and save space compared to vanilla NAR models in long sequence settings.

Ethical Issues. AMLP is designed to speed up the generation of non-autoregressive models, by replacing the inefficient softmax attention with our AMLP module to achieve linear complexity. The potential positive implications imply lower difficulty in deploying NAR models on resource-limited devices, thus increasing the accessibility of NAR models. AMLP also makes positive impacts on extending NAR models to various domains, since it can do both self-attention and cross-attention. Moreover, the high efficiency of AMLP reduces the carbon footprint of training a model and thus brings positive environmental benefits. As such, we do not foresee any immediate negative ethical or societal consequences stemming from our work that are different from those that apply to other fundamental components of the transformer architecture and NAR models.

References

1. Ali, A., et al.: Xcit: cross-covariance image transformers. Adv. Neural Inf. Process. Syst. **34**, 20014–20027 (2021)
2. Bahdanau, D., Cho, K., Bengio, Y.: Neural machine translation by jointly learning to align and translate. In: ICLR (2015)
3. Bao, Y., et al.: Non-autoregressive transformer by position learning. arXiv preprint arXiv:1911.10677 (2019)
4. Bao, Y., et al.: latent-GLAT: glancing at latent variables for parallel text generation. In: Proceedings of the 60th Annual Meeting of the Association for Computational Linguistics (Volume 1: Long Papers), pp. 8398–8409. Association for Computational Linguistics, Dublin (2022). https://doi.org/10.18653/v1/2022.acl-long.575,https://aclanthology.org/2022.acl-long.575
5. Beltagy, I., Peters, M.E., Cohan, A.: Longformer: the long-document transformer. arXiv preprint arXiv:2004.05150 (2020)
6. Bojar, O., et al.: Findings of the 2014 workshop on statistical machine translation. In: Proceedings of the Ninth Workshop on Statistical Machine Translation, pp. 12–58. Association for Computational Linguistics, Baltimore (2014). https://doi.org/10.3115/v1/W14-3302
7. Chang, H., Zhang, H., Jiang, L., Liu, C., Freeman, W.T.: Maskgit: masked generative image transformer. In: Proceedings of the IEEE/CVF Conference on Computer Vision and Pattern Recognition, pp. 11315–11325 (2022)
8. Chen, S., Xie, E., GE, C., Chen, R., Liang, D., Luo, P.: CycleMLP: A MLP-like architecture for dense prediction. In: International Conference on Learning Representations (2022). https://openreview.net/forum?id=NMEceG4v69Y
9. Chen, Z., Gong, M., Ge, L., Du, B.: Compressed self-attention for deep metric learning with low-rank approximation. In: Proceedings of the Twenty-Ninth International Conference on International Joint Conferences on Artificial Intelligence, pp. 2058–2064 (2021)
10. Choromanski, K.M., et al.: Rethinking attention with performers. In: International Conference on Learning Representations (2021). https://openreview.net/forum?id=Ua6zuk0WRH
11. Dosovitskiy, A., et al.: An image is worth 16x16 words: Transformers for image recognition at scale. In: International Conference on Learning Representations (2021)
12. Du, C., Tu, Z., Jiang, J.: Order-agnostic cross entropy for non-autoregressive machine translation. In: International Conference on Machine Learning, pp. 2849–2859. PMLR (2021)
13. Fusco, F., Pascual, D., Staar, P.: pnlp-mixer: an efficient all-mlp architecture for language. arXiv preprint arXiv:2202.04350 (2022)

14. Gardner, M.W., Dorling, S.: Artificial neural networks (the multilayer perceptron)-a review of applications in the atmospheric sciences. Atmosph. Environ. **32**(14–15), 2627–2636 (1998)
15. Ghazvininejad, M., Karpukhin, V., Zettlemoyer, L., Levy, O.: Aligned cross entropy for non-autoregressive machine translation. In: International Conference on Machine Learning, pp. 3515–3523. PMLR (2020)
16. Ghazvininejad, M., Levy, O., Liu, Y., Zettlemoyer, L.: Mask-predict: parallel decoding of conditional masked language models. In: Proceedings of the 2019 Conference on Empirical Methods in Natural Language Processing and the 9th International Joint Conference on Natural Language Processing (EMNLP-IJCNLP), pp. 6112–6121 (2019)
17. Gu, J., Bradbury, J., Xiong, C., Li, V.O., Socher, R.: Non-autoregressive neural machine translation. In: International Conference on Learning Representations (2018)
18. Gu, J., Wang, C., Zhao, J.: Levenshtein transformer. Adv. Neural Inf. Process. Syst. **32** (2019)
19. Guo, J., Tan, X., Xu, L., Qin, T., Chen, E., Liu, T.Y.: Fine-tuning by curriculum learning for non-autoregressive neural machine translation. Proc. AAAI Conf. Artif. Intel. **34**(05), 7839–7846 (2020). https://doi.org/10.1609/aaai.v34i05.6289
20. Guo, J., Xu, L., Chen, E.: Jointly masked sequence-to-sequence model for non-autoregressive neural machine translation. In: Proceedings of the 58th Annual Meeting of the Association for Computational Linguistics, pp. 376–385 (2020)
21. Ho, J., Kalchbrenner, N., Weissenborn, D., Salimans, T.: Axial attention in multidimensional transformers. arXiv preprint arXiv:1912.12180 (2019)
22. Huang, C., Zhou, H., Zaïane, O.R., Mou, L., Li, L.: Non-autoregressive translation with layer-wise prediction and deep supervision. Proc. AAAI Conf. Artif. Intel. **36**, 10776–10784 (2022)
23. Huang, X.S., Perez, F., Volkovs, M.: Improving non-autoregressive translation models without distillation. In: International Conference on Learning Representations (2022)
24. Indyk, P., Motwani, R.: Approximate nearest neighbors: towards removing the curse of dimensionality. In: Proceedings of the Thirtieth Annual ACM Symposium on Theory of Computing, pp. 604–613 (1998)
25. Ito, K., Johnson, L.: The lj speech dataset. https://keithito.com/LJ-Speech-Dataset/ (2017)
26. Karras, T., Aila, T., Laine, S., Lehtinen, J.: Progressive growing of gans for improved quality, stability, and variation. In: International Conference on Learning Representations (2018)
27. Karras, T., Laine, S., Aila, T.: A style-based generator architecture for generative adversarial networks. In: Proceedings of the IEEE/CVF Conference on Computer Vision and Pattern Recognition (CVPR) (2019)
28. Kitaev, N., Kaiser, L., Levskaya, A.: Reformer: the efficient transformer. In: International Conference on Learning Representations (2020). https://openreview.net/forum?id=rkgNKkHtvB
29. Lee, J., Mansimov, E., Cho, K.: Deterministic non-autoregressive neural sequence modeling by iterative refinement. In: Proceedings of the 2018 Conference on Empirical Methods in Natural Language Processing, pp. 1173–1182 (2018)
30. Li, N., Liu, S., Liu, Y., Zhao, S., Liu, M.: Neural speech synthesis with transformer network. Proc. AAAI Conf. Artif. Intel. **33**(01), 6706–6713 (2019). https://doi.org/10.1609/aaai.v33i01.33016706

31. Li, Z., et al.: Hint-based training for non-autoregressive machine translation. In: Proceedings of the 2019 Conference on Empirical Methods in Natural Language Processing and the 9th International Joint Conference on Natural Language Processing (EMNLP-IJCNLP), pp. 5708–5713. Association for Computational Linguistics, Hong Kong (2019). https://doi.org/10.18653/v1/D19-1573,https://aclanthology.org/D19-1573
32. Liu, G., et al.: Don't take it literally: an edit-invariant sequence loss for text generation. In: Proceedings of the 2022 Conference of the North American Chapter of the Association for Computational Linguistics: Human Language Technologies, pp. 2055–2078. Association for Computational Linguistics, Seattle (2022). https://doi.org/10.18653/v1/2022.naacl-main.150, https://aclanthology.org/2022.naacl-main.150
33. Liu, H., Dai, Z., So, D., Le, Q.V.: Pay attention to MLPS. Adv. Neural Inf. Process. Syst. **34**, 9204–9215 (2021)
34. Liu, J., et al.: Task-level curriculum learning for non-autoregressive neural machine translation. In: IJCAI, pp. 3861–3867 (2020)
35. Liu, Z., et al.: Swin transformer: hierarchical vision transformer using shifted windows. In: Proceedings of the IEEE/CVF International Conference on Computer Vision, pp. 10012–10022 (2021)
36. Luong, T., Pham, H., Manning, C.D.: Effective approaches to attention-based neural machine translation. In: Proceedings of the 2015 Conference on Empirical Methods in Natural Language Processing, pp. 1412–1421. Association for Computational Linguistics, Lisbon (2015). https://doi.org/10.18653/v1/D15-1166, https://aclanthology.org/D15-1166
37. Ma, X., et al.: Mega: moving average equipped gated attention. arXiv preprint arXiv:2209.10655 (2022)
38. Ma, X., Zhou, C., Li, X., Neubig, G., Hovy, E.: FlowSeq: non-autoregressive conditional sequence generation with generative flow. In: Proceedings of the 2019 Conference on Empirical Methods in Natural Language Processing and the 9th International Joint Conference on Natural Language Processing (EMNLP-IJCNLP), pp. 4282–4292. Association for Computational Linguistics, Hong Kong (2019). https://doi.org/10.18653/v1/D19-1437
39. Papineni, K., Roukos, S., Ward, T., Zhu, W.J.: Bleu: a method for automatic evaluation of machine translation. In: Proceedings of the 40th annual meeting of the Association for Computational Linguistics, pp. 311–318 (2002)
40. Peng, H., et al.: ABC: attention with bounded-memory control. In: Proceedings of the 60th Annual Meeting of the Association for Computational Linguistics (Volume 1: Long Papers), pp. 7469–7483. Association for Computational Linguistics, Dublin (2022). https://doi.org/10.18653/v1/2022.acl-long.515, https://aclanthology.org/2022.acl-long.515
41. Peng, H., Pappas, N., Yogatama, D., Schwartz, R., Smith, N., Kong, L.: Random feature attention. In: International Conference on Learning Representations (2021)
42. Qian, L., et al.: Glancing transformer for non-autoregressive neural machine translation. In: Proceedings of the 59th Annual Meeting of the Association for Computational Linguistics and the 11th International Joint Conference on Natural Language Processing (Volume 1: Long Papers), pp. 1993–2003. Association for Computational Linguistics (2021). https://doi.org/10.18653/v1/2021.acl-long.155
43. Qian, L., et al.: The volctrans GLAT system: non-autoregressive translation meets WMT21. In: Proceedings of the Sixth Conference on Machine Translation, pp. 187–196. Association for Computational Linguistics (2021)

44. Qin, Z., et al.: cosformer: rethinking softmax in attention. In: International Conference on Learning Representations (2022). https://openreview.net/forum?id=Bl8CQrx2Up4
45. Ran, Q., Lin, Y., Li, P., Zhou, J.: Guiding non-autoregressive neural machine translation decoding with reordering information. In: AAAI, pp. 13727–13735 (2021)
46. Ren, Y., et al.: Fastspeech 2: fast and high-quality end-to-end text to speech. In: International Conference on Learning Representations (2021)
47. Roy, A., Saffar, M., Vaswani, A., Grangier, D.: Efficient content-based sparse attention with routing transformers. Trans. Assoc. Comput. Linguist. **9**, 53–68 (2021)
48. Saharia, C., Chan, W., Saxena, S., Norouzi, M.: Non-autoregressive machine translation with latent alignments. In: Proceedings of the 2020 Conference on Empirical Methods in Natural Language Processing (EMNLP), pp. 1098–1108. Association for Computational Linguistics (2020). https://doi.org/10.18653/v1/2020.emnlp-main.83
49. Saharia, C., Ho, J., Chan, W., Salimans, T., Fleet, D.J., Norouzi, M.: Image super-resolution via iterative refinement. IEEE Trans. Pattern Anal. Mach. Intel. (2022)
50. Tay, Y., Bahri, D., Metzler, D., Juan, D.C., Zhao, Z., Zheng, C.: Synthesizer: rethinking self-attention for transformer models. In: International Conference on Machine Learning, pp. 10183–10192. PMLR (2021)
51. Tay, Y., Bahri, D., Yang, L., Metzler, D., Juan, D.C.: Sparse sinkhorn attention. In: International Conference on Machine Learning, pp. 9438–9447. PMLR (2020)
52. Tolstikhin, I.O., et al.: MLP-mixer: An all-MLP architecture for vision. Adv. Neural Inf. Process. Syst. **34** (2021)
53. Vaswani, A., et al.: Attention is all you need. Adv. Neural Inf. Process. Syst. **30** (2017)
54. Wang, C., et al.: fairseq s2: a scalable and integrable speech synthesis toolkit. In: Proceedings of the 2021 Conference on Empirical Methods in Natural Language Processing: System Demonstrations, pp. 143–152. Association for Computational Linguistics, Online and Punta Cana (2021). https://doi.org/10.18653/v1/2021.emnlp-demo.17
55. Wang, Z., Bovik, A.C., Sheikh, H.R., Simoncelli, E.P.: Image quality assessment: from error visibility to structural similarity. IEEE Trans. Image Process. **13**(4), 600–612 (2004)
56. Wei, B., Wang, M., Zhou, H., Lin, J., Sun, X.: Imitation learning for non-autoregressive neural machine translation. In: Proceedings of the 57th Annual Meeting of the Association for Computational Linguistics, pp. 1304–1312. Association for Computational Linguistics, Florence (2019). https://doi.org/10.18653/v1/P19-1125
57. Xiong, Y., et al.: Nyströmformer: A nyström-based algorithm for approximating self-attention. Proc. AAAI Conf. Artif. Intel. **35**(16), 14138–14148 (2021). https://doi.org/10.1609/aaai.v35i16.17664
58. Zaheer, M., et al.: Big bird: transformers for longer sequences. Adv. Neural Inf. Process. Syst. **33**, 17283–17297 (2020)
59. Zhang, J., Jiang, S., Feng, J., Zheng, L., Kong, L.: Cab: comprehensive attention benchmarking on long sequence modeling. arXiv preprint arXiv:2210.07661 (2022)
60. Zheng, L., Wang, C., Kong, L.: Linear complexity randomized self-attention mechanism. arXiv preprint arXiv:2204.04667 (2022)
61. Zhou, H., et al.: Informer: beyond efficient transformer for long sequence time-series forecasting. Proc. AAAI Conf. Artif. Intel. **35**(12), 11106–11115 (2021). https://ojs.aaai.org/index.php/AAAI/article/view/17325

MASTER: Multi-task Pre-trained Bottlenecked Masked Autoencoders Are Better Dense Retrievers

Kun Zhou[1,3], Xiao Liu[4], Yeyun Gong[4], Wayne Xin Zhao[2,3](✉), Daxin Jiang[4], Nan Duan[4], and Ji-Rong Wen[1,2,3]

[1] School of Information, Renmin University of China, Beijing, China
jrwen@ruc.edu.cn

[2] Gaoling School of Artificial Intelligence, Renmin University of China, Beijing, China
batmanfly@gmail.com

[3] Beijing Key Laboratory of Big Data Management and Analysis Methods, Beijing, China

[4] Microsoft Research, Beijing, China
{xiaoliu2,yegong,nanduan}@microsoft.com

Abstract. Pre-trained Transformers (*e.g.,* BERT) have been commonly used in existing dense retrieval methods for parameter initialization, and recent studies are exploring more effective pre-training tasks for further improving the quality of dense vectors. Although various novel and effective tasks have been proposed, their different input formats and learning objectives make them hard to be integrated for jointly improving the model performance. In this work, we aim to unify a variety of pre-training tasks into the bottlenecked masked autoencoder manner, and integrate them into a multi-task pre-trained model, namely MASTER. Concretely, MASTER utilizes a shared-encoder multi-decoder architecture that can construct a representation bottleneck to compress the abundant semantic information across tasks into dense vectors. Based on it, we integrate three types of representative pre-training tasks: corrupted passages recovering, related passages recovering and PLMs outputs recovering, to characterize the inner-passage information, inter-passage relations and PLMs knowledge. Extensive experiments have shown that our approach outperforms competitive dense retrieval methods. Our code and data are publicly released in https://github.com/microsoft/SimXNS.

Keywords: Dense Retrieval · Pre-training · Multi-task Learning

1 Introduction

Recent years have witnessed the great success of dense retrieval methods [12,43,45,46] in industrial applications, *e.g.,* web search [5,45] and question

K. Zhou—This work was done during internship at MSRA.

© The Author(s), under exclusive license to Springer Nature Switzerland AG 2023
D. Koutra et al. (Eds.): ECML PKDD 2023, LNAI 14170, pp. 630–647, 2023.
https://doi.org/10.1007/978-3-031-43415-0_37

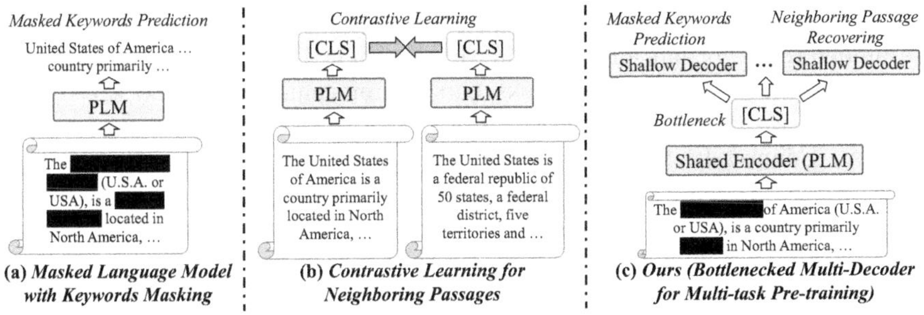

Fig. 1. The comparison of two representative pre-training tasks and our approach. Ours incorporates a bottlenecked multi-decoder architecture that unifies different tasks into the same input format and leverages specific decoders to deal with them separately.

answering [12,25]. These methods typically encode queries and passages into low-dimensional dense vectors and utilize the vector similarity between them to measure semantic relevance. In real-world applications, the dense vectors of a large number of passages will be pre-computed. Then the approximate nearest neighbor (ANN) search techniques [11] can be incorporated for efficient retrieval.

In existing dense retrieval methods, pre-trained language models (PLMs) [4, 44] have been widely adopted as the backbone, showing the superiority to generate high-quality dense vectors. However, general PLMs (*e.g.*, BERT [4]) may not be the best for dense retrieval, as their produced native dense representations (usually the `[CLS]` embedding) are not designed on purpose to compress the information from the input text. To solve it, recent studies [5,20,37] continually pre-train PLMs for improving the `[CLS]` embedding. Typically, they mainly focus on capturing the inner-passage information (*e.g.*, recovering masked tokens) [17,35] or inter-passage relations (*e.g.*, co-occurring passages) [36], and specially design pre-training tasks. After pre-training, the enhanced `[CLS]` embeddings would be fine-tuned on downstream passage retrieval tasks, achieving faster convergence and better performance than general PLMs.

As existing work has shown the effectiveness of capturing the two types of characteristics during pre-training by specific tasks, it is promising to combine these tasks for enhancing the `[CLS]` embedding. Intuitively, by incorporating more tasks to capture more specific useful information, the `[CLS]` embedding would be further enriched during pre-training, helping it generalize better into downstream retrieval tasks. However, due to the divergence of focused characteristics, the available pre-training tasks in existing work may adopt different settings in training objectives and input formats, *e.g.*, contrastive learning with co-occurring passages as positives and sampled negatives, and masked language model with special masking strategies on passages. Such differences make it hard to combine existing pre-training tasks, and an arbitrary integration of these tasks may even cause detrimental interference in the semantics of the `[CLS]` embedding, leading to performance degradation.

To address this problem, we consider integrating multiple pre-training tasks in a unified input format and reducing the divergence of different training objectives. Since most of the NLP tasks can be reformulated as the text-to-text format [27], we can also reconstruct the available pre-training tasks into such a format. Concretely, the tasks for capturing the inner-passage information or inter-passage relations, can be converted as predicting the inner- or inter-passage textual information (*e.g.,* tokens) based on the same input passage. Therefore, we can propose a unified framework for these tasks that adopts the PLM as the shared encoder, and multiple task-specific decoders. As shown in Fig. 1, the shared encoder produces the `[CLS]` embedding for the input passage, and all the decoders mainly rely on the embedding for predicting the specific texts. Such a way constructs an information-bottleneck architecture [17,35,36] where the PLM encoder is forced to inject sufficient task-specific information into the `[CLS]` embedding, for well accomplishing the tasks in decoders.

The proposed bottlenecked multi-decoder architecture provides a flexible way to integrating multiple different tasks for pre-training dense retriever. Based on it, we can combine a diverse range of available tasks for capturing the useful information or relations from different perspectives. Besides the commonly-used inner-passage information and inter-passage relations, we also consider to learn the knowledge from other public generative PLMs (*e.g.,* GPT-2 [26]), for capturing useful information beyond the corpus. Specifically, we devise three types of pre-training tasks for recovering corrupted passages, related passages, and PLMs output, respectively, including a total of five tasks in five decoders. Inspired by the masked autoencoder method (MAE) [9], we perform aggressively masking on the decoders (*e.g.,* masking 50% tokens), hence the deep encoder would be forced to generate compressed high-quality representations to recover them. Finally, we propose **MASTER**, a **m**ulti-t**as**k pre-**t**rained bottlenecked masked autoenc**o**de**r**, that adopts a shared-encoder multi-decoder architecture to integrate the five pre-training tasks in the bottlenecked MAE format. To verify the effectiveness of our approach, we conduct extensive experiments on several text retrieval datasets. Experimental results show that our approach can outperform competitive baselines.

2 Related Work

Dense Retrieval. Dense retrieval approaches [12] typically map queries and documents into low-dimensional dense vectors for evaluating their relevance, which support the efficient approximate nearest neighbor (ANN) search engines, *e.g.,* FAISS [11]. For effectively training dense retrieval models, existing work typically leverages pre-trained Transformers [4] to initialize the dual encoders and then samples high-quality negatives for fine-tuning the encoders. Early work [12] mainly relies on in-batch random negatives and hard negatives mined by BM25. Afterward, a line of work [25,39] picks top-k ranked documents by a trained dense retriever as hard negatives and improves the performance. However, a common problem for such top-k negative sampling strategies is that they are easy to select false negatives, which impedes better performances. To alleviate it, current studies have explored several practical directions, *e.g.*, knowledge distillation [16,25,32], pre-training [5] and negative sampling [45]. Besides, recent work is also exploring more efficient and effective ways for training dense retrievers, *e.g.*, ambiguous negative sampling [45] and neural corpus index [47].

Pre-training for Dense Retrieval. As general PLMs [4] are pre-trained without any prior task knowledge, they are not ready to use for dense retrieval [5,7], especially in low-data situations. To solve this issue, several studies [5,36] are proposed to make the output sentence embedding more informative and discriminative. A type of work relies on the explicit relations between text pairs and designs the pre-training tasks based on the contrastive learning objective [7,29], *e.g.*, inverse cloze task and contrastive span prediction. Another line of work aim to compress the semantic information into the `[CLS]` embedding. They leverage the masked autoencoder architecture that incorporates a deep encoder and a shallow decoder, forcing the `[CLS]` embedding of the input text from the encoders to recover itself [17,36,38] or related texts [35].

3 Preliminary

Task Definition. Given a query q, the dense retrieval task aims to retrieve the most relevant top-k passages $\{p_i\}_{i=1}^{k}$ from a large candidate pool $\mathcal{P}$. To achieve it, the dual-encoder architecture is widely used. It consists of a query encoder E_q and a passage encoder E_p, mapping the query q and passage p into k-dimensional dense vectors $\mathbf{h}_q$ and $\mathbf{h}_p$, respectively. Then, the semantic relevance score of q and p will be computed using dot product as

$$s(q,p) = \mathbf{h}_q \cdot \mathbf{h}_p. \tag{1}$$

Existing work mostly adopts pre-trained Transformers (*e.g.*, BERT [4]) as the two encoders, using the representations of the `[CLS]` token as the dense vectors. In this work, we aim to propose a more effective multi-task pre-training framework specially for the dense retrieval task, which learns to compress more useful information into the `[CLS]` representations. Formally, given a pre-training corpus and a Transformer encoder, we focus on devising several tasks to pre-train the parameters of it. Then, the pre-trained Transformer will be used as the backbone of the query encoder E_q and passage encoder E_p, and can be fine-tuned on downstream dense retrieval tasks.

Fine-tuning Dense Retrievers. In the fine-tuning stage, the learning objective is to pull the representations of a query q and its relevant passages $\mathcal{P}^+$ together (as positives), while pushing apart irrelevant ones $\mathcal{P}^- = \mathcal{P} \setminus \mathcal{P}^+$ (as negatives). Therefore, high-quality negatives are critical to the effectiveness of dense retrievers. Existing work commonly leverages the BM25 negatives [12] or the top-k ranked negatives mined by a well-trained dense retriever [25,39], denoted as $\tilde{\mathcal{D}}^-$. Then, the optimization objective can be formulated as:

$$\theta^* = \arg\min_{\theta} \sum_{q} \sum_{d^+ \in \mathcal{D}^+} \sum_{d^- \in \tilde{\mathcal{D}}^-} l(s(q,d^+), s(q,d^-)), \tag{2}$$

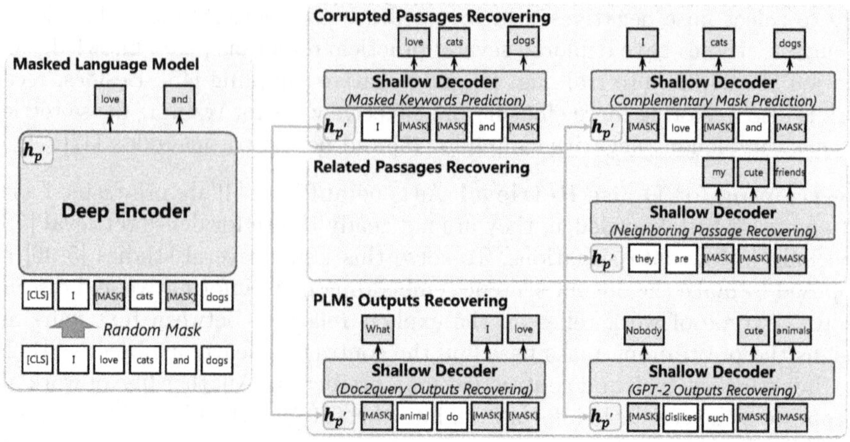

Fig. 2. The overview of MASTER. We adopt a bottlenecked multi-decoder architecture, and design three types of pre-training tasks, totally five decoders for specific tasks.

where $l(\cdot)$ is the loss function. Besides, as the top-k hard negatives may contain false negatives, recent studies [19,25,30] have adopted knowledge distillation strategies to solve it. They rely on pre-learned cross-encoder rerankers to produce soft labels on $\tilde{\mathcal{D}}^{-}$, and minimize the KL divergence between the dual encoders' outputs and the soft labels.

4 Approach

In this section, we present MASTER, an approach to pre-training an effective dense retriever. We first introduce the bottlenecked model architecture (consisting of a PLM encoder and multiple shallow decoders), then describe our adopted three types of pre-training tasks unified as the bottlenecked masked autoencoding manner. Figure 2 shows the overview of our approach.

4.1 Bottlenecked Multi-decoder Architecture

To pre-train the dense retriever for compressing useful information into the dense vectors, we design a bottlenecked multi-decoder architecture. In the architecture, we incorporate a deep Transformer encoder to compress the input text into a dense vector, and five shallow decoders corresponding to different pre-training tasks to capture diverse semantics and relations.

Concretely, the deep Transformer encoder shares the same architecture as BERT [4], and can be initialized with its pre-trained parameters. Given a passage p from the pre-training corpus, we leverage the deep encoder to encode it, and select the output representation of the `[CLS]` token as its dense vector

$\mathbf{h}_p$. Following existing work [5,18], we employ a masked language model task to pre-train the encoder. Formally, a certain percentage $\alpha\%$ of tokens from p will be masked to obtain p', and the encoder needs to predict them as:

$$L_{\mathrm{MLM}} = \sum_{t_i \in \mathcal{M}_{p'}} -\log p(t_i | p'; \Theta_E) \tag{3}$$

where $\mathcal{M}_{p'}$ denotes the masked tokens in p', Θ_E denotes the parameters of the encoder. The multiple shallow decoders are all the 2-layer bi-directional Transformer, and share the embedding matrix and language modeling head with the deep encoder. For each decoder, its input is an aggressive masked text x' (masking rate $\beta \geq 50\%$) that requires to be recovered. Besides, the dense vector $\mathbf{h}_{p'}$ from the encoder will be inserted into the decoder to replace the original `[CLS]` token embedding. In this way, the learning objective of each decoder is:

$$L_D = \sum_{t_i \in \mathcal{M}_{x'}} -\log p(t_i | x', \mathbf{h}_{p'}; \Theta_E, \Theta_D) \tag{4}$$

where $\mathcal{M}_{x'}$ denotes the masked tokens in x', Θ_D denotes the parameters of the decoder. Such a way builds the information bottleneck where multiple decoders rely on $\mathbf{h}_{p'}$ to recover the input, forcing it to reserve more useful information.

4.2 Multi-task Pre-training

Based on the architecture, we devise multiple pre-training tasks, to help dense vectors capture more useful information. Concretely, we adopt three types of tasks to capture the semantic information within passages, relations with other passages, and knowledge from other PLMs, namely corrupted passages recovering, related passages recovering and PLMs outputs recovering, respectively.

Corrupted Passages Recovering. Given a passage p from the pre-training corpus, the corrupted passages recovering tasks (CPR) first mask its contained tokens to compose the inputs of the encoder p' and decoder $\hat{p}'$ according to the mask rates $\alpha\%$ and $\beta\%$ respectively. Then, the output dense vector $\mathbf{h}_{p'}$ from the encoder will be leveraged to help the shallow decoder to recover $\hat{p}'$ into p. Such a way is helpful to compress important semantic information from the passage into the dense vector. To achieve it, we design two pre-training tasks by utilizing special masking mechanisms for the decoder, namely masked keywords prediction (MKP) and complementary mask prediction (CMP).

For MKP, we aim to mask more keywords in the decoder, as they may reflect important semantic information of the passage. Specifically, we rely on the TF-IDF weights [28] to obtain a masked probability distribution about words in the passage, where keywords with low frequencies would receive larger probabilities to be masked. In this way, the input masked passage $\hat{p}'_{\mathrm{MKP}}$ of the decoder will lose most keywords, which will force the dense vector $\mathbf{h}_{p'}$ to well reserve their information for recovering. For CMP, given the passage p, we leverage a complementary mask mechanism in the decoder that masks the unmasked tokens from the input of the encoder p'. As a result, the incomplete inputs of the encoder and decoder will be complementary, and the dense vector $\mathbf{h}_{p'}$ should accurately remember all the unmasked input information from p' for recovering $\hat{p}'_{\text{CMP}}$.

Finally, the pre-training objective of the CPR tasks is given by combining the above two tasks as:

$$L_{\text{CPR}} = \sum_{t_i \in \mathcal{M}_{\text{MKP}}} -\log p(t_i | \hat{p}'_{\text{MKP}}, \mathbf{h}_{p'}; \Theta_E, \Theta_D^{\text{MKP}}) + \sum_{t_i \in \mathcal{M}_{\text{CMP}}} -\log p(t_i | \hat{p}'_{\text{CMP}}, \mathbf{h}_{p'}; \Theta_E, \Theta_D^{\text{CMP}}),$$

where $\mathcal{M}_{\text{MKP}}$ and $\mathcal{M}_{\text{CMP}}$ denote the masked tokens in $\hat{p}'_{\text{MKP}}$ and $\hat{p}'_{\text{CMP}}$, respectively, and Θ_D^{MKP} and Θ_D^{CMP} are the parameters of the two specific decoders.

Related Passages Recovering. The related passages recovering task (RPR) aims to model the semantic relationships between related passages. In this work, we focus on the commonly-used and easily-obtained co-occurrence relation from the pre-training corpus. Based on this motivation, we collect the passage pairs $\{\langle p_i, p_{i+1} \rangle\}$ that are neighbouring spans in a document, and devise the neighbouring passage recovering task (NPR).

In NPR, given a neighbouring passage pair $\langle p_i, p_{i+1} \rangle$, we rely on the mask rates $\alpha\%$ and $\beta\%$ to mask their tokens for composing the inputs of the encoder p'_i and decoder p'_{i+1}, respectively. Next, the output dense vector of p'_i from the deep encoder is utilized to help the decoder recover p'_{i+1}. Such a way encourages the dense vector to retain the information related to the neighbouring passage, capturing the intrinsic token-level correlations across the two passages. Besides, we also rely on the TF-IDF weights of words to mask more keywords in the decoder as MKP, which further increases the difficulty of this task and forces the dense vector to focus more on the key information. The learning objective of the RPR task can be defined as:

$$L_{\text{RPR}} = \sum_{t_i \in \mathcal{M}_{\text{NPR}}} -\log p(t_i | p'_{i+1}, \mathbf{h}_{p'_i}; \Theta_E, \Theta_D^{\text{NPR}}),$$

where $\mathcal{M}_{\text{NPR}}$ and Θ_D^{NPR} denote the masked tokens in p'_{i+1} and the parameters of the decoder specially for the NPR task, respectively. Note that existing work [15,21] has also considered the neighbouring relations and mostly adopts the contrastive learning objective to capture it. In fact, contrastive learning mainly aims to characterize the passage-level semantics and would be affected by the quality of sampled negative passages. As a comparison, the NPR task can capture more fine-grained token-level characteristics, and such a generative way only focuses on modeling the relations between neighbouring passages, avoiding the influence from other passages.

PLMs Outputs Recovering. The above tasks are able to capture the semantic information and relations within the unsupervised pre-training corpus. We further consider to learn the knowledge from other PLMs, to capture more rich information beyond the corpus. Based on this idea, we design the PLMs outputs recovering tasks (POR) that aim to recover the outputs of two generative PLMs, consisting of the doc2query outputs recovering (DOR) and GPT-2 outputs recovering (GOR) tasks.

Given a passage p, we leverage a public well-trained doc2query model [23] to generate k relevant queries $\{q_i\}_{i=1}^{k}$ and concatenate them into a long sentence $s_{(q)}$, as the generated queries have shown effectiveness in previous dense retrieval methods [24]. Besides, we also use p as the prompt to guide the popular autoregressive GPT-2 model [26] to generate a long sentence $s_{(g)}$, as GPT-2 has shown surprising performance in generating informative long text. Then, we aggressively mask the tokens in $s_{(q)}$ and $s_{(g)}$ according to the mask rate $\beta\%$, to obtain the inputs $s'_{(q)}$ and $s'_{(g)}$ of two task-specific decoders. Similar to above tasks, the two decoders also rely on the dense vector $\mathbf{h}_{p'}$ to recover the generated texts, and the pre-training objective of the POR tasks is the combination of the two tasks as:

$$
\begin{aligned}
L_{\text{POR}} = & \sum_{t_i \in \mathcal{M}_{\text{DOR}}} -\log p(t_i | s'_{(q)}, \mathbf{h}_{p'}; \Theta_E, \Theta_D^{\text{DOR}}) \\
+ & \sum_{t_i \in \mathcal{M}_{\text{GOR}}} -\log p(t_i | s'_{(g)}, \mathbf{h}_{p'}; \Theta_E, \Theta_D^{\text{GOR}}),
\end{aligned}
$$

where $\mathcal{M}_{\text{DOR}}$ and $\mathcal{M}_{\text{GOR}}$ denote the masked tokens in $s'_{(q)}$ and $s'_{(g)}$, respectively, and Θ_D^{DOR} and Θ_D^{GOR} are the parameters of the two specific decoders, respectively. In this way, the dense vector is enhanced to capture richer knowledge from other PLMs, and learn more information not included in the corpus. Such a way is similar to the knowledge distillation process that transfers the learned knowledge from PLMs into the dense vector by forcing it to predict the PLMs' outputs.

4.3 Learning

During pre-training, we optimize the parameters in the deep encoder and the multiple shallow decoders using the above pre-training tasks, denoted as:

$$L_{\text{total}} = L_{\text{MLM}} + L_{\text{CPR}} + L_{\text{RPR}} + L_{\text{POR}} \tag{5}$$

During fine-tuning, we utilize the pre-trained deep encoder as the backbone of the query and passage encoders. Following the pipeline in previous dense retrieval methods [7,35,36], we first train the **Retriever$_1$** using the in-batch negatives and BM25 hard negatives. Then, we utilize Retriever$_1$ to mine hard negatives from a large-scale passage pool, and leverage these negatives and in-batch negatives to train the **Retriever$_2$**. Next, we train a cross-encoder reranker model based on the mined negatives from Retriever$_2$. Finally, we distil the knowledge from the reranker into the **Retriever$_{\text{distil}}$** by using it to produce soft labels for both positives and mined negatives from Retriever$_2$. Note that our pre-trained encoder is used to initialize the Retriever$_1$, Retriever$_2$ and Retriever$_{\text{distil}}$.

Table 1. Statistics of the text retrieval datasets.

Dataset	Train	Dev	Test	#Passage
MS MARCO Passage Ranking (MS-Pas)	502,939	6,980	–	8,841,823
TREC 2019 Deep Learning Track (TREC-2019)	–	–	200	8,841,823
TREC-2020 Deep Learning Track (TREC-2020)	–	–	200	8,841,823
Natural Questions (NQ)	58,880	8,757	3,610	21,015,324

5 Experiment

5.1 Experimental Setting

Datasets and Evaluation. We conduct experiments on several text retrieval datasets: MS-MARCO [22], TREC-2019 Deep Learning Track [2], TREC-2020 Deep Learning Track [1], and Natural Questions (NQ) [14]. The statistics of the above datasets are shown in Table 1. MS-MARCO consists of real queries collected from Bing search engine. NQ is an open domain QA dataset.

Baselines. We compare our approach with a variety of methods: BM25 [40] is a widely-used sparse retriever based on exact matching. DeepCT [3] and docT5query [23] enhance BM25 with neural models. ANCE [39], TAS-B [10] and STAR [41] are dense retrieval methods that adopt top-k hard negatives to improve training. RocketQA [25], AR2 [42] and ERNIE-search [19] utilize knowledge distillation technique that leverages a teacher model to guide the training of the dual-encoder retriever. COIL [8], ColBERT [13] and ColBERTv2 [31] utilize multiple representations for text retrieval. SEED [18], RetroMAE [17], Condenser [6], PAIR [29], coCondenser [7], CoT-MAE [36] and SimLM [35] design special pre-training tasks to improve the backbone models.

Implementation Details. During pre-training, we leverage BERT-base to initialize the shared encoder, and all decoders are randomly initialized two-layer Transformers. Following previous work [7,35,36], we leverage the passages in MS-MARCO and NQ dataset as the pre-training corpus of them, respectively. The pre-training steps are setting to 120k. During fine-tuning, we also follow SimLM that progressively trains Retriever_1, Retriever_2, and $\text{Retriever}_{\text{distil}}$, where our pre-trained deep Transformer encoder is leveraged to initialize their parameters. Our all other hyper-parameters are the same as SimLM [35].

5.2 Main Results

Performance on Web Search Datasets. Table 2 shows the results on three web search benchmarks, *i.e.*, MS-MARCO, TREC-2019 and TREC-2020. First, we can see that with or without distillation strategy, the best baselines are both

Table 2. Results on three web search datasets. The best and second-best methods are marked in bold and underlined, respectively. The ✓in the column of "with KD?" means that the model has used knowledge distillation.

Model	with KD?	**MS-MARCO**			**TREC-19**	**TREC-20**
		MRR@10	R@50	R@1k	nDCG@10	nDCG@10
BM25 [40]		18.5	58.5	85.7	51.2	47.7
DeepCT [3]		24.3	69.0	91.0	57.2	–
docT5query [23]		27.7	75.6	94.7	64.2	–
ANCE [39]		33.0	–	95.9	64.5	64.6
STAR [41]		34.7	–	–	68.3	–
TAS-B [10]	✓	34.0	–	97.5	71.2	69.3
RocketQA [25]	✓	37.0	85.5	97.9	–	–
RocketQAv2 [30]	✓	38.8	86.2	98.1	–	–
AR2 [42]	✓	39.5	87.8	98.6	–	–
ERNIE-Search [19]	✓	40.1	87.7	98.2	–	-
AR2+SimANS [45]	✓	40.9	**88.7**	<u>98.7</u>	–	–
COIL [8]		35.5	–	96.3	70.4	–
ColBERT [13]		36.0	82.9	96.8	–	–
ColBERTv2 [31]	✓	39.7	86.8	98.4	–	–
SEED [18]		33.9	–	96.1	–	–
RetroMAE [17]		35.0	–	97.6	–	–
Condenser [5]		36.6	–	97.4	69.8	–
coCondenser [7]		38.2	86.5	98.4	<u>71.7</u>	68.4
CoT-MAE [36]		39.4	87.0	<u>98.7</u>	–	<u>70.4</u>
PAIR [29]	✓	37.9	86.4	98.2	–	–
SimLM [35]	✓	<u>41.1</u>	87.8	<u>98.7</u>	71.2	69.7
MASTER	✓	**41.2**	<u>88.6</u>	**98.8**	**72.7**	**71.7**

pre-training dense retrieval methods, *i.e.*, CoT-MAE and SimLM, even outperforming methods using multiple representations. It indicates that proper pre-training strategies are helpful to the downstream dense passage retrieval tasks. Second, SimLM mostly outperforms other baselines. It employs a bottlenecked architecture that learns to compress the input information into a dense vector, and adopts a replaced language modeling objective to pre-train it. Such a way is more effective to force the dense vector to reserve the important semantics.

Besides, our approach outperforms all the baselines in terms of all metrics on all datasets. Our approach adopts a multi-task pre-training framework that unifies five tasks on recovering of corrupted passages, related passages and PLMs outputs, based on a bottlenecked one-encoder multi-decoder architecture. In this way, we can force the output dense vector from the encoder to be more

Table 3. The performance of Retriever_2 without knowledge distillation on NQ.

Model	DPR	ANCE	RocketQA	Condenser	PAIR	coCondenser	SimLM	MASTER
R@20	78.4	81.9	82.7	83.2	83.5	84.3	84.3	**84.6**
R@100	85.4	87.5	88.5	88.4	89.1	89.0	89.3	**89.4**

Table 4. Zero-shot dense retrieval nDCG@10 performances on BEIR benchmark. Results with * are from our reproduction.

Dataset	BERT	LaPraDoR	SimCSE	DiffCSE	SEED	Condenser	SimLM*	MASTER
TREC-COVID	0.615	0.492	0.460	0.492	0.627	**0.750**	0.637	0.620
BioASQ	0.253	0.308	0.263	0.258	0.308	0.322	0.350	**0.354**
NFCorpus	0.260	**0.335**	0.260	0.259	0.278	0.277	0.323	0.330
NQ	0.467	0.473	0.435	0.412	0.446	0.486	0.477	**0.516**
HotpotQA	0.488	0.495	0.502	0.499	0.541	0.538	0.581	**0.589**
FiQA-2018	0.252	0.314	0.250	0.229	0.259	0.259	0.292	**0.328**
Signal-1M(RT)	0.204	0.231	**0.262**	0.260	0.256	0.261	0.257	0.252
TREC-NEWS	0.362	0.374	0.356	0.363	0.358	0.376	0.326	**0.409**
Robust04	0.351	0.368	0.330	0.343	0.365	0.349	0.368	**0.405**
ArguAna	0.265	**0.469**	0.413	0.468	0.389	0.298	0.421	0.395
Touche-2020	0.259	0.182	0.159	0.168	0.225	0.248	0.292	**0.320**
CQADupStack	0.282	0.288	0.290	0.305	0.290	**0.347**	0.332	0.327
Quora	0.787	0.847	0.844	0.850	0.852	**0.853**	0.773	0.791
DBPedia	0.314	0.338	0.314	0.303	0.330	0.339	0.345	**0.399**
SCIDOCS	0.113	**0.155**	0.124	0.125	0.124	0.133	0.145	0.141
FEVER	0.682	0.646	0.623	0.641	0.641	0.691	0.657	**0.692**
Climate-FEVER	0.187	0.209	0.211	0.200	0.176	0.211	0.163	**0.215**
SciFact	0.533	0.599	0.554	0.523	0.575	0.593	0.588	**0.637**
Avg.	0.371	0.396	0.369	0.372	0.391	0.407	0.407	**0.429**

informative and functional to accomplish these tasks, leading to better representative capacity.

Performance on Open Domain QA Datasets. Table 3 shows the results an open domain QA datasets, NQ. For a fair comparison, we only report the performance of Retriever_2 without performing knowledge distillation. First, we can also see that pre-training dense retrieval methods mostly outperform other methods. It further indicates the effectiveness of pre-training techniques in open domain QA tasks. Besides, coCondenser and SimLM perform better than other methods, the reason is that they both adopt a bottlenecked architecture to compress the information into the dense vectors. Finally, we can see that our approach outperforms all the baselines. As a comparison, our approach can enhance the informativeness of dense vectors by integrating multiple pre-training tasks, which compress the semantic information within passages, model the relations between passages, and learn the knowledge from other PLMs.

Table 5. Comparison with different pre-training dense retrieval methods in three stages of our fine-tuning pipeline on the dev set of MS-MARCO.

Model	coCondenser		CoTMAE		SimLM		MASTER	
	MRR@10	**R@1k**	**MRR@10**	**R@1k**	**MRR@10**	**R@1k**	**MRR@10**	**R@1k**
Retriever_1	35.7	97.8	36.8	98.3	38.0	98.3	**38.3**	**98.8**
Retriever_2	38.2	98.4	39.2	98.7	39.1	98.6	**40.4**	**98.8**
$\text{Retriever}_{\text{distil}}$	40.2	98.3	40.4	98.7	41.1	98.7	**41.2**	**98.8**

Table 6. Ablation and variation study of our approach. We report MRR@10 of the retriever_1 and retriever_2 on the dev set of MS-MARCO.

Model	MASTER	w/o CPR	w/o RPR	w/o POR	+Shared-Dec	SimLM
Retriever_1	**38.3**	37.7	37.6	37.6	37.4	38.0
Retriever_2	**40.4**	39.9	39.8	39.8	39.1	39.1

Zero-Shot Evaluation. We evaluate the zero-shot retrieval performance of our approach on BEIR benchmark [33]. It contains 18 datasets, covering dense retrieval tasks across different domains. Following [33], we fine-tune our approach in MS-MARCO training set and evaluate it on the BEIR benchmark using the official evaluation toolkit. nDCG@10 is chosen as the evaluation metrics. As shown in Table 4, the average performance of our approach surpasses all baselines significantly. Since our approach incorporates multiple pre-training tasks for learning the dense representations, such a way can enrich the informativeness of them and help better adapt into different domains and retrieval tasks.

5.3 Further Analysis

Fine-tuning Performance in Three Stages. To further investigate the effectiveness of our approach, we show the performances of MASTER and other pre-training dense retrieval methods in each stage of our fine-tuning pipeline. Here, the models in the three stages are all initialized by corresponding pre-trained parameters of these methods. As shown in Table 5, the performances of all pre-training methods are consistently improving with the process of the three-stage training. In addition, our approach also outperforms all other pre-training methods in the three stages. It indicates the superiority of our proposed multi-task pre-training strategy.

Ablation and Variation Study. Our proposed approach incorporates a multi-decoder architecture and three types of tasks for pre-training. To verify the effectiveness of each part, we conduct the ablation and variation study on the dev set of MS-MARCO to analyze their contributions. We remove the CPR, RPR and POR tasks individually, and propose a variants that adopts a shared decoder to deal with the multiple tasks. As shown in Table 6, we can see that

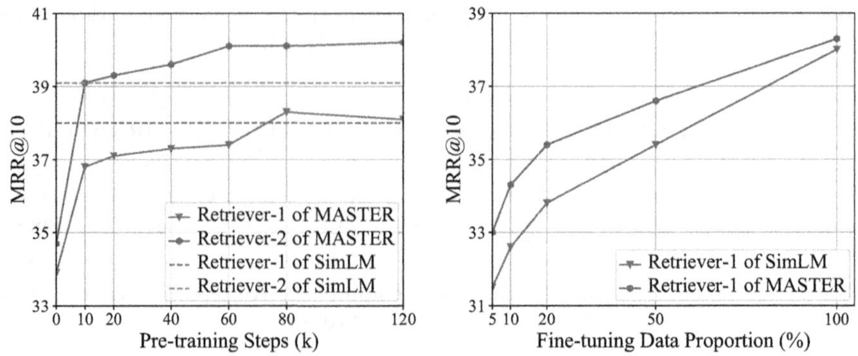

Fig. 3. Performance comparison w.r.t. different number of pre-training steps and data proportions on MS-MARCO.

Table 7. Experimental results on four NLU tasks from GLUE.

Model	CoLA	MRPC	STS-B	QQP
BERT	59.1	87.7	87.8	89.7
Ours	60.7	89.1	88.0	89.8

all the ablation and variation models will lead to the performance degradation. It indicates that all the pre-training tasks and our multi-decoder architecture are useful to improve the performance. Besides, after removing any type of pre-training tasks, our Retriever$_2$ still outperforms the SOTA method, SimLM. It further shows the promising effectiveness of multi-task pre-training for dense retrieval tasks.

Performance w.r.t. Different Pre-training Steps. As a pre-training approach, the number of pre-training steps will affect the performance on downstream tasks. In each step, we optimize the model parameters using a batch of pre-training data by gradient descent algorithm. However, too many pre-training steps are time-consuming and costly. Here, we investigate the performance convergence speed of our approach during pre-training. As shown in Fig. 3(a), we can see that our model performs well with few pre-training steps, especially that the retriever$_2$ of our method achieves the 39.1 on MRR@10 metric (the same as SimLM) after 10k steps. It shows that our approach is more effective to pre-train effective dense vectors, with no need for too many pre-training steps.

Few-Shot Learning. In our approach, as we have pre-trained the backbone via a multi-task manner, the pre-learned dense vectors can be easily adapted into downstream tasks with less data. To validate it, we reduce the training data size into 50%, 20%, 10% and 5%, and compare the performance of our approach with the pre-training method SimLM. As shown in Fig. 3(b), we can see that the performance substantially drops when less training data is used. Additionally,

Table 8. Performance comparison w.r.t. different masked rates in the encoder and decoder. We report MRR@10 of the Retriever_1 and Retriever_2 on MS-MARCO.

Model	30% En-50% De	15% En-50% De	50% En-50% De	30% En-30% De	30% En-70% De
Retriever_1	**38.3**	37.9	37.6	37.5	38.0
Retriever_2	**40.4**	39.9	39.7	39.8	39.9

our approach is consistently better than SimLM in all cases, especially in an extreme sparsity level (5%). It indicates that MASTER is better pre-trained to effectively adapt to downstream dense retrieval task.

Natural Language Understanding Tasks. In our approach, as we integrate multiple pre-training tasks, our model can capture diverse knowledge from these tasks. In this part, we evaluate if our pre-training methods can also benefit for natural language understanding (NLU) tasks. We select the single-sentence and similarity tasks from the GLUE benchmark [34] (*i.e.*, CoLA, MRPC, STS-B and QQP), which focus on predicting the acceptability, similarity and paraphrase of sentences from different domains (e.g., news and misc). We fine-tune our pre-trained model on these tasks. and all the hyper-parameters are following the suggestions of the original BERT paper [4]. As shown in Table 7, our approach improves the performance of BERT on these NLU tasks. It indicates that our multi-task pre-training can also enrich the useful knowledge about NLU tasks.

Hyper-parameter Tuning. The masked rates of the deep encoder and multiple decoders are two important hyper-parameters, as they control the information bottleneck in our approach. Here, we set the masked rate in the encoder to be 15%, 30% and 50%, and that in decoders to be 30%, 50% and 70%. Table 8 shows the evaluation results. First, our model is robust to these different settings. Besides, when the masked rates of the encoder and decoders are set to 30% and 50% respectively, our model performs slightly better than others. Therefore, we apply 30% and 50% as the masked rates of the encoder and decoders.

6 Conclusion

In this paper, we proposed MASTER, a multi-task pre-trained bottlenecked masked autoencoder for dense retrieval task. In our approach, we adopted a bottlenecked multi-decoder architecture to integrate a variety of pre-training tasks, and devised three types of pre-training tasks about corrupted passages recovering, related passage recovering and PLMs outputs recovering. The three types of tasks focused on compressing the information within the passages, modeling relations among passages, and learning the knowledge from external public generative PLMs, respectively, leading to more informative and effective dense vectors. Experimental results have shown the superiority of our approach.

Limitations

A major limitation of our approach is the cost of pre-training. Actually, it is not necessary for researchers or developers to complete the whole pre-training process, as they can directly utilize our publicly released checkpoints for initialization. Besides, in this work, we evaluate our approach mainly on passage retrieval tasks, and do not consider the retrieval of very long documents. Another possible issue derives from that we continually pre-train the parameters of BERT. Since existing works have revealed that BERT might represent biases from the pre-training corpus, such an issue may also be inherited by our approach.

Acknowledgement. Kun Zhou, Wayne Xin Zhao and Ji-Rong Wen were partially supported by National Natural Science Foundation of China under Grant No. 62222215, Beijing Natural Science Foundation under Grant No. 4222027, Beijing Outstanding Young Scientist Program under Grant No. BJJWZYJH012019100020098, and the Outstanding Innovative Talents Cultivation Funded Programs 2021 of Renmin University of China. Xin Zhao is the corresponding author.

References

1. Craswell, N., Mitra, B., Yilmaz, E., Campos, D.: Overview of the TREC 2020 deep learning track. arXiv preprint arXiv:2102.07662 (2021)
2. Craswell, N., Mitra, B., Yilmaz, E., Campos, D., Voorhees, E.M.: Overview of the TREC 2019 deep learning track. arXiv preprint arXiv:2003.07820 (2020)
3. Dai, Z., Callan, J.: Deeper text understanding for IR with contextual neural language modeling. In: Proceedings of SIGIR 2019, pp. 985–988 (2019). https://doi.org/10.1145/3331184.3331303
4. Devlin, J., Chang, M.W., Lee, K., Toutanova, K.: BERT: pre-training of deep bidirectional transformers for language understanding. In: Proceedings of NAACL 2019, pp. 4171–4186 (2019). https://aclanthology.org/N19-1423
5. Gao, L., Callan, J.: Condenser: a pre-training architecture for dense retrieval. In: Proceedings of EMNLP 2021, pp. 981–993 (2021). https://aclanthology.org/2021.emnlp-main.75
6. Gao, L., Callan, J.: Is your language model ready for dense representation fine-tuning? arXiv preprint arXiv:2104.08253 (2021)
7. Gao, L., Callan, J.: Unsupervised corpus aware language model pre-training for dense passage retrieval. In: Proceedings of ACL 2022, pp. 2843–2853 (2022). https://doi.org/10.18653/v1/2022.acl-long.203
8. Gao, L., Dai, Z., Callan, J.: COIL: revisit exact lexical match in information retrieval with contextualized inverted list. In: Proceedings of NAACL 2021, pp. 3030–3042 (2021).https://aclanthology.org/2021.naacl-main.241
9. He, K., Chen, X., Xie, S., Li, Y., Dollár, P., Girshick, R.: Masked autoencoders are scalable vision learners. In: Proceedings of the IEEE/CVF Conference on Computer Vision and Pattern Recognition, pp. 16000–16009 (2022)
10. Hofstätter, S., Lin, S., Yang, J., Lin, J., Hanbury, A.: Efficiently teaching an effective dense retriever with balanced topic aware sampling. In: Proceedings of SIGIR 2021, pp. 113–122 (2021). https://doi.org/10.1145/3404835.3462891

11. Johnson, J., Douze, M., Jégou, H.: Billion-scale similarity search with gpus. IEEE Trans. Big Data **7**(3), 535–547 (2021). https://doi.org/10.1109/TBDATA.2019.2921572
12. Karpukhin, V., et al.: Dense passage retrieval for open-domain question answering. In: Proceedings of EMNLP 2020, pp. 6769–6781 (2020). https://aclanthology.org/2020.emnlp-main.550
13. Khattab, O., Zaharia, M.: Colbert: efficient and effective passage search via contextualized late interaction over BERT. In: Proceedings of SIGIR 2020, pp. 39–48 (2020). https://doi.org/10.1145/3397271.3401075
14. Kwiatkowski, T., et al.: Natural questions: a benchmark for question answering research. Trans. Assoc. Comput. Linguist. **7**, 452–466 (2019). https://aclanthology.org/Q19-1026
15. Lee, K., Chang, M.W., Toutanova, K.: Latent retrieval for weakly supervised open domain question answering. In: Proceedings of ACL 2019, pp. 6086–6096 (2019). https://aclanthology.org/P19-1612
16. Lin, Z., et al.: Prod: progressive distillation for dense retrieval. In: Proceedings of the ACM Web Conference 2023, pp. 3299–3308 (2023)
17. Liu, Z., Shao, Y.: Retromae: pre-training retrieval-oriented transformers via masked auto-encoder. arXiv preprint arXiv:2205.12035 (2022)
18. Lu, S., et al.: Less is more: pretrain a strong Siamese encoder for dense text retrieval using a weak decoder. In: Proceedings of EMNLP 2021, pp. 2780–2791 (2021). https://aclanthology.org/2021.emnlp-main.220
19. Lu, Y., et al.: Ernie-search: bridging cross-encoder with dual-encoder via self on-the-fly distillation for dense passage retrieval. arXiv preprint arXiv:2205.09153 (2022). https://doi.org/10.48550/arXiv.2205.09153
20. Ma, G., Wu, X., Wang, P., Hu, S.: Cot-mote: exploring contextual masked auto-encoder pre-training with mixture-of-textual-experts for passage retrieval. arXiv preprint arXiv:2304.10195 (2023)
21. Ma, X., Guo, J., Zhang, R., Fan, Y., Cheng, X.: Pre-train a discriminative text encoder for dense retrieval via contrastive span prediction. In: Proceedings of SIGIR 2022, pp. 848–858 (2022). https://doi.org/10.1145/3477495.3531772
22. Nguyen, T., et al.: MS MARCO: a human generated machine reading comprehension dataset. In: Proceedings of the Workshop on Cognitive Computation: Integrating Neural and Symbolic Approaches 2016, vol. 1773 (2016). http://ceur-ws.org/Vol-1773/CoCoNIPS_2016_paper9.pdf
23. Nogueira, R., Lin, J.: From doc2query to docttttquery (2019). https://cs.uwaterloo.ca/~jimmylin/publications/Nogueira_Lin_2019_docTTTTTquery.pdf
24. Nogueira, R.F., Yang, W., Lin, J., Cho, K.: Document expansion by query prediction. arXiv preprint arXiv:1904.08375 (2019)
25. Qu, Y., et al.: RocketQA: an optimized training approach to dense passage retrieval for open-domain question answering. In: Proceedings of NAACL 2021, pp. 5835–5847 (2021). https://aclanthology.org/2021.naacl-main.466
26. Radford, A., et al.: Language models are unsupervised multitask learners (2019). https://cdn.openai.com/better-language-models/language_models_are_unsupervised_multitask_learners.pdf
27. Raffel, C., et al.: Exploring the limits of transfer learning with a unified text-to-text transformer. J. Mach. Learn. Res. **21**, 140:1–140:67 (2020). http://jmlr.org/papers/v21/20-074.html

28. Ramos, J., et al.: Using TF-IDF to determine word relevance in document queries. In: Proceedings of the First Instructional Conference on Machine Learning, vol. 242, pp. 29–48 (2003)
29. Ren, R., et al.: PAIR: Leveraging passage-centric similarity relation for improving dense passage retrieval. In: Findings of the Association for Computational Linguistics: ACL-IJCNLP 2021, pp. 2173–2183 (2021). https://aclanthology.org/2021.findings-acl.191
30. Ren, R., et al.: Rocketqav2: a joint training method for dense passage retrieval and passage re-ranking. In: Proceedings of EMNLP 2021, pp. 2825–2835 (2021). https://doi.org/10.18653/v1/2021.emnlp-main.224
31. Santhanam, K., Khattab, O., Saad-Falcon, J., Potts, C., Zaharia, M.: Colbertv2: effective and efficient retrieval via lightweight late interaction. In: Proceedings of the 2022 Conference of the North American Chapter of the Association for Computational Linguistics: Human Language Technologies, NAACL 2022, Seattle, WA, United States, 10–15 July 2022, pp. 3715–3734 (2022). https://doi.org/10.18653/v1/2022.naacl-main.272
32. Sun, H., et al.: Lead: liberal feature-based distillation for dense retrieval. arXiv preprint arXiv:2212.05225 (2022)
33. Thakur, N., Reimers, N., Rücklé, A., Srivastava, A., Gurevych, I.: BEIR: a heterogenous benchmark for zero-shot evaluation of information retrieval models. arXiv preprint arXiv:2104.08663 (2021)
34. Wang, A., Singh, A., Michael, J., Hill, F., Levy, O., Bowman, S.R.: GLUE: a multi-task benchmark and analysis platform for natural language understanding. In: Proceedings of ICLR 2019 (2019). https://openreview.net/forum?id=rJ4km2R5t7
35. Wang, L., et al.: Simlm: pre-training with representation bottleneck for dense passage retrieval. arXiv preprint arXiv:2207.02578 (2022)
36. Wu, X., Ma, G., Lin, M., Lin, Z., Wang, Z., Hu, S.: Contextual mask auto-encoder for dense passage retrieval. arXiv preprint arXiv:2208.07670 (2022)
37. Wu, X., et al.: Cot-mae v2: contextual masked auto-encoder with multi-view modeling for passage retrieval. arXiv preprint arXiv:2304.03158 (2023)
38. Xiao, S., Liu, Z.: Retromae v2: duplex masked auto-encoder for pre-training retrieval-oriented language models. arXiv preprint arXiv:2211.08769 (2022)
39. Xiong, L., et al.: Approximate nearest neighbor negative contrastive learning for dense text retrieval. In: 9th International Conference on Learning Representations, ICLR 2021, Virtual Event, Austria, 3–7 May 2021 (2021). https://openreview.net/forum?id=zeFrfgyZln
40. Yang, P., Fang, H., Lin, J.: Anserini: enabling the use of lucene for information retrieval research. In: Proceedings of the 40th International ACM SIGIR Conference on Research and Development in Information Retrieval, Shinjuku, Tokyo, Japan, 7–11 August 2017, pp. 1253–1256 (2017). https://doi.org/10.1145/3077136.3080721
41. Zhan, J., Mao, J., Liu, Y., Guo, J., Zhang, M., Ma, S.: Optimizing dense retrieval model training with hard negatives. In: SIGIR '21: The 44th International ACM SIGIR Conference on Research and Development in Information Retrieval, Virtual Event, Canada, 11–15 July 2021, pp. 1503–1512 (2021). https://doi.org/10.1145/3404835.3462880
42. Zhang, H., Gong, Y., Shen, Y., Lv, J., Duan, N., Chen, W.: Adversarial retriever-ranker for dense text retrieval. In: The Tenth International Conference on Learning Representations, ICLR 2022, Virtual Event, 25–29 April 2022 (2022). https://openreview.net/forum?id=MR7XubKUFB

43. Zhao, W.X., Liu, J., Ren, R., Wen, J.R.: Dense text retrieval based on pretrained language models: a survey. arXiv preprint arXiv:2211.14876 (2022)
44. Zhao, W.X., et al.: A survey of large language models. arXiv preprint arXiv:2303.18223 (2023)
45. Zhou, K., et al.: Simans: simple ambiguous negatives sampling for dense text retrieval. In: Proceedings of the 2022 Conference on Empirical Methods in Natural Language Processing (EMNLP) (2022)
46. Zhou, K., Zhang, B., Zhao, W.X., Wen, J.R.: Debiased contrastive learning of unsupervised sentence representations. In: Proceedings of the 60th Annual Meeting of the Association for Computational Linguistics (Volume 1: Long Papers), pp. 6120–6130 (2022)
47. Zhou, Y.J., Yao, J., Dou, Z.C., Wu, L., Wen, J.R.: Dynamicretriever: a pre-trained model-based IR system without an explicit index. In: Machine Intelligence Research, pp. 1–13 (2023)

Graph Contrastive Learning

Duplicate Multi-modal Entities Detection with Graph Contrastive Self-training Network

Shuyun Gu, Xiao Wang, and Chuan Shi(✉)

Beijing University of Posts and Telecommunications, Beijing, China
{xiaowang,shichuan}@bupt.edu.cn

Abstract. Duplicate multi-modal entities detection aims to find highly similar entities from massive entities with multi-modal information, which is a basic task in many applications and becoming more important and urgent with the development of Internet and e-commerce platforms. Traditional methods employ machine learning or deep learning on feature embedding extracted from multi-modal information, which ignores the correlation among entities and modals. Inspired by the popular Graph Neural Networks (GNNs), we can analyze the multi-relation graph of entities constructed from their multi-modal information with GNN. However, this solution still faces the extreme label sparsity challenge, particularly in industrial applications. In this work, we propose a novel graph contrastive self-training network model, named **CT-GNN**, for duplicate multi-modal entities detection with extreme label sparsity. With the multi-relation graph of entities constructed from multi-modal features of entities with KNN, we first learn the preliminary node embeddings with existing GNN, e.g., GCNs. To alleviate the problem of extremely sparse labels, we design a layer contrastive module to effectively exploit implicit label information, as well as a pseudo labels extension module to determine label boundary. In addition, graph structure learning is introduced to refine the structure of the multi-relation graph. A uniform optimization framework is designed to seamlessly integrate these three components. Sufficient experiments on real datasets, in comparison with SOTA baselines, well demonstrate the effectiveness of our proposed method.

Keywords: Duplicate enetites · Graph learning · Self-supervised learning · Self-training learning

1 Introduction

Duplicate entities detection, finding all two highly similar or even identical entities from massive data, has become a common and important problem, e.g., face matching [23] and user alignment [37]. In e-commerce scenarios, this problem is more challenging, because entities often have multi-modal features, e.g., texts, images and even videos. Duplicate multi-modal entities detection has urgent and realistic needs, which provides the basic function in many applications. For instance, as shown in Fig. 1 (e.g., similar images and descriptions), some store managers defraud illegal subsidies from e-commerce platforms through registering inveracious duplicate stores. Thus, detecting

© The Author(s), under exclusive license to Springer Nature Switzerland AG 2023
D. Koutra et al. (Eds.): ECML PKDD 2023, LNAI 14170, pp. 651–665, 2023.
https://doi.org/10.1007/978-3-031-43415-0_38

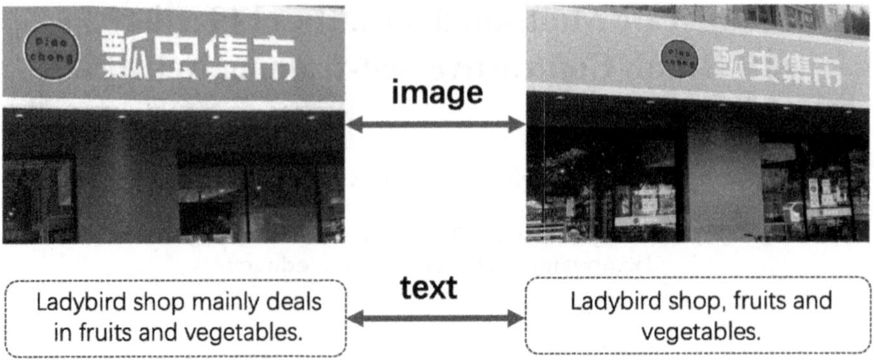

Fig. 1. An example of duplicate multi-modal stores. The images and texts are the outlines and description information of the stores respectively. Because of their highly similar features, they are determined to be duplicate entities.

these duplicate multi-modal entities is an important task for combating fake information and saving cost. In order to solve the above problems, traditional industrial solutions are more inclined to machine learning or deep learning methods [1], making independent decisions for each pair of duplicate entities based on feature engineering, which measures the similarity of entities by feature extraction and feature combination. Nevertheless, these methods have two disadvantages. (1) They do not depict the correlation between entities explicitly. The correlation between entities is important prior knowledge, and thus ignoring them may result in performance degradation. (2) The associations between multiple modals are not considered. Different modals depict entities from distinct perspectives, and thus considering associations between multiple modals may benefit for characterizing entities more accurately.

For solving above disadvantages, a direct solution is to construct a multi-relation graph through employing K-Nearest Neighbors (KNN) [4] on multi-modal features, and then the popular GNN [10,35] can be applied to exploit the structure relations among entities and modals. However, because of the semi-supervised paradigm, this solution faces the extreme labels (i.e., known duplicate entity pairs) sparsity challenge, especially on industrial applications. For instance, an e-commerce platform has tens of millions of offline stores, the proportion of duplicate stores is relatively small. The labels we can obtain also rely on manual annotation. Due to very high labor costs, the known label data may only account for 5% of the duplicate stores, and thus the label data may be no more than 0.05% of all stores.

How to deal with the extreme labels sparsity challenge? A common way is self-supervised learning [32,34] or self-training learning [12,13]. However, these strategies are not easily applied to our problem settings and a single strategy is also not sufficient to solve the above challenge. For self-supervised learning, the conventional process is to generate two augmented views based on a graph, and emphasize the consistency between different views of the same node (i.e., entity) [26,36]. However, in our duplicate multi-modal entities detection scenario, this method of emphasizing the consistency of the same node does not have much benefit to mine whether two nodes is duplicate. As for self-training learning, its main idea is to generate some pseudo labels and train jointly with real labels. In the scenario of duplicate entities detection, we can generate pseudo labels by similarity measurement. However, pseudo labels with different similarities have different influences on the model, so it is difficult to determine a rational threshold for pseudo labels. More importantly, individual self-supervised or self-training learning may be not sufficient to solve the extreme label sparsity, especially in real industry scenorio, which motivates us to effectively integrate more strategies to solve this challenge.

In this paper, we propose a novel graph contrastive self-training network model **CT-GNN**, which solves the challenge of extreme label sparsity by means of seamlessly integrating self-supervised learning and self-training learning. Specifically, after multi-modal feature extraction through pre-training model [5,24], we build a multi-relation graph with KNN method, and learn the node embeddings with GCNs [10] model. In order to exploit implicit label information among graph structure, we propose a novel layer-contrastive module by using the strategy of multiple random walks [11,16,18] to find the others with the most frequency as positive nodes in the topology. At the same time, in order to more fully utilize the feature information of entities, we design a self-training module with a delicate boundary distance, which distinguishes the optimization intensity of labels with different similarities. In addition, the graph structure learning process is introduced to automatically adjust graph structure for iterative representation learning. Finally, a joint optimization function is designed to seamlessly optimize above three components.

We summarize the contributions of this work as below:

- To our best knowledge, we are the first to study the problem of duplicate multi-modal entities detection with extreme label sparsity, which is a basic task in many applications and becoming more important and urgent with the development of Internet and e-commerce platforms.
- We propose a novel graph model named CT-GNN, which seamlessly integrates self-supervised learning, self-training learning and graph structure learning in a uniform optimization framework. In particular, some delicate designs in CT-GNN make it suitable for extreme label sparsity challenge, i.e., layer contrastive module with multiple random walk and self-training module with boundary distance.
- We evaluate CT-GNN by designing both various offline and online experiments. Compared to state-of-the-art alternatives, the improvements of CT-GNN are obvious up to 9.88% in Recall and 7.13% in Precision.

2 Related Work

2.1 Graph Neural Networks

In recent years, Graph Neural Networks (GNNs) has become an extremely important field, e.g., recommendation systems [8,30], fraud detection [15], which learn the node embedding by aggregating the features of neighborhoods [28]. GCNs [10] implements layer-wise propagation to learn the node embedding, and GAT [28] learns different attention scores for neighbors when aggregating neighborhood information. Meanwhile, Some recent models [21] are proposed to deal with heterogeneous graphs which are more practical in reality. RGCN [21] propose to learn node embedding based on multi-relation neighborhoods. Additionally, HAN [31] leverages the attention mechanism under node-level and semantic-level in heterogeneous graphs.

2.2 Self-supervised Learning for GNNs

Recently, motivated by profound success in natural language processing [5] and computer vision [7], self-supervised contrastive learning based graph representation learning attracts considerable attention. Deep Graph Infomax (DGI) [29] learns unsupervised representations for nodes in attributed graphs by the mutual informaton-based learning from Deep InfoMax [9]. GMI [19] is proposed to contrast between center node and its local patch from node features and topological structure. Another line of graph contrastive learning approaches called global-global contrast [20] directly study the relationships between the global context representations of different samples as what metric learning does. In heterogeneous domain,DMGI [17] and HeCo [32] employs network schema and meta-path as two views to capture both of local and high-order structures, and performs the contrastive learning across them.

2.3 Self-training Learning for GNNs

Due to the pressure of sparse supervised signals, some researchers propose that GNNs are not completely suitable for graph semi-supervised learning tasks [13]. Self-training [12] strategy is to first train GNNs with the existing training sets, then selects the samples with high predicting probability as pseudo labels and add them to the training sets, and then continue to train GNNs. The samples selected by self-training should have similar features with the label samples, so that the robustness will be improved after expanding the training sets [38]. These methods have uniform constraint strength for all generated labels, but samples with different prediction probabilities should have different influence on the model.

3 The Proposed Model

3.1 Notations and Definitions

Given entity set $U = \{u_1, u_2, ..., u_n\}$ and feature set $E = \{e_1, e_2, ..., e_n\}$, each entity $u_i \in U$ has a feature $e_i \in E$, in which n is the number of entities and e_i includes multi-modal feature $e_i = \{e_i^{(1)}, e_i^{(2)}, ..., e_i^{(v)}\}$, and v is the number of modals. Without lost of generality, we consider image feature E_{img} and text feature E_{text} in this paper. For these multi-modal features, we can obtain their initial feature (i.e., E_{img} and E_{img}). Through multi-relation graph construction and GNN method, we fully learn node embedding (i.e., $\boldsymbol{X}^{\mathbf{0}}$). Our goal is to mine all suspicious duplicate entities through the similarity calculation of node embedding.

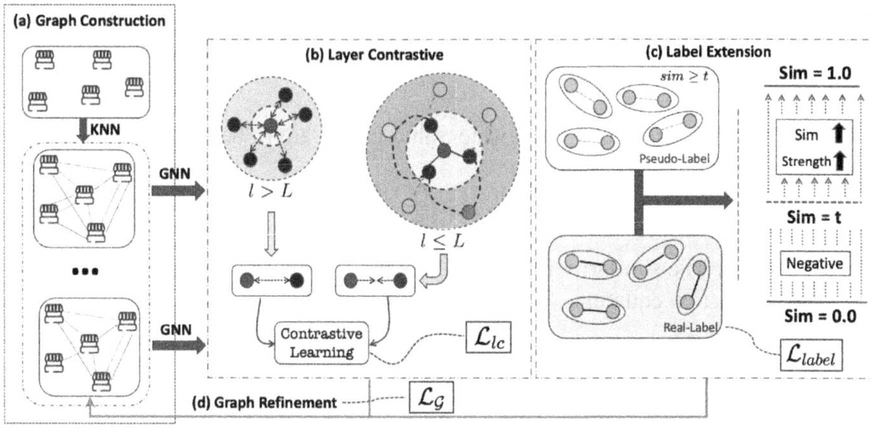

Fig. 2. The architecture of CT-GNN. (a) is the constructing process of multi-relation graph. (b) is the layer contrastive module through multiple random walks. (c) is the self-training learning considering boundary distance. (d) is the graph refinement process.

3.2 Overall Framework

Figure 2 shows the overall framework of our CT-GNN model. After constructing multi-relation graph by multi-modal features, we design a graph contrastive self-training network to solve the extreme label sparsity challenge, including layer contrastive learning, self-training with boundary distance and graph structure learning, in a uniform optimization framework. Concretely, after learning graph embedding with GCNs, we firstly design a layer contrastive module to sufficiently utilize self-supervised information, which uses multiple random walks to find the important neighbors of the central node as positive samples of contrastive learning. Then we introduce a self-training module to flexibly extend label information. Based on the similarity between entities, we smartly generate pseudo labels through a delicate boundary distance loss distinguishing the optimization intensity of labels with different similarities. Meanwhile, in order to refine the graph structure, we further design a graph structure refinement process during iteration.

3.3 Multi-relation Graph Construction

Firstly, we construct a multi-relation graph of entities under the multi-modal features with the KNN method. Without lost of generality, we consider image and text feature. ***Image Feature:*** we employ the pre-training image model VGG [22,24] to acquire the image feature vectors $\boldsymbol{X}_{img} \in \boldsymbol{R}^{n*d}$ and d represents feature dimension. ***Text Feature:*** we use the pre-training language model BERT [5,25] and convert all of the text information for each entity feature vector $\boldsymbol{X}_{text} \in \boldsymbol{R}^{n*d}$.

Based on $\boldsymbol{X}_{img}$ and $\boldsymbol{X}_{text}$, we can construct the K-Nearest Neighbor graph $\mathcal{G}_{img} = (\boldsymbol{A}_{img}, \boldsymbol{X}_{img})$ and $\mathcal{G}_{text} = (\boldsymbol{A}_{text}, \boldsymbol{X}_{text})$, where $\boldsymbol{A}_{img}$ and $\boldsymbol{A}_{text}$ are the adjacency matrix of KNN graphs under images and texts respectively. Specifically, under $\boldsymbol{X}_{img}$ or $\boldsymbol{X}_{text}$, for each sample, we first find its top-K similar neighbors and set edges to connect it with its neighbors. There are many methods to calculate the similarity matrix $\boldsymbol{S} \in \boldsymbol{R}^{n*n}$ of samples. Here we list two common methods for building KNN graph,

- **Cosine Similarity:** It uses the cosine value of the angle between two vectors to measure the similarity:

$$\boldsymbol{S}_{ij} = \frac{\boldsymbol{x}_i \cdot \boldsymbol{x}_j}{|\boldsymbol{x}_i||\boldsymbol{x}_j|}. \tag{1}$$

- **Heat Kernel:** The similarity is calculated by Eq. (2) where t is the time parameter in heat conduction equation.

$$\boldsymbol{S}_{ij} = e^{-\frac{||\boldsymbol{x}_i - \boldsymbol{x}_j||^2}{t}}. \tag{2}$$

Here we uniformly choose the Cosine Similarity. By this way, we can obtain two graphs: $\mathcal{G}_{img}$ and $\mathcal{G}_{text}$, and then combine them to get a multi-relation graph $\mathcal{G} = (\mathcal{V}, \mathcal{E}, \mathcal{R})$, in which $\mathcal{V}$ and $\mathcal{E}$ represent the node set (all entities) and edge set respectively, and $\mathcal{R} = \{image, text\}$ represent all relations between two nodes, i.e., the association between nodes in the image and text dimension.

3.4 Graph Embedding Learning

Now we have built the graph $\mathcal{G}$. The initial node feature are image and text feature, i.e., $\boldsymbol{X}_{img}$ and $\boldsymbol{X}_{text}$. We first learn from the idea of GNNs (e.g., GCNs [10]) to get the embedding of each type of feature, and then integrate them together. The generation method of embedding under image feature is as follows,

$$\boldsymbol{x}_{i_{img}}{}^{l+1} = \sum_{j \in \mathcal{N}_i^{img}} \frac{1}{\sqrt{|\mathcal{N}_i^{img}||\mathcal{N}_j^{img}|}} \boldsymbol{x}_{j_{img}}^l, \tag{3}$$

where $\boldsymbol{x}_{i_{img}}{}^{l+1}$ represents the embedding of node i at the $(l+1)^{th}$ layer under image feature. $\mathcal{N}_i^{img}$ represents the neighbor set of i (including the central node i) under the image feature. The embedding learning method under the text feature is the same as the image feature.

In order to obtain a comprehensive node embedding for subsequent graph learning, we fuse two types of embeddings by a function f, as follows,

$$\boldsymbol{x}_i{}^{l+1} = f(\boldsymbol{x}_{i_{img}}{}^{l+1}, \boldsymbol{x}_{i_{text}}{}^{l+1}), \tag{4}$$

where $\boldsymbol{x}_i{}^{l+1}$ is the embedding of node i after fusion. The common designs of f are concatenation, weighted sum and softmax [14], and we choose concatenation operation in this paper.

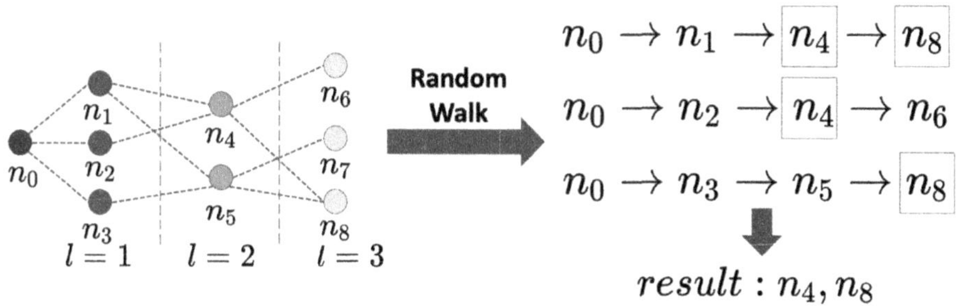

Fig. 3. Positive example selection in layer contrastive module. Three random walks are performed from the central node n_0, and $L = 3$ is limited, and the n_4 and n_8 appear the most times, i.e., n_4 and n_8 are taken as positive samples of n_0.

3.5 Self-supervised Learning with Layer Contrastive

In this section, we introduce a layer contrastive module to alleviate the problem of extreme sparse supervised signals. Traditional graph contrastive learning is to generate two augmented views based on a graph, and emphasize the consistency between different views of the same node, which does not match our goal of predicting whether two entities are duplicate. Because the duplicate entities usually meet the graph structure proximity principle, i.e., the two nodes that meet the duplication condition should be topologically highly related in the graph structure. Therefore, we design a layer contrastive learning module, which implements N random walks within L layer and finds the first top m nodes that appear more times. In this way, we can capture the neighbor (which can be multi-hop) nodes that are more important in the topology of the central node, and take them as positive samples in contrastive learning. As is shown in Fig. 3, starting from node n_0, we generate three random walk paths ($L = 3$). Among all paths, n_4 and n_8 appear the most frequently. We think n_4 and n_8 have the strongest correlation with the central node n_0 in the topology, that is, they are most likely to be duplicate with n_0. Therefore, n_4 and n_8 are used as positive samples of n_0 in contrastive learning. As for the negative samples, we randomly select from outside the Lth layer.

Obviously, the strength of entity repeatability is inversely proportional to the layer and directly proportional to the similarity. Therefore, we hope to use features and layers to constrain embedded learning. After finding the positive and negative examples, we adopt the contrastive loss, InfoNCE [6], to maximize the agreement of positive pairs and minimize that of negative pairs. On this basis, we consider the different effects of layers and similarities on the optimization strength, and update the loss function, as below,

$$\mathcal{L}_{lc} = -\sum_{v \in \mathcal{V}} \sum_{l=1}^{L} \sum_{u^+ \in nebor^l} \frac{sim(\boldsymbol{x}_v, \boldsymbol{x}_{u^+})}{l^\gamma} \\ log \frac{exp\{sim(\boldsymbol{x}_v, \boldsymbol{x}_{u^+})/\tau\}}{\sum_{u^- \in \mathcal{N}} exp\{sim(\boldsymbol{x}_v, \boldsymbol{x}_{u^-})/\tau\}}, \quad (5)$$

where $(\boldsymbol{x}_v, \boldsymbol{x}_{u^+})$ is the the positive pair and $(\boldsymbol{x}_v, \boldsymbol{x}_{u^-})$ is the negative pair. τ is a hyper-parameter, known as the *temperature* coefficient in softmax. We can see that the optimization proportion of positive samples is proportional to the similarity and inversely proportional to the layer l (i.e., the distance between nodes), and the influence intensity of the l is controlled by an intensity coefficient γ.

3.6 Self-training Learning with Boundary Distance

In this section, we introduce a self-training module to further relieve the extreme lacking labels. Conventional methods calculate the similarity between entities, and judge whether are pseudo labels by a boundary (i.e. threshold). However, a popular fixed boundary is not retional, since the pseudo labels with different distances from the threshold have different effects in the optimization process. And thus we design a smart threshold with boundary distance.

We use R to represent the set of real labels and generate pseudo labels with the similarity of nodes. Specifically, we set a super parameter t, and then calculate the cosine similarity between nodes. For two nodes whose similarity is greater than or equal to t, we think they are likely to be duplicated, so we regard them as a pair of pseudo labels. We use P to represent the set of pseudo labels. The generation process of P is formalized as follows,

$$(u, v) \in P, sim(\boldsymbol{x}_u, \boldsymbol{x}_v) \geq t. \tag{6}$$

Obviously, this threshold t can be considered as the boundary between duplicate and non-duplicate entities, and the node similarities in the real labels are far away from t. In order to distinguish the optimization strength of pseudo labels with different distances from t, we design a semi-supervised normal form based on boundary distance, as follows,

$$\begin{aligned}\mathcal{L}_{label} = -\frac{1}{N} \sum_{\substack{(u,u^+)\in P\cup R \\ (v,v^-)\in Neg}} (\frac{sim(\boldsymbol{x}_u, \boldsymbol{x}_{u^+}) - t}{1-t})^{\alpha} \\ log\{\sigma(sim(\boldsymbol{x}_u, \boldsymbol{x}_{u^+}) - sim(\boldsymbol{x}_v, \boldsymbol{x}_{v^-}))\},\end{aligned} \tag{7}$$

in which Neg is the negative sample set. Negative samples are randomly selected from the set whose similarity is less than t. α and σ are the strength-control coefficient and a non-linear activation function, respectively. As shown in Eq. (7), the optimization strength of all pseudo labels (i.e. positive samples) is different, and it decreases with the increase of the distance from the boundary t.

3.7 Graph Structure Learning

In order to ensure the credibility of the graph structure in the model iteration process, we choose to refine the graph structure in each epoch. The method of reconstructing the graph is shown in Sect. 3.3.

Let the graph adjacency matrix of the last epoch be A_{pre}, and that of the current epoch be A_{new}. In order to constrain the stability of nodes embeddings during the training process, we need to constrain the graph structure changes between the two epochs, which is as shown below,

$$\mathcal{L}_{\mathcal{G}} = ||A_{new} - A_{pre}||_2. \tag{8}$$

3.8 Joint Optimization

In order to combine the above modules, we jointly optimize the model, which is as below,

$$\mathcal{L} = \mathcal{L}_{lc} + \lambda_1 \mathcal{L}_{label} + \lambda_2 \mathcal{L}_{\mathcal{G}}, \tag{9}$$

in which λ_1 and λ_2 are hyperparameters to control the proportion of label extension module and graph refinement module, respectively.

4 Experiments

4.1 Datasets

Three datasets are utilized in our evaluation, and can be described as follows:

- **M Stores**: It is an offline stores datasets of Mplatform. It includes multi-modal information (e.g., store outline images and store names). We extracted partial data, including 111,635 entities (stores).
- **M commodities**: M platform maintains a large number of commodities online. When they are released, sellers need to upload multi-modal information of the commodities, such as the appearance images and the commodity names. We extract 125,320 entities (commodities) for experiment.
- **T commodities**: T has a large number of commodities for users to choose. We can obtain multi-modal information of commodities including the image, name and attribute, etc. We obtain 69,911 entities (commodities).

4.2 Experimental Settings

Baseline. We compare CT-GNN with several state-of-the-art methods. The baseline can be divided into three categories: traditional industrial models, graph models and multi-modal models. The traditional industrial models include: XGBoost [2] and MLP [27]. The graph models include GCN [10], GAT [28], RGCN [21] and HAN [31]. The multi-modal models include ITA [33] and HVPNet [3].

Table 1. The **R** (Recall) and **P** (Precision) results under different threshold (**t**) on three datasets.

Dataset	t	M	XGB	MLP	GCN	RGCN	ITA	HVPNet	CT-GNN	Improv.
M Stores	0.85	**R**	0.3633	0.3152	0.3578	0.3756	0.3312	0.3621	**0.4122**	9.74%
M Stores	0.85	**P**	0.7429	0.7093	0.8033	0.8154	0.7645	0.8392	**0.8567**	2.09%
M Stores	0.90	**R**	0.3422	0.2978	0.3420	0.3693	0.3247	0.3529	**0.3923**	6.23%
M Stores	0.90	**P**	0.7803	0.7432	0.8358	0.8492	0.7850	0.8415	**0.8625**	1.57%
M Stores	0.95	**R**	0.3137	0.2765	0.3197	0.3128	0.2933	0.3367	**0.3670**	5.52%
M Stores	0.95	**P**	0.8232	0.7938	0.8552	0.8737	0.8022	0.8639	**0.9245**	5.81%
M commodities	0.85	**R**	0.3278	0.3024	0.3538	0.3793	0.3488	0.3725	**0.3928**	3.56%
M commodities	0.85	**P**	0.5281	0.4933	0.5324	0.5633	0.5384	0.5528	**0.5933**	5.33%
M commodities	0.90	**R**	0.3055	0.2933	0.3228	0.3387	0.3176	0.3495	**0.3582**	2.50%
M commodities	0.90	**P**	0.5468	0.5162	0.5533	0.5966	0.5539	0.5932	**0.6124**	2.65%
M commodities	0.95	**R**	0.2873	0.2734	0.2956	0.3034	0.2753	0.3008	**0.3143**	3.59%
M commodities	0.95	**P**	0.5884	0.5478	0.6055	0.6374	0.5976	0.6123	**0.6534**	2.51%
T commodities	0.85	**R**	0.3256	0.2833	0.3277	0.3328	0.3165	0.3245	**0.3547**	6.58%
T commodities	0.85	**P**	0.5218	0.4908	0.5329	0.5587	0.5180	0.5267	**0.5853**	4.76%
T commodities	0.90	**R**	0.2945	0.2678	0.3002	0.3086	0.2858	0.3224	**0.3290**	2.05%
T commodities	0.90	**P**	0.5468	0.5100	0.5591	0.5933	0.5265	0.5371	**0.6356**	7.13%
T commodities	0.95	**R**	0.2449	0.2208	0.2675	0.2773	0.2508	0.2729	**0.3047**	9.88%
T commodities	0.95	**P**	0.5934	0.5736	0.6093	0.6533	0.5732	0.6262	**0.6603**	1.07%

4.3 Performance Evaluation

In this section, we empirically compare CT-GNN with several state-of-art alternatives and analyze the experimental results. In order to fully evaluate the results, we take $t =$ 0.85, 0.90 and 0.95 respectively. As shown in Table 1, the following major observations can be made.

Obviously, CT-GNN achieves the best performance in the duplicate entities detection task on all datasets. Compared with the second best result, the improvement is up to 9.88% in Recall and 7.13% in Precision. This phenomenon is reasonable. Compared with non-GNN-based methods (i.e., XGBoost and MLP), GNN-based methods can mine high-order information through graph structure. Compared with other GNN-based models (i.e., GCN and RGCN), our model alleviates extreme label sparsity challenge with self-supervised module and self-training module. Note that, compared with the multi-modal based methods (i.e., ITA and HVPNet), our model achieve significant performance improvement because of capturing the correlation among entities and modals.

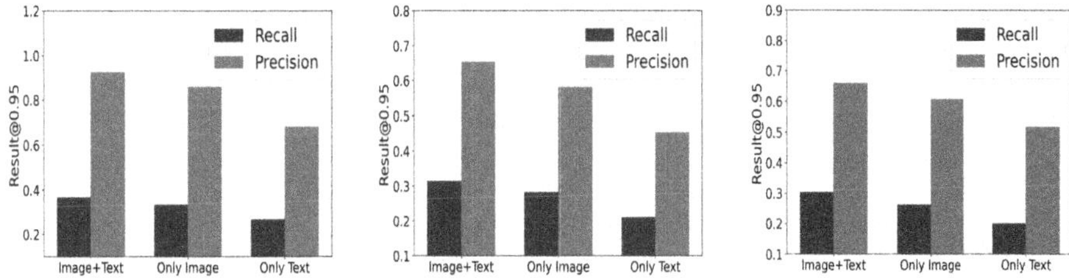

(a) M Stores (b) M commodities (c) T commodities

Fig. 4. The result comparison of removing different information, i.e., removing images or texts. (we set $t = 0.95$).

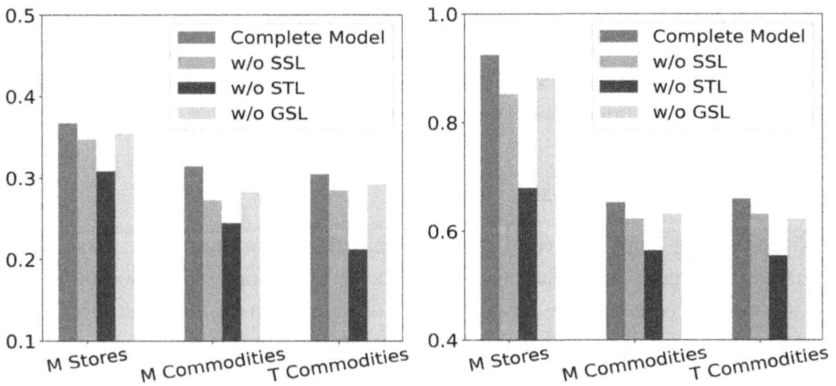

(a) Recall (b) Precision

Fig. 5. The comparison result of removing different modules. SSL is Self-supervised learning. STL is Self-training learning. GSL is Graph structure learning (we set $t = 0.95$).

4.4 Ablation Analysis

In order to extensively validate our model, we conduct the following ablation experiments.

Firstly, we explore the impact of multi-modal information, i.e., images and texts. In order to explore the importance of each kind of information in the model, we remove images and texts respectively, and then test the experimental results. As shown in Fig. 4, without either images or texts, the experimental results are significantly lower than complete CT-GNN model. Through the analysis of experimental results, we found that the two kinds of information, image and text, have different influences in the duplicate entities detection. For example, as shown in Fig. 4(a), the prediction accuracy without image information is far lower than that without text information. It indicates that image information has a greater impact on the detection results.

Secondly, we explore the importance of three modules (i.e., self-supervised learning, self-training learning and graph structure learning) in our model. We remove them respectively, and then compare the experimental results. As shown in Fig. 5, we find that after removing the self-training module, the decline of experimental results is the

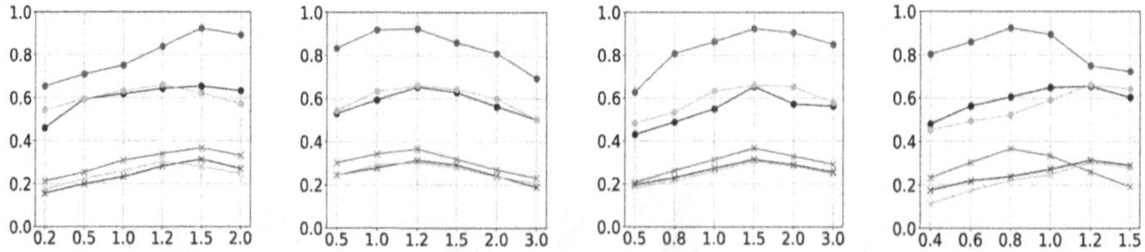

(a) γ (b) α (c) λ_1 (d) λ_2

Fig. 6. Impact of γ, α, λ_1 and λ_2 to the result under three datasets. The red line, blue line and green line respectively represent M stores, M commodities and T commodities. $\times$ is Recall and $\bullet$ is Precision (we set $t = 0.95$). (Color figure online)

most significant, followed by removing the self-supervised and graph structure learning module. It indicates that all three modules play important roles in the result of detection, and the self-training module has the greatest influence.

4.5 Hyperparameter Analysis

In this section, we analyze several important parameters in the model. First, we analyze the two strength control factors γ and α set in layer contrastive module and label extension module respectively. As our model jointly optimizes the three modules with hyperparameter λ_1 and λ_2 in Eq. (9), we then explore the effect of them on the final performance, and their change trends are shown in Fig. 6.

Firstly, we observe two strength coefficients, i.e., γ in Eq. (5) and α in Eq. (7). we tune γ in $\{0.2, 0.5, 1.0, 1.2, 1.5, 2.0\}$ and view the corresponding results. As shown in Fig. 6(a), the index of the experiment increases gradually with γ from 0.2 to 1.5, and reaches the peak at $\gamma = 1.5$. Then it shows a downward trend. Then we tune α in $\{0.5, 1.0, 1.2, 1.5, 2.0, 3.0\}$ and observe the results. As shown in Fig. 6(b), the experimental results can get the maximum value at $\alpha = 1.2$, and decrease at both sides of 1.2. The change trend of this result also verifies the rationality of setting strength parameters γ in Eq. (5) and α in Eq. (7).

Next, we evaluate the impact of λ_1 and λ_2. We perform experiments on three datasets and tune λ_1 in $\{0.5, 0.8, 1.0, 1.5, 2.0, 3.0\}$ and λ_2 in $\{0.4, 0.6, 0.8, 1.0, 1.2, 1.5\}$. As we can see in Fig. 6(c) that when $\lambda_1 = 1.5$, the best experimental results can be obtained on three datasets, and the two sides of $\lambda_1 = 1.5$ show a downward trend, in which we can infer that the label extension module is more important than the layer contrastive module. As for λ_2 shown in Fig. 6(d), the best performance is achieved when $\lambda_2 = 0.8$ on M Stores dataset. While on the other two datasets, the best performance is achieved at $\lambda_2 = 1.2$. It can be seen that the influence of the scale parameter λ_2 of graph refinement on different datasets is different. We speculate that in M Stores dataset, the features of entities are relatively dispersed and the initial graph is relatively accurate. However, in other datasets, the features of entities are relatively dense and the reliability of the graph is low, so the influence of λ_2 is greater.

5 Conclusion

In this paper, we study the multi-modal entities detection under extreme label sparsity. We propose a novel model named CT-GNN, which can alleviate the extreme labels sparsity challenge by two module, i.e., self-supervised learning with layer contrastive and self-training learning with boundary distance. Meanwhile, graph structure learning is introduced to stabilize learning performance. We carry out comprehensive experiments, and the results demonstrate that CT-GNN has significant performance improvement on three datasets compared with SOTA models.

Acknowledgments. We would like to thank the anonymous reviewers for their constructive feedback. This work is supported in part by the National Natural Science Foundation of China (No. 62192784, U1936104, U20B2045, 62172052, 62002029).

References

1. Belgiu, M., Drăguţ, L.: Random forest in remote sensing: a review of applications and future directions. ISPRS J. Photogrammetry Remote Sensing **114**, 24–31 (2016)
2. Chen, T., Guestrin, C.: Xgboost: A scalable tree boosting system. In: Proceedings of the 22nd ACM sigkdd International Conference on Knowledge Discovery and Data Mining. pp. 785–794 (2016)
3. Chen, X., et al.: Good visual guidance makes a better extractor: Hierarchical visual prefix for multimodal entity and relation extraction. arXiv preprint arXiv:2205.03521 (2022)
4. Cunningham, P., Delany, S.J.: K-nearest neighbour classifiers-a tutorial. ACM Comput. Surv. (CSUR) **54**(6), 1–25 (2021)
5. Devlin, J., Chang, M.W., Lee, K., Toutanova, K.: Bert: pre-training of deep bidirectional transformers for language understanding. arXiv preprint arXiv:1810.04805 (2018)
6. Gutmann, M., Hyvärinen, A.: Noise-contrastive estimation: A new estimation principle for unnormalized statistical models. In: Proceedings of the Thirteenth International Conference on Artificial Intelligence and Statistics. pp. 297–304. JMLR Workshop and Conference Proceedings (2010)
7. He, K., Fan, H., Wu, Y., Xie, S., Girshick, R.: Momentum contrast for unsupervised visual representation learning. In: Proceedings of the IEEE/CVF Conference on Computer Vision and Pattern Recognition. pp. 9729–9738 (2020)
8. He, X., Deng, K., Wang, X., Li, Y., Zhang, Y., Wang, M.: Lightgcn: simplifying and powering graph convolution network for recommendation. In: Proceedings of the 43rd International ACM SIGIR Conference on Research and Development in Information Retrieval. pp. 639–648 (2020)
9. Hjelm, R.D., et al.: Learning deep representations by mutual information estimation and maximization. arXiv preprint arXiv:1808.06670 (2018)
10. Kipf, T.N., Welling, M.: Semi-supervised classification with graph convolutional networks. arXiv preprint arXiv:1609.02907 (2016)
11. Lawler, G.F., Limic, V.: Random walk: a modern introduction, vol. 123. Cambridge University Press (2010)
12. Li, Q., Han, Z., Wu, X.M.: Deeper insights into graph convolutional networks for semi-supervised learning. In: Thirty-Second AAAI Conference on Artificial Intelligence (2018)
13. Liu, H., Hu, B., Wang, X., Shi, C., Zhang, Z., Zhou, J.: Confidence may cheat: self-training on graph neural networks under distribution shift. In: Proceedings of the ACM Web Conference 2022. pp. 1248–1258 (2022)

14. Liu, W., Wen, Y., Yu, Z., Yang, M.: Large-margin softmax loss for convolutional neural networks. arXiv preprint arXiv:1612.02295 (2016)
15. Liu, Z., Chen, C., Yang, X., Zhou, J., Li, X., Song, L.: Heterogeneous graph neural networks for malicious account detection. In: Proceedings of the 27th ACM International Conference on Information and Knowledge Management. pp. 2077–2085 (2018)
16. Nikolentzos, G., Vazirgiannis, M.: Random walk graph neural networks. Adv. Neural Inf. Process. Syst. **33**, 16211–16222 (2020)
17. Park, C., Kim, D., Han, J., Yu, H.: Unsupervised attributed multiplex network embedding. In: Proceedings of the AAAI Conference on Artificial Intelligence. vol. 34, pp. 5371–5378 (2020)
18. Pearson, K.: The problem of the random walk. Nature **72**(1865), 294–294 (1905)
19. Peng, Z., et al.: Graph representation learning via graphical mutual information maximization. In: Proceedings of The Web Conference 2020. pp. 259–270 (2020)
20. Qiu, J., et al.: GCC: graph contrastive coding for graph neural network pre-training. In: Proceedings of the 26th ACM SIGKDD International Conference on Knowledge Discovery & Data Mining. pp. 1150–1160 (2020)
21. Schlichtkrull, M., Kipf, T.N., Bloem, P., van den Berg, R., Titov, I., Welling, M.: Modeling Relational Data with Graph Convolutional Networks. In: Gangemi, A., et al. (eds.) ESWC 2018. LNCS, vol. 10843, pp. 593–607. Springer, Cham (2018). https://doi.org/10.1007/978-3-319-93417-4_38
22. Sengupta, A., Ye, Y., Wang, R., Liu, C., Roy, K.: Going deeper in spiking neural networks: VGG and residual architectures. Front. Nurosci. **13**, 95 (2019)
23. Shen, S., et al.: Structure-aware face clustering on a large-scale graph with 107 nodes. In: Proceedings of the IEEE/CVF Conference on Computer Vision and Pattern Recognition. pp. 9085–9094 (2021)
24. Simonyan, K., Zisserman, A.: Very deep convolutional networks for large-scale image recognition. arXiv preprint arXiv:1409.1556 (2014)
25. Tenney, I., Das, D., Pavlick, E.: Bert rediscovers the classical NLP pipeline. arXiv preprint arXiv:1905.05950 (2019)
26. Tian, Y., Sun, C., Poole, B., Krishnan, D., Schmid, C., Isola, P.: What makes for good views for contrastive learning? Adv. Neural Inf. Process. Syst. **33**, 6827–6839 (2020)
27. Tolstikhin, I.O., et al.: MLP-mixer: an all-MLP architecture for vision. Adv. Neural Inf. Process. Syst. **34**, 24261–24272 (2021)
28. Velickovic, P., Cucurull, G., Casanova, A., Romero, A., Lio, P., Bengio, Y.: Graph attention networks. Statistics **1050**, 20 (2017)
29. Veličković, P., Fedus, W., Hamilton, W.L., Liò, P., Bengio, Y., Hjelm, R.D.: Deep graph infomax. arXiv preprint arXiv:1809.10341 (2018)
30. Wang, X., He, X., Wang, M., Feng, F., Chua, T.S.: Neural graph collaborative filtering. In: Proceedings of the 42nd International ACM SIGIR Conference on Research and Development in Information Retrieval. pp. 165–174 (2019)
31. Wang, X., et al.: Heterogeneous graph attention network. In: The world wide web conference. pp. 2022–2032 (2019)
32. Wang, X., Liu, N., Han, H., Shi, C.: Self-supervised heterogeneous graph neural network with co-contrastive learning. In: Proceedings of the 27th ACM SIGKDD Conference on Knowledge Discovery & Data Mining. pp. 1726–1736 (2021)
33. Wang, X., et al.: ITA: image-text alignments for multi-modal named entity recognition. arXiv preprint arXiv:2112.06482 (2021)
34. Wu, J., et al.: Self-supervised graph learning for recommendation. In: Proceedings of the 44th International ACM SIGIR Conference on Research and Development in Information Retrieval. pp. 726–735 (2021)

35. Wu, Z., Pan, S., Chen, F., Long, G., Zhang, C., Philip, S.Y.: A comprehensive survey on graph neural networks. IEEE Trans. Neural Netw. Learn. Syst. **32**(1), 4–24 (2020)
36. You, Y., Chen, T., Sui, Y., Chen, T., Wang, Z., Shen, Y.: Graph contrastive learning with augmentations. Adv. Neural Inf. Process. Syst. **33**, 5812–5823 (2020)
37. Zheng, V.W., et al.: Heterogeneous embedding propagation for large-scale e-commerce user alignment. In: 2018 IEEE International Conference on Data Mining (ICDM). pp. 1434–1439. IEEE (2018)
38. Zou, Y., Yu, Z., Liu, X., Kumar, B., Wang, J.: Confidence regularized self-training. In: Proceedings of the IEEE/CVF International Conference on Computer Vision. pp. 5982–5991 (2019)

Graph Contrastive Representation Learning with Input-Aware and Cluster-Aware Regularization

Jin Li[1], Bingshi Li[1], Qirong Zhang[1], Xinlong Chen[1], Xinyang Huang[1], Longkun Guo[2], and Yang-Geng Fu[1(✉)]

[1] College of Computer and Data Science, Fuzhou University, Fuzhou, China
fu@fzu.edu.cn

[2] School of Mathematics and Statistics, Fuzhou University, Fuzhou, China

Abstract. With broad applications in network analysis and mining, Graph Contrastive Learning (GCL) is attracting growing research interest. Despite its successful usage in extracting concise but useful information through contrasting different augmented graph views as an outstanding self-supervised technique, GCL is facing a major challenge in how to make the semantic information extracted *well-organized* in structure and consequently *easily understood* by a downstream classifier. In this paper, we propose a novel cluster-based GCL framework to obtain a semantically well-formed structure of node embeddings via maximizing mutual information between input graph and output embeddings, which also provides a more clear decision boundary through accomplishing a cluster-level global-local contrastive task. We further argue in theory that the proposed method can correctly maximize the mutual information between an input graph and output embeddings. Moreover, we further improve the proposed method for better practical performance by incorporating additional refined gadgets, *e.g.*, measuring uncertainty of clustering and additional structural information extraction via local-local node-level contrasting module enhanced by Graph Cut. Lastly, extensive experiments are carried out to demonstrate the practical performance gain of our method in six real-world datasets over the most prevalent existing state-of-the-art models.

Keywords: Graph neural networks · Graph representation learning · Contrastive learning · Node classification · Node clustering

1 Introduction

Graph neural networks (GNNs) [14] are regarded as successful expressive models [26] for solving tasks on graphs such as semi-supervised node classification [6,14]

This research was supported by the University-Industry Cooperation Project of Fujian Province, China (2023H6008) and the National Natural Science Foundation of China (12271098). Paper with appendix can be found at https://drive.google.com/file/d/1FVziwZpsq4v5oLvPz9qFr77ozkQwhvFw/view?usp=sharing.

© The Author(s), under exclusive license to Springer Nature Switzerland AG 2023
D. Koutra et al. (Eds.): ECML PKDD 2023, LNAI 14170, pp. 666–682, 2023.
https://doi.org/10.1007/978-3-031-43415-0_39

and graph classification [4]. Compared to other deep neural networks, GNNs can extract concise but meaningful information from both input feature vectors and graph structures into low dimensional hidden representations, *i.e.*, embeddings. Moreover, they can deal with various kinds of graphs including citation graphs, social networks, co-purchase graphs, knowledge graphs, etc. Guided by appropriate supervision, existing GNN models have achieved significant performance gain compared to classic graph tools, *e.g.*, graph kernels [32] and random walk-based methods [25]. But in the real world, data labeling can be very expensive [24] and even suffer from privacy issues [18,24]. Moreover, labels are sometimes noisy and may mislead models. So increasing attention has been attracted to learning representations in an unsupervised manner.

Self-supervised learning (SSL) [3,9] is one of such techniques that can extract correct supervision signals from input and guide models to learn meaningful knowledge. Among many SSL methods in the literature, Contrastive learning (CL) [3] is a successful example that can even outperform its supervised counterparts [31,40]. The key idea of CL is to construct several views via some augmentation tricks [2,38], in which the embeddings of the same part appear similar in different views [5] or a global pooling vector is provided to compare with local embeddings [31]. In addition to making models more robust intuitively, it can maximize mutual information (*i.e.*, MI) between input and output (called *IOMIMax*) or between global and local content (called *GLMIMax*), which theoretically guarantees it can extract meaningful information instead of noise.

In this paper, we focus on Graph Contrastive Learning (GCL) and aim to accomplish the unsupervised graph representation learning task using CL. But unfortunately, there is no specific and clear definition of the mutual information between a random input graph and random vectors. Although GMI [24] provided an example with theoretical consideration, it is not yet explainable whether and why useful information can be captured by their method. This paper presents another example (see Sect. 4) which is more effective and interpretable. We consider this from different perspectives first (e.g., from features and structure individually) and then trade-off them globally, locally, or node-wisely. And to keep it simple, we use a non-parametric encoder[1] to encode structural information.

Yet there is another concern on mutual information maximization on graph even with a well-formed definition: MI maximization can only *capture* and *keep* meaningful information in embeddings but can hardly *organize* and *show* them clearly. In other words, the exacted semantic information might not be *clearly recognized* by a linear downstream classifier due to the following reasons: 1) there are too many semantic clusters even if MI is maximized, *i.e.*, their structure is too complex for a *linear* classifier to capture; 2) the embeddings around the cluster boundary may be still vague and confused, so the classifier could make an unconfident decision only. In order to solve this issue, we cluster embeddings into k parts (here $k << n$, where n is the number of nodes in the input graph) and guide our model via maximizing mutual information between every local node and the global vector summarized from the cluster that accommodates this

[1] *E.g.*, spectral embeddings used in Spectral Clustering [33].

node (called *Cluster-GLMIMax*[1]). Note that Cluster-GLMIMax can not be used without Graph-IOMIMax providing strong semantic signals to guide clustering, since otherwise, the quality of semantic structure may significantly degrade. This is the reason why Graph-IOMIMax is considered as a regularization: it keeps meaningful information in a well-organized form.

Besides, we propose two additional refinements to further improve performance. We use the Silhouette Coefficient to measure the certainty of clustering and discount those unconfident nodes in case of wrong supervision. Moreover, the Metis algorithm is introduced to do graph cutting and favor a local-local contrastive module. Intuitively, it supplements some other prior structural knowledge (*e.g.*, perception of distance and density on graph) and can be seen as an auxiliary improvement of Graph-IOMIMax (See Sect. 4.2).

Extensive experiments are carried out on six real-world benchmarks, and our method achieves competitive performance compared with those supervised counterparts and even outperforms some of them. This indicates the potential of our design on Graph-IOMIMax and the advantage of cluster awareness. We leave as future work on how to combine features and structural embeddings more sophisticatedly. The contributions of the paper can be summarized as follows:

- Propose a novel approach to maximize the mutual information between an input graph and output embeddings (*Graph-IOMIMax*), which can be interpreted as a more simple and effective regularization to capture concise but useful information, resulting in a *semantically well-formed* structure of node embeddings.
- Devise a global-local contrastive module at the cluster level (*Cluster-GLMIMax*), which supplements some relatively global information from corresponding clusters for unconfident nodes and derives significantly clearer decision boundaries.
- Extensive experiments are conducted to demonstrate our method achieving competitive performance compared to existing state-of-the-art models on six real-world benchmarks.

2 Related Works

2.1 Graph Neural Network

Graph neural networks (GNNs) are a kind of neural network that can extract information from graphs into low-dimensional embeddings preserving both attributive and topological information [35]. They are first introduced in [14], which proposed a spectral-based convolutional operation to encode both graph structure and node features. In order to specify the importance of neighbors, GAT [30] leverages masked self-attention layers to measure different weights to different nodes in a neighborhood. SGC [34] reduces the excess complexity of GCN by removing nonlinearities and collapsing weight matrices between consecutive layers. On the other hand, GraphSAGE [6] performs a non-spectral graph

[1] Because we use GLMIMax in *cluster's* level instead of the whole graph.

convolution over a fixed-size set of randomly sampled neighbors to integrate neighbor features. FastGCN [1] also adopts a sampling strategy to reduce the computational complexity of GCN by interpreting graph convolutions as integral transforms of embedding functions. GIN [36] makes use of sum aggregation and MLPs to obtain a maximally powerful GNN. However, these methods mainly focus on supervised settings, which require a large volume of sample annotation. On the other hand, the representations generated by them have limited generalization capabilities in various downstream tasks.

2.2 Graph Contrastive Learning

Contrastive Learning(CL) is a self-supervised method that learns representations by pulling positive pairs together and pushing negative pairs apart. Inspired by its success in Computer Vision and Natural Language Processing, CL has been widely used to solve graph tasks in recent years. DGI [31] first adopts contrastive learning to Graph Representation Learning, which maximizes the mutual information between graph-level and node-level embeddings. MVGRL [7] enhances the contrastive mechanism of DGI with graph augmentation strategies. GMI [24] tries to maximize the mutual information between input and representations of the target node and its neighbors. While GRACE [40], GCA [41], and Merit [10] construct node classification tasks, which focus on feature alignments between the same nodes from different augmented views, instead of exploring local-global relationships. In this paper, we propose three contrastive modules in our framework. Compared to the aforementioned prior works, ours can not only more effectively preserve and well-organize knowledge in input, but also facilitate information sharing in 1) in cluster-level embedding space; 2) in balanced sub-graphs. See Sec. G in Appendix for a more detailed comparison.

3 Preliminaries

3.1 Notation, GCN, and SGC

Let $G = (V, E)$ represent a graph, where V is the set of n nodes $\{v_i\}$, and E is the set of edges. Feature matrix and adjacency matrix are represented by $X \in \mathbb{R}^{n \times f}$ and $A \in \{0,1\}^{n \times n}$, respectively, where $x_i \in \mathbb{R}^f$ denotes the feature vector of v_i and $A_{ij} = 1$ iff $(v_i, v_j) \in E$ and $A_{ij} = 0$ otherwise. $\mathbb{1}(x = y) = 1$ if $x = y$ otherwise 0. GCN [14] in the spatial domain can be described as several stacked aggregation operations, linear transformations, and non-linear activation functions:

$$H^{(0)} = X, \quad H^{(l+1)} = \sigma\left(\hat{A}H^{(l)}W^{(l)}\right) \in \mathbb{R}^{n \times d}, \tag{1}$$

where $l \in [0, L)$, L is the number of layers, and $\sigma(\cdot)$ denotes the non-linear activation function (*e.g.*, ReLU) except the last layer where softmax is deployed.

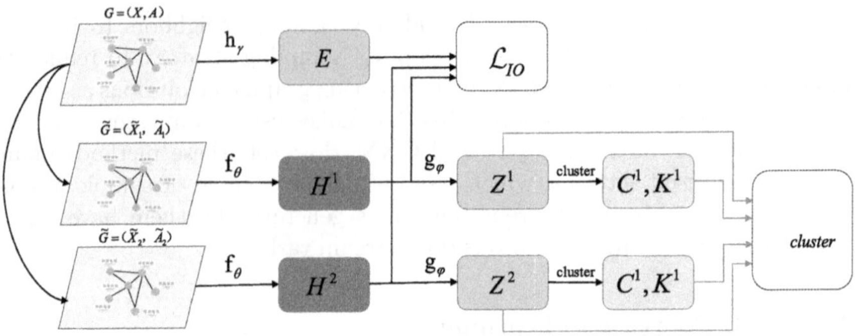

Fig. 1. Comprehensive depiction of our framework. Z^1 and Z^2 are the projected node embeddings of augmented views $\tilde{G}^1$ and $\tilde{G}^2$. Applying the K-means algorithm on Z^1 and Z^2, we can get cluster centroids C^1, C^2 and cluster labels K^1, K^2 which are used to calculate the cluster-level contrastive loss.

$\hat{A} = \tilde{D}^{-\frac{1}{2}}\tilde{A}\tilde{D}^{-\frac{1}{2}}$ is the symmetrical normalized matrix of $\tilde{A} = A + I$ (*i.e.*, adjacency matrix with self-loops) and diagonal matrix $\tilde{D}_{i,i} = \sum_{j=1}^{n} \tilde{A}_{i,j}$. $H^{(l)} \in \mathbb{R}^{n\times d}$ and $W^{(l)} \in \mathbb{R}^{d\times d}$ represent the embedding matrix of nodes and trainable parameters in the l-th layer. SGC [34] simplifies GCN by dropping its non-linear activation functions. Its forward pass can be described as follows:

$$H^{(L)} = \hat{A}^{L}XW \in \mathbb{R}^{n\times d}. \tag{2}$$

3.2 Contrastive Learning and InfoNCE Loss

The target of contrastive learning is to learn a graph encoder $f_\theta : \mathbb{R}^{n\times f} \times \mathbb{R}^{n\times n} \rightarrow \mathbb{R}^{n\times d}$ that generates node embeddings $H = f_\theta(X, A) \in \mathbb{R}^{n\times d}$ by maximizing the agreement of representations between different views.

Specifically, we first generate two graph views by performing random graph augmentation on the input. After that, we employ a contrastive objective that pulls positive pairs together and pushes negative pairs apart. InfoNCE loss [8] has been widely used as contrastive loss, which could be written as:

$$\mathcal{L}_{CL}(Z^t, Z^s, \mathbb{P}, \mathbb{N}) = -\frac{1}{N}\sum_{i=1}^{N}\sum_{j\in\mathbb{P}_i} \log \frac{\exp(sim(z_i^t, z_j^s)/\tau)}{\sum_{k\in\mathbb{P}_i\cup\mathbb{N}_i} \exp(sim(z_i^t, z_k^s)/\tau)}, \tag{3}$$

where Z^t, Z^s represent the embeddings of target nodes and sample nodes, respectively. N is the number of target nodes, $\mathbb{P}$ and $\mathbb{N}$ represent positive and negative sample sets, respectively. $sim(\cdot,\cdot)$ denotes the cosine similarity between two vectors, and τ is a temperature hyper-parameter. Theoretically, minimizing InfoNCE loss equivalently maximizes a lower bound of MI (see *e.g.*, [8]).

Due to limited space, we move the subsection *Clustering and Spectral Embedding* to the Appendix (see Sec. E).

4 Proposed Method

In this section, we describe our **Cluster-aware Regularized Graph Contrastive Learning framework**. See Fig. 1 for a comprehensive depiction. We first augment the input graph to generate two views with two strategies, *i.e.*, removing edges and masking node features randomly. We propose three contrastive objectives to train our GNN encoder: 1) maximizing mutual information between the input graph and output embeddings (*i.e.*, Graph-IOMIMax); 2) maximizing mutual information between every local node and the global vector summarized from the cluster this node belongs to (*i.e.*, Cluster-GLMIMax); 3) employing Graph Cut-favored local-local contrastive learning to supplement some extra structural knowledge. In the following subsections, we introduce each part of our framework in detail.

4.1 Mutual Information Maximization Between Input Graph and Output Embeddings (Graph-IOMIMax)

GMI [24] is a prior example of defining clearly the mutual information between input graph and output embeddings. It focuses on feature vectors first and then injects some structural knowledge into its design via an auxiliary contrastive term. This motivates us to consider features and structural information individually and combine them via a simple global trade-off or in a local-adaptive and node-wise way, which will help our model learn more meaningful and accurate information and effectively alleviate adverse effects from noise in inputs. Sec. G in Appendix enumerates detailed differences between our method and other mainstream previous works including GMI.

MI with Feature Vectors. Recall our motivation for GCL is to learn semantically well-clustered embeddings. Note that the majority of real-world graphs are homogeneous, so their feature vectors can already provide enough information to get not bad results in downstream tasks. Then the distribution of features can regularize our output embeddings to keep similar distribution and form a not-bad initial semantic structure. And later, the graph encoder we train should encode some additional knowledge from the input graph structure and perform careful combination in an implicit way with the knowledge already encoded in the initial distribution, *i.e.*, it should not alter the initial distribution too much. From this perspective, maximizing MI with features can be interpreted as a good regularization, just as mentioned in Sect. 1. Specifically, we maximize MI between input features and output embeddings by minimizing the following loss term:

$$\begin{aligned} \mathcal{L}_{FIO} &= \mathcal{L}_{CL}\left(H^1, E_F, \mathbb{P}, \mathbb{N}\right) + \mathcal{L}_{CL}\left(H^2, E_F, \mathbb{P}, \mathbb{N}\right), \\ E_F &= W_1 X, \quad H^1 = f_\theta(X^1), \quad H^2 = f_\theta(X^2), \end{aligned} \tag{4}$$

where $X^1, X^2 \in \mathbb{R}^{n\times f}$ denote features of different augmented view V^1 and V^2. And $f_\theta \in \mathbb{R}^{f\times d}$ is a GNN encoder generating $H^1, H^2 \in \mathbb{R}^{n\times d}$ as the embeddings of V^1, V^2. $W_1 \in \mathbb{R}^{f \times d}$ is a trainable weight matrix that projects X into the same latent space of embeddings. See Eq. 3 for the definition of $L_{CL}(\cdot)$. Here we treat the samples from the same instance as positive pairs and those from different instances as negative pairs.

MI with Structural Embeddings. In some situations, feature vectors are missing, incomplete, or noisy. So trusting features too much as Sect. 4.1 may provide limited or misleading information. As a result, structural information matters. Here we want to do regularization via input graph structure just as features, but it's difficult to directly exploit graph structure: simply adopting rows of the adjacency matrix A as structural embeddings may not estimate local similarities well because rows of two nodes can be very different while their local environments might be very similar or even isomorphic. In order to capture more accurate information about the local structure for each node, we prefer a non-parameter encoder. To keep it simple, we use classic spectral embeddings inspired by Spectral Clustering [33]. They can be efficiently calculated via eigen-decomposition with partial-SVD [15]. To see the rationals for them to represent structural knowledge, consider: $\hat{A} = U \Lambda U^T = \sum_{i=1}^{n} \lambda_i u_i u_i^T \approx \sum_{i=1}^{f'} \lambda_i u_i u_i^T = U_{f'} \Lambda_{f'} U_{f'}^T = \hat{A}_{f'}$, where eigen-values of $\hat{A}$ satisfy $1 = \lambda_1 \geq \lambda_2 \geq \lambda_3 \geq \cdots \geq \lambda_n \geq 0$ and u_i is the eigen-vector corresponding to the eigen-value λ_i. We want to keep the top f' groups and drop the others (*i.e.*, $U_{f'}$ formed by the first f' columns of U and $\Lambda_{f'}$ is a diagonal matrix containing the first f' elements in the diagonal line of Λ), so $\hat{A}_{f'}$ can be viewed as a low-rank approximation of $\hat{A}$. Denote $T = U_{f'} \in \mathbb{R}^{n \times f'}$ and T_i is the i-th row of T, and we adopt T_i as the structural embedding of node i. We can do link prediction via bi-linear function $h(x, y) = x^T \Lambda_{f'} y$ where $x, y \in \mathbb{R}^{f' \times 1}$ are spectral embeddings of two different nodes. Note that spectral embedding is just a simple example of structural embeddings, and other choices may also be rational. Similar to features, define MI with structural embeddings:

$$\begin{aligned} \mathcal{L}_{SIO} &= \mathcal{L}_{CL}\left(H^1, E_S, \mathbb{P}, \mathbb{N}\right) + \mathcal{L}_{CL}\left(H^2, E_S, \mathbb{P}, \mathbb{N}\right), \\ E_S &= W_2 T, \quad H^1 = f_\theta(X^1), \quad H^2 = f_\theta(X^2), \end{aligned} \tag{5}$$

where $T \in \mathbb{R}^{n \times f'}$ denotes the structural embeddings, $W_2 \in \mathbb{R}^{f' \times d}$ is a trainable weight matrix.

How to Combine them to Represent the Whole Input Graph? In order to consider features and graph structure simultaneously, we give two simple ways to combine them in this subsection. They can effectively extract semantic information from the whole input while avoiding the negative effect of possible noise. Considering combining them with a linear global trade-off directly:

$$\mathcal{L}_{IO} = \beta_1 \mathcal{L}_{FIO} + \beta_2 \mathcal{L}_{SIO}, \tag{6}$$

where β_1 and β_2 are trade-off hyper-parameters. The rationale for this direct trade-off is: when one of them is too noisy to trust, we can discount it by tuning the hyper-parameter. In Sect. 5.1, we will give a Noisy-Feature task to show our method can alleviate noise from features via extracting more useful semantic information in the graph structure. We also give another node-wise combination strategy in the Appendix.

4.2 Cluster-Level MI Maximization Between Global Summarization and Local Embeddings (Cluster-GLMIMax)

We devise a cluster-level global-local contrastive module for a clearer decision boundary. The key idea is, for every node, to obtain shared common knowledge from its cluster (*e.g.*, embedded in cluster centroids), which makes itself more confident. Furthermore, common knowledge can also be distilled from the local environments of every node in a cluster. Formally, a shared projection g_η is used to project embeddings of different views h_i into the space where contrastive loss is applied, *i.e.*, $z_i = g_\eta(h_i)$. With k-means algorithms, we can cluster all projected $z_i \in \mathbb{R}^{n\times d'}$ into K clusters whose centroids are denoted as $C \in \mathbb{R}^{K\times d'}$. Then we minimize this cluster-level MI defined as follows:

$$\mathcal{L}_{CLS} = \mathcal{L}_{CL}\left(C^1, Z^2, \mathbb{P}^1, \mathbb{N}^1\right) + \mathcal{L}_{CL}\left(C^2, Z^1, \mathbb{P}^2, \mathbb{N}^2\right), \tag{7}$$

where C^1, C^2 are the cluster centroids on views V^1, V^2. Similarly, Z^1, Z^2 denote the projected embeddings of V^1 and V^2. For each cluster centroid c_i on view V^1, we select all nodes belonging to this cluster as $\mathbb{P}_i^1$ and naturally treat all left nodes as negative samples of c_i, denoted as $\mathbb{N}_i^1$. Note that $\mathbb{P}_i^1, \mathbb{P}_i^2$ are generated from different graph views V^1, V^2.

Considering Cluster Uncertainty Estimation. For better accuracy of classification, we observe that less attention should be given to nodes near cluster boundaries whose cluster information may be noisy and misleading and can not be confidently trusted. Based on the observation, we utilize the Normalized Silhouette Coefficient $\{S_i\}$ to estimate the uncertainty of every node and adjust the influence on contrastive signals for the training.

$$\mathcal{L}_{CLS} = \mathcal{L}_{CLS}^1 + \mathcal{L}_{CLS}^2,$$
$$\mathcal{L}_{CLS}^1(C^1, Z^2, \mathbb{P}^1, \mathbb{N}^1) = -\frac{1}{K}\sum_{i=1}^{K}\sum_{j\in\mathbb{P}_i^1} S_j^1 \log \frac{exp(sim(c_i^1, z_j^2)/\tau)}{\sum_{k\in\mathbb{P}_i^1\cup\mathbb{N}_i^1} exp(sim(c_i^1, z_k^2)/\tau)},$$

where S_i^1 and S_i^2 denote the Normalized Silhouette Coefficient of node v_i on views V^1 and V^2. $\mathcal{L}_{CLS}^2$ can be defined similarly.

By symbols on clustering in Sec. E (Appendix), $\{S_i\}$ can defined as follows:

$$S_i = \frac{S_i' + 1}{2} \in [0,1], \quad S_i' = \frac{b_i - a_i}{\max(a_i, b_i)} \in [-1,1], \quad \forall\, i \in [1,n],$$
$$a_i = \frac{1}{|C_{k_i}| - 1}\sum_{j\in C_{k_i}\setminus i} d(h_j, h_i), \; b_i = \min_{1\le t\le K, t\ne k_i} \frac{1}{|C_t|}\sum_{j\in C_t} d(h_j, h_i).$$

But in practice, it's often difficult and expensive to calculate the coefficients due to the high time and space complexity. To give an efficient, parallelable, and space-saving implementation, we do some derivations as follows: let $f(i,t) = \sum_{j \in C_t} \|h_j - h_i\|_2^2 = |C_t| \cdot \|h_i\|_2^2 + S^{(norm)}(t) - 2S(t)$ where $S^{(norm)}(t) = \sum_{j \in C_t} \|h_j\|_2^2$ and $S(t) = \sum_{j \in C_t} h_j$. The first term $|C_t| \cdot \|h_i\|_2^2$ can be calculated via a vector outer product, and $\|h_i\|_2^2, S^{(norm)}(t), S(t)$ can be pre-processed with no more than $\mathcal{O}(n \cdot K \cdot d)$ time complexity where $t \in [1, K]$, $h_i \in \mathbb{R}^d$, for all $i \in [1, n]$, and n, k represent the number of elements and clusters, respectively. So we can get the matrix $F \in \mathbb{R}^{n \times K}$ containing all $f(i,t)$ ($\forall\, i \in [1, n], t \in [1, K]$) with $\mathcal{O}(nKd)$ running time and $\mathcal{O}(nd + nK)$ space complexity. Finally, those coefficients can be easily obtained by simply selecting the top 2 elements with $\mathcal{O}(nK)$ complexity.

4.3 Extracting Further Structural Knowledge by Graph Cut

To supplement further additional structural information, we also employ a Graph Cut technique to enhance a local-local node-level graph contrastive learning module, since Graph Cut can divide a graph into several relatively balanced groups efficiently. In particular, Metis Package [11] is introduced to help us choose some appropriate positive or negative node pairs. See the Appendix for more details. It can help our framework perceive distances and densities on the graph in a node-adaptive manner because nodes in dense local environments may need a shorter distance to capture structural knowledge (longer distance may hurt performance), while sparse nodes may need longer distance (shorter distance may not be enough). Thus mutually learning in the same part can simultaneously benefit dense and sparse nodes, which may be hard for the contrastive module in Sect. 4.1. Formally, we minimize the following objective:

$$\mathcal{L}_{GC} = \mathcal{L}_{CL}\left(Z^1, Z^2, \mathbb{P}^1, \mathbb{N}^1\right) + \mathcal{L}_{CL}\left(Z^2, Z^1, \mathbb{P}^2, \mathbb{N}^2\right),$$

where for node v_i, we treat all the nodes in the same part with v_i as $\mathbb{P}_i$, and all the left nodes treated as $\mathbb{N}_i$.

4.4 Overall Loss Function for Our Framework

To learn node embeddings more effectively for various downstream tasks, we jointly optimize both Graph-IOMIMax and Cluster-GLMIMax losses. The overall objective function we hope to minimize during training is defined as follows:

$$\mathcal{L} = \gamma_1 \|W\| + \gamma_2 \mathcal{L}_{IO} + \gamma_3 \mathcal{L}_{CLS} + \gamma_4 \mathcal{L}_{GC}, \tag{8}$$

where γ_is are all hyper-parameters to control the contribution of each loss term, W refers to trainable parameters in Graph-IOMIMax loss, and $\|W\|$ serves as a regularizer to avoid trivial solutions.

4.5 Theoretical Analysis

In this section, we give some theoretical analysis of why our *Graph-IOMIMax* method can maximize the mutual information between the input graph and the output embeddings by deriving a meaningful lower bound with some assumptions on conditional distributions and independence. Some definitions, lemmas, and proofs are moved to the Appendix.

Theorem 1. *For an undirected graph $G = (V, E)$ with adjacency matrix A (or normalized version $\hat{A}$, see Sect. 3.1), and feature matrix $X \in \mathbb{R}^{n\times f}$ where the i-th row of X (i.e., X_i) is the feature vector of node i, $n = |V|$ is the number of nodes. With some assumptions, the following inequality holds:*

$$I(G; H) = I(X, \hat{A}; H) \geq I(X; H) + I(U_d; H) \tag{9}$$

where $H = f_\theta(X, \hat{A}) \in \mathbb{R}^{n\times d}$ is output embeddings by a graph encoder f_θ, e.g., implemented by a GNN model, $\hat{A} = U\Lambda U^T$ is the eigen-decomposition of $\hat{A}$ (suppose the elements of the diagonal line of λ satisfying that $\lambda_1 \geq \lambda_2 \geq \cdots \geq \lambda_n$, and the i-th column of U, i.e., $U^{(i)}$ is the eigen-vector corresponding to λ_i, and if the solution U is not unique, choose the lexicographically smallest one (see Definition 3 in Appendix), and U_d is the first d columns of U.

Corollary 1. *With the same definitions in Theorem 1 and some further assumptions of independence, we can obtain:*

$$I(G; H) \geq \sum_{i=1}^{n} I(X_i; H_i) + \sum_{i=1}^{n} I((U_d)_i; H_i), \tag{10}$$

where H_i and $(U_d)_i$ are the i-th rows of matrix H and U_d respectively.

Corollary 1 indicates a lower-bound of MI between the input graph and output embeddings (*i.e.*, $I(H; G)$), which consists of independent considerations of every node from different perspectives, *i.e.*, features and topology. Thus, we can maximize $I(H; G)$ via maximizing the value of RHS of Eq. 10, which also justifies Eq. 6. However, it is notable that one of the features or topology may sometimes contain possible noise whose effect should be reduced. Therefore, we further introduce two hyper-parameters β_1, β_2 to tune them in practice (see Eq. 6) provided the demonstrated different significance.

5 Experiments

To evaluate the effectiveness of our method, extensive experiments are carried out on six real-world datasets against baseline models on node classification tasks with a GeForce RTX 3090 GPU. The proposed framework is implemented by Pytorch [23] and optimized with Adam Optimizer [12]. For simplicity, we adopt a 2-layer SGC as the backbone graph encoder of our framework. These public benchmarks are widely used for node representation learning,

Table 1. Accuracy Comparison on Node Classification Tasks

Models	Cora	Citeseer	Pubmed	Computers	Photo	lWikiCS
MLP	55.12 ± 0.41	69.80 ± 0.26	71.44 ± 0.34	73.81 ± 0.21	81.81 ± 0.32	71.98 ± 0.42
GCN	81.54 ± 0.68	70.73 ± 0.65	79.16 ± 0.25	86.51 ± 0.54	92.42 ± 0.22	77.19 ± 0.12
SGC	81.00 ± 0.00	71.90 ± 0.10	78.90 ± 0.00	86.94 ± 0.31	92.76 ± 0.25	76.11 ± 0.82
GAT	83.00 ± 0.70	72.60 ± 0.60	79.00 ± 0.30	86.93 ± 0.29	92.56 ± 0.35	77.65 ± 0.11
DGI	82.34 ± 0.71	71.83 ± 0.54	76.78 ± 0.31	83.95 ± 0.47	91.61 ± 0.22	75.35 ± 0.14
GMI	82.39 ± 0.65	71.72 ± 0.15	79.34 ± 1.04	82.21 ± 0.31	90.68 ± 0.17	74.85 ± 0.08
GRACE	81.92 ± 0.89	71.21 ± 0.64	80.54 ± 0.36	87.46 ± 0.22	92.15 ± 0.24	78.19 ± 0.01
GCA	82.07 ± 0.10	71.33 ± 0.37	80.21 ± 0.39	87.85 ± 0.31	92.53 ± 0.16	78.35 ± 0.05
BGRL	81.44 ± 0.72	71.82 ± 0.48	80.18 ± 0.63	89.68 ± 0.31	93.07 ± 0.30	79.36 ± 0.53
MVGRL	83.45 ± 0.68	73.28 ± 0.48	80.09 ± 0.62	87.52 ± 0.11	91.74 ± 0.07	77.52 ± 0.08
Ours	**84.65 ± 0.31**	**73.70 ± 0.20**	**81.90 ± 0.47**	**90.02 ± 0.23**	**93.39 ± 0.23**	**79.45 ± 0.46**

Table 2. Comparison on Link Prediction and Noisy Features

Link Prediction				Noisy Features			
Model	Cora	Citeseer	Pubmed	Model	Cora	Citeseer	Pubmed
VGAE	91.58 ± 0.54	91.21 ± 1.14	96.51 ± 0.14	GCN	54.8	36.1	40.4
ARGVA	92.45 ± 1.11	91.71 ± 1.38	96.62 ± 0.12	SGC	51.9	34.7	41.0
GIC	93.68 ± 0.59	95.03 ± 0.65	93.00 ± 0.36	Pairnorm	56.6	37.5	41.3
GIC+WP	95.90 ± 0.50	95.94 ± 0.53	**98.72 ± 0.10**				
Ours	**96.12 ± 0.08**	**97.98 ± 0.17**	97.49 ± 0.12	Ours	**72.0**	**50.5**	**61.7**

including Cora [27], Pubmed [27], Citeseer [27], Amazon-Photo [28], Amazon-Computers [28] and WikiCS [17], whose statistics and detailed descriptions are presented in Tab. 6 and Sec. D in Appendix, respectively. All hyper-parameters, including the number of epochs, are tuned according to the best results on the validation set. See Tab. 7 in Appendix for detailed hyper-parameter configurations.

5.1 Performance in Different Scenarios

We evaluate the performance of our framework in four prevalent scenarios: Node Classification, Link Prediction, Node Clustering, and Node Classification with noisy features.

Node Classification. To validate the effectiveness of our proposed framework, we compare ours with the following models: 1) four classic supervised and semi-supervised baseline models, namely, MLP, GCN, GAT, and SGC; 2) five GNN-based state-of-the-art self-supervised models, including DGI [31], GMI [24], GRACE [40], GCA [41] and BGRL [29]. Following the evaluation protocol of previous works [41], each model is first trained in an unsupervised manner. Then, the pre-trained embeddings are used to train and test a simple ℓ_2-regularized logistic regression classifier. For the datasets with public train/valid/test splits (*e.g.*,

Table 3. Accuracy Comparison of Node Clustering Tasks

Methods	Cora			Citeseer			Pubmed		
	ACC	NMI	ARI	ACC	NMI	ARI	ACC	NMI	ARI
K-means	49.2	32.1	22.9	54.0	30.5	27.8	59.5	31.5	28.1
GAE	59.6	42.9	34.7	40.8	17.6	12.4	67.2	27.7	27.9
ARGA	64.0	44.9	35.2	57.3	35.0	34.1	66.8	30.5	29.5
ARVGA	64.0	45.0	37.4	54.4	26.1	24.5	69.0	29.0	30.6
GALA	74.5	57.6	53.1	69.3	44.1	44.6	69.3	32.7	32.1
DBGAN	74.8	56.0	54.0	67.0	40.7	41.4	69.4	32.4	32.7
DGI	55.4	41.1	32.7	51.4	31.5	32.6	58.9	27.7	31.5
MVGRL	73.2	56.2	51.9	68.1	43.2	43.4	69.3	34.4	32.3
MERIT	73.6	57.1	52.8	68.9	43.9	44.1	69.5	**34.7**	**32.8**
Ours	**76.2**	**57.8**	**55.6**	**70.5**	**45.6**	**47.2**	**70.0**	33.1	32.6

Cora, Citeseer, and Pubmed), we evaluate the framework on the fixed public split as [37]. For the WikiCS dataset, which provides 20 canonical train/valid/test splits, we directly use the given split. For Amazon datasets, we randomly split the nodes 20 times into (10%/10%/80%) for train/valid/test respectively following [41]. All experiments are performed 10 times and we report average results and standard error. Table 1 shows the node classification accuracy of respective models over six real-world datasets. We can see that our method gets competitive performance compared to existing state-of-the-art models across all these public benchmarks, which verifies the superiority of the proposed contrastive learning framework and shows that our MI maximization between input graph and output embeddings (*i.e.*, Graph-IOMIMax) and cluster-level contrasting module (*i.e.*, Cluster-GLMIMax) effectively guide the training of our GNN backbone and successfully encourage output node embeddings to become semantically well-formed. So the embeddings not only *capture* and *keep* semantic information, but also *organize* it well.

Link prediction is another common and important graph-related task that has broad real-world applications *e.g.*, Recommend System. For this task, we choose three commonly used citation networks and compare our framework with the following methods: 1) baselines: VGAE [13] and ARGVA [20]; 2) state-of-the-art methods: GIC [16] and GIC with WP [19]. The same evaluation protocol in previous work [19] is used for fair comparison: we first train our framework in an unsupervised manner to obtain the embeddings of nodes and then predict the existence of edge (x, y) via Sigmoid activation of dot product after a shared linear transformation, *i.e.*, $p(x, y) = \sigma(W \cdot h_x, W \cdot h_y) \in [0, 1]$, where $h_x, h_y \in \mathbb{R}^d$ are two embeddings of two nodes $x, y \in V$, $W \in \mathbb{R}^{d' \times d}$ is a trainable matrix shared for all nodes in the input graph, and $\sigma(\cdot)$ is the Sigmoid function. We adopt (85%/5%/10%) random dataset split for train/valid/test as [19] and positive

Table 4. Influence of Label Rate

Model	Cora						Citeseer			
	0.5%	1%	2%	3%	4%	5%	0.5%	1%	2%	3%
GCN	56.9	70.7	76.2	81.3	82	82.5	46.9	64.4	68.0	72.7
SGC	50.6	70.8	77.1	77.3	81.6	80.4	46.1	62.5	69.2	72.1
Ours	**65.9**	**80.3**	**81.5**	**83.1**	**84.0**	**84.3**	**65.7**	**69.9**	**70.2**	**72.8**

samples are sampled from existing edges in the graph, while negative ones are sampled from non-existing edges with the same number as positive ones.

We run five times with different initializations for every experiment and report the results including average AUCs and standard deviations for the task in Table 2. It is demonstrated that our framework outperforms the first three counterparts by a large margin while achieving competitive performance compared to the last one. Note that the last counterpart (*i.e.*, GIC with WP) is a magnificent state-of-the-art method that consistently performs better than lots of prior works. This shows the potential of our framework for capturing important structural information because it can reconstruct the adjacency matrix well compared to existing methods.

Node Clustering. For node clustering tasks, we first cluster node embeddings using K-means and then evaluate the results C on three citation networks via three traditional metrics, *i.e.*, ACC, NMI, and ARI (introduced in Sec. F of Appendix). The results are summarized in Table 3. We can see in Cora and Citeseer our framework consistently outperforms those baselines (*e.g.*, K-means, GAE [13] and DGI [31]) and state-of-the-art methods (*e.g.*, ARGA [21], ARVGA [21], GALA [22], DBGAN [39], MVGRL [7] and MERIT [10]) while in Pubmed it can obtain competitive performance, although not necessarily the best in all three metrics. These results show our framework can well organize semantic information and make node embeddings have more clear cluster boundaries, which will generalize well in lots of downstream tasks.

Node Classification with Noisy Features. In this subsection, we carry out the evaluation against the task called Node Classification with Noisy Features. In the task, features of all nodes are substituted by noise sampled from Standard Normal Distribution $\mathcal{N}(0,1)$. This task requires models to capture more useful structural knowledge for alleviating the adverse effect of noise in features. In the evaluation, we regard only structural embeddings in our Graph-IOMIMax module (see Sect. 4.1). On this occasion, it may degrade the performance when using Graph-IOMIMax with features because there can be a wrong alignment between embeddings and features. Anyhow, we nevertheless feed these noisy features into our framework, because in the real world, it is unknown how much noise exists in the features. So we actually tune the trade-off hyper-parameter between input features and the input graph structure. As demonstrated in Table 2, our framework outperforms most of the supervised baselines by a huge margin, indicating it has a better capability of capturing effective structural knowledge even compared with supervised methods.

5.2 Ablation and Hyper-Parameter Studies

To better illustrate the different impacts of individual parts in our framework, ablation studies were done over the three citation networks. In Table 5, it is shown that Graph-IOMIMax is the most effective term and each of these three parts can provide a meaningful supervision signal to guide the training for GNN models. By combining them together, we can further improve the performance due to their different focuses, *e.g.*, Graph Cut can help models perceive distance and density in graphs and may favor some nodes in a sparse local environment to learn more semantic information. Note that Cluster-GLMIMax is also effective because it can improve nearly 9% from 74.7% to 83.6% in Cora. The reason could be that there is some overlap in semantic information between Cluster-GLMIMax and Graph Cut because of possible density-uniformity in common citation networks, provided the majority of papers cite similar numbers of others and density varies not too much from local to local.

We also aim to show how the performance of our framework varies against label rate (*i.e.*, the size of the training set) for node classification tasks in Cora and Citeseer. From the experimental results reported in Table 4, it can be observed that the performance of all modules decreases as the labeling rate decreases. Although our method and the baselines (*i.e.*, GCN and SGC) have similar performance when the label rate is large, the gap between them grows when the label rate decreases. This indicates our framework has consistent superiority of embeddings output overall label rates in the downstream semi-supervised tasks compared to those semi-supervised counterparts.

Table 5. Ablation studies

Method	Cora	Citeseer	Pubmed
w/o. Graph-IOMIMax	74.70 ± 0.65	65.32 ± 1.60	77.38 ± 0.15
w/o. Cluster-GLMIMax	84.38 ± 0.25	73.50 ± 0.21	81.70 ± 0.60
w/o. Graph-Cut	83.62 ± 0.13	73.26 ± 0.32	80.14 ± 0.31
All	$\mathbf{84.65 \pm 0.31}$	$\mathbf{73.70 \pm 0.20}$	$\mathbf{81.70 \pm 0.60}$

6 Conclusion

In this paper, we proposed a novel approach called Graph-IOMIMax to maximize the mutual information between an input graph and output embeddings, aiming to derive a semantically well-formed structure of embeddings via capturing concise (but useful) information. Moreover, regarding the unconfident nodes, we devised a cluster-level global-local contrastive module and obtained a more clear decision boundary in the light of supplementing relatively global information. In addition, we considered the uncertainty of clustering and employed a local-local contrastive module collaborating with graph cut to further improve the performance. Furthermore, we provided a theoretical explanation of why Graph-IOMIMax can maximize the mutual information between input and output. Finally, extensive experiments were carried out comparing our framework with existing state-of-the-art models in six real-world benchmarks, demonstrating its potential in various machine-learning scenarios and tasks.

In the future, we will investigate combining semantic knowledge from features and graph structures in *Graph-IOMIMax* at a more sophisticated node-wise level.

Ethics Statement. We believe in using machine learning responsibly and ethically and in minimizing any potential harm associated with its use. We will strive to ensure the accuracy and reliability of our models. We will always respect applicable laws, regulations, and best practices and will make sure our models are used ethically and responsibly.

References

1. Chen, J., Ma, T., Xiao, C.: FastGCN: fast learning with graph convolutional networks via importance sampling. In: 6th International Conference on Learning Representations, ICLR 2018, Vancouver, BC, Canada, 30 April–3 May 2018, Conference Track Proceedings. OpenReview.net (2018)
2. Ding, K., Xu, Z., Tong, H., Liu, H.: Data augmentation for deep graph learning: a survey. CoRR abs/2202.08235 (2022)
3. Ericsson, L., Gouk, H., Loy, C.C., Hospedales, T.M.: Self-supervised representation learning: introduction, advances, and challenges. IEEE Signal Process. Mag. **39**(3), 42–62 (2022). https://doi.org/10.1109/msp.2021.3134634
4. Errica, F., Podda, M., Bacciu, D., Micheli, A.: A fair comparison of graph neural networks for graph classification. In: 8th International Conference on Learning Representations, ICLR 2020, Addis Ababa, Ethiopia, 26–30 April 2020. OpenReview.net (2020)
5. Grill, J.B., et al.: Bootstrap your own latent-a new approach to self-supervised learning. Adv. Neural. Inf. Process. Syst. **33**, 21271–21284 (2020)
6. Hamilton, W.L., Ying, Z., Leskovec, J.: Inductive representation learning on large graphs. In: Guyon, I., et al. (eds.) Advances in Neural Information Processing Systems 30: Annual Conference on Neural Information Processing Systems 2017, 4–9 December 2017, Long Beach, CA, USA, pp. 1024–1034. Curran Associates Inc. (2017)
7. Hassani, K., Ahmadi, A.H.K.: Contrastive multi-view representation learning on graphs. CoRR abs/2006.05582 (2020)
8. Hjelm, R.D., et al.: Learning deep representations by mutual information estimation and maximization. In: 7th International Conference on Learning Representations, ICLR 2019, New Orleans, LA, USA, 6–9 May 2019. OpenReview.net (2019)
9. Jaiswal, A., Babu, A.R., Zadeh, M.Z., Banerjee, D., Makedon, F.: A survey on contrastive self-supervised learning. Technologies **9**(1), 2 (2021). https://doi.org/10.3390/technologies9010002

10. Jin, M., Zheng, Y., Li, Y.F., Gong, C., Zhou, C., Pan, S.: Multi-scale contrastive siamese networks for self-supervised graph representation learning. In: International Joint Conference on Artificial Intelligence 2021, Paolo, Brazil, pp. 1477–1483. Association for the Advancement of Artificial Intelligence (AAAI), CEUR-WS.org (2021)
11. Karypis, G., Kumar, V.: A software package for partitioning unstructured graphs, partitioning meshes, and computing fill-reducing orderings of sparse matrices. University of Minnesota, Department of Computer Science and Engineering, Army HPC Research Center, Minneapolis, MN 38 (1998)
12. Kingma, D.P., Ba, J.: Adam: a method for stochastic optimization. In: Bengio, Y., LeCun, Y. (eds.) 3rd International Conference on Learning Representations, ICLR 2015, San Diego, CA, USA, 7–9 May 2015, Conference Track Proceedings. Conference Track Proceedings (2015)
13. Kipf, T.N., Welling, M.: Variational graph auto-encoders. Stat **1050**, 21 (2016)
14. Kipf, T.N., Welling, M.: Semi-supervised classification with graph convolutional networks. In: 5th International Conference on Learning Representations, ICLR 2017, Toulon, France, 24–26 April 2017, Conference Track Proceedings. OpenReview.net (2017)
15. Lin, Z.: Some software packages for partial SVD computation. CoRR abs/1108.1548 (2011)
16. Mavromatis, C., Karypis, G.: Graph infoclust: leveraging cluster-level node information for unsupervised graph representation learning. CoRR abs/2009.06946 (2020)
17. Mernyei, P., Cangea, C.: Wiki-CS: a Wikipedia-based benchmark for graph neural networks. CoRR abs/2007.02901 (2020)
18. Olatunji, I.E., Funke, T., Khosla, M.: Releasing graph neural networks with differential privacy guarantees. CoRR abs/2109.08907 (2021)
19. Pan, L., Shi, C., Dokmanic, I.: Neural link prediction with walk pooling. CoRR abs/2110.04375 (2021)
20. Pan, S., Hu, R., Long, G., Jiang, J., Yao, L., Zhang, C.: Adversarially regularized graph autoencoder for graph embedding. In: Lang, J. (ed.) Proceedings of the Twenty-Seventh International Joint Conference on Artificial Intelligence, IJCAI 2018, 13–19 July 2018, Stockholm, Sweden, pp. 2609–2615. ijcai.org (2018)
21. Pan, S., Hu, R., Long, G., Jiang, J., Yao, L., Zhang, C.: Adversarially regularized graph autoencoder for graph embedding. In: Lang, J. (ed.) Proceedings of the Twenty-Seventh International Joint Conference on Artificial Intelligence, IJCAI 2018, July 13–19, 2018, Stockholm, Sweden. pp. 2609–2615. ijcai.org (2018)
22. Park, J., Lee, M., Chang, H.J., Lee, K., Choi, J.Y.: Symmetric graph convolutional autoencoder for unsupervised graph representation learning. In: 2019 IEEE/CVF International Conference on Computer Vision, ICCV 2019, Seoul, Korea (South), 27 October–2 November 2019, pp. 6518–6527. IEEE (2019)
23. Paszke, A., et al.: Pytorch: an imperative style, high-performance deep learning library. In: Advances in Neural Information Processing Systems, vol. 32 (2019)
24. Peng, Z., et al.: Graph representation learning via graphical mutual information maximization. In: Huang, Y., King, I., Liu, T., van Steen, M. (eds.) WWW 2020: The Web Conference 2020, Taipei, Taiwan, 20–24 April 2020, pp. 259–270. ACM/IW3C2 (2020)

25. Perozzi, B., Al-Rfou, R., Skiena, S.: Deepwalk: online learning of social representations. In: Proceedings of the 20th ACM SIGKDD International Conference on Knowledge Discovery and Data Mining, KDD 2014, pp. 701–710. Association for Computing Machinery, New York (2014). https://doi.org/10.1145/2623330.2623732
26. Sato, R.: A survey on the expressive power of graph neural networks. CoRR abs/2003.04078 (2020)
27. Sen, P., Namata, G., Bilgic, M., Getoor, L., Galligher, B., Eliassi-Rad, T.: Collective classification in network data. AI Mag. **29**(3), 93–93 (2008)
28. Shchur, O., Mumme, M., Bojchevski, A., Günnemann, S.: Pitfalls of graph neural network evaluation. CoRR abs/1811.05868 (2018)
29. Thakoor, S., Tallec, C., Azar, M.G., Munos, R., Velickovic, P., Valko, M.: Bootstrapped representation learning on graphs. CoRR abs/2102.06514 (2021)
30. Velickovic, P., Cucurull, G., Casanova, A., Romero, A., Lio, P., Bengio, Y.: Graph attention networks. Stat **1050**, 4 (2018)
31. Velickovic, P., Fedus, W., Hamilton, W.L., Liò, P., Bengio, Y., Hjelm, R.D.: Deep graph infomax. In: ICLR (Poster), vol. 2, no. 3, p. 4 (2019)
32. Vishwanathan, S.V.N., Schraudolph, N.N., Kondor, R., Borgwardt, K.M.: Graph kernels. J. Mach. Learn. Res. **11**, 1201–1242 (2010)
33. Von Luxburg, U.: A tutorial on spectral clustering. Stat. Comput. **17**(4), 395–416 (2007)
34. Wu, F., Souza, A., Zhang, T., Fifty, C., Yu, T., Weinberger, K.: Simplifying graph convolutional networks. In: Chaudhuri, K., Salakhutdinov, R. (eds.) Proceedings of the 36th International Conference on Machine Learning. Proceedings of Machine Learning Research, Long Beach, California, USA, vol. 97, pp. 6861–6871. PMLR (2019)
35. Wu, Z., Pan, S., Chen, F., Long, G., Zhang, C., Yu, P.S.: A comprehensive survey on graph neural networks. IEEE Trans. Neural Netw. Learn. Syst. **32**(1), 4–24 (2021). https://doi.org/10.1109/tnnls.2020.2978386
36. Xu, K., Hu, W., Leskovec, J., Jegelka, S.: How powerful are graph neural networks? In: 7th International Conference on Learning Representations, ICLR 2019, New Orleans, LA, USA, 6–9 May 2019. OpenReview.net (2019)
37. Yang, Z., Cohen, W.W., Salakhutdinov, R.: Revisiting semi-supervised learning with graph embeddings. In: Balcan, M., Weinberger, K.Q. (eds.) Proceedings of the 33nd International Conference on Machine Learning, ICML 2016, New York City, NY, USA, 19–24 June 2016. JMLR Workshop and Conference Proceedings, vol. 48, pp. 40–48. JMLR.org (2016)
38. Zhao, T., Liu, Y., Neves, L., Woodford, O., Jiang, M., Shah, N.: Data augmentation for graph neural networks. In: Proceedings of the AAAI Conference on Artificial Intelligence, vol. 35, no. 12, pp. 11015–11023 (2021)
39. Zheng, S., Zhu, Z., Zhang, X., Liu, Z., Cheng, J., Zhao, Y.: Distribution-induced bidirectional generative adversarial network for graph representation learning. In: 2020 IEEE/CVF Conference on Computer Vision and Pattern Recognition, CVPR 2020, Seattle, WA, USA, 13–19 June 2020, pp. 7222–7231. Computer Vision Foundation/IEEE (2020)
40. Zhu, Y., Xu, Y., Yu, F., Liu, Q., Wu, S., Wang, L.: Deep graph contrastive representation learning. CoRR abs/2006.04131 (2020)
41. Zhu, Y., Xu, Y., Yu, F., Liu, Q., Wu, S., Wang, L.: Graph contrastive learning with adaptive augmentation. In: Leskovec, J., Grobelnik, M., Najork, M., Tang, J., Zia, L. (eds.) WWW 2021: The Web Conference 2021, Virtual Event/Ljubljana, Slovenia, 19–23 April 2021, pp. 2069–2080. ACM/IW3C2 (2021)

Temporal Graph Representation Learning with Adaptive Augmentation Contrastive

Hongjiang Chen[1], Pengfei Jiao[1], Huijun Tang[1](✉), and Huaming Wu[2]

[1] School of Cyberspace, Hangzhou Dianzi University, Hangzhou 310018, China
{hchen,pjiao,tanghuijune}@hdu.edu.cn
[2] Center for Applied Mathematics, Tianjin University, Tianjin 300072, China
whming@tju.edu.cn

Abstract. Temporal graph representation learning aims to generate low-dimensional dynamic node embeddings to capture temporal information as well as structural and property information. Current representation learning methods for temporal networks often focus on capturing fine-grained information, which may lead to the model capturing random noise instead of essential semantic information. While graph contrastive learning has shown promise in dealing with noise, it only applies to static graphs or snapshots and may not be suitable for handling time-dependent noise. To alleviate the above challenge, we propose a novel Temporal Graph representation learning with Adaptive augmentation Contrastive (TGAC) model. The adaptive augmentation on the temporal graph is made by combining prior knowledge with temporal information, and the contrastive objective function is constructed by defining the augmented inter-view contrast and intra-view contrast. To complement TGAC, we propose three adaptive augmentation strategies that modify topological features to reduce noise from the network. Our extensive experiments on various real networks demonstrate that the proposed model outperforms other temporal graph representation learning methods.

Keywords: Temporal graphs · Network embedding · Contrastive learning

1 Introduction

Temporal networks have become increasingly popular for modeling complex real-world scenarios, e.g., citation networks, recommendation systems, and engineering systems [3,7,9,16], where nodes represent interacting elements and temporal links denote their labeled interactions over time. These networks are inherently dynamic, with the topology and node properties evolving over time [32]. However, the real world is often affected by time-varying noise, which can have a significant impact on the network structure and its predictions. For instance, colleagues who work together on a project may interact frequently during the project's duration, but may rarely interact afterwards, leading to a decrease

© The Author(s), under exclusive license to Springer Nature Switzerland AG 2023
D. Koutra et al. (Eds.): ECML PKDD 2023, LNAI 14170, pp. 683–699, 2023.
https://doi.org/10.1007/978-3-031-43415-0_40

in the amount of available information for future interactions. Therefore, it is imperative to investigate techniques for reducing the influence of time-varying noise on temporal graphs in order to improve the accuracy of predicting future interactions.

In recent years, there has been a surge in the development of temporal graph neural networks (TGNNs), which extend the capabilities of neural networks to structured inputs and have achieved state-of-the-art (SOTA) performance in various tasks, such as link prediction. However, one of the key challenges in temporal graph representation learning is the presence of time-varying noise, which can significantly affect the network's evolution. Existing methods [10,11, 17,19,33] have primarily focused on capturing fine-grained information to obtain a more comprehensive node representation. This can lead to overfitting and the capture of random noise, which can obscure essential semantic information in the network as it evolves. Therefore, it is important to explore new approaches that balance the capture of both fine-grained and essential semantic information in order to improve the robustness and generalization ability of TGNNs.

Contrastive learning (CL) has emerged as a promising approach for addressing the aforementioned challenges in temporal graph representation learning by enabling the method to learn more generalized graph representations through the generation of multiple views for each instance using various data augmentations. This process helps reduce the impact of noise and improve method generalization and robustness [36]. However, current graph augmentation methods tend to focus primarily on capturing structural features at the node or graph level, while neglecting the temporal information of edge generation [34]. Incorporating temporal information related to edge generation into graph learning can help capture the dynamic evolution of the graph and improve the accuracy of node representations. Thus, there is a need to develop new approaches that effectively integrate temporal information into CL-based methods for temporal graph representation learning.

Consider the toy example of a temporal network shown in Fig. 1. When using the method of static graph augmentation (e.g., GCA [37]) to improve the temporal graph, the edge between nodes D and E may be inadvertently removed. As a result, TGNNs may not be able to accurately predict future interactions based on the enhanced graph because crucial temporal information has been lost. Specifically, the interaction between nodes D and E at the most recent time t_5 is crucial for accurately predicting future interactions, while the interaction between nodes B and C at time t_2 may be less important. Consequently, the static graph augmentation method fails to capture important temporal information that is essential for accurate predictions of future interactions in temporal graphs. To overcome this issue, incorporating temporal information into data augmentation and node representation can effectively capture the evolution of edge generation and improve the accuracy of future interaction predictions.

In this paper, we propose a novel contrastive model called Temporal Graph representation learning with Adaptive augmentation Contrastive (TGAC). Firstly, we utilize centrality measures to eliminate redundant topological

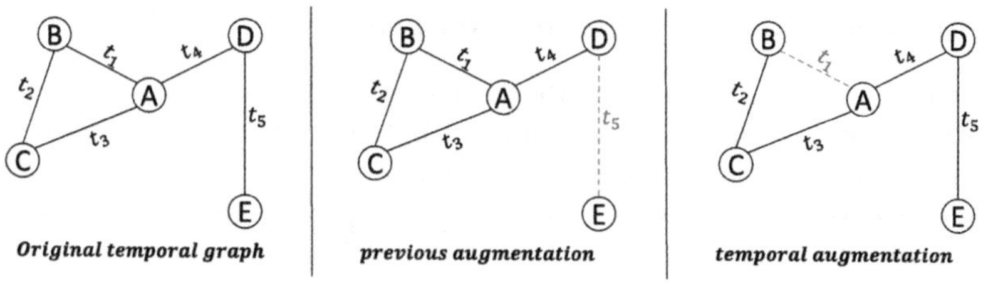

Fig. 1. The toy example illustrates the limitations of the static graph augmentation method when applied to a temporal graph. Specifically, the original temporal network (left) and the resulting loss of temporal information following the application of static graph augmentation (middle) are demonstrated. To address this issue, we propose a novel approach for augmenting temporal graphs by incorporating both topological and temporal information. This approach allows us to eliminate redundant information while preserving vital temporal information (right).

information from the input temporal graph by taking into account both structural and temporal influence. This process enhances the effectiveness of temporal graph augmentation. Subsequently, the pruned graph is subjected to perturbations to generate two distinct temporal views for augmentation. Finally, the model is trained using a contrastive loss function to maximize the agreement between node embeddings in the two views.

Specifically, the main contributions are summarized as follows.

- We present a novel approach for temporal graph contrast learning that incorporates temporal information during edge generation. This enables the model to better capture the structural evolution characteristics of graphs, resulting in improved representation learning.
- We propose a temporal graph augmentation method that leverages both the structural and temporal information of neighborhoods. By doing so, we are able to augment the original graph while preserving important temporal features.
- To further enhance important topology structures and improve node representations, we propose a graph pruning scheme that employs edge centrality measures to remove noisy or redundant connections prior to attention allocation.
- Experimental results demonstrate the superior performance of our proposed TGAC in tasks such as link prediction and node classification, when compared to other state-of-the-art temporal graph representation learning models.

2 Related Work

In this section, we will provide a concise overview of the existing literature on temporal graph representation learning. We will then delve into the topic of contrastive representation learning methods. Finally, we will compare and contrast our proposed method with related works in the field to better understand its unique contributions.

2.1 Temporal Graph Representation Learning

Graph representation learning methodologies are designed to generate embeddings that capture both structural and attribute information at either the node or graph level [4,24,26,31]. For temporal graphs, traditional representations can be expanded to incorporate time-dependency, where the model of temporal dependence is formulated either as snapshot-based or event-based methods [20]. These techniques aim to learn temporal node or graph embeddings that capture the evolution of the graph over time. While snapshot-based paradigms may have merit, our paper focuses primarily on event-based models, which have exhibited superior performance in empirical studies compared to models based on snapshot temporal graphs [27].

Temporal graphs exhibit the time-varying behavior of nodes, which provides distinct insights not present in static graphs. By incorporating historical interaction information, we can distinguish between nodes that have similar local neighborhoods but different structural roles. For instance, JODIE [14] learns the embeddings of evolving trajectories by leveraging past interactions. TGN [25] keeps track of a memory state for each node and updates it with new interactions. CAWs [32] capture the dynamic evolution of networks by using temporally anonymous random walks to extract temporal network motifs. Unfortunately, all of the aforementioned techniques do not take into account the impact of noise in the network, which can be detrimental to the ability to capture valuable temporal information.

2.2 Contrastive Representation Learning

Inspired by recent advancements of CL in computer vision [12] and natural language processing [18] domains, some research has been conducted to apply CL to graph data. For instance, DGI [30] combines Graph Neural Networks with infomax and concentrates on contrasting views at the node level by generating multiple augmented graphs through handcrafted augmentations. GRACE [36] generates two views by randomly masking node attributes and removing edges, while GCA [37] employs a similar framework to GRACE but emphasizes designing the adaptive augmentation strategy.

Although some studies have explored the potential of contrastive learning for temporal graphs, most of them focus on static graphs and snapshot-based temporal graphs [5,22,23]. In contrast, our proposed approach addresses the challenge of noise in temporal graphs by considering the importance of edges with respect to both temporal and topological features, and adaptively augmenting the graphs in an efficient manner. Our approach effectively enhances both the temporal and topological features of the graphs, distinguishing it from existing methods for temporal graph learning and graph contrastive learning.

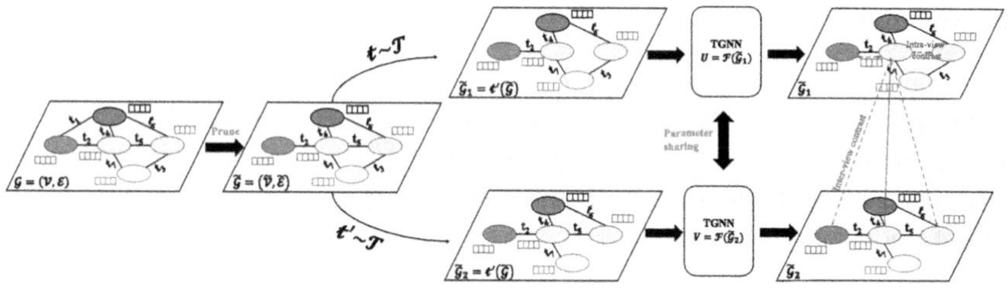

Fig. 2. Our proposed Temporal Graph representation learning with Adaptive augmentation Contrastive (TGAC) model. The input graph $\mathcal{G}$ is first pruned to be $\widetilde{\mathcal{G}}$, then use two augmentation t and t' are generate two temporal graphs $\widetilde{\mathcal{G}}_1$ and $\widetilde{\mathcal{G}}_2$. A shared TGNN $\mathcal{F}$ is employed to obtain two views' node representation. Finally, the model was trained by contrasting positive-negative pairs in both intra-view (in purple) and inter-view (in orange). (Color figure online)

3 The Proposed Method

In this section, we will introduce the notations and definitions used in this paper. Then, we will present the problem formulation and introduce the overall framework of TGAC. Finally, we will provide a detailed description of each component module (Fig. 2).

3.1 Preliminaries

First, we define the temporal graph based on the timestamps accompanying the node interactions.

Definition 1 (Temporal Graph). *A temporal graph is represented as* $\mathcal{G} = (\mathcal{V}, \mathcal{E})$*, where* $\mathcal{V}$ *is the set of nodes and* $\mathcal{E}$ *is the set of sequences of node interactions with timestamps labels. For any edge* $(u, v, t) \in \mathcal{E}$*, there exists a set of timestamps* $\mathcal{E}_{u,v} = (u, v, t_1), (u, v, t_2), \cdots, (u, v, t_n)$*, indicating that nodes* u *and* v *have interacted at least once at each of the corresponding timestamps. Two interacting nodes are referred to as neighbors. It is important to note that in temporal graphs, the concept of interaction replaces the concept of edges, and multiple interactions can occur between two nodes.*

A good representation learning method for temporal networks should be able to accurately and efficiently predict how these networks will evolve over time. In this context, the problem can be formulated as follows.

Definition 2 (Problem formulation). *For any temporal graph* $\mathcal{G} = (\mathcal{V}, \mathcal{E})$*, the task is to learn the mapping function* $f : \mathcal{V} \rightarrow \mathbb{R}^d$ *to embed the node in a* d*-dimensional vector space, where* $d \ll |\mathcal{V}|$*. The node representation is supposed to contain both structural and temporal information and is suitable for downstream machine-learning tasks such as link prediction, and node classification.*

3.2 Overview

The proposed model utilizes graph contrastive learning to capture the structural and temporal features from temporal graphs during the training phase. The model prunes the input temporal graph, generates contrasting views, and uses a loss function that includes both link prediction and contrastive loss to learn effective node representations.

3.3 Temporal Graph Pruning

To ensure effective node representation learning for downstream tasks, it is necessary to remove noisy edges from the original time graph topology. TGAC achieves this by computing the importance of each edge, which takes into account both the node centrality and temporal information. As a result, the pruned time graph provides richer information for TGNN to learn node representations more effectively. The centrality of each edge is assessed based on a combination of node properties, graph topology, and temporal characteristics. By removing noisy links based on their centrality attributes, the pruned temporal graph facilitates improved information use for node representation learning through TGNN.

Node centrality is a common method for measuring the importance of nodes in large-scale complex networks. Various techniques have been proposed to measure node centrality, some of which are outlined below:

- Degree centrality (DE) is considered one of the elementary measures of centrality, which quantifies the number of edges incident to a particular node in a network. It is a widely used and effective approach for evaluating the significance of a node in a network. Specifically, in social networks such as Twitter, nodes represent people, while edges represent the following connections among them. Nodes with a high degree of centrality tend to correspond to more important people.
- Eigenvector centrality (EV) is another important centrality measure that considers not only the number of connections of a particular node but also the centrality of its neighboring nodes. The idea is that if a node is connected to other nodes with high centrality, its own centrality is subsequently augmented. Consequently, a node's eigenvector centrality may not necessarily be high even if it has a substantial degree, in cases where all its connections have low centrality. Subsequent paragraphs, however, are indented.
- PageRank centrality (PR) is a measure of centrality determined by utilizing the PageRank algorithm. This algorithm involves developing a random walk model on a directed graph and calculating the likelihood of visiting each node under specific conditions. The resulting stable probability value of each node is its PageRank value, which serves as an indicator of the node's importance or centrality within the network.

These three methods of calculating node centrality have distinct advantages and limitations. DE is a straightforward and efficient method, making it suitable for datasets that are not very sensitive to node characteristics. EV takes into account both node characteristics and topology and performs well across a wide range of datasets. PR is especially effective for analyzing complex topological networks. Consequently, we can use the notation $\varphi(\cdot)$ to indicate the specific node centrality method used for a given dataset.

Additionally, since temporal graphs contain temporal information that static graphs lack, we need to consider the temporal dimension when measuring the impact of each edge. To achieve this, we define the centrality of each edge as ϕ_{uv}^t, which is determined by the centralities of the two nodes it connects and the time of its occurrence. In undirected graphs, $\phi^t uv$ is computed as the product of the average centralities of its two nodes and the time at which the edge is formed. This can be expressed mathematically as follows:

$$\phi_{uv}^t = (\varphi(u) + \varphi(v))/2 + \alpha t_{uv}. \tag{1}$$

This definition enables us to capture the evolving nature of the temporal graph and obtain more precise node representations that can be used for downstream tasks. In the case of a directed graph, we define the centrality of an edge as the product of the centrality of the node it is pointing to and the time at which the connection is established. This reflects the impact of the edge in directing the flow of information or influences toward the target node, while also taking into account the time factor. Hence, the edge centrality for a directed graph is defined as:

$$\phi_{uv}^t = \varphi(v) + \alpha t_{uv}. \tag{2}$$

After obtaining the centrality score for each edge, we sort all the edges in descending order based on their centrality scores and then select the top k edges to retain while pruning the rest. The value of k is determined by the formula $k = E \times (1 - c)$, where E represents the total number of edges in the temporal graph, and c is the pruning ratio. The temporal graph after pruning is illustrated below:

$$\widetilde{\mathcal{E}} = \left\{u_i, v_i, t_i | \phi_{u_i v_i}^{t_i} \in \text{TopK}(\phi(\mathcal{E}), k)\right\}. \tag{3}$$

This method helps to remove redundant and noisy edges from the temporal graph and obtain a pruned temporal graph that can be used for subsequent training, which facilitates the acquisition of improved representation results.

3.4 Temporal Graph Encoder

The temporal graph encoder is based on TGN [25] and consists of interchangeable and independent modules. Each node in the model has a memory vector that represents its past interactions in a compressed form. When a new event occurs, the mailbox module calculates the message for each related node, which is then used to update the node's memory vector. To address the issue of stale information, the embedding module calculates node embeddings at each time step by using their neighborhood and memory state. In other words, the encoder updates the memory state of each node with new interactions and employs a node memory update mechanism. In the node memory storage module, at time t, the model stores the memory of each node u it has encountered so far in a vector denoted by $s_u(t)$. Whenever a new interaction occurs with a node, its compressed historical information is used to update its memory state. During the message passing and updating phase, the model calculates the memory vectors for the source and target nodes u and v affected by each event. This is done using the msg method, which computes the message sent from the source node to the target node. The message is then used to update the memory vectors of both nodes. We formulate message passing function as

$$m_u(t) = msg\left(s_u(t^-), s_v(t^-), t\right), \tag{4}$$

$$\bar{m}_u(t) = agg\left(m_u(t_1), \ldots, m_u(t)\right). \tag{5}$$

To clarify, the message passing and aggregator part involves calculating the message using the msg method for the nodes u and v affected by each event, where $s_u(t^-)$ represents the information at node u before time t. The message is then aggregated with the information obtained before the node, and the resulting information is then updated to yield the $s_u(t)$ value for node u. This process involves the utilization of a learnable information method, such as MLP, followed by information aggregation techniques, such as RNNs or attention mechanisms, and concluded with information update operations. In scenarios where nodes u and v are affected by an interaction event, their information is updated using a memory cell such as GRU [2] or LSTM [8]. The process can be mathematically formulated as follows:

$$s_u(t) = mem\left(\bar{m}_u(t), s_u(t^-)\right). \tag{6}$$

Finally, after obtaining $s_u(t)$, the node representation is obtained by concatenating it with the current input features of node u at time t, followed by a non-linear transformation to obtain the final embedding $h_u(t)$. Specifically, the concatenation operation is defined as follows:

$$z_u(t) = emb(u,t) = \sum_{v \in \mathcal{N}_u^k([0,t])} h\left(s_u(t), s_v(t)\right), \tag{7}$$

where h is a learnable function. The resulting $z_u(t)$ can be used for downstream tasks such as node classification or link prediction.

3.5 Temporal Contrastive Learning

Contrastive learning aims to learn node or graph representations by bringing positive samples closer and pushing negative samples farther apart. We use a general contrastive learning framework to maximize representation consistency across different views. Two views of the pruned graph are generated using random augmentation operations. Existing methods struggle with topological random disturbances, as selecting positive and negative samples is crucial. After a disturbance, ineffective neighborhood information can make optimizing contrastive targets difficult. We must perturb the graph to preserve its internal mode as much as possible. Our method removes edges randomly with a probability but assigns a weight to each edge to decrease the probability of removing important edges and increase that of removing redundant ones.

To achieve this, we introduce a removal probability for each edge and improve the perturbation process of the temporal graph by considering edge importance. Similar to temporal graph pruning, we compute edge importance based on topology and time information and use it to calculate the removal probability for each edge. However, since the importance values may be relatively large, we first normalize them by setting them to $w_{uv}^t = \lg \phi_{uv}^t$. After normalization, we obtain the removal probability for each edge as follows:

$$p_{uv}^t = \min\left(\frac{w_{max}^t - w_{uv}^t}{w_{max}^t - \mu_w^t} \cdot p_e, p_r\right), \tag{8}$$

where p_e is a hyperparameter that controls the overall probability of edge removal, w_{max}^t and μ_w^t are the maximum and average values of w_{uv}^t, respectively. We set a cut-off probability $p_r < 1$ to prevent the removal probability from becoming too high and corrupting the graph topology. The resulting temporal graph is pruned and looks like this:

$$P\left\{(u, v, t) \in \widetilde{\mathcal{E}}\right\} = 1 - p_{uv}^t. \tag{9}$$

To enhance the quality of node representations, we propose topological perturbations that generate distinct views during each iteration of training, denoted as $\widetilde{\mathcal{E}}_1$ and $\widetilde{\mathcal{E}}_2$. The probabilities of generating these two views are represented by p_e^1 and p_e^2, respectively. To prevent excessive perturbation that may lead to the degradation of the graph topology, we set p_e to 0.7, ensuring that p_r does not surpass 0.7.

3.6 Loss Function

Task Loss: To learn the parameters of TGNN for each view node, we utilize a link prediction binary cross-entropy loss function, define as follows:

$$\mathcal{L}(u, v, t) = -\log \sigma(-{z_u^t}^{\mathrm{T}} z_v^t) - Q\mathbb{E}_{v' \sim P(v)} \log \sigma({z_u^t}^{\mathrm{T}} z_{v'}^t). \tag{10}$$

The loss function aims to maximize the likelihood of the observed edges while minimizing the likelihood of negative edges. Since two views both have this task, the loss for the two views is defined similarly. The overall objective to be maximized is defined as the average over two views, formally given by:

$$\mathcal{L}_{task} = \sum_{(u_1, v_1, t_1) \in \widetilde{\mathcal{E}}_1} \mathcal{L}(u_1, v_1, t_1) + \sum_{(u_2, v_2, t_2) \in \widetilde{\mathcal{E}}_2} \mathcal{L}(u_2, v_2, t_2). \tag{11}$$

Contrastive Loss: We use a comparison objective for the two generated views to differentiate nodes with the same identifier in different views from other embeddings. For any node v_i in one view, its corresponding node u_i in the other view is considered as an anchor, and v_i and u_i form positive sample pairs. All other nodes from both views form negative samples, guiding the model to maximize the consistency of node representations across the two views. The representations of each node in the two views should be similar and distinct from those of other nodes.

Furthermore, we use a two-layer MLP to transform node representations into a feature space for comparison. A similarity function $\theta(u, v) = s(g(u), g(v))$ is used to measure different node representations, where s can be either cosine or Euclidean distance and $g(\cdot)$ denotes the non-linear projection of the MLP. To achieve contrastive learning in multi-view, we use a loss function similar to InfoNCE. For each positive sample pair u_i and v_i, the objective function is defined as follows:

$$\mathcal{L}_{cl} = \sum_{u_i, v_i \in \mathcal{V}} \log \frac{P_i}{P_i + N_i^{inter} + N_i^{intra}}, \tag{12}$$

where $P_i = e^{\theta(u_i, v_i)/\tau}$ is positive pair, N_i^{inter} and N_i^{intra} are inter-view and intra-view negative pairs, respectively, which are given by the following:

$$N_i^{inter} = \sum_{k \neq i} e^{\theta(u_i, v_k)/\tau}, \tag{13}$$

$$N_i^{intra} = \sum_{k \neq i} e^{\theta(u_i, u_k)/\tau}, \tag{14}$$

where τ denotes the temperature coefficient.

Total Loss: The total loss function is a combination of the task loss $\mathcal{L}_{task}$ and contrastive loss $\mathcal{L}_{cl}$. The definition of the total loss function $\mathcal{L}$ is established formally by utilizing Eqs. 11 and 12. Specifically, the total loss function $\mathcal{L}$ is expressed as follows:

$$\mathcal{L} = \lambda \mathcal{L}_{task} + \mathcal{L}_{cl}, \tag{15}$$

where λ is a hyperparameter that balances the weights of the two loss functions. The task loss function $\mathcal{L}_{task}$ evaluates the predictive capability of the model in identifying observed edges in the temporal graph, whereas the contrastive loss function $\mathcal{L}_{cl}$ encourages the consistency of representations of the same node across the two augmented views.

4 Experiments

In this section, we evaluate the performance of TGAC against a variety of baselines on different datasets. We further conduct an ablation study on relevant modules and hyperparameter analysis.

4.1 Experimental Setup

Datasets. We evaluate the performance of TGAC on the tasks of temporal link prediction and dynamic node classification using four public temporal graph datasets, namely, Wikipedia [14], Reddit [1], MOOC [14], and CollegeMsg [15]. A detailed description of the statistical characteristics of these datasets is presented in Table 1.

Table 1. Statistics of the datasets.

Datasets	$\|\mathcal{V}\|$	$\|\mathcal{E}\|$	Feature	Label
Wikipedia	9,227	157,474	172	2
Reddit	10,984	672,447	172	2
Mooc	7,144	411,749	0	2
CollegeMsg	1,899	59,835	0	0

Baselines. To evaluate the performance of TGAC, we compare ten state-of-the-art graph embedding methods on both static and temporal graphs. For static graph embedding methods, including GAE, VGAE [13], GraphSAGE [6] and GAT [29]. For temporal graph embedding methods, including CTDNE [21], JODIE [14], DyRep [28], TGAT [35], TGN [25] and CAWs [32].

Parameter Settings. In the parameter settings, we select the optimizer with the Adam algorithm, the learning rate is 0.0001, and the dropout probability is 0.1. The dimension of both node embedding and time embedding is set to 100, memory dimension is set to 172. The temporal information weight α and contrastive loss weights λ are set at 10 and 0.1. For the baseline methods, we keep their default parameter settings.

4.2 Temporal Link Prediction

For temporal link prediction, we follow the evaluation protocols of TGN [35]. The goal of this task is to predict whether a temporal link will exist between given two nodes at a certain future point in time. We consider two different downstream tasks for evaluation: transductive and inductive link prediction. In the transductive link prediction task, we aim to predict the presence or absence of a link between two nodes that were observed during the training phase. In the inductive link prediction task, we aim to predict the presence or absence of a link between two new nodes that were not observed during the training phase. We divide the ratios of training, validation, and testing are 70%, 15%, and 15%, respectively.

Table 2. ROC AUC(%) and Average Precision(%) for the transductive temporal link prediction on Wikipedia, Reddit, Mooc and CollegeMsg. The means and standard deviations are computed for ten runs.

Task	Methods	Wikipedia		Reddit		Mooc		CollegeMsg	
		AUC	AP	AUC	AP	AUC	AP	AUC	AP
Transductive	GAE	91.47 ± 0.3	91.12 ± 0.1	95.87 ± 1.2	96.57 ± 1.0	87.89 ± 0.6	90.70 ± 0.3	73.15 ± 1.5	70.00 ± 1.17
	VGAE	82.43 ± 1.6	82.50 ± 4.0	92.70 ± 0.4	91.53 ± 0.7	88.21 ± 0.6	$\mathbf{91.00} \pm 0.3$	74.07 ± 0.9	70.66 ± 1.0
	GraphSAGE	92.00 ± 0.3	92.34 ± 0.3	97.75 ± 0.1	97.85 ± 0.1	56.17 ± 0.3	60.63 ± 0.2	62.38 ± 1.3	62.48 ± 0.9
	GAT	92.76 ± 0.5	93.17 ± 0.5	97.90 ± 0.1	97.07 ± 0.1	67.24 ± 0.1	66.66 ± 0.8	78.09 ± 0.5	75.97 ± 0.7
	CTDNE	82.36 ± 0.7	80.86 ± 0.7	85.32 ± 2.0	87.31 ± 1.4	88.37 ± 2.6	89.27 ± 2.0	81.88 ± 0.7	80.25 ± 0.8
	JODIE	94.94 ± 0.3	94.65 ± 0.6	97.62 ± 0.2	97.07 ± 0.4	79.75 ± 2.8	74.85 ± 3.1	59.85 ± 6.0	54.50 ± 4.4
	DyRep	94.22 ± 0.2	94.63 ± 0.2	98.01 ± 0.1	98.05 ± 0.1	80.57 ± 2.1	77.30 ± 2.2	54.75 ± 6.8	51.89 ± 4.8
	TGAT	94.99 ± 0.3	95.29 ± 0.2	98.07 ± 0.1	98.17 ± 0.1	66.02 ± 1.0	63.82 ± 0.9	81.05 ± 0.6	79.16 ± 0.6
	TGN	98.42 ± 0.1	98.50 ± 0.1	98.69 ± 0.1	98.73 ± 0.1	$\mathbf{89.07} \pm 1.6$	86.96 ± 2.1	85.06 ± 5.9	85.38 ± 6.4
	CAWs	98.39 ± 0.1	98.62 ± 0.1	98.05 ± 0.1	98.66 ± 0.1	69.48 ± 5.3	70.11 ± 6.2	90.02 ± 0.2	92.55 ± 0.1
	TGAC-DE	98.85 ± 0.0	98.89 ± 0.0	98.70 ± 0.0	98.73 ± 0.0	85.39 ± 1.0	82.20 ± 1.0	91.39 ± 0.6	92.91 ± 0.5
	TGAC-EV	$\mathbf{98.86} \pm 0.0$	$\mathbf{98.91} \pm 0.0$	98.71 ± 0.1	98.74 ± 0.0	88.54 ± 0.8	86.02 ± 0.8	$\mathbf{91.55} \pm 0.7$	$\mathbf{93.03} \pm 0.5$
	TGAC-PR	98.85 ± 0.0	98.90 ± 0.0	$\mathbf{98.76} \pm 0.1$	$\mathbf{98.76} \pm 0.1$	88.14 ± 1.4	85.47 ± 1.3	91.49 ± 0.7	92.98 ± 0.5
Inductive	GraphSAGE	88.60 ± 0.3	88.94 ± 0.5	94.28 ± 0.4	94.51 ± 0.1	53.68 ± 0.4	55.35 ± 0.4	49.64 ± 1.5	51.83 ± 0.8
	GAT	89.11 ± 0.5	89.82 ± 0.4	94.30 ± 0.4	94.58 ± 0.3	53.43 ± 2.1	54.80 ± 0.9	68.98 ± 1.2	66.22 ± 1.2
	JODIE	92.75 ± 0.3	93.11 ± 0.4	95.42 ± 0.2	94.50 ± 0.6	81.43 ± 0.8	76.82 ± 1.4	51.59 ± 3.2	50.02 ± 2.2
	DyRep	91.03 ± 0.3	91.96 ± 0.2	95.79 ± 0.5	95.75 ± 0.5	82.06 ± 1.7	79.17 ± 1.6	49.05 ± 4.1	49.30 ± 2.6
	TGAT	93.37 ± 0.3	93.86 ± 0.3	96.46 ± 0.1	96.61 ± 0.2	69.09 ± 0.8	67.65 ± 0.7	72.27 ± 0.5	72.53 ± 0.6
	TGN	97.72 ± 0.1	97.83 ± 0.1	97.54 ± 0.1	97.63 ± 0.1	$\mathbf{89.03} \pm 1.6$	$\mathbf{86.70} \pm 2.0$	78.54 ± 3.9	80.77 ± 3.7
	CAWs	98.16 ± 0.2	$\mathbf{98.52} \pm 0.1$	97.56 ± 0.1	97.06 ± 0.1	74.79 ± 2.3	76.02 ± 2.2	$\mathbf{89.11} \pm 1.5$	$\mathbf{91.79} \pm 1.4$
	TGAC-DE	$\mathbf{98.29} \pm 0.0$	98.35 ± 0.1	98.95 ± 0.0	98.98 ± 0.0	84.00 ± 1.3	80.02 ± 1.5	88.42 ± 0.5	90.70 ± 0.4
	TGAC-EV	98.28 ± 0.1	98.35 ± 0.1	98.94 ± 0.1	98.97 ± 0.1	88.23 ± 0.6	85.30 ± 0.7	88.49 ± 0.5	90.75 ± 0.4
	TGAC-PR	98.28 ± 0.1	98.34 ± 0.0	$\mathbf{98.96} \pm 0.1$	$\mathbf{98.98} \pm 0.1$	88.16 ± 1.5	85.16 ± 1.7	88.49 ± 0.5	90.73 ± 0.4

The results of our method and the baseline method on the temporal link prediction task are compared in Table 2. We leverage the Area Under the ROC Curve (AUC) and Average Precision (AP) as performance metrics. On both transductive and inductive tasks, we make the following observations.

- Baseline temporal graph embedding methods outperform static graph embedding methods such as GAE, VGAE, GraphSAGE, and GAT in link prediction tasks on four real-world datasets that include temporal information.
- For the temporal graph embedding methods, compare with the methods which combine time embedding, node features, and graph topology (i.e., CTDNE, TGAT) are worse than the use of a special module to update node embeddings based on temporal interactions (i.e., TGN, TGAC).
- Our method outperforms several existing methods on multiple datasets, although it is not as effective as CAWs on some of them. However, CAWs uses online time random walk sampling to obtain time node representations, which cannot be parallelized on the GPU and therefore require significant processing time. By incorporating prior knowledge into our time map and utilizing message passing, our method improves efficiency compared to TGN and achieves faster processing speeds than CAWs.

4.3 Dynamic Node Classification

For dynamic node classification, we also follow the evaluation protocols of TGN. The goal of this task is to predict the state label of the source node while giving the node link and future timestamps. Specifically, we use the model obtained from the previous transductive link prediction as the pre-training model for node classification. The node classification task trains a classifier decoder separately, such as a three-layer MLP. We evaluate the task on three datasets with dynamic node labels (i.e., Wikipedia, Reddit, and Mooc), excluding the CollegeMsg dataset because there are no node labels.

The results of our method and the baseline method on the Dynamic Node Classification task are compared in Table 3. We leverage the Area Under the ROC Curve (AUC) as performance metrics. Our results demonstrate superior performance on all three datasets, underscoring the effectiveness of our model's use of contrastive learning. By bringing the distance between nodes in one view closer while pushing away nodes in the other view, our model learns more optimized node representations for downstream classification tasks. This approach has proven to be more effective than alternative methods, as evidenced by the superior performance of our model.

Table 3. ROC AUC(%) for the transductive dynamic node classification on Wikipedia, Reddit and Mooc. The means and standard deviations are computed for ten runs. We use bold and underline to highlight the best and second best performers.

	Wikipedia	Reddit	Mooc
CTDNE	84.86 ± 1.5	54.38 ± 7.5	71.84 ± 1.0
JODIE	84.40 ± 0.9	61.51 ± 1.2	70.03 ± 0.5
DyRep	83.25 ± 0.5	60.86 ± 1.7	64.64 ± 1.4
TGAT	84.41 ± 1.5	65.98 ± 1.6	65.79 ± 0.5
TGN	87.56 ± 0.7	65.51 ± 0.8	63.93 ± 0.3
CAWs	84.88 ± 1.3	66.52 ± 2.2	68.77 ± 0.4
TGAC-DE	87.69 ± 0.2	68.54 ± 0.4	$\underline{70.13 \pm 0.2}$
TGAC-EV	$\mathbf{90.13} \pm 0.2$	$\mathbf{71.70} \pm 0.4$	61.83 ± 0.7
TGAC-PR	$\underline{88.85 \pm 0.2}$	$\underline{71.06} \pm 0.8$	$\mathbf{71.10} \pm 0.3$

4.4 Ablation Experiment

We conducted a series of experiments on the CollegeMsg dataset to evaluate the effectiveness of pruning on temporal graphs, using different centrality measures. Our findings, presented in Table 4, indicate a notable enhancement in the model's performance upon the removal of extraneous links through the application of diverse node centrality principles. Herein, "T" refers to the TGNN function,

Table 4. Ablation study result on CollegeMsg for Pruning schemes

	T	T+DE	T+EV	T+PR	T+DE+P	T+EV+P	T+PR+P
AUC	85.06	90.38	90.57	90.58	**92.39**	**92.55**	**92.49**

Table 5. ROC AUC(%) for both the transductive and inductive temporal link prediction on Wikipedia, Reddit, and CollegeMsg.

	Wikipedia		Reddit		CollegeMsg	
	Transductive	Inductive	Transductive	Inductive	Transductive	Inductive
TGAC w/o CL	98.29	98.37	98.54	98.57	85.06	87.41
TGAC w/o Prune	98.32	98.40	98.62	98.65	90.57	87.93
TGAC	**98.53**	**98.64**	**98.82**	**98.86**	**92.71**	**88.79**

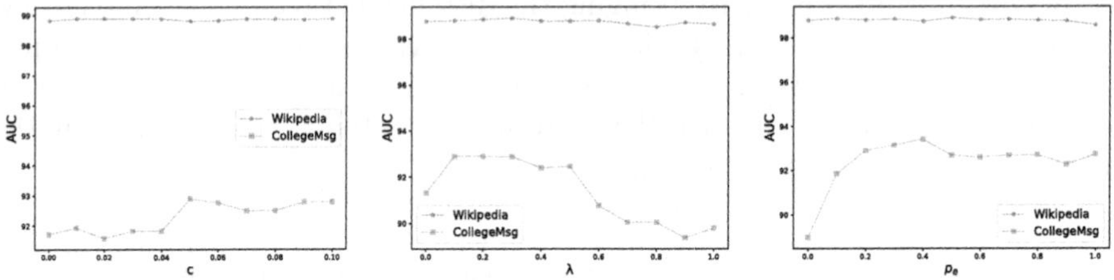

(a) Pruning ratio c (b) Balance weight λ (c) Drop ratio p_e

Fig. 3. Parameter Sensitivity.

while "P" denotes the Prune function. Furthermore, we conducted an ablation study to assess the impact of contrastive learning, and the results are depicted in Table 5. Upon removing both the pruning and contrastive learning aspects, the model became a conventional TGN model. Our findings demonstrate that the absence of pruning and contrastive learning resulted in a significant decline in the performance of the TGN model.

4.5 Parameter Sensitivity

Our proposed method requires a thorough analysis of hyperparameters' impact on temporal link prediction performance on the datasets. These hyperparameters are the temporal graph pruning ratio c, the balance parameter λ, and the temporal graph enhancement factor p_e. We use a range of evaluation metrics to gauge the efficacy of various parameter values. We evaluate them on Wikipedia and CollegeMsg datasets using link prediction as the downstream task. We investigate the impact of the temporal graph pruning ratio on the model's ability to learn effective information. Additionally, we explore the balance between link prediction and contrastive learning. Figure 3 illustrates the sensitivity of our model's performance to various hyperparameters, including c,

λ, and p_e. Our experiments show that the proposed method achieves the best results when $c = 0.05$, $\lambda = 0.1$, and $p_e = 0.4$.

5 Conclusion

This paper introduces a novel temporal graph contrastive learning model named TGAC. The proposed model employs a pruning and adaptive augmentation technique that incorporates topological and temporal information with prior knowledge. This approach leads to the generation of enhanced temporal graph information, which in turn improves the performance of TGNN. The experimental results demonstrate that the TGAC model outperforms state-of-the-art methods on most of the datasets.

Acknowledgments. This work was supported by the Fundamental Research Funds for the Provincial Universities of Zhejiang Grant GK229909299001-008 and GK239909299001-028, Zhejiang Laboratory Open Research Project under Grant K2022QA0AB01, National Natural Science Foundation of China under Grant 62071327.

Ethical Statement. 1. The authors declare that they have no known competing financial interests or personal relationships that could have appeared to influence the work reported in this paper.

2. To the best of our knowledge, this work does not have potential negative social impacts.

3. All authors have already known that they intend to submit to the ecml-pkdd conference, and there is no multiple submission of one manuscript.

4. There is no conflict of interest in this study. Any questions or problems, please feel free to contact us.

References

1. Baumgartner, J., Zannettou, S., Keegan, B., Squire, M., Blackburn, J.: The pushshift reddit dataset. In: Proceedings of the International AAAI Conference on Web and Social Media, vol. 14, pp. 830–839 (2020)
2. Cho, K., et al.: Learning phrase representations using RNN encoder-decoder for statistical machine translation. arXiv preprint arXiv:1406.1078 (2014)
3. Gorochowski, T.E., Grierson, C.S., Di Bernardo, M.: Organization of feed-forward loop motifs reveals architectural principles in natural and engineered networks. Sci. Adv. **4**(3), eaap9751 (2018)
4. Grover, A., Leskovec, J.: node2vec: scalable feature learning for networks. In: Proceedings of the 22nd ACM SIGKDD International Conference on Knowledge Discovery and Data Mining, pp. 855–864 (2016)
5. Gutmann, M.U., Hyvärinen, A.: Noise-contrastive estimation of unnormalized statistical models, with applications to natural image statistics. J. Mach. Learn. Res. **13**(2) (2012)
6. Hamilton, W., Ying, Z., Leskovec, J.: Inductive representation learning on large graphs. In: Advances in Neural Information Processing Systems, vol. 30 (2017)

7. Hamilton, W.L., Ying, R., Leskovec, J.: Representation learning on graphs: methods and applications. arXiv preprint arXiv:1709.05584 (2017)
8. Hochreiter, S., Schmidhuber, J.: Long short-term memory. Neural Comput. **9**(8), 1735–1780 (1997)
9. Holme, P., Saramäki, J.: Temporal networks. Phys. Rep. **519**(3), 97–125 (2012)
10. Huang, C., Wang, L., Cao, X., Ma, W., Vosoughi, S.: Learning dynamic graph embeddings using random walk with temporal backtracking. In: NeurIPS 2022 Temporal Graph Learning Workshop (2022)
11. Jin, M., Li, Y.F., Pan, S.: Neural temporal walks: motif-aware representation learning on continuous-time dynamic graphs. In: Advances in Neural Information Processing Systems (2022)
12. Jing, L., Tian, Y.: Self-supervised visual feature learning with deep neural networks: a survey. IEEE Trans. Pattern Anal. Mach. Intell. **43**(11), 4037–4058 (2020)
13. Kipf, T.N., Welling, M.: Variational graph auto-encoders. arXiv preprint arXiv:1611.07308 (2016)
14. Kumar, S., Zhang, X., Leskovec, J.: Predicting dynamic embedding trajectory in temporal interaction networks. In: Proceedings of the 25th ACM SIGKDD International Conference on Knowledge Discovery & Data Mining, pp. 1269–1278 (2019)
15. Leskovec, J., Krevl, A.: Snap datasets: Stanford large network dataset collection (2014)
16. Liben-Nowell, D., Kleinberg, J.: The link prediction problem for social networks. In: Proceedings of the Twelfth International Conference on Information and Knowledge Management, pp. 556–559 (2003)
17. Liu, M., Liu, Y.: Inductive representation learning in temporal networks via mining neighborhood and community influences. In: Proceedings of the 44th International ACM SIGIR Conference on Research and Development in Information Retrieval, pp. 2202–2206 (2021)
18. Liu, X., et al.: Self-supervised learning: generative or contrastive. IEEE Trans. Knowl. Data Eng. **35**(1), 857–876 (2021)
19. Liu, Y., Ma, J., Li, P.: Neural predicting higher-order patterns in temporal networks. In: Proceedings of the ACM Web Conference 2022, pp. 1340–1351 (2022)
20. Longa, A., et al.: Graph neural networks for temporal graphs: state of the art, open challenges, and opportunities. arXiv preprint arXiv:2302.01018 (2023)
21. Nguyen, G.H., Lee, J.B., Rossi, R.A., Ahmed, N.K., Koh, E., Kim, S.: Continuous-time dynamic network embeddings. In: Companion Proceedings of the Web Conference 2018, pp. 969–976 (2018)
22. Park, N., et al.: CGC: contrastive graph clustering for community detection and tracking. In: Proceedings of the ACM Web Conference 2022, pp. 1115–1126 (2022)
23. Peng, Z., et al.: Graph representation learning via graphical mutual information maximization. In: Proceedings of the Web Conference 2020, pp. 259–270 (2020)
24. Perozzi, B., Al-Rfou, R., Skiena, S.: Deepwalk: online learning of social representations. In: Proceedings of the 20th ACM SIGKDD International Conference on Knowledge Discovery and Data Mining, pp. 701–710 (2014)
25. Rossi, E., Chamberlain, B., Frasca, F., Eynard, D., Monti, F., Bronstein, M.: Temporal graph networks for deep learning on dynamic graphs. arXiv preprint arXiv:2006.10637 (2020)
26. Tang, J., Qu, M., Wang, M., Zhang, M., Yan, J., Mei, Q.: Line: large-scale information network embedding. In: Proceedings of the 24th International Conference on World Wide Web, pp. 1067–1077 (2015)

27. Tian, S., Wu, R., Shi, L., Zhu, L., Xiong, T.: Self-supervised representation learning on dynamic graphs. In: Proceedings of the 30th ACM International Conference on Information & Knowledge Management, pp. 1814–1823 (2021)
28. Trivedi, R., Farajtabar, M., Biswal, P., Zha, H.: Dyrep: learning representations over dynamic graphs. In: International Conference on Learning Representations (2019)
29. Velickovic, P., Cucurull, G., Casanova, A., Romero, A., Lio, P., Bengio, Y., et al.: Graph attention networks. Stat **1050**(20), 10–48550 (2017)
30. Velickovic, P., Fedus, W., Hamilton, W.L., Liò, P., Bengio, Y., Hjelm, R.D.: Deep graph infomax. In: ICLR (Poster), vol. 2, no. 3, p. 4 (2019)
31. Wang, D., Cui, P., Zhu, W.: Structural deep network embedding. In: Proceedings of the 22nd ACM SIGKDD International Conference on Knowledge Discovery and Data Mining, pp. 1225–1234 (2016)
32. Wang, Y., Chang, Y.Y., Liu, Y., Leskovec, J., Li, P.: Inductive representation learning in temporal networks via causal anonymous walks. arXiv preprint arXiv:2101.05974 (2021)
33. Wen, Z., Fang, Y.: Trend: temporal event and node dynamics for graph representation learning. In: Proceedings of the ACM Web Conference 2022, pp. 1159–1169 (2022)
34. Wu, L., Lin, H., Tan, C., Gao, Z., Li, S.Z.: Self-supervised learning on graphs: contrastive, generative, or predictive. IEEE Trans. Knowl. Data Eng. (2021)
35. Xu, D., Ruan, C., Korpeoglu, E., Kumar, S., Achan, K.: Inductive representation learning on temporal graphs. arXiv preprint arXiv:2002.07962 (2020)
36. Zhu, Y., Xu, Y., Yu, F., Liu, Q., Wu, S., Wang, L.: Deep graph contrastive representation learning. arXiv preprint arXiv:2006.04131 (2020)
37. Zhu, Y., Xu, Y., Yu, F., Liu, Q., Wu, S., Wang, L.: Graph contrastive learning with adaptive augmentation. In: Proceedings of the Web Conference 2021, pp. 2069–2080 (2021)

Hierarchical Graph Contrastive Learning

Hao Yan[1], Senzhang Wang[1(✉)], Jun Yin[1], Chaozhuo Li[2], Junxing Zhu[3], and Jianxin Wang[1]

[1] Central South University, Changsha, China
{CSUyh1999,szwang,yinjun2000,jxwang}@csu.edu.cn
[2] Beihang University, Beijing, China
lichaozhuo@buaa.edu.cn
[3] National University of Defense Technology, Changsha, China
zhujunxing@nudt.edu.cn

Abstract. Unsupervised graph representation learning with GNNs is critically important due to the difficulty of obtaining graph labels in many real applications. Graph contrastive learning (GCL), a recently popular method for unsupervised learning on graphs, has achieved great success on many tasks. However, existing graph-level GCL models generally focus on comparing the graph-level representation or node-level representation. The hierarchical structure property, which is ubiquitous in many real world graphs such as social networks and molecular graphs, is largely ignored. To bridge this gap, this paper proposes a novel hierarchical graph contrastive learning model named HIGCL. HIGCL uses a multi-layered architecture and contains two contrastive objectives, inner-contrasting and hierarchical-contrasting. The former conducts inner-scale contrastive learning to learn the flat structural features in each layer, while the latter focuses on performing cross-scale contrastive learning to capture the hierarchical features across layers. Extensive experiments are conducted on graph-level tasks to show the effectiveness of the proposed method.

Keywords: Graph Contrastive Learning · Graph Neural Network · Unsupervised Learning

1 Introduction

Graph Neural Networks (GNNs), with their advantage in learning representations of graphs as non-Euclidean data, have achieved remarkable success in numerous graph learning tasks such as node classification [5,28,36] and graph classification [4,15,29,33]. Most studies of GNNs are conducted under supervision, which requires label information during model training. However, in many real scenarios, label information is difficult and costly to acquire, e.g., determining the pharmacological effects of drug molecular graphs requires living animal experiments [26]. Therefore, how to train GNNs to learn a better graph representation without relying much on labels has naturally become a hot research topic [11,12].

© The Author(s), under exclusive license to Springer Nature Switzerland AG 2023
D. Koutra et al. (Eds.): ECML PKDD 2023, LNAI 14170, pp. 700–715, 2023.
https://doi.org/10.1007/978-3-031-43415-0_41

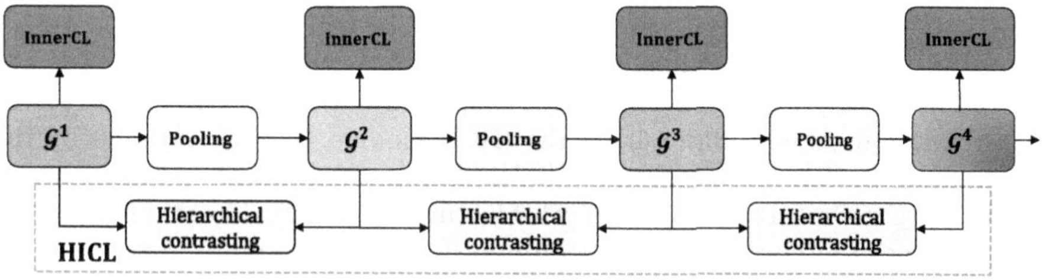

Fig. 1. The framework of hierarchical graph contrastive learning model HIGCL.

Graph contrastive learning (GCL) [24,34,38] is a label-free learning method that has recently achieved great success with a variety of graph data. The basic idea of GCL is to maximize the consistency of the learned representations of graphs relevant to itself (etc., augmented views) while pushing other graphs away from itself, thus allowing the model to capture feature information between the graphs. For different types of graph tasks, GCL typically focuses on representations at different granularities in the graph.

For GCL methods that focus on graph-level tasks, most existing works consider graph-level structural information. For example, GraphCL [34] seeks to maximize the mutual information (MI) between the graph-level representations of two augmented views. However, many graphs contain hierarchical structural properties, such as subgraphs and communities [25]. Such hierarchical structures in graphs may contain significant features for many graph-level tasks and this structural information is not easily mined from the graph-level representation [27]. How to conduct graph-level GCL to capture the hierarchical structural information remains an open problem.

Hierarchical graph pooling methods use a hierarchical architecture to learn graph features at different granularities, yet they all rely on labeling information [4,13,33]. InfoGraph [24] and MVGRL [8] compare graph-level representations with node-level representations to enable the model to capture more fine-grained information in the graph. However, this contrasting objective is associated with higher computational costs and the nodes are difficult to capture the entire graph attribute information. MICRO-Graph [35] performs contrastive learning between subgraph-level and graph-level by mining motif-related subgraphs in the molecular graph. However, it requires strong domain knowledge to design and lacks generalisability.

In this paper, we propose a novel **HI**erarchical **G**raph **C**ontrastive **L**earning model HIGCL as shown in Fig. 1 to effectively fill the gap between hierarchical graph structures and GCL models. HIGCL is technically novel compared with existing GCL models in terms of both contrastive objectives and model architecture. First, unlike existing GCL models which mostly have one contrastive objective, we design two different contrastive objectives, inner-contrasting and hierarchical-contrasting to make full use of the structural information of the graph. Inner-contrasting aims to capture the flat structural information in each layer(granularities) through same-scale contrastive learning(etc., graph versus graph) in the InnerCL module, while hierarchical-contrasting focuses on learning the hierarchical features across layers through cross-scale contrastive learning(etc., graph versus subgraph) in the HICL module. Second, inspired by the hierarchical pooling architecture [13], HIGCL is designed as a multi-layered architecture to capture the hierarchical structures of graphs. The graph of layer l, $\mathcal{G}^l$, undergoes the Pooling module to produce a refined graph of the next layer, which retains the important structural information of the $\mathcal{G}^l$ and reduces the redundant information. Our major contributions are highlighted as follows:

- We propose a novel hierarchical graph contrastive learning model which learns graph representations incorporating hierarchical structural information through a multi-layered architecture. We are one of the early works focusing on the integration of graph hierarchical representation learning with GCL.
- We design two contrasting objectives for graphs at each granularity, which not only fully learn the properties of graphs at different granularities but also capture the correlations across the layers.
- We conduct extensive experiments on nine graph datasets that are extensively used in GCL to validate the effectiveness of HIGCL compared with graph kernel methods, traditional graph unsupervised learning methods, and state-of-the-art GCL methods. Parametric analysis and ablation experiments can further demonstrate that mining hierarchical structural features in graphs is beneficial for the GCL.

The remainder of this paper is organized as follows. Section 2 introduces the related works. Section 3 describes notations used in the paper and presents some preliminary knowledge. Then, we propose the HIGCL model in Sect. 4. Experiments and detailed analysis are reported in Sect. 5. Finally, we conclude the paper in Sect. 5.

2 Related Work

Graph Contrastive Learning. As an effective self-supervised learning approach on graphs, GCL [8,24,34,37,38]has attracted rising research attention in recent years. GCL can train GNNs without relying on labels, which is particularly useful in many real-life scenarios where labels are difficult to obtain [10,24]. Generally, GCL contains three major steps: data augmentation, pretext task design, and contrastive learning. GraphCL [34] is a universal framework designed for GCL at the graph-level, and it incorporates four random data augmentation methods: node dropping, edge perturbation, attribute masking, and subgraph sampling to enhance the performance of GCL. JOAO [38] proposes a bi-level optimization framework for selecting data augmentation strategies based on the graph data domain. SimGRACE [30] abandons data augmentation and directly compares the perturbed encoder with the normal encoder to avoid the semantic information lost. The above are all maximize the agreement between graph-level representations, which makes it hard to capture graph structure information at different granularities. InfoGraph [24] maximizes the mutual information(MI) between node representations at different GNN layers and corresponding graph-level representations. MVGRL [8] uses graph diffusion convolution to generate different semantic views and maximizes the MI between the cross-view representations of nodes and graphs. These two are a kind of cross-scale contrastive learning compared to the former, however, it is difficult for individual nodes to provide valid feature information for graph-level related tasks. On molecular graph data, MICRO-Graph [35] designs a motif-driven GCL framework to compare semantically rich subgraphs with graphs. Different from existing GCL methods, we propose a multi-layered GCL framework to capture the hierarchical structural properties. Two contrastive objectives are also designed to capture the flat structure information within each layer and the hierarchical structure features across layers simultaneously.

Hierarchical Graph Pooling. Hierarchical graph pooling aims to learn the information about the possible hierarchical structure in the graph data by using a hierarchical architecture [4,6,13,14,33]. Recently, hierarchical graph pooling methods can be roughly divided into the coarsening pooling and the node selection pooling [20]. Diffpool [33] belongs to the former and regards the graph pooling problem as a node clustering problem, which generates a coarser graph by learning a clustering assignment matrix in an end-to-end fashion, while this is usually accompanied by high computational costs and poor interpretability. Graph U-nets [6] proposes a node selection pooling method, which calculates the score of each node by a learnable vector and then selects the top-ranked nodes. MuchPool [4] uses the multi-channel framework to combine different types of pooling methods, e.g., coarsening pooling and node selection pooling. [16] finds that the cluster matrix in the coarsening pooling method does not play a major role in graph representation learning. Therefore, in this paper, we adopt node selection pooling method to generate refined graphs of different granularities.

3 Notations and Preliminaries

Graph Representation Learning. We denote a set of graphs as $\mathbb{G} = \{\mathcal{G}_1, \mathcal{G}_2, \cdots, \mathcal{G}_M\}$, where M is the number of graphs. For an arbitrary graph as $\mathcal{G}_i = (\mathbf{A}_i, \mathbf{X}_i)$, where $\mathbf{A}_i \in \{0,1\}^{n_i \times n_i}$ denotes the adjacency matrix, $\mathbf{X}_i \in \mathbb{R}^{n_i \times f}$ denotes the node feature matrix, n_i is the number of nodes and f is the dimension of node feature. Since our model is a multi-layered architecture and the graph structure changes between layers, we further denote the i-th graph fed into the l-th layer as $\mathcal{G}_i^l$ with n_i^l nodes. Then, the adjacency matrix and the hidden node representation matrix are represented as $\mathbf{A}_i^l \in \mathbb{R}^{n_i^l \times n_i^l}$ and $\mathbf{H}_i^l \in \mathbb{R}^{n_i^l \times d}$.

Graph Contrastive Learning. GCL is a recently emerged popular method for training GNNs without relying on labels. It trains GNNs to maximize the agreement between the representations of two positive pairs of the input graph. Existing works design the GCL model from the following three major steps:

(1) Data augmentation. The purpose of data augmentation is to improve the quality of the representation of GNNs, such as robustness, by generating more diverse graph data [8,34]. GraphCL [34] proposes four random augmentations: node dropping, attribute masking, edge perturbation and subgraph sampling. The data augmentation operations in our model follow these four augmentation way.

(2) Pretext tasks design. Differences in pretext tasks are usually represented by differences in the contrasting objectives. For graph-level GCL, most focus on contrasting between graph-level representations in the contrastive learning process. This fails to capture the structural information and hierarchical features of the graph at each granularity.

(3) Contrastive learning. In GCL, increasing the agreement between representations is mostly achieved by maximizing their MI. The MI can be estimated by maximizing the MI lower bound [2,9,19]. When computing the MI of two representations, it is common to go through a projection head (MLP) to produce the positive pairs z_i and z_j in the contrastive space. In this paper, we adopt the widely used NT-Xent loss [19,23] as follows to estimate the MI between two representations

$$\mathcal{L}_{CON} = -\frac{1}{N}\sum_{n=1}^{N}\left[log\frac{exp(sim(z_{i,n}, z_{j,n})/\tau)}{\sum_{n'=1}^{N} exp(sim(z_{i,n}, z_{j,n'}))/\tau)}\right], \tag{1}$$

where $sim(z_{i,n}, z_{j,n}) = z_{i,n}{z_{j,n}}^T/\|z_{i,n}\|\|z_{j,n}\|$ denotes the similarity between the positive pairs. τ denotes the temperature parameter and N denotes the batch-size. $(z_{i,n}, z_{j,n'})$ denotes the negative pairs where $z_{j,n'}$ is the augmented views from the other graphs in the same batch.

4 The Proposed Model

In this section, we introduce the proposed hierarchical graph contrastive learning (HIGCL) model. As shown in Fig. 2, the proposed HIGCL model is a multi-layered architecture that contains the InnerCL module to conduct inner contrasting learning within each layer and the HICL module to conduct hierarchical contrasting learning across different layers. Next, we will introduce the two modules in detail.

4.1 InnerCL Module

In each layer l, the l-th graph $\mathcal{G}^l$ is input into its InnerCL module, which is composed of the l-th GNN f^l, l-th projection head g^l and the augmentation operator. The contrastive learning process in the InnerCL module is similar to the traditional graph-level GCL methods [34]. Traditional graph-level GCL usually develops contrastive learning only at the original graph, while we design

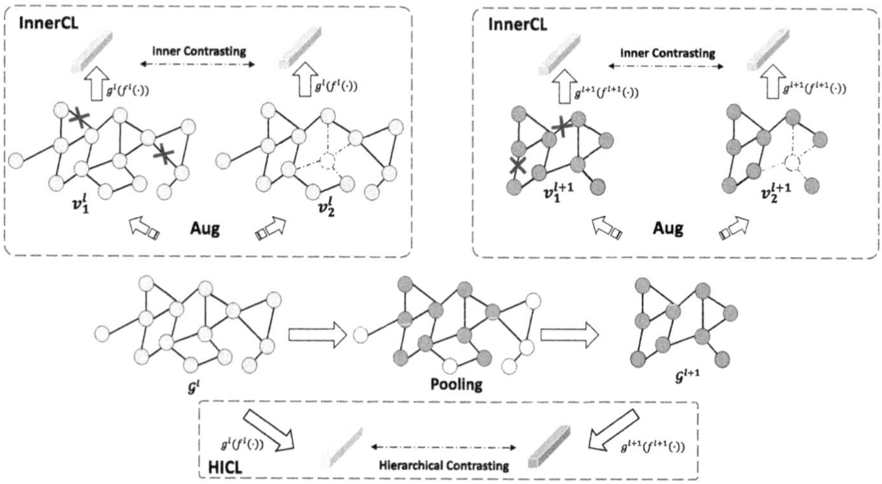

Fig. 2. The illustration of any two layers in the HIGCL. In the InnerCL module, each $\mathcal{G}^l$ learns the flat structural information through the inner-contrasting. Hierarchical features across layers are captured by the hierarchical-contrasting. All the hierarchical-contrasting between different layers forms the HICL module.

the inner contrasting objectives to capture more fully the structural information of the graph at different layers.

Inner-contrasting: We first perform data augmentation for $\mathcal{G}^l$ to produce two diverse augmented views V_1^l and V_2^l. Then the augmented views are encoded by the shared encoder f_l to generate the graph representations $\mathbf{h}_{v_i}^l \in \mathbb{R}^{1\times d^l}, i = 1, 2$. Subsequently, we get the representation $\mathbf{z}_{v_i}^l$ by mapping the graph representation into the contrastive space through the projection head g^l. The MI between the two representations in the contrastive space is maximized by the NT-Xent loss mentioned in Sect. 3. Combining the contrastive loss functions in the InnerCL of each layer, we obtain the total objective function for inner-contrasting as follows:

$$InnerCL_{loss} = -\frac{1}{L}\frac{1}{N}\sum_{l=1}^{L}\sum_{n=1}^{N}\left[log\frac{exp(sim(\mathbf{z}_{v_{1,n}}^l, \mathbf{z}_{v_{2,n}}^l)/\tau)}{\sum_{n'=1}^{N} exp(sim(\mathbf{z}_{v_{1,n}}^l, \mathbf{z}_{v_{2,n'}}^l)/\tau)}\right], \quad (2)$$

where $\mathbf{z}_{v_{i,n}}^l \in \mathbb{R}^{1\times D}, i = 1, 2$. D denotes the dimensions of the vectors in the contrastive space.

4.2 HICL Module

The structure of HICL is shown in Fig. 1 and Fig. 2. HICL has a multi-layered structure and the input of l-th layer are $\mathcal{G}^l$ and $\mathcal{G}^{l+1}$. Hierarchical-contrasting in the HICL is finally conducted between the representations across layers to capture the hierarchical structure information.

Hierarchical Views: In InnerCL we enrich the graph data at each granularity by data augmentation and perform inner contrasting to capture the structural information in each layer. However, such same scale contrasting objectives cannot bridge the different structural layers and thus make it difficult to capture some important hierarchical features. Therefore, we consider the graphs between two adjacent layers (e.g. $\mathcal{G}^l$ and $\mathcal{G}^{l+1}$) as two hierarchical views to perform hierarchical-contrasting.

Hierarchical-Contrasting: This contrastive objective aims to maximize the MI of the hierarchical structure representation $I(\mathcal{G}^l, \mathcal{G}^l + 1)$ across layers, where $I(\cdot, \cdot)$ denotes the MI between the two graphs of adjacent layers. Different from inner contrasting, hierarchical contrasting compares graphs at different granularities. Under this contrasting objectives, encoders at different layers are jointly optimized to enable the model to capture hierarchical structural information. For each layer $\mathcal{G}^l$, the corresponding representation vector $\mathbf{h}^l$ and the representation $\mathbf{z}^l \in \mathbb{R}^{1\times D}$ in contrastive space are obtained with f^l and g^l as shown in Fig. 2.

Then MI between the two graphs of adjacent layers can be calculated by the following formula:

$$HICL^l_{loss} = -\frac{1}{N}\sum_{n=1}^{N}\left[log\frac{exp(sim(\mathbf{z}^l_n, \mathbf{z}^{l+1}_n)/\tau)}{\sum_{n'=1}^{N} exp(sim(\mathbf{z}^l_n, \mathbf{z}^{l+1}_{n'}))/\tau)}\right]. \quad (3)$$

It is possible that with the increase of the layers, the global semantic information of the initial graph may gradually loss due to the heavily refine graph by pooling. That is, the learned substructure information may not be sufficient to the downstream graph-level tasks. To avoid this issue, we also maximize the MI of the two graphs in the first and last layers to ensure global consistency. For uniformity of the formula, we define $\mathcal{G}^{L+1}$ as the original graph $\mathcal{G}^1$. Then the overall hierarchical contrastive loss is the aggregation of all the layer-wise losses as follows

$$HICL_{loss} = \frac{1}{L}\sum_{l=1}^{L} HICL^l_{loss}. \quad (4)$$

where L is the number of layers in HIGCL.

4.3 Hierarchical Graph Representation

Most GCL methods focus on training GNNs with augmented views from the original graph and derive graph representations via a simple readout [34]. These are flat way, and it is difficult to capture the hierarchical structure features of the graph. Therefore, we introduce graph pooling operators to generate refined graphs in different granularities and learn representations of graphs with hierarchical structural information by GNNs at each layer. $\mathcal{G}^l$, f^l represent the graphs and GNNs of the l-th layer, respectively.

Graph Pooling: In this part, we introduce how to obtain $\mathcal{G}^{l+1}$ according to $\mathcal{G}^l$ and f^l. First, $\mathcal{G}^l$ undergoes f^l to learn the node hidden representation matrix

Algorithm 1. Hierarchical Graph Contrastive Learning

Input: Data $\mathbb{G} = \{\mathcal{G}_1, \mathcal{G}_2, \cdots, \mathcal{G}_M\}$, $f, g, \tau, Pool$, L for the number of layers of HIGCL. Note that $\mathcal{G}_n^1 = \mathcal{G}_n$.
for sampled minibatch of data **do**
  for $n = 1, 2, ..., N$, **do**
    for $l = 1, 2, ..., L$, **do**
      Sample q_1, q_2 from τ
      $V^l{}_{n,1} \sim q_1(\cdot|\mathcal{G}_n^l)$, $V^l{}_{n,2} \sim q_2(\cdot|\mathcal{G}_n^l)$
      $\mathbf{h}_{v_{1,n}}^l = f^l(V^l{}_{1,n})$, $\mathbf{h}_{v_{2,n}}^l = f^l(V^l{}_{2,n})$, $\mathbf{h}^l = f^l(\mathcal{G}_n^l)$
      $\mathbf{z}_{v_{1,n}}^l = g^l(\mathbf{h}_{v_{1,n}}^l)$, $\mathbf{z}_{v_{2,n}}^l = g^l(\mathbf{h}_{v_{2,n}}^l)$, $\mathbf{z}^l = g^l(\mathbf{h}^l)$
      $\mathcal{G}_n^{l+1} = Pool^l(f^l(\mathcal{G}_n^l), \mathbf{A}_n^l)$
    end for
  end for
  Compute $\mathcal{L}_{CON}$ with Eq. (2) and Eq. (4).
  Update the parameters of $f, g, Pool$ in each layer with $\mathcal{L}_{CON}$.
end for
return Encoder f and pooling operators $Pool$ in each layer.

$\mathbf{H}^l \in \mathbb{R}^{n^l \times d^l}$. Based on the node selection pooling method [6], we introduce a learnable vector $\mathbf{p}^l \in \mathbb{R}^{d^l \times 1}$ to measure the importance of each node in the latent space and then select the top k ranked nodes to form the refined graph

$$score^l = \mathbf{H}^l \cdot \frac{\mathbf{p}^l}{\|\mathbf{p}^l\|}, \quad idx^l = \text{top-rank}(score^l, \lceil k \cdot n^l \rceil) \tag{5}$$

where idx^l denotes the node index in the l-th layer, and $score^l \in \mathbb{R}^{n^l \times 1}$. Then the generated $\mathcal{G}^{l+1}$ can be represented by the following formula

$$\mathbf{X}^{l+1} = \mathbf{H}^l(idx^l, :) \odot score^l(idx^l, :), \quad \mathbf{A}^{l+1} = \mathbf{A}^l(idx^l, idx^l). \tag{6}$$

where $\odot$ is the broadcasted element-wise product. $\mathbf{X}^{l+1} \in \mathbb{R}^{n^{l+1} \times d^{l+1}}$ and $\mathbf{A}^{l+1} \in \{0, 1\}^{n^{l+1} \times n^{l+1}}$ denote the feature matrix and adjacency matrix of $\mathcal{G}^{l+1}$, respectively. n^{l+1} is equivalent to $\lceil k \cdot n^l \rceil$ where k is a hyper-parameter that indicates the ratio of the reserved nodes.

4.4 Objective Function

Traditional hierarchical graph representation learning uses downstream labeling information to optimize the model [33].

Our proposed HIGCL model uses two contrastive learning losses to optimize the model, thus eliminating the need for label information. The final objective function contains $InnerCL_{loss}$, and $HICL_{loss}$. Then HIGCL performs inner-contrasting and hierarchical-contrasting through optimizing the following objective function

$$\mathcal{L}_{CON} = \beta \cdot HICL_{loss} + (1 - \beta) \cdot InnerCL_{loss}, \tag{7}$$

where β is the trade-off parameter between the two loss terms $HICL_{loss}$ and $InnerCL_{loss}$.

Table 1. Statistics of the 9 graph datasets used in the experiment

Dataset	NCI1	PROTEINS	DD	MUTAG	PTCMR	COLLAB	RDT-B	RDT-M5K	IMDB-B
Graphs	4110	1113	1178	188	344	5000	2000	4999	1500
Vertices	29.87	39.06	284.32	17.93	14.29	74.49	429.63	508.52	19.77
Edges	32.3	72.82	715.66	19.79	14.69	2457.78	497.75	594.87	96.53
Features	37	3	89	7	18	1	1	1	1
Classes	2	2	2	2	2	3	2	5	2

4.5 Fusing Graph Representations of Multiple Layers

As HIGCL is a multi-layered architecture and each layer will produce a graph representation, we need to fuse the graph representations of all the layers to form a final one. The final graph representation can be obtained through aggregating layer-wise representations as follows:

$$\mathbf{h}^l = \text{READOUT}(f^l(\mathbf{X}^l, \mathbf{A}^l)), l \in \{1, ..., L\}$$
$$\mathbf{h}^{final} = \alpha \cdot \mathbf{h}^1 + (1-\alpha) \cdot \frac{1}{L-1} \sum_{l=2}^{L} \mathbf{h}^l, \tag{8}$$

where $\mathbf{h}^l \in \mathbb{R}^{1 \times d}$ and L represent the layers of HIGCL. α is used to tune the degree of contribution of the original and refined graph to the final graph representation. This is mainly considering that different graph data have different degrees of hierarchical structural information. The training algorithms of HIGCL are summarized in Algorithm 1.

5 Experiment

In this section, we perform extensive experiments to evaluate the proposed HIGCL. We will first introduce the datasets, baselines and experiment setup. Then the performance comparison will be performed and the result will be discussed. Finally we will show parameter analysis.

5.1 Experiment Setup

Datasets. We evaluate HIGCL over 9 graph classification benchmark datasets which are widely used for GCL models evaluation. These graph datasets include **NCI1**, **PROTEINS**, **DD**, **MUTAG**, **PTCMR**, **COLLAB**, **REEDIT-BINARY**, **REEDIT-MULTI-5K** and **IMDB-BINARY** collected in TUDataset [17]. In Table 1 we show more details about the 9 graph datasets used in our experiment. These graph datasets can be categorized into biochemical graphs and social networks.

Baselines. We compare HIGCL with three types of baseline methods: graph kernel methods, classic graph unsupervised representation learning methods and

Table 2. Graph classification accuracy comparison among different methods over 9 benchmark datasets in the unsupervised learning setting. In each column, the bold-faced score denotes the best result of all the methods. "–" means that there are no corresponding results in the original papers or running out of memory.

Dataset	NCI1	PROTEINS	DD	MUTAG	PTCMR	COLLAB	RDT-B	RDT-M5K	IMDB-B
GL	66.02 ± 0.12	–	–	81.66 ± 2.11	57.32 ± 1.43	–	77.34 ± 0.18	41.01 ± 0.17	65.87 ± 0.98
WL	80.01 ± 0.50	72.92 ± 0.56	–	80.72 ± 3.00	56.91 ± 2.79	–	68.82 ± 0.41	46.06 ± 0.21	72.30 ± 3.44
DGK	80.31 ± 0.46	73.30 ± 0.82	–	87.44 ± 2.72	–	–	78.04 ± 0.39	41.27 ± 0.18	66.96 ± 0.56
node2vec	54.89 ± 1.61	57.49 ± 3.57	–	72.63 ± 10.20	58.60 ± 8.00	56.10 ± 0.20	–	–	50.22 ± 0.91
sub2vec	52.84 ± 1.47	53.03 ± 5.55	–	61.05 ± 15.80	60.01 ± 6.42	–	71.48 ± 0.41	36.68 ± 0.42	55.26 ± 1.54
graph2vec	73.22 ± 1.81	73.30 ± 2.05	–	83.15 ± 9.25	60.17 ± 6.86	–	75.78 ± 1.03	47.86 ± 0.26	71.10 ± 0.54
InfoGraph	76.20 ± 1.06	74.44 ± 0.31	72.85 ± 1.78	89.01 ± 1.13	61.71 ± 1.42	70.65 ± 1.13	82.50 ± 1.42	53.46 ± 1.03	73.03 ± 0.87
MVGRL	75.13 ± 0.67	70.60 ± 0.42	–	89.35 ± 0.63	62.50 ± 1.71	–	84.51 ± 0.62	-	73.26 ± 0.34
GraphCL	77.87 ± 0.41	74.39 ± 0.45	78.62 ± 0.40	86.80 ± 1.34	59.37 ± 0.82	71.36 ± 1.15	89.53 ± 0.84	55.99 ± 0.28	71.14 ± 0.44
JOAO	78.07 ± 0.47	74.55 ± 0.41	77.32 ± 0.54	87.35 ± 1.02	–	69.50 ± 0.36	85.29 ± 1.35	55.74 ± 0.63	70.21 ± 3.08
JOAOv2	78.36 ± 0.53	74.07 ± 1.10	77.40 ± 1.15	87.67 ± 0.79	–	69.33 ± 0.34	86.42 ± 1.45	56.03 ± 0.27	70.83 ± 0.25
SimGRACE	79.12 ± 0.44	75.35 ± 0.09	77.44 ± 1.11	89.01 ± 1.31	–	71.72 ± 0.82	89.51 ± 0.89	55.91 ± 0.34	71.30 ± 0.77
HIGCL	**80.62 ± 0.53**	**76.44 ± 0.24**	**79.22 ± 0.92**	**90.02 ± 0.80**	**63.86 ± 1.81**	**73.32 ± 0.49**	**89.67 ± 1.01**	**56.28 ± 0.54**	**73.38 ± 0.77**

GCL methods. The graph kernel methods include Graphlet kernel (GK) [22], Weisfeiler-Lehman sub-tree kernel (WL) [21] and deep graph kernels (DGK) [32]. The classic graph unsupervised representation learning methods include node2vec [7], sub2vec [1] and graph2vec [18]. Graph contrastive learning methods include InfoGraph [24], GraphCL [38], MVGRL [8], JOAO [38] and SimGRACE [30].

Implementation Details. We closely follow the experimental protocol of the previous state-of-the-art GCL approaches. For the unsupervised graph classification, we report the mean 10-fold cross validation accuracy after 5 runs followed by a SVM [3]. The SVM is trained by applying cross validation on training data folds and the best mean accuracy is reported. To make a fair comparison, we adopt the basic setting of InfoGraph [24] for graph classification. We conduct experiment with the values of the number of GNN layers, the number of epochs, batch size, the parameter C of SVM in the sets $\{1, 2, 4\}$, $\{10, 20, 40, 60\}$, $\{32, 64, 128, 256\}$ and $\{10^{-3}, 10^{-2}, ..., 10^{2}, 10^{3}\}$, respectively. We use Adam optimizer with learning rate in $\{0.01, 0.001, 0.0001\}$. We adopt GIN [31] as our graph encoder similar with other GCL and set the hidden representation dimension as 128. We use a three-layer HIGCL in the main experiment. The code to reproduce our results is publicly available at Github and there are more detailed parameters set in it.

5.2 Performance Comparison

The performance comparison result of various methods in unsupervised graph classification is shown in Table 2. The best results are highlighted in bold font, and the best result achieved by baselines are underlined. From the two tables, one can have the following observations. First, we can see that graph contrastive learning methods generally outperform traditional graph kernel methods or classical graph unsupervised learning methods, whether on biochemical molecular

Table 3. The result of the weighting parameter α on five datasets.

Dataset	NCI1	PROTEINS	MUTAG	PTCMR	COLLAB	IMDB-B
HIGCL-G	79.04 ± 0.44	76.26 ± 0.20	$\mathbf{90.02 \pm 0.80}$	$\mathbf{62.43 \pm 2.11}$	71.98 ± 0.76	$\mathbf{72.44 \pm 0.45}$
HIGCL-M	$\mathbf{80.62 \pm 0.53}$	$\mathbf{76.44 \pm 0.24}$	89.06 ± 0.97	62.17 ± 2.45	$\mathbf{73.32 \pm 0.49}$	72.22 ± 0.85

graphs or social network graphs. This demonstrates the effectiveness as well as the adaptability of the GCL methods. Then, our proposed model HIGCL achieves the best performance on all datasets, which verifies the superiority of our methods. Further, GraphCL, JOAO, JOAOv2, and SimGRACE are GCL methods for directly comparing graph-level representations, which lack the ability to explore more hierarchical structures in graph data and thus affect the performance of GCL. MVGRL performs node-level and graph-level cross-scale contrastive learning and achieves two suboptimal results on the biochemical graph datasets. However, for larger-scale graph data, which is particularly likely to be found in social network data, MVGRL does not work well due to the high computational cost. Compared to the best results in the baseline, our model delivers an average improvement of 0.81% and 0.53% in the biochemical graph datasets and social network datasets, respectively. In particular, our model delivers the most significant improvement on the PTCMR and COLLAB datasets, with 1.36% and 1.60% respectively. This proves that our methods have a good generalization to graph data at different scales or in different domains, and all achieve effective enhancement with existing graph contrastive learning methods.

Another interesting point is that the proposed HIGCL is rather stable, which means it can achieve the best or comparable to the best results for all the datasets. However, other methods work well on some datasets, but badly on others. For example, graph kernel method DGK performs well on NCI1, PROTEINS, and MUTAG; while on RDT-B and RDT-M5K datasets, the accuracy achieved by DGK are 78.04 and 41.27, which are significantly lower than the results (89.67 and 56.28 respectively) achieved by HIGCL. A similar problem also exists in classic graph unsupervised representation learning methods such as graph2vec and sub2vec as well as GCL methods such as InfoGraph and MVGRL. Generally, GCL methods work better than graph kernel-based methods and unsupervised graph representation learning-based methods.

5.3 Parameter Analysis on α

Due to the different structures of the various graph data, we introduce weights α to align the contribution of the original and refined graph to the final graph representation. We conduct unsupervised graph classification experiments on six datasets in Table 3, where HIGCL-G indicates when $\alpha = 1$, i.e., only using original graph-level GNN, while HIGCL-M indicates a mixture of the GNNs in different layers. We conduct experiments on a 3-layer HIGCL and set the $\alpha = 1/3$ for the HIGCL-M. Observation of Table 3 shows that on the small-scale datasets MUTAG, PTCMR, and IMDB-B, the use of original graph-level

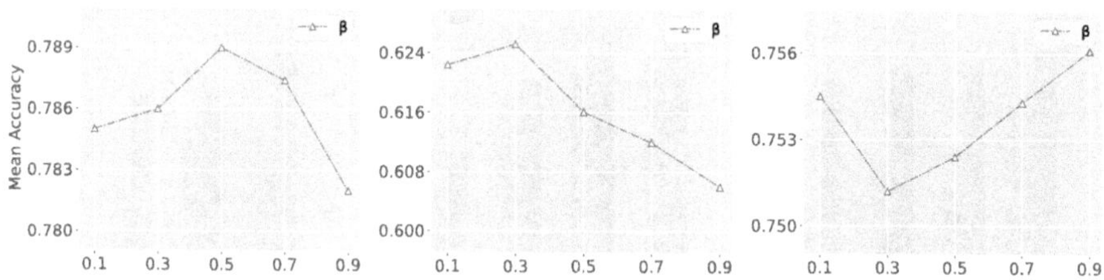

(a) NCI1 (b) PTCMR (c) PROTEINS

Fig. 3. Effect of different β values on HIGCL performance over NCI1, PTCMR and PROTEINS datasets.

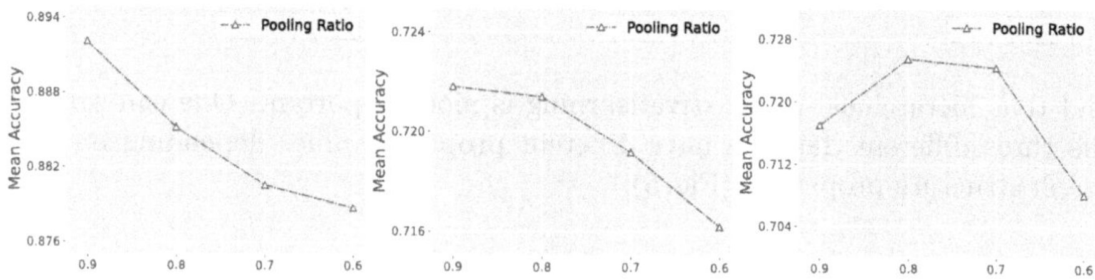

(a) MUTAG (b) IMDB-B (c) COLLAB

Fig. 4. Parameters analyze of the graph pooling ratio k.

Table 4. Ablation study on the InnerCL and HICL modules

Dataset	NCI1	PROTEINS	MUTAG	PTCMR	COLLAB	RDT-B	IMDB-B
w/o I	77.62 ± 0.54	75.36 ± 0.38	88.46 ± 0.82	59.16 ± 2.16	70.98 ± 0.76	89.23 ± 1.45	71.56 ± 0.88
w/o H	78.56 ± 0.54	75.24 ± 0.38	89.32 ± 0.82	61.32 ± 2.16	71.63 ± 0.76	89.12 ± 1.45	72.45 ± 0.88
HIGCL	**80.62 ± 0.53**	**76.44 ± 0.24**	**90.02 ± 0.80**	**63.86 ± 1.81**	**73.32 ± 0.49**	**89.67 ± 1.01**	**73.38 ± 0.77**

GNN is more favorable for generating high-quality graph representations. This is mainly because the hierarchical structure may be less obvious in small graphs and pooling the data at a finer granularity may destroy the structural information in it. On the other hand, the fusion of the different GNNs on larger graphs will be more conducive to representation learning. This is mainly because larger-scale graphs are more complex in structure and the use of multi-level GNNs is more conducive to capturing structural features at different granularities.

5.4 Parameter Analysis on β

HIGCL has a parameter β to control the importance of two modules InnerCL and HICL. We next conduct parameter analysis on β to study how β affects the model performance. Due to space limitation, we only show the result on NCI1, PTCMR, and PROTENS datasets in Fig. 3. One can see that β has a significant impact on the model performance on all three datasets as the performance curves vary remarkably with the increase of the β value. A larger β means a larger $HICL_{loss}$,

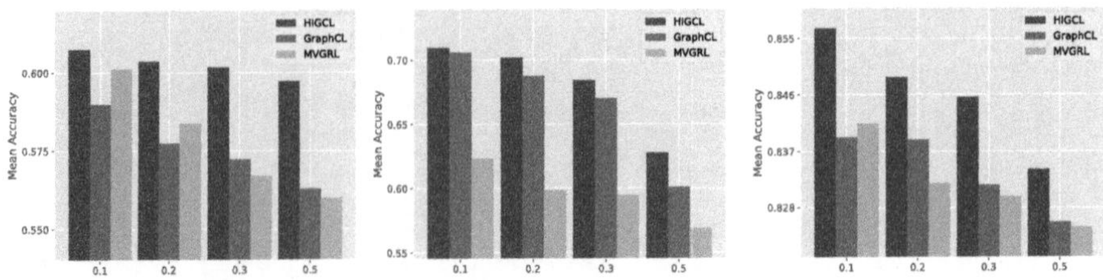

(a) PTCMR (b) IMDB-B (c) MUTAG

Fig. 5. We perform model robustness tests on three datasets, PTCMR, IMDB-B, and MUTAG. The numbers on the vertical axis indicate the ratio of perturbations applied to the datasets.

and thus hierarchical contrastive learning is more important. One can see that the three different datasets have different proper α values depending on their graph structure properties (Fig. 5).

5.5 Ablation Study

Our proposed model HIGCL contains two modules, InnerCL and HICL, and both provide $InnerCL_{loss}$ and $HICL_{loss}$, respectively, for the final optimization objective. To investigate whether these two modules are valid, we explored two variants of HIGCL on 7 datasets, where w/o I denotes the removal of the InnerCL module and w/o H denotes the removal of the HICL module. Observing the results in Table 4 reveals that removing either InnerCL or HICL leads to a decrease in effectiveness. When removing InnerCL, the effect of the model decreased by an average of 1.88% compared to the full version. In contrast, when HICL is removed, the effect of the model decreases by an average of 1.35% compared to the full version. The effect of removing InnerCL is usually greater because when lacking the InnerCL module, the model is unable to fully explore the structural features of each layer and lacks the diversity data to improve the model performance. The best results with the full version are achieved on all datasets. This fully demonstrates the effectiveness of our proposed two modules.

5.6 Parameter Analysis on Pooling Ratio

Most pooling methods require a pre-determined pooling ratio to determine what proportion of the nodes in the original graph are retained by the refined subgraph. Due to space limitations, we only explore the effect of the pooling ratio k on 3 datasets. We perform the analysis on a three layer HIGCL and set the pooling ratio of the two pooling modules used to be equal. The pooling ratio ranges from 0.9 to 0.6. A higher pooling ratio means that more nodes are retained in the refined graph. For the two smaller datasets, MUTAG and IMDB-B, the models usually achieve better results when the pooling ratio is around a larger value. This is mainly because small-scale graphs have less hierarchical structural information in them, and a lower pooling ratio can result in serious corruption of structural information, thus reducing the effectiveness. In the larger datasets COLLAB, the mean accuracy decreases as the pooling ratio first increases, with the best results achieved between 0.8 and 0.7. This indicates that larger-scale graphs contain useful structural features at different granularities (Fig. 4).

5.7 Robustness Experiments

We further demonstrate the robustness of the proposed model. Our experimental setup is similar to that of unsupervised graph classification. After being trained by GraphCL, and MVGRL with our method, we feed the perturbed data into all three methods and use the classification results of the SVM as our robustness evaluation criteria. In this case, we use a combination of edge perturbation and node dropping for our perturbation method. Based on the three graph datasets, it can be seen that as the perturbation increases, the quality of representation decreases more significantly for GraphCL and MVGRL. MVGRL is less robust due to its use of only subgraph sampling as a data augmentation method and usually performs worst when the perturbation ratio goes above 0.3. Our model is augmented with a variety of data augmentation operations in the InnerCL module, and the representational power and robustness of the model are further increased by two different contrasting objectives.

6 Conclusion

In this paper, we propose a novel hierarchical graph contrastive learning model HIGCL. Significantly different from existing GCL methods that generally used one single contrastive objective and a one-layered flat contrastive learning architecture, HIGCL proposes to integrate both inner-contrasting and hierarchical-contrasting objectives and conducts contrastive learning across different graph layers through pooling in a hierarchical way. In this way, the hierarchical features of graphs can be more effectively captured. Evaluations over 9 graph datasets demonstrate the effectiveness of the proposal in the task of graph classification by extensive comparisons with existing SOTA baselines.

Acknowledgement. This research was funded by the National Science Foundation of China (No. 62172443), Open Project of Xiangjiang Laboratory (22XJ02002, 22XJ03025), Hunan Provincial Natural Science Foundation of China (No. 2022JJ30053) and the High Performance Computing Center of Central South University.

References

1. Adhikari, B., Zhang, Y., Ramakrishnan, N., Prakash, B.A.: Sub2vec: feature learning for subgraphs. In: Proceedings of PAKDD (2018)
2. Belghazi, M.I., et al.: Mine: mutual information neural estimation. In: Proceedings of ICML (2018)

3. Chang, C.C., Lin, C.J.: LibSVM: a library for support vector machines. ACM Trans. Intell. Syst. Technol. **2**, 27:1–27:27 (2011)
4. Du, J., Wang, S., Miao, H., Zhang, J.: Multi-channel pooling graph neural networks. In: Proceedings of IJCAI (2021)
5. Fu, X., et al.: ACE-HGNN: adaptive curvature exploration hyperbolic graph neural network. In: Proceedings of ICDM (2021)
6. Gao, H., Ji, S.: Graph u-nets. IEEE Trans. Pattern Anal. Mach. Intell. 1 (2019)
7. Grover, A., Leskovec, J.: node2vec: Scalable feature learning for networks. In: Proceedings of KDD (2016)
8. Hassani, K., Khasahmadi, A.H.: Contrastive multi-view representation learning on graphs. In: Proceedings of ICML (2020)
9. Hjelm, R.D., et al.: Learning deep representations by mutual information estimation and maximization. In: Proceedings of ICLR (2018)
10. Hock, F.J.: Drug Discovery and Evaluation: Pharmacological Assays. Springer, Cham (2016). https://doi.org/10.1007/978-3-319-05392-9
11. Hu, Z., Fan, C., Chen, T., Chang, K.W., Sun, Y.: Unsupervised pre-training of graph convolutional networks. In: Proceedings of ICLR (2019)
12. Kipf, T.N., Welling, M.: Variational graph auto-encoders. In: Proceedings of NeurIPS (2016)
13. Lee, J., Lee, I., Kang, J.: Self-attention graph pooling. In: Proceedings of ICML (2019)
14. Li, M., Chen, S., Zhang, Y., Tsang, I.: Graph cross networks with vertex infomax pooling. In: Proceedings of NeurIPS (2020)
15. Ma, T., Xiao, C., Zhou, J., Wang, F.: Drug similarity integration through attentive multi-view graph auto-encoders. In: Proceedings of IJCAI (2018)
16. Mesquita, D., de Souza, A.H., Kaski, S.: Rethinking pooling in graph neural networks. In: Proceedings of NeurIPS (2020)
17. Morris, C., Kriege, N.M., Bause, F., Kersting, K., Mutzel, P., Neumann, M.: Tudataset: a collection of benchmark datasets for learning with graphs. In: ICML 2020 Workshop on Graph Representation Learning and Beyond (2020). https://www.graphlearning.io
18. Narayanan, A., Chandramohan, M., Venkatesan, R., Chen, L., Liu, Y., Jaiswal, S.: graph2vec: Learning distributed representations of graphs. In: Proceedings of MLG (2017)
19. Van den Oord, A., Li, Y., Vinyals, O.: Representation learning with contrastive predictive coding. arXiv preprint arXiv:1807.03748 (2018)
20. Pang, Y., Zhao, Y., Li, D.: Graph pooling via coarsened graph infomax. In: Proceedings of SIGIR (2021)
21. Shervashidze, N., Schweitzer, P., Van Leeuwen, E.J., Mehlhorn, K., Borgwardt, K.M.: Weisfeiler-Lehman graph kernels. J. Mach. Learn. Res. **12** (2011)
22. Shervashidze, N., Vishwanathan, S., Petri, T., Mehlhorn, K., Borgwardt, K.: Efficient graphlet kernels for large graph comparison. In: Artificial Intelligence and Statistics, pp. 488–495 (2009)
23. Sohn, K.: Improved deep metric learning with multi-class n-pair loss objective. In: Proceedings of NeurIPS (2016)
24. Sun, F.Y., Hoffman, J., Verma, V., Tang, J.: Infograph: unsupervised and semi-supervised graph-level representation learning via mutual information maximization. In: Proceedings of ICLR (2019)
25. Sun, Q., et al.: Sugar: subgraph neural network with reinforcement pooling and self-supervised mutual information mechanism. In: Proceedings of WebConf (2021)

26. Suresh, S., Li, P., Hao, C., Neville, J.: Adversarial graph augmentation to improve graph contrastive learning. In: Proceedings of NeurIPS (2021)
27. Ullmann, J.R.: An algorithm for subgraph isomorphism. J. ACM **23**(1), 31–42 (1976)
28. Veličković, P., Cucurull, G., Casanova, A., Romero, A., Liò, P., Bengio, Y.: Graph attention networks. In: Proceedings of ICLR (2018)
29. Wang, S., et al.: Adversarial hard negative generation for complementary graph contrastive learning. In: Proceedings of SDM (2023)
30. Xia, J., Wu, L., Chen, J., Hu, B., Li, S.Z.: Simgrace: a simple framework for graph contrastive learning without data augmentation. In: Proceedings of the ACM Web Conference 2022 (2022)
31. Xu, K., Hu, W., Leskovec, J., Jegelka, S.: How powerful are graph neural networks? In: ICLR (2019)
32. Yanardag, P., Vishwanathan, S.: Deep graph kernels. In: Proceedings of KDD (2015)
33. Ying, Z., You, J., Morris, C., Ren, X., Hamilton, W., Leskovec, J.: Hierarchical graph representation learning with differentiable pooling. In: Proceedings of NeurIPS (2018)
34. You, Y., Chen, T., Sui, Y., Chen, T., Wang, Z., Shen, Y.: Graph contrastive learning with augmentations. In: Proceedings of NeurIPS (2020)
35. Zhang, S., Hu, Z., Subramonian, A., Sun, Y.: Motif-driven contrastive learning of graph representations. In: Proceedings of AAAI (2021)
36. Zhao, X., et al.: Multi-view tensor graph neural networks through reinforced aggregation. IEEE Trans. Knowl. Data Eng. **35** (2022)
37. Zhu, Y., Xu, Y., Yu, F., Liu, Q., Wu, S., Wang, L.: Deep graph contrastive representation learning. In: Proceedings of ICML (2020)
38. Zhu, Y., Xu, Y., Yu, F., Liu, Q., Wu, S., Wang, L.: Graph contrastive learning with adaptive augmentation. In: Proceedings of WebConf (2021)

Author Index

© The Editor(s) (if applicable) and The Author(s), under exclusive license to Springer Nature Switzerland AG 2023

D. Koutra et al. (Eds.): ECML PKDD 2023, LNAI 14170, pp. 717–719, 2023.
https://doi.org/10.1007/978-3-031-43415-0

Printed in the United States
by Baker & Taylor Publisher Services